Introduction to Forensic Science

Introduction to Forensic Science: The Science of Criminalistics is a textbook that takes a unique and holistic approach to forensic science. This book focuses on exploring the underlying scientific concepts as presented at the introductory college and senior high school levels. Chapters introduce readers to each of the important areas of forensic science, grouping chapters together by discipline and following a logical progression and flow between chapters. This systematically allows students to understand the fundamental scientific concepts, recognize their various applications to the law and investigations, and discern how each topic fits broadly within the context of forensic science.

The writing is accessible throughout, maintaining students' interest – including both science and non-science majors – while inspiring them to learn more about the field. Concepts are demonstrated with numerous case studies and full-color illustrations that serve to emphasize the important ideas and issues related to a particular topic. This approach underscores scientific understanding, allowing the student to go beyond simple rote learning to develop deeper insights into the field, regardless of their scientific background. This book has been extensively classroom-tested to provide the most comprehensive and up-to-date survey of various forensic disciplines and the current state of the science, policies, and best practices.

Key features:

- Presents a wholly new, fresh approach to addressing a broad survey of techniques and evidentiary analyses in the field of forensic science.
- All concepts – and the underpinnings of forensic practice – are explained in simple terms, using understandable analogies and illustrations to further clarify concepts.
- Introduces topics that other introductory texts fail to address, including serology, behavioral science, forensic medicine and anthropology, forensic ecology, palynology, zoology, video analysis, AI/computer forensics, and forensic engineering.
- Highly illustrated with over 1,000 full-color photographs, drawings, and diagrams to further highlight key concepts.
- Suitable for both high school senior-level instruction and two- and four-year university courses for majors, non-majors, and criminal justice students enrolled in introductory forensic science classes.

Support Materials – including an Instructor's Manual with test bank and chapter PowerPoint lecture slides – are available to professors with qualified course adoption.

James T. Spencer is the Laura J. and L. Douglas Meredith Distinguished Teaching Professor, a Fellow of the Syracuse University Center of Excellence, and Founding Executive Director of the Syracuse University Forensic and National Security Sciences Institute (FNSSI) at Syracuse University (SU) in Syracuse, New York, USA. Dr. Spencer has research interests in inorganic chemistry, organometallic chemistry, materials chemistry and solid-state science, new sensor development, renewable energy systems (photovoltaic), and forensic science, and has taught various courses over the years including, most recently, on chemistry in the modern world, general chemistry, organometallic chemistry, forensic science and advanced forensic science, and scientific and career resources in forensic science. He has received numerous awards for his work, including the Chancellor's Citation for Excellence, the highest award for SU faculty and staff, in recognition of outstanding achievement in teaching and scholarship. Dr. Spencer holds a B.A. in Chemistry and a Ph.D. in Inorganic Chemistry from SUNY Potsdam, and has been published widely in many professional and society journals.

Introduction to Forensic Science
The Science of Criminalistics

James T. Spencer

CRC Press
Taylor & Francis Group
Boca Raton London New York

CRC Press is an imprint of the
Taylor & Francis Group, an **informa** business

Designed cover image: shutterstock

First edition published 2024
by CRC Press
2385 NW Executive Center Drive, Suite 320, Boca Raton FL 33431

and by CRC Press
4 Park Square, Milton Park, Abingdon, Oxon, OX14 4RN

CRC Press is an imprint of Taylor & Francis Group, LLC

© 2024 James T. Spencer

Library of Congress Cataloging-in-Publication Data
Names: Spencer, James T. (Professor of forensic sciences), author.
Title: Introduction to forensic science: the science of criminalistics / James T. Spencer.
Description: Boca Raton, FL: CRC Press, 2024. | Includes bibliographical references and index.
Identifiers: LCCN 2024004002 (print) | LCCN 2024004003 (ebook) | ISBN 9781032025179 (hardback) | ISBN 9781032024301 (paperback) | ISBN 9781003183709 (ebook)
Subjects: LCSH: Criminal investigation. | MESH: Forensic medicine.
Classification: LCC HV8073 .S644 2024 (print) | LCC HV8073 (ebook) | DDC 614/.1—dc23/eng/20240208
LC record available at https://lccn.loc.gov/2024004002
LC ebook record available at https://lccn.loc.gov/2024004003

ISBN: 9781032025179 (hbk)
ISBN: 9781032024301 (pbk)
ISBN: 9781003183709 (ebk)

DOI: 10.4324/9781003183709

Typeset in Times New Roman
by codeMantra

Access the Support Material: www.routledge.com/9781032025179

To my family:
Judith, Sarah, Susanne, and Clint
Who always made the adventure together possible, worthwhile, and amazing with their unending love, grace, and support.

To my parents:
Kathryn and Harold,
Who were always there with quiet grace, strong foundation, and loving patience.

And to my friends and colleagues:
John C. Fiset and Michael B. Sponsler,
Who always knew it could be done.

Contents

Preface   ix
Acknowledgments   xi

PART 1   Introduction   1

1   Introduction, Historic Development, and Legal Roles in Forensic Science   3

2   Crime Scene Investigations   29

3   Science, Pseudoscience, and the Law   53

PART 2   Biological Evidence   77

4   Methods for Examining Biological Evidence   79

5   Forensic DNA   113

6   Forensic Serology   154

7   Anatomical Evidence: The Outside Story   189

8   Forensic Medicine: The Inside Story   245

9   Forensic Anthropology   300

10 Forensic Ecology   334

PART 3   Chemical Evidence   383

11 Overview of Chemical Evidence   385

12 Forensic Spectroscopy   423

13 Forensic Toxicology   477

14 Forensic Fire and Explosives   541

PART 4   Physical Properties in Evidence   579

15 Physical Properties: Mineralogical, Soil, Glass, and Paint Analysis   581

16 Firearms, Ballistics, and Impression Evidence   613

17 Forensic Document, Photo, Video Analysis, Voice ID and Linguistics   **650**

18 Forensic Engineering and Computer Science   **687**

PART 5   Behavioral Forensic Evidence   **723**

19 Behavioral Forensic Science   **725**

Index   751

Preface

Forensic science may seem to be an enigma among the sciences, dealing both with solving mysteries and sometimes being a bit mysterious itself in how conclusions are produced from the smallest speck of evidence. But good forensic science cannot be mysterious; it *must* be based on the best possible science derived by applying well-understood established principles and methods to evidence in the quest to illuminate real-life problems. It must be evidence-based, firmly rooted in the scientific disciplines. It spans essentially all fields of human endeavor while striving to maintain a uniformly high level of intellectual thought and scientific rigor throughout. It is also forced, however, to reconcile the often-competing and sometimes seemingly mutually exclusive requirements of the law and science as courts and juries increasingly rely heavily on scientific data and analysis in deciding important legal questions. Nonetheless, many forensic disciplines are under intense scrutiny to employ appropriate scientific standards, while new legal standards are constantly being developed and implemented. In response to these opportunities and challenges, the field is rapidly evolving, making it a truly exciting time for forensic science as new discoveries and advances are rapidly translated into best practices.

This textbook focuses on removing the shroud of mystery from forensic science and exploring its underlying scientific concepts and principles. It is first a book of science, but set squarely in the real world. Scientific methods are radically changing the landscape of our entire criminal justice system. Increasingly, law enforcement and legal proceedings rely on often complex and detailed scientific analyses of forensic evidence. The field now encompasses widely ranging disciplines, from the physical and biological sciences to the social sciences and applied sciences, with new technologies emerging every day. An aim of this text is to provide a comprehensive survey of the field that is both interesting and accessible to students as they delve more deeply into the scientific foundations of the discipline. To achieve this aim, this book first introduces each of the key areas of forensic science and then allows students to logically discover the fundamental scientific concepts behind its application. Concepts are richly illustrated with visualizations, examples, study aids, and case studies that will hopefully serve to emphasize the important ideas and issues related to each topic.

Unlike other introductory texts in forensic science, the topics in this book are logically arranged and presented within their broad scientific disciplines: the biological, chemical, physical, and behavioral sciences. The text opens, however, with several chapters that deal explicitly with the relationships between legal requirements for forensic evidence and the scientific method, which is the foundation of the valid scientific analysis of evidence. These chapters also describe how the disciplines of law and science have found ways to operate effectively at their interface. The manner in which forensic data is collected, analyzed, and interpreted properly, including the use of meaningful statistics, is also presented in these chapters. This opening section ends with a vital discussion on the differences between real science and pseudoscience and how to discern between the two. This is particularly critical for forensic science in the courtroom where, most often, non-scientific juries and judges must grapple with what to believe and what to disregard among the tonnage of evidence presented when reaching their conclusions. But revealing true from false science and evidence-based analysis from false conjecture goes far beyond forensics to encompass our consideration and understanding of the world all around us.

The next large section on biological scientific evidence begins, after a brief excursion into the tools basic to biological investigations, at the smallest (molecular) levels and then proceeds to the largest biological systems (ecosystems). We begin, therefore, by looking carefully at the gold standard of personal identification at the molecular level: DNA. From there, chapters build to successively larger systems through the disciplines of blood chemistry, anatomical evidence (fingerprints, hair, biometrics), forensic medicine, forensic anthropology, and ending with the largest of all, forensic ecology. In this organization, the understanding in each chapter informs that which follows – DNA informs blood studies, medicine informs anthropology, and so on.

The following section on chemical evidence begins with a brief overview of how chemical analysis can provide vital information to forensic investigations. Subsequent chapters explore the ways in which key concepts and techniques of analytical and physical chemistry are applied in forensic analyses. Rather than presenting simply a catalog of techniques and the particular information they may provide, the text attempts to present sufficient background information so that students may actually understand how and why a technique works: a far deeper understanding than just a cookbook approach of simply describing what a technique does. The chapter on chemical toxicology brings together all these concepts and presents an overview of both the basics of toxicology, usually omitted from texts, and how these concepts are applied in forensic investigations regarding drugs, poisons, toxins, and alcohol. The final chapter in this grouping deals with the topics of fire and explosives, areas that typically involve a great deal of chemical evidence and are the outcome of rapid chemical reactivity.

The section on physical properties in forensic evidence begins with an overview of physical properties and measurements before proceeding to investigations that deal largely with these types of information: geology, glass, plastics, paints, and others. The final three chapters in this section focus on specialized fields in which physical measurements form the core of any investigation: firearms, documents, voice recognition, and engineering and computer science.

The final section focuses on the field of behavioral forensic science, specifically forensic psychology and sociology. This field deals with how people function both individually and collectively within larger groups and societies as related to criminal action. This section, usually overlooked in introductory texts, is particularly relevant because the behavioral sciences are now being called upon with rapidly increasing frequency to provide vital information in conducting investigations and deciding legal questions and outcomes.

In presenting such a wide variety of scientific ideas, the text endeavors to present the material in a clear, logical, and progressive fashion, focusing on proven learning strategies for science, based on decades of research. Although frequent and pervasive connections will be made to legal applications, the forensic science techniques are first presented with sufficient background for understanding the science behind them. Throughout the text, the accurate presentation of fundamental scientific principles will be laid out first for understanding, and then their application to criminalistics will be made clear. As described already, the chapters are arranged as a function of logical relationships between techniques rather than being organized confusingly by crime type. This organization results in a smooth transition between topics, and new material builds upon previous concepts as they are developed. This approach avoids fragmented and disjointed explanations of fundamental scientific concepts and certainly aids in making clear connections between techniques. The goal is to provide a deep and meaningful understanding of how forensic science works rather than just offering a cursory "cookbook" phenomenological approach to forensic methods – a far more valuable and versatile type of learning. For example, by first presenting an overview of the fundamentals of spectroscopy, it will be clear how most of these spectroscopic techniques are closely related, allowing them to be readily understood in a unified fashion.

The text has been carefully and thoughtfully designed to provide a more representative coverage of the field of forensic science than is typically found in textbooks. Instructors will no longer be forced to provide extensive supplemental materials to make up for deficiencies in the adopted text. We believe that this textbook is unique in a number of important ways, including:

- Focused curriculum developed through decades of collegiate teaching experience at the introductory level in forensic and general science courses, based on proven learning strategies in the sciences, and tested/revised with the help of tens of thousands of college and senior high school students.
- *Unique coverage* of material that includes topics critical to an introductory level forensic textbook, including key aspects of the sciences, law, and social sciences. In addition, other relevant topics such as mathematics in forensic science and a discussion of the differences between real science and pseudoscience are included.
- *Appropriate depth*, presentation, and coverage are provided for the introductory audience.
- A *creative approach* is employed, designed to engage students from a variety of backgrounds, including both science and "non-science" students, and to excite them about the material presented. The text is written in easy-to-understand language and formatted to provide an authentic, "relatable" learning experience aimed at making connections with students' backgrounds and interests.
- *Learning tools* provided for every chapter include references, cases for further study, a glossary, and questions for practice and mastery. Additionally, study aids, quick summaries, reviews of key concepts, and plenty of examples and cases are provided throughout each chapter.

I hope that this textbook will prove to be exciting for students interested in the vital, dynamic, and rapidly developing field of forensic science. Enjoy the journey!

James T. Spencer
Syracuse, New York
August 2023

Acknowledgments

The author would like to acknowledge Judith A. Spencer (*Textbook Assistant*), Mark Listewnik (*CRC Sr. Editor*), Prof. James C. Dabrowiak (*Syracuse University, DNA*), Prof. Fred. Davies (*Upstate Medical University, Serology*), Dean Cathryn R. Newton (*Dean Emerita, College of Arts and Sciences, Syracuse University*), Dr. Gerald Edmonds (*Director, Syracuse University Project Advance*), Capt. James Krieger (*Fire Department New York (Ret.), Arson and Explosives*), Mr. John C. Fiset (*Associate Director (Ret.), Syracuse University Project Advance*), Dr. Rob Stoppacher, M.D. (*Forensic Medicine*), Dr. Michael Baden, M.D. (*New York City Chief Medical Examiner, Ret., Pseudoscience*), Vice Admiral Robert B. Murret (*USN, Ret.*), Prof. Ann Bunch (*SUNY Brockport, Forensic Anthropology*), Prof. Michael Sponsler (*Syracuse University, FNSSI*), Prof. Kevin Sweder (*Syracuse University (Ret.), Forensic Toxicology*), Mr. Matthew Kurimsky (*Onondaga Co. Forensics Laboratory, Forensic Firearms*), Mr. David Tate (*Onondaga Co. Forensics Laboratory, Forensic Fingerprints*), Dr. Kathleen Corrado (*Exec. Dir., Syracuse University, FNSSI*), and Mr. William Hamilton (*Editing and Research*).

PART 1

Introduction

Introduction, Historic Development, and Legal Roles in Forensic Science

1

1.1 SCIENCE AND THE LAW: *FROM ANCIENT TIMES TO CSI AND BEYOND*

We should be truth seekers who are not partisan, who do not have any interest in the outcome, who call it as we see it no matter the consequences.

Park Dietz (1948–)

LEARNING GOALS AND OBJECTIVES

Today, the prominent role of science in the courtroom is undisputed. We rely upon the scientific analysis and interpretation of key pieces of physical evidence to both exonerate and convict. But this hasn't always been true throughout history. In this chapter, an introduction to the role that forensic science has and does play in criminal justice is presented. In addition, the legal underpinnings of the admissibility, use, and limitations of scientific evidence and testimony in court are explored. After completing this chapter, you should be able to:

- Provide a definition for the terms *forensic science* and *criminalistics*.
- Discern the difference between basic and applied science.
- Understand the relationships among the law, basic science, and applied science.
- Appreciate how forensic science has developed throughout history to arrive at its present state.
- Understand *Locard's Exchange Principle* and *The Principle of Individuality*.
- Understand how fiction has contributed to the development of forensic science and what features

fictional detectives and modern forensic scientists have in common.
- Explain the *CSI Effect* and how it influences scientific evidence in the courtroom.
- Discern how precedent cases pave the way for scientific evidence, analysis, and testimony.
- Explain the key features of the Frye and Daubert cases.
- Identify how the *Joiner, Khumo, Melendez-Dias*, and related cases regulate expert testimony.

1.1.1 Introduction to the Forensic Sciences

Why are we so fascinated by how "detectives" use science to discover hidden secrets that challenge our perceptions of the world? What is it that simultaneously repels and impels us toward investigations of crime and criminals? And why are we so seemingly obsessed with popular forensic science and what it can tell us, not only about *how* a crime was committed, but more intimately, about *why* a crime was perpetrated? Certainly, literature, television, and movies have done much to fuel this interest for generations, but there must be a more fundamental aspect of human nature that drives us to learn about crime and punishment that our popular detective literature simply serves to exploit (Figure 1.1).

There are probably as many answers to such questions as there are people trying to answer them. It may be that by believing we can identify those who commit crimes and then deliver fitting punishments, we gain a sense of security over the vulnerability and, to some extent, the sense of helplessness that we may feel when confronted by a seemingly random crime. It may also give us a chance to explore the darker sides of our human natures in a safe and unthreatening way, much as how we enjoy thrill rides at amusement parks or scary movies by safely facing our fears. Our interest in crime may even arise from a desire to seek collective societal satisfaction and exact a moral judgment upon those who step outside the boundaries of our laws, and in doing so, violate our sense of fairness. A mutually agreed-upon

DOI: 10.4324/9781003183709-2

FIGURE 1.1   A scientist at work analyzing forensic evidence obtained at a crime scene.

Source: Shutterstock.com.

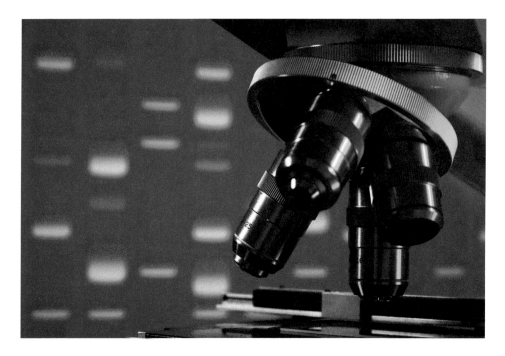

FIGURE 1.2   A close-up picture of a laboratory microscope with a typical DNA gel shown in the background.

Source: Shutterstock.com.

set of laws and customs are, of course, what fundamentally establishes a society in the first place. All sorts of people worldwide certainly know how to manipulate both our fascination with and fear of crime to help achieve their own ends.

It seems that people have also always been inherently interested in mysteries and in finding solutions to puzzling problems. In fact, any basic science seeks to fundamentally unravel the mysteries of the universe around us and to provide answers to the "hows and whys" of nature (Figure 1.2). This is apparently an intrinsic need of humans – the "curiosity killed the cat" syndrome. Forensic science takes this sense of investigation and discovery and applies it to the practical need of providing answers to questions revolving around legal issues (Figure 1.3).

We have long looked to science to inform legal decisions. Historically, advances in forensic science have often occurred not in small steps but in unexpected leaps, either due to changes in the underlying science and technology or because of shifts in legal policy and practice. Recent changes in forensic science continue to be both revolutionary and evolutionary, reshaping the field continually. The entire way we look at the scientific analysis of physical evidence has changed, and the fundamental concepts of the *scientific method* are now applied widely to crime-related investigations. These changes in approach and process provide a solid foundation for how science can offer amazingly detailed and accurate answers, greatly useful for legal deliberations.

Forensic science, by its very nature, lies at the point of convergence between our legal and scientific systems, as illustrated in Figure 1.4. While there are many regions of common purpose, there are, however, three fundamental sources of tension between these two systems involving issues of certainty, time, and truth. In the first issue between these

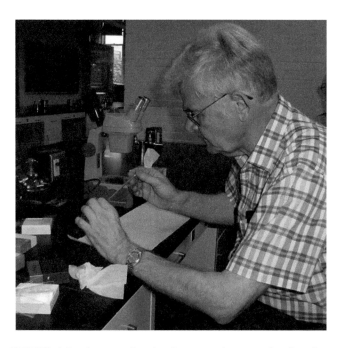

FIGURE 1.3 A research scientist preparing samples for close examination under the microscope. Such careful study is fundamental to good scientific practice.

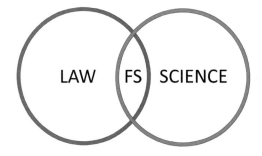

FIGURE 1.4 A Venn diagram illustrating the relationship between the law, scientific inquiry, and forensic science.

systems, the law wants absolute *certainty*: Col. Mustard did it in the hall with a lead pipe. However, science can *only* establish with certainty just the simplest of facts. While science can readily disprove an idea or exonerate a suspect, it cannot prove anything beyond simple facts and can often only provide information as to the *probability* that events may occur in a specific fashion (seen in the famous scientific concept of the *Heisenberg's Uncertainty Principle*, discussed in Chapter 12). Science can, therefore, tell us what the odds are that a particular random occurrence will happen, such as the odds of a DNA 13-loci match between two unrelated and random samples – often as rare as about 1 in 5 trillion – but it lies with juries to ultimately decide what odds are sufficient to convict someone of a crime: it remains a human decision on how to weigh the probabilities in reaching a verdict. All of this is made more difficult by the increasing technical complexity of scientific evidence that non-scientific juries must understand to arrive at a fair and just verdict.

The law and science also differ in their concern for *time*. While both science and the law are best served through "open-ended" investigations leading to greater understanding, science is perpetually revising its understanding of the Universe and never comes to the end of the questions – science just seeks to find a better set of questions to explore further. Stuart Fierstein (2012) has proposed that "human ignorance and uncertainty are valuable states of mind – perhaps even necessary for the true progress of science." The law, however, has a fixed end-point in time when a verdict must be rendered. Legal questions cannot remain indefinitely unresolved, waiting for a new and better set of answers to arise through continued investigation. The accused are constitutionally entitled to a swift resolution of their cases (Sixth Amendment).

Finally, it is also important to recognize that the ultimate goals of the two systems are different: our legal system primarily seeks *justice*, while the scientific world looks for greater understanding through the pursuit of *truth*. Justice may be defined as a *state of being just or fair*. While justice is hopefully based on truth, the fundamental goal of the law is fairness. In contrast, truth may be defined as something that is *generally either in agreement with fact or a fact that is widely accepted as true*. But truth depends on perspective. For example, look at the pictures of the Eiffel Tower shown in Figure 1.5. Which of these pictures represents the "true" picture of the Tower? Of course, they are all "true" pictures of the Tower which simply differ in the perspective and conditions that existed when the pictures were taken. Likewise, truth in a legal context depends on perspective.

But how can juries composed of a variety of non-scientifically trained laypersons sort out real science from pseudoscience? Until about 1923, each court could define for itself what it would allow as valid science in the courtroom. This resulted in very little discrimination between the quacks and charlatans from the true scientists in court – and the person who was most convincing to the juries typically won the day, often the quack who could give "definitive" sounding but wrong answers. In 1923, however, all this changed with the outcome of a case

FIGURE 1.5   *Pictures of the Eiffel Tower from different perspectives.*

Source: Shutterstock.com photos.

involving the admissibility of a lie detector test (it was, by the way, found to be inadmissible but that's irrelevant to what this case did for bringing good science to courts). After the decision in this so-called *Frye Case*, the *bona fide* scientific world, instead of each individual court, was given the responsibility of determining what forensic evidence was based upon good, tried, and true science and allowable in court and what was "fake false" science that was properly inadmissible. This new approach generally worked rather well but it was very slow to admit the results from any new scientific discoveries, often taking decades before new methods were admissible. Then, in 1993, a new standard, called the *Daubert Standard*, placed the responsibility for determining what constituted good admissible science with the judge, but retaining the guidance from the relevant scientific communities. This changed things dramatically by allowing a very rapid transition from a basic laboratory discovery into its direct application in the legal system. For example, in 1985, Alec Jeffries discovered that DNA samples taken from people could be used for individual identification. It took all of 18 months after this discovery before DNA evidence was first used to convict a criminal. However, new standards not only allowed scientific discoveries into the courtroom, they also helped to filter out the pseudo-science, quack testimony, and poorly practiced science. Today, new standards of scientific practice are being applied to all areas

of forensic investigation with the effect that the field is truly developing, across the board, into a defensible, rigorous scientific discipline.

Forensic science, as an applied science, has now developed a valuable relationship with basic scientific research and exploration. It scours the basic research fields and rapidly assimilates recent discoveries into new forensic investigative tools. No discipline appears to be immune from this process of discovery sharing: medicine, chemistry, physics, psychology, anthropology, entomology, and many others push both their own boundaries and those of forensic science through exploration. It also means the effective end of the general, across-the-board criminalist; someone like Sherlock Holmes, who himself knew all that he needed to know from the necessary fields to solve a crime. Today, there is just too much to be known by any one person for them to be expert in every necessary scientific aspect of an investigation such that the field of forensic science has evolved into a variety of complex forensic sub-disciplines with expert specialists. But this does not mean that trained and intelligent investigators have a reduced role in crime solving – quite the opposite, *crimes do not solve themselves*! Someone must take all of the threads provided by forensic science and weave them into a correct solution to the mystery – something that takes skill, experience, knowledge, creativity, collaboration, and intelligence.

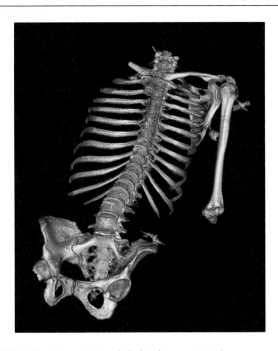

FIGURE 1.6 Computerized skeletal reconstruction.

Source: Used courtesy and with permission of the Institute of Forensic Medicine, University of Bern.

But it also takes top flight science to analyze and interpret the evidence properly (Figure 1.6). Just as you probably wouldn't go to a brain surgeon for a toothache, you also wouldn't go to a dentist for appendicitis – each expert has their own specific sphere of knowledge. Teams of experts may be needed to work together to solve a complex criminal problem: medical examiners, anthropologists, toxicologists, firearms experts, trace analysts, police investigators, lawyers, and many others may be needed depending on the case.

Forensic evidence is often critical in criminal cases. But forensic science also provides equally valuable information in civil trials – although civil trials typically receive less press coverage than their criminal counterparts. Thus, the techniques and underlying science presented in this text cut equally well across both criminal and civil applications.

Sometimes, however, our reliance upon the practice of forensic science has given us a sense of false security: science does have some very real limitations when it comes to finding and analyzing evidence. A recent article has suggested that courts rarely eliminate forensic testimony by experts, even when their error rates are either quite high or, even worse, unknown. While the field of forensic science is rapidly tightening its reliance upon rigorous scientific standards, there remain instances of "less-than-ideal" practices and interpretations of scientific evidence in the courts. There are also times when scientific evidence just can't be found or there is too little to complete the analysis. And, ultimately, it all relies upon the jury understanding the evidence and making the right decisions.

But the proper inclusion of science in the courtroom has also led to another problem that the legal system must continually deal with, a problem largely brought about by the popular

depictions of forensics. Too frequently, juries find cases somehow lacking unless all possible types of scientific data are presented. For example, juries feel that even a truly strong case is somehow weakened unless DNA evidence is provided – even when there is no question of identity or that a suspect was at the crime scene (often by admission of the defendant). Juries also may not have a clue about what the actual forensic evidence can tell them but feel that every possible piece of scientific analysis must be provided. This sometimes leads to silly and expensive uses of forensic testing – such as DNA evidence for shoplifting cases. And sometimes, partial or incomplete knowledge can be a dangerous thing – such as when jury members feel that they have acquired a deep level of understanding of some aspect of forensic science simply by watching television programs that often depict conveniently inaccurate or deeply incorrect science, the so-called *CSI Effect*.

Despite this, however, there are truly remarkable advances in forensic science, resulting from discoveries in the laboratory and allied sciences (Figure 1.7). Science in the courtroom now reaches the highest standards ever seen in history, and each discipline is continually working very hard to tighten up its standards and practices. It stands as a truly respectable applied science, joining the ranks as a full member with the other applied sciences of medicine and engineering. Organizations and agencies, such as the American Academy of Forensic Science (AAFS), the American Society of Crime Lab Directors (ASCLD), the Department of Justice (DoJ), and the United Nations (UN), among others, are all working hard to ensure that the highest levels of scientific standards are employed in all forensic disciplines. Through these efforts, scientists can often provide information that investigators could only dream about just a few

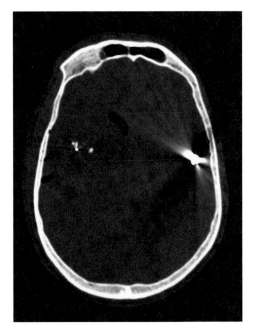

FIGURE 1.7 New frontiers of forensic science – forensic radiology: A Computerized Tomography (CT) scan of a head wound.

Source: Used courtesy and with permission of the Institute of Forensic Medicine, University of Bern.

years ago, and the courts are provided with new ways to decide fairly and justly upon what and who were involved in criminal acts. A strong system of justice requires an equally strong partner in forensic science. It can now be said that the best in criminal justice comes through the best in forensic science.

In order to make sense of where the field of forensic science finds itself today, we must first briefly start near the beginning of its development and provide a brief excursion through the history of forensic science.

1.2 BRIEF HISTORY OF FORENSIC SCIENCE

Forensic science can be defined as the application of scientific methods and principles to the investigation of crimes and criminals. In fact, the word "forensic" is derived from the same Latin root as the word for "forum," since it was in the ancient Roman forum that justice was commonly meted out. Forensic science is founded in the basic sciences, including chemistry, biology, physics, mathematics, and many others. It is also correctly considered to be an applied science since it uses the fundamental principles and methods from many basic disciplines to answer questions of a more practical nature: in this case, it means trying to address questions dealing specifically with legal issues. Forensic science is often closely affiliated with a field called *criminalistics*, defined by the U.S. National Institute of Justice as "the science and profession dealing with the recognition, collection, identification, individualization, and interpretation of physical evidence, and the application of the natural sciences to law-science matters."

Modern forensic science draws upon many aspects of the natural and applied sciences to help answer six basic questions of crime: who, what, when, where, why, and how. Throughout the ages, observant people have used "forensic" techniques to help solve crimes. As far back as thousands of years BCE, it appears that humans recognized the unique character of fingerprints for personal identification in cave paintings and on pottery (Figure 1.8). The early Romans and Greeks clearly used their understanding of the natural world to deduce logical arguments related to criminal prosecutions. In fact, Archimedes is occasionally cited as the "father of forensic science," and there are a number of instances where he certainly used science to unravel difficult legal questions, including his most famous "case" concerned with cheating in the creation of the emperor's golden crown (Chapter 11). The homicide investigation of Julius Caesar employed a detailed autopsy to determine which was the fatal blow, similar to how it is done today. Much later, Quintillian, a Roman attorney, used a bloody handprint to show that someone was trying to frame an innocent blind person in the homicide of his mother.

FIGURE 1.8 Ancient hand paintings at the "Cave of Hands" in Santa Cruz Province, Argentina. The paintings in the cave dates from 13,000 to 9,000 years ago.

Source: Shutterstock.com.

The realm of science can be divided into pure science, or research, and applied science. Basic research seeks to understand the physical world for its own sake; in applied science we seek to use the physical principles discovered to obtain a desired goal. Like medicine or engineering, the forensic analysis of physical evidence is an applied science, resting firmly on a foundation of the basic scientific principles of physics, chemistry, and biology.

(Inman and Rudin, 2001)

The first real attempt at a comprehensive "forensic science textbook," called *Hsi Duan Yu* ("Washing Away of Wrongs" or "Injustices Rectified"), was published around 1248 CE by a Chinese magistrate named Sung T'ze. This book, designed to help magistrates learn to investigate crimes, contained both collected historical cases and his personal experiences in an effort to avoid "injustices" that might lead to bloody acts of revenge and tragic feuds based upon unfounded suspicions and wrong conclusions. His text, published in 55 volumes, details many aspects of forensic science still used today, including examining injuries and wounds, conducting post-mortem autopsies, collecting physical evidence, and the logical analysis of the information gathered. For example, in his text, he reports the first clear use of forensic entomology to solve a murder case where a worker in the nearby rice fields had been murdered by means of a harvesting scythe. Through physical inspection, such as looking for blood and identifying marks, no clear evidence could be found linking any possible assailants with the crime. To solve the case, however, T'ze ingeniously had all the suspects line up before him in the hot afternoon sun while holding their scythes. Curiously, only one of the scythes attracted a swarm of blowflies to the blade – the one with invisible, minute traces of blood remaining on the blade. When confronted, the owner later confessed to the crime. This use of forensic entomology to solve this "dead-end" case was brought about by an understanding of how the natural world works, a basic tenant of forensic science.

BOX 1.1   EARLY DEVELOPMENT OF FORENSIC SCIENCE

- **BCE**: Fingerprints appeared as part of prehistoric paintings and pottery to reflect the individual identity of each artist.
- **2650 BCE**: Grand Vizier Imhotep in Egypt used medical ideas to investigate crimes.
- **44 BCE**: Antistius performed a detailed autopsy on Julius Caesar to help solve his murder.
- **7th Century CE**: Soleiman used fingerprints to validate borrowers and lenders.
- **10th Century CE**: Quintillion used handprints to exonerate a framed person.
- **1248 CE**: Sung T'se published the first manual on criminal investigations.
- **1530**: *Constitutio Criminalis Carolina* (Holy Roman Empire) gave courts the power to investigate crimes based solely upon the facts of the case.
- **1813**: Mathiew Orflia published the first true forensic toxicology treatise.
- **1835**: Henry Goddard (United Kingdom) first used ballistics information in a criminal case.
- **1836**: James Marsh presented the first toxicology test to a jury trial.
- **1856**: Sir William Herschel used fingerprints to identify people in the Indian Civil Service.
- **1883**: Alphonse Bertillon developed a system of anthropometry to help identify criminals by physical features.
- **1891**: Hans Gross published a book describing how science can broadly be used in criminal investigations and coined the term "criminalistics."
- **1896**: Sir Edward Henry developed the fingerprint classification system adopted throughout a large part of the world.
- **1900**: Karl Landsteiner discovered human blood groups and methods to type them.
- **1903**: New York State prison system adopted fingerprinting for inmate identification.
- **1910**: Edmund Locard (FR) established the world's first crime laboratory.
- **1924**: First U.S. Police Crime Laboratory (Los Angeles, California) established.
- **1932**: FBI laboratory founded.
- **1987**: First use of DNA in courtroom.
- **1996**: FBI introduced AFIS computer program for fingerprint comparisons.

The nose, as it cannot be disguised, is extremely important in identification.   The types above, taking them from the
left, show a low, narrow nose, a hooked nose, a straight nose, a snub nose, and a high, wide nose.

FIGURE 1.9   Bertillon's system of anthropometry for classifying nose types.

Source: Retrieved from Wikimedia Commons; used per Creative Commons Attribution.

From the 17th century through the early 19th century, a number of attempts were made to use forensic evidence to aid in criminal cases. The 18th century, however, with the Age of Enlightenment encouraging the use of reason and the burgeoning of scientific thought, brought the focus of science into the area of legal investigation. During that time, all sorts of scientific investigations probed the workings of nature and, not surprisingly, the fruits of these studies began to impact legal cases. Books were written on basic forensic anatomy, document examination, toxicology, and other areas, although the use of these methods in the courtroom was still rather sporadic, unsystematic, and unregulated.

The basis of modern forensic science really began to unfold, however, in the early to mid-1800s. Mathieu Orfila published a very detailed account of his work in forensic toxicology in 1813 and was the first person to attempt to identify blood on pieces of evidence using chemical tests. In 1835, Henry Goddard of Scotland Yard used bullet and firearm comparisons to trace bullets found in victims to the individual weapons that fired them, thereby tying the victim and the weapon together. Shortly afterward, James Marsh used his newly discovered test for arsenic in a jury trial while Jean Servais Stas reported a way to find plant poisons in a person's body. In 1856, Sir William Herschel used fingerprints on Indian Civil Service papers to verify identity for those who were illiterate. His work was followed by others, such as Henry Faulds (Scotland), Juan Vucetich (Argentina), Francis Galton (United Kingdom), Edward Henry (United Kingdom), and Henry DeForrest (United States), who developed systems for classifying fingerprints for personal identification based on similarities in patterns found in each print's details.

By the late 1800s, people increasingly began to recognize that physical traits, such as fingerprints, bones, and blood, could be used to help identify a person. This idea led to the work of the French Police Officer Alphonse Bertillon, who developed a detailed system involving the measurement of anatomical features which he believed could be used to identify a particular person, a field called anthropometry (Figure 1.9). Bertillon also photographed and recorded "mug" shots, tattoos, birthmarks, and scars to provide further identification aids (Figure 1.10). Prior to Bertillon's work (and before fingerprints became widely accepted), it was exceptionally difficult to identify criminals, especially repeat offenders who simply changed their names. Identification at the time was largely based upon eyewitness testimony – a very flawed system. However, despite its innovation, most of Bertillon's system was abandoned by the early 1900s, primarily because of three reasons: two police officers making the same measurement often came up with quite different values, physical features change with age, and the advent of quicker and more reliable fingerprinting systems. Bertillon's system, however, did inspire people to make detailed measurements of the human body – the forerunner of today's field of biometrics.

A few years after Bertillon, in 1889, Alexandre Lacassagne founded the first school to train individuals in developing subfields of forensic science, helping in standardizing practice across the varied disciplines. He contributed to laying the groundwork for a number of forensic areas including blood pattern analysis and firearms examination. This was soon followed by the publication of *Criminal Investigation* by Hans Gross in 1893 – the first book devoted to the application of scientific methods to criminal investigations and the first instance of coining the term *criminalistics*.

In the early years of the 1900s, Edmund Locard served as an assistant to Prof. Lacassagne in Lyon, France, and to Bertillon in Paris, where he applied his training in medicine and law to criminal investigations. In 1910, he left Lacassagne after persuading the Lyon Police Department to give him space in the attic and two assistants to set up what became the world's first police crime laboratory (Figure 1.11). As a result of his research, he formulated the basis for a principle today bearing his name that is fundamental to all of forensic science: *Locard's Exchange Principle*. Edmund Locard wrote:

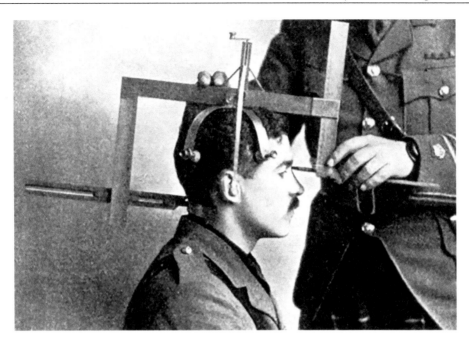

FIGURE 1.10 The taking of Bertillon measurements: measuring the height and reach of criminals at the Palace of Education at the 1904 World's Fair.

Source: Retrieved from Wikimedia Commons; used per Creative Commons Attribution.

FIGURE 1.11 Edmund Locard (1877–1966) in his forensic police laboratory in Lyon, France.

Source: Public Domain.

Wherever he steps, wherever he touches, whatever he leaves, even without consciousness, will serve as a silent witness against him. Not only his fingerprints or his footprints, but his hair, the fibers from his clothes, the glass he breaks, the tool mark he leaves, the paint he scratches, the blood or semen he deposits or collects. All of these and more, bear mute witness against him.

(Paul L. Kirk, 1953)

BOX 1.2   LOCARD'S EXCHANGE PRINCIPLE

Edmund Locard had an intense interest in furthering the use of science in criminal investigations. He believed that "whenever two objects came into contact, physical matter was exchanged between the two." Applying this idea to evidence simply requires the investigator to locate and identify the exchanged material to show that the two objects had indeed come into contact. For example, during the First World War, Locard analyzed stains and dirt from the uniforms of soldiers to help the French Secret Service determine how and where the soldiers had died. Locard also identified metal fragments in the clothing of coin counterfeiters that led to their confessions. He continued his work throughout his life and published his massive, seven-volume *Treatise on Criminalistics* in 1918.

Locard, often called the "French Sherlock Holmes," had much in common with the fictional detective. Locard, just ten when the Holmes series began, often pointed to the methods of Holmes. For example, Locard wrote:

I hold that a police expert, or an examining magistrate, would not find it a waste of his time to read Doyle's novels. For, in the adventures of Sherlock Holmes, the detective is repeatedly asked to diagnose the origin of a speck of mud, which is nothing but moist dust. The presence of a spot on a shoe or pair of trousers immediately made known to Holmes the particular quarter of London from which his visitor had come, or the road he had traveled in the suburbs.

(Edmond Locard, 1930)

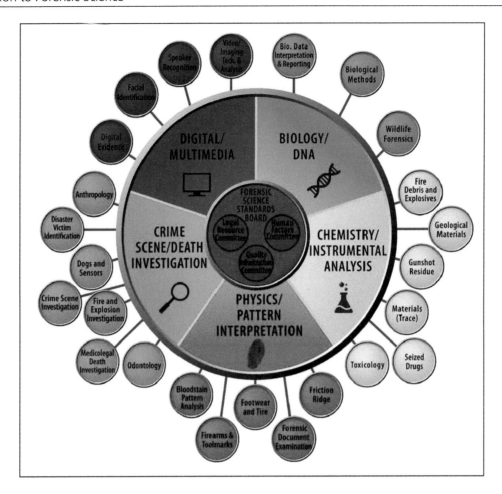

FIGURE 1.12   The organization of forensic disciplines, illustrating their connectedness.

Source: From the Organization of Scientific Committees for Forensic Science (OSAC) of NIST.

Locard used many of Holmes' techniques. For example, he was able to correctly identify the job of 92 of 100 individuals just through an analysis of the dust gathered from their eyebrows ("flour in the baker's, soot in the chimney sweep's, iron filings in the locksmith's," etc.).

The principle, first referred to as the Exchange Principle in 1940, simply states that "a criminal leaves something behind at a crime scene and also takes something away with them": evidence is transferred and exchanged between the scene and the criminal. The difficulty, of course, is to find the transferred evidence and to properly characterize it. Success in this task, however, often sheds light on the central legal issue of placing a suspect firmly at the crime scene. Locard's work led to the establishment of crime labs around the world and the rapid advance in the widespread application of scientific inquiry to criminal cases.

The first crime labs in the United States began appearing in the early 1920s, with the very first lab formally opened in 1924 by the Los Angeles Police Department. The Federal Bureau of Investigation (FBI), founded in 1908 by President Theodore Roosevelt, established their crime lab in 1932. Today,

the FBI crime laboratory is the largest in the world, performing well over 1 million analyses annually and encompassing a great range of scientific disciplines. Other labs around the world soon followed suit and have largely been modeled upon the FBI's structure and organization (Figure 1.12).

BOX 1.3   LOCARD'S CRIMINAL

Crime historian E.J. Wagner points out that Locard also felt that the criminal would "undo" themselves through the "excitement" of the crime. Wagner points to an example of Locard's belief when he wrote:

A recent example is provided by the terrorist who, in May 2010, left a car loaded with explosives in New York City's very busy Times Square. Evidently the "emotion of the moment" caused him to forget all his keys in the vehicle, leaving him unable to access either his getaway car, parked eight blocks away, or his domicile. As he also left his hazard lights on, the attention of the authorities was prompt. Locard, no doubt, would have smiled.

(Wagner, 2010/2011)

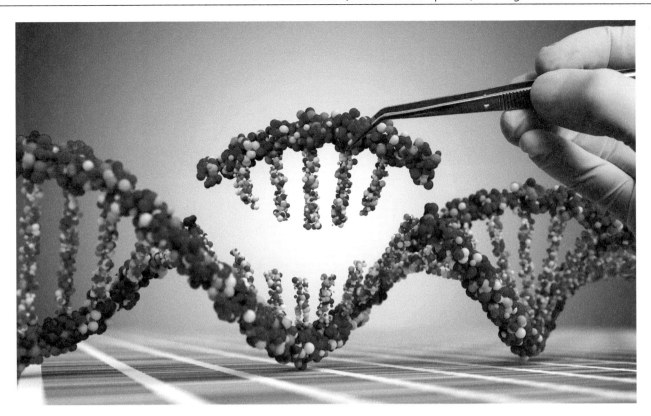

FIGURE 1.13   DNA analysis is often a vitally important component of forensic investigation.

Source: Shutterstock.com.

Crime labs worldwide have experienced rapid growth and development in the past half-century. Especially contributing to this growth has been the worldwide battle against illicit drug use and the advent of DNA technology (Figure 1.13). In the 1960s, large-scale efforts to stamp out illicit drug use through criminal detection and prosecution were initiated. Increased regulation, accompanied by the overwhelming connection of drugs and alcohol with crimes (nearly 80% of all crimes are estimated to have some drug or alcohol connection), has necessitated the rapid and accurate analysis of samples for possible drug content.

In the late 1980s, DNA technology revolutionized personal identification from biological samples. While advances in technology have enormously improved our ability to analyze DNA rapidly and accurately, there remains a mountainous backlog of samples awaiting analysis. With our growing reliance on science to shed light on criminal investigations comes a far greater need for enhanced analytical capabilities, further establishing the centrality of crime laboratories. Today, crime laboratories across the world seek to employ state-of-the-art instrumentation and best practices for evidence analysis. At the same time, laboratories are subject to tighter controls and stricter standards while operating in a highly regulated environment, and with an ever-increasing caseload of work.

More recently, the role of crime laboratories and forensic experts has evolved to encompass both new and "traditional" roles. While analysts are still called upon to examine evidence resulting from criminal behavior, they are increasingly asked to analyze evidence with broader implications. For instance, the FBI's Chemical-Biological Sciences Unit conducts forensic examinations of chemical, biological, radiological, nuclear, and explosive materials (CBRNE) that may be involved in terrorist activities. Additionally, the FBI's Terrorist Explosive Device Analytical Center provides analysis supporting the agency's fight against terrorism. The 21st century brings the inescapable certainty of new challenges and the prospect of far better tools with which to meet them to the world's forensic laboratories (Figure 1.14).

1.3 CRIME DETECTION IN LITERATURE

"I've found it! I've found it," he shouted to my companion, running towards us with a test-tube in his hand. "I have found a reagent which is precipitated by haemoglobin, and by nothing else." Had he discovered a gold mine, greater delight could not have shone upon his features.

(Conan Doyle, 1888)

These were the first words uttered by probably the greatest literature detective of all times, Sherlock Holmes, in the first book in the series: *A Study in Scarlet* (1888).

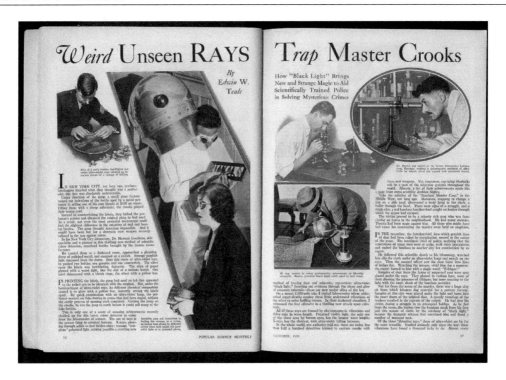

FIGURE 1.14 From an exhibit at *The National Library of Medicine at the National Institutes of Health*: "In the 19th and 20th centuries, glowing newspaper and magazine accounts of forensic technologies, real and imaginary, fueled public support for scientific crime detection." A series of illustrated articles that were published in the 1931 *Popular Science Monthly* by Edwin W. Teale, displays the public's fascination with scientific crime detection. "Working slowly, painstakingly, utilizing every branch of science at hand, modern man-hunters are arriving at astonishing solutions in baffling crimes. Their work is analytical, methodical; but their results are amazing, magical."

Source: NIH.

People have long been fascinated by the fictional accounts of super-sleuths in criminal detection, especially those who employ scientific methods in seemingly miraculous ways for solving baffling crimes and catching the criminals. While it may seem surprising to discuss the accounts and methods of fictional detectives in a forensic science textbook, the connection is both justified and important. Unlike many other fields, the techniques and methods of modern forensic science have often been foretold and even inspired by their first "use" in fictional settings. Fingerprints, chemical analyses for blood, logical deductive reasoning, and aspects of toxicology are just some of the detection techniques employed in fictional literature long before they were widely accepted or even discovered in real-life situations. The criminal justice community has often been awakened to the possibility of using scientific methods to solve difficult problems through the fictional accounts of brilliant detectives, much to the thrilled delight of readers.

Possibly the very first fictional "forensic" detective was C. Auguste Dupin, who first emerged from the pen of Edgar Allan Poe in *The Murders in the Rue Morgue* (1841), *The Mystery of Marie Roget* (1842), and *The Purloined Letter* (1844) (Figure 1.15). The fictional Dupin used a combination of deductive reasoning and insightful imagination to uncover the hidden causes and effects of baffling criminal mysteries – techniques that were not commonly employed by

real investigators during the age when the stories were written. Poe's work came about even before the term detective had been coined. The groundbreaking detective work of the fictional Dupin, a private citizen investigating crime for his own motivations rather than as an official of the police force, proved to be very popular with readers and led to new ways of thinking about solving crimes. Dupin indirectly paved the way for the advent of probably the greatest of all fictional detectives, Sherlock Holmes (Figure 1.16). In fact, some of the "tricks" of mental reasoning and logic so closely attributed to the later Holmes actually first appeared with Dupin. For example, Dupin "reads" the mind of his friend (the story's narrator) by deductively tracing his thoughts through 15 minutes of silence to arrive, seemingly by magic, at the same mental place as his friend – just as Holmes did nearly 40 years later to the incredulous Watson (see Box 1.4). One of Dupin's methods was to imagine himself as the criminal, to "put himself into the criminal's mind," a technique now employed in some areas of forensic psychology, such as in a forensic "psychological autopsy" and criminal profiling. Poe's Dupin established detective fiction as distinct from mystery fiction and focused upon analytical reasoning and logical deduction based on careful observation. In essence, it encouraged a growing popular fascination with the scientific analysis of legal evidence in criminal cases that was just beginning to occur in real life.

FIGURE 1.15 C. Auguste Dupin, a fictional detective created by Edgar Allan Poe, in the case of *The Purloined Letter.*
Source: Public Domain.

FIGURE 1.16 The Sherlock Holmes Museum on Baker Street, one of the famous tourist attractions in London.
Source: Shutterstock.com.

BOX 1.4   THE MIND READING HOLMES?

Excerpt from *The Adventure of the Cardboard Box* by Arthur C. Doyle, 1893.

"Finding that Holmes was too absorbed for conversation, I had tossed aside the barren paper, and leaning back in my chair I fell into a brown study. Suddenly my companion's voice broke in upon my thoughts."

FIGURE 1.17   Silhouette of the Sherlock Holmes statue in London near Baker Street.

Source: Shutterstock.com.

"You are right, Watson," said he. "It does seem a most preposterous way of settling a dispute."

"Most preposterous!" I exclaimed, and then suddenly realizing how he had echoed the inmost thought of my soul, I sat up in my chair and stared at him in blank amazement.

"What is this, Holmes?" I cried. "This is beyond anything which I could have imagined."

He laughed heartily at my perplexity.

"You remember," said he, "that some little time ago when I read you the passage in one of Poe's sketches in which a close reasoner follows the unspoken thoughts of his companion, you were inclined to treat the matter as a mere tour-de-force of the author. On my remarking that I was constantly in the habit of doing the same thing you expressed incredulity."

"Oh, no!"

"Perhaps not with your tongue, my dear Watson, but certainly with your eyebrows. So when I saw you throw down your paper and enter upon a train of thought, I was very happy to have the opportunity of reading it off, and eventually of breaking into it, as a proof that I had been in rapport with you."

But I was still far from satisfied. "In the example which you read to me," said I, "the reasoner drew his conclusions from the actions of the man whom he observed. If I remember right, he stumbled over a heap of stones, looked up at the stars, and so on. But I have been seated quietly in my chair, and what clues can I have given you?"

"You do yourself an injustice. The features are given to man as the means by which he shall express his emotions, and yours are faithful servants."

"Do you mean to say that you read my train of thoughts from my features?"

"Your features and especially your eyes. Perhaps you cannot yourself recall how your reverie commenced?"

"No, I cannot."

"Then I will tell you. After throwing down your paper, which was the action which drew my attention to you, you sat for half a minute with a vacant expression. Then your eyes fixed themselves upon your newly framed picture of General Gordon, and I saw by the alteration in your face that a train of thought had been started. But it did not lead very far. Your eyes flashed across to the unframed portrait of Henry Ward Beecher which stands upon the top of your books. Then you glanced up at the wall, and of course your meaning was obvious. You were thinking that if the portrait were framed it would just cover that bare space and correspond with Gordon's picture there."

"You have followed me wonderfully!" I exclaimed.

"So far I could hardly have gone astray. But now your thoughts went back to Beecher, and you looked hard across as if you were studying the character in his features. Then your eyes ceased to pucker, but you continued to look across, and your face was thoughtful. You were recalling the incidents of Beecher's career. I was well aware that you could not do this without thinking of the mission which he undertook on behalf of the North at the time of the Civil War, for I remember you expressing your passionate indignation at the way in which he was received by the more turbulent of our people. You felt so strongly about it that I knew you could not think of Beecher without thinking of that also. When a moment later I saw your eyes wander away from the picture, I suspected that your mind had now turned to the Civil War, and when I observed that your lips set, your eyes sparkled, and your hands clenched I was positive that you were indeed thinking of the gallantry which was shown by both sides in that desperate struggle. But then, again, your face grew sadder, you shook your head. You were dwelling upon the sadness and horror and useless waste of life. Your hand stole towards your own old wound and a smile quivered on your lips, which showed me that the ridiculous side of this method of settling international questions had forced itself upon your mind. At this point I agreed with you that it was preposterous and was glad to find that all my deductions had been correct."

"Absolutely!" said I. "And now that you have explained it, I confess that I am as amazed as before."

While Dupin was the first, Holmes is certainly the most famous of all fictional detectives, whose technique grew from close observation, detailed measurement, and sharp scientific reasoning – the basis of modern forensic science (Figure 1.17). Holmes was the 1887 creation of Sir Arthur Conan Doyle, a Scottish physician who turned to writing to help fill the empty hours of a relatively unsuccessful medical practice. The fictional Holmes was loosely based on Doyle's medical school professor, Dr. Joseph Bell, from the University of Edinburgh Medical School. As his assistant at Edinburgh, Doyle had the chance to see Bell's remarkable style and brilliance at work close up. Doyle wrote that Dr. Bell would often just sit in his receiving room and "diagnose the people as they came in, before they even opened their mouths. He would tell them details of their past life; and hardly would he ever make a mistake." When later creating the character of Sherlock Holmes, Doyle

> thought of my old teacher Joe Bell, of his eagle face, of his curious ways, of his eerie trick of spotting details. If he were a detective he would surely reduce this fascinating but unorganized business to something nearer an exact science.
>
> *(Arthur Conan Doyle)*

Doyle once wrote to Bell, saying, "I do not think that [Holmes'] analytical work is in the least an exaggeration of some effects which I have seen you produce in the out-patient ward."

The works of Doyle clearly captured the public imagination by solving fictional crimes that had baffled and bewildered the official police force. People would line up for days outside news shops and booksellers awaiting the latest release of the serialized Holmes stories in *The Strand Magazine*. The Holmes saga remains as popular today as it was when it was first released around the turn of the 20th century, with strong book sales, movies, new Holmes-based books by current authors, and worldwide Holmesian Societies celebrating the life and times of the great fictional detective.

While Holmes was purely fictional, essentially an artifact of Arthur Conan Doyle's mind, his methods presaged and inspired many areas of criminal detection, making a lasting and significant contribution to modern forensic science. Sherlock Holmes' use of keen observational skills, coupled with his detached scientific approach, shed light on seemingly

BOX 1.5   A MODEL FOR HOLMES: DR. JOE BELL

Dr. Joseph Bell, a professor of Arthur Conan Doyle's, was an amazing observer who taught his students the power of observation and deductive reasoning. One classic example of Bell in instructing his students provides a glimpse into his methods:

"This, gentlemen" announced Professor Bell, contains a very potent drug. To the taste it is intensely bitter. It is most offensive to the sense of smell. But I want you to test it by smell and taste; and, as I don't ask anything of my students which I wouldn't be willing to do myself, I will taste it before passing it round.

(Arthur C. Doyle, 1924)

Here, he dipped his finger in the liquid and placed it in his mouth. The tumbler was passed around. With wry and sour faces, the students followed the Professor's lead. One after another tasted the liquid; varied and amusing were the grimaces made. The tumbler, having gone around, was returned to the Professor.

"Gentlemen," said he, with a laugh,

I am deeply grieved to find that not one of you has developed this power of perception, which I so often speak about; for if you watched me closely, you would have found that, while I placed my forefinger in the medicine, it was the middle finger which found its way into my mouth.

(From "The Original of Sherlock Holmes" by Dr. Harold Emery Jones, 1904)

intractable criminal problems. Holmes used fingerprints before they were employed in real-life investigations. Additionally, he certainly employed forensic chemistry in many of his "cases" long before the actual chemical analyses existed. Holmes, apart from what some modern detractors might say, was a consummate chemist and scientist. He saw the need for detailed comparative analysis when he described his manuscript on a method for distinguishing "140 types of tobacco by their ashes" and the "anatomy of the human ear." At the time when

FIGURE 1.18 Agatha Christie's brilliant detective, Hercule Poirot, portrayed by Sir David Suchet.

Source: Shutterstock.com.

the Holmes saga began, police agencies were typically rather slow in adopting new methods into their investigations – often taking decades to accept new practices. Holmes' use of fingerprints, chemical analyses, ballistics, handwriting analyses, cryptology, microscopic examinations of trace evidence, and many other methods certainly helped move police agencies to consider these techniques long before they would have under other circumstances.

The exploits of Holmes have served to inspire generations of detectives, both real and imaginary, to employ logical reasoning in their case work, including Edmund Locard. In fact, Sherlock Holmes (and not Arthur Conan Doyle) was inducted in 2002 into the United Kingdom's Royal Society of Chemistry as a Fellow, a very prestigious honor, for his "pioneering work in forensic science." Holmes' famous words from *The Adventure of the Blanched Soldier* (1926) encapsulate his reliance on careful deduction and analytical reasoning based on the scientific method: "The process … starts upon the supposition that when you have eliminated all which is impossible, then whatever remains, however improbable, must be the truth."

While Holmes occupies a central place in the development of modern forensic science, Doyle clearly is not the only author whose work has contributed to the development of the discipline. Characters such as Dorothy L. Sayers' Lord Peter Wimsey and Agatha Christie's Hercule Poirot (Figure 1.18) and Miss Jane Marple have helped lead the way for the use

of deductive reasoning and the application of tenets of the scientific method in actual criminal investigations. These and other authors formed *The Detection Club* in 1930 to help each other with technical and scientific aspects of their crime fiction and to debate new directions for real science to follow in criminal detection. Their stories helped to cement in the public opinion the centrality of science in providing vital information in criminal cases. The works of these authors, in a way, have continued the Holmesian tradition, often through startlingly clear analyses based on knowledge and observation, with no less interest and devotion to their exploits by their readers.

Today, modern authors are continuing this long-standing tradition of science-based fictional super-sleuths. Laboratory-based forensic scientists and Holmesian detectives have made their way into our homes and theaters through television and movies. Detective, true crime, and forensic practitioners are perennially among the most popular shows. *CSI: Crime Scene Investigation*, *NCIS (Naval Criminal Investigative Services)*, *Bones*, *Monk*, *Cold Case Files*, and *House* are just a few of the popular programs that rely heavily on scientific evidence in solving baffling cases, often with unlikely and intriguing twists and turns of the plot. Recently, six of the top ten television shows were, not surprisingly, detective shows. These shows have spun off into a multitude of other fictional programs and movies that follow forensic pathologists, toxicologists, anthropologists, chemists, trace analysts, and many other forensic specialty professions as they go about their work. The general public is now not only comfortable with forensic evidence as never before, but they actually seek out opportunities to test their "forensic skills" with whodunits.

But television shows and movies have also had a much broader impact upon the criminal justice and medical examiner's world in ways far more important to real life than just providing interesting entertainment and education. They raise both the expectation and the demand of the general public regarding the information that forensic science can provide, often by exaggerating to impossible levels the role that forensic science plays in cases. Many legal professionals believe that these programs inspire an unrealistic need and reliance on "high-tech" methods for all cases, in both police work and legal prosecutions. Cases are considered "weak" unless all possible forms of forensic evidence are exhaustively presented during a trial, even if they are irrelevant or unnecessary. For example, in a recent case, the jury asked the judge why a DNA analysis of a blood sample from the crime scene had not been performed to show that it came from the defendant – the reason it had not been done was that the defendant admitted that he had been at the crime scene and that the blood was his. In this case, the DNA analysis would have provided no additional information that the court didn't already have and was, therefore, completely superfluous and certainly not needed – and, therefore, possibly not even admissible. The term "CSI Effect" has been coined to describe the observation that juries now often demand and require forensic evidence in criminal trials, even when unnecessary. This not only raises the prosecution's burden of proof for a conviction to levels that just cannot be delivered by current science, but the defense is also burdened by the jury's exaggerated faith in the reliability of forensic evidence. This demand for more and more forensic analysis has placed increasing workloads on existing forensic laboratories, with associated sky-rocketing costs for analytical equipment, specialized analyst training, and court appearances as experts, which take scientists away from the lab to explain the complex and potentially useless evidence to lay juries. Some prosecutors are even now going to the lengths of bringing in experts to inform juries that they *don't* need certain types of forensic evidence in order to render a verdict and that the absence of this evidence does not weaken a case. The CSI Effect has certainly engendered the public image that forensic science is fast, infallible, and always successful in catching the criminal – things that in reality are not always true. Not all crime scenes deliver testable DNA or other evidence, and evidence can degrade from environmental factors before it even reaches the lab.

Maybe part of the appeal of Holmes and other fictional detectives is that they personify all that we *hope* to see from forensic science – analytic reasoning, brilliant deduction, careful observation, detailed measurements, and supportable conclusions – all this while maintaining the highest ethical standards. But successful fictional characters also retain some of their clearly human traits and quirks that we can personally relate to and which endear them to us: they are, after all, human, and they create a connection between the impersonal and logical realm of forensic science and the real human world. Real-life forensic science certainly also has its human side. Crimes are not solved by science alone; it still takes human intellect combined with experience and creativity to bring it all together. However, despite all this, fiction has certainly been in the vanguard of the application of science to law that is so central to criminal justice today (Figure 1.19).

FIGURE 1.19 Sherlock Holmes, from the case of *The Man with the Twisted Lip.*

Source: First appeared in Paget (1891).

1.4 THE DYNAMIC DUO OF PRINCIPLES

Two basic principles underlie much of forensic science today: *Locard's Exchange Principle* and *The Principle of Individuality.* While often taken for granted, reliance on these basic concepts allows us to fundamentally apply scientific methods to establishing possible relationships between evidence and a criminal act.

1.4.1 Locard's Principle

In Section 1.2, the concept of Locard's Exchange Principle was introduced. This principle is central to all forensic evidence collection and briefly states that *when two objects come into contact, some materials or information are transferred between the two.* If this transferred evidence can be found, then the connection between the two objects may be established. For example, glass shards, pollen, or DNA found on a suspect's clothing can link them directly to a victim or crime scene. Similarly, body fluid, hairs, or fingerprints from a suspect found at the crime scene can likewise link the two. It may even be possible to link cocaine crystals in the fibers of paper money with drug activity (Figure 1.20).

FIGURE 1.20 Locard's Principle says that whenever two objects touch, something is transferred. This picture shows how cocaine may be transferred to paper money and trapped in the fibers through physical contact.

Source: Shutterstock.com.

The common thread that links together evidentiary items with a person or place can be definitive in a case. Locard's principle also goes beyond criminal cases, however, to include applications in civil trials, identification of remains (even if the identification is primarily for remains recovery, such as from combat zones and accidents), authentication of important documents, and other uses. Finding an artist's inadvertent fingerprint (something that they "left behind") on a canvas can verify a painting's authenticity or DNA data that connects a parent to their offspring are all simple extensions of Locard's Principle.

1.4.2 Principle of Individuality

An important idea originating from philosophy states that each person is separate and different from all other people, no matter how similar they may otherwise appear. In forensic science, however, this principle of individuality (or principle of uniqueness) is modified to state that *even though two objects may be indistinguishable, they can never be identical.* This means that while we might not be able to tell the difference between two objects at sight, at some level – maybe even only at the atomic or molecular level – they *must* be different (Figure 1.21). Extending this simple idea should allow us to determine whether or not two samples came from one original source or from two completely separate sources. Once again, this idea is useful in tying together two pieces of evidence when they come from a single, unique source. The main question, of course, is, *do we have the ability to distinguish*

between two objects given the experimental techniques available to us? For example, even identical twins are not exactly identical – one may have a scar or a different fingerprint that serves to distinguish one from the other even though they have the same DNA sequence. In this instance, the method for distinguishing between the two is fairly simple – look for scars and other small physical differences. In forensics, for example, two bullets may be made successively by the same manufacturer at the same time and packaged together but when fired from a gun, differences can be found to distinguish between the two. The application of the principle, in this case, is limited by our ability to find uniquely distinguishing features separating the two bullets. This principle, in theory, allows us to look for similarities and differences to support or refute connections between two pieces of evidence.

Sometimes, additional principles are considered in forensic science besides these two. The *principle of comparison* focuses on measurement of the similarities and differences between two people or pieces of evidence. It typically deals with the necessity to have a standard sample of known origin to compare with an unknown sample to establish a relationship. The *principle of progressive change* states that objects change over time: while it may take a long time to observe these changes, change is nonetheless inevitable and must be considered. The *principle of analysis* states that any scientific analysis can only be as good as the quality of the sample being analyzed.

In Chapter 2, we will examine the characteristics of evidence that can allow us to build upon the principle of individuality in forensic cases by distinguishing evidence by its *class* or *individual* characteristics.

FIGURE 1.21   All objects, even though they may be indistinguishable (or nearly so), are never identical.

Source: Shutterstock.com.

1.5 LEGAL PRECEDENT OF SCIENCE IN THE COURTROOM

Societies are fundamentally based on a mutually agreed-upon set of laws that establish acceptable boundaries of behavior for its citizens and allow for both the punishment of those who step over those boundaries and the protection of innocent members from the criminal actions of others. Without laws, we cannot have a civilized, safe, and just society. Laws are written and decided on through legislative action, but it is up to the courts to find ways to interpret laws in relation to a wide variety of everyday situations.

Legal practice in most common law systems, including in the United States and much of the world, is rooted in the use of *precedent cases* that carve a pathway through the legal forest upon which future cases may travel more smoothly (Figure 1.22). These key cases also serve to translate the intent of our written laws into actual day-to-day practice and to provide consistency between cases. Precedent cases form guides and, in some cases, dictate future court decisions. They provide specific examples and authority for judges to follow when they encounter new cases that are similar to those that have

already been decided. *Black's Law Dictionary* refers to a legal precedent as the "rule of law established for the first time by a court for a particular type of case and thereafter referred to in deciding similar cases." A binding precedent is a decision that binds the actions of lower courts. In a way, this process can speed up the judicial process by not having to "reinvent the wheel" each time a particular legal question arises, such as whether fingerprint or toxicology evidence is admissible. In fact, decisions from higher courts are generally binding to lower courts within a system of justice (something legally called *stare decisis*, from the Latin meaning "to stand by things decided"). For example, U.S. Supreme Court decisions are binding to all lower courts in the federal judicial system, although not necessarily binding to a state court system (unless the state court is ruling on federal law). In other words, courts try to stand by and adhere to legal questions that have already been settled.

The fundamental role of forensic science is to *inform courts* on scientific and technical areas where the courts lack knowledge or expertise. But, in addition, the courts need guidance about what constitutes good science and what does not – court proceedings definitely need to be protected from misleading, improper, incorrect, and unreliable scientific evidence and testimony. As scientific concepts and methods

FIGURE 1.22 Legal precedents help clear the path for future cases.

Source: Shutterstock.com.

become increasingly complex, the gulf between what is good science and the public's understanding of science continues to grow. Historically, in the years leading up to 1923, "scientific" and "expert" testimony was poorly regulated and the decision about what to believe was left entirely up to the jury to decide without any real help or guidance. Self-proclaimed (and often profit-seeking) "experts" could say almost anything they wanted, regardless of whether it was founded in good practice or not, and court records show that some of the most misguided and incorrect testimony was presented alongside good scientific testimony without any guide for distinguishing between the two. Sometimes, defense lawyers presented conflicting ideas through their "experts" simply to confuse juries and steer them away from true scientific findings. Juries were stuck in the middle and often chose to believe what they could understand, or they simply decided based on who had the best presentation – not on the scientific merits of the case. This situation needed to change, and it dramatically did in 1923 with the Frye case (*vide infra*).

Today, the admission of scientific evidence and expert testimony in court proceedings is regulated by a web of precedent cases and rules of evidence (Figure 1.23). The best forensic analysis and testimony are, of course, useless unless they are admissible in court. Admissibility standards have been developed over the years pertaining to exactly how and when scientific evidence can be admitted into court proceedings. A few specific precedent cases, however, have become so important today in determining the admissibility of forensic evidence that it is necessary to examine these central precedent cases in some detail.

1.5.1 First There Was Frye

In November 1920, a notable physician in Washington, DC, Dr. Robert Brown, was shot dead in his own office. Dr. Brown's partner and other witnesses saw the shooting and pursued the attacker until being shot at themselves. The attacker got away. Seven months later, however, James Frye was captured during an armed robbery attempt and confessed to both the robbery and the murder of Dr. Brown. Frye later took back his confession before his trial on the advice of his defender. But Frye's defense case was very weak – no credible alibi that would hold up in court was found, and other evidence against him was strong. In an attempt to build a case, Frye's defense lawyer had a very early version of the lie detector test performed on Frye by psychologist Dr. William Marston (Figure 1.24). The test was very simple – Frye was asked questions and his blood pressure and heart rate were monitored (Figure 1.25). The idea is that your body responds "naturally" to the act of lying by changes in physiology, such as changes in blood pressure, sweating, heart rate, and breathing rate, among others. Probably not surprisingly, Frye "passed" the lie detector test and was declared innocent by the analyst. But when the defense tried to enter this evidence into court, the judge ruled that the evidence was not admissible on scientific validity grounds (the entire debate was held in full hearing of the jury, so they knew the result of the lie detector test anyway). After a four-day trial, Frye was found guilty. The case was appealed, ultimately to the Federal Circuit Court of Appeals in the District of Columbia, on the grounds that the lie detector evidence should have been admitted. The decision to exclude the lie detector evidence was,

FIGURE 1.23 Courts rely on expert testimony to inform the courts in areas where it lacks needed expertise.

Source: iStockphoto.com.

FIGURE 1.24   Early version of the lie detector used by Dr. William Marston in the Frye case, relying on blood pressure and heart rate measurements.

Source: Public Domain.

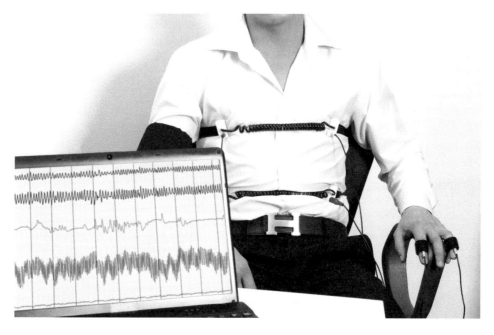

FIGURE 1.25   Modern polygraphs (lie detectors) monitor several types of physiological responses including blood pressure, heart rate, skin conductivity/perspiration, and others.

Source: Shutterstock.com.

however, upheld on the appeal, and the court set the first real precedent for determining when scientific evidence could be admitted in court when they wrote:

> Just when a scientific principle or discovery crosses the line between the experimental and demonstrative stages is difficult to define. Somewhere in this twilight zone the evidential force of the principle must be recognized, and while courts will go a long way in admitting expert testimony deduced from a well-recognized scientific principle or discovery, the thing from which the deduction is made must be sufficiently established to have general acceptance in the particular field in which it belongs.

(Judge Van Orsdel, 1923)

The Frye decision quickly became the standard for the admissibility of all expert scientific testimony in the United States, in both federal and state courts. The key feature of the Frye Standard is that the "relevant field" of science became the decider as to what was admissible and what was not. Under this standard, a potential expert and their testimony must meet the "Frye test" before they are allowed to testify and have their evidence admitted. For example, a toxicologist cannot testify about a surgical procedure as surgery is not their particular field. Similarly, a toxicologist cannot testify about a chemical test that has not been generally accepted by other toxicologists and chemists. The courts were also provided guidance as to how to determine whether or not a particular technique has met this standard. A scientific technique meets the Frye standard by demonstrating that it has appeared in published books and papers, has been accepted in prior judicial decisions, and has been in existence for a long time.

Frye, therefore, set the first standard for the admissibility of scientific evidence in court. However, it is relatively slow and rigid when it comes to admitting newly discovered methods since it requires broad acceptance in the field. Today, about half of the U.S. state courts are still governed by the Frye standard.

1.5.2 A Trilogy of Cases: Daubert and Friends

In the 1990s, a trio of cases helped to revise the Frye standard and set new guidelines on what types of forensic evidence and expert testimony could be admissible in court. In the years between 1923 and 1993, new rules of evidence were passed by Congress, and a great deal of conflicting precedent law had occurred in different courts, leading to some confusion about the admissibility of scientific and expert testimony. These cases defined a new understanding of the admissibility of scientific evidence and eliminated some of the problems encountered with Frye while still giving the courts clear guidance on how to proceed.

Daubert Case: In 1993, a case challenged the centrality of Frye and ended up setting a new standard. In this case, a group of people alleged that a pregnancy "morning sickness" drug, called Bendectin, had caused birth defects in their children. They sued the Merrell Dow Pharmaceutical Company, the manufacturer of the drug, for damages. The case, called *Daubert v. Merrell Dow Pharmaceuticals* (pronounced "Dow-Bert"), was tried in U.S. Federal court. Dow argued that the plaintiffs (people bringing the suit) did not have enough of a case to proceed since Daubert's experts did not present any published scientific link between Bendectin and birth defects, and therefore, there was no link between the drug's use and limb deformations (Figure 1.26). Instead, Daubert's experts presented evidence suggesting that Bendectin *could* cause birth defects, but this evidence was based upon new analytical methods that had not gained widespread acceptance in the scientific community. The court granted a judgment in favor of Dow and said that the Daubert

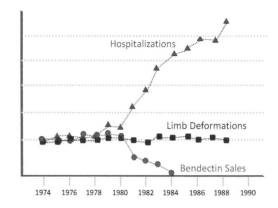

FIGURE 1.26 A plot of *Bendectin* use verses limb deformation.

side had not presented sufficient relevant admissible evidence. The case was ultimately appealed to the U.S. Supreme Court, which reversed the lower court's decision concerning the admissibility of the scientific evidence, ruling that the 1975 *Federal Rules of Evidence* effectively replaced Frye as the new standard:

> If scientific, technical, or other specialized knowledge will assist the trier of fact to understand the evidence or to determine a fact in issue, a witness qualified as an expert by knowledge, skill, experience, training, or education, may testify thereto in the form of an opinion or otherwise.

(Federal Rules of Evidence, Rule 702)

The importance of this new rule, essentially replacing Frye, is that expert testimony does not *require* general acceptance by the scientific community to be admissible in court. Instead, it sets up a series of three standards for scientific evidence and expert testimony:

- **Scientific Basis**: The testimony must be grounded in supported scientific knowledge gained through the application of the scientific method. The method must be based on sufficient facts or data, be the product of reliable methods, and must be properly carried out.
- **Relevance**: The testimony must assist the trier of facts (usually the judge and/or jury) in deciding the issues at hand – there must be a connection between the knowledge being presented and the issue in question – no relevance, no admission to court.
- **Judge as "Gatekeeper"**: The judge is designated as the person who decides whether a particular piece of scientific testimony is sufficiently established and is relevant to the issue at hand. This requires the judge to determine if the "reasoning or methodology underlying the testimony is scientifically valid and whether that reasoning or methodology properly can be applied."

The new Daubert standard, now used in all federal courts and about half of state courts, is more flexible in admitting new types of evidence and relies on the adversarial system of examining and cross-examining witnesses to test the soundness of the scientific principles presented. As in Frye, however, judges still can rely on help from the scientific field by considering the following:

- If the technique or theory has been tested.
- If the technique or theory has been subjected to peer review.
- If the technique's potential error rate is known.
- If there are standards controlling the performance of the analysis.
- If the theory or method has received widespread acceptance within the appropriate community.

The Daubert case provided the needed flexibility that Frye did not have. However, several other cases after Daubert have served to define further and extend the importance of this ruling to key situations.

BOX 1.8   DEFINITIONS AND KEY CASES

Precedent: A legal principle or rule that comes from a court decision that can be used as a point of reference for deciding other cases.

Binding Precedent: A decision from a higher court that must be followed by lower courts in similar cases.

Frye Standard: The 1923 precedent case that sets the standard for admissibility of scientific evidence in court as requiring general acceptance of the scientific methodology in its relevant field.

Daubert Standard: A 1993 precedent case that sets the trial judge as the "gatekeeper" for what scientific testimony is admissible.

Joiner Case: A case that requires experts to limit their opinions to straightforward extensions of the data and imposes limitations on what they can say.

Khumo Tire Case: A case that requires all expert testimony to meet the Daubert standard – not just scientific expert testimony.

Stare Decisis: From the Latin *"stare decisis et non quieta movere"* meaning "to stand by decisions and not disturb the undisturbed," indicating that decisions from higher courts are generally binding on lower courts.

Melendez-Dias: A precedent case where defendants may require analysts to "face" them in court when presenting scientific analyses.

Joiner Case: In 1995, a case called *General Electric Co. v. Joiner* was brought, asserting that, based on loosely-linked animal studies, certain chemicals used by the company caused cancer in a former employee. In the decision, the court limited how far an expert may "stray" from either the data or from commonly accepted practice. They said that:

> conclusions and methodology are not separate. Experts commonly extrapolate from existing data but nothing requires a court to admit opinion evidence that is connected to the data only by the expert themselves.
>
> *(General Electric Co. v. Joiner, 1997)*

This means that the court may conclude that there is too great a gap between the data and the opinion of the expert to allow it into court.

Khumo Tire Case: In 1999, a case was brought against the Khumo Tire Company in which a plaintiff claimed that an automotive tire blowout and subsequent accident resulted from a defective tire and was, therefore, the fault of the tire's manufacturer (Khumo). The "expert" for the plaintiffs relied upon a method that was determined not to be scientifically valid or even previously tested. The judge excluded the invalid testimony. When the case finally reached the Supreme Court, they ruled that the Daubert standard applied to *all* expert testimony – whether scientific or "skill or experience-based." They said that the court must

> make certain that an expert … employs the same level of intellectual rigor that characterizes the practice of an expert in the relevant field.
>
> *(Kumho Tire Co. v. Carmichael, 1999)*

These cases – Frye, Daubert, Joiner, and Khumo – have set the standard for the admission of forensic evidence in the courtroom today and form the basis of how forensic analysis makes its way into trials.

1.5.3 Recent Additions: Melendez-Dias Case

A recent decision by the Supreme Court has added a new wrinkle to the admissibility of forensic evidence and testimony in court. In 2009, the prosecutor in a drug case introduced the chemical analysis from the state's crime lab stating that the material seized by police during an arrest was cocaine. The analysis was performed using standard practice, sworn before a notary public, and submitted in the normal fashion to the court. The defense, however, argued that the *actual individual* who ran the analysis must testify in person using as a basis for their argument the constitutional requirement that a person has the right to face their accusers (Sixth Amendment, U.S. Constitution). The Supreme Court upheld the defense's argument, resulting in the individual analyst who runs a test on a sample to possibly be required to testify in person (Figure 1.27). Concerns about this new requirement include problems connected with taking analysts out of the lab where they do their work and requiring them to participate in lengthy

FIGURE 1.27 The Melendez-Diaz Case found that lab technicians may be required to personally testify about their analyses in court.

Source: Shutterstock.com.

courtroom trials. It also raises the problem of what happens when an analyst is no longer available to testify (e.g., retires, leaves employment, dies, etc.) – possibly the evidence would no longer be admissible.

1.5.3.1 Voir Dire *Process*

An important process in the legal system, with respect to expert testimony, is referred to as *voir dire* (from Old French meaning "speaking [or seeing] the truth"). This process involves a preliminary examination of an expert witness or a potential juror. With respect to expert witnesses, the *voir dire* process is used to establish their expertise and validity to present to the court. Once vetted in this process, including by application of the legal precedents we've talked about in this chapter, the expert is cleared for presenting their testimony.

Through these cases, we now have a pretty clear picture of when and how scientific evidence can be admitted into court. In Chapter 2, we will explore how forensic evidence makes its way from a crime scene into the laboratory.

QUESTIONS FOR FURTHER PRACTICE AND MASTERY

1.1 What is forensic science?
1.2 What is the Daubert standard?
1.3 What is Locard's Exchange Principle?
1.4 What is meant by the "CSI Effect" when it comes to jury expectations during a trial?
1.5 What is the Principle of Individuality?
1.6 What is meant by a "precedent" case? Give examples of precedent cases and explain their significance.
1.7 How did the Frye decision of 1923 impact the admissibility of forensic evidence and testimony?
1.8 What standard replaced the Frye standard, and how did it change the use of forensic evidence at trial?
1.9 List and explain the three parts of the Daubert standard.
1.10 Explain the importance of the Joiner (1995) and Khumo (1999) cases as they pertain to forensic testimony.

GLOSSARY OF TERMS

anthropometry: a detailed system involving the measurement of anatomical features.
binding precedent: a decision from a higher court that must be followed by lower courts in similar cases.
C. Auguste Dupin: the first fictional detective created by Edgar Allan Poe.

criminalistics: (U.S. National Institute of Justice definition) "the science and profession dealing with the recognition, collection, identification, individualization, and interpretation of physical evidence, and the application of the natural sciences to law-science matters."

CSI effect: an empirical theory that proposes that television shows based on crime solving with a heavy reliance on forensic science has made jurors in real-life cases more reluctant to convict when some forms of forensic evidence are neither necessary nor available for the trial.

Daubert standard: a 1993 U.S. Supreme Court ruling that sets the trial judge as the "gatekeeper" for what scientific testimony is admissible.

forensic science: the application of scientific methods and principles to the investigation of crimes and criminals.

Frye standard: the 1923 case that sets the standard for admissibility of scientific evidence in court that required general acceptance of the scientific methodology in its relevant field.

Joiner case: the case that sets the standard that requires experts to limit their opinions to straightforward extensions of the data and places limitations on what they can say in court.

Khumo Tire case: the precedent case that requires an all expert testimony to meet the Daubert standard, not just scientific expert testimony.

Locard's exchange principle: a fundamental principle of forensic science that states that a criminal leaves something behind at a crime scene and also takes something away with them when they leave. This means that evidence is transferred and exchanged whenever two objects come into contact.

Melendez-Dias: the U.S. Supreme Court case that allows defendants to require analysts to "face" them in court when presenting scientific analyses.

precedent: a legal principle or rule that comes from a court decision that can be used as a point of reference for deciding other cases.

principle of comparison: a concept that measures the similarities and differences between people or items of evidence.

principle of individuality (principle of uniqueness): the idea that even though two objects may be indistinguishable, they can never be exactly identical.

Sherlock Holmes: Victorian super-sleuth created by Arthur Conan Doyle.

stare decisis: From the Latin "*stare decisis et non quieta movere*" or "to stand by decisions and not disturb the undisturbed." The meaning is that decisions from higher courts are generally binding to lower courts.

voir dire: a preliminary examination of a potential expert witness or a juror.

BIBLIOGRAPHY

Collin Beavan, *Fingerprints: The Origin of Crime Detection and the Murder Case that Launched Forensic Science*, Hyperion Press, 2002.

Suzanne Bell, *Crime and Circumstance: Investigating the History of Forensic Science*, Praeger Press, 2008.

Stuart Fierstein, *IGNORANCE: How It Drives Science*, Oxford Univ. Press, 2012.

Keith Inman and Norah Rudin, *Principles and Practice of Criminalistics: The Profession of Forensic Science*, CRC Press, 2001.Richard E. McDorman, Liberty and Scientific Evidence in the Courtroom: Daubert v. Merrell Dow Pharmaceuticals, Inc. and the New Role of Scientific Evidence in the Criminal Courts, Organizational Knowledge Press, 2010.

Sidney Paget, "The Man With the Twisted Lip." *The Strand Magazine*, Dec. 1891.

Katherine Ramsland, *Beating the Devil's Games: A History of Forensic Science and Criminal Investigation*, Berkley Trade, 2008.

Nicholas J. Schweitzer and Michael J. Saks, *Jurimetrics*, 47, 357, 2007.

Ronald R. Thomas, *Detective Fiction and the Rise of Forensic Science*, Cambridge University Press, 2004.

E.J. Wagner, *The Science of Sherlock Holmes: From Baskerville Hall to the Valley of Fear, the Real Forensics Behind the Great Detective's Greatest Cases*, John Wiley, 2007.

E.J. Wagner, *Canadian Holmes*, 33(2), 2010/2011.

Wilson Wall, *Forensic Science in Court: The Role of the Expert Witness*, John Wiley, 2010.

Paul L. Kirk, *Crime investigation: physical evidence and the police laboratory*. New York: Interscience Publishers, Inc., 1953.

Edmond Locard, *The Analysis of Dust Traces. Part I*, American Journal of Police Science, Vol 1 (3), 1930, pp. 276–298.

Arthur Conan Doyle, *A Study in Scarlet*, Ward, Lock & Co., 1888.

Edgar Allan Poe, *The Murders in the Rue Morgue*, Graham's Magazine, 1841.

Edgar Allan Poe, *The Mystery of Marie Roget*, W. J. Widdleton Publ., 1842, pp. 213–261.

Edgar Allan Poe, *The Purloined Letter* In *The Gift: A Christmas and New Year's Present for 1845*, Carey and Hart, Publ., 1844.

Arthur Conan Doyle, *Adventure of the Cardboard Box*, Strand Magazine, Jan. 1893.

Arthur Conan Doyle, *Memories and Adventures*, Hodder & Stoughton Ltd., 1924.

Harold Emery Jones, *The Original of Sherlock Holmes*, Collier's Magazine, Jan. 1904.

Arthur Conan Doyle, *The Adventure of the Blanched Soldier*, Strand Magazine, Nov. 1926.

Gerald Hill and Kathleen Hill (Eds), *Nolo's Plain-English Law Dictionary* (1st Ed.), 2009, pp. 109.

Frye v. United States, 293 F. 1013, App. D.C. Dec. 03, 1923.

Federal Rules of Evidence: 28 USC App Fed R Evid Rule 702.

General Electric Co. v. Joiner, 522 U.S., 1997, pp. 136.

Kumho Tire Co. v. Carmichael, 526 U.S.,1999, 137.

Crime Scene Investigations

2

2.1 CRIME SCENE EVIDENCE

This is evidence that does not forget. It is not confused by the excitement of the moment. It is not absent because human witnesses are, it is factual evidence, physical evidence cannot be wrong, it cannot perjure itself...only its interpretation can err.

(Paul L. Kirk, 1902–1970, forensic scientist)

LEARNING GOALS AND OBJECTIVES

Crime scene evidence forms the critical core of forensic investigations. Accurate observations and measurements are key to analyzing these data. Evidence must be legally collected to be useful as forensic evidence. The identification, collection, handling, and storage of evidence from a crime scene is vital to its use in investigations and admissibility in courtrooms. After completing this chapter, you should be able to:

- Describe what physical evidence is.
- Explain when evidence is admissible in court, and what circumstances might render it inadmissible.
- Identify class and individual characteristics of evidence and their uses.
- Understand the types of comparison analyses that can be conducted and when they are used.
- Explain what is meant by probative and prejudicial evidence.
- Identify the important features of the Fourth Amendment to the U.S. Constitution and how it affects evidence collection.
- Determine when and what is required for a search warrant.
- Recognize what legal allowances for warrantless searches are.
- Discuss the outcomes of the key cases regarding evidence collection.
- Describe when and how evidence is inadmissible in court.
- Determine the proper steps for processing a crime scene.
- Identify possible members of an evidence team and their roles.

- Discuss how evidence is properly collected, recorded, and stored.
- Describe what is meant by "chain of custody."

2.1.1 Introduction

What is evidence? In practice, we use forensic evidence to try connecting two things together – a suspect with a crime scene, a weapon to a wound, a computer message with a criminal act, or a poison to a cause of death. Most often, we deal with various types of material evidence; physical items serve in this key linking role. Ideally, the link between the item of evidence and its source should be unambiguous – evidence linking just one person from among all others with one unique crime scene to the exclusion of all other possibilities, although the certainty of the level of connection may not be possible. From *Locard's Principle*, we know that when two objects come into contact there is a transfer of material. We *only* need to discover a way to find, collect, and analyze this transferred material to establish a bridge between the two objects. However, the term "only" in the previous sentence is deceptive. Unfortunately, evidence doesn't come with labels at the crime scene indicating that it is relevant to the case at hand. Instead, it is often lost in a sea of "environmental" items having no particular bearing on the case. Finding the important and relevant evidence may be like finding the proverbial "needle in a haystack." The key ingredient is often our ability to recognize that a particular item may have relevance to the case at hand.

On television and in movies, all too often the lead investigator walks into a crime scene or suspect's home and, in a matter of seconds, locates a seemingly inconspicuous piece of matter and utters the famous words "Ah ha! I've found it!", thereby solving the case and unequivocally linking the suspect with the crime beyond all possible doubt. But, of course, this is fiction, maybe even good fiction, but the world of entertainment is often far from the real world of forensic science. Crime scene investigations take a great deal of hard work, skill, experience, and insight to first find and then link the forensic evidence together to arrive at a logical chain of events. It also takes a finely-honed ability to observe and perceive important pieces of information from among all the background "noise" of the location. The proper processing of a crime scene may require many different skills from specialized experts such as anthropologists, medical examiners, entomologists, fingerprint experts, photographers, firearm analysts, and many others. Each expert brings to the case a refined set of skills that provides insights into what the evidence can provide to the

DOI: 10.4324/9781003183709-3

FIGURE 2.1   Chemical and biochemical analysis of forensic samples, such as blood samples, can help analysts understand the origin and properties of the sample through its chemical and cellular composition.

Source: Shutterstock.com.

investigation (Figure 2.1). In essence, the majority of this book is devoted to showing the value that scientific disciplines, and their practitioners, can bring to criminal investigations.

At its heart, the value of forensic evidence hinges upon what it can tell the "trier of fact," in other words, the court. Unless the evidence can serve in this informing role, it is legally useless, and is, in fact, typically inadmissible. Evidence must also be more probative than prejudicial – meaning that forensic evidence must "probe" the question at hand to provide unbiased information without unfairly prejudicing or confusing the court. These factors all determine the value of forensic evidence in court proceedings.

BOX 2.1   PROBATIVE VS PREJUDICIAL EVIDENCE

Relevant Evidence: Evidence having the ability to make the existence of any fact that is important to the case more probable or less probable (from FRE 401).

Probative: Evidence that has the ability to prove or demonstrate something relevant to the case.

Prejudicial: Evidence that pertains to some matter established previously (such as a prior conviction) or establishes a preconceived bias in a matter being decided. In some ways, all evidence against someone is prejudicial, but it must not be unfairly prejudicial.

In this chapter, we will explore what kinds of information physical evidence can provide, along with how it is properly and legally collected – critically important questions if the evidence is ever to be useful in legal actions.

2.1.2 Types of Evidence

Evidence may be anything that is introduced as part of a trial and may take a number of different forms. Physical evidence is generally recognized to be a material object, such as a weapon, fingerprint, or item of clothing: something that can be observed and measured. It forms part of the broader world of evidence, however, that encompasses many types of forensic evidence including chemical, biological, cyber, linguistic, and behavioral evidence. In successive major sections of this book, we will focus on each of these types of evidence in turn.

Evidence typically can provide two key types of information: identification or comparison analysis.

2.1.3 Identification and Comparison Analysis

An *identification analysis* focuses first on describing, often in great detail, the components or composition of an unknown sample. The goal of this approach is to identify the relevant features of a piece of evidence with as much specificity and certainty as possible, leading to an unambiguous identification of the material and determining its composition (e.g., cocaine, cotton fiber, or lead pipe). For example, the chemical composition of an unknown sample may be required, which can best be provided by forensic laboratory analysis. Samples of evidence materials can come from many places, such as a crime scene, scraped from a weapon, wiped from a suspect's hands, or taken during an autopsy. The analysis usually aims at determining the specific identity of the substance, such as heroin, glucose, or strychnine. In its analysis, the laboratory must carefully consider what type of information is required and how best to obtain useful data. For example, in Chapter 12, we will discuss how light can be used to unambiguously identify the chemical composition of an unknown material to determine if it is an illicit drug, poison or a harmless household compound. Often, multiple methods are employed to verify the correct identification: the more methods that yield similar results from divergent methods, the more confident we are in the result itself.

Comparison analysis, in contrast to an identification analysis, tries to associate a standard reference sample (called an *exemplar*) from a known origin to a sample of unknown origin, usually found at a crime scene or taken from a suspect. Specifically, the goal is to determine if the two samples, both the exemplar and the unknown, have a common origin. For example, does a blood sample recovered from a crime scene and a blood sample taken from a suspect have a common source – the suspect's blood pool? Similarly, does a fingerprint found on a weapon from a crime scene match prints taken by an examiner directly from a suspect? These types of analyses are very common in forensic investigations and are frequently used for the analysis of key types of evidence such as fingerprints, DNA, bullets, bones, patterns, and ecological samples, as shown in Figure 2.2. The ability to make this type of connection between the sample and the exemplar can help place the suspect at a particular location and either refute or support a hypothesis of a particular chain of events.

Typically, two types of comparison analysis are frequently encountered. One process involves matching key features found in an unknown sample with candidates from a very large pool of known possibilities, often many millions of records. This type of comparison is called *one-to-many matching*.

FIGURE 2.3   Differences between one-to-many and one-to-one matching strategies.

Sources: Shutterstock.com.

A very simple example of this is shown in Figure 2.3, where one block is compared with many in a set to see if there is a match. In forensic work, this approach might arise when a fingerprint from an unknown person is found at a crime scene, or the DNA of unknown human remains must be properly identified by comparison to a massive databank. Similarly, a spectrum taken from an unknown chemical may be rapidly compared using a databank containing stored spectra for millions of known compounds to rapidly identify the unknown sample (Figure 2.4). This type of analysis is particularly well-suited to a computer-based searching process using a stored set of records. Using a variety of computer search strategies, the features of the unknown are compared to the stored records of known origin in the database to find the best matches. Fingerprints, DNA profiles, eye iris patterns, handgun firing pin patterns, automotive paint profiles, and biometric information are just a few of the databases frequently employed for this type of searching.

The other type of comparison analysis, sometimes called verification or authentication, focuses on comparing a set of features observed in an unknown sample with either just one reference sample or among a very small number of "standard"

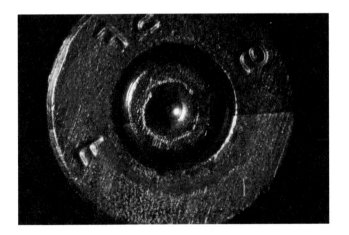

FIGURE 2.2   Forensic ballistics testing: bullet cartridges being compared under a microscope. One half of the image (bottom) shows one cartridge from a test firing, while the other half (top) shows a different cartridge recovered from a crime scene. Unique markings are made as the firing pin of a gun hits the cartridge and as the cartridge recoils from the bullet. The markings can be analyzed and compared to markings on cartridges test-fired from guns suspected of being used in crimes.

Credit: Patrick Landmann/Science Photo Library. Used with permission.

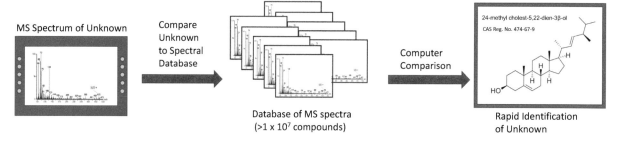

FIGURE 2.4 Chemical analysis by matching the spectrum of an unknown with known spectra stored in a large database.

Source: Used per Creative Commons Share-Alike 3.0 Unported, Attribution Smmudge at the English-language Wikipedia.

FIGURE 2.5 One-to-one matching process using iris patterns for verifying the identity of a person. The person's iris is quickly scanned and the pattern is compared to a previously taken iris scan for the individual. If the two "match," the person's unique identification is verified.

Source: Shutterstock.com.

possibilities. The example in Figure 2.3 shows a comparison of one "unknown" block with a standard block to see if they match. This process is often referred to as *one-to-one matching*. The process usually involves comparing data from an evidence sample with data from one or a small number of previously recorded reference samples. For example, comparing the small scratches (striations) on the sides of a bullet found at a crime scene with those from a test-fired bullet from a suspect's gun can provide support for that particular gun's involvement in a shooting (Figure 2.2). This type of analysis can also be used as part of a biometric security scan (Figures 2.5 and 2.6) or in determining the identity of repeat offenders in the criminal justice system.

In any type of comparison, it is important to determine the chance that a purely random match of the features might occur between two unrelated samples. The more features that a reference sample and an unknown sample have in common (without finding non-matching features), the lower the chances of a random match and the more reliable the analysis. For example, matching two points in a fingerprint pattern

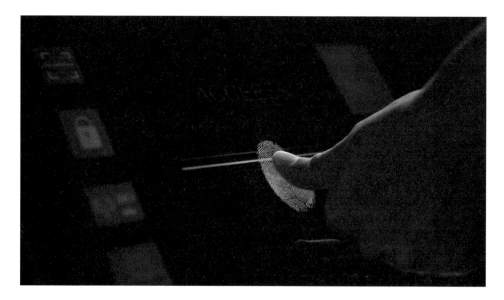

FIGURE 2.6 Personal identification authentication on an automated device using fingerprint recognition to verify a person's identity by matching the scanned fingerprint at the beginning of the transaction with a reference previously taken from the person and stored in a databank.

Source: Shutterstock.com.

between an exemplar and an unknown sample may provide a relatively low level of reliability because of the high chance that a random match will occur. Matching 13 points, however, would have a much higher level of reliability (very low probability of a random match). Similarly, matching two loci (places on a chromosome) in a DNA pattern might give a random match rate of 1 in 500 (1 person in 500 people would be expected to have the same pattern at these two DNA sites), while matching 13 loci may give a random matching probability as high as about 1 in 7 trillion. Probability relates to how often a particular event or set of events, such as finding a matching features, will occur. The chances of random matches occurring are governed by the concepts in the fields of probability and statistics, something that will be discussed in Chapter 3 in more detail. The acceptable number of "matching" data points required to determine "beyond a reasonable doubt" depends on the method used and the consensus of the appropriate scientific community.

When analyzing evidence, the defining characteristics of a sample dictates what kind of information the analysis can provide. Generally, there are two types of characteristics that evidence may possess, class characteristics and individual characteristics.

Class characteristics are those that place the piece of evidence within a particular broad group, such as a lead pipe, a certain model of automobile tire, or a blood type (e.g., AB⁺). *Individual characteristics*, however, relate the sample to a unique and specific origin with a *high degree of certainty*, such as the fine details found in the pattern of a fingerprint or of scratches on a test-fired bullet.

FIGURE 2.7 Games such as "Guess Who" use class evidence charactristics to identify a randomly chosen person through elimination (exclusion).

Source: Shutterstock.com.

BOX 2.2   EVIDENCE CHARACTERISTICS

Class Evidence: Properties of evidence that can only be connected with a broad group rather than with a specific, unique source.

Individual Evidence: Properties of evidence that can connect a sample with a specific common source with a high degree of certainty.

Class evidence allows us to place an unknown sample within a smaller subset of items. A simple example is the children's guessing game shown in Figure 2.7. In this game, each player has the same set of pictures of possible "suspects" placed before them. The goal of the game is for the players to figure out the identity of one of the "suspects" drawn at random from all the possible "suspects" held by the other player. The players do this by asking each other broad questions such as "does the person wear glasses" or "does the person have white hair," to which the other player must respond with either a "yes" or "no". If the answer is no, the player can then eliminate all the people having this feature. Through this process, the players effectively place the people into classes of characteristics, such as all people with glasses or all people with white hair.

Identifying the similarities or differences between samples can greatly help to narrow down the possibilities. For example, identifying a pipe sample as a lead pipe eliminates all other types of pipes except for lead, such as copper, PVC, aluminum, steel, etc. Alternatively, identifying a piece of broken glass as part of a piece of automobile window glass can be very useful. Even blood typing relies on class characteristics. For example, about 0.7% of the world's population has type AB- blood. Finding out this information from a simple blood test can eliminate 99.3% of the population as possible suspects (about 1 in 142 people). Coupling one or more types of class characteristic information can be even more powerful. If it could be determined that the criminal was not only AB- blood type but also was a left-handed, red-haired male, it would further reduce the pool of possible suspects to about 0.0014% or about 1 in 73,000 people.

Class evidence does not, however, usually allow for the direct connection between two individual items with a high degree of certainty, such as between a crime scene sample and a sample taken from a suspect. While using class characteristics to reduce the possibilities can be powerful evidence,

FIGURE 2.8   Two tires of the same make and model. The make and model type represents a form of class information while the wear damage seen along the sides and tread of the tires is a form of individual evidence.

Source: iStockphoto.com, Adisak Mitrprayoon.

it does not provide the one-to-one connection between the evidence and a standard that is often sought after.

Individual evidence, in contrast, usually provides enough distinguishing and unique features to connect two particular pieces of evidence together with a high degree of certainty. For example, two automobile tires can be first placed within a common subset using the class characteristics of make, model, color, tread design, and size. Tires do, however, wear differently by use over time to show unique scratches, marks, and other defining wear and damage features (Figure 2.8).

Finding a distinctive wear pattern from both a tread mark found at a crime scene with matching features on a tire from a suspect's car can connect the two together with a very high degree of certainty. Pieces of plastic, glass, ceramic, paint, or other "broken or torn" materials can sometimes be uniquely pieced back together by matching their individual patterns. For example, the unique shapes of pieces of broken objects can be "fit" back together like a jig-saw puzzle when placed in proper alignment to demonstrate that they were once originally one continuous object, as illustrated by a torn piece of duct tape in Figure 2.9. Similarly, a small glass shard found on a victim of a hit-and-run automobile assault can be a vital piece of evidence. Class characteristics can show that the glass came from a typical car windshield. However, individual characteristics can be used to piece the windshield back together and show that the shard found on the victim

fits uniquely into the complex pattern of only one particular broken windshield (Figure 2.10).

These types of evidence have very important roles in legal investigations. As mentioned earlier, the evidence, once found, must be properly collected and handled in order to be useful legally. This process will be examined in Section 2.2.

2.2 LEGAL EVIDENCE

"Quis, quid, ubi, quibus, auxilius, cur, quomodo, quando?" Sister Fidelma smiled softly at the old man. "Who is the criminal? What is the crime? Where was it committed? By what means? With what accomplices? Why? In what way? When?"

(Tremayne, 2000)

2.2.1 Evidence Collection and the Law

You've probably heard the old saying that a person's "home is their castle". This idea, in fact, has its roots in English law

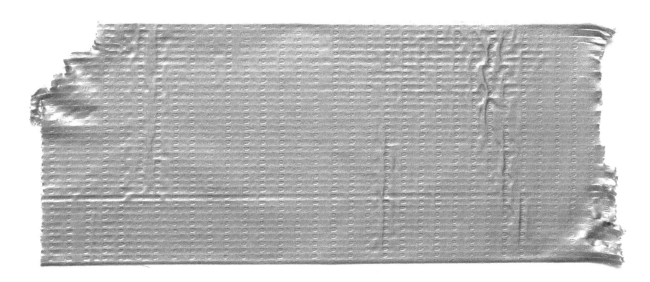

FIGURE 2.9 Individual characteristics of a tear pattern in duct tape shows a highly individual patterns of ripped fibers.

Source: Shutterstock.com.

FIGURE 2.10 Finding a shard of glass from a broken car window in a hit-and-run case can be used to fit into the unique fracture pattern of the windshield.

Source: iStockphoto.com, miljko.

dating back at least to the early 1600s. William Pitt probably summarized it best in 1763:

> The poorest man may in his cottage bid defiance to all the force of the crown. It may be frail – its roof may shake – the wind may blow through it – the storm may enter, the rain may enter – but the King of England cannot enter – all his force dares not cross the threshold of the ruined tenement.

By the mid-1700s, it was fairly well established in a number of nations that a government's rightful abilities to search and seize personal properties were limited and could only happen under certain special circumstances, especially when searching specifically for illegal materials or criminal evidence, and then only when a written "warrant" had been issued stating the goals and purpose of the search. Today, most countries around the world have similar laws to protect the privacy of their citizens but also to allow that there are certain times when it is proper to invade this privacy to look for evidence of criminal activity in the name of justice.

BOX 2.3   FOURTH AMENDMENT TO THE U.S. CONSTITUTION

The Fourth Amendment to the U.S. Constitution, from the Bill of Rights, passed in 1791, states that:

> The right of the people to be secure in their persons, houses, papers, and effects, against unreasonable searches and seizures, shall not be violated, and no Warrants shall issue, but upon probable cause, supported by Oath or affirmation, and particularly describing the place to be searched, and the persons or things to be seized.

In the United States, a person's right to privacy and the protection of their property is guaranteed by the Fourth Amendment to the U.S. Constitution, a notion deeply rooted in 18th Century English Law (see Boxes 2.3 and 2.4). The Fourth Amendment specifically guards against *unreasonable searches and seizures* of both a person and their property by government officials under most circumstances (Figure 2.11). It does, however, provide for times when it has been determined to be in the public's best interest and reasonable for society to allow certain types of privacy intrusions: times when the situation is either so dangerous or fast-moving that there is not sufficient time to obtain a search warrant. These times can be broken down into two main categories: those that require warrants before the search can take place and warrantless searches. Of course, a person can always waive the rights provided in the Fourth Amendment and give their consent to searches of themselves and their property, assuming that they have the proper authority to do that, are aware of what they are doing and are not under duress. Additionally, some types of searches don't fall under the Fourth Amendment provisions at all.

BOX 2.4   FOURTH AMENDMENT RIGHTS

A person's Fourth Amendment protection from unreasonable search and seizure currently only applies to searches by *government officials* (e.g., police officers, court officials, etc.) and *not* to private security guards who currently vastly outnumber police and other government officers. For example, the Fourth Amendment would require a police officer to usually obtain a search warrant before searching a person's backpack in a mall – requiring probable cause and a court-issued warrant. A private security officer, however, can legally search the backpack without a warrant and, if they found something illegal, could call the police and turn the evidence over to the authorities. This would constitute a *legal* search and seizure by the private security officer and the evidence is currently admissible in court.

In a related case, the U.S. Supreme Court said that a police officer cannot probe the outside of an opaque bag that is in public view without a warrant because the person had a "legitimate expectation of privacy" provided by the opaque bag (*Bond v. United States*, 529 US 334, 2000).

FIGURE 2.11   Search and seizures typically require a court-issued search warrant.

Source: Shutterstock.com.

There are times when police and other government officers deem it necessary to search for things that are either illegal to possess or may be material evidence related to a criminal act. In these cases, a *search warrant* is usually required before the search can take place. A search warrant is an order issued by a judge or magistrate that gives officers the authority to conduct a search at a very specific place, time, and for a specific reason. Before a search warrant can be issued, however, the police must first show *probable cause* to an unbiased judge that they are likely to find specific illegal items or criminal evidence in the search. Probable cause is not strictly defined in the U.S. Constitution, but common practice usually requires the police to present to the judge objective facts or evidence supporting that they will find what they are looking for during the search. In other words, a warrant can't be issued on a hunch by the police, but it requires more substantial evidence to overcome the constitutionally guaranteed freedom of privacy.

BOX 2.5   WHAT HAPPENS AFTER AN ILLEGAL SEARCH?

If a court rules that evidence resulting from a search violated someone's Fourth Amendment protections, the evidence may not be admissible in court through two important legal ideas:

Exclusionary Rule: Any evidence resulting from an illegal search cannot be used as direct evidence in court.

Fruit of the Poisonous Tree Doctrine: Any evidence found from an illegal search also cannot be used to find other evidence. For example, an illegally-seized smart phone cannot be used to provide information leading to the discovery of evidence hidden elsewhere – such as an address listed on the phone showing where evidence is hidden.

When can illegally-seized evidence be used? Illegally-seized evidence can actually be used by courts in a few limited circumstances:

- When the judge considers sentencing.
- In civil or deportation cases.
- To attack the credibility of a witness at trial.

A search warrant is issued for a specific place and time, and it describes what items are to be looked for. Officers are then allowed to search the designated place and seize only the items listed in the warrant. The warrant strictly limits what the officers can legally do. For example, if they have a warrant to look in a garage for a stolen truck, they cannot look through the glove compartment of your car parked in the garage – trucks don't fit into glove compartments, and it would be unreasonable to expect to find one there. They could, however, look through a glove compartment to try to find the keys to a missing truck *if that is specifically stated* in the warrant.

It is important to note that the Fourth Amendment only protects a person if they have a "legitimate expectation of privacy"; this is a very important phrase. Police officers do not need a warrant, for example, to seize items that are plainly visible from a place that the officer has a right to be (e.g., sidewalk, roadside, etc.) – this is called the *plain view doctrine*. Items in plain view do not fall under the Fourth Amendment's provisions since the person can have no real expectation of privacy in such circumstances. If a police officer notices a gun or drugs on the seat of a car while standing on the roadside after stopping someone for a legitimate vehicular violation, they do not need a warrant to seize the gun or drugs. However, they cannot search a vehicle's trunk without either consent or a warrant. Investigators cannot put up a surveillance camera in a public bathroom stall without a warrant because society generally holds that someone has a reasonable expectation of privacy in that circumstance.

The plain view doctrine and the concept of an expectation of privacy are often guiding principles for determining the validity of a warrantless search. For example, the Supreme Court has ruled that placing a GPS tracking device on the outside of a person's car, even though it was done without entering the car, violates the Fourth Amendment since we have an expectation of privacy from tracking, even though the plain view doctrine was not violated (see Box 2.6).

BOX 2.6   NEW TECHNOLOGY AND THE FOURTH AMENDMENT

In 2011, the FBI placed a GPS tracking device on the Jeep of Washington, DC, nightclub owner Antoine Jones, which tracked his every move for 28 days, leading to the seizure of 97 kilograms of cocaine and $850,000 in cash. Based upon this evidence, Mr. Jones was convicted and sentenced to life in prison for drug trafficking. The U.S. Supreme Court, however, unanimously overturned his conviction because they ruled that the police needed to obtain a warrant before placing the device. While the decision to overturn the conviction was unanimous, there were several differing opinions as to why a warrant was required. The majority of the court felt that a warrant was needed because it was truly a search and that it violated Mr. Jones' privacy. Others on the court felt that Mr. Jones had a reasonable expectation of privacy against such tracking, and thus, a warrant was required.

In any case, this was a warrantless search that should not have happened. What about cell phone and email origin tracking? What about loyalty card swipes and credit card surveillance? And what about enhanced automotive "black box" recorders, which can monitor a variety of features that now come standard on all new cars? Is information from these sources open to a warrantless search? Clearly, new technologies push our limits and understanding of how they fit into the Fourth Amendment's provisions (Nina Totenberg, 2012).

FIGURE 2.12 Warrantless searches are possible under a number of special circumstances, including during an emergency or when events are moving too rapidly to obtain a search warrant necessary to prevent the destruction of evidence.

Source: Shutterstock.com.

There are some exceptions to the Fourth Amendment's requirement for a prior warrant before a search and seizure can happen. These "special" circumstances that allow warrantless searches include (Figure 2.12):

- **Consent**: If an officer asks and the person says "yes," the officer may search and seize any criminal evidence or contraband that they find in the place identified by the person. It does not open every door, however, and specific consent sometimes needs to be given for different areas. Only adults with some measure of control over the space can give proper consent. For example, a roommate can give consent to have their space and all *common* spaces searched but cannot authorize the search of the other person's private property. Additionally, the person must have ownership or similar rights over the space to grant consented access.
- **Searches during Legal Arrests**: In the course of an arrest, police officers have the right to search your person and the immediate area to seize evidence (including items found after a person has been incorrectly arrested in "good faith"). The surrounding area could be a person's car (not usually the trunk, however, unless they have a probable cause), home or property. The search of a person's home needs to be only a "sweep" to make sure that no threat to the officers or public still exists – more extensive searches still require warrants. The axiom still holds: when in doubt, obtain a warrant.

- **Emergency Circumstances**: When there is an insufficient amount of time to go through the formal process of obtaining a search warrant and where officials must act to protect people from hazard or prevent the immediate destruction of evidence, a warrantless search is justified. For example, officers may enter a smoke-filled building in an emergency and search for people to determine if a threat exists to the public. They may also enter a building when they are in "hot pursuit" of a fleeing suspect or responding to an emergency call. Police can also intervene without a warrant if they believe that evidence is being destroyed, such as drugs being flushed down the drain or alcohol destroyed by the body (see Box 2.7).

BOX 2.7   BODY'S EVIDENCE

The U.S. Supreme Court has ruled that a person may be forced to take a blood alcohol test (Chapter 13) without their consent or need for a search warrant as part of a vehicular investigation. The ground for this decision was that the body, through its normal biochemical processes, works to destroy any alcohol consumed. Since the alcohol in the blood constitutes evidence related to potential criminal DWI (driving while impaired) or DUI (driving under the influence) actions, the body's metabolism of the alcohol actually represents the destruction of evidence. Requiring a person to give blood alcohol evidence (blood sample usually) without a warrant or their consent is, therefore, admissible under the Fourth Amendment.

The important aspect to remember is that evidence found and seized unlawfully cannot be used as direct evidence in court and may, therefore, be legally useless at best and damaging to a case at worst. It is, therefore, especially important for investigators to conduct searches lawfully in order to use the evidence they find in courtroom proceedings.

- **Plain View**: As described previously, this includes items that are visible from a legal viewpoint, such as items seen through a window or out in the open as viewed from a "public" place. Officers may also seize items not listed in an original warrant if they are in "plain view" when conducting a warrant-based search. However, there are plenty of subtleties in the plain view doctrine. For example, the Supreme Court decided that the police were allowed to fly over and observe a person's home from an altitude of 1,000 ft without a warrant, even though the fenced-in yard was not observable in plain view at ground level in order to search for contraband (*California v. Ciraolo*, 1986).
- **Airport, Border, and Sea Searches**: Warrantless searches of a person and their luggage are legal to protect the public from danger at airports, transportation centers, and international borders (Figure 2.13). This can include the scanning of luggage and personal body scans and searches. If agents have reasonable suspicion, a more thorough "non-routine" search can be justified, often without warrants, which could include strip and cavity searches. The main decks of boats may also be searched without a warrant, although interior compartments still usually require probable cause and warrants.
- **"Stop and Frisk"**: If an officer suspects that a person is either engaged in or about to be engaged in a criminal action, has a weapon, or poses an immediate threat to the public, the officer may detain the person and perform a "pat down search" ("frisk"). If the officer feels something on the suspect, such as a weapon, they can reach in and seize it without a warrant.
- **Inventory Searches**: Officials are allowed to search anything seized as part of an investigation or arrest (e.g., automobile, airplane, or boat) when in the process of completing an inventory of the seized item's contents. The inventory is meant to protect both the person's property and the police from false claims of missing or damaged property. But, if illegal materials are found, they can be collected as evidence.

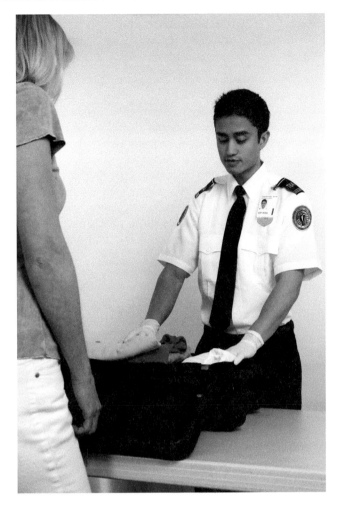

FIGURE 2.13 Agents may perform warrantless searches of people and luggage at transportation centers and borders to ensure public safety.

Source: iStockphoto.com, gchutka.

- **National Security**: Under the USA Patriot Act and similar laws worldwide, email messages, medical and financial records, and other personal information may be searched without a warrant, although other types of surveillance may still require a warrant. Such provisions are enacted by Congress and, thus far, have been allowed by the Supreme Court which may, of course, modify that decision over time. National security searches are also subject to varying rules about when they can be employed, but often the investigators are given wide latitude as to what constitutes a national security-related search.
- **Administrative Searches**: Certain agencies, such as fire, electric, gas, and safety inspectors, may conduct warrantless searches but these searches usually cannot be used to provide evidence in criminal cases. They can, however, alert authorities who can then request a normal search warrant to search and seize the previously observed items.

2.2.2 Precedent Cases for Evidence Collection

Several important cases have helped to set some additional rules governing the practice of how and when forensic evidence may be collected from a crime scene. Especially important among these are the *Mincy* and *Tyler* cases.

Mincy v. Arizona: This was a case of a drug bust that went terribly wrong, resulting in the death of an undercover police officer and the wounding of several others, including the suspect, in the suspect's apartment. After a quick search of the apartment, the responding officers turned the investigation over to homicide detectives who then spent four days opening drawers, ripping up carpet, and searching and seizing 200–300 pieces of evidence from the apartment. This evidence led to the conviction of Mincy on homicide and narcotics charges. The U.S. Supreme Court later ruled that the evidence obtained was inadmissible since it was not obtained properly – no warrant had been issued. While an emergency situation initially existed that allowed the police to quickly search the home, the emergency could not reasonably be thought to exist for four days of searching – in fact, the detailed search did not begin until all the dead and wounded had been removed from the scene. In this case, the police should have obtained a warrant after the emergency had passed to continue their search – a *warrantless search based on an emergency is limited in duration*. It is important to note that, just because they have to stop searching and file for a search warrant, the police do not have to give up control of the crime scene. While a warrant is being sought, the police can close and restrict access to the site until searching can legally begin.

Michigan v. Tyler: In this case, a fire broke out in a furniture store before midnight and was extinguished by the fire department. At 2 AM, an investigation by fire and police officials began that was halted at 4 AM due to darkness, heat, and steam (Figure 2.14). During the following three weeks, investigators returned to the scene repeatedly to collect and remove evidence for a possible arson investigation. Tyler was ultimately convicted of arson. The Supreme Court, once again, said that the evidence was not properly collected and ruled it inadmissible. In this case, they said that

> entry to fight a fire requires no warrant, and that once in the building, officials may remain there for a reasonable time to investigate the cause of the blaze. Thereafter, additional entries to investigate the cause of the fire must be made pursuant to the warrant procedures.

An additional major problem was that the crime scene was not controlled by the police and was left abandoned between searches, allowing someone to potentially add, remove, or tamper with any evidence at the scene (see Section 2.3 for more about this relative to the "chain of custody").

Carpenter v. United States: In this 2018 case, the Supreme Court determined that a person's cell phone records were protected under many circumstances from warrantless searches under the Fourth Amendment. The court determined that the Amendment protects both property and expectations of privacy in the digital age, even though this might not fit neatly within usual precedents. Tracking a person's movements *via* cell-site records is highly intrusive and therefore protected.

Torres v. Madrid: In this 2021 case, two New Mexico police officers attempted to stop the car driven by Roxanne Torres while trying to execute an arrest warrant for another person. When they approached the car, Ms. Torres drove off, claiming later a fear for her safety. The officers shot at the car in an attempt to stop it and, in the process, injured Ms. Torres. The question was whether the unsuccessful effort of the officers to stop Ms. Torres represented a "seizure" of her person.

FIGURE 2.14   The *Michigan v. Tyler* case centered around warrantless search and seizure from a suspected arson fire in Michigan.

Source: Shutterstock.com.

The officers claimed that people are only seized once they are stopped. The Supreme Court determined that the officers did indeed seize Torres, even though she subsequently fled from them. The court went even further stating that "Small intrusions, such as taps on the shoulder, will constitute seizures … if they are intended as a prelude to restraint, even when the tap-ee flees into a crowd." This has important implications on personal seizures and when they are reasonable under the Fourth Amendment.

**BOX 2.8   THE CASE OF THE
*PEOPLE V. ROSARIO***

In 1961, the case of Luis Rosario set a standard that required statements by witnesses who testify (written, recorded, emails, etc.) to be shared between both the defense and the prosecution.

Other laws and rules also bear upon the sharing of evidence between the two sides of a case. The Constitution forbids the prosecution from withholding any evidence related to the innocence of the defendant from the defense. In addition, the states all have statutes governing when and what the prosecution must share with the defense. Usually, during the pre-trial "discovery" phase of a trial, the prosecution must turn over some or all of their evidence to the defense. Additionally, some states require the defense to likewise share the information that they have with the prosecution. (The discovery portion of a legal proceeding is the formal pre-trial process where the defense and prosecution exchange information relevant to the investigation.)

2.3 THE EVIDENCE COLLECTION AND THE EVIDENCE TEAM

2.3.1 Processing the Crime Scene

Now that we understand the legal underpinnings of *when* evidence can be collected, it is now important to consider the skilled work of processing a crime scene – the *how* of evidence collection. The actions of investigators in the field often have profound effects on the later course of a criminal case (Figure 2.15). Crime scene processing involves the proper identification and handling of physical materials associated with criminal actions, including collecting information from witnesses. Failure to do the process correctly will often result in the loss of potentially key forensic information.

BOX 2.9   SOME DEFINITIONS

First Responder: The initial police, fire, or similar trained personnel to arrive at a crime or emergency scene.

Boundary: The border surrounding and including potential physical evidence.

Chain of Custody: The thread that keeps track of the history of a piece of evidence so that its location and handling are documented from the point of its discovery through storage, analysis, and admission into court.

Reference Sample (Exemplar): A sample collected from a verified source for comparison to an unknown (such as a fingerprint taken from a suspect).

FIGURE 2.15   Crime scene processing.

Source: Shutterstock.com.

At the heart of crime scene investigation is the careful observation and proper handling of all potential evidence. Skill, experience, care, and patience all combine to yield the maximum amount of information possible from the evidence at hand.

The proper processing of crime scenes follows certain basic and logical practices and procedures. With training and care, the sequence of steps needed to do this correctly is logical and relatively straightforward. These steps usually include:

- Securing and isolating the scene.
- Recording and documenting the scene.
- Searching and collecting evidence.
- Packaging, transporting, and storing evidence.
- Releasing the scene back to normal use.

Secure and Isolate the Scene: The processing of any crime scene typically begins by securing, controlling, and isolating the scene of the crime. The idea is to first ensure that the scene is safe from all potential threats to responders, victims, and the public, such as criminal actions and physical harm, and that any necessary medical assistance has been rendered. The highest priority must be to ensure the safety of any potential victims, the public and the responders themselves (Figure 2.16). First responders should, in practice, consider the crime to be ongoing from the moment when they first arrive until it is determined to be otherwise. First responders must remain alert, attentive, and observant – recording any person(s) or vehicle(s) leaving the scene and noting anything out of the ordinary. Processing actually begins at the moment of first responder arrival, and attention should be paid to the bystanders: "watch the watchers," as perpetrators may blend into the crowd as observers of their own criminal actions, and

potential witnesses may be noted. Responders need to be alert for any potentially dangerous situations that might arise, such as a gas leak, poisonous substances, explosive materials, or potential chemical, biological, or radiological threats. The first responders may be required to arrest suspects and conduct a preliminary sweep search to make sure that no hidden threats remain, such as criminal accomplices or other victims.

Providing emergency medical treatment has priority over preserving evidence, although usually both ends can be achieved with a little care and cooperation between the police and emergency medical technicians. First responders should assist medical personnel in avoiding evidence destruction as well as documenting the movement of people or physical items by the EMTs. Once proper medical aid has been given and any victims transported off the site, the EMT personnel should not clean up the mess they leave behind – they need to leave it as it is to avoid further contamination of the scene.

Once the scene is determined to be safe, the role of the first responders then shifts to preserving the scene and its evidence in as pristine a state as possible. This usually requires establishing a perimeter large enough to encompass the entire scene and excluding all unauthorized people from the scene, such as bystanders, neighbors, press, and even unnecessary responders and police officials (Figure 2.17). This is sometimes rather difficult to achieve because crimes often bring emotional responses from people who want to see what has happened, including from other police, fire, and EMT personnel. Unfortunately, the more serious the crime, the greater the likelihood of non-essential personnel wanting to gain access to the scene. Only those who have a real need to be at the scene should be allowed to cross the boundary. Suspects, victims, witnesses, medical personnel, and bystanders need to be separated and isolated for later questioning.

FIGURE 2.16 First responders must evaluate and act to secure any potential crime scene, eliminate potential treats, and provide emergency medical assistance.

Source: Shutterstock.com.

FIGURE 2.17   Establishing a secure boundary around the potential crime scene is an important early step in processing a crime scene.

Source: iStockphoto.com, MichaelRLong.

Once the scene is secure, medical attention given, and persons at the scene controlled, a lead investigator must be designated who then defines a crime scene boundary that is determined by the location, extent, and nature of the crime. Usually, larger boundaries are first established that can later be reduced in size as necessary, since expanding the boundary later can be difficult. This is often accomplished by starting at the point where the crime is known to have occurred and then extending outward. Physical barriers, such as the famous "police line" tape, need to be established and the entry of all people and materials in and out of the scene carefully limited and recorded.

Record the Crime Scene: The next key phase involves the complete and careful documentation of the crime scene. This can be an extensive process and is dictated by the size and nature of the scene itself. Investigators need to document the location, condition, and appearance of persons and items within the crime scene. This may include recording the weather conditions, locations of objects within the scene, identification of personal items, and conditions of items (e.g., the television was warm, the oven was on, the room smelled of natural gas, etc.) as well as preliminary interviews with witnesses.

BOX 2.10   THE LOCKERBIE BOMBING CRIME SCENE

On December 21, 1988, Pan Am Flight 103, on its way between London and New York, exploded over the small Scottish town of Lockerbie, killing all 259 people aboard, including 35 Syracuse University students returning to the United States after a fall studying abroad. Additionally, 11 residents on the ground in the town of Lockerbie also died. More than 10,000 pieces of evidence were ultimately found, collected, and preserved during the investigation. The crime scene itself stretched over 845 sq. miles of Scotland and was

intensely scrutinized. Amazingly, a key piece of evidence linking the bomb with suspects from Libya was a very small transistor chip (Figure 2.18) from the radio containing the bomb. This evidence was critical in the conviction of Libyan Abdul al-Megrahi for the bombing.

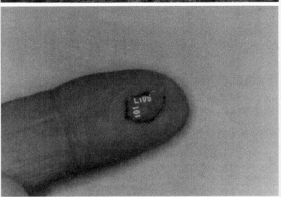

FIGURE 2.18   Photographs of the 1988 Pan Am Flight 103 in Lockerbie, Scotland.

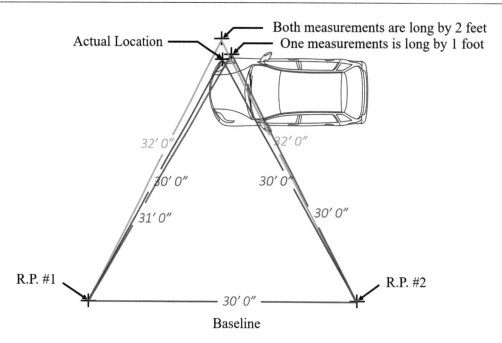

FIGURE 2.19 Triangulation uses the distance of an object from two fixed reference points (labeled RP in the figure) to accurately determine its position in a crime scene.

Several methods have been developed to locate physical items accurately and quickly within the crime scene. These include:

- **Triangulation**: In this process, two fixed points in the crime scene are selected (e.g., the corner of a building, fire hydrant, telephone pole, etc.). Distance measurements (or angles) between an object in the crime scene and the two fixed reference points then serve to establish the position of the object accurately using trigonometry (Figure 2.19).
- **Azimuthal Locating**: This process uses a compass arrangement, similar to that used by surveyors, to locate the evidence by measuring angles and distances to a known geographic point.
- **Coordinate Mapping**: This technique divides the crime scene into a grid of small squares, much like a checkerboard. The contents of each square can then be searched, mapped, and placed within the context of the entire array of squares.
- **Electronic Methods**: With the advantages provided by laser and GPS technology, a number of sophisticated methods may be employed to map an entire crime scene, such as using the "total station" or similar (Figure 2.20).

The measurements from the crime scene and the identity of the items are typically used to construct a detailed "map" of the scene, beginning with a rough sketch prepared while at the crime scene that includes the field measurements. Typically, the data in the rough sketch are then used to generate a detailed finished map using computer-aided design (CAD) techniques

(Figure 2.21). Both two-dimensional and three-dimensional renderings are available using this technology and are often quite helpful in the courtroom to give juries a detailed picture of the crime scene (Figure 2.22).

Crime scenes are also usually documented using photography (Figure 2.23). Photographs of evidence and the crime scene form a permanent record of often ephemeral and short-lived types of evidence. Photographs of fingerprints, footprints, bodies, injuries, bloodstains, tire marks, and many other forms of evidence are often the only record that lasts long enough to be useful in court. Usually, photographers are among the first to enter a crime scene in order to photograph it in as pristine a state as possible. Photographers typically take both overview (wide-angle) photographs to place the item within the context of the entire scene and close-up photos to show the detail of the item.

Search for Evidence: Once the site is "mapped" and recorded, the painstaking task of searching for relevant evidence begins. The investigator in charge usually determines the type, extent, and location of the searches that need to take place. A number of systematic search patterns have been developed that allow for the complete coverage of a search area without missing any areas, as shown in Figure 2.24. These same search patterns can be used effectively for crime scenes of any size, from relatively small areas, such as inside a single room of a house, to very large areas, such as square miles of outside terrain. The goal, of course, is not to miss or damage any potential evidence and to properly record and collect anything relevant to the case that might be found. The difficulty, of course, is to distinguish between "background" environmental items (e.g., items present before the crime occurred or irrelevant to the events) from those that are indeed important.

FIGURE 2.20 A "total station" device used in mapping a crime scene.

Source: Shutterstock.com.

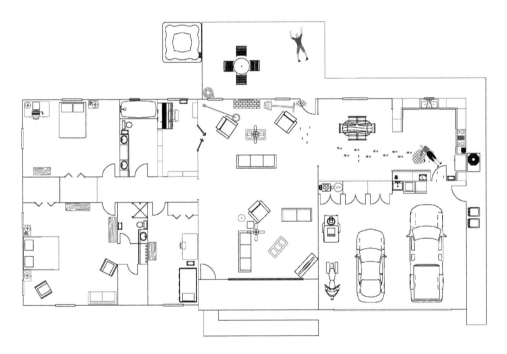

FIGURE 2.21 Diagram of a bird's-eye view and floor plan of a crime scene.

Source: From Baxter (2015).

The ability to make these distinctions usually comes from field experience but it is often better to collect too much than run the risk of missing an important piece of evidence (see Box 2.10).

Police agencies typically develop rather extensive protocols for properly searching areas and determining what to do once a piece of evidence has been located at the scene.

Collection and Preservation of Evidence: Once a piece of evidence is discovered, photographed in place, and located on the site map, it must be properly collected and preserved. The sample must be correctly packaged for transportation to the lab such that contamination does not occur, and it is protected from as much damage and degradation as possible (Figure 2.25).

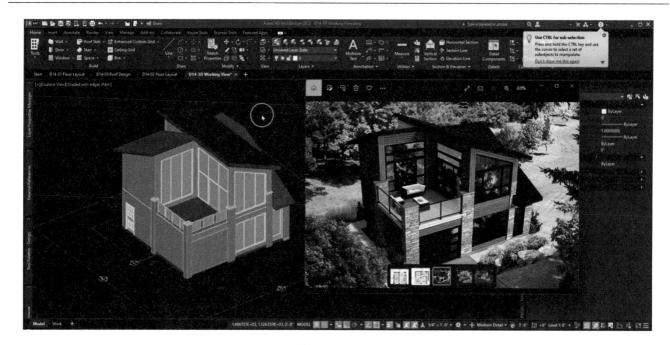

FIGURE 2.22   Computer-aided design software used to generate a detailed three-dimensional map of a crime scene.

Source: Used per Creative Commons Share-Alike 3.0 Unported, Attribution Smmudge at the English-language Wikipedia.

FIGURE 2.23   Crime scene photography used to document the condition and location of pieces of evidence and the overall scene.

Source: iStockphoto.com, Milan Markovic.

Different types of evidence require differing methods of packaging and storage based upon the characteristics of the evidence itself. For example, volatile materials, liquids, and some controlled substances usually need to be packaged in air-tight containers, while moist biological evidence should be placed in a container that would facilitate its drying, such as a cardboard box or paper bag, with the goal of allowing those items to dry under as close to natural conditions as possible. Once again, extensive protocols have been developed on how best to package, preserve, and store important pieces of evidence. A sample of these methods is given in Table 2.1.

A critical piece of the process of collecting and documenting evidence is referred to as the *chain of custody* (CoC). The CoC for a piece of evidence documents its chronological control from the time that it is first discovered until it is needed and admitted into court (and even afterwards). It provides details of every transfer of the evidence, including what is done to the sample (e.g., analysis, storage, transported, etc.), where it is located, when these transfers happen, and who transfers and controls the evidence, to form a continuous and *provable* record of every moment of the evidence's existence after it is found and collected. The key idea is to prove that a particular piece of evidence was truly found at a crime scene and related to the crime without the possibility of it being fraudulently planted, tampered with, or changed before it is presented in court as evidence. A typical chain of custody form is shown in Figure 2.26.

Evidence with breaks in its chain of custody record is highly unlikely to be useful in court since its authenticity can readily be challenged.

The evidence must be stored in a secure, locked location and never out of an identifiable person's control (e.g., never left on a lab bench unattended or transferred an unnecessary number of times without reason). The chain of custody should also contain all of the information regarding the piece of evidence's history: where and when it was found and collected (and by whom), how it was packaged and stored, a physical description of the item along with any identifying numbers.

A chain of custody might not be required for some pieces of evidence – evidence that is so unique that it could not originate any place other than that indicated. For example, an object with a serial number recorded at the crime scene or a vehicle with license plate (and internal serial numbers) may not require the usual chain of custody process and form.

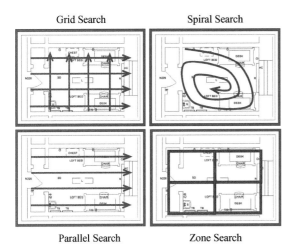

FIGURE 2.24 Types of search patterns for the complete coverage of an area when locating evidence.

Source: Retrieved from Wikimedia Commons; used per Creative Commons Attribution.

BOX 2.11   EVIDENCE PACKAGING GOALS

- Prevents any change in the item after collection.
- Prevents any possible cross-contamination with other samples.
- Preserves the sample as intact as possible.
- Maintains safe environment.
- Ensures proper identification and chain of custody information for the item.

FIGURE 2.25 Components of an evidence collection and packaging kit.

Source: Shutterstock.com.

TABLE 2.1 Selected examples of packaging for different types of evidence

TYPE OF EVIDENCE/SAMPLE	IDENTIFICATION	PRESERVATION	WRAPPING AND PACKING
Blood and body fluids (forensic biology)	On the outside of the box, paper packet, or envelope: type of specimen, date secured, CSI or investigator's initials, case name and number, and where the sample was taken from.	Keep dry.	Tops, ends, and all folds sealed. Never package in plastic. Always use paper.
Stained clothing or fabric	Type of specimen, date obtained, CSI or investigator's initials, case name and number, and owner of garment.	If wet when found, dry under natural conditions. Use no excessive heat to dry.	Each article wrapped separately and identified on outside of package. Place in cardboard box or paper bags, packed to prevent shifting of contents. Always use paper bags, never use plastic bags or containers that do not allow air flow.
Bullets (projectiles, not cartridges)	Seal in container and mark container, not projectile. Place CSI or investigator's initials, date, case name and number on container.	None.	Package to prevent shifting.
Powders, tablets, and capsules	Label or tag on the outside of container. Show type of material, date obtained, CSI or investigator's initials, case name and number.	None.	Seal with tape to prevent any loss.
Hair	Label or tag on the outside of container. Show type of material, date obtained, CSI or investigator's initials, case name and number.	None.	Druggist fold, sealed edges, and openings with Scotch tape or adhesive tape.
Soil	Label or tag on the outside of container. Show type of material, date obtained, CSI or investigator's initials, case name and number.	None.	Paper bags, seal to prevent loss.
Toolmarks	On packaging or on a tag attached to or on the opposite end from where toolmarks appear, CSI or investigator's initials, case name and number.	Cover ends bearing toolmarks with bag and wrap with paper. Never use tape on cut ends.	After marks have been protected, place in strong box and pack to prevent shifting.
Glass fragments	Label or tag on the outside of container. Show type of material, date obtained, CSI or investigator's initials, case name and number.	Avoid chipping.	Wrap each piece separately. Pack in strong box to prevent shifting and breakage. Identify contents.

Source: Adapted using select excerpts from "Evidence Packaging Procedures", Illinois State Police, Division of Forensic Services and Identification Bureau of Forensic Sciences.

2.3.2 Evidence Teams

A number of trained personnel are often needed to properly process a crime scene. The specific types of expertise required mostly depend on the nature of the crime and crime scene itself, although a number of jobs are common to most scenes. Each person on the team has a well-defined set of tasks and responsibilities to minimize duplication of effort (Figure 2.27). A crime scene-processing unit needs to be a well-organized, logic-based operation. A typical crime scene investigative team will usually include:

- **Team Leader**: The team leader assumes control and directs access to the site. They are responsible for the overall operation of the search and recovery of evidence, including determining the site boundaries, the search method, assignment of personnel to various tasks, coordination with all groups involved in investigating the crime and processing the scene (e.g., medical examiners, police responders, investigators, fire personnel, evidence technicians, and various specialists). Since the processing of a crime scene may change as new evidence is found, the team leader must continuously reevaluate the ongoing work and make appropriate changes accordingly. Finally, when the work is completed, they are responsible for releasing the site back to its owners or to public use.
- **Photographer**: The photographer's primary responsibility is to document the site both before

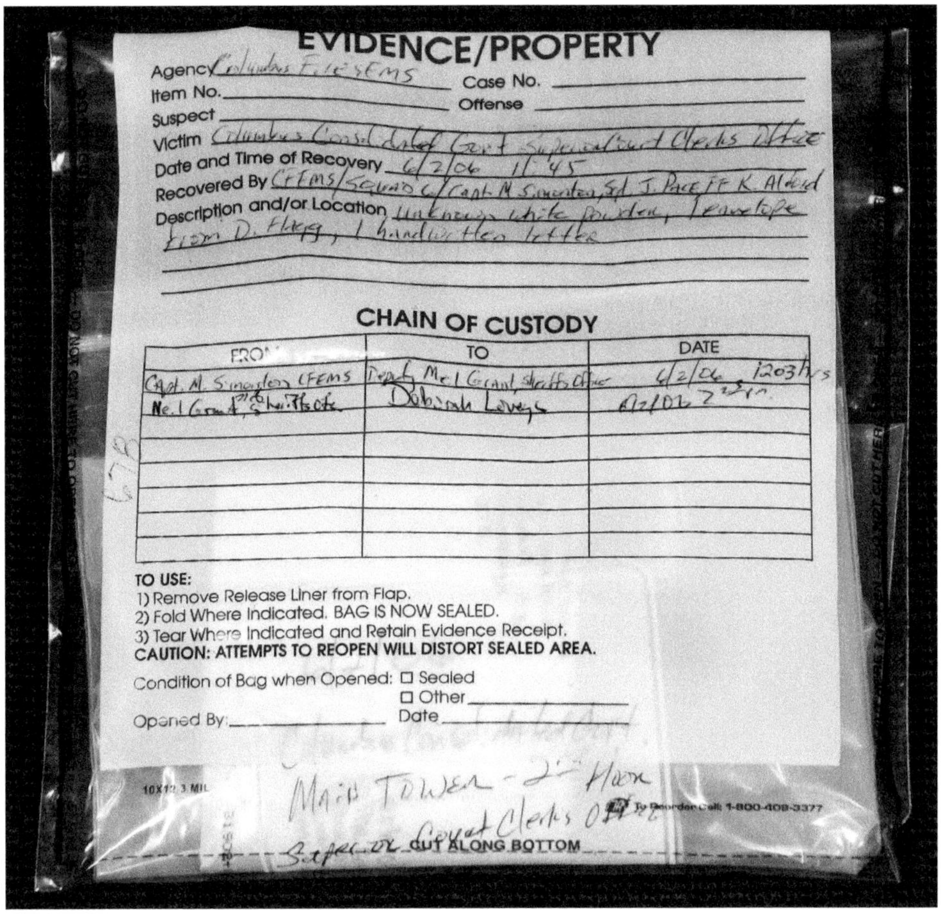

FIGURE 2.26   A typical chain of custody form for a single piece of evidence that records its history, beginning when it is found.

Credit: Richard J. Green/Science Photo Library. Used with permission.

FIGURE 2.27   Personal safety and prevention of contamination are important when searching for and recovering evidence.

Source: Shutterstock.com.

the processing begins and as evidence is collected. This requires both wide-view photographs of large portions of the scene and close-up photographs to show detail. It is important to record a known scale marker, such as a meter stick, coin, or size-grid, in each photograph to provide size information. When a piece of evidence is found, including fingerprints and impressions, it must be photographed before it's collected. Each photograph must be recorded in a log so that it can be placed into the context of the entire scene and entered as part of the evidence. The photographer should also inconspicuously photograph any bystanders or people watching the events – occasionally this will lead to potential suspects and witnesses.

- **Sketch/Map Preparer**: A detailed map of the scene must be prepared using site measurements and evidence location techniques described already. Typically, a rough sketch is first prepared showing the dimensions, orientations, and locations of the evidence. This forms the basis of a finished drawing of the site, usually prepared later and often using computer-based techniques.

- **Evidence Recovery and Recorder Personnel**: These technicians search, locate, collect, and package evidence for transportation to the lab. Each piece of evidence found must be first logged and photographed before collection. The technicians then record a description of the piece of evidence and carefully label the item before it is properly packaged. These technicians also begin the chain of custody record of the item as they hand it over for delivery to the evidence recorder for transportation. Technicians must be keenly aware of any possible hazards associated with the evidence (e.g., biohazard, dangerous chemicals, etc.) and exercise proper techniques for the safe collection of the material.

- **Specialists**: For more complex crime scenes, various experts might be required to deal with specialized evidence (Figure 2.28). These experts can include:

  - Forensic anthropologist (Chapter 9) (Figure 2.29)
  - Medical examiner or medicolegal death investigator (Chapter 8)
  - DNA technician (Chapter 5)

FIGURE 2.28 Crime scenes may require the expertise of specialists, such as at underwater, mountain, or other difficult terrain sites for evidence and remains recovery.

Source: Shutterstock.com.

FIGURE 2.29 A variety of experts may be needed to properly and completely document and recover key evidence from a crime scene on site, such as a forensic anthropologist.

Source: Shutterstock.com.

- Blood spatter experts (Chapter 6)
- Divers and special recovery experts
- Fingerprint/Impression evidence technician (Chapter 7)
- Canine units
- Entomologist (Chapter 10)
- Crime reconstruction engineer (Chapter 19)
- Forensic ecologist (Chapter 10)
- Toxicologist (Chapter 13)

2.3.3 Types of Crime Scenes

Generally, there are three broad types of crime scenes: outdoor scenes, indoor scenes, and "conveyance" scenes.

An outdoor crime scene can range from a relatively small area to one that extends over many square miles of terrain. These scenes present some of the greatest challenges since their processing is most difficult to control adequately and may need to occur under a variety of difficult weather conditions, which may very quickly degrade and eliminate vital forensic information. These scenes often must be processed as quickly as possible to avoid loss.

Indoor scenes are typically easier to control and less subject to environmental conditions. These scenes, of course, present their own set of challenges such as requiring technicians to work in confined areas with potential safety concerns.

Finally, "conveyance" scenes are defined as those involving some form of transportation: cars, planes, trucks, trains, boats, etc. Since vehicles move, it may be necessary to retrace the pathway that a vehicle took to look for evidence ejected from the vehicle – a path often extending over many miles along a path of pursuit.

Proper identification, collection, and storage may be the difference between a strong and weak case. Adhering to well-known and established precedent procedures will certainly minimize errors and problem that can be devastating to a case later in the criminal justice proceedings.

QUESTIONS FOR FURTHER PRACTICE AND MASTERY

2.1   Explain the differences between relevant evidence, probative evidence, and prejudicial evidence.

2.2   Explain what is meant by identification analysis and comparison analysis. Give several examples of forensic techniques used in these types of analysis.

2.3   What is meant by class evidence as opposed to individual evidence?

2.4   What is the basic difference between class characteristics and individual characteristics in terms of establishing a relationship between two pieces of evidence?

2.5   What is the Fourth Amendment to the Constitution, and why is it important to forensic science?

2.6   Who is required to have a warrant to search a person or their property?

2.7   Under what circumstances can illegally obtained evidence be used?

2.8   What is a search warrant? How is one obtained and what must be specified in a warrant?

2.9   Under what conditions may officials conduct a warrantless search?

2.10 Explain the importance of *Mincy v. Arizona* and *Michigan v. Tyler* with respect to the collection of evidence.

2.11 What are the four steps to correctly process a crime scene?

2.12 What are the role and duties of first responders?

2.13 When recording a crime scene, what is triangulation, azimuthal locating, coordinate mapping, and electronic method?

2.14 What are three typical search patterns used in collecting evidence?

2.15 What is the function of a Chain of Custody? Why is it an important document?

2.16 What are the three general types of crime scenes?

EXTENSIVE QUESTIONS

2.17 Evidence can be ruled inadmissible due to an illegal search under either the *Exclusionary Rule* or *Fruit of the Poisonous Tree Doctrine*. Explain what these two terms mean in terms of ruling evidence as inadmissible.

2.18 Extensive protocols have been established for packaging, preserving, and storing evidence. For each of the following, list the identification process, preservation method, wrapping and packing protocols used to best deal with the type of evidence: (a) blood samples, (b) soil, (c) clothing, (d) fibers, (e) biological tissues, (f) minerals, (g) shell casings, (h) skin, (i) hair, (j) fire accelerants, and (k) bullets.

2.19 What are the primary functions of each of the following members of an evidence team? (a) team leader, (b) photographer, (c) sketch map preparer, (d) evidence recovery personnel, (e) recorder personnel, and (f) specialists.

GLOSSARY OF TERMS

azimuthal locating: this process uses a compass arrangement to locate the evidence by measuring angles and distances to a known geographic point(s).

boundary: the border surrounding and including potential physical evidence and/or crime scene.

chain of custody: the written record that keeps track of the history of a piece of evidence so that its location and handling are documented from the point of its discovery through storage, analysis, and use in court.

class characteristics: features that place the piece of evidence within a broad group of similar objects.

comparison analysis: the technique of the association of a standard reference sample (*exemplar*) with a sample of an unknown origin.

coordinate mapping: the technique that divides the crime scene into a grid of small squares or units for effective searching and recording finds.

exclusionary rule: any evidence resulting from an illegal search cannot be used as direct evidence in court.

exemplar: see reference sample.

first responder: the initial police, fire, or similar trained officer to arrive at a crime or emergency scene.

Fourth Amendment to the U.S. Constitution: the Fourth Amendment to the U.S. Constitution states: "The right of the people to be secure in their persons, houses, papers, and effects, against unreasonable searches and seizures, shall not be violated, and no Warrants shall issue, but upon probable cause, supported by Oath or affirmation, and particularly describing the place to be searched, and the persons or things to be seized."

fruit of the poisonous tree doctrine: any evidence found from an illegal search also cannot be used to find other evidence. Any evidence found from information provided by an initially illegal search is itself illegal.

identification analysis: detailed description of the components or composition of an unknown sample.

individual characteristics: features that are of a unique and specific origin with a *very high degree of certainty*.

Michigan v. Tyler: this case further limited the conditions of a warrantless search.

Mincy v. Arizona: this case limited the length of time that a warrantless search was justified under emergency conditions.

one-to-many matching: the process that involves matching key features found in an unknown sample with candidates from a very large pool of known possibilities.

one-to-one matching: the comparison a set of features observed in an unknown sample with either just one reference or among a very small number of "standard" possibilities.

plain view doctrine: items readily observable (plain view) by someone located at a public or legal position do not fall under the Fourth Amendment's provisions since the person can have no real expectation of privacy in such circumstances and visible items can be seized without a warrant.

prejudicial evidence: evidence that may unduly influence the court to decide upon a matter on an improper basis. Evidence must not be unfairly prejudicial to be allowed in court.

probable cause: the common practice that requires the police to present to a judge objective facts or evidence that they will find what they are looking for of a criminal nature during the search.

probative evidence: evidence that has the ability to prove or demonstrate something relevant to the case.

reference sample (or exemplar): a sample collected from a verified source (such as a fingerprint taken from a suspect).

relevant evidence: evidence having the ability to make the existence of any fact that is important to the case more probable or less probable (from FRE 401).

search warrant: an order issued by a judge or magistrate that gives the officers the authority to conduct a search at a specific place, time, and for a specific reason.

triangulation: the use of two fixed points in the crime scene to fix the position of the object accurately.

warrantless search: a search that occurs through well-established exceptions to the Fourth Amendment's requirement where a prior warrant is required, based upon a situation that is either so dangerous or fast-moving that there is not sufficient time to obtain a search warrant.

BIBLIOGRAPHY

Everett Baxter, Jr., *Complete Crime Scene Investigation Handbook*, Taylor & Francis/CRC Press, 2015, 81.

Aric W. Dutelle and Joseph LeFevre, *An Introduction to Crime Scene Investigation*, Jones and Bartlett Publishers, 2010.

Federal Bureau of Investigation, *FBI Handbook of Crime Scene Forensics*, Skyhorse Publishing, 2008.

Jacqueline T. Fish, Larry S. Miller, and Michael C. Braswell, *Crime Scene Investigation* (2nd Ed.), Anderson Press, 2010.

Barry A.J. Fisher, *Techniques of Crime Scene Investigation* (7th Ed.), CRC Press, 2003.

Ross M. Gardner, *Practical Crime Scene Processing and Investigation* (2nd Ed.), Taylor and Francis, 2011.

Robert R. Ogle, *Crime Scene Investigation and Reconstruction* (3rd Ed.), Prentice Hall, 2011.

Peter Tremayne, *Hemlock at Vespers: Fifteen Sister Fidelma Mysteries*, Minotaur Press, 2000.

Tina J. Young and P.J. Ortmeier, *Crime Scene Investigation: The Forensic Technician's Field Manual*, Prentice Hall, 2010.

US Department of Justice, National Institute of Justice, *Crime Scene Investigation Technical Working Group on Crime Scene Investigation*, 2000 [National Council of Justice 17820]. www.ncjrs.gov/pdffiles1/nij/178280.pdf.

Nina Totenberg, National Public Radio, January 23, 2012.

California v. Ciraolo, 476 U.S. 207, 1986.

Science, Pseudoscience, and the Law

3

3.1 A TEST FOR SCIENCE

Science vs Pseudoscience in the Courtroom

Smart people, like smart lawyers, can come up with very good explanations for mistaken points of view.

(Richard P. Feynman, 1999)

LEARNING GOALS AND OBJECTIVES

All legal systems are based on good evidence and scientific practice. Increasingly, evidence is presented with statistical and probability results in order to gauge its reliability and the amount of confidence to place upon the results. Additionally, there is an inherent tension between scientific practice and legal requirements. Throughout the practice of forensic science, practitioners *must* always display the highest standards of professional ethics and unbiased work. After completing this chapter, you should be able to:

- Describe what is meant by good science.
- Explain what is meant by the scientific method and how it operates.
- Discuss how the scientific method applies to forensic investigations.
- Express what is meant by pseudoscience and how it can be identified.
- Explain what is meant by circumstantial evidence and what its strengths and limitations are.
- Discuss what is meant by the terms *probability* and *statistics*.
- Explain how the probability of single and multiple events may be determined.
- Identify the importance of ethics in forensic science.
- Describe what is meant by the terms *statistics* and *probability*.
- Explain what the terms *mean*, *median*, and *standard deviation* represent.
- Understand how to test the validity of data points.

- Discuss how the basics of probability theory work for multiple events.
- Describe what is meant by *ethics* and how it can guide decisions.
- Discuss the possible conflicts encountered in the practice of forensic science.
- Explain what is meant by a *Code of Ethics* for forensic science.

3.1.1 Introduction

Good science can bring amazing insights to legal proceedings, while incorrect and flawed "science" can easily be misleading and cause overwhelming problems for any system of criminal justice (Figure 3.1). The entire foundation of any just legal system rests upon proper evidence supported by the highest level of scientific inquiry and analysis. When arguments are built upon a poor or incorrect pseudoscientific framework, the entire system can collapse. One of the greatest problems that courts face, therefore, is determining what evidence and testimony *are* based on good, accepted scientific practice and what are not. In this chapter, we will explore some of the basic hallmarks of good science and how to test whether new methods and analyses meet acceptable levels of scientific standards.

In previous chapters, we examined the legal underpinning of forensic evidence, analysis, and testimony in courts. Two of the most important cases in U.S. trial law, the *Frye* and *Daubert* cases, focused directly on the problem of differentiating good science from "junk" science. Prior to the *Frye* decision in 1923, each local court could decide almost arbitrarily what they would allow as scientific testimony. Juries, with typically limited scientific backgrounds, were forced to decide for themselves what constituted good science with very little guidance. Needless to say, real problems resulted from their inability to identify false science, often resulting in juries simply believing the "scientific" evidence of witnesses who presented their case with more skill and enthusiasm rather than evaluating the actual merits of the science. After the *Frye* case, however, the courts had a set of legal guidelines for the first time by which they could measure any scientific analysis to see if it met the standards of generally accepted practice. Later cases, such as *Daubert*, *Khumo*, and others, helped to refine these benchmarks for admissible practice, but the issue

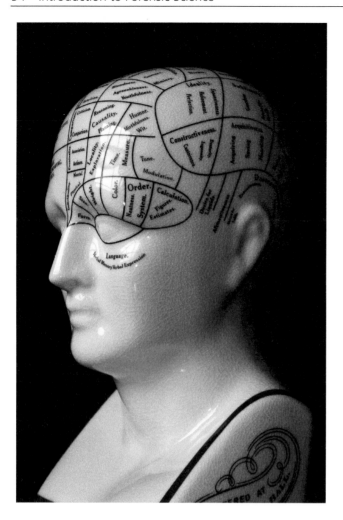

FIGURE 3.1 Courts are required to determine if the scientific evidence presented comes from practices based on the scientific method or from faulty pseudoscience. The field of phrenology, involving the measurement of the head and facial features, was once thought to be a predictor of mental capabilities and character.

Source: Shutterstock.com.

of what is good science remains hotly contested today in courtrooms across the world, leaving juries, judges, lawyers, and investigators with the continuing need to understand for themselves what constitutes good, valid scientific practice and how to present it effectively to juries. This is increasingly problematic as courts are called upon to deal effectively with progressively more complex technological issues that can enormously impact a case's outcome. To sort all of this out and provide a strong system of justice, we need to understand the basics of what constitutes good science.

3.1.2 What Is Science?

Our understanding of science today hinges upon the logical interpretation of systematic observations and experiments. Science is, however, both the collective total of our *knowledge* and understanding and a *process* for discovering new things and refining our picture of the physical world. The word

"science" is derived directly from the Latin word "scientia" meaning knowledge. Today, while our knowledge of important scientific concepts continues to rapidly evolve and grow, the basic approach to understanding these scientific advances remains rooted in critical thinking, analytical problem-solving skills, and the scientific method – all essential components of modern forensic science.

Science also seeks to understand the relationships between things through careful observation, experimentation, and logical analysis. When one action happens, we want to know how that might cause another to occur. Similarly, we often want to understand how one property of a material affects other properties of the material. Science tries to understand at a deep level how things work and what causes them to behave in a particular way under a given set of conditions. Science reasons only with the physical world, dealing exclusively with phenomena that can be perceived, observed, measured, and tested.

When considering the nature of science, it is important to distinguish between the tools of science and science itself. The tools of science include, among others, mathematics, measurement systems, scientific instrumentation, as well as names and definitions for various things. These tools are important for our exploration and communication of scientific ideas and observations, but they are really *not* part of science itself. As the Nobel Prize-winning physicist Richard Feynman illustrated:

> It is not science to know how to change Centigrade to Fahrenheit. It's necessary, but it is not exactly science. In the same sense, if you were discussing what art is, you wouldn't say art is the knowledge of the fact that a 3-B pencil is softer than a 2-H pencil. It's a distinct difference.

(Richard P. Feynman, 1999)

Being able to identify a particular organ as something called a liver really does not tell us anything about the structure, function, and interrelationships it has with other body parts. Names change in different languages but an understanding of how something works is universal. *The name is the tool, the understanding is the science.*

Science is not able to *prove* anything beyond simple facts, so our understanding of science is perpetually in a state of change and refinement. This may seem like a strange statement – what about gravity, relativity, and similar scientific "laws"? Aren't they proven? As we'll see in our consideration of the scientific method, these are examples of scientific ideas that have been tested over and over without finding an exception to their predictions. We, therefore, place a great deal of trust in these ideas as being correct, but they have not been *proven*, just never been found wrong. These are two quite different things. Science can, however, readily *disprove* events and theories. Scientists, including forensic scientists and investigators, must be willing to abandon or modify previously accepted hypotheses and conclusions when faced with new and contradictory data. In addition, scientists must open their experimental findings and analyses up to the scrutiny of others in the much larger scientific community to test, validate, and allow others to build upon their work (Figure 3.2).

"I THINK YOU SHOULD BE MORE EXPLICIT HERE IN STEP TWO."

FIGURE 3.2 Science tries to understand the physical world in reliable, reproducible, and non-arbitrary terms.

Source: Copyright © 2023 by Sidney Harris. http://www.sciencecartoonsplus.com/ used with permission.

BOX 3.1   AN INTERESTING STORY OF SCIENCE

A carpenter, a school teacher, and a scientist were traveling by train through Scotland when they saw a black sheep through the window of the train. "Aha," said the carpenter with a smile, "I see that Scottish sheep are black." "Hmm," said the school teacher, "You mean that some Scottish sheep are black." "No," said the scientist, "All we know is that there is at least one sheep in Scotland, and that at least one side of that one sheep is black" (anon.).

Courts and scientists have many things in common, but one important commonality is that when faced with a claim that is asserted to be true, they both seek evidence and validation to support that claim. In a legal context, the U.S. Supreme Court in the *Daubert* case defined science as "a process for proposing and refining theoretical explanations about the world that are subject to further testing and refinement" and that all "proposed [legal] testimony must be supported by appropriate validation." This clearly holds the science presented in courts to the highest attainable levels of scientific practice and rigor.

3.1.3 The Scientific Method

We are all born with an intuitive "built-in" form of the scientific method: as babies, we constantly observe, seek patterns, experiment, and observe again until we can move beyond simply collecting "facts" to be able to better predict the consequences of our actions. As we continue to grow and develop, our wealth of observations, recognized patterns, and personal "experiments" provide a rich basis for shaping our perception of the world around us and dictating how we interact with it. We also continually make ever more refined "guesses" and predictions based on our evolving ideas and then test these predictions through personal interactions with our environment. Science, defined as systematic knowledge of the physical world gained through the process of observation and experimentation, is quite clearly intimately relevant to all that we see and do as humans. Clearly, the scientific method reflects our own personal growth and developmental process in many ways.

BOX 3.2   THREE HISTORIC QUOTES ON ASPECTS OF THE SCIENTIFIC METHOD FOR FORENSIC SCIENTISTS

- "The strength of a science is that its conclusions are derived by logical arguments from facts that result from well-designed experiments" (Bruce Mahan from *University Chemistry*, 4th Ed., 2000).
- "It is the credo of free men – the opportunity to try, the privilege to err, the courage to experiment anew … experiment, experiment, ever experiment" (Roger Bacon, 1214–1294).
- "Je veux parler des faits" (translation: "Do not rely upon speculation but build upon facts") (Antoine Lavoisier, 1743–1794).
- "When you have eliminated the impossible, whatever remains, however improbable, must be the truth." Arthur Conan Doyle's famous fictional detective Sherlock Holmes (*The Sign of the Four*, ch. 6, 1890).
- "He who loves practice without theory is like the sailor who boards ship without a rudder and compass and never knows where he may cast" (Leonardo DaVinci, 1452–1519).

The *scientific method* may be defined as the *process* by which scientists more formally try to construct an accurate understanding of the things and events around us in reliable, reproducible, and non-arbitrary terms. The scientific method, therefore, aims to use unbiased methods and logical analyses to provide these rational interpretations and new forms of knowledge. It is the way that we conduct scientific work, and understanding this process can clearly help identify valid science from false or pseudoscience.

FIGURE 3.3 A schematic flowchart showing the relationships between the key steps of the scientific method.

Source: Shutterstock.com.

The scientific method is comprised of five key steps: observation, hypothesis formulation, prediction based on the hypothesis, experimentation, and analysis of the results to support, refine, or refute the original hypothesis. These steps are shown schematically in Figure 3.3. However, it all begins with careful observations, measurements, and descriptions.

Step One: Observation. Observation and measurement are rooted in a need to first describe and quantify an object or phenomenon. Lord Kelvin put it well when he said,

> When you can measure what you are speaking about, and express it in numbers, you know something about it; but when you cannot measure it, when you cannot express it in numbers, your knowledge of it is of a meager and unsatisfactory kind.

Observations and measurements are both the starting point and the means forward in any scientific inquiry, including forensic investigations. The methods for measurement and the descriptive vocabulary used in this step are largely established through the standard practices of the relevant scientific community. In Chapter 4, we will examine more closely some of these tools and practices of measurement and description as they specifically relate to forensic science.

Step Two: Hypothesis. Once the initial set of observations and measurements has been made, we try to piece them together into a reasonable *hypothesis* that includes all the data available. A hypothesis is simply a rough statement or explanation made on the basis of the limited data available and serves as a good starting point for further investigation – an informed first guess. For example, you might hypothesize that a lamp does not light because the light bulb is faulty. This would probably lead you to some experimentation: checking and replacing the bulb, checking to see if the lamp is plugged in and the switch is turned on, examining the power cable to see if it's damaged, and other similar "experiments." The major role of a hypothesis is to provide

a logical starting framework to suggest new experiments and observations that would allow you to test, refine, and expand your explanation.

BOX 3.3   ABANDONED HYPOTHESES

Science is filled with examples, large and small, of hypotheses that have had to be abandoned in light of new and compelling data, including:

- The flat world concept.
- The Earth-centered Universe.
- The ability to magically transmute earth into precious metals.
- Nuclear cold fusion.
- Smoking cigarettes is safe.

One common error is to regard the hypothesis as an explanation that does not require further testing. No matter how much "sense" a hypothesis makes, it still *must* be validated and tested.

Step Three: Prediction. Once a reasonable hypothesis has been formulated, it should suggest ways to test its validity. More complex problems often require a detailed experimental plan that serves to both set boundaries around the question to be studied and provide information about the soundness of the hypothesis itself. A well-formulated experimental plan will provide the key information needed to evaluate the accuracy and predictive power of the original hypothesis. For example, we might predict that by changing the light bulb, the lamp will function again. A set of logical, reasonable experiments that bear directly upon the central points of the hypothesis are required – is the bulb broken, is the lamp plugged in, etc.? Putting your fingers directly into the electrical outlet or checking on solar flare activity would not be good or useful starting places for your investigation of the faulty lamp.

However, some types of hypotheses are difficult to use predictively and test directly. Historical events or criminal actions are often unique, one-time occurrences and cannot be directly experimentally observed, tested, or validated. According to Locard, these events do leave behind traces that *can* be scientifically tested to see if they support the hypothesis for the crime. We can also use scientific methods to understand the range of possibilities under a given set of conditions (recreation) to support or refute a proposed chain of events.

Step Four: Experimentation. The experiments designed to test the hypothesis must be made using the best standard practices available. Any interpretation of an experimental outcome can only be as good as the experimental data itself. Ideally, a *series* of experiments should be performed using a variety of different techniques to avoid hidden systematic and random errors (see Chapter 4). It is relatively easy for inadvertent bias to enter experiments, often without being recognized. This bias may be minimized by recognizing the potential sources of bias and through the process of having the experiments repeated by other scientists who presumably would not have the same set of biases as the original experimenter. Additionally, performing experiments using a variety of different techniques to gather the same information further helps to reduce inherent bias.

A common mistake in experimentation is to eliminate data that does not fit the hypothesis being tested. Sometimes, the most important data point is that which seems to be an outlier, apart from the other data, that can lead the way to a better hypothesis. It is important that all data be handled in the same fashion, regardless of whether they support or refute the hypothesis. Statistical and other methods exist for determining if some data are caused by systematic measurement errors and can be justifiably eliminated from further analysis – but these tests must be used to scrutinize *all* data, even those that support the hypothesis (see Section 3.2). A real problem in forensic science is that an investigator or analyst might have a strong bias or expectation about a particular result or outcome. For example, if an officer delivers to the lab a DNA sample taken from a victim's clothes along with a DNA sample taken from the prime suspect and then asks the analyst to show that the two came from the same person, it is likely that the analyst psychologically has a strong bias to find data to support the connection between the two, even if it might not justifiably exist. It is often too easy to discard a data point that does not conform to the hypothesis while not applying the same test to other data that fits into expectations. The converse is also true: an "imaginary" data point might be seen as real if one looks hard enough at the background signal. For these reasons, it is best if the analyst is not informed about any expected outcomes of an experiment before the experiment is completed.

The main idea of testing a hypothesis is actually to try to determine its limitations, seeking to find when it fails. We often learn much more through the failure of an idea than from its successes. Simply seeking confirmatory evidence for a hypothesis without pushing the boundaries of the analysis can readily lead to false confidence in the hypothesis. For example, if we only ever test the switch in the lamp, ignoring all other parts of the lamp, then we end up with a very imperfect understanding of the lamp's operation (see Box 3.4 for another example).

BOX 3.4   AN ELEPHANT OF AN EXPERIMENT

A famous story of unknown origin from antiquity relates the fable about the encounters of six blind men with an elephant.

Six blind men encounter an elephant – although how they knew that it was an elephant the story does not recount. The first touches its trunk and says that an elephant is like a palm tree, another touches its side and says that an elephant is like a rough

FIGURE 3.4   The story of the six blind men and an elephant.

Source: Shutterstock.com.

wall. Another feels its tail and says that an elephant is like a piece of rope. Each comes into contact with a different part of the elephant and is convinced that their own explanation is correct and that the others are wrong. None of them realizes that they are all experiencing just one part of the same elephant and that none of their explanations are complete.

(Knight, 2003)

This story has clear relevance to the proper scope and application of the scientific method. Each blind man, after exploring only one particular facet of the elephant, came up with a view of the animal that, in reality, was very limited and incomplete. If, instead, they had each employed a broader experimental view and shared data, they would have quickly found where their initial hypotheses that the elephant was a palm tree, a wall, or a piece of rope" failed. They would have discovered that the elephant was far more complex than any of their original guesses and recognized the need to revise their hypotheses through more experimentation.

TABLE 3.1   Comparison of scientific attributes to those of pseudoscience

	SCIENCE	*PSEUDOSCIENCE*
Publication	Journals with articles reviewed by experts in the field and subjected to rigorous editorial and experimental control.	General public or media outlets such as newspapers, magazines, online platforms, flyers, brochures, and books. Verification is not required.
Reproducibility	Must provide enough information to be reproducible by others to achieve similar results: full details of the entire experimental method are required so that others can try to duplicate the experiments.	No requirement for reproducible results and few or vague details on the method used are provided – not enough to attempt to duplicate the result without making many guesses.
Claims	Clearly stated and supported by evidence and generally accepted by the discipline.	Vague, untestable, or unbounded claims presented without experimental backup. Sounds often too good to be true (and usually is).
Support	Evidence-based claims with full transparency of how the idea was tested.	Anecdotal evidence, misleading statistics.
Revision	Hypotheses are continually being revised, modified, or even abandoned as new data is found.	Claims and theories are rarely changed from their original introduction.
Experimental plan	Experiments are designed to both provide confirmation and to especially probe for failures or limitations of the hypothesis.	Experiments are designed to give only confirmatory evidence. Reluctance to experiment at all – asks audience to rely on trust.
Contradictory evidence	Evidence that contradicts the hypothesis is included when revising or discarding the hypothesis.	Contradictory evidence is often overlooked or cursorily discarded for unjustifiable reasons.
Future development	Provides a pathway forward to learn more about a phenomenon or topic – leading to the creation of more understanding and new knowledge.	Static, does not provide any further insights into a topic nor move the field forward in understanding.

Some of the key differences between science and false science, often referred to as pseudoscience, are presented in Table 3.1. It is important to note that various systems of belief built upon divine knowledge or revelation are typically not considered pseudoscience since they generally do not claim to be scientific. Science deals only with understanding the physical universe through observation and experimentation and is, therefore, clearly distinguishable from theology. Thus, there is not an inherent conflict between scientific thought and investigation and religious beliefs as long as each is recognized for their origins, methods, and goals.

Of course, careful and complete notes are required to validate any experiments performed, especially in any forensics application. Analyses and experiments in the highly regulated forensic world must also include following all established laboratory protocols that often involve validating experimental

results in very specific ways. Most forensic laboratories have detailed "Standard Operating Procedures" (SOPs) set up for everything they do, including all analyses and procedures that conform to rigorous standards widely accepted as best practices in the field. Any analysis must, therefore, be carried out and validated according to these strict SOPs for it to be routinely acceptable to a court.

Step Five: Analysis and Refinement or Abandonment of the Hypothesis. The data from experiments may support the original hypothesis or might dictate a revision or, if the data requires, the complete abandonment of the original hypothesis in favor of a new "starting" hypothesis. In fact, the scientific method requires that a hypothesis be ruled out and abandoned if its predictions are found to be incompatible with experimental results. If the hypothesis is, however, supported by the data, a new and more refined set of experiments would be designed that would be capable of probing even more deeply into the problem being considered. Through this cyclical process of hypothesis → experimentation → results and analysis → revised hypothesis, an initial hypothesis is continually revised and refined to better describe the phenomenon (Figure 3.5). The more data and experimentation that supports a hypothesis, the more value and credibility we give to the explanation.

When a hypothesis has been tested over and over and found valid in all the circumstances examined, it may take on added importance and is then referred to as a scientific theory or law. The terms "theory" or "law" simply mean that the explanation has been extensively tested and generally accepted as broadly valid by a large number of scientists over a long period of time – it does not mean that it has been proven, just that there have been no known exceptions after a very large amount of data has been accumulated and analyzed. Theories remain theories, however, and unproven in the formal sense. For example, the Law of Gravity or the First Law of Thermodynamics ("conservation of energy") are called laws because we have yet to find an exception to their concepts and predictions: but they are not proven. Nonetheless, few people truly doubt the existence of gravity enough to test this theory by stepping off the top of a high cliff. Science places a great deal of credence and trust in these types of refined explanations and any new experiments that seemingly would refute such well-founded theories would be examined with especially intense scrutiny. A new claim for an antigravity device, for instance, would certainly be open to intense investigation before people would declare it a true exception to the law of gravity.

It is important to note that, while the scientific method describes a very commonly used sequential approach to scientific discovery, in practice the order of the various steps in the process may differ from that presented above. Inspiration or happenstance may "insert" a scientific investigation into any particular step "out of order." The process, however, then typically continues along the course described, simply beginning at a given step, and readily accommodates the scientific thought process.

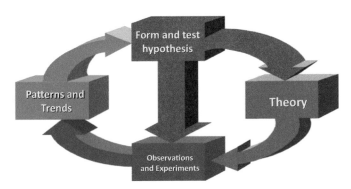

FIGURE 3.5 The cyclical nature of hypothesis, experimentation, results, and revised hypothesis in the scientific method.

3.1.4 The Scientific Method and Forensic Science

Any valid forensic investigation must follow the basic *principles* of the scientific method to be well-accepted by both the scientific and legal communities. In criminalistics, we are usually faced with trying to understand what events have led to an observed result: the crime scene. The investigation must begin, as does the scientific method, with the collection of data – observations, measurements, and descriptions. Once sufficient preliminary information has been amassed, the investigative team usually develops one or several possible hypotheses that can be tested by the forensic data and any other available evidence. The forensic data are then used to support, refine, or refute a particular hypothesis of a crime, including any witness accounts of the happenings. A refined hypothesis can then suggest new avenues of investigation that continue the cyclical investigative process of hypothesis → observation/analysis → results and analysis → revised hypothesis. One important point, as described above in the scientific method, is that investigators should specifically look for evidence that would refute their hypothesis of the crime in addition to looking for confirmatory evidence – simply looking for confirmatory evidence may overlook important insights that would lead to a complete investigation and a proper criminal courtroom outcome.

One major difference between the legal and scientific worlds is that in basic science, the questions examined are open-ended and are continually subject to revision. In the legal system, however, there is usually a definitive end-point – the point at which the jury is presented with the evidence and the hypothesis of the crime, and where they must render a final judgment quickly. At that point, the investigation is over and inquiry is suspended. Another difference is that courts usually seek definitive answers, such as "does this item match a standard" or "did this DNA sample found at the scene come from the suspect." Science, however, can only refute and not prove things. It can, however, state that the DNA sample found at a crime scene is consistent with one taken from a suspect and give an indication of the probability of a random match – such as a 1 in 4 trillion chance of a random match in the general population with the DNA profile. This information provides a measure of the trust and credibility that we can place on a particular piece of evidence (see Section 3.2). It is then up to the judge or jury to decide how much reliance they should place on the evidence in determining the case's outcome.

3.1.5 What Is Pseudoscience?

In most respects, the "opposite" of true science is pseudoscience. The term pseudoscience, sometimes also called "junk," "fringe," "pop," or "alternative" science, refers to the practice or set of beliefs that are not founded in the basics of the scientific method. The term pseudoscience comes from the Greek words "pseudo" meaning "false" and "scientia" meaning "knowledge" so that pseudoscience can be defined as "false knowledge." Typically, pseudoscience is based upon absent, biased, or faulty observations and does not rely upon direct evidence for support. It is often claimed to be "scientific" in its approach but without making use of the scientific method.

BOX 3.5   FAMOUS EXAMPLES OF PSEUDOSCIENCE

There are numerous clear examples of pseudoscience in history that have misled and confused with claims of scientific validity, while actually based on fiction. Some of the more famous examples include:

- Reflexology
- Alchemy
- N-rays
- Engram Theory
- Astrology
- Face on Mars
- Perpetual Motion
- Hollow Earth
- Facilitated Communication
- Extrasensory Perception (ESP)
- Telepathy
- Plant Perception

Throughout history, people have made outlandish and unsupported claims of new theories, quack cures, amazing powers, and incredible technological feats. To a largely non-scientific public and media, these claims have often been believed at face value by unsuspecting or gullible audiences, only to be disappointed later when the claims are proven false. These frauds can also greatly damage the reputation of true scientific work in the public's estimation since pseudoscience masquerades as real science. A recent National Science Foundation (NSF) study reported that the "belief in pseudoscience is widespread" reflecting a basic lack of understanding of how science works.

The real and often vexing problem is how to distinguish valid science from faulty pseudoscience. Probably the best way, of course, is to know as much as possible about the real nature of science itself. Scientists and philosophers are still debating exactly how best to distinguish between science and pseudoscience, but many features are widely agreed upon. Fundamentally, pseudoscience does not rely on the evidence-based scientific method of observation, hypothesis, experimentation, analysis, and revision. *Pseudoscience relies on trust, while science relies on evidence and experimental validation.* Generally, some of the "telltale" features of pseudoscience include:

- **Exaggerated or Untestable Claims**: Pseudoscience tends to present its claims in imprecise and often vague terms that lack measurements or are supported by faulty assumptions. The claims often include convoluted and complicated explanations, manipulating straightforward explanations into complex descriptions that "sound scientific" (see Box 3.6). Pseudoscience also often lacks "boundary conditions" – the conditions under which the theory is valid – and claim broad applicability of their ideas. For example, in Figure 3.6. "Snake Oil" was once claimed to cure "headache, neuralgia, toothache, earache, backache, swellings, strains, sore chest, swelling of the throat, contracted cords and muscles, stiff joints, wrenches, dislocations, cuts, bruises, all aches and pains, deafness, rheumatism, sciatica and other ailments" – too good to believe, literally.

BOX 3.6   THE SHARP LINE OF OCCAM'S RAZOR

Occam's razor, first presented by the English philosopher William of Ockham in the 1400s, is a theory as to how to decide between two competing hypotheses that arrive at the same result. Sometimes, it is summarized by the phrase "when you have two competing theories that make exactly the same predictions, the simpler one is the better." Einstein, however, modified this to say, "Everything should be made as simple as possible, but not simpler." The term "razor" comes from the idea of "shaving away" assumptions to separate two competing theories.

Often, pseudoscientific ideas are surrounded by unfounded and complex assumptions with convoluted arguments, sometimes claiming mutually contradictory things. Occam's razor has been used to try to separate pseudoscientific ideas and explanations from truly scientific ideas.

- **Based on Hearsay**: Pseudoscientific claims are often based on unverifiable or anecdotal evidence, such as newspaper reports, unreachable witnesses, earlier pseudoscientific works, or questionable publications, including referencing themselves in a circle of deceit. For example, someone might claim that their toothache was cured when they took a dose of snake oil, so the snake oil must have been the cause of the "miracle" cure. They make this claim without conducting any controlled experiments to verify this idea. In truth, the snake oil had little or nothing to do with the disappearance

FIGURE 3.6 Pseudoscience "sold" under the misleading guise of real science. Snake oil, while originally a somewhat effective treatment for inflammation made from an extract of a Chinese water snake, later contained no active ingredients or actual snake oil but was still marketed for a variety of medicinal uses. Today, the term means a fraud or quack remedy, used to exploit an unsuspecting audience.

Source: Public Domain.

of the toothache, but it was simply a coincidence that the dose and the disappearance happened "together" – there was no cause-and-effect linkage ("causal relationship"). Pseudoscientific "quack" medical cures, without any real validity, may appeal to people who have not been cured by traditional medical treatments – often with significant harmful effects (Figure 3.7).

- **Reluctance toward Experimentation and Reproducibility**: Pseudoscientific works rarely provide sufficient information or detail to allow others to attempt to duplicate and, therefore, verify their work, while science is based on others duplicating the results reported: reproducibility is very important in science. Proponents of pseudoscientific ideas shun verification studies and claim the failure of attempts at reproducing their results is due to the failure of science or scientists, sometimes leading to wild conspiracy theories. This is in contrast to scientific ideas that are subjected to intense worldwide scrutiny through duplication and refinement by other scientists.

- **Reliance on Confirmatory Experiments rather than Broad, Open Testing**: Explorations of pseudoscientific ideas, when actually tested, rely on confirmatory tests that are designed only to support the tenets of the pseudoscientific idea itself in one instance. Often, the goal of pseudoscience is to rationalize popular ideas and strongly held beliefs rather than to look for alternative possibilities and test them using experimental methods, arbitrarily discarding any alternative explanations. Science especially looks for places where a proposed theory might fail – often, breakthroughs in understanding occur in these moments.

- **Random Disregard of Some Facts or Data**: Evidence that conflicts with pseudoscientific ideas is often simply ignored or explained away as opinion or somehow faulty without legitimate reasons, such as those provided by applying statistical methods to the data. Occasionally, it may even be referred to as a personal attack or a "witch hunt" against the pseudoscience's advocate and a slur upon their character.

FIGURE 3.7 The tension between science and pseudoscience.

Source: Used with permission, © Tony Piro, https://calamitiesofnature.com/.

- **Often Tries to Fill Voids of Scientific Understanding**: Science does not claim to have all the answers but simply tries to find explanations for the physical world: *science has to try to get it right, whereas pseudoscience has no such requirement*. Many times, scientific discoveries do lead to important new applications for real world problems. In areas where science does not yet have explanations, however, pseudoscience often tries to step in and provide rationalizations and answers (Figure 3.8). Just because science does not fully understand a particular phenomenon, does not mean that a scientific reason will not ultimately be found or that somehow the scientific method has failed. One hundred years ago, the role of DNA in heredity was not understood, while today we have a fairly detailed picture of how DNA functions biologically.
- **Pseudoscience may Rely on a False Authority**: Self-proclaimed experts who have little understanding of a particular field may promote a theory that stands in conflict with all that is known in the field, but they are often believed because of an inherent distrust of established groups – established scientific organizations, universities, scientists, governments, and others. Too often, we see TV and movie stars promoting something because they "play a doctor on TV." People tend to believe these people regardless of how unsubstantiated their claims are,

simply because they sound scientific, are familiar, and appear trustworthy. For example, some people believe that "chemtrails," the white streaks that can be seen behind high altitude aircraft, are caused by the government spraying noxious chemicals on the unknowing population ("chemtrails" are actually "contrails" made of condensed water vapor). The popularity of this belief rises every time a celebrity simply mentions it. This is a problem when pseudoscientific forensic "experts" are allowed to promote their own unjustified and untested ideas to a largely unsuspecting jury.

- **Use of New Terminology**: Pseudoscience can often gain an air of scientific acceptability through the use of technical-sounding terminology and jargon. The central idea of pseudoscientific jargon and "technobabble" is to impress, confuse, and mislead listeners rather than to promote precise communication, as is the use of jargon in true science (Figures 3.9 and 3.10). As an example, explore online the term "turboencabulator" as a famous example of "technobabble" – the use of incomprehensible or meaningless terms to impress, mislead, or confuse an audience.
- **Does not Lead to New Discoveries or Knowledge**: Scientific ideas are continually revised and lead to more experimentation that, in turn, leads to more knowledge and a deeper understanding of the idea. Science is dynamic, continually changing, and leads

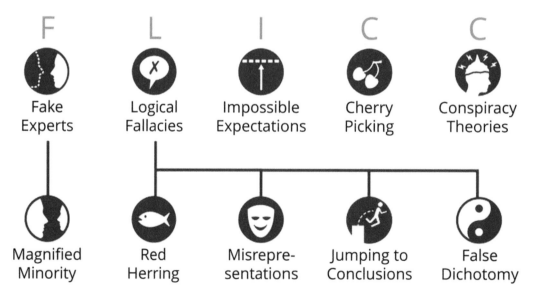

5 Characteristics of Science Denial

F — Fake Experts
L — Logical Fallacies
I — Impossible Expectations
C — Cherry Picking
C — Conspiracy Theories

Magnified Minority
Red Herring
Misrepresentations
Jumping to Conclusions
False Dichotomy

FIGURE 3.8 Pseudoscience may be built upon a scientific fact but then distorts or extends the claims to include entirely non-scientific and unproven ideas.

Source: Used per Creative Commons Share-Alike 4.0 International. User: SkepticalScience, modified by Gregor Hagedorn.

BEWARE of DHMO

This Chemical Is Everywhere In Our Environment!

Locations:
- Acid Rain
- Tumors and Cancers
- Ocean Pollutants
- Poisonous Mixtures
- Industrial Pollution
- Infectious Materials

Threats:
- Toxic Effects
- Carries Diseases
- Erosion
- Death by Inhalation
- Makes Travel Dangerous
- Electrocution Hazard

Uses:
- Nuclear Power Stations
- Fire Suppression
- Government Torture
- Cult Rituals
- Pesticide Delivery
- Chemical Warfare

BAN THE USE OF DHMO!

FIGURE 3.10 False claims, misleading jargon, and distrust of established science may lead to the acceptance of outrageous pseudoscientific ideas – as in the reoccurring dihydrogen monoxide (H_2O) "scares."

FIGURE 3.9 "Instant Success" in tablet form, a common theme in pseudoscientific claims.

Source: Shutterstock.com.

to new insights and discoveries. Pseudoscientific ideas, however, are static and do not change appreciably over time, largely because contradictory evidence is discarded simply because it does not conform to the theory.

Pseudoscientific ideas may be presented as a mixture of true scientific ideas and pseudoscientific components in the courtroom. They may have an appearance of truth on the surface while being built upon an incorrect or flawed foundation. The danger is, of course, when pseudoscientific ideas and practices are accepted as truth in political or legal systems. Pseudoscientific ideas in the courtroom can be very persuasive to lay juries, leading them to rely on faulty reasoning and input when making their important decisions. It is the job of forensic scientists, in conjunction with the entire legal system, to ensure that this doesn't happen through rigorous education, precedent, and practice. Increasingly often, prosecutors are calling upon expert witnesses simply to explain the basis of a scientific method being presented or to refute pseudoscientific claims.

BOX 3.7   TRY THIS AT HOME: IS ASTROLOGY SCIENCE OR PSEUDOSCIENCE?

In a recent Harris Poll, 31% of Americans said that they believed in astrology – the study of the stars and planets in determining a person's traits and destiny. To determine if astrology is science or pseudoscience, try this test yourself. First, consider the criteria for a scientific hypothesis given above to examine the basic ideas of astrology and see if they hold up to the rigor required of the scientific method. Then try this simple experiment:

1. Find a recent newspaper with the horoscope section and cut out the horoscope descriptions.
2. Remove the name signs (e.g., "Libra", "Aries", "Cancer", Capricorn", etc.) from the individual horoscope so that only the descriptions are left.
3. Give all the "nameless" descriptions to a group of people (the more the better) and ask them to identify their own horoscopes for that day from among the 12 choices.
4. Compare their selections with their actual "correct" birth-month sign. What percentage of people correctly identified their own horoscopes?

When this "experiment" is conducted with a large number of people, typically about 8% of the people correctly identify their descriptions. Since there are 12 signs of the Zodiac, a random chance would be about 1 in 12 chances of a "correct" guess – or about 8%. What does this suggest about the scientific validity of horoscopes in providing people with reliable information about their destinies? (Table 3.2).

FIGURE 3.11 The Astrological Zodiac.

Source: Shutterstock.com.

TABLE 3.2   Relative levels of certainty to legally admissible levels of proof

			LEVELS OF CERTAINTY AND PROOF			
LEVEL OF CERTAINTY	GUESS OR INSTINCT	PROBABLE CAUSE	PREPONDERANCE OF THE EVIDENCE	CLEAR AND CONVINCING EVIDENCE	BEYOND A REASONABLE DOUBT	SCIENTIFIC NEAR-CERTAINTY
Evidence required	No physical evidence but a guess	Reasonable facts to act	Something is more likely than not	Firm conviction that it is highly probable	No other reasonable explanation that can come from the evidence	Based on repeated experiments that describe the range of natural phenomena
Certainty	Unknown	Possible	Hypothesis		Theory Construction	Rare
Legal Action	Suppressed	Probable cause	Civil standard of proof	International standard of proof	Criminal law standard of proof	Rarely employed
Investigation	Beginning of investigation	Required for a search warrant	Required in civil case (50%)	Required in important civil cases	Required in criminal conviction	Rarely employed

Source: Adapted from Ward and Osterburg (2000).

3.2 STATISTICS AND PROBABILITY IN FORENSIC SCIENCE

While the individual man is an insoluble puzzle, in the aggregate he becomes a mathematical certainty. You can, for example, never foretell what any one man will be up to, but you can say with precision what an average number will be up to. Individuals vary, but percentages remain constant. So says the statistician.

(Arthur Conan Doyle, The Sign of the Four, 1890)

3.2.1 Introduction

The field of forensic science is becoming more and more reliant upon mathematical methods and quantitative analysis to verify and validate evidence. The fields of probability and statistics are two areas in particular that provide critical tools for modern forensic investigations. Evidence placed in a mathematical context can provide clear insights as to its strength, reliability, and utility, while poor statistical arguments can render an otherwise valuable piece of evidence worthless. For this reason, a secure mathematical underpinning of the validity of a piece of evidence is becoming a commonplace expectation in legal settings.

BOX 3.8   SAMPLE VS POPULATION

Often, in forensic science, we are asked to analyze the properties of a sample taken from a larger population. For example, we measure the physical characteristics of a hair sample taken from the thousands of hairs on a suspect's head. Sample and population are key terms since we need to have representative samples that reflect the properties of the entire population.

A population is the full set of data or objects that make up the whole. A sample is a smaller subset taken from the population. A representative sample is a small amount of the whole that retains the properties reflective of the entire population.

While the terms of statistics and probability are often used together, they usually deal with different problems, although they share much in common (Figure 3.12). Statistics in the forensic setting is focused upon the collection, handling, validation, and interpretation of data. Probability, however, deals with representing the likelihood that a particular event or set of events will occur based on a set of reference data. Statistics often seeks to learn about the properties of a larger population from studying a small subset or sample of the population, while probability tries to learn about a particular smaller sample given knowledge about the larger population. Both have

important places in forensic science, and in this section, we will explore just a few of the most basic ideas of statistics and probability central to forensic analysis.

3.2.2 Statistics in Forensic Science

Forensic science is based on experiment, measurement, and analysis. However, whenever measurements are made, there is an inherent variability and uncertainty in the measurement. For example, any time that we measure the length of an object, at some level, there will always be variation in the measurement – even measurements made by the same person using the same measuring device. Statistical methods can be used to understand and quantify this variability. In forensic science, we particularly need to know the magnitude of the variability to gauge the level of trust that we may place in a particular piece of evidence.

Statistics may also be used to relate the known properties of a small subset of a large population to the properties of the entire larger population itself, without the difficulty of measuring the entire population. For example, we might take a small blood sample from a person to determine their blood alcohol level. Using statistics, we can use the analysis of the small withdrawn blood sample to say that it reflects accurately the blood composition in a person's entire body. Similarly, we can measure the refractive index of a small shard of glass from a broken windshield to determine the properties of the entire windshield. However, to do this in a valid manner, we need to understand the statistical tools used to make the connections between a small sample and the complete population.

One key use of statistics is to provide a mathematical description of an entire set of data from a relatively small sample. There are a number of useful quantities that may be reported to provide critical information about a piece of evidence or analysis. These include:

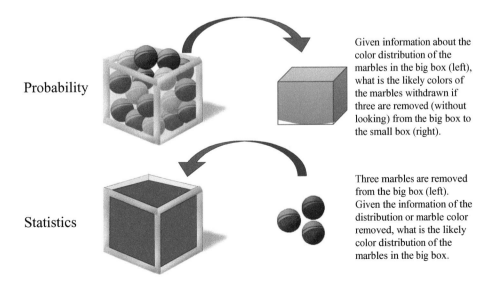

Given information about the color distribution of the marbles in the big box (left), what is the likely colors of the marbles withdrawn if three are removed (without looking) from the big box to the small box (right).

Three marbles are removed from the big box (left). Given the information of the distribution or marble color removed, what is the likely color distribution of the marbles in the big box.

FIGURE 3.12 An example of the relationship between statistics and probability.

- **Average or Arithmetic Mean**: The average or mean is the sum of the values of each of the individual data points divided by the total number of data points in the set. This tells us something about the tendency of the data points toward a center (Figure 3.13), particularly when combined with the standard deviation (see p. 67). For example, to determine the mean height of all professional basketball players, we would simply add together the heights of each individual player and divide by the number of players in the sample. This is illustrated in Figure 3.14.

- **Median**: The median is the halfway point in the data; half of the data points have greater values and half have lesser values than the median. The median is found by lining up all the data in increasing magnitude and then finding the halfway point (Figure 3.15). There are times, especially involving outlying data points in small-sized samples, when the median may be more useful than the mean in describing an entire population from a small sample, as illustrated by the non-symmetric curve in Figure 3.15. For example, when most of the values within a group are clumped close together but it

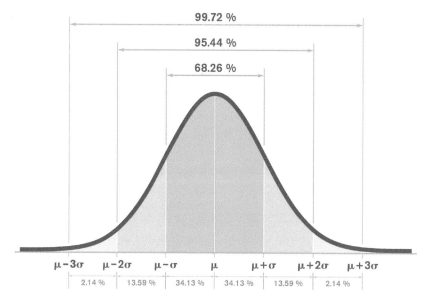

FIGURE 3.13 A plot showing the mean and its relationship with standard deviation for a standard bell-shaped curve.
Source: Shutterstock.com.

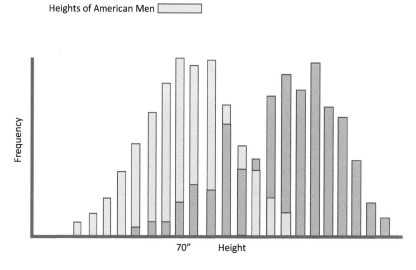

FIGURE 3.14 The distribution of the heights of American men in the general population and the heights of professional basketball players in the NBA.

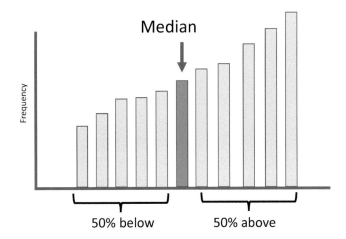

Median

50% below   50% above

Mode (Most Common)

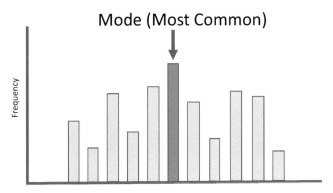

FIGURE 3.15   Graphic examples of median and mode.

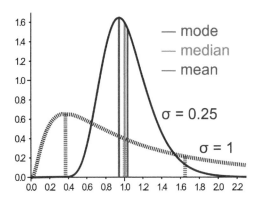

σ = 0.25

σ = 1

— mode
— median
— mean

FIGURE 3.16   An example of when the mean and median are far apart.

Source: Used per Creative Commons Share-Alike 3.0 Unported. User: Cmglee.

contains a few that are very much larger, the mean would be skewed to higher values from the few largest outliers. In this case, the median would be more representative of the entire group.

• **Mode**: The mode is that value that occurs most frequently in a data set (Figure 3.15): the most "popular" value. The mode may be very different from the median and mean for any given data set, as shown in Figure 3.16.

• **Distribution**: A statistical distribution is the way that the data points are spread out over all possible values, showing the number of times that each answer occurs in a data set. A special term, *normal distribution* (sometimes called the "bell-shaped" or Gaussian distribution), describes the most common random distribution pattern found in statistics (and forensics). In a normal distribution, the values tend to "cluster" around a mean value and are "symmetrical" around the mean or mode (highest point). An example of an ideal normal distribution is shown in Figure 3.13, while an actual normal distribution showing the heights of groups of people can be seen in Figure 3.14.

• **Standard Deviation** (σ or SD): The mean and median by themselves really don't provide much information about how the values are distributed in a set – how *often* each possible value appears in the data. A very useful value that tells us much more about what the distribution looks like and which provides an idea of its "shape" is the standard deviation (sometimes denoted as σ, called "sigma"). A standard deviation is a numeric value, given by Equation 3.1, that gives an indication of the breadth of the distribution – how "flat" or "sharp" the curve appears. A small standard deviation value means that the data points are all clustered close to the median (a "sharp" appearing curve), while a large SD indicates a much wider spread of the data points (a "flatter" appearing curve), as illustrated in Figure 3.17 for four normal distributions, all of which have the same mean and median but have very different standard deviations. A unit equal to one standard deviation extended on each side of the median contains about 68% of the data, while a span of two standard deviations includes about 95% of the data (Figure 3.13). The standard deviation is also used to give an indication of the confidence in a conclusion reached from a statistical data set. To calculate the standard deviation (Equation 3.1), the difference between every point and the mean is determined and then squared. This is done for each data point in the sample, and the results are all added together. Finally, this sum is divided by the number of points in the sample, and the square root of the result is taken to obtain the standard deviation. An example is shown in Box 3.10.

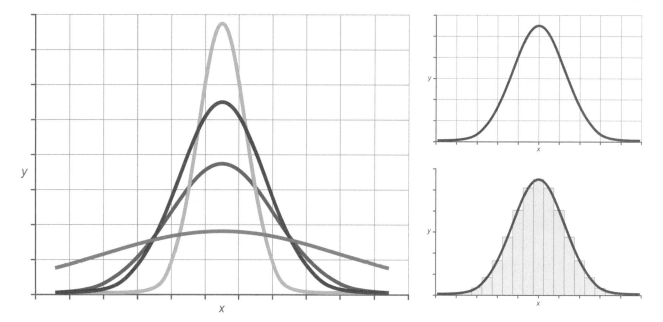

FIGURE 3.17 Comparison of four curves with different standard deviations (s). The green curve has a smaller standard deviation than the red curve. The standard deviations for the four curves are: $s_{green} < s_{red} < s_{blue} < s_{yellow}$.

Source: Shutterstock.com.

BOX 3.9 EQUATION FOR STANDARD DEVIATION

$$SD(\sigma) = \sqrt{\frac{\sum(x - \bar{x})^2}{n}} \qquad (3.1)$$

(where x is the value of a data point, $\bar{x}$ is the mean, Σ is the sum for all of the data points, and n is the number of data points.)

BOX 3.10 CALCULATING A STANDARD DEVIATION

First, let's assume that we have a data set containing the following 11 values:

2, 3, 3, 5, 5, 7, 9, 9, 11, 11, 12

The mean of this set is:

$$Mean = \frac{2+3+3+5+5+7+9+9+11+11+12}{11} = 7.0$$

Next, the difference between each of these values and the mean is determined and then squared:

$(2-7)^2 = 25$ $\qquad$ $(7-7)^2 = 0$
$(3-7)^2 = 16$ $\qquad$ $(9-7)^2 = 4$
$(3-7)^2 = 16$ $\qquad$ $(9-7)^2 = 4$

$(5-7)^2 = 4$ $\qquad$ $(11-7)^2 = 16$
$(5-7)^2 = 4$ $\qquad$ $(11-7)^2 = 16$
$\qquad\qquad\qquad\qquad$ $(12-7)^2 = 25$

Finally, the standard deviation, given by Equation 3.1, is calculated by adding all these individual values together, then dividing by the total number of data points, and finally taking the square root of the result:

$$SD = \sqrt{\frac{25+16+16+4+4+0+4+4+16+16+25}{11}} = 3.4$$

This means that ~68% of the data would fall between (7.0 – 3.4) and (7.0 + 3.4), or between 3.6 and 10.4 (one SD on each side of the mean, or 7.0 ± 3.4).

- **Error Bars**: In a plot of measured data, it is often convenient and important to show directly on the plot the standard deviation information to give a quick indication of the distribution and reliability of *each* data point. This is often done through the use of error bars – small brackets or bars extending through the point to show the span of one standard deviation unit, as shown in Figure 3.18.
- **Frequency**: The statistical frequency is the number of times that a particular value or event shows up in a data set.
- **Range**: The difference between the lowest and highest values in a set of data is the range.

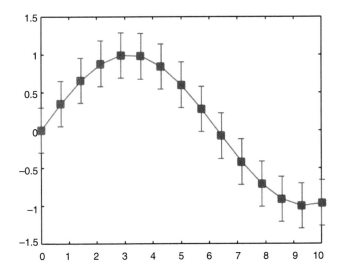

FIGURE 3.18 Examples of error bars showing one standard deviation unit for each measurement.

- **Q-test**: Sometimes, a data point seems to lie far enough from the rest of the data to suggest that it is an erroneous or invalid point and should be discarded. Unless the analyst knows for certain that an error occurred (such as the instrument malfunctioned or a scale was misread), it is difficult to justify ignoring the data point simply because it doesn't "fit" with the others. In fact, many of the great discoveries of science have arisen from looking at "erroneous" data and finding some new phenomena or explanation for its outlying characteristics. Statistics, however, provides a rough test, called the Q-test (or sometimes Dixon's Q-test), that can be used to justify ejecting an outlying data point from a set. A Q-test calculation works best when evaluating between three and ten data points – the typical number of samples in a forensic analysis (for more points than this, another test that is quite similar, called the G or Grubbs test, is most frequently used). Q is calculated by the formula given in Equation 3.2 (where x_0 is the data point in question, $x_{nearest}$ is the data point nearest in value to the disputed point, x_{max} and x_{min} are the largest and smallest data points in the set):

$$Q = \frac{|x_0 - x_{nearest}|}{x_{max} - x_{min}} \qquad (3.2)$$

A sample Q calculation is given in Box 3.11. The value of Q determined from this equation is then compared to a value from a "critical table" for Q for the number of data points in the sample (Table 3.3). If the Q value calculated for a data point is less than the Q value from the critical table, then the data point must be kept in the data set, if it is larger than the critical Q value, it can be justifiably eliminated.

BOX 3.11   DISCARDING A DATA POINT

The Q-test can be used to decide whether we are justified in discarding a data point that is far from the others that have been measured.

For example, if we made three analytical measurements that were 9.1, 12.3, and 12.4, it seems that the 9.1 value is an outlier to the other two, and we might be justified in discarding it. To determine this, we need to perform a Q-test on the point as follows:

Using Equation 3.2, we can calculate a Q (the median of the set is 11.3) of 0.67.

$$Q = \frac{|x_0 - x_{nearest}|}{x_{max} - x_{min}} = \frac{|9.1 - 11.3|}{12.4 - 9.1} = 0.67$$

If we look on the critical Q-table (Table 3.3) for three data points, we find that we'd need a Q value of >0.941 to discard the point. Since the calculated value is only 0.67, we cannot justifiably eliminate the data point from the set.

TABLE 3.3 Q-test values for different numbers of samples (CL = confidence level)

N	Q_{CRIT} (CL AT 90%)	Q_{CRIT} (CL AT 95%)	Q_{CRIT} (CL AT 99%)
3	0.941	0.970	0.994
4	0.765	0.829	0.926
5	0.642	0.710	0.821
6	0.560	0.625	0.740
7	0.507	0.568	0.680
8	0.468	0.526	0.634
9	0.437	0.493	0.598
10	0.412	0.466	0.568

Three other key statistical concepts will be discussed in more detail in Chapter 4: the precision, accuracy, and uncertainty in a measurement,

In forensic analysis, it is often only possible to measure a small number of samples from the entire population – we look at a few hairs instead of all the hairs on the suspect's head. It is, therefore, possible that the mean and standard deviation from the small number of samples is not reflective of the entire population. When dealing with small numbers of samples, the median may be more valuable than the mean. For example, if three measurements from an analysis were 9.1, 12.3, and 12.4, the mean would be 11.3, while the median would be 12.3. Since two values are close to the median (12.3 and 12.4), the use of the median of 12.3 seems more justifiable than the mean. We strive, however, to obtain a small sample that is representative of an entire population to measure. But, the larger the number of samples measured, the more likely it is to reflect the properties of the larger population. So, often a balance must be found between finding a representative sample, where more data points are better, and the need to measure as few data points as necessary.

3.3.3 Probability in Forensic Analysis

Probability refers to the chance of a particular occurrence happening. There are two types of probabilities that can be calculated: theoretical and experimental probabilities. Theoretical probabilities are calculated when all possible outcomes are equally likely, such as the probability of drawing a four of hearts from a pack of cards or tossing a "4" on a single die. Experimental probabilities are calculated when the possible outcomes are not all equally probable – for example, when a die has been tampered with to make certain rolls more likely than others or when not all Short Tandem Repeats (STRs) repeat lengths at a locus are possible in the DNA of a population. In this case, theoretical calculations will fail to predict accurately the chances of a particular outcome occurring. Theoretical probabilities can be calculated using simple mathematical methods. Experimental probabilities must be calculated from a large pool of experimental data rather than from simple calculations only. In forensics, we typically focus on theoretical probabilities since we consider all possible random outcomes as equally probable.

BOX 3.12   ADDITIONAL PROBABILITY DEFINITIONS

Outcome: Outcomes are the possible results from an experiment. Outcomes from rolling a single die are a one, two, three, four, five, or six.

Event: An event is one particular experimental outcome, often from among several choices.

Calculating Theoretical Probabilities: When all possible outcomes are equally likely, as is often the case in certain areas of forensic analysis (e.g., blood typing, fingerprinting, etc.), the probability of certain events happening can be accurately calculated by dividing the number of ways that a particular event might occur by the total number of possible events (Equation 3.3):

$$\text{Probability} = \frac{\text{number of occurrences of a selected event}}{\text{total number of possible events}} \quad (3.3)$$

For example, the probability of rolling a four on one six-sided die will be $1/6$ (~16.7%), since there is one four out of six possible numbers that could be rolled, as illustrated in Figure 3.19. Drawing a four of hearts from a full deck of cards would be 1/52, since there is just one four of hearts card in a deck of 52 cards. Drawing a four card of any suit, however, would have a probability of 4/52 since there are four different four cards in each of the four suits in the deck (e.g., 4♥, 4♣, 4♠, and 4♦).

Often in forensic science, we would like to calculate the probability of two independent events happening together (or sequentially). For example, what would be the probability of rolling one die twice and rolling a four on each roll? The probability of two independent events happening together is determined simply by multiplying the probability of each separate event together. This can be done using as many independent events as are needed. For two events, the math looks like:

Probability of events A and B happening together = (Probability of event A) (Probability of event B)

In the example of rolling two fours on two dice, the probability of this happening is simply the probability of rolling a four on die number one ($1/6$) and a four on die number two ($1/6$) multiplied together:

$$\textit{Probability of rolling two fours} = \left(\frac{1}{6}\right)\left(\frac{1}{6}\right) = 1/36 \ \left(\text{or } 0.028\right)$$

Sometimes, there is more than one way that a given result can occur; for example, there are three ways to roll a *total* of four using two dice: rolling a 1 + 3, a 2 + 2, and a 3 + 1 (note that 1 + 3 and 3 + 1 are separate occurrences – see Figure 3.19). Therefore, the probability of rolling a combined *total* of four on two dice is 3/36 (36 is the total number of possible outcomes or 6 possibilities on one die times six possibilities on the second die). This relates especially to DNA probabilities since you can have a given sequence on either one chromosome *or* the other, making two ways to inherit a particular sequence.

Likelihood Ratio (LR): In criminal proceedings, juries are usually required to decide between two competing hypotheses – one presented by the prosecution and one presented by the defense. A model for aiding the courts in making decisions in these types of situations has been developed, called

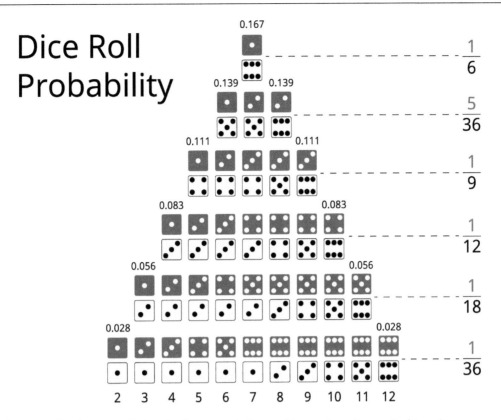

FIGURE 3.19   Chart showing the probabilities of rolling a particular combined value of one roll of two dice.

Source: Shutterstock.com.

TABLE 3.4   Evidential values based upon Likelihood Ratios (LR)

LIKELIHOOD RATIO	VALUE OF EVIDENCE IN SUPPORT OF HYPOTHESIS
<1	Does not support
1	No support or refutation
1–10	Weak support
10–100	Limited support
100–1,000	Strong support
>1,000	Very strong support

the Bayesian model, that defines something called a likelihood ratio (LR); the ratio of the probability that one of two hypotheses is more likely correct than the other. Mathematically, it might be stated for forensic science as:

$$\text{Likelihood ratio} = \frac{\text{Probability of Prosecution Hypothesis}}{\text{Probability of Defense Hypothesis}} = \frac{P[P]}{P[D]}$$

For example, if the likelihood ratio for the case of the prosecution relative to the case for the defense is large, then it is more likely that the defendant committed the crime (prosecution's hypothesis is more likely correct). Each piece of evidence presented into the proceedings affects the ratio by supporting one side over the other. If a piece of evidence is supportive of the prosecution, the ratio is multiplied by a value greater than one, and if it is more supportive for the defense, then a value less than one is multiplied. At the end of the case, the total LR then

can be used to help decide the outcome. Mostly, this concept has been used intuitively, but it can be stated more accurately in mathematical terms (Table 3.4).

Evidence can be given a likelihood ratio to convey information about its evidential value. For example, one way of presenting DNA evidence is to present its likelihood ratio – the ratio of the assumption (or hypothesis) that the DNA came from the suspect versus coming from a random person in the population. Table 3.4 provides an indication of how DNA likelihood ratio data can be used. This concept of LR and similar probability and statistical ideas relative to DNA will be presented in greater detail in Chapter 5.

Probability and statistics clearly provide critical estimates of the value of evidence and ways of determining when it does and does not support the various hypotheses presented in court. As these tools become increasingly valued by courts, forensic scientists must also increasingly provide these statistical benchmarks for their work – all to the good of the science itself.

3.3 ETHICS AND BIAS IN FORENSIC SCIENCE

He that would make his own liberty secure must guard even his enemy from oppression.

(Thomas Paine, 1737–1809)

3.3.1 Ethics in Forensic Science

Scientists are supposed to be unbiased, detached observers who seek simply to understand the physical world through observation, experimentation, and interpretation. They are not supposed to "take sides" by supporting any one particular hypothesis while performing experiments or analyzing the results. They are expected to impartially evaluate the data, revise, or abandon a hypothesis based on the results, and then continue to explore the possibilities through new rounds of experimentation and analysis. Similarly, forensic scientists are expected to follow the evidence wherever it might lead them in an investigation without any preconceived or biased notions of the potential outcomes. All scientists are expected to conform to the highest standards of their professions and adhere to the process of the scientific method. This, of course, includes experimentation and the concept of *falsifiability* – the possibility that a hypothesis can be shown to be false by reproducible

observation or experiment. In other words, a forensic scientist must both seek evidence that a hypothesis is correct but also look to see if other explanations could be true and if the original idea or assumption is incorrect or incomplete. For example, a comparison of a suspect's fingerprint with an unknown fingerprint must not only look for similarities between the two prints but also disclose any differences that might show that the two prints are not from a common source (the suspect's fingers). Forensic science must, therefore, look toward experiments to show that a hypothesis is incorrect as much as to support the theory being tested. We are and must be held to a very high standard of ethics in all scientific endeavors (Figure 3.20).

Ethics is a part of philosophy that deals with questions surrounding our understanding of right and wrong, helping us decide in difficult cases which is the better pathway to follow. It does not provide absolute answers, just guidance. In forensic science, ethics helps to keep our system of justice fair and accurate and provides a framework for how science can operate effectively and correctly to inform legal questions. It helps protect both the rights of the individual and those of society fairly in areas of potential conflict – conflicts that often result in court cases.

Much has been written about ethics in science, and specifically in forensic science, such that now a reasonably deep foundation exists for considering these issues. A full and necessary treatment of this vast area, however, is well beyond the scope possible here so selected issues will be simply presented.

A number of important organizations dealing with forensic science have established an agreed upon set of ethical and moral practices that help guide forensic experts and laboratories in their work. The American Academy of Forensic Science (AAFS), the largest professional organization for forensic science, has established such a set of ethical guidelines to help

FIGURE 3.20   Code of conduct for forensic scientists involves ethics, respect, code, honesty, and integrity.

Source: Shutterstock.com.

promote the highest standards of practice in the field. Similar guidelines have been established by many other organizations dealing with various aspects of forensic science such as the American Society of Crime Lab Directors (ASCLD), the National Association of Medical Examiners (NAME), the American Board of Criminalistics (ABC), the Society of Forensic Toxicologists (SOFT), and others. As a representative example, the AAFS guidelines include:

- Every forensic scientist is expected to adhere to the standards of practice established by the Academy by "promoting education for and research in the forensic sciences, encouraging the study, improving the practice, elevating the standards and advancing the cause of the forensic sciences."
- No forensic scientist "shall materially misrepresent his or her education, training, experience, area of expertise."
- No forensic scientist "shall materially misrepresent data or scientific principles upon which his or her conclusion or professional opinion is based."

Forensic scientists are, therefore, expected to always act ethically and professionally throughout their work. The *National Commission on Forensic Science* of the U.S. Department of Justice (DoJ) has established a "National Code of Ethics and Professional Responsibility for the Forensic Sciences." This Code requires practitioners to:

- Accurately represent their personal scientific qualifications and to avoid any potential conflicts of interest.
- Pursue professional competency through training, proficiency testing, certification, and continuous learning in their disciplines.
- Promote the incorporation of new technologies into practice and resist the use of unvalidated methods.
- Maintain the integrity, proper handling, safe storage, and analysis of evidence.
- Ensure the impartiality of the examination with as little bias as possible and resist external pressure to deliver any particular outcome.
- Provide a true and accurate representation of data and work performed.
- Prepare clear, concise, and complete documentation of their work and always communicate honestly and fully.
- Remain impartial during testimony, provide the highest level of scientific analysis possible, and avoid conclusions that are outside their expertise.
- Maintain confidentiality and provide only legally acceptable disclosures of data and analysis.
- Report colleagues who act in unprofessional and/or unethical ways to the appropriate person.

The stakes can be very high in forensic science such that ethics requires that every action be done to the highest standard. Evidence must be collected, stored, analyzed, and interpreted with the utmost care since failing to do so can potentially destroy the lives of all those involved in the case.

Forensic science, in contrast to much of basic science, is often placed in the difficult position at the interface between science and the legal process. Science and the law, while having important mutual goals, also have some very significant differences. As mentioned in previous sections, science cannot prove anything beyond simple facts. The law, on the other hand, needs definitive answers to come to timely and just decisions. Some of the tools presented in this chapter, specifically the scientific method and mathematical constructions, can help lessen the conflict necessarily caused by these potentially incompatible needs and outcomes. An established code of ethics can help inform and guide scientists on how to balance the responsibilities of science with the demands of a legal case.

Complicating the picture, of course, is the reality that public forensic science laboratories are more closely associated with the prosecution than the defense in a criminal case – they receive samples from the police, report analytical results to the district attorney, and appear in court often for the prosecution. In some cases, the crime laboratory even reports to and is directly controlled, including financially, by law enforcement. The problem for the forensic scientist in this situation, of course, is to maintain impartiality while performing their expected role in support of legal practice.

3.3.2 Bias in Forensic Science

Bias in forensic science, either knowingly or unknowingly applied, usually refers to an unfair prejudice or practice either for or against a particular person or outcome. All people hold biases of some sort, so we must be vigilant against introducing personal biases in both scientific and legal work. Most broadly, there are two types of biases encountered in forensic science: motivational bias and cognitive bias.

Motivational biases are probably the easiest to understand and guard against since they involve intentionally and consciously favoring one particular outcome or person for personal reasons. Sometimes, this might be considered to constitute a conflict of interest. For example, a forensic lab that reports to the District Attorney might be swayed by personal relationships to favor a particular opinion or analysis.

Cognitive bias usually relates to an unconscious tendency to "see what you expect to see." This type of bias may be further divided into several specific types. *Contextual bias* arises when the data being analyzed is embedded within other information that is usually not related to the data itself but may influence the thinking of the analyst. For example, if a firearms analyst also received a fingerprint report tying the suspect to the crime, they might be more likely to match test-fired bullets from the suspect's weapon with the crime scene bullet than if the fingerprint evidence had not been supplied. In a published study, while forensic examiners recognized the potential for contextual bias in their work, they denied that it played a role in their work. Curiously, even though people may be trained specifically in recognizing contextual bias, the study found that they were still highly ineffective in recognizing their own biases in their work. To help overcome this, the President's Council of Advisors on Science and Technology encouraged forensic examiners to be "blinded" to other information in their work to prevent the potential bias of any contextual information.

Expectation bias arises when a person subconsciously expects a particular outcome prior to having all the data necessary to form an appropriate conclusion.

Selection bias refers to not choosing a correct sample that represents the greater population. This frequently arises when witnesses are asked to choose a suspect from a lineup of possible people. The choice of which people to include in the lineup, besides the suspect, can influence the choice made by the witness.

Confirmation bias is an unconscious tendency to look for and interpret data in ways that are consistent with the examiner's own preexisting beliefs. A basic part of unconscious human nature is to find support for our beliefs, leading us to select like-minded friends and look for support and validation for our ideas. However, this becomes a problem when applied to forensic science. For example, the personal confirmation bias of witnesses has been shown to alter both their perceptions and memories of crime scene events.

Research is now focused on finding ways of determining and eliminating the presence of these forms of bias in forensic investigations. Among the key elements of this is education in recognizing bias and establishing protocols for limiting access to other information when performing an analysis.

The Federal Rules of Evidence, the set of rules and practices that control all aspects of the use of evidence in court, require that all forensic "results and reports" must be made available to the defense upon request (Rule 16). The question that often arises, however, is how this rule is actually applied. Typically, it has been used by the courts only for final reports and conclusions and not for information about the methods employed, laboratory notebooks and comments, or other records made during the investigation. The defense also usually does not have an automatic right to test or retest the evidence presented. Currently, laboratories usually do not have a legal obligation to permanently preserve records or even retain the physical evidence itself, potentially for later retesting.

legal practices to best serve both the scientific responsibilities and the legal needs demanded of the forensic community. While great strides continue to be made, much work is yet to be done – a challenge the forensic community is clearly up to.

QUESTIONS FOR FURTHER PRACTICE AND MASTERY

3.1 The length of a shard of glass recovered from a crime scene was measured repeatedly. Given the following data set of these measurements, what is their mean, median, mode, and standard deviation?
1.4, 1.5, 1.5, 1.6, 1.7, 1.7, 1.7, 1.7, 1.9
3.2 Four data points were measured in a blood alcohol determination. These were: 0.024, 0.091, 0.089, and 0.110 g of alcohol per 100 mL of blood. Using a Q-test calculation, can the point at 0.024 be eliminated from the data set?
3.3 What are the major aspects of the scientific method, and how do they work together to form an unbiased picture of an aspect of the physical universe?
3.4 What are some of the hallmarks used to distinguish pseudoscience from real science?
3.5 What is the role of each of the following in the scientific method: (a) Observation, (b) Hypothesis, (c) Prediction, (d) Experimentation, (f) Analysis, and (g) refinement or abandonment of hypothesis?
3.6 What is Occam's razor?
3.7 What is a pseudoscience?
3.8 Give several examples of pseudoscience?
3.9 What are some of the "telltale" features of a pseudoscience?
3.10 What is meant by the term "probability"?
3.11 What is standard deviation? What does the value of the standard deviation tell us about our data?
3.12 What is a Q-test?
3.13 What is the American Academy of Forensic Science?

3.4 CONCLUSION

In 2009, the National Research Council (NRC) of the National Academies of Science presented a report entitled "Strengthening Forensic Science in the United States: A Path Forward." This in-depth study, still actively discussed today, concluded that many aspects of forensic science practice were deficient and needed careful attention to uniformly bring the practices of the entire forensic community up to the highest levels of scientific inquiry. Since the publication of this report, numerous groups and organizations have been tackling the difficult task of raising scientific standards, establishing strong ethical codes, and implementing changes to laboratory and

EXTENSIVE QUESTIONS

3.14 Give a detailed explanation of the scientific method.
3.15 Given the following blood alcohol levels, determine the standard deviation (given in g of alcohol per 100 mL of blood): 0.019, 0.020, 0.021, 0.024, 0.018, 0.023, 0.030, 0.032, 0.028, 0.026, 0.025.
3.16 Explain the difference between the median, mode, and mean in the following set of points: 9, 12, 14, 10, 18, 20. Under what conditions might the median be more indicative of a general population than the mean?

3.17 A forensic scientist measures the amount of arsenic in four hair samples. She determines the amount of arsenic in the sample to be 2.0×10^{-6} mg, 5.2×10^{-6} mg, 7.2×10^{-6} mg and 6.4×10^{-6} mg. Can she discard the 2.0×10^{-6} mg measurement as being an outlier?

3.18 What is the probability of drawing three sixes of any suit consecutively from a shuffled set of three decks of standard playing cards?

3.19 Using the Q-table from the text, determine if the 6.2 g measurement in the following set of masses can be discarded: 6.2 g, 8.8 g, 9.9 g, 10.4 g, 11.6 g.

GLOSSARY OF TERMS

bias: an unfair prejudice or practice either for or against a particular person or outcome that may be either knowingly or unknowingly applied.

confirmatory test: an experiment designed to simply support the tenets of the original hypothesis or idea itself rather than to be a broad-based inquiry.

distribution (statistical): the way in which the data points spread out over all possible values.

error bars: a line through a data point on a plot indicating the standard deviation for each data point.

ethics: a part of philosophy that deals with questions surrounding our understanding of right and wrong, helping us decide what is the better pathway to follow in difficult cases.

event: one particular outcome from an experiment, often from among several or many choices. For example, an event would be rolling a four on a die.

falsifiability: the possibility that a hypothesis can be shown to be false by a reproducible observation or experiment.

frequency: the number of times that a particular value or event shows up in an experiment.

hypothesis: a statement or explanation made based on the limited data available that serves as a starting point for further investigation.

likelihood ratio (LR): the ratio between the probability of two competing hypotheses pointing to which of the two is most likely to be correct.

mean: the sum of the values of each of the individual data points divided by the total number of data points in the set.

median: the halfway point in the data, where half of the data points have greater and half have lesser values than the median.

mode: the most frequent value in a data set.

outcome: one possible result from an experiment.

probability: the field that deals with representing the likelihood that a particular event or set of events will occur given a set of reference data.

pseudoscience (or "junk", "fringe", or "alternative" science): the practice or set of beliefs that are not founded upon the scientific method.

Q-test (or Dixon's Q-test): a rough test to justify ejecting an outlying data point from a set.

range: the difference between the lowest and highest values in a set of data.

science: the collective total of our knowledge and understanding, and a process for understanding the physical world based on logical investigation, measurement, and observation.

scientific method: the process by which scientists more formally try to construct an accurate understanding of the things and events around us in reliable and non-arbitrary terms, involving the cyclical process of: (1) observation, (2) pattern recognition, (3) hypothesis formulation, and (4) renewed experimentation.

standard deviation: a numeric value that gives an indication of the breadth and the distribution of data in a set.

standard operating procedure (SOP): a set of rules and procedures for performing an analysis or experiment that conforms to a rigorous standard widely accepted as best-practice in the field.

statistics: the field that focuses on the collection, handling, validation, and interpretation of data.

theory: an explanation that has been generally accepted by a large number of scientists as valid and is supported by a large amount of experimental evidence.

BIBLIOGRAPHY

Robin T. Bowen, *Ethics and the Practice of Forensic Science*, West Virginia University, Morgantown, USA Series: International Forensic Science and Investigation, CRC Press, 2009.

Charles J. Cazeau, Jr. and Stuart D. Scott, *Exploring the Unknown*, Plenum, 1979.

Itiel E. Dror, "Biases in forensic experts", *Science*, 360(6386), 243, 2018. https://doi.org/10.1126/science.aat8443.

Morris Goran and A.S. Barnes, *Fact, Fraud and Fantasy*, 1979.

Allison B. Kaufman and James C. Kaufman (Eds.), *Pseudoscience: The Conspiracy against Science*, MIT Press, 2019.

Chris Knight, *The Blind Men, the Elephant and the Zoo*.

Jeff Kukucka, Saul M. Kassin, Patricia A. Zapf, and Itiel E. Dror, "Cognitive bias and blindness: A global survey of forensic science examiners", *Journal of Applied Research in Memory and Cognition*, 6(4), 452–459. https://doi.org/10.1016/j.jarmac.2017.09.001.

D. Radner and M. Radner, *Science and Unreason*, Wadsworth, 1982.

Richard H. Ward and James W. Osterburg, *Criminal Investigation: A Method for Reconstructing the Past*, Anderson Publishing, 2000.

Feynman, Richard P., *The Pleasure of Finding Things Out: The Best Short Works of Richard P. Feynman*, Perseus Books, 1999, p. 240.

Arthur Conan Doyle, *The Sign of the Four*, Lippincott's Monthly Magazine, Feb. 1890.

Peer Knight, *Conspiracy Theories in American History: An Encyclopedia*. ABC-CLIO, 2003, pp. 45.

PART 2

Biological Evidence

Methods for Examining Biological Evidence

4

4.1 METHODS FOR BIOLOGICAL EVIDENCE – MEASUREMENT

The eye of a human being is a microscope, which makes the world seem bigger than it really is.

(Khalil Gilbran, 1883–1931)

LEARNING GOALS AND OBJECTIVES

Biological evidence often forms a vital core of forensic investigations. Accurate observations and measurements are essential to analyzing these types of evidence. After completing this chapter, you should be able to:

- Describe units, accuracy, and precision in measurements and how measurements are taken.
- Discuss the limitations of our senses and how this affects our interpretation of the world around us.
- Define what is meant by electromagnetic radiation and how we perceive and measure it.
- Explain what the SI system of measurement is and how it works, including prefixes and scientific notation.
- Demonstrate how the uncertainty of a measurement is estimated and indicated.
- Illustrate what is meant by the accuracy and precision of a measurement.
- Describe how a lens works to create a magnified image.
- Describe the basic principles of light microscope operation.
- Illustrate what is meant by resolution, magnification, numerical aperture, and related terms;
- Discuss the different types of optical microscopy and how they work, including bright field optical microscopy, dark-field microscopy, polarized light microscopy, phase-contrast microscopy, fluorescence microscopy, infrared microscopy, stereo microscopy, and comparison microscopy.

- Diagram how electron microscopy works, including both scanning and transmission electron microscopy.
- Describe what other techniques of microscopy are available and when they are best used.

4.1.1 Introduction

Biological evidence, whether from humans or from the vast array of other living organisms representing all sizes, shapes, and complexities that share the Earth with us, forms a central core of modern forensic evidence. The ability to detect, analyze, and understand biological evidence is, therefore, a foundation of forensic science: from uniquely describing the identity of someone from their personal molecular signatures written in DNA's ink, to the anatomical features that help illuminate a specific chain of events, to the actions and reactions of the living environment around us that are silent witnesses to our presence and actions. We must, however, be circumspect about the ways that we use the forensic evidence that comes from living organisms such that it is complete, accurate, and able to reveal as much detailed information as possible. In this chapter, we will first explore the various tools that forensic science uses in dealing with the study of the complexity and variety of biological evidence. Once armed with these tools, succeeding chapters will explore how and why biological evidence is so valuable in forensic science, beginning with the smallest forms of evidence (molecular) and successively moving to larger (anatomical) and larger (ecological) systems.

4.1.2 Observation, Measurement, and Forensic Science

It probably comes as no surprise that accurate, reliable, and meaningful observations and measurements are fundamental to biological evidence. These observations can be either quantitative, involving detailed measurement, or qualitative, involving careful descriptions. Lord Kelvin, a famous 19th-century scientist whose name we still commemorate in a unit of thermal measurement, once said, "to measure is to know." It is certainly true that our scientific understanding of the world around us must begin with observation and measurement.

DOI: 10.4324/9781003183709-6

Probably the simplest and most straightforward way to describe something comes from direct observation. Using our senses, with or without aids designed specifically to "extend" our senses (*vide infra*), we can describe the shape, color, contours, and other features of an object, person, or place. We can also describe certain comparative relationships that may be important between two objects such as "larger," "darker," "near," or "to the north." Simple observations, while clearly a necessary starting point, often form a rather incomplete way of describing an object and present some rather challenging problems and difficulties. While these direct observations may allow us to identify whether two objects are similar or different, in scientific inquiries, we must often look for more accurate, reliable, and reproducible methods of describing objects that can be used to delineate even the tiniest detail of an object. Turning to Lord Kelvin again, he noted that:

> when you can measure what you are speaking about, and express it in numbers, you know something about it; but when you cannot measure it, when you cannot express it in numbers, your knowledge of it is of a meager and unsatisfactory kind; it may be the beginning of knowledge, but you have scarcely, in your thoughts, advanced it to the stage of science.

BOX 4.1   OBSERVATION VS MEASUREMENT

Look at the below figure and, using *only* your eyes, determine the relationship between the lengths of lines A and B:

1. line A = line B
2. line A > line B
3. line A < line B

Now, take something to measure the lengths of lines A and B with and see what the correct "measured" answer is. Are they the same?

Observation vs. Measurement

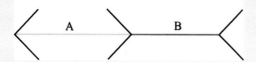

FIGURE 4.1   How measurement and observation are both important.

Careful measurement is the way to more completely and quantitatively describe the size or magnitude of an object's features, such as its length, mass, color, and so on. In order to do this, people for millennia have designed "standards" for these features that can be used to compare with the object. For example, standard units of length have included the breadth of someone's hands (sometimes called a *span*), the distance from a king's nose to his fingertip or the length of his foot (*yard* and *foot*, respectively), or the distance from one fingertip to the opposite fingertip of outstretched arms (*fathom*) (Figure 4.2). Once an agreed-upon

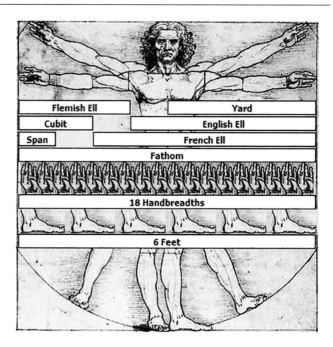

FIGURE 4.2   Historical units of length related to a human scale.

Source: Retrieved from Wikimedia Commons; used per Creative Commons Attribution.

set of standards for each type of measurement is established, all that needs to be done is to compare the unknown object with the established standard. As long as other people employ the same standards, they can accurately reproduce the dimensions of our unknown object without ever seeing it in person.

While talking about observation and measurement methods may not seem to be the most exciting topic in the world, it will be central to many of our future discussions of forensic science. If we can understand how measurement works, including the *limitations* of our measurements, we can better understand the value and limitations of scientific evidence.

Today, we use much the same comparative process of measurement as was used millennia ago: comparing an unknown quantity with an agreed-upon standard. In modern science, the set of standards for all types of measurement generally accepted around the world is the *SI System* (from the French *Système International d'Unités*, Figure 4.3). In this system, there are seven basic units of measurement, from which all others can be derived:

- **Length**: The basic unit of length is the meter (m), defined as the distance traveled by a photon of light in a vacuum during 1/299,792,458th of a second. Roughly, it is approximately the length of an adult arm (similar to the yard in the ancient English system).
- **Mass**: The basic unit is the kilogram (kg), which was once defined as the mass of a cubic decimeter of water, but today, a platinum/iridium cylinder kept in France serves as the worldwide standard.
- **Temperature**: The Kelvin (K), honoring Lord Kelvin, is defined as 1/273.16th of the temperature between absolute zero and the triple point of water

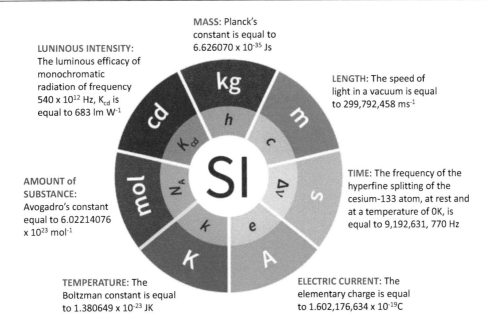

FIGURE 4.3   The SI System, its units, what they measure and how they are defined.

Source: Image used per Creative Commons Share-Alike 3.0 IGO. User: Bureau international des poids et esures, International Bureau of Weights and Measures (BIPM), extracted from https://www.bipm.org/en/publications/si-brochure/ (Tab: The International System of Units – 9th edition – Complete text in English and French).

(the point where liquid, gaseous, and solid water are in equilibrium – about 0°C or 32°F). 1 K is equal to 1°C (note the word "degree" is not used with Kelvin).

- **Time**: The fundamental unit is the second (s), a unit we are all familiar with. The second is scientifically defined, however, as the amount of time it takes for a very large number (9,192,631,770) of certain kinds of vibrations (back and forth motions) in the ^{133}Cs nucleus (sometimes called the "atomic clock").
- **Quantity** (chemical): The mole is the basic unit of matter historically referred to as the number of atoms in 12 g of ^{12}C, a quantity referred to as *Avogadro's Number*. As of May 2019, however, Avogadro's Number has been defined simply as the exact value *of* 6.02214076 × 10^{23} (an important number, somewhat like the "chemist's dozen"). A mole can refer to about 6.02 × 10^{23} of any set of objects: stars, grains of sand, molecules, toasters, etc. (we'll describe the mole in more detail in Chapter 11).
- **Electric Current**: The basic unit of electrical current is the ampere (A) and is defined as the electrical charge flowing through a surface at the rate of 1 C/s (a coulomb is the charge of 6.24151 × 10^{18} protons).
- **Light Intensity**: The basic unit of luminous intensity is the candela (cd) and refers to the power of light emitted in one given direction. For reference, a typical candle emits about 1 cd of light intensity.

While some of these definitions may seem strange and arbitrary, they describe very accurate standards that are reproducible quantities for use at *any place in the world* without the need to travel to a central repository to make copies of one fixed standard. They are typically refinements of the units that have long been in use. For example, the second was originally determined by taking the length of one solar day and dividing it into 24 hours, each hour into 60 minutes, and each minute into 60 seconds. This was certainly good enough for much of our history, but it was found that the length of the solar day is gradually lengthening, making this definition inaccurate for some modern scientific needs. Thus, the second is now defined much more accurately by using a large, but countable number of a particular type of oscillations of the cesium-133 nucleus rather than a subdivision of a solar day on Earth. An important feature is that any scientist with the right equipment can accurately measure a second without ever having to rely upon a standard kept far away.

The fundamental SI units are not, however, always the most convenient to use in their simplest forms, particularly for either very large or very small quantities. In order to deal with this problem, a set of prefixes has been developed that can be placed before the "base" SI unit to increase or decrease the size of the unit. For example, it would be very difficult to measure the size of a single red blood cell with a meter stick. Likewise, it would be tedious and very prone to error to measure the distance from New York City to London in meters. So, in these cases we combine the basic SI unit with a multiplier prefix: we use a "micrometer" (μm) that is 1/1,000,000th of a meter when measuring red blood cells and a kilometer that is 1,000 m for measuring the distance between the two cities. So, the size of a red blood cell can be expressed as 7.8 μm rather than 0.0000078 m. Some of these multiplier prefixes and their meanings are given in Table 4.1.

TABLE 4.1 Prefixes for SI units

Prefix	Symbol for Prefix		Scientific Notation
exa	E	1 000 000 000 000 000 000	10^{18}
peta	P	1 000 000 000 000 000	10^{15}
tera	T	1 000 000 000 000	10^{12}
giga	G	1 000 000 000	10^{9}
mega	M	1 000 000	10^{6}
Kilo	k	1 000	10^{3}
hecto	h	100	10^{2}
deka	da	10	10^{1}
----	--	1	10^{0}
deci	d	0.1	10^{-1}
centi	c	0.01	10^{-2}
milli	m	0.001	10^{-3}
micro	μ	0.000 001	10^{-6}
nano	n	0.000 000 001	10^{-9}
pico	p	0.000 000 000 001	10^{-12}
femto	f	0.000 000 000 000 001	10^{-15}
atto	a	0.000 000 000 000 000 001	10^{-18}

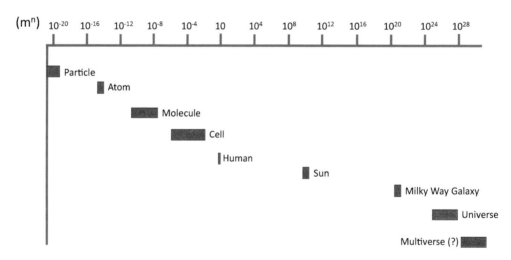

FIGURE 4.4 Some objects in various size ranges as expressed in SI units.

For instance, by adding the prefix *atto* to the base SI unit of mass, the gram, we describe an extremely small measurement that is 1/1,000,000,000,000,000,000th of a gram. When the prefix *exa* is combined with gram, the resulting amount is a very large measurement, 1,000,000,000,000,000,000 g. Between the attogram and the exagram is an amazingly large range of 10^{36} g, conveniently described simply by using the two different prefixes. Using these SI units, expressed as factors of 10^{n}, we can readily display an enormous range of properties, from the size of a subatomic particle ~10^{-20} m to the size of the Universe at 10^{28} m, as illustrated in Figure 4.4.

Another convenient feature of the SI system is that, using just these seven basic units, we can readily derive all other units that we might ever need to measure things. For example, a unit of force that we'll need in later chapters of this text, called the newton (N), is really the combination of three of the basic SI units, such that 1 N equals the force of 1 kg moving at a velocity of 1 m/s² (1.0 N = 1 kgm/s²).

We still frequently encounter, however, the use of a variety of non-SI units that have achieved widespread and long-standing use, particularly units of measure from the *English System*. These units include the foot, inch, and mile for distance measurements, the ounce, pound, and ton for units of mass, the ounce, quart, and gallon for units of volume, the degree Fahrenheit for temperature determinations, and the minute, hour, and day for time measurement. There are also parts of the metric system in common usage that employ non-SI measurements, including the liter and milliliter for volume measurements and the degree Celsius in temperature measurements. Luckily, there are usually rather easy ways to convert between the SI units of measure and these non-SI forms. Nonetheless, forensic reports frequently are found to contain a mixture of these systems of measurement, and juries rarely are comfortable with all of the SI units.

4.1.3 Estimating the Reliability of Measurements

When conducting experimental observations and measurements, there is *always* some error in our determinations, albeit very small. This is a basic feature of the universe – in fact, it's part of a foundational principle of science, called the *Heisenberg Uncertainty Principle*. Paraphrased, this extension of the principle says that we can never measure without error or estimation that comes simply from the act of measuring itself. Given the fundamental concept of uncertainty in all measurements, we need to be able to understand and communicate just how good a particular measurement actually is along with an estimate of how much error we believe is in that particular measurement. To do this, scientists have defined several types of errors and have developed methods to relate how reliable we think a measurement really is.

Errors in measurement generally occur in two ways: systematic and random errors. These are illustrated in Figure 4.5. A *systematic error* is one that occurs when a measurement is consistently off by a certain amount, often due to instrumental or operator errors. For example, a systematic error arises from shooting at a target with the gun's sights adjusted improperly, causing the gun to consistently shoot a bit to the left even when the sights appear to be perfectly aligned on the center of the target. Another example occurs when weighing objects on a balance that doesn't start at zero but begins at 1 g – every measurement on that balance ends up being 1 g too high. Operator errors also contribute to systematic errors when a person consistently misuses or misreads the output of a measuring device.

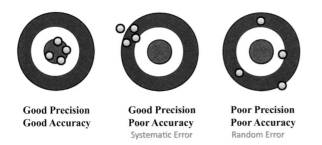

Good Precision
Good Accuracy

Good Precision
Poor Accuracy
Systematic Error

Poor Precision
Poor Accuracy
Random Error

FIGURE 4.5 Depiction of random errors, systematic errors, accuracy, and precision.

Closely associated with systematic errors is the concept of *accuracy*. Accuracy refers to how close a measurement is to the true value of the feature being measured. The presence of systematic errors reduces the accuracy of the measurement by offsetting it from the correct value. The trick, however, is that when conducting an experimental measurement, we usually don't know the "true" value (that's probably why we were making the measurement in the first place). One way scientists try to detect, if not reduce, systematic errors is by using several different methods to measure the same thing. For example, weighing an object using various types of balances and scales (e.g., equal-arm balance, spring balance, triple-beam balance, etc.) and consistently obtaining the same results suggests that systematic errors are minimized since it's unlikely that all the balances used would suffer from the same systematic errors. Figure 4.6 illustrates how using different measuring tools can affect the accuracy of a measurement.

A *random error* is one that is caused by unknown, irregular, or unpredictable forces acting to affect the measurement. These types of errors are randomly scattered and are often averaged "out" if a large number of measurements are taken. For example, when shooting at a target, as in the example in Figure 4.5, random errors could include variations in any crosswind, changes in temperature and air density, motion of the target, or even the pulse of the shooter. If the results from many firings were averaged, however, the effect of these random variations in measurement might well be averaged out of the result. Random errors are *always* present in any measurement, although they can be minimized by controlling the known variables of a measurement as much as possible (e.g., shooting inside to eliminate crosswinds, using a mechanical trigger to eliminate heart pulse unsteadiness, etc.). Sometimes, however, we don't even know what the variables are that randomly affect a measurement – that's when multiple measurements are particularly important.

Closely associated with random error is the concept of *precision*. Precision refers to how closely measurements within a group are to one another and is a measure of the degree of random error in the measurement. In the example in Figure 4.5, the poor precision of the far-right target shows widely spaced shots while the center target shows good precision with a tight bunching of the shots. The "scatter" of the shots in the right target arises from random errors affecting the process.

Given that all measurements have built-in errors and approximations, a key question is: how do we relate to someone else the uncertainty and, therefore, the reliability and limitations of our measurement? As it turns out, this is done in a rather straightforward fashion using something called *significant figures* (Figure 4.7). When we communicate a measured value, the number of significant figures (or significant digits) that we use indicates how reliably we know those figures. For example, if we report the mass of an object is 6.15 g, we are actually saying that we know the "6" and "1" with very high certainty and that we estimate the last number of "5" with an error estimated at ±1, or more accurately, the value is 6.15 ± 0.01 g. This means that the last significant figure reported is

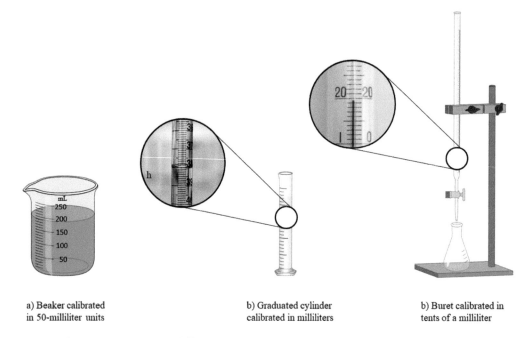

a) Beaker calibrated
in 50-milliliter units

b) Graduated cylinder
calibrated in milliliters

b) Buret calibrated in
tents of a milliliter

FIGURE 4.6 Accuracy of measurements using different sized measuring devices.

Source: Images courtesy Shutterstock.com.

FIGURE 4.7 How many numbers should be reported when doing a measurement – the answer lies with significant figures.

Source: Shutterstock.com.

the one that we are letting people know that we have estimated. Figure 4.6 shows the measurement of a particular volume of liquid using three different measuring devices, each containing *exactly* the same amount of liquid. Using the beaker, we can report the volume as 28 mL, indicating the measurement is accurate to about ±1 mL. While using a graduated cylinder (center), we can report the volume as 28.3 mL, indicating the measurement is accurate to about ±0.1 mL. Finally using the buret (right), we can report the volume as 28.32 mL, indicating

±0.01 mL as the accuracy. Simply by writing these three values, 28, 28.3, or 28.32 mL, we quickly let everyone know how accurately we feel we have measured the volume of the liquid: ±1, ±0.1, and ±0.01 mL, respectively.

BOX 4.2   BRIEF ON MEASUREMENT

- Measurements may be qualitative (observation-based) or quantitative (measurement-based).
- In science, the SI units and their derivatives are used as references for measurements.
- All measurements have errors associated with them.
- Some errors are random (non-reproducible), and some are systematic (an artifact of how we do the measurement).
- Precision and accuracy deal with types of errors that occur during measurements and relate to how much error is present.
- Significant figures quickly relate to others how much reliance to put on the measurements.

A series of rules has been established to determine which numbers in a value are certain and which are estimated: in other words, which figures are significant and which are not. These rules include:

- All non-zero digits are significant (e.g., 1, 2, 3, 4, 5, 6, 7, 8, and 9).
- Zeros between non-zero digits are significant (e.g., the zero is significant in 1503 and 1.07 but probably not in 150 – see the last rule below for the "probably" part).

- Zeros to the left of the leftmost non-zero digit are not significant (e.g., the zeros in 0.00001 and 0015 are not significant but 500001 has six significant figures).
- Zeros at the end of a number but to the right of a decimal point are significant (e.g., the zeros are significant in 12.500).
- The zero may or may not be significant when a number ends in a zero when no decimal point is used (e.g., 1,410; the zero may or might not be significant. This problem is overcome by expressing the number in scientific notation, where the zero is significant in 1.410×10^3 but not in 1.41×10^3).

When determining the number of significant figures, it becomes clear when the number is converted into scientific notation. In scientific notation, 30,000 is denoted as 3×10^4 and has one significant figure while 30,000. is written as 3.0000×10^4 in scientific notation and has five significant figures.

BOX 4.3 "SIG FIG" EXAMPLES

3.573 has 4 significant figures
0.073 has 2 significant figures
3.070 has 4 significant figures
0.003 has 1 significant figure
30001 has 5 significant figures
30000 has 1 significant figure
30000. has 5 significant figures

By applying these rules consistently, we can easily communicate how accurately we have made the measurement. It may seem like we're making a lot of fuss about some minor point, but it really *does* matter – it tells everyone how precise our measurement is and how much trust to put in the details of the numbers we report. Sometimes, this can make a huge difference. For example, to say that a suspect was 100 m from another person or 100.0 m is a big difference. The first says the person was 100 ± 10 m ($\pm \sim 30$ ft), the second says 100 ± 0.1 m (about ± 4 in.). In the forensics world, this can matter a great deal! (Note: generally, we'll try hard to use metric (SI) units throughout this text – although some fields (and countries) still use a combination of SI and other measurement systems.)

4.2 BIOLOGICAL EVIDENCE AND MICROSCOPY

4.2.1 Tools for Understanding Biological Evidence

When making observations and measurements, we perceive the world only indirectly through the faculties of our senses of sight, touch, taste, hearing, and smell. The perception of our environment is only indirect because it first occurs through the stimulation of various sensory organs in our bodies, which then transmit biochemical signals to our brains where they are translated into meaning. We must learn to consciously interpret these signals into meaning through connections made by our experiences as we grow up. For example, simply restoring sight to someone blind since early childhood requires that they spend adult years learning to connect visual signals with meaning; otherwise the signals have no meaning to them even though they can technically see.

As effective as they are, our perceptions of the world are also quite limited by these "biochemical" senses. For example, our "visual detectors," our eyes, are limited in that they can only detect a very small part of the vast electromagnetic spectrum, known as the "visible" portion. This "visible region" accounts for less than about 1.5% of the entire solar spectrum (Figure 4.8). Additionally, we can only see objects down to about the size of the wavelength of light that we are using to see them – with the maximum theoretical resolution (the ability to see two close objects as distinctly separate) being half the wavelength of the light employed. In other words, if we use visible light, the smallest object that we could ever hope to see would be about 400–700 nm – about the size of a bacterium. In reality, however, we are not able to directly observe objects this small with the unaided eye but can only resolve objects down to about 0.1 mm (100,000 nm) or about 250 times larger without mechanical help. This is often good enough for describing larger objects, but sometimes evidence is of a much smaller size – especially structures of biological importance such as cells, fine details of fingerprints, pollen, small scratches, hair, fibers, soil samples, and many others.

BOX 4.4   ON FACTS AND ACCURACY

(Written in 1957, but still very valid.)

There still remains the sorry spectacle of opposing factions in politics and medicine (to mention only two of the most obvious cases) who bolster up their respective cases by statistics in the confident hope that 'figures cannot lie' or, as they often hope, that 'you can't dispute' the figures.
    It is true that it is extremely difficult to interpret figures when they relate to some concrete problem. It is equally true that it is extremely easy to do arithmetic. Herein lies the real difficulty. Averages can be calculated to nineteen places of decimals with astonishing ease. When the job is done it looks very accurate. It is an easy and fatal step to think that the accuracy of our arithmetic is equivalent to the accuracy of our knowledge about the problem in hand. We suffer from 'delusions of accuracy'. Once an enthusiast gets this disease, he and all who depend on his conclusions for their welfare are damned.

(Moroney, 1957)

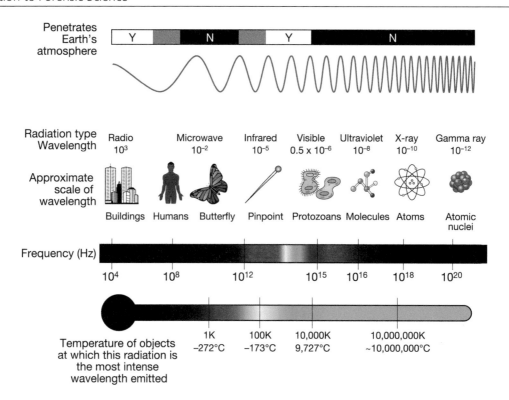

FIGURE 4.8 The electromagnetic spectrum. The diagram shows the properties of electromagnetic (EM) radiation. The scales indicate (top to bottom) atmospheric penetration, wavelength, frequency, and temperature. The visible spectrum, the part of the spectrum that our eyes can detect, is only a small portion of the entire electromagnetic spectrum.

Source: Science Photo Library. Used with permission.

In order to to access the richness of information available beyond our direct senses, we have developed tools to extend and enhance these senses (Figure 4.9). For example, we have developed lenses and microscopes to extend our sense of sight to see very large and very small objects. We have also developed chemical detectors, such as spectrometers, to greatly extend our human biological sensors used for taste and smell. We have also developed a variety of physical and mechanical devices to extend our senses of touch and hearing, allowing us to sense the smallest vibrations, detect slight imperfections in a surface, and perceive exceptionally weak electrical signals.

In this section, we will explore tools that have specifically been developed to *extend our sense* of sight using microscopy. In later chapters, we will focus on chemical and physical detectors that are effective in extending our other senses.

4.2.2 Microscopy Basics

In order to understand how a microscope works, it is very helpful to first understand how our own visual detectors, our eyes, work. When light enters our eyes, the image is focused by the lens and cornea onto the back lining of the eyeball, called the retina (Figure 4.10). Muscles attached to the lens delicately change its shape from more spherical to less spherical to bring this image into sharp focus. Light from the focused image falls on the retina at the back of the eye and interacts with two different kinds of cells there: the rod and cone cells. Rod cells determine the brightness of the light (not color), while the cone cells distinguish different colors of light (not brightness). The intensity and color information from these two types of cells are then converted into electrical signals that are passed along the optic nerve into the brain for processing into a pattern that we can recognize. The eye can detect a very large range of light intensities and distinguish between very close wavelengths of light in the visible region, allowing us to see over 10 million different colors and perceive both bright sunlight and very darkly lit situations.

There are limits, however, on how much we can change the shape of the lens of our eyes to bring close objects into focus on the retina. This focusing ability limits how small an object can be "seen" by our unaided eyes. It turns out that about 25 cm (10 in.) is about as close as an object can come to our eyes and still remain in focus. Closer than that renders the object increasingly blurry, and we are unable to resolve fine detail in the image.

By at least several millennia ago, people realized that they could see things closer when looking through round droplets of water, clear crystals of minerals or pieces of glass. It appears that the Romans took this important technological step

FIGURE 4.9   Our senses have been extended using specially designed devices: lenses and microscopes to extend our sight, chemical detectors, spectrographs and spectrometers to extend our senses of taste and smell, and physical/mechanical devices to extend our senses of touch and hearing.

Source: Image courtesy Shutterstock.com.

forward by discovering that looking through a smooth piece of glass that was thicker in the middle than at the edges (convex) allowed them to see clearly smaller objects than they could otherwise. This happens through a process of bending light rays by *refraction* – where light is slowed and, therefore, bent a bit when it enters something denser than air, such as glass. The Romans referred to such a magnifier as a "lens," since they were shaped similarly to the lentil (Latin for lentil is *lens lentis*), a type of small bean. In the 16th century, however, microscopes were invented that incorporated two or more carefully made glass lenses for greater magnification. The development of the microscope allowed Anton van Leeuwenhoek (1632–1723), often called the "father of microbiology," to first describe a new world of single-celled organisms along with a whole range of previously unknown biological structures. Some representatives in the development of the microscope from Leeuwenhoek to modern microscopy are shown in Figure 4.11.

4.2.3 How a Magnifying Lens Works

When we look through a lens, the image of the object in view is "spread out" across our retina, making it appear as though the object is much larger than it really is. In a way, this tricks our eyes into thinking that the object is much closer by creating something called a "virtual image" (notice the size of the image of the object on the retina in the two cases in Figure 4.12). By moving the lens closer to the object, the virtual image is smaller (appears less magnified) but by moving the lens closer to our eyes and away from the object, the virtual image appears larger and therefore, the greater the magnification. When the lens moves closer to our eyes, the image of the object is actually spread across a greater portion of our retina, making the object appear larger to us. Notice that the virtual image is "beyond" the actual object and larger than the original object.

Human Eye Anatomy

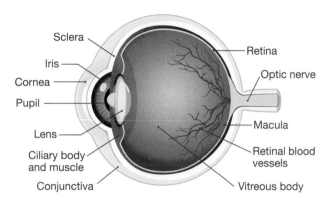

STRUCTURE OF THE RETINA

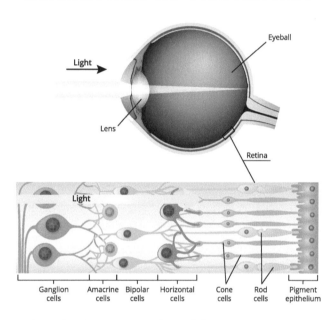

FIGURE 4.10 How our eyes detect light.

Source: Shutterstock.com.

4.2.4 How a Microscope Works

In microscopy, we typically employ several magnifying lenses working together, but they still operate in a similar way to the single lens system described above. A compound microscope is a device built to allow us to put two or more lenses in alignment to obtain much higher magnification. This works as illustrated in Figure 4.13. The object (in the figure, the small letter "G") is projected by the first lens onto the second lens as an inverted image to create Image 1 as a *real* image (real images are similar to those projected onto the screen in a movie theater). The second lens then creates an enlarged *virtual* image (Image 2) of the letter "G," just like the single magnifying lens we've already discussed. Our eyes (labeled "eye lens") perceive this second image as a greatly magnified version of

the original. In essence, the first lens projects an image onto another lens that is then magnified again to give a total magnification greater than any one lens could give alone.

A good way to understand the difference between real and virtual images is to look into a shiny spoon (Figure 4.14). When you look into the inside of the bowl (concave surface), you see an inverted image of yourself *in front* of the mirror. This is a *real* image, just like that produced by the first lens of the microscope. When you look at the outside of the spoon's bowl (convex surface), however, the image is a right-side-up *virtual* image, where it appears that the image is actually *behind* the surface of the spoon. The optical pathways of the light in these two instances are shown diagrammatically as dashed lines in Figure 4.14. While microscopes typically employ convex lenses, the use of the real and virtual images is the same as in the spoon example (see Box 4.5).

BOX 4.5   IS IT REAL OR VIRTUAL?

What's the difference and significance of the distinction between a real and a virtual image? Real images are formed where light rays actually converge to form an image through a focal point and are always upside down. On the other hand, virtual images seem to originate from places behind an object and come from diverging rays of light – for example, the image in a mirror appears to come from behind the plane of the mirror – this is a virtual image. A virtual image cannot be projected since light rays never converge to form the image, while a real image can be projected. It's confusing, but an important distinction in optics.

In a typical compound light microscope, light first passes up through the sample and is projected as an enlarged image by an objective lens onto a second lens, the ocular (or eyepiece) lens, which then creates a further enlarged virtual image that our eyes observe as a greatly magnified image of the original object. In actual practice, the objective lens is most often composed of a series of lenses designed to make various corrections to keep the image well-focused and of the correct color. The tube part of the microscope simply serves to keep the various lenses in proper alignment.

The main components of a typical light microscope, as illustrated in Figure 4.15, include:

- **Arm and Base:** The parts of the microscope that provide the mechanical support to hold all the components of the microscope in the correct position and alignment to produce the magnified image.
- **Illumination System:** Usually employs either reflected or transmitted light depending upon the thickness of the sample and the location of the light source. Reflected light is used for opaque samples (non-transparent) where the light is bounced off the sample, while transmitted light passes up through the transparent sample.

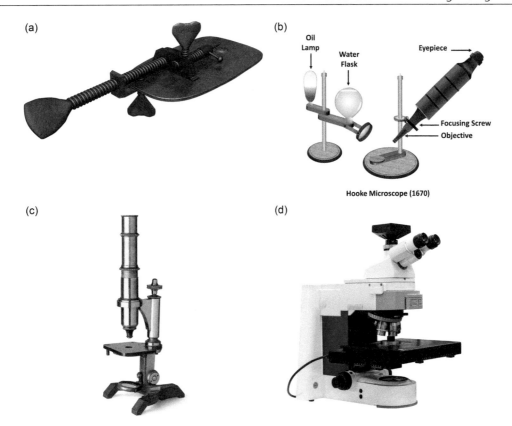

FIGURE 4.11 Illustrative historical microscopes in the development of optical microscopy: (a) the microscope of Anton van Leeuwenhoek from the late 1600s that helped him to discover *animalcules*, (b) Robert Hooke's microscope from 1670 that allowed him to first describe and name "cells," (c) a 19th-century microscope showing many refinements over Hooke's, and (d) a modern microscope.

Source: Images courtesy Shutterstock.com.

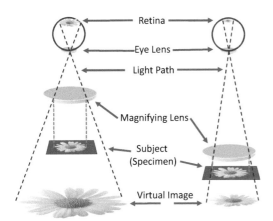

FIGURE 4.12 Magnifying ability of a magnifying lens and the effect that changing the position of the lens relative to the viewer has on the magnification power (the size of the virtual image and how it is spread across the retina).

- **Condenser:** Collects and concentrates the light from the illumination system and directs it onto the sample.
- **Sample Stage:** The horizontal platform holds the sample firmly in place while allowing it to be smoothly moved around mechanically in two dimensions horizontally to bring different parts of the sample into the viewing area of the lenses.
- **Objective Lens:** Often a series of lenses within a single housing to provide magnification while correcting for color and focus problems. Typical microscopes have several objective lenses on a rotating turret (nosepiece) with magnifications of 4×, 10×, 40×, and 100×. These lenses can be quickly exchanged one for another simply by turning the revolving turret.
- **Tube/Body:** The tube separating the objective lens from the ocular (eyepiece) lens and designed to allow focus and magnification to happen properly.
- **Focus Adjustment** (fine and coarse): These knobs focus the image by raising and lowering the sample stage relative to the microscope body and lenses (alternatively, the microscope body tube can be moved relative to the sample stage).
- **Ocular (eyepiece) Lens**: The lens closest to the viewer's eye, providing magnification and individual adjustment for each person' eyesight.

Several terms are important when considering microscopy. The *resolving power* (resolution) of a microscope is its ability to discern two very closely spaced objects as separate items.

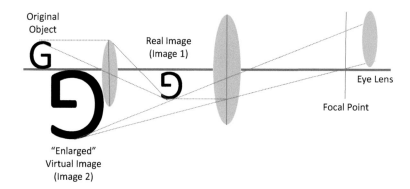

FIGURE 4.13   Two lenses of a compound microscope combine to create the greatly magnified image as perceived by our eyes. The second lens "enlarges" the image created by the first lens (Image 1) to create a new virtual image (Image 2). Our eyes, shown on the far right and labeled "eye lens," then "sees" the enlarged virtual image (Image 2).

(a)

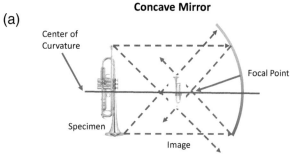

(b)

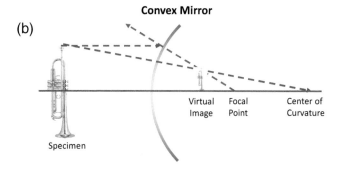

FIGURE 4.14   *Real* and *Virtual* images produced by looking into the different surfaces of a spoon (a) and mirror (b), showing how these surfaces produce real and virtual images.

Credit: (a) Andrew Lambert Photography/ Science Photo Library. Used with permission.

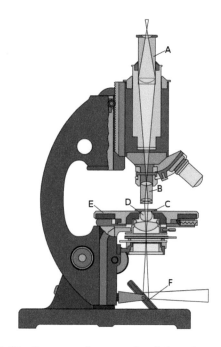

FIGURE 4.15   Cutaway diagram of a light microscope showing the light path (yellow) through the sample, into the objective lens, and through either the eyepiece lens or the camera lens (top). Labeled components: (A) ocular lens, (B) objective lens, (C) sample holder, (D) illumination lenses, (E) stage, and (F) illumination mirror.

Source: Used per Creative Commons Share-Alike 3.0 Unported. User: Tomia.

If two objects are closer than the resolving power for the microscope, then the two objects will blur into one (Figure 4.16). *Magnification power* (magnification) refers to the ability of a lens or microscope to make things appear larger. Magnification is quite separate from resolving power – you can enlarge something greatly with lenses, but if the resolving power is insufficient, the image will look blurry.

The total magnification of a microscope can be easily calculated simply by multiplying together the magnifying powers of each of the individual lenses. For example, when a ten times (10×) ocular lens is combined with a 40 times (40×) objective lens, the total magnification of the combined two-lens setup will be ten times forty or 400 times.

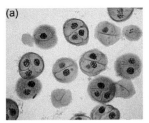
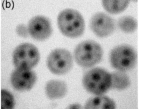

Good Resolution   Poor Resolution

FIGURE 4.16 Pollen grains from light microscopic images with good resolution (a) and poor resolution (b).

Credit: (a) Ikelos GMBH/ Dr. Christopher B. Jackson/Science Photo Library. Used with permission.

Besides magnification, lenses also have an intrinsic value, called *numerical aperture* (NA), which provides an indication of the ability of the lens to gather light and resolve fine details. The larger the NA, the greater the lens' ability to resolve closely spaced features. Typically, objective lenses are marked with their magnification followed by the NA. However, the total NA of a microscope also must include the NA of the light condenser together with the NA of the various lenses.

The *field of view* for a specific set of lenses refers to how much of the sample you can see. For example, if the total magnification of a microscope is 40×, the field of view might be about 4 mm. Increasing the magnification to 400×, however, reduces the field of view to about 0.4 mm. As the magnification increases, the field of view decreases. The useful field of view, however, depends upon the resolution of the lenses – decreasing the field of view without somehow also increasing the resolution will yield a blurry image.

Depth of focus (or depth of field) refers to the thickness of a sample that can be simultaneously viewed in focus and depends upon the magnification. The depth of focus improves when the magnification of the lenses increases.

Contrast refers to the difference in brightness between the features of an object and the surrounding areas. Contrast can be adjusted by changing the amount of illumination hitting the sample. Sometimes decreasing the illumination increases contrast (usually at lower magnification), while at other times, just the opposite works best (at higher magnifications).

Microscopes come in a variety of designs and arrangements of the main components, while the general operating principles discussed above remain the same for all these systems. One common variation is either monocular (one eye piece) versus binocular (two eyepieces) arrangements. Often, a camera can be added to the microscope to allow for a permanent photographic record of the images. Numerous ways have also been designed to properly illuminate the sample, correct for color and lens distortions in the image, and correct for other optical problems.

One way to classify microscopes is to organize them based on the way that they illuminate the sample. In the following sections, therefore, we will focus on two main types of microscopes: those that use some form of light (electromagnetic radiation) and those that use an electron beam to "see" the sample.

4.3 OPTICAL MICROSCOPY

4.3.1 Optical Microscopy

The most common, and certainly the oldest, form of microscopy uses visible light to illuminate the sample so that our eyes can directly "see" the magnified image. Generally, this form of microscopy is called **optical microscopy**. However, there are a number of important variations on this theme that form the core of forensic microscopy. To place optical microscopy in context, Figure 4.17 demonstrates the relative size of

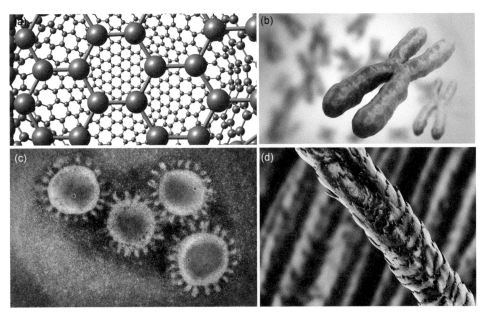

FIGURE 4.17 Ranges of relative size resolution of different types of microscopies. (a) Atomic force microscopy, (b) electron microscopy, (c) optical stereomicroscopy and (d) optical microscopy.

Source: Image courtesy Shutterstock.com and iStockphoto.com.

objects that the various types of microscopy can resolve. All these microscopic systems employ the basic principles that have already been described but have unique advantages and disadvantages that make them useful for specific purposes. In this section, the most generally useful of these methods will be presented.

4.3.2 Bright Field Optical Microscopy

When you simply think of microscopy, you're probably thinking of bright field microscopy. It is the most basic form of light microscopy, where the sample is illuminated by white light, usually from below, which then passes directly through the sample on its way through the magnifying lenses to our eyes (Figure 4.18). The ability to distinguish the various parts of the sample (contrast) arises from the different light absorbances of the various components in the sample. In other words, the light is absorbed or scattered differently by the various chemical compounds contained within the features of the sample – some places absorb a lot of light and appear darker, while other areas absorb less light and appear relatively lighter to our eyes. Since light that does not pass through the sample is absorbed the least and appears brightest to our eyes, the term bright field microscopy is, therefore, used to indicate that the background appears the brightest in the view, while the sample appears relatively darker in comparison. This technique typically is useful in observing objects in the range of 1 μm (1,000 mm) to 0.5 mm (a strand of human hair is typically about 20 mm in thickness). An example of a bright field micrograph of a cotton stem is shown in Figure 4.19.

The great advantage of this approach is its simplicity of use and easy sample preparation. It has, however, several limitations that arise from problems relating to sample transparency, image resolution, and contrast. Bright field microscopy typically has relatively low contrast for biological samples since most biological materials do not absorb light very well. When a sample is colored, however, it provides much better contrast. Some ways of improving contrast have been

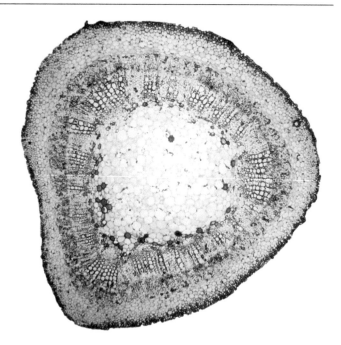

FIGURE 4.19 Light microscopic image of the cross section of a cotton stem at 10× magnification.

Source: Used per Creative Commons 4.0 International. User: Eugeenia Wen.

developed, foremost among these is staining the sample (*vide infra*). Sometimes, instead of white light, colored light can be used to more successfully visualize the details of the sample. Contrast can also be improved by adjusting the amount of light entering the sample using a condenser that focuses and controls the light from the source falling onto the sample. Nonetheless, bright field microscopy provides a basic tool for visualizing small features of both biological and non-living samples.

A variety of modifications of this technique have been developed to enhance contrast by changing the setup of the microscope or by modifying the type of light used, as described in the following sections.

4.3.3 Dark Field Optical Microscopy

Sometimes in bright field microscopy, staining or other contrast enhancing techniques are insufficient to allow us to see the details in a sample. One alternative technique for enhancing contrast that is relatively easy and often effective in these circumstances is referred to as *dark field microscopy*.

In this technique, a physical light block is used to stop all the light that would travel in a straight line from the light source into the lenses. The *only* light that enters the lens in this setup, therefore, is the light that has been scattered into the lens *by the sample*. This is shown schematically in Figure 4.20. In dark field microscopy, light is aimed only from the edges of the condenser lens onto the sample in such a way that it would miss the lens entirely unless the path of the light is changed by the sample (scattered). If you were to look into a dark field microscope without a sample under the lens, you would see a

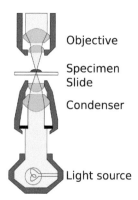

FIGURE 4.18 Light path (optical path) used in bright field microscopy.

Source: Used per Creative Commons Share-Alike 3.0 Unported. User: Egmason.

black field (background) – no light would enter the lens since it is blocked by the annular light stop (Figure 4.20). When a sample is present, however, it deflects some of the light into the lens so that it appears illuminated against a black background, hence the name dark field microscopy. Figure 4.21 shows a comparison of a sample as seen under bright field and dark field conditions. Color is sometimes seen in dark field microscopy that does not appear in the sample under normal illumination, further aiding contrast.

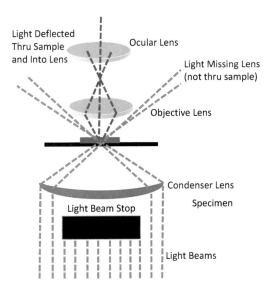

FIGURE 4.20 Schematic drawing showing how a dark field microscope works. In dark field microscopy, a beam stop blocks any light that would go directly through the sample so that only light that is scattered from the sample can enter the lenses.

Advantages of the dark field method include an enhanced ability to see details in biological samples that do not have enough contrast to be seen well in bright field microscopy and the fact that the technique is experimentally quite simple and inexpensive. An important disadvantage, however, is that the sample often appears to have a high degree of glare, leading to the image showing up in silhouette rather than as a clearly defined bright object.

4.3.4 Polarized Light Microscopy

Light, as electromagnetic radiation, is made up of both electrical and magnetic waves that each oscillate as they move through space. These two kinds of waves are perpendicular to one another, as shown in Figure 4.22, and allow energy to travel through a vacuum. Visible light, radio waves, X-rays, microwaves, and WiFi are all just forms of electromagnetic radiation that differ principally in their wavelengths.

Generally, a light source emits tiny packets of light, called *photons*, in all directions. Therefore, a beam of light contains photons with their waves vibrating in all possible orientations (unpolarized light). It is possible, however, to remove all the photons *except* those vibrating in just one direction by passing the light through very tiny, thin rectangular slits, as shown in Figure 4.23. The only photons that can pass through the slit are those in which their plane of oscillation (wave action) lines up with the long direction of the slit. This geometry produces something called *plane polarized light* – light oscillating in only one direction. If you put a second set of slits after the light is polarized (Polarizer 2 in Figure 4.23), two

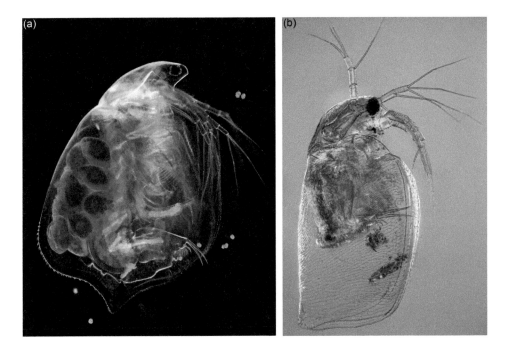

FIGURE 4.21   Dark field (a) and bright field (b) micrographs of a *Daphnia* (*Daphnia pulex*).

Credit: (a) Frank Fox/Science Photo Library, (b) Marek Mis/Science Photo Library. Used with permission.

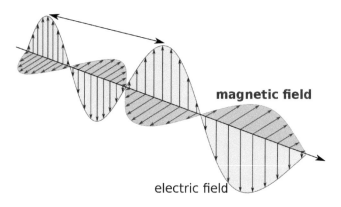

FIGURE 4.22 *Perpendicular oscillating electrical and magnetic waves make up electromagnetic radiation (EM).*

Source: Retrieved from Wikimedia Commons; used per Creative Commons Attribution.

possibilities exist. If the second set of slits lines up with the first set, then the light can pass through, and we see light on the other side. If, however, the second polarizer is lined up in another fashion, the polarized light is cut out – it can't make it through the slit.

A simple analogy for this comes from an old-fashioned comedy movie gag where a person carrying a long board horizontally tries to go through a vertical door. If the board is repositioned to line up with the door, they can pass through; if not, they are blocked. This is similar to how plane polarized light works: "horizontally" vibrating light waves cannot pass through a "vertical" slit opening. This is exactly how polarized sunglasses operate (see Box 4.6).

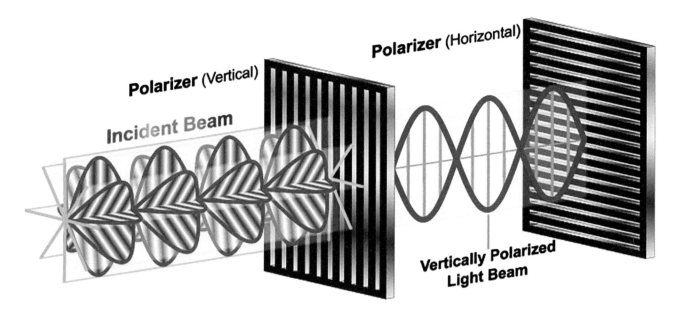

FIGURE 4.23 *How plane polarized light is formed.*

Source: Shutterstock.com.

BOX 4.6   POLARIZED LIGHT APPLICATIONS

A common form of polarizing lenses comes in the form of polarized sunglasses. These lenses are actually made up of tiny parallel slits that only allow light of one orientation through – plane polarized light. These lenses are very good at blocking reflected light that tends to be horizontally polarized and does not align well with the vertical direction of the slits in the lenses of the glasses. This greatly reduces glare from reflections on water, roads, or other shiny surfaces.

Polarized light is also used to produce a 3D effect in movies. When you put on the "magic 3D glasses," images seem to jump off the screen. This is because the slits in the right and left lenses of the glasses are oriented perpendicular to one another. The movie then projects two images simultaneously on the screen that are polarized 90° to each other (one projected image is horizontally polarized and the other vertically polarized). Each lens of the glasses admits only one of the two polarized images while blocking the other. In this way, each eye sees a slightly different image, giving the illusion of 3D.

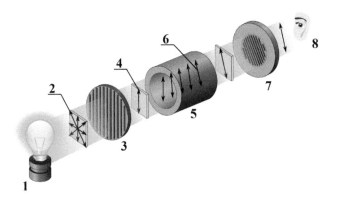

FIGURE 4.24 Polarized light may be "twisted" or rotated by chemicals in the sample. A polarimeter for measuring this optical rotation includes: (1) light source, (2) unpolarized light, (3) linear polarizer, (4) linearly polarized light, (5) sample tube containing the molecules under study, (6) optical rotation due to the molecules, (7) rotatable linear analyzer, and (8) detector.

Source: Used per Creative Commons Share-Alike 3.0. User: Kaidor.

Polarized light can play an important role in forensic microscopy. In this application, the light that passes through the sample is first polarized by a polarizing lens. Some chemical compounds, however, have the ability to "twist" or rotate the plane of polarized light when they interact with it. When the polarized light encounters these molecules, the plane of the light is twisted into a new orientation (Figure 4.24). The light passing through the sample is then passed through a second polarizing lens that can be rotated to determine the orientation of the newly "twisted" light – all other light that is not "twisted" is excluded since it is misaligned with the second polarizing lens and cannot pass through.

Polarized light microscopy works particularly well when molecules that "twist" the light are present in the sample. This is very common for minerals, but living samples also can contain many such molecules. The contrast when these compounds are present can be very striking, as shown in Figure 4.25. The technique is often employed for forensic samples to identify the compositions of fibers, minerals, soils, and biological materials.

4.3.5 Phase Contrast Microscopy

One major problem in bright field microscopy is that most biological samples are colorless and do not absorb enough light to provide suitable contrast to clearly show the features in the sample. *Phase contrast microscopy* is a technique that can be used to enhance the contrast in these types of samples.

When light passes through a substance, it is slightly slowed relative to its speed in air. Our eyes cannot detect this very small amount of slowing, but we can use this phenomenon to enhance contrast. The light that has been slowed by the sample

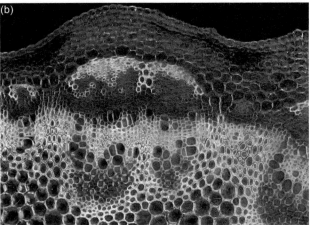

FIGURE 4.25 Polarized light microscopic images: (a) crystals of a common painkiller acetaminophen (Paracetamol) and (b) a transverse section through the stalk of a fleabane plant (*Erigeron* sp., magnification 93×).

Source: (a) Shutterstock.com. Marek Mis/Science Photo Library. Used with permission (b) Used per Creative Commons Share-Alike 3.0. User: Kaidor.

is *out of phase* with light that bypasses the sample: when recombined, the waves don't match up properly, as shown at the bottom of Figure 4.26. Out of phase indicates that similar points on two waves, for example, the two high points, do not align when they are superimposed. This would be similar to two runners on a track who are initially running at the same speed shoulder-to-shoulder. Then, one runner is just momentarily slowed by a bad piece of track. After the slowing, the two runners are once again moving at the same speed, but they are no longer shoulder-to-shoulder – they are "out of phase" compared to when they were initially "in phase." Similarly, when two "out of phase" light waves are added together, the resulting new wave shows a lower peak height (amplitude) than if they were added when "in phase." When two waves are completely out of phase (when the highest point of one wave lines up exactly with the lowest point of a second wave), they cancel each other out entirely, and no light is observed at all.

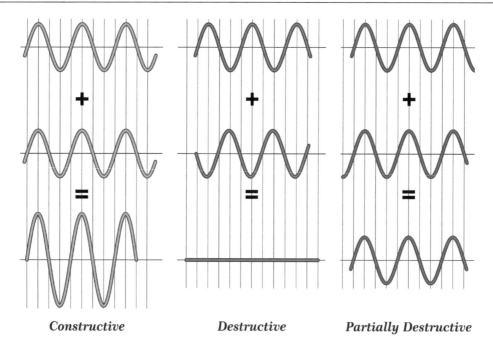

Constructive   *Destructive*   *Partially Destructive*

FIGURE 4.26 Constructive addition from waves in phase (aligned) and destructive addition of out of phase waves.

Source: Shutterstock.com.

In phase contrast microscopy, light that has been slowed by the sample is recombined in a special way with light that has not been slowed by the sample. When this happens, the waves partially "destructively" cancel each other, causing a darkened image for the sample resulting in enhanced contrast. This enhancement is illustrated in Figure 4.27 with a phase contrast image of a protozoan.

4.3.6 Fluorescence Microscopy

In the search for ways to enhance the contrast in samples, the technique of fluorescence microscopy has become one of the most intensely explored methods in forensic optical microscopy. In order to understand how it works, it is first necessary to understand how fluorescence itself operates.

When light shines on a molecule, it can excite electrons in some of the molecule to a higher energy condition (excited state). In some special molecules, when they absorb light to become excited, they can later re-emit the light but only at a slightly longer wavelength than the original excitation light, as shown in Figure 4.28. In this example, blue light, first absorbed by the molecule, excites it to a higher energy state. Then, after the molecule loses some energy through one of several ways, such as vibration, the molecule re-emits the remaining energy as lower energy green light: blue light in, but green light out. This three-step process is termed fluorescence. It is possible to filter out the wavelength of the original exciting light so that you only "see" the fluorescence emission. This process is particularly noticeable when the compound is excited by "invisible" ultraviolet light but emits visible light. You probably have seen this "glow-in-the-dark" effect when "black lights" are used to

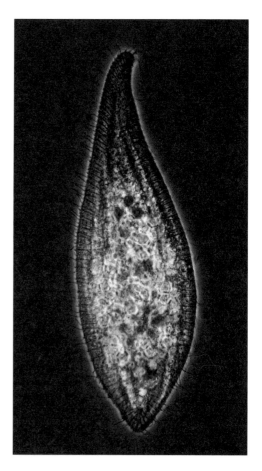

FIGURE 4.27 Phase contrast light micrograph of single living cell of *Loxophyllum*, a predatory ciliate (Protozoa), showing the cilia and extrusomes.

Source: Shutterstock.com.

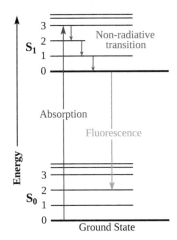

FIGURE 4.28 Fluorescence emission through the absorption of shorter wavelength light (higher energy) to excite electrons followed by the emission of longer wavelength light (lower energy): blue light in and green light out.

Source: Retrieved from Wikimedia Commons; used per Creative Commons Attribution.

FIGURE 4.29 Fluorescent strip embedded in a U.S. 20-dollar bill.

Source: Retrieved from Wikimedia Commons; used per Creative Commons Attribution.

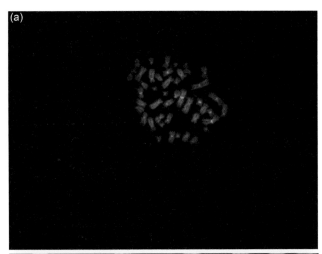

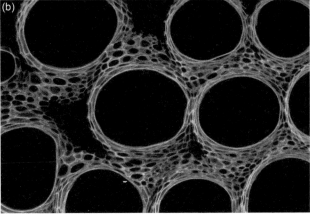

FIGURE 4.30 (a) Fluorescence micrograph *in situ* of human chromosomes in blood and (b) a micrograph of pumpkin stem tissue infused with a red fluorescent dye.

Source: Images courtesy Shutterstock.com.

make items such as clothing, posters, or minerals glow. The U.S. treasury, for example, embeds a fluorescent strip in 20-dollar bills that can only be seen using ultraviolet lamps (black lights) as a method to detect counterfeit bills (Figure 4.29).

Some naturally occurring chemicals fluoresce under ultraviolet radiation, including some body fluids, such as semen and the residues from fingerprint. Specially designed fluorescent compounds may also be added to a forensic sample that bond specifically with certain chemicals to help with visualizing biological structures. For example, a fluorescent dye which binds specifically with certain biological structures, such as the nuclei in sperm cells, may be added. Light is then shone on the sample to excite the dye molecules and then the wavelength of the original light is filtered out before

it reaches the viewer. The only light that is seen, therefore, comes from the fluorescent glow from the dye in the sperm cell nuclei.

In forensic investigations, fluorescence microscopy has found a number of very important uses. One use involves analyzing evidence from rape investigations. Sperm cells are often difficult to differentiate from other cells through other microscopic techniques. As mentioned above, using an appropriate sperm-specific fluorescent stain, these cells readily stand out from all other cells, as shown in Figure 4.30. Many fluorescent dyes have now been developed that bind to specific biological structures and are used to readily visualize these structures.

In art fraud cases, the determination of the authenticity of older works of art can be supported through fluorescence studies. Older paints and pigments usually do not contain fluorescent chemicals, but modern paints and pigments very often contain chemicals that fluoresce under ultraviolet light. This is especially true of the brighter colors, where fluorescent dyes are added to make them stand out better because the ultraviolet portion of ambient sunlight makes them emit visible light – the paints are actually glowing a little bit in the sunlight, making them seem more brilliant. The same happens with "whiteners"

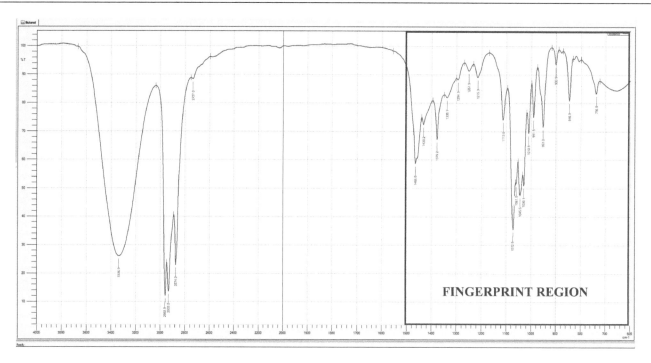

FINGERPRINT REGION

FIGURE 4.31   Infrared transmittance spectrum showing the characteristic IR "fingerprint" region used to identify the compound (on the right side of the spectrum).

Source: Shutterstock.

added to laundry detergent to make the "colors brighter" by helping them emit visible light in the sunshine.

Limitations on fluorescence microscopy relate to reduced resolution and the requirement that the sample be rather thin. This latter requirement is circumvented in more recent forensic work through the use of two-photon fluorescence microscopy (using two photons of light to excite the molecule instead of just one).

4.3.7 Infrared Microscopy

Light that has a wavelength between about 700 nm and 1,400 nm, referred to as infrared radiation (IR), is not visible to the unaided eye. Many compounds of forensic interest, however, readily absorb light in this region. For example, many drugs, fibers, pigments, and dyes have specific "signatures" in the IR spectrum, most often in a part of the IR spectrum called the IR "fingerprint" region: between 500 and 1,500 cm (Figure 4.31). Comparing the pattern from this region of an unknown with a standard may allow the unknown compound to be identified unambiguously.

In infrared microscopy (called infrared microspectrophotometry if we use it to identify specific compounds), IR light is shone on the sample and an IR-sensitive detector, is used to allow us to "see" the sample since our eyes cannot detect IR light. The way certain very small regions of the field of view absorb infrared light (called absorbance) can be chemically analyzed to help identify the material (see Chapter 12 on spectroscopy). This technique allows for the non-destructive analysis of an image by microscopically "mapping" the chemical composition of the entire sample.

In this fashion, specific inks, drugs, gunshot residues, explosives, and even fingerprints have been determined from very tiny, microscopic samples. Figure 4.32 illustrates how IR microspectrophotometry was used to prove that a painting was a forgery by determining that the acrylic chemical composition of a brush fiber found embedded within the paint was not known to exist at the time the painting was claimed to have been done.

4.3.8 Stereomicroscopy

In the types of microscopy presented thus far, the light travels from the source, directly *through* the sample, and finally to the viewer's eyes or detector (transmitted light through the sample). It is also possible, however, to use scattered and reflected light that *bounces off* the sample to look specifically at its surface. A stereomicroscope, sometimes called a dissecting microscope, does just that using separate lenses for each eye to provide a low magnification 3D image of the sample's surface. This is essentially similar to using two magnifying lenses, one for each eye, to obtain a magnified 3D look at a sample. This technique allows us to look at samples that are far too thick or opaque to see using transmitted light microscopy and allows us to focus on surface structures and features.

Stereo microscopes are relatively simple in design, as shown in Figures 4.33 and 4.34. These microscopes consist of two optical pathways, one for each eye, which collects light bouncing off the surface of the sample at a different angle. Each pathway's view is from a slightly different perspective,

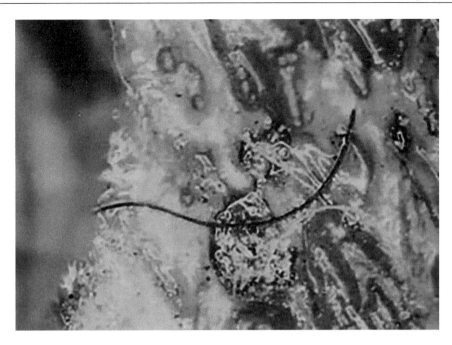

FIGURE 4.32 IR microscopy was used to identify the fiber embedded in this image as an acrylic fiber coming from a paint brush of the type that was first used in the 1960s. This determination shows that this painting could not have been painted in 1937, as was claimed.

Source: www.jackiefreemanphotography.com/specialist_photography.htm. Used with permission.

giving a 3D view of the surface. This allows us to see fine surface details, as shown for a coin surface in Figure 4.35.

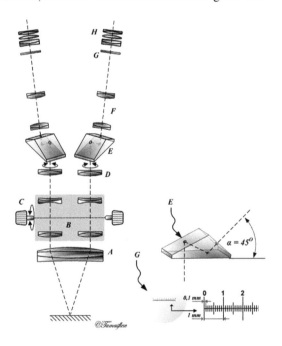

FIGURE 4.33 Optical paths for the two "views" provided by a stereo microscope, one to each eye showing slightly different images of the same sample to obtain a 3D image of the surface of a sample.

4.3.9 Comparison Microscopy

In forensic investigations, it is often useful to compare the fine details of two samples, often an unknown collected at a crime scene to be compared with a reference sample of known origin. This could be done, of course, by looking at the samples one at a time through the microscope. However, it is far more convenient and accurate to use an apparatus that allows us to look at both samples *simultaneously* and to compare them side-by-side at once. This is accomplished very effectively using a comparison microscope.

In essence, a comparison microscope consists of two separate and complete microscopes joined together at the eyepiece, as shown in Figure 4.36. In this fashion, the image from one microscope is viewed in one eyepiece, while the image from the other microscope is seen through the other eyepiece. This allows us to simultaneously view two different samples and to move them around independently to achieve the best comparative orientation for both. Alternatively, the two separate right and left images are juxtaposed on a computer screen to facilitate the comparison.

The comparison microscope has become essential in many types of forensic investigations, including firearm, questioned document, counterfeiting, arson, hair and fiber, soil, and theft cases, among others. For example, when a bullet is fired from a weapon, the scratches and imperfections that are always present in the barrel of the gun are "imprinted" onto the bullet as striations: small scratches and grooves. These striations are unique to an individual firearm, arising both from

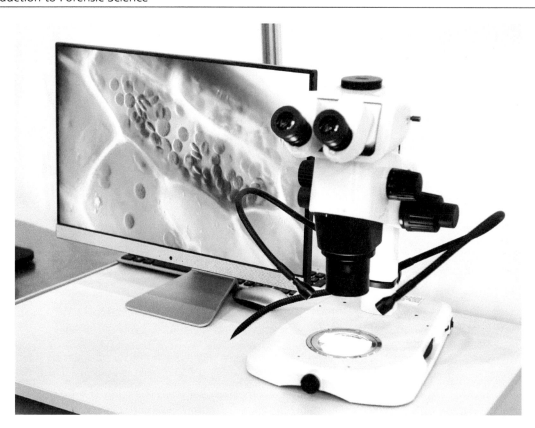

FIGURE 4.34 Design of one type of stereo microscope.

Source: iStockphoto.com, sergeyryzhov.

FIGURE 4.35 Stereo micrographic image of a Deutsche Mark coin, showing wear and die striation marks.

Source: Used per Creative Commons Share-Alike 3.0 Unported. User: SecretDisc.

its manufacturing process and through wear by use. When a bullet is recovered from a crime scene, investigators are often very concerned about which particular weapon fired

the bullet found. If a gun is recovered, then a test bullet of the same brand of ammunition as the recovered bullet can be fired from the suspect gun. The crime scene bullet and the test-fired bullet can then be examined in a comparison microscope to look for microscopic similarities and differences in the striations present. In this process, the two bullets are placed on the two different microscope stages and rotated independently to try to see if the striations and markings on two bullets match up, indicating a high probability that they were fired from the same weapon. Similarly, a recovered casing (the container that originally held the bullet and gunpowder) can be microscopically compared with one obtained by test firing. An example of this is shown in Figure 4.37 for two bullet casings. You should notice that the fine striations between the two casings match up very well, indicating the likelihood that both were fired from the same weapon.

Comparison microscopes are also commonly employed in forgery and questioned document cases. In this use, the exemplar (known) and questioned (unknown) documents are viewed side-by-side under the microscope to see if they match up.

Biological samples can also be compared using this technique. In Figure 4.38, a known wool fiber and an unknown fiber are compared side-by-side.

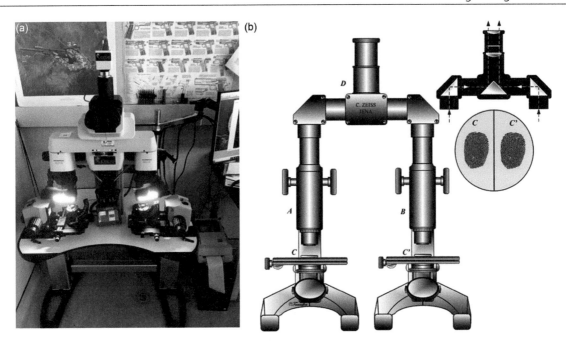

FIGURE 4.36 Comparison microscope showing the two "separate" microscopes joined together such that the left eyepiece displays the image from the left microscope, and the right eyepiece shows the image from the right microscope.

Source: (a) Courtesy of Matthew Kurmisky. (b) Used per Creative Commons Share-Alike 3.0 Unported. User: Tamasflex.

FIGURE 4.37 Comparison micrograph showing the striations (small scratches and grooves) on a bullet recovered from a crime scene compared to a bullet test-fired from a suspect's gun. Note: These two images are joined by a faint line in the center of the picture.

Source: Courtesy of Matthew Kurimsky, Onondga Co. Crime Lab.

4.3.10 Staining Techniques in Microscopy

As described before, many biological samples do not provide sufficient contrast between their structural features to be easily seen. In the preceding sections, we discussed a variety of microscopic techniques that have been developed to enhance this contrast using optical tools. It is also possible, however, to enhance the contrast by modifying the sample itself through *staining* techniques.

Staining simply refers to adding colored or light absorbing chemicals that bind selectively to specific parts of a sample to allow us to see its various features more readily.

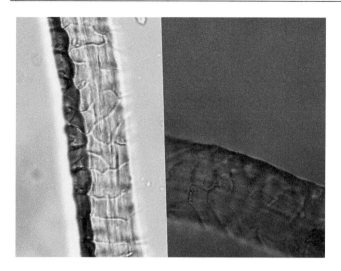

FIGURE 4.38 Known wool fibers and an unknown fiber sample are shown side-by-side using a comparison microscope.

Source: Shutterstock.com.

TABLE 4.2 Examples of stains used in microscopy

STAIN	STRUCTURE
Carmine	Stains glycogen molecules red
Crystal violet	Stains cell walls purple
Fuchsine	Stains bacteria, collagen, smooth muscle, and mitochondria magenta
Malachite green	Stains bacteria and spores blue-green
Neutral red	Stains neurons red
Osmium tetroxide	Stains lipids black
Rhodamine	A fluorescent stain for proteins
Safranin	Stains nuclei red

Numerous dyes have been developed that are useful for imparting color to biological materials, several of these are listed in Table 4.2. Ideally, the stain used will specifically localize only in the structure that you wish to see. For example, iodine will bind to starch and color it dark blue, while methylene blue is used to stain animal cell nuclei blue. Multiple stains can also be combined to give greater enhanced contrast. Fluorescent stains, as already mentioned, are specifically quite good in visualizing biological features, as illustrated in Figure 4.39.

4.3.11 Other Forms of Optical Microscopy

There are many other types of optical microscopy, including numerous variants of those described here, but these have largely not yet made their way into widespread use in forensic investigations.

The techniques described here may seem like a bewildering array of methods, but each microscopic technique provides an important tool in the arsenal to explore the very small features of forensic samples. Table 4.3 is an attempt to summarize the main features, advantages, and limitations of the different microscopic techniques presented in this chapter to aid in understanding their place in scientific examinations.

In this section, we have focused on microscopy that uses "light" (actually electromagnetic radiation of a variety of wavelengths) as the means for illuminating the sample. In the next section, however, we explore the important use of another type of "illumination" for a sample: electrons.

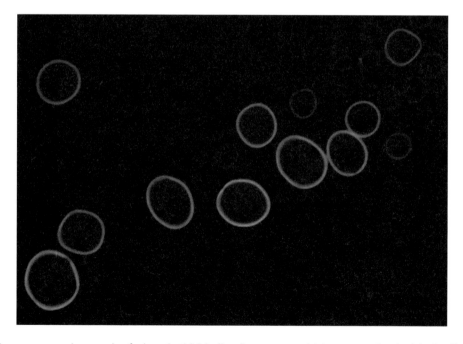

FIGURE 4.39 A fluorescence micrograph of phosphatidylcholine liposomes, which were stained with the fluorochrome acridine orange (1,250-fold magnification).

Source: Used per Creative Commons Share-Alike 4.0 International. User: ArkhipovSergey.

TABLE 4.3 Comparison of selected features of the different types of microscopy

TYPE OF MICROSCOPY	OPERATION AND USES	SOURCE	ADVANTAGES	DISADVANTAGES	MAG.	RESOLUTION (NM)
Bright field optical microscopy	Uses visible light absorbed by parts of a sample to provide contrast	Visible light	Easy, rapid, and most readily available instrument	Difficult to see many types of samples due to poor contrast, especially biological samples; light must go through the sample	100×–1,000×	~500
Dark field optical microscopy	Displays only light refracted or scattered by the sample	Visible light	Allows improved contrast of some biological samples	Limited improvement in contrast; light must go through the sample	100×–1,000×	~500
Polarized light microscopy	Uses plane polarized light to enhance contrast	Visible light	Allows improved contrast of some biological/ mineral samples	Limited improvement in contrast; light must go through the sample	100×–1,000×	~500
Phase contrast microscopy	Uses phase differences between light passing through the sample and light bypassing the sample to enhance contrast	Visible light	Allows improved contrast of some biological samples	Limited improvement in contrast; light must go through the sample	100×–1,000×	~500
Fluorescence microscopy	Uses dyes added to the sample or natural fluorescence in the sample to enhance contrast	Visible light	Allows improved contrast of some biological samples	Limited improvement in contrast; light must go through the sample	100×–1,000×	~500
Stereo microscopy	Uses scattered and reflected light to provide a 3D image of the sample	Visible light	View surfaces of samples in 3D	Limited magnification and images only the surface	10×–100×	~0.01
Comparison microscopy	Two tandem stereo microscopes	Visible light	Able to compare surfaces of two samples simultaneously	Limited magnification and images only the surface	10×–100×	~0.01
Scanning electron microscopy (SEM)	Contrast created by electron scattering from sample	Electron beam	View surfaces of very small samples with high resolution	Non-living samples; view only scattered electrons from the surface	~100,000– 1,000,000×	0.2–2
Transmission electron microscopy (TEM)	Contrast by electron transmission through sample	Electron beam	View internal structure of very small samples with high resolution	Non-living samples; view only internal structure	Up to ~5,000,000×	0.5–10

BOX 4.7   MICROSCOPY AND THE DC SNIPERS

For three weeks in October 2002, the metro-Washington, DC, area was on edge. During this time, an unknown sniper shot and killed ten innocent people and wounded a number of others in a seemingly random and lunatic rampage. It seemed to be the top story in every newspaper, TV news show, and radio broadcasts. The crime spree finally ended with the arrest of two men, John Allen Muhammad and Lee Boyd Malvo, who were apprehended while they were sleeping in their car at an interstate rest stop in the DC area.

Forensic microscopy played a significant role in the identification, tracking, and later conviction of the two men in this killing spree. Using comparison microscopy, the bullets from the various shootings were examined to link many of the crimes together and, later, to the gun found in Muhammad's car along with links to other shootings around the country. Additionally, microscopy also helped to provide critical early leads in the case.

Early on in the shooting spree, the sniper had taunted police by saying that he had been involved a month earlier in the murder of two women in Montgomery, Alabama. This was the break investigators were hoping for. They were able to quickly identify the crime that the sniper described and found the ballistic evidence from the Alabama case that matched the microscopic evidence from the DC area. Fingerprints were also found on the Alabama bullet magazine and, by searching the national fingerprint database, a match was found – teenager Lee Boyd Malvo. Malvo had been previously arrested but, more importantly, another name also surfaced with Malvo's previous record of arrest in Tacoma, Washington – that of John Allen Muhammad. FBI agents quickly located a target "practice" tree stump associated with Muhammad in a yard in Tacoma, Washington, and microscopy was again used to link this Tacoma evidence to the Alabama and DC shootings. Now the police had two key suspects – and the license plate number for Muhammad's blue Chevy Caprice with New Jersey plates: NDA-21Z. ATF records also showed that Muhammad had a Bushmaster gun in his possession, the same type of gun used in the DC shootings. It only took one day after a media blitz of this information for the car to be spotted and the two suspects to be arrested.

Comparison microscopy of ballistic evidence played a key role both in identifying and convicting the two men responsible for the shootings. Muhammad and Malvo were convicted, and Muhammad was executed on November 10, 2009, in Virginia.

4.4 ELECTRON MICROSCOPY

4.4.1 Electron Microscopy Basics

The limit for the resolution of a microscopic technique ultimately depends upon the wavelength of the illumination used to "see" the sample. In theory, that limit is about half the wavelength of the radiation used. In optical microscopy using visible light, the maximum resolution would be about 300 nm, although in practice, the working limit is much larger. The resolution, of course, dictates how much we can magnify an object, so the maximum magnification in optical microscopy is typically 1,000–2,000 times. In order to visualize smaller objects, we need to employ radiation with much smaller wavelengths.

BOX 4.8   WAVELENGTH OF PARTICLES?

As it turns out, believe it or not, everything has some wave-like properties: everything! That certainly includes not only electrons and atoms but also baseballs, toasters, cars, and planets. The governing principle is that the wavelength of an object is $\lambda = h/mv$ (where λ is the wavelength, h is a constant, m is the mass, and v is the velocity). Using this equation, we can calculate the wavelength for a variety of particles (see the table below) and find that the wavelength goes up as the mass of the particle goes down. From this, we can also see that by the time a particle gets big enough for us to see with our unaided eyes, the wavelength is nearly infinitesimally small. So, don't worry, your new car won't start oscillating from quantum mechanics – or at least not so that you can tell.

PARTICLE	MASS (Kg)	VELOCITY (M/S)	WAVELENGTH λ (pm)*
Earth	5.9×10^{24}	$\sim 3.0 \times 10^{4}$	$\sim 3.7 \times 10^{-75}$
Car	1,000	10	6.6×10^{-38}
Baseball:			
Fast ball	0.1	20	3×10^{-22}
Slow ball	0.1	0.1	7×10^{-20}
He Atom	7×10^{-27}	1,000	90
Electron	9×10^{-31}	1×10^{5}	7,000

Note: *1 pm is 10^{-12} m.

According to discoveries in the field of quantum mechanics, *all* particles have both wave and particulate properties, a feature often called the *duality of nature*. This means that every object, even those that we might think of only as particles, also have wave properties to their nature. The wavelength of any particle can be calculated using a simple relationship: $\lambda = h/mv$, where λ is the wavelength of the radiation, h is Planck's constant, m is the mass of the particle, and v is the particle's velocity. Most objects that we can see with our eyes have relatively large masses, at least when considered next to the mass of an atom, and so have very, very tiny wavelengths, far below what we could ever detect with our eyes. But as the mass of the particle gets smaller, its wavelength becomes larger. For example, the wavelength of an electron (with a mass of about 9.12×10^{-31} kg and a kinetic energy of 2 eV) is about 0.8 nm. If we could somehow use an electron to "view" a sample, much as we use visible light photons in optical microscopy, we could have greatly increased resolution, and therefore, much higher magnifications would be possible. For example, using an electron beam to illuminate a sample, the ultimate resolution with a 0.8 nm wavelength electron would be about 0.4 nm or approaching 1,000 times better than optical microscopy. The wavelength of the electron can also be made even smaller by increasing its velocity so that its wavelength can be up to about 100,000 times smaller than visible light, allowing ultimate magnifications of up to several million times!

Electron microscopes in practice employ a tiny beam of fast-moving electrons that is aimed at the sample. However, the beam that interacts with the sample must be focused, much like what is done with light in optical microscopes. The focusing "lenses" in electron microscopy are made up of electrical and magnetic fields rather than optical glass lenses, but they work in principle very much the same. Since electrons are also readily absorbed by air molecules, the samples and the electron beam must be placed in a high-vacuum chamber where all air is removed for the technique to work. This means that it is not possible to observe living samples using electron microscopy and occasionally requires the use of specialized sample preparation techniques. Depending upon the specific electron microscopic technique employed, the electrons either pass through the sample (transmission) or interact with the sample's surface (scanning) to give a greatly magnified image.

The use of electrons to microscopically observe samples provides amazingly detailed views of the miniature world, such as the snowflake, as shown in Figure 4.40. Electron

FIGURE 4.40 Electron micrograph of a columnar snow crystal.

Source: U.S. Department of Agriculture.

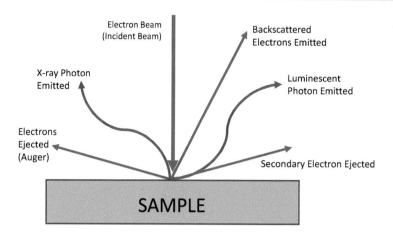

FIGURE 4.41   Electrons and X-rays are ejected from the surface of a sample in a scanning electron microscope (SEM).

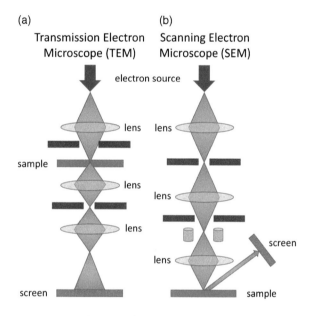

FIGURE 4.42   Schematic drawing of the operation of transmission (a) and scanning (b) electron microscopes.

microscopy has been used extensively in forensic investigations to examine evidence such as gunshot residue (GSR), biological samples, paint particles, fibers, and many others. Two main techniques have been employed in this work: scanning electron microscopy and transmission electron microscopy.

4.4.2 Scanning Electron Microscopy (SEM)

Scanning electron microscopes (SEM) use a tightly focused beam of electrons aimed at the surface of the sample. When the electrons hit the surface, both electrons and X-rays are ejected from the sample, which can then be detected (Figure 4.41). The SEM detector collects the scattered electrons and converts them into a greatly magnified image on a viewing screen. The tiny spot of the electron beam is rapidly scanned across the surface of the sample, ultimately sweeping across every part of

the sample. All of these "spot" images are put together to form the final completed image. The setup of an SEM microscope is shown schematically in Figure 4.42. In some ways, the SEM is analogous to the optical stereomicroscope in that it uses radiation that does not pass through the sample but looks only at the radiation scattered from the surface of the sample.

Samples for the SEM sometimes need to be specially prepared. Since electrons are shot at the sample, the surface receives a significant amount of incoming negative charge. If the sample conducts electricity, this excess negative charge simply flows off the sample, and no net charge is built up. If, however, the sample is non-conductive, it must first be coated with a very fine layer of conductive material to channel away the excess charge that would otherwise build up and interfere with the formation of an image by repelling further incoming negatively charged electrons.

SEM images provide exceptionally detailed 3D pictures of the surface, as seen in Figure 4.43. They provide excellent depth of field, allowing the different depths of the sample to be in focus simultaneously. As shown in the figure, this technique is used in a wide variety of investigations. Forensic applications often include firearms analysis (gunshot residue, see Figure 4.44), palynology (e.g., identification of pollen and dust), hair and fiber analysis, forgery and counterfeit detection, controlled substance identification, accident reconstruction, tool mark analysis, paint chip analysis, and in post-mortem examinations (e.g., diatom identification in drowning victims), among many others. Each of these topics will be discussed in later chapters of this text.

Besides the electrons given off by the sample, X-rays are also produced when the electron strikes the sample. The energy of an X-ray given off is unique to the element that produced it. For example, X-rays produced by iron atoms have different energies than X-rays produced by sodium atoms. Each element produces X-rays with unique characteristic energies. By analyzing the different X-ray energies given off in the SEM experiment, we can identify the elemental composition in different parts of the sample. This technique is referred to as EDXA (energy dispersive X-ray analysis) or X-ray microanalysis. An elemental composition "map" can be made to show the distribution of the elements in the SEM image, as shown in Figure 4.45.

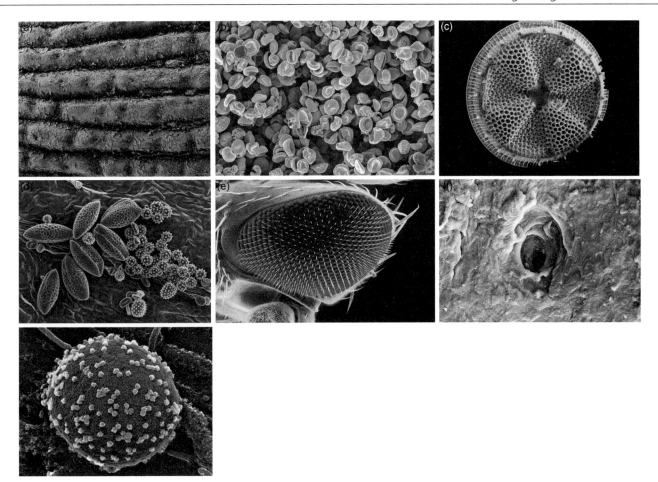

FIGURE 4.43 Scanning electron micrographs (SEM) of: (a) Fingerprint (Source: Steve Gschmeissner/Science Photo Library. Used with permission), (b) malaria parasite (Source: Shutterstock.com), (c) diatom (Source: Shutterstock.com), (d) pollen grains (Source: iStockphoto.com, Jannicke Wiik-Nielsen), (e) *Drosophila* eye (Source: Shutterstock.com), (f) sweat pore on a human finger (Source: Dr. Jeremy Burgess/Science Photo Library. Used with permission), and (g) a coronavirus on a cell.

Source: Science Photo Library used with permission. Retrieved from Wikimedia Commons; used per Creative Commons Attribution.

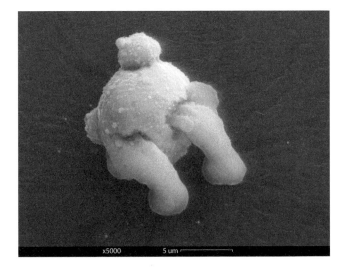

FIGURE 4.44 A scanning electron microscopic image of gunshot residue. This type of residue is deposited in the vicinity of a firearm being discharged. Analysis of the direction and amount found will indicate how far a firearm was from a victim when the gun was discharged. The criteria most commonly used in this determination are the presence or absence of gunshot residue, the pattern diameter, and the type and distribution of gunshot residue.

Source: Edward Kinsman/Science Photo Library. Used with permission.

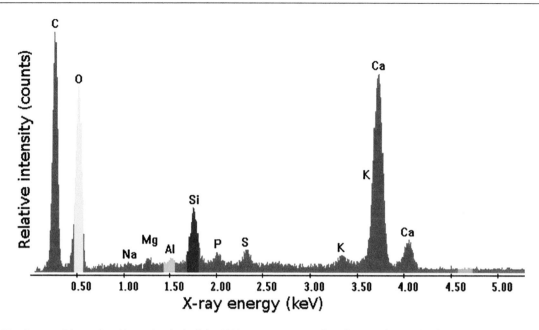

FIGURE 4.45   Energy-Dispersive X-ray Analytical (EDXA) spectroscopy showing qualitatively the elemental composition of a poppy seed.

Source: Used per Creative Commons Share-Alike 4.0 International. User: FDominec.

4.4.3 Transmission Electron Microscopy (TEM)

If scanning electron microscopy is conceptually related to stereomicroscopy in light microscopy, transmission electron microscopy (TEM) is most similar to bright field microscopy. In TEM, the electrons aimed at the sample travel directly *through* the sample, just as light passes through a sample in bright field microscopy (Figure 4.42). Some of the electrons, however, are scattered by the sample and don't make it to the viewing screen. This results in a relative darkening of the image in places where the scattering occurs. In this way, a "shadow" image is produced from the sample resulting from the differences in density throughout the sample. A typical TEM instrument is shown in Figure 4.46, while several examples of TEM images are shown in Figure 4.47.

The TEM makes it possible to see exceptionally small features, sometimes even down to a few angstroms in size [1 Å = 0.1 nm = 10^{-10} m; for comparison, ten atoms lined up in a row would be about one angstrom (Å)].

In forensic investigations, TEM and SEM images are both used to look at the shapes of very small particles, identify unknown materials and pathogens (agents that cause disease), determine an object's chemical compositions, and visualize the minute structures of materials (Figure 4.48). For example, very fine mineral samples from a suspect or crime scene can be identified readily using SEM and/or TEM, sometimes even allowing them to be traced to their site of origin with a remarkably high degree of certainty.

FIGURE 4.46   Transmission electron microscope.

Source: Shutterstock.com.

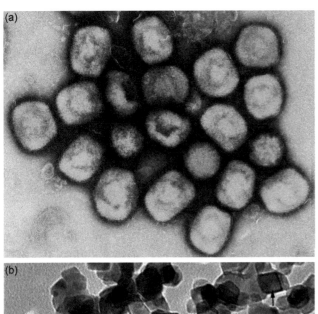

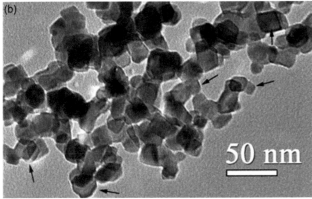

FIGURE 4.47 Transmission electron micrographs (TEM): (a) colorized TEM image of monkeypox virus particles (green), cultivated and purified from cell cultures (Used per Creative Commons Attribution 2.0 Generic. User: NIAID), and (b) TEM image showing primary crystallites of titanium dioxide nanoparticles (TiO$_2$).

Source: U.S. EPA.

4.4.4 Conclusions

Armed with these methods for examining the microscopic world, in the following chapters, we will explore how these and other tools are used by forensic investigators, beginning first at the smallest level of inquiry: the unique molecular signature of life – DNA. In later chapters, we

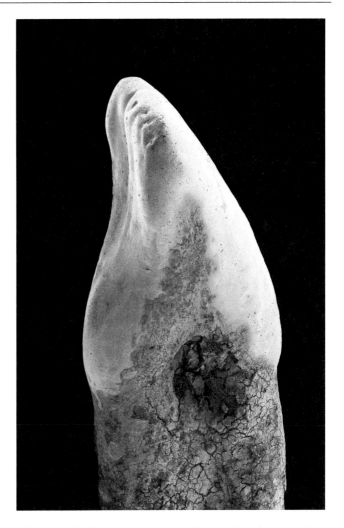

FIGURE 4.48 Tooth decay: colored scanning electron micrograph (SEM) of a cavity (lower center) in a human incisor. Cavities are caused by dental plaque (brown), a film of bacteria embedded in a glycoprotein matrix. The matrix is formed from bacterial secretions and saliva. The bacteria feed on sugars in food, producing acid as a waste product. This acid corrodes the teeth's enamel coating, resulting in cavities.

Source: Steve Gschmeissner/Science Photo Library. Used with permission.

will progressively explore increasingly larger systems, ending with the largest systems in forensic science: forensic ecology.

BOX 4.9   NOT TOO HOT IN THE FURNACE?

A paper in the *Journal of Forensic Science* describes how electron microscopy can help uniquely identify a person from remains that have been incinerated at very high temperatures. It seems that about 40 million root canals are done in the United States each year alone. Using electron microscopy, coupled with an EDXA elemental microanalysis, it is possible to identify many of the components used in the root canal procedure. These components stand up remarkably well to high-temperature incinerations (900°C for ~5 hours). Given that extensive records often exist when such a process is done, it is likely that an endodontic "fingerprint" may be particularly useful in post-mortem identification from fire, incorrect cremations, and acts of terrorism. Much work remains to be done, however, in establishing a reference database for root canal fillings for use in identification.

QUESTIONS FOR FURTHER PRACTICE AND MASTERY

4.1   What are the seven SI units of measure, and what are they used for?
4.2   Give the metric prefix indicated by the following:
(a) 10^{-3} (b) 10^6 (c) 10^{-9} (d) 10^{-2} (e) 10^1 (f) 10^{-12} (g) 10^3
4.3   What is the difference between accuracy and precision?
4.4   How many significant figures are there in each of the following:
(a) 0.0245 (b) 3.010 (c) 0.0030 (d) 7,000
4.5   What is the difference and significance of the distinction between a real and a virtual image?
4.6   Define resolving power, magnification power, numerical aperture, field of view, depth of focus, and contrast.
4.7   What are the relative size resolution limits for: (a) unaided eye, (b) optical microscopy, and (c) electron microscopy?
4.8   What is polarized light?
4.9   What is a systematic error?
4.10   What is random error?
4.11   Which size can the human eye discern objects down to: (a) 0.1 nm, (b) 0.1 cm, (c) 0.1 m, (d) 0.1 mm?
4.12   What is refraction?
4.13   What happens to the field of view as the magnification increases in a microscope?
4.14   What are some of the limitations of bright field microscopy?
4.15   What methods are used to improve contrast in bright field microscopy?
4.16   What is dark field microscopy, and how does it work?
4.17   What is a photon?
4.18   What is plane polarized light?
4.19   How is polarized light used in forensic identification of a sample?
4.20   What is a stereo microscope, and how is it employed in forensic investigations?
4.21   What is a comparison microscope? What is it used for?
4.22   What is the principle known as the *duality of nature*?
4.23   What is the wavelength of an electron with a mass of 9.12×10^{-31} kg traveling at 1.0×10^8 m/s (Planck's constant is 6.63×10^{-34} Js)?
4.24   How does the wavelength of a particle change as the mass of the particle gets smaller?
4.25   How many times greater is the magnification of an electron microscope compared to an optical microscope?

EXTENSIVE QUESTION

4.26   List the operation and uses, advantages, disadvantages, and resolution of each of the following: phase contrast microscopy, fluorescence microscopy, infrared microscopy, stereo microscopy, comparison microscopy, scanning electron microscopy, and transmission electron microscopy.

GLOSSARY OF TERMS

absorbance: a measure of how much light is absorbed by a sample.
accuracy: a measure of how close a measurement is to the true value of the feature that is being measured.
amplitude: the height of a wave from the center of its oscillation to the extreme of its movement.
angstrom (Å): a unit of measure that is one ten-billionth of a meter (1 Å = 0.1 nm = 10^{-10} m).
bright field microscopy: a form of microscopy in which the light passes directly through the sample and through lenses to the viewer and where the background appears the brightest in the view, while the sample appears relatively darker in comparison.
comparison microscope: a form of microscopy that consists of two separate and complete microscopes joined together at the eyepiece, allowing a simultaneous view of two different samples.
concave: an inner rounded surface, such as the inner portion of a bowl (inward curving).
condenser: a device on a light microscope that collects and concentrates the light from the illumination system and directs it onto the sample.
cone cells: Light receptor cells in the eye responsible for color vision and operate best in bright illumination.
contrast: the difference between a feature of a microscopic sample compared with other features, such as the background.
convex: an outer rounded surface, such as the outer portion of a bowl (outward curving).
dark field microscopy: a form of microscopy in which a physical light block is used to stop all the directly transmitted light traveling in a straight line from the light source, through the sample and into the lenses. The *only* light that enters the observing lens is light that has been scattered into the lens by the sample.
density: an intrinsic physical quantity of mass per unit volume.
depth of field (depth of focus): a term that refers to the thickness of a sample that can be simultaneously viewed in focus and depends upon the magnification, where

the depth of focus increases when the magnification of the lenses increases.

duality of nature: A basic principle of quantum mechanics where all matter has both wave and particulate properties.

EDXA (Electron Diffraction X-ray Analysis): an analytical technique that measures the energy of X-rays given off from an irradiated sample to give the elemental composition of the sample.

electromagnetic radiation: radiation that is made up of perpendicular electrical and magnetic waves that oscillate as it movea through space.

electron microscopy: a form of microscopy that uses an electron beam to "illuminate" a sample, allowing magnifications of up to several million times.

English system (measurement): a system of measurement that has achieved widespread and longstanding use and includes units of the foot, ounce, quart, degree Fahrenheit, and the minute. Today, in most places and throughout science, it has been replaced by either the metric or SI systems.

field of view: the amount of sample area that is visible through the microscope's lens.

fluorescence: the physical property displayed when a substance absorbs light at a shorter wavelength (higher energy) and then emits light at a longer wavelength (lower energy).

fluorescence microscopy: a form of optical microscopy where a sample is irradiated with light that excites molecules in the sample to emit fluorescent light that is then detected.

focus: the point where beams of light converge.

frequency: in electromagnetic radiation, the number of waves that pass a fixed point in a given amount of time. In light, the relationship that exists between wavelength and frequency is: $c = l\nu$ (where c is the speed of light, λ is the wavelength, and ν is the frequency).

gunshot residue (GSR): the burnt and unburnt components, mostly very small particles, expelled from a firearm upon firing.

Heisenberg Uncertainty Principle: a basic principle of quantum mechanics that says that it is impossible to know both the exact position and the momentum (related to velocity) of a particle at the same time.

illumination system: the components of a microscope that directs light onto the sample.

infrared light: The portion of the electromagnetic spectrum with wavelengths longer than visible light and shorter than radio and microwaves in the range of ca. 750 nm to ~1 mm.

lens: a curved optical component, usually made from glass or other transparent materials, which is used to form an image by focusing light beams.

magnification: the process of making an object appear larger.

microscope: the optical instrument, comprised of lenses held in alignment, used for magnifying small objects.

microspectrophotometry: the technique of measuring the light absorbed by the components of microscopic samples that can be used for the chemical identification of the components in the sample.

nanometer (nm): one billionth of a meter (1 nm = 10^{-9} m).

numerical aperture: a measure of the resolving power of a microscope.

objective lens: the lens in a microscope closest to the object being viewed.

ocular lens (eyepiece): the lens in a microscope closest to the viewer.

optical microscopy: the type of microscopy, often called light microscopy, that uses visible light to observe and magnify a small object.

phase contrast microscopy: a type of light microscopy that uses small differences in the phase shift of the light transmitted or reflected by the sample to form the image.

plane polarized light: light in which its electric field oscillates in just one direction (in a single plane).

polarizing lens: an optical lens that produces plane polarized light by filtering out all light *except* that vibrating in just one plane.

precision: a measure of how closely repeated measurements are grouped together, sometimes called reproducibility.

random error: chance errors with a random distribution (no particular pattern) that lead to inconsistent values in repeated measurements.

real image: an image produced from an object when the light from the object passes through a single point.

resolving power: the ability of an optical system, such as a microscope, to separate images that are close together.

retina: the layer of cells at the back of the eye that converts light energy striking the cells into an electrical impulse that passes into the brain.

rod cells: the visual receptor cells at the back of the eye that are particularly sensitive to dim light (peak sensitivity ca. 498 nm).

sample stage: the component of the microscope that holds and moves the sample being observed.

scanning electron microscopy: a microscope that forms an image by moving a focused beam of electrons across a sample and detecting the electrons scattered by the sample.

SI System (Système International d'Unités): an internationally agreed upon set of measures, based on the metric system, and including the following as the standard units: length (m), mass (kg), temperature (K), time (s), quantity (mol), electrical current (A), and light intensity (cd).

significant figures: the digits in a number that are known with a high degree of certainty.

staining: a chemical, such as a dye or pigment, used to selectively color or otherwise increase the contrast/resolution of microscopic features.

stereo microscope: a type of light microscope that has a separate set of optics for each eye to give a three-dimensional appearance to a microscopic sample. The microscope uses reflected or scattered light rather than light transmitted through the sample.

systematic error: an error in a measurement that is not introduced by random chance and affects all measurements similarly.

transmission electron microscopy: a microscopic technique that employs an electron beam passed directly through a sample to produce a cross-sectional image with very small feature resolution.

virtual image: an image produced by reflected or refracted light that diverges, such as an image seen in a typical mirror.

visible light: electromagnetic radiation that can be detected by the human eye, typically between about 280 and 750 nm.

wavelength: The distance measured between like points of successive waves, such as the distance between the crest of one wave to the crest of the following wave.

BIBLIOGRAPHY

John J. Bozzola and Lonnie D. Russell, *Electron Microscopy* (2nd Ed.), Jones and Bartlett Learning, 1999.

William J. Croft, *Under the Microscope a Brief History of Microscopy*, World Scientific Publishing Co., 2006.

Alberto Diaspro, *Optical Fluorescence Microscopy: From the Spectral to the Nano Dimension*, Springer, 2010.

Julian P. Heath, *Dictionary of Microscopy*, Wiley, 2005.

Joseph R. Lakowicz, *Principles of Fluorescence Spectroscopy* (3rd Ed.), Springer, 2006.

Jerome Mertz, *Introduction to Optical Microscopy*, Roberts and Co. Publishing, 2009.

M.J. Moroney, *Facts from Figures*, Penguin Books, 1957, 2–3.

Doulgas B. Murphy, *Fundamentals of Light Microscopy and Electronic Imaging*, Wiley-Liss Publishing, 2002.

Stephen J. Pennycock and Peter D. Nellist (Eds.), *Scanning Transmission Electron Microscopy: Imaging and Analysis*, Springer, 2011.

Nicholas Petraco and Thomas Kubic, *Color Atlas and Manual of Microscopy for Criminalists, Chemists, and Conservators*, CRC Press, 2003.

Ludwig Reimer and Peter W. Hawkes, *Scanning Electron Microscopy: Physics of Image Formation and Microanalysis*, Springer, 2010.

Barbara Wheeler and Lori J. Wilson, *Practical Forensic Microscopy: A Laboratory Manual*, Wiley, 2008.

Lord Kelvin (William Thomson), *Electrical Units of Measurement*, Popular Lectures and Addresses, Vol. 1, 1889 (delivered May 1883).

Forensic DNA

5

5.1 DNA: THE GENETIC RECORD

With the exception of nuclear DNA analysis, however, no forensic method has been rigorously shown to have the capacity to consistently, and with a high degree of certainty, demonstrate a connection between evidence and a specific individual or source.

(National Research Council, 2009)

LEARNING GOALS AND OBJECTIVES

The use of DNA evidence has become the "gold standard" of forensic investigations, and there is a wealth of information that can be gained from forensic DNA studies. When you complete this chapter, you should be able to:

- Describe the chemical structure of DNA, and how it holds genetic information.
- Explain the transcription and translation processes of DNA.
- Discuss the parts of DNA science are involved in forensic examinations.
- Define the meaning of variable number tandem repeats (VNTR) and short tandem repeats (STR).
- Explain how the Restriction Fragment Length Polymorphism (RFLP) method works.
- Define what a mutation is and what SNPs are.
- Outline how the polymerase chain reaction (PCR)/ STR method of DNA typing works.
- Explain how DNA fragments are separated.
- Describe how the frequency of occurrences of STRs in a population is determined and used.
- Explain what is meant by CODIS.
- Illustrate how mitochondrial DNA can be used in forensic investigations.
- Review how DNA typing is being used in plants and other living organisms.

5.1.1 Introduction

In the search for compelling scientific evidence, the criminal justice system has frequently looked to advances in basic scientific research to lead the way to new forensic techniques. Nowhere has this progress been more dramatic than in the application of modern biochemical methods in linking evidence gathered from crime scenes directly with potential individual persons. The explosive growth in creative work and new discoveries in biochemistry has led to the addition of many important new forensic tools. These methods, such as DNA analysis and biometrics, are so powerful in providing the critical linking information that they have become the "gold standards" of forensic evidence (Figure 5.1). Juries have especially come to depend upon DNA evidence as an integral part of all cases, regardless of what other evidence is available.

The rapid advance of DNA evidence, from its first courtroom appearance in 1987 to its commonplace use in investigations today, is unprecedented in criminalistics. The discovery in 1985 that biological DNA samples can be uniquely traced to a single human, followed by its first use in a forensic investigation just one year later, was truly a monumental achievement.

Humankind has long sought a way to uniquely identify one person from another: our appearance, signature, and fingerprints have all been used with varying degrees of success. However, it is with our DNA that we find the ultimate personal "signature." In fact, each person's DNA is unique among the DNA of all other humans who have ever lived – no one (except possibly an identical twin) has ever had the exact same DNA composition as you.

In this chapter, several of the most important forensic bioanalytical techniques are described, especially as they apply to courtroom applications. First, we need to answer the question "what is biochemistry and molecular biology?" Biochemistry and molecular biology are commonly thought of as closely related fields of science that involve the study of chemical compounds and reactions that occur in living systems. Biochemistry is the point at which biology is reduced to its most fundamental level – the level of atoms and molecules. At this level, we are usually most concerned with how molecules are formed and then function to control all the processes that we collectively call life. Thus, simply stated, biochemistry is a study of the "chemistry of life."

FIGURE 5.1   DNA: the blueprint of life.

Source: Shutterstock.com.

FIGURE 5.2   New York City, Ground Zero. DNA analysis was critical in the identification of remains from the World Trade Center attack in 2001.

Source: National Archives, Photographer Paul Morse.

In this chapter, we will explore how modern biochemical tools are being applied to forensic problems (Figure 5.2). How did a seemingly abstract laboratory discovery that there are repeated sections in our DNA makeup, mostly without known purpose, lead to the development of one of the most important methods in the forensic toolbox? How can the presence of certain chemicals contained in our blood be used to determine biological ancestry and lineage? How can we obtain uniquely identifying information from incredibly tiny biological samples collected at the crime scene? These are just a few of the basic questions that will be addressed in this chapter in which we will explore the basic forensic chemistry of DNA.

BOX 5.1   CASE HISTORY: COLIN PITCHFORK AND THE DNA DRAGNET

On November 21, 1983, 15-year-old Lynda Mann never returned home from a friend's home in Narborough, England. When her body was found the morning after her disappearance, it was learned that she had been sexually attacked before being murdered. Analysis of biological samples collected from the victim showed that the attacker must have been a young male who belonged to a relatively rare blood type, referred to as A/PGM+. Despite their best efforts, the police quickly came to a dead end in their investigation.

Almost three years later, in 1986, the strikingly similar attack and murder of 15-year-old Dawn Ashworth occurred in the same area of Narborough. This time the police had a suspect that they thought could be linked to both crimes: 17-year-old Richard Buckland, who came forward and voluntarily confessed. This unusually large, intellectually limited youth appeared to have more information about the murder than had been released to the public. After two days of incoherent admissions and ramblings, he signed a confession for the murder of Dawn Ashworth, but he maintained his innocence of the Lydia Mann attack. Since police believed that the same person committed both crimes, they turned to Dr. Alec Jeffreys of the University of Leicester for help in trying to connect these two cases with Buckland.

The analysis, based on Jeffreys' longtime DNA research, confirmed that one man had indeed been responsible for both crimes, but it also wasn't Buckland! This was the first time that an innocent person was exonerated by DNA evidence. Dr. Jeffreys was quoted as saying, "I have no doubt whatsoever that he would have been found guilty had it not been for DNA evidence." It is now believed that Buckland had witnessed the murder of Ashworth from a distance.

Faced with this dilemma and no other leads, the police launched a massive campaign to screen more than 5,000 local males for blood type and DNA profile. This mass screening, however, came up without a match until a local bakery worker was overheard in a pub saying that he had been paid by a co-worker, Colin Pitchfork, to provide a blood sample for him. The police quickly brought in Pitchfork and obtained an authentic blood sample: it matched. Pitchfork later confessed and was charged with the rape and murder of both Lynda Mann and Dawn Ashworth. He was quickly convicted after a trial that lasted just one day.

FIGURE 5.3   Dr. Alec Jeffreys of the University of Leicester in England led the 1985 DNA investigation of the Colin Pitchfork Case.

Source: NIH.

This case clearly illustrates the enormous strength of DNA evidence: it both exonerated an innocent suspect while locating and convicting the real attacker.

5.2 DNA: HOW DNA WORKS

5.2.1 Introduction

Unraveling the secrets of DNA as the biochemical blueprint governing the chemistry of life certainly ranks as one of the greatest accomplishments of modern civilization. This one amazing molecule is common to all living things and is arguably the best studied and single most important molecule on Earth. It governs our chemical makeup, our biological functions, and even determines whether we will have brown hair or green eyes. It determines whether an organism will develop into a dog, a tree, or a human being. It can even determine whether an organism will be healthy or carry a biochemical disorder. The more we learn about this one molecule, the more we come to see how fundamentally dominant it really is in all of life's biological processes. Our intimate knowledge of the inner workings of DNA has changed our lives in both subtle and dramatic ways, from the development of new diagnostic and therapeutic drugs to the designed modification of life forms, such as bacteria, through recombinant techniques.

Using a very simple analogy, DNA can be thought of as the massive biochemical cookbook that contains the instructions for making all the compounds that we require for life. Inside each one of our more than 60 trillion cells resides one complete and identical copy of our DNA cookbook. Each recipe in our book, called a gene, contains specific directions for making just one biochemical item, such as a protein or enzyme. If we look closely at a typical written cookbook, we see that each recipe contains arrays and sequences of letters that are recognizable to us as words, which we can, in turn, understand and translate into an action, such as measure, mix, or bake. So, by the careful arrangement and combination of the 26 letters of the alphabet, we can completely and fully describe how to prepare every item that we wish to make. On a conceptual level, DNA works much the same way as a cookbook, except that it uses just four "letters" instead of the 26 alphabetic letters, and all of the DNA "words" are only three letters long. The DNA instructions are just as clear and precise as the best cookbooks. Our DNA is different, however, in that the DNA "recipes" (genes) are separated by long stretches of seemingly random letters that form a uniquely different pattern from person to person, forming the basis of how DNA forensic identifications work.

We begin by describing the basic chemical features of DNA and how it works to direct the chemistry of life. This is followed by the specific uses of DNA in forensic investigations. As a note, the field of forensic DNA is heavily laden with highly technical jargon that serves to convey very precise information between specialists both quickly and efficiently. However, this language is often quite daunting and confusing to those encountering it for the first time. In the following discussions, the highly technical vocabulary of forensic DNA will be kept to the absolute minimum needed to understand the important concepts of the field.

TABLE 5.1   A brief timeline on the development of our understanding and application of DNA science and a summary of key discoveries on DNA

TIMELINE OF DNA	BRIEF ON DNA
1868 Miescher "discovers" DNA. 1953 Watson and Crick report double helix structure. 1977 First human gene cloned. 1985 Jeffreys reports VNTR DNA sequences. 1985 First report of PCR method. 1986 Jeffreys uses DNA to solve first murder case (Pitchfork case). 1987 First conviction in the United States based on DNA evidence (Andrews case). 1991 STRs first reported. 1998 FBI starts CODIS database. 2005 2.5 million DNA "fingerprints" in FBI database.	1. DNA is composed of nucleotide building blocks that are connected together into chains. 2. Nucleotides contain phosphate, sugar, and nitrogen base units. 3. Phosphate and sugar units form the DNA backbone chain and nitrogen bases "hang" from the backbone. 4. Pairing of nucleotide bases holds two strands of DNA together by hydrogen bonds. 5. Bases pair such that only adenine (A) pairs with thymine (T), and guanine (G) pairs only with cytosine (C).

5.2.2 DNA Background

In recent years, forensic investigations have increasingly relied upon DNA evidence both to convict and exonerate suspects. DNA (deoxyribonucleic acid), the genetic "cookbook" of life, often provides vital information about crimes and suspects. While the fundamental structure of DNA had been known since 1953, it had no significant place in the courtroom until the discovery by Alec Jeffreys in 1985 that biological samples taken from people could be used for their individual identification. In fact, prior to this work, DNA was thought to have very limited forensic use because organisms generally don't tolerate any deviations from the standard genetic code well. In other words, variations in the genetic DNA code usually lead to non-viable offspring. For example, if a cookbook recipe called for one cup of sugar and instead, we used one cup of salt, the product of our work would certainly be inedible. Similarly, changing one "letter" in a DNA code could easily render a critical protein biochemically useless, leading to death. Luckily for forensic science, the regions between DNA's "recipes" provide unique markers that can be used to establish "beyond a reasonable doubt" a connection between a specific person and a biological sample collected at a crime scene. In order to understand how DNA is employed in forensic settings, however, an understanding of some of the basics about DNA itself is first necessary.

5.2.3 DNA Structure

DNA, along with carbohydrates and proteins, is one member of a class of important biomolecules referred to as *biopolymers*. These biopolymers are compounds formed by linking together small molecular building blocks (monomers) in a repeating fashion to form much larger molecules. This conceptually resembles forming a long railroad train by linking together individual cars to produce a far longer assembly. The properties of the resulting biopolymer depend directly on the identity and chemical features of the basic building blocks that make up the biopolymer. The properties also depend on how the building blocks are connected together, such as in a straight chain like a train or branched like a tree.

Historically, the discovery of DNA itself has been attributed to Johann Miescher, a 19th-century Swiss chemist (Table 5.1). Prior to his work, it was believed that cells were made up largely of proteins; large biopolymer molecules made up of long chains of small linked amino acid building blocks. Miescher, however, found that certain extracts from the pus cells he was studying could not "belong among any of the protein substances known hitherto." He showed that these fractions were not made up of protein at all since they were not digested by protease enzymes (enzymes that specifically break down *only* protein molecules). These particular extracts were also shown to arise solely from the nuclei of the cells and were, therefore, named "nuclein." Later work on nuclein by another chemist, Albrecht Kossel, showed that nuclein was built of long chains of only four very similar building blocks (nucleic acid units) and was later renamed a nucleic acid (DNA) by Richard Altmann. The structure that we recognize today as the famous double helical arrangement of a long, twisting biopolymer was finally explained in 1953 by James Watson and Francis Crick, work for which they received the 1962 Nobel Prize in Medicine, along with Maurice Wilkins (Figure 5.4). Their work, however, would not have been possible without the pioneering X-ray studies done by Dr. Rosalind Franklin (Figure 5.4). Although her seminal work was not recognized by the Nobel Prize in 1962, since she died four years before the prize was awarded (Nobel Prizes are never awarded posthumously), she has more recently been recognized for the vital contributions that she provided, not just in our understanding of the structure of DNA, but also to our understanding of RNA (ribonucleic acid), viruses, coal, and graphite.

DNA, at its most fundamental level, is made up of repeating units called *nucleic acids* (Figure 5.5) connected in a polymeric fashion. The term "polymer" (from "poly" meaning many and "mer" meaning unit) indicates a large molecule formed by linking together many smaller units (monomers) into larger arrays. In DNA, one nucleic acid unit is linked to another to form a long, linear chain, much in the way that alphabet letters are linked together to form words, respectively. These nucleic

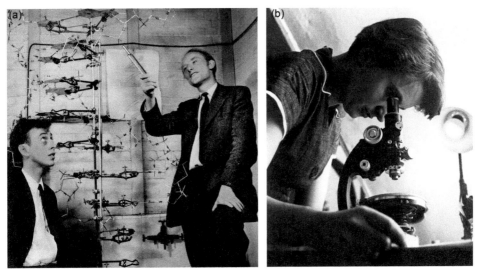

FIGURE 5.4 (a) James Watson and Francis Crick with a model of the DNA double helix, and (B) Rosalind Franklin, whose seminal X-ray work led to the discovery of DNA structure.

Source: (a): A. Barrington Brown, © Gonville & Caius College/Colored by Science Photo Library. Used with permission. (b): Used per Creative Commons Share-Alike 4.0, International, User: MRC Laboratory of Molecular Biology.

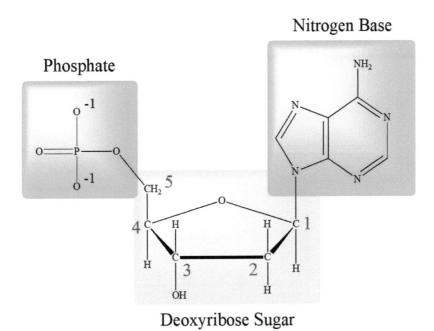

FIGURE 5.5 Nucleic acid (nucleotide) unit [the numbers on the deoxyribose sugar ring denotes the numbering scheme used for the ring system).

acid building blocks are themselves composed of three simpler components (Figure 5.5): (1) a phosphoric acid residue (PO_4^{2-}), (2) a five-carbon sugar unit (specifically, DNA uses a deoxyribose sugar, such as that shown at left in Figure 5.6), and (3) a nitrogen-containing base. Together, these three components form what is known as a *nucleotide* (just the deoxyribose sugar and the nitrogen base together are called a nucleoside) – make sure that you understand what a nucleotide is because it will be used quite often throughout this chapter. The phosphates and

deoxyribose sugars of the nucleotides, when linked together in an alternating fashion, form a straight chain backbone for the DNA polymer. Attached to this backbone are the nitrogen bases, somewhat similar to the way that clothes are hung on a clothesline. Maybe surprisingly, DNA uses only four different nitrogen base units: adenine (A), guanine (G), cytosine (C), and thymine (T) (Note: RNA, a close relative of DNA and a molecule important in the transfer of information from DNA into biochemical action, uses uracil instead of thymine). These

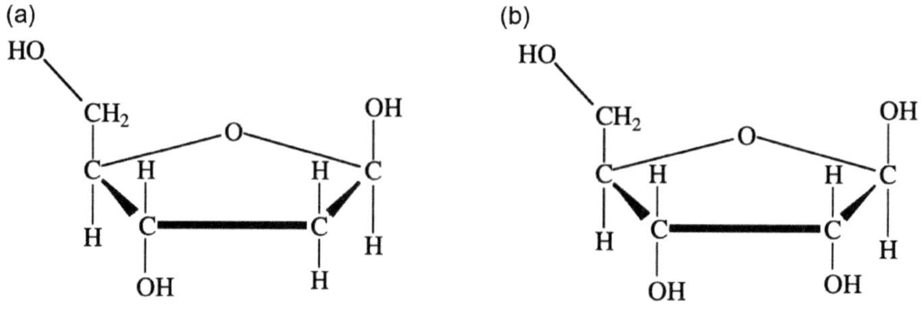

(a)   (b)

FIGURE 5.6   Deoxyribose (a) and ribose (b) sugars.

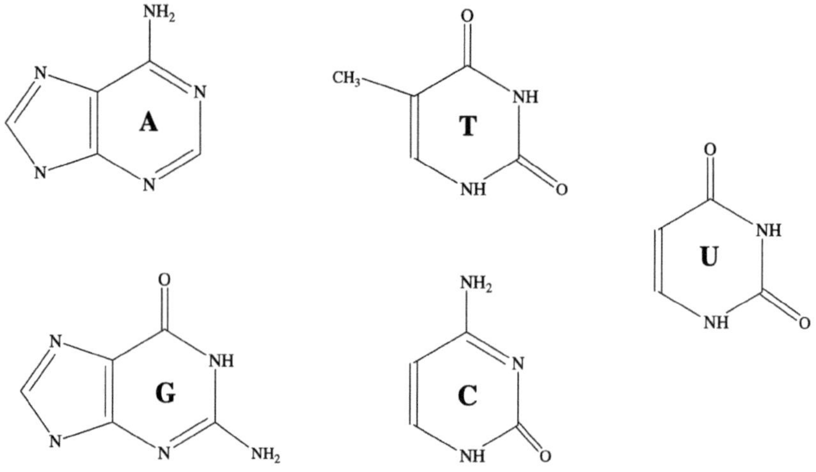

FIGURE 5.7   Nitrogen bases used in DNA (*clockwise from upper left*): adenine (A), thymine (T), cytosine (C), and guanine (G). Uracil is shown at far right and is only used in RNA.

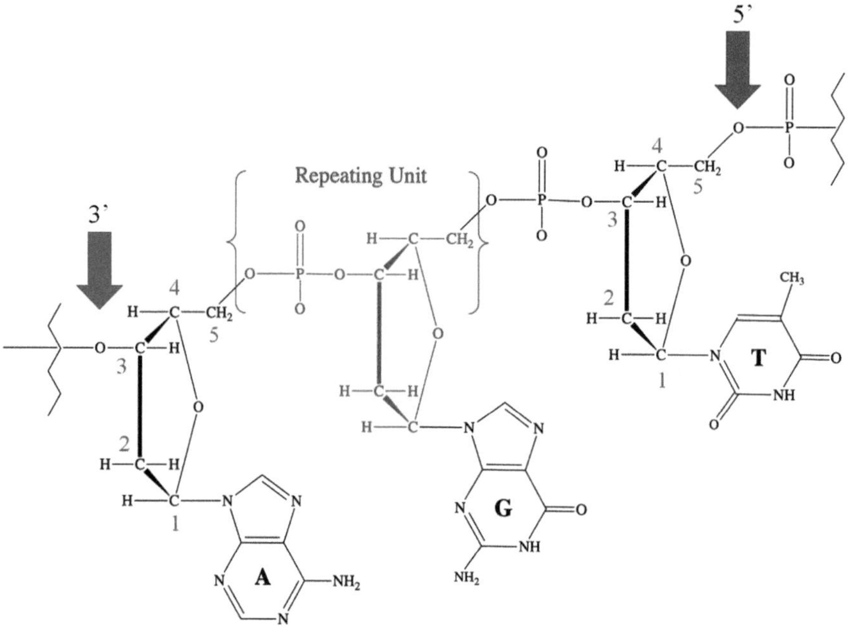

FIGURE 5.8   Structure of the DNA polymer: the sugar-phosphate backbone with pendant adenine nitrogen bases. The 5′ and 3′ ends of the polymer are notated.

four bases are shown in Figure 5.7. All the repeating units of the DNA backbone are completely identical (alternating phosphate and sugar units), while the pendant nitrogen bases are chosen from among this small group of four bases (A, T, G, and C). The entire fundamental structure of a strand of DNA thus consists of repeated phosphate-sugar-nitrogen base building blocks that come together to form the observed complete DNA structure as illustrated in Figure 5.8.

The order of the nucleotide units in the DNA chain can be readily specified by simply writing the order of the nitrogen bases in the chain since all the other components are always the same. The sequence shown in Figure 5.8 is "AGT" since the three bases shown are adenine, guanine, and thymine, while a much larger, 18-nucleotide DNA sequence, might be completely defined as "AGTCGTAACGTCGGTAAA." Translated, this means that this latter DNA chain consists of an adenine nucleotide unit, followed by a guanine unit, followed by a thymine unit, followed by a cytosine unit, and so on until the end of the chain is reached. Also, the two ends of the DNA strand are inherently different and are denoted as either the 3′ or the 5′ end. This is based on the numbering scheme of the deoxyribose ring, as shown in Figure 5.5. If the phosphate group is bonded to the 5-carbon of the deoxyribose sugar as the chain's connection point, it is labeled the "5′-end", as illustrated in Figure 5.8. The other end, closest to the 3-carbon, then must be the "3′-end".

In a typical strand of the DNA polymer, huge numbers of nucleotide units are strung together consecutively to form an extremely long chain. DNA strands in the nuclei of human cells may contain over 3 billion nucleotide pairs. These strands of the DNA polymer are usually found in nature not as individual strands but rather as *complementary pairs* of strands, meaning that two DNA chains are required to come together in a very specific way to form the observed complete double helical DNA structure. These strands don't just come together in any random fashion; instead, they are fit together through highly specific chemical interactions between the two chains. To form the double-strand arrangement, one nitrogen base on *each* chain must fit perfectly together to form a close electrostatic attraction, called a *hydrogen bond*. Only specific pairs of bases can interact in this fashion as dictated by their chemical structures. In this way, only cytosine and guanine are chemically built to allow this close interaction – close enough to form a hydrogen bond that electrostatically holds the two bases together and, therefore, also holds the two DNA chains together. This is something like snapping together two toy building pieces that have matching arrangements of holes and studs. However, you can't put together one piece with three holes with another piece with just two studs; they just don't fit. The orientations of the holes and studs don't line up properly. This is very similar to how the nucleic acids "fit" together to form a hydrogen bond. Cytosine and guanine "fit" together just right while adenine and thymine properly align to form a hydrogen-bonded unit. These interactions are illustrated in Figure 5.9 for the only two possible combinations: C with G and A with T. If, however, cytosine and thymine or guanine and adenine are forced to come together, no hydrogen bond can be formed since their structures do not allow for the proper electrostatic "fit." This would be like trying to plug a three-pronged electrical cord into a two-pronged outlet; it just doesn't work. When every adenine (A) on one DNA strand is adjacent to a thymine (T) on the other strand of the pair and every cytosine (C) is matched with a guanine (G), the two strands are said to have a *complementary sequence* of bases. Having a complementary sequence on the two DNA strands allows for the formation of a

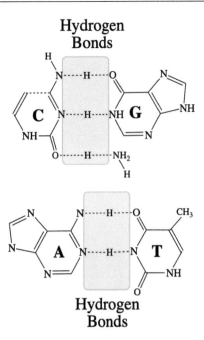

FIGURE 5.9 Hydrogen bonds formed between the DNA base pairs cytosine and guanine and also between adenine and thymine (C = cytosine, G = guanine, A = adenine, T = thymine). Conversely, G does not "fit" with either adenine or thymine and adenine does not "fit" with either guanine or cytosine.

new double chain that is effectively "pinned together" at every nucleotide through the hydrogen bonding of the nitrogen base pairs. This is shown schematically in Figure 5.10. When these two complementary strands of DNA come together, they form the well-known double helical structure (similar to a twisted flight of stairs, Figure 5.11).

BOX 5.2   HELPFUL REMINDERS

Nucleotide: The building block of DNA, consisting of a sugar, a phosphate group and a linked nitrogen base (e.g., adenine, thymine, cytosine, and guanine).

Gene: A small sequence of nucleotides along the DNA chain that codes for a protein.

Chromosome: A long chain of DNA (and proteins) containing many genes and spacers (non-coding) that resides in the nucleus of a cell.

Genome: The entire DNA component of an organism, in humans it includes 24 chromosomes.

RNA (ribonucleic acid): An analog of DNA that transfers genetic information into the cell, where the thymine is replaced by the uracil base (it also serves as the genetic component of some viruses).

Ribosome: The cellular structure where the genetic code copied from the nuclear DNA directs the synthesis of a protein.

Tandem Repeat: A specific pattern of nucleotides in DNA that is repeated back-to-back.

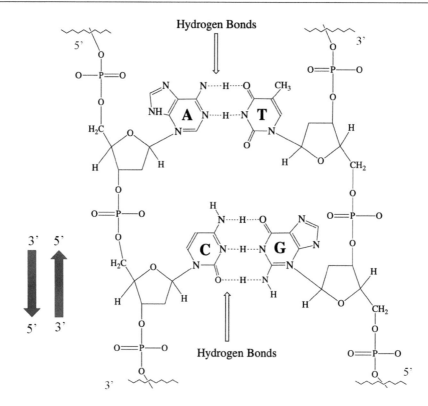

FIGURE 5.10 Hydrogen-bonded base pairs holding two strands of DNA together (C = cytosine, G = guanine, A = adenine, T = thymine).

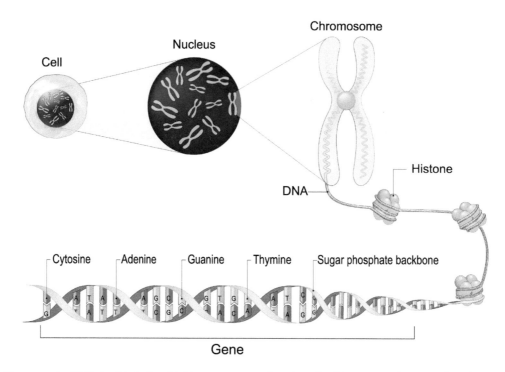

FIGURE 5.11 Close-up of a DNA double helix with histones, sugar-phosphate backbone, guanine, cytosine, thymine, adenine nucleotides and a gene depicted. A gene is a sequence of nucleotides along the DNA chain that codes for the synthesis of a specific protein.

Source: iStockphoto.com, ttsz.

The sequence of nitrogen bases in the DNA polymer is the fundamental basis for controlling all of life's cellular processes, just as the order of letters on a page allows us to correctly read a recipe. The basic DNA unit that determines which characteristics are transmitted to succeeding generations (the "recipe") is called a *gene*. A gene is simply a portion of the DNA strand, composed of a highly specific sequence of nucleic acids, that contains the DNA-encoded message for something inherited (Figure 5.11). Each gene regulates the preparation of a specific protein within the cells of the body, ultimately leading to the direct regulation of all of life's biochemical processes. At the simplest level, our genes are really just chemical "addresses" where we find a needed message written. The basic genetic language of this message consists of just four letters (adenine, thymine, guanine, and cytosine) that provide all the chemical information necessary to exactly prepare a specific molecule. Thus, the genetic region of the DNA strand forms a blueprint for making a molecule. The location of a gene on a DNA strand is referred to as its *locus* (the plural is loci) with the genes residing along very specific stretches of the DNA chain (Figure 5.12).

BOX 5.3   DNA, GENE, CHROMOSOME, GENOME

It may seem confusing, but there's a relatively straightforward explanation. DNA is a polymeric molecule composed of a specific sequence of nucleic acids. A particular length, or sequence, of DNA is called a gene – a "word." The genetic and non-genetic lengths of DNA together form a strand of DNA – a "sentence." A long chain of DNA that is part of the entire DNA complement of a cell is called a chromosome – a "chapter." All 23 human chromosomes taken together make up the genome – the entire "book."

A particularly important discovery for forensic science was made in 1985 when it was learned that the relatively short coding regions of DNA (genes) are usually found separated from each other by long stretches of DNA that do not seem to encode for anything known. These separating regions are called "non-coding" or *hypervariable* regions (sometimes also incorrectly called "junk" DNA in the popular press). The relationship between coding and non-coding DNA regions is illustrated schematically in Figure 5.13 using the cookbook analogy. In this analogy, the first part of the strand of letters is meaningless to us until we reach a section of the cookbook that encodes for words that we do understand ("spread jelly on bread"), called the coding region. After this understandable section follows another nonsense region (non-coding region) until we reach another understandable region ("add water and lemon"). In a similar

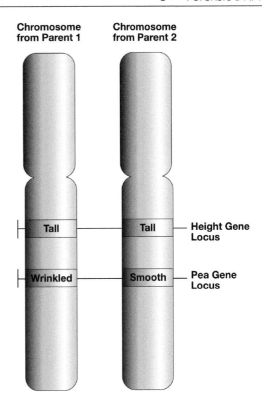

FIGURE 5.12 Chromosomes in nuclear DNA showing two plant genes, their loci and alleles.

fashion, DNA has long non-coding regions located between the smaller genetic coding regions. This will become important later when considering how our DNA can uniquely identify one person from another.

BOX 5.4   IS JUNK REALLY JUNK: NO!

For decades, it was thought that possibly up to 98% of our DNA was genetically unimportant and simply acted as spacers between the genes. Recently, however, scientists at the ENCODE Project (Encyclopedia of DNA Elements) have come to think that a least "some kind of biochemical activity" can be ascribed to as much as 80% of our DNA code and includes important "molecular switches" responsible for regulating the activity of the genetic portions of DNA.

The DNA of an organism is found most of the time coiled up in the form of *chromosomes* in either the nucleus (nDNA) or in the mitochondria (mtDNA) of the cell (Figures 5.12 and 5.14). All cells of an individual organism have an identical set of DNA strands, so it doesn't matter what cell the DNA originates from when considering the individual's DNA

Recipe Book (DNA)

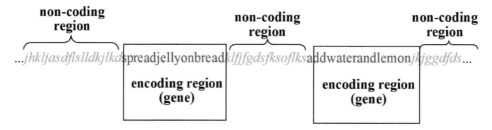

FIGURE 5.13   Coding and non-coding regions of an interesting recipe book.

CHROMOSOME

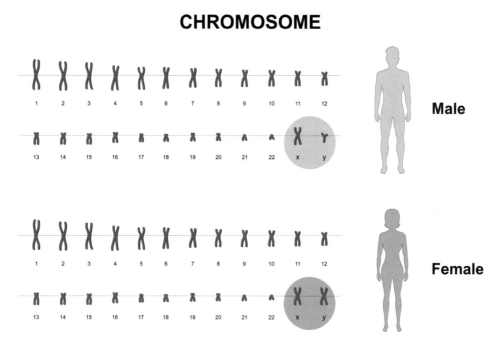

FIGURE 5.14   Human chromosomes showing the 23 pairs in the human genome (computer artwork) composed of DNA (deoxyribonucleic acid) that provides the information necessary for the cell to make the necessary proteins.

Source: Shutterstock.com.

code. Chromosomes are similar to the chapters of a book: they are convenient ways to "package" a large part of the story into smaller, more readily handled units. In humans, the DNA in most of our cells is arranged into 23 pairs of chromosomes identified by their characteristic sizes and shapes (Figure 5.15). One pair is referred to as the sex chromosomes and can either be of a larger variety (the "X" chromosome) or a smaller version ("Y" chromosome). Females genetically have two "X" chromosomes, while males have a size mismatched "X" and "Y" pair. One-half of our genetic information comes from our mothers, and the other half comes from our fathers, with the "Y" chromosome inheritable only from fathers to sons.

5.2.4 DNA Functioning: Coding for Life

So how do we get from the basic chemical sequence of nucleotides in DNA to the color of our eyes? And can we track backward from a known DNA sequence to discover if the owner of that DNA code had green eyes? The pathway that leads from DNA's "letter" sequence to the synthesis of cellular proteins that regulate life employs two very important processes called *transcription* and *translation*. In a very brief summary, DNA's cellular control works something like this. In the first process, called *transcription*, a portion of the DNA double helix is first

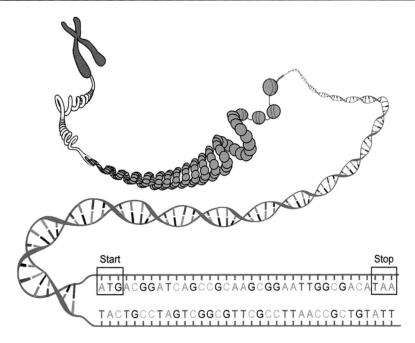

FIGURE 5.15   The coiling of DNA helices to form nuclear chromosomes.

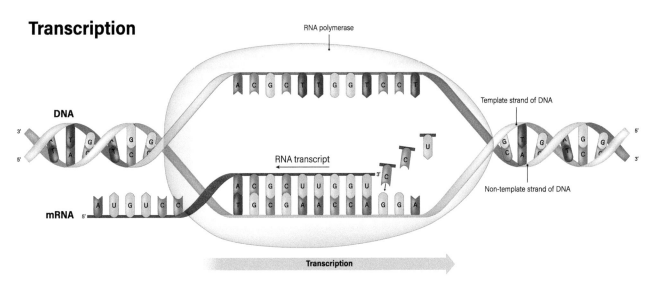

FIGURE 5.16   Schematic drawing showing the transcription of DNA to mRNA (red "ribbon" near the bottom).

Source: Shutterstock.com.

unraveled into single strands in the region that codes for the needed cellular compound (the gene). A brand-new complementary nucleic acid strand forms, this time an RNA strand, with A's pairing with U's (since this is RNA, it uses U in place of DNA's T) and G's pairing with C's between the original template and the newly forming strand. The new strand, called messenger RNA or mRNA, is an exact complementary match to the original DNA template in which every C in the original is matched to a G in the new RNA strand and so on, as shown in Figure 5.16. This process can really move along very quickly, with an estimated 90,000 bases properly added in sequence per minute.

The mRNA is somewhat like a negative image in photography that is formed from an actual (positive) scene. The "negative image" carries all the original visual information of the scene but only in reverse. Just as the original positive photographic image can easily be regenerated from the negative, so can the original DNA sequence be "regenerated." The newly formed mRNA, once prepared through transcription, moves out of the nucleus and onto an organelle in the cell's cytoplasm called a *ribosome*. On the ribosome, each group of three adjacent nitrogen bases in the mRNA strand uniquely designates one specific amino acid that will be placed into the growing protein polymer molecule being synthesized on the ribosome.

These amino acids are sequentially linked chemically together into a new polymeric chain to form the protein in a process known as *translation*. This process is shown schematically in Figure 5.17. For example, the mRNA code "GGG" translates directly into the command that a glycine amino acid needs to be placed in the growing protein chain while an "AAA" code specifies that a lysine amino acid be placed next in line. In this manner, the mRNA sequence "AAAAAAGGGAAA" would translate to a small protein composed of two glycines, Gly (AAA-AAA), followed by a lysine, Lys (GGG), and ending with another glycine unit (AAA), or a protein composition of Gly-Gly-Lys-Gly. It's important to understand that the sequence of the bases in the DNA molecule is ultimately preserved and translated into a very specific sequence of amino acids that are linked together to form a new protein molecule. This is conceptually quite similar to translating a coded message into equivalent words in a language. In this analogy, the letters in the word "yes" in English are translated uniquely into the letters of the word "oui" in French. Analogously, "GGG" in DNA is translated into "glycine" in the forming protein. In DNA, however, all "words" have just three letters so that exactly three nitrogen bases (chosen from A, T/U, G, and C) are needed to specify one specific amino acid unit in

the protein chain. Protein composition, structure, and function (including enzymes, structural proteins, and many others) are, therefore, uniquely dictated by the DNA base ordering. Since the chemical and physical properties of a protein are determined fundamentally by the order of its linked amino acid units, DNA ultimately controls all our protein synthesis and, in turn, cellular processes.

5.2.5 Human Genome and DNA Tandem Repeats

In 2003, researchers around the world completed the largest scientific undertaking in history, called the Human Genome Project (HGP). This project completely determined the DNA base sequence in all the approximately 30,000 human genes: in other words, the *precise order* of nearly 3 billion A, T, G, and C nucleotides in human DNA was figured out – a truly amazing accomplishment! One significant discovery was that we share about 93% of our DNA genetic code with the fruit fly and roundworm: there is a commonality in all of life. Much more surprising, however, was the finding that there is only about one-third the total number of genes that were originally predicted. The size of individual genes also varies quite a bit, but an average gene contains about 3000 bases, with the largest known gene having about 2.4 million bases (dystrophin). Quite surprisingly, only about 1.5% of the DNA in our bodies actually codes for compounds! This means that the vast majority of the human DNA polymer does not code for any known proteins. Our DNA, therefore, contains far more seemingly random "data" than the amount contained within the coding portions of the DNA. This would be like a book with only one sentence out of a hundred having any discernible meaning.

Our genes appear to be concentrated in areas along the chromosomes, with vast expanses of non-coding DNA lying between the genes (hypervariable or "non-coding" regions). Stretches of up to 30,000 repeating C and G bases tend to

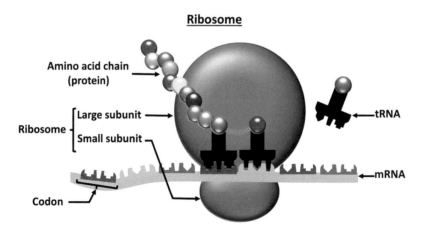

FIGURE 5.17   Translation process, based on a sequence of DNA nucleotides, in the formation of a protein.

Source: Shutterstock.com.

occur near the concentrations of genes, forming a "barrier" between the genes and the more random hypervariable DNA, while "gene-poor" regions are predominantly formed from A and T nucleotides. These non-coding portions may either have once had a function in the past but are now not necessary, or they may have arisen by other means such as mutation or viral insertions, both well-known processes. Some researchers, however, believe that these hypervariable regions may play a critical role in gene expression and regulation. In any case, it is these "non-coding" repetitive regions that are at the heart of modern forensic DNA analysis.

Scientists have discovered that, within the non-coding regions, certain short sequences of nucleotide "letters" (A, T, C, and G) are repeated back-to-back numerous times throughout the DNA chain, as shown in Figure 5.18, where the short sequence "ACCT" is repeated multiple times. In fact, while we don't yet understand why this occurs, it appears that more than 50% of human DNA is composed of these repeating sequences. Repeated sequences that are arranged consecutively along the DNA chain are called *variable number tandem repeats* (VNTR) and are centrally important to one type of DNA forensic test described later, the RFLP method. VNTR sequences usually consist of 7–27 nucleotides linked to one another in up to 50 tandem repeats (tandem here simply means connected one to another just as railroad cars connect together to form a train). These VNTR sequences show a great deal of variability in the *number of repeats* for each location (locus) on the DNA chain. For

example, one person may have a particular DNA sequence repeated ten times in a row, while someone else has the same sequence repeated 20 times in a row at the same DNA locus. Another type of repeated pattern is very similar to the VNTR's, except that it is made up of both much *shorter* repeated sections (fewer "letters") and with fewer tandem repeats. These shorter patterns are called *short tandem repeats* (STR) (Figure 5.18). The use of STR sequences is the basis of much of the current human forensic DNA testing procedures.

Since protein structure and function derive directly from the ordering of the nitrogen bases in DNA, very small changes in the base ordering in the genetic regions of DNA may cause catastrophic changes in the protein's function. One base unit incorrectly placed can mean the difference between disease or no disease or even life versus death. For example, the substitution of a single nitrogen base for the correct base in the gene regulating hemoglobin production leads to one misplaced amino acid (switching one valine for a glutamic acid) out of the entire 146 amino acids within the hemoglobin molecule. This very simple change, however, may result in a person having sickle cell anemia. Within a species such as humans, there is very little variation of the DNA code within genes (more than 99% of our *genetic* DNA is the same from person to person worldwide). Importantly, however, there can be very large differences from person to person in our non-genetic (non-coding) DNA since there is no survival difference by changing the code in these regions – these regions do not code for any biomolecules.

Changes in the order of the nitrogen bases in the DNA chain (called *mutations*) are usually not well tolerated and typically do not result in viable offspring. Since the genetic (coding) portions of the DNA for each healthy human are essentially the same, if we were to look at these regions, we'd find very little difference to distinguish one person from the next. The genetic coding regions are, therefore, not really helpful in individual forensic identifications – we're all essentially the same in our genes. Changes in the non-coding DNA regions that separate the genes, however, usually make no difference in the survival of an individual organism since these parts of the DNA code play no role in regulating

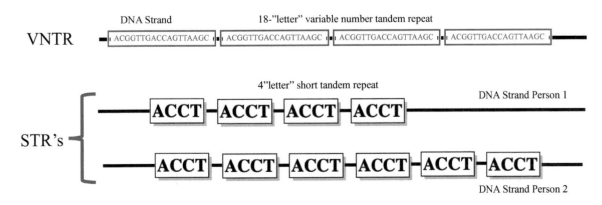

FIGURE 5.18 Short tandem repeats (STR) along a DNA chain. The top sequence consists of four consecutive STR units while the bottom consists of six STR units.

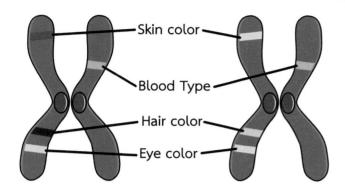

FIGURE 5.19 Allele vs gene. A gene is a sequence of nucleotides along the DNA chain while an allele is one of several possible variations of a gene.

Source: Shutterstock.com.

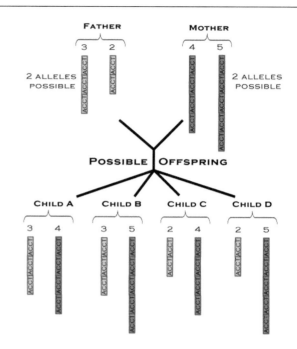

FIGURE 5.20 Inheritance pattern of STR alleles from parents to offspring.

cells or making needed proteins. Over time, these nonsensical regions have become quite diverse, such that essentially no two people have exactly the same DNA codes in these inter-gene regions (including possibly identical twins). The differences in our non-coding DNA sequences are called *polymorphisms* (or many forms). The basis, therefore, of forensic DNA testing is not to look at the genes but rather to look at the DNA in these inter-gene regions.

In a more detailed examination of these polymorphisms, variations are possible at specific loci along the DNA chain. For example, at a particular locus, there may be several tandem repeats of an "ACCT" nucleotide sequence. This simple STR repeat may occur two times in a row, three times, or more. Each of these possible forms is referred to as an *allele* (see Box 5.7, Figure 5.19). In Figure 5.20, the inheritance pattern for a simple STR sequence at a particular DNA locus is illustrated. If, for instance, the father has the "ACCT" sequence repeated three times on one chromosome and only two times on the paired chromosome, he has two alleles at this specific locus (called *heterozygous* if the two alleles are different and *homozygous* if they are the same). It's important to remember that we're talking just about the non-coding regions of the DNA. The father's allele composition in Figure 5.20 can be simply referred to as 3,2.

If the mother, however, has four and five repeats on her two chromosomes at the same DNA position, she is denoted as 4,5. Four allele combinations are, therefore, mathematically possible for any offspring arising from these parents: (3,4), (3,5), (2,4), and (2,5).

BOX 5.7   ALLELE VS GENE

A gene is a particular sequence of nucleic acids at a particular place along the DNA chain. An allele, on the other hand, is one of several possible variations of a gene.

Humans differ in their DNA compositions at many loci in the human genome. Therefore, to measure a person's individuality, we simply need to look at the differences in their allele compositions at specific loci along the non-coding parts of their DNA chains.

BOX 5.8   CASE HISTORY: CHIMERISM AND THE MISSING MOTHER

In 2002, Lydia Fairchild was pregnant with her third child when she applied for child support. In order to receive the support, however, she was required to provide DNA paternity evidence to show that her estranged partner was the father of her children. The DNA results came back with some startling news: while the partner was essentially shown to be the father, Fairchild could not be the children's biological mother. Fairchild was promptly charged with fraud for claiming support benefits by using other people's children. When her third child was born, court ordered, administered, and witnessed blood tests were performed on both Fairchild and the newborn in the hospital. These DNA tests also amazingly showed that Fairchild was not the biological mother of the child she had just delivered before witnesses.

FIGURE 5.21   A chimeric calico Scottish fold cat or tortoiseshell and white cat.

Source: Shutterstock.com.

The answer to this strange dilemma came when a similar case in Boston was discovered to be a case of chimerism. Chimerism arises when a person has two separate cell lines within their bodies, each with its own entirely different set of chromosomes. This is thought to occur when two separate embryos are physically mixed, each with its own DNA complement. During development, different tissues within the body develop from different original cell strains.

Further DNA tests on Fairchild showed that samples from her skin did not match her children, but samples from her cervical tissue did indeed match. It is now thought that natural chimerism, previously believed to be very rare, may be more common than had been presumed. If so, how might this change the role of DNA in legal proceedings? Chimerism is well-known to be fairly common with other animal species. For example, pictured in Figure 5.21 is a chimeric cat showing multiple fur patterns from different genetic sources.

5.3 FORENSIC APPLICATIONS OF DNA

5.3.1 Introduction to Forensic DNA

Forensic DNA profiling, sometimes referred to as DNA fingerprinting or typing, relies upon the uniquely individual nature of the "non-coding" or hypervariable regions of DNA. Looking at this region allows us to distinguish a DNA-containing sample of one person from another and has often provided the "smoking gun" evidence long sought for in judicial proceedings.

In forensic DNA typing, the first thing to understand is that the sequence of "letters" (nucleotides) in the DNA sample is most often not actually "read." This would be a more difficult, expensive, and time-consuming task than required. Instead, we look at just the regions of DNA that contain the most differences observed between people. Second, DNA evidence is very good at ruling out a potential suspect as contributing a particular biological sample found at a crime scene. Third, DNA evidence cannot prove that a suspect *did* contribute a sample found at a crime scene, but it can tell us that we cannot *exclude* a suspect based upon DNA evidence and that there is a measurable probability of an "accidental" random match in the population. We then leave it to the jury to decide what is the right level of certainty in connecting the sample with the suspect.

Two general methods of DNA typing have emerged since it was first introduced into the forensic toolbox in 1985. These are referred to as the *RFLP* (restriction fragment length polymorphism) and *PCR*-based (polymerase chain reaction) *STR* methods of DNA testing. Both of these techniques have their advantages and disadvantages, although the PCR method is used almost exclusively in current human forensic investigations and newer methods are now also finding increased usage.

Between these two approaches, the RFLP method requires a larger sample size than the PCR technique, but RFLP is a more direct technique. Older or even partially degraded DNA samples are, however, often rendered unsuitable for RFLP methods. In contrast, the PCR method can use very small samples, even badly damaged and degraded samples, but is an indirect method that is especially sensitive to handling and contamination problems. Techniques have now been developed that allow for the rapid analysis of forensic DNA samples, allowing such evidence to become nearly ubiquitous in the courtroom. Many variations of these two primary techniques, including combinations of the two, have been developed for a wide range of investigations beyond simple human sample identification to now include plant, animal, and microbe testing.

Each of these techniques is described in more detail in the following sections, with more recent developments presented later in this chapter. The RFLP method is presented here both for historical reasons and since it is related to several other methods, especially in plant and animal DNA testing. The RFLP method, however, has essentially been replaced by the PCR-based and other methods in the realm of human DNA analysis for courtroom proceedings.

5.3.2 DNA Typing: Restriction Fragment Length Polymorphism (RFLP)

The fundamental concept behind the RFLP (restriction fragment length polymorphism) method is that a strand of DNA can be readily cut into small segments of varying sizes by severing the chain at very specific places along the DNA polymer using special enzymes. These smaller pieces of DNA can then be arranged by size and the resulting size patterns are compared between different samples to find similarities and differences. The key idea here is that individual people differ from one another not so much in the genetically coding DNA regions but mostly in the hypervariable regions between the genes. Using the differences in the hypervariable regions that exist from person to person, size distributions of fragmented DNA samples collected from different places, such as from the crime scene or directly from a suspect, can be readily compared.

In our DNA, we all have very similar repeated sections of DNA in the non-coding regions of the strands. The RFLP method begins, after isolation and separation of the DNA in the sample, by cutting the DNA into many smaller segments. The chain is not cut randomly; however, it is instead cut at *very specific* locations (loci) along the DNA strand. In essence, this process cuts at the locations in DNA that have certain recognizable sequences. The cutting is performed by a special enzyme, called a restriction endonuclease enzyme, usually just called a *restriction enzyme*, that recognizes just one very specific nucleotide sequence. It is somewhat similar to marking a text every time that the word "because" appears. The enzyme recognizes only one certain sequence of DNA "letters," just as we recognize words from a sequence of letters, and then cuts the DNA at this place. For example, one particular restriction enzyme, called "Hae III," recognizes only the "GGCC" sequence and none others. When it finds this sequence along the DNA chain, it cuts it between the "G" and the "C" nucleotides of each and every "GGCC" sequence it finds – *and nowhere else*. Another restriction enzyme, called "apa I," recognizes the "GGGCCC" sequence and no others, and cuts between the first and second "C" nucleotides in the sequence. The action of a restriction enzyme on DNA is shown schematically in Figure 5.22. Over

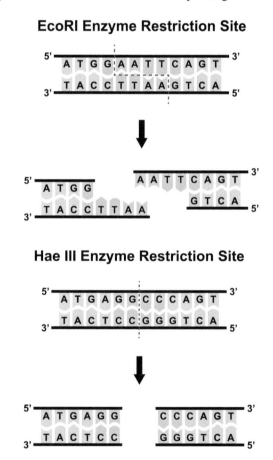

EcoRI Enzyme Restriction Site

Hae III Enzyme Restriction Site

FIGURE 5.22 Schematic of the cutting action of restriction enzymes on a portion of DNA that it "recognizes." At the left is shown the cutting pattern for the enzyme EcoRI and at the right is the different cutting pattern for the Hae III enzyme.

Source: Shutterstock.com.

BOX 5.8   BRIEF ON RFLP DNA TYPING

1. RFLP uses restriction enzymes to cut DNA into different-sized segments at specific places (loci).
2. Fragmented segments are separated by electrophoresis based on their sizes.
3. Smaller DNA fragments move faster.
4. Fragment distributions are compared to population distributions or between samples.

the years, a large number of these restriction enzymes have been developed, each with a different specific DNA sequence that it recognizes and cuts along the strand.

The DNA from a relatively large number of cells, typically several thousand, is required for the RFLP analysis. However, because the DNA from all cells within an individual is identical, all the DNA in the sample will be cut in exactly the same places along the chain. When the cutting process is complete, the original DNA molecule has been cut into many smaller lengths. Due to the variability in the DNA non-coding regions from person to person, the array of different lengths of DNA fragments can be unique to a particular person. For example, in Figure 5.23, two strands of DNA (Chromosomes A and A′) are shown. Each strand has a number of "GGCC" repeated units but differs in the total numbers and spacings of these sections between the two strands. When the strands are cut *only* at the "GGCC" sequence (between the two "C"s) by the restriction enzyme "Hae III", fragments of different lengths will be formed. The lengths of the cut fragments in reality can be quite long, up to thousands of base pairs (kilobase pairs) with many different-sized fragments generated. In the example shown in Figure 5.23, chromosome A is cut by the enzyme into four pieces with sizes of 2.5, 4, 5, and 6 kbp (kilobase pairs or thousand(s) of nucleotides). Chromosome A′, in contrast, is cut into only three pieces of 4, 6, and 7.5 kbp lengths. When the fragments are separated by lengths and compared, as shown on the right-hand side in Figure 5.23, clear differences and similarities between the two strands are easily noticed. The difference between the two sequences in the figure arises solely from the presence of one additional "GGCC" unit on chromosome A that is not present on chromosome A′. This simple change, however, leads to striking differences that are clearly identifiable in the fragment length plot.

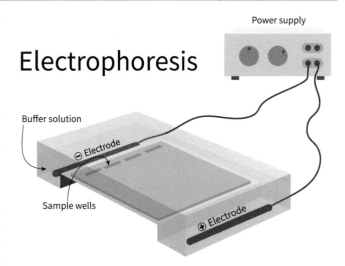

FIGURE 5.24 Experimental gel electrophoresis setup.

Source: Shutterstock.com

The success of our entire DNA typing process depends upon our ability to separate, sort by size, and visualize the fragments after they have been cut. Luckily, this can be readily done using one of several common techniques involving a method called *electrophoresis* (Figure 5.24).

One of the first electrophoretic methods used for separating large molecules by their charges and size is *gel electrophoresis*. The basic idea behind this method is that a sample mixture of different-sized fragments can be size-sorted by placing the mixture on a gel and applying an electrical current. The gel used in this analysis is usually quite similar to the gelatin used in many common food products. The molecules of the mixture move through the gel at differing

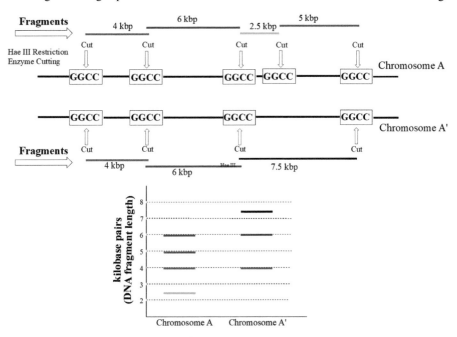

FIGURE 5.23 At the top are shown possible "ACCT" repeat patterns and the sites of action for a restriction enzyme on two DNA strands, A and A′ (kbp stands for 1,000 base pairs). At the bottom is shown a plot of the size distributions arising from the two cut DNA samples.

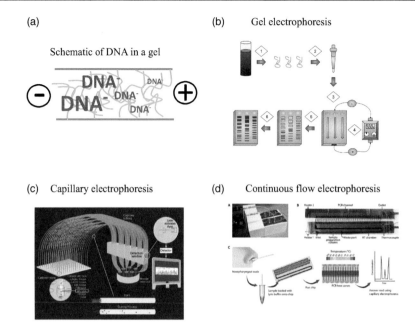

(a)

Schematic of DNA in a gel

(b)   Gel electrophoresis

(c)   Capillary electrophoresis

(d)   Continuous flow electrophoresis

FIGURE 5.25 (a) The illustration shows how a polymeric gel impedes the progress of DNA fragments along the gel based on their size, with smaller fragments traveling faster than larger fragments. (b) The illustration shows a biological sample, such as blood, undergoing a gel electrophoresis experiment to yield forensic identification information. The steps include (1) DNA extraction, (2) mixing the sample with a restriction enzyme to cause fragmentation and amplification with PCR, (3) adding the fragmented/amplified mixture to the wells of the gel, (4) application of an electric current to move the negatively charged DNA along the gel, (5) separation of the fragments based on length, and (6) staining the bands to show the location and amounts of the separated DNA fragments. (c) The illustration shows a schematic for the techniques of capillary electrophoresis and (d) continuous flow electrophoresis.

Credits: (b) Used per Creative Commons Share-Alike 4.0, International. User: Jennifer0328. (c) U.S. Department of Energy. (d) Used per Creative Commons 2.5 Generic. User: Qingqing Cao, Madhumita Mahalanabis, Jessie Chang, Brendan Carey, Christopher Hsieh, Ahjegannie Stanley, Christine A. Odell, Patricia Mitchell, James Feldman, Nira R. Pollock, Catherine M. Klapperich.

rates depending upon their relative sizes and charges, with smaller and higher-charged components moving most rapidly through the gel (Figure 5.24). The size separation occurs because frictional forces slow the larger molecules as they move through the pores in the gel much more than the smaller molecules. The entire process is shown schematically in Figure 5.25 a, b. The DNA fragments in the buffer solution have an overall negative charge due to the presence of their charged phosphate backbones. These charged fragments move through the gel when an electric current is applied at a rate depending upon their lengths. In DNA, the longest fragments travel the least and are found nearest to the starting point, while the shortest fragments move the most and are found furthest from the start. One analogy that has been used is that gel electrophoresis is like a stream with many nets stretched across it (the stream's current is analogous to the electrical charge running through the gel). These nets, however, have holes in them of all different sizes: from small holes to larger holes. The smallest fish in the stream pass through the nets most easily, barely slowed by the nets and fitting through all the holes quite easily. These smallest fish will emerge downstream the fastest. Larger fish travel

through the netting obstacles more slowly and, therefore, emerge at a later time. In a similar fashion, the smallest DNA fragments pass through the gel fastest and travel the farthest (Figure 5.25). Larger fragments travel more slowly and are found closer to the starting point. Many "bands," groups observed in the gels with the same lengths, are typically observed and display a fingerprint-like pattern that may be unique to a particular person (Figure 5.26).

Several methods have now supplanted the gel electrophoresis method and include capillary electrophoresis (CE) and continuous flow electrophoresis (CFE) (Figure 5.25). These will be described later, but they all share the process of separating DNA fragments based on their sizes and charges.

In an actual RFLP DNA analysis, the DNA sample is first digested with the restriction enzyme to selectively cut up the strand. The mixture containing all the different-sized fragments is then put into a buffer solution placed in a porous gel in an electrophoresis instrument, and finally, the electrical current is turned on. The DNA fragments move toward the positive pole of the chamber, with the relative distance that each fragment moves dependent primarily upon the size of the fragment (number of nucleotides). Finally, the distribution

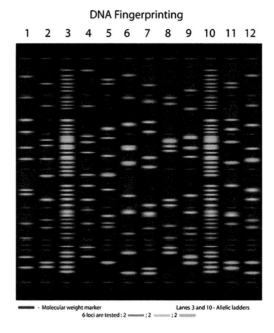

DNA Fingerprinting

Molecular weight marker   Lanes 3 and 10 - Allelic ladders
6 loci are tested : 2 ▬▬ ; 2 ▭▭ ; 2 ▭▭

FIGURE 5.26 Autoradiogram from the gel electrophoresis of ten individual samples showing DNA fragmentation patterns.

Source: Shutterstock.com.

Note: Lanes 3 and 10 are simply markers used to establish the locations of known length fragments.

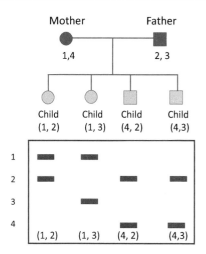

FIGURE 5.27 Inheritance of markers through two generations of one family.

of the fragments along the gel is visualized and compared to other samples being considered. The visualization is done through a process known as blotting and hybridization. Once the fragments have moved down the gel, they are transferred to a nylon sheet (blotting). The fragments on the sheet either contain from the outset or are then typically treated after the gel separation with a radioactive marker or an attached dye. This process of linking the markers to the DNA fragments is called *hybridization*. The labeled sheet is finally placed near photographic flim or a photosensor, which, when developed, shows the location of each fragment along the gel as a band.

A typical result from the electrophoresis of a number of samples is shown in Figure 5.26. This image illustrates the fragmentation pattern for ten individuals. Comparison of the sorted fragments between samples can readily reveal their level of similarity.

Besides simply comparing DNA samples between a suspect and a sample collected from a crime scene, other kinds of forensically useful information can be gained through RFLP DNA typing. One example is tracing a person's family tree for inheritance, immigration, or paternity claims. In this application, molecular probes are usually employed that bind to only one place in a person's non-coding DNA makeup. The probe will attach itself to DNA fragments that have been cut at different places by the restriction enzyme. These cutting sites are inherited by people in the same way genes are inherited, half from the mother and half from the father. In Figure 5.27, one family's inheritance through two generations is shown. A total of four variations in the DNA code at a particular locus on a chromosome are seen in the plot. While all the children have one marker from each parent, they may have an overall composition different from one another (e.g., 1,2; 1,3; etc.). Multiple probes and suitable samples readily allow this technique to track ancestries back for generations.

BOX 5.9   CASE HISTORY: THE BACTERIAL TRAIL

DNA typing can also be used for tracing plants, such as crops, to establish breeder's rights, as well as animals and bacteria, besides people. Millions of dollars can be at stake from a determination of where a biological sample originated. For example, the use of DNA typing can trace the source of an individual bacterial infection.

In 2002, 68-year-old Patricia Pfoutz began to experience intense diarrhea that ultimately led to acute kidney failure. She died one week later, leaving the doctors in Ohio without a clear answer for the cause of her death. The Centers for Disease Control and Prevention investigated and found that Ms. Pfoutz died from a severe infection by a strain of *E. coli* bacteria. Most interesting, however, was the fact that the DNA from the *E. coli* that killed Ms. Pfoutz matched the DNA from an outbreak of *E. coli* at a meatpacking plant in Greeley, Colo., nearly 1,300 miles away. Ms. Pfoutz must have been infected through foodborne contamination.

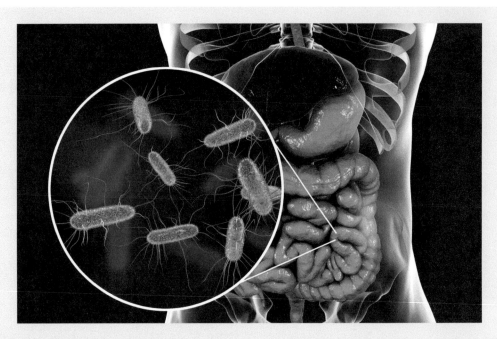

FIGURE 5.28   Intestinal microbiome: an illustration showing the anatomy of the human digestive system and enteric bacteria *E. coli*, colonizing the jejunum, ileum, and other parts of the intestine.

Source: Shutterstock.com.

DNA testing provides a definitive way to trace food contamination, often back to its sources, even to a location far distant from the outbreak. In Ms. Pfoutz's case, a lawsuit was filed that was eventually settled for a multi-million-dollar amount.

5.3.3 DNA Typing: Polymerase Chain Reaction (PCR-STR) Methods

Among the most problematic features of the RFLP method is that it requires samples containing relatively large amounts of undamaged DNA and is relatively slow. Often, however, samples from crime scenes are either very small or are partially, or even badly, degraded. To overcome these difficulties, a technique involving a process known as the *polymerase chain reaction* (PCR) was developed. PCR can take extremely small quantities of incomplete DNA strands and prepare enough duplicates of portions of the original DNA to allow for an accurate analysis. This duplication process, known as *amplification*, makes many, many copies of specified pieces of DNA molecules. In fact, within a few hours, an automated PCR instrument can theoretically make many millions of copies of just the DNA target region from a single source molecule! This method has essentially replaced the RFLP method for routine samples.

The PCR technique involves a process that is very similar to what happens naturally in cells when DNA is copied in the transcription process. It is not a DNA forensic test in itself, however, but rather it is instead a process that provides enough copies of duplicate DNA fragments to allow for typing to occur. PCR is actually used in association with a number of other DNA methodologies to perform the analysis.

The PCR process employs several simple steps that beautifully mimic the natural duplication of DNA. It is important to note at the outset that it is not necessary to copy the entire DNA strand in a sample. Luckily, it is necessary just to copy only the small portions of DNA required to establish a person's identity uniquely (just the parts that are different from person to person, parts of the polymorphic hypervariable or non-coding regions).

So how does this "molecular copy machine" work? Like the paper copy machine, the PCR process involves repeated cycles of a small set of steps or chemical reactions. Each cycle copies only a selected target region of the DNA, much as our paper copy machines copy only one page of a book at a time rather than copying the entire book. As long as the copied page has the information we need, we're in great shape. Similarly, with the right biochemical tools, we can copy just the DNA information we need for the analysis. Unlike copy machines, however, each PCR cycle doubles the amount of the DNA sequence that was present at the start: $1 \rightarrow 2 \rightarrow 4 \rightarrow 8 \rightarrow 16 \rightarrow 32 \rightarrow 64 \rightarrow 128 \rightarrow 256 \rightarrow 512 \rightarrow 1024 \rightarrow$ etc.

There are four main steps in each cycle of our PCR "biological copy machine": denaturation, annealing (primer addition), extension, and ligation. The overall goal is to make many copies of an STR that we will later use to determine how many repeats are in a specific STR.

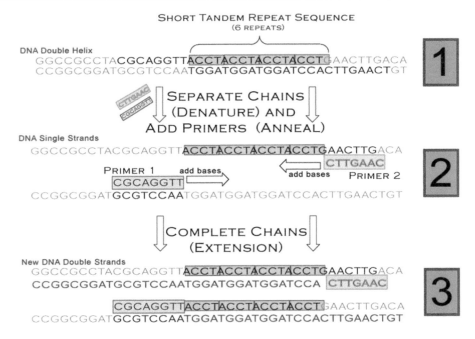

FIGURE 5.29 Steps in one cycle of PCR duplication (amplification of a DNA target sequence). In "real life", the primers used are up to about 30 nucleotides long. Stage 1 → 2 shows the denaturation (separating strands) and annealing (adding primers) steps. Step 2 → 3 shows extension (adding complementary nucleotides) and ligation process (linking the new nucleotides).

The first step in the PCR process, called *denaturation*, involves unraveling the DNA double helix into its two separate strands (Figure 5.29). This can be quite simply done by briefly heating the DNA to 94°C. Once separated into individual strands, each strand can then serve as a template upon which to rebuild a new double strand of DNA through base pairing (just as in transcription described before).

In the second step, the temperature is lowered to about 60°C, and small, specially constructed pieces of DNA called *primers* are added. These primers are carefully designed to mark the boundaries of the stretch of DNA that will be duplicated, much in the way that paper clips or "sticky" notes might be used to mark the exact pages to be copied from a book. The primers work by binding to the beginning and end of the portion of the DNA that will be copied. These chemical markers are used to signal enzymes where to begin to match base pairs to convert the single strands into new double strands. The overall process is shown schematically in Figure 5.29. Let's say that we want to make many copies of a short region of DNA, as labeled in the figure with the "Short Tandem Repeat Sequence" (STR). In the first line of the figure (labeled step "1" at the right-hand side), we start with a complete double strand of DNA containing a target STR region, in this case, an "ACCT" sequence that is repeated four times ["ACCTACCTACCTACCT"]. The double helix strands are then separated by heating to give two single strands. In step two of Figure 5.29, two different primers ["CGCAGGTT" and "CTTGCCA"] are added that have been designed to exactly "fit" near the beginning and end of the target STR repeated sequence (like paper clip markers). For example, Primer 1 is exactly the right sequence of bases to match a little bit of the DNA sequence that is just to the left of the target STR region

to be copied. When Primer 1 is added to the mixture of separated strands, it will bind (a process called *annealing*) to the complementary DNA strand just before the STR target region. Primer 2, however, is made up of a complementary version of the sequence that occurs just to the right of the target STR region on the other single strand. So, when Primer 2 is added to the separated strands, it will bind just to the right of the STR repeats in the top strand. By adding these two primers, we have marked out the beginning and the end of the STR section that we want to copy.

In the final steps of this cycle, another enzyme (called a DNA polymerase) first finds the primers and then fills out the *double* strands of the two DNA *single* strands in a complementary fashion (places an "A" when it finds a "T", and so on). This process is called *extension*. Lastly, the newly added and sequenced nucleotides are hooked together (something like knitting) in a process called *ligation* to form the two complete sections of the double strands of DNA. This entire process is shown schematically in Figure 5.30 for many cycles.

There are several important things to recognize about this PCR process. First, after completing a cycle (denaturation, annealing, extension, and ligation), we have now taken one double strand and have made two identical DNA double strands in the region copied, which can serve as templates for the next cycle of the PCR process. In short, we have doubled the amount of DNA we had when we began by selectively copying the target STR region. When the cycle is run for a second time, we end up with four DNA double strands, each of which can again serve as starting templates. After cycle three, we have eight strands, and after four cycles, we have 16. This exponential increase continues with each cycle. Since each

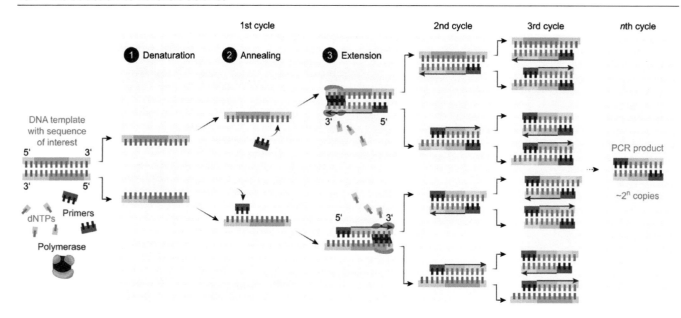

FIGURE 5.30   Production of target STR region copies by PCR.

Source: Used per Creative Commons Share-Alike 4.0, International. User: Enzoklo.

BOX 5.10   BRIEF ON PCR

1. Generates many, many duplicates of selected short regions of DNA containing STRs.
2. The first step separates the DNA double strand into two single strands (denaturation).
3. The second step adds markers (primers) to show where to start and stop copying the DNA strand (hybridization).
4. The third and fourth steps complete the strand by filling in complementary bases starting at the primers (extension and ligation).
5. The cycle (steps 1 through 3) is repeated until many copies of targeted DNA sequences have been made.
6. Every cycle doubles the amount of DNA.

---

cycle can be completed in just a few minutes, within hours we can produce millions and millions of copies of the targeted DNA STR regions. For example, running 32 cycles could theoretically create over 1 billion copies of a targeted DNA region in a few hours! Another important feature to note is that not all the DNA copies made in the PCR process are the same size, as shown in Figure 5.30. For example, after three cycles, there are four copies of just the targeted STR region and four larger sections. As more cycles are completed, the relative amount of *only* the targeted STR region becomes very large compared to the earlier copied larger sections. This is particularly beneficial because we ultimately want to copy just the portions of DNA needed for a forensic analysis: the region with the short tandem repeats.

The PCR method differs from the naturally occurring DNA transcription process in cells in that it copies *only* selected small regions of DNA, typically fewer than 1,000 nucleotides, rather than duplicating the large regions necessary to code for a protein (a gene). However, this effectively restricts current PCR methods from being applied to VNTR

(and RFLP) techniques because VNTR/RFLP uses relatively large segments of DNA.

The PCR technique is readily performed in the laboratory using specialized instrumentation. Usually, the DNA sample to be amplified is added to a "soup" of biochemical reactants including the chosen primers, nucleotides (A, T, C, and G nucleotides), buffer, and several necessary enzymes. The steps are then carried out automatically by cycling the temperatures of the mixture: heating to 92°C for denaturation, then cooling to 60°C for annealing, and finally warming to 72°C for extension. Every time the temperature is cycled, another cycle of the PCR amplification process is completed. Experimentally, it's almost as simple as pushing the copy button on the copy machine!

The PCR method allows us to generate the relatively large amounts of DNA needed for accurate typing from very tiny samples. It must be coupled, however, with another technique to complete the DNA typing analysis. This is most commonly done by looking more closely at the STR fragments that have been amplified in the PCR process.

5.3.4 DNA STR Typing

As described previously, DNA contains repeated sections known as VNTRs, which are repeated consecutive sequences all connected together. These VNTR sections usually consist of rather large repeated segments of DNA. The problem with using VNTR analysis, therefore, is that long DNA segments are relatively easily degraded and are difficult to copy using PCR methods. This means that we need a relatively large sample in order to get enough DNA to complete the analysis. The shorter STR segments, however, work quite well with PCR amplification methods. These *STRs* are typically made up of short sequences of only two to six nucleotides that are repeated usually between 7 and 20 times (as opposed to the maximum of about 50 repeats in VNTRs). Since STRs are much shorter than VNTRs, they can be easily duplicated quickly using PCR methods (the FBI uses only STRs with four nucleotides). This allows both very small samples (such as contact DNA which requires as little as a few cells) and badly degraded and broken samples of DNA that only contain short intact pieces to be successfully analyzed.

A PCR-STR analysis begins with a PCR amplification where the DNA is first denatured, and the chosen primers are added. The "forward" primer is, however, attached to a small molecular dye that fluoresces (gives off light) when excited by an external beam of suitable wavelength light. The reason for this fluorescent "tag" is that it allows us to very easily visualize where the different-sized STR pieces are located once separated without having to use the difficult radioactive labels used in gel electrophoresis. When we shine light on the sample, the dye molecules fluoresce (Chapter 12), such that we can find the locations of the STR fragments to which they are attached by looking for the telltale light that they emit. The PCR process provides a huge number of copies of the targeted STR region with the fluorescent dye molecules attached needed for the analysis.

Once copied and labeled with dye, the STRs can then be separated using a rapid electrophoresis technique, such as *capillary electrophoresis*. This technique is used to separate the STRs by length (number of repeats), similar to gel electrophoresis, except that it uses a very narrow charged glass capillary tube instead of a gel plate. This allows for a much faster analysis with higher resolution. The different-sized STR fragments are carried down the tube by a buffered solvent at rates that depend upon their charges and sizes, with smaller segments of the same charge moving faster. The smallest fragments will, therefore, reach the end of the capillary tube first, with the largest fragments coming out last. Over the length of the capillary, the fragments are separated into distinct *bands* that contain DNA segments of the same length. As each band of like-sized STR pieces moves to the end of the capillary tube, it passes a light source and a detector, recording the fluorescent light emitted by the small dye molecules attached to the STR fragments. In this way, it can be determined when each of the STR fragments passes through the capillary tube. A typical capillary electrophoresis setup is shown schematically in Figure 5.31.

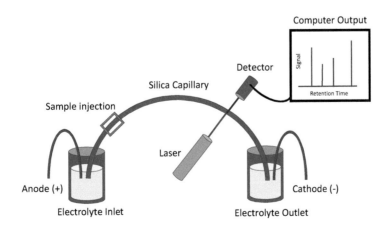

FIGURE 5.31 Schematic of capillary electrophoresis.

Capillary electrophoresis using an array of different-colored fluorescent dyes tagged to different primers or biomarkers allows for the simultaneous determination of many PCR amplified regions. This means that we can rapidly analyze for many STRs located at different loci at the same time by detecting different fluorescent wavelengths or retention times. This is often referred to as capillary electrophoresis-based multiplex PCR technology.

In large populations, there are many possibilities for the number of times that a particular nucleotide sequence, such as "ACCT" in Figure 5.18, is repeated within the DNA code. It is often quite desirable from a forensic perspective to know how often any given number of tandem repeats at a locus (PCR fragment size) is found within a population, especially because we'd like to know what the odds are that a person selected from the population at random would show a particular STR repeat pattern in their DNA. It is quite different to say that there is a one-in-a-hundred chance (1%) that two randomly chosen people will have the same pattern of fragments than a one-in-a-trillion chance (0.0000000001%). To help provide an estimate of these odds, databases obtained from large numbers of people have been built that show how common a particular DNA STR repeat number at a locus is within a population. How often a particular repeat is observed within the database is called the **population frequency**. For example, if the frequency of two different tandem repeat numbers in a population, such as 8-repeats and 10-repeats at a particular locus, happens to each be one-in-four (25% of the population or a 0.25 probability), then the probability of randomly finding two people in the population with both of these two repeat numbers (8 and 10) is $^1/_4 \times ^1/_4$ or 1-in-16 (6¼%) (see Chapter 3 for probability calculations). The chance of a random match goes down very rapidly as more STR loci are considered and can be figured out simply by multiplying the population frequency for each of the repeat lengths together. In our simple example, if each repeat number has a 1-in-4 chance, then the total probability is equal to $(0.25)^n$ (where n is the number of different fragments considered). For example, the probability of matching 10 STR repeat numbers, each found in 25% of the population, is $(0.25)^{10}$ or a 1-in-1,048,576 chance (~0.0001%). In other words, the probability of picking two people at random that had the same ten matching STR repeat numbers at a 25% population frequency would be slightly less than one in a million. Increasing the number of fragments considered from 10 to just 16 means that statistically you would likely not find another random match on Earth (about a 1-in-4.3 trillion chance of two randomly chosen people having the same 16-STR tandem repeat profile).

In order to determine the probability of someone having a particular STR profile, the key piece of information is how many repeats of the particular STR sequence are present at a given locus on a person's DNA. For example, using one DNA locus that the FBI has decided to examine (called locus D13S317), there are ten repeat-number possibilities that have been observed at this locus in humans consisting of 5, 7, 8, 9, 10, 11, 12, 13, 14, and 15 repeats of the "TATC" sequence. The worldwide frequency of the occurrences of these STR possibilities (each possibility is called an allele) is presented in Table 5.2 for a few select populations. For instance, the five-repeat pattern is essentially unknown in the United States but does occur in about 0.5% of people living in China. In contrast, the 15-repeat pattern occurs in about 3.3% of Americans but is essentially unknown in the German population (North Bavaria). The most common patterns in all human populations are the 11 and 12-repeat versions (alleles), accounting for about a third of the population each.

The success of the STR analysis relies upon comparing an observed STR repeat pattern at a particular locus in a forensic sample with how often it randomly occurs in a population. Figuring out the odds of a random DNA STR match with a forensic sample is much like figuring the odds when playing cards. For example, if you were dealt one card from a full deck of cards, the chance that it would be a red card would be 50% (26/52 or 0.50): on average, you'd get a red card half of the time. The odds that a second dealt card would also be red would similarly be about 50% for that one event (actually, it would be 25/51, but we'll use 0.5 here for simplicity). However, the odds that you would be randomly dealt two red cards in a row would be 0.50 times 0.50, or 25%. Using the same idea, what would be the chances of getting five red cards dealt in a row? The answer would be the chance of each separate event multiplied together or approximately $0.50 \times 0.50 \times 0.50 \times 0.50 \times 0.50$ or $(0.50)^5 = 0.031$ or 1 in about 32 times (again simplifying to 0.5 for each draw, rather than $26/52 \times 25/52 \times 24/52$, etc.). Likewise, we can calculate the odds of being dealt one specific card, such as the four of hearts. The probability of this happening is calculated in the same way as before by multiplying the probability of each separate event together. In this case, the chance of getting dealt a heart card is one-in-four (13/52 = 0.2500) and being dealt a four is 1-in-13 (1/13 = 0.0769), so the probability of being dealt the four of hearts is (0.2500) × (0.0769) = 0.0192 or 1-in-52. This is the same as if we knew that there was only one 4 of hearts in a deck of 52 cards, or a 1-in-52 chance (1/52).

The probability of any particular random set of DNA STRs is determined in exactly the same way as calculating

TABLE 5.2 World distribution of the D13S317 STR fragments

POPULATION	5	7	8	9	10	11	12	13	14	15
Australia	0.0000	0.0016	0.1433	0.0609	0.0556	0.3211	0.2938	0.0883	0.0359	0.0016
Germany	0.0000	0.0000	0.1500	0.0620	0.0650	0.2810	0.2920	0.0960	0.0540	0.0000
United States	0.0000	0.0000	0.1026	0.0762	0.0662	0.3377	0.2682	0.1093	0.0364	0.0330
China	0.0053	0.0020	0.2713	0.1572	0.1372	0.2341	0.1556	0.0314	0.0059	0.0000

Source: John M. Butler, 2006 [WWW/MedFak/Serology/DNA-Systeme/d13s317.htm].

card probabilities. Suppose, for instance, that one of your chromosomes, say at the D13S317 locus (Table 5.2), has nine "TATC" repeats and the other chromosome at the same locus has 11 "TATC" repeats (remember you have a pair of chromosomes so you have two possible repeat numbers, or alleles, at a particular site). Using the data in Table 5.2, it can be determined that the probability of someone chosen at random from the population of the United States as having this same 9 and 11 repeat pattern would be 0.0762 times 0.3377 times 2 or 0.0514 (5.14%). The final multiplying factor of two simply comes from the fact that since there are two chromosomes, the 9 and 11 repeats STR could occur on either chromosome, either in a 9, 11 or an 11,9 arrangement, which gives the same pattern but just uses different chromosomes; hence, a multiplier of two is needed.

As more and more STR regions on different chromosomes in the sample are used in the analysis, the probability of a random match drops very quickly. For this reason, we usually look at 13 or more STR loci when completing the DNA analysis. For example, using the 13 STR regions employed in the O.J. Simpson DNA analysis, it was determined that the odds of someone randomly matching his DNA profile would be about 1-in-7 trillion.

It is important to note that the odds of a random match depend both on what the repeat numbers are *and* which population we choose. So, for the above example using the D13S317 locus, suppose we chose the eight and nine-repeat variants and compare the Chinese and Australian populations. For the Chinese population, a random match would be 0.2713 (for the eight-repeat version) times 0.1572 (for the nine-repeat version) times 2 for a combined random match probability of 0.0852 or 8.52%. For Australia, it would be 0.1433 times 0.0609 times 2 for a combined probability of 0.0175 or about 1.8%. Thus, it would be almost five times more likely to find a random match between a forensic sample with the 8,9 repeat versions in China as it would be in Australia. Also, in Australia, the 11,12 combination is nearly 37,000 times more common than the 7,15 version in the same population.

The ideal for a forensic case would be to decrease the chance of a random match to an infinitesimally small value by examining as many STR sequences as possible. Fortunately, it is relatively easy to look at many STR locations all at once for a DNA sample. This is done by first carefully choosing and using a set of primers that will copy different non-overlapping STR regions so that we can duplicate *different STR regions simultaneously* through PCR amplification. This process, called *multiplexing*, is illustrated in Figure 5.32. In this example, three locations on the DNA strand (labeled D3, vWA, and FGA) are amplified simultaneously and tagged with a blue fluorescent dye. At the top of Figure 5.32 is shown a set of three bars depicting the different sizes of the three *non-overlapping* STR locations. The horizontal axis in this figure shows the number of nucleotides in the STR fragment, given as a size of the DNA fragment. The middle plot shows all the possibilities of repeat numbers for each STR location. So, the D3S1358 locus has 8 possibilities (12–19 repeats), vWA has 11 possibilities (11–21 repeats) and the FGA locus has 14 possibilities (18–30 repeats). It is important to note that for a "real" person, there can be either one or two fragment sizes (alleles) seen for any given STR locus: one arising from each member of a pair of matched chromosomes. This arises because we inherit one allele (number of repeats) from our mother and one from our father. If both the mother and father "donate" chromosomes which contain the same number of repeats at the STR locus (homozygous), then only one band is seen. If, on the other hand, the inherited STRs are different from the mother and father (heterozygous), then two bands are observed.

One way to look at many STR regions at a time is to use different-colored fluorescent dyes attached to the primers. By combining these two ideas – different primers targeting non-overlapping regions coupled with different-colored dyes – we can look at many STR regions simultaneously. This is shown in Figure 5.33 using five different fluorescent dyes. By employing these concepts, the odds of a random match between a forensic sample and a population can often be reduced to a one-in-a-trillion chance, often good enough to convince a jury of the connection between two biological samples.

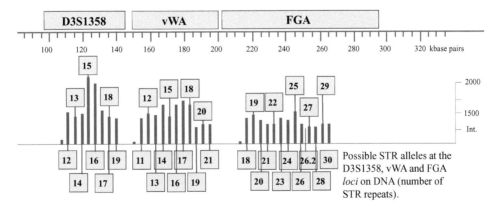

FIGURE 5.32 The possible number of STR repeats at three different loci on the DNA strand: D3S1358, vWA, and FGA.

Source: Based on work reported in Dror and Hampikian (2011).

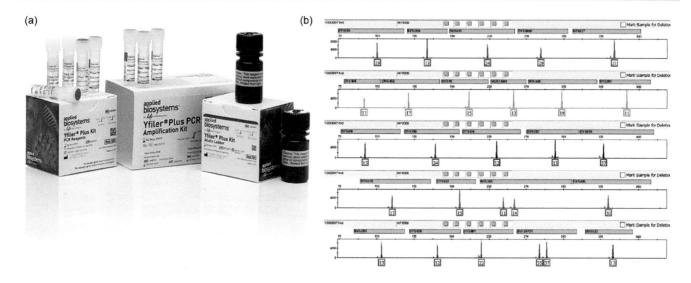

FIGURE 5.33 (a) Applied BiosystemsTM AmpFLSTR™ Identifiler™ Plus PCR Amplification Kit; (b) The output for a 1:1,000 male:female mixture, amplified using the Yfiler Plus kit and 30 cycles on Applied Biosystems™ 3500 Series Genetic Analyzer.

Source: Copyright and used with permission and courtesy of ThermoFisher, Inc.

TABLE 5.3   Comparison between the RFLP and STR DNA typing methods

	RFLP	STR
Sequence size	Employs restriction enzymes to cut the DNA strands at specific locations to yield fragments.	Employs short tandem repeats (STR) with two to six nucleotides repeated consecutively 7–30 times that are copied many times using the PCR method.
Sample size	Relatively large amounts of DNA are required (ca. 100 mg: equivalent to the DNA from several thousand cells).	Relatively small amounts of DNA are required (in practice, about 1 ng from as little as seven to eight cells is required).
Sample quality	Requires good quality (undegraded) DNA samples.	Works well on fragmented or partially degraded DNA.
Reliability	Relatively reliable and compares forensic sample with exemplar.	Based on probabilities of random match in a populationd, it epends on comparison with proper population and availability of statistical data.
Speed	Relatively slow.	Can be a very rapid analysis.
Other advantages and problems	Requires relatively large amounts of DNA, but it is relatively insensitive to impurities.	Only needs very small DNA samples that can be partially degraded and can be automated by multiplexing and PCR processing. The technique is sensitive to contamination.

To summarize the two DNA typing systems discussed, RFLP and STR methods, Table 5.3 compares some of the major features and differences for the two types of analysis.

5.3.5 Mini-STR and SNP DNA Profiling

Unfortunately, some biological samples of great interest may be badly degraded from age, exposure, bleaching, or other factors. Using a technique called mini-STR, useful DNA forensic evidence can still sometimes be obtained from these damaged samples. This technique employs much smaller fragments of DNA for the analysis, the mini-STRs. The main difference in

using mini-STRs occurs during the PCR amplification steps in which the primers (the markers that tell the enzymes where to begin or end copying the DNA strand) are moved much closer to the repeated STR regions, as illustrated in Figure 5.34. A complete set of mini-STR primers has been developed that allows for the closest approach of the primers to the actual STR *loci* for all 13 CODIS STRs. This technique has been especially useful in the identification of remains from the World Trade Center attacks and similar cases involving damaged DNA samples.

Current work is moving beyond even the mini-STR techniques to look at micro-STR and SNP technologies. A technique that has gained in forensic use involves exploring DNA differences that appear as single nucleotide polymorphisms (*SNPs*, usually pronounced "SNiPs"). SNPs are actual variations in

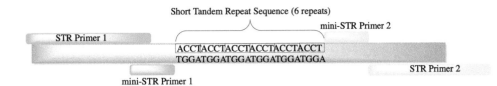

Short Tandem Repeat Sequence (6 repeats)

STR Primer 1

mini-STR Primer 2

ACCTACCTACCTACCTACCTACCT
TGGATGGATGGATGGATGGATGGA

STR Primer 2

mini-STR Primer 1

FIGURE 5.34 Mini-STR primers relative to typical STR primers.

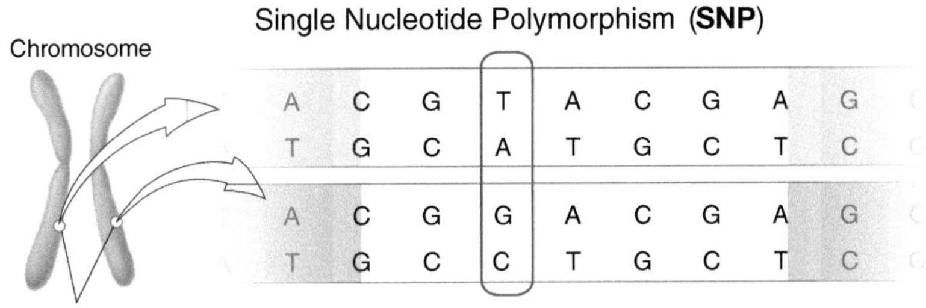

Single Nucleotide Polymorphism (**SNP**)

Chromosome

| A | C | G | T | A | C | G | A | G |
| T | G | C | A | T | G | C | T | C |

| A | C | G | G | A | C | G | A | G |
| T | G | C | C | T | G | C | T | C |

FIGURE 5.35 Single nucleotide polymorphism (SNP).

Source: NIH.

the DNA sequence that occur when one base pair is changed from what is typically found in a population, as illustrated in Figure 5.35. Forensic uses of SNPs are significantly different from the other DNA typing techniques presented so far in that the SNP technique looks directly at the DNA sequence itself, rather than focusing on DNA fragment lengths or numbers of tandem repeats. For example, one person might have a sequence "AATCGGGACC," while someone else has "AAACGGGACC" at the same *locus*. In this example, there is a SNP at the third position where a "T" in the first person has been replaced by an "A" in the second person (highlighted in red). These SNP point changes are actually rather common, typically found every 100–300 base pairs along the DNA strand. Because of the high frequency of SNPs, forensic analysis requires examination of many SNP variations and may be rather complicated and time-consuming. While it appears that SNPs may not soon replace STR-based analysis, SNPs are playing a valuable role in some forensic applications such as mitochondrial DNA (mtDNA) testing, ancestry informative markers (AIMs), Y-SNPs as lineage markers, and other potential applications.

BOX 5.12   THE LIGHTEST TOUCH: TOUCH DNA (CONTACTOR TRACE DNA)

One advance in the forensic application of DNA involves the use of a technique known as "touch" or "contact" DNA analysis. In July of 2008, this technique proved crucial in clearing JonBenét Ramsey's family in her death and has now gained relatively widespread use, especially in the field of "cold cases." The success of touch methods in both this and other more recent cases has led to similar analyses in a number of difficult or cold cases. In response to this, DNA laboratories have reported more than a 20% increase in the use of the touch DNA technique.

In "touch" DNA, tiny samples are obtained from surfaces that the suspect contacts, including food, utensils, clothing, tables, glasses, and the like, in order to isolate enough DNA-containing material for the analysis. Importantly, the "touch" DNA approach has been used to recover viable DNA samples from surfaces that do not show a visible stain. As little as seven to eight cells, or even less, has been used in this type of analysis, although such small sample sizes bring new problems related to statistical and probabilistic sampling.

In the JonBenét Ramsey case, her parents lived under suspicion for years after her death. Initially, it took police investigators seven years to send the DNA sample found in JonBenét's undergarments out for analysis, primarily due to problems with the DNA sample that was recovered. This sample had been deemed to lack the quality needed to enter it into the law enforcement databases for comparison. Using the "touch" DNA method, this sample was identified as belonging to an unknown male, thus exonerating the Ramsey of culpability.

The initial DNA sample analyzed was from a small drop of blood found on JonBenét. The "touch DNA" technique was used years later to analyze the clothing that JonBenét was wearing. Analysts have matched the DNA from skin cells found on the waistband of the murdered child's long underwear to the DNA in the blood sample from her underpants. The "touch DNA" analysis points to the presence of an unknown male, putting an end to a 12-year nightmare for John Ramsey. Unfortunately, JonBenét's mother, Patsy Ramsey, died two years earlier of ovarian cancer with the cloud of suspicion cast by the media and the police still over her head.

5.3.6 Familial DNA

With the explosion of ancestry services that use our DNA to trace back through time along our family trees, there has been an increasing interest by law enforcement in using very similar methods to trace unknown DNA from a crime scene along family lines to discover the identity of the criminal.

When you submit your DNA to an ancestry service, they compare your DNA information with that from millions of other people compiled in vast databases, and often your DNA also becomes part of these same databases. Your DNA, for obvious reasons, most closely resembles that of your biologically closest relatives: parents, grandparents, siblings, and so on. For example, you share half of your DNA with each of your parents and a quarter with your grandparents, as given in Table 5.4. So, if investigators have a DNA profile from an unknown person for which they can find no *exact* match in the DNA databases, they can then look for *close* similarities in the hopes of finding a relative of the criminal: the closer the similarities, the closer the relative. Once a closely similar profile is located, investigators can then use that known similar person to construct a family tree for the person. Presumably, the unknown source of the forensic DNA sample would then be located somewhere on the family tree.

State and federal authorities have collected huge DNA databases from convicted criminals, and increasingly, states are now collecting DNA for the databases from those simply arrested and/or charged with a crime. When governmental databases are considered along with existing ancestral databases, a vast number of DNA records are available for the familial search process. The FBI alone has over 20 million records, and just one ancestry service reports >16 million records.

As an important note, while law enforcement officials are finding a powerful tool in familial DNA searches, its use remains controversial as a potential invasion of privacy and violation of the U.S. Constitution's 4th Amendment. Some states have put significant restrictions on familial DNA

searching, such as limiting it to the most violent crimes and those without leads, while others have legalized its use. While the technique is not used nationally, the federal government is largely leaving it up to individual states to decide whether or not to use familial DNA for themselves.

One of the most famous cases involving familial DNA was the identification of the "Golden State Killer." In 2018, an arrest was made in a 30-year-old case involving at least 13 murders, 50 rapes, and 120 burglaries between 1973 and 1986. The perpetrator, Joseph James DeAngelo, was found by comparing the unknown DNA sample from the perpetrator collected from victims with information found in open access DNA databases to search for close relatives. Once a distant relative was located, the thread was ultimately traced back to the criminal. This was, however, no small feat since the relative was DeAngelo's third great grandparent and the work required constructing 25 family trees to ultimately find the culprit. It has been estimated that between 50% and 90% of Americans now have at least a third cousin in a DNA database, and that number is rapidly increasing, potentially allowing investigators to link essentially everyone to someone in a DNA database.

5.3.7 DNA Phenotyping

As we continually learn more about how gene expression controls our outward appearance, a natural extension has been to use genetic information to create a biological profile of a person just from their DNA alone. While this is less well-developed than many other aspects of DNA science, significant advances have been made in this technique, especially in the area of facial reconstruction.

Creating a biological profile, including a person's facial features, from their DNA code has been called *DNA phenotyping*. A person's phenotype refers to their biochemical features that have been determined by both their genetic makeup and environmental influences. These can include blood type, hair and eye color, skin color, stature, facial shape, and thousands of other features. DNA phenotyping is, therefore, the prediction of a person's physical features based on their DNA genetic code. An example is shown in Figure 5.36.

In this process, millions of specific SNPs that are associated with human physical features are typically tested and then put into a mathematical predictive model to generate a person's profile. For example, one of the first predictive models used was for eye color, which is largely determined based on six SNPs in pigmentation genes. Examining these six SNPs was shown to predict eye color in some populations with >90% accuracy. While much work remains before this can be a fully accurate predictive tool, it has been used by law enforcement officials in generating new leads in cold or difficult cases. Particularly promising is the technique's potential to generate investigative leads from crime scene DNA, decide between a small group of possible suspects, and identify remains from missing persons, among others.

TABLE 5.4   Amount of DNA shared with relatives

RELATIONSHIP	AVERAGE PERCENT OF DNA SHARED (%)
Identical twin	100
Parent	50
Sibling	50
Grandparent	25
Aunt, uncle, step sibling	25
Great grandparent	12.5
Second great grandparent	6.25
First cousin	12.5
Second cousin	3.13
third cousin	0.78
Fourth cousin	0.20

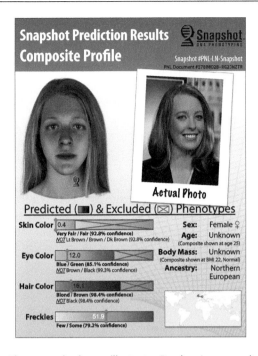

FIGURE 5.36 Phenotype DNA analysis. The example shown illustrates Parabon's composite software program Snapshot®.

Source: Copyright and used with permission and courtesy of Parabon NanoLabs, Inc. https://parabon-nanolabs.com.

5.4 MITOCHONDRIAL DNA AND Y CHROMOSOMAL TYPING

5.4.1 Mitochondrial DNA

The DNA we've looked at so far is found in the nuclei of cells, but a "second genome" exists within each cell. A small, circular portion of DNA is found outside of the nucleus in cellular structures called mitochondria (referred to as mtDNA or mitochondrial DNA). It's thought that at one time, mitochondria were separate bacterial organisms that eventually became permanent residents within cells, providing the cell with a means to readily convert food stocks and oxygen into usable energy in return for a rich supply of nutrients. Typically, each cell has many, many mitochondria, each with its own identical copy of this small loop of DNA, as shown in Figures 5.37 and 5.38.

Unlike nuclear DNA, the DNA in mitochondria is predominantly inherited *only* from mothers – matrilineal inheritance (although recent work has shown that in some instances mitochondria are inherited from both parents in a dominant/ recessive fashion). This is shown schematically in Figure 5.39. At fertilization, one-half of the chromosomes in the nucleus comes from the sperm cell and the other half from the egg. The egg cell outside the nucleus may have 100,000 or more mitochondria distributed throughout the cell while the sperm has only a few hundred mitochondria that are located primarily at the base of the flagellum. The flagellum and, essentially,

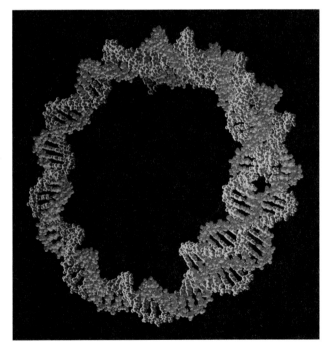

FIGURE 5.37 Circular mitochondrial human DNA inherited from the maternal line.

Source: Alfred Pasieka/Science Photo Library. Used with permission.

all the sperm's mitochondria typically do not penetrate the egg at fertilization, leaving just the mother's mitochondria in the fertilized cell. This is shown schematically in Figure 5.40.

The absence of mixing of paternal and maternal DNA in the mitochondria means that the mtDNA may be inherited over hundreds of generations without any changes along the mother's bloodline. Thus, mtDNA typing cannot typically distinguish between people along the same matrilineal descent but can identify members of the same bloodline.

In instances where nuclear DNA material is either scarce (e.g., bones, hair, teeth), badly damaged, or entirely absent (such as in our mature red blood cells and hair shafts that do not contain nuclei), it is possible to examine mtDNA for forensic information. While each cell has only one copy of nuclear

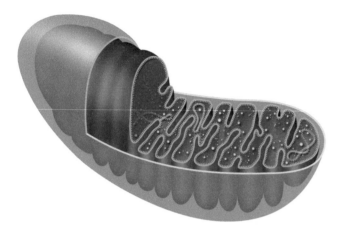

FIGURE 5.38 Artist's depiction of a mitochondrion. The mitochondrion is a double-membrane-bound organelle found in most eukaryotic organisms and responsible for cellular respiration (energy production).

Source: Shutterstock.com.

DNA, it may contain tens of thousands of copies of mtDNA. This means that it might be possible to obtain an mtDNA profile from the DNA found in a single cell.

Most of the mitochondrial DNA codes directly for important proteins needed for respiration and there is comparatively little non-coding DNA in mtDNA (Figure 5.41). For instance, human mtDNA contains a total of 16,569 nucleotides (compared with about 3 billion in nDNA) and all but about 1,200 of these code for proteins. Most of these 1,200 non-coding bases are located together in a region known as the control region.

In forensic mtDNA typing, about 610 nucleotides within the control region are sequenced and compared with a standard sequence. Differences between the standard sequence and that of the sample are then recorded and analyzed. Currently, mtDNA analysis is difficult, time-consuming, and expensive. Thus, its use has been limited to cases in which other DNA methods are not possible or maternal lineage information is particularly needed.

5.4.2 Y-Chromosome Typing

Just as mitochondrial DNA is inherited solely from mothers, the Y chromosome in the nucleus is inherited only from fathers. Thus, looking specifically at STRs on the Y chromosome can be used to trace paternal lineage and identify unknown male samples through paternal relatives. This information is particularly valuable in missing persons, sexual assault, and paternity investigations. The analysis can be very rapid and can often distinguish between single and multiple male donors in sexual assault cases. Additionally, the primers for the Y STRs ignore

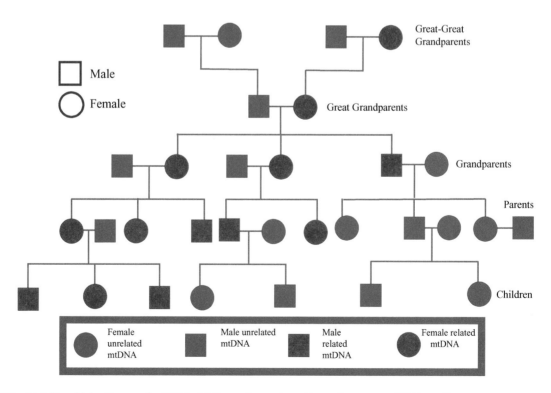

FIGURE 5.39 Matrilineal inheritance of mtDNA. All those shown in red have the same mtDNA profile.

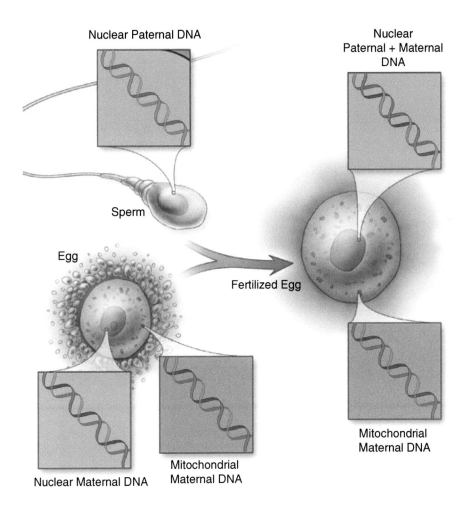

Nuclear Paternal DNA

Nuclear
Paternal + Maternal
DNA

Sperm

Egg

Fertilized Egg

Nuclear Maternal DNA

Mitochondrial
Maternal DNA

Mitochondrial
Maternal DNA

FIGURE 5.40   Inheritance of mtDNA.

Source: NIH.

DNA from females entirely so that separations of male from female cells prior to PCR is not usually necessary, eliminating a great deal of hard work. Identifying Y STRs from samples taken at different locations at a crime scene can also be used to establish where blood samples from males are present.

Y STR analysis has only recently been employed in forensic work since it was originally thought that there was less variability in this chromosome. However, it has now been established that up to 60% of the Y chromosome is composed of repetitive DNA that lends itself to this type of analysis.

5.4.3 Plant and Animal DNA Typing

DNA is the common thread binding all life forms together. It is as important to plants, animals, and microbes as it is to humans. It controls all their biochemical processes down to the simplest molecular level. The fundamental nature of DNA in all life forms, therefore, can be useful in providing forensically valuable information. Techniques have now been

developed and upheld in court, for obtaining DNA profile data that has proved useful in the identification of non-human subjects. Plant evidence has been used to place suspects at a crime scene, tie a drug dealer to his crop, and detect smugglers. Viral and bacterial DNA or RNA profiles have been equally successful in catching an attacker who murdered with the HIV (AIDS) virus and to trace soil samples to their local origins through the bacteria they contained. Animal DNA evidence has been used to place a suspect with a victim through pet hairs and animal-based fabric fibers, such as wool, mink, rabbit, and fox. Additionally, the illegal exploitation of animals and animal products can also be tracked using DNA (wildlife forensics).

Non-human DNA profile data has been used not only in criminal trials but also in civil proceedings. For example, plant breeders often spend a great deal of time and money developing new and improved strains of crops. It has been particularly difficult, however, for these breeders to protect the new strains that they have developed. These issues can be readily resolved using DNA plant profiling techniques by "registering" the DNA profile of a new breed.

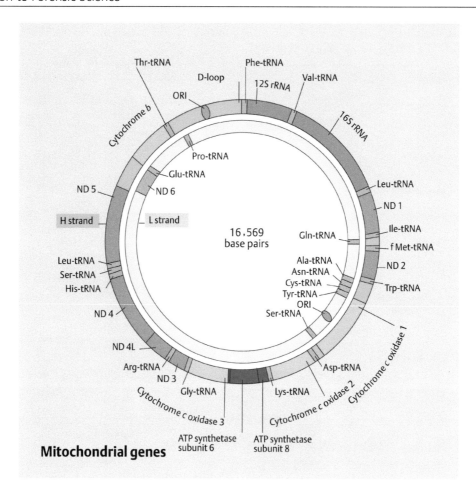

FIGURE 5.41   Mitochondrial DNA inheritance and structure.

Source: Shutterstock.com.

BOX 5.13   AFRICAN LEMBA LINEAGE

A southern African tribe, the Lemba, believe that they are direct descendants of the Jewish line of Abraham. At the same time, a group of Jews, called the Cohanim, wanted to confirm that they were direct descendants of Aaron, brother of Moses and direct descendant of Abraham. A big difference between these two groups, however, is that the Cohanim group had a written record tracing back millennia that was missing for the Lemba.

To answer both these questions, DNA tests using Y-chromosome markers were performed on people of the Cohanim, Lemba, and other faith communities as a comparison population. It was found that one particular Y-chromosome marker was present in 50% of the Cohanim males, 10% of all other Jewish males, and essentially unknown for those of other faiths. DNA tests of the Lemba tribal leaders likewise showed that 50% of these leaders also carried the Y-marker, while the marker was found in 10% of the remainder of the tribe, similar to the entire worldwide Jewish population and different from all non-Jewish populations tested. It seems that the claims of the Lemba tribe are quite reasonable, and they now learn Hebrew and study to become Rabbis.

5.5 DNA DATABANKS: CODIS AND BEYOND

5.5.1 CODIS (Combined DNA Index System)

Many different STR regions are available for the type of analysis described in the previous sections. In order to standardize the choices for comparisons, in 1998, the FBI launched a system called CODIS or the Combined DNA Index System. Similar systems are also used around the world by other organizations.

In the CODIS system, the FBI chose a standard set of 13 STR *loci* that are all "four-letter" sequences. In addition, one locus on each of the X and Y chromosomes was also chosen to determine gender, specifically the *amelogenin* gene that codes for tooth enamel. The choice of which of the many STR possibilities to include in the data set was carefully made and arranged such that the STR sequences were as discriminating between people as possible. The locations of these STR sequences on our chromosomes are shown in Figure 5.42. As of 2024, ~17 million

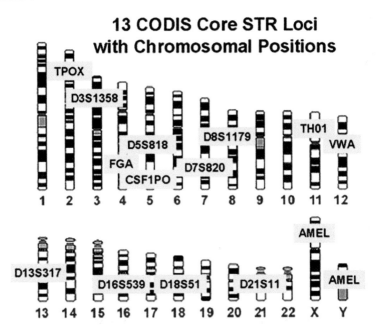

FIGURE 5.42 The chromosomal positions of the 13 STR regions (loci) used by the FBI for the CODIS databank.

Source: FBI/NIST.

offender profiles, 5.4 million arrestee profiles, and 1.3 million forensic DNA CODIS profiles are on record at the FBI, making it one of the largest DNA databanks in the world. CODIS has been enormously successful in aiding investigations with over 500,000 hits and assisting in more than 500,000 investigations.

CODIS contains several databases (called indices) including convicted offender, arrestees, forensic samples collected from crime scenes, missing persons, and their relatives. There is an increasing push to have more and more DNA profiles placed in the CODIS system. For example, military personnel, convicted felons, and many law enforcement officers are currently required by some states to be DNA-profiled. Legislation is also pending in many states to have the DNA profile for anyone arrested to be included in this database. Many states also currently maintain their own DNA databanks that may be used in conjunction with the CODIS system.

In these computer-based DNA database systems, the number of tandem repeats of the chosen DNA STRs are easily converted into sets of numbers. A computer-searchable code listing the specific STR followed by the number of repeats

found at that *locus* is prepared. For example, the code "FGA 21,22" would indicate that someone is heterozygous at the FGA locus with two alleles present: one with 21-repeats and one with 22-repeats. This process is then completed for all 13 STR sites and the amelogenin site on the X and/or Y chromosome to form the complete CODIS profile. New leads in hundreds of thousands of "cold cases," many leading to convictions, have now arisen from the use of these powerful DNA databanks. In addition, DNA databases have provided clear links between cases in which no obvious connection had been made before.

CODIS does not provide any additional information about the sample other than a sample identifier and the coded STR information. As mentioned earlier, concerns have arisen, however, surrounding the ethical, legal, and societal implications of an ever-increasing DNA database. Since DNA dictates our biochemical makeup, DNA information may provide sensitive information about an individual such as susceptibility to disease, behavioral disorders, lineage, and abilities. Additionally, complicating the issue is the proliferation of private DNA databases from ancestral and genealogical companies and

BOX 5.14   ROYAL RUSSIAN FAMILY: CZAR NICHOLAS ROMANOV

In 1917, the reign of the Russian Czars came to an abrupt end when the Bolsheviks dethroned and imprisoned Czar Nicholas II and his family. In July 1918, the family was believed to have been unceremoniously murdered, and their bodies buried in a shallow swamp outside Yekaterinburg.

In 1991, the bodies believed to be those of Nicholas, Alexandra, and three of their children (along with the royal physician and three servants) were found and exhumed. DNA, especially mtDNA, bone samples, and other information, were used in 1998 to identify the remains. Samples were compared with known origin samples, including a sample from Prince Philip of England, maternally related to the Czarina, along with samples from maternal relatives of the Czar. Curiously, the remains of the heir, Alexei, and daughter Anastasia, were determined not to be among the remains. In 1998, the royal remains were buried in St. Petersburg, and the Czar and Czarina were canonized in 2000.

FIGURE 5.43   Czar Nicholas II of Russia and family.

Recently, questions have been raised by Alex Knight and Joanna Mountain of Stanford about the validity of the earlier DNA testing in 1994. Their concerns arise from forensic inconsistencies and recent DNA testing of known relatives of the Romanovs that contradict the earlier DNA analysis.

organizations. When and how samples are stored or destroyed and who has access to the data in these records is an area of significant legal and ethical debate.

5.5.2 Innocence Project

"Innocence Project" was established in 1992 by lawyers Barry Scheck and Peter Neufeld in an attempt to use DNA evidence to exonerate wrongly convicted suspects. The Project handles cases where post-conviction DNA analysis could possibly lead to "conclusive proof of innocence." According to the Innocence Project, over 250 people in 32 states have been exonerated

through DNA testing by 2024, including 21 of these exonerees who had previously been sentenced to death.

5.5.3 Summary

DNA techniques are among the most powerful tools in modern forensic science. Careful analysis of biological samples can both exonerate and connect suspects with crimes. Recent explorations of these techniques have vastly expanded the utility of DNA analysis to include essentially all living organisms, enhanced database searching, and genetic phenotyping, among many others.

BOX 5.15   THE CASE OF THE PALO VERDE TREE

On May 3, 1992, the strangled body of Denise Johnson was found underneath a Palo Verde tree outside Phoenix, Arizona. An eyewitness told police that they had seen a white pickup truck speeding away from the area at about the time of the crime. Near the body, a pager was found that led investigators directly to Mark Bogen. Bogen admitted to picking Denise

FIGURE 5.44 Palo Verde tree (*Cercidium floridum*).

Source: Shutterstock.com.

up as a hitchhiker and that, after an argument, he had kicked her out of the car. He also claimed that she had stolen several of his things, including his wallet and pager.

Police searched Bogen's car and found, among other items, two seedpods from a Palo Verde tree. At the crime scene, several Palo Verde trees were identified, including one that appeared to have been hit by a vehicle. Police contacted researchers at the University of Arizona to see if it was possible to trace the DNA of the seedpods. A DNA profile was run on the seedpods found in the suspect's truck and on samples obtained from the damaged tree found at the crime scene: they matched. This strongly supported Bogen's vehicle being at the crime scene.

The problem was that plant DNA evidence had never been used in court before. In order for this new DNA evidence to be admissible, it had to first be proven to be statistically meaningful. In other words, can individual plants be traced by their DNA? After a study of other Palo Verde trees, it was established that indeed each Palo Verde tree is statistically unique in its DNA profile. Bogen was then convicted of first-degree murder, a verdict upheld by the U.S. Court of Appeals.

5.6 ADVANCES AND DEVELOPMENTS IN DNA, RNA, AND RELATED ANALYSIS

5.6.1 Overview

DNA and RNA remain the most studied molecules in all human history. The pace of new discoveries and the development advanced methodologies continues unabated at an exceptional rate. Today, an enormous amount of research is currently underway in academic, governmental, and corporate laboratories to build upon the enormous potential of these analyses for forensic applications. A few of the many developments that are either currently in use or likely soon to have a significant impact on future criminal investigations are briefly described here.

5.6.2 Microbial Forensics

We all carry around with us enormous amounts of bacteria, mostly of the harmless or even beneficial type. Recent estimates have suggested that the number of bacterial cells in and on us is about equal to the number of human cells that make up our bodies, or about 40×10^{13} cells from both bacterial and human sources. It has now been shown that the types of bacteria growing on us, especially on skin and fingertips, may be used to distinguish one person from another since we each carry personally unique bacterial communities. By analyzing such bacterial DNA, it is possible to identify these bacteria and, in turn, potentially identify the human source of these communities.

But a new and broader field, called *microbial forensics*, has arisen that goes far beyond the analysis of our uniquely personal human biome. Microbial forensics has been defined as work related to a biocrime, bioterrorism, or an inadvertent

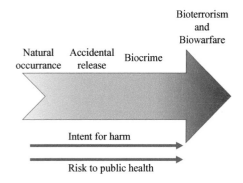

FIGURE 5.45   The types and relative risks from biological agents and the need for microbial forensics.

or natural microorganism release. These biological agents may pose substantial dangers not just to an individual but more broadly to public health, the environment, and even the health and economies of entire nations and the world (Figure 5.45). An example of the global political and economic impact of a biological agent comes from the recent SARS-CoV-2 pandemic of 2020 (Note: viruses are typically not considered to be living organisms, but they are nonetheless often classified as microorganisms for forensic purposes). The intentional use of bioagents may arise from purely criminal reasons or from

bioterrorist acts with religious, political, economic, or environmental goals. But it is believed that the vast majority of the threats or uses of biological agents over the past century have arisen from purely criminal intentions, such as extortion, revenge, intimidation, and murder.

One of the key goals of microbial forensics is to determine the scientific attribution of the microorganism release. *Attribution* in this context has as its goal to find out where and when the agent was prepared (where does it come from), where it was first released and who was responsible. Microbial DNA analysis may be particularly useful in identifying whether a sample was the result of an intentional bioterrorist attack or arose from an inadvertent or natural occurrence with the further key goal of identifying the original source of the pathogen – who carried out the act and where did it originate. Information from microbial forensics may even provide complementary confirmation of bioagent exposure *via* epigenetics (see below). The subdisciplines of biosecurity, public health surveillance, and microbial-based foodborne outbreaks also play important roles in today's society, and all have forensic components. In bioterrorism, the great concern arises especially because a very small amount of material may be able to do a great deal of damage, both lethal or nonlethal, with the net result being similar to the release of highly dangerous chemical weapons. In addition, bioagents may be "engineered" to make them more deadly, infectious, or dangerous in other ways.

BOX 5.16   MICROBIAL FORENSICS IN WARFARE

Unfortunately, microbes have been used for probably millennia as intentional agents of destruction and warfare. The detection, analysis, and attribution of these agents form the core of microbial forensics. Some of the most infamous biocrime and biowarfare uses of microbial agents and/or their toxins in the past have included:

- **1348**: Tartars catapulted plague-infected bodies (*Yersina pestis*) over the wall of Caffa (now in Ukraine): this single act may have led to "Black Death" outbreaks in Europe from 1348 to 1351, estimated to have killed between 75 and 200 million people.
- **1495**: The Spanish mixed the blood of leprosy patients with wine that was then sold to their French enemies.
- **1710**: Russian soldiers catapulted bodies of plague victims into Swedish cities.
- **1763**: British soldiers distributed smallpox-infected (*variola virus*) blankets to Native Americans, resulting in a smallpox outbreak in the Ohio River Valley.
- **1797**: French soldiers flooded the Italian plains around Manuta to spread malaria and weaken the Italian forces.
- **1863**: Dr. Luke P. Blackburn, a Kentucky-born physician and American Confederate agent, distributed yellow fever-infected (*Flavivirus spp.*) clothing to northern cities, Union soldiers, and even clothing aimed toward President Lincoln (the plot failed mostly because a co-conspirator told the plot to U.S. authorities).
- **1914**: Germany shipped anthrax (*Bacillus antracis*) and glanders (*Pseudomonas pseudomallei*) infected horses to the United States of America and elsewhere as part of World War I efforts.
- **1932–1945**: Japanese scientists and soldiers experimented on prisoners of war using biological pathogens, including meningitis (*Neisseria meningitidis*), cholera (*Vibrio cholerae*), Shigella (*Shigella* spp.), and plague (*Yersinia pestis*), with more than 10,000 deaths arising from these infections.
- **1995**: Sarin gas attack in the Tokyo subway system.
- **2001**: "Amerithrax", intentional mailing of anthrax-laden letters after the 9/11 terrorist attacks to several media outlets and U.S. senators, killing 5 people and infecting 17 others.

Forensic scientists, public health care workers, and law enforcement must initially work together in dealing with any pathogenic microbial release. The initial need is to locate the source, identify the pathogen or its toxins, and contain its further spread as much as possible. Rapid response and correct answers are required to be effective in these goals. However, while protecting the public health is the primary concern, microbial forensics has the additional requirement of providing valid and legally defensible evidence for later criminal investigations. It should also be noted that humans are not the only potential target of biocrime and bioterrorism: agricultural targets and water supplies may be targeted in order to make them unusable for food.

The CDC has defined categories to help classify and understand bioterrorism agents, somewhat similar to the "schedules" used in determining the response to illegal drugs. They have defined three categories, ranging from A to C:
Category A:

- Easily disseminated and transmitted from person to person.
- High mortality rates with great potential for major public health impact and disruption.
- Requires special action for public health preparedness.
- Examples include anthrax, botulism, smallpox, tularemia, and viral hemorrhagic fevers (e.g., Ebola, Marburg, Lassa).

Category B:

- Moderately easy to disseminate and transmit.
- Moderate morbidity and low mortality rates.
- Requires specific diagnostic capacity and disease surveillance.
- Examples include brucellosis, salmonella, glanders, ricin, typhus, cholera, viral encephalitis, and others.

Category C:

- Emerging pathogens, engineered for mass dissemination with ready availability, ease of production and dissemination.
- Potential for high morbidity and mortality rates and major health impact.
- Examples include Nipah virus and hantavirus.

Much work, both scientifically and organizationally, needs to be done, but microbial forensics is expected to be an increasingly important field in the future.

5.6.3 New Directions and Opportunities in Forensic DNA and RNA

DNA Transfer and Persistence: One of the big questions in forensic DNA is how a particular DNA sample was transferred to a piece of evidence, and how long it might have been there. In some cases, the presence of DNA on evidence from a particular person is not disputed, but the activity that led to it being found there is in question. In other words, does the DNA sample found correlate with part of a criminal act or was it transferred innocently or accidentally? Scientists are, therefore, working to better understand the processes involved in the transfer, persistence, prevalence, and recovery of DNA from evidence, referred to as *DNA-TPPR*. Knowing better how a person's DNA ended up on a piece of evidence, or why it was missing when it was expected to be found, has become very relevant in criminal investigations. This concern also extends to considerations of how long an identifiable DNA sample can persist on different materials and under varying environmental conditions. Studies are also focused on methods to understand and improve DNA collection and preservation methods in order to maximize the useful laboratory analysis of these materials.

Next Generation Sequencing (NGS) is a new approach that involves a massively parallel sequencing process for DNA, used to rapidly determine the actual order of nucleotides in large portions, even entire strands, of DNA or RNA. This method provides extremely fast sequencing of nucleotides by first breaking the DNA strand into millions of small fragments and then sequencing the many fragments simultaneously (called massively parallel sequencing). Once the fragments have all been sequenced, they can then be reassembled to give the entire sequence of the original intact DNA strand. One large question that needs to be addressed, however, is how information from NGS sequencing will be made compatible with the existing STR databases, such as those found in CODIS.

Artificial Intelligence (AI), the use of computers to aid in information collection and problem-solving by accessing and processing huge amounts of available data, is expected to have an enormous future impact in many aspects of human life. In forensic DNA, AI is expected to aid in identifying forensically useful alleles, understanding fine details of individual DNA profiles, assigning the number of contributors to complex DNA mixtures, and addressing other important problems.

Epigenetics involves changes in the way that genes are controlled and expressed without changing the sequence of the DNA itself. One common way that this may be accomplished involves methylation of the DNA sequence upon exposure to environmental, genetic, or other factors. Methylation involves the attachment of chemical methyl groups ($-CH_3$) to the "outside" of a DNA strand, thereby changing the activity of the methylated portion of the DNA without changing the actual DNA nucleotide sequence (Figure 5.46). By identifying the locations of epigenetic methyl markers found on a DNA strand, we may be able to determine if a person was environmentally exposed to certain chemicals, such as explosives, gunpowder, drugs, or poisons since these exposures would lead to understandable patterns in DNA methylation. Since the methylation occurs at the molecular level, it is very unlikely that the presence of these markers in evidence collected at a crime scene can be altered or purposefully planted.

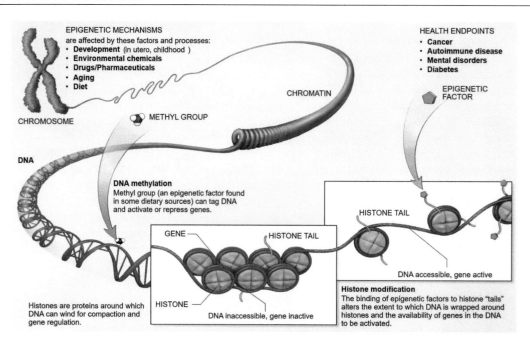

FIGURE 5.46 Epigenetic marking of DNA (methylation) is affected by development in childhood, environmental chemicals, drugs and pharmaceuticals, aging, and diet. DNA methylation (adding methyl groups to the "outside" of a DNA strand) can tag DNA and activate or repress gene expression.

Source: NIH.

There is also an effect often referred to as the epigenetic clock that may be useful in determining the age of a person who contributed a DNA sample. Recent research has shown that these markers from a DNA sample may be accurate in predicting a person's age to within ±3.6 years. Additionally, although identical twins have identical DNA sequences, they would not likely have the same epigenetic profile since they would be expected to have been exposed to different environmental conditions over time, providing a ready way to distinguish identical twins.

Body Fluid Analysis: Sometimes, it is important to establish what type of biological material contributed to the DNA sample. For example, did the sample come from saliva, sweat, vaginal secretions, blood, or others? Recently, it has been shown that the origin of body fluid samples can be uniquely identified using DNA methods with an overall accuracy of 89.9%.

RNA Analysis: The analysis of RNA from a victim in a medicolegal investigation has been proposed to be useful in determining the cause and mechanisms of death in forensic pathology. In addition, it may be possible to determine the age of wounds and injuries on a victim as well as an estimate of the post-mortem interval (PMI) by examining the role of RNA in gene expression and the extent of degradation of different types of RNA.

X Chromosome Analysis: As described previously, the Y chromosome has found use in forensic DNA for a variety of cases. The X chromosome, however, has seen less forensic application. Recently, however, scientists have begun to use STR markers on the X chromosome as complementary to analyzing Y-chromosome markers in cases of incest rape, paternity without a mother's comparison sample, and in complex mixture cases.

Complex DNA Mixtures: One significant challenge that has vexed DNA analysis in the past has been deciphering samples that contain contributions from multiple people. But, using a variety of new approaches, including computer (machine and AI) and sequencing methods, researchers are increasingly able to tease out the DNA contributions from different people mixed together into individual components.

Tracking and Surveillance: Using DNA databases from plants, especially pollen, and bacteria gathered from all over the world, scientists have successfully tracked shipments of contraband and weapons with amazing accuracy. When an object is moved over large distances, it typically becomes coated with the local microscopic fauna and flora, specifically local pollen and bacteria. By analyzing the DNA of these materials and comparing results to extensive pre-established geolocated DNA databases, it can be possible to find the site of origin and/or track the route that an object took during shipment. Thus, illegal drugs and weapons may now be tracked back to their local origins for further investigation *via* DNA.

These are only a few of the creative ways that DNA and RNA analyses are being employed to facilitate criminal investigations. It is certain that this steady development track will continue into the future with exciting new opportunities and applications for forensic science.

5.6.4 Interesting DNA Cases for Further Study

Snowball the Cat: In 1994, Shirley Duguay was found murdered on Prince Edward Island in Canada. The prime suspect was her former husband, Douglas Beamish, who was living nearby in his parent's home. The evidence collected included a leather jacket stained with Shirley's blood and containing 27 strands of white hair: cat hair. The Mounties found a white cat named Snowball that lived in Beamish's parent's home. A DNA study connected hair from Snowball with the hair fibers found on the victim.

Green River Killer: In the early 1980s, the Green River Killer was believed to have murdered as many as 50 women near Seattle, Washington. At the time of the murders, DNA technology was not sufficient to provide information in the case. In 2001, Gary Ridgway was arrested as he was leaving the factory where he worked. DNA evidence had been used to definitively link him to four of the murders. Two years later he pleaded guilty to 48 murders, although estimates place the number of his murders higher.

Kenniwick Man: The remains of an ancient man found in the Pacific Northwest raised a variety of scientific and cultural issues. The remains predated the arrival of European settlers, but DNA testing also showed that he is significantly different from Native American populations. The question revolves around who are his descendants and who should control his remains?

Argentina's Children: During a repressive military regime in Argentina in the 1970s, many people were kidnapped and murdered. After the fall of this regime, stories surfaced of children either born in prison or kidnapped from their parents and then given to childless military families. Several years later, when children started showing up to register for school with "suspicious" documents, the "grandmothers of the Plaza de Mayo" began to ask difficult questions. mtDNA testing was used to trace the families of some of these "missing" children and over 50 have been restored to their biological families.

King Louis XVII: After the death of King Louis XVI and Marie Antoinette in 1793, their young son Louis-Charles de France remained in prison until his reported death in 1795. Recently, royalists have speculated that the "Lost Child King" managed to escape from the Revolution. In 1999, a DNA sample from the presumed heart of Louis XVII was removed, and an mtDNA profile obtained. This profile was then compared with DNA samples from other known members of the royal family, both living and dead, including a sample from a lock of Marie Antoinette's hair (Louis' mother). These analyses confirmed the heart to belong to a person of royal descent.

Additional Cases:

Jefferson/Hemings Paternity
NFL Souvenir Footballs (animal DNA verification)
Jack the Ripper (partial/degraded DNA)
Josef Mengele (DNA confirmation of identity)
JonBenét Ramsey, cleared John Mark Karr (exonerated confession)
Tomb of the Unknowns (Vietnam MIA identified in DC tomb)
World Trade Center (remains identification)
Golden State Killer (2018, Joseph James DeAngelo)
Fawn Cox (2020).

QUESTIONS FOR FURTHER PRACTICE AND MASTERY

5.1 Regions of DNA that do not code for any known protein are called _____.

5.2 The genetic information within our DNA is used to create a(n) molecule in the nucleus which then moves to the ribosome for protein synthesis.

5.3 A permanent alteration or change in the sequence of nucleotides in the DNA of an organism is called a(n) _____.

5.4 In DNA, the base adenine always pairs with while guanine always pairs with _____.

5.5 Transcription is process that occurs within the nucleus and forms a _____ molecule from a template

5.6 DNA with different genetic information at the same locus are called _____.

5.7 The sequence of DNA nucleotides that provides the genetic information corresponding to a single characteristic is a _____.

5.8 In the RFLP method of DNA analysis, fragments of DNA created by the restriction enzyme can be separated according to their size by the technique called.

5.9 The PCR technique is used for _____.

5.10 A forensic scientist was conducting a genetic investigation and identified a satellite (STR sequence) on a chromosome and constructed the primer CTTGCTTGGAAAATTCCGTGGAC. What is the corresponding template DNA sequence?

5.11 What are the limitations in the use of forensic DNA profiling?

5.12 A nucleotide is composed of three units: _____, ___, and a __ unit.

5.13 Given the data in Table 5.2, what is the probability that someone from China would be homozygous for seven repeats of the D13S317 STR fragment _____.

5.14 Why are probability calculations so important in forensic applications of DNA analysis?

5.15 Provide a short definition for each of the following:

(a) STR
(b) RFLP Analysis
(c) Mitochondrial DNA

5.16 The process of copying a portion of nuclear DNA to form a mRNA molecule is referred to as _____.

5.17 How do the VNTR alleles (variable number tandem repeats) in the hypervariable regions of human DNA used for forensic investigations often differ from each other?

5.18 The basic building block in DNA, consisting of a phosphate, a sugar, and a nitrogen base, is called a _____.

5.19 In PCR, describe each of the following steps:

(a) denaturation
(b) annealing
(c) extension
(d) replication
(e) polymerization

5.20 DNA is *a(n)*: (a) protein, (b) starch, (c) nucleic acid, (d) enzyme, (e) sugar.

5.21 Describe the use of capillary electrophoresis in PCR-STR analysis.

5.22 When the Amelogenin locus shows two peaks in the DNA analysis, does the profile come from a male or female?

5.23 What is CODIS?

5.24 How many different nitrogen bases are used in the makeup of a DNA molecule?

5.25 Given the forensic DNA pattern for a bloodstain found at a crime scene, how can a suspect be eliminated from further consideration?

5.26 Describe the pattern of inheritance of mitochondrial DNA.

5.27 Why has STR analysis mostly replaced RFLP DNA typing?

5.28 Write below, side by side, a BRIEF description comparing the differences between nuclear DNA typing and mitochondrial DNA typing (compare the differences between these two techniques).

NUCLEAR DNA TYPING	MITOCHONDRIAL DNA TYPING

5.29 What are the three components of a nucleotide?

5.30 What are the four nitrogen bases in DNA?

5.31 What are the base pairings for the hydrogen bonds that join the two complementary DNA strands?

5.32 What is a gene?

5.33 About what percent of human DNA "codes" for known proteins?

5.34 What is VNTR? What is STR?

5.35 Why aren't the coding regions of DNA used to forensically identify an individual?

5.36 What is meant by polymorphism?

5.37 What are the two primary methods of DNA typing?

5.38 List the advantages and disadvantages of RFLP and PCR testing methods.

5.39 What does a restriction enzyme do?

5.40 How do gel electrophoresis and capillary electrophoresis differ?

5.41 What is amplification in the PCR process?

5.42. What is epigenetics?

5.43 How does the "touch" (or "contact") DNA process differ from other DNA methods?

5.44 How is mitochondrial DNA different from nuclear DNA?

5.45 When would mtDNA analysis be a better choice than nuclear DNA analysis?

5.46 In what types of cases would Y-chromosome typing be useful? When would X chromosome typing be useful?

EXTENSIVE QUESTIONS

5.47 Explain what "coding" and "non-coding" means with respect to the sequencing of genes.

5.48 Explain the translation and transcription processes.

5.49 Explain how restrictions enzymes work.

5.50 Explain the steps in the PCR process.

5.51 Explain how STR repeat patterns in a sample can be used to determine the probability that the sample would match another sample in the population.

5.52 Compare the RFLP and STR DNA typing with respect to sequence size, reliability, and speed.

GLOSSARY OF TERMS

allele: one of several possible variants of the genetic code at a specific location (locus) along the DNA molecule.

annealing: the pairing of nucleotides in complementary DNA strands together by forming hydrogen bonds in the PCR process.

base pairing: when two nitrogen bases in complementary strands connect to form a hydrogen bond, holding the two DNA strands together. In DNA, adenine (A) pairs only with thymine (T) and guanine (G) pairs only with cytosine (C).

capillary electrophoresis: a technique separating DNA fragments by their electrophoretic mobility using an applied voltage. This essentially separates the fragments by size (length).

chromosome: the strand of DNA and its associated proteins found in the nucleus of a cell that carries genetic information.

CODIS (Combined DNA Identification System): developed by the FBI to store DNA information in a searchable computer database.

complementary DNA: a strand of DNA in which the sequence of bases matches those of another strand of DNA according to pairing rules. Thus, if the original strand contains an "A" nucleotide at a particular location, the complementary strand would have a "T" nucleotide at the equivalent location. Similarly, C and G nucleotides occupy equivalent locations on complementary DNA strands.

denaturation: the process of separating the two strands of double helical DNA into individual single strands.

DNA (deoxyribonucleic acid): the basic genetic molecule of living organisms composed of repeating nucleotides, with each nucleotide contains a phosphate, a deoxyribose sugar, and a nitrogen base.

enzyme: a protein that catalyzes a chemical reaction by affecting the rate of a chemical reaction without being consumed by the reaction.

extension: completing a complementary DNA strand from a template strand in the PCR process.

gel electrophoresis: the process of separating DNA fragments based upon their charge and size. Charged DNA fragments are placed in a gel bed and moved through the medium by applying an electric current. Shorter fragments move fastest and farthest through the gel, while longer fragments move the least.

gene: a region of a DNA strand that provides coding information for the synthesis of proteins.

hybridization: the process of joining together complementary strands of DNA through base pairing.

hypervariable DNA (also called "junk", "non-coding" or "nonsense" DNA): a region of DNA that shows a great degree of variability in a population and does not code for any known protein but may have a role as molecular switches in regulating genes.

locus (plural "loci"): a specific position on the DNA strand.

microbial forensics: related to a biocrime, bioterrorism, or an inadvertent or natural microorganism release.

mitochondrial DNA (mtDNA): a small ring of DNA that resides outside the nucleus in the cellular mitochondria, coding for proteins needed for respiration. mtDNA is only inherited from mothers and passed to all offspring.

mutation: an inheritable change in the base sequence of DNA.

nucleotide: the basic building block of DNA, consisting of a phosphate, a deoxyribose sugar, and a nitrogen base.

PCR (polymerase chain reaction): a laboratory method for the rapid replication of specific regions of DNA.

population: a specific group of people defined by geography, race, of other defining features.

restriction enzyme: a protein that locates a specific DNA sequence and cuts the DNA strand at that location.

RFLP: restriction fragment length polymorphism.

RNA (ribonucleic acid): similar to DNA and composed of repeating nucleotides (except RNA uses uracil instead of DNA's thymine). Important in transcription and translation processes and as the genetic code in viruses.

STR (short tandem repeat): a region of DNA in which a small sequence of nucleotides (2 to 6 nucleotides) is repeated multiple times in a row.

VNTR (variable number tandem repeat): a region of DNA in which a larger sequence of nucleotides (up to fifty nucleotides) is repeated multiple times consecutively.

X chromosome: one of two sex chromosomes; females have two X chromosomes and males have an X and a Y chromosome.

Y chromosome: the chromosome inherited only through the father and passed along only to male offspring.

BIBLIOGRAPHY

Bruce Budowle, Tamyra Moretti, Jenifer Smith, and Joseph DiZinno, *DNA Typing Protocols: Molecular Biology and Forensic Analysis*, Eaton Publishing, 2000.

National Research Council. *Strengthening Forensic Science in the United States: A Path Forward.* Washington, DC: The National Academies Press, 2009 [https://doi.org/10.17226/12589].

John Butler, *Forensic DNA Typing: Biology and Technology behind STR Markers*, Academic Press, 2001.

John M. Butler, Yin Shen, and Bruce R. McCord, "The development of reduced size STR amplicons as tools for analysis of degraded DNA", *Journal of Forensic Sciences*, 48, 1054, 2003.

S. Debus-Sherrill and M.B. Field, "Familial DNA searching – An emerging forensic investigative tool", *Science & Justice*, 59(1), 20–28, 2019. https://doi.org/10.1016/j.scijus.2018.07.006.

Itiel Dror and Greg Hampikian, "Subjectivity and bias in forensic DNA mixture interpretation", *Science & Justice*, 51(4), 204–208, 2011.

Shiyu Luo, C. Alexander Valencia, Jinglan Zhang, Ni-Chung Lee, Jesse Slone, Baoheng Gui, Xinjian Wang, Zhuo Li, Sarah Dell, Jenice Brown, Stella Maris Chen, Yin-Hsiu Chien, Wuh-Liang Hwu, Pi-Chuan Fan, Lee-Jun Wong, Paldeep S. Atwal, and Taosheng Huang, "Biparental inheritance of mitochondrial DNA in humans", *Proceedings of the National Academy of Sciences*, 115(51), 13039–13044, 2018. https://doi.org/10.1073/pnas.1810946115.

Helena Machado and Rafaela Granja, "Emerging DNA technologies and stigmatization", *Forensic Genetics in the Governance of Crime*, Palgrave Pivot, 2020 [ISBN 978-981-15-2428-8].

David A. Micklos and Greg A. Freyer, *DNA Science: A First Course*, Cold Spring Harbor Laboratory Press, 2003.

Dragan Primorac and Moses S. Schanfield, *Forensic DNA Application: An Interdisciplinary Perspective* (2nd Ed.), CRC Press/Taylor & Francis Group, 2023.

Norah Rudin and Keith Inman. *An Introduction to Forensic DNA Analysis*, CRC Press, 2002.

Rob Sender, Shai Fuchs, and Ron Milo, "Revised estimates for the number of human and bacteria cells in the body", *PLoS Biology*, 14, 2016. https://doi.org/10.1371/journal.pbio.1002533.

John M. Butler, *Genetics and Genomics of Core Short Tandem Repeat Loci Used in Human Identity Testing*, J Forensic Sci, Vol. 51, No. 2, Mar. 2006 [doi:10.1111/j.1556-4029.2006.00046.x]

Forensic Serology

6

6.1 INTRODUCTION TO FORENSICS SCIENCE

Forensic Serology, Blood, and Immunoassay: The Fluids of Life

Yet who would have thought the old man to have had so much blood in him?

([Lady Macbeth] William Shakespeare, 1564–1616)

LEARNING GOALS AND OBJECTIVES

The study of body fluids, especially blood, both regarding its biochemical composition and its physical fluid properties, can yield information of importance to forensic investigations. After completing this chapter, you should be able to:

- Understand what is meant by the term serology.
- Describe how blood functions in our bodies and recognize its various components.
- Explain what is meant by presumptive and confirmatory tests.
- Summarize how blood can be detected and identified as human blood.
- Discuss how different immunoassays work.
- Identify the various blood types and illustrate what this means biochemically.
- Explain what is meant by hereditary patterns of blood types.
- Discuss what is meant by blood pattern analysis.
- Illustrate how events can be understood through blood pattern analysis.
- Identify how other body fluids can be used in forensic science.

6.1.1 Introduction

Blood is our most precious life-giving fluid. It flows continuously in each person through a closed-loop of nearly 60,000 miles of arteries, veins, and capillaries, efficiently providing our nearly 40 trillion cells with vital nourishment while removing unwanted byproducts (Figure 6.1). It bathes all our tissues in a constant and complex supply of the materials necessary to deliver sustenance, provide protection, and even lend some physical structure to our bodies. These components must deliver oxygen, recognize, and fight off outside invasion, remove chemical byproducts, transport cellular materials, and yet remain fluid (Figure 6.2). Blood must squeeze through the tiniest of capillaries, where individual red blood cells must twist and distort to even go through in single file, and without requiring so much fluid backpressure as to damage other sensitive tissues and vessels. When blood flow is interrupted for even a very brief time, our cells quickly wither and die. When a breach in our blood delivery system occurs, such as through injury or illness, components within the blood must react very quickly as first responders to try to stop blood and pressure loss and to effectively repair the breach. In short, blood truly is a miraculous substance, wonderfully suited to the many tasks it is called upon to perform.

But blood is also often a very visible part of criminal events. A hundred years ago, the legal world was desperately seeking some unique marker that could unambiguously tie a particular individual to a biological sample collected at a crime scene. The best technique at the time for doing this,

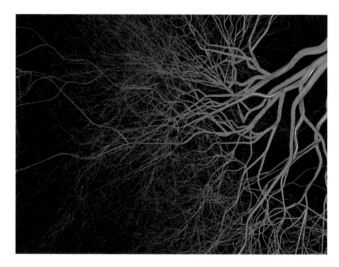

FIGURE 6.1 About 60,000 miles of blood vessels, including arteries, veins, and capillaries, carry blood throughout the body to infiltrate our tissues, thereby supplying them with necessary nutrients, exchanging gases and performing a host of vital functions.

Source: Shutterstock.com.

DOI: 10.4324/9781003183709-8

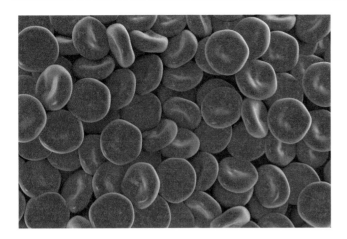

FIGURE 6.2 Red blood cells, called erythrocytes, are the disc-shaped cells that primarily transport gases throughout the body.

Source: Shutterstock.com.

fingerprinting, had both its successes and serious limitations (Chapter 7). Many times, interpretable fingerprints were not found at the crime scene, while biochemical tissues and fluids were abundantly available. After a landmark discovery by Karl Landsteiner in 1901, however, attention turned to the analysis of blood to hopefully provide such vital connections between evidence and suspects. Through careful scientific investigation, blood analysis quickly reached an impressive level of detail that was able to provide the needed links between forensic samples, often with millions-to-one odds of random matches. This analysis remained the gold standard for forensic identification until DNA typing became the method of choice in the late 1980s. Today, blood analysis still provides an enormous amount of unique information to a forensic investigation, shedding light on both questions of "who" and "how."

Since Landsteiner's discoveries, advances in understanding biological fluids have coupled with the development of new biochemical techniques to produce an arsenal of compelling forensic probes. Since blood is such an integral part of our immune system, immunological methods in blood analysis have become centrally important. Simple but vital questions such as "is this blood," "is this blood human," and "what biochemical markers may be found in the blood" can now be very quickly answered, even at the crime scene itself. More sophisticated immunological studies of a forensic sample in the laboratory can further provide a dazzling amount of information from these easily collected specimens.

Blood analysis remains one of the most powerful tools for understanding samples of forensic interest. Blood assays can often be performed in a matter of minutes using relatively inexpensive instruments and techniques. These analyses may serve as a first screen for whether or not to employ the more instrument-intensive DNA typing or, in some cases, to provide independent laboratory corroboration for the conclusions derived from the DNA data.

Equally important, however, is the biochemical analysis of blood and the things that it carries, since this may provide information for forensic medical and toxicological investigations not obtainable in any other fashion. Understanding some key features about blood chemistry is, therefore, important not just for personal identification and crime scene analysis but also in determinations such as cause of death, post-mortem interval, the presence of drugs and alcohol, and many others. The concepts of blood chemistry discussed in this chapter will, therefore, be fundamental in considering several other chapters including forensic medicine (Chapter 8), forensic toxicology (Chapter 13), and forensic psychology (Chapter 19).

Blood and other biological fluids are frequently found at crime scenes in relatively large amounts, especially in crimes of violence. Because of their seriousness, these are also usually the crimes for which we *must* have the best and most detailed information.

Besides information about the chemical composition of a blood sample, the patterns and locations of fluid samples can provide investigators with a great deal of information about how a crime might have been committed and the sequence of events that occurred.

Serology is broadly defined as the study of serums, or body fluids and liquids (the plural for serum can be either serums or sera). While there are many different types of serums in the human body that we will touch upon in this chapter, we will focus most of our attention here on the forensic application of blood analysis: both biochemical and physical.

In this chapter, we will begin by examining the basic features of blood and body serums and how such detailed information can be used in forensic investigations. We will also explore how the physical patterns of blood and other biological fluids at a crime scene can provide information about the sequence of events leading to the observed crime scene.

BOX 6.1   CASE HISTORY: LUDWIG TESSNOW

In early July of 1901, two young brothers, aged 6 and 8, did not return home after a day of playing together on Rugen Island in northern Germany. The next day, a full-scale search was mounted when their dismembered bodies were found spread over a wide area of the island. A local carpenter remembered seeing the boys talking with another local resident, Ludwig Tessnow, early on the day that they disappeared. Investigators went to Tessnow's home where they found his freshly laundered work clothes with unusual stains that could have been bloodstains. Tessnow, however, quickly explained that these were wood dye stains, not unusual for a carpenter of the time. In addition, a local farmer identified Tessnow from a line-up as the man who was seen dismembering seven of his sheep and tossing their legs around a field. When considering the case, an alert local magistrate remembered that, in another case, three years earlier and 300 miles to the east, Tessnow had also been a prime suspect in a dismembering and had used the same reasons to explain similar stains found on his clothing then. In that earlier case, two young girls of Osnabruck, Germany had been found dismembered in a similar fashion to the two Rugen boys. The problem, however, was that there was no other evidence connecting Tessnow with any of the crimes, and it was impossible at the time to determine if the stains on his clothing came from wood dye, sheep's blood, or human blood.

The answer to this dilemma came from Prof. Paul Uhlenhuth at the nearby University of Greifswald. Dr. Uhlenhuth had just developed a new test that could be used to differentiate human blood from other stains, even from other types of animal blood. In his work, he had injected hen's blood into rabbits and then isolated the serum (liquid portion) from the rabbit's blood. When this same rabbit serum later came in contact with hen's blood, a reaction occurred, causing a solid precipitate to immediately form. When the blood from other animals was placed in the rabbit serum, however, no reaction was found. He further demonstrated that he could use similarly prepared animal serums to distinguish uniquely the blood of one animal from all other species of animals, including humans. Thus, when human blood was injected into another animal and the serum from that animal was isolated, now called human anti-serum, it reacted *only* with human blood and none other to form a solid.

In the Tessnow case, Prof. Uhlenhuth examined the overalls taken from Tessnow and determined, using his human anti-serum, that besides the wood dye, the clothing conclusively contained many traces of both human and sheep's blood. Tessnow's explanation immediately fell apart, and he was quickly convicted at trial and executed in 1904 for his crimes.

This case demonstrated the first use of an immunological test to determine the presence of human blood in a forensic sample. However, the significance of this case goes well beyond the Tessnow case: it served to strengthen the importance of forensic science in the courtroom and to place science as a powerful ally in crime detection and legal prosecution.

6.2 BLOOD AND IMMUNOASSAY

6.2.1 Background and History of Blood Analysis in Crime Detection

Blood consists of an amazing collection of cellular, biochemical, inorganic, and liquid components that perform an enormous array of life-sustaining functions. It is the fragile link that nourishes, supports, and defends our cells. It is also all too often shed in the commission of crimes and, therefore, leaves a trail of valuable evidence to be considered.

For centuries, investigators have longed for the ability to learn the secrets hidden in the blood found at crime scenes. Even simple questions of whether or not a stain was really blood remained elusive until the 20th century. Simple observations such as the color, smell, and texture of a suspected bloodstain are unreliable indicators. Dried blood, for example, may appear as red, brown, or even greenish-yellow depending on the sample's age and history. The difficult problems of blood analysis even surfaced in Arthur Conan Doyle's 1887 book "A Study in Scarlet" when Sherlock Holmes, the quintessential detective, complains about the inadequacies of then-existing blood tests and demonstrates his own "new" procedure.

By the late 1800s, a series of chemical tests had been developed that could provide an indication of whether blood was present. Most relied upon an observable color change when a standard reagent came into contact with a suspected blood sample. One of the first of these was the Guaiacum test, in which a plant extract turned blue when brought into contact with blood.

A modification of this test is still employed diagnostically today as a colon cancer screen to determine if invisible, minute quantities of blood (called "occult blood") are present in fecal materials. The forensic problem with this test is that it gives many false positives and cannot distinguish human from animal blood. Another test, also still in use, is called the Kastle-Meyer test. This method uses a chemical called phenolphthalein that, when mixed with hydrogen peroxide and blood, changes in color from colorless to pink. Like the Guaiacum test, the Kastle-Meyer test cannot discriminate between human blood and animal blood and gives false positives from potatoes, horseradishes, and a number of other natural materials. Other color-change tests have been developed, but all suffer from similar problems. Criminals could simply claim that the positive test arose from the fact that they had come into contact with animal blood, raw meat, or even that they had eaten horseradish. The problem was that these claims could not be easily disproven.

Around the turn of the 19th century, a series of discoveries began to change the face of blood analysis. In 1879, Louis Pasteur was working on understanding cholera in chickens. He noticed that when he accidentally injected a deteriorated cholera sample into some chickens, they became sick but ultimately recovered fully from this usually fatal disease. When he later tried to reuse these recovered chickens in his work, he found that he could not infect them with even the strongest strains of cholera. These chickens had developed an immunity to cholera. He then extended his work in a similar fashion to include animal immunizations for anthrax and rabies. Pasteur's work, in which a weakened or "dead" strain of a disease is first injected to cause immunity to the full-strength contagion, actually built upon the much earlier work of Edward Jenner who, in 1796, used cowpox injections in people to give them immunity from the terrible smallpox disease (Figure 6.3).

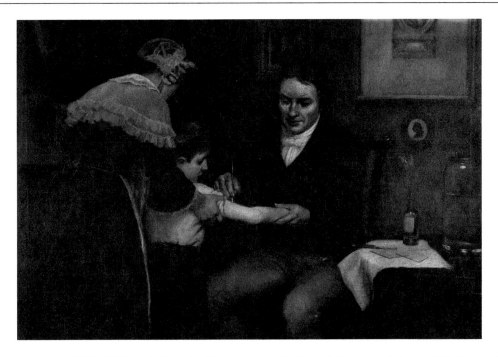

FIGURE 6.3 Edward Jenner (1749–1823), a British physician, is shown in the painting inoculating a child. Jenner first developed a vaccine for the often-fatal smallpox infection. He investigated common folk stories about how people who had survived the milder cowpox infection became immune to smallpox. In 1796, he inoculated a healthy child with pus from a cowpox sore on a dairymaid's finger. Weeks later, he exposed the child to the smallpox contagion (definitely not something practiced today in medical research), but the child did not develop the disease. This immunization process was named vaccination after the name of the cowpox virus (*variola vaccinia*). Smallpox was declared extinct outside of laboratories in 1980 due to extensive vaccine work.

Jenner coined the word vaccination for the process from the Latin name for the cowpox virus (*variola vaccinia*). Later, in 1892, Emil von Behring found that animals exposed to a toxin of diphtheria developed a resistance to the disease in the *blood*. A huge advance for blood forensic analysis finally came in 1900 when the Uhlenhuth serum-based test, first demonstrated in the Tessnow case (see Box 6.1), was found to be specific for a particular type of blood – human blood. This new "precipitin test" could readily distinguish human blood from all others. In fact, specific tests were later developed to distinguish between blood samples for many different species of animals based on the precipitin test.

But now that it was possible, using the precipitin test, to establish that a sample truly contained human blood, the next important question became "whose blood?" Was it even possible to say with any certainty that a particular blood sample originated from a given person?

The roots to answering this question lie in medieval times. For centuries, people had sought for ways to quickly replenish the blood supply of people who had lost significant quantities of blood through accidents, injuries, or diseases. The main idea was to take blood from a healthy person or animal and give it to the injured person to restore some of the lost blood until their body could replenish the supply itself (Figure 6.4). While this was occasionally successful, it more often resulted in the death of the recipient. Sparked by these failures, human blood transfusions were banned by the early 1700s across much of

(a)   (b)

Clysmatica nova 1667   Attempted early blood transfusion from lamb to man

FIGURE 6.4 Historical Blood Transfusions. (a) 17th-century artwork of a patient during a blood transfusion, taken from the 1667 book by Johann S. Elsholtz (*Clysmatica nova*), and (b) 17th-century artwork showing Richard Lower (1631–1691) transfusing blood into a man's arm from a lamb. The tubes used to transfer the blood are shown at the top left. These transfusions were often fatal for the patients due to blood incompatibilities, leading to coagulation and cell rupture. In 1901, Karl Landsteiner discovered the ABO blood groups. After the discovery of other blood groupings (e.g., M, N, and P groups) in the 1920s, and the Rhesus factor in the 1930s, transfusions became generally safe to practice.

Europe. Experiments with animals, however, showed that it was sometimes possible to transfer blood from one animal to another without significant problems. The important question then became why this process was not similarly successful in human patients?

The first answers to why fatalities happened in humans came in 1875 from the work of Leonard Landois when he observed that when blood from two different humans was mixed, the cells often clumped together and sometimes were even ripped into pieces. This "clumping" process resulted in the formation of very many blood clots throughout the body, often leading to kidney damage, shock, cardiac arrest, and, ultimately, to death. In 1901, Karl Landsteiner provided the first landmark understanding of why this happens and, most importantly, how to avoid it from happening during transfusions. He discovered what we know today as the ABO system of blood typing. He found that people had a variety of possible proteins associated with their red blood cells. His work allowed the determination of the incompatibility of mixtures of human blood before a transfusion took place, saving countless lives and setting the stage for the forensic individualization of blood samples.

In the 1920s, researchers found that blood type can often be determined from other body fluids besides blood, meaning that an actual blood sample was not required to determine blood type. In 1949, it was learned that the gender of an individual could also often be determined from the presence of a characteristic structure (Barr body) within white blood cells. Since then, we have learned how to glean increasingly *individualized* information from blood, rather than just class evidence.

But can additional, forensically valuable, information be determined from blood – such as a physical record of how a violent crime took place? References as far back as the Bible and even before describe the importance of blood in understanding unobserved but violent events (Gen. 4:10: "Your brother's blood cries out to me from the ground"). In recent years, the science of blood dynamics and blood pattern analysis has developed into an integral part of investigations involving blood evidence.

Thus, blood can provide us with a wealth of forensic insight – victims and their assailants can speak clearly to investigators through the blood record. Blood evidence can tell us if the sample is human or animal, it can lead us to the individual whose blood it is, it can tell us about diseases in the blood donor, it can provide a trace of lineages, and it can even tell us about the events involved in the distribution of blood around a crime scene.

6.2.2 General Definitions

The field of blood and bloodstain pattern analysis encompasses several well-established areas including serology, immunology, pathology, and fluid dynamics. Each has information to contribute that completes a picture of the people and events that led to the observed scene.

Serology is the area of science that deals specifically with the study of serums (body fluids), such as blood, saliva, urine, semen, blisters, sweat, and others. However, it often focuses on blood serum since that is the most abundant serum in the body. Serology also deals with antibody-antigen reactions within the blood, and clinically it may involve the diagnostic identification of antibodies found in body fluids.

Immunology is the broad branch of science that deals with aspects of the immune system. This huge field is broken into several subfields including clinical immunology, diagnostic immunology, immunotherapy, evolutionary immunology, and others. In diagnostic immunology, the unique selectivity of the interactions between antibodies and antigens has led to the development of an array of detection methods for a variety of substances that are of interest to forensic investigators. For example, immunoassay tests for blood types, microbes, drugs, toxins, and diseases have revolutionized the detail of forensic information available. These tests are often fast, inexpensive, highly selective (with few false positives and negatives), and extremely sensitive for the target component.

Fluid dynamics, located at the intersection of physics and engineering, deals primarily with the behavior of liquids and gases in motion. In blood analysis, it focuses on how blood flows and may involve calculations of density, velocity, surface tension and viscosity. The field may also consider questions such as how blood flows *within* the body and the mechanisms of how it can be spread around a crime scene.

Blood pattern analysis considers bloodstains found at a scene and attempts to provide an understanding of how they were formed. It brings together aspects of chemistry, physics, fluid dynamics, and other disciplines to help provide this information. Questions such as the speed of the weapon causing the injury, the relative location of the victim and assailant during the attack, the order of attacks, and the physical characteristics of the weapon used in the attack are among the answers sought from this type of analysis.

In order to understand more fully how blood analysis can provide such information to investigators, a deeper understanding of the nature and properties of blood itself is first required.

6.2.3 Blood Chemistry

Blood is composed of many different components, each with a function to perform. In this section, we will describe the most important features of these components and discuss how they function in living systems. For forensic purposes, red blood cells and blood plasma, described below, are probably the most important types of evidence. From these two components, a complete blood typing profile can be made.

6.2.3.1 Liquid Components of Blood

Blood is medically classified as a *circulating tissue* in the body that comprises about 7% of our total weight, or about 4–6 L

FIGURE 6.5   Three different blood products: the unit on the left shows whole blood containing red blood cells, white blood cells, and platelets suspended in a liquid plasma, the unit in the center contains a concentrated solution of platelets, used to aid in blood clotting, and the unit on the right contains blood plasma.

Source: Images courtesy Shutterstock.com.

(four to six quarts). Maintaining a normal blood volume is critical for maintaining life functions. The loss of only about 10% of our blood volume causes an increase in blood pressure and other symptoms. Loss of 25–30% of the effective blood volume, however, leads to a state of shock with a dangerous drop in blood pressure and irregular heartbeats. If prolonged or followed by further blood volume loss, coma and death usually occurs.

Blood consists of a complex mixture of cellular, biochemical, and inorganic components, all in a water-based solution. The liquid portion of blood comprises about 55% of its volume and is known as *plasma*. If the blood is first allowed to clot, however, followed by removal of the solids by centrifugation (rapid spinning of the sample), a slightly yellow solution known as blood *serum* is obtained. The main difference between plasma and serum is that the serum contains none of the clotting factors found in plasma (principally fibrinogen and platelets). These factors are effectively removed when the blood clots and the liquid portion is separated from the clotted solids. The three types of blood solutions often used medically, including plasma, are shown in Figure 6.5.

The blood plasma rapidly carries nutrients, such as glucose, amino acids (protein building blocks), lipids, salts, and fatty acids to all the cells in the body at up to ~12 ft/s (~3.6 m/s). It consists of about 92% water, 8% blood proteins, and very small amounts of other compounds. Also contained within the plasma are important "messenger" compounds, such as hormones, that provide regulatory and signaling information for the body. The blood also serves to very effectively regulate body temperature, removing excess heat from overheated areas and providing more warmth to cold regions. For example, after you've been outside on a cold day, your body sends an increased blood supply to the exposed tissues, seen as a blush, to help restore proper temperature. Our blood is also slightly basic (alkaline), which helps our bodies maintain a proper acid-base (pH) balance. Blood carries immunoglobulins (antibodies) and blood-clotting factors (fibrinogen) to sites where they're needed to ward off infection and repair damaged tissues.

Whole blood has about the same density as water (1.06 g/mL) but about three times the viscosity (resistance to flow), meaning that the internal friction of blood is significantly higher than water. Generally, as more cells are found in the blood,

the greater the internal friction. The result of this is that blood is more resistant to flow than water but is still a relatively free-flowing liquid (e.g., olive oil has about 20 times the viscosity of blood). The forensic implications of this will become apparent when we consider bloodstain pattern analysis.

Significant problems arise when the blood supply is interrupted to our tissues, even for a very brief time. This rapidly results in a shortage of the oxygen necessary for respiration (cellular energy production) and a buildup of toxic waste products (mainly carbonic acid, CO_2, and lactic acid). You might experience rapid lactic acid buildup in a limited way as a burning sensation when vigorously exercising – at these times our bodies cannot deliver enough oxygen to its tissues for sufficient respiration to occur so it uses another mechanism to produce energy that ultimately generates lactic acid. When the blood supply is cut off to a tissue or organ, it is medically referred to as *ischemia* and, unless rapidly corrected, usually results in tissue damage and cellular death.

6.2.3.2 Cellular Components of Blood

There are three primary types of cells found in whole blood: red blood cells (erythrocytes), white blood cells (leucocytes of various types), and platelets (thrombocytes). Drawings of these three cell types are shown in Figure 6.6.

Red blood cells (RBCs) account for about 96% of the cellular portion of blood and appear as flexible, disc-shaped cells that are concave on both sides. Their primary function is to carry oxygen from the lungs to the cells and return waste carbon dioxide from the cells back to the lungs. The red color comes from the main chemical component of RBCs, the oxygen-carrying protein-iron complex called hemoglobin, which accounts for about 90% of the dry weight of a mature RBC. The unusual biconcave disc shape of RBCs arises because this is the most efficient shape for gas exchange between the cell's interior, where the hemoglobin is located, and its environment. When fully oxygenated, blood is bright red (absorbs mostly blue light), but when deoxygenated and loaded with carbon dioxide, it appears as a darker red color. A common misconception is that deoxygenated (venous) blood is actually blue. This is, however, an "illusion" based on the fact that when white light,

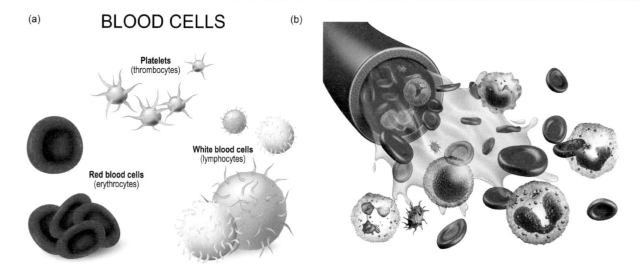

FIGURE 6.6   Human blood cells: (a) a drawing illustrating the different types of blood cells, and (b) a drawing showing the various types of arterial blood cells in plasma. Red blood cells are disc-shaped and contain hemoglobin, a chemical that combines reversibly with oxygen, allowing them to transport oxygen from the lungs to the tissues. Platelets are produced in the bone marrow and are involved in the process of blood clotting. White blood cells are involved in the human immune system response.

Source: Image Sources courtesy Shutterstock.com.

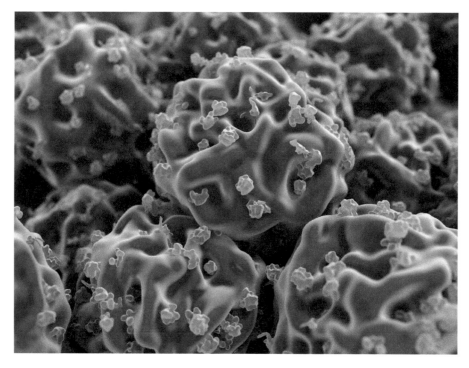

FIGURE 6.7   Scanning electron micrograph (SEM) showing fetal blood stem cells. Stem cells are *pluripotent*, meaning that they are able to differentiate into any type of blood cell through a process called hemopoiesis.

Source: Shutterstock.com.

containing all visible wavelengths, shines on our skin, the longer wavelength red light can easily travel through the skin to be absorbed by the hemoglobin, while the shorter wavelength blue light is mostly reflected to our eyes by the skin.

The proportion of blood made up of RBCs is called the *hematocrit*, which usually ranges between 40% and 50% in a healthy adult male and between 35% and 45% for a female. Typically, there are about 200–400 million RBCs in every drop of our blood.

RBCs are formed, as are most of the cellular components of blood, in the bone marrow from stem cells at a rate of about 2 million new cells per second (Figure 6.7). A unique feature of RBCs is that, as they mature, they expel their nuclei and all their organelles, including their mitochondria. This renders RBCs useless for forensic DNA profiling. As RBCs have no nucleus or organelles, they cannot repair themselves and, therefore, typically last for only about 120 days on average before they die and are removed from the system by the spleen or liver. Other waste products in the blood are also removed primarily by the liver and kidneys.

RBCs function to transport oxygen and carbon dioxide in the body primarily by the red protein, hemoglobin (Figure 6.8). Each blood cell contains about 270 million hemoglobin molecules, each molecule equipped with four iron-based heme groups – the center of oxygen and carbon dioxide transport. When the blood is in the high-oxygen environment of the lungs, the heme groups in the RBCs reversibly pick up oxygen molecules to become oxyhemoglobin. The oxygen-rich RBCs then travel throughout the body *via* the arteries, releasing oxygen to our cells in the oxygen-poor environment of our tissues. The release of oxygen is actually aided by the presence of carbon dioxide in the cells (a bi-product of respiration) through a complex series of chemical reactions. In return, the oxygen-poor

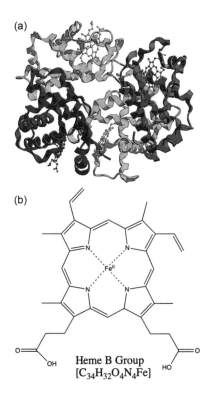

FIGURE 6.8 Hemoglobin: (a) a model of the hemoglobin molecule that transports oxygen around the body within red blood cells, and (b) the heme subgroup in hemoglobin. The hemoglobin molecule has four heme subgroups surrounded by four globular protein chains and coils (each protein subunit, containing one heme unit, is shown in a different color in the picture). Each protein subunit is wrapped around a heme group, protecting it from being destroyed by the oxygen it is intended to transport and allowing it to function properly. The iron atom of each heme group reversibly binds to oxygen and carbon dioxide in the blood to transport these gases throughout the body.

Source: (a) Shutterstock.com.

RBCs pick up the waste carbon dioxide molecules and travel *via* our veins back to the oxygen-rich lungs where they release the carbon dioxide before beginning the process all over again.

The capacity of RBCs to transport O_2/CO_2 can be dramatically affected by disease or the presence of other chemicals in our bodies. In an example all too common in forensic investigations, a common gas in automotive exhaust, carbon monoxide (CO), also binds very easily to the heme groups of the RBCs, in fact, to the exclusion of oxygen. Carbon monoxide readily displaces oxygen from hemoglobin and forms carboxyhemoglobin, a molecule that is 140 times more stable than oxyhemoglobin, causing it to bind very strongly and to be released only very slowly. As a result, breathing only 0.1% CO in air for four hours converts 60% of our hemoglobin into carboxyhemoglobin! This means that 60% of our hemoglobin is essentially unavailable for oxygen transport, potentially leading to asphyxiation. Luckily, CO binding is reversible, although slowly, and if the patient can be removed from the CO source in time into an oxygen-rich atmosphere, they often can recover fully.

White blood cells, or leukocytes (shown in Figure 6.9), are actually a large and diverse group of cell types that differ from RBCs primarily in that they have nuclei and organelles and perform different functions in our bodies. They are typically round to irregularly shaped cells, accounting for about 3% of the total number of blood cells. Their primary responsibility is to fight off disease and infection and to effect cellular repair. A single drop of whole blood typically contains between 10,000 and 25,000 white blood cells. The shape of these cells can radically change, however, in response to activation by chemicals or invaders in the blood. These cells are found in a number of places besides in the blood, including in the lymph system, spleen, and liver.

White blood cells are formed in the bone marrow at the rate of about 100,000 new cells per second. Recent studies have suggested that the skin may also play an important role

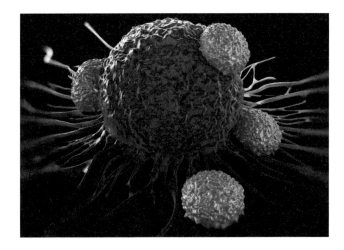

FIGURE 6.9 Composite micrograph of T-cells attacking a cancer cell. T-cells are a type of white blood cell (lymphocyte) that develop from stem cells and form a key part of the immune system. Lymphocytes, mainly T-cells and B-cells, recognize foreign antigens and destroy attacking viruses and bacteria.

Source: Shutterstock.com.

in white blood cell formation. Occasionally, it may be possible to determine how soon after an injury an organism died by determining the extent of leukocyte attack on infection (see Chapters 8 and 9 on forensic medicine and anthropology, respectively).

Among the many types of white blood cells are neutrophils, B-cells, T-cells, monocytes, and natural killer (NK) cells. Neutrophils represent our primary defense mechanism against bacterial infections. Pus, the whitish-yellow substance formed at infection sites, is made up of both living and dying neutrophil cells involved in the fight. These neutrophils break down and release chemicals that kill invading bacteria and also signal other white blood cells to join the fight. B-cells and T-cells are responsible for making antibodies and coordinating immune responses, respectively. The natural killer cells roam the body and kill cells that do not display the correct "do not kill" signal, often infected or cancerous cells. Finally, monocytes are our cellular "vacuum-cleaners," eliminating infected cells.

Blood platelets, or thrombocytes, account for about 1% of blood cells and play a particularly important role in blood clotting and self-repair processes of blood vessels. Like RBCs, "resting" platelets have no nucleus and are smooth, disc-shaped cells, although much smaller in size than the RBCs (Figure 6.10). Unlike RBCs, They do contain some RNA and other cellular structures.

Platelets originate in bone marrow and are very short-lived, typically lasting only about eight to ten days before they are removed from circulation by the spleen. Platelets come into action when they detect a breach in a blood vessel from injury or disease. They quickly transform in shape and initiate a complex chain of biochemical reactions resulting in the release of sticky fibrin strands and a clumping together of the platelets with other blood cells (Figure 6.10). This action forms a blood vessel "plug" that then contracts to further tighten the seal. Aspirin and a variety of other compounds interrupt platelet function, which might not return until new platelets are generated.

6.2.3.3 Other Blood Components

Blood contains hundreds of other chemical components beyond those described thus far, including fibrinogen, salts, proteins, glycoproteins, carbohydrates, antibodies, hormones (e.g., insulin, testosterone, estrogen, adrenaline, epinephrine, etc.), albumin, and dissolved gases. The most common protein in our plasma is albumin, which is responsible for maintaining a proper fluid balance between our tissues and the rest of our bodies. Blood also contains waste products from cellular reactions, viral impurities, cell fragments from immune battles, invading parasites and microbes, and substances that we add to our systems (e.g., drugs, alcohol, poisons, etc.).

6.2.3.4 Blood-Based Diseases

Diseases found in the blood can also provide useful information in forensic analysis. These conditions can arise

(a)   (b)   (c)

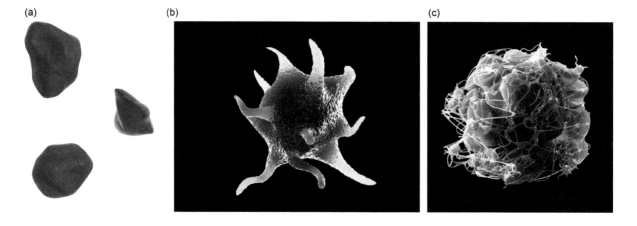

FIGURE 6.10   (a) Image of non-activated blood platelets (thrombocytes). These platelets are formed from bone marrow cells (megakaryocytes), circulate within the blood, and are responsible for blood clotting. (b) Image of activated platelets. Activated platelets have long dendritic "fingers" that allow them to clump together if they detect a break in a blood vessel. (c) A thrombus in the bloodstream, a blood clot formed from activated platelets and fibrin.

Source: Images courtesy Shutterstock.com.

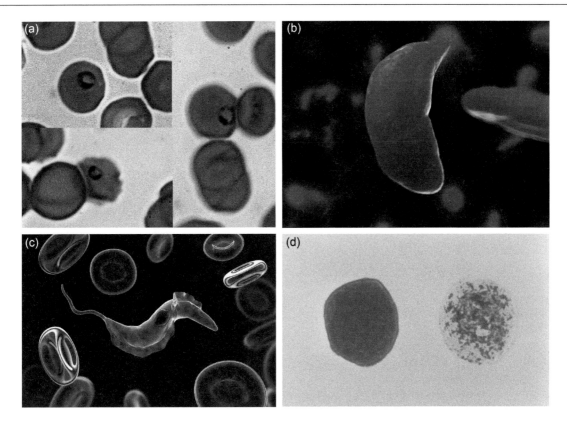

FIGURE 6.11 Common diseases found in blood cells: (a) malarial parasites, *Plasmodium*, form inside red blood cells (Used per Creative Commons Share-Alike 4.0, International. User: Dr. Graham Beards), (b) medically accurate illustration of sickle cells (Source: Shutterstock.com), (c) *Trypanosoma cruzi* parasite illustration, a protozoan that causes Chagas' disease transmitted to humans by the bite of triatomine bug (Source: Shutterstock.com), and (d) HIV vs Normal RBC (shown is a red blood cell diagnostic test for an HIV infection; 'clumping' indicates a positive result).

Source: Used per Creative Commons Attribution 3.0, Unported. User: CSIRO.

from genetic disorders (e.g., sickle cell anemia and hemophilia), diseases (e.g., leukemia and cancer), viral and bacterial infections (e.g., HIV, SARS-CoV-2, and Lyme), and parasitic invasions (e.g., malaria, sleeping sickness, etc.) (Figure 6.11). For example, sickle cell anemia results when the hemoglobin protein in the RBCs has one amino acid changed from the normal variant. People with this disease make *hemoglobin S* instead of the normal *hemoglobin A* molecules. Hemoglobin S carries a smaller negative charge than hemoglobin A, causing it to clump together more readily than hemoglobin A when it loses oxygen. This results in the observed sickle-shaped RBCs (Figure 6.11) that are fragile, short-lived, and inefficient at oxygen transport under lowered oxygen levels. The sickle cells are rigid and sticky, leading to clogged arteries and dehydration. Carriers of the sickle cell allele are, however, more resistant to malaria because the malarial parasites are killed inside sickle-shaped blood cells.

Often, traces of chemicals added to a person's body for medical treatment or as drugs of abuse can be detected in their blood. Identifying these compounds, along with their concentrations and likely sources, can be an enormous aid to an investigation. This information is often gained through a chemical toxicological study of a person's blood and will be discussed in Chapter 13.

6.2.4 Blood Testing

6.2.4.1 Three Questions of Blood

So, now that we know more about the basic chemistry of blood and how it functions in our bodies, we can begin to answer more fully the questions posed earlier such as "is it blood?"; "is it human blood?"; and ultimately "whose blood is it?" In this section, we will take these questions one at a time, beginning with "presumptive" blood tests.

6.2.4.2 Question One: Is It Blood?

In the late 1880s, investigators were not able to determine if a suspicious stain was blood or something else, especially since bloodstains can appear as anything from red to green. Fruit juices, dyes, and other compounds can give stains that look remarkably similar to bloodstains. To help ascertain whether a stain was indeed a bloodstain, a series of tests were developed to provide a quick visual indication of the presence of blood. The advantage of these *presumptive tests* is that they are fast and relatively sensitive. The great disadvantage is that they can give false positive readings – a positive reading when blood is not actually present in the sample, but the test says it is. In presumptive tests, if a test is negative, the blood is believed most likely to be absent, but if the test gives a positive result, then blood is probably, although not definitely, present. Thus, a presumptive test is an analysis that suggests that blood could be present in a sample. Today, these tests are used as effective screens to determine whether or not additional, more conclusive (confirmatory) testing is warranted. A *confirmatory test* is an experiment that can indicate the presence of a particular chemical in the sample, in this case blood, with a very high degree of certainty.

One of the first presumptive tests developed was the Guaiacum test, in which a solution turns blue in the presence of a blood sample. Due to significant problems associated with the accuracy and ease of the Guaiacum test, a variety of other presumptive color-change tests were developed, including the benzidine (Adler test), leucomalachite green, and *ortho*-tolidine tests. While these procedures still retain some limited use, they have fallen out of general use because they involve either toxic, cancer-causing, or difficult-to-handle chemicals. These tests have now mostly been replaced by the tetramethylbenzidine (TMB) and Kastle-Meyer tests (Figure 6.12). In the *Kastle-Meyer* procedure, the most commonly employed presumptive field blood test, a suspected sample is collected on a swab with alcohol, and a few drops of phenolphthalein are added followed by a few drops of hydrogen peroxide (H_2O_2). If blood is present, the swab immediately turns pink (Figure 6.13). One important advantage of this test is that it is typically non-destructive, allowing further tests to be run on the sample if needed, including DNA analysis.

These presumptive color-change tests rely on the catalytic behavior of the heme group in blood to catalyze the oxidation of a colorless material, such as phenolphthalein, to a colored material by an oxidant, such as hydrogen peroxide (Figure 6.12). If you've ever put hydrogen peroxide on a cut to disinfect it and noticed that it bubbled profusely, you've probably observed this same reaction. The bubbling comes from the release of oxygen gas (O_2) due to the decomposition of hydrogen peroxide (H_2O_2) to water and oxygen caused by the hemoglobin. The Kastle-Meyer test, like all other presumptive tests, however, cannot distinguish human blood from animal blood and can give false positive results from non-blood components also in the sample, such as horseradish and potatoes (or anything that behaves as a biochemical *peroxidase*, an enzyme that catalyzes the oxidation of another compound by the decomposition of a peroxide). In fact, the presence of any naturally occurring peroxidase compound will give a positive test *but*, to an observant analyst, the color change seen from these "false positive" compounds is often noticeably slower to develop than for a blood sample. These tests are often successful on dried and old samples, including a recent report of a successful blood test from the uniform of a wounded officer from the War of 1812.

At crime scenes, it may be important to find the locations of suspected blood residues that cannot be seen by the unaided eye. For this purpose, two reagents, called luminol and fluorescein, are usually employed. While their modes of action are quite different, both reagents provide a visible glow where very minute residues of blood are found. The use of these reagents can reveal patterns, such as shoeprints and drag stains, that would otherwise be undetectable to the unaided eye.

In the luminol procedure, a weak solution of the chemical luminol (with an activator) is sprayed where the blood is suspected. The iron from trace amounts of hemoglobin catalyzes

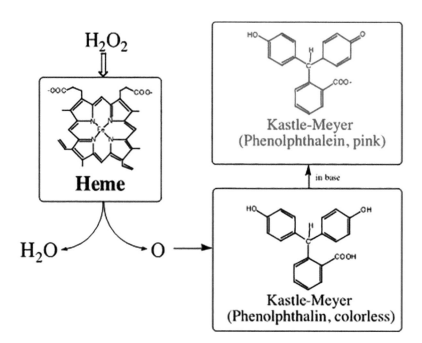

FIGURE 6.12 Kastle-Meyer test involving the catalytic oxidation of the colorless phenolphthalein indicator to pink by the heme groups in hemoglobin.

when illuminated by UV light. Fluorescence is quite different from the chemiluminescence process of luminol and occurs when a molecule absorbs light at one wavelength and then emits light at a different wavelength (Chapter 12). With fluorescein, the oxidized molecule absorbs light in the ultraviolet region that our eyes cannot see and then emits light in the visible region, producing a blue glow.

Sometimes, it is also desirable to enhance weakly visible bloodstains, for example, to make bloody footprints, fingerprints, and other patterns more visible. Luminol and fluorescein can be used for this, but they tend to blur the pattern's detail. Instead, a solution of a dye, such as Leucocrystal violet, can be used very effectively. It is an extremely simple procedure; simply spraying the reagent on the stain immediately produces a permanent dark purple color. Similar results can also be obtained using a variety of other dyes (e.g., Hungarian red, amido black, Crowle's Stain, Coomassie Blue, etc.).

All the tests described so far are presumptive tests, suggesting whether or not blood is present in the sample, helping to decide whether to move to more detailed studies (confirmatory tests).

A variety of confirmatory tests have been developed over the past century to determine conclusively if a stain contains blood. One group of these tests is called "crystal tests" because, when treated with a specific chemical, blood uniquely forms identifiable crystals under the microscope. For example, in the Takayama test, a solution containing pyridine and glucose is added to the sample and, only if blood is present, beautiful red crystals are formed. Similar crystal tests involving other reagents have also been developed (e.g., Wagenhaar and Teichmann tests).

Many of these tests have now been replaced with methods that not only determine if blood is present but also whether the blood is human. These methods usually involve a process called immunoassay.

6.2.4.3 Question Two: Is It Human Blood?

The method for figuring out whether a blood sample is human blood or whether it comes from another animal is usually answered in a manner quite similar to the way our bodies recognize and attack invading substances, such as bacteria and viruses. When our bodies detect an invader, they swing into action and ultimately develop antibodies very specific for defeating the invader at hand, attacking only where needed. These antibodies destroy the source of the infection and effectively remove it from the system. In other terms, our bodies react to an outside *antigen* (a virus or bacterium, for instance) and generate a specific *antibody* just for that one, and only, antigen. An antigen is any substance that can stimulate the production of antibodies, and an antibody is a Y-shaped protein molecule that can combine with a foreign antigen to disable or destroy it. A quite similar process can also be used to determine if a blood sample is human or not.

Our blood serum contains numerous proteins unique to humans. If human blood serum is injected into a rabbit, the rabbit's system must identify and destroy the human

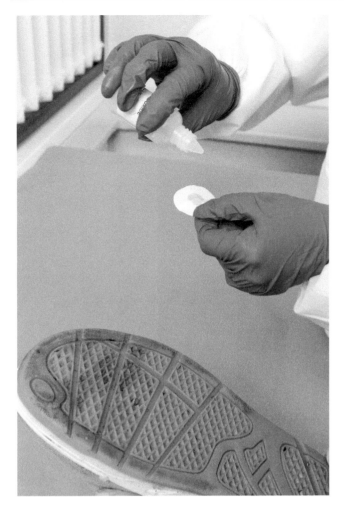

FIGURE 6.13 Forensic officer performing a blood verification test on a stain on the sole of a shoe. During the test, a swab is treated with chemicals and then wiped over the stain. If the stain is blood, the chemicals react and the swab changes color. The test being used is the Kastle-Meyer presumptive blood test. If blood is found on the shoes, its DNA can be later extracted and analyzed.

Source: Jim Varney/Science Photo Library. Used with permission.

a series of chemical reactions that ultimately cause the luminol to briefly glow in the dark through a process called *chemiluminescence* (emission of light from chemical reactions without the emission of heat). The blue glow, lasting for up to a minute, can be readily seen and photographed in a darkened room (Figure 6.14). This technique is very sensitive to even very small trace amounts of blood. Luminol has, however, some significant problems with its use. It also glows in the presence of copper, horseradish, bleach, fecal matter, certain plant enzymes, and animal blood. While not proven, luminol is also a suspected carcinogen.

Fluorescein is similarly applied to a suspected area, and the area is illuminated by an ultraviolet light (often called an *alternate light source*, ALS). The iron of the heme group catalyzes the oxidation of the solution, which will then fluoresce

FIGURE 6.14   After spraying a suspected bloodstain area with luminol, a glow indicates the possible presence of blood.

Source: Shutterstock.com.

BOX 6.3   IS IT BLOOD: THE SHROUD OF TURIN

Since at least 1350, faithful pilgrims have made their way across Europe to view a piece of cloth claimed by many to be the final burial shroud of Jesus. Probably the most striking feature of this remarkable 14' by 4' cloth is a photographic-quality image of a presumably crucified man imprinted in the fabric. Throughout its long history, there have been both strong supporters and critics of the shroud's authenticity, including the Catholic Church's official skepticism for hundreds of years. In recent years, a variety of scientific methods have been used to determine if the shroud

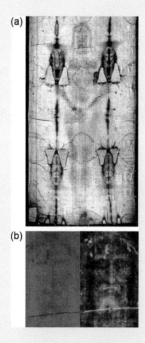

FIGURE 6.15   Images of the Shroud of Turin: (a) one-half of the Shroud and (b) a close-up of the facial region of the Shroud.

Source: Retrieved from Wikimedia Commons; used per Creative Commons Attribution.

is a medieval forgery or a 2,000-year-old relic, with mostly inconclusive and even contradictory results. Studies in the 1980s using radiocarbon dating methods dated the cloth to the mid-1300s, but recent reports have shown that the fibers studied originated from a medieval patch and not from the true shroud, such that the real date of the cloth still remains to be established (Rogers, 2005).

One part of the image contains what appear to be bloodstains where the nails were used for crucifixion. Several spectroscopic and presumptive tests have now indicated that the material is likely blood. Blood proteins and heme groups have been detected in the bloodstains but not in other regions of the cloth. While much more needs to be learned about the shroud, it does appear that, at least, the bloodstains are likely genuine.

invaders (antigens) to survive. The rabbit's body responds by producing antibodies against the foreign human proteins, called *anti-human serum* antibodies, since they specifically bind to human serum proteins. If this anti-human serum is then removed from the rabbit, it will still attack any human blood it encounters, causing a "precipitin reaction" to occur. As the name implies, when a *precipitin* reaction occurs between an antigen and an antibody, a visible precipitate or solid will form. So, in a forensic setting, a suspected blood sample (antigen serum) is brought into contact with anti-human serum (from the rabbit), and if a precipitate forms, then the sample is not only blood but must also be human blood. The process of using specific antibodies to identify biological samples is called *immunoassay*.

Anti-sera can be developed in a very similar fashion for essentially any protein antigen from any animal species, as the antigen-antibody reaction is a uniquely species-specific interaction. Thus, human blood will not react with chicken or horse anti-serum, only with anti-human serum.

Several variants of the precipitin test have been developed over the years to take advantage of the specificity of this antigen-antibody reaction. In general, they involve exposing a solution containing the human anti-serum to a second solution containing the suspected blood sample. If there is a reaction, a precipitate is noticed at the juncture of the two solutions. The *ring precipitin test*, for example, simply places the anti-human serum in a small test tube and the bloodstain extract is then carefully layered on top of the anti-human serum (Figure 6.16). The dissolved antigens and antibodies then diffuse toward each other and a precipitate is formed at the interface between the two solutions *only* if human blood is present. Variations on this general method employ gels, glass plates, electrophoresis, and other methods, but the basic concept remains the same for all.

This same idea of using antibodies specific to a certain biological substance to uniquely identify it can be extended to the analysis of both blood and non-blood substances, including drugs and poisons. Two particularly powerful immunoassay techniques, called Enzyme Multiplied Immunoassay Technique (EMIT) and Enzyme Linked Immunosorbent Assay (ELISA), have been developed for these types of analyses.

6.2.4.4 EMIT (Enzyme Multiplied Immunoassay Technique)

In this analytical method, the biological compound or drug that we wish to analyze for is first attached to a protein and then injected into an animal such as a rabbit or rat. As with any foreign protein, the animal makes antibodies to this

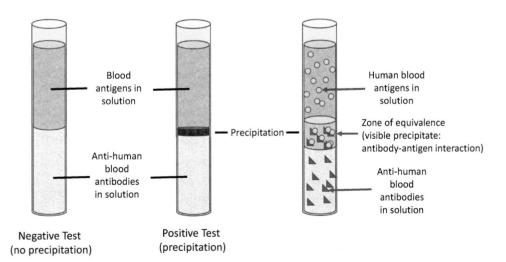

FIGURE 6.16 Ring Precipitin Test. At the bottom of the test tube is the solution containing anti-human blood antibodies in solution. The solution at the top is the test solution containing the suspected blood serum (antigen). A ring develops at the interface between these solutions from an antibody-antigen reaction if blood is present, as shown in the center. The image on the right illustrates what happens during a positive test.

protein-linked antigen that can be isolated from the animal's serum. In the case of a drug/protein antigen, we have now prepared an anti-drug serum that will react specifically with the drug we are interested in. When used to determine if that particular drug is present in someone's urine or blood, for example, a sample of urine or blood is first mixed with a sample of anti-drug serum. Any drug present then completely reacts with the anti-drug serum (antibodies). In the final step, a carefully measured amount of the same drug bound to an enzyme is added. Any unreacted anti-drug serum that is still in the solution will react with this added "extra" drug/enzyme complex. By measuring how much unreacted drug/enzyme complex remains at the end of this reaction, it is possible to determine how much of the anti-serum was used up in reacting with the drug in the original sample, as shown in Figure 6.17. For example, if a solution contained 100 molecules of anti-methadone antibodies and we added to it a solution of urine or blood that contained 60 molecules of methadone, all the methadone would react with the antibodies to form 60 methadone/anti-methadone complexes. This leaves, however, 40 free antibodies after all the methadone is used up. If we now add to this another solution containing 100 molecules of a new methadone/enzyme complex (and we know there are exactly 100 present), 40 of these enzyme complexes will react with the remaining unused anti-methadone antibodies left over from the earlier reaction. This leaves 60 methadone/enzyme complexes unreacted in the solution that we can measure simply by determining the remaining enzyme activity (only 60% of its starting activity remains if 40 have been bound to the drug). Thus, by some simple math, we can work backward to determine that there must have been 60 methadone molecules in our original sample. So, in a conceptually similar example, if you gave a cashier a dollar (100 cents) and got back 60 cents in change, you would know that the item that you purchased cost 40 cents without ever looking at the price tag. The entire EMIT process may be done in a single step, allowing the drug in the sample to compete with the drug/enzyme complex for a limited amount of the specific antibodies. In this way, we have an accurate and very sensitive method for determining

how much of a particular drug is in a sample, information that may be important to medicolegal investigations (see Chapters 8 and 13).

A variant of this method is called *radioimmunoassay* (RIA). Instead of using an enzyme linked to the drug in the final step, the drug is instead linked to a radioactive tracer. By measuring the radioactivity level, it is similarly possible to determine the quantity of a specific drug or protein antigen in the sample. Other methods have been developed that use optical, fluorescence, and magnetic labels to determine the amount of antigen/antibody binding in the EMIT experiment.

> **BOX 6.4   BRIEF ON CONFIRMATORY AND IMMUNOASSAY BLOOD TESTS**
> 1. Confirmatory blood tests indicate the presence of blood in the sample with a very high degree of certainty.
> 2. Older tests involve the crystallization of blood.
> 3. Immunoassay methods capitalize on the specific nature of antibody-antigen reactions.
> 4. Using specific antibodies, we can test for blood components or blood-based chemicals (e.g., drugs, poisons, toxins, etc.).

6.2.4.5 ELISA (Enzyme Linked Immunosorbent Assay)

Another important immunoassay technique is known as the ELISA method (Figure 6.18). In this method, the antibodies specific to a particular protein or drug are made as before but then are attached firmly to the plastic surface of a small reactor. The solution containing the drug or protein (antigen) to be tested for, such as methadone or blood albumin, is then added to the reactor. If any of the specific drug or protein is present in the sample, it binds tightly to the antibodies attached to the wall of the reactor. After washing away everything but the tightly bound antibody and antigen, another solution containing the same antigen-specific antibody is added, except that this second antibody is attached to an enzyme – something like a biochemical flag. These new antibody-enzyme complexes bind only to where a drug is already attached to an antibody stuck to the wall of the reactor. After again washing away anything that is not bound to the reactor's walls, any antibody-enzyme complex found remaining in the reactor **must** be attached to a drug-antibody stuck to the reactor wall. We then simply look for the "flags" (or enzymes) attached to the "stuck" drug to determine how much drug (or protein) was in the original solution. Here's a simple analogy that might be helpful. Say that we had an unknown number of darts, dipped in sugar, that we threw at a target *in the dark* (presume all hit the target). Since we can't visually see how many darts we threw, we need an indirect method to figure this out. So, we next release a group of fireflies that are attracted to the sugar on the darts (say only

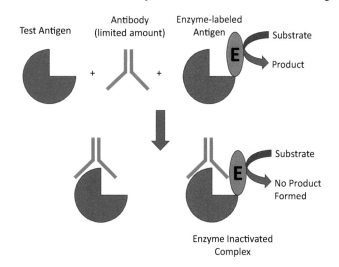

FIGURE 6.17   EMIT: Enzyme Multiplied Immunoassay Technique.

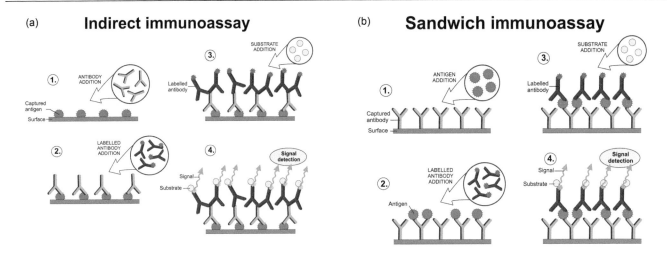

FIGURE 6.18 (a) An indirect immunoassay is used to measure the concentration of antigen. The basic components of the test are antigen, labeled antibody, and substrate. (b) A sandwich immunoassay similarly measures the concentration of antigen. The basic components of the test are antigen, labeled antibody, and substrate.

Source: Images courtesy Shutterstock.com.

one firefly per dart). Now, since we can "see" the glow from each firefly in the dark, we simply count the number of fireflies glowing, and we can determine the number of darts that were thrown. This is essentially what happens in ELISA – the drug/antigen (the dart) is fixed onto the plastic immobilized antibody (the dartboard), and visualizing the second "flagged" antibody (fireflies) allows us to determine how much drug/antigen was in the sample (the number of darts fixed to the dartboard). Several variants of the ELISA method have also been developed.

One problem with all these analyses for drug detection is that there can be positive reactions for other compounds having chemical structures similar to the drug being investigated.

Both EMIT and ELISA have significant similarities and differences. The chemicals for both the EMIT and ELISA experiments last a long time, and the procedure can be performed with minimal training and experience. EMIT is primarily used for small molecules such as drugs, drug metabolites, and hormone analyses. ELISA measurements, however, are primarily used in analyzing larger molecules, such as protein antigens and antibodies, and are used for diagnosing infectious diseases and blood immunoglobulins. The EMIT method tends to be faster, but ELISA-based methods have greater sensitivity.

6.2.4.6 Monoclonal Antibodies

When our bodies produce antibodies to attack an invading substance, they actually prepare a whole range of antibodies that target different parts of the invader (called polyclonal antibodies). This is similar to what real armies do; they have infantry, cavalry, artillery, and other specialties that target different parts of the same enemy. While this works well for armies and our bodies, it can also cause significant problems if we want antibodies that can reliably target just one particular molecule for the immunoassay techniques already described. Luckily, a powerful technique involving the use of something called

monoclonal antibodies has been developed to deal with this very effectively. A *monoclonal antibody* is an antibody that is more uniform than our natural antibodies and attacks and binds to only one site on a chosen antigen. These monoclonal antibodies can be used to protect against diseases, diagnose illnesses, and detect the presence of drugs and other abnormal chemical compounds in the blood.

Most of these methods first require the preparation of very specific antibodies. Monoclonal antibody technologies allow us to efficiently prepare pure antibodies in very large quantities. In summary, as shown in Figure 6.19, the antigen of interest (e.g., blood protein or protein-linked drug) is injected into a mouse to form specific antibodies against the injected antigen. Instead of isolating the antibodies produced, as was done in the previous techniques, this time we actually remove the spleen cells from the mouse that produce the antibodies themselves. This process is like removing the factory that produces the antibodies in the mouse's body. These spleen cells are then fused with fast-growing cancer cells to form a new hybrid cell (hybridoma). These new cells can be screened to select only the best producers of the antibody we want. These champion producers, called "immortal cells," are then cultured and grown to make a continuous and permanent supply chain of pure antibodies for use in immunoassays. This is analogous to creating a permanent antibody-growing factory to supply a continuous stream of the desired antibody forever.

6.2.4.7 Question Three: Whose Blood Is It?

The question of individualizing a biological sample uniquely to one particular person has long been a central goal. Blood analysis held out the first real hope that this type of specific connection was possible; a hope that was ultimately fulfilled by DNA typing. Nonetheless, individual information, at times approaching the specificity of DNA typing, has been achieved through careful blood typing studies.

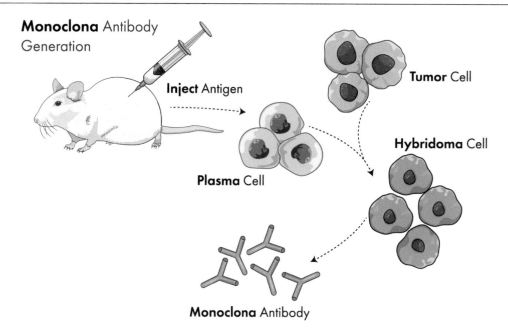

FIGURE 6.19   Hybridoma technology of monoclonal antibody production.

Source: Shutterstock.com.

In 1901, Karl Landsteiner discovered what we know today as blood groups. His immediate concern at the time was to find a safe and reliable way to know when blood from a donor can be safely given intravenously to a patient in need. He found that blood of one type of donor, which he called type A, could be safely mixed with some blood samples without agglutination (clumping) but not with others, for example type B donors. Type B donors, in turn, could be mixed with blood from other type B donors without problems but could not be mixed with type A. Further experiments allowed him to ultimately classify blood into the four different types we know today as the ABO system.

sugar components attached) that is found sticking to the surface of RBCs. These glycoproteins contain one of three different chemical ends, just like "snap-on" attachments that fit onto the end of a tool. The "basic" version of the glycoprotein ends with a certain sugar (fructose) exposed, and this entire unit is referred to as the H antigen (Figure 6.20). The presence of only the H antigen on the RBC gives rise to the O blood type. If we "snap-on" an additional sugar (acetylgalactose amine) to the end of the H antigen, the A antigen is formed, which gives rise to the A blood type. If instead, we "snap-on" a different sugar (galactose), then the B antigen is formed, which leads to the B blood type. Since we inherit one gene from our mothers and one from our fathers, six possible combinations from these three antigens are possible: HH, HA, AA, HB, BB, and AB. Since A and B are genetically co-dominant (have the same genetic "strengths" for inheritance), these six possibilities lead to the four observed blood types in the ABO system: A (*AA or AH*), B (*BB or BH*), AB (*AB only*), and O (*HH*). This is shown schematically in Figure 6.20 and summarized in Table 6.1.

As we've learned already, blood plasma contains substances called antibodies that target very specific proteins, such as the glycoproteins found on the surface of our RBCs. Within the plasma of a person with type A blood is contained antibodies against the B antigen (anti-B). These antibodies are present even before there is contact with B type blood, possibly due to the fact that some bacteria and plants also have these antigens so that we develop antibodies to them from a very young age. Similarly, the plasma of a person who carries the B antigen on their RBCs (B type blood) contains antibodies against the A antigen (anti-A). If we mix type A blood samples with plasma from a person with B type blood, an immune reaction will occur and the RBCs will clump together in a process called *agglutination*. This is shown in Figure 6.21. Note

BOX 6.5   BRIEF ON BLOOD TYPING

1. Different proteins (antigens) are present on the surface of RBCs and are inherited.
2. The presence or absence of different red blood cell (RBC) antigens leads to different blood types.
3. The most commonly employed blood groups involve the ABO and Rh systems.
4. Agglutination occurs when antibodies in the plasma specific for an RBC antigen react to "clump" cells together.
5. Four possible blood types exist in the ABO blood system (A, B, AB, and O).
6. More than 600 RBC antigens are known.

Our DNA carries a gene that dictates the formation of one of three possible forms of a glycoprotein (a protein with

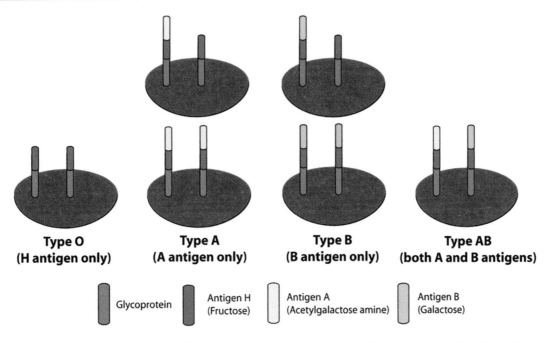

FIGURE 6.20 The antigens giving rise to the different ABO blood types. In O type blood, there is no "additional" sugar cap on the end of the glycoprotein. In types A and B, there are other sugars capping the H-end sugar. In type AB, both A and B sugars are present. Note that there are two genotypic ways to have either type A and type B blood.

TABLE 6.1 Blood type antigens and antibodies

END GROUP (ATTACHMENT)	ANTIBODY PRESENT IN BLOOD	FREQUENCY (%)	GENOTYPE
N-acetylgalactosamine	Anti-B	42	AA or AO
D-galactose	Anti-A	10	BB or BO
Both N-acetylgalactosamine and D-galactose	None	4	AB
L-fructose	Both anti-A and anti-B	44	OO

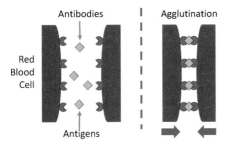

FIGURE 6.21 The drawing on the left shows two red blood cells with the surface antigens (small green shapes) and the yellow serum antibodies (small diamonds) indicated. The antibodies bind with the antigen, causing the red blood cells to clump together through agglutination.

that agglutination refers to the clumping of RBCs together due to antigen-antibody reactions while *coagulation*, or clotting, is the process of converting blood into a jelly-like substance from the action of activated thrombocytes sticking blood cellular material together. A sample of type O plasma contains antibodies against *both* A and B (anti-A and anti-B), while type AB blood plasma contains *neither* of these antibodies. This is why type AB blood is often referred to as the universal

acceptor blood type since it does not contain antibodies against either the A antigen or the B antigen. These people can usually receive RBCs from any of the ABO blood types without problems. Type O blood is called the universal donor since it contains neither A nor B antigens on the RBCs, while type AB is the universal donor for blood plasma. There is no known antibody against the H antigen.

Determining the ABO blood type of a particular sample simply requires mixing the sample blood separately with anti-A and anti-B sera. If the A antigen is present in the blood sample (from either type A or AB blood), then an agglutination reaction occurs when mixed with Anti-A serum. If the B antigen is present (from either type B or AB blood), then no reaction occurs with the anti-A serum but agglutination does occur when mixed with anti-B serum. If no reaction is observed with either anti-A or anti-B sera, then the blood is type O. Examples of this process are shown in Figure 6.22.

The ABO system is only one of at least 29 known blood group systems. A complete blood type description for a blood sample, although very rarely done, would potentially include an analysis for the full set of substances found on the surface of the RBCs. In the 29 blood group systems, well over 600 different blood antigens are known. A person's *complete* blood

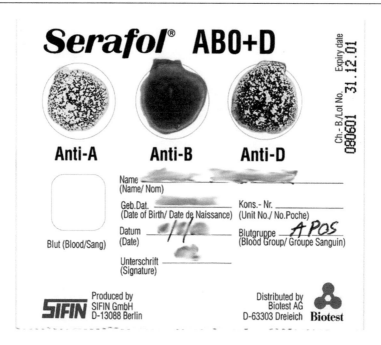

FIGURE 6.22 The blood group test card for a type A+ blood sample. The blood grouping card shows agglutination of blood with anti-A and anti-Rh(D), but not with anti-B.

Source: Used per Creative Commons Attribution 2.0 Generic. User: Apers0n at English Wikimedia.

Note: D refers to the Rh factor.

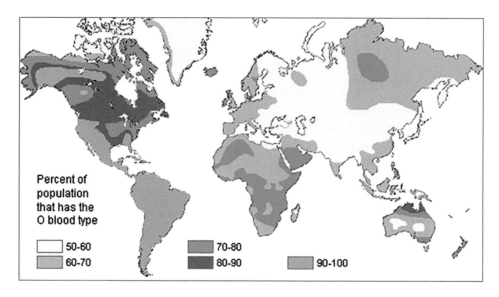

FIGURE 6.23 Distribution of the type O blood in native populations of the world.

Source: Used per Creative Commons Attribution Share-Alike 3.0, Unported. User: anthro palomar.

type would be one of the many, many possible combinations of these blood group antigens. Many of these combinations, however, are very rare or limited to certain ethnic groups. The ethnic distribution of particular blood antigens can, in some instances, provide useful forensic information. For example, one Rhesus antigen is present in less than 0.5% of Caucasians but present in 40% of West Africans. In contrast, the Kell antigen is essentially only found in Caucasians, and the Diego antigen is absent from Caucasians yet present in blood from most Japanese and Chinese people. The percentage of two different

populations for two blood group systems (ABO and Rhesus) is given in Table 6.2, and the variation in the frequency of the O blood type around the world is shown in Figure 6.23. The rarest blood type known is the "Bombay" type that is present in about 0.0004% of the population (about four people in a million) (the Bombay type is missing the H antigen entirely).

Besides the ABO system, the other most common blood group is the Rhesus blood group (Rh). Named for its first isolation from the Rhesus monkey, blood labeled Rh positive contains the D antigen on the surface of RBCs, while Rh-negative

TABLE 6.2 Blood type frequencies

BLOOD TYPE (ABO AND RH)	POPULATION % IN S. KOREA	POPULATION % IN US
A positive	34.4	35.7
A negative	0.1	6.3
B positive	26.8	8.5
B negative	0.1	1.5
AB positive	11.2	3.4
AB negative	0.05	0.6
O positive	27.4	37.4
O negative	0.1	6.6

blood lacks the D antigen. In typical blood transfusion work, the ABO and Rh systems are both determined to establish the compatibility of the blood.

6.3.5 Blood Type Inheritance and Parental Testing

Since blood types are determined through the actions of our genes, blood types are inherited from our parents and do not change throughout our lives. A person's ABO blood type, for example, is determined by which alleles they inherit: the H (often just called O), A, or B antigens. Both the A and B alleles are dominant over O and co-dominant to each other (co-dominant means equal genetic "strength" in determining inheritance). This means that when only one O allele is present, the other allele dictates the blood type. A person who is AO will have an A blood type. It takes the combination of two O alleles to produce the O blood type. The combination of one A and one B allele results in the AB blood type. This is summarized in Table 6.3.

The Rh system is far more complex than the ABO system, with over 35 different possibilities from each parent. Generally, these possibilities fall into what are referred to as positive or negative groups (see above), with the positive dominant over the negative. Because of the complexity of this grouping, however, it is possible for two Rh-positive parents to produce an Rh-negative child.

TABLE 6.3 ABO blood type allele contributions

		FATHER'S ALLELE CONTRIBUTION		
		A	B	O
Mother's allele contribution	A	AA (type A)	AB (type AB)	AO (type A)
	B	BA (type AB)	BB (type B)	BO (type B)
	O	OA (type A)	OB (type B)	OO (type O)

Blood typing can help identify the father in paternity cases, usually by conclusively ruling out possible fathers (Table 6.3). For example, two type O parents cannot have a type A or B child. Similarly, two type A parents cannot have a type B or AB child. Adding other blood tests, such as Rh, MN, and others, can provide a greater certainty in the result. The final positive determination of paternity in the United States and most other countries is no longer, however, established on blood typing but is now based on DNA typing. According to the American Association of Blood Banks, 27.9% of men accused of paternity that are tested are not the biological fathers (see Box 6.6). In addition, about 15% of men named on a birth certificate are not the biological fathers based on DNA typing. Many states assume that a woman's husband is the father, allowing her to sue for child support. The accused father then carries the burden of proof to show that he is not the true father.

BOX 6.6   DISPUTED PATERNITY: CHARLIE CHAPLIN AND BLOOD TESTS

In 1945, Charlie Chaplin was accused by his young actress protégé, Joan Barry, of being the father of her new baby daughter, Carol Ann. The case was tried in California state court for disputed paternity since Charlie denied that he was the father. He was also simultaneously charged in federal court for paying to transport Barry and her daughter across state lines to her home in Nebraska – a violation of the Mann Act. He was convinced that he was not the father and innocent of the paternity claim, so blood tests were ordered. Chaplin was found to be type O blood while Joan Barry was determined to be type A. The child, however, proved to be type B blood; conclusively proving that Chaplin could not have been the father.* At the time, however, blood typing was relatively new in the California legal system and was not required as a paternity test. Complicating things for the jury was the fact that Chaplin was notoriously "unfaithful" and had a particularly bad local reputation with women. Chaplin was found innocent of the Mann Act charges but, in spite of the conclusive blood evidence, the California state jury declared him the father of the child. He was forced to pay child support for 18 years for a child that was certainly not his. It is believed that the sentence came about both because the jury was confused

FIGURE 6.24   Charlie Chaplin (1889–1977).

Source: Retrieved from Wikimedia Commons; used per Creative Commons Attribution.

by the scientific evidence and by their desire to "teach Chaplin a lesson," a clear case of jury negation that should have required the judge to set aside the guilty verdict and order a new trial. Note: with this information, Chaplin must have had the genotype of OO, Barry must have been AO, and the Child must have been BO.

BOX 6.7   THE SECRET OF THE BLOOD

In 1992, a Canadian doctor, Dr. John Schneeberger, was accused of sexual assault by drugging the victim during a medical examination. The victim had physical proof of the hospital attack: semen samples were found and collected from the victim's clothing. Dr. Schneeberger voluntarily provided a blood sample, but the analysis showed that there was no match with the semen, and he was eliminated as a suspect. Still convinced, but unable to convince authorities to look further, the victim hired a private investigator who managed to obtain the lip balm of Dr. Schneeberger. The DNA analysis from the lip balm this time showed a match with the semen sample. However, since the balm was obtained without a warrant, it was not admissible as evidence. It did, however, convince the court to seek another DNA sample. Interestingly, this second time drawing Dr. Schneeberger's blood, the technician found it hard to get enough blood from the procedure and noticed that the blood appeared to be very "old." The DNA analysis once again showed no match with Dr. Schneeberger, so the case was dismissed.

The case went dormant for several years until Dr. Schneeberger's wife found out that he was raping his 15-year-old step-daughter, while she was drugged. This discovery, along with various other incriminating evidence, convinced Canadian authorities to obtain more DNA samples, this time from multiple sources: blood, saliva, and hair. This time, however, there was found to be a "match" between Dr. Schneeberger's DNA and the samples from the victims. Dr. Schneeberger was convicted in 1999 for his crimes and deported.

But how did Dr. Schneeberger avoid DNA detection through his blood samples on the first two occasions? It turns out, he did it by first secretly collecting blood from one of his male patients and then implanting a plastic tube containing the patient's blood within his own arm. When the blood samples were taken from Dr. Schneeberger's arm, they were actually extracting the blood that he had collected from his male patient. So, obviously there was no match. But blood cells die over several months, as observed by the second technician from Dr. Schneeberger's drawn blood. Dr. Schneeberger also later confessed to giving the victims the powerful drug, Versed, that immobilized them during the attacks. Dr. Schneeberger was tried, convicted, and sentenced to six years in prison along with having his medical license revoked and being divorced. Upon release from prison, he was stripped of his Canadian citizenship and deported to South Africa (where he had permanent citizenship), because he lied that he was not under any police investigation at the time of his Canadian citizenship hearing.

6.3 BLOOD PATTERN ANALYSIS

6.3.1 Introduction

The wealth of information provided by blood evidence is not solely confined to its biochemical makeup. Blood is first and foremost a fluid that flows under pressure throughout the body, and its observed physical behavior is controlled by the predictable forces of nature. When a breach in a blood vessel occurs through injury, blood is often distributed in the vicinity in a way that provides telltale clues as to *where* the assault occurred, *how* the injury was caused, and *what* were the actions that followed. Careful observation of bloodstain patterns at the scene provides an unmistakable record of activity. This is fundamentally different from many other types of physical evidence that focuses on identifying *who* was at the crime scene (e.g., DNA, fingerprint, blood chemistry, impressions, etc.), but it instead largely focuses on the *where*, *what*, and *how*. In this section, we will consider some of the fluid properties of blood and how to use the bloodstain record to gain insights for crime scene interpretation (Figure 6.25).

The typical human has between 4 and 6 l of blood in the body, making it possible for relatively large amounts of blood to be found at violent injury scenes. As previously discussed, blood is a complex liquid with about the same density but roughly three times the viscosity of water. *Viscosity* is the resistance of a liquid to flow through a capillary under stress or pressure. For example, water, which has relatively low viscosity, flows readily through a small tube at room temperature, while motor oil, with relatively high viscosity, flows very slowly. *Surface tension*, another physical property of a fluid, is the tendency of the molecules at the surface of a liquid to behave as if they were part of an elastic membrane, making molecules at the surface of a droplet cling to one another tightly and thereby reducing the exposed surface area to a minimum. This behavior arises from the molecules within the liquid attracting one another and dictates how blood droplets, both in the air and on surfaces, form and are shaped.

These properties help to dictate where and how bloodstains are distributed throughout a scene.

So, what kinds of things might be possible to learn by examining bloodstains? Among the information that can be gained includes:

1. The locations and distribution of the bloodstains, suggesting where the crime occurred, the positions of the victim and assailant(s), the locations of nearby objects, and any movements of people or objects after the attack.
2. The manner of formation of the observed stains (e.g., passive, active, and transfer stains).
3. The point (area) of origin and travel directions of the droplets.

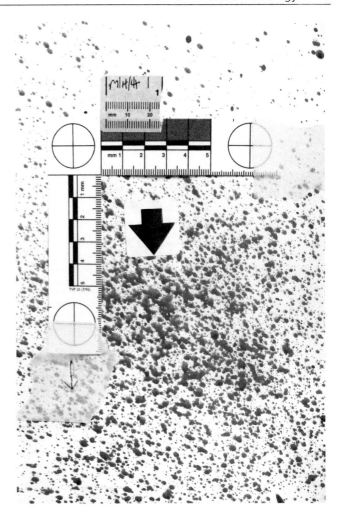

FIGURE 6.25 Bloodstain on a surface, surrounded by scale bars. Bloodstain patterns are analyzed to help investigators potentially determine: (1) the wound orgin on the body, (2) the weapon used and the number of blows, (3) the relative position of the victim and assailant and (4) the sequence of events. In impact patterns, the length and width of each drop is measured and the angle at which they struck the surface calculated. This indicates the direction the blood was traveling and the speed at which it traveled. The convergence point (area) of the droplets indicates the location of the blood source.

Source: Jim Varney/Science Photo Library. Used with permission.

4. The type of weapon used in the attack, the weapon's velocity, and the minimum number of impacts.
5. The sequence of events leading up to the observed crime scene.
6. The likelihood of the stories given by suspects, witnesses, and victims.

Many times, the answers gained from bloodstain analysis are not entirely conclusive but can still provide a consistent and corroborative picture of events.

6.3.2 Bloodstain Patterns Analysis

The first job where bloodshed is known or suspected is to identify and fully locate all the blood droplets at the scene. The
locations of bloodstains can usually be readily seen visually,
but sometimes, the stains have either been cleaned away, contain only trace amounts of blood, or the body/object has moved
from its original location. In these cases, the extremely sensitive luminol and fluorescein techniques can be particularly
helpful in locating the patterns (see Section 6.2.4). Where blood
is suspected, a complete and thorough search of an extended
area is usually needed. Any traces must be carefully recorded
and, where possible, samples taken for further analysis.

The careful examination of bloodstains and the application of certain aspects of several fields of science are usually
referred to as *bloodstain pattern analysis* or BPA. Patterns of
bloodstains at a crime scene are often classified into one of three
groups: passive, active, and transfer. These terms refer primarily
to the mechanism of forming and distributing the droplets.

6.3.2.1 Passive Bloodstains

Passive bloodstains are defined as the residue of blood droplets, flows, and pools formed *solely* under the control of gravity.
These stains can form through blood flow directly from a wound
or by dripping off objects and weapons (Figure 6.26). Generally,
passive bloodstains are further divided into passive drops (simple droplets falling vertically onto a surface), drip patterns (droplets falling directly into other blood), flow patterns (bloodstains
arising from the movement of blood on a surface influenced by
either gravity or the movement of an object), and pool patterns
(from pooled blood on a surface that does not move for a time).
Observing the blood pattern can help determine whether the
body has been moved by noting an unexplained change in the
direction of blood flow within the stain.

The bloodstain can also reveal the angle that the droplet
originally fell onto a surface. Blood droplets tend to form a perfectly spherical shape as they move through the air, primarily from the effects of surface tension, until something causes
them to disperse into smaller droplets. A droplet impacting a
surface at a 90° angle will usually form a completely round
spot. Changing this angle of impact will result in a progressively elongated droplet pattern (discussed in further detail
under active bloodstains). Additionally, satellite mini-droplets
(small droplets "splashed" outward from the initial impact of
the liquid with the surface, Figure 6.26a) can provide information about the height that the blood is dropped from and the
nature of the surface that the droplet hits. Hard and smooth
surfaces tend to form clean, sharp stains while rougher or softer
surfaces tend not to form sharply defined satellites. Blood droplets falling from higher levels form more broadly dispersed satellite droplets due to a greater speed of impact with the surface.
At a height above the surface of about 8 ft and more, no differences are observed since the terminal velocity of about 25 ft/s
is reached for a single blood droplet at that point.

Careful observation of passive bloodstains can provide
clues about how much time has elapsed since the stain was

(a)

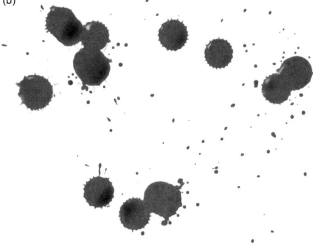

(b)

FIGURE 6.26   Passive bloodstains formed from a blood droplet
falling onto a surface solely under the influence of gravity. The
droplets fall as spherical droplets (a) and tend to produce round
and relatively large spatter patterns (b).

Source: (a) iStockphoto.com, Credit: tstajduhar; (b) iStock-
photo.com, Credit: Eshma.

formed. Blood dries at a rate that can be reasonably estimated
by considering the surface material holding the blood, the
amount of blood present, and the prevailing environmental
conditions at the time (e.g., temperature, relative humidity,
wind speed, sunlight, and other factors). Control experiments
measuring the time necessary to recreate an observed state of
dryness under known conditions can be very useful and help
corroborate a post-mortem interval (PMI) determined by other
means (e.g., autopsy, vitreous humor, algor mortis, etc.).

Bloodstains dry from the perimeter of the stain toward the
center, and if enough blood is present, clotting can be observed
in the center before drying is complete. The pools or droplets
form an outer crusty ring very quickly, often in less than one
minute of air exposure. Wiping clean the droplets after this
time will leave behind a ring that is rather difficult to remove.
This can provide information regarding the timing and movement of the victim by determining whether the bloodstain was
disturbed after it had been initially formed and partially dried.

The nature of the surface that the droplet lands on greatly affects the appearance of the bloodstain. When a droplet falls on a smooth surface, such as glass or linoleum, the stain has sharp edges with relatively little distortion. If instead the droplet falls on a rough surface, such as carpeting, concrete, or wood, the bloodstain pattern is distorted to a variable extent.

6.3.2.2 Active Bloodstains

Active bloodstains are defined as those that are formed by the action of a force in addition to gravity. These bloodstains may arise through the force of an attack, by blood flung from a weapon in motion, or by the blood pressure of the body expelling blood through a wound.

Bloodstains formed in the course of an impact from a weapon or projectile can be classified on the basis of the velocity of the impacting object. It is important to note that the velocity here refers to the velocity of the impacting object, not the velocity of the blood droplets flung through the air because of the impact. Velocity also refers to both a speed *and* a direction, since velocity is a vector quantity (Figure 6.27).

Low-velocity impact spatter is found when the impact occurs at speeds up to about 5 ft/s (1.5 m/s). The droplets observed are rather well-formed and typically are larger than 3–4 mm in diameter (Figure 6.27, a). This pattern might arise from a walking or running person, from a relatively slow assault (e.g., fist attack), or from a very short fall. A *medium velocity impact* spatter arises when the velocity of the striking object is between 5 and 100 ft/s (1.5 m/s to 30 m/s). The droplets found here typically range in size between 1 and 4 mm in diameter (Figure 6.27, b). These types of patterns usually come from blunt and sharp force trauma injuries, assaults, and accidents. The final type of pattern, *high-velocity impact*, is usually observed when the striking object moves at speeds of greater than 100 ft/s (>30 m/s) or faster (Figure 6.27, c). The resulting bloodstain pattern often appears as a fine mist with droplet sizes smaller than 1 mm. These types of patterns arise from bullet wounds, explosives, sneezing, coughing, or injuries from high-speed machinery (e.g., cars, power tools, etc.).

Blood patterns resulting from blood forced out through a person's nose or mouth are called expired patterns and can sometimes be distinguished from other patterns by the presence of the amylase enzyme and cheek cells in these samples that come only from the nose and mouth. Active bloodstain patterns can also be formed as blood is ejected from an arterial wound under the force of a person's blood pressure. This is frequently called arterial gush or spurt and is apparent from the characteristic inverted V-shaped pattern caused by the rise and fall of the blood pressure as the heart beats (Figure 6.28). A person's average blood pressure is equivalent to the pressure caused by a column of mercury almost a meter high or about 2 pounds per square inch. This exerts significant backpressure on the blood so that when a breach in an artery occurs, blood can shoot out several feet from the body.

Blood can also be flung from a blood-coated object as it moves quickly or stops suddenly, such as occurs in a knife attack. These patterns are sometimes referred to as cast-off and

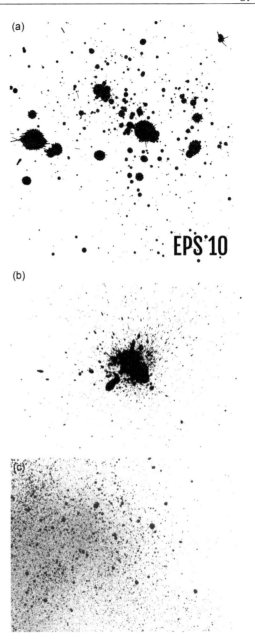

FIGURE 6.27 Active bloodstains: (a) low-velocity impact blood spatter [5 ft/s; 1.5 m/s], (b) medium velocity impact blood spatter [5–100 ft/s; 1.5–30 m/s], and (c) high-velocity impact blood spatter [>100 ft/s; >30 m/s].

Source: All images from iStockphoto.com (a) writerfantast, (b) Marat Musabirov., (c) stuartbur.

cessation bloodstains, respectively. Since blood cast-off from a weapon travels in line with the motion, these types of patterns are easily recognized and are particularly useful in determining the direction of the movement of the weapon. It can also be useful in figuring out the minimum number of impacts that occurred in the assault with one line of blood for each impact.

It is possible to determine from active bloodstains the direction of the droplets and backtrack to their 3D point of origin. As blood moves through the air, the droplets assume a spherical shape. If they hit a wall or floor at 90°, a perfectly spherical shape is observed. As the angle that the blood hits the

FIGURE 6.28   Arterial gush pattern on wall.

Source: James et al. (2005).

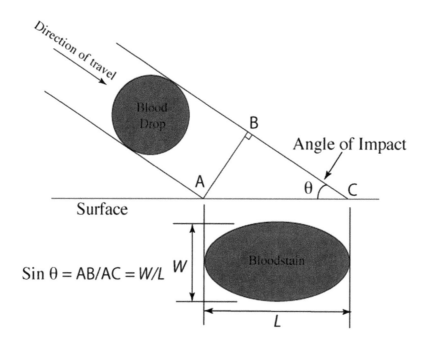

FIGURE 6.29   Angle of impact calculations for a blood droplet.

surface decreases (called the *angle of impact*), the bloodstain assumes an increasingly elongated shape. By simply measuring the length and width of the bloodstain, the approximate angle of the droplet's impact can be easily determined. The width of the bloodstain corresponds to the diameter of the spherical droplet just before it hit the surface. The length of the stain provides information about the angle of impact as illustrated in Figure 6.29. Using these two measurements, a simple right triangle can be formed with the width of the bloodstain (w) equal to the length of the line AB, and the length of the stain (l) corresponding to another side of the triangle, the line AC. The impact angle (θ) can then be simply calculated from trigonometry as: $\sin \theta = AB/AC = w/l$. The value of θ is only approximate, however, since it assumes that the droplets travel in a straight line and, in reality, they travel in an arc due to the influence of gravity.

BOX 6.8   BRIEF ON BLOOD IMPACT ANALYSIS

1. Bloodstains may be classified as passive, active, and transfer.
2. Passive bloodstains are formed under the influence of gravity only.
3. Active bloodstains are formed by a force in addition to gravity and are divided into low-velocity, medium-velocity, and high-velocity impact stains.
4. Transfer stains contain imprint information such as footprints and handprints.
5. Blood-containing evidence must be collected and preserved properly.

The direction that a blood droplet travels can be determined from the shape of the bloodstain. When a blood droplet hits a surface, it forms a teardrop-shaped stain with the narrow end "pointing" in the direction of travel of the droplet (Figure 6.30). This is true for a stain where a droplet directly hits a surface, but if the stain is large enough, secondary stains can result from smaller droplets splashed out from the original droplet. In these smaller satellite droplets, the narrow end points toward the point of original impact of the larger droplet with the surface, as shown at the right in Figure 6.30. When a blood droplet is directed back toward the source of the force that caused the spatter, it is referred to as backspatter.

By knowing the direction of travel and the angles of impact of a series of blood droplets, it is possible to determine their common starting points, or more accurately, their area or *point of origin or convergence*. For example, if lines are drawn from each droplet back along their travel path and at the determined angle of impact, the origin must lie near or along that line. If enough droplets are considered, the point (area) at which all the lines intersect is where the blood spatter originated. This is shown for a complex series of bloodstains in Figure 6.31. Because of some uncertainty in the exact trajectory of the droplets due to gravity and environmental conditions, it is probably best to talk about an area of origin rather than a single point of origin. The field of BPA, however, tends to refer to the point of origin. A single well-formed drop of blood can fix the line of origin, but at least two or more droplets are required to fix with any certainty the point (area) of origin. Using this approach, it is also possible to determine if there were multiple points of origin, possibly from multiple separate attacks, and help develop a sequence of events taking place in the assault (Figure 6.31b). The movement of the victim and the attacker can also be followed and even the order of the blows determined. This is valuable information in confirming or refuting the victim's (if available) and suspect's accounts of the events.

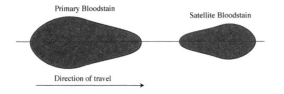

FIGURE 6.30 Relationship of shapes between primary and secondary (satellite) bloodstains.

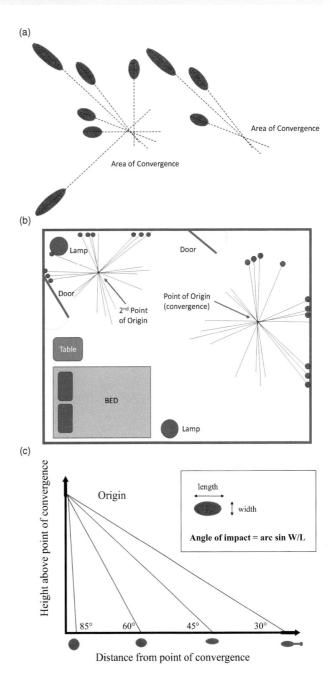

FIGURE 6.31 (a) Lines through the central axes of the individual stains cross at the point (area) of convergence, (b) crime scene drawing showing the arrangement of blood patterns in the space, and (c) a plot used for the determination of point (area) of origin from angles of impact.

BOX 6.9   BLOOD WITNESS: GRAHAM BACKHOUSE AND THE TELLTALE BLOOD RECORD

In 1984, a car bomb explosion in Horton, England, critically injured Margaret Backhouse. The belief at the time was that the attack was intended for her husband, Graham Backhouse, who had been the subject of a series of apparent hate crimes. Backhouse had received hate letters and threatening telephone calls, and ultimately, a decapitated sheep's head with a warning attached, "You Next." After nine days of around-the-clock surveillance of his farm, Backhouse installed a direct alarm to the local police station and the surveillance was called off. About two weeks later, the alarm sounded and police rushed to Backhouse's farm to find a neighbor, Colyn Bedale-Taylor, shot dead with a bloody knife in his hands and Backhouse seriously wounded with knife cuts to his chest and face.

The account Backhouse provided was that Bedale-Taylor had come that evening to the Backhouse farm and a heated argument ensued. He said that the neighbor had confessed to the hate crimes and then attacked him with the knife in the kitchen. After a violent struggle, Backhouse was able to break free and run down the hall to get his shotgun. After warning Bedale-Taylor to stop, Backhouse shot him.

Forensic investigations centered on the bloodstain pattern analysis of the crime scene. The results, however, pointed to clear discrepancies between Backhouse's story and the blood evidence present including: (1) too little blood found in the kitchen, (2) a lack of bloodstains consistent with a violent struggle, (3) the knife Bedale-Taylor held contained only his blood, suggesting it had been placed there after the shooting, (4) the presence of blood smears from Backhouse on the top of a kitchen chair but not on the gun (inconsistent with his sequence of events), (5) the discovery of blood droplets under upset pieces of furniture (consistent only with the furniture being upset after the struggle), (6) the presence of blood drops from Backhouse that were consistent with those only coming from a stationary person (passive), and (7) the absence of a blood trail down the hallway to the gun.

A more consistent story based on the blood pattern evidence was that Backhouse had killed Bedale-Taylor and tried to cover up his crime by self-inflicting some wounds and staging the scene to look like an attack. The real motive was that Backhouse was trying to murder his wife to collect the large life insurance policy on her to offset his large debts. He was trying to implicate Bedale-Taylor in Margaret's attempted murder in order to shift the suspicion from himself to Bedale-Taylor.

Backhouse was tried in 1985, convicted, and sentenced to two life terms in prison.

6.3.2.3 Transfer Bloodstains

Transfer bloodstains arise when objects containing wet blood touch a surface and transfer a print-like pattern of the object directly onto the surface. Fingerprints, handprints, shoe tracks, and hair marks from both the victim and attacker can leave unmistakable patterns that can be invaluable in determining both the identity and movements of the participants (Figure 6.32). Examination of the imprint from a transfer

FIGURE 6.32   Transfer bloodstain of a bloody footprint found at a crime scene.

Source: Shutterstock.com.

pattern can indicate the direction of motion. The shape of the contact print can leave behind a recognizable imprint that can be used to identify the object that created it (see Box 6.10). Occasionally, round or cylindrical bloodied objects that are rolled, such as a baseball bat or piece of furniture, may leave behind a series of repetitive bloodstains. The distance between similar points in adjacent stains approximates the circumference of the rolled object. Repetitive footprint stains can be used to calculate the length of the person's stride and whether they were walking or running, along with the direction of their travel. If the bloody object impacts a surface with some force, blood can be ejected from the object, and "spines" are often observed radiating from the imprint. The size and extent of this can suggest the approximate force of impact.

Tracing bloody footprints can visibly follow the movements of an attacker. Once an object is contaminated with blood, every time it is brought into contact with something else, such as the floor or furniture, some of the blood rubs off and decreases the amount left on the object. The pattern then becomes fainter with every step. Very small, invisible trace amounts of blood, however, can continue to be followed using luminol and fluorescein. Thus, long after a visible trace is gone, the movements of the attacker can still be followed.

6.3.3 Collecting and Preserving Blood Evidence

Properly collecting and preserving blood-containing samples presents some unique challenges. Blood can carry many diseases that can survive outside the body for days, months, and even years. Studies have shown, for example, that the HIV virus that causes AIDS can survive in dried blood samples outside the body for at least 15 days, while the Hepatitis A virus can survive for months and still transmit infection. It is, therefore, wise to treat all blood samples with extreme caution and handle them as if they carried disease.

Blood patterns and their locations at the crime scene should first be photographed from a variety of angles, and measurements should be taken before samples are collected. Samples containing wet blood on clothing or other artifacts collected at crime scenes must be air-dried to avoid decomposition and putrefaction. They should be stored in a dry paper bag and labeled as a biohazard, not in a sealed plastic bag. Items that are very wet, however, should be initially placed briefly in a sealed plastic bag for transportation to the laboratory for drying. Once dried, samples should be refrigerated to avoid further decomposition. Of course, proper chain of

---

BOX 6.10   FATAL IMPRESSION: LINCOLNSHIRE AXE MURDERS

In 1991, the body of Fred Maltby was found in his home just outside Lincoln, England. By examining the wounds, the blood spatter around the room, and, most importantly, the blood imprints of the weapon on a nearby sofa and pillows, it was quickly determined that the attack had been carried out using an old axe. A second similar murder occurred in Lincolnshire in January 1993. An axe head was found shortly afterwards in a local pond by two teenage boys. A comparison of the axe head with the bloody imprints on the furniture, along with inductively-coupled plasma atomic emission spectroscopy (ICP AES, Chapter 12) of paint samples from the axe head, definitively tied the axe to the two murders and led to the conviction of the suspect in the crime.

(a)   (b)

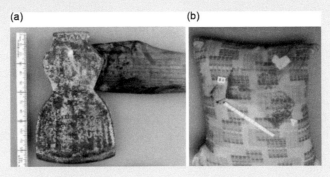

FIGURE 6.33   Imprints of the murder weapon on a nearby sofa and pillows in the Lincolnshire Axe Murder Case: (a) hand axe found near the crime scene identified from transfer blood patterns and paint analysis, and (b) cushion with bloodstains from the axe head.

Source: Released image Lincolnshire Police, UK.

---

custody documentation must always be completed. Blood can be decontaminated with a 10% bleach solution, and all equipment and personal clothing that come into contact with even traces of blood should be decontaminated before leaving the crime scene.

In 1983, the International Association of Bloodstain Pattern Analysts (IABPA) was formed to "promote the science

of bloodstain pattern interpretation [and to] standardize the scientific techniques of bloodstain pattern interpretation." In 2002, the FBI established a *Scientific Working Group on Bloodstain Pattern Analysis* (SWGSTAIN) that helps focus scientific work in this area and support the development of common practices and terminology across the field.

6.4 SEROLOGY AND OTHER BIOLOGICAL FLUIDS

6.4.1 Introduction

While blood is certainly the most abundant fluid in the body, a variety of other fluids are both present in the body and may prove valuable in investigations. In this section, we will briefly examine several of these other body fluids or serums.

Some individuals are referred to as secretors, meaning that they secrete the same RBC antigens (such as A and B) in other body fluids besides blood. About 80% of a typical population are secretors. This means that blood typing can be determined not just from a secretor's blood but also from their other body fluids, such as sweat and saliva.

BOX 6.11   BRIEF ON OTHER SEROLOGICAL FLUIDS

1. A variety of body fluids can be used in forensic investigations including saliva, semen, urine, sweat, bile, vitreous humor, and others.
2. Saliva can be used to determine improper contact and provide DNA samples.
3. Semen and vaginal fluids are involved in many sexual assault cases, and a series of presumptive and confirmatory tests have been developed.
4. Urine is especially useful for the qualitative identification of drugs, toxins, and disease.
5. Vitreous humor (eyes) can be used both for a PMI estimation and confirmation of drug use and disease.

6.4.2 Saliva

Saliva is about 99% water mixed with small amounts of proteins, enzymes, mucus, electrolytes, and other components. It is secreted by three glands located in the mouth, with the average person producing between about 0.7 and 1.5 L (~quarts) of saliva each day. Its primary function is to aid with the digestive process by lubricating and cleansing the mouth, initiating the first steps of the chemical breakdown process of food, and assisting in the mechanical processes necessary to swallow our food.

An old belief is that licking a wound helps it heal faster, presumably by killing bacteria. Interestingly, saliva does contain several natural compounds that have some antibacterial properties (e.g., IgA, lactoferrin, and others), but our mouths also contain a great many bacteria that are not killed by saliva, some of which can cause severe illness through bite wounds. Saliva also contains an enzyme called salivary amylase (also known sometimes as ptyalin) that begins the breakdown of

starch and glycogen in foods into smaller component sugars. This starch breakdown is completed in the small intestines by the related pancreatic amylase (amylopsin). While amylase is present in the saliva of humans, it is not present in the saliva of many other mammals, such as dogs, horses, and cats.

Saliva can be important in a variety of forensic settings. If detected, it can support allegations of improper sexual contact or attacks. It has been recovered from discarded coffee cups, cigarette butts, stamps, and even bite marks to help connect a suspect with a crime, especially through the use of DNA typing and serological testing. Residues from the back of stamps have helped provide information related to hate crimes and have even been used to reinvestigate the identity of the notorious Jack the Ripper 120 years after the crimes were committed in 1888.

Presumptive tests have been developed to detect the presence of saliva in a sample. These tests usually rely on detecting the presence of either the amylase enzyme or the squamous epithelial cells that are continually shed from the insides of our mouths. Saliva testing is becoming increasingly common, and many drugs can now be readily identified in saliva samples, including marijuana, cocaine, PCP, heroin, amphetamines, ketamine, LSD, Rohypnol, and others.

A positive test for amylase in a wound can indicate a human bite rather than a dog bite, for instance. The test is rather simple and relies on the breakdown of starch by any amylase in the test sample. The suspect sample is first mixed with a small amount of starch solution. Then, an iodine solution is added (iodine turns black in the presence of starch). If amylase is present in the sample, it breaks down the starch into its smaller units, mainly to glucose, and the solution does not turn black. If amylase is not present, all the starch remains intact, and the solution turns a characteristic blue-black color upon exposure to iodine. The problem with this test, however, is that certain proteins in other common body fluids, such as blood and semen, can react with iodine to give false positive results. A more common test employs starch molecules attached to a blue dye molecule in microcapsules (Phadebas reagent). If amylase is present, the starch is broken down, and the dye is released from the microcapsules into solution to generate a visible color (Figure 6.34). Amylase is also present elsewhere in the body, although usually in lower concentrations than found in saliva. This can also give rise to false positive test results.

Squamous cells from the inside of a person's mouth can usually be identified microscopically. These cells from the mouth lining are extremely flat, often so flat that the nucleus causes a noticeable bulge in the center of the cell. While the body does have other squamous cells besides those found in the mouth, they are not typically found in saliva samples. If these cells are present, DNA typing can aid in the identification of the donor.

6.4.3 Semen

Semen is a semi-fluid produced by the male reproductive system and serves as the carrier for sperm cells (spermatozoa) in sexual reproduction. It is a complex mixture of cells, proteins,

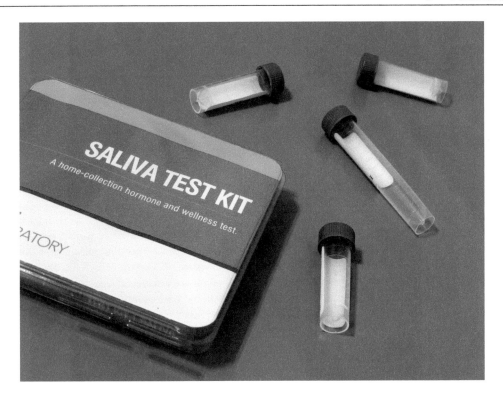

FIGURE 6.34 Saliva test strips tubes containing water and the Phadebas Reagent. Saliva is added to the test tubes for testing.

Source: Shutterstock.com.

amino acids, hormones, carbohydrates, and a variety of other inorganic and organic compounds. About 3–6 mL is ejaculated during sexual intercourse and typically contains over 100 million sperm cells (spermatozoa) per mL (~20 droplets per mL). A variety of factors, including drugs, alcohol, disease, and vasectomy, can drastically decrease the sperm count (azoospermic means semen without sperm cells).

Spermatozoa are unique cells that have long whip-like flagellar "tails" that propel them through body fluids. The whip-like action usually lasts for between three and six hours after discharge. The head of the sperm cell contains its DNA complement along with a wealth of enzymes that help it cut through the cell membrane of the egg during fertilization. The sperm cells contain only half the normal cellular DNA complement of other body cells since they carry just the male genetic information that will combine with an egg to form a complete double-stranded complement of DNA in the fertilized egg.

Semen has preeminent importance in forensic cases involving sexual assault. Only one presumptive test is widely used and has become the method of choice for identifying semen. This test involves the identification of high levels of an enzyme, seminal acid phosphatase (SAP), found in semen. After puberty, the male prostate produces concentrations of SAP that remain relatively high throughout life, although the level usually begins to decline after about age 40. Importantly, this enzyme is present even when sperm cells are absent due to disease, drugs, or surgery. The method involves the use of a dye-containing solution, called Brentamine Fast Blue B, that turns purple in the presence of semen.

The most convincing confirmatory test for the presence of semen in a forensic sample is the microscopic identification of sperm cells. This identification can be aided using sperm-specific dyes, such as Nuclear Fast Red and picocarmine. In the absence of identifiable spermatozoa, a second confirmatory test that involves the identification of prostate-specific antigen (PSA or p30) in the sample may be used. This test is effective even when a vasectomy has eliminated sperm cells from the semen. It is usually coupled with an SAP presumptive test to provide a convincing analysis.

Several relatively new techniques have also been used to confirm the presence of semen in a forensic sample. One method, called Y-Detect™ (Reliagene Tech., Inc.), uses a modified PCR method to detect the presence of male DNA from sperm (Y chromosome). The advantage of this system is that it is very sensitive, highly specific (presence of female components does not interfere with the analysis), and all types of human cells can be used, not just sperm. A second technique, called the Rapid Stain Identification test (RSID), uses monoclonal antibodies specific for seminal fluid (human semenogelin antigens) that do not react with any other body fluids.

The collection and proper handling of evidence from suspected sexual assault cases are of great importance. Since most rape cases occur in private, the only witnesses to the crime are the people directly involved. This places a large burden on the forensic investigation. Each year, over 200,000 rape kits are analyzed in the United States alone. Timely work by trained medical professionals operating within strict protocols is essential to ensure an acceptable process in handling sexual assault cases. Among the evidence usually collected are blood samples, clothing, swabs (oral, vaginal, and cervical), and body hairs.

6.4.4 Urine

Urine is used by the body to eliminate soluble waste products and to regulate ion concentrations. It is composed mostly of water and salts (Figure 6.35) and is formed in the kidneys, stored in the bladder, and excreted through the urethra. Its main use in forensic studies has been to search for the qualitative presence of added compounds, such as drugs, poisons, and alcohol, since the kidneys are quite efficient at collecting and concentrating these compounds and their metabolites in the urine.

Composition of urine

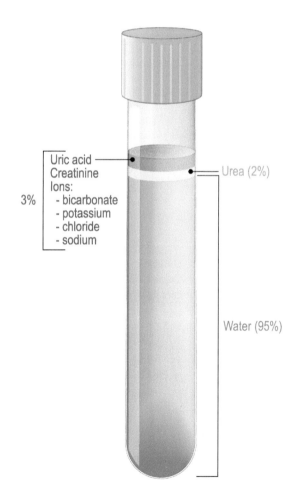

FIGURE 6.35   Urine is mainly made of water, salt, urea and uric acid. Its composition is approximately: water (95%), urea (2%), chloride (0.6%), potassium (0.6%), sulfate (0.18%), phosphate (0.12%), and ammonia (0.05%).

Source: Shutterstock.com.

Presumptive tests for urine are relatively rarely performed due to a lack of sufficient sensitivity and difficulties encountered in distinguishing urine from other body fluids. Most existing tests measure levels of urea $[(NH_2)_2CO]$ and creatinine $[C_4H_9N_3O_2]$ in the sample. While these compounds are also found in other body fluids (e.g., blood, semen, sweat, saliva), they are typically most concentrated in the urine. Even given their relatively high concentrations, they are often difficult to detect in stains since urine readily evaporates and is rapidly absorbed and spread throughout porous materials such as fabric. The DNA analysis of urine is also challenging since the concentrations of cellular materials are typically very low.

Urine is principally used for the *qualitative* analysis of drugs and alcohol. In other words, it is used to determine *if* a drug has been consumed but not *how much* was consumed. This is primarily due to the fact that the concentration of drugs and alcohol in urine depends on many factors, such as how much liquid has recently been consumed (level of hydration or dehydration), how recently the bladder has been emptied and a person's physical state.

6.4.5 Other Body Fluids

A variety of other body fluids have varying forensic usefulness. These include sweat, bile, vaginal fluids, vitreous humor (eye), and others.

Sweat is mostly a saltwater solution, mostly composed of sodium chloride, secreted by sweat glands in an attempt to cool the body through evaporation. It also contains hormones and proteins and, as mentioned earlier, can be used to determine ABO blood types if the person is a secretor. It has been shown to be possible to measure various amino acids and metabolites in sweat to develop a profile that is unique to a particular person.

Bile is a yellow or green fluid secreted by the liver and stored in the gallbladder, primarily to aid digestion of lipids. It is discharged into the intestines after eating. Bile has been used almost exclusively for the determination of drugs and poisons in post-mortem samples (see Chapter 13 on toxicology).

Vitreous humor is the gelatinous fluid filling the eyeball behind the lens and has been used forensically in several ways: post-mortem determination of diseases, detection of drugs and poisons, and in the estimation of the PMI. It is frequently used in post-mortem examinations because it is easier to collect than cerebrospinal fluid and degrades much more slowly than blood.

The concentrations of a variety of forensically interesting compounds remain relatively constant in the body after death. For example, measuring sodium, urea, or creatinine can suggest a post-mortem diagnosis of renal failure, severe dehydration, or excessive water intake. Measuring hydroxybutyrate and certain enzyme levels can suggest antemortem diabetes and alcoholism, respectively. Many drugs and their metabolites (including alcohol) can be measured post-mortem, although reproducibility has been a significant problem with certain of these analyses. PMI estimations have also been successfully made based primarily on potassium and calcium levels.

6.5 INTERESTING BLOOD-RELATED CASES FOR FURTHER STUDY

- Shriver House
- Jesse Watkins
- Jeannie Donald
- Joseph Williams
- Arthur Hutchinson
- Lindy Chamberlain
- War of 1812 Bloodstain
- Sam Sheppard Case
- Pierre Voirbo

QUESTIONS FOR FURTHER PRACTICE AND MASTERY

6.1 Describe the nature and importance of the components of blood plasma.

6.2 What is typically the percent blood volume loss that would lead to irreversible shock?

6.3 Which is *false* about red blood cells (*hint*: figure out which statements are true and the remaining one must be the answer): (a) they do not have a nucleus, (b) they do not have a spherical shape, (c) they do not contain hemoglobin, (d) they do not produce antibodies, (e) they do not live long (<120 days).

6.4 Which type of blood cell is involved in blood clotting?

6.5 When the antibodies are removed from the liquid portion of blood through clotting, what is the remaining solution, after filtering, called?

6.6 If blood plasma is found to contain both A and B antibodies, what is the blood type in the ABO blood system?

6.7 If a blood sample was found in the laboratory to contain both the A and B antigens, what is its blood type in the ABO blood system?

6.8 What are monoclonal antibodies, and how are they used in immunoassay?

6.9 Charlie Chaplin was type O blood and was accused of fathering a type B child with a type A mother. Could he have been the father (not *was* he, but *could* he have been based on blood typing)? Why? Why do you think he was convicted?

6.10 To determine whether a blood sample is *human* blood, which test(s) would you employ? What would influence your decision?

6.11 True or false: blood falling from a wound *only* under the influence of gravity is referred to as blood spatter.

6.12 When a blood droplet is directed toward the source of the force that caused the spatter, what is it called?

6.13 True or false: a blood spatter pattern that consists primarily of very tiny droplets, forming a mist-like appearance might be expected from a velocity impact.

6.14 In the blood spatter droplet, what does the narrow end of the droplet point toward?

6.15 Is the fluid portion of unclotted blood?

6.16 What antigens and anti-antibodies are found in Type-B blood?

6.17 What was Karl Landsteiner's contribution to our understanding of blood?

6.18 What is the difference between blood plasma and blood serum?

6.19 What is medically known as ischemia?

6.20 What are the functions of red blood cells, white blood cells, and platelets?

6.21 What is the hematocrit?

6.22 Why aren't red blood cells used for DNA analysis?

6.23 What is meant by the term activated platelet?

6.24 Describe the Kastle-Meyer test. What are its limitations?

6.25 What is the difference between fluorescence and chemiluminescence?

6.26 What are the EMIT and ELISA tests?

6.27 What is the distinction between active and passive bloodstains?

6.28 What are the parameters used for classifying a blood spatter as low, medium, or high-velocity impact? How does the appearance of the blood spatter differ from one classification to the other?

6.29 What are transfer stains?

6.30 Why must all blood samples be treated with precaution when handling?

6.31 What type of cell is usually used to identify the presence of saliva?

6.32 What is the one presumptive test for semen? What is the most convincing confirmative test for semen?

6.33 What is the vitreous humor, and what can be determined from it in a post-mortem analysis?

6.34 What is cast-off?

EXTENSIVE QUESTIONS

6.35 Briefly describe the following areas of bloodstain analysis:

Serology
Immunology
Fluid dynamics
Blood pattern

6.36 Explain the oxygen-carbon dioxide transport process of hemoglobin in red blood cells.

6.37 Explain the function of each of the following white blood cells.

Neutrophils
B-cells, T-cells
Monocytes
Natural killer cells

6.38 Explain the process of immunoassay in identifying a blood sample as human.

6.39 Explain the ABO blood typing system.

6.40 What are some of the important information that can be gained from a complete study of a bloodstain pattern?

GLOSSARY OF TERMS

active bloodstains: bloodstains acted upon by a force in addition to gravity.

albumin: the major plasma protein in human blood (~60% of plasma proteins) that is soluble in water and salt solutions. It coagulates by heat and is responsible for maintaining plasma osmotic pressure (fluid balance) and transporting biomolecules.

amylase: an enzyme that breaks down starch and glycogen into its component simple sugars (mainly glucose).

angle of impact: the angle formed between the pathway of a moving blood droplet and the plane of the surface that it strikes.

antibody: a "Y-shaped" protein molecule that can combine with a foreign antigen to disable or destroy the antigen.

antigen: any substance that can stimulate the production of antibodies.

bile: a yellow or green fluid secreted by the liver and stored in the gall bladder, primarily used to aid in the digestion of lipids.

blood pattern analysis (BPA): the analysis of bloodstains found at a crime scene that attempts to provide an understanding of how the observed blood patterns were physically formed.

bone marrow: the soft, spongy tissue found in the center of bones that produces most of the cellular components of blood from stem cells.

catalyst: a substance that accelerates a chemical reaction without being consumed in the reaction.

chemiluminescence: the emission of light from chemical reactions without the emission of heat.

confirmatory test: an experiment that can indicate the presence of a particular component in the sample with a very high degree of certainty.

ELISA: an immunoassay technique in which antibodies specific to a particular antigen are first attached firmly to the plastic surface of a small reactor. A solution containing the antigen is then added, whichbinds tightly to the antibodies on the wall of the reactor. After washing, only bound antibody and antigen remain. Another solution containing an enzyme-labeled antibody is then added. The antibody-enzyme binds only to where an antigen is already attached to an antibody stuck to the wall of the reactor.

EMIT: an immunoassay technique in which antibodies for a specific antigen are made and isolated from a test animal's serum. A sample is mixed with the appropriate anti-serum, and any antigen present in the sample then completely reacts with the anti-serum. Measuring the amount of the antigen bound to an enzyme tells how much antigen was in the original sample.

enzyme: a protein that catalyzes a specific biochemical reaction without being consumed in the reaction.

fluid dynamics: the branch of science that deals primarily with the behavior of liquids and gases in motion. In blood analysis, it focuses on how blood flows and may involve calculations of density, velocity, viscosity, and others.

fluorescein: a chemical that is oxidized by hydrogen peroxide when hemoglobin is present to emit light through fluorescence (activated by ultraviolet light at 365 nm and emits light at 450–490 nm).

fluorescence: the phenomenon that occurs when a molecule absorbs light at one wavelength and then emits light at a different wavelength.

glycoprotein: a protein with covalently bonded sugars attached at specific amino acids (primarily serine, threonine, and asparagine). Found in plasma membranes and in most secreted proteins.

hemoglobin: a globular protein containing four iron-based heme subunits that carries oxygen from the lungs to the body's tissues and carbon dioxide from the tissues to the lungs.

high-velocity impact spatter (HVIS): a bloodstain pattern caused by an impact to a blood source, observed when the striking object is moving at speeds of 100 ft/s (30 m/s) or faster.

immunoassay: a technique for identifying and measuring the amount of a substance in the blood primarily through antigen-antibody interactions.

immunology: the broad branch of science that deals with all aspects of the immune system.

ischemia: a low oxygen state in tissues primarily due to an obstruction or otherwise decreased blood flow in tissues.

Kastle-Meyer test: a presumptive blood test using phenol-phthalein and hydrogen peroxide. If blood is present, the solution turns pink.

low-velocity impact spatter (LVIS): a bloodstain pattern caused by an impact of a blood source, caused by striking at speeds up to about 5 ft/s.

luminol: a chemical that is oxidized by hydrogen peroxide when hemoglobin is present to emit light through chemiluminescence.

medium velocity impact spatter (MVIS): a bloodstain pattern caused by an impact with a blood source, usually when the velocity of the striking object is between 5 and 25 ft/s.

monoclonal antibody: an artificially prepared antibody that is more uniform than our natural antibodies and that attacks and binds to only one site on a chosen antigen. Prepared using spleen cells that have been activated to produce antibodies and then fused to fast-growing cell strains that are selected and cultured to generate the antibody.

passive bloodstain: a bloodstain where the droplet moves primarily by the action of gravity alone.

Phadebas reagent: the presumptive test reagent for saliva through detection of amylase.

plasma (blood): the liquid portion of blood that comprises about 55% of its volume and consisting of a complex mixture of cellular, biochemical, and inorganic components in a water-based solution.

platelets (thrombocytes): the cellular component of blood accounting for about 1% of blood cells that are important in blood clotting and self-repair processes of blood vessels. Platelets have no nucleus but do contain some RNA and other cellular structures.

peroxidase: an enzyme that catalyzes the oxidation of a compound from the reduction of hydrogen peroxide.

presumptive test: an analysis which can screen for, but not confirm with certainty, the presence of a particular substance in a sample.

protein: an organic polymer molecule made up of a linear chain of amino acid building blocks. They are essential to living organisms and their sequence of amino acids is dictated by the DNA genetic code.

radioimmunoassay: a technique that is similar to the EMIT immunoassay technique except a radioactive tracer is linked to the final antigen for analysis.

red blood cells (erythrocytes, RBC): the flexible, biconcave disc-shaped cells that account for about 96% of the cellular portion of blood. Their primary function is to carry oxygen from the lungs to the cells and return waste carbon dioxide from the cells back to the lungs. The main chemical component of an RBC is a protein called hemoglobin, which accounts for about 90% of the dry weight of a red blood cell.

ring precipitin test: an immunoassay test in which a soluble antigen reacts to form a precipitate when it combines with a specific antibody.

saliva: a body fluid produced by the salivary glands of the mouth that is comprised mostly of water with small amounts of proteins, enzymes, and other substances.

satellite spatter: the small droplets of blood distributed around a larger drop of blood and formed from the force of the droplet's impact with the surface.

secretor: a person who secretes blood antigens in other body fluids besides blood.

semen: the seminal fluid containing cells, proteins, amino acids, hormones, carbohydrates, and a variety of other inorganic and organic compounds. It is produced by the male reproductive system primarily to carry sperm.

seminal acid phosphatase: the enzyme found in high levels in semen.

serology: the field of science that deals specifically with the study of serums (sera) and other body fluids, such as blood, saliva, urine, and semen. It includes the diagnostic identification of antibodies found in the serum and other body fluids.

serum (blood): a slightly yellow solution obtained by first allowing blood to clot and then removing the solids by centrifugation. Differs from plasma since it contains none of the clotting factors (principally fibrinogen and platelets) found in plasma.

Sickle cell anemia: the disease caused by a change of a single amino acid in hemoglobin (replacement of a glutamic acid for a valine). As a result, the red blood cells change to a sickle-shape under low oxygen levels, often clogging arteries and leading to anemia. Imparts some resistance to malaria.

sperm: the male reproductive cell.

substrate: a substance upon which an enzyme works.

surface tension: the tendency of molecules at the surface of a liquid to behave as if they were part of an elastic membrane.

sweat: a mostly saltwater solution secreted by sweat glands in an attempt to cool the body by evaporation.

transfer bloodstains: a pattern created when a wet, bloody surface comes in contact with another surface to form a print-like pattern.

transfusion: the addition of blood or blood components from a donor directly into the blood stream of a recipient.

urine: the solution comprised mostly of water and salts, used by the body to eliminate soluble waste products and to regulate ion concentrations.

viscosity: the resistance of a liquid to flow under stress.

vitreous humor: the gelatinous fluid filling the eyeball behind the lens.

white blood cells (leucocytes): the cellular component of blood that consists of a large and diverse group of cell types containing nuclei and organelles. They are round to irregularly shaped cells, accounting for about 3% of the total number of blood cells, whose primary responsibility is to effect cellular repair and fight off disease and infection.

REFERENCES AND BIBLIOGRAPHY

Tom Bevel and Ross M.Gardner, *Bloodstain Pattern Analysis* (2nd Ed.), CRC Press, 2002.

Ira S. Dubey, *A Study of the Impact of the Physical Properties of Blood on the Interpretation of Bloodstain Patterns in Forensic Investigations*, ProQuest Dissertations Publishing, 2019.

Maurice Aalders and Leah Wilk, *Investigating the age of blood traces: How close are we to finding the holy grail of forensic science?*, *Emerging Technologies for the Analysis of Forensic Traces*, Springer International Publishing AG, 2019, 109–128.

Ross A. James, Paul A. Hoadley, and Brett G. Sampson, *Determination of postmortem interval by sampling vitreous humour*, American Journal of Forensic Medicine and Pathology, 18, 158–162, 1997.

Stuart H. James and William G. Exkert, *Interpretation of Bloodstain Evidence at Crime Scenes* (2nd Ed.), CRC Press, 1999.

Sturt H. James, et al., *Principles of Bloodstain Pattern Analysis: Theory and Practice*, CRC Press, 2005.

Alwin Kienle, Lothar Lilge, I. Alex Vitkin, Michael S. Patterson, Brian C. Wilson, Raimund Hibst, and Rudolf Steiner, *Why do veins appear blue? A new look at an old question,* Applied Optics, 35, 1151, 1996.

Herbert L. MacDonell, *Bloodstain Patterns*, Golas Printing, 1997.

Alan R. McNeil, Andrea Gardner, and Simon Stables, Simple method for improving the precision of electrolyte measurements in vitreous humor, Clinical Chemistry, 45, 135–136, 1999.

G. Paul Neitzel and Marc K. Smith, United States Office of Justice Programs, *The Fluid Dynamics of Droplet Impact on Inclined Surfaces with Application to Forensic Blood Spatter Analysis*, Office of Justice Programs, 2017.

B rittany C. Novelli, *A Review of Substances Reported to Cause False Positives and Negatives in Forensic Blood Identification Tests*, ProQuest Dissertations Publishing, 2020.

Raymond N. Rogers, *Thermochimica Acta*, 425(1), 189–194, 2005.

Miranda L. Shaine, *Optimization of the Forensic Identification of Blood Using Surface-Enhanced Raman Spectroscopy*, ProQuest Dissertations Publishing, 2020.

Anita Y. Wonder, *Blood Dynamics*, Academic Press, 2001.

Anita Y. Wonder, *Bloodstain Pattern Evidence: Objective Approaches and Case Applications*, Elsevier Science, 2011.

Anatomical Evidence
The Outside Story

7

7.1 ANATOMICAL EVIDENCE: THE OUTSIDE STORY

Each one of you has something no one else has, or has ever had: your fingerprints, your brain, your heart. Be an individual.

(Jon Bon Jovi)

LEARNING GOALS AND OBJECTIVES

Forensic evidence directly from the human body can provide a variety of forensic information. This chapter helps us gain a deeper appreciation of how external anatomical structures provide essential forensic information.

Fingerprints have been used for centuries as a unique mark of just one particular person. We now recognize that each person has a set of ridges on their fingers that sets them apart from all others and, therefore, allows their fingerprints to be used to potentially identify their involvement in events. After studying this chapter, you should be able to:

- Describe what makes up our skin and how it functions.
- Discuss the biological formation of friction ridges along with their structures and features.
- Identify the main patterns of fingerprints: loops, whorls, and arches.
- Explain the identification and use of minutiae and other detailed features for identification.
- Indicate the meaning of visible, latent, and plastic fingerprints.
- Describe the methods for visualizing, lifting, preserving, and comparing latent fingerprints.

- Discuss the development of IAFIS and similar systems.
- Explain the basic steps in a biometric identification.
- Recognize the use of other biological structures for identification (e.g., lips, ears, skin, etc.).
- Discuss current and future types of biometric measurements.
- Describe the advantages and limitations of various biometric identifications.

In addition to fingreprints, hair and fiber information can provide valuable forensic information on the origin and history of the sample. By exploring this section on how hair analysis can be used, you should be able to:

- Describe the chemical composition and structure of hair and how it grows.
- Show how we can tell human hair from that of other animals.
- Describe how information about the treatment of hair can be obtained.
- Show how hair can be used in toxicological studies.
- Discuss how hair samples are collected and analyzed.
- Describe the types of natural and manmade fibers, including their composition and formation.
- Explain how fibers in cloth can provide production and historical information about the cloth.

7.1.1 Introduction

An understanding of the key physical characteristics of the human body in criminal investigations has a long and interesting history. For well over 2,000 years, people have looked to the bodies of victims and suspects to reveal the connections between people, personal identification, and the sequence of actions that occurred as part of the commission of a crime. Today, information from our bodies can provide unique and

DOI: 10.4324/9781003183709-9

unambiguous identification of a person for both criminal and security applications alike. Thus, if we know where and how to look for it, Locard's Principle tells us that we should be able to find evidence left behind by and on our physical bodies themselves.

In previous chapters, we have primarily focused on the smallest types of biological evidence: the molecular and cellular components of biological systems. This approach has provided us with insights useful for identifying the origin of biological samples on the smallest scales. In this and the following two chapters (Chapters 8 and 9), our perspective now shifts to the examination of increasingly larger, multi-cellular arrays of tissues and structures of our bodies: our organs and anatomical structures. We will specifically examine how the evidence of our bodies can be used, along with closely associated materials (e.g., fibers, cloth, etc.), to either uniquely connect a particular person with the evidence or unambiguously identify a person.

The types of evidence that we'll consider in this chapter fall within a broad definition of evidence called *trace evidence*. Typical types of trace evidence include fingerprints, hair, fibers, glass, soil, and explosives, among others (Figure 7.1). One definition of trace analysis involves comparing small pieces of evidence with a standard (called an *exemplar*) in an attempt to see if the evidence's origin or method of use can be identified. Examples of trace evidence might include a small glass chip identified as coming from a particular headlight, a fingerprint connected with a particular person, or a bone chip arising from a particular bone of the body.

Studied carefully, the human body provides an amazing array of individual characteristics that can ideally be used to uniquely identify one person from all other humans. Patterns on our hands and feet, in our eyes, and on our faces can all contribute to our identification. The fast-growing field of biometrics, measuring body features, aims to find rapid and highly reliable methods of correlating these features with a person's recorded identity. Biometric identification has therefore increasingly become an integral part of both forensic investigations and security analysis. In fact, this chapter could well be subtitled "Biometrics in forensic and security applications" since this is the direction in which both fields are rapidly moving.

We will begin this chapter focusing on the exterior of our bodies and explore several topics: fingerprints, hair, and fiber analysis. Each of these types of evidence shares the commonality of involving the examination of structures and organs of the body itself, rather than evidence arising from the actions of our bodies or evidence at the molecular-cellular level. In addition, they share a close developmental connection as well. Very early in our embryonic growth, three germinal layers form that eventually give rise to all the organs and structures in our bodies. The outermost of these germ layers, called the *ectoderm*, specifically gives rise to our epidermis: skin, hair, eyes, and nervous system. These "outermost" tissues are particularly important in biometrics and are therefore grouped together in this chapter, along with the closely associated topic of fiber analysis. Finally, these tissues share the common feature that they are found on the part of our bodies that directly faces the environment – the outside – making them readily accessible for observation. In the following chapter (Chapter 8), we will explore the internal structures and organs of the body, examining both how medicine can inform us about the history of a person and what information our internal organs can provide.

FIGURE 7.1 Fingerprinting for personal identification.

Source: Shutterstock.com.

7.2 FINGERPRINTS

7.2.1 Background and Introduction

The use of fingerprints for personal identification has been around, in one form or another, for millennia. In the ancient world, fingerprints were regularly used in China, Japan, Babylon, and other places to certify business transactions and as a personal sign for important contracts. By the 3rd century BC, the evidence is clear that people in China understood the individual nature of fingerprints and used them as personal identifiers in official documents. Even before that, however, potters and artists from across the ancient world left their indelible marks on their works with thumbprints, possibly to uniquely identify work as their creations (Figure 7.2).

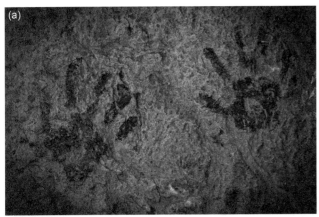

For example, fingerprints have been identified on Stone Age ceramic artifacts, monuments, and lithographs; an indication that people far back into our pre-history at least peripherally understood the uniquely personal character of fingerprints. Ceramic and forensic experts have recently worked with archaeologists to try to use fingerprints on unearthed ancient pottery to learn how many potters may have been responsible for producing the artifacts found at a particular site.

Possibly the first recorded case of the legal use of fingerprints, however, comes from medieval Rome where the 10th-century Roman attorney Quintilian was able to show that bloody handprints found at a crime scene were meant by the true criminal to frame a blind man for the murder of his mother. In the 1600s, there were several important fundamental developments in understanding the unique nature of fingerprints. In 1684, the Dutch scientist Nehemiah Grew reported his studies of the ridges and sweat pores found on human hands and fingers, features he called "little fountains." His work was elaborated upon in 1686 by Prof. Marcello Malpighi from the University of Bologna, when he provided a more detailed picture of the ridge patterns found on fingers. An interesting recent discovery from this time period came when modern renovators were remodeling a room at Hampton Court in England and found 17 complete hand and fingerprints in the underlying plaster from workmen who "signed" their work when the room was last remodeled in 1690 for King William III (Figure 7.3).

By the early 1800s, naturalists clearly had begun to understand the origins and individuality of fingerprints. In 1823, Prof. John Evangelist Purkinje of the University of Breslau

FIGURE 7.2 (a) A pair of aboriginal ochre handprints on a rock in Queensland, Australia, and (b) a finger pressed into the wet clay to form an individualized ceramic object from between 43 and 410 CE.

Source: (a) Shutterstock.com. (b) Used per Creative Commons Attribution 2.0, Generic. Credit: Lincolnshire County Council.

FIGURE 7.3 Right palm imprint in plaster, Hampton Court, London, 1689–1690.

Source: Ed. Henry et al. (2001). Chapter 1 by J. Berry and D.A. Stoney. Figure supplied by Nicholas John Hall, M.F.S., Hertfordshire.

published a thesis on different types of fingerprint patterns, and in 1858, Sir William Herschel, Chief Administrative Officer in Bengal, India, followed a local Indian custom and used fingerprints to sign contracts with local workers. Herschel also realized from his observations spanning six decades that the fingerprint pattern we are born with persists throughout life, and he referred to this important concept as the *Principle of Persistency*. This principle says that once our fingerprints are formed during prenatal development, these patterns then remain unchanged throughout our lives and often last even well beyond death to the latter stages of decay.

One of the big problems in the criminal punishment system of the 19th century that Herschel and others were particularly concerned about had to do with recognizing repeat offenders. Like today, 19th-century societies wanted to levy more severe punishments on a criminal who repeated their offenses. The problem was how to be sure that it was the same offender each time (see Box 7.1). Photographs were not reliable, especially over time, and a system of measurements of our physical features, known as the *Bertillon System* (e.g., distance between the eyes, size of nose, length of fingers, etc.), was highly problematic and later abandoned completely. However, Herschel saw the clear advantages of using fingerprints to identify repeat criminals and advocated fingerprint use in the personal identification records of prisoners.

While Herschel sought to use fingerprints to identify convicted criminals, what was really needed for fingerprints to become useful in forensic investigations was some system for the classification of the lifelong ridge patterns so that large numbers of prints and files could be quickly and easily compared. One of the first attempts at this task came from the work of Dr. Henry Faulds, British Surgeon-Superintendent of the Tsukiji Hospital in Tokyo, who developed the first systematic method of classification. Dr. Faulds also clearly recognized the potential use of fingerprints in forensic investigations when he wrote:

> when bloody fingerprints or impressions on clay, glass, etc. exist, they may lead to the scientific identification of criminals ... There can be no doubt as to the advantage of having, beside their photograph, a copy of the forever unchangeable finger furrows of important criminals.
>
> *(Faulds, 1880)*

He recognized the value of latent prints, those not visible to the unaided eye, and used his expertise to exonerate a staff member at his hospital who had been incorrectly charged with robbery. Dr. Faulds is generally recognized today as the "father of fingerprinting," although this recognition didn't come until nearly half a century after his death.

In *Life on the Mississippi* (1883) and later works, Mark Twain brought to literature the use of fingerprints in criminal justice. In real life, however, Juan Vucetich of the Argentine Police in 1891 was one of the first to use fingerprints to identify a woman who had murdered her two sons and then took her own life in an attempt to frame someone else. Her bloody handprint, however, was found on the doorpost, thereby both exonerating the framed person and showing the woman as the true murderer. At about the same time, Sir Francis Galton

published a book entitled *Fingerprints* that reiterated the individuality (uniqueness) and permanence (persistence) of fingerprints and presented an alternative to Dr. Faulds' classification system. Galton's system, however, was soon replaced in 1896 by Sir Edward Henry's fingerprint classification system. This system, first adopted by Scotland Yard in 1901, is essentially the same system that is still used in most places today.

Fingerprint use as personal identifiers in the United States began in 1902, when the New York Civil Service Commission and, in 1903, the New York State Prison system began using fingerprints for the identification of convicted criminals. At about the same time (1902) in a related development, R. Fischer presented his related work on the furrows of the human lips for individual identification, a field known as *cheiloscopy*. This work culminated in 1968 when the lip prints of over 1,300 people were examined at Tokyo University with the conclusion that lip prints, like fingerprints, are also unique to an individual and persist.

BOX 7.1   THE CASE OF THE WILLS WEST

In 1903, Will West was admitted to the Leavenworth Federal Penitentiary in Kansas. As part of his induction, a series of measurements were taken to see if he was a repeat offender, and, sure enough, a card listed someone as William West with essentially the same set of measurements and photographic likeness (Figure 7.4). But with a little more examination, it was learned that William West was *already* at Leavenworth serving a life term for murder! The fingerprints of the two men, however, were clearly quite different. While this is an interesting case, it probably didn't play a particularly important role in establishing fingerprint analysis in the United States as an important basis of criminal identification.

In 1977, the FBI began using its *Automated Fingerprint Identification System* (AFIS) using digital scans of fingerprints (Figure 7.4). This system was upgraded in 1996 to allow for the computerized searches of the entire AFIS fingerprint database, and then modified again in 1999 with the formation of the *Integrated Automated Fingerprint Identification System* (IAFIS), which provided for the automated digital computer submission, storage, and search of the national FBI fingerprint database. In 2011, the new *Next Generation Identification System* (NGI) was introduced to ultimately replace IAFIS. Today, federal and state agencies can receive answers to requests for matching criminal fingerprint patterns from a massive fingerprint database within just hours of submission.

One point of distinction, before we delve further, is that sometimes the term "fingerprint" is differentiated from the term "fingermark." In this usage, fingerprint is meant to denote a rolled print (exemplar), while fingermark is a collected print, such as what might be obtained from a crime scene. In this chapter, however, we will predominantly use the term "fingerprint" for both usages, since this remains the most common and inclusive practice in the field.

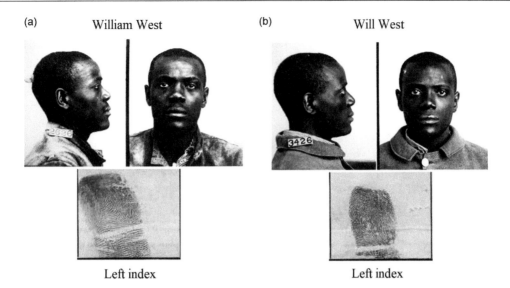

(a) William West   (b) Will West

Left index   Left index

FIGURE 7.4   Photographs of Will West (a) and William West (b), from 1903 Leavenworth Federal Penitentiary in Kansas.

Source: Retrieved from Wikimedia Commons; used per Creative Commons Attribution.

BOX 7.2   BRIEF ON FINGERPRINTS: TIMELINE

- **>3000 BC**: Ancient fingerprints on pottery.
- **300 BC**: Chinese use of fingerprints for personal identification in legal documents.
- **1100 AD**: Quintilian uses fingerprints to solve a murder case.
- **1684**: Nehemiah Grew reports studies on ridges and pores.
- **1823**: J.E. Purkinje describes ridge details.
- **1858**: Herschel reports persistency of fingerprint detail throughout life.
- **1880**: H. Faulds proposes fingerprint use in forensic investigations *via* latent prints and proposes a classification system.
- **1891**: J. Vucetich uses fingerprints to solve a murder-suicide case and exonerate a suspect.
- **1892**: F. Galton expands on the use of fingerprints and proposes a classification system.
- **1896**: E. R. Henry develops classification system that is still in use.
- **1902**: First American criminal use of fingerprints.
- **1977**: FBI begins computerized AFIS system.
- **1999**: FBI begins completely digital fingerprint system for submission, storage, and search (IAFIS).
- **2018**: FBI's Next Generation Identification (NGI) system logs 300,000 searches per day.
- **2020**: U.S. Department of Homeland Security (DHS) has >120 million fingerprints on record.

7.2.2 Skin: The Amazing Organ

Our skin is the largest organ system in the human body weighting, on average, 25 pounds and covering an area of about 20 ft². Our skin is part of the larger *integumentary system* that forms the outer "boundary" of our bodies and also includes our hair and nails, which are considered "derivatives" of our epidermis. It consists of an array of various tissues and structures that function together for the protection and regulation of underlying organs and receives about one-third of all the oxygenated blood that leaves the heart. In particular, the skin helps to regulate the temperature of our bodies in the face of constantly changing thermal environments, controls moisture loss, protects us from physical impact and wear, provides a barrier to the entry of unwanted substances and agents into our bodies (e.g., dirt, bacteria, and viruses), and serves as a highly sensitive sensory organ for the body. It allows us to feel the lightest touch and yet withstand some pretty significant impacts and abrasion forces. It's tough, durable, and constantly being repaired and replaced.

The skin contains a variety of specialized cells and structures (Figure 7.5). Our skin has three major layers, although each is often broken into smaller sublayers. The lowest layer is referred to as the *subcutaneous layer* (or more accurately called the *hypodermis*) and is composed largely of fat and connective tissue that contains larger blood vessels and nerves. The middle layer, referred to as the *dermis*, is composed mostly of collagen (protein) fibers, elastic tissue, and reticular fibers (cross-linked fibers that form a fine supporting meshwork). The dermis is also the place where the hair follicles, sebaceous (oil) glands, eccrine (sweat) glands, apocrine (scent) glands, and hair erector muscles are found. Additionally, smaller blood vessels and nerves run through this layer that transmit information about temperature, touch, pressure, and sometimes pain to our brains. More will be presented later about hair and how it grows from the follicles located in these dermal layers. The main structural function of the dermis is to support and nurture the layer lying above it. The outermost layer of our skin is called the *epidermis* and ranges in thickness from very thin on our eyelids (about 0.05 mm) to rather thick on the palms of our hands and the soles of our feet (around 1.5 mm thick). It is this layer that also contains *melanin*, the

HUMAN SKIN ANATOMY

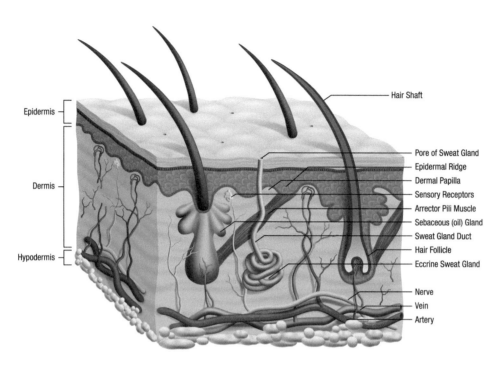

FIGURE 7.5 Human skin anatomy: structure of skin and fingerprint ridges.

Source: Shutterstock.com.

pigment responsible for skin coloration. At the lowest portion of the epidermis, often referred to as the "generating layer" (*stratum basale*), column-like cells constantly divide and push previously formed cells toward the surface, causing these cells to flatten out and ultimately die in the process. The very top layer of the epidermis (*stratum corneum*), the part directly in contact with the outside world, is composed of about 25 layers of dead cells that stay at the surface for about two weeks before being shed and replaced from layers below.

7.2.3 Development and Structures of Fingerprints

On certain surfaces of our skin, particularly our hands and feet, a tightly packed series of ridges are formed early in our development. These regular patterns of ridges usually begin to be observed between the third and fifth months of our pre-natal development and grow in complexity as the fetus develops. Once established, these patterns of ridges stay with us unchanged throughout life, simply expanding uniformly to a larger size as we grow and develop. These "friction" ridges serve to greatly increase the skin's surface area and, therefore, increase the gripping ability of our hands and feet, especially on smooth and wet surfaces, and to increase the sensitivity of our touch sense (Figure 7.6). These ridges are believed to

FIGURE 7.6 Color scanning electron micrograph (SEM) of part of a human finger, showing details of skin ridges in the outer epidermis. The small circular openings on the ridge tops are the sweat glands. Epidermal ridges also occur on the soles of feet and palms of the hands, forming distinct patterns. Each fingerprint pattern is unique to an individual. Even identical twins have different fingerprints.

Source: Steve Gschmeissner/Science Photo Library. Used with permission.

originate during our prenatal development from the buckling of the basal cell layer of the fetal epidermis as the cells in this layer grow rapidly and do not have sufficient space to spread out. Consequently, the layer ends up permanently bending and buckling to form the ridges that we see at the surface of the skin. This process is somewhat similar to how submerged rocks at the bottom of a shallow stream cause surface ripples to appear in the water.

The tops of the individual patterns on our fingers are called *ridges*, and the adjacent lower valleys are called *furrows*. The surface of these ridges is dotted with the openings for sweat glands that are located deeper in the dermal layers and serve to help remove cellular waste products, including salt and urea, and to regulate body temperature. Each ridge unit, of the 2,700 ridge units per square inch of friction skin, contains a sweat gland. The observed pattern of our fingerprints arises from our epidermal layer, although the pattern is formed deeper at the interface between the top of the dermal layer and the lowest epidermal layer, the *stratum basale* or "base layer" of the epidermis (Figure 7.5). Because the pattern of our ridges arises from these lower levels, fingerprint patterns cannot be easily altered, even when the epidermal layers of the skin are injured. An injury must penetrate and change the deeper dermal layer to make a lasting impact on someone's fingerprint pattern. Fingerprints may, however, be affected by deep trauma or disease. For example, eczema, psoriasis, dermatopathia pigmentosa reticularis (DPR), or a disease called scleroderma may lead to either distorted or even the complete lack of fingerprints (Figure 7.7). Additionally, treatment with a common anti-cancer drug, Capecitabine, in some instances leads to the disappearance of a person's fingerprints.

7.2.4 Fingerprint Patterns

The ridges on our fingers form interesting, regular, and unique patterns that can be classified into overall broad groupings and further into sets of smaller identifiable characteristics. Several systems of classification exist, although the *Henry System* was the most commonly encountered until relatively recently. While the Henry System has now largely been replaced by digital automated systems, many of the general features of the system remain important in identifying and comparing fingerprints.

Fingerprint classification systems typically begin by identifying three basic patterns: the *loop*, the *arch*, and the *whorl*, shown in Figure 7.8. An *arch* pattern, found in about 5% of all fingerprints, has ridges beginning at one side of the fingerprint and running completely to the other side of the fingerprint without a backward turn. In contrast, *loop* patterns, found in about 60%–70% of fingerprints, contain ridge lines that enter on one side of the fingerprint, run toward the middle, and then curve backward to exit on the same side that they entered the pattern. *Whorls*, found in about 25%–35% of fingerprints, contain ridges that complete at least one 360° "circuit" within the pattern, although not always forming a regular circular pattern (e.g., a double whorl pattern).

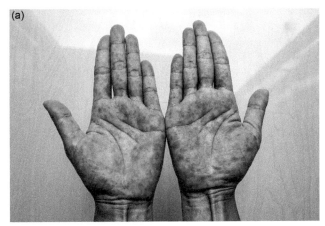

FIGURE 7.7 (a) Atopic dermatitis (AD), also known as atopic eczema, is a type of inflammation of the skin (dermatitis) of the hands and (b) a scarred fingerprint.

Source: Images used courtesy Shutterstock.com.

Two important additional features of fingerprints help to readily define these three basic patterns: the *delta* and the *core*. These two features are probably most easily understood by examining more closely a loop pattern, such as that shown in Figure 7.9. Where a loop pattern reaches its farthest point toward the middle of the print and begins to turn backward, the innermost ridge of the curve is referred to as the *core*. If, instead, we look at the ridge lines that enter the print from the side opposite from where the loop enters and exits, we see that where these ridges encounter the looped ridges, they must move either downward or upward to go around the looped ridges. This is similar to the effect observed in a flowing stream that encounters a rock in the middle of its path: some of the water is deflected to the left and some to the right. The point of ridge divergence, where the upward and downward deflected ridges meet the looping ridges (the point at the rock in the stream), forms a *delta* (a small triangular region). Often, a small island is also observed at the center of the delta. If a line is drawn from the top of the core to the delta point, it intersects a number of ridges between these two features. The number of ridges between these two features is known as the *ridge count*. The three basic patterns of arch, loop, and whorl are also defined specifically by their core and delta features. Loop

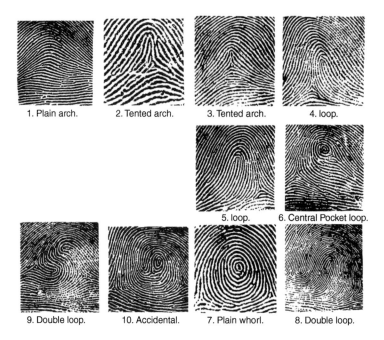

FIGURE 7.8   Examples of the different types of fingerprint patterns: arch (plain and tented arch), loop (plain, radial, and ulnar), and whorl (double loop, pocket, plain, or mixed/accidental).

Source: FBI.

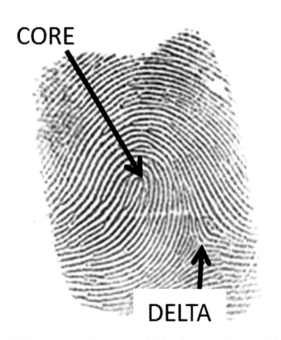

FIGURE 7.9   Fingerprint core and delta features illustrated for a loop pattern. The number of ridges that are between the core and the delta defines the ridge number of the print.

Source: Used per Creative Commons Attribution-Share Alike 2.0 Generic. User: Vivien Rolfe.

patterns show one delta and one core feature, whorl patterns have at least two deltas, and plain arches have no deltas.

These broadest three patterns are, however, often broken down into several more detailed groups. Arches are often

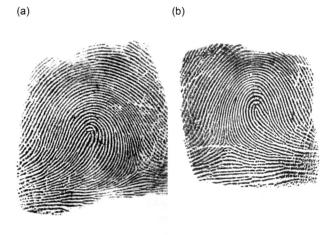

FIGURE 7.10   Ulnar loop (a) and radial loop (b) from a right hand.

Source: Images used courtesy Shutterstock.com.

broken down into plain and tented arches. The ridges in a plain arch pattern flow relatively smoothly across the print, while a tented arch has a significantly "upward" pushed pattern that resembles a tent pole, and where one ridge stands up at least at a $45°$ or greater angle (and usually contains a delta). Loops can be plain, radial (where the starting, open part of the loop points toward the thumb – nearest the radial arm bone), or ulnar (where the open part of the loop points away from the thumb – or toward the ulnar bone), as shown in Figure 7.10 [an easy way to remember where the radius bone joins the hand is to remember "*Teddy Roosevelt*" – the *T*humb and *R*adius are on the same side]. Radial loops are very uncommon and usually found only on the index finger. Finally, whorls can be broken down into plain whorls, double-loop whorls, accidental (mixed) whorls, and central pocket (pocket) loop whorls.

Upon closer examination of the patterns made by the ridges on our fingers, we find that they are often not just simple lines but are far more complex. The lines vary in length and thickness, branch, and fuse together, end and start abruptly, and form a rich level of detail within the general loop, arch, and whorl patterns. The information obtained from fingerprints is often divided into three levels of detail. The first level (not surprisingly, called level 1) describes the overall structural information found in the pattern (e.g., arch, loop, double-loop whorl, etc.). Level 2 contains information about how the individual friction ridges are arranged in terms of their starting and stopping, fusing, branching, and other features – referred to as *minutiae* and pattern *paths*. The final level (level 3) describes the finest details about individual ridges, such as their thicknesses, edge shapes, location of pores, and other fine detail information.

There are a number of minutiae features that can be identified in a fingerprint, a few of which are shown in Figure 7.11. For example, the point where a single ridge splits into two ridges is called a *bifurcation*, while a single friction ridge that simply ends is called a *ridge ending*. A short ridge enclosed by other ridges is referred to as either an *island* or a *ridge dot* (when the ridge's length is approximately the same as its width, it's called a dot). Many other types of minutiae exist and help define the individual characteristics of a fingerprint. Both the type and location of each of these minutiae features are important in characterizing and comparing fingerprints.

The most detailed level of a fingerprint (level 3) looks at the fine characteristics of an individual ridge unit (e.g., edges, textures, pore positions, etc. of the ridge). This level of detail is typically not currently included in most forensic identification methods but is gaining increased use in digital personal identification systems based on biometrics – a method for uniquely identifying specific people based on measurable and permanent physical traits.

7.2.5 Comparing Fingerprints

Most often, fingerprints are used to compare an unknown sample, such as prints taken at a crime scene or from someone of unknown identity, with fingerprints obtained from a known source (reference or exemplar). In this fashion, the unknown prints may often be assigned to identify one individual person (Figure 7.12). The process usually involves both the general classification system (level 1) and the identification and location of minutiae within the prints (level 2). Generally, the more matching features found when comparing two sets of prints, without the addition of any unique features found *only* in one print, the more confidence that can be placed in the comparison. The exact number of matches necessary for a valid identification, however, continues to spark debate. Usually, most fingerprint experts seek to identify at least 12 matching points to place a reasonable level of trust in the comparison, although European courts typically requires 16 matching points for a comparison to be considered valid. However, in North America, the generally accepted threshold for the number of matching points is the "examiner's determination that sufficient quantity and quality of detail exists in the prints being compared" (International Association for Identification, IAI).

No two fingerprints, including the minutiae features, have ever been found to be identical, even those obtained from identical twins. Early on in the use of fingerprints for

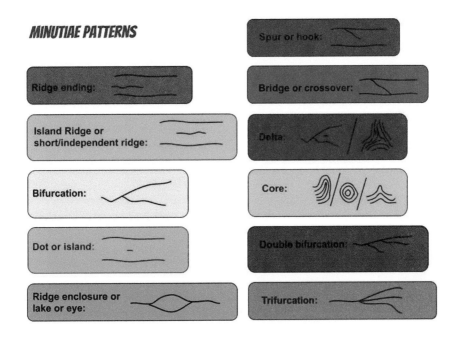

FIGURE 7.11   Common fingerprint minutiae patterns.

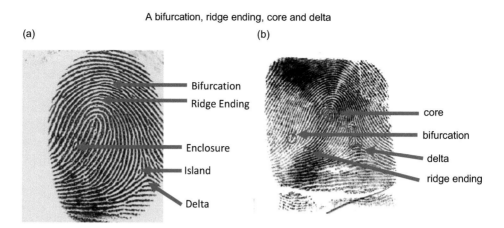

A bifurcation, ridge ending, core and delta

(a)   (b)

Bifurcation
Ridge Ending
Enclosure
Island
Delta

core
bifurcation
delta
ridge ending

FIGURE 7.12   Comparison of several minutiae features between two separate fingerprint samples. Twelve or more points, without any unmatched features, are often needed to consider the two prints "matched" with a high degree of certainty.

Source: (b) NIST.

identification, Galton conservatively estimated the number of possible fingerprints at over 64 billion. That would mean that the chance of two random prints being identical would conservatively be estimated at $(1/64,000,000,000)^2$ or about a 1 in 4×10^{21} chance of two matching identical prints – an astronomically small chance. Adding in the third level of detail increases this number astronomically.

BOX 7.3   ACE-V

ACE-V refers to a process in the identification of friction ridge impressions that follows the steps of: Analysis, Comparison, Evaluation, and Verification. This approach has been likened to the process of the scientific method itself, which employs the steps of: (1) observing and collecting data, (2) recognizing empirical relationships in the data, (3) forming a hypothesis to explain these relationships at a deeper level, and (4) testing and refining the hypothesis through carefully designed experiments.

In the ACE-V process, analysts typically begin by initially examining a fingerprint in question to identify overall flow and recognizable features, such as loops, bifurcations, etc. Once these features have been "located," the print can then be compared with a reference fingerprint to identify both similarities and differences. Once this comparison is completed, the degree of the "match" between the unknown and the reference print can be evaluated. Finally, another analyst verifies the degree of match or non-match between the two prints to ensure the objectivity of the analysis.

The use of this approach has, however, come under some legal scrutiny, and it has been argued that this approach would "guarantee precision of application, [but] not accuracy of conclusion." This doubt has been reinforced by a court decision which found that the ACE-V method has not yet met the Daubert standard itself [U.S. v. Plaza, Acosta and Rodriguez, 2002]. It remains, however, the primary method used for fingerprint analysis (see SWGFAST).

In fingerprint comparison, the ridge line patterns are usually first compared at all locations between a pair of fingerprints to determine the general pattern features (e.g., arch, loop, or whorl). Cores and deltas are also identified and located within the print to help orient the two prints for comparison. Minutiae are then similarly identified and located within the "map" of the print to complete the full picture. It is occasionally possible, however, to go beyond this level of detail and to resolve pore features and locations in the ridges and also identify imperfections in edges of the ridges, usually from electronic scanning methods rather than other sampling methods (see Section 7.2.6). Work is in progress to use this third level of information in a way similar to how minutiae are employed in print comparison. Some features, such as scars and creases, can be used, but they are often changeable over time and are, therefore, of limited use. There also appears to be some relationship between fingerprint patterns and ethnicity, with those of European and African descent displaying relatively high incidences of loop patterns and Asians and Australian Aborigines showing greater amounts of whorls.

BOX 7.4   THE PRINTS OF THE MASTER: DA VINCI UNKNOWN TREASURE?

Have all Da Vinci's works been found and cataloged almost 500 years after his death in 1519? According to some, at least one recently discovered work is an unknown masterpiece of Leonardo Da Vinci's that somehow missed everyone's attention. The work, entitled *La Bella Principessa*, is a beautiful piece of ink and chalk on vellum (treated animal skin), shown in Figure 7.13. But how to determine if it truly is a lost masterpiece?

As it turns out, the artist of the questioned work left a partial fingerprint in the upper corner of the drawing. This partial print has been compared to fingerprints left on an early verified Da Vinci work in the Vatican collection called *St. Jerome*. The problem is the quality of the print on *La Bella Principessa*.

FIGURE 7.13 *La Bella Principessa* (the Beautiful Princess), attributed to Leonardo Da Vinci, is a colored drawing in chalks and ink on vellum showing a young girl in profile wearing a renaissance dress (1490s) whose authenticity is disputed. Fingerprints have been discovered on the drawing that some have ascribed to Da Vinci.

Source: Retrieved from Wikimedia Commons; used per Creative Commons Attribution.

At this point, experts agree that there is indeed a fingerprint on the questioned work, but disagree as to any match between the *Principessa* print and those found on Da Vinci's *St. Jerome* painting; some say yes but others disagree. The stakes, however, are very high upon any identification. The work was purchased in 1998 at auction for $19,000 but has been estimated to have a value of $150,000,000 if it is indeed an unknown Da Vinci work. But for now, the question still remains undecided.

7.2.6 Computerized Methods: IAFIS, NGI, and Beyond

In the past, fingerprint comparisons involved long and laborious manual visual identification and comparison of features. This has largely changed, with most comparisons now done using computer-assisted methods. In the United States, the FBI maintains an electronic database containing the fingerprints of millions of people in its IAFIS, the largest such database in the world, with over one hundred and ten million fingerprints currently in the system and growing daily. These computer-based methods quickly and efficiently compare fingerprint features between an unknown print and millions of records in the database, known as a *one-to-many matching* process, and are able to provide information about the individual person found with any matching fingerprints (e.g., prior criminal record, gun purchases, etc.). The system is frequently used in employment background checks, verifying legitimate firearms purchases, identifying remains, and in criminal investigations. The system is heavily used and has performed as many as 100,000 matches in a day.

The FBI is replacing IAFIS with an enhanced automated system, called the *Next Generation Identification System* (NGI), that will integrate many types of personal identification data, including fingerprints, eye-scans, and facial imaging methods, to permit expanded capabilities for the extremely fast identification of people for both criminal and security purposes (Figure 7.14).

The process of entering fingerprint information into either the IAFIS and NGI systems uses a technique for either taking high-resolution prints directly from a subject or digitally scanning previously taken prints (Figure 7.15). The process is similar to how digital cameras take pictures. In either case, the prints are digitized and the computer locates the patterns and minutiae in the print for comparison with other prints in the database. Traditionally, fingerprint analysis has been performed using 2D images, but recent advancements in 3D imaging technology have allowed for more detailed and accurate analysis using 3D images, allowing the observation of ridge depths, fingerprint contours, pore placement, and other highly detailed information for more accurate identifications (Figure 7.16). Often, prints that carry similar features to the sample being compared are provided by the computer search along with some measure establishing the degree of certainty in the comparison. The system has an estimated error rate of about 2%. Importantly, once a computer comparison is done, a human analyst must still make the final comparison.

7.2.7 Uses of Fingerprints: Identification vs Authentication

Fingerprint information is typically used for one of two main tasks: *identification* or *authentication* (Chapter 2). While these may sound very similar, the process and ultimate answers provided can be quite different.

Identification specifically refers to using fingerprints to identify an unknown person from a set of prints. The main issue here is to uniquely identify a set of "unknown" fingerprints by matching their features with candidates in a large pool of possibilities, often many millions of records, called *one-to-many matching*. In forensic work, this may arise when a fingerprint is found at a crime scene and needs to be attributed to one person. This method is also commonly associated with determining the identity of unknown human remains.

Authentication (sometimes called verification) using fingerprints, in contrast, focuses on comparing a set of fingerprints from a person with either just one reference set or to a very

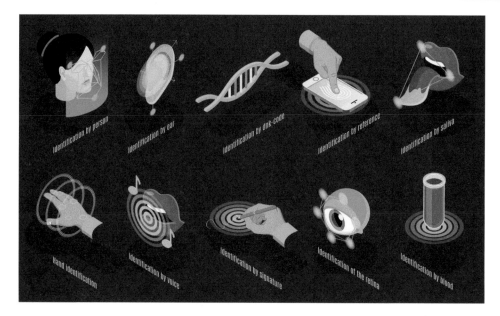

FIGURE 7.14 Isometric biometric identification information for NGI with fingerprint, face, ear, DNA, reference saliva, hand, voice, signature, retina, and blood recognition data, among others.

Source: Shutterstock.com.

FIGURE 7.15 Digital fingerprint scanner.

Source: Use per Creative Commons Attribution-Share Alike 3.0. Unported. User: Rachmaninoff.

7.2.8 Observing Fingerprint Patterns

Fingerprint impressions are classified into one of three major types, depending on how the print is formed and visualized. These types are usually referred to as *visible* prints, *latent* prints, and *impression* (or plastic) prints.

7.2.8.1 Visible Prints

As the name implies, visible prints are those that are readily seen by the unaided eye. These are typically made by the transfer of the print using a visible medium, such as ink, paint, blood, or dirt, to a surface where it is directly observed. This process is very similar to a printing process where the ridge patterns serve as the "type" to transfer the "ink" to the paper. It is also the method used when preparing "rolled" reference prints for later comparisons, as shown in Figures 7.18 and 7.19. Visible prints can also be found at crime scenes where a person's hands or fingers come in contact with the visible substance and then the pattern is transferred by touching a smooth surface, as shown in Figure 7.20.

7.2.8.2 Latent Prints

When we touch an object with our fingers, some of the oils, water, and amino acids on the tops of the ridges can be transferred to the object. This process imparts an invisible pattern of chemicals to the surface that, with proper techniques, can be made visible. These prints are called *latent prints*, or prints "waiting" to be made visible. These deposited chemicals from our fingers are essentially non-volatile and have been shown to remain in place when undisturbed for decades, rendering clear fingerprint patterns.

small number of "standard" possibilities, called *one-to-one matching*. This can be used as part of a biometric security scan at a border or building or for the identification of repeat offenders in the criminal justice system. The process usually begins when a "known" person provides their fingerprints to form a biometric reference template that is linked to their previously established "known" identity. Then, at a later time, when their identity needs to be confirmed, such as to log into a computer or bank account, a new scan is taken and compared only to their single reference record on file. A match then allows the person access to the restricted account or "authenticates" their identity (Figure 7.17).

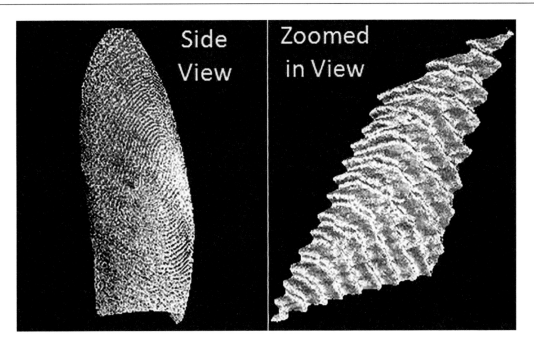

FIGURE 7.16 3D scanned digital fingerprint.

Source: Retrieved from Wikimedia Commons; used per Creative Commons Attribution.

FIGURE 7.17 Using finger scans at Walt Disney World, where the data is converted to a "unique numerical value to determine if the same person uses an admission ticket on different days."

Source: Creative Commons Attribution-Share Alike 3.0 Unported. User: Raul654.

Numerous techniques have been developed to help visualize latent prints. One of the simplest techniques is to simply "dust" a very fine powder across the surface containing the prints using a delicate brush (Figure 7.21). The fine powder sticks to the oils and moisture in the latent prints. When the excess powder is removed from the area, only the places where the oils and moisture trapped the dyed powder remain behind to show the detailed fingerprint. Many types of powders with different colors and properties are available (Figure 7.22) and are chosen to accentuate the latent print from

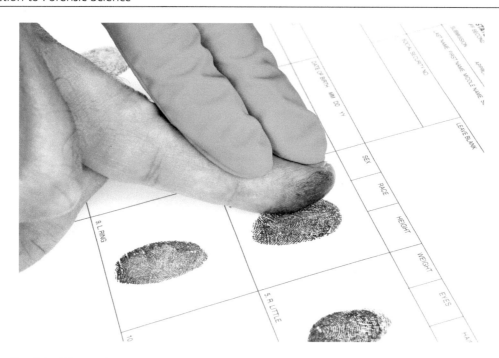

FIGURE 7.18   Rolling inked fingerprints.

Source: Shutterstock.com.

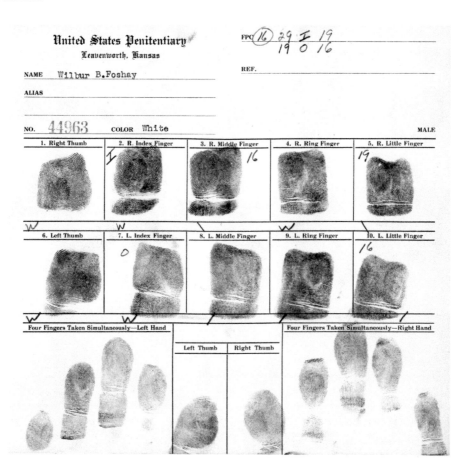

FIGURE 7.19   Fingerprints obtained by rolling inked fingers on a standard collection card. This is a historic fingerprint card of Wilbur Foshay when he started his term in Leavenworth Federal Prison. Fingerprint cards have largely remained the same today (although they are being replaced by digital scanners).

Source: U.S. National Archives and Records Administration.

FIGURE 7.20 Visible hand and fingerprints in blood on a wall.

Source: Used per Creative Commons Attribution-Share Alike 2.0 Generic. User: Adam Jones from Kelowna, BC, Canada.

FIGURE 7.22 Application of fine magnetic powders for latent print visualization. The colored powder adheres to the moisture and oils transferred from the ridge tops of the fingerprints to the surface. The magnet then removes the loose powder, rendering the observable fingerprint.

Source: Shutterstock.com.

FIGURE 7.21 Fingerprint brush (dactyloscopy brush) for applying fine powders for visualization of latent prints.

Source: Shutterstock.com.

FIGURE 7.23 Fingerprint made visible using a fluorescent powder and illuminated with an ultraviolet light.

Source: Shutterstock.com.

the background material. Some powders contain a fluorescent dye that can visualize the fingerprint using ultraviolet light (Figure 7.23) to make the print visibly "glow."

A very similar method employs very fine magnetic powder that similarly adheres to the oils and moisture in the latent print. The excess powder, however, is cleanly removed by passing a magnet across the surface to extract any unadhered powder from the print, as shown in Figure 7.22.

Another important way to visualize latent prints is to react the oils, amino acids or salts in the transferred fingerprint with some chemical reagent that allows us to see the print. Many such methods have been developed but four are particularly interesting and useful.

One such method involves spraying a chemical called *ninhydrin* onto the surface containing the print. The ninhydrin

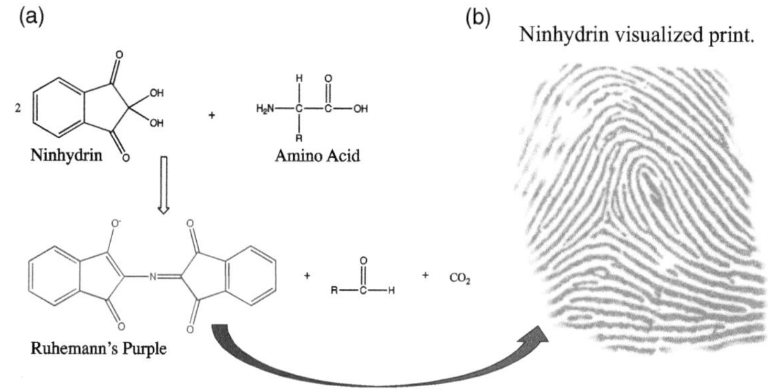

(a)

Ninhydrin

Amino Acid

Ruhemann's Purple

(b)

Ninhydrin visualized print.

FIGURE 7.24 The reaction of ninhydrin (a) with amino acids to yield a purple color (Ruhemann's Purple). A fingerprint visualized by ninhydrin (b).

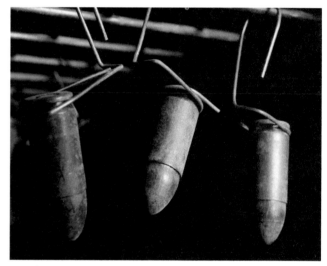

FIGURE 7.25 Cyanoacrylate (super glue) "fuming" chamber for developing latent fingerprints.

Source: Shutterstock.com.

FIGURE 7.26 Unfired bullets hanging in a cyanoacrylate fuming cupboard. Latent fingerprints are transferred to objects from chemicals exuded through skin pores. The cyanoacrylate (super glue) is heated in a sealed chamber and forms a gas that reacts with amino acids in the latent fingerprints to form a visible white solid. These unfired bullets were from a handgun found at a crime scene.

Source: Mauro Fermariello/Science Photo Library. Used with permission.

reacts with the amino acids found in the print and, upon gentle heating to speed up the otherwise slow chemical reaction, forms a purple/blue-colored pattern of the fingerprint (Figure 7.24).

Another common reagent used in a similar fashion is *iodine*. Elemental iodine (I_2) reacts readily with the oils left behind from our fingers to form a somewhat transient, but observable, brown color where the finger oils were deposited. In much the same fashion, silver nitrate ($AgNO_3$) reacts with chloride ion from the salts sweated from the finger pores to form the black silver chloride compound ($AgCl$) that shows the print. Finally, a very common reagent used in this method is cyanoacrylate, commonly known as super glue. In this technique, the object suspected of containing fingerprints is placed in a closed "fuming" chamber (Figure 7.25) where it is exposed to a vapor of cyanoacrylate. The cyanoacrylate then reacts with the amino acids in the print to form a clearly observed white residue, as shown in Figure 7.26.

The success of making latent prints visible largely depends on the nature of the surface to which they have been transferred. Smooth, non-porous surfaces, such as glass, metal, plastic, or polished stone, usually provide an excellent opportunity to visualize the print. Porous or irregular surfaces, such as wood, Styrofoam, or granular surfaces, usually present difficulties, although useful prints can be sometimes obtained from such surfaces. Progress has been made, however, using methods including vacuum metal-vapor deposition (e.g., sputtering, CVD, MOCVD) and gel lifters in developing fingerprints from non-porous surfaces. Latent prints of attackers have even been successfully lifted from the bodies of human victims.

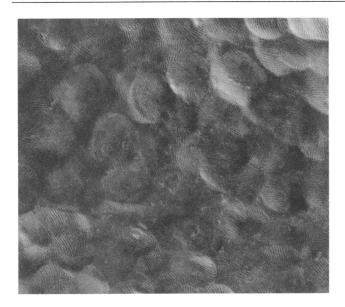

FIGURE 7.27 Plastic fingerprints in window putty (plasticine).

Source: Shutterstock.com.

7.2.8.3 Impression (Plastic) Prints

When someone touches a soft, pliable surface, such as clay, putty, wax, or wet paint, they may leave behind an impression of the ridge pattern of their fingers. These patterns are often clearly visible to the unaided eye. An example is shown in Figure 7.27 where fingerprints can occasionally be observed in break-in robberies in window putty.

Interestingly, other mammals also have fingerprints similar to those found in humans. Monkeys, apes, and even koala bears show fingerprints.

7.2.9 Preserving Visualized Fingerprints

Once a fingerprint has been found, developed, and visualized, it is important to preserve and record the evidence. Typically, once the visualization is completed, the prints are photographed and digitized to form a permanent record. It is often desirable, however, to preserve the fingerprint intact for later study and storage. Several techniques have been developed over the years to "lift" fingerprints from the surfaces on which they are originally found.

One very common method used for "lifting" fingerprints involves using cellophane tape. The tape is carefully placed over the visualized print and then rubbed to ensure that the adhesive on the tape makes full contact with the print (Figure 7.28). Subsequently, the tape is slowly peeled away from the surface and applied to a card for permanent storage. One advantage of the cellophane tape method is its ability to bend to conform to an irregular surface. Additionally, it is inexpensive, easy to use, and preserves the fingerprint as it originally appears, rather

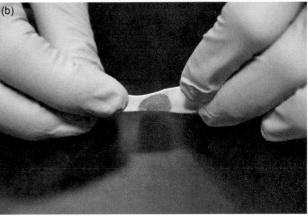

FIGURE 7.28 Dusting with powder (a) and then lifting fingerprints using clear adhesive tape (b).

Source: (a) Used per Creative Commons Attribution-Share Alike 3.0 Unported. User: Arnij at Dutch Wikipedia. (b) NIST.

than in reverse. A variety of other techniques have been developed, such as casting and the use of color-coded maps to rapidly display the quality of the print (Figure 7.29).

7.2.10 Legal Challenges to Fingerprint Evidence

Fingerprint evidence has been used in courtroom proceedings for personal identification for over a century, with the first U.S. murder conviction based on fingerprint identification evidence occurring in 1911. The comparison of latent prints not only determines who made the prints with a high degree of certainty but may also indicate where that person has been, for example, at the crime scene.

Recently, however, the use of fingerprint information in court has come under intense legal scrutiny. Most of these challenges have arisen from questioning the accuracy rate of the examiners, the average accuracy rate of the profession, and

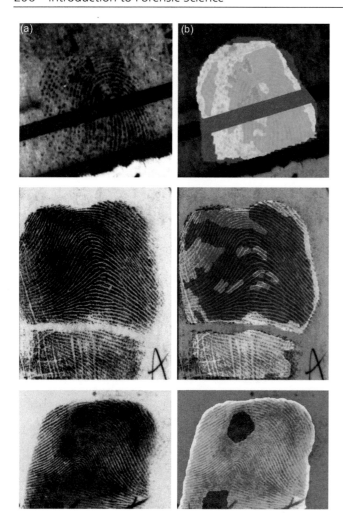

FIGURE 7.29 Examples of fingerprint images (a) on which a color-coded quality map has been superimposed (b). The color coding provides forensic examiners with a means of marking the quality of the data that can be obtained from the friction ridge details seen in the images. Blue areas are excellent, green are satisfactory, yellow may potentially contain false or missed features, and red have no evidentiary value at all.

Source: NIST.

even the scientific underpinnings of the technique. The ultimate question is, of course, whether fingerprint evidence and testimony meet acceptable legal evidence standards. The U.S. *Scientific Working Group on Friction Ridge Analysis, Study, and Technology* (SWGFAST) has stated that forensic friction ridge impression examination "is an applied science based upon the foundation of biological uniqueness, permanence, and empirical validation through observation" and is, therefore, an accepted scientific discipline that meets the requirements set forth in the Federal Rules of Evidence.

Most often, the main issue in courtroom use of fingerprints is whether fingerprint examiners can accurately determine the identity of a latent print found at a crime scene. This issue partially arises because latent prints are often incomplete; the average size of a latent print from a crime scene was shown to be only ~22% of that of a reference print. Latent prints may

also be distorted by the surface upon which they are found and/or the method of contact, adding further uncertainty to the comparison between two prints. It is certainly true that fingerprint testimony is not completely infallible and an unquestioned reliance on this type of evidence cannot be justified. But it is generally believed that the problems lie mainly with the testimony of identity itself and not with problems in the basic premise that fingerprints are both unique and permanent records of a person's identity.

Errors in analysis do occur, with a recent estimate placing the error rate at about 0.8%, or a little less than 1 in 100 comparisons, while another investigation placed the error rate somewhat higher. There have unfortunately been several highly prominent cases of mistaken identity using fingerprints, accentuating these concerns. One of these cases involved the Portland, Oregon lawyer, Brandon Mayfield, whose file prints were matched with fingerprints obtained from the 2004 Madrid, Spain railcar bombing. Experts matched Mayfield's fingerprints with those from a bag carrying the explosives in Madrid, with the FBI calling the match "100 percent positive" and an "absolutely incontrovertible match." Mayfield was jailed for two weeks based upon this evidence before the Spanish National Police examiners showed the error in the analysis, and he was released and exonerated.

BOX 7.5   THE CERTAINLY MISTAKEN FINGERPRINT

In 1997, the body of Marion Ross was found murdered in her home in western Scotland. David Asbury, a handyman who had previously worked in Ross's home, became the prime suspect. At least one fingerprint from her home was identified as Asbury's, but surprisingly, a second print, a bloody thumbprint found in a doorway of the house, was identified as belonging to Police Constable Shirley McKie. The only problem was that McKie denied ever having been in the Ross home, and none of the many police officers processing the crime scene remembered having seen her there. Eventually, however, McKie was fired, arrested, and tried for perjury.

During the trial, four Scottish fingerprint examiners testified that there was no doubt that the fingerprint at the crime scene belonged to Constable McKie. Two fingerprint experts from the FBI were then asked to examine the prints, and they found that the prints conclusively did *not* match McKie's. Eventually, a member of the Scottish parliament invited 171 expert fingerprint analysts from around the world to examine the prints, and *none* found that they matched McKie's, despite the Scottish analysts saying that the match was "100% certain."

Eventually, McKie was cleared of all charges, awarded £750,000 in damages, and received an official apology, but not before her reputation and career were destroyed. However, because McKie was cleared based on faulty fingerprint analysis in the case, doubt then fell on the fingerprint analysis of David Asbury's prints by the same four Scottish examiners. As a result of this, Asbury's conviction was overturned and the case remains unsolved.

A governmental inquiry later found that the Scottish fingerprint examiners were "ill-equipped to reason their conclusions as they are accustomed to regarding their conclusions as a matter of certainty and seldom challenged" and determined that "fingerprint evidence should be recognized as opinion evidence, not fact."

Nonetheless, fingerprint evidence remains a powerful investigatory and courtroom technique that is generally relied upon as scientifically valid, reliable, and trustworthy when applied in a rigorous manner. It has withstood significant Daubert challenges so far and thus remains an important part of forensic investigations and courtroom proceedings.

7.2.11 Palm- and Footprint Evidence

Fingers are not the only portions of our bodies covered with epidermal friction ridges. Ridges are also found on the palms of our hands and on the soles of our feet, displaying many of the same pattern characteristics that are so important in fingerprint analysis. While palm and foot ridge pattern analysis are less well developed relative to fingerprint analysis, the information derived from palm- and footprint pattern analysis can still be very useful.

The patterns observed on our palms and feet not only contain patterns of friction ridges but also show complex patterns of *flexion creases* – places where the skin flexes or folds to cause breaks in the observed ridge patterns. The major creases are formed prenatally and are places where the epidermis and dermis of the skin are very firmly anchored together, necessary because of their rugged use. Generally, our palms show three prominent creases and numerous smaller creases (Figure 7.30). One major crease runs in our palms "underneath" our fingers, called the *distal transverse crease* ("distal" meaning farther from the main part of our body and "transverse" meaning that it runs perpendicular to the axis of our hands). A second crease runs parallel to this first crease but closer to the arms and is called the *proximal transverse crease* ("proximal" meaning closer). The final main crease runs along the boundary of our thumbs in the palm and is called the *radial transverse crease* ("radial" since it is close to the radius bone not that it radiates). These three creases break the palm into three separate regions for more detailed analysis. In addition to these major creases, our palms and feet show many very fine, thin creases that break up the ridge lines.

The ridges in our palms contain sweat pores like the fingers but our palm ridges do not contain any hair or oil glands. Like fingerprints, however, the ridges on our palms and feet show a variety of fine minutiae features that can be

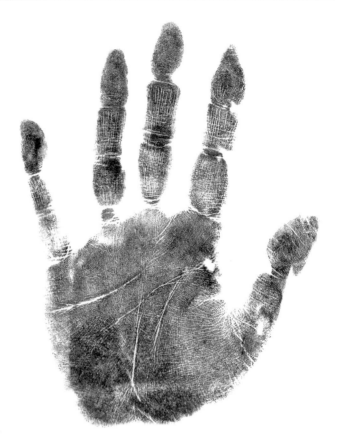

FIGURE 7.30 Palmprint regions with ridge patterns showing major creases (*distal transverse crease, proximal transverse crease*, and *radial transverse crease*).

Source: Daniel Sambraus/Science Photo Library. Used with permission.

classified, identified, and located for analysis and comparison. These provide a unique set of patterns that can be used to identify the prints in a very similar fashion to that described earlier for fingerprints (both using one-to-one and one-to-many matching methods). A typical fingerprint pattern contains about 100 minutiae features, while a palmprint may contain as many as 800 minutial features. Palmprint identification will be an important component of the FBI's new NGI system, since it is estimated that about 30% of prints recovered from crime scenes are palm- and not fingerprints.

The patterns on our feet and hands appear to be persistent throughout life and form entirely unique patterns that are individual to each person, as do fingerprints. The use of palm- and footprints does, however, suffer from the same problems encountered in fingerprint use: incomplete images, poorly resolved features, smudges, and small recovered areas of the prints. Palm- and footprints carry the added difficulty of the numerous complex patterns of fine creases and lines interrupting the ridge patterns, causing difficulties in automated identification of the prints.

Nonetheless, analysis of our palms and foot ridge and crease patterns is expected to become increasingly important as we understand more about how to analyze these features.

7.2.12 Ear and Lip Pattern Evidence (Pinnascopy and Cheiloscopy)

The use of lip marks and ear shape patterns has been proposed as another way of linking a biological feature to a particular person. In order for any technique to be employed, it must first be demonstrated that it provides unique information and that the information is permanent (does not change over time or by design).

Lips have been shown to contain many "elevations and depressions" along their surfaces (sometimes called grooves), although these do not have direct biological similarity to the ridges found in fingerprints (Figure 7.31). It was proposed as early as 1902 that the patterns formed by these grooves could provide a means of personal identification. A number of methods for identifying lip mark features have been developed, although none has gained general acceptance.

A number of studies have been undertaken to determine whether *cheiloscopy*, the study of lip groove patterns, meets the requirements of scientific validity to define legal uniqueness, persistence, and permanence. Cheiloscopy has been used in several court proceedings with mixed admissibility results. One study in Japan measured the lip marks of over 1,300 subjects, including several identical twins, and found them uniquely different. Researchers then followed a number of subjects for several years and noted that the patterns did not appear to change. However, the scientific validity of the technique remains unverified, and a great deal of work is needed before this method can find acceptable use in forensic investigations and courtroom proceedings.

In a similar fashion, the shapes of people's ears have shown significant variation and have been used to link a particular person with a "found" earprint (pinnascopy), such as on a window, door, or mirror (Figure 7.32).

7.3 HAIR ANALYSIS

7.3.1 Introduction

In the early stages of human embryonic development, both the skin and hair form from the ectoderm (the outermost layer). As such, hair and skin not only share a strong biological connection, as hair is considered a derivative of our skin, but also, more simply, both of these tissues are primarily found on the outside of the organism. Therefore, hair and skin are the components of our bodies that directly interact with the environment and can easily leave lasting and identifiable forensic evidence. Because of the similarity between hair and fibers in their form and forensic function, we will consider them together in this section, beginning with a discussion of hair.

Hair and fiber samples are among the most durable of all biological materials and retain much of their forensic value for many years. While most biological tissues quickly degrade after death, hair samples have been known to persist virtually unchanged for even thousands of years. These samples can provide both structural and chemical clues as to both their individual origin and the underlying biochemistry that formed them. Similarly, durable fibers, both natural and manmade, found throughout our society in cloth and other items, can also provide useful information about their origin, composition, form, and use.

7.3.2 Hair and Fur

Hair is a complex appendage that grows from a follicle in the skin of mammals only. One of its main purposes is to help regulate the body temperature of an organism by either trapping

FIGURE 7.31 Typical pattern of grooves found on lips.

Source: Used per Creative Commons Attribution 2.0 Generic. User: Tania Saiz.

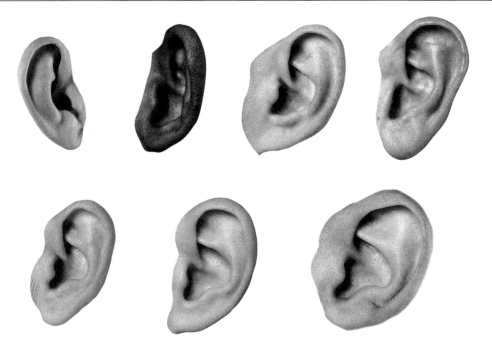

FIGURE 7.32 Examples of the variety of known ear shapes.

Source: Shutterstock.com.

or releasing warm air near the skin's surface. The protective function of hair and its exposure to extreme conditions require it to be physically strong, highly flexible, and chemically durable.

Hair exhibits enormous diversity of form, both between different species of organisms and from individual to individual. Traditionally, hair that comes from non-human mammals is referred to as *fur* rather than hair, but the structures are very similar.

7.3.2.1 Composition of Hair

Hair is composed of about 80–90% protein, mostly *keratin* and *melanin*, and between 8% and 15% water, with the remainder mostly as lipids. Keratin is a tough, durable, fibrous protein composed of long chains of amino acids and typically found as a structural component of hair, nails, horns, and claws. Melanin, however, is a pigment polymer derived mostly from the amino acid called tyrosine that imparts the color to a hair sample. Generally, the darker the hair coloration, the more melanin it contains. There are, however, several types of melanin commonly found in hair. The dark pigment called *eumelanin* colors black and brown hair, while the pigment called *pheomelanin* is the main coloration chemical found in red hair. Blonde hair simply has lower amounts of melanin overall, while gray hair typically lacks melanin completely. All hair samples have very similar chemical compositions, which limits the use of chemical analysis in the individualization of a hair sample as coming from a particular person.

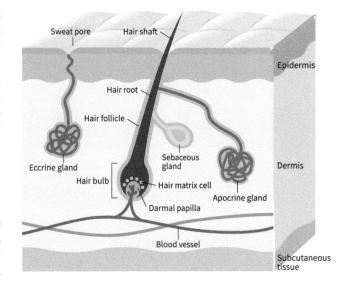

FIGURE 7.33 Skin and hair follicle anatomy with the apocrine, sebaceous, and eccrine glands along with other details of hair structure.

Source: Shutterstock.com.

7.3.2.2 Hair Structure

Hair grows from a hair follicle, a tiny hole in the skin located within the outermost layers of the skin, as shown in Figure 7.33, and consists of a root, shaft, and tip. The hair shaft grows from the base of the follicle in an area known as the dermal papilla

(a)
HAIR STRUCTURE - HAIR SHAFT

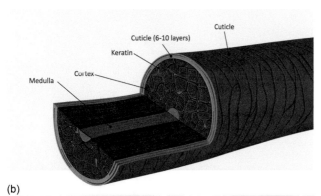

(b)

FIGURE 7.34   (a) Hair shaft structure and (b) scanning electron micrograph (SEM) of hair shafts growing from the surface of human skin.

Source: (a) Shutterstock.com. (b) Steve Gschmeissner/ Science Photo Library. Used with Permission.

to form a rapidly elongating hair bulb. The growing hair root is fed by its own blood supply with new cells pushing the previously formed cells upward. When the hair shaft grows, the follicle deepens into the skin layers while the shaft grows out of the follicle. As the shaft elongates, the hair begins to form

several layers as cells die (Figure 7.34). The portion of the hair shaft that extends beyond the surface of the skin is, therefore, composed mostly of dead keratinized (cornified) material. The only living portion of a hair is the portion that is located in the follicle.

It is important to note that since the cells in the shaft are dead and keratinized, it is almost never possible to extract nuclear DNA from a hair shaft. Mitochondrial DNA, however, can often be found in the shaft and is stable for long periods of time. It is possible to collect nuclear DNA from a hair sample only if the sample contains some of the living cells from either the hair root or from the follicle itself. This is common if a hair has been forcibly removed and some of the tissue from the follicle is pulled out with the hair fiber.

The follicle has associated with it sebaceous glands that produce *sebum*, an oily material that protects, lubricates, waterproofs, and helps to inhibit the growth of microorganisms on the hair. The follicle is also attached to a muscle (arrector pili muscle) that serves to elevate and lower the hair fiber in response to environmental conditions. Contraction of the erector pili muscles also produces what are commonly known as "goosebumps." Thus, when it's cold outside, the erector muscles contract to raise the hair shaft, trapping a layer of warm air next to the skin to help keep us warm and conserve body heat. Each mature hair fiber is typically made up of three components: the cuticle, cortex, and the medulla.

The outermost translucent layer of a hair shaft is called the *cuticle*, which appears similar to the shingles on a roof or the outer scales of a snake's skin, with the exposed portion of the "scale" aimed toward the tip of the shaft (Figures 7.36 and 7.37). You can sometimes feel this directionality of the cuticle scales by first running your pinched fingers along a hair shaft from your head toward the end of the hair and comparing it with running your fingers in the opposite direction from the tip. It often feels rougher when moving from the tip toward the scalp since this is moving against the "grain" of the cuticle scales toward your head. This relatively thin layer, usually just six to ten cells thick, protects the hair by forming a waterproof and rather chemically resistant layer that coats and protects the entire shaft.

The pattern formed by the overlapping cuticle cells is very distinctive and can be easily used to determine the species of animal that produced the hairs (Figure 7.37). The three general types of scale patterns most commonly observed, shown in Figure 7.36, are the coronal ("crown-like"), spinous ("petal-like"), and imbricate ("shingle-like") patterns. The coronal pattern, common in small rodents, appears similar to an arrangement of stacked "crowns" or circular bands. The spinous pattern, found in the hairs of cats and mink, appears like triangular "petals" that often project away from the shaft of the hair. The imbricate pattern, found in human hair, appears as flattened scales.

Since the cuticle is the part of the hair directly exposed to the environment, it is susceptible to damage by sunlight, wear, and the way that people treat and style their hair.

BOX 7.6 COPERNICAN HAIR?

Nicolaus Copernicus (1473–1543) was a Renaissance church canon and astronomer who forever changed our perception of the Universe and our place in it. Prior to his work, the prevailing attitude was that the Earth was the center of the Universe and everything else revolved around it. Copernicus, however, argued that the sun was instead the center and that the earth and all planets moved around it. Historians often point to his seminal work as the beginning of the scientific revolution and modern science. But until recently, the remains of this influential scientist were missing.

When he was buried in Frombork Cathedral, Poland on May 24, 1543, beneath the altar floor, the place of his internment was not marked and ultimately lost to history. In 2005, however, a skull and some remains were unearthed, after an intensive five-year search of the Cathedral, which archaeologists thought might be those of Copernicus. Scientists were able to extract some mtDNA from one of the teeth in the skull and a femur bone, but the problem was what to compare it with?

As it turns out, key evidence came from an unlikely place. In the Stoefler Almanach Copernicus library in Uppsala, Sweden, two hairs were amazingly found in a 16th-century astronomy reference book that had definitely belonged to the great astronomer. Mitochondrial DNA extracted from the hair samples was found to match well with the mtDNA extracted from the bone fragments, providing very strong evidence that the skeletal remains found in the cathedral were those of Copernicus.

Using facial reconstruction techniques on the skull, scientists created a reconstruction of Copernicus' face that corresponds remarkably well with existing portraits of the astronomer. On May 25, 2010, his remains were reburied with full honors beneath the altar where they were found.

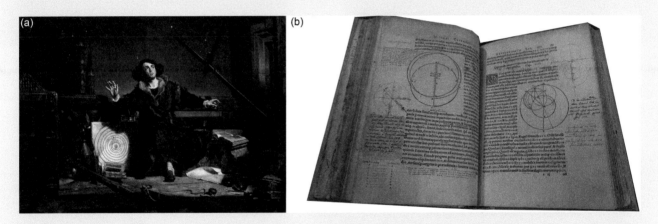

FIGURE 7.35 (a) Astronomer Nicolaus Copernicus, from the painting entitled *Conversations with God* made in 1873 by Jan Matejko (in the background is Frombork Cathedral where he is buried), and (b) Nicolaus Copernicus' famous treatise, entitled *De revolutionibus orbium coelestium* (translated as "On the Revolutions of the Heavenly Spheres"), published in Nuremberg in 1543 and was the first to offer an alternative explanation of the workings of the Universe with the sun as the center of rotation.

Source: (b) Used per Creative Commons Attribution-Share Alike 4.0 International license. User: Sam.Donvil.

For example, dyeing, drying, and styling hair can permanently damage this layer.

If we could peel back the outer cuticle layer, as shown in Figure 7.38, the underlying *cortex* layer would be exposed. The cortex makes up most of the bulk of the hair shaft and gives the hair its characteristic elasticity, stretching up to 30% of its length without breaking. The cortex is primarily made up of long, twisted, and coiled protein fibers, like a spiral staircase, that easily bend and stretch when the long molecules slide past one another (Figure 7.38). When stretched, these molecules can uncoil like a spring, and when released, the molecule can reform its original coiled structure, giving hair its observed elasticity. Pigment molecules, giving hair its color, are also largely found in the cortex layer.

Occasionally, small structures are observed within the cortex of a hair fiber, providing additional comparative information. For example, air bubbles (known as *cortical fusci*), pigment bodies (small areas of pigment concentration), and

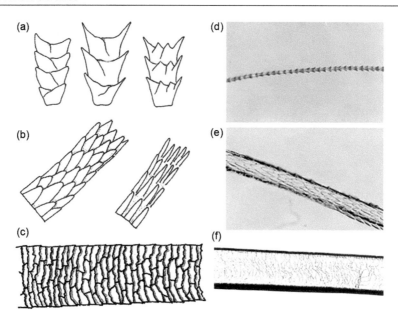

FIGURE 7.36   a–c Cuticle hair patterns: coronal, spinous, and imbricate, and (d) coronal scales of Free-Tailed Bat Hair (*Tadarida brasiliensis*), (e) spinous proximal scales of mink (*Neovison vison*), and (f) imbricate distal scales of mink (*Neovison vison*).

Source: FBI.

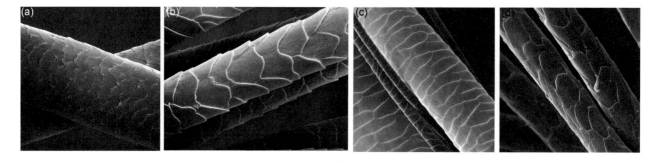

FIGURE 7.37   Cuticle patterns for several animal species; (a) human hair (*Homo sapiens*), (b) dog hair (*Canis lupus familiaris*), c. reindeer hair (*Rangifer tarandus*), and (d) camel hair (*Camelus dromedarius*).

Source: Power and Syred/ Photo Library images. Used with permission.

ovoid bodies (larger pigment-containing structures with regular boundaries) are observed. Ovoid bodies, often found in dog hair but only occasionally in human hairs, are shown in Figure 7.39.

The third and innermost component of hair is the *medulla*. This part of the hair is characterized by either very spongy cells or no cells at all, forming a canal-like structure in the center of the shaft, often called the *medullary canal*. Melanin can sometimes be found in this layer, contributing to the color of the hair. The medulla in human hair can form a continuous canal, be interrupted by areas without a medulla, or be missing altogether (Figure 7.40). The medulla pattern for some animals can be rather complex showing ladder-like or lattice-like patterns.

The ratio of the diameter of the shaft to the diameter of the medulla can be defined as the *medullary index* (MI), which can be used to help distinguish human hair from that of other animals. In many animals, the MI is greater than 0.5, while in humans it is typically found to be less than 0.3.

Hair varies greatly depending on its location on the body. As a fetus, our entire body is covered with very fine colorless hair, called Lanugo. During early childhood, however, this lanugo hair is lost, and the majority of our body is covered with fine short hairs, called *Vellus* hair or sometimes referred to as "peach fuzz". During puberty, humans develop longer, thicker, colored hair on various parts of the body, besides the scalp and eyebrows, called *terminal hair*, which forms part of our secondary sex characteristics. Terminal hair includes hair

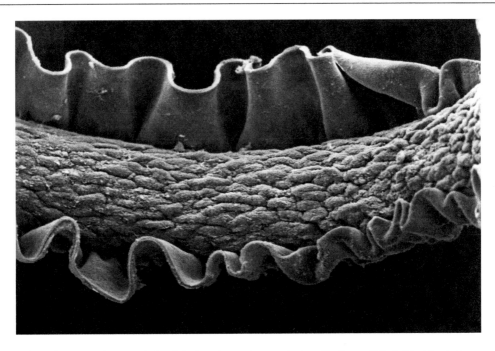

FIGURE 7.38 Scanning electron micrograph (500x) showing a human hair with the cuticle folded back to reveal the underlying cortex layer.

Source: Natural History Museum, London/Science Photo Library. Used with permission.

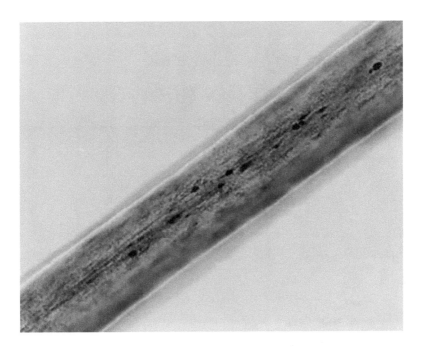

FIGURE 7.39 Photomicrograph of Ovoid Bodies: the presence, abundance, and distribution of these pigment-dense regions can be useful points of comparison.

Source: FBI.

found on our scalps, in armpits, on legs, as chest hair, and in the pubic area.

Usually, a single hair follicle produces only one type of hair, but sometimes a follicle can change to produce a different type of hair. For example, until puberty, the facial follicles on a male produce only fine vellus hair. During puberty, these follicles change to produce a characteristic male beard made up of thicker, longer terminal hair. Similarly, follicles on the

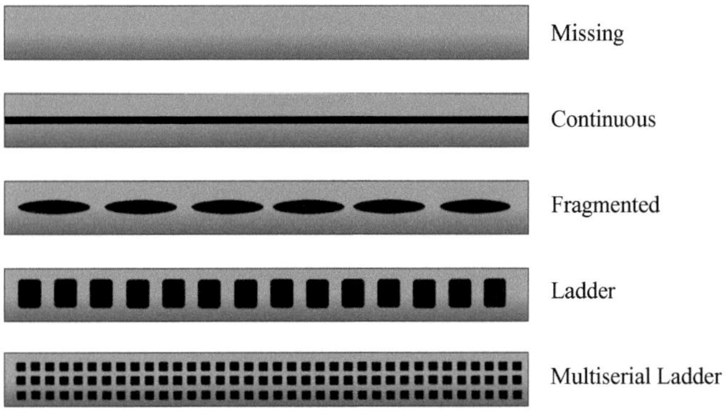

Missing

Continuous

Fragmented

Ladder

Multiserial Ladder

FIGURE 7.40   Patterns observed in hair medulla.

scalp usually produce only terminal hair, but in some instances (e.g., androgenetic alopecia), the follicle can change to produce short, thin, lightly colored hair.

Most animal hairs are divided into three basic types: guard hairs (from the outer coat for protection), fur (from the inner coat for insulation and temperature regulation), and tactile hairs (for sensing, such as whiskers). Human hair, however, is not so well-differentiated, resembling animal fur most closely.

The overall shape and length of a human hair can give information about where on the body it originated, such as the scalp, face, pubic area, or elsewhere. For example, scalp hair is usually long with cut or split tips and a relatively narrow

medulla, while pubic hairs are typically short, with a tapered or rounded tip, and contain a relatively broad medulla. Because of the variation of hair structures, even on one individual person, it is often necessary to collect many hair fibers in order to get a representative sample. This variation in a single individual makes it very difficult to determine if a particular hair fiber originated from a particular person.

7.3.2.3 How Hair Grows

Hair growth occurs in a cycle composed of three main stages: the anagen, catagen, and telogen phases (Figure 7.41). The lengths of these cycles are genetically programmed and can vary greatly from person to person and from place to place on the body. For example, an entire cycle can take four to five years for scalp hair, while the cycle is completed in three to four months for eyebrow hair. In humans, these stages do not occur at the same time for all the follicles – each follicle has its own timetable. This, however, is not true for other animals in which the phases may be timed to occur simultaneously accompanied by the shedding of hair, for example, when a rabbit changes its hair from the darker summer coat to the white winter coat of hair (Figure 7.42).

The *anagen* phase is the part of the cycle in which active growth occurs. During this phase, the cells at the base of the follicle rapidly divide and push "upward" to produce the new hair shaft. The cells in the base of the growing hair

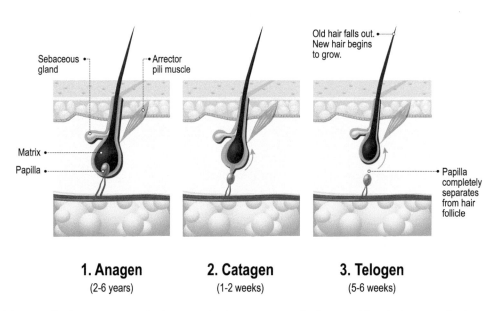

FIGURE 7.41   Hair growth phases: anagen is the growth phase, catagen is the transitional phase, and telogen is the resting or quiescent phase.

Source: Shutterstock.com.

FIGURE 7.42   Winter (a) and summer (b) coats of a snowshoe rabbit (*Lepus americanus*) as an example of correlated hair growth phases.

Source: Images courtesy Shutterstock.com.

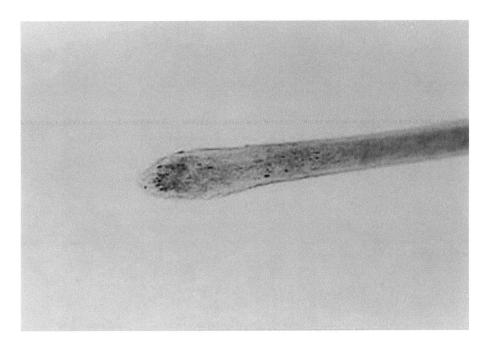

FIGURE 7.43   Naturally shed hair fiber showing the characteristic "club" end shape.

Source: FBI.

bulb are the second fastest-growing cells in the body (after the blood-producing cells of the bone marrow). In humans, this phase can last between several months and many years, depending on where the hair is growing.

Generally, a hair fiber grows about ½ in. (~1 cm) per month (0.3–0.4 mm/day). Thus, the tip of an individual hair that is a foot long began growing within the follicle about two years earlier.

The *catagen* phase can best be thought of as a transitional phase and usually represents about 3–5% of all body hairs at any given time. It is during catagen that hair growth stops, and the portion of the follicle surrounding the hair root shrinks

by about two-thirds through cell death and detaches from the root, forming a "club"-shaped end (Figure 7.43). This process results in major destruction of the lower part of the hair follicle, including the cells that produce the keratin and melanin that form the hair. Usually, the catagenic phase lasts several weeks for all types of hair.

The final phase, the *telogen* phase, is a resting period for the follicle. In this phase, the detached club root has completely formed. The bulb on the dead hair helps to keep the hair in the follicle tube but the hair eventually falls out since it's no longer strongly "connected" to the follicle. This phase can last from a few months to years, depending on its location on the body and usually about 10–15% of all hairs are in the telogen phase at any given time. On average, a typical person has between 100,000 and 150,000 hairs on their head and loses between 50 and 100 hairs every day due to the normal hair growth cycle.

A fourth phase, the *exogen* phase, is sometimes considered, although it is associated with the hair fiber itself rather than with the follicle and simply has to do with the loss of the hair shaft from the follicle. This process is poorly understood, however, but it is believed to be important in the timing of the restart of a new anagen phase of hair growth for the follicle.

These phases typically continue over the entire lifespan of a person. Sometimes, however, this pattern is either interrupted or the follicle is destroyed by medications, radiation, genetics, accidents, or other causes.

BOX 7.7 CAN YOUR HAIR TURN WHITE OVERNIGHT WITH FRIGHT?

There are plenty of stories throughout history where someone, faced with extreme fear or a severely traumatic experience, reportedly has their hair turn completely white overnight. Legend has it that the hair of some famous people, such as Sir Thomas More (1535), Henry of Navarre, later Henry IV of France (1572), and Marie Antoinette (1793), went white overnight when faced with imminent death.

These tales, however, do not have a basis in current scientific research. White hair arises from fibers that do not contain any melanin pigments. When someone goes "gray", it simply means that they have a mixture of colored and uncolored (white) hair. Since the amount of pigment in a hair fiber is fixed at the time it forms within the follicle, even if a hair follicle stopped producing melanin overnight, the hair fiber beyond the follicle would still remain pigmented since the hair is dead. Thus, if all the follicles on a person's head stopped producing melanin at once, the hair would still be largely pigmented. Additionally, there is no research evidence that shows that stress can significantly cause hair to stop producing melanin or go white; it's largely determined by a person's genetics, age, or access to bleach.

There is, however, a fairly rare autoimmune disease (a disease in which your body's immune system turns against itself) called *alopecia areata* in which hair follicles are very rapidly destroyed, even over a few days. There is a particularly rare form of this disease, however, that seems to attack only the pigmented hair follicles, leaving a person with only unpigmented or white hair. Assuming that all the pigmented hair fell out immediately, the remaining white hair would remain, giving the appearance of a rapid transformation from colored or gray hair to white hair – but this certainly would not happen overnight.

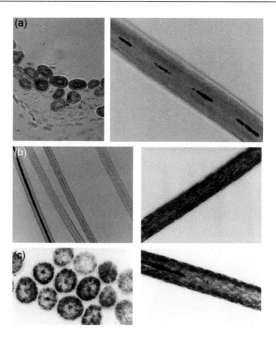

FIGURE 7.44 Ethnic differences in hair structures in cross-section: (a) Caucasian, (b) African, and (c) Asian.

Source: FBI.

7.3.2.4 Sex and Ancestry Differences in Hair Structure

Occasionally, ancestry differences can be seen in hair samples (Note: race does not provide an accurate representation of human biological variation). This will be described in more detail in the chapter on forensic anthropology, but occasionally, some information regarding ethnicity may be gained by examining hair samples, as shown in Figure 7.44.

Hair of Asian ancestry tends to be round in cross-section with a greater diameter than other types, although generally less dense than hair of other ethnicities. This tends to lead to hair that is thicker, straighter, and more difficult to curl than hair of other origins. Caucasian hair tends to be oval in cross-section and more physically durable to bending and stretching than hair of other ancestral types. It is also often relatively straight but flexible so as to form loose curls easily. African hair tends to be oval to relatively flat ("ribbon-like") in cross-section, allowing it to form tight curls readily while remaining very strong across the width of the fiber. Additionally, the fiber tends to vary greatly in its thickness and twists along the length of the shaft in contrast to other ethnicities.

It is typically very difficult to determine the age or sex of an individual from hair samples. It is sometimes possible, although rarely done, to recover follicle cells from the root of forcibly removed hairs. These cells can be stained and examined under the microscope to reveal specific sex-related characteristics, such as the Barr body for females or a Y body for males.

7.3.2.5 Hair Treatment

Hair has important cultural significance beyond its necessary biological functions. People style, condition, shampoo, color, cut, and modify their hair in innumerable ways. Today, over 50% of people in the United States report that they color their hair, with red being the most popular choice. Each process we do to our hair can be "recorded" in the fibers, and this record can help to individualize a fiber by marking the history of its treatment. These modifications can, therefore, be used to advantage to help identify a particular hair and to learn something about its past.

The color of hair can be readily altered through the use of dyes and rinses. To permanently change the color of hair, however, pigment molecules must pass through the outer cuticle layer and be deposited within the cortex. When pigment molecules adsorb only on the outer cuticle layer, the color may be vibrant, but it is also readily removed by simple washing. This is the case with temporary coloration methods such as certain rinses, sprays, and foams.

For a more permanent coloration, the pigment molecules must first penetrate the tough outer cuticle. This requires a modification of the cuticle to make it permeable to the pigments since its primary function is to protect the cortex from the environment, and it, therefore, resists the movement of pigment into the hair. In order for permanent coloration to occur, the cuticle must be chemically treated to open up its scale-like structure, requiring relatively harsh chemical processing. This usually employs an oxidizing agent, an alkaline (basic) agent, and a conditioner in addition to the dye. An oxidizing agent is something that removes electrons from a molecule, such as hydrogen peroxide (H_2O_2). An alkaline agent is a basic chemical, such as ammonia (NH_3), that can react with acids. In the permanent dyeing process, ammonia is often used to chemically open up the cuticle, thereby allowing the dye to penetrate into the cortex, and to catalyze coloration reactions in the cortex. This process also breaks the majority of the sulfur-sulfur bonds holding the inner keratin strands of the hair together, releasing the characteristic odor of hydrogen sulfide and causing the hair to "relax". The hydrogen peroxide is used to remove the pre-existing natural color of the hair and facilitate the reformation of the sulfur-sulfur linkages. Finally, a conditioner is used to try to close the scale-like structure of the cuticle after the process is completed. Often, however, this harsh chemical process results in a damaged cuticle layer that can be helpful in forensic investigations by telling a story about any recent treatment of the hair, as seen in Figure 7.45.

It is occasionally possible to determine a rough timeline of when the dyeing process may have occurred by observing cuticle damage that is found some distance along the fiber but not at the base of the shaft (the youngest part of hair). By noting the distance from the base of the fiber to the beginning of the damaged area, a rough indication of how long ago the dyeing process occurred can be estimated given the average rate of growth of the hair and knowing that hair grows only from its root. Additionally, observing a sharp color change near the root end of the hair fiber, with color that is dense and relatively even throughout the cortex, is evidence that the hair has been dyed.

Hair can also be modified by curling, waving, or straightening through a process often called permanent curling or "perming." About one-quarter of the keratin in hair, the major protein component that gives hair its characteristic shape, is composed of cysteine, a sulfur-containing amino acid. The keratin chains in hair are linked together by connecting the sulfur atoms on two adjacent chains, forming *disulfide bonds*. These linkages largely fix the shape of the strand in much the

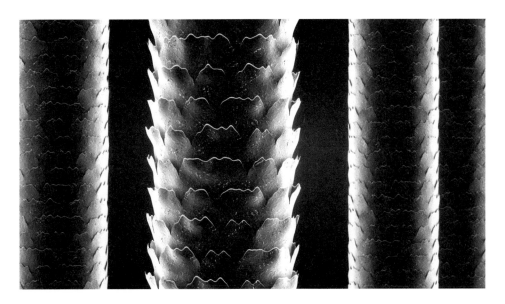

FIGURE 7.45 Micrographs of a damaged cuticle (center) from the hair treatment processes.

Source: Nobeastsofierce/Science Photo Library image. Used with permission.

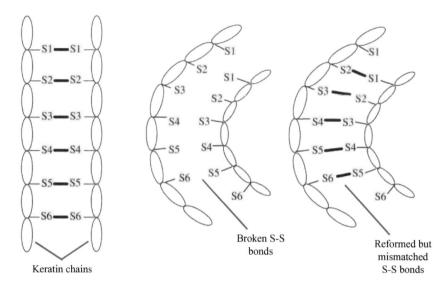

FIGURE 7.46   Disulfide bond breakage and "mismatched" reformation during the "perming" process in hair to create a permanent curl.

same way that the rungs of a ladder hold the two vertical poles together to give rigidity and structure to the ladder, as shown in Figure 7.46. When hair is chemically "permed," a chemical (such as sodium thioglycolate) is first used to break about 30% of the disulfide bonds between the keratin strands. As the hair is placed in the desired shape, the keratin strands are now free to slide past each other to assume the new shape. Then, another chemical, such as hydrogen peroxide or a similar oxidizing agent, is applied to reform the disulfide linkages between adjacent cysteine units. In this final step, however, there is now a new pattern of pairing between adjacent cysteines, thereby permanently locking the keratin strands into the new shape. This would be something like "unzipping" the rungs of a ladder, moving the two poles to a new orientation relative to each other, and then "re-zipping" the rungs together to "fix" the new arrangement of the poles. The curl is permanent only on the portion of hair existing when the permanent was done, and as new hair grows or the old hair is cut, the effect of the permanent gradually disappears.

People also commonly clean and style their hair through regular cleaning and the application of hair products. Several forensically interesting pieces of information can be gained by considering the types of cleaning and styling chemicals used on the hair fibers. Information about any recent washing can be revealed microscopically. Additionally, chemical analysis of the surface or rinsing of the fiber can also show residues of particular types of treatments (see Chapter 12).

Cutting hair, either to maintain a desired hairstyle or through accident, injury, or assault, can provide information on the history of a hair sample. Examples of this type of information from hair fibers can be seen in Figure 7.47.

7.3.2.6 Diseases Involving Hair

Since everyone's basic hair chemistry is about the same, it is difficult to individualize chemically a particular hair

sample sufficiently to connect it with one individual person. Therefore, scientists try to find ways that do individualize a hair sample. One way is to identify the hair as associated with a disease, abnormality, treatment, or infestation. For example, a deficiency of certain vitamins or minerals, such as a zinc deficiency, can result in abnormal hair growth that can be detected in the hair. If a suspect suffers from a similar deficiency, a better link can be made between the recovered sample and a hair sample of known origin. Abnormalities in metabolism, hormone levels, or other biochemical irregularities can also be detected in hair samples (see Section 7.2.3.7).

Abnormalities in hair structure can also help in characterizing a hair sample. One example of many is the striking *pili annulati* hair abnormality which arises from an unusual process in forming the keratin of the hair fiber. This condition results in a cortex that is not solid but rather contains air pockets in a regular pattern along the length of the fiber. These air pockets effectively reflect light so that the hair appears to be banded (Figure 7.48). This distinctive condition is genetic in some circumstances while the cause is unknown in other instances.

Occasionally, it is possible to detect hair infestations, such as mites (arachnids – related to spiders, not insects), lice (insects), and others, as illustrated in Figure 7.49. These can help provide both a connection with a known person and information about the history of the sample.

7.3.2.7 Hair Toxicology

When hair grows within a follicle, certain biochemical conditions existing in a body can be chemically recorded directly within a growing hair shaft. Chemicals can be transferred from a person's bloodstream to the follicle and then deposited in the growing hair. As the shaft continues to grow, the chemical record contained in the living portion of the hair is pushed out of the follicle and becomes a permanent snapshot of what was going on in a person's biochemistry at the time

FIGURE 7.47 Hair patterns from treatment or injury. (a) hair root naturally fallen out, (b) hair cut by razor, (c) naturally knotted hair, (d) split ends, (e) hair with dandruff, and (f) post-mortem root band.

Source: (a) istockphoto.com, Jan-Otto, (b, c, d, and e) Shutterstock.com, (f) FBI.

FIGURE 7.48 Photomicrographs of *Pili Annulati* (banded hair).

Source: FBI.

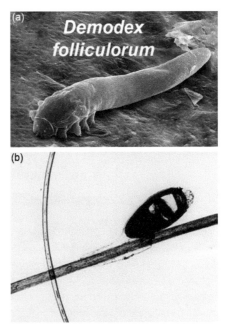

FIGURE 7.49 (a) Follicle mites (*Demodex folliculorum*) emerging from a hair follicle and (b) lice (*Pediculus humanus*) case attached to a hair fiber.

Source: (a) Used per Creative Commons Attribution 4.0 International, Attribution: © Palopoli et al.; licensee BioMed Central. 2014. (b) FBI.

that portion of the fiber was formed. Once the newly formed portion of the hair shaft leaves the follicle and dies, this record can last for a very long time. For example, certain drugs or

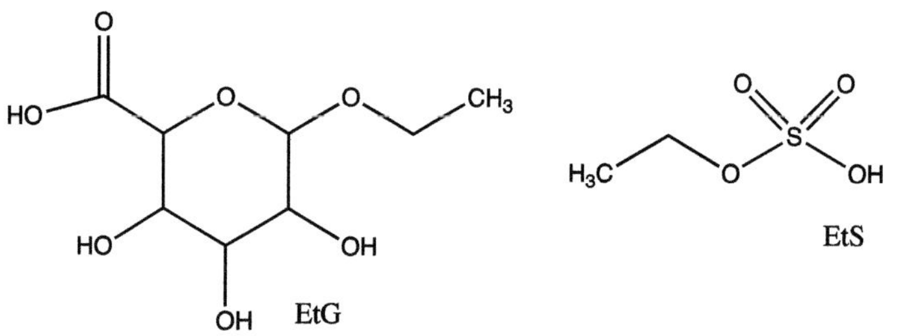

FIGURE 7.50 Structure of ethyl glucuronide (EtG) and ethyl sulfate (EtS).

their metabolites (chemicals that the body transforms the drug into), such as cocaine, heroin, amphetamines, and others, are deposited from a person's bloodstream to the growing hair fiber, providing a long-lasting record of drug use.

Some drugs, particularly those that are bases, bind tightly to the melanin since melanin is acidic. Therefore, the darker the hair, generally the more melanin and the more drug binding found. Neutrally charged drugs tend to enter the hair more easily. Some drugs get into the hair through the sebum (sweat), especially when the cuticle is damaged. Of concern, however, is that chemicals from the surrounding environment (e.g., dirt, smoke, etc.) can also make their way into the hair and affect any later chemical analysis to detect drugs.

Since hair grows at a rate of about ½ in. (~1 cm) per month, a rough timeline of drug or poison intake event(s) can be estimated by chemically analyzing different portions of the hair along the length of its shaft. This form of analysis has become an important part of drug surveillance programs for people on parole, checking to see if a patient has been complying with therapeutic drug therapy, or verifying the reliability of a person's statement regarding their drug use. Besides serving as a record of drug use, this toxicological information can also aid in determining if two fibers have a common source, for example, one found at a crime scene and one taken from a suspect. Hair can also serve as strong evidence showing a person's long-term use of alcohol. When alcohol is consumed, the body produces fatty acid ethyl esters (FAEE), ethyl glucuronide

(EtG), and ethylsulfate (EtS) (Figure 7.50). While alcohol is not deposited in hair, these three metabolites of alcohol (ethanol) are permanently deposited in growing hair fibers, making a lasting record of its use – even for years.

There are a number of both important advantages and challenges when considering toxicology information from hair samples. Hair is usually a readily available, non-invasive, inexpensive, and long-lasting medium for analysis. In addition, chemical analyses have been developed for trace levels of compounds found within hair fibers. But hair analysis also has some significant difficulties. For example, darker and coarser hair fibers retain drug information longer than lighter and finer hair. This may lead to a different drug use profile determined from hair for two people with identical usages. False positives may also present significant problems, such as in the determination of alcohol abuse through EtG analysis. For example, in one study, it was surprisingly shown that a false positive can come from a person using an alcohol-containing hand sanitizer before the analysis. There are also problems in establishing a relationship between the amount of a drug found in a hair sample with how much was in a person's blood system. Other problems currently being addressed include: (1) use of hair from different places on the body, (2) ethnic differences in drug absorption and retention in hair, and (3) the effects of cosmetics on chemical composition. Nonetheless, the use of hair analysis for drug and toxin exposure is increasing and forms an important forensic tool.

BOX 7.8   THE END OF AN EMPEROR: TELLTALE HAIR?

Napoleon Bonaparte (1769–1821) is one of the most studied, despised, and revered figures in history, with tens of thousands of books published on his life and exploits, and thousands of new titles appearing every year. He is certainly a person of intrigue and mystery, but one of the greatest mysteries regarding this enigmatic figure is the cause and manner of his death.

After Napoleon lost the Battle of Waterloo in 1815 and later surrendered to the British, he was exiled to the remote tropical island of St. Helena in the South Atlantic, still one of the most isolated places on Earth. He and his retinue of about 20 friends and associates lived for six years on the island under the close watch of the British commander until his death in 1821. Upon his death, an autopsy was performed by British surgeons and the cause was determined to be a perforated ("bleeding") stomach ulcer that had become cancerous. But today, nearly 200 years later, controversy still remains surrounding his death.

During his exile, Napoleon often thought of escaping and his relations with the British commander on St. Helena, Sir Hudson Lowe, were very poor, indeed. Lowe deeply distrusted Napoleon and had sentries posted constantly to monitor Napoleon's every movement. Napoleon, in turn, ultimately retreated to his home and grounds, Longwood House, and did everything possible to remain out of the sight of his guards – he even had sunken walkways dug on the grounds to enable him to walk outside without being seen by the sentries.

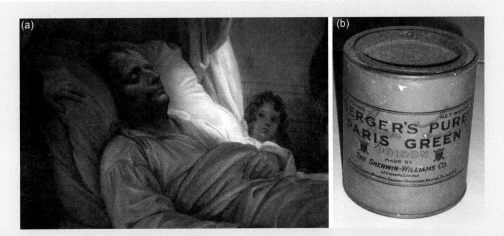

FIGURE 7.51 (a) Painting of the death of Napoleon (Charles Steuben) and (b) Paris Green, an arsenic-containing pigment.
Source: (b) Used per Creative Commons Attribution-Share Alike 3.0 Unported. User: Chris Goulet at English Wikipedia.

During his exile, Napoleon often wrote and said that he was being "murdered by the British Oligarchy." His relatively rapid decline, along with the type of illness and symptoms he reported, has prompted speculation ever since that he was murdered, and theories have abounded about how, who, and why he was murdered. But new insights have come from, of all places, locks of Napoleon's hair.

One theory of his death is that he was poisoned by arsenic – a well-known 19th-century poison. It was noticed that some of the symptoms of Napoleon's demise closely resembled arsenic poisoning. But how to prove this since Napoleon's body, removed from St. Helena in 1841 to a crypt in Paris, is not available for tissue analysis to look for arsenic? As it turns out, something almost as good *is* available – Napoleon's hair.

As part of an old custom, Napoleon bequeathed locks of his hair to his friends and family upon his death. Since hair provides a long-lasting record of toxins in the body, analysis of his hair sample should show high levels of arsenic if this was indeed the cause of his death. A *bona fide* Bonaparte hair sample was ultimately found, and an arsenic analysis was performed. The analysis showed that there were indeed significantly higher levels, nearly 100 times higher, than normal arsenic levels in the former Emperor's hair. But was he poisoned? Some say yes, while other theories have been proposed to account for the arsenic levels.

In 1980, Dr. David Jones proposed that Napoleon was actually suffering from Gosio's disease, a chronic arsenic poisoning from exposure to a common 19th-century pigment – Scheele's or Paris green. Scheele's green contains copper arsenite that, under certain circumstances of high humidity and mold, gives off arsine gas (AsH_3). Almost miraculously, Dr. Jones found what is believed to be an actual piece of Napoleon's wallpaper from Longwood House that clearly had Paris green pigment (note the painting of Napoleon's deathbed in Figure 7.51 that shows the green star pattern on the walls). A chemical analysis of this wallpaper pigment showed that it definitely contained arsenic. But was it the cause of death? And why was Napoleon the only one affected?

As it turns out, others in Napoleon's party complained of illnesses and the "bad air" at Longwood, including the butler who also died. But for a normally healthy person, the level of arsenic might not have been enough to cause severe illness. But to someone already in a compromised health state, such as Napoleon with a problematic ulcer, the added effect of the arsenic might have been enough to significantly contribute to his cause of death (proximate cause of death, Chapter 8). Interestingly, when they exhumed Napoleon's body nearly 20 years later, it had not decayed and was perfectly preserved, even in the warm tropical environment – further suggestioning the presence of arsenic.

So, what caused Napoleon's death? At this point, the evidence is not fully conclusive. and we await more information while the debate continues. What do you think?

7.3.2.8 Hair Comparison and Identification

Probably the most important aspect of examining a hair sample is the observed microscopic structure of the medulla and cuticle of the sample. An individual hair fiber, however, cannot be individualized through its chemical composition or usually even from its structural features. The shaft of a mature human hair does not contain nuclear DNA so that only mitochondrial DNA analysis is possible for such samples. Often, however, tissue from the follicle may remain at the root of a hair sample, such as fibers forcibly removed from the scalp, allowing for a nuclear DNA analysis. Apart from DNA analyses significant error rates are associated with the microscopic comparison of two hair samples. When comparing these samples, the color, length, and diameter of the hair fiber are particularly important.

7.3.3 Fingernails

Fingernails and toenails, like hair, are considered appendages of the skin and are closely chemically related to the claws, hooves, and horns found in other animals. Like hair, nails are made up of the durable protein keratin. The importance of nails in forensic cases usually arises in assault or other violent cases in which pieces of an attacker's or victim's fingernail become lodged in clothing or skin. Finding and analyzing the nail can be valuable evidence.

Nails primarily serve to protect the very sensitive ends of our fingers and toes. The tips of our fingers and toes are among the most sensitive portions of our bodies, through which we sense a great deal of information regarding the shape of the world.

7.3.3.1 Fingernail Growth

Like hair, the majority of nails are dead keratinized material. The only living portion is the nail root, or *germinal matrix*, that extends under the skin opposite to the end of the nail and is where the nerve, blood supply, and lymph vessels are found (Figure 7.52). The nail grows continuously from the root as long as it is healthy and nourished, growing an average of 0.5–1.2 mm/week. Fingernails actually grow much faster than toenails, typically taking about six months to completely regrow a new fingernail while it may take up to two years to fully regrow a toenail.

As new nail cells are produced, they are pushed out of the root area as white, opaque round cells. These newly formed cells are visible near the root of the nail as a crescent shape, called the lunula ("small moon"). The lunula appears largest on the thumb and gets smaller toward the little finger, where it is often not visible at all. As the cells are pushed further

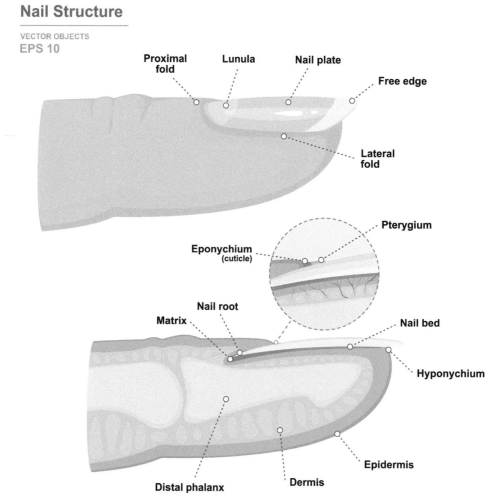

FINGERNAIL ANATOMY
Nail Structure

VECTOR OBJECTS
EPS 10

Proximal fold • Lunula • Nail plate • Free edge • Lateral fold • Pterygium • Eponychium (cuticle) • Nail root • Matrix • Nail bed • Hyponychium • Distal phalanx • Dermis • Epidermis

FIGURE 7.52   Finger and fingernail anatomy and structures.

Source: Shutterstock.com.

away from the root area, they are flattened, compacted, and ultimately die, turning translucent, such that the pink blood capillary bed lying beneath the nail becomes visible. The nail plate, the actual nail itself, rides on the nail bed as it is pushed away from the root. At the sides of the nail is the cuticle, or eponychium, formed from the flap of skin that folds over the nail and forms a waterproof seal with the nail.

The shape and structure of nails can tell us about a person's health. Nails that are discolored, spotted, brittle, or grooved may indicate an underlying disease process before other symptoms appear. For example, pitting may indicate psoriasis, white nails may suggest hepatic failure (liver), or a blue coloration may suggest circulatory problems.

BOX 7.9   A VERY COLD CASE: AN ARCTIC MYSTERY

In 1871, Captain Charles Hall led a congressionally backed expedition on the ship *Polaris* in search of the North Pole. When the expedition came within 500 miles of the pole in late fall, Captain Hall decided to set anchor and winter aboard the *Polaris*, much to the distress and outrage of several crew members. One day in late October, after drinking a cup of coffee at anchor, Captain Hall became quite ill and thought he had been poisoned. He died in early November before help could be arranged. He was buried in Greenland, and a later medical examination found that he had died of natural causes.

The case rested here until 1968 when Hall's body was located, exhumed, and an autopsy performed onsite. Hair and fingernail samples were also taken for later chemical

FIGURE 7.53   Capt. Charles Hall (1821–1871).

analysis. A neutron activation analysis (see Chapter 12 on chemical analysis) was done on these samples, and high levels of arsenic were found. The problem was, however, that the surrounding soil in Greenland was also found to be high in arsenic. But quite importantly, it was found that Hall's nails and hair showed that he had received a large dose of arsenic about two weeks before his death and that arsenic levels were low elsewhere in the samples. This differential location of the arsenic in the nails strongly suggests that he was poisoned. If the arsenic had come from the Greenland soil, a uniform distribution of arsenic in the entire sample would be expected rather than what was found.

Given the high arsenic levels in Hall's nails in some places and not others, coupled with the symptoms that he reported before his death, it suggests that homicide should be the true manner of his death. There remains, however, little evidence to tie any particular person with this crime.

7.3.3.2 Forensic Nails Use

Fingernails can be used forensically in a number of ways. In one case, a broken fingernail was found in the clothing of a suspect. This fingernail was matched with a broken fingernail on the victim, both in lengthwise striations and in the irregular tearing of the broken nail from the victim's nail plate. Work has also shown that the striations in fingernails do not change over a person's lifetime (persistence) and are similar to a unique "barcode" for a person's nails (Figure 7.54).

Fingernails are often found with tissue fragments attached to them when they have been forcibly removed. The attached tissues can yield viable DNA samples. This technique has been successfully used in many cases, and the resulting evidence has led to numerous convictions. Additionally, like hair, fingernails can "record" biochemical information as they grow. There are reported cases that use the analysis of nails to show the non-uniform presence of toxins, such as arsenic, along the length of the nail, suggesting that the toxin was administered at specific times to the victim.

BOX 7.10   DO FINGERNAILS CONTINUE TO GROW AFTER DEATH?

Many people believe that fingernails continue to grow after death and exhumed bodies appear to have much longer nails than expected. It turns out this is actually an illusion based on our normal "living" expectations.

The growth of the nails does indeed stop at death. However, after death, the tissue surrounding the nails shrinks and dehydrates, making it appear that the fingernails are longer. Since we are used to seeing fingernails grow and fingers remain the same size in life, we interpret what we see after death similarly – we assume that the finger tissue has remained the same size when it actually shrinks.

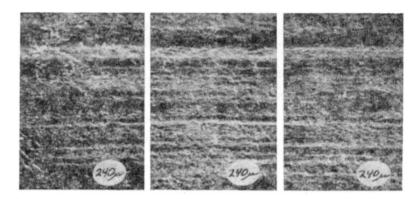

FIGURE 7.54   SEM micrographs showing that fingernail striations remain unchanged over five years.

Source: Used and with permission Herb McDonald.

7.4 FIBER ANALYSIS

7.4.1 Introduction

While manmade and natural fibers, other than hair and fur, are not formally biological materials derived from skin, they are often quite similar in their overall structure and function to hair. Fibers, however, are frequently woven together into cloth and other objects to form both insulating and protective layers that lie adjacent to our skin, enhancing the capabilities of our skin in some respect. But our uses for fibers go well beyond our needs simply for cloth. Fibers are twisted into ropes, embedded within other materials to form composites, pressed into sheets of hardboard, paper, or felt, spun into building materials, and employed in biomedical applications from surgical dressings to artificial skin. Because we use fibers for so many everyday functions, they often find their way into forensic investigations and are employed as evidence similarly to the way that hair evidence is typically considered. For these reasons, fibers will be considered in this chapter along with skin and hair analysis.

7.4.2 What Are Fibers?

Fibers can be defined simply as long, thin filaments with lengths that are very much greater than their widths, typically at least 100-fold greater. Fibers can be classified into one of three main groupings depending on how they are produced: (1) natural fibers, (2) regenerated (sometimes called reconstituted) fibers, and (3) manmade or synthetic fibers. Examples of each of these types are illustrated in Figure 7.55.

7.4.3 Natural Fibers

Natural fibers are very common and were the first type of fibers to be extensively used by humans to make objects for

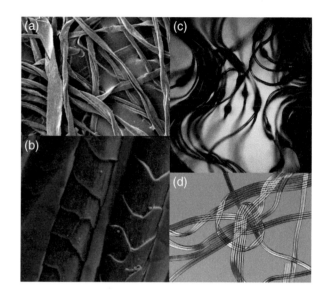

FIGURE 7.55   Natural, regenerated, and synthetic fibers: (a) cotton fibers, (b) wool fibers, (c) nylon fibers, and (d) polyurethane fibers.

Sources: (a) Used per Creative Commons Attribution 3.0 Unported. User: Featheredtar, (b) Used per Creative Commons Attribution-Share Alike 3.0 Unported. User: Gerry Danilatos, (c) Used per Creative Commons Attribution 2.0 Generic. User: Picturepest, and (d) Used per Creative Commons Attribution-Share Alike 4.0 International. User: Photon 400 750.

skin protection and insulation. Wool and dyed flax fibers that were used by early people have been found that date back over 35,000 years. These natural fibers come from many different sources including plants, such as cotton in cloth, wood in paper, and hemp in rope; from insects, such as in silk; from animals (besides hair and fur), such as catgut and spider's silk; and from inorganic materials or minerals, such as asbestos found in older types of home insulation and glass in fiberglass and spun glass materials. Several examples of natural fibers are shown in Figure 7.56.

Plant-based fibers may be either carbohydrate-based or protein-based. Many plant-derived fibers are composed

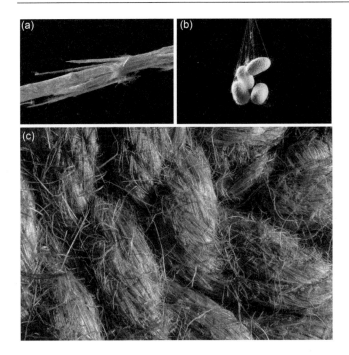

FIGURE 7.56 Examples of natural fibers: (a) asbestos fibers, (b) silk fibers from silkworm cocoons, and (c) jute rope fibers.

Source: Images used courtesy Shutterstock.com.

largely of the carbohydrate polymer cellulose, a complex sugar or polysaccharide molecule ("poly" meaning many and "saccharide" meaning sugar). The chemical structure of cellulose, shown in Figure 7.57, consists of many smaller sugar units (the six-membered rings) strung together to form a very long chain. These long chains can intertwine and chemically bond to one another through hydrogen bonds between adjacent strands to give a strong and sturdy fiber (Figure 7.58).

Animal-derived fibers are typically composed largely of protein, such as keratin or the silk-related proteins. Like cellulose, these proteins are polymeric materials built from smaller units linked together, except in this case using amino acid building blocks. These fibers can be both very strong physically and highly resistant to chemical damage. Some can be remarkably elastic. Probably the most common animal protein fiber is silk, obtained from the cocoons of silk moths. Silk proteins, mostly fibroin and sericins, are largely built from the amino acid glycine, making up to about 50%, which provides the highly desirable strength, sheen, and texture of silk.

Mineral fibers, such as asbestos, have a variety of compositions and are primarily used for composites and building components. They are so ubiquitous that they often appear in forensic investigations.

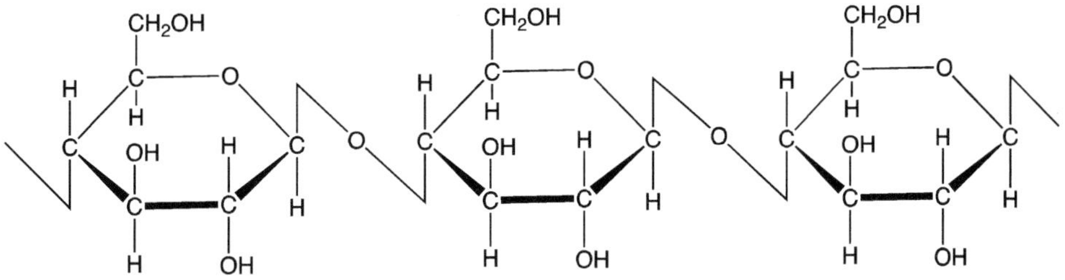

FIGURE 7.57 Structure of cellulose $[(C_6H_{10}O_5)_n]$.

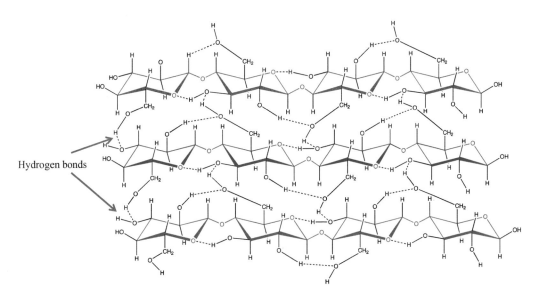

Hydrogen bonds

FIGURE 7.58 Hydrogen bonds (dashed lines) holding together three strands of cellulose polymer (each cellulose strand is shown in a different color).

7.4.4 Regenerated Fibers

Regenerated fibers are those made by chemically processing naturally occurring materials into fibers with new shapes and designed structures. Rayon and acetate are two very common examples of regenerated fibers made from cellulose (Figure 7.59).

Regenerated fibers can be classified as deriving from either cellulose-based or protein-based starting materials, both typically processed from plants. The first commercial regenerated fiber was rayon, originally called "artificial silk". It was discovered in 1855 and later produced on a large scale beginning in the 1890s. However, the early artificial silk was far different from the material we use today; through chemical modifications in the production process in 1924, a very stable, durable, and desirable form of rayon silk was first introduced to the market.

In the production of rayon and its analogs, cellulose from trees and other plants is first dissolved or suspended in a solvent and chemically purified and treated before being formed into new threads and fibers through a variety of manufacturing processes. In one common process for forming these fibers, the wood from trees is first chopped into small pieces that are chemically treated to remove all non-cellulose components and bleached to eliminate any coloration from the material. The cellulose is then dissolved in a basic solution, bathed in carbon disulfide (CS_2), extruded from a showerhead-like device (spinneret), and ultimately stretched to produce the characteristic thin threads. The final stretching process helps to realign the long cellulose molecules along the length of the fiber.

There are a number of new and increasingly important regenerated fibers that originate from plant or animal proteins rather than from cellulose. For example, the protein from corn (seins), soy (glycins), peanut (mainly arginine), or milk (casein) can be used to form strong, stable, and occasionally biodegradable fibers (Figure 7.60). A good example is soybeans, which form smooth, light, and soft fibers, similar to the natural fiber of cashmere. Some of these fibers have the advantage of being produced in an environmentally friendly fashion.

FIGURE 7.59 The preparation of changed forms of regenerated cellulose fibers from dissolved cellulose in a solution of Schweizer's reagent.

Source: Used per Creative Commons Attribution-Share Alike 4.0 International. User: Perwincz.

7.4.5 Synthetic Fibers

Synthetic fibers are entirely prepared from small molecules, often petrochemicals (oil), rather than from natural fiber sources, and are formed through polymerization reactions that lead to long-chain molecules. Common synthetic fibers include nylon, polyethylene, acrylic polyesters, PVC fiber, and polyurethane. The properties of synthetic fibers are controllable by design and vary widely in structure.

Some synthetic polymers have special elastic properties and are called *elastomers* (e.g., spandex, polyurethane, neoprene, and others). Silicones, compounds composed of chains

(a)

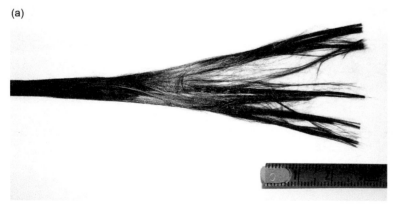

(b)

FIGURE 7.60 (a) Regenerated carbon fiber and (b) regenerated cotton and synthetic polyurethane fibers woven together to form an elastomer.

Source: (b) Susumu Nishinaga/Science Photo Library. Used with permission.

of silicon, carbon, and oxygen atoms, make particularly good elastomers since the chemical backbone chain is very flexible. Lycra (spandex) is a polyurethane polymer that has both rigid and flexible subunits repeated in its chain structure. The combination of these subunits provides a material with strength from the rigid parts *and* elasticity from the flexible units that can "unwind" (Figure 7.60b).

Synthetics are among the strongest of the known fibers. Additionally, many regenerated and synthetic fibers are *thermoplastic* – they melt or soften easily. This allows them to be easily molded into a variety of shapes by heating and then cooling (e.g., pleats, creases, containers, solid objects, and many more). A *plastic* material, by definition, is simply *something that can be shaped or molded*. Today, however, the term plastic has become synonymous with synthetic thermoplastics.

7.4.6 Polymers

In Chapter 4 on DNA, the general idea of polymeric molecules was presented. Fibers, whether natural, regenerated, or synthetic, are typically composed of long polymer molecules, of which DNA is just one very important specific example.

Polymers are, by definition, long-chain molecules that are built by stringing together many smaller subunits, called monomers. These chains are typically very long. To get a sense

of this, a typical polymer made up of 10,000 monomers strung together would be comparable in length-to-thickness ratio to a 6-in.-thick rope (15 cm) that was over a mile long (1.6 km).

Importantly, polymers and plastics are everywhere we look today and, therefore, are very frequently part of crime scenes, emergency medical apparatuses to aid victims, and numerous other aspects of forensic investigations.

One convenient way to subdivide the vast array of known polymers already described is to consider natural polymers and synthetic polymers. Chemically, natural polymers include biopolymers, such as proteins, polysaccharides, nucleic acids, and inorganic polymers, such as asbestos and graphite. Synthetic polymers are most often prepared by linking together a variety of small organic monomers.

Polymers display an amazing array of properties that are put to an equally enormous variety of uses, ranging from soft pliable materials to extremely hard, structural components. Polymers now fulfill needs that *no* other materials can, from artificial skin to high-strength composites. There are, however, a few key features that dictate the observed properties of a polymer. Understanding these features helps us identify the specific polymer that might have played a role in a crime.

Probably the most important feature is the identity of the small monomer molecules that are linked together to form a polymer strand. The chemical structure of the individual monomers dictates what is possible in the full polymer. A few

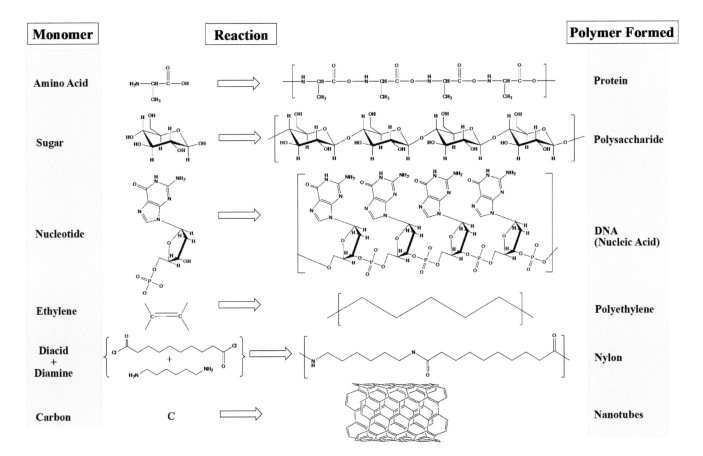

FIGURE 7.61 Various monomers that combine to make polymers (unlabeled junctures between the lines indicate carbon atoms).

examples of monomers, along with the polymers that they form, are shown in Figure 7.61 and include:

- Amino acids, which form proteins.
- Sugar molecules (such as glucose), which form polysaccharides.
- Nucleotides (composed of a phosphate, sugar, and nitrogen base), which form DNA and RNA.
- Ethylene, which forms polyethylene.
- An organic di-acid molecule coupled with a diamine, which forms nylon.
- Carbon, which forms diamond, buckminsterfullerene, and nanotubes.

Today, most of our synthetic polymers are composed of just five monomers: ethylene, vinyl chloride, styrene, propylene, and terephthalic acid (when reacted with ethylene glycol). The structures of these five small molecular monomers and some of the objects made from them are shown in Figure 7.62. The first four of these monomers form long chains through the formation of direct monomer-to-monomer linkages, a chemical process called polymerization that is brought about by *catalysts* (special chemical reagents that can cause a chemical reaction to occur or to accelerate without being ultimately changed itself). These reactions are often called *addition* reactions since the net result is to simply add the monomers together without the loss of any portion of the monomer. These reactions account for millions of tons of polymers produced annually in the United States alone, with polyethylene being the number one polymer produced.

The other most common way to form a polymer from monomers occurs through a reaction called *condensation*, a reaction that involves the loss of a small molecule, such as water, from the reaction. For example, the reaction of terephthalic acid with ethylene glycol results in the elimination of H_2O to form the condensation polymer polyethylene terephthalate (Figure 7.63). To say that this type of reaction is important in forming needed biopolymers would be a huge understatement. Condensation reactions are used to build proteins from amino acid building blocks, polysaccharides from simple sugars, and DNA from individual nucleotides (Figure 7.64). Clearly, without this single type of polymerization reaction, life would not be possible as we know it.

Overall, the properties of polymer molecules are controlled by several chemical features including:

- Chemical composition of the monomers.
- Formation of straight or branched chains.
- Length of the chains.
- Orientation of the monomers within the chains.
- Bonding between the chains.
- Introduction of co-polymers.

Some monomers can only link to form a straight chain, like a railroad train, while others can branch out, forming tree-like structures. Their ability to branch strongly affects the chemical and physical properties of the resultant polymer. For example, high-density polyethylene (HDPE) is made up almost entirely of straight chains. This allows the chains to stack together very well to form dense, tightly packed materials, similar to the way

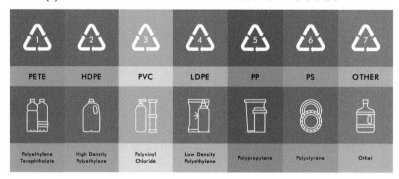

FIGURE 7.62   (a) The most common monomers for making synthetic polymers today are (Clockwise from Upper Left): ethylene, vinyl chloride, styrene, propylene, and terephthalic acid. (b) Some of the plastic items made from these monomers.

Source: (b) Shutterstock.com.

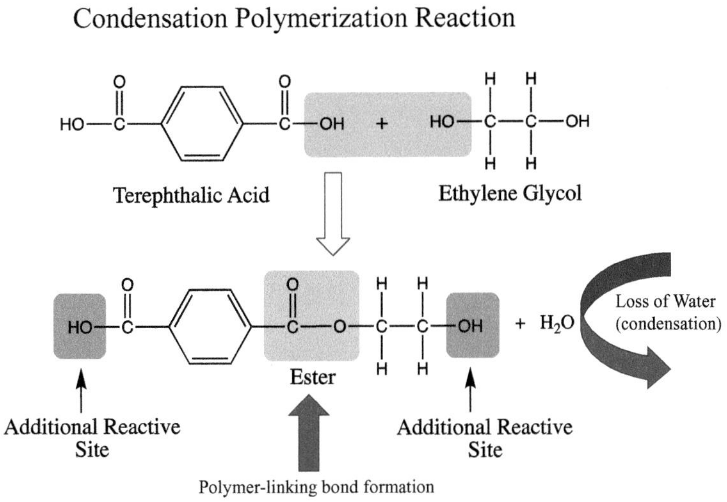

Condensation Polymerization Reaction

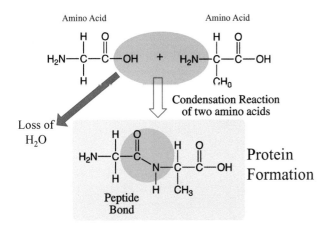

FIGURE 7.63 Formation of a polyester: the polymer polyethylene terephthalate is produced from a condensation reaction through the loss of water and the formation of an ester bond (R-O-C(=O)R′ where R and R′ are organic chemical groups).

FIGURE 7.64 Formation of a peptide bond, the bond linking amino acids together, to form a protein biopolymer.

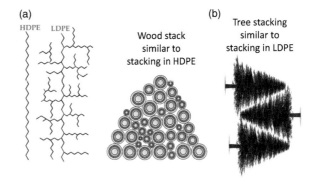

FIGURE 7.65 (a) Schematic of the polymer stacking in high-density polyethylene (HDPE) *versus* low-density polyethylene (LDPE) and (b) a comparison with the analogous stacking of logs *versus* branched trees.

long boards in a lumberyard or straight logs can be efficiently stacked in a pile (Figure 7.65). Low-density polyethylene (LDPE), on the other hand, is made up of branched chains that do not allow the individual chains to pack together very tightly. This would be similar to trying to stack trees with all of the branches still attached, resulting in an inefficient stack with lots of open airspaces between the tree trunks. The result of these kinds of packing is that HDPE forms very rigid, dense, and high-strength materials, used in applications such as water pipes, snow boards, and storage sheds, while LDPE forms softer, low-density, flexible, low-melting polymers, found frequently in plastic bags, milk containers, and plastic laminate.

With some monomers, the two "ends" of the building blocks where they connect together have different chemical components. When they are assembled into a polymer, there are two main ways that the building blocks can be assembled: head-to-head or head-to-tail, as illustrated in Figure 7.66. These two possibilities lead to different chemical and physical

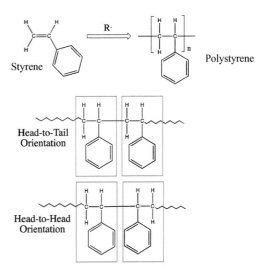

FIGURE 7.66 Orientation differences in forming synthetic polymers: head-to-tail versus head-to-head connections.

properties of the polymer, although head-to-tail arrangements are far more common.

The properties of polymers can often be changed by building bridges between adjacent chains through a process called *cross-linking*. This process is what usually happens when a resin or polymeric precursor is cured or hardened after it is applied in a soft or liquid form. During the hardening process, the bridges are created between the polymeric strands to form a three-dimensional lattice of interwoven strands and linkages throughout the material (Figure 7.67). These bridges can also occur at several size levels. Most commonly, cross-linking is considered at the molecular level, but larger strands can also be cross-linked at the macroscopic level to give a three-dimensional web-like structure, as shown for a cross-linked styrene-based polymer in Figure 7.68. The degree of cross-linking imparts important features to the polymer. For example, permanent press fabrics have relatively few cross-linkages, resulting in a soft and pliable fabric but one that can retain its shape. Rigid polymers, such as Bakelite (the world's first synthetic plastic, used to produce clocks, car parts, washing machines, and kitchenware), are heavily cross-linked, forming exceptionally hard, inflexible, and brittle materials.

Polymers can also be made from a blend of different monomers. The resulting polymer is referred to as a *copolymer*, in contrast to a *homopolymer* which is a polymer made from just one type of monomer. The very popular plastic wrap, used for preserving food because of its very low permeability to gases and moisture that would speed up food spoilage, is an example of a copolymer made from polyvinylidene chloride and other monomers such as acrylic esters. Many variations on the copolymer idea have been developed for specific applications.

7.4.7 Forming Polymer Fibers

Many methods have been developed over the years to form reconstituted or synthetic polymers into useful fibers. Probably the most common, however, involves some type of extrusion process (Figure 7.69).

In this technique, the polymer(s) in a pliable form, such as in a solution or as a viscous liquid, is forced through the small openings of a showerhead-like device called a spinneret. The spinneret may have from just a few to hundreds of holes of varying shapes. Often, the shapes of the small openings dictate the cross-sectional shape of the fiber produced (polyurethane fibers in Figure 7.55). As the fiber is pushed out through the holes, it solidifies to produce the filaments. Often, the fibers are stretched while they are hardening to align the polymer molecules along the length of the fiber, producing a stronger fiber.

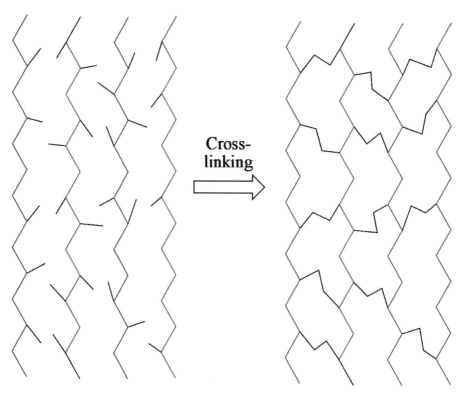

Free Polymer Strands   **Cross-linked Polymer Strands**

FIGURE 7.67 Cross-linking of individual polymer molecules.

(a)

(b)

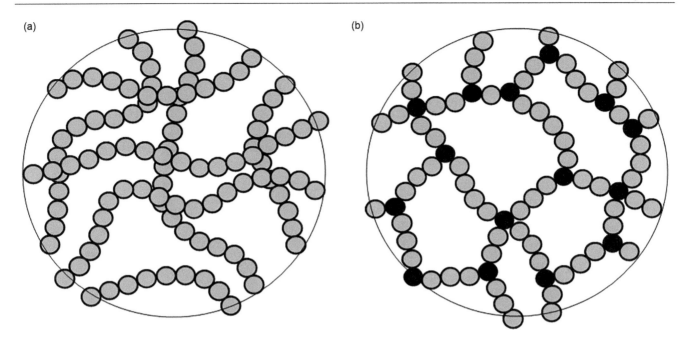

FIGURE 7.68   Cross-linked polymers: (a) linear chains of thermoplastic polymer, and (b) a three-dimensional cross-linked thermosetting polymer (cross-linking points are shown as black circles). Such networks are usually insoluble and do not melt (the dimension of a circle (monomer unit) is approximately 1 Å).

Source: Used per Creative Commons Attribution-Share Alike 3.0 Unported. 3.0. User: Cjp24.

FIGURE 7.69   Fiber extrusion process (e.g., nylon, polyester, etc.) using two different polymers which, when extruded together, produces structured fibers with properties differing from the original fibers.

Source: Used per Creative Commons Attribution 3.0 Unported. User: CSIRO.

7.4.8 Forensic Analysis of Fibers

There are several important questions that are often asked as part of forensic investigations when considering fibers, including

- *What is the composition of the fiber?* This can often be answered through a chemical analysis of the fiber using the analytical tools described in later chapters. The goal is to determine the chemical components that make up the fiber (the component monomers) and to determine the specific features of the molecular structure of the chains. This would involve discovering the identity of the monomer(s) employed, whether the sample is a copolymer or homopolymer, the relative orientation of the monomers to each other, and the degree of cross-linking formed between the chains. The chemical analysis would also determine the presence of plasticizers and other additives included in the polymer to help it be more pliable or stable. A simple flow chart has been developed to aid in describing the chemical/structural composition of fiber, as shown in Figure 7.70.

- *What are the physical properties of the fiber?* This typically involves determining the melting properties (e.g., softening temperature, melting temperature, glass transition temperature (T_g), and the sharpness of the melting point), the degree of crystallinity, the refractive index, and the chain length in the polymers in the fiber. Other information of interest might involve features such as birefringence (whether the refractive index is the same in all directions of the fiber) and opacity (whether light can pass through the fiber).

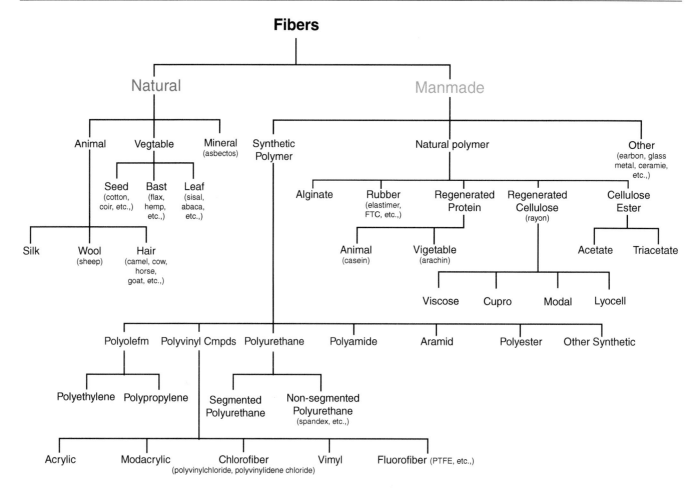

FIGURE 7.70 Flow chart for determining the classification of fibers.

- *What is the shape of the fiber?* This can usually be best answered by observing the structure of the fiber at the microscopic level. Both light and electron microscopic investigations are possible, including comparison microscopic techniques to evaluate the similarities and differences between two fibers.
- *Is the fiber part of a larger piece of evidence?* This refers to the possibility of the fiber being part of a particular collection of fibers, such as a piece of cloth, with the likelihood of dyeing and/or coloration of the fiber as part of a pattern or design on the cloth.
- *Are there any uniquely identifying features of the fiber?* This involves looking for unique features of the fiber or cloth that would separate it from all other similar samples, such as striations, cutting marks, torn features, extrusion shapes, and other considerations.

7.4.9 Collections of Fibers in Larger Pieces

One of the key reasons why fibers are of such utility and so commonly found in forensic investigations is their fabrication into larger collections to form cloth, rope, paper, and many other items. Of particular importance is the use of fibers to form cloth.

Cloth, or textile, is a network of fibers that can be shaped into a two-dimensional layer for a variety of uses. While these two terms are often used interchangeably, they have subtly different meanings; a textile is a material made from interlacing fibers while the term cloth refers to a fabric that has been made into a finished piece such as a shirt or pants. Typically, textiles are made from yarns, long segments of fibers that are twisted or grouped together to form a relatively strong, interlocking array. Yarns are often formed by twisting shorter lengths of fibers together such that the manner of twisting can help identify a particular yarn. For example, the yarn can be characterized by whether it is twisted clockwise or counterclockwise (Figure 7.71), how tightly it is twisted (e.g., number of twists per inch), the number of fibers in the thickness of the yarn, and how it is colored. Importantly, yarns are often made by blending together different types of fibers. For example, a textile used in clothing might be a blend of 20% cotton, 30% wool, and 50% synthetic polymer.

Yarns may be made stronger by taking smaller yarns and twisting them together to make even thicker units. For example, taking two previously formed yarn strands and twisting them together makes a thicker, stronger, 2-ply yarn. The "ply"

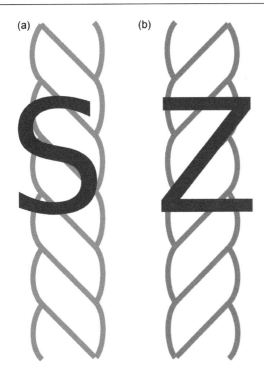

FIGURE 7.71 Types of twists in yarn production: The "twist" in spun yarns or ropes is often labeled S-twist (a) and Z-twist (b). To determine the "handedness" of the twist, look down the length of the yarn and the direction of the twist *as it progresses away from you* reveals its handedness.

Source: Retrieved from Wikimedia Commons; used per Creative Commons Attribution.

number indicates how many single spun yarns are twisted together to make the thicker yarn.

Yarns are often woven together in intricate patterns to form cloth. An analysis of these weaving patterns can readily show that two samples are not from a common origin if they have different weaves. There are hundreds of known weave patterns; just a few are illustrated in Figure 7.72.

Yarns of different colors can be woven to give pattern and design to the fabric, such as seen in plaids, stripes, and similar arrangements. It is also common, however, for yarns to be woven together first to form an unpatterned cloth and then a design incorporated into or onto the fabric using dyes, pigments, and other forms of coloration. This can be done by printing, resist dyeing, tie-dyeing, and many other methods. Colored thread can also be stitched into the final cloth (embroidery) to provide intricate overlay patterns. In effect, each of these added treatments helps to individualize the piece of cloth as to its origin and use.

Besides patterns in coloration, there are other ways that cloth can be individualized to yield information about a crime. Occasionally, a piece of cloth is ripped or otherwise damaged before or during a crime. It may be possible to fit these torn or damaged pieces together.

Many other objects made of fibers and polymers may also play a role in forensic investigations. Rope, twine, cord, paper, fiberboard, and other materials can transfer fibers, *a la* Locard's Principle. Rope is simply a thicker, and therefore stronger, version of cord, both are composed of fibers that can be characterized using the methods described above. Various designs of rope, cord, and thread are possible and their forensic analysis is very similar to that described for yarns. Additionally, polymeric materials, including sheet plastic and tapes (with and without added fibers), can carry unique markings, such as striations formed during the manufacturing process, that can individualize a sample (Figure 7.73).

BOX 7.11   TWO CASES HANGING BY A FIBER

THE WAYNE WILLIAMS CASE

From 1979 to 1981, the City of Atlanta, Georgia was plagued by a number of unsolved murders that appeared to be the work of just one person, and were referred to as "child murders" although not all of the victims were children. The victims were murdered in a variety of ways including being shot, bludgeoned, stabbed, asphyxiated, and traumatized. A number of the later bodies had been pulled from nearby rivers, leading desperate investigators to use night surveillance of area bridges in the remote hopes of catching the murderer disposing of their most recent victim's body. On May 21, 1981, an officer stationed under the Chattahoochee River Bridge was fortunate to hear both a splash in the river and a car drive by. The car, driven by Wayne Williams, was stopped by officers near the bridge and, after several hours of interrogation and a search of his car, he was released. Several days later, however, the body of a victim was found downstream from the Chattahoochee Bridge and all attention was refocused upon Wayne Williams.

The case was complex and difficult, with much testimony and various types of evidence. The key pieces of evidence, however, turned out to involve fibers. Expert fiber testimony connected several types of carpet fibers found in Williams' home with fibers found on several of the victims. Additionally, some of the victims were found with fibers linked to the trunk liners of two cars of the Williams' family. The difficulty was that these types of fibers were common in carpeting used both in homes and cars in the Atlanta area. Prosecutors had to show that the fibers found on the victims had a high probability of coming from Williams' home and car. Investigators examined the structure and colors of the fibers and determined how common these fibers were in Atlanta, and determined the odds of a random match of these fibers at about 1 in 30,000,000. In the end, they were able to convince the jury that there was enough of a link between the two sets of fibers to convict Wayne Williams of two of the homicides.

There remain for many people, however, unanswered questions in this case. It appears that the car from which the matching fibers were obtained was not available to Williams at the time of the crimes. The fibers were also commonly found in hotels, homes, and other residential buildings. And Williams himself has maintained his innocence throughout his imprisonment.

JEFFREY MACDONALD CASE

Early on the morning of February 17, 1970, military police on Fort Bragg were called to a reported violent attack. When they arrived at the home of Captain Jeffrey MacDonald, a doctor on the base, they found a violent scene with MacDonald's wife and two small children dead. The MacDonalds had been violently attacked and repeatedly stabbed and beaten. MacDonald was found wounded, but none of his wounds were life-threatening.

The case quickly centered upon Dr. MacDonald as the prime suspect since investigators felt that Dr. MacDonald's account did not seem to match the physical evidence. MacDonald's account was that intruders had broken into his home and carried out the crime.

A great deal of evidence was collected in this complex case, but once again, fiber analysis proved to be key. Investigators found fibers from MacDonald's pajama tops in several places at the crime scene and identified a number of holes in the cloth of his pajamas. He said that he had wrapped his pajama top around his hands to help ward off the blows from the ice-pick-wielding attacker. The tears in the cloth, both in location and in the smooth nature of the holes, were, however, thought not to be consistent with a defensive posture but more consistent with MacDonald attacking his wife with the pajama top laid over her.

Captain MacDonald was convicted on August 29, 1979, and sentenced to life imprisonment. Captain MacDonald continues to declare his innocence and has lodged a number of unsuccessful appeals. Subsequent DNA analysis has failed to turn up any connection with someone other than a member of the MacDonald household.

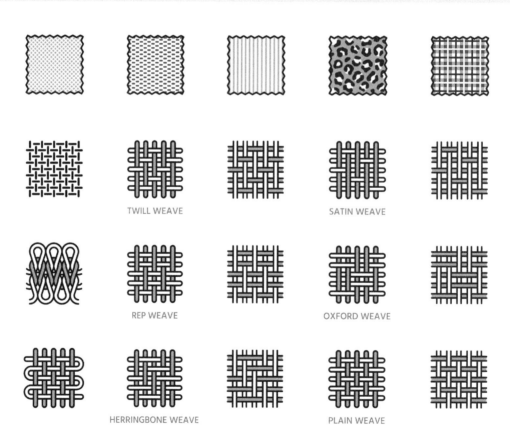

FIGURE 7.72   Examples of various weave patterns found in cloth.

Source: Shutterstock.com.

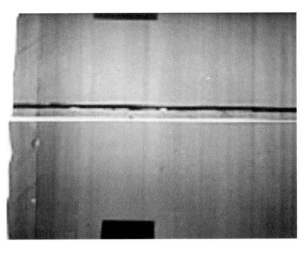
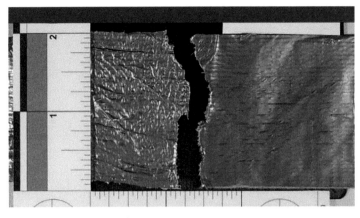

FIGURE 7.73 Striations in plastic polymer bags and in the polymer backing of duct tape can be important when compared between known and questioned samples.

Source: Used with permission and courtesy New Jersey State Police, Office of Forensic Science.

7.5 BIOMETRICS

7.5.1 History of Biometrics

The unique identification of a particular person has long been a significant problem in both criminal justice and security settings. In criminal applications, it is important to be able to identify a wanted person, detect someone in disguise, determine if a person is a repeat offender, or just to keep track of a particular person of interest. In security applications, such as protecting sensitive information, equipment, or areas from unauthorized use, it is equally important to discover a person's identity to determine if they should be allowed access. In the past, solutions to these security problems have taken the form of either physical identifiers, such as keys, ID cards, driver's licenses, and badges, or through some shared secret information, such as passwords or access codes. These means of personal identification can, however, be readily lost, stolen, or hacked. Besides simply losing access to the secure items when these forms of ID are lost or stolen, personal identifiers can be used by someone else to gain unauthorized access to these secure items.

Since we have become so reliant upon electronic forms of communication and access in every part of our lives, we are required to use increasingly complex forms of authentication. For example, in order for an electronic account password to be reliable, it must be complex enough to avoid random guessing, never be written down, and changed frequently. It is not unusual today for someone to need dozens of passwords and user IDs that may rarely be used and must be changed frequently. This is particularly problematic given the inconvenience and expense associated with forgotten or lost passwords. So, more sophisticated, reliable, and intimately personal forms of identification are required that cannot be easily forgotten, lost, stolen, or transferred. Today, billions of

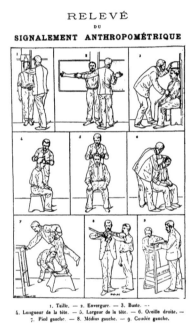

FIGURE 7.74 Bertillon System for identification based on human body measurements (not used today).

Source: Retrieved from Wikimedia Commons; used per Creative Commons Attribution.

dollars of banking and investment transactions occur daily by electronic means that require rapid and assured authentication. To meet this challenge, science has increasingly turned to the use of identifying features of our own bodies to uniquely identify us from everyone else.

In the late 1800s, Alphonse Bertillon developed a system called "Anthropometry" or the Bertillon System, which was proposed to identify a person based upon simple measurements of body features such as head length, the length of the middle finger, the distance between a person's eyes, tattoos, and foot size (Figure 7.74). While this method was soon supplanted by other far more reliable, and scientifically-based methods, it did form the first attempt to base personal identification on measurable body traits.

As presented earlier in this chapter, fingerprints have been a powerful tool for uniquely identifying people for well over 100 years. Increasingly, however, other forms of recognition based on various aspects of the human body are being used for identification.

7.5.2 Biometrics Basics

Biometrics is the application of statistical methods to biological data and is based on finding some measurable individual trait of a person that can distinguish them from all others. These traits can be biological, such as a fingerprint or iris pattern, or behavioral in nature, such as how a person acts, lives, or even as subtle as how they type on a computer. But all forms of biometric identification, in order to be useful, must meet a specific set of criteria that includes *Universality*, *Uniqueness*, *Permanence*, *Measurability*, and *Ease of Use*.

- **Universality**: In order to be useful, the trait must be something that all people to be authenticated have in common. The analysis must be based on common biological structures or developed behavioral patterns. For example, a biometric marker based on how someone types on a computer keyboard makes sense only for populations where keyboard use is common but of limited use in "computer-less" populations. In contrast, an analysis based on iris patterns in the eye would be generally useful for the entire human population.
- **Uniqueness**: A biometric feature must be able to differentiate between people needing authentication. An analysis based on the number of fingers on a person's right hand is based on a common biological trait but is not very useful in distinguishing between most people. An analysis based on fingerprints, however, is far more able to separate two people. It is important to realize, however, that any such analysis must be based on an understanding of the statistics involved; in other words, how probable it is that two people would randomly have the same measured value such that the test could not determine the difference between them. In the chapter on DNA, we said that the chance of two people having the same DNA profile of 14 loci markers is often one in several trillion, making it a very reliable tool for personal ID. A biometric analysis based on ABO blood typing, however, might have a random match rate in the percent range, making it far less useful when compared to DNA as a biometric tool.
- **Permanence**: Any biometric tool must persist unchanged for a very long time in a person, ideally for an entire lifetime. Most biological biometrics such as DNA, eye iris patterns, and fingerprints typically don't change over a lifetime. Some biological and behavioral markers do change, however, with age, illness, accident, growth, or learned patterns, such as voice pattern and writing patterns. These changes do not render the method useless,

however, but care must be taken to understand the possibility for change and account for it in the analysis.
- **Measurability**: Any biometric tool must employ a trait that can be measured reliably, rapidly, and with straightforward measuring devices. If a trait cannot be measured, it cannot be used in ID systems.
- **Ease of Use**: There are many types of probes that could be used in a biometric method that are impractical, expensive, or difficult to use. Preferred methods employ measurements that are easy and quick and give highly reliable data for comparison. So, for most ID applications, DNA analysis is not suitable due to cost and time.
- **Circumvention**: This refers to how easily the biometric trait can be "defeated" or gotten around through the use of a substitute, such as a fingerprint casting or a contact lens with a false iris pattern.

7.5.3 Biometric Methods

Biometric methods typically try to establish someone's identity by answering one of three specific questions: (1) who are you, (2) what information do you possess, or (3) what items do you own?

The first question "who are you?" deals specifically with the use of physical or behavioral traits to identify a person by determining if a person's body features can be used to identify them. The second question, "what information do you possess?" involves the use of passwords, secret questions, and similar information to establish your identity. Finally, the question "what do you possess?" answers the identity problem through the use of physical devices such as keys, cards, and multi-factor authentication (do you have multiple features/devices for independent verification). Often, however, combinations of these methods are employed to gain a higher level of reliability in establishing identity.

There are two quite distinct ways in which biometric information may be employed: identification and authentication (or verification). When we considered the use of fingerprints for identification, these two terms were first presented. *Identification* refers specifically to using biometric information to identify an unknown person from among a very large pool of possibilities. This could involve thousands or even many millions of records through a *one-to-many matching* process. **Authentication** (verification), however, compares biometric information from one person with either just one reference or from among a special group of possibilities. This *one-to-one matching* process tries to identify a person as a match (or not) with a known biometric identity. For example, in cybersecurity systems, an iris scan can be compared to a password and user ID to prove that the person trying to gain access is indeed the person entering the password. Biometric verification is usually much faster and more reliable than biometric identification since fewer comparisons are needed.

Essentially, all biometric forms of authentication have in common the same basic steps: (1) initial *enrollment* or registration, (2) characteristic information *storage*, and (3) a *comparison* process.

The first step in a biometric analysis typically begins with measuring and storing a given biological or behavioral trait and then connecting this information with a particular person. For example, a fingerprint is first scanned and then linked directly to a person's name and individual personal or criminal record. This enrollment forms the basic data set to be used later linking an unknown person to a file. The second step involves recording the new data from a person trying to gain entry in a digital form. Most often, entire images, complete scans, or entire measured data sets are not stored but rather just the minimum number of salient features needed to form a *unique* identifier for that person. Reducing the data to the smallest set necessary to obtain a unique identifier speeds up analysis and reduces the amount of data needing to be stored. The final step usually involves a computer program that compares the new measurement with stored data to determine the similarities and differences between the two data sets. As mentioned before, a measure of the reliability of the match is key to understanding the usefulness of the comparison results.

In a typical biometric system, a sensor is used to measure the needed data. The sensor can take many forms including cameras, scanners, tablets, keyboards, microphones, and even chemical detectors.

7.5.4 Types of Biometric Traits

There are many biological and behavioral traits that might be useful in biometric analysis. Some, such as fingerprints, palmprints, and DNA, have already been considered in detail. Others are useful for varying levels of reliability, ease of use, and uniqueness. Some have been in use for years, while others are still being developed. A sampling of some of the more common methods is summarized here.

7.5.4.1 Hand and Finger Geometry

The shapes of our hands and fingers can vary enough between people to form a low-level biometric trait. For example, the relative lengths and thicknesses of our fingers and the shapes contained in our hand can be used in verification of a person's identity. The process is very simple, usually just a photograph of our hands when they are placed on a flat surface. The digitized image of several key features is then compared to similar stored data for the person needing to have their ID verified. There are two downsides to this analysis: there is only limited variation between people's hands, and our hands can change their geometries with age, weight, accident, illness, or hydration – even within the span of a single day. Nonetheless, this is a rather non-threatening and easy, low-level verification technique that has been adopted in a number of "quick-check" situations such as schools, theme parks, and businesses.

7.5.4.2 Writing and Typing Analysis (Processed Dynamic Data)

For centuries a person's signature and their handwriting have been used for identification on legal documents. While the topic of questioned document analysis will be covered in a later chapter, it is appropriate to mention it briefly here in connection with biometric analysis since the types of information gained in the two approaches may be quite different.

In questioned document analysis, the shapes of the letters and the visual patterns of words they make on the page are very important in determining the authenticity of the document. While a signature or writing can sometimes be learned and forged, it is much more difficult to forge the physical *way* in which people write. For example, the speed, pressure, pen angle, direction changes, and rhythm with which a group of words is written can tell more in terms of identification than the actual shapes of the words and letters themselves. The physical process of typing on a keyboard can also be used to differentiate individuals, just as playing of the same musical piece by two different pianists can often be distinguished by someone attuned to listening carefully; the notes are the same but the method of producing them varies. Similarly, the biometric analysis of writing and typing processes can help to identify the person making the patterns.

7.5.4.3 Vein Geometry Biometric Analysis

This method works by identifying the patterns that our blood vessels make below the surface of the skin in our fingers, hands, and elsewhere (Figure 7.75). The pattern from these small veins

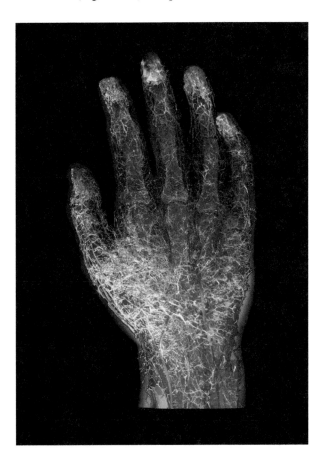

FIGURE 7.75 Cast of the blood vessels of the human hand superimposed on a computed tomography (CT) scan.

Source: Zephyr/Science Photo Library. Used with permission.

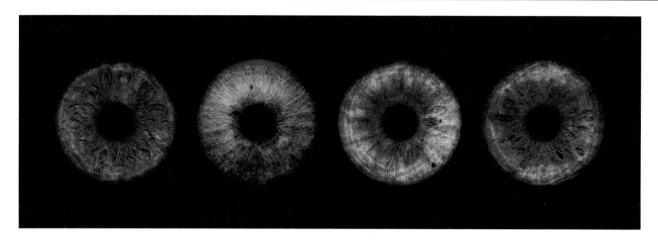

FIGURE 7.76   Close up of the iris of the eye for several different people.

Source: Shutterstock.com.

and capillaries is believed to be unique to each person, similar to fingerprints and DNA. In addition, our vein patterns differ from left to right sides, and even twins do not have identical patterns. In this method, near-infrared light shone onto a hand is absorbed by the hemoglobin. Using an infrared-sensitive detector, the pattern of the veins can be recorded and compared with a known pattern previously recorded.

7.5.4.4 Eye Biometrics

If you've ever watched a spy movie, you've certainly seen eye measurements used for ID verification. Our eyes are complex light-harvesting and sensing organs, designed to collect light from the outside, focus it onto highly specialized cells, and convert the light into an electronic signal that our brains recognize as an image. Two structures of the eye, however, carry information that can be specifically used in a biometric application.

The iris of our eye is a thin membrane whose main job is to control the amount of light allowed to enter the eye through the pupil (Figure 7.76). Muscles attached to the iris expand or contract the hole, or pupil, through which light enters the eye. Pigments in the iris are responsible for our eye colors. However, the detailed "fibrous ridge" structure, coloration, and blood vessel pattern of the iris itself are highly variable and unique to a particular person. A detailed "picture" of the cornea and iris of a person's eye can be readily taken, and the patterns can be compared to a known standard for verification.

The other main type of biometric eye scan involves looking at the retina, the thin membrane that covers the back of the eye. This membrane contains specialized cells and molecules that can capture the energy of a photon, a packet of light, and ultimately convert it into electrical signals that the brain can process. The blood capillaries embedded within the retina form a very complex pattern that is unique to each person in placement and shape. Importantly, this pattern of

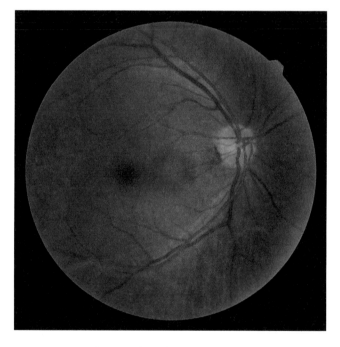

FIGURE 7.77   View inside a human eye showing the retina, optic nerve and macula. Retinal scans show the unique pattern formed by the blood capillaries in the back surface of the eye.

Source: Shutterstock.com.

blood capillaries doesn't change over the course of a person's lifetime, although some diseases, such as diabetes and various degenerative eye diseases, can affect these blood vessels. A retinal scan can be easily and quickly done by shining a beam of infrared light onto the retina where the blood vessels absorb this light more strongly than the surrounding tissue, as shown in Figure 7.77. In this fashion, a detailed map of the pattern of the capillaries can be generated and compared to reference data sets.

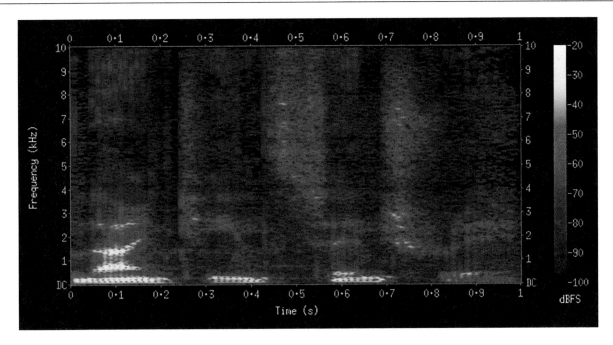

FIGURE 7.78   Digitally produced spectrogram of a male voice saying "nineteenth century."

Source: Retrieved from Wikimedia Commons; used per Creative Commons Attribution.

7.5.4.5 Voice Analysis

Our voices are different due to variations in our vocal and nasal cavities, our vocal cord properties and a number of other features where small changes can make detectable differences in the voices we produce.

In biometric voice analysis, a voiceprint is made by having a person speak certain words or phrases into a microphone. The data is converted into a plot of sound frequency versus time, as shown in Figure 7.78. This spectrogram is then compared with a stored version of the same spoken word for a particular person to complete the analysis. More on this topic will be presented in Chapter 17.

7.5.4.6 Face Image Data

Facial recognition methods are certainly one of the oldest human ways of recognizing a person. The faces of our parents are imprinted on our brains at a very early age so that we can readily recognize them. Face image data, however, is both easily obtained but difficult to use reliably. Our faces also change with age, emotion, disease, photographic conditions, and a variety of other factors. Nonetheless, the technique is being used with increasing frequency. But faces can be very revealing. Current work has shown success in determining a person's potential threat level, mood, and intent by analyzing their facial features.

In a typical facial recognition process, a photographic analysis of a face is "coded" into a number of important points, as shown in Figure 7.79. The size, distance, and relative orientation of these different features then form the basis for comparison with a standard data set.

7.5.4.7 New Methods

New approaches to biometric measurement are rapidly evolving, and new methods and technologies continue to emerge. Below are a few of the more recent entries to this dynamic field.

- **Ear Canal Biometrics**: The fine details of our ear canals vary from one person to another. This variation can be used as a biometric trait to tell us apart. For example, have you ever wondered who you were talking to when you made a phone call or wanted to be sure that you were talking to the person you intended to (if not, then there are times that you *should* definitely wonder)? This problem could be aided using ear canal biometrics. In this application, the phone could send out a very tiny pressure wave when it is held up to someone's ear, which could map the ear canal of the person holding the receiver. This pattern could then be used in comparison with the known ear canal profile of a person on file to verify to whom you are talking.
- **Odor**: Scientists are exploring the possible use of an "odorprint" to help establish both individual identity and to determine when a person is lying. This has been the basis for the use of dogs, such as bloodhounds, which have a keen ability to detect a person's unique odors and track them over long ranges. Every person emits an array of organic chemicals that contain an odor, and the ability to detect these chemicals and their relative abundances could lead to sensitive new probes for biometric analysis.

FIGURE 7.79   Facial points used in a biometric analysis of face pattern for biometric identification.

Source: Shutterstock.com.

- **Palatal Rugae** (palatoscopy): The palatal rugae are the ridges on the inner parts of the roof of our mouths, closest to the upper teeth. These patterns differ from person to person and can persist even throughout life (Figure 7.80). There is still considerable debate, however, about the reliability of using these structures for biometric identification.
- **Electrocardiogram**: An electrocardiogram is the measurement of the electrical signals from the heart. These signals have been shown to vary in detail from person to person and may provide continuous authentication and surveillance of a person's physical and psychological state.

7.5.5 Automated Biometric Identification System (IDENT)

The U.S. Department of Homeland Security, in cooperation with several other agencies is working to develop a comprehensive system using biometric data to link a particular person rapidly with biographic information, such as criminal arrests, personal identification, and travel restrictions, for security and law enforcement work. The IDENT system provides verification capabilities to a wide range of government programs that collect biometric data and compile personal biographical information. Recently, the IAFIS fingerprint system has been incorporated into the broader IDENT system.

Countries all over the world are faced with the increasing need for identification and authentication of people in the spheres of both criminal and security threats. Thus, the use of biometric data is expected to grow rapidly in the near future as one of the best ways to rapidly and accurately connect a person with critical biographic information about them.

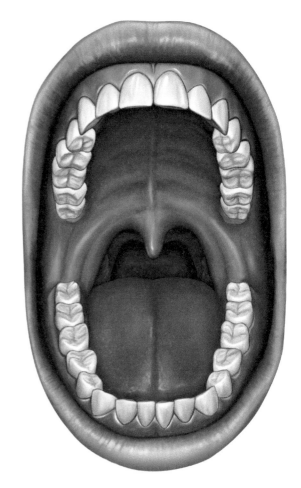

FIGURE 7.80   Anatomy of the mouth showing palatal rugae. The palatal rugae are the inner ridges on the upper hard palate of the mouth.

Source: Shutterstock.com.

QUESTIONS FOR FURTHER PRACTICE AND MASTERY

7.1 Hair, fibers, and fingerprints are examples of what type of evidence?

7.2 Who is considered the "father of modern fingerprinting?"

7.3 What is IAFIS?

7.4 Define the following terms used in fingerprint identification: core, delta, bifurcation, ridge line, and island.

7.5 What is often considered the minimum accepted number of matching points needed to place a reasonable level of trust in deciding two fingerprints are a match? What is the legal standard?
(a) 6   (b) 8   (c) 10   (d) 12   (e) 14

7.6 What is the difference between identification and authentication methods?

7.7 What are some of the legal questions that have arisen in the use of latent prints in court cases?

7.8 What are the three general scale patterns on a hair shaft?

7.9 What are the three layers in a hair fiber?

7.10 In order for a hair dye process to be effective (last longer than a rinse), what must the hair stylist do to the cuticle layer of the hair shaft?

7.11 How does a "perm" work?

7.12 What forensic information may be gathered when examining a dyed or 'permed' hair shaft?

7.13 What are the three main groupings of fibers?

7.14 Plant fibers are typically _____ based, while animal fibers are typically _____ based.

7.15 What is a regenerated fiber? What is a synthetic fiber?

7.16 What property do thermoplastics have that makes them desirable polymers?

7.17 What are the two main polymer synthetic reactions?

7.18 What are the criteria that any biometric identification must satisfy?

7.19 Which of the following could not be used as a means of biometric analysis and why? (a) fingerprints (b) vein geometry (c) iris scan (d) face imaging (e) right-hand digit count

EXTENSIVE QUESTIONS

7.20 Explain the basis for classifying a fingerprint as an arch, a loop, or a whorl.

7.21 Explain the difference between visible, latent, and plastic fingerprints.

7.22 Describe the anagen, catagen, and telogen phases of hair growth.

7.23 Describe the classification most often used for fibers.

7.24 What are the important forensic questions that are asked when examining a fiber found at a crime scene?

7.25 Explain the following biometric criteria:

Universality
Uniqueness
Permanence
Measurability
Ease of use

GLOSSARY OF TERMS

addition reactions (polymers): a chemical reaction where the net result is to simply add monomers together without the loss of any significant portion of the monomer.

AFIS: a fingerprint database; abbreviation for Automated Fingerprint Identification System.

anagen phase: the active growth period for hair formation.

apocrine gland: the scent glands (viscous sweat production).

arch pattern: the fingerprint pattern that has ridges beginning at one side of the fingerprint and running completely to the other side of the fingerprint without a backward turn.

authentication: the process of comparing a set of fingerprints or other biometric features from a person with either just one reference set or with a very small number of "standard" possibilities.

automated biometric identification system (IDENT): the U.S. Department of Homeland Security's comprehensive system for using biometric data to link a particular person rapidly with biographic information, such as criminal record, personal identification, and travel restrictions, for security and law enforcement work.

bifurcation: the point in a fingerprint pattern where a single ridge splits into two ridges.

biometrics: a branch of biology and computer science that analyzes statistical biological data. Forensic applications of biometrics are based upon finding individualized traits that can statistically distinguish one person from all others.

catagen phase: the transitional phase in hair growth when the hair stops growing, and the portion of the follicle surrounding the hair root shrinks considerably.

catalysts: chemical reagents that can cause a chemical reaction to occur or to accelerate without being ultimately changed or consumed itself.

cellulose: a carbohydrate polymer molecule found in many plant-based fibers.

cheiloscopy: the furrows of the human lips used for individual identification.

condensation reactions: a chemical reaction that involves the loss of a small molecule, such as water, from the reaction and couples together the two starting molecules.

core: the feature formed where a loop pattern reaches its farthest point toward the middle of the print and begins to turn backward, constituting the innermost ridge of the curve.

cortex: the inner portion of a hair fiber that makes up most of the bulk of the hair shaft and gives the hair its characteristic elasticity.

cuticle: the outermost translucent protective layer of a hair shaft that appears as overlapping plates.

delta: the point of ridges in a fingerprint pattern where the upward and downward deflected ridges meet the looping ridges, forming a triangular-shaped intersection.

dermis: the middle skin layer that is composed mostly of collagen (protein) fibers, elastic tissue, and reticular fibers.

disulfide bonds (biopolymers): the chemical linkages between sulfur atoms (primarily in cysteine) in different keratin molecules that create keratin chains, thereby giving rigidity and structure to the hair fiber.

eccrine glands: the sweat glands (watery sweat production).

ectoderm: the outermost developmental germ layers of the human body that give rise to the epidermis (skin), hair, eyes, and nervous system.

elastomers: synthetic polymers with special elastic (stretch) properties.

epidermis: the outermost protective layer of our skin that ranges in thickness from very thin on our eyelids (about 0.05 mm) to rather thick on the palms of our hands and the soles of our feet (~1.5 mm).

eumelanin: the dark pigment that colors black and brown hair.

fibers: small structures defined as long, thin filaments with lengths very much greater than widths (at least 100-fold).

fingermark: see fingerprint.

fingernails: hard protective structures at the ends of fingers, composed primarily of keratin, that are considered to be an appendage of the skin and are closely chemically related to the toenails, claws, hooves, and horns found in other animals.

fingerprint: the impression made on a surface by the unique set of friction ridges found on a person's fingers and used for the individual identification of an individual. Sometimes differentiated from fingermark, where in this usage fingerprint means a rolled print and fingermark is a collected print.

fingerprint lifting: the process of preserving fingerprints by using cellophane tape (or similar materials) that has been carefully placed over the print and then rubbed to ensure that the adhesive on the tape is in full contact with the print. The tape is then removed and carries the pattern of the fingerprint when it is lifted from the surface.

friction ridges: raised surfaces forming furrows in the skin that result in the observed pattern of our fingerprints and serves to both greatly increase the skin's surface area and increase its gripping ability.

fuming fingerprint visualization (also cyanoacrylate or super glue fuming): a technique where an object suspected of containing fingerprints is placed in a closed "fuming" chamber where it is exposed to a vapor of cyanoacrylate under which conditions the fingerprints show up as a white residue.

furrows: the adjacent lower valleys next to the ridges of fingerprints.

hair: the complex appendage, composed largely of keratin, that grows from a follicle in the skin only of mammals and is a derivative of the skin's epidermis; it functions mainly to regulate the body temperature of an organism by either trapping or releasing warm air near the skin's surface.

Henry system: an early system of classifying fingerprint patterns.

hypodermis: see Subcutaneous Layer.

IAFIS: a revised automated fingerprint database; abbreviation for Integrated Automated Fingerprint Identification System.

identification: the process of using fingerprints or other features to identify an unknown person from among a large set of possibilities.

impression prints (Plastic): fingerprints left in a soft, pliable surface, such as clay, putty, or soil.

integumentary system: rhe biological system that forms the outer "boundary" of our bodies and includes our skin, hair and nails.

iodine: a chemical element that reacts readily with the oils left behind by fingers to form a somewhat transient, observable, brown color where the finger oils were deposited.

keratin: a tough, durable, fibrous protein composed of long chains of amino acids (mainly cysteine) and typically found as a structural component of hair, nails, horns, and claws.

latent fingerprints: fingerprints are not observable to the unaided eye but are present as residual oils and amino acids that have been left behind on a surface when touched by a finger. These may later be developed to become visible.

loop pattern: the fingerprint pattern that contains ridge lines that enter on one side of the fingerprint, run toward the middle of the print, and then curve backward to exit on the same side from which they entered the pattern.

medulla: the central part of the hair fiber that is characterized by either very spongy cells or no cells at all, forming a canal-like structure in the center of the shaft (medullary canal), when present.

medullary canal: see Medulla.

medullary index (MI): the ratio of the diameter of the shaft to the diameter of the medulla.

melanin: a pigment derived mostly from the amino acid tyrosine that imparts color to a hair sample.

minutiae: the fine details of fingerprint patterns.

monomers: the small molecular building blocks that make up polymers.

natural fibers: fibers come from many different naturally occurring sources including plants, animals and inorganic materials.

ninhydrin: a chemical that reacts with the amino acids found in a fingerprint and, upon gentle heating, forms a characteristic purple/blue-colored pattern of the fingerprint.

palmprint: patterns left by the complex patterns of flexion creases and ridges found in the palm of the hand (similarly with the sole of the foot).

pheomelanin: the pigment that is the main coloration chemical found in red hair.

pinnascopy: the patterns of ear shapes and feature used for individual identification.

polymers: long-chain molecules that are composed of smaller units, called monomers, strung together.

principle of persistency: the principle that refers to a biological feature that, once formed, remains unchanged throughout our lives and may often last even well beyond death into the latter stages of decay.

regenerated fibers: fibers that are made by chemically processing naturally occurring materials into new fibers of a desired shape and structure.

ridge: the top of the fingerprint ridge pattern on our fingers.

ridge count: the number of ridges between two features in a fingerprint pattern.

ridge ending point: the point in a fingerprint pattern where a single friction ridge ends.

sebaceous glands: glands in the skin that produce sebum, an oily material that protects, lubricates, waterproofs, and helps to inhibit the growth of microorganisms on the hair.

stratum basale: the lowest layer of the skin's epidermis.

stratum corneum: the topmost layer of the skin's epidermis.

subcutaneous layer (hypodermis): the skin's lowest layer, composed largely of fat and connective tissue, that also contains larger blood vessels and nerves.

synthetic fibers: fibers that are prepared from chemical feedstocks and are typically formed through controlled polymerization reactions that create long-chain molecules.

telogen phase: the resting period for the follicle in the hair growth cycle.

thermoplastic: synthetic fibers that melt or soften easily at lower temperatures.

trace evidence: evidence that includes fingerprints, hair, fiber, glass, soil, and gunpowder, among others. Trace analysis often involves the comparison of small pieces of evidence with a standard in an attempt to see if the origin or use of the evidence can be identified.

vellus hair: the fine short hairs that cover the majority of the human body.

visible fingerprints: fingerprints readily observable by the naked eye.

whorl pattern: the fingerprint pattern where the ridges complete at least one 360° "circuit", although not always forming a regular circular pattern.

BIBLIOGRAPHY

Fingerprint References

Christophe Champod, Chris J. Lennard Pierre Margot, and Milutin Stoilovic, *Fingerprints and Other Ridge Skin Impressions* (International Forensic Science and Investigation), CRC Press, 2004.

M. Hawthorne, *Fingerprints: Analysis and Understanding.* CRC Press, 2009.https://doi-org.libezproxy2.syr.edu/10.1201/9781420068658

Brian Innes, *Fingerprints and Impressions*, M.E. Sharpe Publ., 2007.

Miroslav Kralik and Ladislav Nejman, *Journal of Ancient Fingerprints*, 1, 2007.

Henry C. Lee and Robert E. Gaensslen (Eds.), *Advances in Fingerprint Technology* (2nd Ed.), CRC Press, 2001.

Davide Maltoni, Dario Maio, Anil K. Jain, and Salil Prabhakar, *Handbook of Fingerprint Recognition*, Springer, 2009.

H. Moses Daluz, *Fundamentals of Fingerprint Analysis* (2nd Ed.), CRC Press, 2018. https://doi-org.libezproxy2.syr.edu/10.4324/9781351043205

Peter Silverman, *Leonardo's Lost Princess. One Man's Quest to Authenticate an Unknown Portrait by Leonardo Da Vinci*, Wiley, 2010.

Cliff Wang, Ryan M. Gerdes, Yong Guan, and Sneha Kasera(Eds.), *Digital Fingerprinting*, Springer Nature, 2011.

U.S. v. Plaza, Acosta and Rodriguez, United States District Court for the Eastern District of Pennsylvania, Cr. No. 98-362-10,11,12, March 13, 2002, pp. 48.

Hair and Fiber Analysis References

Richard E. Bisbing, "The Forensic Identification and Association of Human Hair", Richard Saferstein (Ed.), *Forensic Science Handbook*, Prentice Hall, 1982.

D.R. Cousins, "The use of microspectrophotometry in the examination of paints", *Forensic Science Review*, 1(2), 141–162, 1989.

B.D. Gaudette, "The forensic aspects of textile fiber examinations", R. Saferstein (Ed.), *Forensic Science Handbook*, Vol. II, Prentice Hall, 1988.

B.D. Gaudette, "Probabilities in human pubic hair comparisons", *Journal of Science*, 21(3), 514–517, 1976.

B.D. Gaudette and E.S. Keeping, "An attempt at determining probabilities in human scalp hair comparison", *Journal of Forensic Sciences*, 19, 599–606, 1974.

James Robertson, *Forensic Examination of Human Hair*, Taylor & Francis, Inc., 1999.

J.R. Robertson and E. Brooks, *A Practical Guide to the Forensic Examination of Hair: From Crime Scene to Court*, CRC Press, 2021. https://doi-org.libezproxy2.syr.edu/10.4324/9781315210650

James Robertson and Michael Grieve (Eds), *Forensic Investigation of Fibres*, Taylor & Francis, Inc., 1999.

J. Robertson, C. Roux, and K.G. Wiggins, *Forensic Examination of Fibres* (3rd Ed.), CRC Press, 2017. https://doi-org.libezproxy2.syr.edu/10.1201/9781315156583

John D. Wright, *Hair and Fibers* (Forensic Evidence), Sharpe Focus, 2007.

John D. Wright and Jane Singer, *Hair and Fibers*, Routledge, 2009.

Biometrics References

R. Das, *The Science of Biometrics: Security Technology for Identity Verification*, Routledge, 2018. https://doi-org.libezproxy2.syr.edu/10.4324/9780429487583

Henry Faulds, *On the Skin-Furrows of the Hand*, Nature, 22, 605, 1880.

Ronald Hall, *Biometrics 100 Most Asked Questions of Physicological and Behavioral Biometric Technologies, Verification Systems, Design, Implementation and Performance Evaluation*, Emereo Publ., 2008.

Anil Jain, Ruud Bolle, and Sharath Pankanti, *Biometrics: Personal Identification in Networked Society*, Kluwer Academic Publ., 1998.

Anil K. Jain, Patrick Flynn, and Arun A. Ross (Eds.), *Handbook of Biometrics*, Springer Scientific, 2008.

Anil K. Jain, Arun A. Ross, and Karthik Nandakumar, *Introduction to Biometrics*, Springer Science, 2011.

M. Smith, M. Mann, and G. Urbas, *Biometrics, Crime and Security*, Routledge, 2018. https://doi-org.libezproxy.syr.edu/10.4324/9781315182056

Forensic Medicine
The Inside Story

8

8.1 FORENSIC PATHOLOGY AND MEDICINE

Hic locus est ubi mors gaudet succurrere vitae.
(A motto often found where autopsies are performed meaning "This is the place where death rejoices to help those who live").

(Att. Giovanni Morgagni, 18th physician)

LEARNING GOALS AND OBJECTIVES

Forensic medicine and anatomical evidence from a body itself can provide crucial information about the events leading to someone's injury, illness, or death. This information can be obtained through a variety of means, including external examination and internal examination, often involving an autopsy. This chapter will help you understand the stories that bodies can tell. After studying this chapter, you should be able to:

- Describe various aspects of medicine that are involved in medicolegal practice.
- Explain the duties and training required for coroners and medical examiners (pathologists).
- Define what is meant by manner of death, cause of death, and mechanism of death.
- Explain the classifications for manner of death and how they are determined.
- Define post-mortem interval, rigor mortis, livor mortis, and algor mortis.
- Discuss when autopsies are needed or required.
- Show what information can be gained from an autopsy and how they are performed.
- Describe the major organ systems of the body investigated during an autopsy and the types of information that can be learned from each.
- Summarize the major types of trauma and how they may be characterized.

8.1.1 Introduction

For as long as accidents, violence, and disease have plagued humans, we have looked to the body itself to provide important clues as to what happened and how it occurred, especially when the victims cannot tell their stories with their own voices. When a body is unable to "speak" with its own voice, it can still convey volumes about what happened if we know how and where to look. In fact, the word autopsy comes from the Greek, meaning "seeing for oneself" – a reference to the medical process where the body reveals its injuries and illnesses to a trained pathologist through careful examination. Finding telltale physical trauma or injury in a body, when coupled with a medical understanding of how these may be caused, can shed light on the sequence of events that took place during a crime or accident.

In the previous chapter, we examined the types of forensic information that can be gained from the external biological structures of the body, such as hair, skin, and biometric anatomical features. In this chapter, however, we will specifically look more carefully both inside and outside of the body to allow it to "tell" us medical information of legal importance. The focus of this chapter will be on the forensic information that our organs and soft tissues can provide. Evidence relating to our bones and teeth, and the accompanying issues of burial and post-mortem fate (taphonomy) of human remains, is presented in the following chapter on forensic anthropology.

The field of forensic pathology is the branch of medicine charged with understanding the "how and why" of a person's death, injury, or disease. In death investigations, the main focus of this chapter, when trying to answer the central question of how a person died, we must look more closely at the information gained directly from both external and internal physical examinations of the body, and indirectly through biomedical imaging techniques.

8.1.2 History of Medicolegal Death Investigations

The use of medical expertise and "surgical" techniques for examining dead bodies in an attempt to learn more about their deaths dates back thousands of years. The ancient Egyptians

DOI: 10.4324/9781003183709-10

clearly connected medical observations with legal questions when the Grand Vizier Imhotep was appointed by Pharaoh Zozer to investigate deaths that occurred under suspicious circumstances around 2650 BC. Imhotep probably also wrote the very first medical texts in history, used medical ideas to investigate crimes, and experimented with new medical treatments that were quite remarkable for his time.

One of the first detailed written reports of a medicolegal death investigation comes from the Roman physician Antistius who performed an autopsy on Julius Caesar after Caesar's assassination in 44 BC. Caesar was brutally attacked and left to die on the floor of the Curia in Pompey by a group of between five and ten conspirators. When Caesar's body was carried home three hours later, Antistius identified 23 distinct stab wounds to Caesar's body, but found that just the second wound, an upward-thrusting chest wound between the first and second ribs, proved fatal. Another report from about the same period describes when the Roman physician Germanicus in 19 AD was employed to determine if a particular death was natural, as one group had claimed, or due to deliberate poisoning, as claimed by the other side, on the basis of the fact that the victim's heart would not burn – both sides claiming that this fact supported their views.

While ancient and medieval records report medical dissections were done in particularly important legal cases, they appear to have been relatively rare and in many places were entirely banned due to religious beliefs. In 13th-century China, however, an important book by Sung T'zu, entitled *Hsi Yüan Lu* (sometimes translated as "washing away of wrongs," subtitled "Instructions to Coroners," Figure 8.1), was published in which a relatively comprehensive set of instructions for death investigation was provided. This book apparently was based upon centuries of earlier practice and was even routinely used well into the 20th century in China. This book stressed the complete and careful examination of the entire body and its wounds to see if they were consistent with witness statements, emphasizing cataloging the locations and types of wounds, identifying possible indicators for poisoning, and even using the observed state of the body's decomposition and forensic entomology to arrive at a rough estimation of the time of death – relatively sophisticated considerations even by modern standards.

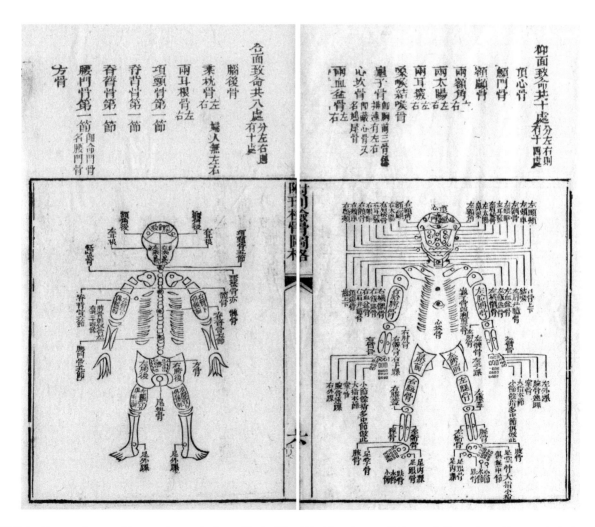

FIGURE 8.1 Nomenclature of human bones in Sung T'zu's "The Washing Away of Wrongs" (Sung T'zu: Xǐ-yuān lù jí-zhèng, 1843 edition, edited by Ruǎn Qíxīn). This 13th-century manuscript was the first forensic medical textbook in the world.

The use of a "crowner," later to evolve into our modern term of coroner, in death investigations dates back well over a thousand years to medieval England. By the time of King Richard I (1189–1199), the duties of the coroner were fairly well defined and included the physical examination of the bodies of all people who had died unexpectedly. It was deemed a responsibility of the crown since the death formally deprived the king of the services of that person. Crowners rarely had any medical training or experience and autopsies were banned in England and most of Europe at the time due to prevailing religious beliefs. It was not until 1240 when the Holy Roman Emperor Frederick II opened the door to human dissection by first passing a law that a body could be dissected once every five years for teaching medical students, those dissections began to be a more generally accepted medical practice.

In medieval and Renaissance Europe, medical investigations appear to still have been relatively uncommon and typically reserved only for cases of unusual importance. The first recorded post-mortem dissection of a suspicious death was performed by Bartolomeo da Varignana of Bologna in an autopsy of the nobleman Azzolino in 1302 after he had collapsed and died suddenly after eating. Azzolino's body quickly became bloated, turned an olive color, and then ultimately became black. Azzolino had many enemies at the time, and it was believed by some that he was poisoned. Bartolomeo, however, performed the autopsy and determined that the manner of death was from natural causes due to blood accumulation in the liver (probably hepatic veno-occlusive disease). Even though dissections were carefully controlled by law in Renaissance Europe, there was quite a significant hidden market for bodies destined for secretive dissection by medical students and artists. This market was supplied by grave robbers (sometimes called "resurrectionists"), a practice that still, unfortunately, thrives today in various places worldwide (see the case of journalist and famous TV personality Alistair Cooke in 2004).

In 1530, an important set of laws called the *Constitutio Criminalis Carolina* was adopted, aiming to unify the often vastly different criminal laws then existing throughout the Holy Roman Empire. The *Constitutio*, brought about several important changes relative to medicolegal investigations: it emphasized the importance of physicians in legal cases involving bodily injury, it dictated certain circumstances when medical information was required in court proceedings (e.g., murder, hanging, poisoning, drowning, and abortion), and for the first time, it gave courts the power to investigate crimes based solely upon the facts of the case and not be restricted solely to the verbal claims of the litigants. Prior to the *Constitutio*, the courts could only deal with accusations from the litigants without the chance to explore the claims further. In other words, in 1530, the courts were given inquisitorial powers, a fact that still often affects medicolegal practice worldwide.

In the 16th century, the French barber-surgeon Ambroise Paré revolutionized surgical practice, primarily through his work in treating battlefield wounds and through his influence as the royal court physician. He felt strongly that anatomical knowledge was critically important to physicians and published widely on his autopsies and dissections. His published case reports of medicine used in legal contexts, including specific directions on how

FIGURE 8.2 Anatomical theater for autopsies from the University of Padua, built in 1594 to teach anatomy. Dissections were performed on the central table while students stood in the steep balconies and watched.

Source: Retrieved from Wikimedia Commons; used per Creative Commons Attribution.

to present medicolegal information to courts, became the first widely recognized texts on legal medicine. After his death, his work led to King Henry IV of France appointing skilled medical experts to make medicolegal investigations and report on all deaths in all cities and royal jurisdictions.

The study of anatomy, aided by careful dissections, became much more common in the 17th and 18th centuries (Figures 8.2 and 8.3) when medical practice became more fundamentally rooted in scientific observation and reasoning. As medicine matured, so did its application to legal questions. Forensic medicine began to be recognized as its own separate specialty. Giovanni Morgagni, considered by many as the founder of modern anatomic pathology, wrote an extensive work on pathology in 1769 called the "Seats and Causes of Disease Investigated by Anatomy." In the late 18th century, the first textbooks arrived on the scene to guide medically trained investigators, aided by Francois-Emanuel Fodoeré's three-volume treatise on legal medicine in 1799 and *The Principles of Forensic Medicine* by John Gordon in 1821. These works helped lead the way to understanding how injury could leave a set of observable features on a body that might be traced to a specific sequence of events while excluding other mechanisms for causing the observed trauma.

Today, forensic medicine is a well-established subdiscipline of medicine that has developed extensive standards and methods that work to ensure uniform practice based on rigorous scientific principles.

8.1.3 Medicolegal Practice

Medicolegal practice today represents a very broad range of work involving the application of medicine to inform many different types of legal proceedings. These applications can

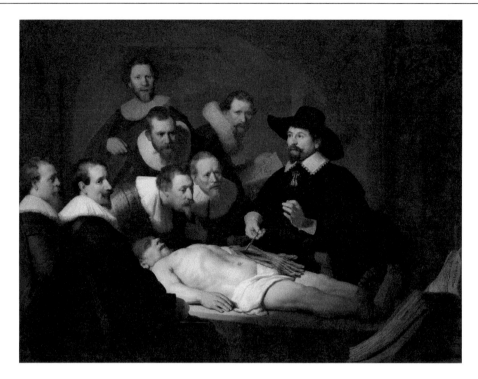

FIGURE 8.3   Rembrandt van Rijn's 1632 painting "The Anatomy Lesson of Dr. Nicolaes Tulp" shows a 17th-century public autopsy.

Source: Retrieved from Wikimedia Commons; used per Creative Commons Attribution.

be quite legally complicated and include patient rights protection, malpractice liability, advance healthcare directives, mental competence, and injury and death investigations, among many others. The use of the term in connection with forensic science, however, is most commonly associated with medical investigations involving personal injury and the determination of the cause and manner of death. The distinction is often made, however, between clinical forensic medicine, where the victim is still living, and forensic medicine in which the victim has died. Examples of clinical forensic medicine include cases of non-accidental injury, abuse, assault, and rape (Figure 8.4). In many cases, the medical examiners first and foremost job is protecting public health.

Pathology is the study of the causes and effects of disease and disorders and is divided into two main branches: clinical and anatomic pathology. Clinical pathology deals with the diagnosis of disease and is most often based on laboratory tests of body fluids and tissues. Anatomic pathology deals largely with the determination of disease or trauma based on physical examination of the organs and tissues of the body. Forensic pathology is an important sub-specialty of anatomic pathology and usually focuses on determining the cause and manner of death of a body.

In the United States and many places in the world, there are two systems of death investigation in common use: coroners and medical examiners. Coroners, as described previously, date back more than a thousand years to 10th-century England and derive from a crown officer ("crowner") entrusted with the oversight of all investigations involving human deaths, especially to ensure that the death taxes were paid to the King. Today, coroners are usually elected officials,

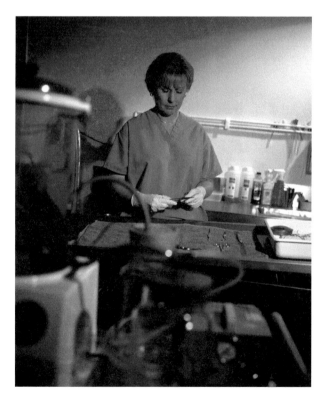

FIGURE 8.4   Forensic pathology laboratory: a forensic pathologist checking medical instruments. Forensic pathology is the branch of medicine that determines, among other jobs, the cause and manner of death of a person who has died in unexplained circumstances. A post-mortem autopsy, the dissection and examination of a dead body, is often required.

Source: John Mclean/Science Photo Library. Used with permission.

generally in more rural locations, who are not typically required to have any specific medical or forensic training but who are legally responsible for overseeing some aspects of death investigations. Coroners are not able to perform autopsies and their quasi-judicial actions are usually controlled by local and state regulations. In some locations, they can convene special inquests with juries to investigate and render a determination of the manner of an unknown or suspicious death. Occasionally, the duties of a coroner are coupled with other governmental positions such as that of a sheriff, district attorney, county health commissioner, or other official who performs the duties of the coroner in conjunction with their other responsibilities. In some locations, coroners are sworn law officers with the right to arrest suspects, issue subpoenas, and carry firearms, but this appears to be relatively uncommon. Currently, ten states use only coroners as their death investigation officials and about another 30 employ a combination of coroner and medical examiner systems, depending on the specific location in the state.

In the larger jurisdictions of cities and states in the United States, however, the medical examiner (ME) system has often replaced the older coroner system. A medical examiner must first be a physician, and almost always with special credentials as a board-certified forensic pathologist. These highly trained physicians are able to perform autopsies to determine the cause, time, and manner of death. In the United States, about 50% of the population is served by medical examiners, and there were approximately 750 board-certified forensic pathologists currently working in 2023. Any autopsies that need to be performed in a county with a coroner system are usually contracted out to nearby places with certified medical examiners. Unlike the frequent images depicted in TV shows, medical examiners do not typically go to death scenes themselves. Specially trained medicolegal death investigators (MDI) often go to the actual location, take photographs, examine the body, and take charge of the remains before bringing it back to the medical examiner's office along with any associated evidence including drugs and medications, weapons, suicide notes, ligatures, and any other materials associated directly with the body. These investigators often serve as the liaison between the medical examiner's office, the families of the deceased, witnesses, and law enforcement investigators.

BOX 8.1   HOW TO BECOME A FORENSIC PATHOLOGIST?

Forensic pathologists are highly trained physicians with deep knowledge of both medicine and various aspects of forensic science and the law.

The typical training to become a forensic pathologist begins with four years of undergraduate studies followed by four years of medical school. After this, the new MD must spend four years, usually at a hospital, serving in something like an apprenticeship in clinical and/or anatomic pathology. Then, they need to spend a year or more pursuing a forensic pathology internship or fellowship in a medical examiner's office, working under the supervision of a trained forensic pathologist. During this time, they perform autopsies and the other jobs of a medical examiner. Finally, they need to pass a comprehensive examination to become a board-certified forensic pathologist. The entire process from entering college to board certification usually takes about 13 years of post-high school study and practice.

BOX 8.2   WHAT'S IN A NAME?

The National Association of Medical Examiners (NAME) is an organization for medical examiners engaged in the investigation of "sudden, violent and suspicious deaths, deaths related to public health and who perform autopsies," along with other medicolegal death investigators and administrators. The group seeks to practice "medicine in the finest tradition of preventive medicine and public health by making the study of the dead benefit the living."

The investigation of the cause and manner of violent, suspicious and untimely deaths can help to resolve both civil and criminal legal disputes. Even when the cause and manner of a person's death may seem obvious, an autopsy may be necessary to confirm the absence of foul play, to assist in any related police/legal investigation, or in relation to the transfer of assets of the deceased. For example, even though a gunshot wound may seem to be the obvious cause of death, an autopsy can confirm that a specific wound was the cause of death, recover bullets, collect vital trace and toxicology evidence and determine the trajectories of the bullets to aid in the investigation and crime reconstructions. Autopsies are also performed to ensure high-quality medical care, educate young physicians and aid in the identification of public health disease threats. A recent study has shown that about one-third of autopsied patients had significant discrepancies between their clinical diagnoses made while they were living and the diagnosis at autopsy that would have made a difference in their ultimate survival. Understanding trauma from autopsies has also led to new and more effective methods for treating trauma patients and improving their survival rates. Finally, autopsies have helped to discover new diseases or groups of diseases that have led to significant advances in public health and safety. For example, between 1950 and 1983, over 80 new diseases were discovered from autopsies.

8.1.4 Medical Death Investigation

The purpose of a death investigation is ultimately to determine how and why a person died. There are three important medicolegal questions that must ultimately be answered in any death investigation: the manner, the cause, and the time of death. Autopsies form only a part of the process of gaining sufficient information to answer these important questions. Other valuable information can be learned from a person's medical history, details of the circumstances surrounding the death, items found near the body, the state of the body (e.g., rigor mortis), and interviews with family and witnesses, among other details.

Probably the two most important terms in the vocabulary of death investigation are *cause of death* and *manner of death*. These have very precise medical and legal definitions and it is important to understand the differences between these two terms.

8.1.4.1 Manner of Death

The term manner of death relates specifically to a determination of the intent or series of events that brought about the death and is classified into one of only just a few possible categories. These categories typically include homicide, suicide, accidental, natural, and undetermined. Some places also add therapeutic complications as a manner of death, although this is not available in all jurisdictions, and where it is not an option, deaths from medical procedures are often placed in the natural category. It is important to note that the determination of the manner of death is primarily a *legal* determination, not a strictly medical issue, although it is decided by a medical examiner or coroner. A typical distribution of deaths among the major categories from the National Institutes of Health (NIH) is shown in Figure 8.5. The main manners of death are described in more detail below.

Homicide is defined as a death caused by another individual, whether by intent, through negligence, or inadvertently. In legal proceedings, we differentiate between the level of intent used to bring about someone's death by deciding whether it was on purpose, leading to murder and homicide charges, or without intent, usually leading to manslaughter charges if the offender was determined to be negligent. For example, the planned shooting or drowning of someone would lead to a murder charge, while someone bringing about a fatal heart attack through abduction or by the unexpected discharge of a firearm could be charged with manslaughter. Nonetheless, the manner of death in *all* these cases is simply homicide – a death brought about by the actions of someone else for any reason.

Suicide is a death brought about intentionally by the person who dies themselves in an effort to end their own lives. Suicide is illegal, as is usually assisted suicide facilitated by another person. It may be difficult to determine, however, whether a death was a suicide or brought about by another manner of death, but information about a person's background, medical history, and mental state at the time of death can help provide important clues. Suicides vary greatly depending upon age groups, as shown in Figure 8.6. There are some conventions that are typically used by medical examiners where an apparent suicide might be classified as an accident or natural. For example, the death of a person who knowingly engages in dangerous and reckless behavior and then dies from a fall is usually classified as an accident, while a terminally ill patient who refuses to eat and dies of malnourishment is usually classified as a natural death. In both these examples, it could be argued that the person's death arose from knowingly engaging in actions that would bring about their own deaths and could, therefore, be classified as suicides. Typically, fewer than one-third of intentional suicide victims leave notes about their deaths.

Accidental deaths arise from a violent, unexpected death that was not caused by any natural, intentional, or criminal act by another person. Accidental deaths are, unfortunately, very common, and Table 8.1 exhibits the leading causes of accidental death in the United States. Accidental deaths account for about one-fourth of all deaths for people 25–44 years old and over one-third of all deaths of children. Poisoning, primarily from drug overdose, and traffic-related deaths are by far the largest two causes of accidental deaths (Figure 8.7). In the United States, there were about three accidental deaths every ten minutes in 2018. Additionally, deaths from natural disasters are considered natural deaths.

The category of a *natural* death accounts for the largest overall number of deaths by far and is the result of a naturally occurring illness or disease such as heart disease (~25% of all deaths), cancer (~23%), stroke (~6%), birth defects (classified as such even if the decedent died at an old age), SIDS, influenza, and other viruses, among many others. Figure 8.8 shows the ten major causes of death, with nine of the top ten coming from natural causes. Natural deaths comprise between 90% and 95% of all deaths (averaged over all age groups, 2009 CDC statistics).

Occasionally, it is very difficult or impossible to determine the manner of death, either due to lack of evidence or as a result of very complicated issues associated with the

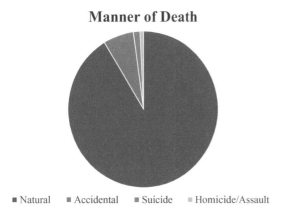

Manner of Death

■ Natural   ■ Accidental   ■ Suicide   ■ Homicide/Assault

FIGURE 8.5 Typical data for the four leading manners of death for all age groups (2020 NIH).

(a) Number of suicides for females, by age group and means of suicide: United States, 2016

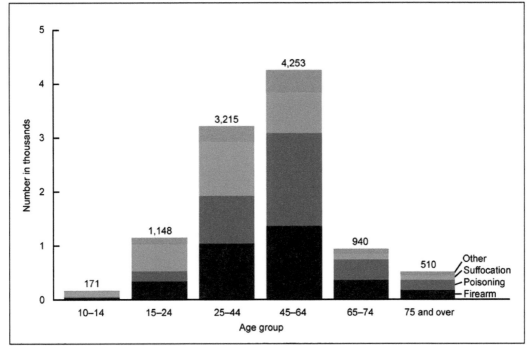

NOTES: Suicides were identified using *International Classification of Diseases,10th Revision*, underlying cause-of-death codes: U03, X60–X84, and Y87.0.
Suicides were categorized by the means of suicide based on the underlying cause-of-death codes: firearm (X72–X74), suffocation (X70), poisoning (X60–X69),
and other means (U03, X71, X75–X84, and Y87.0). Access data table for Figure 4 at: https://www.cdc.gov/nchs/data/databriefs/db309_table.pdf#4.
SOURCE: NCHS, National Vital Statistics System, Mortality.

(b) Number of suicides for males, by age group and means of suicide: United States, 2016

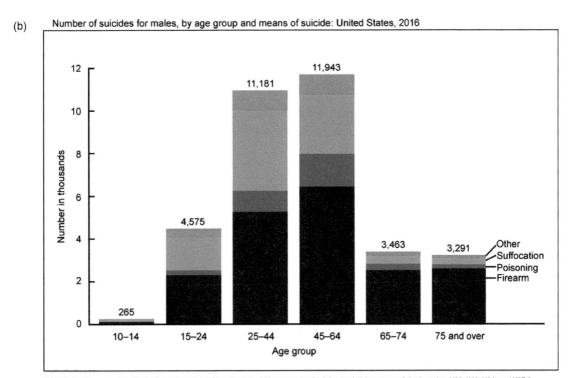

NOTES: Suicides were identified using *International Classification of Diseases,10th Revision*, underlying cause-of-death codes: U03, X60–X84, and Y87.0.
Suicides were categorized by the means of suicide involved based on the underlying cause-of-death codes: firearm (X72–X74), suffocation (X70), poisoning
(X60–X69), and other means (U03, X71, X75–X84, and Y87.0). Access data table for Figure 5 at: https://www.cdc.gov/nchs/data/databriefs/db309_table.pdf#5.
SOURCE: NCHS, National Vital Statistics System, Mortality.

FIGURE 8.6 (a) Number of suicides for females, by age group and means of suicide in the United States, and (b) number of suicides for males, by age group and means of suicide in the United States (all data from the CDC, 2016).

Source: NCHS, National Vital Statistics System, Mortality.

death, such as when there is more than one factor at work. In these cases, the manner of death may be listed as *undetermined* when a classification cannot be reasonably made. The determination of a manner of death often has important legal consequences, including criminal charges, such that a medical examiner may choose to wait for more evidence and use this classification until the case becomes clearer. Many medical examiners feel that it is better to have the manner of death remain undetermined for a period of time, in some cases even indefinitely, rather than change a classification of the manner of death later on. However, the medical examiners and courts always have the right and responsibility to change the manner of death as more information becomes available since there is no statute of limitations for human deaths.

In some places, the additional category of *therapeutic complication* (sometimes referred to as "medical misadventure") is used to indicate that a death occurred due to known and often predictable side effects from appropriate medical procedures. It is important to note that cases in which a person dies because of the misapplication of standard medical

TABLE 8.1 Leading causes of accidental deaths in the United States in 2017

LEADING CAUSE	PERCENT
Poisoning (including overdoses)	38.2
Motor vehicle crashes	23.7
Falls	21.4
Suffocation by ingestion/inhalation	3.1
Drowning	2.1
Fires and burns	1.7
Mechanical suffocation	1.0
Heat/cold	0.7
Machinery	0.3
Firearms	0.2

Source: CDC, National Vital Statistics Report (2019).

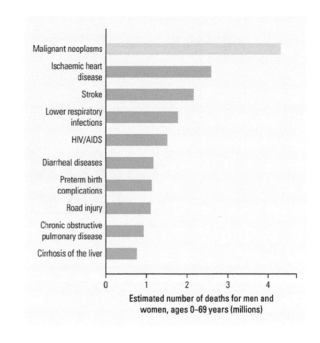

FIGURE 8.8 Top 10 Causes of Death Worldwide (NIH, 2015).

Source: Gelband et al. (2015). License: Creative Commons Attribution, BY 3.0 IGO.

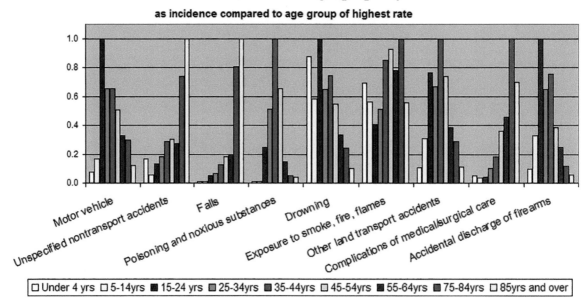

FIGURE 8.7 Typical distribution of accidental deaths by age group.

Source: Mikael Häggström, National Vital Statistics Report Col. 50 (15)(2002).

practice are not part of this category and should be classified as homicides. Also excluded from this category are cases in which well-intentioned mistakes, including incorrect diagnoses, lead to death: these are properly classified as arising from a natural manner of death. Where this classification does not exist, the medical examiner must decide whether it should be classified as a natural death or a homicide: usually these deaths are classified as natural deaths. In the United States, it is estimated that about 50,000–100,000 deaths would fall into this therapeutic complication category annually (NIH).

8.1.4.2 Cause of Death

In contrast with the manner of death, the cause of death is the *medical* reason for the death and relates to the disease or injury that actually brings about the death of the person.

It is important to note that the causes of death vary greatly by age groups. For example, the leading cause of death in young adults is mainly from accidents, while those for older adults are primarily from natural causes (Figures 8.9 and 8.10).

The *mechanism of death* is the actual biochemical or physiological means by which a person dies. For example, if a person sustains multiple impact injuries from an automobile accident, the cause of death could be determined to be blunt force trauma with the mechanism of death being exsanguination (loss of blood). The independent issue of manner of death could be determined to be homicide, accidental, or suicide in this case, depending upon other

evidence. Occasionally, a pathologist may identify a *contributing cause of death* or *proximal cause of death* to provide additional information about the death. For example, our accident victim could have had seizures causing them to "black out" which might have started the chain of events that led to the death. The contributing cause, in this case, could be epilepsy. Finally, in a cause of death determination, the term *pertinent negative* may also be important and refers to a negative finding (not observing something specifically) that is relevant to the death.

It is important to know that, in our legal system, injuries always take precedence over disease for determining the cause of death. For example, a person could have severe heart disease long before they might have been mildly assaulted. In a normal person, the assault might have caused little more than a bruise, but in this case, it could have triggered a heart attack that led to the person's death. The cause of death in this instance would be determined to be from blunt force trauma (the assault), with heart disease as a contributing cause, and the manner of death determined to be a homicide. Since there is no statute of limitations on homicide, injuries sustained in an attack might not result in death for many, many years and still have the death determined to be a homicide. For example, if a person is shot and recovers but dies from a brain aneurysm 20 years later, it might be determined that the death was caused by the older gunshot injury weakening the blood vessel in the brain, with the aneurysm as the contributing cause leading to a manner of death determination of homicide.

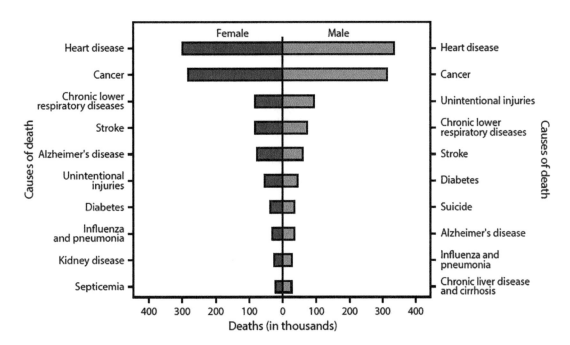

FIGURE 8.9   In 2015, heart disease and cancer were found to be the top two causes of death for both sexes. The ten leading causes of death accounted for approximately three-quarters of all reported deaths.

Source: CDC (2015); Credit line: QuickStats: Number of Deaths from 10 Leading Causes, by Sex — National Vital Statistics System, United States, 2015. MMWR Morb Mortal Wkly Rep 2017;66:413.

10 Leading Causes of Death by Age Group, United States – 2018

Rank	<1	1-4	5-9	10-14	15-24	25-34	35-44	45-54	55-64	65+	Total
					Age Groups						
1	Congenital Anomalies 4,473	Unintentional Injury 1,226	Unintentional Injury 734	Unintentional Injury 692	Unintentional Injury 12,044	Unintentional Injury 24,614	Unintentional Injury 22,667	Malignant Neoplasms 37,301	Malignant Neoplasms 113,947	Heart Disease 526,509	Heart Disease 655,381
2	Short Gestation 3,679	Congenital Anomalies 384	Malignant Neoplasms 393	Suicide 596	Suicide 6,211	Suicide 8,020	Malignant Neoplasms 10,640	Heart Disease 32,220	Heart Disease 81,042	Malignant Neoplasms 431,102	Malignant Neoplasms 599,274
3	Maternal Pregnancy Comp. 1,358	Homicide 353	Congenital Anomalies 201	Malignant Neoplasms 450	Homicide 4,607	Homicide 5,234	Heart Disease 10,532	Unintentional Injury 23,056	Unintentional Injury 23,693	Chronic Low. Respiratory Disease 135,560	Unintentional Injury 167,127
4	SIDS 1,334	Malignant Neoplasms 326	Homicide 121	Congenital Anomalies 172	Malignant Neoplasms 1,371	Malignant Neoplasms 3,684	Suicide 7,521	Suicide 8,345	Chronic Low. Respiratory Disease 18,804	Cerebro-vascular 127,244	Chronic Low. Respiratory Disease 159,486
5	Unintentional Injury 1,168	Influenza & Pneumonia 122	Influenza & Pneumonia 71	Homicide 168	Heart Disease 905	Heart Disease 3,561	Homicide 3,304	Liver Disease 8,157	Diabetes Mellitus 14,941	Alzheimer's Disease 120,658	Cerebro-vascular 147,810
6	Placenta Cord. Membranes 724	Heart Disease 115	Chronic Low. Respiratory Disease 68	Heart Disease 101	Congenital Anomalies 354	Liver Disease 1,008	Liver Disease 3,108	Diabetes Mellitus 6,414	Liver Disease 13,945	Diabetes Mellitus 60,182	Alzheimer's Disease 122,019
7	Bacterial Sepsis 579	Perinatal Period 62	Heart Disease 68	Chronic Low Respiratory Disease 64	Diabetes Mellitus 246	Diabetes Mellitus 837	Diabetes Mellitus 2,282	Cerebro-vascular 5,128	Cerebro-vascular 12,789	Unintentional Injury 57,213	Diabetes Mellitus 84,946
8	Circulatory System Disease 428	Septicemia 54	Cerebro-vascular 34	Cerebro-vascular 54	Influenza & Pneumonia 200	Cerebro-vascular 567	Cerebro-vascular 1,704	Chronic Low. Respiratory Disease 3,807	Suicide 8,540	Influenza & Pneumonia 48,888	Influenza & Pneumonia 59,120
9	Respiratory Distress 390	Chronic Low. Respiratory Disease 50	Septicemia 34	Influenza & Pneumonia 51	Chronic Low. Respiratory Disease 165	HIV 482	Influenza & Pneumonia 956	Septicemia 2,380	Septicemia 5,956	Nephritis 42,232	Nephritis 51,386
10	Neonatal Hemorrhage 375	Cerebro-vascular 43	Benign Neoplasms 19	Benign Neoplasms 30	Complicated Pregnancy 151	Influenza & Pneumonia 457	Septicemia 829	Influenza & Pneumonia 2,339	Influenza & Pneumonia 5,858	Parkinson's Disease 32,988	Suicide 48,344

Data Source: National Vital Statistics System, National Center for Health Statistics, CDC.
Produced by: National Center for Injury Prevention and Control, CDC using WISQARS™.

Centers for Disease Control and Prevention National Center for Injury Prevention and Control

FIGURE 8.10   Ten leading causes of death in the United States (all races, both sexes).
Source: CDC.

BOX 8.3   TWO-MINUTE MYSTERY

Case: A motorcycle accident leaves a man with a fractured tibia that is set in the hospital, and the person ultimately recovers. Over several years, however, an undetected infection of the broken bone sets in that ultimately develops into a cancer in the open space left in the bone after treatment in the hospital by the original accident. The cancer goes undetected for years and is identified only after it metastasizes (spreads) elsewhere in the body. The cancer eventually kills the man more than 20 years after the original motorcycle accident.

   Problem: If you were the pathologist in this case, what would you determine to be the cause, manner, and mechanism of death (and contributing cause if possible) in this instance (answer at the end of the chapter)?

Time of death: Time of death is a valuable piece of information in any death investigation, one determined by understanding the many post-mortem changes in the body upon death (Figure 8.11). A variety of methods have been developed, and new techniques are on the horizon for improving our estimates of the time of death when it is uncertain. Several physical and biochemical markers, such as body stiffening, ion concentration in the vitreous humor of the eye, and protein release into the bloodstream, are useful indicators of the *Post-Mortem Interval* (PMI), the time between the actual death and the time that the body was found. The use of indicators such as insect life found on or around the body and the stage of decomposition of the remains may be very useful for determining longer periods of time, up to months and even years (Chapter 10). Nonetheless, forensic pathologists are often called upon to use evidence from the body to determine the time of death, especially in the first 72 hours after death.

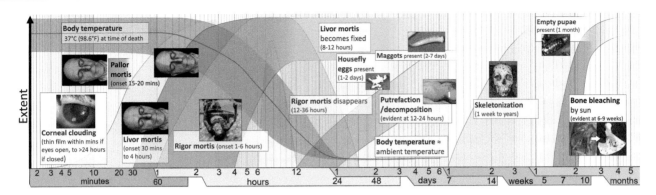

FIGURE 8.11 Changes upon death in a body during the post-mortem interval (PMI).

Source: Creative Commons Attribution 4.0 International. User: Mikael Häggström, M.D.

Using a PMI determination and the known time that the body was discovered, you can back-calculate to determine the actual time of death. Forensic pathologists have methods that can be fairly accurate in determining the PMI within about the first 72 hours of death. These methods especially include *rigor mortis*, *algor mortis*, and *livor mortis*. The time of death, however, is usually presented as a range of times – the longer the PMI, the larger the range (or the uncertainty of the actual time of death).

Rigor mortis, probably the best-known measure of the PMI that is found throughout the popular literature, is stiffening of the muscles of the body after death, as illustrated in Figure 8.12.

While there is a fair amount of variation depending on the individual and conditions, some important trends are helpful in determining the PMI from rigor mortis observations. Rigor usually begins about four to six hours after death, reaches a maximum between 12 and 24 hours after death, followed by a gradual relaxation. The lingering effects from *rigor* can last for as much as 72 hours before the tissues are fully relaxed again. The effects of rigor are first observed in the smaller muscles, such as the jaw, fingers, and toes, before becoming noticeable in the larger muscles of the arms and legs. Rigor mortis also affects the muscles of the skin and hair follicles, producing "goosebumps" (called *cutis anserine*); their presence does *not* reflect the temperature of the surroundings at the time of death. As rigor is released, the muscles relax in the reverse order; the larger muscles soften first, followed by the smaller ones. Observing these differences can help determine how long *rigor* has been in effect.

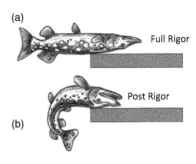

FIGURE 8.12 Illustration of *rigor mortis* in fish: the fish overhanging the table on the (a) is in full rigor (stiffened), while the fish on the (b) is not. The same process happens in humans.

Source: Fish images courtesy Shutterstock.com.

Unlike when we flex our muscles, *rigor mortis* does not occur through the shortening of muscle tissues. When we flex our muscles, small structures in our muscles called sacromeres contract by causing the long protein filaments of actin and myosin to slide by each other, shortening the sacromere (Figure 8.13). Energy is then required to overcome this shortened arrangement by forcibly moving calcium ions around to relax the sacromeres in the muscle back to their starting point. In the case of *rigor mortis*, however, the energy needed to "unlock" the sacromeres and allow them to relax is not available after death, and the sacomeres become "locked" in the "on" (shortened) position. It is only after the proteins themselves decompose sufficiently that the muscles begin to relax, and *rigor* passes off the body.

Livor mortis, also known as lividity, is observed as dark red to purple discolored areas of the skin and internal organs that arise after death (Figure 8.14). It is caused by the blood settling into the lowest parts of the body due to the effect of gravity on the blood after the heart stops pumping, producing the discoloration. The effect occurs because the tiny blood capillaries in the skin dilate (open up) after death. If pressure is put on parts of the body where the blood is pooling, such as when lying against the floor or a solid object, the blood will not settle there, and the skin will appear lighter ("blanched") relative to the surrounding tissues. During the first 8–12 hours

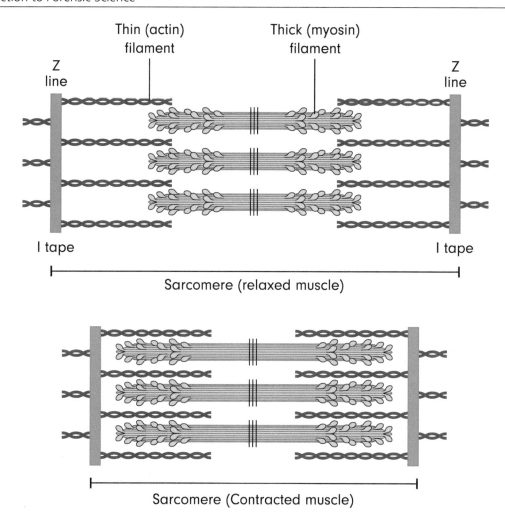

FIGURE 8.13 A sacromere, made up of actin and myosin filaments interwoven, produces contraction and lengthening of muscles.
Source: Shutterstock.com.

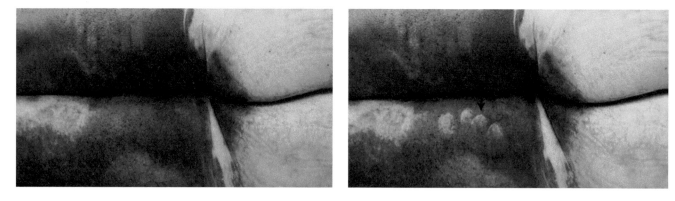

FIGURE 8.14 Livor mortis: the pooling of blood in the lowest regions of the body. Unfixed livor shows blanching of the coloration. Note the finger marks caused by pressing the blood away from the skin surface of the right thigh.
Source: Catanese (2016).

after death, the blood is free to move and resettle somewhere else if the body is shifted or pressure is put on a region of lividity. After this time, however, the color becomes "fixed" due to the congealing of the blood and constriction of the tiny capillaries, such that the blood no longer moves freely if the body is placed into a new position. The presence of "fixed" lividity that doesn't match up with the position of the body can indicate that the body was moved well after death.

Lividity may be decreased or even absent in cases of extreme blood loss or anemia (decrease in the number of red blood cells). Lividity may also be difficult to observe in people with dark skin pigmentation.

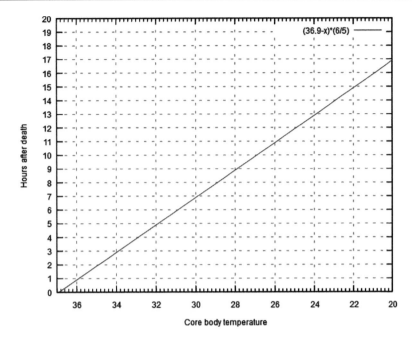

FIGURE 8.15   Plot showing the decrease in body temperature from *algor mortis* after death.

Source: Retrieved from Wikimedia Commons; used per Creative Commons Attribution.

Algor mortis is the slow cooling of the body after death. The normal body temperature is ~98.6°F (37°C), which is typically higher than the ambient temperatures of most surroundings. Once someone dies, the body begins to cool because there are no longer any biochemical reactions operating within the body to maintain the living body's temperature, until it reaches thermal equilibrium with its surroundings (when the body temperature and the surrounding temperature are about the same). If we know how fast a body cools and because we know the temperature of the body at the moment of death (usually), we can estimate roughly the time it took to cool to the observed temperature, giving a good estimate of the PMI. The temporary heat generated through decomposition can slow down this return to ambient temperatures.

Generally, the body cools at a rate of about 2.0–2.5°F (1.1–1.4°C) per hour for the first few hours, with an average rate of about 1.5–2.0°F (0.8–1.1°C) per hour averaged over the first 12 hours, slowing to about 1.0°F for the following six hours. Many factors contribute, however, to significant variations in this cooling rate, such as clothing, the surroundings (e.g., temperature, moisture, humidity, sunlight), the amount of body fat, diseases (especially fever), location of the body (e.g., in water, buried, in the sun, etc.), and insect activity. An example in Figure 8.15 illustrates the cooling of the body over time. Algor mortis is certainly a useful indicator for determining the time of death but is only a rough guide and can be affected by many conditions that are hard to quantitatively account for.

8.1.5 When Are Autopsies Performed?

The internal organ systems of the body can provide vital information needed to determine the causes and manner of death. When this is necessary, a pathologist examines the body closely and collects samples for appropriate laboratory tests to provide the missing information. An autopsy, as defined by the National Association of Medical Examiners (NAME), is "primarily a systematic external and internal examination for the purposes of diagnosing disease and determining the presence or absence of injury [including the] chemical analysis of body fluids for medical information as well as analysis for drugs and poisons." An autopsy occurs under a very specific set of circumstances when the dissection of a person's remains is required to provide information about the circumstances surrounding their deaths that cannot be determined through other means. Sometimes, it may be decided that sufficient information is available to answer these questions without an autopsy. Local and state laws typically govern when autopsies are required. The usual conditions when autopsies are legally required often include:

- Any unattended or unexplained death when a physician is not available or is unwilling to sign a death certificate.
- Any unexpected death that takes place under unusual, unexplained, or suspicious circumstances suggesting foul play.
- Any death resulting from homicide, suicide, or certain types of accidents (e.g., vehicle accidents, falls, drowning, burning, ingestion of poisons, etc.).
- Any death from a disease or other agent that could pose a risk to public health, including contagious diseases and toxins.
- Any death that occurs while the person is in legal custody, incarceration, or in confinement.
- Any employment or occupational-related death.
- Any death of an institutionalized person for reasons other than illness or known disease.

- Any death from a standard "lower-risk" medical procedure (e.g., anesthesia, routine surgery, dental procedures, standard therapies, etc.).
- Any hospital death when the person is pronounced dead on arrival or occurs within the first 24 hours of being admitted to the hospital unconscious.
- Any death that appears to be the delayed result of a previous injury, especially when the injury resulted from criminal actions against the person (e.g., assault resulting in seizures, pulmonary embolism, heart attack, poisoning, etc.).
- Any death where the body will be cremated and not available for future exhumation.

There are, of course, other circumstances when an autopsy is performed. For example, it might be desirable for a family to learn more about the medical cause of a particular death to confirm the diagnosis of a suspected disease or illness impacting the long-term health of the living. This could provide information about the presence of inherited diseases such as cancer, kidney disease, heart disease, or Alzheimer's disease. In this instance, the family can request an autopsy to focus on providing this potentially useful information.

There are also times when, due to religious, cultural, or ethical grounds, a family might *not* wish to have an autopsy done. Medical examiners certainly try to accommodate these wishes as far as it is possible legally, but when the law requires an autopsy, the legal requirement for autopsy almost always takes precedence. Sometimes, the extent of the autopsy can be limited as a compromise. For example, the autopsy might be limited to just the chest organs or only the brain. The

pathologist tries to make it such that the effects of the autopsy can be concealed so that an open casket funeral or other religious ceremonies may still be possible.

Relatively few deaths actually legally require autopsies. Typically, autopsies are performed on between 10% and 20% of all *investigated* deaths. Autopsies are most common for younger people (Figure 8.16) and for those involved in violent crimes (Table 8.2).

TABLE 8.2   Percentage of autopsies for selected causes (CDC)

LEADING CAUSE	PERCENT
Assault (homicide)	91.8
Legal intervention (e.g., police shooting)	81.7
Accidental poisoning and exposure to noxious substances	72.5
Accidental drowning	63.7
Accidental firearm discharge	60.7
Pregnancy and childbirth	60.3
Transportation accidents	54.6
Intentional self-harm (suicide)	51.8
Accidents (unintentional injuries)	43.7
Chronic liver disease and cirrhosis	7.4
Diseases of the heart	6.2
Influenza and Pneumonia	4.2
Septicemia	4.1
Diabetes mellitus	2.7
Cerebrovascular diseases (brain)	2.0
Chronic lower respiratory diseases	2.0
Malignant neoplasms (cancer)	1.3

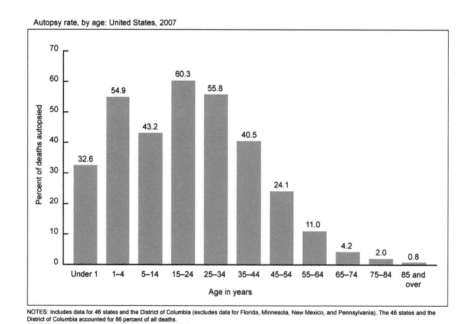

FIGURE 8.16   Percentage of deaths for which autopsies were reported in the United States by age group.
Source: CDC.

8.1.6 Information from an Autopsy

It has been proposed that an autopsy may be considered something like an interrogation, where the pathologist seeks to discover answers to six important questions from the deceased (Dr. Lester Adelson). In essence, it involves asking the body to reveal its information. These key questions are as follows:

1. **Who are you?** One of the first questions that needs to be answered is who the body belonged to. This is usually determined through a number of methods that include (in approximate order of increasing reliability): (1) visual identification by a friend or family member, (2) identifying materials found on the body (e.g., ID card, jewelry, passport, or other papers), (3) physical markings on the body, such as scars, birthmarks, and tattoos, (4) comparison of X-ray or similar biomedical scans (e.g., dental X-ray, chest X-ray, MRI, CAT, etc.), (5) fingerprint comparison, and (6) DNA comparison analysis. Visual identification and items found on the body are often remarkably unreliable and are rarely used today as the sole means of identification and may be omitted entirely. The best identification, of course, involves DNA testing, but there are some limitations of DNA uses already discussed in Chapter 5, especially when there is a lack of a known DNA sample from the suspected person suitable for comparison. This can especially arise if the person is completely unknown rather than using DNA to verify a suspected identification.

BOX 8.5   WHY DO SAILORS GET TATTOOS?

Getting a tattoo is a common experience that sailors throughout naval history share. The origin of this "tradition," however, comes from the straightforward need to provide a ready method for identifying the bodies of sailors after horrific sea battles. These battles involved closely confined quarters and very destructive cannons, frequently resulting in severe trauma that necessiated an easy means of body identification – if nothing more than to keep track of who died. Tattoos provided an easy, decorative, highly personalized, and inexpensive permanent marking on a sailor's body to provide a degree of permanent identification. This practice of personalized tattoos today still provides medical examiners with useful pieces of evidence in post-mortem body identification.

2. **When did you become ill or hurt and when did you die?** Answers to these questions can come from a variety of sources such as those previously discussed, including *rigor mortis*, *livor mortis*, and *algor mortis*. Other physical markers can also be used to inform us of when an injury occurred. For example, bruises (contusions) can help determine when an injury might have occurred since bruises typically change color as they heal, often progressing from a purple/red color (injury to 18 hours), through a blue/brown color (~1–2 days), then to green (~2–5 days), and finally to a yellow color (~5–10 days) before fading completely, assuming a healthy person (Figure 8.17). Signs of healing of a wound and how far the healing has progressed could indicate how much time might have elapsed between the injury and death. Additionally, the stage of digestion of the contents of a person's stomach can also indicate when their metabolism was stopped by death, suggesting the length of time between the last meal and death. These findings during the autopsy can be reinforced or brought into question by information that is not determined at the autopsy but comes from other sources, such as the person's last known sighting and chemical analysis (e.g., eye vitreous, proteins, etc.).

3. **Where did you get hurt and where did you die?** A great deal of information regarding this question can come directly from the death scene rather than from the autopsy, but the information often informs the pathologist's investigation. Incident reports, hospital records, and emergency medical accounts can provide valuable information. Information provided by the medical examiner, however, can certainly help to confirm or refute theories. For example, unusual *livor mortis* patterns that are inconsistent with how the body was found can help show that the body was moved some hours after death. Finding unexpected items within the body cavity can also suggest a place of death. For example, pollen found

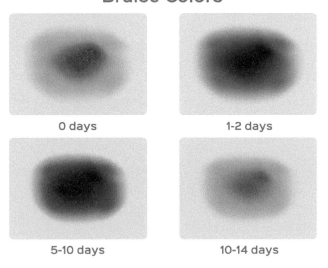

Bruise Colors

0 days

1-2 days

5-10 days

10-14 days

FIGURE 8.17   Typical color changes observed during the healing of a bruise (contusion).

Source: Shutterstock.com.

in the sinus cavity can be compared with plants in the area to suggest a possible location that the person visited recently. The field of forensic taphonomy, covered in Chapter 9 on forensic anthropology, deals with how remains decay and are moved, distributed, or otherwise disturbed after death.

4. **Did you die as a result of an accident, violence, natural causes, or some combination of reasons?** The answer to these questions results in the determination of manner of death with much of the key information coming from the autopsy itself. Each organ, wound, and injury is carefully examined during the autopsy, with the intent of determining the manner and mechanism of death. Evidence from the autopsy can also be deemed consistent with or differing from a suspected cause of death.

5. **If violence was completely or partially responsible for your death, was it from suicide, accident, homicide, or other reasons?** In this question, the pathologist focuses upon any wounds or injuries found on the body. They begin by determining the type (e.g., laceration, incised or cut wound, puncture, abrasion, contusion, or gunshot), size (e.g., length, width, depth), and location of the wound. The direction of the wound is also important and can often be determined from the shape of the wound or injury.

6. **If someone killed you, who did it?** This is often not the role of the pathologist, but they can provide important clues for other investigators that can support or refute a suspect's story of the events.

Answers to each of these questions provide an important piece of the puzzle in determining how someone died. In the next section, we'll explore what happens during an autopsy and how valuable information can be discovered through this process.

8.1.7 The Autopsy

A complete autopsy proceeds along a series of well-orchestrated steps to systematically examine the body, inside and outside. An autopsy can involve the entire body or be restricted to just one area, such as the head or chest. Throughout the autopsy process, plenty of photographs and notes are taken by the pathologists, which provide a key to their ability to use the autopsy evidence in court. And, of course, during the autopsy, the safety and protection of the pathology team from injury and infection is of paramount importance.

This section presents the generalized steps often employed during a complete autopsy. Sometimes, there is variation in the order and extent of the steps due to the condition of the body or the specific information sought.

BOX 8.6   COMMON TERMS INVOLVED IN AN AUTOPSY

Decedent: the person who has died.

Laceration: occurs when pressure splits open the skin to produce uneven wounds, such as from a blunt force impact.

Contusion: a bruise usually caused by an impact that damages blood vessels and causes them to leak into the surrounding tissue.

Hematoma: a blood tumor with a significant amount of blood collection.

Blunt force trauma: trauma caused by the impact of a non-penetrating object, such as a bat, a car, or by hitting the floor with force.

Sharp force trauma: trauma caused by a sharp object such as a knife, often a form of penetrating trauma.

Incision: a cut wound that is longer than it is wide, usually caused by drawing a sharp object across the skin.

Stab or puncture wound: a cut or piercing wound that is wider than long, caused by a stabbing motion with a pointed object.

Abrasion: a wound caused by rubbing or scraping an object across the skin – usually involving just the outer layers of the skin.

Gunshot: penetrating wounds created by a high-velocity projectile expelled from a firearm or similar device.

Ligature: a thread, rope, or cord, such as used in strangulation.

Embolism: the obstruction of a blood vessel.

Edema: swelling from fluid accumulation.

Step 1 – Access and Control of the Remains: Truly, the process of autopsy begins at the scene. While not in a physical sense, without information from the death scene it is very difficult to correctly determine the manner of death for a person. In fact, it's

been estimated that manner of death determinations may be incorrect up to 80% of the time without information available only from the scene. This information includes the arrangement of the physical surroundings, the orientation and setting of the body, information from first responders, witnesses, and family, among other information.

This may seem like an obvious step, but especially in a criminal investigation, the body is itself considered to be physical evidence and subject to a rigorous chain of custody process. Typically, the body is placed into a new "body bag" at the death scene and sealed with "tamper-proof" tags to ensure that it arrives at the medical examiner's office intact and untouched. As with all evidence, proper records, photographs, and narrative are important for keeping track of the evidence. If there is a gunshot possibility, the decedent's hands are often covered to prevent contamination or loss of residue evidence. Care is also taken at the crime scene to recover potentially valuable evidence closely associated with the body itself, such as clothing, fluids, medications, etc.

Step 2 – **External Examination**: Before any cutting begins, a very careful external examination of the entire body is made. The overall health and description of the person (e.g., sex, hair color, weight, length/height, eye color, ethnicity, age, etc.), including any clothing, penetrating objects, and stains, are detailed first. All marks, scars, tattoos, signs of trauma and other visible features are recorded and photographed. Wounds and injuries are located on the body and measured, including the direction of any penetrating wounds. If emergency medical intervention or hospital procedures were performed, the results of these actions are also carefully preserved and recorded. Often, the fingernails are scraped, hands tested for gunshot residue (GSR), fingerprints rolled, fibers collected, and samples of any other relevant materials on the body are taken (e.g., glass fragments, paint chips, soil samples, etc.). X-ray images are usually taken, and increasingly, other biomedical scans are employed, such as MRI and CT scans. These methods of biomedical imaging will be discussed in greater depth later in this chapter.

Step 3 – **Opening the Thoracoabdominal (thorax and abdomen) and Brain Cavities**: In this step, the pathologist typically begins by making a "Y-shaped" incision across the chest, starting near

each shoulder, coming together at the sternum, and then down the abdomen to the pubis (missing the navel), as shown in Figure 8.18. Bleeding from these cuts is very small since the blood moves only in response to gravity but may also be congealed (fixed) in *livor mortis*. The skin is then folded back to expose the ribs and sternum (breastbone). The sternum and the front parts of the ribs are then removed, often with a Stryker saw; a motorized saw specifically designed to efficiently cut through bone (Figure 8.19). This type of incision provides good access to the chest cavity and neck without disturbing the face, arms, and hands.

The brain cavity is then opened by making an incision behind one ear and then across the top of the skull to the same point behind the other ear (Figure 8.18). The flaps of skin of the scalp are separated by pulling one flap forward over the face and the other backward over the nape (sometimes only one flap is used). The skull is then cut along the nape, joining the cuts behind the ears. The cut skull cap can then be removed to expose the brain. The brain is first observed in place and then removed for further study.

Step 4 – **Removing Organs**: Once the chest and thorax have been opened, the organs are removed for measurement and examination. The organs can be

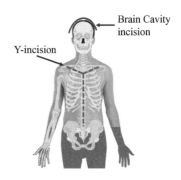

FIGURE 8.18 Y-incision to open the thoraco-abdominal cavity.

Source: Retrieved from Wikimedia Commons; used per Creative Commons Attribution.

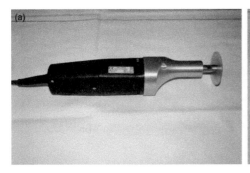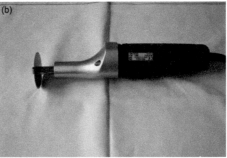

FIGURE 8.19 Electric portable swinging saw used to cut bone during an autopsy.

Pomara and Fineschi (2020).

removed one at a time or all together in a "block." Each of the organs is weighed, measured, carefully inspected, and dissected for signs of disease or trauma. During this process, the pathologist usually takes many samples of tissue and fluid from numerous places for later examination and chemical analysis.

The careful evaluation of the major organs of the body forms an important part of the internal autopsy examination. These major organ systems will be considered shortly in terms of their function and evaluation during an autopsy.

Step 5 – Evaluation and Analysis of Samples: One of the most time-consuming, and often most valuable, steps of an autopsy involve the careful examination and analysis of the tissue and fluid samples recovered during the procedure. Tissue samples are processed into microscopic samples and studied for abnormal shapes and structures, indicating conditions such as cancer, congenital defects, and diseases. The fluids are usually analyzed for controlled substances, toxins, alcohol, proteins, and other chemical compounds, depending on the suspected cause of death.

Step 6 – Closure: At the end of the autopsy, the pathologist usually places the organs back into the body cavity, replaces the sternum and skull cap, and the incisions are stitched up so as to show as little evidence as possible of the procedure (using a "baseball" stitch). This usually allows funerals, including open casket services, to proceed without noticeable signs of the autopsy. Samples removed from the body must be preserved properly and stored (chain of custody) for extended periods, sometimes up to 25 years or more by law. After all samples have been recovered and the procedure completed, the body can then be released to the family or mortician for burial or cremation.

8.1.8 Major Organ Systems Examined

As described above, the major organ systems are typically removed from the body during the autopsy and subjected to careful examination. Pathologists are particularly concerned with identifying any structural abnormalities, diseases present, or signs of injury or violence that could have contributed to the person's death. These major organs studied include:

- **Heart**: The heart is the center of our circulatory system and is responsible for pumping about 1,900 gallons (7,200 L) of blood throughout the entire body each day! It beats about 100,000 times every day and requires only about 20 seconds to pump a portion of

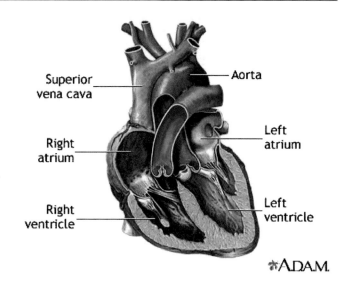

FIGURE 8.20   Anatomy of the heart.

Source: Shutterstock.com.

blood through the entire circulatory system. A typical adult heart weighs about 300 g and is somewhat larger than the size of a clenched fist (Figure 8.20). During the autopsy, it is removed and separated from the lungs, weighed, and inspected – especially the blood vessels on the outside of the heart (coronary arteries). If the heart is unusually large, it can indicate the presence of a condition known as hypertension or high blood pressure – a condition where the heart must work extra hard to pump blood through the blood vessels. The heart is usually dissected to examine the inner structures, and the dissection occurs in the order of blood flow, from the right atrium to the right ventricle to the left ventricle and ending with the left atrium. Throughout the process, the pathologist looks for anything unusual relative to a normal, healthy heart and searches for evidence of infection, damaged tissue and valves, and blocked arteries, especially in the coronary arteries. Any potential damage to the large veins and arteries around the heart, such as the aorta and vena cava, is also explored.

It is obvious from this that the pathologist must have a very detailed understanding of the structure of both a normal heart as well as how the organ changes with disease or injury. This, of course, is also true for the other organs of the body.

- **Lungs**: The lungs are responsible for both oxygenating and removing carbon dioxide from the blood. The lungs exchange these gases between our blood system and the outside air, exchanging over 2,000 gallons (7,500 L) of air in a day. The lungs are composed of an intricate network of blood vessels and mucus-lined air passageways, arranged like the branches of a tree (Figure 8.21).

HUMAN LUNG ANATOMY

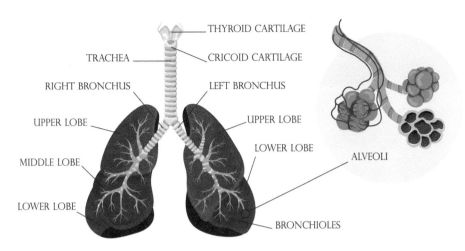

FIGURE 8.21 Anatomy of the lungs and alveoli, the air spaces in the lungs through which oxygen and carbon dioxide are exchanged. Source: Shutterstock.com.

They are organized with one lung on either side of the heart (the left lung is slightly smaller than the right due to the placement of the heart). Once removed, the pathologist inspects the lungs for fluid, foreign materials, growths, and discolorations. Lungs are also inspected for embolisms; an object, such as a blood clot, that moves through the body and blocks blood flow in a vessel. Often, these emboli form in the veins of the legs, arising from extended bed rest, disease, or trauma to the legs, and move to the lungs where they can produce fatal blockages. The pathologist also looks for signs of infection, pneumonia, smoking-related diseases, and tumors.

- **Liver and Gall Bladder**: The liver is a very large organ with multiple functions that include glycogen storage (an energy reserve molecule made when our bodies have excess glucose so that our cells can be powered even when we are not actively taking in any calories, such as when we sleep), removal of waste products from the blood, protein production, and other key biological functions. A typical healthy adult liver weighs about 1.5 kg (~3 lbs) and is bright red (Figure 8.22 Top). Some diseases, such as cirrhosis, which can arise from chronic alcohol consumption, cause the liver to become very fatty, yellow, hardened, and dysfunctional (Figure 8.22 Bottom). A number of other serious conditions of the liver, including cancer, necrosis (dying tissue), hepatitis, and others, can be found upon liver examination. The liver also produces bile, a chemical that aids in the digestion of fats and lipids in the body. Excess bile is stored in the gall bladder when not needed for digestion. The gall bladder can become

inflamed, infected, carry "gall stones," or develop a variety of other problems that can be revealed during an autopsy.

- **Stomach and Intestines**: The stomach is a key organ of the digestive system that continues the digestion of food that begins in the mouth and starts the absorption of nutrients into the bloodstream (Figure 8.23). The small intestines are attached to the stomach (about 6 m, or 20 ft, long) and lead into the large intestines (about 1.5 m, or 5 ft, long). During an autopsy, the contents of the stomach are examined to learn both what the person last ate and to gain a rough indication of how long after eating they died. Pill casings, poisons, and toxins can sometimes be found in the stomach and intestines, suggesting a possible suicide or drug overdose. Various diseases, such as cancer, ulcers, and blockages, are also looked for during the examination. As part of the autopsy, the intestines are removed and the entire length examined for obstructions, disease, or trauma.

- **Kidneys, Bladder, and Urinary System**: The pair of kidneys, each weighing about 150 g and about 10 cm (4 in.) long, form a key part of the urinary system, although they also play important roles in blood chemistry regulation, hormone secretion, and control of the body's blood pressure (Figure 8.24). Healthy kidneys appear dark red with a very smooth surface. As with the liver, they are dissected to look for any signs of disease, blockage, or trauma that might be observed. The bladder holds urine until it is released from the body through the urethra. Urine is usually sampled for later toxicological studies.

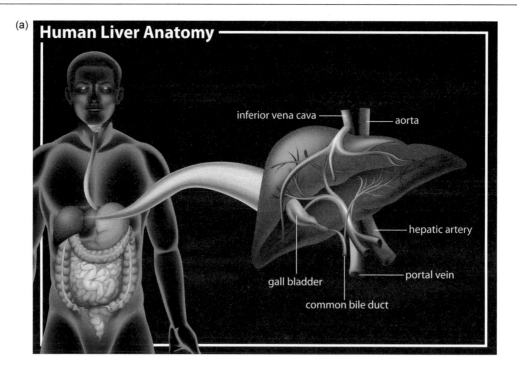

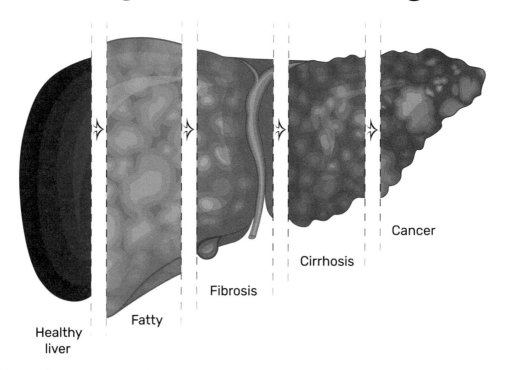

FIGURE 8.22 (a) Human liver anatomy, and (b) the effects of various liver diseases, from fatty liver to cancer.

Source: Images courtesy of Shutterstock.com.

- **Spleen and Lymph System**: The spleen is an important part of our lymph system, which also includes the lymph nodes, tonsils, thymus, and bone marrow. The spleen is central to the production of both red and some types of white blood cells. The spleen is sensitive to trauma and is often compromised or ruptured from impact trauma such as car accidents, leading to internal blood loss through hemorrhaging (Figure 8.25). The lymph nodes are also checked for possible signs of cancer.

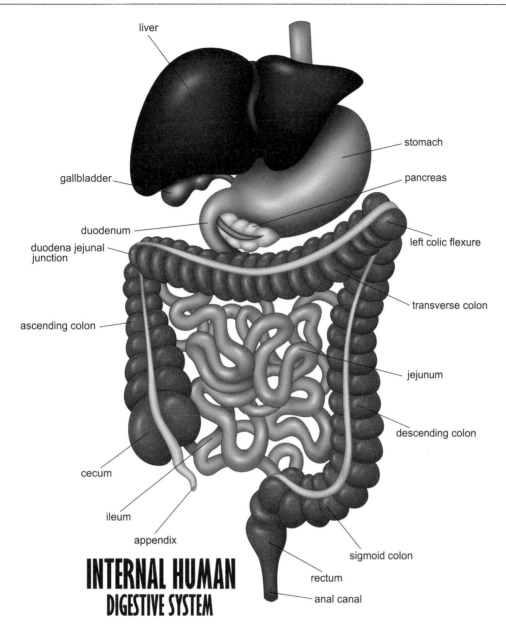

liver

stomach

gallbladder

pancreas

duodenum

left colic flexure

duodena jejunal
junction

transverse colon

ascending colon

jejunum

descending colon

cecum

ileum

appendix

sigmoid colon

rectum

anal canal

**INTERNAL HUMAN
DIGESTIVE SYSTEM**

FIGURE 8.23   Anatomy of the human digestive system: stomach and intestinal tract.

Source: Shutterstock.com.

- **Pancreas**: The pancreas is about 5 in. long in an adult and is located "behind" the stomach, toward the spine (Figure 8.26). Its primary function is the production and regulation of insulin and several digestive enzymes that are required to convert our food into cellular energy. Failure of the body to produce sufficient insulin, or an inability to properly respond to insulin, results in diabetes. Long-term diabetes that has not been well controlled can result in a variety of severe problems including heart disease, nerve damage, weight loss, and many others. Recently, an estimate of between 15% and 20% of all autopsies involved patients with diabetes. Other diseases of the pancreas, including cancer, pancreatitis (an inflammation of the pancreas), and cystic fibrosis would be detected at autopsy.

- **Neck**: The organs of the neck, especially the esophagus, larynx, tongue, epiglottis, and thyroid may be removed and examined (Figure 8.27). The pathologist looks for unusual growths, malformations, or cancers. In addition, if strangulation is suspected, the small and somewhat fragile hyoid bone in the neck is often found to be broken and is checked to see if it is damaged.

- **Sex Organs**: The utcrus in women and the prostate in men are removed and dissected to see if

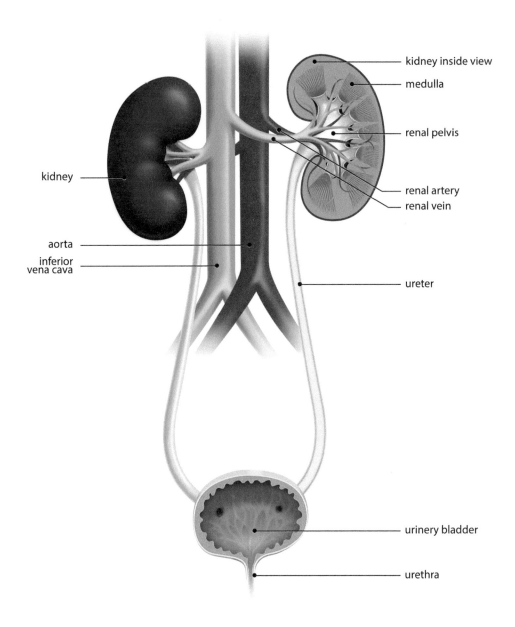

FIGURE 8.24   Human urinary tract, showing both kidneys and urinary bladder.

Source: Shutterstock.com.

any tumors or other unusual features are present. Additionally, undetected pregnancies are looked for. These organs are usually not weighed.

- **Brain**: The adult brain, weighing around 1.4 kg (3 lbs), usually appears smooth and near-white on the inside and gray on the outside portions with numerous blood vessels crisscrossing throughout (Figure 8.28). Once removed, the brain is usually preserved in fixative for a week or more to firm it up prior to dissection. Blunt trauma, including car crashes and other head injuries, can lead to hemorrhaging of the blood vessels in the brain. Elsewhere in the body, a region surrounding any hemorrhage can

easily swell to relieve the pressure buildup from the accumulating fluid. Think, for example, of a swollen lip or ankle after an injury; the tissue surrounding the injured area is able to expand to accommodate the fluid buildup. In the brain, however, the inflexible, rigid skull bones prevent this expansion from happening. This tightly restricted space stops the body's ability to freely swell around a brain hemorrhage, allowing it to swell only about 8–10% before being stopped by the skull. This restriction can lead to a dangerous buildup of pressure in the brain, causing blood supplies and vessels to be compressed and even completely shut off, leading to tissue

LYMPHATIC SYSTEM

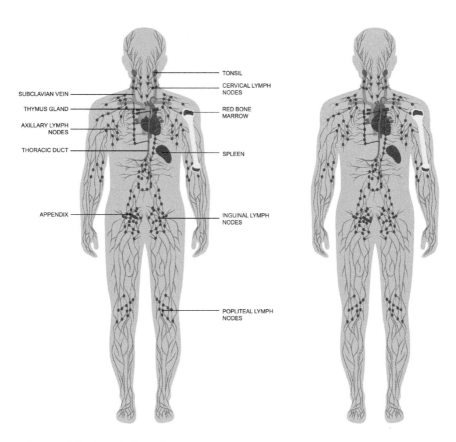

FIGURE 8.25 Human spleen and the lymphatic system.

Source: Shutterstock.com.

HUMAN PANCREAS

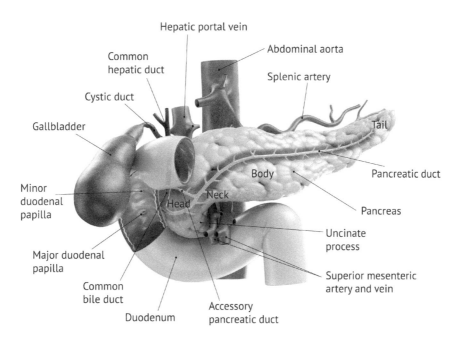

FIGURE 8.26 Human pancreas with gallbladder, duodenum, and corresponding blood vessels.

Source: Shutterstock.com.

death. This general effect is referred to as *compartment syndrome* and is a rapid-onset, life-threatening problem common with brain injuries. A similar effect can be seen with brain aneurysms ("ballooning") or ruptures of weakened blood vessel walls in the brain. Brain tumors can also be readily seen as smooth and distinct from the surrounding brain tissue. Autopsies remain the best current method to confirm a diagnosis of Alzheimer's disease in older patients (Figure 8.29). Gunshot wounds to the brain can lead to blackened and torn tissue along the path of the projectile, allowing the pathologist to track the bullet's path.

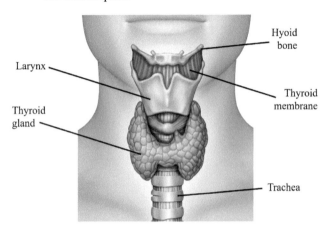

FIGURE 8.27 Anatomy of the neck and thyroid gland.

Source: Shutterstock.com.

8.2 TRAUMA, INJURY, AND SUDDEN DEATH

8.2.1 Types of Trauma

Some types of injuries are so common that they require a separate detailed description. Generally, injuries can be broadly divided into two large groups that revolve around whether they are penetrating or non-penetrating wounds. Penetrating wounds include *projectile wounds*, such as from bullets, arrows, and flying debris, and *sharp force trauma* wounds, such as those that may arise from knives, glass, and similar cutting objects. Non-penetrating wounds are primarily *blunt force trauma*, such as injuries sustained in vehicular accidents, falls, or assaults, and instances where asphyxia occurs, such as from strangulation or suffocation.

1. **Firearm Injuries**: Firearms vary greatly in terms of size, shape, and force that a projectile can impart to a body when struck at high velocity. Details about firearms themselves will be presented in much greater detail later in Chapter 16, but a special consideration of the types of wounds that they inflict is important in forensic pathology. The term *terminal* (or wound) *ballistics* is usually applied to the path and effects of a high-speed projectile, such as a bullet, when it impacts a body. There are several mechanisms by which tissue damage occurs from a

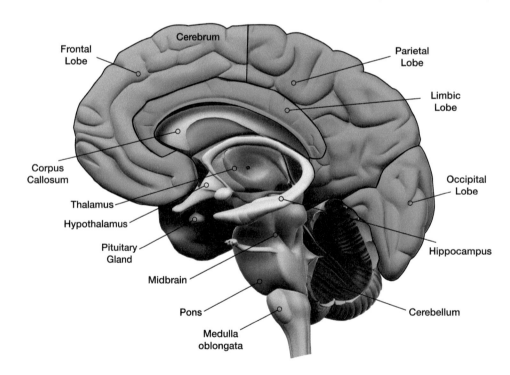

FIGURE 8.28 Structures and anatomy of the brain.

Source: Shutterstock.com.

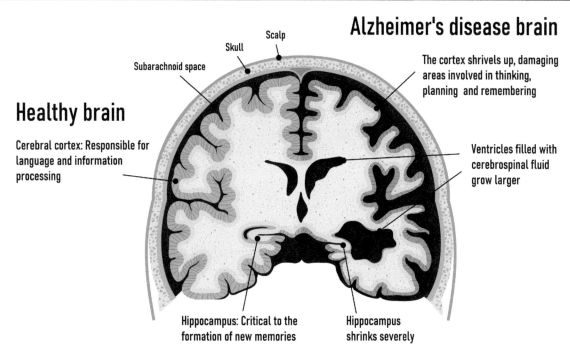

FIGURE 8.29   Changes in the brain from a healthy brain (Left) to one with Alzheimer's disease (Right).

Source: Shutterstock.com.

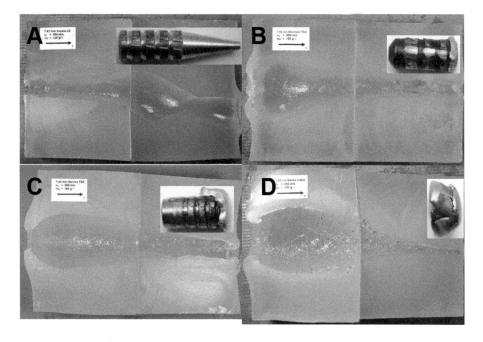

FIGURE 8.30   Cut soap blocks for different bullet types after passing through the blocks (exiting bullet fragments are shown as inlay). Seen are the permanent cavities from the bullet trajectory.

bullet strike (Figure 8.30). The first is the obvious direct impact of the bullet on tissue directly in front of its path as it travels through the tissue (sometimes called "tissue crush" or "permanent cavity damage"), illustrated in Figure 8.31. The second damage mechanism, often referred to as temporary cavitation (or tissue stretch), arises from the cavity briefly formed behind the bullet as it moves at high velocity through tissue by pushing the tissue outward and away from the bullet's path, as seen

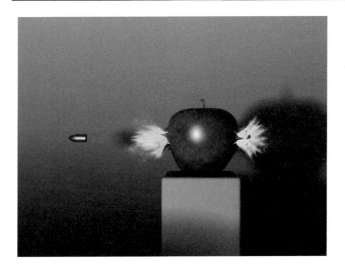

FIGURE 8.31 Bullet passing through an apple showing crush and stretch "wounds". Notice the tissue being pushed outwards by the bullet as it passes through.

Source: Shutterstock.com.

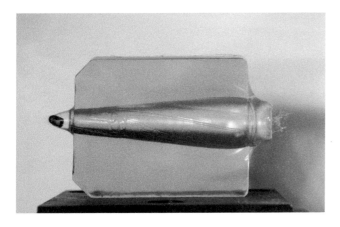

FIGURE 8.32 A 0.22 caliber bullet passing through ballistic gelatin, a substance whose density is similar to that of human flesh, at ~1,000 ft/s. Temporary cavitation can be seen from the bullet moving through the gelatin.

Source: Edward Kinsman/Science Photo Library. Used with permission.

in Figure 8.32. Note that the "sonic wave" from a bullet may not, however, have any real impact on tissue damage (consider that the therapeutic lithotripter used to break up kidney stones with sonic waves is 2,000 times stronger than a bullet's sonic wave without any tissue damage). The sonic wave, shown in Figure 8.33, can have a neurological effect upon the victim, causing shock and disorientation. The amount of damage from temporary cavitation depends upon what tissue it affects; stretchy tissues, such as the lungs and skin, can show little damage from temporary cavitation while solid organs, such as the liver, aorta, heart, and kidneys, can show great damage. Larger and slower bullets typically

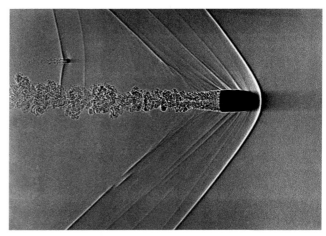

FIGURE 8.33 Shock wave: A bullet traveling at about 1,100 mph (500 m/s). When the bullet breaks the sound barrier, shock waves are created (the curved line at the front edge of the bullet). Other shock waves can be seen alongside the bullet, and a turbulent wake behind it.

Source: NASA.

crush more tissue than smaller, faster projectiles with the same kinetic energy, while the faster bullet will stretch more tissue with relatively less direct (crush) damage.

A bullet can impart a significant amount of energy to the body as it moves through the tissue due to its kinetic energy (KE), which depends on the mass and velocity of the bullet (KE = $\frac{1}{2}mv^2$, where m is the mass of the projectile and v is its velocity). The kinetic energy of a bullet, therefore, increases as the mass or velocity of the bullet increases. If a bullet is stopped entirely by the "target", then all of its kinetic energy is delivered to the target. Bullets, therefore, vary in the amount of kinetic energy they can deliver, with a 0.50 caliber bullet delivering about 12 times the energy of a 0.22 caliber bullet with just a doubling of the diameter of the projectile. Once a bullet impacts bone or tissue, it may not follow a straight path due to tumbling and yawing (rotation around the long axis of the bullet) motions. When the bullet passes through bone, the entrance and exit wounds of the bullet can often be determined by the beveling of the bone it passes through (Figure 8.34). The amount of tissue damage observed is a complex combination of projectile features that include its shape, velocity, pathway through tissue, whether it deforms on impact, and many other features.

Details of gunshot wounds can be used to identify an entrance from an exit wound (if it does exit at all), providing information about the direction of the shot. Entrance wounds are typically much smaller than exit wounds, although not always. Because of the tumbling or yawing that a bullet may experience after striking tissue and the elasticity of the skin, it

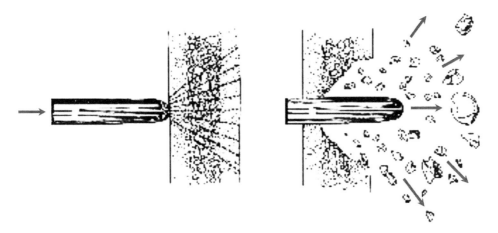

FIGURE 8.34 Bone beveling on the exit side of the bone damage. When a bullet penetrates a bone, it leaves a small hole on the side from which it enters and a larger crater, or bevel, on the side that it exits from.

Source: **Retrieved from Wikimedia Commons; used per Creative Commons Attribution.**

FIGURE 8.35 Hot gases, burning gunpowder, and unburned materials expelled from the muzzle of a handgun, can burn skin from a close range shot causing stippling.

Source: **Shutterstock.com.**

is usually not possible to determine the size (or caliber) of the bullet from the size of the flesh entrance wound. There is great variation in the size and shape of gunshot wounds, depending on the corresponding size, shape, velocity, and trajectory of the bullet when it strikes the body. There are four general types of entrance wounds: contact, intermediate range, distant range, and atypical wounds.

Contact wounds occur when the muzzle of the gun is either placed directly on or very close to the skin (<2 in.). This type of wound often leaves visible soot and searing of the skin with a possible muzzle impression left behind on the skin. Intermediate range wounds come from the muzzle placed between 2 in. to 2 ft from the victim and usually leave a stippling effect on the skin (small "spots" from burning or hot unburned gunpowder from the shot, Figure 8.35). It may be possible to estimate the range of the shot from the diameter of the stippling pattern. Distant shots are considered to occur from shots at ranges greater than 2 ft and usually can leave clean, star-shaped wounds. Atypical wounds occur from grazing, surface lodged, or other unusual types of impacts.

FIGURE 8.36   Different sizes of shot often used with shotguns.

Source: Used per Creative Commons Attribution 3.0, Unported. User: Andrew Davidhazy.

Exit wounds are often irregular, large, and lacerated. Exit wounds can sometimes be differentiated from entrance wounds by looking at bone beveling – the exit side of the bone will show a "crater" of larger diameter than the entrance side (Figure 8.34).

Shotguns produce quite different wounds from single projectile weapons (e.g., rifle, handgun). Shotguns often use many smaller projectiles (typically pea-sized or smaller, Figure 8.36) in a single burst that disperse once they leave the barrel of the gun. The body can show a circular pattern of wounds, and the diameter of the wound pattern can be used to estimate the distance between the gun and the victim.

2. **Drowning/Asphyxia**: Death by asphyxia, lack of oxygen, can occur from drowning, accidental or intentional suffocation, and strangulation, among others.

Drowning deaths are usually caused by fluids entering the lungs, preventing the normal lung gas exchange function. In the United States, drowning is the second leading cause of death for children under 12. Deaths in water can occur from natural causes other than drowning, such as heart attack, seizure, prior injury, or injury while in the water. Drowning usually involves a victim initially holding their breath, which increases their blood carbon dioxide levels and triggers involuntary breathing. The victim then swallows water leading to convulsions, loss of consciousness, and death within three to four minutes. Drowning can occur with relatively little water found in the lungs. This can happen from

FIGURE 8.37   Scanning electron micrograph (SEM) of tiny diatoms found in water. The diatoms are a group of photosynthetic, single-celled algae containing about 10,000 species. The characteristic feature of diatoms is their intricately patterned, durable glass-like cell walls, or frustules.

Source: Steve Gschmeissner/Science Photo Library. Used with permission.

sudden cardiac arrest or a laryngeal spasm (tight closing of the larynx in the throat) upon the shock of falling into the water. Near-drowning, when someone is revived while unconscious, can also be fatal and presents a serious medical threat. Occasionally, diatoms (small organisms with hard skeletons found in water, Figure 8.37) or other water-borne matter can be found in the lungs, sinuses, or elsewhere, indicating that drowning is the cause of death.

3. **Blunt Force Trauma**: Blunt force trauma, probably the most common type of injury, refers to injuries arising from the forceful action of non-penetrating objects on a body, such as from a fist, foot, bat, hammer (Figure 8.38), pipe, fall, or similar. The amount and type of injury depend on the amount of force delivered (Force = ma, where m is mass and a is acceleration), how quickly the force is delivered, where on the body the injury occurs, and the health of the victim. Types of blunt force trauma also include abrasions, contusions, lacerations, and fractures, discussed previously (Figure 8.39).

4. **Sharp Force Trauma**: This type of penetrating trauma refers to injuries arising from stabbing, cutting, and incisions that enter the body, such as those that arise from a knife, rod, or other sharp object. Both stabbing and cutting (incised) wounds involve slit-like injuries but an incised wound is usually longer than wide or deep and a stab wound is deeper than long. The normal elasticity of the skin can often make it very difficult to determine much about the weapon used to cause incised wounds, although some important inferences can be made, especially whether a particular weapon is capable of producing observed wounds on a victim. Careful dissection can often tell the depth, width, and direction of a stab. Of particular concern in assaults is the presence of defensive wounds – wounds usually on the hands and arms as the victim tried to shield themselves from the attacker by extending their hands and arms outward.

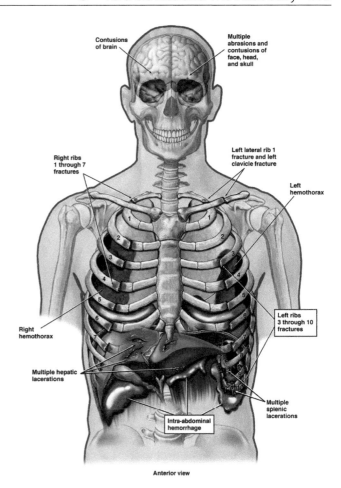

FIGURE 8.39   Examples of blunt force trauma.

Source: Used with permission and courtesy Nucleus Medical Media, Inc.

5. **Vehicular Trauma**: Vehicular trauma can be thought of as a special case of blunt force trauma to drivers, passengers, and pedestrians resulting from the injuries received involving a motor vehicle. Worldwide, this type of trauma accounts for more than 1.2 million deaths annually. The evaluation of vehicular trauma involves consideration of often complex human, vehicular, and environmental factors, such as biological effects from drug use, psychological issues such as depression and suicide, vehicle repair, and driving conditions. The most common types of injuries encountered are brain/head injuries and broken bones.

6. **Fire-Related Injuries**: Deaths associated with fire are typically handled as suspicious until evidence suggests otherwise, although the majority of house fires are accidental. Burns are classified into first-, second-, and third-degree burns depending on their depth and severity (Figure 8.40). Third-degree burns can be very deep and involve charring of the skin. In cases of death by burning, bodies largely consumed by fire typically assume a "pugilistic attitude" – a boxer-like pose where the knees and elbows are

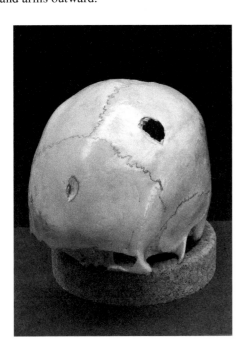

FIGURE 8.38   Skull showing blunt force hammer trauma.

Source: US Armed Forces Institute of Pathology.

VARYING DEGREES OF BURN INJURIES

NORMAL HEALTHY SKIN

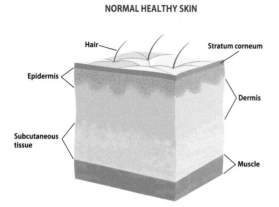

FIRST DEGREE BURN INJURY

Involves of skin

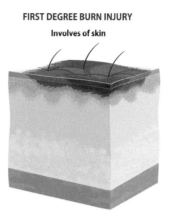

SECOND DEGREE BURN INJURY

Involves top of skin and dermis

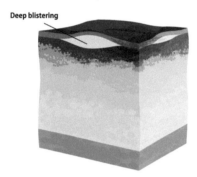

THIRD DEGREE BURN INJURY

charred dermis and subcutaneous tissue

FIGURE 8.40   Types of burns and damage levels.

Source: Shutterstock.com.

bent and the hands clenched, caused by dehydration of the body tissues. Internally, the organs may show signs of extreme heat damage. The lungs at autopsy might show significant damage from smoke inhalation, while toxicology reports might show higher than normal CO_2 or CO levels in the blood. Toxicology and autopsy results are also important in determining if the person died before the fire, such that the fire could disguise the true cause of death.

7. **Sudden and Unexplained Deaths:** This category is not a true form of trauma but involves the same type of careful detective work by the pathologist as used in death investigations from trauma. Sudden, unexpected, and unexplained deaths (SUD) encompass a great deal of medical territory. Generally, they are defined as those that arise either from a brief illness resulting in death before a diagnosis can be made or from a longer illness that does not have a satisfactory diagnosis. Usually, no apparent trauma is externally visible. Upon autopsy, these types of deaths can be found to arise from many different causes. An autopsy involving SUD deaths can also often provide valuable medical information to the living by indicating the presence of hereditary or congenital diseases. These types of deaths are relatively uncommon in both the young, who typically die from either well-known health problems or through accidental deaths, and the old, who often die from longstanding, well-diagnosed chronic problems. Thus, they are most commonly observed in adults from 25 to 65 years old. The list below presents just a very few possibilities for SUD that can be discovered during autopsy.

- *Cardiovascular Problems*: This category represents the predominant cause of sudden and unexplained deaths through cardiac arrest, myocardial infarction, atherosclerosis (thickening of blood vessel walls), hypertension (high blood pressure leading to an enlarged and inefficient heart), and other heart and circulatory problems.

- *Intracranial Lesions*: These include epilepsy, aneurysms (weakening of a blood vessel's wall, often leading to the rupture of the blood vessel and hemorrhaging), brain malformation (e.g., hydroencephaly, hydranencephaly), trauma or disease-induced hemorrhage (loss of blood from the circulatory system), tumors, meningitis, and others.

- *Respiratory Causes*: These include severe bronchitis, emphysema, asthma, pulmonary tuberculosis, lung cancer, pulmonary embolism (blockage), pneumonia, influenza, pneumothorax (collapsed lung), and others.
- *Metabolic Disorders*: This encompasses many disorders including diabetic coma, hormone problems, insulin shock, and others.
- *Psychiatric Patients*: This category includes delirium syndrome, choking, and others.
- *Urogenital, Gastrointestinal, and Spleen*: This includes problems involving kidney tumors, bladder cancer, peptic (bleeding) ulcer, perforated ulcer, peritonitis (inflammation of the inner lining of the abdomen), and others.

- *Miscellaneous*: This category is very large and includes SIDS (sudden infant death syndrome), tubal pregnancy, artery erosion, undiagnosed tumors, and others. There are certainly instances when, even after completion of an autopsy and exhaustive laboratory analysis, the medical cause of death remains a mystery.

Once the autopsy and death investigation have been completed, the medical examiner must communicate their findings to both the family and governmental officials (e.g., law enforcement, prosecutors, health department, etc.) through a formal death certificate. This document provides, besides identification, information of the victim, details about where, when, and the cause and manner of death of the person. Additionally, in the case of a finding of homicide or suicide, the medical examiner may be called upon to testify in court about their work.

BOX 8.7 DEATH OF A COMIC

Steve Allen, one of the most famous comics in the early days of television and the first host of the *Tonight Show*, died unexpectedly in 2000. On the way to his son's home in California for dinner one evening, he had a very minor "fender-bender" automotive accident. There were no apparent injuries and, after exchanging insurance information with the other driver, he arrived safely at the dinner party. Shortly after arriving, however, he said he felt unwell and went to take a brief rest. He was found unconscious a short time later and was pronounced dead, from a presumed heart attack, at a local hospital.

The autopsy found that the cause was not a heart attack. Apparently, the minor accident had ruptured a blood vessel in Allen's chest that allowed blood to leak into the sack surrounding Allen's heart, called the pericardium. As the sack filled with blood, it placed pressure on the heart, leading to inefficient pumping of blood and, ultimately, death. Without the autopsy, the wrong cause of death would have been listed. What do you think should be the correct manner of death in this circumstance (it was ruled accidental by the coroner in LA)?

FIGURE 8.41 Comedian Steve Allen (1921–2000).

Source: Used per Creative Commons Attribution 2.0, Generic; Photo by Alan Light.

8.2.2 Mass Disasters (DMORT)

On rare occasions, medical examiners may be called upon to deal with situations that involve more than one death from a particular event, such as a hurricane, earthquake, flood, transportation crash, explosion, and act of terrorism, among others. Mass disasters are defined in several ways but most commonly simply as a manmade or natural disaster that *exceeds the local capacity to deal with it*. In rural places, even two or three simultaneous deaths may, therefore, be determined to be a mass disaster.

In the United States, there are a number of both public and private agencies that deal with disaster relief. In terms of forensic pathology, the *Disaster Mortuary Operational Response Team* (DMORT) is a Federal governmental response unit that works with local coroners and medical examiners to assist in their work of recovery, identification and death investigation of human remains. These teams are composed of forensic, medical, dental, mortician, and other death professionals who aid local work in many ways including search and recovery, mobile morgue operations, forensic examinations, sample acquisition, burial, and family assistance.

BOX 8.8   DEATH FROM A "SMALL BALL": LINCOLN AUTOPSY

On the day that Abraham Lincoln died, April 15, 1865, his body was autopsied at noon in the White House, in what is now the president's dining room. The partial autopsy focused solely on his brain. During the procedure, the skull was opened, and the brain was carefully removed. When the brain was lifted out, however, the round bullet, having traveled from behind the left ear to just behind the right eye, dropped out. Eight government officials were in attendance that day, and during the procedure, Mrs. Lincoln requested that the doctors remove a lock of the president's hair for remembrance, a common tradition of the time (that's where our term "locket" comes from, a place to preserve a lock of a loved one's hair). An excerpt from the official report of the surgeon, Dr. Joseph J. Woodward, stated:

> There was a gunshot wound of the head around which the scalp was greatly thickened by hemorrhage into its tissue. The ball entered through the occipital bone about one inch to the left of the median line and just above the left lateral sinus,

FIGURE 8.42   Death Mask of Abraham Lincoln (1809–1865), U.S. President (1861–1865).
Source: Shutterstock.com.

which it opened. It then penetrated the dura matter, passed through the left posterior lobe of the cerebrum, entered the left lateral ventricle and lodged in the white matter of the cerebrum just above the anterior portion of the left corpus striatum, where it was found.

The wound in the occipital bone was quite smooth, circular in shape, with beveled edges. The opening through the internal table being larger than that through the external table. The track of the ball was full of clotted blood and contained several little fragments of bone with small pieces of the ball near its external orifice. The brain around the track was pultaceous [soft consistency] and livid [angry] from capillary hemorrhage into its substance. The ventricles of the brain were full of clotted blood. A thick clot beneath the dura matter coated the right cerebral lobe.

(Joseph J. Woodward in Maloney 2014)

Curiously, in recent years, some physicians and historians have argued quite persuasively and with reasonable evidence that Lincoln was dying at the time of the assassination from a hereditary cancer and that he would have died very soon of natural causes anyway. Both Marfan Syndrome and Multiple Endocrine Neoplasia have been suggested based on the death mask and period photographs of Lincoln that show an increasing dissymmetry of his face and skull. Current theories strongly favor Multiple Endocrine Neoplasia as the culprit, which often presents in facial changes, especially lip shape, accompanied by gastrointestinal problems, conditions well-known to have been present for Lincoln. This theory could be confirmed from a tissue sample from Lincoln but his body is entombed safely behind tons of cement after an 1876 attempt to steal his body for ransom from his vault in Springfield, Ill., making a tissue sample unavailable for analysis.

8.3 FORENSIC RADIOLOGY AND VIRTOPSY

LEARNING GOALS AND OBJECTIVES

Biomedical imaging has long held a central place in clinical diagnostic medicine. X-rays have been routinely used for well over 100 years to examine internal structures and gather anatomic evidence from a body. Newer techniques, such as CAT, MRI, ultrasound, and other imaging methods, now make significant contributions to radiologic medicine. Relatively recently, these imaging techniques have joined the arsenal of tools available in forensic biomedical investigations, including in the new methodology of virtopsy. After having studied the material in this section, you should be able to:

- Describe what is meant by radiology and biomedical imaging.
- Explain the basic principles underlying the major methods in biomedical imaging, including X-ray, magnetic resonance imaging (MRI), computerized axial tomography (CAT), and ultrasound.
- Discuss how radiographic techniques may be used in forensic investigations.
- Explain what is meant by the term virtopsy and how this technique may aid forensic investigations.

8.3.1 Introduction to Forensic Radiology

Physicians have long desired a detailed view of the inner workings of a patient's body without having to resort to potentially risky, and certainly painful, surgical techniques. In recent decades, this wish has increasingly come true with the advent of an amazing array of techniques that provide an incredibly detailed and informative picture of our inner biological structures and their workings (Figure 8.43). New techniques and advances in existing methods of biomedical imaging are providing an ever-evolving level of detail and accuracy that is

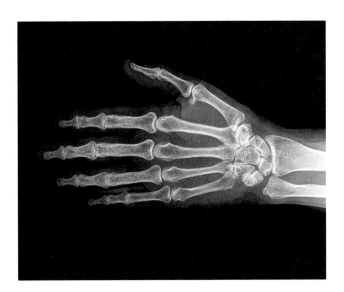

FIGURE 8.43 Hand X-ray image.

Source: Shutterstock.com.

now routinely available to doctors and, increasingly, to forensic pathologists. In fact, because of the advances in radiology, traditional invasive surgical procedures have decreased by 95% in the last 15 years!

An important area in medicine is known as *radiology* which deals with the use of a variety of body-penetrating radiation, such as X-rays, for the accurate diagnosis and treatment of disease and injury. Many of these techniques started out simply as interesting discoveries in research laboratories but ultimately have made their way into medical applications. These techniques have revolutionized modern medicine, and some, primarily X-ray imaging, have long been employed by forensic pathologists.

BOX 8.9   MILESTONES IN RADIOLOGY

1895: Discovery of X-rays by Röntgen
1905: First good chest X-ray produced
1956: Medical use of ultrasound begins
1962: Emission tomography first used (PET and SPECT)
1967: First clinical use of MRI
1972: CT invented by Godfrey Hounsfield
1977: First human MRI scans produced
1984: Widespread use of MRI
2001: Virtopsy patented

8.3.2 History of Biomedical Imaging

Biomedical imaging can trace its unexpected roots to a chance discovery made in late 1895 by Wilhelm Röntgen. At the time, Röntgen was the newly appointed leader of the University of Würtzburg in Germany and was interested in cathode rays: beams generated by applying an electrical voltage across metal plates in an evacuated tube. By chance, one day as he was working with the cathode rays, he noticed that a screen across the lab was glowing strangely. Since there was no visible source, Röntgen presumed the glow was generated by the rays from the cathode tube. This was quite surprising since cathode rays were thought not to travel far outside of the evacuated chamber used to create them. Once he had confirmed that the glow was indeed connected with his cathode rays, he immediately understood the potential importance of his discovery, and for six weeks, he shut the world out entirely to focus on his work in the laboratory. After this brief but intense period of work, he produced arguably the most important photograph in medical history: a picture of the bones and ring of his wife's hand (Figure 8.44).

When he announced his discovery of a new ray in December of 1895, first termed Röntgen Rays and later renamed X-rays ("x" because it was an unknown quantity), the worldwide reaction was immediate and intense. These "rays" became all the scientific rage at the time, and scientists were

FIGURE 8.44   The picture that changed medicine: the first X-ray taken by William Röentgen showing the bones and ring of his wife's hand.

Source: Used per Creative Commons Attribution 4.0, International. Source: Wellcome Images, a website operated by Wellcome Trust, a global charitable foundation based in the United Kingdom.

intent on discovering what they were and how they behaved under a variety of conditions. Within just a few months of this ground-shaking announcement, doctors around the world were using the easily generated X-rays to accurately locate broken bones, kidney stones, diseased organs, and foreign objects lodged in human bodies. His simple discovery more broadly also helped to rekindle a waning interest in physics and chemistry, spurred medical discoveries using his invention, and led to the birth of the new field of medical radiology. For his work, in 1901 Röntgen received the first Nobel Prize ever given in Physics.

Röntgen's initial discovery spurred an enormous amount of research that quickly led to both diagnostic and therapeutic uses of various types of radiation in medicine. Early work by Marie and Pierre Curie, Henri Becquerel, and many others greatly expanded our understanding of radiation and radioactivity, especially how it interacts with matter and living tissues.

BOX 8.10   MARIE SKLODOWSKA-CURIE

Marie Curie is probably the best known of all women scientists. She made enormous and lasting contributions to the scientific and, ultimately, medical worlds. Through her pioneering, incredibly difficult, and courageous work, she achieved many firsts, including:

- In 1903, she became the first woman to win a Nobel Prize for Physics (shared with Pierre Curie and Henri Becquerel) for the discovery of radioactivity.
- The discovery of the elements polonium (named after her native Poland) and radium.
- She was a professor at Sorbonne University in Paris (1906).
- In 1911, she won an unprecedented second Nobel Prize (in chemistry for her discovery of radium). She was the first person ever to receive two Nobel Prizes.

She was also the first Nobel Prize–winning mother of a Nobel Prize winner; her daughter, Irene Joliot-Curie, won the Nobel Prize in Chemistry in 1935.

Unfortunately, because of the unknown effects of radiation on the body at the time of her work and her intense study of radioactive materials, she died at the age of 66 in 1934 from *aplastic anemia*, caused by damage to her bone marrow from radiation exposure. In 1995, her remains were exhumed and reburied in a lead-lined coffin in the Paris Panthéon, along with her husband: she is the first woman to receive this honor on her own merits. Her laboratory notebooks, and even cookbooks, are still stored in a lead vault because of their intense contamination with radioactive materials.

FIGURE 8.45   Marie Sklodowska-Curie (1867–1934).

Source: Retrieved from Wikimedia Commons; used per Creative Commons Attribution.

But it was discovered early on that the use of X-rays for medical imaging was not without its problems and significant risks. Many of the early researchers died of severe radiation burns and cancers arising from ionizing effects of X-rays on living tissues, since they didn't understand the dangers of radiation exposure (Figure 8.46). Röntgen himself, however, was spared this fate since his research with X-rays was only very brief, he only published three papers on X-rays in his career, and he took unusual precautions for the time period by wearing lead aprons and avoiding exposure to the beams. Eventually, however,

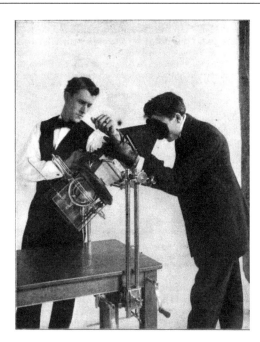

FIGURE 8.46   Photograph of an early X-ray procedure around 1910. No precautions to minimize radiation exposure were taken since the dangers of X-rays were not known at the time. The caption read: 'A physician examining the bones of the arm by means of X-rays.'

Source: Retrieved from Wikimedia Commons; used per Creative Commons Attribution.

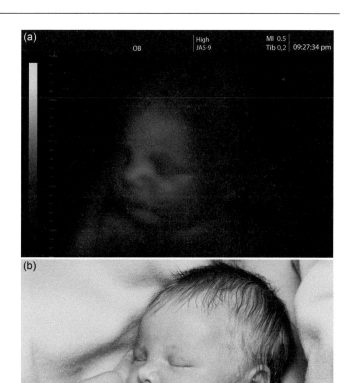

FIGURE 8.47   Image of seven-day-old newborn baby (b) and the 3D ultrasound of the same baby unborn *in utero* (a).

Source: Shutterstock.com.

scientists understood the potential dangers of X-ray exposure and were able to minimize the risk while steadily improving the quality of the images. But scientists have continued their search for new techniques that provide enhanced views inside our bodies with fewer risks and side effects.

The use of sound waves for detecting unseen objects has long been known, beginning with work in the 18th century showing that bats navigate primarily by sound rather than by sight. Sound waves in water had been employed as early as World War I to detect enemy ships and later icebergs, something of increased interest after the sinking of the Titanic.

It was found that sound waves can readily travel through a material, such as water, air, and living tissue, and bounce off an object in its path to be reflected back to the wave's source, providing information about the shape of the object. In the 1940s, researchers sent high-frequency sound waves, called *ultrasound*, through tissues to study the internal organs of animals; the first clinical uses (often called medical sonography) on humans were reported in the 1950s. Today, ultrasound offers very low-risk imaging and is one of the most common biomedical imaging techniques encountered, with 3D and holographic techniques providing early detection of cancer and images of babies *in utero* (Figure 8.47), among many other uses.

One particularly important advance in biomedical imaging came in 1972 when Godfrey Hounsfield invented *computerized tomography* (CT) imaging. In this technique, a computerized 3D image is "built" from a series of 2D images

taken at slightly different angles. With this approach, 3D images can be quickly and accurately assembled to provide amazingly detailed pictures of internal anatomy, as illustrated in Figure 8.48.

Advances in methods of diagnostic medicine, such as magnetic resonance imaging (MRI, see Section 8.3.7), Computerized Axial Tomography (CAT), and Positron Emission Tomography (PET), among others, now provide an array of tools with which the physician can visualize the internal structure and function of tissues within the body without resorting to invasive surgical methods.

In recent years, many of the tools commonly employed in medical diagnostic radiology have found their way quite successfully into forensic investigations. These methods not only provide information supportive of discoveries made during autopsy examinations but also can provide data not readily available through autopsies. This is leading the way for a relatively new method, sometimes referred to as *virtopsy* (or "virtual autopsy"), to make its way into forensic investigations.

The following section will focus on X-ray and magnetic resonance imaging methods, since these are primarily the techniques used in modern forensic medicine.

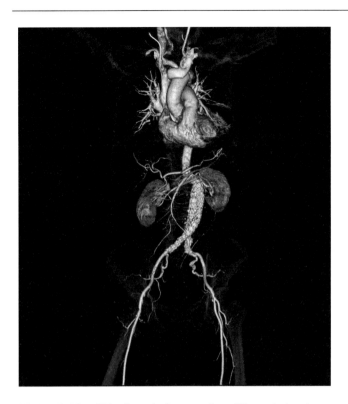

FIGURE 8.48 CTA of a whole aorta in a 3D rendering image showing the arteries with abdominal aorta stent graft, generated from a CT scanner.

Source: Shutterstock.com.

BOX 8.11 THE AMAZING "LIFE" OF A PHOTON

Photons are the basic units of electromagnetic radiation. Curiously, however, while they can sometimes appear to behave as solid particles, at other times they can display wave-like properties, like a wave on a pond. This strange, schizophrenic behavior, referred to as the Wave-Particle Duality, is clearly outside our everyday experience – things either behave as a wave or as a particle. In truth, however, a photon always displays both types of behavior simultaneously; we just can't measure both of these properties at once. This reality becomes even odder when we consider other features of photons that are central to the field known as quantum mechanics. If you really want to explore some surprising ideas, look up the "two-slit" experiment – one of the most baffling, yet most fundamental, of all experiments in chemistry and physics.

8.3.3 Radiology in Forensic Investigations

When a medical examiner begins their work in determining the cause and manner of a death, typically one of the first things they do is X-ray the body, often while it is still encased in the body bag. This not only provides a permanent record of the body's structures but also is useful in quickly finding foreign objects, such as bullets, glass, and medical devices, within the body. But X-rays, and more recently magnetic resonance imaging (MRI) techniques, have been used in new ways to provide a wealth of previously unattainable physical information.

8.3.4 X-Ray Imaging Methods

X-ray radiation, like visible light, is a form of electromagnetic radiation carried in small packets called photons. Photons carry energy, have no mass, are always moving, and, in a vacuum, travel at the speed of light. These photons come in a variety of energies, and the amount of energy they carry allows us to classify them into different "types" within the electromagnetic spectrum, such as radio, microwave, infrared, visible, ultraviolet, gamma rays, and X-rays.

All electromagnetic radiation can be thought of as a wave, similar to sound waves or ocean waves, and can be defined by their wavelengths, the distance between the tops or crests of adjacent waves. These waves travel at the speed of light ($\sim 3 \times 10^8$ m/s) in a vacuum and obey the simple relationship of $c = \lambda \nu$ (where c is the speed of light, λ is the wavelength of the light, and ν is the frequency, or number of waves that pass a given point per second). Since the speed of light is a taken as constant, the equation tells us that as the wavelength gets larger, the frequency must get smaller so that their product always equals the constant number, c. We will talk more about the properties of electromagnetic radiation in a later chapter on spectroscopy (Chapter 12).

The basic difference between X-rays and visible light is that X-rays carry far more energy than visible light waves. An important property of all light is that as its wavelength gets smaller, both its frequency and its energy increases ($E = hc/\lambda$ where E = energy, h and c are constants and λ is wavelength). X-rays, in comparison with visible light, have much shorter wavelengths, around 0.01–10 nm, and carry between about 10,000 and 100,000 times the amount of energy of a typical visible photon of light. It is this high-energy feature of X-rays that allows them to penetrate through the tissues of the body and to be useful in visualizing internal structures.

X-rays are also invisible to our eyes. In fact, our eyes are "tuned" to "see" only a very small portion of the total electromagnetic spectrum, typically only radiation with wavelengths between 390 nm (violet) and 750 nm (red). Usefully, this wavelength "tuning" of our eyes sensitivity corresponds to the wavelengths predominantly emitted by the sun.

BOX 8.12 BRIEF ON X-RAYS

- X-rays are high-energy photons ("packets" of light) with more than 10,000 times the energy of visible photons.
- X-rays are generated by "shooting" high-energy electrons at a metal target.

- X-rays can penetrate through our bodies but are attenuated (e.g., absorbed, diffracted, etc.) by more dense materials.
- Bones and other dense objects (e.g., teeth, metal) block much more of the X-radiation than living soft tissues.
- Looking at an image formed from X-rays penetrating the body can show the shape and structure of internal anatomical features.
- 2D "slices" of X-ray images can be combined by a computer to form a 3D representation of the body (CT scanning).

When light shines on atoms and molecules, it can be absorbed, reflected, or transmitted. In atoms and molecules, electrons occupy different energy levels around the nuclei, called orbitals (more on this in Chapters 11 and 12). Light can be absorbed by molecules if it has an energy that corresponds exactly to the difference in energy between two of these energy levels or orbitals (Figure 8.49). Typical X-rays carry far too much energy to be efficiently absorbed by the soft tissues of our bodies since they are composed primarily of the lighter elements of hydrogen, carbon, oxygen, and nitrogen whose differences in electron energy levels are just not large enough to match the very high energy of the X-ray photon. The much heavier elements, such as the calcium and phosphorus found in bones and metal atoms in manmade objects, such as knives and surgical implants, are able to absorb, block, or scatter X-ray photons. These heavier atoms have electron energy level differences sufficient to absorb the X-ray photon and excite an electron to a higher energy level. Thus, when an X-ray beam is directed at a person's body, the beam largely goes through unaffected by the soft tissues but is absorbed or scattered by the bones and other similarly dense materials. In this way, X-ray beams penetrate through the body to provide "negative" images of our bones and any dense foreign objects, where the soft tissues appear brighter than those areas that absorb the radiation, which appear darker on the image.

X-rays also have enough energy to knock electrons completely away from the atoms that make up our tissues. This process is called *ionization*, which can result in severe damage to these tissues, especially the sensitive and life-critical DNA molecules.

There are typically two ways that X-rays are produced for medical imaging. Inside an X-ray imaging machine, a very large electrical current is passed through a metal plate, called the cathode, that is heated to very high temperatures. When this happens, the cathode emits a beam of electrons (Figure 8.50) that are accelerated toward a second metal plate, called the anode, making it highly electrically positive. These electrons then forcefully strike the second metal plate in the machine. When these high-energy electrons strike the anode, they can do one of two things. In the first case, the accelerated electrons can knock away a low-energy electron that lies close to the nucleus of the anode's metal atoms, much as a cue ball knocks another billiard ball when they strike. The removal of this electron from the metal leaves a vacant space in the metal's electron arrangement that is then filled by other electrons falling from higher levels to fill in the lower-level void. This would be similar to removing the bottom box from

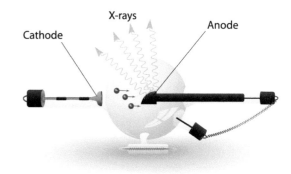

X-RAY TUBE

FIGURE 8.50 Schematic diagram of an X-ray tube that could be used for radiation therapy, medicolegal forensic radiography, and airport security.

Source: Shutterstock.com.

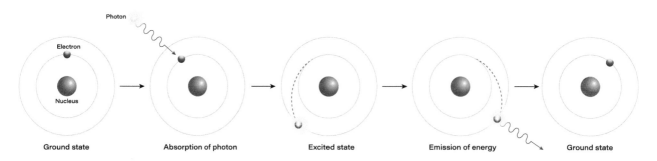

FIGURE 8.49 From ground state to excited state; absorption and emission processes of an atom.

Source: Shutterstock.com.

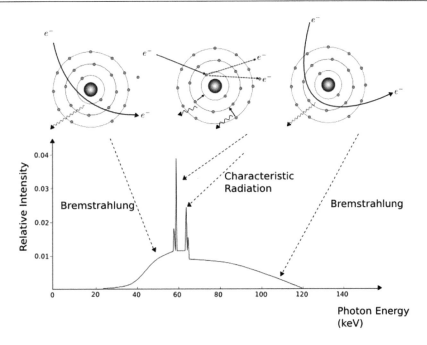

FIGURE 8.51   How X-rays are generated by a braking (or Bremsstrahlung) process.

Source: Used per Creative Commons Share Alike 4.0, International. User: Berger et al. (2018).

a stack of many boxes – the higher boxes would move down ("fall") to fill the void that the bottom box had once occupied. In atoms, however, when a higher-level electron "falls" to fill the void, energy is emitted equal to the energy difference between the two energy levels – the starting level and the ending level. This process results in the generation of an emitted X-ray photon. This type of X-ray production is called *characteristic* radiation since the emitted X-ray photon energy is characteristically unique to just one particular element. The other way that X-rays are formed happens when an accelerated electron from the cathode passes very near to a nucleus. Nuclei of atoms are very positive and can cause the accelerated, negatively charged electrons to dramatically slow down, much as a person is slowed when walking into a very strong wind. When this happens, the slowing electron releases energy as an X-ray photon and heat. This slowing process generates what is called *braking radiation* (or most commonly, the German word *Bremsstrahlung* is used). Braking radiation is much more common and accounts for most of the X-rays formed in a typical X-ray generation machine. These two methods of forming X-rays are shown in Figure 8.51.

After X-rays are formed, the X-ray machine focuses the photons into a narrow beam directed toward a person's body to produce an image of its internal structure. A camera, placed on the opposite side of the patient from the beam, records the X-ray photons which pass through the body.

Doctors typically view the pattern that the X-ray beam makes on the film as a negative – places where the most X-rays pass more easily through the body appear light, such as the soft tissues, while those areas that block or absorb more of the beams, such as bone and foreign objects in the body, show up darker.

8.3.5 Forensic Uses of Medical X-rays

One of the very first medical uses of X-rays came shortly after their discovery in 1895 when a bullet in the leg of a gunshot victim was located through an X-ray examination. Since then, X-rays have been a standard part of post-mortem examinations.

X-ray radiographs are typically taken at the outset of a physical examination of a body and assist in locating foreign objects within the body and in helping to determine the manner of death. Information from the X-ray scan can warn the pathologist that an unsuspected death may actually be suspicious and needs a more complete evaluation. These images may also help the pathologist determine the best way to carry out the autopsy so as to get the most information possible from the procedure.

However, additional uses for X-ray images in forensic settings have also been developed. X-rays are an important part of many medical treatments and form a permanent record of the course of treatment and the advance or healing of an illness or injury. When a person dies after injuries or illness, the deceased clinical X-ray images provide a picture of the progression of the problem in the patient and whether it led to their death. These same images are also forensically useful when a patient survives their injuries and assault charges are brought against a suspect. The documentation of these injuries can show whether the sustained injuries are consistent or inconsistent with the type of trauma expected from the way the attack occurred. For example, a particular cranial fracture seen on an X-ray scan can be shown to be inconsistent with an accidental fall as described by a suspect.

Smugglers of drugs and contraband occasionally try to conceal drugs or weapons within their bodies. Figure 8.52 shows an X-ray scan of a person carrying 38 capsules of cocaine in their stomach and intestines. These capsules were ingested before crossing the border and were not apparent from the typical border search. Of course, a big problem results when one or more of these containers ruptures or becomes lodged in a person's gastrointestinal tract, leading to other types of medical emergencies and forensic investigations.

X-ray images can also aid in the identification of human remains. This is usually done by comparing antemortem and post-mortem radiographs of unique anatomical features that can be matched. For example, radiographs can show the location of long-healed broken bones, congenital abnormalities, such as fused ribs, bone spurs, or disease processes, such as osteoporosis (Figure 8.53). They may also show the results of medical procedures and the presence of prosthetic devices within the body, such as rods and screws from broken bones, tooth implants, metal plates, replacement joints, and pacemakers (Figures 8.54 and 8.55). These features may be difficult to locate at autopsy. The X-ray images showing these features, taken at the time of autopsy, provide a permanent record that can be compared long after the examination has been completed with antemortem images that are later found.

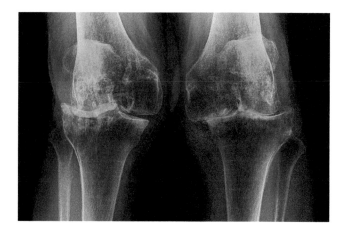

FIGURE 8.53 Knee osteoarthritis. Colored X-ray of the knees of an 87-year-old male patient with severe osteoarthritis. Osteoarthritis is a common degenerative disease characterized by a loss of the cartilage that lines the joints between bones.

Source: Dr. P. Marazzi/Science Photo Library. Used with permission.

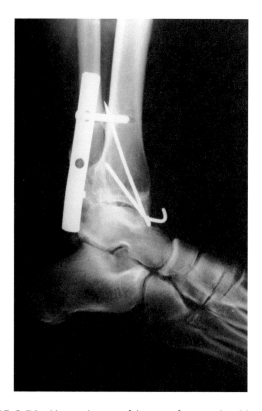

FIGURE 8.54 X-ray picture of human fractured ankle with a metal plate and screws to help the bone heal.

Source: Shutterstock.com.

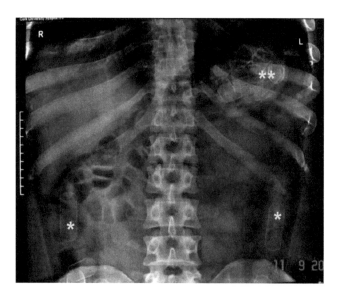

FIGURE 8.52 Radiograph of the abdominal area of a drug courier showing multiple capsules containing drugs in the intestines (the yellow markers **). The courier swallowed 38 capsules containing cocaine.

Source: Used per Creative Commons Attribution 2.0, Generic according to Pubmed central, Author: Jaqueline Kelly, Mark Corrigan, Ronan A. Cahill, and H.P. Redmond.

X-ray images can also be used to confirm the presence of diseases or injuries that either partially contributed to or were the cause of death of an individual. Some diseases that can be discerned from a radiograph include Marfan's syndrome (see

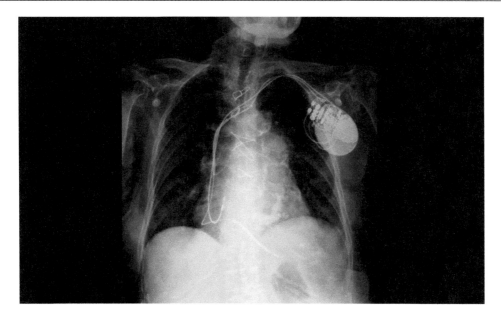

FIGURE 8.55 A chest X-ray of a patient who underwent surgical implantation of an artificial cardiac pacemaker device for creating heart impulses as needed.

Source: Shutterstock.com.

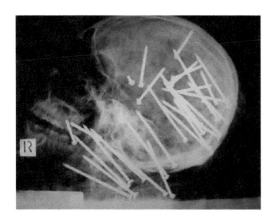

FIGURE 8.56 X-ray image of a homicide using a nail gun.

Source: **Photograph released to public by Sydney police department; from DiMaio (2015).**

FIGURE 8.57 X-ray image of an automatic weapon.

Source: Shutterstock.com.

Lincoln inset box), genetic diseases, and undiagnosed diseases (e.g., cancer, bone diseases, blood clots, etc.). Radiographs from a homicide using a power construction nail gun show the potential force of such a tool (Figure 8.56).

X-rays also provide information in forensic investigations beyond bodies. They are commonly used to visualize the inner mechanisms of firearms (Figure 8.57), to look inside sealed boxes and containers in search of explosives and contraband (Figure 8.58), and to inspect for damage to structures, even as large as buildings and bridges. X-ray analysis can also determine the compounds present in a sample, such as a paint chip, and whether a material has been chemically tampered with, as in chemically modified gemstones.

8.3.6 CT Imaging

An X-ray-based imaging method, called computerized tomography (CT) or sometimes computerized axial tomography (CAT), provides 3D X-ray images with remarkable detail. In this technique, a large number of "normal" 2D X-ray images are taken with slightly different orientations and then "stacked" in sequential order by a computer to recreate a detailed 3D picture of the structure of the body. This is similar to creating a 3D image of a loaf of bread by taking individual slices and stacking them in the correct sequence to "reconstruct" the original complete loaf of bread (Figure 8.59). The technique works similar to other X-ray imaging processes in which the X-ray beams are blocked by denser structures of the body. The various images used to create the final 3D pictures are generated by rotating the X-ray source and detectors around the body by small increments and taking a 2D X-ray image at each

angle to capture the different internal views ("slices of bread"). After these images are taken, the 3D picture is generated by computer reconstruction, a process known as tomography, and displayed as either a series of 2D or 3D images (putting the bread slices back together to make a 3D loaf). A typical CT image displaying a blunt force injury to the skull is shown in Figure 8.60.

FIGURE 8.58 X-ray display of pipe bomb.

Source: FAA. Photo from Security Training and Technical Resources.

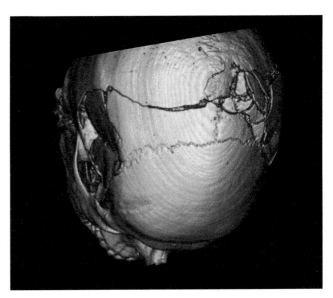

FIGURE 8.60 3D computed tomography (CT) scan of a skull with multiple traumatic fractures due to a traffic accident. The skull has fragmented at the vertex (upper right) and over the right temple (center left) with a crack running between these two areas.

Source: Zephyr/Science Photo Library. Used with permission.

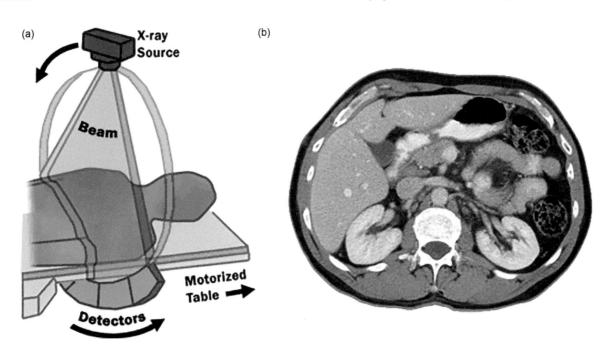

FIGURE 8.59 (a) Drawing of CT fan beam and patient in a CT imaging system, and (b) CT image of the abdomen.

Source: FDA.

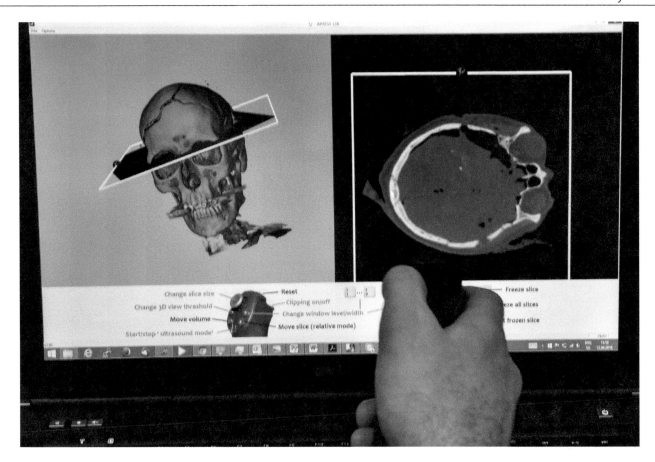

FIGURE 8.61   A 3D surface CT scan imagery to allow forensic analysis of a murder victim. The scans show a clear presentation of bullet entry and exit wounds, and the bullet's trajectory through the head.

Source: Zephyr/Science Photo Library. Used with permission.

A CT scan can provide a far more detailed image of the internal structures of the body than a simple 2D X-ray radiograph. The technique is particularly well suited for quick searches for internal injuries from trauma and for providing a permanent record of injuries. It can also provide the radiologist and forensic anthropologist with rapid and accurate information about bone damage and trauma, as shown in Figures 8.61 and 8.62. Additionally, a CT scan more accurately reveals the pathway of a projectile through the body by tracing its path through the various "slices," thereby helping in the reconstruction of the events of the crime.

In living patients, dyes can be injected into the blood to provide a better image of the blood vessels, which helps to show blockages, tumors, injuries, and other problems where blood vessels are involved more clearly. Recent work has even used these dye contrast agents in post-mortem examinations with good results.

8.3.7 Magnetic Resonance Imaging (MRI)

While the techniques employed in performing an autopsy have changed little in decades, new radiologic methods have the potential to become key tools in forensic pathology in the future. One of the most important of these techniques in forensic investigations involves something called *magnetic resonance imaging* (MRI). While MRI has in recent years become an essential tool in diagnostic medicine for the living, it is now finding its way into forensic work for the dead. The technique is a comparable newcomer when compared with X-ray scans, with the first MRI scan taken in 1977. Today, they are quite common, with a recent estimate of about 100 million scans performed worldwide annually, and the number is rapidly growing.

For living patients, the MRI imaging process clearly has some significant advantages over many other imaging techniques, such as X-ray methods, in that it does not employ potentially damaging ionizing radiation to form the image and is more sensitive than X-ray and CT scanning for soft tissues. Additionally, MRI is a non-invasive technique that can be performed as frequently as necessary, for example, to monitor the progress of treatment or the evolution of a disorder. Of particular value to both antemortem and post-mortem work is the feature that MRI images primarily show soft tissues; not only can internal structures (anatomy) be seen more clearly, but also biological functions (physiology) can be evaluated (see functional MRI, fMRI). Recent advances in computer

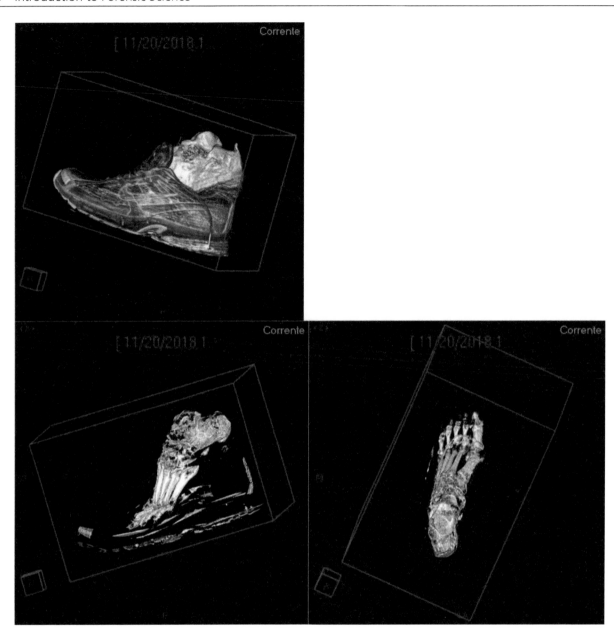

FIGURE 8.62   VR CT reconstruction showing skeletal segment (left ankle and footbones) in "running" shoe with loose laces.

Source: Pomara and Fineschi (2020).

processing speed and new superconducting magnetic materials are leading the way to less expensive instruments and even greater routine use of MRI imaging methods. In recognition of the importance of MRI scans to medicine, the 2003 Nobel Prize in Medicine was awarded to two researchers who were central to the development of the MRI technique for diagnostic medicine.

The application of MRI methods is now making significant contributions to forensic investigations, especially in characterizing and permanently recording physical injuries and internal anatomy. The technique is also being used, often in conjunction with X-ray/CT data, for rapid facial reconstructions that can lead to the identification of unknown discovered remains. To understand the growing role of MRI methods in forensic investigations, however, some understanding of the fundamental principles of the technique itself is necessary.

Underlying the MRI technique is a phenomenon usually referred to by scientists as nuclear magnetic resonance (NMR). The NMR technique has been used for chemical and biochemical investigations for many decades and has its own place in chemical forensic toxicology. Both the MRI and NMR techniques are based on the same principle: observing the magnetic properties of an atomic nucleus, most often hydrogen.

BOX 8.13   THE STORY OF A PROTON

A proton is one of the three elementary particles that make up an atom (along with the neutron and electron). The proton has a positive charge, which is equal and opposite to the electron's charge. It is about the same size as the electrically uncharged neutron and about 1,800 times more massive than the electron. Protons, along with neutrons, form the nucleus of an atom and are held together by very strong forces known as the *strong nuclear force*. When a proton is closely associated with a single electron, it forms a hydrogen atom, the most abundant element in the universe, constituting about 75% of all matter. Removing the electron to leave only the lone proton generates the positive hydrogen ion (H⁺).

Our bodies are principally composed of molecules that incorporate large amounts of hydrogen atoms within their chemical structures, such as proteins, carbohydrates, fats, and, of course, water (about 60% of an adult's body weight comes from water). These hydrogen atoms have a nucleus that consists solely of a single spinning, positively charged proton. From physics, we know that a spinning charged particle, such as a proton, generates its own tiny magnetic field. This proton spin may be considered to occur either in a clockwise or counterclockwise direction, as is shown in Figure 8.63. The result of these two spinning arrangements is the generation of small magnetic north and south poles pointing in opposite directions. In the absence of any magnetic field applied from outside of the nucleus (called the *external field*), all the hydrogen nuclei, regardless of the direction of their spins, are at the same energy, and these tiny magnets wobble randomly

around in every direction. When placed in a strong external magnetic field, however, things change, and the two different proton spins (clockwise and counterclockwise) end up at quite different energy levels. This is shown schematically in Figure 8.64. In the presence of this strong outside magnetic field (shown as a large red arrow in the figure), the individual little proton magnets may either align their own tiny magnetic poles roughly with (parallel) or against (antiparallel) this strong external field (actually, they wobble around the direction of the magnetic field like little wobbling tops). As might be expected, most of the proton magnets align themselves *with* the external field, but some opt for the higher energy arrangement and align themselves such that their little magnetic fields are against the external field. In a very simple analogy, the individual hydrogen nuclei magnets may be considered to act like little canoes. When a canoe is paddled on a windless day across a lake, it may move in any direction on the surface of the lake with equal ease. This is equivalent to the behavior of the little hydrogen magnets without any outside applied magnetic field. When our canoes are placed in a rapidly moving stream, however, the only two stable arrangements for the canoes are either paddling directly upstream or downstream. We know from experience that these two arrangements, while stable (e.g., the boat doesn't upset), also require very different energy input from the paddlers. Similarly, the proton magnets aligned *with* the external field (similar to paddling downstream with the current) are at a lower energy level than those aligned against the external field (similar to paddling upstream against the current). In the typical MRI setup, the energy difference between these two arrangements (ΔE, which is the difference in energy between the two "paddling" or magnetic arrangements) corresponds to the energy of radio frequency radiation. This means that "shining" radio frequency radiation on a little proton magnet aligned with the field (lower energy state) can cause it to "flip" its spin to the higher energy arrangement by absorbing the energy in the radio wave. When this spin "flip" occurs and the radio energy is absorbed, the nuclei are said to be in resonance with the applied radiation, hence the name nuclear magnetic resonance. The amount of energy required to perform this spin "flip" primarily depends upon the strength of the outside magnetic field that the individual hydrogen nucleus feels. A small external field strength corresponds to less energy required for the "flip" to occur while a larger

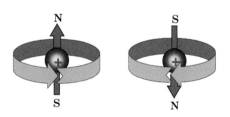

FIGURE 8.63   Generation of magnetic fields by oppositely spinning hydrogen nuclei.

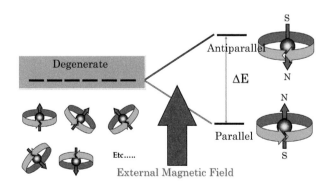

FIGURE 8.64   Energies of spinning protons before and after the introduction of a strong external magnetic field (large red arrow).

external field requires more energy to cause the spin "flip". In our canoe analogy, it's easier to change directions (upstream or downstream) in a stream with a slow current than with a swift current. It's actually a good deal more complicated than this simple description implies, but this picture presents a good approximation for understanding the basics of the MRI experiment.

BOX 8.14   BRIEF ON MRI

- Protons (hydrogen nuclei) are charged, spinning subatomic units.
- When a charged particle spins, it creates a magnetic field – the hydrogen atom forms a tiny magnet.
- Magnetic Resonance Imaging (MRI) probes the spin of hydrogen nuclei in the molecules containing hydrogen in our bodies.
- To gain an image, the body is placed in a very strong magnetic field, causing most of the magnetized hydrogen atoms to align with the external field.
- Radio frequency "light" is used to "bump" the tiny hydrogen magnets out of alignment and the amount of energy required for this provides information about the hydrogen-containing chemicals in the body.
- Using computer techniques, a 3D image of the soft tissues of the body is obtained (bone has little hydrogen so it is largely not involved in the image).

In real hydrogen-containing molecules, such as those found in the human body, the little hydrogen magnets often do not feel the full force of an applied external magnetic field due to the presence of other small nuclear magnets in their molecular vicinity. The 3D chemical structure of the molecule containing the hydrogen nucleus that we are observing controls the arrangement between the hydrogen atom we're measuring and all the other nuclear magnets surrounding it. In turn, this 3D chemical structure then determines how much of the external magnetic field penetrates to any particular hydrogen nucleus. A simple analogy for this would be if we were driving in a car without a windshield. In this case, we'd feel the full force of the wind upon us. But with the windshield in place, it blocks or screens some of the wind from reaching us, so that we feel a much-reduced wind force. In a similar fashion, neighboring atoms (tiny magnets) block some of the external magnetic field from reaching the hydrogen nucleus that we're measuring. Since the strength of the external field that a particular hydrogen feels determines how much energy is necessary to flip its spin, we can learn a great deal about the chemical "neighborhood" of the hydrogen by measuring how much energy is required to do the spin flip. If this energy measuring is done with 3D resolution, we can build up a detailed 3D picture of the different hydrogen-containing chemical environments within the body, particularly of the soft tissue. Detailed pictures of human anatomy and physiology can be developed using this method, leading to remarkable images, as shown in Figure 8.65.

BOX 8.15   WHAT'S WITH MR. IMAGING?

The term chemists and physicists use for magnetic resonance imaging (MRI) is nuclear magnetic resonance (NMR), since it looks at the magnetic properties of the nucleus. The medical world, however, has dropped the word "nuclear" from the title since this term scared some patients unnecessarily. Nonetheless, the two terms describe just about the same phenomenon.

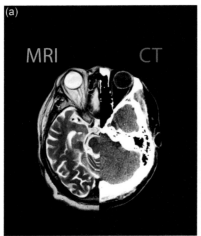
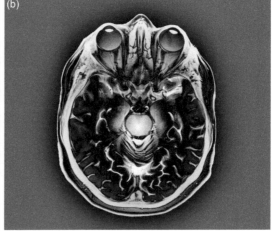

FIGURE 8.65   A comparison of a magnetic resonance image (a) and CT image (b) of a person's head. The MRI image provides a significantly better level of detail of the brain's soft tissues, while the CT provides greater detail of the bone structure.

Source: (a) Shutterstock.com. (b) Louise Murray/Science Photo Library. Used with permission.

In the real world, the MRI scan takes place in a machine where the body is placed in a long tube that moves it into a very strong magnetic field. A radio transmitter and receiver then use radio waves to look at the chemical "neighborhoods" of the different hydrogen atoms in the body and record the 3D information from these locations, much like a "molecular GPS". It is, of course, very important that no metal objects (e.g., watches, ferric implants, jewelry, etc.) are brought near the imager since the strong magnetic field will pull these objects toward it with a very strong force. Finally, a computer puts all the scanned information together to create the completed 3D scan of the body.

The application of MRI methods to forensic investigations has focused on four main areas: (1) supporting and extending autopsy work, (2) measuring and preserving biological information, (3) forming anatomical reconstructions, and (4) estimating the time of death.

The first of these areas involves MRI as a diagnostic tool in forensic pathology, either applied to a living patient (trauma victim) or for a minimally invasive autopsy (Figure 8.66). This is often desirable both from a time and information standpoint. For a living patient, it is sometimes necessary to accurately evaluate and document a person's internal injuries, especially brain and abdominal injuries from trauma. Trauma from assault or vehicle accidents is often best visualized by MRI. MRI is also an important tool when examining deceased individuals where tissues may be in a poor state of preservation or so highly decayed and fragile that a physical autopsy may not reveal the fine details of anatomical structures present.

MRI has also proven to be superior to autopsy in certain cases involving cranial, skeletal, or tissue trauma.

The second use of forensic MRI revolves around the technique's ability to provide an accurate and reliable method for measuring and presenting forensic pathology findings. MRI images can be used to visualize both internal and external structures and show very accurately the medical considerations often necessary in a criminal case (such as the trajectory of a gunshot projectile or the exact pathway of knife wounds through a body). MRI scans provide a permanent record of the anatomical, biological, and chemical data necessary to document pathology data. The technique can also quickly visualize organs that may be harder to get to during an autopsy, such as the brain. An example is shown in Figure 8.67. This may be particularly useful as an investigation evolves and heads in new directions, and also when a case is brought to trial (Figure 8.68).

A third forensic use of MRI involves 3D surface scanning as a basis for anatomical structure reconstructions. This is increasingly used in biological descriptions and facial reconstructions where the identity of a body is otherwise unknown or difficult to determine. When a badly decomposed body or bones are found, often the first problem is to determine the identity of the person. This challenge also arises in cases when the murderer has purposely destroyed facial features to thwart the identification of the body. In one older method used to identify unknown remains, the unidentified skull or its cast is used as the basis for a sculpted likeness of the person. This is done by applying layers of clay over the skull using clay thicknesses derived from measurements of human models (Chapter 9).

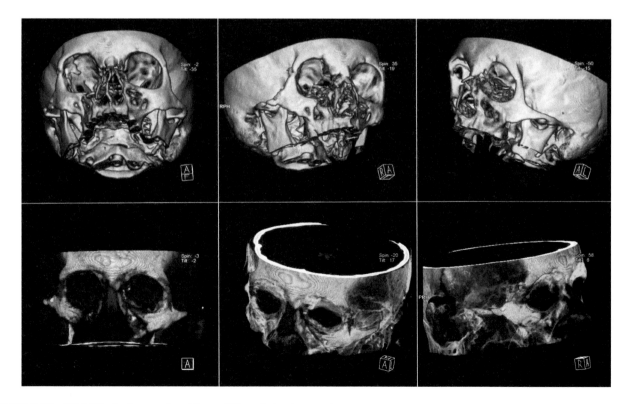

FIGURE 8.66 3D MRI of a human head from different viewing angles.

Source: istockphoto.com, Suljo.

Best guesses are made from available information, such as hair color, to prepare a final image that might hopefully be matched with a picture and description of a missing person. This is often a rather long, difficult, and costly process, requiring the talents of a skilled sculptor to render a reasonable likeness.

Recent methods, however, either employ X-ray CT or MRI data (or some combination of both together) in facial reconstruction. Using these computerized methods, a reasonable reconstruction may be accomplished within a few hours on a computer without extensive artistic skill. The method first 3D images the head and any remaining tissue. Tables of human facial tissue thicknesses and structures are combined with the 3D model of the scanned head. Textures are then mapped onto the model to provide color and other aesthetic features to render the final likeness. As an interesting example to illustrate the computerized reconstruction approach, a facial reconstruction of a 2,300-year-old mummy has been completed (Figure 8.69).

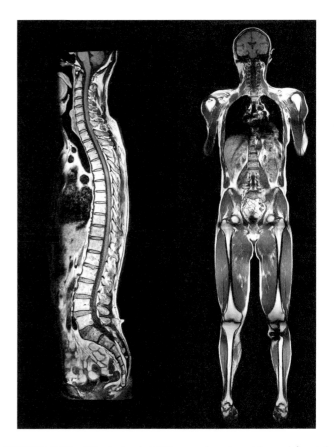

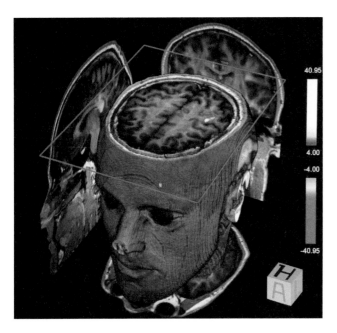

FIGURE 8.67 Advanced MRI brain scans. These magnetic resonance imaging (MRI) scans of a normal head and brain are: coronal (background), sagittal (left), 3D (center) and axial (below 3D model).

Source: Phillipe Psaila/Science Photo Library. Used with permission.

FIGURE 8.68 Whole-body MRI scan showing side and frontal images.

Source: Shutterstock.com.

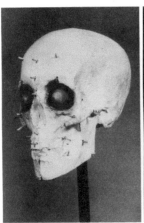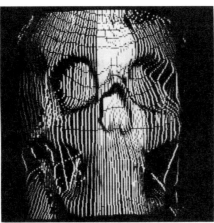

FIGURE 8.69 Reconstruction of the facial features of an Egyptian mummy by CT methods. The top picture is the mummy head in its current state of preservation. The pictures below the mummy head show the various stages of the computer-generated reconstruction, including mapping tissue onto the scanned skull and the addition of surface textures onto the reconstruction.

Source: Used with permission Elsevier. Vanezis (1989).

Finally, the MRI experiment can be used in some instances to provide and validate times of death by looking at post-mortem biochemical profiles within the remains. While still a controversial method, it has been used as an additional piece of information to support other more conventional time of death estimates.

BOX 8.16   THE COMING WAVE?

A variant of MRI is called functional MRI (or fMRI). Studies suggest that a person's emotional state can be determined by looking at fMRI images of the brain. One recent report suggests that these images can even reveal whether a person is being truthful or lying. While this type of analysis has yet to be admitted as evidence, attorneys are working to get fMRI data into court proceedings. The scientific evidence for the use of fMRI data in lie detection is still, however, under debate.

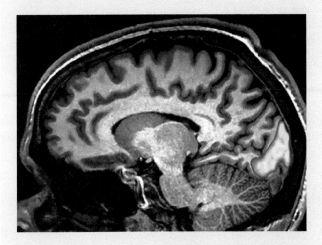

FIGURE 8.70   Functional MRI (fMRI) was obtained during the presentation of a visual stimulus to the subject while in the MRI unit. There is an observable activation of activity in the occipital brain lobe which is the primary visual cortex.

Source: Living Art Enterprises/Science Photo Library. Used with permission.

BOX 8.17   THE DANGEROUS OFFICE

In a recent case, a 50-year-old person had a history of upper neck pain diagnosed *via* MRI as resulting from a herniated cervical disk. It was successfully treated with steroid injections. Then, while sitting in a typical office swivel chair, it collapsed, and he fell backward, landing on his upper back. The person's neck pain recurred, but this time it was not treatable with injections, and he ultimately had to undergo surgery with vertebral fusion and metal plating. The case was brought, arguing that the

surgery resulted from the fall and defective chair. The defense team contended that it was merely the normal progression of a preexisting condition.

An MRI scan taken one year before the accident was compared with one right after the fall. The patient's legal team was able to demonstrate that the disc herniations were much worse afterward and not consistent with a normal disease progression expected during the short time elapsed between images. The patient was successful in their legal suit. A MRI scan of a typical neck region wth spinal stenosis is shown below.

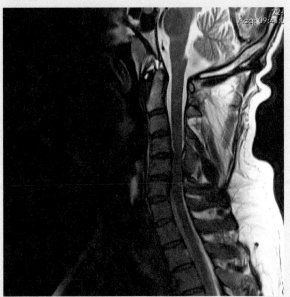

FIGURE 8.71   Neck MRI. The image shows a spinal stenosis – constriction of the nerve in the neck – near the top of the throat.

Source: Used per Creative Commons Share Alike 3.0, Unported, Attribution © Nevit Dilmen.

8.3.8 Virtual Autopsy: "Virtopsy"

A procedure has been developed, referred to as a virtual autopsy or "virtopsy," which is now widely used in forensic examinations. Its goal is to combine biomedical imaging techniques, such as CT and MRI, to form a permanent, highly detailed, and accurate representation of both external and internal structures, along with a biochemical profile of a body. The most comprehensive system currently utilizes a robot-guided process to map the body's external features, a CT scanner to visualize the denser internal parts of the body (e.g., bone, teeth, metal objects, etc.), and an MRI scanner to visualize the internal soft tissues and biochemical markers.

The virtual autopsy provides several useful features to the medical examiner including:

- A permanent 3D record of the anatomical, biological, and biochemical features of the body that can be revisited and reexamined even long after burial.
- Rapid assessment of the body for feedback to investigators before a complete autopsy can be accomplished.
- Opportunity to readily visualize difficult-to-see features that might be overlooked by a conventional autopsy.
- Estimate and validation of biochemical information such as the time since death (PMI).
- Clear information regarding the placement and trajectory of projectiles through the body's tissues.
- Detailed 3D surface "map" of the body for forensic reconstruction that can aid in the development of models to validate crime reconstructions.
- An acceptable way around the occasional objections to autopsies on religious, cultural, or conscience grounds without having to go to court to obtain permission (families and others have not been able to object to virtopsies).

Virtual autopsies form part of the permanent record of the body that stays behind long after the physical remains are gone. Once a medical examiner has completed their work through the destructive autopsy process, it is usually impossible to go back and either provide additional documentation or to reexamine specific portions of the body. With a virtual autopsy, however, the 3D scans preserve the evidence for reexamination at any time in the future, including providing the opportunity to go back to look more carefully at places that might take on added importance as an investigation continues.

BOX 8.18   THE VIRTUAL AUTOPSY TABLE

In an amazing advance of technology, a touch-interactive table has been developed that allows users to access CT and MRI data at the touch of a hand. By touching the table in a variety of ways, users can display imaging data from any orientation and as 3D images or 2D slides. Using this technique, pathologists can rapidly examine the body and discover conditions difficult to see with a conventional autopsy.

Medical imaging can be effective in showing a jury the extent and nature of injuries, sometimes far better than photographs taken at autopsy. Photographs from the autopsy are 2D images that sometimes can be difficult for a jury to understand, as well as potentially gruesome to their inexperienced eyes. The virtual autopsy provides complete 3D views that can be seen from any angle, slice, or orientation. In addition, the 3D anatomically accurate models of the person can be placed in a "virtual" crime scene to determine if the injuries are consistent with the story of the crime. For example, in a pedestrian-automobile accident, the highly accurate scan of the body can be placed in

various orientations relative to a scanned suspect car to see if the observed injuries are consistent with the proposed positioning. Another example could be positioning an anatomically accurate scan of a person's jaw and skull relative to bite mark injuries preserved on the MRI image.

The images can also be enhanced by angiography, injecting dye into the blood vessels to allow them to be very clearly seen (Figure 8.72). This approach is important in determining the cause of death from conditions such as stroke, heart disease, cerebral edema (swelling), blood embolism (blockage), trauma to the blood vessels, and other causes.

A virtual autopsy can sometimes serve as a good compromise between the legal need for evidence obtained from an autopsy and the wishes of the family against an autopsy based on religious or moral beliefs. Thus far, no legal objections to a virtopsy have been successful.

The virtual autopsy process can be very rapid. This can help alleviate the tension between the crime scene evidence unit, which wants to complete their site investigation before the autopsy, and the family and police, who would like the autopsy results as soon as possible. A virtopsy can provide preliminary findings or, in some cases, render a complete autopsy unnecessary.

As described in preceding sections, a virtual autopsy can reveal things that are normally difficult for a medical examiner to see. One study reported that a virtual autopsy was far better than the traditional autopsy for revealing some types of cranial, skeletal or tissue trauma. For example, emboli (tiny air bubbles in the bloodstream that can enter from a wound) are very difficult to observe visually and are destroyed during the autopsy. However, emboli can easily be seen and preserved as evidence in a virtual autopsy. Virtopsies can also be used to visualize water in the lungs, possibly from drowning, indicating that the person entered the water while still alive.

It is hoped that the virtual autopsy technique will increase the value of pathology evidence in court as well as lead to new autopsy techniques, such as "minimally invasive" autopsies (similar to "key-hole" minimally invasive surgical techniques now common in therapeutic medicine). However, virtopsy is far from a perfect technique and is very unlikely to soon replace the physical examination and autopsy. Many things uncovered by the pathologist at an autopsy are difficult to see in a virtual autopsy, such as poisoning, heart failure, and infarction.

Answer to the two-minute mystery: Assuming that all of the things mentioned in the case brief could be *proven*, then: (1) Manner: accidental; Primary Cause: metastatic cancer; Contributory Cause: fracture and chronic osteomyelitis [infection]; Mechanism: would be determined from the final few days of life and what was going on with the metastatic cancer (e.g., cardiac arrhythmia, dehydration, etc.). Also, in some jurisdictions, the manner determination of "therapeutic complications" is possible and may then be used here. Note, if the link between the event and the illness cannot be proven, then the manner would be natural. As a thoughtful ME once said: "As forensic pathologists, in the end, he who opines must prove."

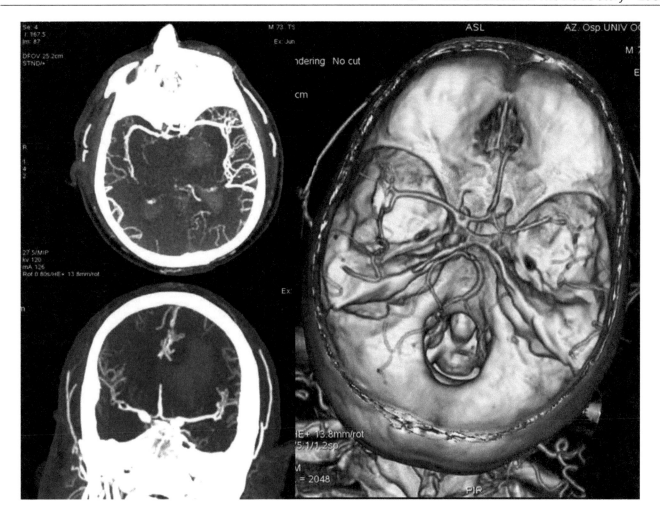

FIGURE 8.72   MRI reconstructions with the presence of contrast medium.

Pomara and Fineschi (2020)

QUESTIONS FOR FURTHER PRACTICE AND MASTERY

8.1   What is the difference between the cause of death and manner of death as determined by a forensic pathologist?

8.2   A body is discovered hanging in a home from an interior doorway. The victim has a pronounced blue skin color, burst blood vessels in the eyes, and inflated lungs. Forensic pathologists examine the rope marks on the neck and determined that they did NOT contain inflamed and bruised edges. The rope marks on the victim's neck are examined and found that they matched the rope found at the scene of the crime. What might you determine as the cause and manner of death? Explain your reasoning.

8.3   In the United States, we have both coroner and ME systems in operation. This has been a subject of intense debate. Describe the advantages and disadvantages of these two systems. Would you advocate for one system over the other; why or why not, which one and why?

8.4   Describe very briefly the chief functions of the following organs/organ systems. For each of these indicate one abnormality that might lead to a cause of death determination.
(a) heart
(b) liver
(c) pancreas
(d) gall bladder
(e) spleen
(f) pulmonary
(g) skeletal
(h) digestive

8.5   What are the six questions "posed" during an autopsy and how might they be answered?

8.6   What is the difference between blunt force and sharp force trauma?

DEFINITIONS. Questions 8.7–8.12: Provide a brief synopsis/description for each of the following. Focus on the forensically useful information.

8.7   Livor mortis, algor mortis, rigor mortis.
8.8   Forensic taphonomy.
8.9   Virtopsy.
8.10   Steps in an autopsy.
8.11   Cause, manner, and mechanism of death.
8.12   SIDS.
8.13   What are the two main branches of pathology?
8.14   What are the differences between a coroner and a medical examiner?
8.15   What are the medicolegal questions that must be answered in a death investigation?
8.16   What are the five categories typically used in a *manner of death* classification?
8.17   What is the distinction between murder and manslaughter?
8.18   Under what conditions might a medical examiner classify a manner of death as undetermined rather than assign a specific category?
8.19   What is the distinction between cause of death and mechanism of death?
8.20   What is a proximal (or contributory) cause of death? Give an example.
8.21   What is PMI?
8.22   What is rigor mortis? What muscles are affected first? When does it begin? How long does it last?
8.23   What is livor mortis?
8.24   For how long after death may the blood move freely in the body?
8.25   What is algor mortis? What is the average rate of body cooling over the first 12 hours post-mortem?
8.26   Under what circumstances would an autopsy be required?
8.27   What is a laceration?
8.28   What constitutes a penetrating wound?
8.29   What does the term *temporary cavitation* describe?
8.30   What are the four general types of entry wounds? What parameters are used to classify these entry wounds?
8.31   What is represented meant by bone beveling?
8.32   What is the difference between blunt force trauma and sharp force trauma? Give several examples of each.
8.33   Why is an autopsy of the lungs important when a victim is found underwater or at a fire scene?
8.34   What does the acronym DMORT stand for and what is the function of a DMORT team?
8.35   What is a virtopsy?
8.36   What is the difference between characteristic radiation and braking radiation?
8.37   What are some of the advantages of MRI over X-rays and CT scans?

8.38   What are the main areas of forensic investigations in which MRIs are used?
8.39   What are the advantages of a virtopsy over an autopsy?
8.40   What is meant by the term stippling?

EXTENSIVE QUESTIONS

8.41   Briefly describe the steps of an autopsy.
8.42   During an autopsy, a medical examiner will remove and examine the internal organs of the victim. Briefly describe what the medical examiner is looking for when examining the heart, the lungs, the liver and the kidneys.
8.43   Briefly describe the following imaging techniques: X-rays, CT scan, and sonography.
8.44   List some of the forensic uses of X-rays.

GLOSSARY OF TERMS

abdomen: the cavity in the human body that lies between the neck and the top of the pelvic cavity and is enclosed by the ribs and spine.

abrasion: a wound caused by rubbing or scraping an object across the skin, usually involving just the outer layers of the skin.

accidental death: the death of a person by unexpected, unintended or unusual external actions.

algor mortis: the cooling of the body after death.

Alzheimer's disease: a disease of progressive mental degeneration in later life due to degeneration of brain tissue.

anode: the positively charged electrode.

antemortem: the time prior to death.

artery: the part of the circulatory system that consists of muscular, elastic tubes that carry the blood away from the heart to the body.

asphyxia: a medical condition arising from a shortage of oxygen to tissues.

autopsy: a post-mortem examination of a body in an attempt to learn the cause and manner of death.

biomedical imaging: various techniques developed to visualize internal organs, structures, and tissues, usually noninvasively.

bladder: the organ that stores urine until it is released during urination.

blunt force trauma: a wound trauma that is caused by the impact of a non-penetrating object, such as from a bat, a car, or the fist.

brain: the controlling organ of the central nervous system.

cathode: the negatively charged electrode.

cause of death: the specific medical reason, agent, or event that causes a death.

circulatory system: the system of blood vessels that transports blood and lymph throughout the body (the lymph system is usually considered part of the circulatory system).

compartment syndrome: the medical condition that results from an increase in pressure within a confined portion of the body with restricted space, such as the brain confined within the skull.

computerized axial tomography (CAT): an imaging technique that employs multiple X-ray scans from slightly different perspectives that are assembled using computer methods to produce detailed images, including 3D images, of internal organs and tissues.

contact wound: the wound arising from a gunshot that occurs while the muzzle of the weapon is in direct contact with the body when fired.

contributing cause of death (proximal cause of death): the disease or injury that started the chain of events that ultimately leads to the death of a person.

contusion: a bruise that is usually caused by an impact that damages blood vessels and causes them to leak into the surrounding tissue.

coronary arteries: blood vessels that supply blood to the heart tissues themselves.

coroner: an official whose primary function is to investigate deaths. In the United States, this is usually an elected official without the requirement of medical or forensic training.

cranium: the skull.

decedent: the person who has died.

distal: farther away from the "center."

drowning: a death by submersion/immersion in water.

edema: a swelling from fluid accumulation.

electromagnetic radiation: radiation that consists of waves composed of oscillating perpendicular electric and magnetic fields. Electromagnetic radiation includes visible, infrared, ultraviolet, X-ray, radio, and other types of radiation.

embolism: an obstruction of a blood vessel.

entrance/exit wound: the location of the entry and exit points as a projectile travels through a body.

gall bladder: the saclike organ, connected to the liver, that stores and delivers bile.

gunshot: a penetrating wound from a high-velocity projectile ejected from a firearm or similar device.

heart: the organ that pumps blood through the body's circulatory system.

hematoma: an injury with a significant amount of blood collection outside of blood vessels.

homicide: the killing of one human being by another, whether by accident or on purpose.

incision: a cut wound that is longer than wide, usually caused by drawing a sharp object across the skin.

kidney: the urinary organ that helps regulate the body's water balance and clear unwanted chemicals from the body by excreting urine into the bladder.

kinetic energy: the energy associated with a moving mass that is equal to one-half of the object's mass times its velocity squared ($KE = \frac{1}{2} mv^2$): energy of motion.

laceration: a wound that occurs by tearing or when pressure splits open the skin to produce uneven wounds, such as from a blunt force impact.

large intestines: the lowest portion of the digestive tract, made up of the cecum, colon, and rectum, and located between the small intestines and the anus, that is primarily involved with waste elimination and water reabsorption.

ligature: a thread, rope, or cord.

liver: the large organ that is primarily involved in processing digestive waste products, filtering blood, formation of glycogen, and other metabolic processes.

lividity: the coloration in tissues from blood accumulation.

livor mortis: discoloration of parts of the body after death from the settling of the blood.

lungs: the large saclike organ that exchanges gases between the air and the blood through tiny blood capillaries.

magnetic resonance imaging (MRI): an imaging technique that uses a very strong magnetic field and radio waves to generate a detailed internal image of the organs, structures, and tissues of the body.

manner of death: the fashion and circumstances that resulted in a death, usually categorized into homicide, suicide, accidental, natural, or undetermined manners of death (possibly also therapeutic complications).

medical examiner: a specially trained medical physician charged with investigating deaths to determine the cause and manner of death.

medicolegal: the intersection of medical and legal practice, sometimes referred to as medical jurisprudence.

natural death: a death caused by natural processes, such as disease or old age.

pancreas: the organ that secretes digestive enzymes, especially insulin.

pathology: the study of diseases and how they change or harm tissues.

perimortem: The interval at or around the time of death.

permanent cavity damage (tissue crush): the injury and tissue damage that result from the direct impact of a projectile on tissue along its path as it travels through the tissue.

emission tomography: an imaging technique that employs radioactive tracers that emit a positron (opposite of an electron or beta particle). When emitted, the positron quickly encounters an electron and the two annihilate each other to create a pair of gamma photons that can be detected to locate the radioactive tracer in the body. The technique is used to create a detailed 3D image of internal organs and tissues.

post-mortem: the time after death.

post-mortem interval (PMS): the time elapsed between an actual death and the time that the body is found.

proximal: closest to the "center."

puncture wound: a cut or piercing wound that is wider than long, caused by a stabbing motion with a pointed object.

radiograph: the image produced on a detector or film from radiation passing through an object, such as a body.

radiology: the study and use of various types of radiation for the observation, diagnosis, and treatment of disease and injury.

reproductive system: the organs involved in sexual reproduction by producing and delivering gametes and their later development into a new organism.

rigor mortis: a stiffening of the muscles and joints in the body after death.

stab wound: see puncture wound.

sharp force trauma: the penetrating injury caused by an object having a sharp edge.

small intestines: the part of the digestive tract, located between the stomach and the large intestines, where nutrients from digested food are absorbed into the bloodstream.

spleen: the organ that is involved in the production and removal of the various blood cells; part of the immune system.

stomach: the organ primarily involved in the initial digestive processes of food.

suicide: the action of killing oneself with the intent to die as a result of the action.

taphonomy: the study of processes that affect decomposition of remains after death, such as the extent of burial, post-mortem movement or disturbance of the remains, or the effect of environmental conditions on decomposition.

temporary cavitation damage: the injury and tissue damage that arise from the briefly formed cavity behind a projectile as it moves at high velocity through tissue by pushing the tissue outward and away from its path.

therapeutic complication: a death or injury that results from unexpected medical outcomes or from deviations from normal medical practices.

thoracoabdominal cavity: the largest cavity in the human body that lies between the neck and the top of the pelvic cavity, surrounded by the abdominal muscles and the vertebral column.

thorax: the cavity in the human body that lies between the neck and the diaphragm, surrounded by the abdominal muscles and the backbone.

ultrasound imaging: the use of high-frequency sound waves to image internal structures of the body.

urinary system: the body's organ systems that are involved in the elimination of urine, including the kidneys, ureters, bladder, and urethra.

v: the part of the circulatory system that consists of tubes that carry the blood toward the lungs.

virtual autopsy (virtopsy): a non-invasive autopsy method that uses various types of biomedical imaging to produce and manipulate both external and internal images of the body.

X-ray: a high-energy form of electromagnetic radiation with wavelengths in the range of 0.01–10 nm.

Y-incision: a commonly employed initial cut to open the body cavity for an autopsy examination.

BIBLIOGRAPHY

Lester Adelson, *The Pathology of Homicide*, Charles C Thomas Publisher Ltd., 1974.

Kenneth Alonso and Carmen Alonso, *Forensic Pathology: An Overview*, Allegro Press, 1997.

M. Berger, Q. Yang, and A. Maier, Chapter 7: X-ray Imaging. In: Andreas Maier, Stefan Steidl, Vincent Christlein, and Joachim Honrnegger (Eds.), *Medical Imaging Systems: An Introductory Guide*. Cham: Springer, 2018.

Robert Calaluce and Jay Dix, *Guide to Forensic Pathology*, CRC Press, 1999.

Charles A. Catanese, *Color Atlas of Forensic Medicine and Pathology*, CRC Press, 2016.

Claire Datnow and Boris Datnow, *The Final Diagnosis: What Autopsies Reveal about Life and Death*, Media Mint Publishing, 2010.

Vincent J.M. Di Maio, *Gunshot Wounds: Practical Aspects of Firearms, Ballistics, and Forensic Techniques* (3rd Ed.), Taylor & Francis and CRC Press, 2015, 251.

Vincent Di Maio and Suzanna E. Dana, *Handbook of Forensic Pathology* (2nd Ed.), CRC Press, 2006.

Dominick Di Maio and Vincent Di Maio, *Forensic Pathology* (2nd Ed.), CRC Press, 2001.

Jay Dix, *Forensic Pathology: A Color Atlas*, CRC Press, 1999.

David Dolinak, Evan Matshes, and Emma O. Lew, *Forensic Pathology: Principles and Practice*, Academic Press, 2005.

John Gall and Jason Payne-James, *Current Practice in Forensic Medicine*, Wiley, 2011.

Helen Gelband, Prabhat Jha, Ramanan Laxminarayan, and Susan Horton (Eds.), *Cancer. Disease Control Priorities* (3rd Ed), volume 3, World Bank, 2015. http://dx.doi.org/10.1596/978-1-4648-0349-9

Felix Gremse, Oliver Krone, Mirko Thamm, Fabian Kiessling, Rene H. Tolba, Sigfried Rieger, Carl Gremse, "Performance of lead-free versus lead-based hunting ammunition in ballistic soap", *PLoS One*, 9(7), e102015, 2014. https://doi.org/10.1371/journal.pone.0102015; https://journals.plos.org/plosone/article?id=10.1371/journal.pone.0102015

Mehmet Y. Iscan and Richard P. Helmer (Eds.), *Forensic Analysis of the Skull: Craniofacial Analysis, Reconstruction, and Identification*, Wiley-Liss, 1993.

Kenneth D. Kochanek, Sherry, L. Murphy, Jiaquan Xu, and Elizabeth Arias, Source: Deaths: Final Data for 2017. *National Vital Statistics Reports* 68(9). Hyattsville, MD: National Center for Health Statistics, 2019.

Angela D. Levy and H. Theodore Hackle, Jr., *Essentials of Forensic Imaging: A Text-Atlas*, CRC Press, 2010.

John J. Miletich and Tia L. Lindstrom, *An Introduction to the Work of a Medical Examiner: From Death Scene to Autopsy Suite*, Praeger Press, 2010.

Arialdi M. Miniño, Elizabeth Arias, Kenneth D. Kochanek, Sherry L. Murphy, Betty L. Smith, National Vital Statistics Report, Vol. 50, No. 15, September 16, 2002.

Jason Payne-James, Richard Jones, Steven Karch, and John Manlove, *Simpson's Forensic Medicine* (13th Ed.), Hodder Arnold Publishers, 2011.

Cristoforo Pomara and Vittorio Fineschi, *Forensic and Clinical Forensic Autopsy* (2nd Ed.), CRC Press, 2020.

Cristoforo Pomara, Steven B. Karch, and Vittorio Fineschi (Eds.), *Forensic Autopsy: A Handbook and Atlas*, CRC Press, 2010.

Michael J. Shkrum and David A. Ramsay, *Forensic Pathology of Trauma*, Springer, 2006.

Werner U. Spitz and Daniel J. Spitz, *Spitz and Fisher's Medicolegal Investigations of Death: Guidelines for the Application of Pathology to Crime Investigation* (4th Ed.), Charles C Thomas Publisher Ltd., 2005.

Michael J. Thali, Mark D. Vinter, and B. G. Brogdon, *Brogdon's Forensic Radiology* (2nd Ed.), CRC Press, 2010.

Peter Vanezis, R.W. Blowes, A.D. Linney, A.C. Tan, R. Richards, and R. Neave, "Application of 3-D computer graphics for facial reconstruction and comparison with sculpting techniques", *Forensic Science International*, 42, 69–84, 1989.

David J. Williams, Anthony J. Ansford, David S. Priday, and Alex S. Forest, *Forensic Pathology (Colour Guide)*, Churchill Livingstone, 1998.

Joseph J. Woodward In William J. Maloney, *The Medical Lives of History's Famous People*, Bentham Science Publishers, 2014. [ISBN 9781608059379].

Forensic Anthropology

9

9.1 FORENSIC ANTHROPOLOGY: THE ENDURING RECORD

LEARNING GOALS AND OBJECTIVES

Forensic anthropology can provide valuable answers in an investigation involving human remains. After studying this chapter on forensic anthropology, you should be able to:

- Label the structures and explain the functions of the bones of the human body.
- Discuss how to determine if an object is bone or not.
- Show how to determine if a bone is human bone.
- Explain how the age of a bone might be determined.
- Describe how to construct a biological profile from skeletal remains.
- Discuss how an expert might prepare a facial reconstruction from a skull.
- Discuss how to gain insight into how someone died by examining their bones.
- Explain how to process a crime scene containing skeletal remains.
- Discuss what is meant by forensic taphonomy.

9.1.1 Background and Introduction

The field of anthropology deals specifically with the study of human societies, cultures, and civilizations. This broad field has been divided into several sub-disciplines, including biological (or physical) anthropology, archaeology, cultural anthropology, linguistics, and, most recently, applied anthropology. Biological anthropology deals with understanding the physical features of human beings through the study of human adaptation, variability, genetics, and evolution. Cultural anthropology looks at the cultural and organizational aspects of human civilizations, while linguistics seeks to understand more fully the various ways that humans communicate, both across cultures and across time. Archaeology uses artifacts to understand past human activities and societies. Applied anthropology cuts across many of these sub-disciplines to inform contemporary human problems. Since much of forensic science deals specifically with human behavior, it should not be surprising that several branches of anthropology have become particularly valuable in understanding the interface between humans and the laws of their culture.

While anthropology can indeed help inform legal issues, the field of forensic anthropology has come to primarily focus on the analysis of human skeletal remains for personal identification and understanding unexplained deaths. This quite natural fit arises from the need for anthropologists to intimately understand the human skeleton in investigations of past peoples and civilizations. Typically, when scientists seek to unravel the secrets of long past civilizations, only the artifacts and human bones from these peoples remain. Archaeologists have developed a superb set of tools and techniques for excavating, cataloging, and understanding these artifacts and bone remains. There is a close similarity in intent, approach, and technique between their investigations of ancient burial sites and modern homicide investigations. Thus, many of the tools used by forensic anthropologists today are directly "borrowed" from the tools employed in archaeological investigations.

BOX 9.1   BRIEF ON ANTHROPOLOGY

1. Anthropology is the study of humans and their cultures and civilizations.
2. Anthropology is divided into five sub-disciplines: biological, cultural, linguistics, archaeology, and applied anthropology.
3. Forensic anthropology is the application of anthropological methods and techniques to legal questions and is largely focused on understanding human skeletal remains.
4. Forensic anthropology employs tools from several disciplines, including archaeology and biological anthropology.

DOI: 10.4324/9781003183709-11

9.1.2 Information Provided by Forensic Anthropology

Human remains in varying states of decay, especially in their skeletonized state with only the bones and teeth remaining, are often all that investigators have available to try to piece together the sequence of events leading to the death of the individual. These remains are often accidentally discovered by hunters or hikers, during digging projects for new building and road construction, and in a variety of other unexpected places. The questions that investigators would like answered when faced with skeletonized remains are very similar to those posed by forensic pathologists during an autopsy (Chapter 8): who do these remains belong to, when did they die, how did they die (cause), if violence was involved, what was the cause of death, and who did this to the person?

So, what's first? Before these questions about human remains can be considered, we need a more detailed understanding of bones and teeth themselves. Forensic anthropologists have an intimate working understanding of the development, morphology (shapes and sizes), function, and variation of human bones across human cultures.

9.1.3 Human Skeletal Anatomy

The hard and rigid human skeleton provides the mechanical and structural framework necessary to support the rest of the human body. The beauty of our internal skeletal system (endoskeleton) lies in the fact that, while providing this rigid "architectural" structure and protection for our internal organs, it is also amazingly lightweight and allows for easy movement, flexibility, and resiliency. Bones come in an enormous variety of shapes and sizes, tailored to their specific location and function within the body. They are superb examples of form fitting their required function. In addition to their structural importance, bones also produce blood cells, store minerals, protect against excessive acid-base shifts in our blood, and even help in our hearing.

Bones are not simply solid rods forming an internal framework; they are actually complex organs composed of an array of different tissues and components, each contributing a necessary feature to the form and function of the bone. A bone is not a "dead" component but a vibrantly alive organ. The largest component of bones is the mineralized osseous tissues - tissues that have become hardened by a process of mineralization (formation of inorganic minerals). These "matrix" tissues are composed primarily of a form of calcium phosphate, called hydroxyapatite [$Ca_{10}(PO_4)_6(OH)_2$], and comprise about 70% of the mass of a typical bone (a matrix is a material in which something may be attached, embedded, or enclosed). This material gives the bone its enormous strength and structural rigidity. The bone matrix also contains an organic portion called collagen (Figure 9.1). Collagen is the most abundant protein in the body (about 25% of the body's protein content) and forms long, dense fibers extending through the bone matrix, adding to the bone's structural strength. Collagen,

FIGURE 9.1 Compact bone lamellae. A scanning electron micrograph of bony lamellae in the femur (thigh bone). These structures are found in compact bone and are made of compacted collagen fibers and ground substances. The cells responsible for compact collage fiber production are known as osteoblasts. During bone formation, osteoblasts lay down a bone matrix in a lamellar, sheet-like form which is subsequently mineralized by the formation of calcium phosphate crystals. Most of these lamellae are concentrically arranged around pre-existing blood vessels.

Source: Prof. P. Motta/Dept. of Anatomy/University "La Sapienza," Rome/Science Photo Library. Used with permission.

however, also imparts a significant amount of elasticity, or ability to deform without breaking, to the bones. Bones also consist of living cells and tissues embedded throughout this inorganic calcium phosphate and collagen matrix.

BOX 9.2   FORENSIC ANTHROPOLOGY BONE TERMS

DIRECTIONS (ANATOMICAL)

Proximal: toward or closer to the head or trunk of the body.

Distal: away or farther from the head or trunk of the body.

Superior (cranial): upper.

Inferior (caudal): lower.

Anterior (ventral): front.

Posterior (dorsal): rear.

Matrix: a material in which something may be embedded, enclosed, or attached.

Medial: toward the midline.

Lateral: away from the midline.

Longitudinal: aligned in a head-to-foot fashion.

Sagittal: from front to back.

Superficial: toward the surface.

Deep: away from the surface.

BONE-RELATED PARTS

Diaphysis: shaft of a long bone.

Epiphysis: part of a bone naturally separated from the main body of the bone.

Metaphysis: part of the bone lying between diaphysis and epiphysis.

Cartilage: tough, smooth, flexible connective tissue often found lining joints.

Foramen: opening in the bone.

Sinus: cavity in the bone.

Crest: a ridge.

Process: a projection or bump.

The outer portion of a bone, comprising up to 80% of the bone's total mass, consists of a relatively dense packing of the matrix to form compact bone (sometimes called cortical bone). This *compact bone* is very hard and composed of tightly packed layers with relatively few spaces between layers (Figure 9.1). The interior of a bone is, by contrast, considerably less dense and provides spaces for cellular components and blood vessels. This less dense bone is often called *spongy bone* (also called *trabecular* or *cancellous bone*, Figures 9.2 and 9.3). This honeycomb-like material provides a strong, rigid structure while remaining lightweight. It also provides plenty of open spaces where bone marrow, blood vessels, and other cellular components may reside.

The spongy bone contains blood vessels and *osteocyte* cells, the mature bone cells. These osteocytes have the primary functions of both forming mineralized bone and maintaining healthy bone, a continuous lifelong process of "remodeling" bone. Two other types of cells are important in bone development: osteoblasts and osteoclasts. *Osteoblasts* are responsible for the formation of new bones, while *osteoclasts* are responsible for the removal (resorption) of the bone. There is a continuous transfer of

materials between the blood, the bone's cellular components, and the matrix. Throughout life, the osteoclasts continually remove old bone, while the osteoblasts reform new bone in its place, a continual process of removal and reformation.

The interior spongy bone contains two additional types of cellular tissue: yellow and red marrow. The red marrow, mostly found at the end of the bones nearest to the trunk of the body (proximal), forms the body's red blood cells, platelets, and a large portion of the white blood cells. Because of this, bone marrow is very important to our circulatory and immune systems (Chapter 6). The yellow marrow, found throughout the long shafts of bones, is composed of fat and blood cells that also engage in the production of white blood cells (Figure 9.4). A typical leg bone alone may contain over 400 billion marrow cells!

Bones are formed early in the development of a fetus by the mineralization of newly formed cartilage. A child is born with about 300 bones, many mostly made up of cartilage. Over time, many of these ultimately harden (ossify) and fuse together during childhood and adolescence, resulting in the 206 bones of an adult human. Bones are generally categorized into one of five types (Figure 9.5).

1. **Long Bones**: Where the length is much greater than the width. Most of the bones of our arms, legs, ribs, fingers, and toes are these types of bones (except the wrist, ankle, and kneecap). They generally are mostly compact bone with less spongy bone and marrow than other types. They grow by elongation of the shafts and are capped at the ends with epiphyses that usually fuse and stop growing by adulthood.

2. **Short Bones**: Bones that are about as wide as they are tall and appear as roughly spherical or cubic shaped bones, such as in the ankle and wrist, composed mostly of spongy bone with a thin layer of compact bone on the outside.

3. **Flat Bones**: Typically curved and flat. These bones have primarily either a protective or an attachment function, such as the skull, pelvis, and scapula (shoulder blade). In adults, this is where most of a person's red blood cells are manufactured.

4. **Sesamoid Bones**: This type of very specialized bone, named for its resemblance to a sesame seed, is embedded within tendons and functions to cover a joint. The kneecap (patella) is an example of this type of bone.

5. **Irregular Bones**: These are bones that don't easily fall into one of the other categories. Like the flat bones, these are mostly spongy bone with a thin compact outer bone layer. They are used for support and protection, such as in the vertebrae, or the attachment of muscles, such as the sacrum and hyoid bone (connection of the tongue to the body).

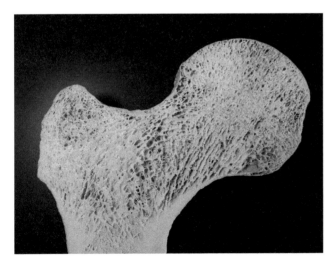

FIGURE 9.2 An inner view of a leg bone (femur) shows that it is made of two different types of bone. The outside edges are compact bone, and the inside part is composed of spongy bone.

Source: Wikipedia/MAKY.OREL.

The skeleton is often divided into two main groupings: the *axial* skeleton, involving the head, neck and trunk, and the *appendicular* skeleton that includes the limbs (Figure 9.6). These bones function structurally through a complex system of

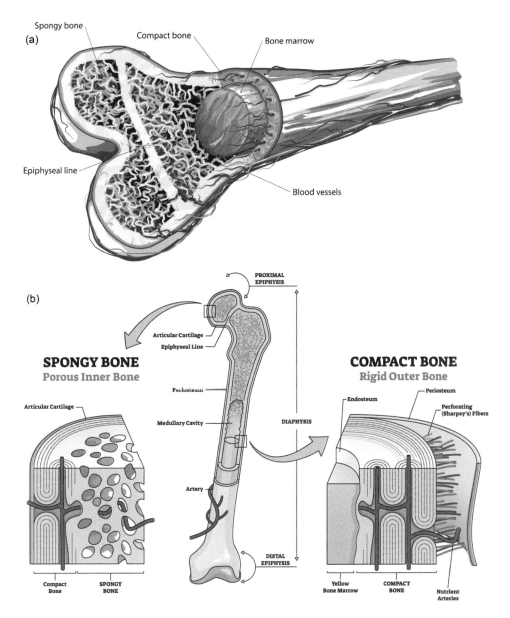

FIGURE 9.3 (a) Structure and anatomy of a typical human bone, and (b) close-up structure of spongy and compact bone.

Source: Images courtesy Shutterstock.com.

connective tissues and muscles. The bones meet at joints, held together by very strong *tendons* (connecting muscles to bone) and *ligaments* (connecting bone to bone), to provide mobility, stability, and flexibility. These strong connective tissues are composed primarily of collagen. Cartilage, also largely made up of collagen and other proteins, is a smooth, slippery substance that allows bones to glide past each other easily, and is usually found at the junctions of bones, cushioning the points of contact. Muscles are tissues that can expand and contract to produce motion of the skeletal framework and compose about 40–50% of the total mass of an adult male and 30–40% for an adult female.

The forensic anthropologist first needs to understand the form and function of each bone in a healthy person in order to gain useful information relevant to a forensic setting.

9.1.4 Five Central Questions of Forensic Anthropology

When faced with an unknown object that is suspected to be a bone and, therefore, of potential forensic interest, investigators and medical examiners often turn to the forensic anthropologist to provide answers to five critical questions: (1) Is it bone? (2) Is it human bone? (3) How old is it? (4) Whose bone is it? and (5) How did they die? The path of the legal investigation often hangs upon finding answers to these key questions.

QUESTION ONE: Is It Bone? One of the first questions that often needs to be answered when examining a recovered item from a crime scene is whether it is bone, tooth, or another hard material. While this sounds like an easy question

SYNOVIAL JOINT

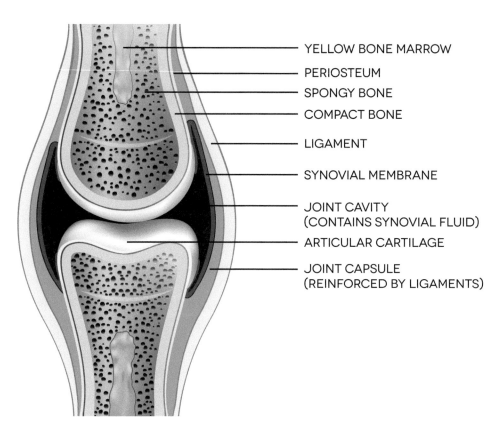

YELLOW BONE MARROW
PERIOSTEUM
SPONGY BONE
COMPACT BONE
LIGAMENT
SYNOVIAL MEMBRANE
JOINT CAVITY
(CONTAINS SYNOVIAL FLUID)
ARTICULAR CARTILAGE
JOINT CAPSULE
(REINFORCED BY LIGAMENTS)

FIGURE 9.4   Bone joint structure, showing bone marrow and cartilage.

Source: Shutterstock.com.

to answer, it can pose some difficult challenges. If the bone is relatively complete and intact, the question may be quite easily resolved simply by comparing the size, shape, and structure of the object with known human bones. The observation of compact and spongy bone, along with some other telltale features such as joints, cartilage, or processes (projections), may provide useful information. Remains that have been weathered for some time or have been subjected to physical damage by the elements, fire, or animals, however, are often broken and fragmented into very small pieces. In this case, a weathered bone may look a great deal like stone, pottery, or other non-bone materials. Simple comparisons, in this case, are not particularly helpful and may even be misleading.

So, how can an anthropologist answer the question of whether a small shard of material is truly bone? Probably the best way is to examine the microscopic features of the material to see if it contains structures identifiable as unique to bone. As shown in Figure 9.7, bones have detailed microscopic structures, such as blood vessels, bone cell groupings (osteons), and layers of bone, that are lacking in other materials. By examining a cross-section of the material in question, it is usually possible to learn if it is bone or not.

QUESTION TWO: Is It Human? Once an object has been identified as a bone, the next issue is to resolve whether it is

human bone or not. Often it is not necessary to determine which specific animal a bone comes from but just whether or not the fragment is of human origin.

BOX 9.3   THE CASE OF THE "COBBLER'S BASEMENT"

In 1943, a Cincinnati cobbler was accused of luring a young girl into his basement shop and brutally killing her. In the course of the ensuing investigation, the earthen basement shop floor was excavated, and a large collection of bones were recovered – at least 18 recognizable bones and a collection of ribs were found (similar to those shown in Figure 9.8). This array of bones seemed to incriminate the cobbler in a number of other recent unsolved crimes in the area, especially since the pervasive thinking at the time was that crimes of this nature tended to be repeated, further "implicating" the cobbler. An eminent anthropologist at the University of Chicago, Prof. Wilton M. Krogman, was asked to examine the remains and determine the identity and origin of the bones. He identified them as coming from a cow, five sheep, a turkey or goose, a rat, a pigeon, and an owl – none were found to be human.

TYPES OF BONES

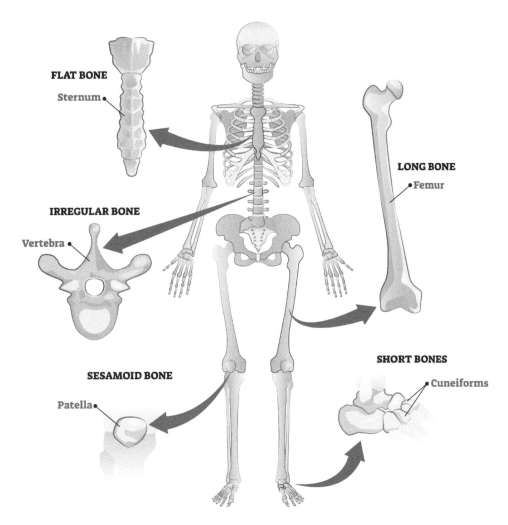

FLAT BONE
Sternum

IRREGULAR BONE
Vertebra

SESAMOID BONE
Patella

LONG BONE
Femur

SHORT BONES
Cuneiforms

FIGURE 9.5   Structures of various types of bone.

Source: Shutterstock.com.

In general, there are at least two reliable methods used in determining whether a bone is human or not: macroscopic and microscopic examination. An examination of the large-scale, macroscopic features of a bone includes observing a bone's size, shape, and structure, usually by visual inspection. An expert trained in the intricacies of the human skeleton, such as a forensic anthropologist, can often quickly eliminate bones as not belonging to humans, especially if the bone contains a joint. It is rather common, however, for non-experts to be fooled into thinking unearthed remains are human and require a police investigation. For example, the de-clawed "hands" of the black bear are remarkably similar in skeletonized form to those of a human. These remains frequently cause alarm when found in trash or in the woods since they arise when hunters "field clean" a fresh hide in the woods by skinning the animal. In this process, they typically sever the hands and feet from the body but keep them attached to the hide, leaving the delicate job of removing the hands and feet for later. At home, they complete the process by removing the hand and foot bones and simply discarding them without the claws. The similarity of the bear "hand" bone to human hand bones can be seen in Figure 9.9.

There are times, however, when the piece of bone of concern is either of ambiguous origin or the fragment is too small to make a clear identification based simply on the gross physical structure of the bone. In this case, a microscopic examination can usually eliminate non-human from human bones. While it can be difficult to determine which particular animal a bone belonged to, its identification as a human bone can be relatively certain - and this is usually good enough for the investigators. An example is shown in Figure 9.10 comparing a human bone, bird bone, and cow bone in microscopic cross-section. Work, however, remains to be done to allow this system of identification to be foolproof.

QUESTION THREE: How Old Is the Bone? Once a bone has been determined to be of human origin, the next question often is, "Are these remains of current legal concern?" For example, human bones are occasionally discovered when

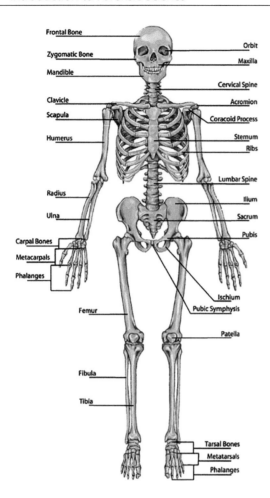

FIGURE 9.6 Anterior (front) view of adult skeletal bones. The axial (framework) bones include the spine and skull, while the appendicular bones are those attached to this framework, such as leg, arm, collar, and pelvic bones.

Source: Shutterstock.com.

digging in the garden or at a construction site. The immediate issue is often whether these bones are of historical or current legal interest. Bones are an enduring legacy of the human body and can remain intact for many centuries when buried under certain conditions. Thus, dating the remains becomes of interest. These "accidental" discoveries often arise because in earlier times, or through neglect of burial sites, burials might not have been marked or the markers have been lost or destroyed. These remains are usually not of legal interest but could be of keen interest regarding legal ownership of the remains. The question is then, how can these older bones be differentiated from more modern remains?

One particularly useful tool is to evaluate the context of the remains; where were they found? Sometimes, objects found with the remains give clear clues. Buttons, tools, coffin nails, and other durable artifacts can often be dated to provide burial timelines. For example, one investigator noticed that green stains were sometimes found on skulls of presumed older burials. These green stains were later determined to arise from a colonial American practice of wrapping the body for burial with a long cloth sheet that was fastened with a copper clip at

the head. Over time, the copper clip oxidized completely away, leaving only the characteristic green stain behind, similar to the color seen on the "skin" of the Statue of Liberty.

BOX 9.4   INDIGENOUS NATIVE AMERICAN SKULL AT A CONSTRUCTION SITE

In 2007, construction workers in California were excavating for a new home foundation when they exposed a human skull. The Los Angeles County Coroner's Office was called, and a "skeletal" team with professional forensic anthropologist, Prof. Beth Miller, was sent to investigate. Dr. Miller was able to determine that the skull was not recent but rather was "prehistoric" remains and not of medicolegal forensic interest. This was determined by examination of the remains' condition (e.g., brittleness, color, etc.), tooth wear from a prehistoric diet, scene context, and facial characteristics. The best guess was that the remains were of an indigenous Chumash Native American from <1,000 years ago.

Sometimes, the remains are just so brittle or decayed that only the passage of a very long time could have caused this level of deterioration. Occasionally, remains of discarded archaeological "souvenirs" or medical samples are found and cause concern. These discoveries, however, can usually be differentiated, and the investigation brought to a quick close (e.g., clean saw marks and clasps on the skull for medical student education). Other clues arising from the bones themselves can be quite helpful in determining the time since death, such as: the odor of the bones and its intensity, the presence of any remaining "soft" parts attached to the bone, the presence of vegetation growing in, on, or through the bone, tooth marks, stains/bleaching of the bones, and the presence of insect life around the remains (see Chapter 10 on forensic ecology).

QUESTION FOUR: **Whose Bone Is It? Biological Profile**. Once a bone has been determined to be of relatively recent human origin, the investigation quickly focuses on the identity of the person. Investigators often don't have a good idea regarding the identity of remains when they are found. Given the strengths of DNA science in answering such identification questions, one might first think to simply employ DNA profiling to provide these answers. When usable DNA is available, DNA analysis is a powerful tool. However, this may not be possible due to a lack of suitable DNA for analysis, either nuclear or mitochondrial, and/or a lack of a known profile to compare the DNA data with. In the absence of DNA confirmation, it's up to the forensic anthropologist to interpret the clues that will help lead investigators to the person's identity.

Depending upon the number and condition of the bones being studied, anthropologists seek a variety of clues about the individual. They start by attempting to answer a number of relatively specific questions about the physical make-up of the person, in other words, to create a *biological profile* of the person. Questions such as how tall, how old at death, and which

Dimensional diagram bone structure

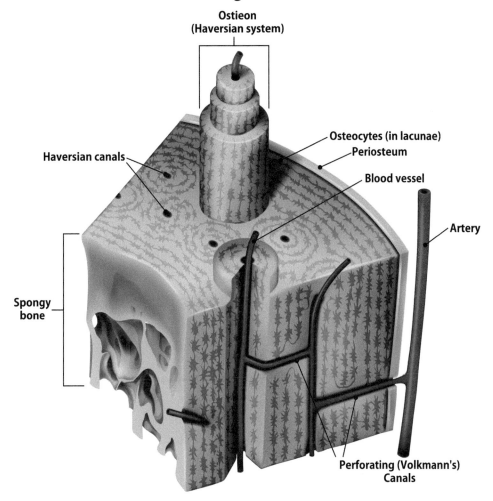

FIGURE 9.7 Microscopic bone structure.

Source: Shutterstock.com.

FIGURE 9.8 Examples of various animal bone fragments that might be confused with human bones.

Source: Used per Creative Commons Share-Alike 4.0, International. Credit: The Portable Antiquities Scheme/The Trustees of the British Museum.

sex help to build a composite picture of the unknown person for comparison with missing person descriptions. Each answer helps to limit the scope of possibilities until, ideally, only one possibility remains. While this is often not fully acheivable, it remains a primary goal of the work.

It is useful to consider here the legal role of forensic anthropology in establishing the identity of remains as those of a particular person. The most common type of analysis is to determine, or exclude, the possibility that a particular set of remains could have belonged to a specific person. As you will see below, this can often be done by developing a biological profile of the remains that is then compared to the biological profile for the known person. This is sometimes called "circumstantial identification." In some cases, however, it may be possible to go beyond the biological profile to uniquely identify the remains (often improperly called "positive identification") by finding features or artifacts in the remains unique to only one person.

General Description: Anthropologists and artists have long been particularly concerned with the variability of the human body. Through careful study, they have found that

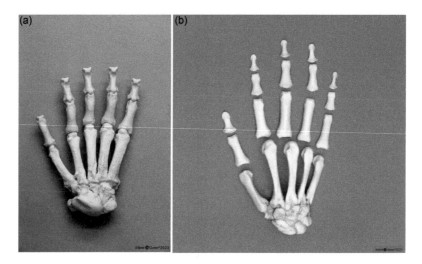

FIGURE 9.9 (a) Comparison of Bear hand skeleton and (b) bones of the human hand.

Source: Figures used with permission and courtesy ©Bone Clones, www.boneclones.com.

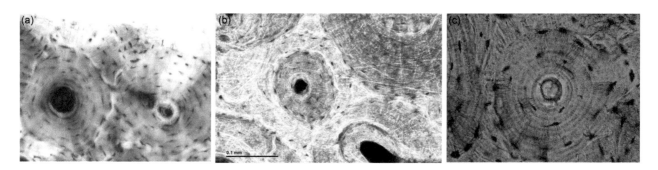

FIGURE 9.10 Magnified images of cross-sections of: (a) human compact bone tissue, (b) typical bird bone, and (c) cow (bovine) bone.

Source: (a) Shutterstock.com. (b) Used per Creative Common Share-Alike, 3.0 Unported. User: Doc, RNDr. Josef Reischig, CSc.

certain relationships exist that are fairly constant in all humans between the relative sizes of body parts and, therefore, the underlying bone structure (Figure 9.11). For example, artists generally use the idea that a human body is about eight "heads" tall and that the limbs and other body components are proportional to one another. From these observations has arisen a detailed understanding of the relationship of the size of a particular bone to the overall physical stature (height) of the person; these correlations are referred to as *allometric* relationships. They allow anthropologists to estimate the stature of a person in life from their skeletal remains (see Box 9.5).

The success in estimating stature, along with other biological information, depends on the completeness of the recovered skeleton and, in the case of partial remains, which bones are available for study. The most straightforward and accurate method involves simply laying out a complete skeleton, allowing for the natural spaces between bones and the missing soft tissues, and then measuring the height of the individual (Figure 9.12).

However, when complete skeletons are not available, anthropologists must rely upon the known relationships between the size of particular bones and an individual's

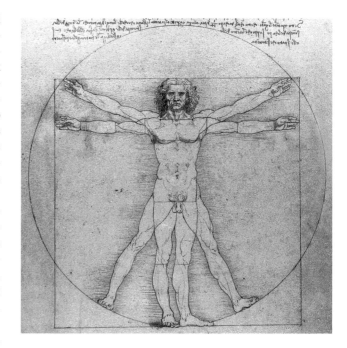

FIGURE 9.11 *Vitruvian Man*, drawn by Leonardo daVinci in 1487, shows the relatively constant proportions found in human anatomy.

FIGURE 9.12   Complete skeletons are most useful in determining stature. This skeleton is from a soldier of the Second World War.

Source: Shutterstock.com.

FIGURE 9.13   A forensic scientist examining human remains in a forensic anthropology laboratory. The anthropologist is measuring the length of a femur to establish the height of the individual as an aid in the investigative process.

Source: Lewis Houghton/Science Photo Library. Used with permission.

overall stature. These estimates are most reliable when working from the largest long bones in the body, such as the femur, tibia, humerus, and others. The process involves measuring the length of the bone (Figure 9.13) and then using that measurement in a mathematical formula to calculate the approximate stature. These formulae have been developed for a number of human populations based on extensive fieldwork in measuring bone lengths and knowing the overall stature for comparison. The process of measuring bones is called *osteometry*.

BOX 9.5   STATURE ESTIMATES FROM OSTEOMETRY

A partial skeleton was found and determined to be that of an adult Caucasian male. Investigators needed a stature estimate to help determine the identity. While only a few long bones were found, anthropologists were able to measure the length of the femur bone at 49.29 cm. They then used the reported formula for this population:

$$\text{Stature}(\text{cm}) = 2.26(\text{femur}) + 66.38\,\text{cm}(\pm 3.72)$$

The measured femur length is then substituted into the formula:

$$\text{Stature} = 2.26(49.29) + 66.38\,\text{cm}(\pm 3.72) = 177.77\,\text{cm}\left(\text{or about}\,5'10'' \pm 1.5''\right)$$

The stature would then be estimated as between about 5′9″ and 5′11.″

Stature estimates from bone remains are not exact and must be given as a range, such as a stature of between 5′3″ and 5′6″. Stature relationships also vary depending upon bioaffinity (also called ancestry) and sex; different formulas are used for different worldwide populations and sexes. It is also important to note that the stature of a living human actually varies both throughout their life and even throughout a given day – we're typically taller in the morning than in the evening. Additionally, it can be problematic when comparing stature estimated from skeletal remains with reports of a "missing" person since the measurement of stature of a living person is prone to error arising from how the measurement is done. Comparisons are further complicated by the tendency of people, especially males, to record their heights incorrectly on official documents, such as passports, driver's licenses, and work records.

Sex of the Decedent: Sex is an important determination for skeletal remains both since it narrows the potential pool of people by half and because the determination of other information, such as stature and age, relies upon knowing the sex of the individual.

The determination of the sex of the remains depends on the subtle differences between male and female skeletons, called *sexual dimorphism*. While both male and female skeletons contain the same bones and there is not one individual marker that completely and unambiguously identifies a skeleton as male or female, observations from several key bones can lead to a reliable determination. The most important bones for sex determination are the pelvic bones, the skull, and the long bones, in that order of accuracy.

The pelvis contains the most telltale bones in the human body relative to sex determination. The bowl-shaped pelvis, however, is actually a collection of several bones that form the intersection between the lower axial and appendicular parts of a human skeleton; the point connecting the legs to the framework of the skeleton. The pelvis is comprised of four bones: two hip bones, the sacrum, and the coccyx (Figure 9.14).

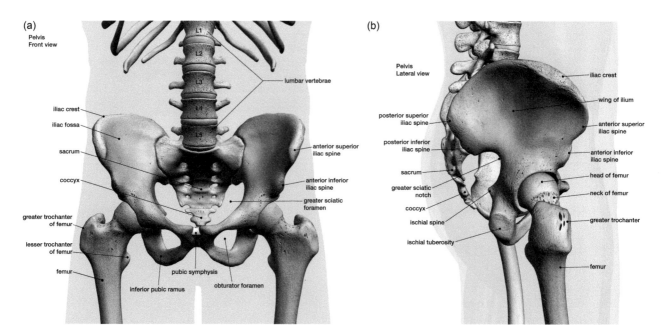

FIGURE 9.14   (a) Front view and (b) side view of human pelvic bones.

Source: Images courtesy Shutterstock.com.

Each hip bone is formed from the earlier adolescent fusion of three other bones; the ilium, the ischium, and the pubis. Their juncture point, the acetabulum, forms the socket where the ball of the leg bone connects.

In general, the pelvic bones of a female are less massive, less sloped, and wider than those of a male. The cavity in the center, called the aperture, is larger and more circular than that of a male, providing space for the birth canal. These are, however, relative determinations and are defined by the averages for males and females. There is great variation not only between females and males but also among members of the same sex. For example, there are female pelvises that are more massive than some males and vice versa. This means that determining sex from skeletal remains is approximate; as more "markers" are found pointing toward one sex, the more secure is the determination. Additionally, skeletal changes between males and females only begin during puberty so sex determinations from bones in prepubescent children are particularly difficult.

One of the most important differences between males and females can be observed at the front of the pelvis; an area called the *pubic symphysis*, which is the front point of connection between the two hip bones (where the pubic bones meet and are held together by cartilage). In males, the arch formed at this point of juncture is rather sharp and narrow (typically less than 90°), while that for a typical female is much broader and less narrow (typically greater than 90°), as shown in Figure 9.15. Other differences between males and females can be observed at the sciatic notch, ventral arc (front), and auricular surfaces. An example of the differences in the sciatic notch in the pelvic bones is shown in Figure 9.16. Occasionally, marks associated with giving birth can also be found on female pelvic bones. These are sometimes seen as small pits inside the pelvis but are not observable in all cases.

Recently, researchers have used 3D imaging techniques to measure more than 20 "landmarks" of the pelvic bones to determine the sex of the decedent. Several advantages of this method include being able to complete the determination even if only

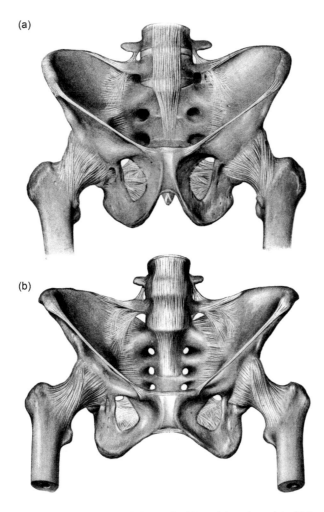

(a)

(b)

FIGURE 9.15 Illustrations of the bones and ligaments of the male (a) and female pelvis (b) bones and the hip joint, as seen from the front. The left and right halves of the pelvic bones are connected to the central sacrum by strong ligaments. In males, the pelvic opening (pubic arch) is narrow, whereas in females, it is broader. At the midline of the pelvis, the pubic angle is wider in the female compared with the male pelvis.

Source: Microscape/Science Photo Library. Used with permission.

15% of the pelvis is found, a >90% accuracy rate, and the use of quantitative data rather than just a qualitative determination.

The skull is another place where differences between male and female skeletons can be observed. Like the pelvis, the skull is composed of a number of bones, normally about 22 bones in all (Figure 9.17). The male skull tends to be more massive and solid, while the female skull is less angular and smaller. The points of attachment of muscles to the skull, the ridges, are typically more pronounced and larger in males, and the jaws of males tend to be more square with a larger and thicker jawbone.

While the pelvic and skull bones are usually considered to be the best in determining the sex of the remains, other bones of the body may also be used (sometimes they are all that is available). These long bones are, however, more prone to uncertainty. The long bones, such as the femur and humerus, have been studied most extensively, although the sternum, clavicle, and scapula have also been used. As with other bones, the long bones of the male body tend to be larger, thicker, and stronger since they typically have to bear greater weight. The sex differences in the femur tend to be more readily observed. The female bones tend to be lighter with less pronounced muscle attachment ridges and with a more nearly right angle between the shaft and neck of the bone. Additionally, the two "knobs" at the bottom of the femur (the femoral condyles) tend to be shaped differently between the sexes, with the notch wider for females than for males.

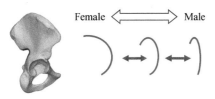

Female ⟵⟶ Male

FIGURE 9.16   Differences in the sciatic notch in the pelvic bones between males and females (seen from the side view), the sciatic notch at left is show outlined in red.

Source: Retrieved from Wikimedia Commons; used per Creative Commons Attribution.

As mentioned, there is great variation in these features within a sex and a population (ancestry/bioaffinity), so care must be taken when using these skeletal bones in the determination of sex.

Age of the Decedent: The age of a person at the time of their death is a particularly useful piece of information in identifying the remains. While our bones undergo constant change from birth until death, the type of change varies as we age. For example, from our earliest childhood through puberty, our bones continue to grow, morph, and merge until a person is around 25 years old; at about this time, growth essentially stops, and a slow degenerative process tends to begin. Unlike the other information determined from bones, the most useful bones in figuring out the age of a person vary based on the age of the person being studied. For example, in young children, tooth development and the ends of long bones are particularly important, while the pubic bones are most valuable in aging older adults. To some extent, the bones used in determining age also vary by the sex of the individual.

When we first develop as a fetus, our bones are mostly cartilage. This cartilage is gradually replaced with hard bone during development through childhood and puberty. This process, called *ossification*, follows a relatively straightforward sequence of events, leading to adult bone structures by the end of puberty, as shown in Figure 9.18. In long bones, for example, the bone shafts (called diaphysis) begin the ossification process first followed by secondary centers at the ends of the bones (called epiphyses). These secondary centers develop until, eventually, they fuse with the long ossified shaft to form one complete adult bone. Importantly, the fusion of the main shaft with the secondary centers tends to be completed at different times during our childhood development, depending on the specific bone. The order of fusion in the bones in our bodies follows a fairly well-understood sequence and timing that allows us to estimate the age at death of the person by examining the extent of ossification and fusion. For example, from Table 9.1, it can be observed that complete fusion of the humerus begins when a person is about 17 years old. Fusion is dependent on the specific

(a)   (b)

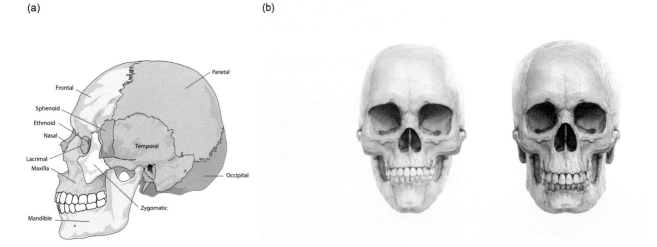

FIGURE 9.17   (a) The adult skull is normally made up of 22 bones joined together by sutures, semi-rigid connections formed by bone formation (except for the mandible), and (b) differences between female and male skulls (male on right and female on left).

Source: (b) Shutterstock.com.

GROWING BONES

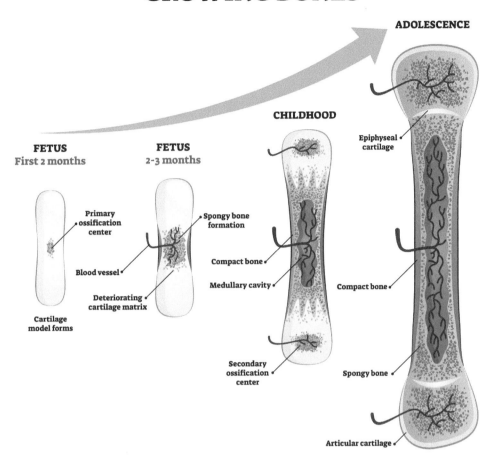

FIGURE 9.18   Bone development and growth from fetus through childhood to adolescence.

Source: Shutterstock.com.

TABLE 9.1   Fusion times (in years) of epiphyses in humans

BONE	COMPLETE FUSION MALE	EARLIEST FUSION MALE	COMPLETE FUSION FEMALE	EARLIEST FUSION FEMALE
Distal tibia and fibula	19	14–16	16	12
Humerus (proximal)	25	17	25	17
Humerus (distal)	21	16	21	16

bone, sex, nutrition, medical history, and bioaffinity (ancestry) of the decedent. Humans have 800 ossification centers as a fetus that then fuse to about 405 centers at birth which then ultimately fuse further into our 206 adult bones.

Our skulls also undergo a bone fusion process as we develop. In between most of the bones of the skull are tiny juncture lines called *sutures*. When a child is born, the sutures are rather loose, and in some places, the bones may not even touch, sometimes called the baby's "soft spots" or *fontanelles* (Figure 9.19). This provides the necessary expansion space as our brains grow within the confinement of our skull. As we develop, however, these sutures become progressively more rigid and eventually fuse together sometime in early adulthood. These sutures can be effectively used to determine the age of younger people, depending on the nature and extent of the suture fusion.

Probably one of the best methods for dating the remains of a young person involves looking at their teeth. In our lives, we have only two sets of teeth: *deciduous teeth* (also known as "baby" or *temporary* teeth) and *permanent teeth*. The deciduous teeth of a newborn are located just below the skin but begin erupting at about six months. This eruption process occurs in a regular sequence until all 20 deciduous teeth have erupted (Figure 19.20). During this time, the 32 permanent teeth form below the deciduous teeth and eventually push them out, replacing them (Figure 9.21). The front teeth are usually the first deciduous teeth to be lost and the first permanent teeth to erupt. The third molars in the back of the mouth, sometimes called wisdom teeth, are usually the last to erupt at about 18 years of age – sometimes these teeth never erupt.

SKULL OF A NEWBORN

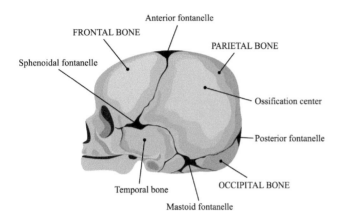

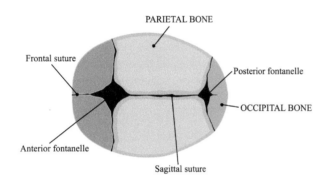

FIGURE 9.19 Skull and cranial sutures of a newborn.

Source: Shutterstock.com.

Calculating the age of a young decedent at death using teeth requires determining which teeth have and have not erupted. For example, using the approximate eruption times shown in Figure 9.20, if it was found that a person's permanent upper first premolar had erupted, which typically occurs at 10.2 years, and that the adjacent upper second premolar had not erupted, which typically erupts around 11.1 years, then the age of the person would be estimated to be between these two ages, somewhere between 10.2 and 11.1 years old. By bracketing the ages using approximate eruption times, a good approximation of the age of the young decedent can be obtained. It is important to note that these are approximate times and orders of eruption and that variations are found in actual practice.

Once a person reaches adulthood, however, changes are more gradual and less certain in terms of onset time, and teeth eruptions can no longer be used as all teeth have erupted by then. One of the best indicators, however, involves looking at the surfaces of the bones in the pelvis, specifically the pubic symphysis and auricular surfaces. As a person ages, these surfaces gradually change from relatively smoothly contoured and "billowed" to a more flattened, rough, and porous appearance. Researchers have developed models that can be used to estimate age based on comparing the bones in the remains to a set of "standards," as shown in Figure 9.22. It is important to note, however, that as a person ages, the estimated age range widens considerably. It is often only barely possible to assign an older adult to within one decade of life, while assigning a child's age might be accurate to within a year or two.

Other changes in bone and cartilage occur as a person grows older and can be used to help determine age. In general, bones lose density gradually as we age, especially for postmenopausal women. This bone loss is very dependent on factors such as sex, size (weight), and nutrition.

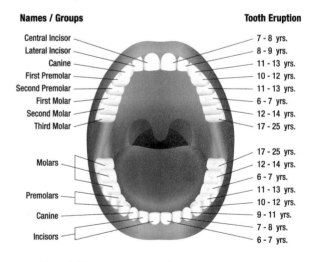

FIGURE 9.20 Tooth development of (a) deciduous (baby or temporary teeth) and (b) permanent teeth.

Source: Images courtesy Shutterstock.com.

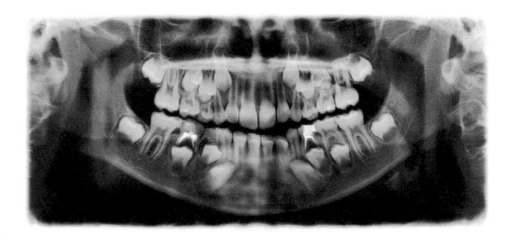

FIGURE 9.21   Panoramic dental radiograph (X-ray) of the upper jaw (maxilla) and lower jawbone (mandible) for a seven-year-old child showing the deciduous teeth with the permanent teeth below these "baby" teeth (the adult teeth are at the edges of the X-ray).

Source: Shutterstock.com.

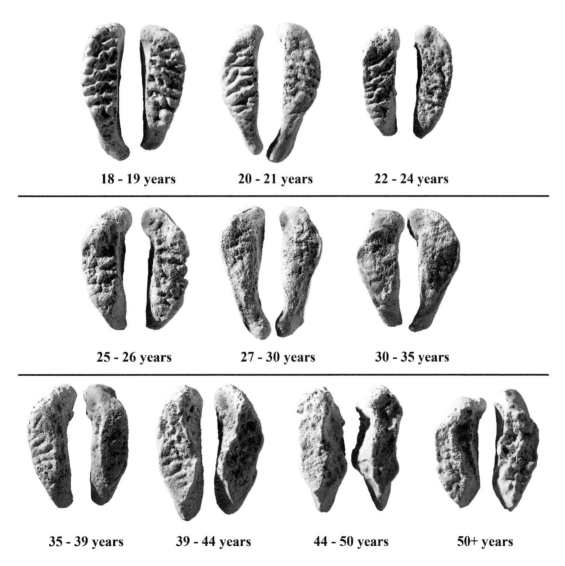

FIGURE 9.22   Changes in the pubic symphysis with aging.

Source: Figure generated for use specifically within the book, copyright and used with permission courtesy of Pieter Folkens. © Pieter Folkens.

Osteoarthritis (OA) and Rheumatoid arthritis (RA), caused by the degradation of the cartilage in joints, can also be seen in the bones. Osteoarthritis can occur in any joint but is most commonly found in the knee, elbow, shoulder, hip, and spine (Figure 9.23). This condition is rather rare in individuals under 40. While OA and RA may yield similar bone degradation, osteoarthritis is caused by mechanical wear and tear on joints, while rheumatoid arthritis is an autoimmune disease where the body's own immune system attacks the joints, leading to cartilage degradation and bone erosion.

Another technique for dating individuals uses something called the "bomb curve." In the 1950s and early 1960s, extensive above-ground testing of nuclear weapons occurred, resulting in relatively high levels of atmospheric radiocarbon-14 (^{14}C) that quickly spread and equalized across the entire globe. This testing ended in 1963, and since then both the ^{14}C levels and its worldwide spread have dropped. Since carbon is incorporated into all living organisms and the ½-life of ^{14}C is relatively long (5,730 years), some ^{14}C is also incorporated into every living human body. By comparing the ^{14}C content found in a person's tooth enamel or bones with the extensive atmospheric record for ^{14}C ("bomb curve"), it may be possible to estimate the person's birth date to within one year. This is possible because the amount of ^{14}C is fixed when the tooth or bone was formed.

Bioaffinity/Ancestry of the Decedent: One of the most difficult jobs forensic anthropologists are called upon to

occasionally perform is a determination of the ancestry of a decedent. All humans are members of the same species, *Homo sapiens*, but anthropologists in the past have recognized different races as being ethnically important. Due to migration and the merging of populations, skeletal differences attributed to particular ancestral groups are, at best, a vague guess. Even members of the "same" population group often show a wide range of differences in their skeletal remains. While such information may still occasionally be sought by investigators, the concept of distinct human races in a biological sense is now obsolete. In 2019, the *American Association of Biological Anthropologists* stated: "Race does not provide an accurate representation of human biological variation. It was never accurate in the past, and it remains inaccurate when referencing contemporary human populations."

In the past, when examining skeletal remains in an attempt to gain some ancestral information, anthropologists most commonly examined the nose, face, head shape, stature, skull, teeth, and body proportions (Figure 9.24). For example, some populations generally tend to have broader nasal openings, while others tend to show unique shapes on the rims of their incisor teeth. Additional features can help lead to a particular "educated guess," but it is usually not based on any single skeletal feature and the determination is being increasingly discounted.

Occupations and Habits: Sometimes it is possible to learn about the possible lifelong occupations or habits of people

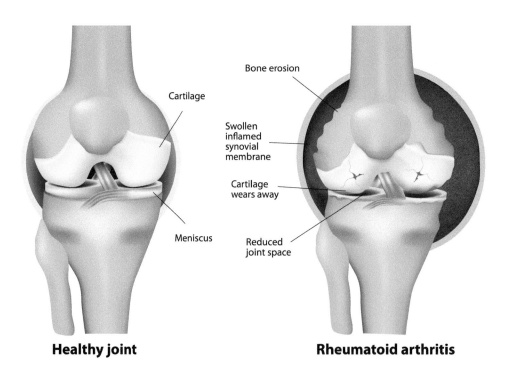

FIGURE 9.23   Rheumatoid arthritis (RA) is a type of inflammatory autoimmune disease that usually affects knees by degradation of the cartilage with severe bone erosion of the knee. The body's immune system mistakenly attacks its own healthy tissue.

Source: Shutterstock.com.

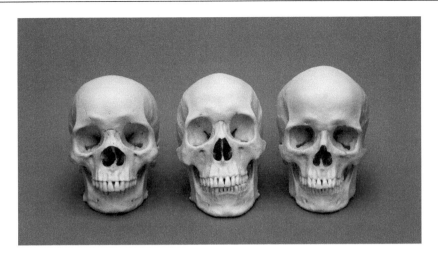

FIGURE 9.24 Comparison of skulls of different ancestries.

Source: Figure used with permission and courtesy ©Bone Clones, www.boneclones.com.

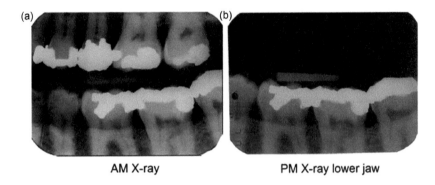

FIGURE 9.25 Comparison of antemortem (a) and post-mortem (b) dental X-rays showing matching structure and restorations.

Source: Image generated by Alex Forrest. Used courtesy Health Support Queensland Forensic and Scientific Services (HSQ FSS) and the Queensland State Coroner, with permission.

from their skeletal remains. If a person engages in stressful, repetitive motions for very long periods, such as in a lifelong physical job, there may be observable wear and stress marks found on the skeleton. For example, a long career involving computer typing can lead to observable wear on the bones of the arms and hands, while a career as a laborer using a shovel can result in spinal, shoulder, and arm wear that is not normally observed otherwise. Repetitive motions may also lead to arthritic conditions observable in the remains.

Long-term habits may also leave their marks on the bones. It may be possible to determine if someone is right- or left-handed using this same approach if they greatly favored the use of one arm over the other. The skeletons of athletes or people chronically overweight also often show wear or thicker-than-usual bones, especially in the bones that carry most of the athletic strain or weight. Therefore, the leg and foot bones of such people are often noticeably thicker, with particular wear at the ends of the bones.

Medical History (pathology): A person's medical history may be clearly reflected in their skeletal remains. The most obvious example of this comes from a person's dental history, as discussed earlier. The arrangement of the teeth, missing teeth, and any subsequent wear or dental repairs (restorations) are usually noted carefully by dentists when the patient is still living, occasionally with detailed molds or X-ray records of a person's dentition. Comparison of these records with the dentition of the remains can lead to an individual identification with a very high degree of certainty, as seen in Figure 9.25. In addition, if the person needed highly personalized dental appliances, such as bridges, dentures, implants, and braces, these items may be found in the remains and compared with dental records.

Sometimes people have either congenital defects or injuries that leave lasting records on the skeleton. For example, broken bones can easily be spotted and compared with "in-life" X-rays and medical histories. Prosthetic devices are sometimes required to repair damage or wear, such as hip replacement, implants, and metal plates from injuries. These devices often have durable serial numbers engraved on them that can lead to a definitive identification. For example, the identification of a skeleton can be made from the serial numbers of an implanted replacement hip (Figure 9.26).

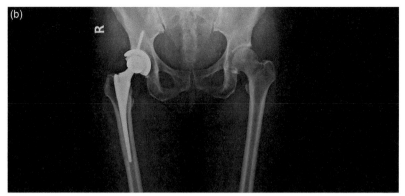

FIGURE 9.26 (a) Close-up of a hip replacement prosthetic implant, and (b) X-ray image of a total hip replacement in a patient with osteoarthritis in the hip joint.

Source: Images courtesy Shutterstock.com.

Some diseases can be detected in the bones and compared with the known medical histories of patients. Tuberculosis, osteoporosis, Paget's disease, syphilis, cancer, and others change bones in well-understood ways and may be diagnosed from remains (Figure 9.27). For example, anemia in children can be detected in the skeletal remains by observing Harris lines (bone growth lines appearing as alternating rings of abnormal bone hardening) or *Cribra orbitalia* (bony lesions/pores in the eye sockets – orbits).

Facial Reconstructions: In identifying remains, it is sometimes very helpful to try to construct a facial image of what a person looked like when they were alive. This aids in matching possible missing persons with their remains. The goal is to use the skeletal remains, coupled with the biological profile of the person and our understanding of the human body, to build a graphic likeness of the unknown person. Several techniques have been used to aid in this process, including photographic overlays, 2D drawings, 3D modeling, and computer-aided reconstructions.

Overlay Process. In the overlay process, a photograph of a person from life is scaled to the same dimensions as a photograph of the skull (or fragment) obtained from the remains. The trick is to have the two scaled photographs taken from the same perspective. The two pictures are then superimposed, and the extent of overlap and agreement between the features of the two photographs may be used to support or refute the identification of the remains made using other information. For example, as shown in Figure 9.28, the partial skull remains of a missing soldier are compared with a photograph taken shortly before his disappearance. From this comparison, it can be seen that there is generally good agreement between the somewhat unusual features of the recovered cranial bone and the soldier's picture, supporting the identification of the remains. This method is most effective when the person's skull has some unique features of size or structure that can be seen in the photograph taken in life.

2D Facial Reconstruction. A second method involves using either the actual skull or a 3D copy of the skull and adding tissue depth markers in positions on the skull from anthropological tables. A photograph of the skull with the tissue depth

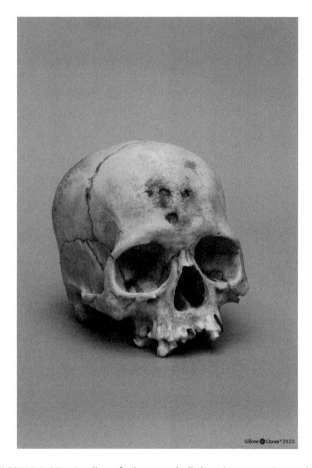

FIGURE 9.27 Replica of a human skull showing extensive syphilis damage.

Source: Figure used with permission and courtesy ©Bone Clones, www.boneclones.com.

markers then is used as a template for an artist who constructs a drawing matching the depth markers and completes the likeness based on pictures of a suspected person from life. An example of this is shown in Figure 9.29. The upper left shows the skull with the tissue depth markers in place. A piece of tracing paper was then laid over the picture, and the person's profile

(a) (b) (c)

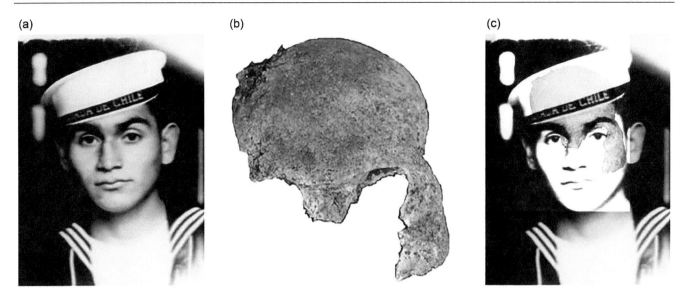

FIGURE 9.28 Superposition of a photograph of missing soldier Gerardo Olivares with a recovered cranial fragment. (a) Picture of a soldier antemortem. (b) Photograph of the frontal cranial fragment and (c) the superimposition of the left and center images. The unique bone shape of his nose particularly helped with the identification.

Source: FBI.

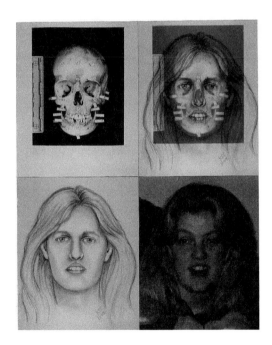

FIGURE 9.29 Examples of 2D hand-drawn facial reconstruction on a photograph of a 3D skull compared with the actual skull and photograph of the suspected victim.

Source: Taylor (2000).

was constructed. Consequently, using the known photograph (bottom right) and the traced profile, the artist draws a composite consistent with both the skull and the known photograph.

3D Facial Reconstruction. This process begins similarly to that used in creating a 2D likeness using either the skull or a digital 3D image of the skull (such as from a CT scan). The process then builds up tissues either by using clay applied by a sculptor or digitally in the computer (see below). In either process, typically at least 20 tissue depth markers are used to build up the missing

tissues based on what is known about the person (e.g., sex, ancestry/bioaffinity, weight, etc.). By gradually adding facial muscles using the built-up tissues, the underlying structure of the face can be created. Finally, the skin and other surface features (e.g., wrinkles, skin tone, hair, and eyes) can be added. An example is shown in Figure 9.30 (top images), preparing a 3D facial reconstruction for comparison with a photograph of a missing person. While not exact, this approach does provide a method to access the overall similarity of the skull with the missing person.

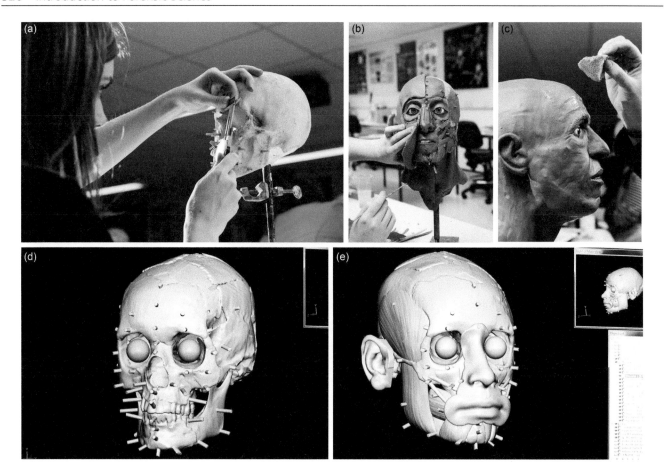

FIGURE 9.30 Top images showing a facial reconstruction using clay applied onto an unknown skull using tissue depth markers: (a) the skull with standard tissue depth markers being added according to tables of average depths at various locations on the face, (b) using the markers and anatomical features, clay is added to develop the contours of the face, and (c) the final steps to create a realistic model of the decedent. Bottom images show a computer-based facial reconstruction: (d) image shows the scanned skull in the computer with initial tissue depth markers established and (e) the addition of muscles and tissue depths on the model.

Source: (a–c) Lewis Houghton/Science Photo Library. (d,e) Louise Murray/Science Photo Library. Used with permission.

Computer-Based Digital Facial Reconstruction. Today, computer-based digital methods are mostly replacing the older clay methods to create a model of the unknown person. In this process, a detailed 3D scan of the skull is digitized in the computer. Then, using specialized software and haptic feedback tools, "digital clay" is applied to the computer model using tissue depth markers, facial muscle, and anatomical information. An example is shown in the bottom images of Figure 9.30. The basic methodology employed in either the physical model or the computer-based reconstruction is essentially the same for each approach, combining anatomical information and soft tissue thickness guides to create an authentic image for identification. One important advantage of using a computer to complete the process is that it can be done relatively rapidly from digitized skull images to provide a complete three-dimensional rendering.

Problems with Facial Reconstructions. Facial reconstructions are currently among the more subjective and controversial of forensic techniques. One problem with these reconstructions

is that available tissue depth information, upon which these reconstructions are built, is incomplete, sometimes questionable, and highly variable from person to person and among ethnic, sex, and age groups. Another problem is that some facial features have very little skeletal basis for creating an accurate reconstruction. For example, very little information regarding the shape and size of a person's nose, lips, and ears comes from the skull, and the reconstruction of these features is primarily the artist's best guess. Further complicating the utility of these likenesses is the fact that often a person's nose, ears, eyes, lips, hair, and similar features are the least reliably reconstructed but are the most readily remembered features of a person.

Because of these difficulties, facial reconstructions are typically not admissible in court for the identification of remains. While facial reconstruction appears often in the world of TV and movies, it is used far less often in actual forensic investigations. However, the technique still has a place as an investigative tool.

QUESTION FIVE: How Did They Die? Pathology and Cause of Death. Sometimes anthropologists are asked by medical examiners or coroners to assist in their quest to find out how someone died. Their primary concern, of course, is to discover whether the person died by the action of someone else or by "natural" causes. This, however, may be one of the toughest questions to answer from the skeletal record.

BOX 9.6 BRIEF ON FIVE CENTRAL QUESTIONS

1. Is it bone?
2. Is it human bone?
3. How old is the bone?
4. Whose bone is it (bioprofile)?
5. How did they die (pathology)?

In trying to piece together the clues to help determine how someone may have died, the forensic anthropologist typically seeks to answer several more focused and specific questions: (1) What can be found in the bone record (e.g., type of injury)? (2) When did the injury occur? (3) What was the cause of the injury? and (4) Was the injury the cause (or contributing cause) of death?

What can be found in the bone record: type of injury? The anthropologist's job here is to carefully examine the remains to simply look for signs of damage, particularly damage that might have resulted from significant trauma. If trauma was isolated solely in the soft tissue, then little or no evident damage might be recorded in the bones. Trauma of a more violent nature, however, such as from an assault, gunshot, stabbing, or automobile injury, can often leave behind a bone record of this injury. The nature and extent of bone scars and fractures can help to inform this and other questions. Note that the term "trauma" is applied to injury only to a living victim, while the term "damage" refers to post-mortem changes.

When did the injury occur? This question is quite different from the question already posed of how old the bones are. In this case, we look to see if we can learn if the injuries found on examination of the remains occurred before the time of death (antemortem trauma), at about the time of death (perimortem trauma), or after death (post-mortem trauma). Typically, injuries either before or after death are of less immediate concern in determining if a crime had been committed than those that occur near the time of an unattended death. Post-mortem damage can, however, have important lessons to teach an investigator about the crime itself (see forensic taphonomy later in this chapter).

During a person's life, they may experience a number of events that may leave a record in the bones. In the United States, for example, a recent health survey showed that the *annual* rate of bone fracture is almost 2.4% of the population, about 6.3 million fractures per year! Accidental bone fractures, even when long healed, can still be detected at a site of fracture. The process of healing of bones is a relatively slow, long-term process. The rate of healing also varies a great deal with age, nutrition, and overall health, with children having an amazing ability to repair bone tissues.

The pathway to bone healing is a wonderfully complex process, as illustrated in Figure 9.31. Immediately after a break in a bone, blood surrounds the affected site and forms a large blood clot (hematoma) around the break. Within a few weeks, the blood cells in the clot die and are replaced by a fibrocartilage callus that serves to weakly "splint" the broken bones together but is not strong enough for full use of the bone. During this time, capillary blood vessels reform in the callus, and the dead blood cells are cleaned up. Over the following several months, this initial cartilage callus is slowly replaced by a bony callus, forming a strong reunion of the bone pieces. The final steps in bone healing take place over about the following year in which any excess bony callus is removed, compact bone is deposited, and the surface of the bone is smoothed and reshaped, referred to as *bone remodeling.*

If a broken bone is found in human remains, an assessment of the extent of healing can indicate how long healing had progressed before death, and therefore, provide an estimate of the post-mortem interval (PMI). Thus, if a bone fracture is found to be completely healed and remodeled, then the injury that caused this fracture must have taken place long before the death of the person and is unlikely to be a significant factor in the person's death.

Completely healed bone may still be of forensic interest, however. If a series of bone fractures, at various stages of healing, are found, this may indicate a case of systematic physical abuse over a long period of time. Old fractures can also be used, like dental records, to match a known medical history with the remains.

Unlike trauma to soft tissue, it is usually not possible to determine the exact point of death relative to bone healing since the timeline of bone restoration is so long. Bone injuries at the time of death would not show healing, but such injuries are often difficult to differentiate from post-mortem bone damage (taphonomy, Section 9.2). Some types of post-mortem bone damage, however, can be differentiated from trauma. For example, if the remains were scavenged by animals, such as coyotes, rodents, pets, or birds, then telltale marks from their actions are often found on the bones (see Section 9.2.2). It is also occasionally possible to determine if the body had been dismembered and even what type of instrument had been used in the process, as shown in Figure 9.32. In these images, the clear striations show that tools had been used for the dismemberment.

BOX 9.7 YOU BE THE SLEUTH: TWO-MINUTE MYSTERY

The skull shown in Figure 9.33 was found at a digging site and was carefully measured and excavated. What do you think these wounds can tell you about the cause of death? (Answer at the end of the chapter.)

FRACTURE REPAIR

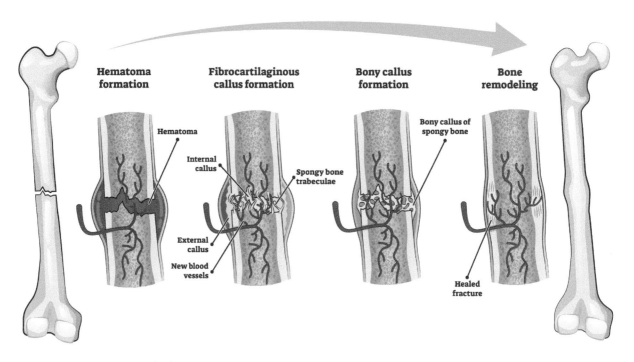

FIGURE 9.31   Healing process of a fractured bone. The process includes (left to right): formation of a hematoma (blood clot), forming a callus at the break site, generation of a bony callus, and finally, bone remodeling.

Source: Shutterstock.

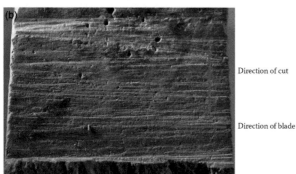

FIGURE 9.32   Photographs of bone damage by tools: (a) damage to the bone caused by a hacking or chopping action, and (b) kerf wall damage in dental stone caused by a saw.

Source: Sue Black et al. (2017).

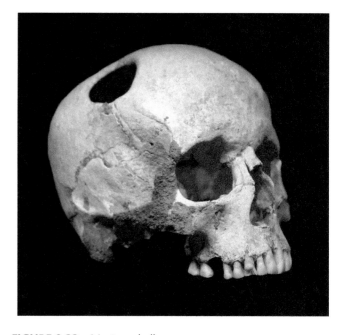

FIGURE 9.33   Mystery skull.

Source: Creative Commons Share-Alike 3.0, France. User: Rama.

What was the cause of the injury? By examining bone damage, it may be possible to shed light on how the injury might have happened, or especially sometimes how it could not have happened (Figure 9.33). It's all a matter of a careful examination of the bone record.

Skeletal trauma is often divided into two broad categories: blunt force trauma (BFT) and sharp force trauma (SFT). As mentioned in Chapter 8, BFT or non-penetrating trauma occurs when a blunt object strikes a person with sufficient force to cause physiological damage. This type of trauma may occur from a personal assault (e.g., fist, foot), leveraged assault (e.g., baseball bat, gun stock, or furniture), massive assault (e.g., automobile injury, airplane crash), or from a gunshot impact. SFT, or penetrating trauma, may result from an attack with a knife or other sharp object. These two types of trauma may leave marks on the bones, and they can look quite different from one another.

Gunshot wounds are common examples of forensic blunt force trauma. With bullet wounds, it is often necessary to first confirm that the wound came from a gunshot and second to determine things such as the bullet's trajectory, the sequence of multiple gunshots, and the type of gun and bullet employed. An important goal is to determine the entrance and the exit sites of the bullet. Typically, an entrance wound of a bullet is smaller with sharp edges in contrast to exit wound, which is usually large and irregularly shaped, but there are situations in which this can be misleading. The best evidence for the direction of the bullet, however, comes from looking for beveling of the bone (see Chapter 8). Beveling occurs on the side of the bone away from the approach of the bullet and appears as a concave crater away from the entrance side. Thus, a bullet entrance wound in a skull, for example, would show beveling on the *inside* of the cranial chamber, and the exit wound would show beveling on the *outside* of the skull.

Information regarding the trajectories of the bullets can be deduced by lining up the entrance and exit wounds (Figure 9.34b). The order of bullets can sometimes be determined by looking at the fracture lines from bullets in the bones and applying similar reasoning to that used for determining the order of bullets through a pane of glass: the cracks (fracture lines) from a later bullet do not cross already existing fracture lines from earlier bullets (Chapter 16). In this fashion, the sequence of events, such as the presence of multiple shooters, the order of attack, and the relative positions of the shooter and victim, can be built up in

a way consistent with the bone evidence. The evidence can, of course, also "shoot" holes in false alibis.

Scientific studies have shown that we usually cannot determine the caliber of a bullet by inspecting the wound, although a shotgun wound can usually be distinguished from other gunshot wounds. Bullets from rifles may apply so much force that the bones are shattered too extensively to allow for any type of reconstruction (Figure 9.34a). Gunshot damage essentially always shows a characteristic entrance hole, but other types of blunt force trauma can also exhibit deceptively similar hole formation. Only experience and careful observation can help to distinguish between the origins of these types of trauma.

In examining other types of blunt force trauma damage to bones, it may be possible to arrive at a general description of the weapon used in the assault. For example, a physical assault with someone's fist cannot cause the type or extent of damage possible by an assault with a baseball bat. The amount of energy necessary to cause a particular type of injury can be estimated and determined to be either consistent or inconsistent with a description of the events. Additionally, it may be possible to provide a picture of the irregular shape of an object used in the assault. Figure 9.35 illustrates an example of the type of bone injury seen from an attack with a hammer.

BFT typically begins with in-bending of the bone at the impact site followed by a fracture that begins on the side *away* from the impact site. As an impact continues or is stronger, the fractures then radiate *into* the point of contact between the bone and the weapon. If insufficient force is applied, the fracture may never reach the actual site of the impact and can be misleading, especially in attacks involving the skull.

SFT may result in bone chipping, scoring, or scraping. As with BFT, the damage may also lead to a description of the weapon that caused the wound. One characteristic of a SFT is that it tends to be very rapid and active in nature. Additionally, SFT wounds tend to be more commonly hinge and radiating, rather than concentric, fractures. Examples of the cut marks and wounds on bones from knife SFT are shown in Figure 9.36.

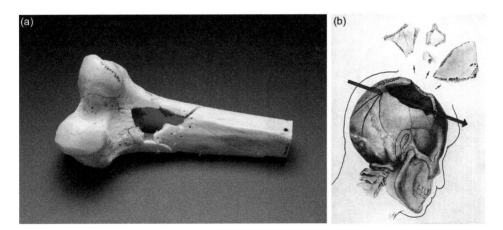

FIGURE 9.34 (a) Human distal femur shot with a mini-ball fired from a 0.58 caliber Springfield Model 1862 rifle. (b) Diagram showing the trajectory of the bullet through President John F. Kennedy's skull (skull fragments not drawn to scale).

Source: (a) NIH. (b) Made by medical illustrator Ida G. Dox and published as Figure 29 on page 125 of volume 7 (Medical and Firearms Evidence) of the Appendix to Hearings Before the Select Committee on Assassinations of the U.S. House of Representatives (1979).

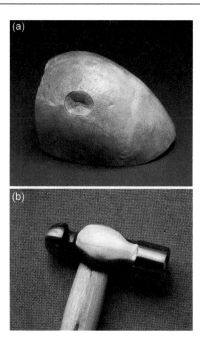

FIGURE 9.35 (a) Skull showing ball-peen hammer trauma and (b) a ball-peen hammer.

Source: (b), NIH.

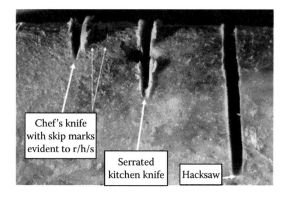

Chef's knife with skip marks evident to r/h/s

Serrated kitchen knife

Hacksaw

FIGURE 9.36 Sharp force trauma on bones from various knives (class characteristics): (Left to Right) a Chef's knife, a serrated kitchen knife and a hacksaw on a porcine (pig) femur.

Source: Black et al. (2017).

Was the injury the cause (or contributing cause) of death? Determining the cause of death, or discovering the way in which someone died, from skeletal remains is, at best, difficult. For example, people have been known to survive a massive assault with multiple fractures and other bone injuries only to die from other causes. In contrast, trauma that may lead to either very little or no observable bone damage can easily cause death. There are times, however, when severe bone damage is clearly inconsistent with life and must be associated with the death of the individual. Gunshot wounds to the skull or massive cranial fractures can usually be placed in this latter category.

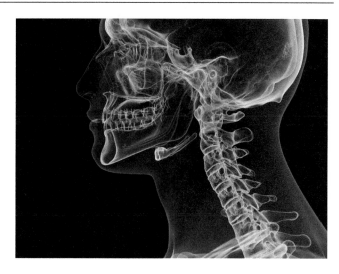

FIGURE 9.37 Hyoid bone and cartilage attachment, situated in the neck.

Source: Shutterstock.com.

An example of fairly definitive bone evidence leading to a determination of the cause of death is in the case of strangulation. In our necks, there is a small bone, the hyoid bone (Figure 9.37), that is the only bone in our bodies not directly associated with another bone. It has many functions, including anchoring the tongue and facilitating speech, respiration, chewing, and swallowing. This bone is held in place by cartilage and muscle and helps give our throats and tongues their observed large degree of motion and flexibility. It is, however, a rather delicate bone that is easily broken in the process of strangulation. While not always present, the observation of a broken hyoid bone leads to the strong suggestion that strangulation probably occurred.

BOX 9.8   THE MISSING KING

On August 22, 1485, during the Battle of Bosworth Field, King Richard III became the last English monarch to die in battle. His loss in this battle ended the English civil war, the War of the Roses, between the Houses of York and Lancaster, marking the beginning of the new Tudor line of kings and queens. Perhaps more importantly, many believe that this battle marked the end of the English Middle Ages. After Bosworth Field, however, Richard's naked body was taken to nearby Leicester and buried in a humble, unmarked grave. His legacy lived on through the play by William Shakespeare, who depicted Richard as a badly deformed man, "rather like a spider," resorting to murder and treachery to secure the throne, including the famous murders of his two nephews in the Tower of London.

The question of what happened to the remains of Richard III has intrigued people for centuries. His final burial site was lost until 2012 when researchers worked to locate the site of the vanished Greyfriars Church, demolished during Henry VIII's time, where it was believed that Richard might have been buried. Astonishingly, in 2012, the foundation of the church was located under a modern city car park. Upon excavation, skeletal remains were very quickly found, coincidentally directly under an *R* painted on the pavement (meaning *Rex*, coincidence?).

When forensic anthropologists examined the remains, they found many features suggesting that, against all odds, this was the skeleton of Richard III. The body was determined to be that of an adult male with severe scoliosis of the spine. Additionally, ten wounds were identified comprising several injuries to the skull including a shallow wound, most likely caused by a dagger, and a depression to the skull, most likely caused by a bladed weapon such as a sword. Also, on the bottom of the skull was a large hole, presumably where a halberd had entered the cranium, the ultimate cause of death. Any doubt that this was actually Richard III's body, however, was removed when mitochondrial DNA evidence showed his royal ancestry. Richard's remains were ultimately carried in procession to the Leicester Cathedral and reburied there on March 26, 2015 (Figure 9.38).

As mentioned before, the observation of multiple bone wounds (e.g., fractures, assaults, etc.) in various stages of healing suggests that long-term abuse might have occurred.

While the anthropologist can shed light on what might have happened around the time of death of a person, it is ultimately the job of the medical examiner to make the final determination of the cause of death.

9.1.5 Crime Scene Processing with Skeletal Remains

Ideally, in a forensic investigation involving skeletal remains, a trained forensic anthropologist would have the responsibility of properly excavating and processing the site. While fieldwork by a trained forensic anthropologist is desirable, it is often not possible. More commonly, an anthropologist is called in to examine remains that have already been recovered by the police or medical examiner's office.

When work at the site of the discovery of the remains is possible, anthropologists use well-developed methods of archaeology to conduct the recovery (Figure 9.39). Proper excavation, collection, and treatment of bones are key steps to a good investigation. The most important rule at the site is to prevent any further damage from occurring to the remains. This involves careful search, survey, documentation, labeling, and field storage of the specimens before transportation to the laboratory for later study. A careful map is prepared that shows the location and orientation of each individual bone and fragment recovered – such information can often be quite helpful in recreating the sequence of events that led to the observed crime scene. Care must be exercised to ensure that small bones, such as teeth, that have become loose are also recovered. Sometimes, work in the lab will suggest that an important bone or tooth is missing, requiring a return to the site to search for the missing item.

When the remains are brought into the laboratory, the work usually begins with a careful examination and cataloging of the remains, making special note of any flesh, cartilage, soil, plants, insects, and other materials that are associated with the remains – especially if the anthropologist has not been part of the recovery team. In skeletonized remains, it is important to also note any odor, discoloration, or bleaching of the bones since this can give clues as to their age.

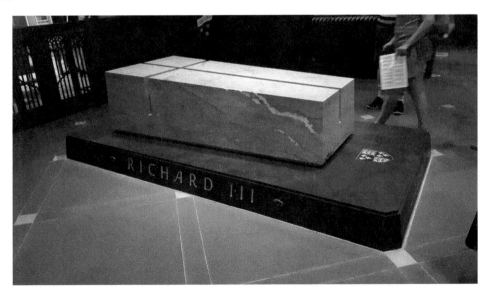

FIGURE 9.38   Tomb of King Richard III of England (1452–1485) in Leicester Cathedral.

Source: Retrieved from Wikimedia Commons; used per Creative Commons Attribution.

FIGURE 9.39   A worker helps excavate the site of the El Mozote massacre (1981), where an El Salvadoran army battalion killed about 800 villagers, almost half of them children. This massively co-mingled remains site presents exceptionally complex problems of recovery and identification of the individual remains.

Source: NIH, photo by Mercedes Doretti, EAAF.

FIGURE 9.40   Reconstruction of skeletal remains.

Source: NIH, photo by Stephen Ferry.

Once these materials have been examined and samples removed for later study, it is often desirable to completely clean the bones of any remaining flesh and preserve them to allow for a close examination of the bones themselves. This can be accomplished in a variety of ways, including the use of insects, bacterial decomposition, and manual cleaning. Once the flesh has been removed, the bones can be dried, and in some instances preserved by applying a resin coating, to protect the clean bones. Occasionally, it's desirable to try to restore the bones in order to better understand how they might have been broken or damaged (Figure 9.40).

Sometimes the remains of multiple people or remains of people mixed with animal remains are found together, referred to as *co-mingled remains* (Figure 9.39). The first task here is to determine how many individuals are present in the collection of bones. One approach is to determine the number of corresponding bones present (e.g., the number of right humerus bones); this gives an estimate of the *minimum number of*

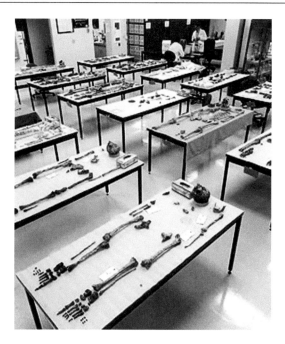

FIGURE 9.41   Reassembling co-mingled remains into individual skeletons.

Source: Defense Department laboratory in Hawaii.

individuals (MNI) present in the collection. Sometimes, this MNI value underestimates the number of people represented in the collected remains so a different number, the *most likely number of individuals* (MLNI), can be alternatively used. A larger MLNI may be chosen, for example, if a manifest or passenger list is available that suggests more individuals must be present than are found for the MNI estimation.

The next task is to arrange the remains so that the bones for each individual person are separated from those of the others (Figure 9.41). This can be a daunting and time-consuming task but can often be accomplished by careful study of the remains. For example, the human body is remarkably symmetric such that comparable bones on the left and right side should be about the same size and shape. For example, a person's right humerus is about the same size and a mirror-image shape as their left humerus. Other aids used to differentiate the bones of different individuals include the stature, age, sex, medical history, and other indicators that have been previously described.

In some investigations, a forensic odontologist is brought in to assist the medical examiner and anthropologist by examining dental remains. Their area of expertise is especially important in identifying any dental restorations or dental appliances found.

It is important to meticulously keep track of all work and observations when dealing with the remains. This meticulousness is necessary because these observations and conclusions are part of a larger legal investigation. This marks the departure between a historical archaeological investigation and a forensic investigation. In forensic work, an anthropologist may be called into court to present and explain their work and observations. Careful notes, adherence to acceptable practices, and considerations of the chain of custody are certainly important for allowing the testimony into legal proceedings.

BOX 9.9   MOZART'S LAST OPUS?

Wolfgang Amadeus Mozart, born in 1756, is an enigma both in his life and in his death. His life was short and tumultuous, but filled with splendid music, dazzling virtuosity, and missed opportunities. Many of his works are recognized today as among the greatest achievements of Western music. He died just before his 36th birthday in 1791, leaving behind over 600 compositions and a whole raft of rumors about his demise. He succumbed to a miserable death after a relatively short illness of several weeks; his body so swollen that he could hardly move, racked with fever, suffering from black vomit, and other terrible symptoms. The "medical" report indicated his death was from "severe military fever," a diagnosis that could mean almost any type of infectious disease. He was buried in a communal grave, but rumors ran wild about the "true" cause of his death, ranging from murder to political assassination for his slander of the Free Masons in his opera *Die Zauberflote* (The Magic Flute).

In the cemetery where Mozart was buried, the tradition at the time was to dig up the graves after ten years and remove the bones; rich people had their bones labeled and stored while the poor had their bones crushed and reburied to make way for more bodies. The sexton who oversaw the burial of Mozart, however, claimed to have tied wire around his corpse so he could find it when later exhumed. When the ten years had passed, he claimed to have found the body and saved Mozart's skull from the crusher. This skull passed from person to person over the years until it was finally given to the International Mozarteum Foundation in Salzburg in 1901, where it remained on display until 1955. In 2006, a forensic investigation was launched to try to determine if the skull indeed belonged to Mozart. Overlay images, correlations with Mozart's reported dental records (he had only a reported seven teeth), and the observance of a hematoma on his skull all have supported the claim. A recent DNA study, however, proved inconclusive in identifying it as Mozart's skull. So, the jury is still out as to if it is indeed his skull.

A curious footnote to this is that other famous composers have experienced a bit of Mozart's fate. The skulls of Beethoven, Haydn, Schubert, and Liszt have all been "collected" and put on display from time to time.

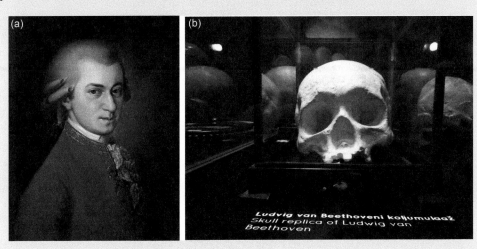

FIGURE 9.42   (a) Posthumous portrait of Wolfgang Amadeus Mozart (1756–1791, Otto Erich Deutsch 1965) and (b) replica of Ludwig van Beethoven's skull (1770–1827).

Source: Used per Creative Commons Share-Alike 4.0 International. User: Ijon.

9.2 FORENSIC TAPHONOMY

9.2.1 Background and Introduction

The field of taphonomy involves the study of the decay and post-mortem processes of an organism. When specifically applied to forensic investigations, it deals not only with how animal and plant remains decay but also with how they may be buried, moved, distributed, or otherwise changed after death. It considers how the environment, including other organisms, may have affected the post-mortem remains. Understanding these post-mortem processes can shed valuable light on a crime scene investigation. Remains are not only changed by the environment, the local environment is also changed by the introduction of the remains. The soil becomes enriched and disturbed, the layers of soil may shift in the burial process, scavengers may visit and change the site, and other natural features may be modified due to the presence of the remains. Sometimes these changes to the environment persist for a very long time, as often observed in historical archaeological excavations. Thus, forensic taphonomy deals with all events that occur around remains specifically during the PMI.

Taphonomic investigations typically consider the perimortem time through the PMI up to the discovery of the remains.

All events, beginning with the death of the organism, that occur to affect and change the remains found at discovery are part of the investigation. This raises a real problem, however, as it is often difficult to clearly distinguish between the events that occurred at the time of death and those that occurred either before or after death, especially when the PMI, the time between death and discovery, becomes long and the remains have a greater chance to decompose and be exposed to outside action. This problem of distinguishing events right at the time of death from later changes is illustrated by the common usage of the term perimortem (at or around the time of death); a pathologist may mark this period in a matter of minutes, while for an anthropologist, it may stretch into years, since it may take years for skeletal remains to be observably changed.

Once the post-mortem period becomes longer than just a few days, the forensic pathologist often has difficulties accurately estimating the time of death. As this time stretches from days into weeks, other methods of determining the PMI, such as forensic entomology (Chapter 10), may become useful. The difficulties in determining the PMI as the time lengthens further are compounded by the increased opportunities for the action of the weather and other organisms to change the remains in a multitude of ways. It becomes increasingly difficult to separate any perimortem trauma that may have been the cause of a person's death from any post-mortem damage to the remains caused by the environment. Finally, as the PMI time grows longer, even these methods become less useful, and we are left with only the skeletal remains from which to seek answers.

9.2.2 Post-mortem Modifications

When examining remains, one of the first jobs of the anthropologist is to catalog which bones are present and to locate and describe any observed damage to the bones, with an eye to determining the cause of death and other forensically useful information. But, as mentioned above, the environment around the remains is rarely passive and works to change the remains in often quite significant ways. So, the job also involves determining what damage to the remains occurred at the time of death (or even before) and what changes have occurred afterward during the PMI. Sometimes this is rather straightforward. For example, if carnivores scavenged the remains, their tooth marks and the observed pattern of damage can clearly identify their work (*vide infra*). Certain kinds of bone fractures, particularly spiral fractures (Figure 9.43), are usually identified as antemortem while others, such as extreme crushing fractures, may be marks of post-mortem damage. The action of the weather and the result of insect and microbial decomposition are often quite recognizable as post-mortem damage.

Researchers have categorized the forces that cause observed taphonomic changes as arising from individual, cultural, and environmental sources. Individual factors refer to features of the decedent themselves, such as size, age, weight, and cause of death. Cultural features are those arising from the action of other humans, as dictated by their traditions, cultures, and behaviors. Cultural factors include burial rituals (e.g., cremation, burial locations, embalming, etc.), unusual events (e.g., war casualties, genocide, suicide), and abnormal behavior (e.g., dismemberment, attempted destruction of the remains). Environmental factors are those arising from the locale of the remains such as temperature, precipitation, soil composition, carnivore and plant action, and placement of the body (e.g., water, desert, pavement, etc.). Additionally, factors such as the victim's clothing (e.g., winter clothing vs bathing suit, tight vs loose), microclimate (e.g., sunny vs shady), and access to the remains by other organisms can be important.

As noted above, the presence of scavengers can serve to both damage the bones and spread the remains over a wide area, depending on the species. The pattern of tooth marks

Types of Bone Fractures

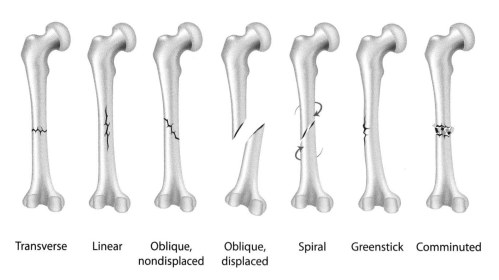

Transverse   Linear   Oblique, nondisplaced   Oblique, displaced   Spiral   Greenstick   Comminuted

FIGURE 9.43 Types of bone fractures.

Source: Shutterstock.com.

can be very informative; dogs and cats leave pointed marks on the remains and typically follow a set pattern of consumption (head/face first followed by chest to the lower extremities, etc.). Rodents leave a very different pattern (Figure 9.44). Carnivores tend to leave conical holes, while rodents leave concave scrapings (often showing as two or three tooth grooves) in the bone. These animals also attack the bones in characteristic patterns and may strew the bones about the investigation site.

The accidental breakage of bones may occur by being trodden upon by larger animals, especially common where farm animals are found. Damage also occurs from simple weathering as the bones become progressively more brittle and fragile upon exposure to the elements.

One piece of useful information from a taphonomic investigation might be whether the site of death was different from where the remains were found. This can arise from the transportation of the body from the site of death to a distant burial site or from an initial burial followed by an exhumation of the body and reburial elsewhere. Clues to the occurrence of these actions can often be read from a careful examination of soil and plant evidence. Plant and animal evidence can also shed light on the season of the year that the remains were deposited. For example, skeletal remains were found after a long winter, but the date of death was unknown and important to determine. It was noted that the remains were found lying over top of a species of crushed wildflowers. These flowers must have, therefore, been in bloom when the remains were deposited. Knowing the brief blooming season for the flowers during the previous summer allowed for a fairly accurate determination of the date that the remains were deposited.

Several types of actions in the PMI require some special consideration. If the burial is in water, the order and timing of post-mortem events can be quite different from land-based decomposition and is dependent upon water temperature, composition (salt or freshwater), depth, movement (e.g., tides, stream action, lakes, etc.), and the action of water organisms.

Another taphonomic action involves the burning or attempted burning of the remains. One important question frequently asked is when did the burning occur, and was it perimortem or post-mortem? The answer to this difficult question

often hinges on the state of the remains and is dependent upon the temperature, length of burning and the state of the body at the time of incineration. If the bones are badly damaged, a definitive answer might not be possible. In some instances, it may be possible to determine if the body had been disarticulated (taken apart) before the firing.

Thus, a careful consideration of the taphonomic evidence can give valuable information to a forensic investigation involving human remains.

BOX 9.10   MURDER AT HARVARD, BUT WHERE'S THE BODY?

In 1849, Harvard University was the scene of an interesting case of forensic taphonomy. Prof. John Webster, a professor of chemistry and geology, was once a wealthy person who fell on hard times and was forced to borrow money from a Boston-area merchant, Dr. George Parkman. In November 1849, Dr. Parkman entered Harvard's Medical College to demand repayment of his loan to Dr. Webster – and was never seen again. All searches for Parkman, and of Webster's apartment, failed to turn up any information as to his whereabouts. The janitor, however, began to grow suspicious, especially from an unusually hot fire that Webster had stoked in the furnace, so hot that the wall on the other side of the furnace was hot to the touch. Eventually, a search was made of the furnace and a variety of human remains were found, including some that were identified as certainly belonging to Dr. Parkman. Dr. Webster was eventually convicted of the murder and was hanged on August 30, 1850.

FIGURE 9.45 Prof. John Webster (1793–1850) (Stringer 2024).

Source: Retrieved from Wikimedia Commons; used per Creative Commons Attribution.

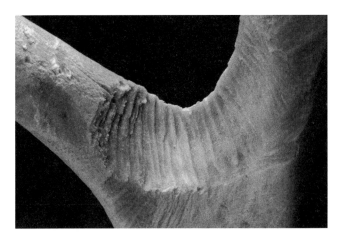

FIGURE 9.44 Post-mortem rodent damage done to a white-tailed deer antler.

Source: Shutterstock.com.

BOX 9.11   SPOTLIGHT ON FORENSIC ANTHROPOLOGY

Dr. Douglas H. Ubelaker,

Smithsonian Institution and Former President of the American Academy of Forensic Science (2011–2012)

Dr. Douglas H. Ubelaker is a curator in the Department of Anthropology at the National Museum of Natural History, Smithsonian Institution in Washington, DC, and a professional lecturer in the departments of anatomy and anthropology at George Washington University. He has been a consultant in forensic anthropology to the FBI since 1978, reporting on more than 800 cases. He is a member of a number of national forensics and anthropology organizations, including Diplomate, American Board of Forensic Anthropology and Fellow of the American Association for the Advancement of Science. His numerous awards include the FBI Director's Award for Exceptional Public Service (2002), the FBI special recognition award (2004), and the T. Dale Stewart Award by the Physical Anthropology Section of the American Academy of Forensic Sciences (2001).

Education: B.A. and Ph.D. from the University of Kansas.

Why did you decide to go into this field? Following an initial fieldwork experience, I became fascinated with all one could learn from the study of skeletal remains. As an undergraduate, I participated in original research and took courses that expanded my knowledge base. Basically, I entered the field because I was intellectually engaged in the subject matter and realized that I thoroughly enjoyed it.

What background, training, certification is required to become a forensic anthropologist? An expert in my field typically has an advanced degree in physical anthropology, broad exposure to the field of anthropology, and experience in skeletal analysis and with archeological techniques. The primary certification is Diplomate status granted by the American Board of Forensic Anthropology (ABFA).

Are there any professional organizations in forensic anthropology? The primary professional organization is the American Academy of Forensic Sciences. Other key organizations include the American Association of Physical Anthropology, the Society of American Archaeology, and the International Academy of Legal Medicine.

What is your most interesting case? The cases that hold the greatest interest for me are those with the strongest intellectual challenge. Of particular interest are those cases that presented problems that could not be adequately and fully resolved with existing methodology. Such cases have stimulated research, thought and design, leading to new published information.

What do you like most about forensic anthropology? I enjoy the research process and publishing the results in scholarly journals. Forensic anthropology also offers friendly, supportive and productive colleagues, international perspective and opportunities for participation, and the chance to apply our knowledge and techniques to real problems of contemporary society.

What is the most difficult part of your profession? Time-management. With so much important work to be done, it can be challenging to devote the necessary time to meet deadlines and effectively contribute to diverse activities.

What advice would you give to someone who is considering pursuing this field? It is important for people entering this field to have a broad, yet focused education on topics relevant to forensic anthropology. Important skills include writing and speaking. It is also important to obtain practical experience working with someone actively engaged in the field.

FIGURE 9.46   Dr. Douglas H. Ubelaker.
Source: Photo used per Douglas Ubelaker.

Interesting Forensic Anthropology Cases for Further Study

- Donner Party (1847, California)
- President John F. Kennedy Assassination Case
- John Wayne Gacy Case
- Dr. Josef Mengele War Crimes Trial

- John Emil List Case (facial reconstruction)
- Paul Revere's identification of Gen. Joseph Warren from the battle of Bunker Hill by a dental prosthesis that he had made

- The identification of Agrippina, Emperor Claudia's wife by a tooth
- John Wilkes Booth body identification by his brothers from gold tooth filling

Answer to Box 9.7 **You Be the Sleuth: Two-Minute Mystery** (see Figure 9.33): The cranial opening in this skull was healed as the result of an ancient trepanation – opening the skull to relieve a mental illness or as part of a spiritual rite.

QUESTIONS FOR FURTHER PRACTICE AND MASTERY

9.1 Forensic anthropology involves the application of the data, theory, and methods of which subdiscipline of anthropology to legal questions?

9.2 All of the following are examples of typical anthropological physical evidence from a human burial EXCEPT: (a) decomposing human remains, (b) clothing, (c) perimortem trauma (e.g., gunshot wounds, knife marks), (d) handwriting, (e) projectile.

9.3 Perimortem trauma refers to injuries sustained when?

9.4 What type of information can typically be determined by a forensic anthropologist when examining a complete set of skeletal remains?

9.5 How can information about the sex of a decedent be gained from the examination of a person's pelvic bones?

9.6 How can each of the following be estimated for decedent from skeletal remains?
(a) stature, (b) sex, (c) age, (d) occupation, (e) weight, (f) cause of death.

9.7 Describe what is meant by taphonomy and how it is a part of a forensic investigation.

9.8 What is meant by *minimum number of individuals* (MNI)?

9.9 Give three examples of blunt force trauma.

9.10 Give three examples of sharp force trauma.

9.11 Describe how the hyoid bone can give evidence of a cause of death.

9.12 A mandible was found with all deciduous teeth except for the eruption of a permanent first incisor. Using the data in the text, what would you estimate as the age at death for this person?

9.13 What is meant by co-mingled remains?

9.14 What chemical is responsible for giving bones their strength and rigidity?

9.15 What is the most abundant protein in the body?

9.16 What is the difference between a tendon and a ligament?

9.17 What is cortical bone?

9.18 How does the interior material of bone differ from the outer material?

9.19 What is the function of red marrow? What is the function of yellow marrow? Where are they typically located in bones?

9.20 What property does collagen give to bone?

9.21 What are the two main bone groupings when considering a skeleton?

9.22 What methods are used to determine if an unknown object is a bone?

9.23 How is a bone determined to be human?

9.24 What methods are used to determine how old a bone fragment may be?

9.25 What is a biological profile? How does it help establish the identity of the remains?

9.26 What are allometric relationships?

9.27 What is osteometry?

9.28 What part of the skeleton provides the most information for determining the sex of remains?

9.29 What are the general differences between the pelvis of a female and that of a male?

9.30 What is the pubic symphysis? How does its appearance differ between males and females?

9.31 What are some of the dimorphic differences between male and female skeletons, in especially the skulls?

9.32 What are some of the observed differences between the femurs of males and females?

9.33 What are deciduous teeth? How many teeth does an adult typically have?

9.34 What bones are typically used to try to determine the ancestry of a descendant?

9.35 What are some of the difficulties inherent in the reliability of facial reconstruction using a skull?

9.36 What are some of the inherent problems faced when using skeletal remains to determine how a victim died?

9.37 What are the steps the body takes when healing a broken bone?

9.38 How can the location of bone beveling help determine the direction a bullet traveled through a body?

9.39 What bone is associated with determining death by strangulation?

9.40 What is the expertise of an odontologist?

9.41 What are some of the difficulties a forensic pathologist faces as the PMI (post-mortem interval) increases?

9.42 A forensic pathologist observes that remains have a fresh spiral fracture. Is this fracture most likely antemortem or post-mortem?

EXTENSIVE QUESTIONS

9.43 Explain the following forensic anthropology terms: distal, superior, proximal, inferior, lateral, sagittal, anterior, posterior, medial, longitudinal, superficial, and deep.

9.44 Explain the characteristics of the five categories of bones.

9.45 What are the five central questions a forensic anthropologist tries to answer when given an unknown object?

9.46 What are the differences in the following facial reconstruction processes? (a) overlay, (b) 2D facial reconstruction, (c) 3D facial reconstruction?

9.47 Given the table in the text, consider the following problem. Two bones were found at a crime scene. Bone A was determined to be a fibula from a male with incomplete fusion of epiphyses, while Bone B, from a female, had complete fusion. What can be concluded about the ages of the male and female?

9.48 Using the following osteometric standard equations, determine the stature of each of the following:

Stature
3.26 × (humerus) + 62.10 = stature ± 4.43 cm
3.42 × (radius) + 81.56 = stature ± 4.30
3.26 × (ulna) + 78.29 = stature ± 4.42
(there will be two calculations for stature, based on the upper and lower standard of error)

a. a humerus measuring 47.42 cm
b. an ulna measuring 17.54 cm
c. a radius measuring 16.55 cm

GLOSSARY OF TERMS

allometric relationship: a relationship of the size of a particular bone to the overall physical stature.

antemortem trauma: injury that occurs before the time of death.

anterior (ventral): front.

anthropology: the field that focuses on the physical, cultural, and social organization of humans.

appendicular skeleton: the portion of the skeleton that includes the limbs (legs and arms) and their points of attachment (pelvis, shoulder) – the parts of the skeleton that "hang" on the central (axial) support column.

axial skeleton: the portion of the skeleton that includes the spine and head that provides the primary vertical support to the skeleton.

archaeology: the branch of anthropology that explores past human life by studying the remaining physical evidence.

beveling: the bone wound that appears as a concave crater.

biological profile: a description of the biological properties of a person from the skeletal remains and frequently includes stature, age, sex, ancestry, and medical history.

blunt force trauma (BFT): the injury that occurs when a blunt object strikes a person with sufficient force to cause physiological damage.

bone: a strong tissue that provides support for the body and is made up primarily of calcium phosphate (hydroxyapatite) and organic components, especially collagen. Classified into long bones, short bones, flat bones, sesamoid bones, and irregular bones.

cartilage: the tough, smooth, flexible connective tissue often found lining joints, largely made up of collagen and other proteins that allow bones to glide past each other smoothly.

collagen: the tough, fibrous protein that is used for strength and attachment in multiple places in the body.

co-mingled remains: remains from more than one individual mixed together at a single site.

compact bone: the dense part of the bone made up of a hard matrix, primarily hydroxyapatite and collagen.

crest: the top of a ridge.

deciduous teeth: baby, or temporary, first teeth that are eventually lost and replaced by permanent teeth.

deep: away from the surface.

diaphysis: shaft of a long bone.

distal: away from the head or trunk of the body.

endoskeleton: an internal skeleton.

epiphysis: the part of a bone separated from the main body of the bone, primarily at the ends of long bones.

facial reconstruction: the creation of a likeness of the face of a person from their skeletal remains.

foramen: an opening in a bone.

hematoma: a blood clot.

hydroxyapatite: a form of calcium phosphate $[Ca_{10}(PO_4)_6(OH)_2]$ which is a primary component of bone.

hyoid bone: a small "U"-shaped bone found in the neck that supports the muscles of the tongue.

inferior (caudal): lower.

lateral: away from the midline.

ligaments: tough fibrous tissue that connects bones to other bones.

linguistics: the study of language.

longitudinal: along a line that runs from head to foot.

marrow: the soft tissue inside a bone that is responsible for red blood cell production.

medial: toward the midline.

metaphysis: the part of the bone lying between the diaphysis and epiphysis.

morphology: the form or structure of an object.

ossification: the process of bone formation primarily from the calcification of soft tissue.

osteoarthritis: a disease resulting from the chronic breakdown of the cartilage in the joints.

osteocyte cells: mature bone cells.

osteometry: the process of measuring bones.

pelvis: the intersection of the axial and appendicular skeleton; comprised of the two hip bones, sacrum, and coccyx.

perimortem trauma: an injury that occurs at about the time of death.

posterior (dorsal): toward the rear.

post-mortem trauma: an injury that occurs after the time of death.

process: a projection or bump.

proximal: the direction toward the head or trunk of the body.

remodeling bone: the process of reshaping bones by resorption and deposition of new bony material.

sagittal: from front to back.

sexual dimorphism: differences in shapes or structures between male and female anatomical features.

sharp force trauma (SFT): injury that occurs from an attack with a knife or other sharp object.

sinus: a cavity in the bone.

spongy Bone: the more open, porous bony tissue that makes up the inner portions of a bone.

superficial: toward the surface.

superior (cranial): upper.

suture: the line where two bones come together, such as between two flat bones of the skull.

symphysis pubis: the front point of connection between the two hip bones.

taphonomy: the study of how remains decay and are moved, distributed, disturbed, or otherwise changed after death. The field also examines how the environment is affected by the remains.

tendon: a tough fibrous tissue that connects muscles to bone.

BIBLIOGRAPHY

William Bass and Jon Jefferson, *Death's Acre: Inside the Legendary Forensic Lab the Body Farm Where the Dead Do Tell Tales*, Berkeley Trade Publisher, 2004.

Sue Black, et al., *Criminal Dismemberment: Forensic and Investigative Analysis*, CRC Press, 2017.

Karen R. Burns, Forensic *Anthropology Training Manual*, Prentice Hall, 2006.

Steven N. Byers, *Introduction to Forensic Anthropology*, Prentice Hall, 2010.

Steven N. Byers and Susan Myster, *Forensic Anthropology Laboratory Manual*, Allyn & Bacon, 2011.

Angi M. Christensen, Nicholas V. Passalacqua, and Eric J. Bartelink, *Forensic Anthropology, Current Methods and Practice*, Elsevier Inc., 2019.

Heather M. Garvin and Natalie R. Langley (Eds.), *Case Studies in Forensic Anthropology: Bonified Skeletons*, CRC Press, 2019. https://doi-org.libezproxy2.syr.edu/10.4324/9780429436987

William D. Haglund, *Forensic Taphonomy* in *Forensic Science: An Introduction to Scientific and Investigative Techniques* (2nd Ed), Stuart H. James and Jon J. Nordby (Eds.), CRC Press, 2009.

William D. Haglund and Marcell H. Song, *Advances in Forensic Taphonomy: Method, Theory, and Archaeological Perspectives*, CRC Press, 2001.

William D. Haglund and Marcella H. Sorg (Eds.), *Forensic Taphonomy: The Postmortem Fate of Human Remains*, CRC Press, 1997.

Angela Libal, *Forensic Anthropology*, Mason Crest Publisher, 2005.

Myriam Nafte, *Flesh and Bone: An Introduction to Forensic Anthropology*, Carolina Academic Press, 2009.

Thomas D. Stewart, *Essentials of Forensic Anthropology*, Charles Thomas, Publisher, 1979.

Karen T. Taylor, *Forensic Art and Illustration*, CRC Press, 2000.

Douglas Ubelaker and Henry Scammell, *Bones: A Forensic Detective's Casebook*, M. Evans and Co., 2000.

Tim D. White, Michael T. Black, and Peter A. Folkens, *Human Osteology* (3rd Ed.), Academic Press, 2011.

Caroline Wilkinson, *Forensic Facial Reconstruction*, Cambridge University Press, 2008.

Otto Erich Deutsch (Posthumous portrait of Wolfgang Amadeus Mozart) *Mozart: A Documentary Biography*. Stanford: Stanford University Press, 1965.

Stringer & Townsend, "Trial of Professor John W. Webster for the Murder of Doctor George Parkman," *OnView*, accessed June 5, 2024, https://collections.countway.harvard.edu/onview/items/show/6608.

Forensic Ecology

10

10.1 FORENSIC ECOLOGY

By a sample we can see the whole.

(Tremayne, 2008)

LEARNING GOALS AND OBJECTIVES

Forensic ecology is becoming an increasingly important part of forensic science. In order to show a deeper understanding of the potential uses and limitations of the field of forensic ecology, after completing this chapter you should be able to:

- Define forensic ecology and describe the subfields that are most often employed in forensic work.
- Explain what is meant by forensic entomology, zoology, botany, mycology, and palynology.
- Discuss what constitutes an ecosystem and how a particular ecosystem can be identified from its proxy indicators.
- Describe the classification system used for all life.
- Describe the types of information the sub-disciplines of ecology can provide to forensic investigations.

Forensic entomology has potential uses and limitations of insect life in legal proceedings, and, after completing the chapter, you should be able to:

- Discuss the general features, classification, and morphologies of insects.
- Describe the three areas of study in forensic entomology.
- Show how insects form part of the complex ecosystem of decaying remains.
- Recognize the features of the different stages of decay after death.

- Explain what factors affect insect colonization and development in remains.
- Describe the key features of insect succession in the decomposition of a body.
- Discuss the stages of insect growth and development.

10.1.1 Introduction

The Earth's biosphere forms a complex and dynamic fabric, teeming with an amazing diversity of living organisms that have somehow found a way to survive and even thrive in often harsh and uninviting physical environments. These organisms interact in a multitude of ways throughout their lives, and even after death as they enrich the habitat with their remains. As humans, we cannot escape the company of our natural world companions; animals, plants, fungi, protists, bacteria, and others. The field of ecology (also called bionomics) focuses on the relationships that exist between organisms and their environment. The term ecology even derives from a fusion of the Greek words for "dwelling place" and "study" (Figure 10.1).

Since forensic science often seeks to establish interrelationships, a study of the interaction of the all-encompassing living world around us can yield unique forensic information. By understanding what the "silent witnesses" from the natural world and the environment can tell us, we hope to reveal their unmistakable stories.

10.1.2 Overview of Forensic Ecology

Forensic ecology focuses on studying organisms and their environments and using these relationships to look for observable changes or altered patterns that can provide unique legal information. The basic underlying principle of forensic ecology is that organisms are found in recognizable and predictable environments and live within complex, interrelated biological communities. These complex communities exist within the larger context of the surrounding habitat involving the climate, non-living components (e.g., soil, water, minerals), and light conditions. When taken together, the living community with its habitat forms an *ecosystem* (Figure 10.2). Each ecosystem comes complete

DOI: 10.4324/9781003183709-12

FIGURE 10.1 Ecology depicts the distribution and interrelationships between organisms in the living environment and their habitats, as illustrated by the painting entitled "Peaceable Kingdom" by Edward Hicks (1780–1849).

Source: National Gallery of Art, Washington, DC.

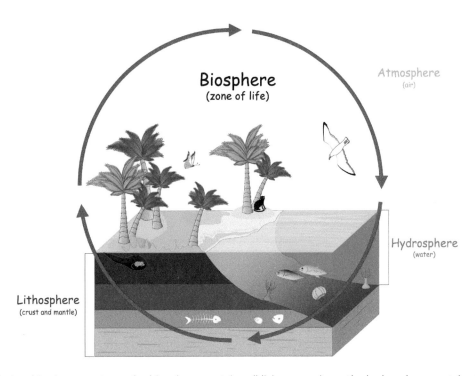

FIGURE 10.2 Relationships in ecosystems: the biosphere contains all living organisms, the hydrosphere contains the water environment, the atmosphere contains the air, and the lithosphere includes the Earth's surface, crust, and a portion of the upper mantle.

Source: Shutterstock.com.

with its own unique set of interrelationships between and among its living (biotic) and non-living (abiotic) parts. Unlike the focus in previous chapters on molecules and aspects of *individual* living things, such as organs, bones, fingerprints, and retinal patterns, forensic ecology focuses its attention on larger patterns formed *between* organisms

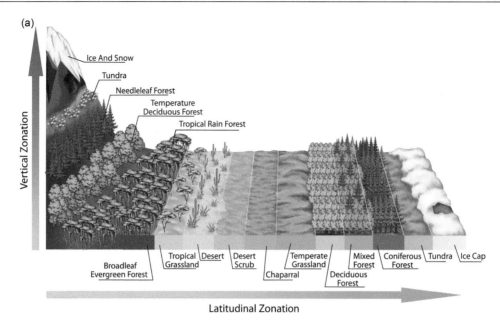

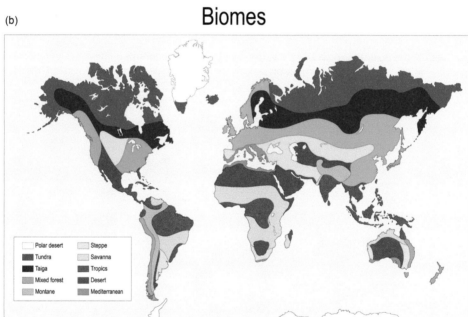

FIGURE 10.3 Biomes: the world's major types of ecosystems. The biomes are distributed across the Earth and vary by (a) altitude and (b) latitude (the north-south position on Earth).

Source: Images courtesy Shutterstock.com.

and their environs – even on worldwide ecosystems, often called *biomes* (Figure 10.3).

Forensic ecology is a rapidly evolving and developing field with enormous potential to broadly impact forensic investigations. The information that can come from ecological studies may influence many types of legal investigations, including:

- Estimating the post-mortem interval (PMI) – the time elapsed between the actual death of an organism and the discovery of its remains.

- Locating human remains and determining whether the remains have been moved (finding and differentiating burial from death sites).
- Determining the relationships between people and specific places (e.g., if a person recently visited a particular site or traveled along a specific pathway).
- Determining if a crime site has been disturbed (e.g., has something been hidden, removed, changed, or buried at a given place) and when these changes occurred.
- Validating or disproving disputed events (e.g., has a person lain or kneeled on a particular patch of

ground or what did someone last eat as determined from plant remains in the stomach).

- Recreating a timeline of events that occurred in the commission of a crime.

Forensic ecology encompasses several important sub-disciplines of study including:

- **Entomology**: The study of insect life.
- **Zoology**: The study of animal life.
- **Botany**: The study of plant life.
- **Palynology**: The study of pollen, spores, and similar materials along with trace amounts of organic matter, inorganic minerals, and soils.
- **Mycology**: The study of fungi (e.g., mushrooms, molds, etc.).
- **Soils and sediments (geology and sedimentology)**: The study of the organic and inorganic matter found in soils, minerals, and rocks.

Each of these areas will be discussed in more detail in this chapter, with the exception of soils and sediments, which will be presented separately later (Chapter 15).

10.1.3 Application of Ecology to Forensic Investigations

In the application of ecological concepts to forensic problems, scientists are often called upon to use relatively small amounts of plant, animal, and other materials to describe in detail where they originated. This is often possible through the use of something called *proxy indicators*. Proxy indicators are small amounts of identifiable material from an ecosystem that can indicate with relatively high accuracy, information about the *entire* ecosystem from which they originated (Figure 10.4). For example, tiny pieces of wood, leaves, seeds, pollen, lichen, or soil can, when identified and taken together, indicate with amazing accuracy which type of ecosystem they originated from. Some species of plants, for instance, are found only in dry, arid desert environments while others are found only in woodlands, and yet others grow only in alpine meadows. Similar relationships between the ecosystem and its components are true for animal life, bacteria, fungi, soils, and other components. If traces of these materials are found during an investigation, they may provide information about the places of their origin. These proxy indicators may be picked up by a suspect directly, such as on their clothes or person, or on other pieces of evidence that can ultimately be traced back to a particular source location with confidence.

With appropriate knowledge, it is possible to visualize the place from which a set of proxy indicators originated. While finding pollen on someone's clothes from a particular species that only grows along stream banks may suggest a particular site of origin, the greater the number of indicators found, the more complete the picture of the place of origin will be. Therefore, the accuracy of predicting the site of origin depends

on the number of indicators found. Thus, a dozen proxy indicators identify their common origin site with much greater reliability than just a few. Often, however, diligent collection and analysis can uncover dozens of indicators that connect a piece of evidence with just one specific geographic location. Often, no other type of evidence can provide such clear and evident linkages between just one site and a particular piece of evidence.

Proxy indicators can be any organism, part of an organism, or environmental component (e.g., soil, mineral, etc.) that is part of a larger ecosystem. They may also range from single-celled organisms to large animals and plants. There are obviously huge, almost infinite, variations possible in the combinations of proxy indicators that can be found in nature. With a sufficiently detailed catalog of indicators present, forensic ecology may one day reach a level of site identification similar to the current ability to identify a particular person with a great deal of certainty based on the uniqueness of their DNA patterns.

BOX 10.1 SHERLOCK HOLMES ON PROXY INDICATORS

Long before this term was known or used by anyone and it couldn't be put it better:

"From a drop of water," said the writer, "a logician could infer the possibility of an Atlantic or a Niagara without having seen or heard of one or the other. So, all life is a great chain, the nature of which is known whenever we are shown a single link of it." From an article quoted by Holmes in *A Study in Scarlet* (Arthur Conan Doyle, 1888).

Ecosystems merge and overlap in nature, forming transitional communities. This great potential for variation can mean that every single location may be fundamentally distinct from every other on the planet, even those just a few meters apart. While there may be great similarities in the proxy indicators found between two locations, it is exceptionally unlikely that any match between the two will be complete and exact.

Prof. Patricia Wiltshire, a founder of the field of forensic ecology, has pointed out that "no two oak woodlands are identical, and identification of a specific oak woodland (or an area within that woodland) requires detailed profiles of proxy indicators relating to the specific microsite." Therefore, a detailed understanding of the ecological communities for the places in question is required. This type of information can be derived only through detailed sampling and identification of the species and materials present at each location. But consideration beyond just the identification of the species present is needed; an understanding of the interrelationships *between* the species and materials found is also important for a successful investigation.

Forensic ecology can be equally successful when applied to indoor and outdoor environments. The actual path taken by

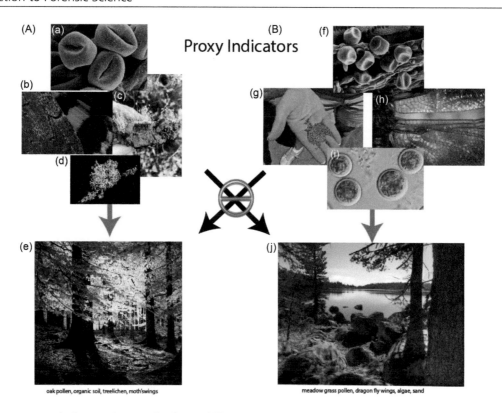

FIGURE 10.4 Four proxy indicators from each of two different ecosystems that identify their respective ecosystems from among other possibilities. For the temperate forest (A), oak pollen, forest soil and moss, forest tree lichen, and forest-dwelling moth wing point strongly to the forest environment. The lake meadow ecosystem (B) is indicated by the presence of meadow pollen grains, beach sand, dragonfly wing, and algae.

Source: Image Credits Top Left image grouping: (a) Dr. Jeremy Burgess, Science Photo Library. Used with permission. (b) Used per Creative Commons Attribution 2.0 Generic, User: Geoff Gallice from Gainesville, Florida. (c) US Department of Agriculture, (d) Used per Creative Commons Attribution-Share Alike 4.0 International, User: Hubertl. (e) Used per Creative Commons Attribution-Share Alike 3.0 Unported, User: Marlene Thyssen. Top Right image grouping: (f) Dr. Jeremy Burgess, Science Photo Library. Used with permission. (g) Used per Creative Commons Attribution-Share Alike 3.0 Unported. User: Corwin Hee, (h) Used per Creative Commons Attribution 3.0 Unported. User: Miguel Varona. (j) Used per Creative Commons Attribution 2.0 Generic. User: Rick Cooper.

a criminal can be "tracked" both inside and outside by looking for key ecological indicators. For example, an outdoor pathway taken is often limited by the terrain (e.g., hills, ravines, streams, bridges, fences, etc.), and the plants along the actual path taken can readily show signs of having been disturbed (e.g., broken twigs, impressions in the leaves and ground, etc.). In fact, not only can the pathway be discovered in this fashion, but also a rough idea of how long ago it was used can be made from the damage and regrowth patterns of the plants along the path – remember plants "heal" in predictable patterns and times just as a person's wounds heal, as considered in the pathology Chapter 8. Native "trackers" worldwide have long known this and have used it with often startling results to effectively track prey and enemies across enormous distances and widely differing terrains. Indoor ecology, often containing molds, spores, plants, insects, dust, and other materials, can be treated similarly to an outside ecosystem.

Some species may only be found within a geographically limited range while other species are much more commonly distributed across broad ranges. Knowing where different species are found and the limits of their range and habitat is important in forensic ecology. For example, shown in Figure 10.5 is a case where a number of different plant species are found within a fairly small area of Yosemite National Park in California. From this map, it can be seen that the Quaking Aspen tree (*Populus tremuloides*, green on the map) is found almost exclusively in the western region of the park, while the Oregon White Oak (*Quercus garryana*, dark red on the map) is found exclusively in the eastern side of the park. Finding the leaves from one of these species associated with a piece of evidence would suggest that it may have been connected with just a few limited locations within the park. Additionally, the plants encountered along one path can be very different from those found along a nearby but different pathway. Ranges can be likewise established for animal species and other types of flora and fauna, along with the locations of rock outcrops and soil types. For example, the San Juan Antelope Squirrel is found only along the California

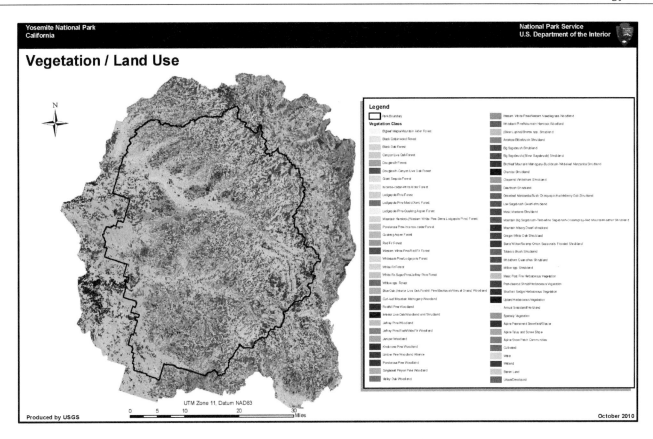

FIGURE 10.5   Vegetation distribution in Yosemite National Park in California. The different colors correspond to park locations where specific species of plants can be found.

Source: U.S. Department of the Interior.

Pacific coastline portion of the Antelope Squirrel range, while the Texas Antelope Squirrel is found only in western Texas (Figure 10.6).

But geographic distribution is only one aspect of useful ecological evidence that can be based upon a particular species. Some plants, for example, that are very common in many places and, therefore, of limited use for narrowing the source location of a piece of evidence because they are so common, can still be useful forensically depending on how their seeds and pollen are distributed (Figure 10.7). Plants that are pollinated by the wind typically produce a great deal of pollen that is broadcast across a very wide area. In this way, even the pollen of a relatively rare plant may be commonly found in the environment many miles from the original plant. This result may make pollen evidence from this particular plant species open to misinterpretation when determining a location of origin. In contrast, the pollen from a plant that is spread by insect action *only* can be much more geographically restricted in its distribution and relatively rare to find in the environment or on evidence, even for a very common plant. This type of pollen is particularly useful as a geographical marker. Thus, it is important not only to consider the species total range but also the range of that plant's pollen in interpreting where a piece of evidence picked up the traces from a plant source.

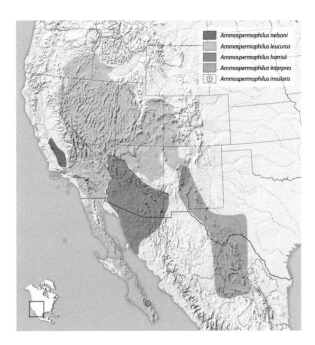

FIGURE 10.6   Distribution map of different species of antelope squirrels (genus *Ammospermophilus*).

Source: Used per Creative Commons Share-Alike 3.0, Germany. Credit: NordNordWest/IUCN Red List of Threatened Species.

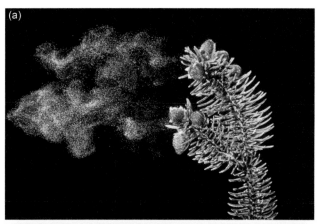

FIGURE 10.7   (a) Wind-borne pollen from the Norway Spruce (*Picea abies*) and (b) insect-borne pollen by a bee.

Source: (a) Jerome Wexler/Science Photo Library. Used with permission. (b) used per Creative Commons 2.0 Generic. User: coniferconifer from Japan.

Urban, suburban, and indoor environments are also home to an enormous variety of "artificial" ecosystems – ecosystems that are either partially or wholly constructed from non-native materials that may be transported from places far from their origin, to create complex transplanted environments (Figure 10.8). For example, home gardens and public landscapes often contain plants from around the world to create decorative landscapes. Flowers and shrubs such as the torch lily (South Africa), Hyacinth (Iran), Nasturtium (Mexico), Gladiolus (Mediterranean), Fuchsia (South America), and Eucalyptus (Australia), among thousands of others, are found in gardens and groupings never found naturally. This complexity, however, can prove to be an advantage in forensic investigations. Finding traces of plants, lichen, fungi, and organic matter on a piece of evidence from a collection of species that are never found together in the wild can uniquely lead to a very localized garden or landscaped area. Look, for example, at home gardens found on almost any suburban street, and you will quickly find that no two gardens are alike in terms of the species planted together. This type of evidence, for example, has been used to determine the validity of disputed events in assaults, kidnappings, and other cases.

10.1.4 Classification of Life

All life on Earth has been divided into groups based on their common features. This allows for easier study and organization of both the similarities and differences between living organisms. This field is often called systematics or taxonomy. These groupings are especially important in the study of forensic

FIGURE 10.8   The manmade flower garden at the Bethesda Terrace, overlooking The Lake in New York City's Central Park, is an excellent example of how people create complex transplanted environments.

Source: Shutterstock.com.

ecology since it is necessary to be able to recognize individual organisms as part of a well-recognized group – such as a Douglas Fir tree (*Pseudotsuga menziesii*), gray wolf (*Canis lupus*), or a common blue dragonfly (*Enallagma cyathigerum*) from a conifer forest.

The groupings or classifications of living organisms are similar in design to a branched tree – the most basic features that organisms have in common form the trunk and variations of these features divide the different organisms into progressively smaller and smaller groups until we can uniquely identify a group containing only one type of organism by its features – a species (Figure 10.9). The broadest classification level is the kingdom and all life is now divided into kingdoms: monera, protists, fungi, plants, and animals, as shown in Figure 10.10. Kingdoms are distinguished by whether an organism has a nuclear membrane or not, whether they are unicellular (one-celled) or multicellular (many cells), and how they derive their nutrition. Each of these kingdoms is further broken up into phyla, classes, orders, families, genera (*plural* for genus), and species. In biology, an organism is uniquely

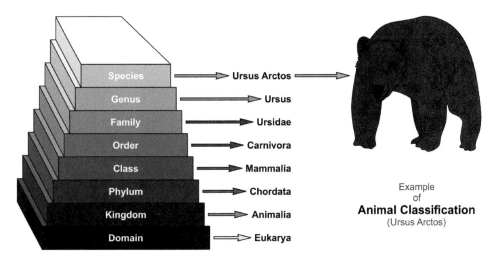

FIGURE 10.9 Classification system of life into kingdom, phylum, class, order, family, genus, and species. The classification is shown for a brown bear (*Ursus arctos*).

Source: Shutterstock.com.

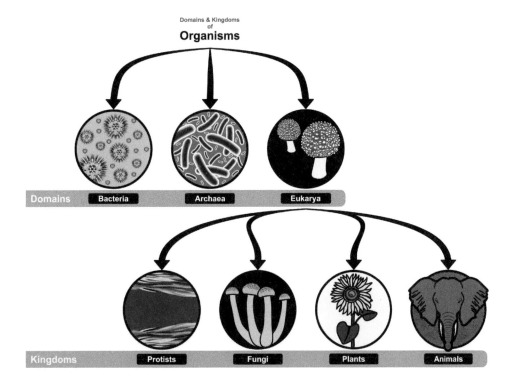

FIGURE 10.10 Classification of life into kingdoms: *monera* (prokaryotes: bacteria and archaea), *protista* (eukaryotes not in other kingdoms), *fungi* (yeasts, molds, mushrooms), *plantae* (plants), and *animalia* (animals).

Source: Shutterstock.com.

named simply by giving their genus and species (remember that if organisms are in the same genus they must also be in the same family, order, class, phylum, and kingdom). For example, the brown bear in Figure 10.9 is denoted by the name *Ursus arctos*, while the black bear is *Ursus americanus* – both have the same genus but differ only in species name. Therefore, with just two words, we can unambiguously talk about the brown bear apart from all other living organisms – even its closely related "cousins," the black, polar, or any other bear species. Later in this chapter, this classification system of living organisms will be employed as part of forensic investigations.

In the following sections, we will explore some of the more common applications of sub-disciplines of ecology to forensic investigations, beginning with probably the best-developed field, forensic entomology.

10.2 FORENSIC ENTOMOLOGY: MUTE "WITNESSES"

10.2.1 Background and History

Since all organisms on Earth are part of a highly interactive biosphere, it's not surprising that forensic science has begun to look carefully at the relationships between organisms and their environments in the hopes of finding useful information. Nowhere has the development of this idea been clearer than in the field of entomology, to the point that it is now a powerful investigative tool.

Our living world is divided most broadly into five general groupings or kingdoms into which all organisms fit (taxonomy): animals, plants, fungi, protists, and monerans. This system has arisen from an attempt by scientists to organize and help understand the relationships among all living things. The largest and most complex of these broadest groupings is the animal kingdom. Within the animal kingdom, organisms are known that range in size from just a few cells linked together to the massive blue whale, the largest creature to have ever lived on Earth. The most diverse form of animal life, in fact, the most diverse and numerous of all life forms, is found in a subgroup (phylum) referred to as the arthropods. This diverse phylum contains the crustaceans, spiders, centipedes, insects, and their relatives. It is within this grouping that forensic entomology is focused.

So, what is forensic entomology? First, entomology is the field of science that deals specifically with the study of insect life. Insects are truly and undisputedly the most successful branch of organisms in the animal world, with well over 900,000 species known, representing over 80% of the Earth's known species of living organisms. But this seems to be just the tip of the iceberg. Scientists estimate that fewer than one-half of all insect species have been so far identified, with estimates ranging from 2 to 30 million for the true number of insect species on the planet. Insects probably also represent the largest biomass on the planet, with an estimate of 10^{19} individual insects alive at any given time or about 200 million insects *per person*. This has been calculated to equate to about 300 pounds of insects per person. Two recent studies have estimated that 1 acre of soil in North Carolina would contain about 124 million insects, and a study acre in Pennsylvania could contain as many as 425 million individual insects, a truly astonishing number.

Historically, insects have been dominant on Earth, beginning with their first appearance over 400 million years ago. Some insect species, such as the cockroach, have remained relatively unchanged for hundreds of millions of years.

Insects are defined as having three pairs of legs and segmented bodies that are divided into a head, thorax, and abdomen (Figure 10.11). They are relatively small, air-breathing arthropods that often have true wings (not modified arms and legs as are found in birds and bats). Adult insects have their skeletons on the outside in the form of an *exoskeleton*, mostly made of a hard material called chitin (a polymeric sugar molecule). Most insects hatch from eggs and go through a series of stages (molt) before finally reaching their final adult form. The insect phylum ranges from the ants and earwigs to butterflies, dragonflies, and beetles, but it does not include many species commonly called insects, such as spiders, scorpions, and centipedes, among others. While these latter organisms do have some similarities with insects, such as segmented bodies and exoskeletons, they do not have the six legs required to be classified as insects.

Insects occupy almost every climate, region, and environment in the world. They fly, burrow, walk, crawl, and swim. Every aspect of human life is intimately intertwined with insect life, from the moment of birth to well past the point of death. Insects are responsible for much of the food we eat, the products we consume, and ultimately for the process of recycling dead organisms to provide the basic resources needed for the next generations of life. All these processes, however, can also provide forensic information to a variety of investigations.

Forensic entomology uses what is known about insects to answer questions of legal importance such as time of death, product storage integrity, drug and toxin identification, and the

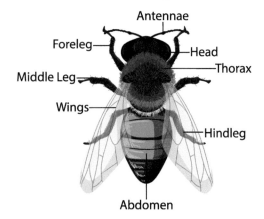

FIGURE 10.11   External Anatomy of an insect (Honey Bee).

Source: Shutterstock.com.

connection of crime scenes with suspects and victims. The use of insect information in legal settings has a very long history. As far back as at least the mid-13th century in China, the value of the insect record in law was appreciated. The Chinese judge Sung T'zu wrote a book in 1247 called *The Washing Away of Wrongs*, the oldest known handbook of forensic science for judges and lawyers. In his book, he tells of one investigation of a murder that took place near a local rice field. Upon examining the body, he determined that the likely weapon was a scythe – a long-handled blade that was used on farms for harvesting grass and grain. No other clues as to the identity of the attacker could be gained, however, from the crime scene or through his interviews of suspects. In a clever attempt to identify the assailant, however, he had all the suspected field workers line up with their scythes and stand in the hot noonday sun … and he waited. Before long, the scythe of only one man had attracted a large number of flies, presumably from invisible remains of human blood and tissue on the scythe. When confronted with the evidence, the man confessed to the crime and "knocked his head on the floor." This is the first recorded use of forensic entomology to quite literally "sniff out" a murderer.

Since the time of Sung T'zu, the use of insects in legal settings has made slow but steady progress. One important step came in 1626 when Francesco Redi (Figure 10.12) showed that maggots (larvae of flies) did not "spontaneously arise"

from the organic matter in rotten meat but only came from eggs deposited by adult flies on the meat.

A landmark case came in 1850 when the body of a small infant was found behind a fireplace mantle in an apartment building near Paris. Since the apartment had been occupied continuously by four different sets of tenants in the preceding few years, it became important to determine how long ago the infant died in order to suggest a possible suspect. A local physician with forensic interests, Dr. Bergeret d'Arbois, was called in. By carefully determining the insect activities and the state of the remains, he was able to conclude that the body had been there since 1848, clearing one set of tenants and throwing suspicion on others. Later, in 1894, J. P. Mégnin published the first textbook on how entomology could be used in forensic investigations (*La Faune des cadavres: Application de l'entomologie à la médicine légale* translated as "The Fauna of corpses: Application of entomology to forensic medicine"). In the first half of the 20th century, several important scientific studies of the lifecycles of insects, especially flies, provided a necessary foundation for understanding what a forensic insect record could tell (Figure 10.13). Interest really took off, however, in the 1970s with a series of cases in which insect evidence was used to great effect in several murder investigations. Since then, forensic entomology has developed into a well-respected and often important forensic tool.

BOX 10.2 CASE HISTORY: DR. RUXTON AND THE FLIES

On September 29, 1895, two young women were gazing over the side of a small bridge near Edinburgh, Scotland, when they noticed what appeared to be a human leg. The police were called, and after carefully examining the vicinity, they found the remains of two people "surgically" cut into many small fragments, some wrapped in newspaper and badly decomposed.

The bodies were later identified as those of Mrs. Isabella Ruxton and her housekeeper, Mary Rogerson. The identity of Mrs. Ruxton was aided by overlaying a scaled photo of Mrs. Ruxton onto a similar scaled photo of one of the recovered skulls (a).

The prime suspect in the murder of Mrs. Ruxton was her husband, Dr. Buck Ruxton (c). Dr. Ruxton, formerly Gabriel Hakim from India, first arrived in Scotland in 1927 to attend medical school. He soon married Isabella Kerr and, by 1935, they lived with their children and housekeeper in Lancashire, England, 100 miles south of where the bodies

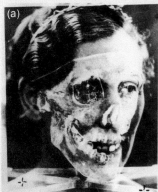 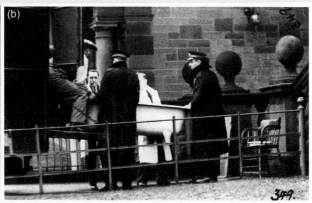 

FIGURE 10.14 (a) Superimposed photographs of Mrs. Isabella Ruxton and "skull no. 2, 1935" [investigators laid a photo-transparency of this skull over Mrs. Ruxton's portrait to establish that the skull belonged to Mrs. Ruxton], (b) Photograph of Dr. Ruxton's bath, where he dismembered his victims, and (c) Dr. Buck Ruxton, 1935.

Source: NIH.

were found (a place now locally known as "Ruxton's Dump"). Dr. Ruxton, who was known to have a particularly violent temper and a deeply suspicious nature, frequently suspected his wife of infidelity. Police were often called to the Ruxton household to settle family disputes. On one occasion, he even told the police officer, "Sergeant, I feel like murdering two persons ... my wife is going out to meet a man."

The prosecution built its case upon the plausible scenario that Dr. Ruxton had confronted his wife with charges of adultery after a trip that she had made alone to Edinburgh. The confrontation turned violent, and he killed his wife. Unfortunately, their housekeeper, Mary Rogerson, must have witnessed the murder and was also killed by Dr. Ruxton to silence her. The evidence had identified the bodies and determined that they were surgically dismembered to try to remove all traces of their identities, including the removal of fingertips. In investigating Dr. Ruxton, bloodstains were found throughout the Ruxton home; he had even asked a patient to help clean up the mess (b). However, the prosecution's case needed to accurately determine the time of death in order to convict Dr. Ruxton. For this, they turned to forensic entomology. Dr. A.G. Mearns identified a species of blowfly (*Calliphora vicina*) on the remains and determined their stage of development. He was able to say that Mrs. Ruxton had died between 12 and 14 days before her body was recovered. This evidence agreed with other scientific testimony and led directly to the conviction of Dr. Ruxton for murder. After an unsuccessful appeal, he was hanged in 1936 in Strangeways Prison in Manchester, England.

FIGURE 10.12 1664 book by Francesco Redi (*Osservazioni intorno alle vipere* translated as "Observations about vipers") disproving the theory of spontaneous generation and showing that maggots grow from eggs produced by adult flies.

10.2.2 Forensic Entomology Basics

Forensic entomology involves the use of insects in law and has been broken down into three distinct areas of study: urban, medicolegal, and stored product issues. Urban entomology is focused on the relationships between man and insects, most often centered upon insect pests and their eradication. This area includes considerations of the damage, disease, and elimination of insect species such as termites, mosquitoes, wasps, fleas, ticks, and many other "pest" insect species. Medicolegal uses of entomology tend to focus on insects that feed directly upon human remains, often called *necrophagous insects*.

This type of insect data can provide information about the time of death, the cause of death (including the presence of drugs and toxins), whether a body has been moved, and who might have been involved in the crime. Often, insects are the sole remaining "witnesses" of a violent crime, able to shed light on the sequence and timing of events. Interpreting this record correctly may help to either confirm or cast doubt on the testimony of suspects and victims. Analyzing insect life on a cadaver can provide a more accurate estimate of time of death than a medical examiner's estimate in the several days to several weeks range. This is often a crucial time period in understanding criminal events where medical pathology cannot usually provide definitive answers. The final area, stored product forensic entomology, deals primarily with insect pests that can contaminate and destroy commercial products, such as food, water, medicine, and building supplies.

In this section, however, we will deal mostly with medicolegal uses of forensic entomology.

10.2.3 Medicolegal Forensic Entomology

The human body, after death, is an amazingly nutrient-rich but fleetingly ephemeral object. Its nutritional resources are vigorously contested by a huge variety of living organisms, each having carved out specific niches that give them a competitive advantage for a particular aspect of the remains. Some thrive due to their early arrival on the remains, some flourish by focusing on certain tissue types for nourishment, and some succeed by scavenging the residue at the end. Other species prey on organisms that feed on the remains, while yet other species only use the body as a convenient environment to live upon.

Arthropods can generally be placed into one of four groups of organisms that are part of the ecosystem of the remains:

1. *Necrophagous species* (species that feed directly on the remains) – e.g., blowflies, flesh flies, skin beetles, carrion beetles, etc.

FIGURE 10.13 Stages of fly development (counterclockwise from bottom left; eggs, first, second, and third instar larvae, puparium, and adult).

Source: Shutterstock.com.

2. *Predators and parasites* (feed on the necrophagous species, not the remains) – e.g., rove beetles, wasps, some fly species, etc.
3. *Omnivorous species* (feed both on the remains and the resident species) – e.g., wasps, ants, and some beetles.
4. *Adventive species* (use the remains as part of their habitat) – e.g., springtails, spiders (incidental predators), etc.

Some species fall into different groups as they progress through their life cycles. For example, some fly larvae begin by feeding solely upon the remains (necrophagous) but become predatory at later stages of their development.

Within a short time after death, a complex ecosystem is rapidly established on and around the body, with its own unique set of inter-species relationships and a recognizable progression of species that are successively active over the time of decay (*faunal succession*). In the end, the chemical resources contained within the body are efficiently returned to the biosphere to support new generations of life; in this sense, insects perform an absolutely necessary biochemical recycling function for our planet. The vital part that insects play in this ecosystem and the profound effects of their action on animal

remains are illustrated in Figure 10.15, in which the decomposition of an animal is shown both with and without exposure to insects.

BOX 10.3   BRIEF ON INSECTS AND DECAY

1. Four types of species found on dead remains: those that feed directly on the remains (*Necrophagous*), those that feed on the necrophagous species but not the remains (*Predators and Parasites*), those that feed both on the remains and the resident species (*Omnivorous species*), and those that use the remains as part of their habitat (*Adventive species*).
2. Five stages of decay: fresh, bloated, decay, post-decay, and dry.
3. Duration of stages depends on environmental and other factors.
4. Insects are often central to the decomposition of remains.

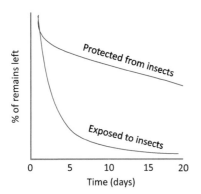

FIGURE 10.15 Plot showing the effect of exposure of animal remains to insects.

Source: Adapted from Payne (1965).

A mammal, such as a human, undergoes a series of identifiable stages of decay after death. This predictable series of stages, shown for a pig in Figure 10.16, are often referred to as the fresh stage, bloated stage, decay stage, post-decay stage (or advanced decay stage), and dry stage. The time of onset and duration of each of these stages may be highly variable and depend on a variety of chemical and environmental conditions, such as weather conditions (e.g., temperature, rainfall/snowfall, wind speed, humidity, sunlight, etc.), location (e.g., temperate, semi-tropical, arid, forest, apartment, urban, etc.), position of the body (e.g., lying on the surface, underwater, partially buried, etc.), body composition (e.g., size, age, health, presence of drugs and toxins), and other factors. For example, the dramatic effect of seasonal temperature and weather conditions on the duration of these stages is shown in Figure 10.17; the entire first three stages take less time to complete in the summer than just the first stage in winter. Also, the decomposition of bodies in freshwater may occur at less than half the rate of remains found on land. Some species of flies cannot penetrate shallow buried remains, while others have been found in deeply buried coffins. Bodies located indoors or tightly wrapped with cloth or plastic may also be inaccessible for insect colonization. An understanding of the stages of decay is important for the accurate interpretation of insect evidence. These stages are:

The *fresh stage* of decay starts at the point of death and may last for up to several days. During this stage, there may be few outward signs of change, and the person may appear to be simply "sleeping." However, significant biochemical changes are occurring at the cellular and organ levels within the body. The body first slowly cools to match the temperature of its surroundings (*algor mortis*). During this time, the cells begin to undergo a carefully programmed death cycle that produces enzymes catalyzing the breakdown of proteins, carbohydrates, and fats in the body (*apoptosis*). The muscles stiffen due to the chemical decomposition of glycogen and the formation of lactic acid (*rigor mortis*). The stiffening process is usually noticeable within 6 to 8 hours of death and may last two to three days, depending on conditions. Bacteria proliferate and further break down internal tissues and organs while producing gases as byproducts of the decomposition process (e.g., ammonia, carbon dioxide, hydrogen sulfide, and others). Ectoparasites, such

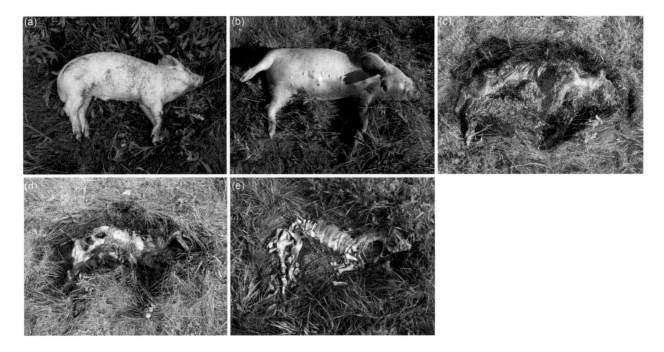

FIGURE 10.16 Stages of decay and entomological succession: (a) fresh stage, (b) bloated stage, (c) decay stage, (d) post-decay stage, and (e) dry stage.

Source: (a–e) Used per Creative Commons Attribution-Share Alike 3.0, Unported. User: Hbreton19.

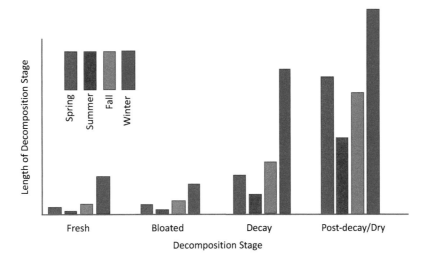

FIGURE 10.17 The effect of seasonal differences on the duration of the decay stages.

Source: Adapted from Reed (1958).

as fleas, lice, and ticks, typically leave the body relatively soon after the death of their host organism. If environmental conditions are favorable and the body is accessible, blowflies can quickly locate the body from extremely faint decay odors and deposit their eggs (*oviposition*) in all available body orifices. This can occur under optimal conditions within just a few minutes after death. The eggs are laid around the nose, ears, mouth, eyes, anus, genital openings, and any puncture wound areas on the body. The location of these latter types of sites, wound areas, can become important since the locations of "hidden" trauma on badly decayed bodies (not readily observable with normal physical examinations) can sometimes be found by noting where the insects have penetrated into the body, such as through gunshot or knife wounds. Eggs are also deposited in other dark and moist places such as folds of clothing, skin, or underneath the edges of the body. For the flies to be active and find the body, however, the air temperature must be within a relatively narrow range (too hot or too cold prevents their activity), and conditions must permit insect flight (e.g., it must not be too windy or raining heavily to preclude flight). Certain species of flies are attracted preferentially to the remains of different animals – some insects prefer small mammals while others focus on human-sized remains. Some species also have additional requirements; for example, Bluebottle flies strongly prefer shady settings while the closely related greenbottle flies prefer sunny locations. This difference is dramatically illustrated by the following quote from a World War I trench-warfare veteran: "In the shade afforded by the deep portion of the trench, round the traverses, any moist patch of chalk wall would be hidden by a dense, indigo-colored cluster of *Calliphora* [Bluebottle fly], large as a soup plate ..., whereas, where the trench was shallow or blown in [sunny locations], the green shimmer of *Lucilia* [Greenbottle fly] was everywhere" (see Box 10.6). The species distribution may, therefore, indicate whether a body had been lying in direct sunlight or in more shady conditions. Blowflies also typically do not lay eggs at night, so remains must wait until morning to be colonized.

BOX 10.4 CASE HISTORY: THE FLY NOSE

In Indiana, a dead body was deposited down an abandoned well after the homicide. The shaft of the well was then filled with rubble, thereby burying the body under tons of debris. Additionally, to cover their tracks, the well itself was camouflaged by mounds of dirt, tires, and old junk. When following some leads for the missing person, investigators at a farm in the vicinity noticed swarms of blowflies on the concealing mound of tires. Curious at this observation, eventually the investigators uncovered and excavated the well and found the missing body. Even though the blowflies could not directly reach the body itself, they were strongly attracted to the odor from the decay.

Insects are not immediately and equally attracted to all tissues and organs after death. For example, exposed liver (such as that found at a slaughterhouse) typically remains untouched for about the first three hours, while kidneys and entrails are usually attractive to flies immediately. This may be due to the fact that some tissues are too acidic for the flies immediately after death but become less acidic with time. The fresh stage ends when the buildup of gases becomes visible, leading to the bloated stage.

In the *bloated stage*, putrefaction begins, and the large amount of gas produced from anaerobic bacterial action inflates the body cavities, especially the intestines and abdomen. This stage typically lasts from two to six days, depending on environmental conditions. External insect activity also becomes very noticeable and active during this stage. The body begins to change dramatically in its external appearance, with pronounced discoloration caused by blood pooling at the lowest spots of the body due to gravity (*livor mortis*). During this stage, blowflies continue to lay eggs, but other species, including flesh flies and cheese skippers, make their

FIGURE 10.18   Maggot mass on a decomposing Virginia Opossum (*Didelphis virginiana*).

Source: Retrieved from Wikimedia Commons; used per Creative Commons Attribution.

first appearance and begin egg-laying and feeding. Feeding maggots are clearly visible on the outside of the body during this period. Maggots representing several stages of development, from freshly hatched to larger, later stages of growth, are found mixed together.

As mentioned before, the insect species that inhabit decaying remains have developed unique traits that allow them to compete effectively for the rich nutritional resources contained within the body. While blowflies are usually the first to arrive on-site and lay eggs, the later-arriving flesh flies make up for the apparent disadvantage of their late arrival by depositing live larvae rather than laying eggs on the remains that take time to hatch. Some species compensate by becoming predators on other larvae at later stages of their development. These competitive factors play an important role in the type (species), number, and sizes of the larvae found on the remains.

The *decay stage* begins when the abdominal wall ruptures, allowing the built-up gases to escape and the carcass to collapse and flatten. This is an exceptionally busy time for insect life on the remains. While adult blowflies no longer visit, large numbers of maggots can be found throughout the body, feeding both internally and externally. The number of maggots can become so large that the internal temperature of the body can be raised dramatically, often by tens of degrees Celcius, from the combined heat generated by the *maggot mass* (Figure 10.18). The mass, in reality, creates its own microenvironment, causing changes in the developmental rates of the larvae themselves. Maggots from the inner portions of the mass may occasionally move to the edges of the mass to cool because the temperature in the center of the mass has risen too high. The large number of feeding larvae also attracts other insect species that parasitize or prey directly upon the

larvae, such as wasps and fly parasites. Some wasp species, for example, lay their eggs directly within the fly pupae. When the wasp eggs hatch, they consume the fly larvae as food from the "inside." The decay stage may last about a week or more and continues until the moist tissues of the remains have been largely depleted, leaving mostly skin, cartilage, bones, hair, and teeth.

During the next stage, referred to as the *post-decay* stage, the remains continue to dry out more fully. The larvae have consumed most of the soft tissues and have reached the developmental stage where they leave the body to pupate. New species arrive, including varieties of beetles, that continue the decomposition process. This stage can last several weeks or even months.

The final stage, or *dry stage*, can last for months or even years, depending upon body placement and environmental conditions. It is often difficult to use this stage to accurately determine the age of the remains, except within very broad ranges. Insects that have evolved mechanisms for digesting keratin (a tough, insoluble protein found in hair, fingernails, skin, and other resistant tissues) are the primary inhabitants of the body during this last stage. These include the dermestid beetles, clothes moths, and sap beetles. At the end of the process, very little besides bones and teeth remains of the body.

The variation of insect species through the stages of decomposition provides information about how long the body has been decomposing. Figure 10.19 and Table 10.1 list some specific species found during the different decay stages. Representative pictures showing each of these insect types are found in Figure 10.20. For example, finding dermestid beetles on the remains suggests that the body is in the final stage of decomposition, while finding *silphidae* insects (Carrion

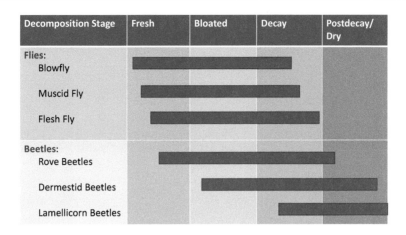

FIGURE 10.19 Succession of adult insect species on human remains over time.

TABLE 10.1 Selected insect arrival times during decay

DECOMPOSITION STAGE	EXAMPLE INSECT SPECIES
Fresh	Blowflies (*Calliphoridae*), Flesh Flies (*Sarcophagidae*), Horse and House Flies (*Muscidae*), Small Dung Flies (*Sphaeroceridae*)
Bloated	Blowflies (*Calliphoridae*), Flesh Flies (*Sarcophagidae*), Horse and House Flies (*Muscidae*), Small Dung Flies (*Sphaeroceridae*), Rove Beetles (*Staphylinidae*), Scuttle and Coffin Flies (*Phoridae*), Cheese Flies (*Piophilidae*), Scavenger Flies (*Sepsidae*)
Decay	Blowflies (*Calliphoridae*), Flesh Flies (*Sarcophagidae*), Horse and House Flies (*Muscidae*), Rove Beetles (*Staphylinidae*), Cheese Flies (*Piophilidae*), Carrion Beetles (*Silphidae*)
Post-Decay	Rove Beetles (*Staphylinidae*), Cheese Flies (*Piophilidae*), Checkered Beetles (*Cleridae*)
Dry Stage	Sap Feeding Beetles (*Nitidulidae*), Skin Beetles (*Dermestidae*)

Source: Adapted from Cleveland Natural History Mus., Invertebrate Zoology Research Collection.

Beetles) suggests an age within the earlier decay stage. A careful understanding of the climate and the presence of any drugs is necessary, however, in order to properly interpret the timing. For example, the presence of cocaine, a stimulant, in the body can accelerate the entire larval development process dramatically. Also, bodies deposited outside during winter are typically not accessible to blowflies. In this case, beetles are often the primary colonizers of the remains without the usual pattern of insect faunal succession since the remains dehydrate before being consumed by flies.

As mentioned previously, burial or submersion in water changes the decomposition characteristics of a body, often quite significantly. Burial virtually eliminates aerobic bacteria and many commonly found insect species associated with surface decay. Some species of bacteria and insects, however, are still able to reach and flourish on buried remains, depending primarily upon the depth of burial. The effects of burial, even from a shallow burial under an inch of soil, are to significantly lengthen the time necessary for decomposition relative to that for remains found on the surface since fewer species can reach the remains. Finding blowfly larvae on buried remains can often indicate that the burial was not immediate after death but was delayed long enough for the blowflies to colonize the remains.

Submersion in water usually also results in different organisms involved in the decomposition and may include crustaceans, caddis-flies, and other aquatic species, depending upon the local environment (e.g., salt or freshwater, water temperature, currents, etc.). If a body floats, the exposed parts can be colonized by typical surface species such as blowflies and beetles. When the remains sink, however, the fly larvae and beetles either migrate away from the body or are drowned. After sinking, the decomposition process is usually completed by bacteria, fungi, and carnivorous aquatic larvae.

The activity of vertebrate scavengers can also dramatically affect the sequence and timing of the decay process (Figure 10.21). By opening alternative pathways into a body or by scattering the remains, they may provide earlier than typical access to insects into the interior of the body. This process also causes the remains to dry out faster, leading to an earlier start of later decomposition stages than would normally be expected. Larger scavengers can also slow the process by partially or even completely burying or transporting the remains. Their action, however, can often be discovered by a careful physical examination of the remains (e.g., tooth marks, bone abrasions, unusual tissue shearing/tearing, etc.).

Different regions of the world exhibit a diversity of species involved in the decay process. It is crucial to

FIGURE 10.20 Insect types commonly found during decay stages [clockwise from top left]: (a) *Calliphoridae* (blowfly), (b) *Sarcophagidae* (flesh fly), (c) *Muscidae* (house fly), (d) *Phoridae* (Scuttle and Coffin Flies), (e) *Piophilidae* (cheese fly), (f) *Sepsidae* (scavenger fly), (g) *Staphylinidae* (Rove Beetle), (h) *Dermestidae* (skin beetles,), and (i) *Silphidae* (carrion beetle)].

Sources: (a) Used per GNU Free Documentation License, Version 1.2. User: Muhammad Mahdi Karim. (c) Used per Creative Commons Attribution-Share Alike 3.0, Unported. User: Toby Hudson. (c) Used per Creative Commons Attribution-Share Alike 3.0, Unported. User: Alvesgaspar. (d) Used per Creative Commons Attribution-Share Alike 2.5, Generic. User: James Lindsey at Ecology of Commanster. (e) Used per Creative Commons Attribution 3.0, Unported. Created by user Dick Belgers at waarneming.nl. (f) Used per Creative Commons Attribution-Share Alike 2.5, Generic. User: Bruce Marlin. (g) Used per Creative Commons Attribution-Share Alike 4.0, International. User: URSchmidt. (h) Use per Creative Commons Attribution-Share Alike 3.0, Unported. User: Aiwok. (i) Used per Creative Commons Attribution-Share Alike 4.0, International. User: WanderingMogwai.

FIGURE 10.21   Examples of vertebrate scavengers: (a) red fox (*Vulpes vulpes*), (b) turkey vulture (*Cathartes aura*), and (c) coyote (*Canis latrans*).

Sources: (a) Used per Creative Commons Attribution-Share Alike 2.0 Generic. Gunilla G from Örnsköldsvik, Sweden. (b), Used per Creative Commons Attribution 4.0 International. User: Anja J. (c) Used per Creative Commons Attribution-Share Alike 3.0 Unported. User: Yathin S Krishnappa.

know the local insect fauna at the site of any remains to accurately interpret the insect record. One of the most important pieces of information the insect record can provide is the length of time that the body has been dead: the post-mortem interval.

10.2.4 Estimating Post-Mortem Interval (PMI)

After a human body has been dead for more than just a few days, many of the tools that the medical examiner has available for estimating the time of death (*rigor mortis, algor mortis, livor mortis*) are no longer useful. The most important time period that needs to be defined in a typical forensic investigation is referred to as the *post-mortem interval* (PMI), or the length of time from the actual death of the organism to the time that the remains are found. By knowing the PMI, it is possible to calculate backward from the time of the discovery of the body to determine the approximate time of death.

The determination of a PMI estimate using entomology starts with several reasonable assumptions. First, it is assumed that the flies have ready access to the body beginning at the time of death and that conditions are right for them to both find the remains and to deposit eggs quickly. To evaluate the validity of this assumption requires knowing the weather patterns at the time of death (e.g., temperature, wind speed, rainfall, etc.) and an estimate of the first point in time at which the flies had free access to the body. If access has been in some way limited, then the PMI needs to be adjusted accordingly. Access can be limited not only by weather patterns but also by underground burial, submersion in water, wrapping the body in cloth or plastic, or depositing the body in an enclosed space. For example, an investigation of a murder crime scene found evidence of a burglary, with the body found near the open window entry point. Pathology suggested a PMI of at least 24 hours, but the insect life found on the body, however, suggested that it had not been exposed to the outdoors for very long at all, no more than just a few hours. It was later determined that the person reporting the crime had actually committed the murder on the previous day in a closed apartment (no insect access) but had subsequently returned to the crime scene the next day, opened the window, and set the scene to make it appear as though a burglary had occurred. The murderer then called the police to report the crime after resetting the scene. Once the proper sequence of events was established, all the physical and entomological evidence then fit clearly within the same timeline.

Second, PMI estimates assume that the succession of insect colonization on the body follows a predictable course of faunal succession. Noted exceptions to the usual succession, once understood, can provide additional evidence about whether the body had been moved and where the original crime scene might be located.

A third assumption in making a PMI estimate presumes that the course of insect development follows a predictable pattern and timeline (e.g., egg → larvae → pupae → adult). This requires a sufficiently detailed understanding of the stages of development for *each species* present along with an understanding of how climate conditions affect insect growth and development. Luckily, much is known about the lifecycles and growth patterns for many of the insects particularly important to PMI evaluations.

Finally, an accurate estimate of PMI requires that environmental conditions at the body site can be reasonably estimated beginning at the suspected time of death and running continuously through the time when the remains were found. This can often be estimated by obtaining climatological data from the nearest weather station and then estimating the local conditions at the body site (microclimate). This information is necessary since the rate of insect development, including the time for each developmental stage, is very strongly affected by the environment.

Probably the most useful insect in determining a PMI, especially during the first few weeks following death, is the fly. The life cycle of a fly, such as the blowfly or housefly, proceeds through a series of well-defined stages, as illustrated in Figure 10.22. It begins with the deposition of eggs by an adult female fly (oviposition) in a dark and sheltered place. These eggs hatch to form tiny maggots, or fly larvae, that are about 2 mm long (about the size of two grains of salt). This freshly hatched larval form is referred to as the *first instar* stage of development. A maggot is really little more than an efficient eating machine, equipped with a simple intestinal digestive tract, salivary glands, a hook on the "front" end to allow it to stuff food into its "mouth," and structures on the posterior end (called *spiracles*) that allow it to breathe when "head-down" in tissue feeding, shown in Figure 10.23. The presence of this "rear-end" breathing tube allows the maggot to continuously immerse its head in the semi-fluid mixture it feeds upon. When the maggot reaches about 5 mm in length, it can no longer continue to grow within the confines of its original skin. In order to continue its growth, the maggot molts or sheds its first skin to reveal a larger skin underneath. This begins the *second instar* stage of its development. During this stage, it grows to about 10 mm (the size of a small marble) before molting again for the *third instar* stage. This final instar stage continues until the maggot grows to about 20 mm (about the length of a penny) before migrating away from the body as a prepupa. Once well away from the body in a dry and well-protected place, the larva forms a *puparium* in which the outer skin of the prepupal larva hardens and darkens to form the outer pupal case. Inside this protective casing, the final transformation of the larva into an adult fly occurs. This is biochemically a very complex time as the tissues of the larva are completely rearranged to form the structures, organs, and tissues of the adult fly. The pupae are very durable and the insect may remain in this stage until environmental conditions are right for it to emerge as an adult, such as over the winter or through droughts, although under optimal conditions they may emerge as adults within about a week. Only the adult stage insect has wings and, after emerging from the puparium, they fly off to repeat the cycle.

An adult fly typically lives between two to four weeks, but during this time, an adult female fly can lay thousands of

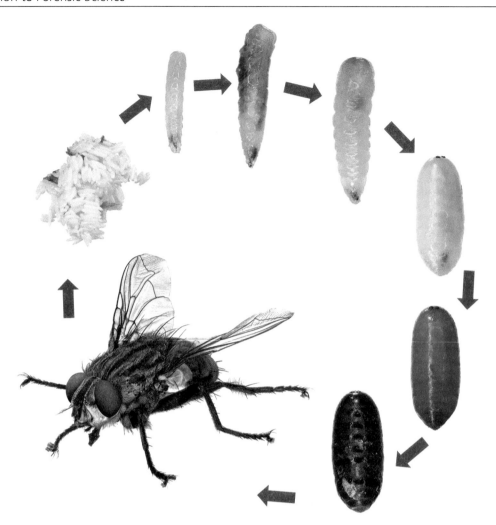

FIGURE 10.22   Life cycle of a blowfly [*Calliphoridae*].

Source: Shutterstock.com.

eggs, usually in clumps of 50–100. It has been estimated that if a single pair of flies began non-stop egg-laying in April, they would have about 2×10^{20} descendants by August if all the offspring lived. This, of course, does not occur, but it gives an indication of the prolific nature of fly egg deposition.

While this is the general pattern for a fly lifecycle, there are notable variations. For example, the flesh fly gives birth to live larvae on the remains instead of laying eggs. Other insect species important to PMI estimates, such as beetles, also have varying lifecycles and stages.

There are two primary tools for helping entomologists determine the PMI: species succession and developmental stage. The range and type of insects present are particularly important for determining the age of remains that are more than a month old while individual insect developmental information is typically most useful in narrowing down the timeline within the first month.

The first tool, insect succession, involves identifying the various insect species found on the remains. As discussed before, insect species arrive and depart at different stages of the decay process in a typically well-ordered and overlapping procession (or more accurately called succession) of species.

Observing which species are present, therefore, provides an opportunity to estimate how long it would take for that stage of insect infestation to occur. The succession times are correlated with the observed condition of the remains (bloated, decay, post-decay, etc.). For example, egg-laying by flies typically stops when the maggot population becomes sufficiently large, usually within a few days. Maggot growth also slows as the food supply runs short and the remains begin to dry significantly. Once the moist food supply runs short, the maggots usually move away from the body, while at the same time, the beetle population increases. While these are overlapping events, clearly understandable patterns can be observed, as illustrated in Figure 10.24. It is useful to note that the shape of each population curve in the figure becomes more elongated as time progresses. The first few stages may completely occur within a few days, while later stages may extend over weeks, months, or even years. This broadening of time ranges at later stages also leads to more uncertainty and less accuracy in PMI estimates as the time increases. The stages of insect succession can also be interrupted, or even eliminated, when the body has been moved between different environments. For example, a body deposited in an arid climate may become dried out so

FIGURE 10.23 Scanning electron micrograph (false color) of a maggot (2 hours old) of the common greenbottle fly, or green blowfly (*Lucilia caesar*) feeding on a piece of raw beef. The mouth end (not visible) tapers into a thin wedge with two mouth hooks to stabilize the maggot. Secreted enzymes breakdown and liquefy the food tissue which can then be absorbed.

Source: Dr. Jeremy Burgess/Science Photo Library. Used with permission.

quickly as to virtually eliminate the possibility of colonization by flies, leaving the beetles as the primary insect decomposers. Other possibilities already mentioned, such as burial,

submersion in water, and depositing the remains outside in winter, can strongly influence the pattern of insect succession.

The second tool for establishing a PMI estimate relates to the age and developmental stage of the individual insects found on the remains, especially the largest and, presumably (but not always), the oldest larvae. The particular stage of development for a maggot can usually be determined by measuring its size and, in some instances, measuring the spiracles (breathing tubes). Each stage of the fly's development lasts for a specific amount of time that depends principally upon the local temperature and available food resources, as illustrated in Figure 10.25, which shows the growth rates at different temperatures. Insects grow faster in warmer environments than in colder settings, within limits. Therefore, as the temperature around the larvae goes up, the time necessary for each stage decreases, and conversely, as the temperature decreases, the development slows. If it is too cold or too warm, larval growth is greatly limited or even stopped entirely. The temperatures for these upper and lower thresholds vary from species to species but have been measured for many insects of medicolegal importance.

Insects require a certain total amount of heat to develop to the next developmental stage. This is often referred to as *accumulated degree-days* (ADD or °D), or sometimes *degree-hours* (ADH), for development. Degree-days/hours refer to the total amount of heat accumulated by a larva between its upper and lower growth thresholds, as shown in Figure 10.26. Different species require different ADDs to complete their development. For example, the Greenbottle Fly (*Phaenicia sericata*) needs about 200 total ADD to complete its development, while the Bluebottle Fly (*Calliphora vomitoria*) requires over 700 ADD to reach the same stage of development. The total accumulated degree-days can be calculated using a variety of methods, but it is proportional to the area of the curve between the two thresholds (shown in yellow in Figure 10.26). For example, the lower threshold for the Blue Bottle Fly is 6°C. If the temperature were to be held at 7°C for 24 hours, the insect would experience one degree of temperature above the lower threshold for a total of 24 hours, and 24 degree-hours would be accumulated

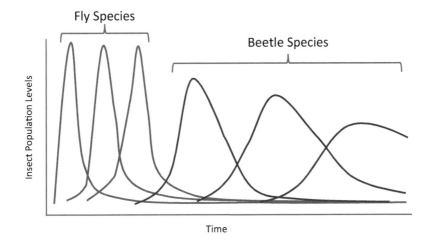

FIGURE 10.24 Overlapping insect succession and development stages.

(1 ADD). The Green Bottle Fly, which has a higher threshold of 10°C, would not accumulate any ADD at that same temperature of 7°C, and therefore would show no growth. This information is important in determining the age of specimens collected from the remains (see below).

Once it is known when the first opportunity for egg-laying occurred, the next step is to determine the age of the oldest larvae on the remains. There are two primary methods for determining the age of insect larvae found on a body. The first, and probably simplest, relies upon collecting live larvae at the scene and then rearing them to adults. By controlling the conditions in the laboratory and measuring the accumulated

degree-days needed to raise the larvae to adulthood, it is then possible to estimate the ADD that was required for the larvae to have accumulated during their time on the body. This is done simply by subtracting the amount of ADD found from the laboratory rearing experiment from the total ADD known to be needed for this species to develop from egg to adult, shown schematically in Figure 10.27. For example, if it was found to require 240 ADD to raise a collected Bluebottle larva to adulthood in the laboratory, then the number of ADD that occurred before collection can be calculated by subtracting the lab ADD from the total of 740 ADD known to be needed for the complete lifecycle of the Bluebottle. Therefore, about 500 ADD

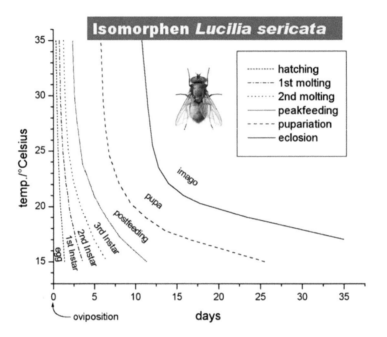

FIGURE 10.25 Development of fly stages (*Lucilia sericata*) from hatching to pupation as a function of ten different temperatures, called an isomorphen diagram. Arrows indicate first and second molting.

Source: Used with permission Forensic Science International (2001).

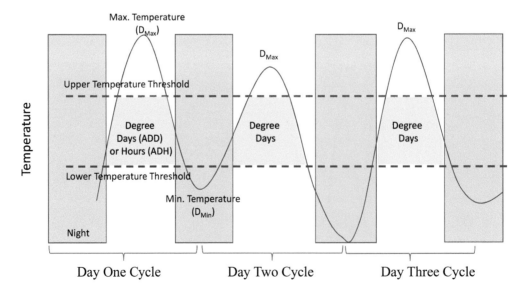

FIGURE 10.26 Accumulated degree-days between upper and lower temperature thresholds.

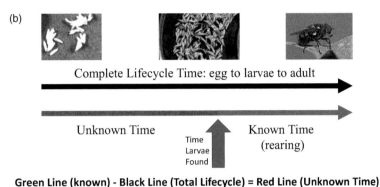

Species	Lower Threshold (°C)	ADH	ADD
Phaenicia sericata	10	4140 - 5812	173 - 242
Phormia regina	10	4038 - 6100	168 - 254
Calliphora vomitoria	6	17678	737
Cynomyopsis cadaverina	6	5511	379

Complete Lifecycle Time: egg to larvae to adult

Unknown Time

Time Larvae Found

Known Time (rearing)

Green Line (known) - Black Line (Total Lifecycle) = Red Line (Unknown Time)

FIGURE 10.27 (a, b) Determining PMI from controlled rearing of insects using ADD measurements.

Source: Images (b, left) Creative Commons Attribution 3.0, Unported. Credit: Clemson University – USDA Cooperative Extension Slide Series. Bugwood.org. (b, center) Creative Commons Attribution-Share Alike 2.0 Generic. User: Cory Doctorow. (b, right) Used per GNU Free Documentation License, Version 1.2. User: Muhammad Mahdi Karim.

occurred before the maggot was collected. In general, this is the most accurate method for estimating the PMI but requires the obvious, but often overlooked, need for the collection of live specimens at the crime scene.

The second method of estimating the age of a larva involves the use of an *isomegalen diagram*. An isomegalen diagram is a plot that shows the relationships between the time necessary for a larva to grow to a given size and the temperature of its surroundings. An example of an isomegalen diagram is shown in Figure 10.28 for the Green Bottle Fly (*Lucilia sericata*). In this method, the largest maggots are measured and the isomegalen plot is used to determine their age. The general assumption here is that the largest larvae found on the remains are also the oldest and, therefore, developed from the first egg-laying cycle that occurred. These larvae can be used, therefore, to provide a reasonable estimate of the amount of time that the body has been colonized by flies. For example, if the largest maggots on the remains were found to be 8 mm, the curve for 8 mm is first located on the isomegalen diagram (note: there is a different curve for each maggot size). From weather estimates, the maximum temperature (T_{max}) and minimum temperatures (T_{min}) for the site are estimated for the period in question. From where the T_{max} and T_{min} lines intersect the 8 mm curve, the range of days necessary for the larvae to reach the observed size can be estimated. For this example, let's assume that the T_{max} was 24°C and the T_{min} was 16°C for the time period in question. By using the isomegalen plot for the correct species of fly collected, the T_{max} of 24°C line intersects the 8 mm curve at about 1.5 days (red dotted line). This is the least amount of

time necessary for an 8 mm larva to be formed. The T_{min} line at 16°C intersects the 8 mm curve at about 4.5 days (purple dotted line), the maximum amount of time necessary for a larva to grow to this size. Thus, a time estimate for this size of larvae would be between 1.5 and 4.5 days, with an average of 3.0 days ± 1.5 days (green dotted line).

It is important to search the scene for and locate any pupal cases from larvae that might have already migrated from the body in their quest for a dry and safe place to pupate. These pupal cases can help both identify the species of insect present and determine the time necessary to reach this stage of development (including how many "generations" of flies have been reared on the remains).

A variety of complicating factors have already been discussed in using these methods for determining the PMI, including weather and insect accessibility to the remains. Additionally, during the decay stage, there is an enormous increase in the maggot population on the remains, leading to a maggot mass. Some of the heat from this enormous amount of metabolic activity is released to the surroundings. As more and more maggots come together, the maggot mass formed may considerably raise the temperature around the larvae, up to 50°C higher than the surroundings. This increase in temperature results in significantly shorter development times. It is very difficult to accurately estimate the effect of the heat generated by a maggot mass on development, leading to relatively large uncertainties in PMI estimates. Neglecting the heat generated by the maggot mass, especially in cooler environments, may lead to a significant overestimation of the PMI.

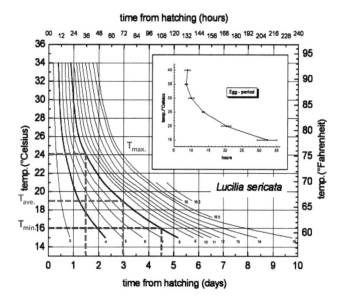

FIGURE 10.28 Isomegalen diagram for a species of blowfly (*Lucilia sericata*). Time is plotted against temperature and each line represents an identical larval length (mm).

Source: Used with permission Forensic Science International (2001).

Another complicating feature relates to the assumption that the largest larvae are also the oldest. Some species have a faster developmental growth rate than others, such that the larvae from one species may quickly overtake and grow larger than an older larva from another species. This makes species identification of each larva necessary. Competition for food between species or the drying of the remains, reducing access to the moist tissues, also yields smaller larvae than would be expected, leading to underestimates of PMI times.

The presence of drugs or toxins in the body may have a profound influence on the growth rate and even the mortality of the larvae. For example, a body containing cocaine (a stimulant) may greatly increase the development rate of the larvae, while heroin may slow the growth. Poisons are often bioaccumulated within the tissues of the maggots as they feed, and this may further slow the growth or even kill the larvae. This bioaccumulation, however, has been used to good effect in toxicological studies to determine the presence of drugs or poisons in a decayed body since the concentrations of these substances may be much higher in the insects than in the body itself.

Additional complications in PMI estimates may arise from: (1) a need to better understand the activity of insects at night and during rainfall, (2) regional adaptation of insects to environmental conditions, (3) the effects of the maggot mass on different body sizes, and (4) the possibility of insect hibernation triggered by short days and cool temperatures.

While the focus in PMI estimates tends to be on flies and beetles, a variety of other insect and arthropod species may visit remains, and their presence can assist in PMI determinations. These species can include butterflies (Figure 10.29), moths, bees, and ants.

FIGURE 10.29 The Southern Pearly-eye (*Enodia portlandia*) may often be found at death scenes since they can feed on body fluids. Their presence may help in estimates of the PMI.

Source: Retrieved from Wikimedia Commons; used per Creative Commons Attribution.

10.2.5 Other Aspects of Medicolegal Forensic Entomology

An understanding of the insect species that inhabit a particular location can indicate whether the body was found at the original crime scene or whether it had been moved after death. This has been used to detect the transportation of remains over large distances where species and sub-species vary by geographic location. For example, identifying species of insects found primarily in an urban environment on a body that was found in the rural countryside indicates that the crime may have occurred in the city but that the body was later moved to the country. It may also be possible to determine if the remains had been disturbed after death by looking for interruptions or unexplained changes in the development cycles of the insects.

Insects that feed directly upon dead flesh often make no distinction between fresh, decaying, and even cooked tissue. These insects can colonize unclean and infected wounds in living people and animals. Cases of abuse (harmful treatment) or neglect (failure to provide proper care or treatment) have been shown by noting insect infestation, especially involving the treatment of the elderly and young children. This usually happens when files are attracted to the smell of urine, defecation, or open wounds on a person and then lay their eggs in surrounding clothing and directly on the affected tissue. Young children and the elderly are often not capable of taking care of their bodily functions themselves and require others to provide this care. If a child or elderly person has not been cared for properly, blowflies can arrive and lay their eggs that will develop into larvae that feed on open sores and wounds, ultimately eating away the tissues. These irritated and wounded tissues can then become infected, a process known as *myiasis* (the disease arising from the infection and feeding of fly larvae directly on a host's tissues). These infestations can occur wherever conditions are suitable for insect development, especially warm and damp locations with dead tissue to feed upon. While blowfly larvae will feed only on dead tissue and are, therefore, usually not an immediate threat to a person's health, other insect species may be present that feed on still living tissue. The presence of particular species and their stage of development can clearly indicate for how long the abuse has continued, possibly when it began, and the type of physical abuse inflicted.

Myiasis is not limited to humans but may also be involved in cases of animal cruelty. In these cases, insect evidence is often the best type of evidence since animals are not able to communicate verbally with us. These cases typically arise from an owner's failure either to treat wounds or provide a suitable state of cleanliness for the animal. In animals, this condition is usually called "blowfly strike." Both domestic and wild animals are prone to this disease if not properly cared for.

Insects that do not feed upon remains may also have a story to tell. One suspect was caught when investigators noticed that his legs were badly attacked by small insects found near the crime scene that was known to be infested by small biting insects. Another suspect was convicted of sexual assault by finding a cocklebur on the clothing of the suspect and identifying the insect inside as found only near the crime scene.

Finally, even small changes related to each insect species can be noted and used as evidence. For example, the green bottle blowfly colonizes remains in sunny and warmer locations while the blue bottle prefers shady, cooler areas. Finding primarily green bottle larvae on remains in a secluded, shady spot suggests that the remains were moved after the insects initially colonized the remains (see Box 10.6).

BOX 10.5   LARVAL HEALERS

Fly larvae (maggots) have recently been used to help heal difficult medical problems and wounds (larval biotherapy). In the past, when people had tissue that had died due to trauma or decreased blood flow (e.g., in the feet of diabetics), surgical amputation was a common treatment. Recently, however, the medicinal use of maggots to eat away the dead tissue *without* harming the living tissue has proven to be a very effective treatment for these types of problems, much cleaner than the surgeon's knife. Maggots have also been used to treat "super-bug" bacterial infections (Methicillin-resistant *Staphylococcus aureus*, MRSA), with cures averaging three weeks instead of the typical 28-week conventional treatment course. This treatment, however, goes back to ancient times when people used maggots to keep infected wounds clean and to fight gangrene infections.

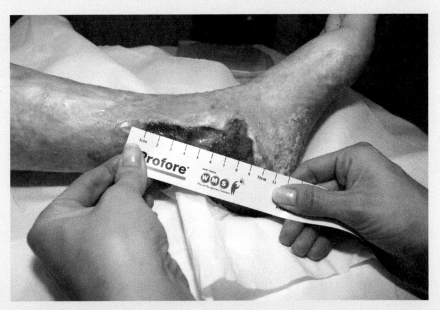

FIGURE 10.30 Maggot therapy. Medical staff measuring a patient suffering from a leg ulcer before treatment with live surgical maggots. Larvae (maggots) of the greenbottle fly (*Lucilia sericata*) are able to clean wounds by eating dead, or dying flesh, and leaving healthy areas untouched. The maggots prevent the growth of harmful bacteria in the wound by altering the acidity and releasing an antibiotic compound. This is a more efficient method for wound healing and prevention of gangrene or septicemia than drugs or other treatments.

Source: Louise Murray/Science Photo Library. Used with permission.

An amazing story comes from a WWI soldier's diary describing the difficult life in the trenches of France. The veteran, in describing the trench, wrote that on one sunny morning the top of the trench was a beautiful, shimmering, iridescent green color while in the darker, lower portions of the trench, the color shifted to a beautiful indigo-blue color. This is an excellent example of different species of blowfly seeking their own optimal conditions. The green bottle fly (*Lucilia illustris*, (a)) prefers sunnier and warmer locations (the top of the trench), while the blue bottle (*Calliphora vicina*, (b)) prefers the lower, darker portions of the trench.

FIGURE 10.31 (a) Green Bottle Fly (*Lucilia illustris*), and (b) Blue Bottle Fly (*Calliphora vicina*).

10.3 FORENSIC BOTANY

10.3.1 Introduction

Botany is the study of plant life. With more than 400,000 known species of plants and more being identified almost daily, the field encompasses an enormous range of life forms, from the tiniest of plants, such as the Columbian Watermeal (*Wolffia columbiana*) that is smaller than the head of a pin (1 mm) but still a flowering plant, to the world's largest single (genetically identical) living organism, by mass, believed to be the fully-connected Aspen grove in Utah (*Populus tremuloides*), nicknamed Pando, that covers over 107 acres (0.43 km²) and weighs about 6 million kg (ca. 13 million lbs) (Figure 10.32) (although a fungus, Honey fungus (*Armillaria ostoyae*), probably covers the greatest space of a single organism at 2,384 acres and is at least 2,400 years old).

Scientists have organized this immense field to look at it from several different perspectives: the identification of plant species (taxonomy or systematics), the biological internal and external structures of the plant (plant anatomy and morphology), the biochemical features and function of the plant (physiology and biochemistry), plant genetics (inheritance), paleobotany (ancient plants), and phytopathology (plant diseases). Each of these areas of study can be used to provide clues regarding criminal actions.

10.3.2 Forensic Botany

Plants play vital roles in every aspect of our lives, including food, shelter, medicines, clothing and in so many other areas. In fact, the field of ethnobotany specifically focuses on the complex relationships between humans and plants (see Chapter 13 on Toxicology). Plants are also found in every type of climate and habitat on Earth, and we often take them with us whenever we move about and more permanently when we relocate to new areas in the form of gardens, landscapes, crops, and in a variety of functional uses (e.g., house structures, implements, tools, etc.). Many parts of plants are very long-lasting in the environment, some persisting relatively unchanged for even thousands of years. Plant cell walls contain cellulose (a polymer of glucose) and lignin (long-chain complex biopolymers) that are very durable and highly resistant to decomposition. Because of this, plant-based materials are found all around us (and even *in* us) and can, therefore, provide clues in a forensic investigation. The important underlying principle in forensic botany is that *plants have predictable life cycles and patterns of growth*. Being able to recognize and understand these patterns is basic to the usefulness of the field as a forensic discipline.

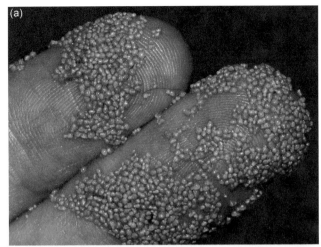

FIGURE 10.32 (a) Columbian Watermeal (*Wolffia columbiana*) on a finger and (b) the Pando Aspen (*Populus tremuloides*) Grove in Utah.

Source: (a) Used per Creative Commons Attribution-Share Alike 3.0, Unported. User: Christian Fischer; (b) U.S. Department of Agriculture, Forest Service.

Plants and parts of plants have been used in many types of forensic investigations, including: (1) tracking a suspect's or victim's movements, (2) validating (or refuting) alibis and proposed timelines of events, (3) determining how long someone has been dead, (4) dealing with issues of plant-based poisons and toxicology, (5) deciding on whether a particular wooden tool has been used for a particular purpose related to the crime, and (6) investigating food adulteration cases. Plant-based evidence may include the whole organism or just parts of the plant such as its seeds, leaves, roots, stem, bark, or pollen.

A common use of forensic botany is to determine the site of origin of plants and, therefore, where the evidence that contains the plant matter has traveled from. This type of evidence points to common linkages between a crime site and the piece of evidence – placing the evidence at some point in time at the crime scene. This process typically involves two discrete steps: identification and comparison. The first task is often the identification (classification) of the species present in or on the evidence. This involves careful sampling of the evidence and preservation of the material. Identification of the

BOX 10.7   TELLTALE SEEDS

Dr. Shirley Graham describes her work using plant seeds to connect a murderer with a gravesite. The gravesite of two murdered children was found at the edge of an Ohio cemetery. The best suspect at the time was the children's stepfather who had claimed that he had never been near the gravesite. On a blanket and on the clothes of the father, however, investigators found seeds of a variety of plants found together at the gravesite. These seeds were of the type with hooks and barbs that fasten the seed onto the fur of any animal (or human) passing by to distribute the seeds. The stepfather, however, had claimed that the seeds came from around his home. His farmyard, however, was not a suitable environment for these types of plants to grow, and none of these plants were found near his home. The father was ultimately convicted of the two murders, partially upon the strength of this key botanical evidence.

FIGURE 10.33 The hooked seeds from the catchweed plant (*Galium aparine*) were found adhered to the murderer's clothing and at the clandestine gravesite, but not near the murder's home, helping to identify him as the assailant.

Source: Thomé (1885).

species from a taxonomic analysis (genus and species) is based on observable plant features (morphology). Plant species often differ in large-scale structure and microscopically in cell wall shapes, sizes, and patterns. This often allows identification of the plant species with a high degree of certainty from just small pieces of the whole plant. In order to connect the plant material found on the evidence with a particular geographical location, a botanical survey of the location must be completed, exhaustively collecting and identifying all species found at the site. Of course, the methods of collection and analysis must be strong in order to stand up to the scrutiny of the court. The site survey focuses on what and how much of each plant species is present, along with whether any damage to the vegetation can be seen. The final step is to compare the plant survey with the plant information found on the evidence in an effort to connect the two to a common origin. As a note, the identification of microscopic components or pollen of plants typically falls into the area of palynology and will be described in more detail in Section 10.4.

Sometimes, it is difficult to completely identify a piece of plant matter as to its correct species with absolute certainty. Increasingly, DNA analysis is being used to unambiguously provide this complete identification for plants but, apart from a few commonly encountered plant species, such as marijuana, the general use of DNA analysis for plant identification has not been sufficiently developed nor commonly employed in forensic practice thus far. The problem most often encountered is that plant DNA databases are not particularly well developed or extensive enough to be useful for the identification of a wide variety of species. Additionally, DNA methods are still rather expensive and slow compared with the visual identification process employed by a knowledgeable botanist.

Sometimes, instead of species identification, it would be highly desirable to use DNA techniques for identifying an *individual* plant just as we now use forensic DNA to identify an individual person (see the case involving the Palo Verde tree [*Parkinsonia florida*] in Chapter 5). This would require the development of suitable DNA markers (small DNA pieces with complementary sequences near STRs of interest) for the particular species examined along with a large enough database of these same markers for *individual organisms* to form a valid comparison. Thus far, not enough work has been done to show that there is sufficient variability in the DNA of a given plant species to make DNA analysis a reliable method for separating one individual plant from all others. Complicating this method further is the fact that, unlike in animals, plants often form clones with identical DNA makeup through non-sexual reproductive means. These identical clones may then be spread over a very large geographic region, even hundreds of square miles or farther. For example, many grape plants are genetically identical clones derived from just one individual plant that has been propagated by humans for thousands of years. The clover plants from a meadow may all be genetically identical to one another just as a grove of Aspen trees may truly be called one individual. Plants also readily hybridize (e.g., mating of two different species to form a new genetic hybrid of the original two species) and may be polyploidic (contain additional

chromosomes, such as cells that contain four or more copies of a particular chromosome), complicating the DNA analysis. These new hybrids are often stronger than the parent plants, leading to an ecological advantage for the hybrid species but confusing DNA identification of individual plants. Examples of plant hybridization are the Loganberry (cross between a raspberry and a blackberry, peppermint (cross between spearmint and water mint), and the grapefruit (cross between an orange and pomelo).

Artificial plant combinations in gardens and landscapes provide very distinctive "unnatural" combinations of plants that can be used to identify with a high degree of certainty which garden a plant species profile originates from. In Section 10.1.2, we discussed how species distribution and pollen distribution are important in determining how plant material is distributed across the landscape. Because of the enormous number of combinations of plants possible, every location has a distinctive and recognizable "biological signature" that distinguishes it from all others. The trick is identifying the unique characteristics of these differing site "signatures" and recognizing the connections between the site and the physical evidence. Gardens and artificial landscapes often provide a clearly recognizable signature that is distinct from the native plants nearby. A detailed knowledge of the distribution of plant species, both native and imported, is required (some plants are widespread while others are localized). Finding plants with limited distribution gives better information, which can help suggest a likely place to look for evidence by tracing where a suspect has been.

Occasionally, forensic botany has been used to aid in the reconstruction of a sequence of events associated with a crime. In this case, botanical evidence can be used in conjunction with other physical evidence to validate or refute a particular hypothesis or storyline. For example, if the stomach contents of an autopsied person contain certain plant materials, it can show what the victim's *last* meal was, which can be compared with eyewitness accounts of when the person was last seen. Plant structures, such as seeds, leaves, fruit, roots, and stems, can often be easily identified, providing a detailed "menu" of the last meal eaten. The degree of digestion of the plant and animal material in the stomach and intestines can also provide support for a time of death established by other biological and chemical indicators. Plant material, containing cellulose, is often slow to decompose relative to other materials, such as meat and animal-based proteins. By estimating the relative degree of decomposition of the plant and animal matter, an estimate can be made as to how long ago the food was consumed.

Once several days after death have elapsed, the forensic pathologist must turn to the forensic entomologist or ecologist to help determine the PMI. We've seen how insects can be used to provide an estimate of the PMI, and plants can also provide useful information concerning the time of death. Like insects, plants have predictable life cycles, growth patterns, growth responses, and developmental responses to environmental changes and patterns. If an object falls onto a plant bed, such as a tool or a body, the developmental stage of the plants lying underneath the object can give a clear indication of the season when the object was placed upon it. For example, a body was found many months after it was deposited at a site on top of a female stinging nettle plant (*Urtica dioica*) that had unripened fruit. The presence of the fruit, combined with the fact that it had not yet ripened, placed the date when the body fell on the nettle as between late July to early August. Any earlier and the fruit would not have been developed; any later and the fruit would have ripened. This is a very narrow window of just a few weeks and was more accurate than any other method for estimating such a long PMI.

If the ground around a body is disrupted as part of the crime, such as during a burial or dragging a body across vegetation, any new growth observed at the site must have begun after the time of the crime. By estimating how long the new plants took to reach the observed stage of regrowth on the disturbed ground, a reasonable PMI can be established. The particular species present may also be helpful since plants tend to colonize open or disturbed soil in a regular pattern of plant species, referred to as *plant succession*. In addition, identifying plant matter found on a suspect's clothing may provide clues as to their travels in burying a body or other aspects of the crime.

Finding broken plants (e.g., stems, leaves, branches) at a crime scene coupled with information about the state and rate of a plant's "recovery" (regrowth) from the injury can indicate how long ago the plant was broken and therefore when and where someone traveled a particular path. This is similar to how the degree of healing of human wounds can be used to indicate the date of the injury. An object placed on plants will leave an impression for weeks afterward.

When the remains consist of only bones, it is often difficult for entomology to determine with any accuracy how long ago the body was placed there. Forensic botany, however, may provide information even when very long timelines are involved. For instance, the field of dendrochronology uses the annual rings of trees and woody shrubs to date the year when each ring was formed, often to an exact calendar year (Figure 10.34). Each year, a woody plant produces new xylem – the layer of living cells just below the bark that is responsible for transporting water and nutrients from the roots to the leaves of the plant. As this layer matures, the cell walls become thicker with lignin, forming holes where the water can move from cell to cell, and the internal protoplasm dies to form water "tubes." The thickness of these cells varies during each growing year to form a visible annual ring – typically becoming smaller as the growing season progresses and growth conditions of late summer become less favorable. The thickness of the ring also reflects the overall yearly growing conditions for the tree; thicker rings are usually associated with better growing conditions and thinner rings from years with less favorable growing conditions (e.g., drought, hotter temperatures, etc.). Using correlations of the ring patterns of unknown age trees with trees of known age in the region allows for the accurate age determination of the wood. Imported wooden objects may sometimes be traced to their origin by knowing the historical weather patterns that affect ring development. Additionally,

when graves are dug, plant roots are often injured. It is sometimes possible to determine the number of growth rings formed after the injury, giving an estimate of the number of years since the burial took place.

Wood, as a strong and durable material, finds many uses in everyday implements, such as hammers, ladders, furniture, and decorative objects. Unfortunately, these items also find their way into crime scenes, used as weapons or in other ways that aid in the commission of the crime. Occasionally, it is important to identify a particular wooden artifact as connected with a criminal action. Identifying the species of wood, and occasionally its age and region of origin through dendrochronology, can be helpful in this work.

Tree ring analysis can be very important in determining the authenticity of significant wooden objects, such as paintings or a musical instruments. Many painters throughout history have preferred to paint their masterpieces on wood. Because of this, their paintings not only endure but are also often accurately dated from the tree rings. For example, it was shown that a work by the famous Flemish artist Peter Paul Rubens (1577–1640), originally dated 1616, could not have been painted before 1626. Another of his works, *Samson and*

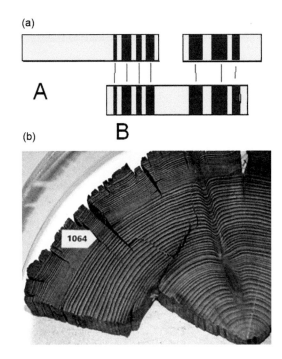

FIGURE 10.34 (b) Determining the age of a wood sample (dendrochronology) by studying the varying patterns of the tree growth rings. In this process, a sample from wood is taken with a hollow drill. This sample of unknown age (B in the figure) is then compared with other samples from trees in the area that have partly different ages (A in the figure). Portions of the unknown sample's growth ring pattern are then matched to similar patterns in trees of known age. (b) Variations in tree growth ring thicknesses: one ring represents a full year's growing season.

BOX 10.8   THE TRUE CASE OF THE CENTURY: THE LINDBERGH KIDNAPPING

THE CASE FOR TREE RING PATTERNS

It can be argued that the most important case of the 20th century was the kidnapping of the 20-month-old infant son of Charles Lindbergh in 1932. Charles Lindbergh was certainly one of the most famous people of the time worldwide as the first person to cross the Atlantic on a solo, non-stop flight in 1927. On a March evening in 1932, however, Lindbergh's fame came from a different direction – Lindbergh's son was kidnapped from his second-floor bedroom in the family's quiet New Jersey home. The child was quickly and unsuccessfully ransomed for $50,000 paid by the family, but two months later his body was found just a few miles from the Lindbergh home.

As part of the crime, the kidnapper used a crudely built wooden ladder to gain access to the child's room. The ladder was left behind at the house and later became a key piece of evidence. In an attempt to gain clues from the ladder, a member of the U.S. Forest Service, Arthur Koehler, carefully examined the ladder and later testified in court about his findings – the first botanical evidence used in an American court.

FIGURE 10.35   The ladder, leaning against the Lindbergh home, used to abduct Charles Lindbergh, Jr. The wood from the ladder was found to have matching tree rings with the Hauptman attic floorboards in Bronx, NY.

Source: US Forest Service.

Koehler was able to determine the species of wood in the ladder, identified where the wood was produced locally by the milling marks left in the wood, and identified and located nail holes in the planks. It also appeared that the wood was relatively coarse and unweathered, presumably protected by its use in an unfinished area in an interior location, such as a barn, attic, or elsewhere.

The case soon came to a near halt from lack of clear suspects and connecting evidence. After two years without a viable suspect, some of the marked ransom money finally turned up at a local gas station in 1934 from a Bronx, NY carpenter: Bruno Hauptmann. Hauptmann was arrested and thousands of dollars of the ransom money were later found stashed in his garage. But the key evidence came, however, when the police searched his attic. There they found attic floorboards clearly missing. Koehler's careful work finally paid off. The nail holes exactly lined up with corresponding nail holes in the ceiling joists where floorboards were missing. The species of wood for the ladder and floorboard also matched, as did the milling marks. But quite importantly, the tree rings of at least one of the ladder boards matched exactly with the tree rings of the attic boards – tree ring analysis had paid off. Hauptmann was convicted on kidnapping and murder charges and then executed in 1936.

Delilah (Figure 10.36), was properly dated to about 1609, dispelling claims by some art historians that it dated from much later based on stylistic considerations.

Many musical instruments were originally crafted from wood because of the relative ease of forming instruments with complex shapes and designs, giving rise to unique musical

FIGURE 10.36 The painting *Samson and Delilah* by Peter Paul Rubens (1577–1640) was dated to 1609–1610 by dendrochronology.

Source: Retrieved from Wikimedia Commons; used per Creative Commons Attribution.

sounds. For example, two violins were inherited and claimed to be the works of the master craftsman Antonio Stradivari, making them worth enormous amounts of money. However, analysis of the tree ring structures present in the woods of the violins showed that they could not have been made before 1910, while Stradivari worked in the 17th century.

If skeletal remains are found with roots, stems, or other growing parts of trees or shrubs penetrating into the bones or other physical evidence, it may be possible to determine the age of the plant and infer that the plant came after the body/evidence was deposited on the site. This means that the item must have been placed there before the plants grew *into* the evidence. The age of pioneer plants (first colonizers of a new area) growing in disturbed soil, such as graves or places where things have been dragged across the ground, can also provide an estimate of when the event occurred. For shorter periods of time, the new growth of grasses and other small plants can be used as an estimate of the PMI, as illustrated above by the stinging nettle case. If leaf litter is found *under* a body or in a grave, this may indicate the season of burial and, in some cases, the pathway used to move the body to the gravesite by noting the species found among the leaves and plant material.

Wooden objects can, to some extent, be located geographically by correlating the ring patterns observed with those of different locations. Pollutants can be trapped within the growing wood and later chemically analyzed to determine the dates

and nature of the pollution – potentially providing information for lawsuits on pollution events or when fires occurred.

Plants produce a number of chemicals to cope with their environment. They produce dyes to absorb light, cellulose to form strong structures, hormones to promote and regulate growth, waxes to regulate water loss and retention, and toxins to defend themselves from plant and animal invaders. Chemicals produced in plants also form an array of powerful drugs when used in humans, including antitumor agents, depressants, stimulants, hallucinogens, narcotics, and many more, as shown in Table 10.2.

Plants also produce chemicals that may be highly toxic to animal species. This toxicity often varies greatly from one animal species to another. For example, the Yew berry is highly toxic to humans but completely non-toxic to birds and mice (see Chapter 13 on chemical toxicology). It also matters what part of the plant is eaten and whether it has been cooked or not. For example, rhubarb stalks are safely eaten by humans, but the high concentrations of oxalic acid in the leaves may render them harmful to some people. Plant poisons have, not surprisingly, found their way into homicide cases for millennia as natural poisons, such as strychnine, ricin, cyanide, myristicin, and many others.

Plant derivatives are also of forensic importance as controlled substances. For example, marijuana (genus *Cannabis*), produces a chemical called tetrahydrocannabinol (THC) that is

TABLE 10.2 Some common drugs derived from plants

DRUG	CLINICAL USES	PLANT SOURCE
Aspirin (acetylsalicylic acid)	Analgesic (pain reduction, NSAID)	*Salix sepulcralis* (Weeping Willow) and many others
Caffeine (1,3,7-trimethylpurine-2,6-dione)	Central nervous system stimulant	*Camellia sinensis* (Chinese Camellia – tea plant)
Camphor (1,7,7-trimethylbicyclo[2.2.1] heptan-2-one)	Rubefacient (produces redness of skin by dilating capillaries and relieves pain)	*Cinnamomum camphora* (Camphortree)
Cocaine ($C_{17}H_{21}NO_4$)	Anesthetic (insensitivity to pain)	*Erythroxylum coca* (Coca)
Codeine ($C_{18}H_{24}NO_7P$)	Analgesic (pain reduction), antitussive (cough relief)	*Papaver somniferum* (Opium Poppy)
Digitalin ($C_{41}H_{64}O_{14}$)	Cardiac stimulant	*Digitalis purpurea* (Foxglove)
Kheltin ($C_{14}H_{12}O_5$)	Bronchodilator	*Ammi visnaga* (Toothpickweed)
Methyl salicylate (methyl 2-hydroxybenzoate)	Rubefacient	*Gaultheria procumbens* (Boxberry or Wintergreen)
Nicotine (3-(1-methyl-2-pyrrolidinyl)pyridine)	Insecticide	*Nicotiana tabacum* (Tobacco)
Quinine ($C_{20}H_{24}N_2O_2$)	Anti-malarial	*Cinchona ledgeriana* (Quinine Bark)
Salicin (precursor to aspirin)	Analgesic	*Salix alba* (white willow)
Strychnine ($C_{21}H_{22}N_2O_2$)	Central nervous system stimulant	*Strychnos nux-vomica* (Strychnine Tree)
Taxol ($C_{47}H_{51}NO_{14}$)	Antitumor agent	*Taxus brevifolia* (Pacific Yew)
Theobromine (3,7-dimethyl-1H-purine-2,6-dione)	Diuretic, vasodilator	Theobroma cacao (Chocolate)
Vascine (RNA)	Cerebral stimulant	*Vinca minor* (Periwinkle)

BOX 10.9   PLANT TOXINS: MURDER BY UMBRELLA

Georgi Markov was a writer in Bulgaria in the 1960s before he defected to the West in 1969. At first, he hoped that the political climate at home would change and he would be able to return to his native Bulgaria, but his works were removed from Bulgarian libraries and he was even sentenced to prison *in absentia* for treason. Eventually, he decided to remain in the West and found work as a journalist and broadcaster for the BBC and Radio Free Europe while maintaining his writing career.

A strong anti-communist, Markov openly and frequently criticized the Bulgarian government and its president, Todor Zhivkov. Apparently, this finally became too much for the Bulgarians, and in 1978 they asked the Soviet secret police, the KGB, to help them eliminate Markov for good. Twice the Bulgarian secret police tried unsuccessfully to assassinate him and sent him telephone death threats. Finally, in September, 1978, while Markov was waiting for a bus, he felt a slight pain

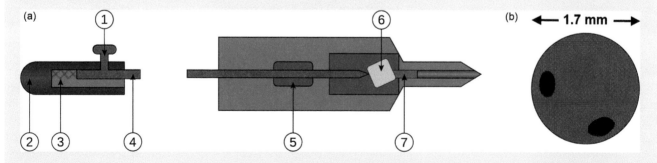

FIGURE 10.37   (a) Diagram of the firing mechanism of the umbrella used to assassinate Bulgarian dissident Georgi Markov [(1) trigger in umbrella handle, (2) umbrella handle, (3) spring to push the linkage system, (4) linkage system connecting the trigger to valve, (5) cylinder of compressed air, (6) switch to activate the valve, and (7) valve that fires the ricin pellet through the 'barrel' of the umbrella]. (b) Drawing of the pellet that was used to assassinate the Bulgarian exile Georgi Markov in London in 1978 (based on the photo of the pellet).

at the back of his right thigh akin to an insect bite. When he turned around, he saw a man pick up an umbrella, say "I'm sorry" in a foreign accent and dash across the street to a waiting taxi. By the time he reached his office, the pain had not subsided, and a small red "bite" mark was evident on his thigh. That evening he developed a high fever, was admitted to the hospital but died three days later. The cause of his death was determined to be from ricin poisoning delivered by a small metal pellet, later recovered during the autopsy. The pellet was the size of a pinhead that had been injected into his thigh from the umbrella. No traces of ricin were ever found on the pellet or in his body, but the use of the potent plant poison was deduced by a variety of medical means. Ricin, an extremely toxic poison derived from castor bean plant, is a protein that can kill half of adults with a dose of about the size of a small grain of salt with no known antidote (LD_{50} = 22 µg/kg). Further support for the ricin explanation came from an unsuccessful assassination attempt of another Bulgarian dissident in Paris just ten days before Markov's murder using a similarly small ricin-containing pellet.

a psychoactive drug. Other plant-based controlled substances of abuse include heroin, cocaine, dimethyltryptamine (DMT), and others. The forensic botanist may be called upon to identify plant material seized – sometimes a challenging problem due to the many available variants of these plants. Exact identification is required where laws designate a particular species as illegal to possess. In the case of marijuana, however, some places have changed older laws to outlaw the entire genus of *Cannabis* rather than specifying a specific species, while other locations are removing legal restrictions.

Plant forensics also finds applications in international law and economics. For example, hybrid species of plants developed for use as crops may be patented by the companies that develop them. These companies invest heavily in developing "improved hybrids that have economic advantages" such as improved resistance to pests, enhanced flavor, and nutrition, and greater resilience to drought and cold conditions. The company then can legally patent and own these hybrid species, controlling their use and distribution. Occasionally, these hybrids are stolen, just as any other patented items can be infringed upon and stolen. For example, hybrid tomato and strawberry variants have been produced containing a gene from the flounder fish to make the fruit less susceptible to cold temperatures. The "theft" of these hybrid species can result in significant financial losses to the original developer, resulting in lawsuits that require the expertise of a botanist.

Finally, there are plant species that are illegal to transport across state or international borders. This can arise from attempts to protect native species, prevent the theft of patented crop strains, and stop the import of drug-related plant matter. The forensic botanist is typically called upon to identify these species for legal proceedings.

10.4 FORENSIC PALYNOLOGY AND MYCOLOGY

10.4.1 Forensic Palynology

Palynology refers to the study of pollen, spores, soil, and other very small particles, including both recently living and fossil organic and inorganic materials. These tiny particles range in size from about 5 to 500 µm, where 5 µm is just about the thickness of a spider's thread and 500 µm is a bit thinner than an average credit card. Some of the amazing variation in the shapes and sizes of just pollen and spores can be seen in the micrographs shown in Figure 10.38. In fact, the term *palynology* is derived from the Greek word "to sprinkle," such as in fine flour. These very small objects are everywhere around us (and in us) and typically are very resistant to decay. Importantly, due to their small sizes, these particles can readily become embedded in cloth, plastic, and other everyday items that are transported away from where they were originally found. Finding these site-specific particles can provide an unambiguous connection between a crime scene and a piece of physical evidence or a suspect.

The most abundant type of *palynomorphs*, or small particles, is plant pollen and spores. Pollen is produced by both flowering (seed-bearing) and non-flowering (cone-bearing) plants. In contrast, spores are produced by algae, fungi, ferns, mosses, and others. Both pollen and spores are involved in the reproductive cycles of the parent organism, where pollen carries the male reproductive cells while spores carry the asexual bodies. Pollen and spores are generally produced during very specific seasons of the year and can also help provide a timeline marker when found.

Pollen grains are made up of many cells, including both vegetative cells (non-reproductive) and reproductive cells. The entire pollen grain is surrounded by an inner wall (intine), primarily composed of tough cellulose, and an outer wall (exine), composed primarily of very durable *sporopollen* (Figure 10.39). This extremely tough outer wall is typically very intricate, forming patterns unique to one particular species that allow for the identification of the plant species that produced it. These durable outer walls have been found well preserved for thousands and even millions of years to the degree that the plant species can still be readily determined.

Spores are reproductive cells formed by a variety of organisms including bacteria, algae, fungi, and plants, and released into the environment. They are also very durable and tough, capable of lying dormant for long periods of time during unfavorable growing conditions. Once the conditions have changed to be favorable for growth again, the spore can then leave this dormant state and rapidly develop into a fully-formed organism.

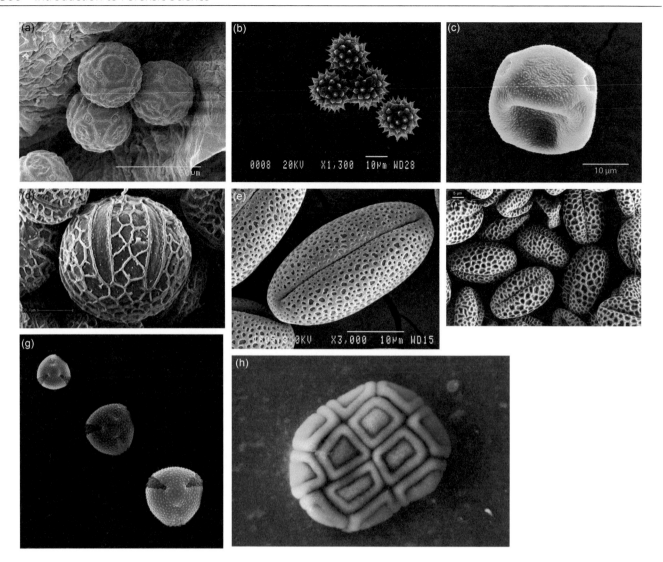

FIGURE 10.38   SEM Photomicrograph of various pollen and spores (a) dwarf holly (*Ilex vomitoria*), (b) daisy (*Bellis perennis*), (c) alder (*Alnus* sp.), (d) java tea (*Orthosiphon aristatus*), (e) redbud, (*Cercis canadensis*), (f) lilac (*Syringa vulgaris*), (g) columbine (*Aquilegia vulgaris*), and (h) acacia (*Acacia* sp.).

Sources: (a) Shutterstock.com, (b) Shutterstock.com, (c) Used per Creative Commons Attribution-Share Alike 4.0, International. User: ToniVakiparta. (d) Used per Creative Commons Attribution-Share Alike 3.0, Unported. User: Mogana Das Murtey and Patchamuthu Ramasamy. (e) Used per Creative Commons Attribution-Share Alike 3.0, Unported. User: Kleopatra. (f) Used per Creative Commons Attribution 4.0, International. Userr: Yapryntsev A.D., Baranchikov A.E. and Ivanov V.K. (g) Used per Creative Commons Attribution 4.0, International. User: Andrey Erst. (h) Used per Creative Commons Attribution 3.0, Unported. User: CSIRO.

Pollen is very abundant, and a single plant anther (male reproductive structure in a flower) may produce up to 100,000 grains of pollen at a time. Pollen and spore palynomorphs may be quite localized or widely distributed by the action of air, water, soil, animals, or insects. These tiny structures may adhere to surfaces they land upon and then be transferred to other objects that come into contact with these surfaces – another superb example of Locard's Principle. Once transferred, however, pollen and spores will stick to a person and clothing for a relatively long time. Pollen sticks especially well to synthetic fabrics and plastic, largely due to static electricity. Almost everyone carries pollen on them all the time, especially in their hair. However, pollen and spores from the last place visited typically are the predominant types found on an item. The location on a person where these palynomorphs are found may indicate how the material was transferred to them. For example, simply walking through an open forest setting would transfer pollen and spores from the ground directly onto shoe soles, while walking through a grassy meadow might transfer pollen up to the ankles. Walking through a tall garden might deposit pollen and spores up to a person's waist, while moving through shrubs might cover a person's entire body, from foot to head, in pollen and spores. Finding palynomorphs on a person may also indicate specifically where a person has lain or kneeled on the ground, based on where the pollen is found on their clothes. For example, finding grass pollen or ground spores on someone's jacket would support the story that they had been lying on their back on the

Grain of Pollen

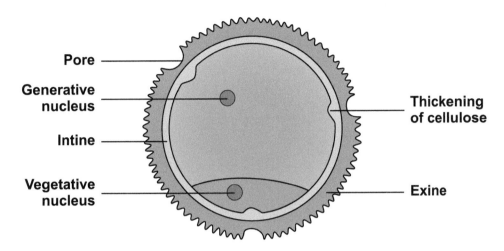

Pore
Generative nucleus
Intine
Vegetative nucleus
Thickening of cellulose
Exine

FIGURE 10.39 Structure of pollen.

Source: Shutterstock.com.

ground during an assault. It may also differentiate where within a particular field the assault had taken place based on the species of plants found.

BOX 10.10   TINY WITNESSES

In 1959, a missing person in Vienna, Austria was believed to have been murdered while on a trip along the Danube River. The problem was that, even though there was a very credible suspect, there was no body. Without some proof linking the suspect to either the body or the suspected crime scene, there was no case.

To help with the case, Dr. Wilhelm Klaus, a noted geologist, was asked to examine some mud-caked boots found at the suspect's home. In the mud, he found pollen grains from several local trees including spruce, willow, and alder trees. Importantly, however, he also found 20-million-year-old pollen from ancient hickory trees in the mud. From his experience and samples that he had taken along the Danube, he was able to identify the specific area that had produced the mud pollen he had found on the suspects shoes, an area 15 miles north of Vienna along the Danube. When the suspect was confronted with this detailed evidence and information of where he had been, he confessed to the murder and led police to the site of the buried body – exactly where the pollen had predicted it would be. The suspect was convicted of the murder, primarily on the strength of the pollen evidence.

Every place has its own unique palynological profile (type and amount found in the area), sometimes called its "pollen fingerprint." This uniqueness may not, however, be easy to demonstrate and requires careful work. The key initial task is the correct identification of the origin of the palynomorphs found in the evidence, specifically the identification of the species that produced the pollen or spores. Fortunately, the intricate and ornate outer walls of pollen and spores can result in the identification of the genus, and in some cases, species, of the plant parent.

In order to connect a particular site with a suspect or piece of evidence on which the palynomorphs were found, a large number of proxy indicators are needed. This, in turn, requires large numbers of identified palynomorphs. Connecting palynomorphs from a forensic sample with a particular site is a *comparative* process. This means that the types and quantities of palynomorphs found on a forensic sample are compared with surveys listing the types and quantities of palynomorphs found at many specific places. The profiles of these sites must be different enough to distinguish between them, as described earlier in Section 10.1.2.

The geographic distribution of plants and their abundance can play an important role in palynology. Finding pollen from rare plants, or even better, rare combinations of plants, can place a suspect at a very specific site. Finding pollen and spores for even common plants, however, can be rare and depends on how their pollen is distributed. Pollen that is wind-distributed (anemophilous plants) can be spread over vast areas, while plants that utilize insect pollinators (zoogamous plants) can be rare to find at a location, even if it is from a common plant. Insect pollinators typically do not spread the pollen very far beyond the individual plant. Clover and willow are relatively common plants but, since their pollen is insect-distributed, it would be considered rare to find pollen from one of these species on someone who had not had direct contact with these plants. Wind distribution is a hit-and-miss affair and is not terribly efficient – so plants that use this type

FIGURE 10.40   Released pollen of the European Spruce (*Picea abies*). Pollen of different sizes sink to the ground at different rates.

Source: Used per Creative Commons Attribution-Share Alike 4.0, International. User: Uoaei1.

FIGURE 10.41   Photograph of dust patterns from the sole of a shoe on a tile floor.

Source: Shutterstock.com.

of distribution tend to produce very large amounts of pollen that may be spread across miles and miles of terrain. Some plants are self-pollinating (autogamous plants) and are very efficient at pollination – producing as little as 100 pollen grains per anther.

Another feature that affects the distribution of pollen and spores in an area relates to how fast the pollen falls to the ground, sometimes referred to as the *sinking rate* (Figure 10.40). Very small and light pollen, such as from marijuana and birch, falls

to the ground rather slowly (ca. 2 cm/s). Other types of pollen that are much larger and more dense, such as corn or hickory pollen, fall to the ground much faster (>30 cm/s). Because of their different sinking rates, marijuana would be expected to have a much wider area of distribution than corn pollen.

Of course, palynology also includes the analysis of soil and mineral dust, tiny animal parts (primarily insect parts and microorganisms), and other small particles but these will be described in other areas of this text (Figure 10.41).

BOX 10.11   TELLTALE POLLEN

In November 2000, a 16-year-old English schoolgirl, Leanne Tiernan, was kidnapped and murdered less than a mile from her home. After an exhaustive search, her body was ultimately discovered buried in a shallow grave in dense woods very near a busy parking lot. The autopsy revealed that the body had not been there long but had first been carefully wrapped and stored at low temperature before being buried. After following many leads, the police focused their investigation on John Taylor, who lived less than a mile from Tiernan's home. As part of the evidence, Patricia Wiltshire, a noted forensic botanist, was asked to examine the evidence (see highlight on Dr. Wiltshire at the end of the chapter). Dr. Wiltshire was able to demonstrate that Leanne had been in Taylor's garden just before she was killed. This conclusion came from a detailed examination of Tiernan's nasal cavity, skin, and hair where pollen samples were found that uniquely placed her specifically in Taylor's garden. The pollen evidence, given below, showed that the palynomorphs found on the victim did not come from the victim's home or garden but matched rather well with the materials collected in the suspect's garden. Based upon this and a variety of other evidence, Taylor confessed and was sentenced to two life terms in prison.

Species	Victim's hair	Suspect's Garden	Victim's Garden
Lilac	3.5	11.0	4.2
Non-native plants	2.8	2.0	0
Plum/cherry	1.1	2.1	0
Goosefoot	8.2	7.5	.1
Nettle	3.0	3.1	0
Dandelion	1.0	2.0	5.3
Poplar	5.1	8.1	0

FIGURE 10.42   The distribution of pollen types in the Leanne Tiernan case.

Although the use of palynomorphs can provide key forensic information, there remain some significant challenges in using palynology. Actual field samples often contain a great deal of unidentifiable material, with pollen and spores in poor states of preservation. This makes identification of the types of pollen and spores present in the sample very difficult. DNA has not been effectively used in pollen and spore identification due to a lack of development of suitable methods for plants. Sampling techniques and contamination of samples are also areas of great concern. Nonetheless, the field has the potential to provide powerful information in forensic investigations.

10.4.2 Forensic Mycology

Mycology is the study of *fungi*. This huge group of organisms, estimated at 1.5 million species worldwide (of which only about 100,000 species have been classified), includes molds, mildews, mushrooms, lichens, and yeasts. This enormous range of species, coupled with the fact that they are often found abundantly and in all environments of the Earth, provides a great deal of potential markers for forensic work.

For example, one particular, well-researched location has been shown to contain between 1,000 and 3,500 fungal species.

The use of fungi in forensic investigations has so far been focused upon three types of investigations: (1) helping to explain the causes of death from poisons and toxins derived from fungi, (2) using fungi to determine the actual location and time of death (PMI), and (3) using fungi to place a person or piece of evidence at a particular site at a given time.

Fungi have long been known to have potent effects on humans, including hallucinations and death, and have a long history of causing both intentional and accidental deaths (see Box 10.12). Many species of mushrooms are considered to be edible delicacies and can fetch exceedingly high prices as food – recently a single Italian White Alba Truffle (*Tuber magnatum*, Figure 10.43) sold for more than $330,000! The problem, however, is that many highly poisonous mushrooms look a great deal like edible mushrooms. For example, the immature "Death Cap" (*Amanita phalloides*) and the "European Destroying Angel" (*Amanita virosa*) mushrooms look very much like non-poisonous puffballs and other edible mushrooms (Figure 10.44). As the deathly names imply, bad things arise from eating the Death Cap or Destroying Angel mushrooms and these two mushrooms account for most of the deaths from fungi

FIGURE 10.43 World's most expensive food, the Italian White Alba Truffle. Recently, one of these, weighing slightly less than 3 lbs (1.4 kg), sold for $330,000.

Source: Used per Creative Commons Attribution-Share Alike 3.0, Unported. Author: Marco Plassio, Wikimedia Commons.

FIGURE 10.44 Poisonous and edible mushrooms often look very similar: (a) highly poisonous immature Death Cap mushroom (*Amanita phalloides*) and (b) Destroying Angel mushroom (*Amanita virosa*) look a great deal like (c) the edible Common Puffball (*Lycoperdon perlatum*).

Sources: (a) Used per Creative Commons Attribution-Share Alike 3.0, Unported. User: Mars 2002. (c) User per Creative Commons Attribution 3.0 Unported. User: Henk Monster.

worldwide (eating half of a Death Cap is enough to kill an adult human)! There are generally no known antidotes to the toxins from mushroom poisoning, although there are some medical treatments that improve survivability. Most ultimately lead to liver failure and produce death within days of ingestion.

Some species of fungi have been cultivated as toxins for biological weapons, such as a number of *Fusarium* spp. (especially *Fusarium solani*), which produces the highly poisonous T2 toxin that can be sprayed on troops, causing keratitis, onychomycosis, peritonitis, and cellulitis. Sprays containing fungi have also been developed to primarily kill crops rather than people, including destroying drug crops without harming the local population.

Fungi have been used to help locate burial sites and to assist with PMI determinations. For example, some species of mushrooms (Figure 10.45) are particularly associated with disturbed ground, such as the "Shaggy Ink Cap" (*Coprinus comatus*). The "Corpse-Finder" mushroom (*Hebeloma radicosum*) has likewise often been associated with buried bodies and has been used to help find missing human remains. Finding these mushrooms may indicate where the soil has been disrupted as part of a struggle or a pathway through undergrowth.

Because fungi, like plants and animals, have predictable life cycles, the stage of development of fungi found on a body may provide useful information in determining the PMI. Fungi and fungal sheaths, a compact and dense fungal layer, may be found on bodies deposited in water and used to indicate both the amount of time the body has been in the water and the location from which it was deposited based on species.

FIGURE 10.45 (a) The "corpse-finder" mushroom (*Hebeloma radicosum*) and (b) Shaggy Mane mushroom, or Shaggy Ink Cap, (*Coprinus comatus*) grow on disturbed ground.

Source: (a) Used per Creative Commons Attribution-Share Alike 3.0, Unported. Author: Dragonòt. (b) Used per Creative Commons Attribution-Share Alike 3.0, Unported, Author: A. Uciechowska.

BOX 10.12   THE FUNGUS MADE ME DO IT!

A POSSIBLE CONSIDERATION OF THE SALEM WITCH TRIALS OF 1692

A dark chapter in American history that has long sparked literary interest and historical speculation surrounds the Salem Witch Trials. The classic text, *The Crucible* by Arthur Miller, is a fictionalized dramatization of the events that occurred during the 1692 trials in the Colony. Authors have debated for decades, however, what the true causes of those tragic events were, and theories have included fraud, hysteria, political gain, paranoia, psychological illness, and others. Another interesting theory, however, was put forward by Linda Caporael and is still actively debated.

The "case" began in Salem in late 1691 with a number of people, especially young women, who developed alarming symptoms that included hallucinations, psychosis, sensations of "crawling of the skin," and more. Eventually, these were attributed to the effects of witchcraft, and hundreds of people were imprisoned in early 1692. Following a series of chaotic and bizarre summer trials, 19 people were ultimately convicted and executed by September of 1692, while hundreds of others awaited trial and probable execution. And then, something unexpected happened. In the few weeks that followed these trials, all returned essentially to normal: no more trials, everyone was released from prison, and the afflicted returned to normal. So, by the end of 1692, this dark chapter was closed, never to be repeated to date. But what was behind these strange events?

According to Caporael's theory, the story might well be told, however, beginning long before Salem in the art of a well-known painter, Hieronymus Bosch (1450–1516). Bosch often painted people with apparent medical disorders and diseases. One particular illness that appears in several of his works, including the famous *Temptation of St. Anthony* (1501), has been recently ascribed to ergotism, a terrible epidemic disease of the time referred to as "St. Anthony's Fire" or "The Holy Fire." There are three forms of this disease: gangrenous, convulsive, and hallucinogenic. The symptoms of the convulsive form include "crawling sensations in the skin, tingling in the fingers, vertigo, tinnitus aurium, headaches, disturbances in sensation, hallucination, painful muscular contractions leading to epileptiform convulsions, vomiting, and diarrhea," and "mental disturbances such as mania, melancholia, psychosis, and delirium." The hallucinogenic version of ergotism also adds the symptoms of vivid hallucinations, physical and nervous excitement, and strange compulsive and convulsive "dances" leading ultimately to collapse and exhaustion. These are all symptoms described by the young girls affected in Salem in early 1692. But where does this disease come from, and how does is possibly relate to Salem?

The proper medical term for this disease is ergotism and it occurs when a chemical produced by the ergot fungus (*Claviceps purpurea*) enters the bloodstream. This particular fungus grows especially well on rye grain and is known to have been well established in the New World on wild rye long before western colonization. The new colonists, however, also brought rye with them, and it rapidly became a staple crop of the colony, growing in abundance around Salem. There certainly must have been some ergot in the rye crops of the time, but typically not enough to cause a problem – unless the weather turned out to be just right, as it seemingly did in the spring and summer of

(a)

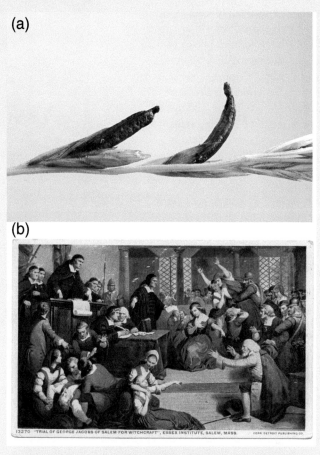

(b)

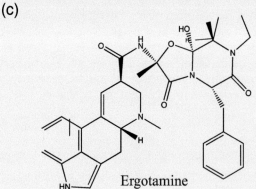

(c)

Ergotamine

FIGURE 10.46   (a) Ergot fungus (*Claviceps purpurea*), (b) painting of the *Trial of George Jacobs, Sr. for Witchcraft* in Salem, Mass. (1855), and (c) the chemical structure of Ergotamine.

Source: (a) Shutterstock.com.

1691. The spring of 1691 was quite unusual – very warm, wet, and stormy, followed by cool and damp – perfect conditions for a large "bloom" of the fungus. Ergot also grows best on rye found in low-lying, wet fields, and some of the most noteworthy symptoms came from people who were living close to rye fields growing in exactly such conditions.

Typically, rye seeds were sown in April, harvested in August, and threshed by the young women in November. This timing lines up well with the Salem events. The first symptoms were reported in December of 1691, shortly after the threshing started, and the entire affair ended in the fall of 1692 – just weeks after the new harvest (presumably not heavily contaminated with ergot). It is important to note that the spring and summer of 1692 were "normal" and not particularly conducive to the growth of the ergot fungus.

In any case, the active ingredient that causes ergotism is the compound ergotamine. This compound is a strong vasoconstrictor and restricts blood flow to certain parts of the body, causing the observed symptoms. It is also the direct precursor to LSD, a very strong hallucinogenic compound (see toxicology chapter). While LSD is not made directly from ergotamine in bread, the ergotamine derivatives, related to LSD, in the bread could have produced hallucinations and other psychological symptoms in Salem.

One episode which might have sparked the blaze of witchcraft trials involves making a witch cake. This cake was made of rye flour and the urine of an afflicted person and then fed to a dog. While we don't know the specific outcome in Salem, if the dog experienced convulsions, the colonists would have taken this as a clear and definitive sign of witchcraft in the person whose urine was added to the cake.

The main support for ergotism as a contributing cause of the Salem mania includes: (1) the known presence of ergot in Salem's rye, (2) the weather patterns of 1691 and 1692, (3) the type and nature of the symptoms shown by the people of Salem, (4) the correlation of symptoms with the locations where the most amount of the ergot would be expected to be found, and (5) the timing of the series of events. In looking for additional support for this theory of ergotism underlying the events in Salem, support may come from medieval Europe. Numerous witchcraft trials there are presumed to have occurred in areas strongly affected by ergotism.

But, of course, the role of ergot in Salem cannot be proven after these hundreds of years, and this theory is still debated. Nonetheless, it forms an interesting argument for what might have sparked a waiting fire into life. What do you think?

As with plants and pollen, fungi and their spores may be transferred from a particular location to a suspect or piece of evidence. Identifying the presence of the fungi on the evidence and comparing it to the profile of a site can help to place the evidence at a crime scene. Unlike plants, however, fungi can grow directly on rocks (lichen), bricks, wood, plastic, and other manmade materials.

Fungi also have a key place in environmental forensics. For example, mold and fungi are often associated with indoor air quality and moisture conditions. These molds, as shown in Figure 10.47, may require extensive renovation or demolition of buildings and can cause severe illness in humans. Identifying the type and source of such fungal invasions can have important legal implications, including construction malpractice and insurance claims.

Forensic mycology is a new field that is just beginning to find application in criminal investigations. Ongoing work is certainly needed to reach the enormous potential that this new field has for forensic work.

FIGURE 10.47 Removal of black fungus (*Aspergillus* sp.) in an apartment.

Source: Shutterstock.com.

10.5 FORENSIC ZOOLOGY

10.5.1 Introduction

Zoology relates to the study of the structures, biological functions, and behavior of animals. Animals and their actions can play valuable roles in forensic investigations, ranging from providing information about how and when a crime was committed to the results of their actions in changing and disturbing a crime scene or evidence (taphonomy) to being victims of crimes themselves. Many aspects of zoology as it relates to forensic science have already been covered in previous sections. However, a few topics that focus on animals in criminal investigations require brief further discussion.

10.5.2 Forensic Veterinary Medicine

A relatively new discipline has arisen that deals with animals in forensic settings: Forensic Veterinary Medicine. This specialty of animal medicine deals specifically with legal cases involving animal health and welfare, causes of animal death, age and parentage of a particular animal, and where the animal originally came from (e.g., ownership, importation, etc.). In many ways, the forensic veterinarian acts as a medical examiner but just in animal, rather than in human, medicine. The main work involves investigating cases of animal cruelty, neglect, and violations of animal conservation/importation laws.

10.5.3 Forensic Animal Cruelty Investigations

Unfortunately, animals are frequently the victims of careless neglect, intentional injury, and even death as a result of human actions. Laws are becoming stricter regarding the ethical treatment of animals, and severe penalties may now result from animal cruelty charges.

The investigations leading to criminal charges against a person for animal cruelty-related crimes require the same

degree of careful analysis, proper procedures, and attention to detail as are employed in human-related forensic cases. Animal crime investigators are often called upon to employ the tools of forensic pathology, ballistics, chemical trace analysis, DNA, and other forensic disciplines, just as they are used in human cases, to solve animal-related crimes and bring criminals to justice.

One problem, however, is that there are typically not enough regulators and inspectors to investigate such cases. The USDA has only 90 inspectors nationally who oversee and inspect more than 30,000 breeders, dealers, and exhibitors of wildlife (Figure 10.48).

10.5.4 Forensic Wildlife Investigations

Most countries in the world have strict laws dealing with the capture, sale and transportation of animals or animal products. This is especially critical in efforts to protect endangered species from extinction due to over-hunting, mistreatment, and capture. Many animal species are highly prized as "pets," and some are hunted solely for their organs or pelts. For example, tiger pelts, rhinoceros

FIGURE 10.48   USFWS Wildlife Forensic Laboratory investigating suspicious animal deaths and the trafficking of illegal animal products.

Source: U.S. Fish and Wildlife Service.

FIGURE 10.49 A ranger in Mozambique looks at the confiscated feet of poached elephants. Elephants are classified as endangered, with only about 40,000–50,000 remaining in the wild.

Source: Shutterstock.com.

horn, bear gall-bladders, and whale products bring large sums of money in some places of the world. Ivory from elephants and exotic feathers for sale worldwide may possibly have come from a protected animal illegally killed (Figure 10.49); some are more valuable, ounce-per-ounce, than gold. Nearly 20 million Americans alone own exotic pets, amounting to an annual $20B market (third only to weapons and drugs), according to a recent National Pet Owners Survey.

It can be very difficult to determine if an animal or their products come from legal or illegal sources. For example, bear gall bladder may be ground and used as a "medicine" or dietary supplement. From this ground sample, it is nearly impossible to determine whether it was derived legally or illegally. Legal caviar looks a great deal like illegal caviar – and in some places, legal caviar is even labeled as illegal caviar to increase its value! All of this makes the work of forensic animal investigators very difficult.

In the United States, the U.S. Fish and Wildlife Services (USFWS) runs a forensics laboratory, the first in the world, dedicated to bringing progressive forensic tools to criminal investigations involving animals. This laboratory assists in investigations around the world and helps determine the cause of death of animals and works to link animal-related crimes to suspects. The analyses can include bones, fur, tissue, and any other parts of an animal that are available. These investigations are very similar to those described in previous chapters for human victims.

10.5.5 Animal Parentage and Behavior

In some cases, it is necessary to determine the ancestry of a living animal. For example, thoroughbred horses and certain breeds of dogs and cats may be particularly valuable based on their parentage. DNA has been used successfully in such instances to verify or refute the claimed provenance (ancestry) of an animal.

Animal behavior may also provide valuable clues as to how the animal was treated in the past and even where it originally came from. Occasionally, knowledge of an animal's behavior patterns is important in deciding whether injuries caused by an animal to either another animal or a human were caused by negligence or were provoked. Forensic animal behavior is a new field that is just beginning to be employed in legal settings.

10.5.6 Human Fauna Possibilities

Our bodies are typically teeming with microscopic animal organisms, from tiny eyelash mites (Figure 10.50) to harmless, but sometimes harmful, parasites in our intestinal tracts, not to mention microbial "riders" on and in us. Someday it may be possible to use the array of these person-specific indicators to identify a particular human's involvement in a crime, although, at this point, this has yet to be developed.

FIGURE 10.50   Tiny, harmless eyelash mites (*Demodex folliculorum*) infesting human hair follicles, as many as 25 per follicle, including eyelash follicles. They feed off of oil secretions and dead cells and give rise to a condition called demodectic mange or red mange.

Source: Shutterstock.com.

BOX 10.13   THE ADVENTURE OF SLIVER BLAZE AND THE SILENT DOG

One of the most famous of Sir Arthur Conan Doyle's novels about his great detective duo, Mr. Sherlock Holmes and Dr. John Watson, spins the tale of the mysterious disappearance of the thoroughbred racehorse Silver Blaze and the murder of his handler, John Straker (Figure 10.51). In this story, the favorite at the upcoming Wessex Cup horse race disappears in the middle of the night, and the body of his trainer, Straker, is found on the moors of Dartmoor dead from blunt force trauma to the head. Apparently, the stable boy had been drugged with opium in his food, and the horse was led out in the middle of the night, presumably to be killed or injured. It was suspected that Straker, discovering the plot as it unfolded, was killed as the victim of the crime while protecting Silver Blaze. Two curious features of the case relating to animal behavior, however, led Holmes to a different solution. First, the watchdog at the stable did not bark during the night that Silver Blaze was taken, presumably by an ill-intentioned stranger. Second, three sheep had recently gone lame unexpectedly at the farm.

As it turns out, these animal behavioral clues were key. The reason that the dog didn't bark was that Straker himself, well known to the dog, took Silver Blaze from his stall and led him to the moor. In Holmes' words:

> I had grasped the significance of the silence of the dog, for one true inference invariably suggests others … Obviously the midnight visitor was someone whom the dog knew well. It was Straker who removed Silver Blaze from his stall and led him out on to the moor.
>
> *(Arthur Conan Doyle, 1892)*

Straker's motive was to subtly injure the horse, in such a way that could not be detected but yet was severe enough to cause him to lose the race – by nicking a tendon in the horse's leg. Straker was deeply in debt and had gambled everything he had on Silver Blaze's rival to win – a long shot who was only sure to win if Silver Blaze was out of the running. However, during the attempt to injure his tendon, Silver Blaze sensed something was wrong and lashed out with his hoof, striking Straker in the head and killing him instantly. The murderer was, therefore, Silver Blaze acting in "self-defense."

The importance of the lame sheep, of course, was that Straker needed to practice the delicate process of laming Silver Blaze. He did this by practicing the operation on the sheep until he had the procedure perfected.

FIGURE 10.51 Drawing by Sidney Paget of *Silver Blaze,* from Arthur Conan Doyle's Sherlock Holmes book *The Case of Silver Blaze and the Silent Dog* (1892).

Source: Retrieved from Wikimedia Commons; used per Creative Commons Attribution.

BOX 10.14   SPOTLIGHT OF FORENSIC ECOLOGY

Dr. Patricia Wiltshire is internationally renowned for her research and expertise in the area of archaeological palynology and for her contributions toward establishing the new discipline of forensic palynology. She is actively engaged in forensic botany and palynology, as well as environmental and ecological profiling. Dr. Wiltshire serves as a consultant for a number of police forces in England, Wales, Ireland, and Scotland, applying her expertise to cases involving theft, murder, rape, and abduction. She specializes in locating clandestine burials and estimating the time of deposition of corpses, as well as linking objects to places, using palynological, ecological, and botanical methods.

Wiltshire collaborates with scientists from the Forensic Science Service, Forensic Science Service Specialist Advisors, and Specialist Advisors of the National Police Improvement Agency (NPIA) in the United Kingdom and is a member of the International Homicide Investigators Association. She has taught at King's College, London University; the Institute of Archaeology, University College London, where she established the Institute's master of science program in forensic science; and is currently a Research Fellow at the University of Aberdeen and a Research Associate at the University of Gloucestershire.

Education: Ph.D. in Botany, King's College, London University; Honorary higher doctorate (D.Sc.), University of Gloucestershire.

Why did you decide to go into this field? *As* a palynologist (study of pollen and spores) and botanist, I have worked on high-profile archaeology digs in the area of environmental reconstruction. I examine soils and sediments that contain pre-historical, and historical evidence. This evidence mainly includes pollen grains and plant spores, although fungal spores are also valuable.

One day, a criminal investigator asked me to apply my expertise to a murder case. I used my skills to produce sufficient evidence for the police to arrest and convict a gang of criminals. Since that first case, I have worked to develop the discipline of forensic palynology in Great Britain.

What background, training, experience, and/or certification does someone typically need to become an expert in your field? A Ph.D. and experience in routine palynology. Also, study botany and ecology, with special emphasis on soils. Fieldwork in the area of paleoecology (environmental reconstruction) and archaeology helps one acquire basic techniques and learn to cope with difficult samples. It is also essential to be familiar with plants exotic to one's own country or research area.

Are there professional organizations in your field? The Forensic Science Society and the American Association of Sedimentary Palynologists are two organizations that lend credibility to one's expertise in this area. But there are so few of us in the field of forensic palynology, it would be difficult to have a professional organization just for this discipline.

FIGURE 10.52 Prof. Patricia Wiltshire and Dr. David Hawksworth.

Source: Used with permission.

What was your most interesting case? One of the most satisfying cases was where I was able to prove who put a baby's body in a bag and deposited it in a dirty stream. It turned out the culprit was the boyfriend of the child's mother. They lived in a very poor part of Birmingham (UK). The range of exotic pollen I obtained from the suspect matched that which was found around the stream. The results were quite bizarre because the vegetation around the stream was poor. However, I found split plastic bags of rotting plant material at the site, garden waste that had been dumped along the stream. The "compost" had spread over the site and it was rich in pollen. The suspect had walked through this on his way to the stream.

What do you especially like about working in this field? I like the fact that I can apply my training, and the wealth of experience I have accumulated over the years, to a good use for society. It is also satisfying that every single case is unique and challenging. The actual work of processing samples, and identifying and counting pollen grains and spores, is very tedious. But, interpreting the results and realizing that they are meaningful to a case, is very exciting.

What is the most difficult part of your profession? There are no written instructions to help with what I do, and much of the information in the literature is not helpful. Another issue is dealing with police, pathologists, and other (more conventional) forensic scientists who find it difficult to understand or accept that something as old-fashioned as botany can help solve cases. It is also very difficult dealing with rotting corpses, gut contents, feces, and other items that most people would never encounter. One needs to have a robust character and a strong stomach.

What advice would you give to someone who is considering pursuing this field? Obtain a degree in botany and study as much ecology – plants, microbes, and animals – as possible. The knowledge will help one interpret complex patterns at crime scenes, in the mortuary, and under the microscope. It is utterly imperative to be a good field ecologist. In order to identify anomalies at crime scenes and other places, one must know what is normal.

Dr. David Hawksworth, scientific associate for the National Museum in London, is a biologist who has applied his expertise in mycology (study of fungi) to worldwide forensic investigations, including the use of fungal growth and spores to estimate PMI, field evaluation and identification of fungi and spores (including lichens), and differentiation of poisonous and hallucinogenic fungi. He has taught at the University of Gloucestershire and served 14 years as director of the International Mycological Institute in Kew and Egham. He is the recipient of numerous awards, including Commander of the British Empire (1996) for services to science.

Education: Honorary Higher Doctorate, Umeå University, Sweden. D.Sc., Ph.D., and B.Sc. from Leicester University.

Why did you decide to go into this field? I became involved in forensics investigations in 2006 when I was asked to identify fungal spores found in palynological preparations made in connection with a murder case. Since then, I have assisted in about 15 cases in the United Kingdom.

What background, training, experience, and/or certification does someone typically need to become an expert in your field? A Ph.D. in some aspect of systematic mycology followed by fieldwork to identify fungi from diverse habitats around the world.

Are there professional organizations in your field? Many countries have mycological societies, though these tend to concentrate on larger fungi. There are also international associations concerned with various aspects of the subject, however, none issue any formal qualification or certifications.

What was your most interesting case? There are really two. One case involved an alleged rape. We used fungal spores along with trace evidence of pollen to identify the sites where the alleged crime occurred. The findings led to a confession. The second case involved the growth of fungi on a carpet soaked with body fluids following a murder. Through experiments, it was possible to estimate the time and day of death.

What do you especially like about working in this field? I enjoy applying knowledge I've accumulated over many years to resolve serious crimes and obtain convictions of those responsible. It is a contribution to society that I had never contemplated as something that I could do with my expertise.

What is the most difficult part of your profession? Getting to know the fungi and their ecological requirements. It is also difficult to keep up with the growing amount of literature available in the field. I continue to find spores that I have never encountered. We probably have only named about 5 to 6 percent of all the fungi on Earth.

What advice would you give someone who is considering pursuing this field? First, obtain a Ph.D. in some aspect of fungal taxonomy that involves the study of microscopic features, and then spend time learning about the fungi that occur in the region where you expect to work through fieldwork and by working alongside other mycologists.

QUESTIONS FOR FURTHER PRACTICE AND MASTERY

10.1 What can forensic entomology *typically* can be used for.

10.2 What are the most important forensic insects in PMI determinations.

10.3 Describe the most important stages and the events associated with each stage in the decomposition of a body.

10.4 Using the plot in the text for Lucilia sericata, the largest larva removed from a body was found to be 4 mm. If the temperature for the previous week was constant at 60°F (15.5°C), what would be the age of this larva? What would happen if the temperature during this period were 70°F (21.1°C) instead of 60°F (15.5°C)?

10.5 Describe the life cycle of a blowfly and how this might be used to determine a PMI.

10.6 Describe the first insect species to typically arrive at a body after death and those species that subsequently arrive. What is faunal succession?

10.7 What is/are the factor(s) that affect the rate of maggot growth and development on a body the most?

10.8 Using the blowfly development plot, how long would you expect it to take for a maggot to grow to 8 mm at 15°C?

10.9 What are the most important factors in determining the PMI from blowfly maggot growth and development?

10.10 When and where do blow flies usually lay their eggs?

10.11 Briefly describe how pollen and fungi can be used in a forensic investigation.

10.12 What is meant by the term biome?

10.13 What are some of the limitations of palynology in a forensic investigation?

10.14 Cite one case (from the internet) where forensic zoology formed an important aspect of the case.

10.15 What is ecology?

10.16 What are proxy indicators?

10.17 What is taxonomy?

10.18 On which phylum does entomology focus?

10.19 What defines an insect?

10.20 What is a necrophagous insect?

10.21 What are the classifications of arthropods associated with the ecosystem of a dead animal?

10.22 How quickly after the death of an animal will blowflies deposit their eggs?

10.23 How long does the bloated stage typically last? What is primarily responsible for the bloating?

10.24 What signals the onset of the decay stage?

10.25 What effect can the maggot mass have on the remains?

10.26 What parts of the animal are typically left at the end of the decay stage?

10.27 How long does the post-decay stage usually last and how/why does this vary?

10.28 How does burial impact the decay process?

10.29 How might vertebrate scavengers impact the decay process?

10.30 When using insect cycles to set PMI, what factors must be considered?

10.31 What is myiasis?

10.32 What is the important underlying principle of forensic botany?

10.33 How does a forensic botanist link evidence to a particular site?

10.34 What factors go into a botanical survey of a location?

10.35 What are some of the difficulties in using DNA to track particular plant species?

10.36 What identification difficulties and advantages are presented by plant cloning and plant hybridization?

10.37 What is the most abundant palynomorph?

10.38 What is the difference between pollen and spores?

10.39 How can the presence of pollen or spores found on a victim or on a suspect help a forensic botanist in an investigation?

10.40 What are the differences between anemogamous plants, zoogamous plants and autogamous plants?

10.41 What is "sinking rate"?

10.42 Fungi have well-known growth cycles. Explain how this can help in determining PMI.

10.43 What are some of the responsibilities of a forensic zoologist?

EXTENSIVE QUESTIONS

10.44 Explain what each of the following areas of ecology study: entomology, botany, zoology, palynology, and mycology.

10.45 List the scientific classifications of life from the broadest category to the narrowest.

10.46 Explain the five decay stages. What factors can affect the timeline of this process?

10.47 A forensic entomologist identifies the presence of eggs from a Green Bottle fly in human remains found in a shady cove. What conclusion can be drawn about the remains?

10.48 Describe how the type of plant life and its condition at a crime scene can help determine PMI (post-mortem interval).

10.49 A forensic entomologist removes the largest maggot from some remains found in the woods. The maggot measures 10mm. The temperature over the past week has had a high of 80°F (26.7°C) and a low of 65°F (18.3°C)? Using the Isomegalen chart in the text, what is the range for the age of the maggot?

GLOSSARY OF TERMS

adventive species: insect species that use dead animal remains as part of their habitat.

algor mortis: the cooling of the body after death.

animals: multicellular organisms that are members of the kingdom *Animalia*.

anther: the part of the flower's stamen that produces pollen.

beetle: an insect with a hard exoskeleton, hard forewing covers that protect the flight wings, and belonging to the order *Coleoptera*.

biome: a large community of plants and animals that occupy a habitat in the natural world.

biosphere: the living part of the Earth.

blowfly: an insect from the family *Calliphoridae* with two sets of wings and deposit their eggs on the remains; one of the most important species in forensic entomology.

botany: the scientific study of plants.

chitin: a hard material composed of a polymeric sugar molecule from which the exoskeleton of insects is formed.

ecosystem: a complex system of interrelated living organisms and their environment.

entomology: the scientific study of insects.

exoskeleton: the external covering, typically hard, that supports and protects an insect.

faunal succession: the concept that different plants and animals follow each other in a predictable sequence. For example, blowflies arrive first at decaying remains, followed by beetles.

fungi: the group of living organisms, belonging to the kingdom *Fungi*, that live by decomposing and absorbing nutrients (e.g., mushrooms, molds, yeast).

insect: animals, belonging to the class *Insecta*, that have bodies divided into three parts (head, thorax, and abdomen), three sets of legs, usually two sets of wings, and an exoskeleton.

instar: a larval stage in the development of an insect.

isomegalen diagram: a plot that shows the relationship between temperature and the time necessary for a larva to grow to a given size.

maggot mass: a collection of large numbers of feeding maggots in one place.

medicolegal forensic entomology: the branch of forensic entomology that deals with its juncture with medicine and the law.

monerans: prokaryotic organisms, belonging to the kingdom *Monera*, that includes bacteria, blue-green algae, and other primitive species.

mycology: the scientific study of fungi.

myiasis: the disease arising from blow flies feeding directly on a living host's tissues.

necrophagous insects: insects that feed directly upon dead remains.

omnivorous species: organisms, such as insects, that feed both on the remains and resident species.

oviposition: the deposition of eggs by an insect.

palynology: the study of pollen, spores, and similar very small materials.

palynomorph: a very small particle, typically between 5 and 500 μm, such as pollen, microfossils, or similar.

parasite: an organism that lives off of another organism (host) without providing any advantage to the host.

phylum: the second most general biological subdivision, just below the kingdom level, and includes organisms with similar biological organizations.

plants: organisms belonging to the kingdom Plantae that produce their nutrition by photosynthesis and have rigid cell walls.

pollen: the fine reproductive material discharged from the male part of a flower or cone.

post-mortem interval (PMI): the length of time from the actual death of the organism to the time that the remains are found.

protists: simple one-celled organisms belonging to the kingdom Protista.

proxy indicator: evidence that points to a particular biological organism, habitat or similar.

puparium (puparia): the larvae form of insect in which the outer skin of the pre-pupae larvae hardens and darkens to form the outer pupal case.

rigor mortis: the muscle stiffening that occurs after death, caused by the chemical decomposition of glycogen and the formation of lactic acid.

segmented body: the divisions of an insect's body into the head, thorax, and abdomen.

sinking rate: the rate at which pollen falls under the influence of gravity.

spiracles: a respiratory opening in the body of an insect larva or through the exoskeleton of an adult insect.

spore: the minute reproductive unit that can grow into a new organism without sexual fusion.

taxonomy: the science of description and classification of living organisms based on their similarities.

BIBLIOGRAPHY

Forensic Ecology, Botany, Palynology and Mycology

David L. Hawksworth, and Patricia E.J. Wiltshire, "Forensic mycology: The use of fungi in criminal investigations", *Forensic Science International*, 2010.

Heather Miller Coyle, *Forensic Botany: Principles and Applications to Criminal Casework*, CRC Press, 2004.

Heather Miller Coyle, Cheng-Lung Lee, Wen-Yu Lin, Henry C. Lee, and Timothy M. Palmbach, "Forensic botany: Using plant evidence to aid in forensic death investigation", *Croatian Medical Journal*, 46(4), 606–612, 2005.

Ruth M. Morgan, Patricia Wiltshire, Adrian Parker, and Peter A. Bull, "The role of forensic geoscience in wildlife crime detection", *Forensic Science International*, 162, 152–162, 2006.

H.B. Reed, *American Midland Naturalist*, 59, 213, 1958.

Maryalice Walker, *Entomology and Palynology: Evidence from the Natural World*, Mason Crest Publisher, 2005.

Patricia E.J. Wiltshire, "Chapter 2: Forensic Ecology", Peter White (Ed.), In *Crime Scene to Court: The Essentials of Forensic Science* (3rd Ed.), Royal Society of Chemistry, ppg 54-85, 2010.

Patricia E.J. Wiltshire, "Chapter 9: Forensic ecology, botany, and palynology: Some aspects of their role in criminal investigation", K. Ritz et al. (Eds.), *Criminal and Environmental Soil Forensics*, Springer Science Business Media B.V. 2009.

Patricia E.J. Wiltshire, "Consideration of some taphonomic variables of relevance to forensic palynological investigation in the United Kingdom", *Forensic Science International*, 163, 173–182, 2006.

Patricia E.J. Wiltshire, "Hair as a source of forensic evidence in murder investigations", *Forensic Science International* 163, 241–248, 2006.

Patricia E.J. Wiltshire and Sue Black, "The cribriform approach to the retrieval of palynological evidence from the turbinates of murder victims", *Forensic Science International* 163, 224–230, 2006.

Arthur Conan Doyle, *A Study in Scarlet*, Ward, Lock & Co., 1888.

Thomé, O. W., "Illustration botanique du Gaillet gratteron (Galium aparine)." In "Flora von Deutschland, Österreich und der Schweiz in Wort und Bild für Schule und Haus", Gera-Untermhaus: Verlag von Ernst Günther, 1885.

Forensic Entomology

Jens Amendt, M.L. Goff, Carlo P. Campobasso, and Martin Grassberger, *Current Concepts in Forensic Entomology*, Springer, 2010.

Martin Benecke, "A brief history of forensic entomology", *Forensic Science International*, 120, 2–14, 2001.

Martin Benecke, "Forensic entomology special issue", *Forensic Science International*, 120(1–2), 1–160, 2001.

Jason H. Byrd and James L. Castner, "Forensic Entomology: The Utility of arthropods in Legal Investigations", CRC Press and Taylor & Francis, 2009. ISBN: 9780849392153.

Dorothy Gennard, *Forensic Entomology: An Introduction*, Wiley, 2007.

M. Lee Goff, *A Fly for the Prosecution: How Insect Evidence Helps Solve Crimes*, Harvard University Press, 2000.

Leonardo Gomes and Claudio J. Von Zuben, "Forensic entomology and main challenges in Brazil", *Neotropical Entomology*, 35(1), 001–011, 2006.

D. Janzen, "Why are there so many species of insects?", *Proceedings of XV International Congress of Entomology*, 8494, 1976.

Kenneth G.V. Smith, *A Manual of Forensic Entomology*, Cornell University Press, 1986.

Peter Tremayne, *Prayer for the Damned*, Minotaur Books, 2008.

Sung Tz'u (Translated by Brian E. McKnight), *The Washing Away of Wrongs*, University of Michigan Press, 1981.

Arthur Conan Doyle, *The Adventure of Silver Blaze*, The Strand Magazine, 1892.

Reed HB. "A study of dog carcass communities in Tennessee, with special references to the insects", *Am Mid Nat*. 59, 213–245, 1958.

Jerry A. Payne, "Plot showing the effect of exposure of animal remains to insects", *Ecology*, 46, 592–602, 1965.

Martin Grassberger and Christian Reiter, "Effect of temperature on Lucilia sericata (Diptera: Calliphoridae) development with special reference to the isomegalen- and isomorphen-diagram", *Forensic Science International*, 120, 2001, Pages 32–36.

PART 3

Chemical Evidence

Overview of Chemical Evidence

11

11.1 OVERVIEW OF CHEMICAL EVIDENCE

Je Veux Parler Des Faits ("Do not rely upon speculation but build upon facts").

(Antoine Lavoisier [1743–1794], *The "father of modern chemistry"*)

LEARNING GOALS AND OBJECTIVES

Chemical evidence forms the core of many forensic investigations. Accurate observations and measurements are key to analyzing these data. After completing this chapter, you should be able to:

- Explain what is meant by quantitative and qualitative chemical analysis.
- List the main questions in deciding upon a particular analytical method.
- Discuss what is meant by precision and accuracy in measurement.
- Explain the SI system of measurement and how significant figures work.
- Elaborate on the basic concepts underlying modern atomic theory.
- Describe the *Law of Conservation of Mass*.
- Show how balanced chemical reactions are employed in analytical chemistry.
- Describe what is meant by the mole and how it is used.
- List several chemical and physical properties of matter.

- Describe pure compounds, homogeneous and heterogeneous mixtures, and how mixtures are separated into their components.
- Explain how chromatography works.
- Discuss what is meant by chemical (classical) analytical methods.
- Describe how gravimetric and volumetric analyses are carried out.

11.1.1 Introduction

Sometimes, it is important to know the detailed chemical composition of an unknown material. Identifying the components – atoms and molecules – of an unknown substance, along with how much of each component is present, can be prime questions in an investigation. For example, when an unknown material is found, it may be necessary to know whether it is a controlled substance, a poison, an explosive, or a routine household chemical. The identity of the substance may also play a key role in any emergency medical treatment required for a victim; the course of medical treatment or a medical examiners inquiry may depend upon what and how much of the substance a person consumed. Medical examiners routinely look to the chemical analysis of body fluids and tissues both for the presence of non-natural components (e.g., poisons, toxins, infectious agents, etc.) and naturally occurring substances that might have contributed to the cause of death. For example, high potassium levels suggest kidney failure while high creatine phosphokinase (CPK) levels may indicate a heart attack.

The field of *analytical chemistry* deals specifically with providing answers to questions such as what is the elemental or molecular composition of a sample and how much of each component is present. The field, therefore, focuses on the separation, purification, characterization (identification), and quantification (how much) of the components that make up a sample (Figure 11.1). In this and the next chapters, the concepts and techniques of analytical chemistry will be presented with a focus on answering these key questions.

FIGURE 11.1 "Sherlock Holmes working hard over a chemical investigation" by Sidney Paget (1892) to Illustrate Arthur Conan Doyle's "Adventure of the Naval Treaty."

Source: NIH (PD).

11.1.2 Analytical Chemistry

According to the American Chemical Society (ACS), the world's largest organization of chemists, analytical chemistry is "the science of obtaining, processing, and communicating information about the composition and structure of matter." The work of analytical chemists impacts many aspects of our everyday lives. Chemical analysis provides assurance and oversight relating to food safety issues, pharmaceutical production, forensic investigations, environmental studies, medicine, petroleum-based product manufacture, bulk materials preparation (e.g., paints, solvents, etc.), scientific and biomedical research, and many other areas. It is through the application of analytical methods that product safety is determined; when someone takes a medicine, there is confidence that it actually is what it claims to be because of carefully performed analytical procedures.

People have long sought answers to what a particular object was made of. Before the advent of modern scientific analytical methods, "touchstones" were used by ancient merchants to roughly determine the identity and purity of a metal (Figure 11.2). When an item was rubbed on a touchstone, the color of the streak left behind gave an indication of its purity (similar to our modern color tests, Section 11.4). In this manner, the difference between 16- and 20-karat gold items could be quickly and easily determined. These touchstones constituted one of the first analytical methods in history.

FIGURE 11.2 Touchstones, today called "streak plates", are used to quickly identify the composition and purity of minerals and jewelry. The plate on the left shows the characteristic streak color for pyrite (fool's gold, FeS_2) while that on the right shows rhodochrosite ($MnCO_3$).

Source: Used per Creative Commons Share-Alike 3.0 Unported. User: Ra'ike.

One of the most famous early examples of a chemical test, however, comes from the work of Archimedes in determining if a new crown created for the King of Syracuse was made of pure gold or whether it was just a gold-plated fraud (see inset box: Archimedes' Great "Eureka"). Many of the first chemical tests were aimed at keeping both the persons and the properties of kings and queens safe and secure. Among the greatest concerns in the Middle Ages was the possibility of arsenic poisoning. Arsenic has been known since ancient times as an easy-to-obtain, simple-to-administer, difficult-to-detect, and nearly impossible-to-prove method of poisoning. The first true chemical toxicological analysis, not surprisingly, was the Marsh test of 1836, which was designed specifically to detect arsenic (see Box 11.2).

BOX 11.1   ARCHIMEDE'S GREAT "Εὔρηκα" ("EUREKA")

Or "be watchful while bathing."

A story was told by the 1st-century writer Marcus Vitruvius Pollio (~80 to 15 BCE) about one ancient form of chemical analysis. In about the 3rd century BCE, the King of Syracuse was Hiero II who reigned for over 50 years. It was during his reign that he commissioned the construction of a new gold crown, possibly to adorn the statue of a favorite god or goddess. When it was delivered, however, he suspected that the goldsmith had cheated him and had replaced some of the gold in the crown with silver or another less valuable metal. Hiero II asked Archimedes, the local genius, to determine whether the wreath was truly pure gold or whether it was a fraud. The only problem, however, was that the wreath could not be harmed since it was destined for holy use – the problem required a non-destructive form of analysis. The solution came to Archimedes when he stepped into his bath one day, causing it to overflow. This moment of discovery inspired him to develop the method needed to determine the volume of an irregularly shaped object by determining the amount of water that the object (e.g., his foot) displaced (the colorful version of the story says that at this point, when Archimedes realized his discovery, he was so excited that he ran immediately from the baths and through the streets to his home – naked and exclaiming "Εὔρηκα, εὔρηκα," or "Eureka, Eureka," which sort of means "I've found it!" It might have been quite a scene)

The ability to accurately determine the volume of space that the crown occupied allowed him, for the first time, to determine the density of the crown, since density is simply mass divided by volume. Mass is easy to determine, but the volume of an irregularly shaped object had presented a very difficult problem. In the experiment described by Vitruvius, Archimedes put a gold object equal in weight to the crown and known to be pure into a bowl which was completely filled

FIGURE 11.3 Statue of Archimedes (287–211 BCE) in Haifa, Israel, in a bathtub, demonstrating the principle of buoyant force. His discovery that water displacement could be used to accurately measure the volume of an irregularly shaped object was an important breakthrough.

Source: Shutterstock.com.

with water, displacing a volume of water equal to the volume of the object, which then became the standard. Then, the pure gold standard was removed, and the same process repeated by immersing the king's new crown in the same bowl of water. If the crown was as pure as the standard, it would occupy the same volume and displace the same amount of water as the standard. However, if it was made of a lighter (less dense) material, the increased bulk of the crown would take up more space and cause the water in the bowl to overflow.

There is some doubt as to whether Archimedes actually performed this experiment as Vitruvius describes it or if he relied on his principle of buoyancy, which might be more likely. In any case, the goldsmith probably had a hot time after Archimedes' work, and his punishment can only be imagined (Virtuvius says "manifestum furtum redemptoris" or "caught in the act of theft," which usually meant capital punishment involving the "caput" or head).

BOX 11.2   A POTENT CUP OF COFFEE

In 1832, Scottish chemist James Marsh was called to testify in the case against John Brodie. Brodie was accused of poisoning his grandfather's coffee with arsenic, the so-called "inheritance powder." Arsenic in food is very difficult to detect by victims since it tastes like garlic, and its effects mimic many other illnesses, including bacterial food poisoning. Marsh's test clearly showed arsenic in the victim's coffee and body, but the chemical residue proving it didn't last long enough to show to a jury. Brodie, who later confessed, was acquitted – much to the distress of chemist Marsh. Marsh then became focused on developing his analytical method so that its result could stand up in court.

Marsh's improved test was first used in the case of the LaFarge poisoning in 1840: the first successful use of a forensic chemical test in a court case. In this case, Marie LaFarge was accused of poisoning her husband Charles LaFarge with arsenic. The circumstantial evidence was strong: Marie had bought arsenic-containing poison to "kill rats," and there were eye-witnesses who saw Ms. LaFarge mixing a white powder in her husband's food and drink. Marsh's test on the husband's exhumed body, however, proved to be incontrovertible when it showed the presence of arsenic. Marie LaFarge was convicted and sentenced to life imprisonment, largely on the "Marsh Arsenic Test."

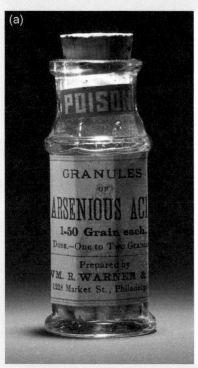 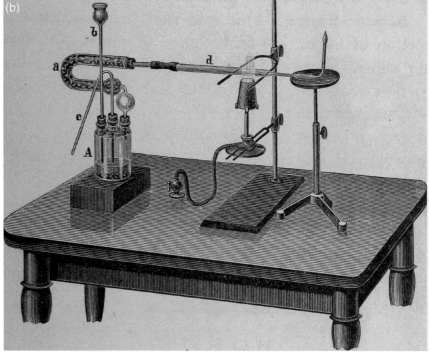

FIGURE 11.4   (a) Arsenic-based medicine of ~1900 and (b) the apparatus for performing the Marsh test for arsenic.
Source: (a) NIJ; (b) Steel (1887).

Analytical chemistry can be broken down into two main areas of analysis: classical (wet chemical) methods and physical (property and instrumental) analysis. This chapter will focus on classical methods, while Chapter 12 will cover methods of instrumental analysis. Before delving into the specific classical methods in use today, we need to first explore a few important concepts briefly in analytical chemistry and separation science.

11.2 METHODS IN ANALYTICAL CHEMISTRY

11.2.1 Types of Analysis

Analytical chemistry primarily focuses on two central questions: what is the identity of a substance and how much of it is present? Today, many analytical techniques have been developed that can quickly and accurately answer these questions, each with its own unique set of advantages and limitations. The trick is often choosing just the right analytical method from among a wide array of possibilities, balancing the type of information needed with the best way to obtain it.

Surprisingly, modern analytical chemistry owes much to the ancient alchemists (Figure 11.5). While they certainly were not scientific in their work by today's standards, they were meticulous in their observations and tireless in their trial-and-error methods, leading to many discoveries that laid the foundations for the later birth of modern chemistry in the late 18th century. Through their experiments, they inadvertently found a wealth of methods for purifying and analyzing many previously unknown chemical compounds.

In choosing the best analytical method for a particular need, a number of preliminary questions must first be answered. These include:

1. **Is the technique qualitative or quantitative?** Often, the first question that needs to be answered in choosing the best analytical technique is whether we need to know the identity or how much of a particular substance is present in the sample, or both. Determining the identity of a particular substance is called *qualitative analysis* – referring to the qualities of the material. The determination of how much of a component is present is referred to as *quantitative analysis* – what is the quantity of the substance in question. This difference between these types of analyses is illustrated by the analogy using Figure 11.5 and summarized in Table 11.1, where several qualitative and quantitative features of a painting are given.

   In a forensic setting, qualitative information often focuses on determining whether a

FIGURE 11.5 The Alchymist, in Search of the Philosopher's Stone Discovers Phosphorus (1771) by Joseph Wright. Oil on canvas.

Source: Retrieved from Wikimedia Commons; used per Creative Commons Attribution.

particular chemical is present in the sample. For example, simply finding compounds known to come from marijuana in a urine sample collected at a competitive athletic event provides all that is needed to be known; the person either has or has not used the drug. How much was used is not important: the important determination is that the substance was used at all. Frequently, as we'll discuss in Chapter 13, the actual compound that we're testing for is destroyed by the body very rapidly, but metabolites (compounds that remain after the body breaks down the original material) can be identified and provide a definite link to the original drug.

In contrast, when testing for alcohol in the blood, it is not sufficient to simply identify that alcohol was consumed; an accurate determination of the amount of ethanol per deciliter of blood is required to show levels of intoxication that could lead to possible legal penalties. Similarly, the presence of amphetamine in a blood sample would be expected for someone known to have a legitimate

TABLE 11.1   Consider the *The Alchymist, in Search of the Philospher's Stone Discovers Phosphorus* painting, what are the qualitative and quantitative aspects of the picture?

QUALITATIVE	*QUANTITATIVE*
The canvas is relatively large.	The picture is on a canvas 50 × 40 in.
The painting appears to be very old.	The painting was completed in 1771 by Joseph Wright.
The painting is very realistic and shows skillful technique.	The painting utilizes a specific style called the *Chiaroscurro* effect.
The painting is heavy.	The painting weights 25.2 lbs

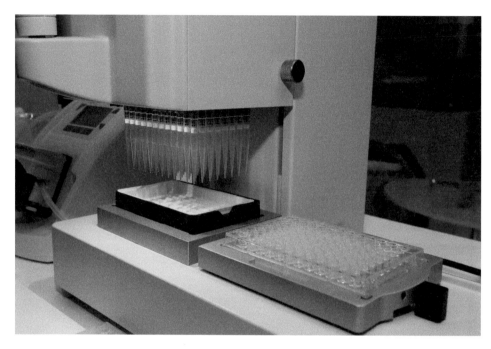

FIGURE 11.6   Robotic workstation for sample preparation and analysis can perform steps such as filtration, extraction, and dilution automatically.

Source: Shutterstock.com.

prescription for the drug but quantitative analysis showing a higher-than-expected concentration of that drug may indicate that an overdose could have contributed to their cause of death.

2. **What sample size is needed?** Some analytical methods require relatively large samples to complete the analysis (100–500 mg or about the size of a Tylenol tablet), while others only require samples that are so small that they are even difficult to see with the unaided eye. If only a small amount of material is available, this can limit the choices of analytical method. For example, a typical combustion analysis may require up to 100 mg (0.1 g) to figure out an empirical formula, while a mass spectrometric analysis can be done on samples as small as 1 ng (1×10^{-9} g). Of course, many times sufficient sample size is available, so that this may not be an important consideration, such as with drug-related arrests.

3. **What type of sample preparation is required?** Sample preparation can range from using the compound as received all the way to extensive, painstaking procedures to render the sample suitable for the ultimate analysis. Probably the most common sample preparation requires the separation of the original sample into its individual components, if it is composed of a mixture of several things. In this process, each component is analyzed separately. Sometimes, separation techniques are not an independent step but are part of the analytical method itself, such as in GC-mass spectrometry. When preparatory steps need to be repeated often, robotic devices may help to speed up the process (Figure 11.6).

4. **What level of analysis is required?** This question relates to how precise a determination must be. For example, do you need to know the percent phosphorus in a sample to within ±1% or to within ±0.0001%? If an answer that is accurate to ±1% phosphorus composition will suffice, then there may be no need to employ a method that can give you a much higher level of analysis, especially since the cost of an analysis tends to increase exponentially as a higher level of precision is required. Further, it may be necessary to run the analysis in duplicate or triplicate to get a defensible result, requiring more sample overall.

5. **What are the detection limits (analytical concentrations) of the method?** What is the lowest concentration or sample size that can be used and still provide an accurate determination of the composition of a substance? For example, if you are analyzing for an element that is present at the 0.01% level, then a rather sensitive technique must be used.

6. **Is the technique destructive or non-destructive?** During the actual performance of the analysis, some techniques consume the sample while others do not alter the sample, and it can be recovered after the measurement. Many times, such as in drug testing, there is no problem if the sample is consumed during the course of the analysis. But, if the sample forms part of an object that cannot be destroyed, such as a painting or a valuable piece of artifact, a non-destructive analytical method is required. For example, it is not likely that a piece of canvas from a questioned rare painting will be allowed to be burned in a combustion analysis to determine if it's a forgery; you might figure out the answer to the forgery question, but the painting would be lost in the process. In this instance, a spectroscopic method that has no physical impact on the sample would be a far better analytical choice.

7. **Is the instrument available?** The instrument needed to complete various determinations varies with each analytical technique. Necessary equipment can range from simple flasks, beakers, and inexpensive chemical reagents to sensitive instruments costing more than $1 million and requiring extensive maintenance and dedicated staff. As a result, different laboratories will have varying testing capabilities and options concerning the choice of what type of analysis will be performed. The actual choice may certainly have both financial and availability constraints to consider.

8. **Is it admissible in court?** One feature unique to forensic analysis, not encountered in other areas of analytical chemistry, is whether the technique and, therefore, the data obtained from it, are admissible in court. To meet this requirement, several considerations must guide the selection of analytical technique, as illustrated in Figure 11.7, and legal admissibility may differ from scientific acceptability.

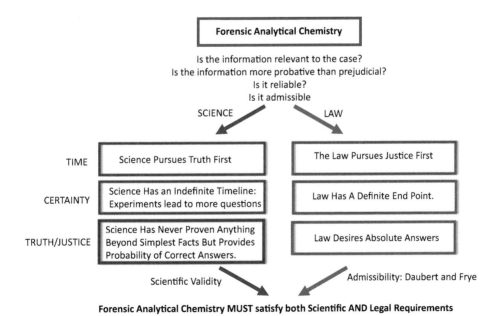

FIGURE 11.7 Analytical chemistry must satisfy both scientific and legal requirements to be admissible and useful in court.

First, the technique must provide information to the court that is more probative than prejudicial, as discussed in the opening chapters of this text. In simple terms, the data must provide the court with *useful and relevant* information that informs its decision-making process. For example, the chemical analysis of a lead pipe showing that it contains lead and a variety of trace materials is only useful if the inquiry revolves around whether the pipe is made of lead or of some other metal. If the question involves comparing two lead pipes, however, there must be suitable differences in the chemical composition between lead pipes from different batches or manufacturing companies to uniquely identify the source of the one pipe in question. This means that there must be sufficient compositional variation between all known lead pipes to link the unknown sample with a reference sample *to the exclusion* of all other lead pipes. An analysis can be enormously detailed, backed up by good scientific methods, and properly done, but if it provides the court with no useful information in determining where the pipe came from, it is inadmissible.

Second, any analytical technique must typically also meet the requirements of either the Frye or Daubert standard (or other similar admissibility standards), depending upon which court is hearing the case and the rules of evidence they employ. Frye requires long-standing general acceptance of a technique, while Daubert is more flexible. The technique must be grounded in good science, reliably executed according to established operating procedures, have known error rates, and be interpreted properly.

9. **Cost of the analysis?** While this is not a true chemical consideration in some sense, cost often plays a deciding role in choosing the technique. Laboratories, as real-world organizations, must operate within budgetary constraints. The cost of an analysis must be justified by the importance of the information that it provides. For example, an expensive immunoassay experiment might not be justified in a simple shoplifting case.

10. **Are there any interferences expected?** Some chemicals or elements present in the sample may interfere with the determination of the component that you are interested in. For example, the Marsh test previously mentioned for arsenic works very well, but if antimony is present in the sample, it can lead to vastly incorrect answers. Antimony, in this case, is referred to as an *interference* in the Marsh test, and another method is required to determine arsenic in the presence of antimony.

11. **How are analytical results verified?** If an analytical result is a key piece of evidence, it is often desirable to use two quite different analytical techniques to run complementary tests. If both techniques, using different approaches, come back with the same answer, then we have a much higher level of confidence in the result. For example, if the concentration of arsenic in a sample is determined by both a chemical method *and* by a spectroscopic method (using light), and the two independent methods provide answers that are found to agree, then the answer can be regarded as much more reliable. Using multiple, experimentally unlike techniques helps to eliminate systematic errors in the analysis.

This series of preliminary questions may seem like a daunting list to consider when selecting the proper analytical method for a particular application, but it's really not as bad as it seems. Standard methods of analyses have now been developed for many of the forensically important substances that are frequently encountered, such that most or all of these questions have already been answered for many types of determinations. For example, the analysis of alcohol in blood is most often done by either mass spectrometric or spectrophotometric analysis, while the identification of a fiber is frequently performed by infrared microspectrophotometer. However, the analyst must know the strengths and limitations, as well as the answers to these questions, for any method that they employ. Table 11.2 gives a summary of some of the most common analytical methods used in forensic analysis along with some advantages and limitations of each method.

Analytical tests can also be considered either *presumptive* or *confirmatory*. Presumptive tests (Figure 11.8), first introduced in the chapter on serology, provide a rapid screening process to determine the likelihood of a particular chemical's presence in the sample. These tests are most often used to determine whether or not additional, more conclusive testing is warranted. One of the disadvantages of presumptive tests is that they can give rise to either false positive or false negative readings. A *confirmatory test* is a measurement that can indicate the presence of the substance in the sample with a very high degree of certainty, vastly reducing false readings. For example, the Marquis test (presumptive) can indicate that a substance is likely to contain the drug Ecstasy. However, a complete GC-mass spectrometric analysis (confirmatory) is required to verify the presence of the drug in the sample to the standards required for courtroom evidence.

TABLE 11.2 Analytical features for several types of classical and instrumental methods

METHOD OR TECHNIQUE	QUALITATIVE VS QUANTITATIVE*	SAMPLE SIZE REQUIRED	DETECTION LIMITS	DESTRUCTIVE METHOD	INSTRUMENTAL AVAILABILITY
Chemical (Classical) Methods (Chapter 11)					
Combustion Analysis	Quantitative*	50–100 mg	~0.1%	Yes	Easy
Gravimetric Analysis	Quantitative*	20–50 mg	~0.5%	Yes	Easy
Titrimetric Analysis	Quantitative*	1–10 mg	~0.1%	Yes	Easy
Physical (Instrumental) Methods (Chapter 12)					
Mass Spectrometry	Qualitative and quantitative (with GC)	1×10^{-9} g	10^{-12}– 10^{-15} g	Yes	Moderate
Infrared Spectrophotometry	Qualitative and semi-quantitative	0.001 g	~0.02%	Maybe	Moderate
UV-visible Spectrophotometry	Quantitative	0.001 g	~0.02% but variable	Maybe	Moderate
Atomic Emission Spectrophotometry	Qualitative and semi-quantitative	10 mg	10^{-4} g/L	Yes	Moderate
Atomic Absorption Spectrophotometry	Qualitative and quantitative	10 mg	10^{-4} g/L	Yes	Moderate
Neutron Activation Analysis	Quantitative and quantitative*	0.1 mg	10^{-4} g/L	Minimally	Difficult

Note: *Some of these techniques can also be adapted into quantitative methods, although their current use is primarily qualitative.

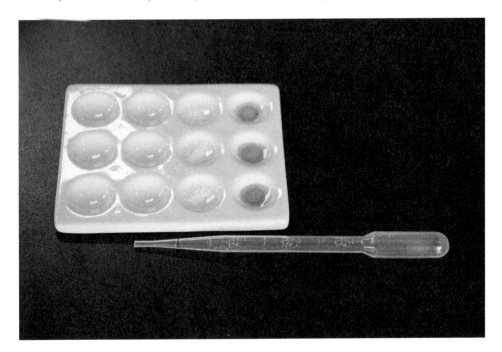

FIGURE 11.8 Presumptive field drug testing.

Source: Retrieved from Wikimedia Commons; used per Creative Commons Attribution.

Finally, let's define a few terms to help simplify the conversation about analytical chemistry later. An *analyte* is the target substance for which the analysis is being done. *Concentration* refers to the amount of material dissolved in a given amount of solvent. For example, the concentration of a solution might be 10 g of NaOH in 100 mL of solvent. Later in the chapter we will define a key concept, molarity, which provides a very useful relative measure of concentration.

11.3 ATOMS, MOLECULES, AND SEPARATION SCIENCE

In order to grasp the basic principles underlying analytical techniques, it is first necessary to briefly review some fundamental features of atoms and molecules. While we have never directly "seen" atoms, we have developed a detailed understanding of their properties and behavior through over a century of careful experiments designed to probe their inner workings.

11.3.1 Basic Atomic Theory

At a fundamental level, matter can be broken down into atoms, the simplest units of chemical importance. Atoms themselves are composed of collections of atomic building blocks or particles, including protons, neutrons, and electrons (Figure 11.9).

The protons and neutrons, called nucleons, are grouped together to form the atom's dense central nucleus, while the much smaller electrons move around outside the nucleus. To put this in relative human terms, if the nucleus were about the size of a golf ball (~2.5 cm or 1 in. in diameter), it would weigh more than 2.5 billion tons (2.2 trillion kg), and the electron would move within a space of about 200 m (~200 yards) in diameter. This analogy illustrates both the enormous density of the nucleus and the fact that atoms are mostly empty space.

The two primary nuclear particles, neutrons, and protons, are about the same size and are either electrically neutral (neutron) or positively charged (proton). The electron, with a mass about 1/2,000th that of a proton or neutron, carries an equal but opposite charge (negative) and moves rapidly around outside the nucleus. The number of protons in an atom is referred to as its *atomic number*, and the total mass of an atom is referred to as its *atomic mass* or weight. Atomic masses are determined by adding up the masses of the individual nuclear particles that it contains. Since atomic particles are so incredibly small, it's not very convenient to talk about their masses using the standard kg unit that was designed to weigh far heavier objects. For this reason, a relative mass unit, called the *atomic mass unit* (amu), was defined as 1/12th the mass of a carbon atom containing six protons and six neutrons, or about the mass of a single proton or neutron (~1.66×10^{-27} kg). Using this unit, the mass of a lithium atom, with three protons and four neutrons,

FIGURE 11.9   Drawing of the structure of an atom, including the positively charged protons, neutral neutrons and negatively charged electrons. Note: the electrons do not travel in circular paths around the nucleus and are about 1/2000th the size of a proton, and the atoms are mostly empty space – not drawn to scale.

Source: Shutterstock.com.

would be about 7 amu while a hydrogen atom, with just one proton in its nucleus, would weigh just about 1 amu.

Neutral atoms contain equal numbers of protons and electrons such that the overall charge on the atom balances out to zero. There are times, however, when these charges don't balance out and the atom carries a net charge. Atoms with fewer electrons than protons carry an overall positive charge and are called *cations*, while those that have more electrons than protons carry an overall negative charge and are called *anions*. Together, cations and anions are collectively known as *ions*, which are atoms that have an overall net charge (similarly for molecular ions, especially important in mass spectrometry, as discussed in Chapter 12).

Elements are composed of all atoms with the same atomic number (the same number of protons) and are the smallest units that retain their characteristic chemical properties. Elements cannot be broken down into simpler substances by normal chemical means and, therefore, are the most basic building blocks for constructing compounds (molecules) and materials found in nature. For example, all carbon atoms have exactly six protons while all gold atoms have 79 protons. Adding just one proton to a carbon nucleus would "transform" it into a nitrogen atom; this transformation is actually exceedingly difficult to perform and can only be achieved through nuclear reactions. Today, 118 elements are known that can be conveniently displayed according to their increasing atomic numbers in the *periodic table* (Figure 11.10). It is called a "periodic table" largely because the elements in the vertical columns share many physical and chemical features – in other words, these properties repeat periodically as you progress through the list of elements. The periodic table simply displays and emphasizes the relationships between the elements that share these common properties by lining them up in vertical columns.

While all carbon atoms must have exactly six protons, individual carbon atoms may contain differing numbers of neutrons. For example, carbon atoms are known to contain between five and eight neutrons, although the most stable and common arrangement has six protons and six neutrons. Atoms that vary in the number of neutrons while keeping the same number of protons are called *isotopes*, as illustrated in Figure 11.11. This feature is very important in some forms of chemical analysis – especially the forensic workhorse techniques of mass spectrometry and radioisotope analysis (e.g., dating, geographic mapping, etc.). Chemists have developed a shorthand for quickly indicating important compositional information about an individual atom. In this shorthand, the element is denoted by an atomic symbol using letters, such as "C" for carbon or "Au" for gold, with the atomic mass and atomic number shown as a superscript and subscript, respectively.

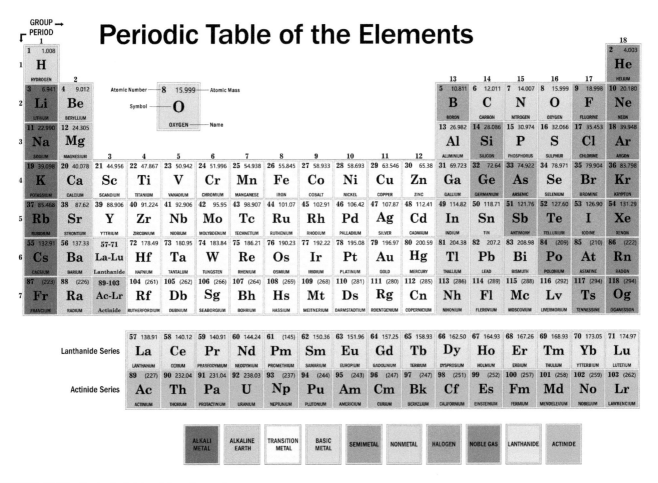

FIGURE 11.10   Periodic table of the elements.

Source: Shutterstock.com.

ISOTOPES OF CARBON

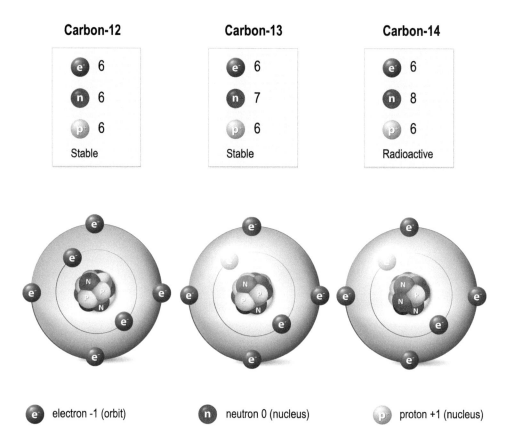

FIGURE 11.11   Three of the possible isotopes of carbon. Carbon-12, on the left, is the most common isotope while the radioactive Carbon-14 isotope is used for the radio-dating of artifacts.

Source: Shutterstock.com.

11.3.2 Molecules and Compounds

Atoms can come together to form more complex units, called *molecules* (Figure 11.12). We indicate this through the use of *chemical formulas*, where the number and type of each atom in the molecule are listed. For example, ethyl alcohol is denoted as C_2H_6O, meaning that two carbon, six hydrogen, and one oxygen atoms come together to form the molecule.

When two or more atoms come together, they can bind to each other in very special ways to form compounds with properties that can be quite different from those of the individual atoms. For example, chlorine (Cl_2), a toxic gas, and sodium (Na), a highly reactive metal, can come together to form solid sodium chloride (NaCl): ordinary, life-sustaining table salt. Additionally, the specific arrangement and interconnections between the atoms of a molecule dictate its properties; the same array of atoms can often be arranged in alternative ways to form a variety of molecules with quite different chemical and physical properties. Arranging the same set of atoms together in different ways produces new substances called *isomers*.

For example, two isomers with the molecular formula C_2H_6O, shown in Figure 11.13, are ethanol and dimethyl ether – two compounds with very different chemical and physical properties. Ethanol, consumed in alcoholic beverages, has a boiling point of 78°C, is completely soluble in water (miscible), and has an LD_{50} of 10.3 g/kg (a measure of its toxicity, Chapter 13), while dimethyl ether has a boiling point of −23.6°C, is only partly soluble in water, and has an LD_{50} of 1.2 g/kg. Simply organizing the atoms in alternate ways in the two compounds changes the boiling point by over 100°C and increases the toxicity tenfold.

In 1805, John Dalton came up with a series of statements about matter that formed the beginning of our modern concept of atoms and molecules. Several of his ideas remain central to our understanding of chemistry today. Among these, his refinement of the *Conservation of Mass* idea, first put forward by Lavoisier, states that the total amount of material present before and after a chemical reaction is the same. Another way to say this is that the total number of atoms of each element is not changed when a chemical reaction occurs. Knowing this allows us to keep track of all the atoms of each element as they

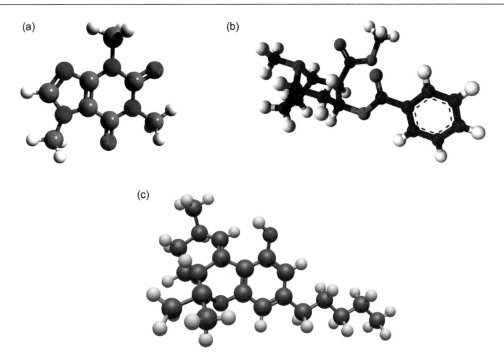

FIGURE 11.12   Atoms can bind together in unique configurations, dictated by the number and type of each element in the collection, to form molecules, such as (a) Caffeine ($C_8H_{10}O_2N_4$), (b) Cocaine ($C_{17}H_{21}NO_4$) and (c) THC ($C_{21}H_{30}O_2$) [white spheres are hydrogen, black are carbon, red are oxygen, and blue are nitrogen atoms]. The chemical formula tells the number of each type of atom (element) in the compound.

Source: (a) Used per Creative Creative Commons 3.0 Unported. User: Giorgiogp; (c) Used per Creative Commons Share-Alike 4.0 International. User: Mplanine.

(a)   (b)

Both have the same chemical formula: C_2H_6O

Ethanol   Dimethyl ether

FIGURE 11.13   Isomers of C_2H_6O: (a) ethanol and (b) dimethyl ether – two very different compounds with the same chemical formula: CH_3O.

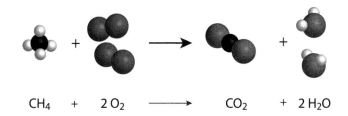

CH_4 + $2 O_2$ ⟶ CO_2 + $2 H_2O$

FIGURE 11.14   Combustion reaction of methane with oxygen to form carbon dioxide and water.

Source: Shutterstock.com.

go through a chemical reaction – a central idea of analytical chemistry. We conveniently keep track of these atoms through the use of *chemical equations*. Thus, a chemical equation contains all the atoms in the reacting molecules or elements, called *reactants*, and the atoms in the resulting new molecules, called *products*. A chemical equation uses an arrow to show the predominant "direction" of the reaction as it proceeds from reactants to products, but a chemical equation can also correctly be thought of as a mathematical equation where the number of each type of atom on both sides need to balance. Thus, the arrow in a reaction can be conceptually replaced by a mathematical equal sign. For example, in the reaction of the combustion of methane, shown in Figure 11.14, one molecule of methane (CH_4) reacts with two molecules of oxygen (O_2) to yield molecule of one carbon dioxide (CO_2) and two molecules

of water (H_2O). There are the same number of carbon, hydrogen, and oxygen atoms on each side of the arrow. This can, however, be more conveniently and simply written in the form of a chemical equation, as shown below.

$$CH_4(g) + 2O_2(g) \rightarrow CO_2(g) + 2H_2O(l) \qquad (11.1)$$

$CH_4(g)$	$2 O_2(g)$	---->	$CO_2(g)$	$2 H_2O(l)$
1 Carbon		=	1 Carbon	
4 Hydrogen		=		4 Hydrogen
	4 Oxygen	=	2 Oxygen	2 Oxygen

This simple equation shows that there are four hydrogen atoms, one carbon atom, and four oxygen atoms on each side of the arrow, indicating that the equation is *balanced*; all atoms are accounted for, and no additional atoms are listed. This exacting relationship for keeping track of the atoms of the reactants and products in a chemical reaction is referred to as the *stoichiometry* of the reaction. The stoichiometry of a chemical reaction also tells us how many molecules of each type of reactant combine to form exactly how many molecules of each product.

11.3.3 The Mole

Chemical equations are truly very useful in keeping track of the overall stoichiometry (reacting ratios and quantities) involved in a chemical reaction and form a key part of forensic analytical chemistry. However, it is impossible to count out the actual number of reactant molecules needed when setting up a chemical reaction; atoms and molecules are far too small to allow for that, and the numbers involved are far too large. Additionally, the same number of different types of atoms have different weights. For example, there are vastly different numbers of atoms in 10 g of gold when compared to 10 g of carbon or 10 g of hydrogen. This same small 10 g sample of hydrogen (H_2) contains over 3×10^{24} H_2 molecules (that's more than 3,000,000,000,000,000,000,000,000 H_2 molecules) – and that's a relatively small amount of hydrogen in human-scale terms! So, a more useful system for dealing with

the very large numbers of atoms and molecules encountered when working with chemical reactions was needed. This system was provided by the introduction of a unit called the *mole*. The mole, like any other counting unit, represents a certain number of items. Other common counting units, such as a dozen (12 items), a gross (144 items), and a ream (500 items), are convenient ways to denote larger numbers and are simply shorthand for a particular number of items. Similarly, the mole is simply shorthand for a very large number of items: 6.02×10^{23} items, called *Avogadro's number*. When balancing chemical equations, we worry about the relative numbers of atoms involved, but moles provide us with a way of keeping track of the numbers of atoms in real-life, large-scale samples. Thus, 10 g of H_2 can also be expressed as 5 mol of H_2; much simpler and of far greater utility than using 3×10^{24} H_2 molecules. It is important to realize that a mole always contains 6.02×10^{23} of any item, whether it be H_2 molecules, Au atoms, electrons, toasters, cars, etc. The mass and volume of material in 1 mol of several different elements are shown in Figure 11.15; each contains exactly the same number of atoms (6.02×10^{23}), but they all have different weights and volumes [Note: 1 mol used to be defined as the number of atoms in 12 g of C^{12} but is now defined just as the number 6.02×10^{23}]. Notice that the mass in grams of 1 mol of carbon is the same as its atomic number: 12. This relationship holds for each of the elements; there is 1 mol of atoms in 1 g of H^1, 7 g of Li^7, and 197 g of Au^{197},

FIGURE 11.15 Comparison of 1 mol of several different substances: (starting at the upper left, clockwise) 270.3 g of iron (III) chloride ($FeCl_3$), 249.7 g of copper sulfate ($CuSO_4$), 166.0 g of potassium iodide (KI), 291.0 g of cobalt nitrate ($Co(NO_3)_2$), 158.0 g of potassium manganate (K_2MNO_4), and 58.5 g of sodium chloride (NaCl). In each case, they all contain 6.02×10^{23} atoms.

Source: Andrew Lambert Photography/Science Photo Library. Used with permission.

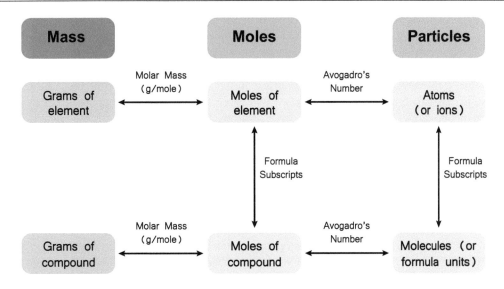

FIGURE 11.16   Method to interconvert between grams, moles, and the number of atoms or molecules.

Source: Shutterstock.com.

respectively. The weight that correlates with 1 mol of the element is referred to as the *molar mass* and is defined as equal to the atomic mass of the substance. In the case of molecules, the molar mass is replaced by the term *molecular or formula weight*, something which will be explained in a later section. Using these relationships, it's very easy to convert between grams (mass), moles, and the number of atoms or molecules (Figure 11.16). The number of moles in a sample of a substance is equal to the number of grams of the substance divided by its atomic or molecular weight:

$$\text{Moles} = \frac{\text{grams of substance}}{\text{molecular weight}} \qquad (11.2)$$

Now, we are able to convert something that is easily (grams), into moles, which show the correct ratios and quantities of substances involved in any chemical reaction.

BOX 11.4   USING MOLES

One common question that needs to be answered is how many moles of a substance are in a certain sample. It turns out that this is pretty easy to calculate. For example, how many moles (mol) of carbon are in 8.0 g of carbon?

To figure this out, we simply take the 8.0 g of carbon present in the sample and divide it by its atomic weight [remember that moles = grams/(atomic or molecular weight)]:

Moles = grams/(atomic or molecular weight)
Moles of carbon = 8.0 g/12 (g/mol) = 0.75 mol

And remember, 1 mol contains 6.02×10^{23} of whatever it is that we are counting. Chemists find this number so important that we celebrate it annually on "Mole Day" at 6:02 AM every October 23rd (10/23).

BOX 11.5   M&MS COUNT

Using the mass of a sample to figure out how many atoms or molecules it contains is similar to counting M&M candies. For example, if a manufacturer of M&Ms wanted to ship a big box containing 100,000 M&Ms, they certainly couldn't take the time to count them by hand, or even by computer – that would simply take far too long. Instead, manufacturers of small things that are sold in large numbers, such as candies, pins, screws, and many other items, use weight to determine the count. For example, if a 1 lb pound bag has about 1,000 "regular" M&Ms, then the big box would need to be loaded with the equivalent weight of 100,000 M&M's × 1 lb bag/1,000 M&Ms or 100 bags. So, to have 100,000 M&Ms, the manufacturer needs 100 lbs of M&Ms.

$$100{,}000\,\text{M\&Ms}\left(\frac{1\,\text{one-pound bag}}{1{,}000\,\text{M\&Ms}}\right) = x\,\text{one-pound}$$
$$\text{bags} = x\,\text{pounds on M\&Ms}$$

Cancel M&M on the top and bottom of the left-side of the equation gives:

$$100{,}000\,\text{M\&Ms}\left(\frac{1\,\text{one-pound bag}}{1{,}000\,\text{M\&Ms}}\right) = x\,\text{on-pound bags}$$

100 one-pound bags = 100 pounds of M&Ms

Moles work the same way. If we wanted 6.02×10^{23} atoms, we'd need a specific mass of that element, its molar mass. For molecules, this is the molecular mass. It's also true that the molar mass changes for each different substance – just as if we switched from "regular" M&Ms to peanut M&Ms, each would have its own mass per 1,000.

The concept of the mole has particular value when combined with chemical equations and allows us to: (1) predict the amounts of products produced from any scale of reaction, (2) determine the amount of reactants needed to produce a specific amount of products, (3) determine chemical formulas from analytical data, (4) formulate unknown compounds, (5) identify unknown compounds, and (6) other uses.

It is important to note that the multiplier in front of each chemical in a balanced equation (called its coefficient), such as the 2 before the O_2 in the reaction of 2 O_2 with 1 CH_4, is the ratio of the moles involved in the reaction (Equation 11.1). Thus, we can say that 1 mol of methane reacts with 2 mol of oxygen to form 1 mol of carbon dioxide and 2 mol of water. Using moles, we can interconvert between grams and the number of atoms or molecules present in a specific sample, as illustrated in Figure 11.16. We can use this convenient interconversion to determine how many grams of a reactant or product are consumed or produced in a chemical reaction by comparing the number of moles of each and, therefore, determine just the right amount of each used or formed in the reaction.

11.3.4 Chemical Formulas

Another chemist at the time of Dalton, Joseph Louis Proust (and later restated by Dalton), first presented another fundamental idea of chemical analysis, called the law of *Constant Composition*, which states that for any compound, the number and type of atoms that make it up are *always* the same. In other words, all water molecules in the Universe have the same ratio of hydrogen atoms to oxygen atoms fixed at 2:1. If this ratio changes to anything else, such as 1:1 or 3:1, then the molecule becomes a *different* compound, hydrogen peroxide or the hydronium ion, respectively. This also means that the formula of a molecule does *not* depend on how it's made or where it's found: water is always H_2O. This may sound like stating the obvious, but it is sometimes not so obvious to everyone (see Box 11.6).

BOX 11.6   WHICH WOULD YOU RATHER HAVE?

If you were given the choice of taking one of two vitamin C tablets (ascorbic acid) of the *same* purity, one extracted from all-natural rose hips in the sunny highlands of Italy by friendly farmers and the other prepared in an automated chemical production laboratory in a five-step pathway from glucose, which would you choose? The law of constant composition says that, from a chemical perspective, it doesn't matter at all; ascorbic acid is ascorbic acid, no matter the source (as long as the purity is the same). As writer Gertrude Stein once wrote "a rose is a rose is a rose" – a somewhat fanciful statement of the law of identity, a "thing is what it is …"

This concept can have important applications to both the development of new pharmaceuticals and our ability to identify unknown compounds. For example, a native healing remedy, derived from natural sources, can be isolated and found to have valuable medicinal properties. The natural sources, however, usually cannot provide enough of a compound to supply all the people who need it. In this case, a lab synthetic method is developed to provide enough of the compound without jeopardizing the natural environment. The synthetic compound has exactly the same properties as the pure, naturally-obtained drug. Look up *taxol* for a good example of this process.

So far, we have used chemical formulas for molecules to indicate how many of *each* type of atom must come together to form a specific compound. This type of formula is called a *molecular formula* since it represents the actual type and number of each atom in the molecule. Sometimes, such as in a chemical analysis, we are only able to determine the lowest whole number ratio of all the atoms present. For example, the molecular formula of glucose is $C_6H_{12}O_6$, meaning, of course, that 6 carbon, 12 hydrogen, and 6 oxygen atoms are contained in the actual glucose molecule. The $C_6H_{12}O_6$ formula does not, however, represent the smallest whole number ratio of the atoms: for $C_6H_{12}O_6$, that ratio would be CH_2O. This reduced formula is called the *empirical formula* and is usually the type of information that we obtain from classical chemical analytical methods. If we did an elemental chemical analysis of glucose, such as through a combustion analysis, we would determine that the ratio of C:H:O was 1:2:1. Thus, the empirical formula for $C_6H_{12}O_6$ is simply CH_2O. It is important to note that many compounds may have the same empirical formula. For example, the very different structures of acetylene (C_2H_2) and benzene (C_6H_6) have the same empirical formula (CH), while fullerene (C_{60}) and nanotubes (Cn) both have the same empirical formula: C (Figure 11.17). But sometimes, the empirical and molecular formulas for a compound are the same: the empirical and molecular formulas for sucrose – common table sugar – are both $C_{12}H_{22}O_{11}$.

When considering atoms, we described their mass in terms of an atomic mass. When considering molecules, we similarly define a term called the molecular mass, or more commonly *molecular weight*. The molecular weight of a compound is calculated simply by adding up the atomic masses for every atom in the molecule. For example, in glucose, $C_6H_{12}O_6$, the molecular mass is the sum of six times the atomic mass of carbon added to 12 times the atomic mass of hydrogen and that all added to six times the atomic mass of oxygen, as shown in the equations below:

6 (C atomic mass) + 12(H atomic mass) + 6 (O atomic mass) = molecular weight of $C_6H_{12}O_6$

6 (12.01 amu) + 12 (1.01 amu) + 6 (16.00) = molecular weight of $C_6H_{12}O_6$

72.06 amu + 12.12 amu + 96.00 amu = molecular weight of $C_6H_{12}O_6$

180.18 amu = molecular weight of $C_6H_{12}O_6$

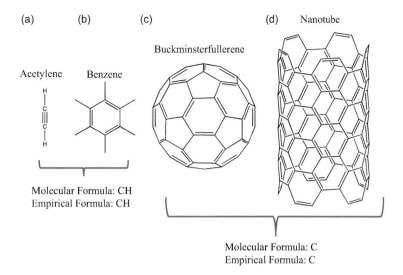

FIGURE 11.17   Structures of (a–d): acetylene, benzene, buckminsterfullerene, and a carbon nanotube. The empirical formulas for both acetylene and benzene are CH while the empirical formula for both buckminsterfullerene and a carbon nanotube is simply C.

It is useful to note that chemically, some compounds are not made up of small, independent molecules but rather are extended repeating patterns of stacked atoms (ions), such as NaCl. In this case, the chemical formula used for these extended, infinitely repeating compounds is referred to as the formula weight rather than the molecular weight (Figure 11.18).

When an elemental analysis is done on a compound, the result is usually expressed in terms of an elemental *percentage composition*. We'll discuss how this is done later in this chapter but the data is the percent, by mass, that each element contributes to the total mass of the compound. For example, if we completed an elemental analysis on a 100 g sample of glucose, we would find that it contained about 40.0 g of carbon, 6.7 g of hydrogen, and 53.3 g of oxygen. Converting this to percent (amount in 100 g) would give about: C = 40.0%, H = 6.7%, and O = 53.3%.

We can use this elemental analytical information to determine an empirical (reduced) formula for the compound, often leading to a preliminary identification of the material. This is done through the application of the relationships and definitions already presented. The process has several steps, starting with the percent elemental composition data:

1. *Assume* a 100 g sample; this allows us to convert percent data directly into grams.
2. *Convert* the percent of each element into grams: 15% C means that there would be 15 g carbon in a 100 g sample.
3. *Convert* the grams of each element into moles by dividing the grams present by the element's atomic weight.

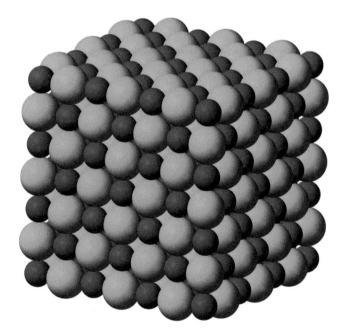

FIGURE 11.18   A lattice of Na⁺ and Cl⁻ ions forming the NaCl (sodium chloride) compound. Since there is no simple molecule but rather an infinite array of atoms (ions), we use the formula weight for NaCl rather than a molecular weight.

Source: Retrieved from Wikimedia Commons; used per Creative Commons Attribution.

4. *Calculate* the mole ratio of the elements; divide all the moles calculated by the smallest number of moles then multiply all these numbers by a factor to find the nearest whole number ratio of the elements.

These steps are illustrated for a forensic sample in Box 11.7.

BOX 11.7   IT'S ELEMENTARY, WATSON

A sample of a pure white substance was obtained from a routine traffic stop. The compound was brought into the forensic lab and an elemental combustion analysis was performed (see Section 11.3.5). The results showed that the sample contained 68.3% carbon, 6.2% hydrogen, 3.8% nitrogen, and 21.7% oxygen by weight. To provide a preliminary identification of the compound, determine the empirical formula for this compound?

Using the method illustrated below, the compound's empirical formula can be quickly determined. Here are the steps:

1. Assume a 100 g sample (since percent is defined as the amount in 100, this is easy to do – just change the "%" symbol with "grams").
2. Convert percent to grams:
   Carbon = 68.3% carbon = 68.3 g carbon
   Hydrogen = 6.2% hydrogen = 6.2 g hydrogen
   Nitrogen = 3.8% nitrogen = 3.8 g nitrogen
   Oxygen = 21.7% oxygen = 21.7 g oxygen
3. Convert to moles:
   Carbon = 68.3 g carbon = 68.3 g/12.0 amu = 5.69 mol carbon
   Hydrogen = 6.2 g hydrogen = 6.2 g/1.0 amu = 6.2 mol hydrogen
   Nitrogen = 3.8 g nitrogen = 3.8 g/14.0 amu = 0.27 mol nitrogen
   Oxygen = 21.7 g oxygen = 21.7 g/16.0 amu = 1.35 mol of oxygen

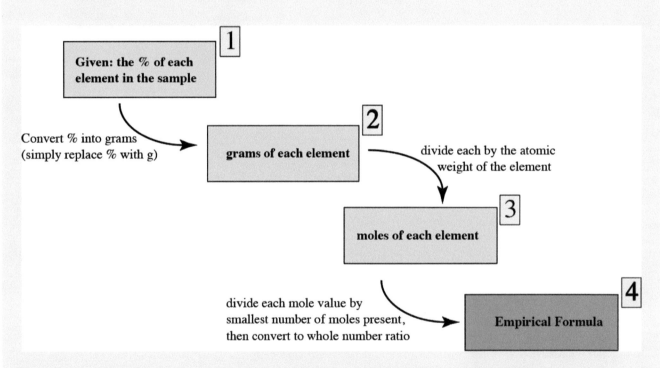

FIGURE 11.19   Step-by-step method for finding an empirical formula from elemental percent composition data.

4. Calculate mole ratio to find empirical formula:
   Since nitrogen is present in the sample in the smallest molar quantity (0.27 mol), we divide each of the other molar quantities by 0.27 mol:
   Carbon = 5.69 mol/0.27 mol = ~ 21
   Hydrogen = 6.20 mol/0.27 mol = ~ 23
   Nitrogen = 0.27 mol/0.27 mol = 1.0
   Oxygen = 1.35 mol/0.27 mol = 5.0

Therefore, the empirical formula for the unknown is $C_{21}H_{23}NO_5$. By looking through published tables of chemical empirical formulas, we see that this is the same empirical (and molecular) formula for heroin. A preliminary identification of the compound would therefore be consistent with *heroin*.

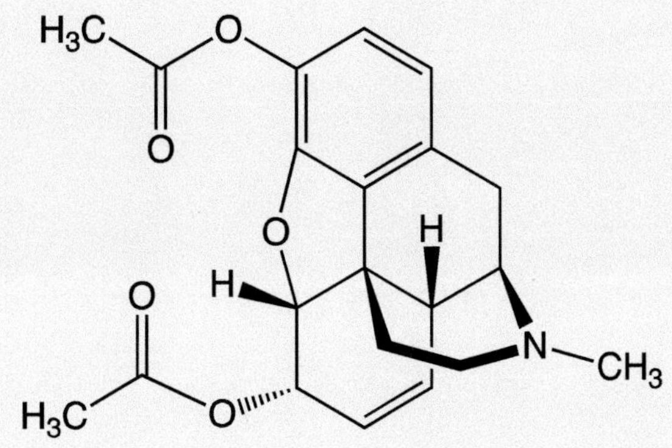

FIGURE 11.20 Structure of Heroin (empirical and molecular formulas are the same: $C_{21}H_{23}NO_5$).

11.3.5 Properties and States of Matter

Under normal conditions, matter comes in three *states* or *phases*: gas, liquid, or solid (Figure 11.21). Each of these states has a distinctive set of characteristic properties that sets it apart from the others. A *gas* has no fixed shape or volume but expands to fill the shape of the container holding it. The molecules in a gas move very fast and have only relatively weak interactions with each other – bouncing off the walls of the container and each other randomly. In contrast, a *liquid* has a fixed volume but no fixed shape. In liquids, the molecules are still moving about fairly rapidly but they also interact more strongly with one another than in gases, somewhat restraining their movement. While liquids are very difficult to compress without extreme pressures (fixed volume), they can easily slip past each other to flow to conform to the shape of their container. Finally, a *solid* is defined by both a fixed volume and a fixed shape. In a solid, the molecules are usually held in position quite tightly by fairly strong interactions with their neighbors, allowing relatively little motion of the molecules. These tight connections force the solid to retain its shape, similar to the arrangement of atoms shown in NaCl in Figure 11.18.

Every compound has a unique set of properties that separates it from all other compounds. This characteristic collection of properties can be used to help identify the compound. These properties can be defined as falling within two general types: physical properties and chemical properties. *Physical properties* are those that can be measured without changing the compound chemically into something else. For example, the properties of state described above define a physical property of a substance. Additionally, color, melting point, boiling point, index of refraction, and density are other physical properties. In each case, the compound remains the same after the measurement is performed. For example, in measuring the boiling point of water, the molecules of water are not changed into another compound through the boiling process but are simply changed from one state of water – liquid – into another

state of water – steam (gas). Notice that water's molecular form does not change in this process of measurement, just its apparent physical form. *Chemical properties*, on the other hand, involve changing the molecule into something chemically different through a chemical reaction. Chemical properties measure *change*. For example, a chemical property of iron is that it rusts to form iron oxide. Some examples of physical and chemical properties are shown for four common substances in Table 11.3.

Finally, some properties are dependent on how much material is present in the sample, while other properties are not. *Intrinsic* (or intensive) *properties* do not rely on how much sample is involved. For example, density, melting point, and color are intrinsic properties – we obtain the same answer whether the sample is tiny or massive. *Extrinsic* (extensive) *properties*, however, depend on the sample size. For example, mass, volume, and heat are extrinsic properties.

11.3.6 Solution Chemistry

Often in analytical chemistry, we must deal with solutions of substances. Usually, it is important to know how much of a compound, called the *solute*, is dissolved in a certain volume of a liquid *solvent*. This refers to the concentration of the solute in solution. Concentration is usually expressed in terms of the number of moles of the compound that is dissolved in 1 L of solvent, called the *molarity* of the solution. To determine the molarity of a solution, we simply take the number of moles of the substance dissolved and divide it by the volume of solution used (in liters). For example, if we dissolved 0.5 mol of NaCl in enough solvent to make 250 mL (or 0.250 L) of solution, then the molarity of the solution would be molarity $(M) = (0.5$ mol NaCl)/(0.250 L solution) = 2.0 molar (abbreviated M).

Using this simple relationship, $M = $ mol/vol, we can figure out how many moles of a compound are present in a given volume of a solution if we know the molarity. These ideas will become important when we discuss the topic of titrametric analysis (Section 11.4).

State of Matter

Solid   Liquid   Gas

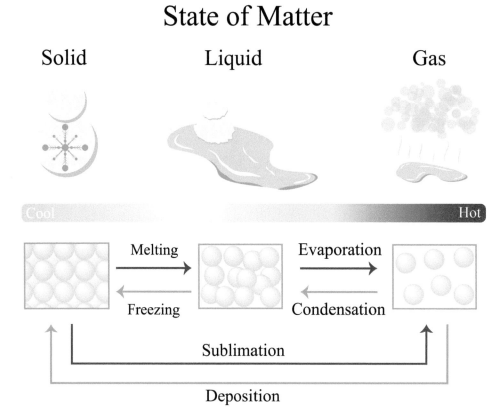

FIGURE 11.21   States of matter and the processes of their interconversion.

Source: Shutterstock.com.

TABLE 11.3   Selected physical and chemical properties of common substances (room temperature state or phase)

COMPOUND	PHYSICAL PROPERTY	CHEMICAL PROPERTY
Iron	RT state = solid Color = metallic Density = 7.874 g/cm³ Melting point = 1,538°C Boiling point = 2,862°C Hardness = 4 (Mohs)	$Fe(s) + \frac{1}{2} O_2(g) \longrightarrow Fe_2O_3(s)$ $2\,Fe(s) + 3\,Cl_2(g) \longrightarrow 2\,FeCl_3(s)$
Water	RT state = liquid Color = colorless Density = 1.0 g/cm³ Melting point = 0°C Boiling point = 100°C	$2H_2O(l) + 2Na(s) \longrightarrow 2NaOH(s) + H_2(g)$ $CO(g) + H_2O(l) \longrightarrow CO_2(g) + H_2(g)$ $H_2O(l) + H^+(l) \longrightarrow H_3O^+(l)$
Hydrogen	RT state = gas Color = colorless Density = 0.09 g/L Melting point = −252.9°C Boiling point = −259.1°C	$H_2(g) + O_2(g) \longrightarrow 2\,H_2O(g)$ $2H_2(g) + CO_2(g) \longrightarrow CH_4(g) + O_2(g)$
Diamond	RT state = solid Color = yellow to colorless Density = 3.53 g/cm³ Melting point = 1,538°C Hardness = 10 (Mohs)	$C(s) + O_2(g) \longrightarrow CO_2(g)$ $C(s) + 2H_2(g) \longrightarrow CH_4(g)$

TABLE 11.4   Homogeneous and heterogeneous mixtures

	HOMOGENEOUS MIXTURE	*HETEROGENEOUS MIXTURE*
Gas	Air Anesthesia gas	Smoke (gas and solid) Cloud (gas and liquid)
Liquid	Salt water Soft drink Gasoline	Water/oil mixture Liquid suspension
Solid	Metal alloys: brass, bronze, 12 karat gold. Paint (dried)	Iron filings and salt Bag of M&Ms Bleu cheese (solid)

11.3.7 Pure Substances and Mixtures

Nearly everything that we encounter in the world is a mixture of substances and not just a single, pure compound or element. Quantitative analytical methods, however, typically first require that we separate mixtures into their individual components and then go about analyzing each component separately. For very complex mixtures, this can be a daunting task. Luckily, however, many methods have been devised to separate complex mixtures into their components.

Mixtures occur when we combine together two or more compounds that don't chemically react but retain their own individual properties. There are two types of mixtures that we consider: homogeneous and heterogeneous mixtures. A **homogeneous mixture** appears uniform throughout the sample. For example, air is a homogeneous mixture of mostly nitrogen (N_2) and oxygen (O_2) with smaller amounts of carbon dioxide, helium, argon, and other gases. Solutions containing dissolved compounds, such as when salt is dissolved in water, are also homogeneous mixtures. While each compound or element is still present and retains its own identity in the mixture, we can't readily distinguish the individual components. Homogeneous mixtures may also exist in any of the three phases (states) of nature. Table 11.4 gives some examples of both homogeneous and heterogeneous mixtures for different phases.

Heterogeneous mixtures are those that are non-uniform throughout the sample. For example, a mixture of iron filings and sea salt is a mixture in which we can still see the individual components clearly.

A number of simple flowcharts, such as the one shown in Figure 11.22, have been developed to allow us to quickly and easily classify substances into pure compounds, pure elements, homogeneous mixtures, and heterogeneous mixtures.

11.3.8 Purification Methods

Many methods have been developed to separate mixtures into their pure components. These methods are generally divided into two main types: physical and chemical separation methods. This shouldn't be too surprising since we classified the properties of substances as either chemical or physical

properties, and we'll use these different properties to separate the components of a mixture.

11.3.9 Physical Separations

Physical separations rely upon the differences in the physical properties of each of the different components in the mixture. Since the components of mixtures retain their individual properties, we can make use of any differences between them to cause a separation to occur, such as density, boiling point, or freezing point.

11.3.9.1 Density Separations

Heterogeneous mixtures are often the easiest to separate. One property that may effectively be used to separate them into pure components is density. Density is defined as the mass of a material per unit of volume, usually expressed as g/cm^3. If two substances have different densities, they may be separable using a liquid of intermediate density. For example, if a substance has a greater density than a liquid, it will sink through the liquid. If another substance has a lesser density than the liquid, however, it will float. Placing the mixture into various liquids with different densities will then cause the two components to separate. For more complex separations, a gradient tube can be used, as will be described in greater detail in Chapter 15. Gradient tubes have several liquids (or gels) placed in a tube where the density varies from the highest density at the bottom and the lowest density at the top, allowing the separation of several fractions with different densities. This method is commonly used when separating out mineral and biological samples, such as blood cells from serum and different glass samples, as shown in Figure 11.23.

11.3.9.2 Solubility

Another common method for separating mixtures takes advantage of any difference in the solubility of the components. If one component is soluble in a liquid, such as water, while the other is insoluble, it is a simple process to dissolve the one component, leaving the other behind. The liquid is then filtered to

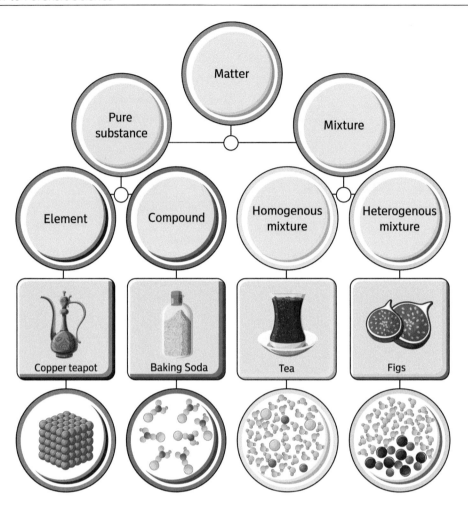

FIGURE 11.22 Flowchart of pure substances and mixtures.

Source: Shutterstock.com.

capture the insoluble component. The remaining liquid, after it passes through a filter, can then be removed by evaporation to give the pure soluble component.

11.3.9.3 Boiling Point/Melting Point

Differences in the boiling or melting points of the components of a mixture can also be used to effect a separation. In a process called *distillation*, a liquid mixture is slowly heated. When the boiling point of one of the components is reached (the one with the lowest boiling point), it boils (turns into a gas) and bubbles out of the mixture. This vapor can be collected and condensed to obtain the pure liquid sample. A typical laboratory distillation apparatus is shown in Figure 11.24. The process can be continued by allowing the temperature of the mixture to rise until the boiling point of each fraction of pure compound is reached. The process of separating multiple liquids from a mixture in this way is called fractional distillation. For example, if a mixture contains three different liquids with boiling points of 50°C for compound (A), 75°C for compound (B), and 90°C for compound (C), fractional distillation can be used to separate them. When the temperature in the flask reaches 50°C, compound A will boil out (and the temperature

of the mixture will remain at 50°C until all of A has boiled away). Then, after all of A has been removed, compound B will boil out at 75°C and can be collected separately. Finally, compound C can be collected when the flask reaches 90°C.

Melting points can also be used in a similar fashion, this time usually by lowering the temperature of the solution. As the temperature of the solution becomes low enough, one component may crystallize out as a solid from the solution. The solid may be filtered off to give a pure sample of the compound. Multiple compounds may be obtained from the mixture through the process of fractional crystallization, a process very similar to fractional distillation except brought about by lowering the temperature.

Differences in other physical properties of the mixture's components, such as magnetic and electrical properties, are also used to separate mixtures.

11.3.10 Chromatography

One of the most powerful and commonly encountered of all purification or separation techniques, and one that has a central place in forensic chemistry, is chromatography. While

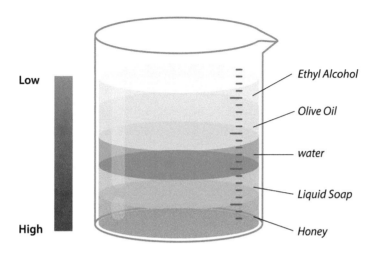

LIQUID DENSITY

FIGURE 11.23   Use of a density gradient tube to separate out the various components in heterogeneous mixtures. The tube has different densities from the bottom to the top of the column. In biological samples, when cell components are placed at the top, they move to the level that about matches their density.

Source: Shutterstock.com.

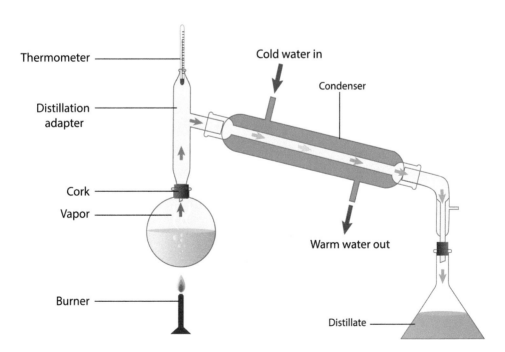

FIGURE 11.24   Typical apparatus for separating liquid components from a homogeneous mixture (solution) by fractional distillation. The mixture to be separated is placed in the flask (left) and heated. Each component boils off at a different temperature and is collected sequentially in the cooling condenser as a pure fraction.

Source: Shutterstock.com.

there are many forms of chromatography, they all employ the same general principles.

Chromatography is fundamentally based on how two compounds interact with one another. For example, when two compounds come into close contact, they can be attracted to each other, repel each other, or display something in between. For example, one molecule may have a strong attraction with the components in paper while another molecule might have only a very weak interaction with the same paper. The molecule with the strong interaction would bind tightly with the paper and only occasionally come off the paper (dissociate). The weakly interacting molecule, however, would spend relatively little time bound to the paper and is easily displaced. In chromatography, the mixture is placed onto a common substance, for example, paper. Some carrier, such as water, another solvent or even a gas, is then used to push the components of the mixture across the paper. The molecule which binds tightly to the paper doesn't move very fast. In contrast, the weakly binding component spends relatively little time bound to the paper and moves rapidly along. After a time, the two components of the mixture have separated apart on the paper. The common substance – the paper in this example – is called the *stationary phase*, while the carrier containing the mixture components is called the *mobile phase*.

A beautiful analogy of how chromatography works is given by a hornet-honey bee idea, illustrated in Figure 11.25. In this example, a person has a jar holding a mixture of hornets and honey bees, and they would like to separate the two types of insects into separate jars but avoid being stung in the process. The idea is to use a field of flowers to affect the separation. The mixture of hornets and bees is released on one side of the field. The honey bees fly from flower to flower, stopping at each one in order to collect nectar. The hornets, however, have little interest in the flowers so mostly fly straight across the flower bed – stopping only occasionally. A person then simply has to stand at the other side of the field from where they were released with a net and two jars and wait. The hornets will reach the collector first, with no honey bees in sight. The hornets can then be collected, and the person then has only to wait for the slower honey bees to arrive later and collect them separately. The flower bed has effectively served as a *stationary phase*, interacting with the two insect species differently. The *mobile phase* is the air (or the wings) that moved the insects across the flower bed, allowing them to interact differently with the flowers and delivering them separately to the collector.

Chromatography works quite similarly to the hornet-honey bee situation. The mixture to be separated is added to the beginning of the stationary phase. The mobile phase then carries the components across the stationary phase, causing the separation to occur. Ultimately, the different components, collected in fractions, arrive at the detector to be measured at different times. An example of this is shown in Figure 11.26 for paper chromatography. Hundreds of variations in the types of stationary phase and mobile phase have been developed. However, four very common methods are summarized in Table 11.5.

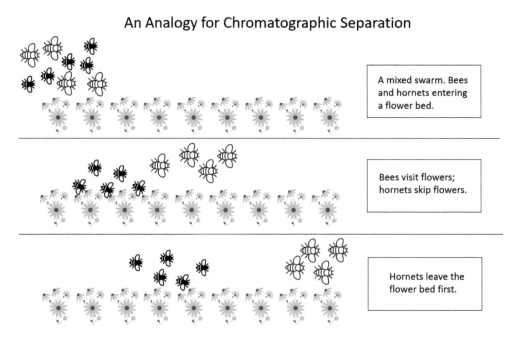

An Analogy for Chromatographic Separation

A mixed swarm. Bees and hornets entering a flower bed.

Bees visit flowers; hornets skip flowers.

Hornets leave the flower bed first.

FIGURE 11.25 Hornet-honey bee analogy for how chromatography works.

Source: Original illustration adapted from image by Dr. Frederick Senese. https://antoine.frostburg.edu/chem/senese/101/matter/chromatography.shtml.

Paper Chromatography

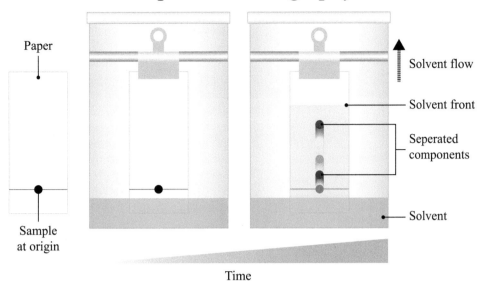

FIGURE 11.26 Paper chromatography for a mixture of dyes, in which the paper is the stationary phase and the solvent is the mobile phase.

Source: Shutterstock.com.

TABLE 11.5 Selected types of chromatography

	STATIONARY PHASE	MOBILE PHASE	USES
Paper chromatography	Paper	Liquid solvent (e.g., water, alcohol, organic solvent).	Separate wide variety of soluble compounds.
Gas chromatography	Glass or a coated column (e.g., coated with paraffin, mineral oil, organic chemicals, etc.).	Gas (e.g., air, argon, helium, nitrogen, etc.).	Separate efficiently wide variety of organic compounds. Can use elevated temperatures.
Liquid chromatography (HPLC)	Silica gel (SiO_2), alumina (Al_2O_3), plastics, coated solids, etc.	Liquid solvent (e.g., organic solvents).	Rapid, high-performance separation, including of larger quantities.
Gel chromatography	Gel	Liquid	Separates molecules based on their relative sizes and shapes.

Some chromatographic techniques are particularly valuable when combined with other analytical techniques, such as mass spectrometry (Chapter 12), to form GC/Mass spectrometry: the workhorse technique in modern forensic chemistry. As shown in Table 11.5, gas chromatography (referred to simply as GC) uses a gas to push the components of a mixture through a hollow tube, either of glass or a tube coated in a special compound to aid separation. Over time, each component interacts with the walls of the tube differently, eventually separating them by the strength of this interaction. This is illustrated in Figure 11.27.

It is often helpful to have a measure of how quickly a compound passes across the stationary phase. As described before, the stronger the adsorption of a compound on the stationary phase, the slower it moves. The strength of this interaction is often referred to as the *affinity* of the compound for the particular stationary phase. In chromatography that employs a solid stationary phase, such as paper and liquid chromatography, the term is called the *retention factor*, R_f. The R_f value for a compound is defined as the distance a component moved down the column or paper strip divided by the distance moved by the pure solvent (called the solvent front). This is shown schematically in Figure 11.28. The two compounds shown in the figure each have different R_f values. The R_f value for a compound is reported *under a very definite set of conditions*. The R_f for a compound changes when either the mobile or stationary phase is changed. For example, compound 1 may have an R_f value of 0.24 on silica gel (stationary phase) using hexane as the mobile phase, but it might have an R_f value of 0.85 when the hexane is replaced by methylene chloride (CH_2Cl_2).

In some types of chromatography, the R_f value is replaced by a related term called the *retention time*, especially in gas

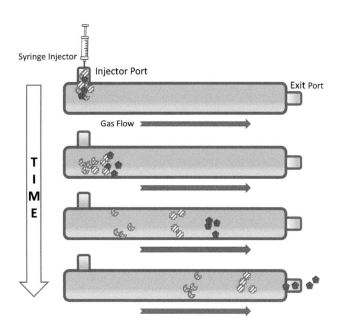

FIGURE 11.27   How gas chromatography (GC) works.

chromatography. Retention time is simply the amount of time that it takes a compound to emerge from the end of the column, starting from the moment it is placed on the column. Retention times for three compounds are shown in a typical gas chromatogram in Figure 11.29. As with R_f, the retention time is defined under a very specific set of conditions (e.g., column length, gas flow rate, temperature, etc.). Changing any of these parameters in turn changes the retention time. It is a very useful value to know, however, when running many analyses for exactly the same compound and using exactly the same set of operating conditions. Under identical conditions, a particular compound will consistently come off the column (elute) at the same time, every time, after it is injected onto the column. It is quite useful to note that a comparison of the areas under each peak in the GC gives the relative amount of compound present. From a comparison of the relative areas of the peaks, the ratio of the quantity of the compounds in the original sample can be determined.

Sometimes, a chromatographic separation can be affected based on the differing sizes and shapes of the component molecules. In this so-called size exclusion chromatography, as

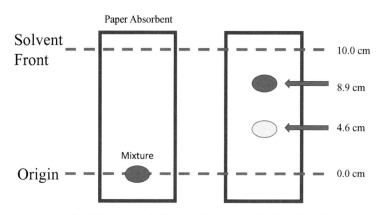

R_f = Distance traveled by spot / distance traveled by solvent front
R_f (blue spot) = 8.9 cm / 10.0 cm = 0.89
R_f (yellow spot) = 4.6 cm / 10.0 cm = 0.46

FIGURE 11.28   Chromatographic R_f values for two compounds in thin-layer chromatography.

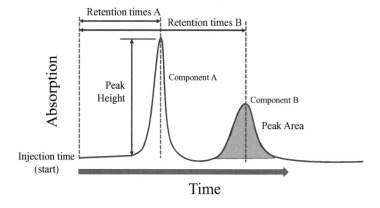

FIGURE 11.29   Retention time for compounds in gas chromatography.

Column

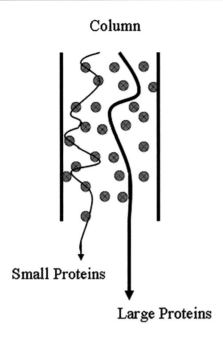

Small Proteins

Large Proteins

FIGURE 11.30 Size exclusion chromatography.

shown in Figure 11.30, smaller molecules are able to fit into tiny pores in a column packed with particles and travel relatively slowly down a column because of the time that they are delayed inside the pores. The larger molecules are not able to fit into these pores, however, and travel more rapidly.

Another method, known as gel electrophoresis chromatography, also separates molecules based on their differences in size and is described in much more detail in Chapter 5, since it is often an important step used in forensic DNA analysis.

11.3.11 Chemical Separations

We can also use simple chemical properties to separate mixtures. In such processes, one component of the mixture might be reactive toward an added reagent, while the other components do not react. For example, a mixture of gold and iron can be separated with acid because iron reacts with mineral acid, while gold does not. Reacting the sample with mineral acid would then remove all the iron, leaving the pure gold behind. Similarly, a reactive polymer can be designed to react only

---

BOX 11.9   THE TRUTH OF HITCHCOCK'S *THE BIRDS* MOVIE

THE CASE OF THE "AMNESIAC SHELLFISH MYSTERY"

The 1963 horror film *The Birds* by Alfred Hitchcock depicted crazed birds attacking a small town in California. The movie revolves around the brief but violent avian attacks on the community. But is the movie solely fiction?

In 1961, just a few miles from where Alfred Hitchcock was vacationing, a group of normally docile birds (shearwaters) really did attack the town of Capitola, California, apparently without reason or precedent. Sixteen years later, in November of 1987 on Prince Edward Island (PEI) in Canada, a seemingly unrelated incident occurred that was later connected to the California avian onslaught through an amazing piece of forensic chemistry sleuthing centered around the use of chromatography.

In the Prince Edward Island (PEI) incident, 153 people became ill with some rather strange symptoms after eating a meal of cultured blue mussels. The symptoms included diarrhea, headaches, and vomiting, often followed by confusion, loss of memory, seizures, coma, and, in some cases, death – not the normal symptoms for simple food poisoning. Alarmingly, however, about one-quarter of the victims had permanent dementia and loss of their short-term memory capabilities. Loss of short-term memory means that essentially you cannot learn anything new; victims could remember nothing forward from the poisoning incident ... ever! Permanent brain damage of this type had never been seen in food poisoning cases.

Immediately, investigators sought the cause of the outbreak. Most of the likely candidates were quickly ruled out, including agents such as pathogens, viruses, pollution, etc. Luckily, the investigators did find a test (called an assay) to detect samples containing the poison; when injected into mice, the blue mussel toxin caused the mice to persistently scratch their shoulders with their hind legs! A most surprising thing.

Ultimately, investigators decided to look for the chemical culprit by continually dividing a contaminated sample of the shellfish in half using various separation methods described in this chapter. They hoped to narrow down the huge initial number of possible compounds to just the one compound that caused the disease. For example, they first extracted the sample with methanol and then the part that dissolved and the part that did not dissolve were separately tested. The mice injected with the dissolved fraction scratched their shoulders while the others didn't. That meant that the poison was in the dissolved fraction. They subsequently did more extractions (solubility-based separations), column chromatography, liquid chromatography and paper-based chromatography. Eventually, after all this, only one fraction of a pure compound caused the scratching, the sample that contained domoic acid ($C_{15}H_{21}NO_6$).

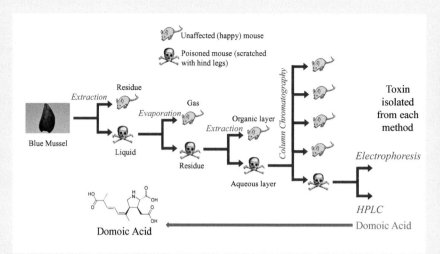

FIGURE 11.31   Procedures for separating and identifying the domoic acid from the tainted shellfish.

Source: Retrieved from Wikimedia Commons; used per Creative Commons Attribution.

At first, they weren't sure they had the right chemical because domoic acid is found in foods elsewhere without causing problems. It turned out, however, that the mussels in PEI delivered more than ten times the dose compared to what other foods deliver.

Domoic acid makes nerve cells fire electrical signals that are received by our brains. Normally, nerve cells are activated by glutamic acid. The problem is that domoic acid turns these neurotransmitters on very effectively but *does not* turn them off, as glutamic acid does. The result is that domoic essentially burns out the neural pathways permanently, essentially killing neurons and destroying pathways and memories. It appears that the excess domoic acid, which was also linked to the outbreak of the bird attacks in 1961 in California, came from small organisms called diatoms, that produce the domoic acid and contaminated the mussels, birds, and people who ate the mussels. Today, governments carefully test seafood for domoic acid to prevent future outbreaks. An amazing piece of forensic sleuthing.

with one component of a mixture. When exposed to the reactive polymer, only one component reacts and "sticks" to the surface, allowing the other component to be washed away and isolated. Other chemical reactions can likewise be used for the separation of mixtures.

BOX 11.10   REWRITING HISTORY: THE HITLER DIARIES

In 1983, the editor of *Stern* magazine decided to buy 27 volumes of the previously unknown Adolph Hitler Diaries, covering the period of 1932–1945 for millions of dollars. Surprisingly, before this transaction, no one even knew that Hitler had kept handwritten diaries. Most importantly, however, was that the diaries told a very different picture of the war, including that Hitler was unaware of the Holocaust. The diaries were supposedly recovered from a plane crash in East Germany after the war and eventually found their way into the possession of an antiques dealer in West Germany.

To verify the authenticity of the volumes, *Stern* magazine commissioned three handwriting experts and two WWII historians to examine the diaries. All agreed that they were authentic.

When news of the history-changing diaries broke, doubts quickly surfaced. The definitive analysis showing that they were fakes, however, came from a paper and ink analysis of the diaries. Using chromatographic techniques, the inks and paper treatment were found to include chemicals not found in inks and papers from Hitler's lifetime. Other support later surfaced showing that the diaries were fakes.

So how did all five of the well-respected experts get it wrong? It turns out that when they were commissioned to examine the volumes, they were asked to compare the diaries with *bona fide* "authentic" Hitler writing samples – standard practice even today. The problem was that the documents they used for the comparison, obtained from museums and collectors across the world, had also been forged by the same person – Konrad Kujau. So, while the experts were correct in saying that the same hand had written both sets of documents, they were incorrect in saying that the hand belonged to Adolph Hitler.

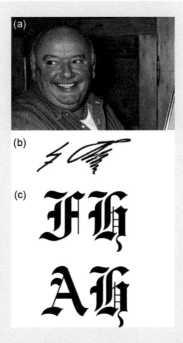

FIGURE 11.32 Hitler Diaries: (a) photograph of Konrad Kujau, forger of the Hitler Diaries, (b) the forged signature of Hitler by Konrad Kujau (Used per Creative Commons Share-Alike 3.0 Unported. User: Achim Necker), and (c) the initials "FH" and "AH" in Engraver's Old English normal font, as used by Konrad Kujau for the Hitler diaries (the initials FH, top row, were used mistakenly by Kujau in the diaries, instead of AH, bottom row).

Source: Retrieved from Wikimedia Commons; used per Creative Commons Attribution.

The broker and the salesman were both tried and, largely on the basis of the forensic separation analysis, were convicted and sentenced.

11.4 CLASSICAL METHODS IN ANALYTICAL CHEMISTRY

11.4.1 Introduction to Classical Chemical Analysis

Numerous qualitative and quantitative analytical methods have been developed to answer questions about the identity and amount of a particular chemical present in a sample. These methods may be divided into two general types: physical and classical (wet chemical) methods of analysis. The simplest type of physical methods deals with the measurement of properties such as the density and refractive index of a sample. Often, these are the quickest methods for the identification of certain kinds of substances, such as glass and minerals, and will be explored in detail in Chapter 16.

Instrumental analysis, usually considered a type of *physical analysis*, deals with using specially designed, and often complex, instruments to measure and analyze the physical properties of a sample. Many of these methods explore how the atoms and molecules in the sample interact with light – giving us both qualitative and quantitative information in the process. Others measure how molecules fall apart after being bombarded with energetic particles and light. These methods, however, will be the focus of Chapter 12.

In contrast, *classical methods*, sometimes called wet chemical analyses, are based upon well-known chemical reactions of the compounds being studied (analyte) and are often referred to as classical methods since many were first developed in the 19th century. These chemical techniques involve two main types of analysis: gravimetric and volumetric (titrimetric) analysis.

Instrumental methods have become the most common laboratory analyses in forensic investigations since they typically require far less sample, are very reproducible, and can be run very rapidly on many samples. Classical methods, however, retain an important place in forensic analysis as they are very accurate, quickly adaptable, far less expensive, and, on occasion, less sensitive to impurities. Importantly, within this classical group of methods are included a variety of field tests that are very convenient to use away from the laboratory as a quick indication of the nature of a substance: a presumptive test. For example, a field officer may find an unknown sample suspected to be a controlled substance. Rather than immediately send it to the lab and wait for an analysis (which might take days), a simple test can be quickly run in the field

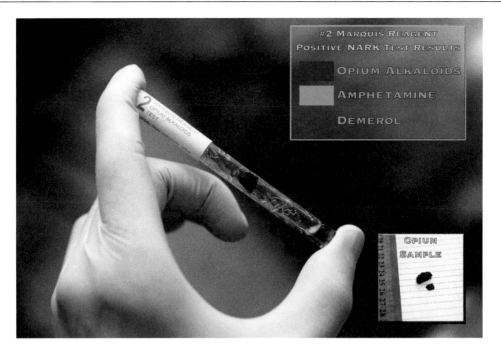

FIGURE 11.33 Colors of the presumptive Marquis field-testing kit of an unknown substance. The photo shows a positive result using the Marquis reagent with an unkonwn sample. The test is conducted by placing a small sample of unknown material in the vial containing concentrated sulfuric acid with formaldehyde. The dark brown final color of the liquid is indicative of a positive presumptive test for opioid.

Source: Used per Creative Commons Attribution 2.0, Generic. User: Jack Spades.

by mixing prepackaged reagents (chemicals) with a small portion of the substance and observing any color change. One of the most common presumptive field tests is the Marquis test, employing a prepackaged reagent kit (containing formaldehyde [CH_2O], sulfuric acid [H_2SO_4], and often methanol [CH_3OH]), that is mixed with the unknown substance. If the initially colorless Marquis solution changes to dark purple, it may be MDMA (ecstasy) if it turns deep red, it could be heroin (Figure 11.33), while if it turns brown it is an opioid. Presumptive tests require confirmation in the laboratory by more specific methods if a positive field test is observed, but field tests give a very quick and inexpensive indication of what might be in the sample (probable cause).

Classical analytical methods may require the pre-purification of the sample into its constituents prior to the analysis. This is done using the techniques presented in the previous section.

11.4.2 Spot or Color Tests

Spot tests are typically very quick and simple presumptive tests, such as the Marquis test, to indicate the presence of a particular element or substance. They rely on a chemical reaction that occurs *only* if the element or molecule is present in the sample to form a new product. This new product may be brightly colored, form a precipitate (solid), bubble from the reaction, or give some other observable indication of its presence. Importantly, if the element or chemical is not present in the sample, no change should be observed. These tests can often be done on very small samples and usually don't require any pre-purification steps.

Spot tests are used in a wide range of applications including food safety testing, blood testing, pesticide and environmental testing, swimming pool testing, and, of course, forensic drug testing, among many others. Two of the most common biomedical spot tests involve testing blood samples from a diabetic person to determine their blood-glucose level and home body-fluid testing kits (e.g., COVID-19, pregnancy, *H. pylori*, etc.). The well-known litmus test is another example of a spot test where a drop of solution is placed on a piece of litmus paper and, depending on the color change, the unknown substance can be identified as either an acid or a base. One of the earliest analytic tests developed used a piece of paper impregnated with silver carbonate; when the paper came into contact with uric acid, the formation of pure silver from the reaction turned it brown-black. Today, hundreds of reagents have been developed as spot test reagents that are used extensively in field testing.

11.4.3 Gravimetric Analysis

Gravimetric analysis focuses on mass measurements from chemical reactions to determine quantitatively how much of something is present in a sample. In a typical procedure, an unknown is dissolved in a solvent and then allowed to react completely with an excess of another dissolved chemical to form a solid product (precipitate). If the dried solid formed in the reaction is weighed, it can be determined exactly how much of the substance was present in the original material. For example, if we needed to know the amount of chloride in a sample, we might use the following chemical reaction:

$$Ag^+(aq) + Cl^-(aq) \longrightarrow AgCl(s)\downarrow \text{ (the down arrow}$$
$$\text{means a precipitate)}$$

If we run the reaction with an excess of silver ion, all the chloride in the sample will be converted into the solid silver chloride that precipitates from the reaction. By filtering and carefully measuring the mass of the AgCl present after the reaction is complete, the amount of chloride that was present in the original sample can be accurately determined (remember the conservation of mass idea – the amount of chloride afterward equals the amount of chloride before the reaction, we just changed it from dissolved in solution to part of the solid silver chloride precipitate). As long as we know the chemical reaction, this method can be very accurate.

Gravimetric methods find many uses in chemical analysis. For example, gravimetric analysis is used to determine the amount of sulfur dioxide (SO_2) in foods and air pollution, the presence of certain inorganic or ionic toxins in samples, and whether a body has been moved post-mortem (taphonomy) by mineral and soil analysis.

11.4.4 Combustion Analysis

Combustion analysis is a very common type of gravimetric analysis. In this method, a pure organic compound is completely burned with an excess of oxygen (O_2) to ensure that the original sample is completely consumed. This process converts all of the organic chemical to carbon dioxide (CO_2) and water (H_2O) according to the equation:

$$C_xH_y + \text{excess } O_2(g) \longrightarrow X\,CO_2(g) + \tfrac{1}{2}Y\,H_2O(g)$$

(*Note: the subscripts x and y in the organic reactant on the left are directly related to the amount of CO_2 and H_2O formed in the reaction as dictated by the balanced equation.*)

The exact amount of CO_2 and H_2O formed in the reaction is determined using an apparatus such as shown in Figure 11.34. In a typical analysis, a stream of oxygen is forced across the sample, held at high temperatures, and then through several canisters. The first canister ensures all of the carbon is converted to carbon dioxide by using a catalytic converter. The next canister selectively collects all of the H_2O while the final canister collects all of the CO_2 by absorbing those molecules onto appropriate packing materials. The H_2O and CO_2 canisters are weighed carefully before and after the reaction is complete. In this fashion, the amount of H_2O and CO_2 collected from the reaction can be easily determined by subtracting the weight of each empty canister before the reaction from their weights after the reaction is done. By knowing the exact amount of H_2O and CO_2 that is formed, we can use the balanced chemical reaction to exactly determine the amount of carbon and hydrogen that was in the original sample. Using the method presented earlier (see Box 11.7 and Section 11.3), we can determine the empirical formula of the original compound to help identify the unknown substance.

Combustion analysis requires a pure compound for the method to work and, therefore, usually involves a pre-purification step using one of the techniques described in the previous section. The technique also works best on organic samples (those containing mostly carbon and hydrogen) and requires a relatively large sample size. Nonetheless, it has a useful role in the arsenal of analytical forensic techniques.

11.4.5 Volumetric (Titrametric) Analysis

A volumetric analysis involves determining the amount of an analyte (the unknown we're interested in) found in a solution by reacting it completely with a known amount of another solution. The reaction is carried out until all the analyte is exactly reacted to form a product. The point at which all of the analyte is exactly consumed in the reaction, no more no less, is called the *equivalence point*. The exact amount of the reactant solution of known concentration is determined by using a burette through a process called *titration*, a process where a measured volume of a solution with an unknown concentration is added to a known volume of another solution just until the reaction between them is exactly complete, as illustrated in Figure 11.35. A burette, shown in Figure 11.36, is a glass

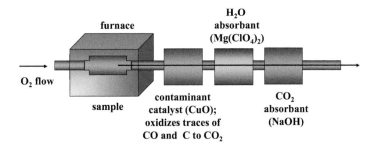

FIGURE 11.34 Schematic drawing of a typical setup for the combustion analysis of an unknown organic sample.

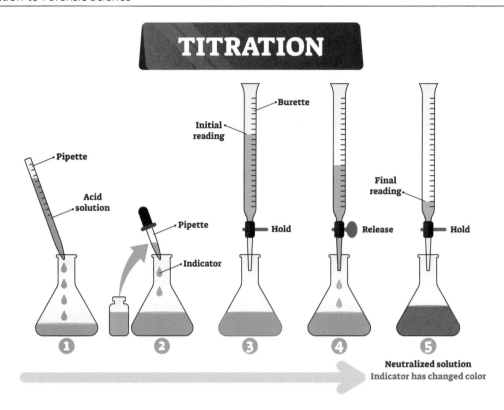

FIGURE 11.35 Titration of an unknown acid with a basic solution of known concentration using a colored indicator. The exact point of complete neutralization is called the equivalence or end point.

Source: Shutterstock.com.

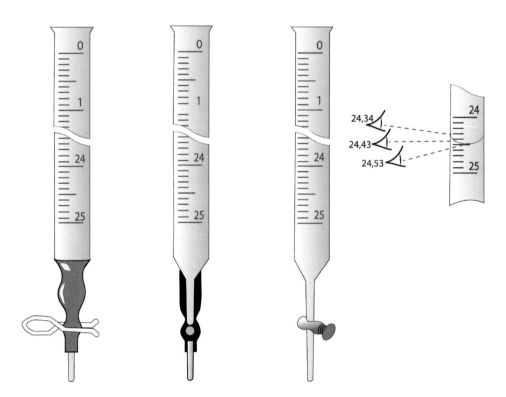

FIGURE 11.36 Burettes used for titrametric analysis. The image at right shows how to correctly read the volume by locating the bottom of the meniscus (the curved surface of the liquid in the tube).

Source: Shutterstock.com.

tube with a stopcock at the bottom that allows the addition of the known concentration reactant to the unknown concentration solution. The markings along its length of the burette tube allow the determination of the volume of reactant used to reach the equivalence point – the exact point of neutralization.

If we know both the amount of the reactant used to reach the equivalence and the balanced chemical equation point for the reaction, it is simple to calculate the amount of the analyte in the original unknown solution. The basic idea is, therefore, to use a chemical reaction to determine the amount of analyte present by measuring how much of the known reactant it took to complete the reaction. For example, if we wanted to determine how much of compound A is present, we can react A completely with an exactly known amount of B according to the equation:

$$A + B \text{------>} C$$

By determining the exact amount of compound B needed to consume all of compound A, we can use the chemical equation just like a mathematical equation and state that the amount of $A = B$ at the equivalence point.

An example of this process is the determination of the unknown amount of hydrochloric acid in a solution. Using titration, the HCl solution reacts with a solution of a base with a known concentration, following the balanced chemical equation below:

$$HCl(aq) + NaOH(aq) \text{------>} H_2O(l) + NaCl(aq)$$

In this case, an unknown amount of HCl is carefully titrated drop by drop with a known concentration of NaOH solution until all the HCl is consumed, reaching the *end point* of the reaction (the point of equivalence). At this end point, the amount of NaOH added to reach the equivalence point can be readily determined. Using the balanced chemical reaction, the amount of HCl in the unknown solution can then be calculated.

One of the most important parts of any titrametric analysis is to determine when we have reached the equivalence point. Most often, two colorless solutions are added such that no visible change can be seen at the end point. To determine the end point, therefore, some observable signal must be employed to indicate its arrival and several techniques have been developed for this purpose. Probably the most common involves the addition of a chemical that causes a visible color change exactly at the endpoint, referred to as a colorimetric method. The compound used that changes color at the end point is called an *indicator*. Hundreds of indicators have been developed, especially those that change color upon acid-base changes, and several are listed in Table 11.6. For example, a small amount of a chemical called phenolphthalein can be added to a reaction. Phenolphthalein is sensitive to the presence of acid and changes color as a solution moves from basic to neutral to acidic. In a vinegar example (see Box 11.11), a little bit of phenolphthalein is added to the acetic acid solution at the outset to form a colorless solution. When titrated with a base, at the point where all the acid has been reacted, the further addition of then one additional drop of base changes, the solution to basic and the phenolphthalein turns instantly from colorless to a bright pink/red.

TABLE 11.6   Properties of selected acid-base indicators

INDICATOR	COLOR OF ACIDIC FORM	COLOR OF BASIC FORM	PH TRANSITION POINT
Phenolphthalein	Colorless	Pink/red	8.3–10.0
Bromothymol blue	Yellow	Blue	2.8–4.6
Methyl red	Red	Yellow	4.2–6.3
Litmus	Red	Blue	4.5–8.3
Methyl violet	Yellow	Violet	0.0–2.0

BOX 11.11   CHEMISTS HAVE SOLUTIONS

Problem: A forensically valuable sample contains a solution of vinegar (acetic acid, $HC_2H_3O_2$). We need to determine the concentration of the vinegar in the solution. We decide to use the known reaction of vinegar with NaOH, employing the balanced chemical equation:

$$HC_2H_3O_2(aq) + NaOH(aq) \text{------>} H_2O(l) + NaC_2H_3O_2(aq)$$

When the analysis is completed, we find that a 2.50 mL sample of the vinegar consumes 34.9 mL of a standard 0.0960 M NaOH solution to reach the equivalence point (remember, M represents molarity, see below). We need to determine, however, how many grams of acetic acid are in 1 L of the vinegar?

Solution: In this problem, we can calculate the moles of NaOH used to react completely with the acetic acid (aa) since we're using a solution of known molarity (moles/volume). Since there is a 1:1 reacting ratio in the balanced chemical reaction between the acetic acid (aa) and NaOH, we know that the number of moles of aa must equal the number of moles of NaOH. From this, we can obtain the number of grams of aa in the sample and also in 1 L of the solution.

We first need to calculate the number of moles of NaOH consumed in the reaction. For this, we use the equations described in Section 11.3:

$$\text{Molarity } (M) = \frac{\text{moles}}{\text{volume}}(l) \text{ and rearranging Moles} = \text{Molarity } (M) \times \text{Volume } (l)$$

Therefore, the number of moles of NaOH used = Molarity of NaOH x volume used (in liters)

moles of NaOH used = (0.0960 M NaOH) x (0.0349 l NaOH used)

moles of NaOH = 0.00335 mol

Since the number of moles aa equals the number of moles of NaOH (based on the balanced chemical reaction), we know that the number of moles of aa in the sample is 0.00335 moles.

We can now determine the concentration of aa (moles per liter) in the original sample by dividing the number of moles of aa by the volume of the original aa solution.

Molarity of aa solution (M) = (0.00335 mol aa)/(0.0025 l aa solution) = 1.42 M aa

To figure out the number of grams of aa in 1 L, we simply multiply the molarity by the molecular mass (weight) of aa (MW aa = 60.0):

grams of aa in 1 L = (1.42 M aa)(60.0) = 85.2 g acetic acid in 1 L of vinegar.

A handy guide to converting between moles, grams, and molarity is demonstrated below.

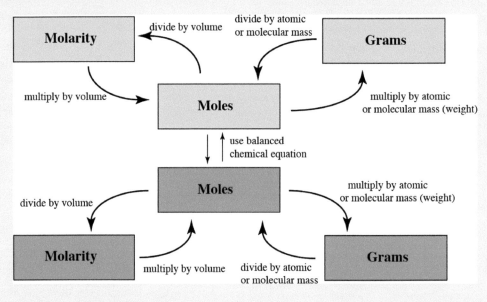

FIGURE 11.37 The relationships between moles, grams, and molarity.

Many types of indicators have been developed besides those that simply change color. Some indicators glow (fluoresce) at the end point, while others are determined by monitoring the electrical conductivity of the solution.

11.4.6 Immunoassay

Increasingly, forensic labs may use techniques based on immunoassay to determine the concentration of biologically important materials, including metabolites, toxins, and drugs in body fluids. Immunoassays rely on monitoring immune-like reactions (antibody-antigen interactions) that are highly specific to a particular material. For example, an antibody specifically designed to bind to heroin can be developed that fluoresces differently after binding. By monitoring the fluorescence, the presence and quantity of heroin in the sample can be determined. This technique was discussed in greater detail in Chapter 6 (on Serology).

11.4.7 Conclusions

Chemical analysis of unknown samples forms a critical part of modern forensic evidence analysis. In this chapter, we have explored the basic ideas of chemical analysis and

BOX 11.12 NATURAL INDICATORS

A variety of naturally occurring substances can be quite effectively used as indicators to determine if we've reached the equivalence point in titrations. For example, boiling red cabbage produces a red/purple-colored solution. This solution can be employed to detect changes in acidity, indicating an end point in a titrametric reaction.

Below figure illustrates a color variation of red cabbage as the pH (acidity) of the solution changes (ranging from very acidic on the left to very basic on the right).

FIGURE 11.38 Colors of red cabbage juice depending on the acidity of the solution. The juice solution is deep red when acidic, blue/purple when neutral, and green/yellow when basic.

Source: Used per Creative Commons 3.0, Unported. Used with permission by User: V. Belkhir, site de l'Académie de Nantes.

measurement, focusing on classical (chemical) methods. In the following chapter, our focus will shift to instrumental methods that employ light and particles to probe molecules to obtain analytical forensic information.

QUESTIONS FOR FURTHER PRACTICE AND MASTERY

11.1 What is the smallest particle of an element that can exist and still retain its identity as that element?

11.2 What is the mobile phase employed in gas chromatography?

11.3 Define an isotope.

11.4 What is the *Law of the Conservation of Mass*?

11.5 What is analytical chemistry?

11.6 What are the two main areas of analysis common in analytical chemistry?

11.7 What is the difference between qualitative analysis and quantitative analysis?

11.8 When deciding which analytical process to use to analyze a sample, what questions must be answered first in order to choose the correct procedure to be employed?

11.9 What are the Frye and Daubert standards for chemical evidence admissibility?

11.10 In terms of analysis, what is meant by an "interference"?

11.11 What is an analyte?

11.12 What is an anion and a cation?

11.13 What is the difference between an empirical and a molecular formula?

11.14 In terms of shape and volume, differentiate between solids, liquids, and gases.

11.15 What are intrinsic (intensive) and extrinsic (extensive) properties?

11.16 What is the difference between a homogeneous and a heterogeneous mixture?

11.17 What are some methods used to physically separate a mixture? How are mixtures separated chemically?

11.18 What is fractional distillation?

11.19 What is meant by the retention factor, R_f?

11.20 Explain gravimetric and volumetric analysis.

11.21 What is a *spot* and a presumptive test?

11.22 What information is learned about a sample by computing the relative areas under the peaks of a gas chromatogram?

EXTENSIVE PROBLEMS

11.23 Determine the molecular masses for each of the following: (a) $CaCO_3$ (b) $C_{21}H_{23}NO_5$ (c) $CuSO_4 \cdot 5H_2O$

11.24 How many moles are present in: (a) 27.84 g of CH_4 (b) 5.22×10^{-5} g of H_2O (c) 9.6×10^4 g of NH_3?

11.25 Balance the following equations:

(a) $C_3H_8(g) + O_2(g) \rightarrow CO_2(g) + H_2O(l)$

(b) $Al_2(SO_4)_3(aq) + Ag_3PO_4(aq) \rightarrow AlPO_4(aq) + Ag_2SO_4(aq)$

(c) $Cu(s) + HNO_3(aq) \rightarrow Cu(NO_3)_2(aq) + NO_2(g) + H_2O(l)$

11.26 Identify the following as heterogeneous or homogeneous mixtures:

(a) sand

(b) strawberry pie filling

(c) root beer

(d) blood

(e) fog

(f) sugar dissolved in water

11.27 A sample of purple ink is to be separated using paper chromatography. The ink is dissolved in methanol, and a strip of chromatography paper is dipped into the solution. Identify the stationary stage and the mobile phase. After 20 minutes a blue mark is found 1 cm from the solution, and a red mark is 1.5 cm from the point of origin on the paper. Which color has the stronger attraction for the paper? If the solvent moved 2.00 cm, what are the R_f values for the blue and red components?

11.28. A 2.00 mL sample of benzoic acid, C_6H_6, a monoprotic acid, is to be titrated with a 3.00×10^{-1} M NaOH solution. The equivalence point is reached after 3.00 mL of the base is added. What is the molarity of the starting benzoic acid solution? How would your calculation differ if the acid had been citric acid, $H_2C_6H_6O_6$, a diprotic acid?

11.29 Two solutions were tested using the indicators methyl red and bromothymol blue. Solution A was red in methyl red and yellow in bromothymol blue. Solution B was yellow in methyl red and yellow in bromothymol blue. Using the information given in Table 11.6, what is the possible pH range for both solution A and solution B?

11.30 Given the following chemical reaction:

$2 C_4H_{10} + 13 O_2 \rightarrow 8 CO_2 + 10 H_2O$

How many moles of CO_2 are produced by the complete combustion of 0.50 mol of C_4H_{10}? By 2.0 mol of C_4H_{10}? By 58 g of C_4H_{10}?

11.31 A 0.740 g sample of an unknown organic compound that consists of C, H and O is burned in oxygen to produce 1.76 g of CO_2 and 0.900 g of H_2O. What is the empirical formula of the unknown organic compound?

GLOSSARY OF TERMS

analytical chemistry: the branch of modern chemistry that deals with the separation, purification, identification, and quantification of chemical substances.

anion: a negatively charged ion.

atom: the basic chemical unit of an element that retains the chemical properties of the element.

atomic mass (weight): the mass of an atom expressed in the standard unit of atomic mass units (amu): approximately equal to the sum of the number of protons and neutrons in the atom.

atomic mass unit (amu): the unit of mass that weighs 1/12th the mass of a carbon atom containing six protons and six neutrons. Used to express atomic and molecular weights.

atomic number: the number of protons in the nucleus of an atom.

cation: a positively charged ion.

chemical analysis: the process of determining the composition of a substance.

chemical equation: a symbolic representation of a chemical reaction showing the reactants combined to form particular products.

chemical property: the property of a substance characterized by a chemical reaction and causing a change in the starting substance during the measurement.

chromatography: the process of separating the components of a mixture that relies on the different affinities of the various components with some medium, such as a solid, gas or liquid.

classical analysis: direct chemical methods, sometimes called wet chemical analysis, for the analysis of a substance.

combustion analysis: the method to determine the composition of a substance by reacting it with oxygen in a combustion reaction and quantitatively characterizing the products formed. Primarily used for carbon and hydrogen analysis of organic compounds.

concentration: the amount of solute dissolved in a specific quantity of solvent, usually given in moles of solute in 1 L of solution (molarity).

confirmatory test (chemical): an analytical procedure used with a high degree of certainty to identify a substance or the components of a mixture.

conservation of mass (law of): the physical law that states that matter cannot be created or destroyed using chemical methods.

constant composition (law of): the principle that states that a pure compound always contains the same elements in exactly the same relative proportions.

density: the mass of a substance per unit volume.

destructive analysis: a chemical process where the sample is destroyed during the analytical procedure.

detection limit: the smallest amount of a substance that can be distinguished with certainty from the background.

electron: the small, stable subatomic particle carrying a negative charge equal and opposite to the positive charge on the proton.

element: a substance that cannot be separated into simpler substances by chemical means, consisting of atoms with the same number of protons.

empirical formula: the formula of a substance that shows the relative proportions of the elements present but not necessarily the actual molecular composition of the substance.

end point: the point of a titration where the reaction is exactly completed.

equivalence point: the point in a titration when the reactant added is stoichiometrically equal to the amount of analyte in the solution.

extrinsic properties: physical properties that depend upon the amount of substance present, such as heat and mass.

gas: a substance that moves freely to fill all available space, without a definite shape or volume.

gravimetric analysis: a chemical analytical technique that measures the weight of the product of a known chemical reaction to determine the composition of the starting material.

heterogeneous mixture: a mixture composed of two or more components that does not result in a uniform composition, appearance, or properties.

homogeneous mixture: a mixture composed of two or more components that results in a uniform composition, appearance, or properties.

immunoassay: a chemical analysis that relies upon the binding of an antibody with its antigen to identify and quantify the substance.

indicator: a chemical that changes properties, such as color or conductivity, when the end point or equivalence point of a titration is reached.

instrumental analysis: the area of analytical chemistry that performs an analysis using scientific instruments such as spectrophotometers or spectrometers.

interference: a chemical substance that obstructs or interferes with the chemical analysis of another substance in a mixture.

intrinsic properties: physical properties that do not depend upon the amount of substance present, such as density, color, and chemical composition.

ion: a charged particle or molecule.

isomers: chemical compounds with the same molecular formula but with different arrangements of the atoms, displaying different properties.

isotope: atoms with the same number of protons but different numbers of neutrons.

liquid: a substance that lacks a definite shape but has a fixed volume.

mobile phase: in chromatography, the component that moves the solute past a fixed medium.

molarity: the number of moles of a solute in 1 L of solution.

molecular formula: the chemical formula that shows the number and kind of each atom present in a molecule.

molecular weight: the mass of a molecule expressed in the standard unit of atomic mass units (amu). Determined from the sum of the atomic masses of all the atoms that make up the molecule.

mole: a chemical unit of measure equal to the number 6.022×10^{23} items (e.g., atoms, molecules, ions, etc.).

neutron: a subatomic particle with about the same mass as a proton but without an electrical charge.

non-destructive analysis: a chemical process where the sample is not destroyed during the analytical procedure.

reactant: a substance that reacts during the course of a chemical reaction and is changed into a different substance.

percent composition: a chemical analysis that provides the percentage by mass of each element in the compound.

periodic table: a table of all the known chemical elements arranged in order of their increasing atomic numbers, with elements having similar chemical properties lined up in (usually) vertical rows.

physical properties: properties used to characterize a substance, such as boiling point and density, that does not require a chemical reaction to define them.

presumptive test: a preliminary test to determine the presence of a substance in a sample with reasonable certainty.

product: a substance that is the result of a chemical reaction.

proton: a subatomic particle with about the same mass as a neutron but with a positive electrical charge equal and opposite to that of the electron.

quantitative analysis: the measurement of the amounts of the components in a substance.

qualitative analysis: the determination of the identities of the components in a substance.

retention factor (*R*~f~): a measure of the degree of interaction of a substance in chromatography with the stationary phase. Determined by dividing the distance the substance traveled by the distance the mobile phase traveled during a period of time.

solid: a substance that has both a definite shape and a fixed volume.

solubility: the degree to which a solute (solid) will dissolve in a solvent.

solute: the substance dissolved in a solvent.

solvent: the liquid used to dissolve a solute.

spot test (also color or presumptive test): a rapid chemical test used to show the presence of a chemical or component in a sample.

stationary phase: in chromatography, the component that remains fixed (does not move) during the separation.

stoichiometry: the relative quantities of reactants and products in chemical reactions.

BIBLIOGRAPHY

Suzanne Bell, *Forensic Chemistry* (2nd Ed.), Pearson, 2012.

Gary D. Christian, *Analytical Chemistry* (7th Ed.), Wiley, 2013.

Hyman Davidsom Gesser, A. B. Bass, and Bradley Myers, *Forensic Chemistry and the Expert Witness*, Nova Science Publ. Inc., 2012.

Daniel C. Harris, *Quantitative Chemical Analysis* (9th Ed.), W.H. Freeman, 2015.

Seamus P. Higson, *Analytical Chemistry*, Oxford University Press, 2004.

JaVed I. Khan, Thomas J. Kennedy, and Donnell R. Christian, Jr., *Basic Principles of Forensic Chemistry*, Springer, 2012.

Lawrence Kobilinsky, *Forensic Chemistry Handbook*, Wiley, 2011.

B. Mahan, *University Chemistry*, Pearson, 1987.

Douglas A. Skoog, Donald M. West, F. James Holler, and Stanley R. Crouch, *Principles of Instrumental Analysis* (9th Ed.), Brooks Cole, 2013.

J. Dorman Steel, *Popular Chemistry*, AS Barnes Company, 1887.

Forensic Spectroscopy

12

12.1 INTRODUCTION TO FORENSIC SPECTROSCOPY

LEARNING GOALS AND OBJECTIVES

Spectroscopy provides chemical information on the atomic and molecular composition of a variety of forensic samples. Spectroscopic analysis is often the method of choice because of its speed, reliability, availability, and flexibility. Because of this, spectroscopic methods are used for the analysis of drugs, biological tissues and fluids, residues, poisons, toxins, metals, and many others. After completing this chapter, you should able to:

- Describe electromagnetic radiation and some of its properties (λ, ν, c, etc.).
- Explain what is meant by quantization and the duality of nature.
- Show what is meant by atomic and molecular energy levels and how they relate to quantum mechanics and standing waves.
- Describe how the absorption and emission of electromagnetic radiation relate to atomic and molecular energy levels and how this explains atomic line spectra.
- Discuss the underlying principles of atomic emission, absorption, and fluorescence spectra and how these techniques may be used for forensic analysis.
- Explain how neutron activation analysis may provide elemental composition data.
- Describe what is meant by molecular spectroscopy.
- Explain why molecules form, what a chemical bond is, and what is meant by the terms atomic and molecular orbitals.
- Discuss how electronic and vibrational spectroscopies work based on quantum mechanics.
- Describe the basic principles of forensic mass spectrometry and how it can provide useful forensic information.
- Discuss what is meant by radioactive decay and how it can be used to date an object.

12.1.1 Introduction

A white substance is found during a traffic stop, a fire is suspected of being started on purpose, a medical examiner suspects poisoning as the cause of death, or a cloth fiber found at a crime scene is believed to be from a suspect's torn clothing. These situations, and many more like them, all have in common the need to identify an unknown substance: is the confiscated white powder a controlled drug, was an accelerant used in the fire, is there poison in a person's blood, and what types of fibers are in the cloth sample? Analytical chemistry, and more specifically spectroscopy, may provide answers to these important forensic questions by furnishing information regarding the elemental or molecular identity of a substance and how much of it is present.

Some of the most powerful methods we have for identifying chemical compounds quickly and accurately are based on measuring how electromagnetic radiation interacts with matter. Chemical compounds may absorb and emit light (Figure 12.1), and in doing so, they reveal information about the identity and nature of the compound itself. Today, the field of spectroscopy focuses specifically on exploring these light-matter interactions and provides a unique set of tools to forensic scientists.

Two terms commonly found in this field are spectroscopy (or spectrophotometry) and spectrometry. Spectroscopy is generally considered to be the study of the interactions of matter with light and other forms of radiation, especially the absorption and emission of radiation by matter. Spectrometry is the actual quantitative measurement of aspects of this matter-radiation interaction (measuring a spectrum). Over time, however, there has been a broadening and blurring of these terms. For example, the term spectrometry is also used to indicate measurements without the use of light, as in mass spectrometry.

In the previous chapter, we explored a variety of ways to identify the composition of a material based primarily on its chemical properties – how an unknown substance reacts with another chemical to reveal some information about itself. In this chapter, however, the measurement of physical properties of a compound (properties that can be determined without changing the compound into something else) will be presented to help identify its chemical composition and structure. Since the measurement of these physical properties typically involves relatively complex instrumentation, the subject is sometimes referred to as *instrumental analysis*. In this chapter, the instruments we will be focusing on are spectrophotometers, also often called spectrometers, that allow us to carefully probe

DOI: 10.4324/9781003183709-15

FIGURE 12.1 Fingerprints visualized on a glass dusted with a fluorescent powder and visualized using ultraviolet light.

Source: Department of Defense. Credit: Airman 1st Class Micaiah Anthony (USAF).

the details of the interplay between electromagnetic radiation and matter.

Spectroscopic analysis is conveniently broken down into two broad types based on the nature of the matter studied: atomic and molecular spectroscopy. In this chapter, we will begin by exploring the spectroscopy of the simplest structures, atoms, before moving on to systems of increasing complexity, from small molecules to much larger polymers and biological molecules. We will end the chapter by examining several related techniques that provide ways of probing atomic and molecular structure: mass spectrometry and radioisotope analysis.

12.1.2 Spectroscopy

Scientists, artists, and philosophers have long been intrigued by the unique aspects of the interplay of light and matter. From earliest times, people have marveled at and wondered about rainbows and reflections, inspiring prophets and poets to write of their beauty and significance. Artists have tried to capture the patterns of light falling on matter in paintings and photographs, while scientists have probed light's inner workings and tried to harness some of its properties. But it was Sir Isaac Newton in 1666 who was the first to really understand, on a fundamental footing, something of the rainbow's scientific secrets. Newton was able to build the first true spectrometer that took ordinary white light from the sun and broke it up into a seemingly continuous band of colors from red to violet: an "artificially" produced rainbow (Figure 12.2). This was done using a prism, a triangular-shaped piece of glass, to spread

out a thin beam of light into the individual colors that collectively make up the sun's white light. Newton also first coined the term *spectrum* to describe the observed color dispersion (spectrum derives from the word meaning "to look at"). In fact, the epitaph composed by Alexander Pope that appears on Newton's tomb in Westminster Abbey reflects Newton's fascination and discoveries with light when he wrote "Nature and Nature's laws lay hid in night: God said, 'Let Newton be!' and all was light" (March 20, 1727).

Newton's work opened the door to many who followed with an interest in understanding more of the basic nature of light. In 1800, William Herschel discovered that there is more to solar radiation than meets the eye. When he passed white light through a prism, he observed the visible rainbow just as Newton had. But, almost by accident, he placed a thermometer in the darkness just beyond the red part of the spectrum. He was surprised to see that the temperature rose "outside" of the visible rainbow and determined that there must also be an invisible component to light, called infrared radiation, that was just beyond the red end of the visible region ("infra" means below, so infrared means "below the red"). Quickly, the idea of invisible light was extended to the opposite side of the spectrum – the ultraviolet region, discovered just beyond the violet end of the rainbow in 1801 ("ultra" means beyond). Then, a really illuminating discovery for analytical science occurred: Joseph Fraunhofer found in 1814 that the solar spectrum, when spread out enough, actually was not a continuous band of colors but had some dark bands running through it at specific places – "missing" colors – that were later shown to be due to the absence of some wavelengths in the solar spectrum (Figure 12.3). The reason for this, however, was

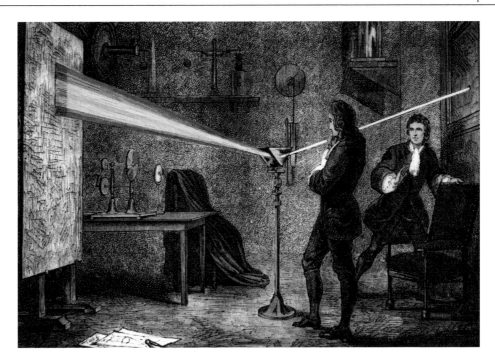

FIGURE 12.2 The English physicist Sir Isaac Newton (1642–1727) conducting his famous experiment on separating light into a rainbow. He used a prism to refract the beam of light from a hole in the shutters over a window to split the beam into different colors. Newton carried out this experiment while at Cambridge University, but the results were not known until he published the book *Opticks* in 1704. Newton is also famous for his general theory of gravitation and for his mathematical discoveries.

Source: Science Photo Library. Used with permission.

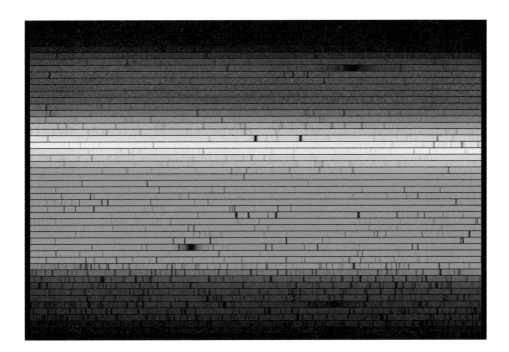

FIGURE 12.3 Visible spectrum of a star showing black lines in the otherwise continuous rainbow of colors in the spectrum. At bottom left is the shortest wavelength visible, around 400 nanometers (nm). Wavelengths increase from left to right along each strip, and from bottom to top. The longest wavelength visible light (700 nm) is at top right.

Source: N.A. Sharp/Noirlab/NSF/AURA/Science Photo Library. Used with permission.

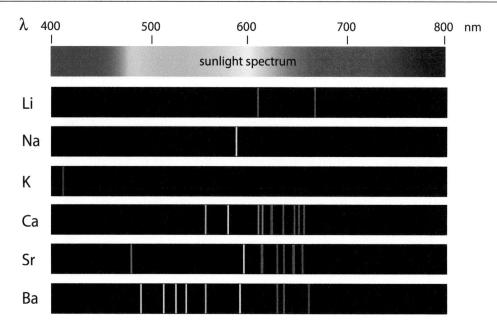

FIGURE 12.4 Line spectrum for several hot gases.

Source: Shutterstock.com.

a mystery at the time. Fifty years later, the dark lines were finally explained by Gustav Kirchhoff, and later expanded by Robert Bunsen, when they showed that chemical substances either produced or absorbed a unique spectrum of their own. This discovery was the beginning of analytical spectroscopy and is the basis of using light to unambiguously identify unknown chemicals.

It was also discovered in the mid-1800s that light of different colors, and therefore different wavelengths, was emitted when a gas became very hot. The light emitted consisted of a series of lines at various wavelengths that depended on the composition of the gas (Figure 12.4). Scientists very carefully measured the wavelengths of these lines and found that the patterns of lines formed unique "signatures" that were different for each element (Figures 12.5–12.7). It was also shown that the wavelength of the light emitted from the hot gas was also the same wavelength that was absorbed by the cold gas – so there must be a connection, but what?

Then, in 1888, through essentially a trial-and-error method, a Swiss schoolteacher, named Johann Balmer found an amazingly simple mathematical formula for the complex pattern that predicted accurately the wavelengths of all the lines in a series (λ is the wavelength):

$$\frac{1}{\lambda} = R_H \left(\frac{1}{n_1^2} - \frac{1}{n_2^2} \right)$$

[where $n_1 = 2$ and $n_2 = 3, 4, 5,...$ with the constant $R = 1.097 \times 10^7$ m^{-1}.]

It turns out that this formula successfully predicted the wavelengths of the lines in the spectra more accurately than they had ever been previously measured, and it also predicted lines that had not been discovered yet but that were experimentally found later. This was truly a handy formula, but what was the physical meaning of the different terms of this seemingly *too* simple equation? Did the form of the equation tell us anything about the fundamental nature of light? The solution to this problem took another 60 years to be answered, and in the process, changed forever all of physics and chemistry through the development of an entirely new field called *quantum mechanics*. Today, quantum mechanics forms the basis for all our understanding about atomic and molecular spectroscopy and allows us to use powerful tools to answer questions of forensic importance. But quantum mechanics goes even deeper than that; it provides our best explanation for all atomic and molecular behavior and, in the process, presents some pretty startlingly unexpected ideas about our world.

Before presenting the individual spectroscopic tools used by forensic chemists today, we need to begin by revisiting atomic theory for just a bit – specifically, we need to look more carefully at some energy considerations for atoms and molecules. In this process, we will need to dabble a bit in some ideas basic to quantum mechanics to explore the nature of light and particles.

12.2 SPECTROSCOPY BASICS: THE STRANGE WORLD OF QUANTUM MECHANICS!

The "paradox" is only a conflict between reality and your feeling of what reality "ought to be".

Richard Feynman (1918–1988)

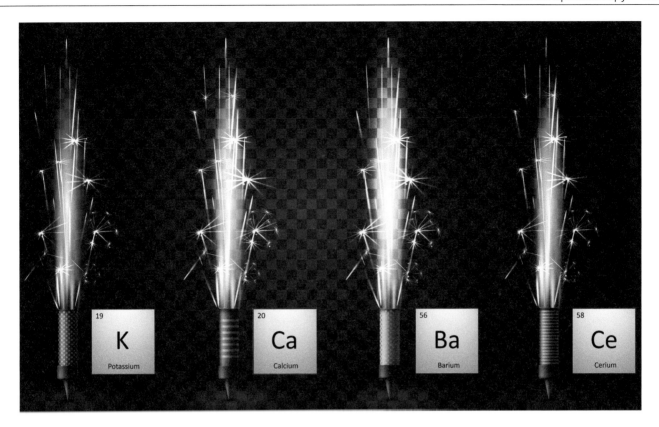

FIGURE 12.5 Light emitted from hot gases produced in firework displays.

Source: Image source courtesy Shutterstock.com.

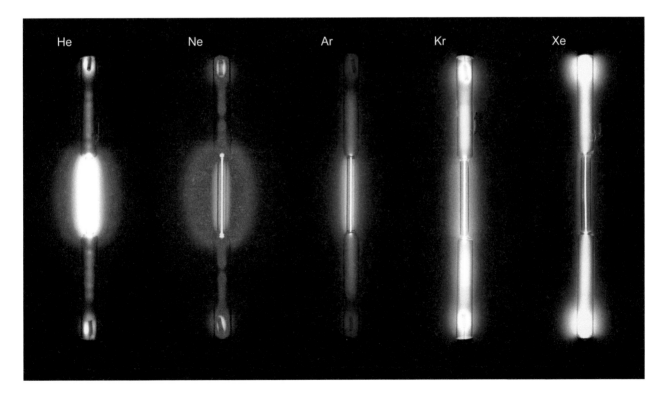

FIGURE 12.6 Gas discharge tubes showing a spectral range of colors, produced from the emission of different wavelengths of light from electrically excited noble gases: helium (He), neon (Ne), argon (Ar), krypton (Kr), and xenon (Xe).

Source: Used per Creative Commons Attribution, NonCommercial NonDerivative 3.0 (U.S.). User: Alchemist-hp www.pse-mendelejew.de.

FIGURE 12.7 "Neon Sign": the different colors are produced using a variety of gases filling the electrified tubes.

Source: Used per Creative Commons Attribution-Share Alike 4.0 International, Author: Q0ywo.

12.2.1 Light and Quantum Mechanics!

In order to understand how chemical compounds absorb and emit light, which forms the basis of forensic spectroscopy, we first need to grasp some of the fundamental properties of light itself. What we call light, or more accurately visible light, is just a small portion of a much broader electromagnetic spectrum. Electromagnetic radiation encompasses many types of radiation that you might be familiar with, such as microwaves, X-rays, ultraviolet, infrared, and visible light. Each of these names simply refers to a particular range of wavelengths found within the entire electromagnetic spectrum (Figure 12.8). The wavelengths of electromagnetic radiation range from very long radio waves, with wavelengths on the order of a kilometer, to very small gamma rays, with incredibly small wavelengths about the size of an atom.

12.2.2 Electromagnetic Radiation

Electromagnetic radiation is a form of energy that consists of two basic components put together: an electric field and a magnetic field. These two components oscillate in magnitude (amplitude) and are perpendicular to one another, as illustrated in Figure 12.9. Each "packet" of electromagnetic radiation (EMR), called a *photon*, is defined by its wavelength, frequency, and amplitude. *Wavelength* refers to the distance between two similar points on adjacent waves. For example,

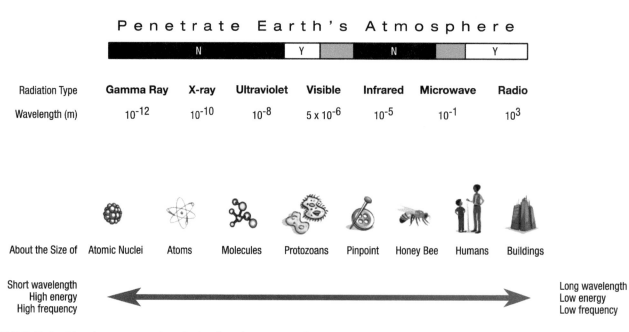

FIGURE 12.8 The electromagnetic radiation (EMR) spectrum, showing a relative size scale of the wavelengths and the energy of the radiation.

Source: NASA.

ELECTROMAGNETIC WAVES

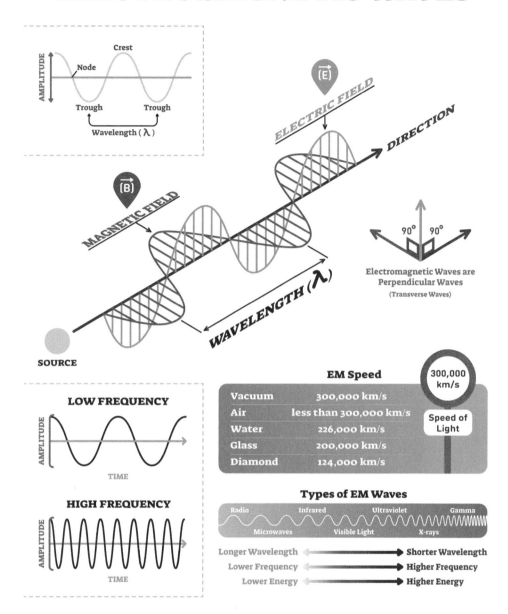

FIGURE 12.9 Electric and magnetic waves making up electromagnetic radiation and selected properties.

Source: Shutterstock.com.

the distance between the tops of two adjacent waves corresponds to the wavelength (Figure 12.9, Top Left). Amplitude is described as the height of each wave above or below the central baseline. At this point, we can think of light simply as an ordinary wave, similar to the waves upon a pond. In this analogy, the distance between the crests of two adjacent waves would define its wavelength while the height of the wave describes its *amplitude*, from a tiny ripple to a tsunami. Additionally, if you were to sit on a pier in the lake and count the number of waves that moved past you in one second, that would define a third feature of light referred to as its *frequency*. The units of frequency are Hertz, or cycles

per second. All electromagnetic radiation moves at the same speed in a vacuum: the speed of light (denoted mathematically as c and equals about 3×10^8 m/s). At this speed, it takes a photon of light a bit over eight minutes to travel from the Sun to the Earth, a distance of about 150 million km (93 million miles).

Since light moves at a constant speed, there is a simple but useful relationship between the features of light: $c = \lambda v$ (where λ, pronounced "lambda," is the wavelength and v, pronounced "nu," is the frequency). Since this equation requires that a photon's wavelength and frequency multiplied together must always equal a constant (the speed of light), then λ and v

are inversely related – simply meaning that as the wavelength becomes larger (longer), the frequency must become smaller (faster) (Figure 12.10). This relationship should make sense when you consider that as the wavelength of a wave traveling across a lake becomes larger or longer, the number of waves that pass by your stationary observation point on the pier per second decreases. For example, if the wavelength of the radiation is 1,000 m (1 km; AM radio waves), the calculated frequency would be about 300 kiloHertz (kHz, 1,000 waves per second). Decreasing the wavelength to just 1 m increases the frequency to 300,000 kHz (300 MHz; TV waves) – an inverse relationship (Figure 12.11).

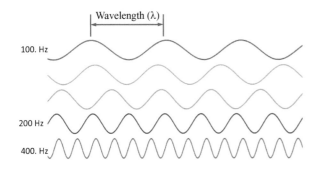

FIGURE 12.10   Relationship between frequency and wavelength for electromagnetic radiation (frequency in kHz).

12.2.3 What Is Quantum Mechanics?

The field of quantum mechanics emerged in the early 20th century, initially as a practical way to explain certain "problematic" features of light by making some rather strange and surprising assumptions. Later, these assumptions were found to be unnecessary, as the phenomena could be explained by a more fundamental consideration of the interconnectedness of matter and energy *without* making any assumptions. The effort to mathematically explain the properties of light ultimately gave rise to something called the wave equation, put forward independently by Erwin Schrödinger and Werner Heisenberg (although it wasn't clear at first what Heisenberg had done, since his math was so complex). These relationships defined by the wave equation are now central to understanding analytical spectroscopy.

A fundamental concept that came out of quantum mechanics is the idea that energy is *quantized*. In 1900, a scientist named Max Planck explained a very vexing problem in spectroscopy when he stated that the energy of emitted electromagnetic radiation could only have certain allowable values: in the language of physics, he said that the emitted energy was *quantized*. In fact, the word quantum simply means a "fixed amount." We can understand quantization by considering a few "life-sized" analogies. For example, a piano is quantized in its production of music while a trombone is not quantized. This means that you can play only certain notes on the

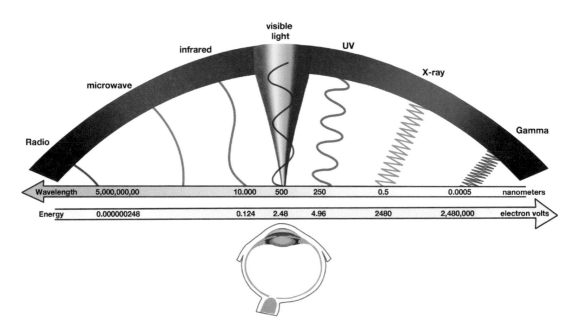

FIGURE 12.11   The wavelength of electromagnetic (EM) radiation, shown by the trace along the bottom with the corresponding frequencies in meters shown along the top. At the longer wavelength end (left) of the EM spectrum are radio waves, microwaves and infrared radiation. At the shorter wavelength end (right) are gamma rays, X-rays and ultraviolet light. Visible light, at center, is a mid-range of wavelengths that can be seen by the human eye.

Source: Spencer Sutton/Science Photo Library. Used with permission.

TABLE 12.1 Everyday analogies for quantization

QUANTIZED	NON-QUANTIZED
Piano	Trombone
Stair steps	Ramp
Typewriter	Pencil and paper
Dollar bill	Exchange rates
Football game score	Long jump distance
Light switch (on/off)	Dimmer switch
Energy	
Matter	

Piano keyboard (Quantized)   Trombone (non-quantized)

piano – while you can play a C and a C#, you can't play halfway *between* a C and C# on a piano, or halfway between adjacent keys. In contrast, on a trombone, you can, in theory, play any note at all just by moving the slide to different positions along its "glide path" (the proof of this non-quantization comes from listening to a group of beginning trombonists playing "together"). Similarly, a light switch is quantized with only two possible states, on and off, while a good dimmer switch is essentially non-quantized; you can dial up almost any level that you desire. Other examples to consider are given in Table 12.1.

Planck's science-changing discovery, therefore, was to show that the energy of the light emitted from a glowing hot object was quantized, and he even determined what the smallest possible quantized "chunk" of energy was. The energy of all electromagnetic radiation is quite simply made up of multiples of that smallest Planck unit – just as a dollar can be thought of as made up of 100 pennies, but you can't get to $1.0001 using pennies; pennies and dollars are quantized and

only certain values are allowed ($1.0001 is not one of them while $1.01 is possible).

Planck's discovery led to a number of important ideas in spectroscopy since it showed us that there is a remarkably simple relationship between the energy of a photon of light and its frequency (and, therefore, its wavelength) through the equation: $E = h\nu$ (where E is the energy of the photon and h is a constant, named after Planck). This means that as the frequency of the radiation gets smaller (and the wavelength gets longer), the energy of the photon decreases. This is why infrared light has less energy in it than ultraviolet light (see Box 12.1). Gamma rays, with very short wavelengths, pack a powerful energetic punch while long radio waves carry very little energy.

About the same time as Planck's work, it was theorized by people such as DeBroglie and Einstein that the Universe surprisingly has a dual nature: *all* things have both wave-like and particle-like properties; the simultaneous existence of these two properties is called the *duality of nature*. This concept was presented earlier in Chapter 4 on microscopy when we considered the use of an electron, with its wave-like properties, in electron microscopy. Making this connection between the two types of behavior allowed scientists to explain a great deal about experiments with light and matter. The key idea for forensic spectroscopy in this duality, as illustrated in Figure 12.12, is that all things, including photons and electrons, have both wave-like *and* particle-like properties. From this duality principle comes the concept that electromagnetic radiation can sometimes act as a wave and sometimes act as a particle, depending on how the *measurement* of the experiment is set up. This statement simply means that if we set up an experiment to measure the particle-like behavior of light, then the light will behave as a particle in our experiment (a photon acting as a particle of light). But if we set up a different experiment to measure its wave-like properties, then it will display its wave-like properties in the experiment. The strange thing here, of course, is that the *experiment itself* dictates the outcome of the measurement – something very disconcerting to scientists whose goal is to design experiments such that they are unbiased, passive observers. In science, we try very hard *not to change the outcome* of the experiment *by doing the measurement*. In quantum mechanics, the idea is that by simply "watching" or observing an experiment, the course of the experiment itself is fundamentally changed – very strange! The problem here is that we would like to make measurements of light and matter, but if the outcome is changed by an unknown amount simply by making the measurement, then how can we ever hope to make valid measurements? This sounds like a glitch in the Matrix!

This enigma was formalized by Werner Heisenberg in one of the most important ideas of quantum mechanics and spectroscopy, now known as the *Heisenberg Uncertainty Principle*. The Uncertainty Principle states that we can never know simultaneously both the position and the speed (actually the momentum) of an object with complete certainty. In other words, the more accurately we measure the position of a particle, the less accurate will be the measurement of its speed (momentum).

(a)
Light: Dual Properties

Light has both wave-like and particle-like nature

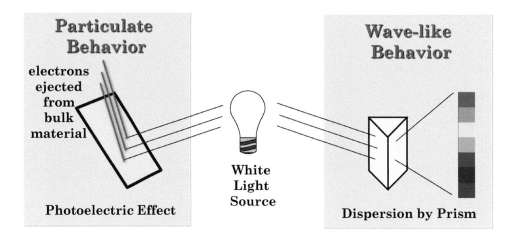

(b)
Matter: Dual Properties

Matter has both wave-like and particle-like nature

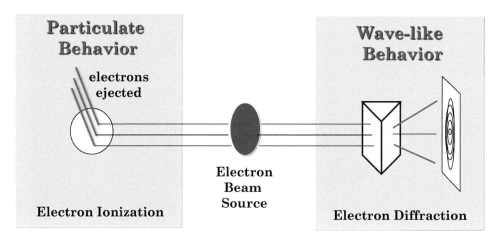

(c)
Hydrogen Emission Spectrum

656.3 nm   486.1 nm   434.0 nm   410.2 nm   364.6 nm

Red   **Blue**   **Ultraviolet**

FIGURE 12.12   Duality of nature. (a) A light wave can act as a wave, as in dispersion, or as a particle, in the photoelectric effect. (b) A particle, such as an electron, also has a dual nature and can act as a wave in diffraction or a particle in electron ionization (collisions). (c) Line spectrum of hydrogen.

BOX 12.2   HEISENBERG MAY HAVE SLEPT HERE?

Werner Heisenberg was clearly a genius. He became a full professor at 25 and received the Nobel Prize at age 32 for his work, which took people decades to fully unravel. In his *Uncertainty Principle*, he said that, in order to "see" an electron, you would have to bounce light off of it with a shorter wavelength than the wavelength of the particle itself. When you do that, however, you give some unknown amount of energy to the particle, changing just the thing that you wanted to measure. He quantified this by saying:

$$\Delta x m \Delta v \geq \frac{h/2\pi}{2}$$

(where *x* is the position, *v* is the velocity, and *h* is Planck's constant.)

This equation can be "translated" as the uncertainty in the measurement of the position of the electron (Δx, pronounced "delta *x*") times the uncertainty in its velocity (Δv, pronounced "delta nu") is equal to or greater than a constant (~ Planck's constant). You can never know both quantities exactly. This uncertainty is not from the instruments used in the measurement but a fundamental barrier to all measurements themselves.

As an analogy to the Uncertainty Principle, consider a pinwheel blowing in the wind. If we photograph the pinwheel with a very fast shutter speed (the shutter opens only very briefly, stopping the action), we see a sharp image of the pinwheel. In this image (on the left-hand side of the photograph), we can measure the position of the parts of the pinwheel very accurately, since it looks like it has stopped, but we know very little about its actual speed – it could even be standing still; we just don't know. In contrast, if we use a very long shutter speed to take the picture (the shutter stays open a long time, image on the right in Figure 12.13), we get a blurred image. This blurred image tells us relatively little about the position of the pinwheel parts but does tell us much more about its speed; we certainly know that it's moving. Thus, as we know more about its speed, we can know less about its position. The Uncertainty Principle works like this at the scale of an electron; the more we know about its speed (momentum), the less we know about its position, and vice versa.

FIGURE 12.13 Images of the same spinning pinwheel, moving at exactly the same velocity in each picture, but taken with different shutter speeds, from very fast shutter (on the left) to much slower (on the right).

Source: Used per Creative Commons Attribution-Share Alike 3.0 Unported, © Nevit Dilmen.

12.2.4 The Bohr Atom and Forensic Spectroscopy

Finally, all the pieces were in place for Niels Bohr to propose a new model for the atom, modified and refined by many others in the following years, that pulled together these new ideas of waves, particles (electrons), energy, quantization, and light into a new scientific understanding – one that finally allows us to understand forensic spectroscopy. Modern atomic theory, as it relates to spectroscopy, retains the idea of a nucleus containing the protons and neutrons in the center with the electrons moving about it in the surrounding empty space. The electrons are held in the "neighborhood" of the nucleus by an electrostatic attraction – the positive charge of the nuclear protons attracts the negatively charged electrons. Because the electrons are

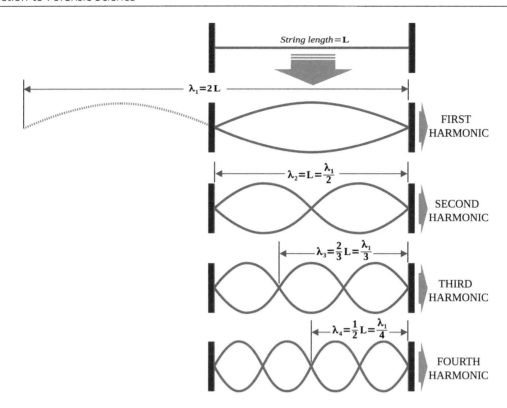

FIGURE 12.14   Standing waves using a jump rope (or "string") and illustrating various standing wave patterns from a jump rope with two fixed ends and different energy levels (first harmonic<second harmonic<third harmonic, etc.).

Source: Shutterstock.com.

constantly moving, however, they don't simply crash into the nucleus but move about with a fixed amount of energy; they have quantized energies (allowed energy states). Bohr's big leap was that he said that the electrons can only have certain allowed "quantized" energies and that they don't continuously radiate energy and spiral into the nucleus as they move around (a pretty controversial idea at the time). Bohr's theory went much farther, however, by saying that the electron, because it has wave-like properties, must move about the nucleus in what amounts to a standing wave. A standing wave is a wave that doesn't appear to change or move over time, as illustrated by the jump ropes in Figure 12.14. Additionally, just like a jump rope, there are different energy levels that a wave can display. For example, it's easy to make the jump rope move relatively slowly with ½ of a wave between the two ends (top of drawing in Figure 12.14), but it becomes successively harder (more energy is required) to make it show two or more peaks (lower portion of Figure 12.14). Figure 12.15 shows Bohr's idea of an "allowed" (quantized) electron energy state as a standing wave [Note: current theory says that the electron wave is really a probability wave – a wave that tells us the probability of finding the electron in a particular place, rather than a real physical standing wave, but that's not key to our understanding of spectroscopy at this point]. The picture shows a wave that takes exactly four complete wavelengths to move around the nucleus and arrive exactly back at the same starting point. There are other possibilities with 4, 5, 6, and so on wavelengths in other

standing wave patterns, but an integral whole number of waves is required to form a stable standing wave (Figure 12.16). These possibilities form a pattern of allowed (quantized) energy levels, or shells, as shown in Figure 12.17. The circular paths drawn for the electrons are illustrative; electrons do not move about the nucleus in spherical orbits, like the planets around the sun; remember Heisenberg's idea of not being able to determine the path of an electron exactly. Luckily, all we need to know is that the electron occupies fixed, quantized energy states.

So, now we're finally armed with enough information about quantum mechanics to understand the emission spectrum of hot atoms, and why Balmer's "way too simple" equation actually works amazingly well to explain the missing wavelengths in the solar spectrum and the characteristic bright spectral lines emitted from hot gases. Our quantum model of the atom has the nucleus in the center with the electrons moving about it with certain fixed, quantized energy levels. These electrons have many possible energy states available to them, just as there are many possibilities for making standing waves with a jump rope, each possibility with a different energy. Once in these energy levels, the electrons are stable and neither gain nor lose energy. *Here's the key to spectroscopy*: the electrons in an atom can *jump* between different energy states given the right opportunity. Furthermore, when they jump between levels, they change their energies, just as you can jump from one stair-step to another and thereby change your

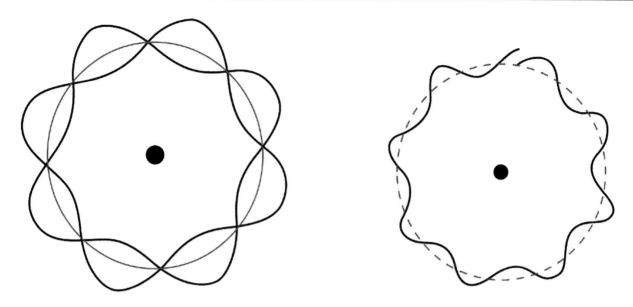

FIGURE 12.15 Electron standing wave in an atom proposed by Bohr. The standing wave on the left exactly fits together and hence represents an "allowed" energy level whereas the standing wave on the right does not "fit" (ends don't match) and therefore is not an "allowed" energy level.

Source: Used per Creative Commons Attribution-Share Alike 3.0 Unported, Author: CK-12 Foundation.

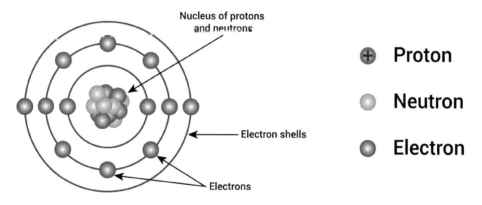

FIGURE 12.16 Multiple "standing" waves, each at a different energy level, in an atom.

Source: Shutterstock.com.

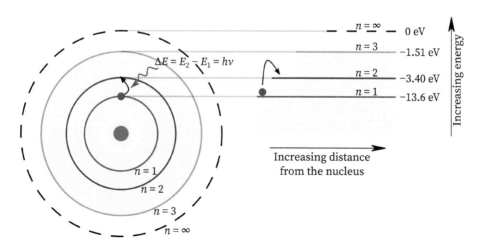

FIGURE 12.17 Different quantized energy levels in an atom. Electrons jump from lower energy to higher energy in hydrogen when the right amount of energy is absorbed. Similarly, when an electron emits energy it moves from a higher to to a lower quantized level.

Source: Shutterstock.com.

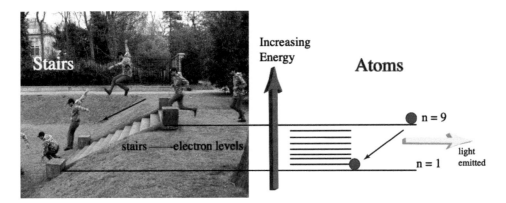

FIGURE 12.18 Conceptual similarity of jumping between stair steps, on the left (quantized "allowed" positions), and atoms, on the right, to change "allowed" energy states.

Source: Photograph source Flickr; © Dr. Ahmed Al-Numairy.

potential energy level in the process (Figure 12.18). In atoms, when an electron jumps from a lower energy to a higher energy level, it must gain energy from somewhere, such as by absorbing a photon of light that carries the exact energy needed to make the jump: exactly the energy difference between the two levels. However, if an electron jumps from a higher to a lower energy level, then it needs to shed the energy difference between the two levels. It can do this by simply emitting a new photon with exactly the energy contained in the difference between the two energy levels. Whether emitting or absorbing light, it takes the same amount of energy: the *difference between the two allowed energy states*. This process of adding or removing energy from something to make it move to different levels is similar to the process of moving a book between the floor and the top of a bookcase. In order for a book to move from the floor to the top shelf, the book must be acted upon by some energy: the energy you must expend in moving the book. The exact energy used to move the book to a higher level now gives the book a new level of potential energy that is exactly equal to the energy required to raise it to its new height. If the book falls from the top of the bookcase to the floor, however, it releases its potential energy and lowers its energy state. It's the same with electrons and photons in atoms and molecules; the book corresponds to the electron and you correspond to the photon supplying or receiving the energy transferred. If an electron moves to a higher energy level, called an *excited state*, the exact amount of energy needed to do this can be provided by *absorbing* the energy of a photon. When an electron moves from a higher energy state to a lower state, it must lose energy and does this by *emitting* a photon whose energy exactly corresponds to this difference. This is shown schematically in Figure 12.19 for a simple atom with six possible energy levels (denoted as $n = 1$ through $n = 6$) – remember wavelength can be equated to energy. The lowest energy state in an atom or molecule is called the *ground state*.

If you remember Balmer's simple equation for predicting the wavelengths of the lines emitted from hot gaseous atoms, such as hydrogen, it was in the form:

$$\frac{1}{\lambda} = R\left[\frac{1}{2^2} - \frac{1}{n^2}\right]$$

where $n = 3, 4, 5,\dots$ and the constant $R = 1.097 \times 10^7$ m^{-1}.

From Figure 12.19, we can now see where all the parts of Balmer's equation come from. The $1/2^2$ term comes from the lower energy level ($n = 2$) that the excited electrons fall into to make the visible series of emission lines, called the Balmer series (those lines we can see with our eyes). The $1/n^2$ term comes from the various possible *higher* energy states for the electrons; for each bright spectral line, the electron starts at a different higher energy level ($n = 3, 4$, or higher) but they all end in the same $n = 2$ level. The difference between any two energy levels, multiplied by the constant R (called the Rydberg constant), gives us the energy of the transition. This energy is expressed as the wavelength of the line. But there's more! According to our theory, there's no reason that a transition must end at $n = 2$ – why not end at $n = 1$ or $n = 3$ or 4 instead of just ending at $n = 2$, as Balmer's equation uses? It turns out that the transitions can indeed end in places other than the second level and, not surprisingly, other sets of lines with different ending levels were discovered once people knew where to look. So, really, Balmer's original equation is just one special case of a more general equation that simply takes the difference between the two energy levels involved in the transition and converts that energy into wavelengths. Other series of lines, named the Lyman, Paschen, and Pfund series, were discovered in the infrared and ultraviolet regions of the spectrum for the hydrogen atom and the Balmer equation worked perfectly to calculate the exact wavelengths in each series. The generalized form of the equation that can be used with any starting and ending levels then looks like:

$$\frac{1}{\lambda} = R\left[\frac{1}{n_{final}^2} - \frac{1}{n_{initial}^2}\right]$$

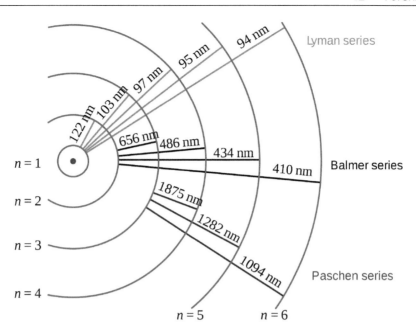

FIGURE 12.19 Electron energy levels in an atom (n = 1–6) and the energy emitted or absorbed as an electron moves between these levels:

- **Lyman series**: comes from electrons dropping from higher energy levels into the n = 1 level (the lowest possible level). These lines form the highest energy series of lines since they drop the farthest (all the way to the "ground" floor or ground state) and are, therefore, found in the highest energy region – the ultraviolet.
- **Balmer series**: comes from electrons dropping into the next to the lowest level (n = 2) with emission lines in the visible light spectrum.
- **Paschen series**: found in the lower energy part of the spectrum – the infrared spectrum – and comes from electrons falling from higher energy levels into the n = 3 level.

Source: Used per Creative Commons Attribution-Share Alike 3.0 Unported. Author: Szdori.

(where n_{final} is the ending energy level, and $n_{initial}$ is the starting energy level.)

The various wavelengths of light emitted by different types of atoms can also now be easily explained with this model. Each atom has its own special set of allowed energy levels, different from other atoms, mainly determined by the number of protons in the nucleus and the number of electrons around the nucleus. Since the differences between allowed energy levels are unique to each atom type, each element gives a characteristic "signature" of lines at specific wavelengths. The more electrons and the more energy levels there are to jump between (like stair steps), generally the more lines are seen in the spectrum. This effect can be seen for several elements in Figure 12.20, where hydrogen has only a few lines while nitrogen (seven electrons) has many lines. Additionally, since the set of lines is unique for each element, it is possible to distinguish between more than one element within a sample by looking at the observed lines for a sample. Also, shown in Figure 12.20 is the relationship between emission and absorption spectra for an atom – they are at the same energy.

At the core of forensic spectroscopy is the concept of moving electrons between quantized energy levels in atoms or molecules and tracking the energy added (absorbed) or lost (emitted). The foundation of all this is quantum mechanics, which turns out to be an incredibly powerful theory that can be used to predict and explain very complex phenomena, including spectroscopy. It has provided explanations for experiments and has directed scientists toward new discoveries, from understanding black holes to using quantum dots for a new generation of computing, as well as detecting toxins and poisons in blood.

So now we've done it – provided a working model for understanding how light is absorbed and emitted by atoms and molecules. These concepts form the basis for understanding the spectroscopy presented in the following sections. Once you grasp these ideas, all of spectroscopy falls into place by simply considering the absorption or emission of light as arising from electrons moving between energy levels in an atom or molecule.

In Section 12.3, we begin with the simplest systems, atoms. Later, we will extend these same ideas to more complex molecules.

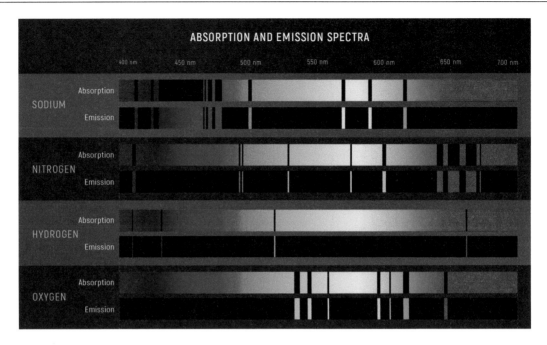

FIGURE 12.20   Absorption and emission spectra of several gaseous elements.

Source: NASA.

12.3 ATOMIC SPECTROSCOPY

12.3.1 Introduction

Forensic scientists are frequently tasked with answering analytical questions, such as determining the chemical composition of a particular sample, identifying whether a sample is a
mixture or a pure substance, and quantifying the amount of
each component present in a sample. Luckily, spectroscopic
methods can often quickly and easily provide answers to these
types of questions. Using the basic understanding of spectroscopy developed in the previous section, we begin by exploring
what are often the simplest of these problems: determining the
elemental composition of a substance. Knowing the elemental
makeup of a sample provides useful insights into the origins,
identity, and history of forensic samples.

There are two main types of analytical information that
can be determined for an unknown sample: quantitative and
qualitative data. As discussed in Chapter 11, quantitative analysis provides information about how much of a component
is present in the sample, while qualitative analysis, identifies
whether a specific component is present or absent. If the sample is a pure substance, quantitative information can be used
to determine its empirical formula (Chapter 11.3), thereby,
moving toward a definitive identification of the material.
Sometimes, simply determining the presence of a particular
element in the sample qualitatively is all that's needed: finding
arsenic in food suggests poisoning, identifying lead in paint
suggests legal problems with the product, or discovering iron

in certain inks suggests forgery. In other instances, we need to
know quantitatively exactly how much of each component is
present: is the alloy found in a bullet recovered from a crime
scene identical to that found in the chamber of a suspect's gun,
how much cocaine is contained in a seized sample, or what
is the concentration of beryllium in a tissue sample to aid in
determining the cause of death.

As the name implies, atomic spectroscopy deals with
the identification and quantification of the different elements,
rather than the molecules, that make up a sample. Each element, under the right conditions, either absorbs or emits light
of different energies, allowing us to discover the elemental
composition of the substance. In this section, we will focus on
light and atoms.

**BOX 12.3   USEFUL TERMS
IN SPECTROSCOPY**

- **Ground State**: The lowest energy state of an
atom or molecule.
- **Excited State**: States with more energy than
the ground state in an atom or molecule.
- **Emission**: When an electron in an excited
energy state falls to a lower energy state with
the energy difference between the two states
emitted as light.
- **Absorption**: When electrons become excited
by moving from a lower to a higher energy
state by absorbing energy.

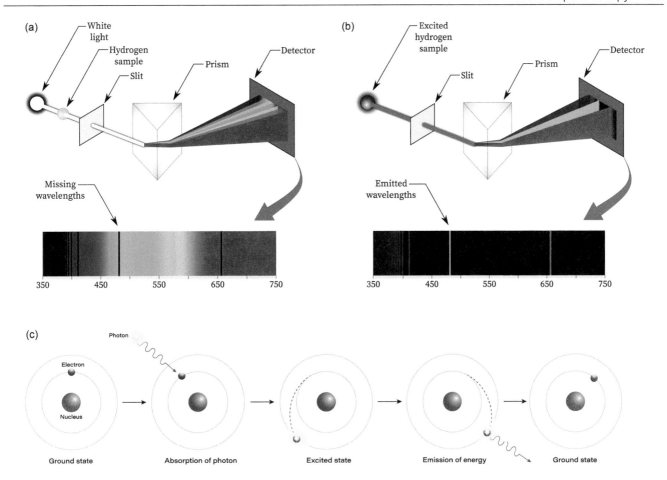

FIGURE 12.21 Schematic drawing of atomic emission spectroscopy (b) for hydrogen atomic absorption spectroscopy (a). A comparison of the output from these two similar types of spectroscopy is shown at the bottom (c).

Source: Images courtesy Shutterstock.com.

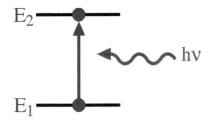

FIGURE 12.22 Electron transition from a lower (E_1) to a higher (E_2) energy level by absorbing light hv atomic absorption spectroscopy.

Source: Retrieved from Wikimedia Commons; used per Creative Commons Attribution.

12.3.2 Atomic Absorption Spectroscopy (AAS)

Atomic absorption spectroscopy, based on discoveries first made in the late 19th century, measures the light absorbed by the atoms of a sample and provides both quantitative and qualitative elemental information. In this method, the atoms, in the form of a gas (Figure 12.21), absorb light energy, which excites the atom's electrons from their lowest energy state, called the ground state, to a higher energy level, called an excited state. This type of energy transition is shown schematically in Figure 12.22. The energy of the photon absorbed by the atom must match *exactly* the energy needed to excite the electron from a lower to a higher energy level. Just as when you walk up stair steps, you must put in exactly the right amount of energy to make it to the next step; too little energy and you don't make it to the next step, and too much energy does not put you on the next step either. Furthermore, you can't step only halfway or three-quarters of the distance to the next step; you must put in just enough energy to make it *exactly* to the next quantized step. In atoms, the photon absorbed must likewise provide exactly the right amount of energy to promote an atom's electron to a higher energy level.

When white light, containing a continuous spectrum of all the visible wavelengths, is used to excite the atoms in the sample, the wavelengths of light that the atoms absorb show up as "missing" wavelengths, or dark lines in the spectrum (Figure 12.20). These "missing" wavelengths correspond exactly to the energy required for the electronic "steps" between energy levels in the atom. For example, shown in

(a)

(b)

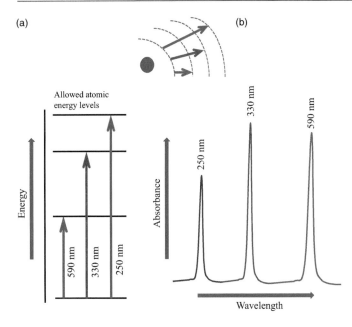

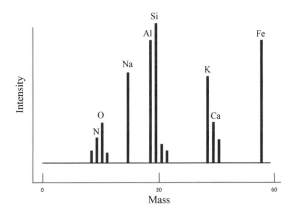

FIGURE 12.24 Typical atomic absorption spectra showing absorption peaks for a variety of elements including sodium (Na), aluminum (Al), potassium (K), and iron (Fe).

FIGURE 12.23 (a) Three electronic transitions for the sodium atom showing the wavelengths for each transition. (b) The three sodium atomic transitions show up as different wavelengths of light absorbed by the sodium atoms with energy exactly equal to the energy difference between the two levels involved in the transition.

Figure 12.23 are three transitions (or "steps") possible between the four different sodium electron energy levels, each requiring a different amount of energy to cause them to occur (shown by the arrows). These three transitions give rise to the sodium absorption spectrum (shown on the right in Figure 12.23) consisting of the three wavelengths corresponding to the three different energy steps or transitions.

Since each element in the periodic table has its own uniquely different set of energy levels, measuring the wavelengths of the light absorbed by a sample using atomic absorption can tell us which elements are present (called the *characteristic wavelengths* for that element), as shown in Figure 12.24. Additionally, the area under a peak for an element in the spectrum can give information on how much of the element is present in the sample. This means that, under the right conditions, atomic absorption analysis can be both qualitative *and* quantitative.

In the atomic absorption method, the compounds present must be first broken down into individual atoms and placed into the vapor phase (atomized). This can be done in a variety of ways, but most commonly, the sample is dissolved in a solvent that is then injected into a flame, plasma, or other hot reactor. This provides enough energy to decompose the compounds into charged atoms, but not enough to electronically excite the electrons to a higher energy level – the vast majority of atoms remain in the ground electronic state.

Once the sample is atomized, light covering the spectrum from the ultraviolet (~200 nm) to the near infrared (~900 nm) is then shone through the relatively cool, gaseous sample (by cool we mean on the order of *only* 2,000–3,000°C). The

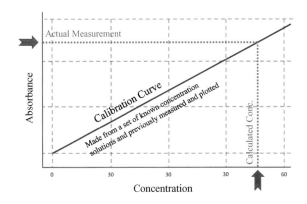

FIGURE 12.25 Use of a calibration curve to find the concentration of an unknown in solution.

various elements in the vaporized sample each absorb light at their characteristic wavelengths, based on their individual atomic energy levels. A special detector is then used to determine which wavelengths of light have been absorbed and, therefore, which elements are present. This method works well for the qualitative detection of the elements present and can detect the majority of the elements in the periodic table simultaneously.

Atomic absorption spectroscopy can also be used to quantitatively measure how much of each element is present in the sample. When this is done, the amount of light absorbed at a particular wavelength is compared with the previously measured absorptions of a set of standard solutions of that element made at different known concentrations but measured at the same wavelength. The absorptions from the set of known concentration solutions are plotted to form a calibration curve, shown in Figure 12.25. Then, the amount of light absorbed by the unknown solution is measured and plotted on the calibration curve to determine how much of the element is present in the unknown sample. The relationship between the concentration of an element in the unknown sample and the amount of light it will absorb is given by a rather simple equation (called the Beer-Lambert Law) that says

$$A = abc$$

This equation means that the amount of light absorbed by the sample (A, absorbance) is equal to a constant for the element (a, called the absorptivity) multiplied by the length of the sample that the light has to pass through (b, path length) multiplied by the concentration (c).

BOX 12.4 MORE TERMS IN SPECTROSCOPY

- **Absorbance**: A measure of the amount of light at a specific wavelength absorbed by the sample.
- **Characteristic Wavelengths**: The wavelengths of light absorbed by atoms of a particular element. The wavelengths depend on the energies of the different allowed levels in the element.
- **Transmission**: The amount of light passing directly through a sample that is not absorbed.

12.3.3 Uses of Atomic Absorption in Forensic Science

Atomic absorption spectroscopy has found its way into forensic investigations in a variety of analyses including gunshot residue, food purity, environmental pollution, and medicolegal investigations.

One of the major uses of atomic absorption spectroscopy is in firearms investigations. When a weapon is fired, there is often a large and instantaneous burst of vaporized material coming from the bullet, gunpowder, and casing materials that is expelled from the weapon. Often, this vapor is transferred to the hands and clothing of both the shooter and the victim. If someone is suspected of firing a weapon, their hands and clothing can be swabbed and analyzed by AAS to determine the presence of unusual amounts of lead, antimony, and bismuth in the sample – all elements found in bullets, gunpowder, and casings. Additional clues as to what happened can come from where the different gunshot residues are found. For example, if residues are found mostly on the back of a person's hands or on their non-firing hand in the case of a rifle shot (the hand used to steady a rifle), then that person is likely the shooter. If, instead, the residues are found primarily on a person's palms or forearms, it suggests either a defensive position of the victim or else some other person has handled the weapon. While positive findings are valuable corroborating evidence, failure to find such evidence does not exonerate someone; the method has a significant false-negative rate due to sampling problems. Additionally, the sampling needs to be performed soon after firing and before a person has had a chance to wash their hands, thereby eliminating the residue.

AAS analysis is also commonly used for soil and environmental analysis. When soil samples are found on evidence or directly on a suspect's clothing, adhered to shoes, on tires, or coating plant materials, investigators often try to trace the soil to its geographical source. One way to do this is to measure the elemental composition of the sample and compare it to known soil compositions measured from various locations.

Atomic absorption is also useful in analyzing biological samples. Trace elements, such as As, Ca, Fe, Hg, Pb, and others, can be readily determined in hair, blood, skin, under fingernails, and in body organs and fluids. Recently, for example, AAS was used to show that an injury was caused by an electrical discharge by identifying trace amounts of copper and aluminum in wounds on the skin.

BOX 12.5 DEATH BY CHOCOLATE?

In the classic fictional detective novel from the "Golden Age" of crime fiction, called *The Poisoned Chocolates Case* by Anthony Berkeley, six "armchair" detectives provide six very different solutions to an apparent poisoning from a "doctored" box of chocolates.

Real-life poisonings throughout history have used just about every conceivable type of food or candy to convey the poison to the victim, and sometimes the assailant at the same time. Atomic spectroscopy can be very effective in identifying elemental poisons, such as arsenic, phosphorus, radium, plutonium, and others.

12.3.4 Advantages and Limitations of Atomic Absorption Spectroscopy

AAS allows for the rapid detection of very small quantities of over 60 elements of the periodic table, with very few interferences (something in the sample that gets in the way of the desired measurement of an element). The instrumentation is relatively simple and straightforward to operate.

The technique has a few disadvantages. Probably chief among these is the need to construct a calibration curve when doing a quantitative analysis for each element. Quantitative analysis also limits the method to the determination of one element at a time, requires the use of special light sources (usually made of the element being detected), and cannot readily measure non-metals. Nonetheless, AAS remains a useful forensic tool in specific circumstances.

12.3.5 Atomic Emission Spectroscopy (AES)

Atomic emission spectroscopy (AES) can be thought of as the exact complement to atomic absorption spectroscopy. In AES, electrons *start* at a higher energy level, an excited energy state, and then fall down into an empty lower energy state. When this happens, the atom must emit a photon of light to "shed" the "extra" energy that is exactly equal to the size of the energy step, shown in Figure 12.26. This is precisely the opposite of what happens in atomic absorption where the electrons start at the *lower* energy state and then absorb a photon to become excited and move to a higher energy level. Since the atomic

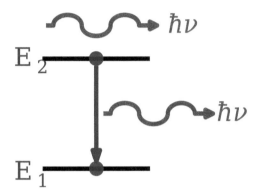

FIGURE 12.26 Drawing of an electron going from a higher energy state to a lower energy state with the emission of a photon of light in atomic emission spectroscopy.

Source: Retrieved from Wikimedia Commons; used per Creative Commons Attribution.

energy levels involved in both of these processes (absorption and emission) are exactly the same, the energy differences between these possible "steps" or transitions are also the same. This means that the wavelengths of the emission lines are exactly the same wavelengths as the absorption lines, as illustrated in Figure 12.27.

In many ways, we are already familiar with the phenomenon behind atomic emission spectroscopy. For example, fireworks, the aurora borealis ("northern lights"), and the glowing colors from "neon" electric signs are all examples of excited atoms losing energy through the emission of visible light (Figure 12.28a). In fireworks, a very energetic explosion excites the atoms from the different elements present into their excited energetic states. These atoms then quickly lose energy from these excited states to fall to lower energy levels by emitting the beautifully colored lights that we see: sodium produces yellow, calcium produces orange, strontium produces red, and blue comes from copper; each element emitting light at its own characteristic wavelengths in a process that is the exact reverse of atomic absorption (Figure 12.28b). In essence, the emission spectrograph simply enables a fireworks-like process to occur inside the instrument while we measure the wavelengths of the light generated. If, while watching fireworks, you were to look through a prism that spread out the spectrum, you would see the many emission lines from all the elements present in

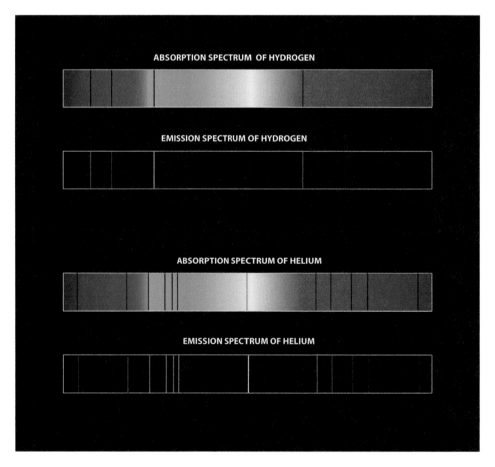

FIGURE 12.27 The wavelengths of light from atomic emission and absorption for a given atom are exactly the same since they arise from the same electronic "steps" or transitions in the atom. Shown are the AES and AAS for hydrogen and helium.

Source: Carlos Clarivan/Science Photo Library. Used with permission.

FIGURE 12.28 The various colors in the *aurora borealis* (northern lights, (a) taken over Canada by NASA astronauts) and fireworks (b) come from different elements emitting light at their characteristic wavelengths from excited atoms as they drop back to lower electronic energy levels.

Source: (a) NASA; (b) NASA/H. Zell.

the explosion. These emission lines correspond exactly to the characteristic energies of those elements displayed through atomic emission spectroscopy.

In AES, samples must first be converted into a gas of atoms, much like in atomic absorption methods. This is typically done using high-energy sources such as electrical discharge, plasmas, or laser beams. Once in the beam, the high-energy process breaks apart any molecules present and places the individual atoms from the molecules into a highly excited gaseous state. Then, just as in fireworks, the excited atoms rapidly lose energy by emitting characteristic photons of light as they transition into lower energy states. Using AES, it is possible to simultaneously detect the presence of about 60 different elements in the sample.

It is important to note the difference between the AAS and AES experiments. In absorption spectroscopy, a bright white light is used to shine *through* the sample to excite the atoms. The resulting spectrum shows "black" lines at "missing" wavelengths that are absorbed by the sample. In emission spectroscopy, no outside light source is used: the sample

is energized to excite the electrons in the atoms. The light is then emitted from the sample *itself* as the electrons fall back to lower energy levels. This light appears as bright lines on a black background at the energy levels characteristic of the elements in the sample. Because light emission is weaker than absorption in these experiments (because, even at high energy, most of the atoms are not excited above the ground state so relatively few atoms emit light at any given moment), the atomic absorption method is more sensitive than emission.

The intensity of the light emitted in AES is proportional to the number of atoms present in a sample. This provides the ability to quantitatively determine how much of a given element is in the sample. Emission spectroscopy has a number of advantages, including a high throughput rate (many samples can be analyzed in a relatively short amount of time), high resolution (providing the ability to measure elements separately), good stability (the results are reproducible), and the relative ease of operation of the instrument.

12.3.6 Uses of Atomic Emission in Forensic Science

Atomic emission spectroscopy is a reliable, simple, and inexpensive method for determining the elemental composition of an unknown sample. It is used in forensic analysis to provide accurate composition information about soil, glass, biological, metal alloy, elemental poison, and other evidence.

Occasionally, it is necessary to measure the composition of metallic and glass samples to determine whether they are similar to a known reference standard, such as comparing a piece of glass found on a victim with that taken from a suspect's car. When glass is manufactured, very small amounts of trace elements (the tiny amounts of other elements besides silicon, oxygen, and boron found in glass) can be incorporated into the glass from the raw materials, furnace, or handling technique used in the process. The inclusion of very small amounts of impurities can easily vary significantly from batch to batch and between manufacturers. Measuring the amounts of these trace elements in a glass sample can help to demonstrate whether a particular sample was or was not produced by a specific manufacturer or as part of a specific batch of glass. There has even been work to try to determine *when* a particular glass sample was made using this trace elemental composition data. Currently, the AES analysis of ten elements in glasses (Al, Ba, Ca, Fe, Mg, Mn, Na, Ti, Sr, and Zr) is regularly employed on milligram-sized samples with very good analytical precision. Reports have shown that it is possible using AES to identify the intended use of a glass sample, such as window glass or headlight glass.

Similarly, metals, such as steel, aluminum, copper, gold, and others, typically contain a relatively large number of trace elements resulting from the mining, refining, and manufacturing processes. AES data can help identify the manufacturer, the geographic source of the ore, or compare two metal samples to attempt to show that they came from the same source.

Biological forensic samples have also been analyzed using AES. For example, thallium, arsenic, and mercury poisoning have been confirmed by AES data from liver samples recovered at autopsy.

12.3.7 Atomic Fluorescence Spectroscopy (AFS)

Atomic fluorescence (AFS) spectroscopy can be thought of as similar to atomic emission spectroscopy in several key ways. In atomic fluorescence, the electrons of atoms are first excited to higher energy levels, just as in atomic emission. However, rather than immediately emitting their characteristic wavelength of light to return to a lower energy state as in emission, in fluorescence, the atoms first lose some of their energy *without* emitting light, typically through low-energy vibrations or some other similar non-radiative process (meaning without the production of light). This drops the energy of the atom down a small amount but *not* to the ground state. After losing an amount of its energy through vibration, the atom can then emit a photon of light to get to the ground state, but a photon of lower energy (longer wavelength) than in atomic emission. In other words, it absorbs light energy to get to an allowed excited state and then later emits a lower energy photon of light. This is shown schematically in Figure 12.29. This process is actually quite similar to the way fluorescent lights used in homes and offices work. By measuring the amount of light later emitted by the atom, it is possible to both qualitatively and quantitatively identify the elements present in the sample that fluoresce.

The experimental setup for AFS is shown in Figure 12.30. In this case, a bright white light (all visible wavelengths) is shone on vaporized atoms, and the fluorescence is measured to the side of the direct path of the white light beam. This allows for the accurate measurement of the longer wavelength of the fluorescent emission without interference with the exciting white light beam that also includes the fluorescent wavelength.

Finally, Figure 12.30 also presents a summary of AAS, AES, and AFS spectroscopies is presented, illustrating the relationships between these types of atomic spectroscopy.

12.3.8 Uses of Fluorescence Spectroscopy in Forensic Science

Atomic fluorescence has its place in forensic investigations particularly in the analysis of elements that prove difficult using other methods. Important among these are the analysis

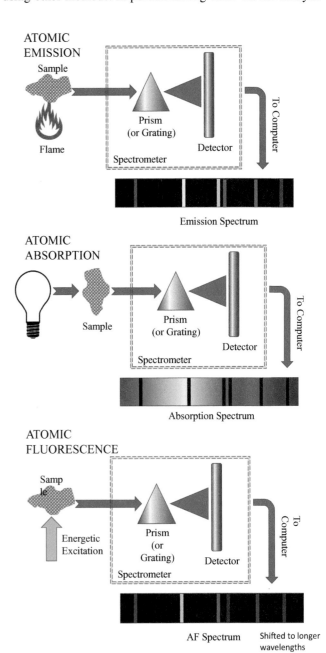

FIGURE 12.30 Schematic experimental arrangement and spectral comparison for atomic absorption (AAS), atomic emission (AES), and atomic fluorescence (AFS) spectroscopy.

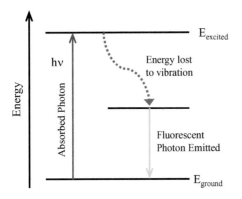

FIGURE 12.29 Energy diagram showing how light is emitted in atomic fluorescence spectroscopy. The red arrow is the energy of the photon absorbed, the green arrow shown the amount of energy lost through vibration or a similar process – it is still quantized but invoving vibrational levels. The yellow arrow is the ultimate energy of the emitted photon.

of mercury and lead. Additionally, AF is used in microscopy to map elemental compositions in a sample.

12.3.9 Neutron Activation Analysis (NAA)

Some experimental techniques for examining samples on the atomic level involve the emission of light through mechanisms other than those described above. For example, small particles, such as electrons, neutrons, and even small atoms, can be aimed at the atoms in a sample. These particles may collide with low-energy electrons in atoms, knocking electrons completely away from the atom. This is similar to the way one ball can knock another ball away through a direct collision. This collision leaves behind a "hole" in the inner electronic structure of the atom, which is then filled by the cascading of the higher energy electrons down to fill the place of the ejected electron. This would be similar to removing a piece from the

FIGURE 12.31 Removing pieces at the bottom of a stack in this game will ultimately result in pieces falling from higher levels to replace the removed lower pieces, similar to how the removal of a lower-energy electron results in a cascade of electrons falling to lower energy levels, in turn producing the emission of electromagnetic radiation.

bottom of a stack of game pieces, as shown in Figure 12.31. When lower pieces are removed, ultimately higher-lying pieces will fall into the place formerly occupied by the missing piece. A similar process happens in this form of emission spectroscopy; electrons fall into lower-lying energy levels vacated by the collisional removal of an electron, resulting in the emission of light corresponding to the energy difference between the starting and ending energy levels for each electron in the cascade. The wavelengths and intensity of this emitted light can then be measured to determine which elements are present by their characteristic emitted light.

One of the analytical techniques that involves photon emission from the collision of particles with atoms is called neutron activation analysis (NAA). In this method, thermal neutrons (relatively slow, low-energy neutrons) from a nuclear reactor are aimed at a sample of unknown elemental composition. An atom in the sample can absorb an additional neutron into its nucleus, becoming one neutron heavier. This altered nucleus, however, is not very stable and quickly emits a gamma ray to lose some of its added energy. Gamma radiation is a form of very high-energy electromagnetic radiation. Each gamma photon carries $\sim 10^5$ times the energy of a visible photon. This emission results in a somewhat more stable, but still radioactive nucleus (see Section 12.6 for more about radioactivity). This radioactive nucleus then undergoes a nuclear decay process by first emitting a beta particle (a beta particle is simply an electron) to "convert" a neutron into a proton, followed by emitting a second gamma ray to produce a stable, non-radioactive nucleus, one proton heavier than the original atom (e.g., converting As^{33} into Se^{34}). This is shown schematically in Figure 12.32.

In neutron activation analysis (NAA), the energy of the second gamma ray that is emitted (the "delayed gamma ray") can be analyzed to reveal the identity of the original target nucleus; all atoms emit gamma rays with different characteristic energies (the first gamma ray can also be analyzed, but less commonly). It is important to note, however, that the gamma ray emitted in NAA does not come from the movement of electrons between energy levels but arises from energy level shifts *within* the nucleus itself. The gamma ray that is emitted has a much shorter wavelength of <0.001 nm than visible light (visible light is ~400–750 nm), so special detectors are needed. The amount of radiation given off can also be used to determine how much of each element is present in the sample. For example, an NAA spectrum displaying the trace elemental composition of scrapings underneath a human fingernail of a suspect showed the presence of high aluminum levels, which were later correlated with the job of the suspect as a machinist.

Neutron activation analysis has some particular advantages and disadvantages over other types of spectroscopic elemental analyses. The advantages include: (1) non-destructive analysis of the sample, (2) extreme sensitivity to very low concentrations (up to parts per trillion), (3) simultaneous analysis of many elements to give a total elemental composition of the sample, and (4) insensitivity to any chemical interferences in the sample (e.g., chemical state, molecular form, or physical properties). The principal disadvantage of the method is that it

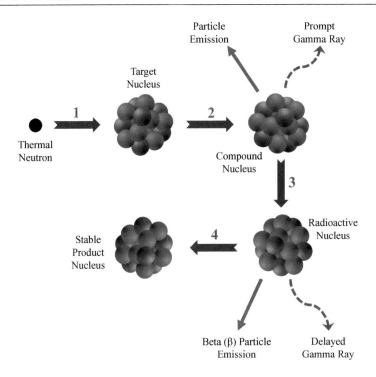

FIGURE 12.32 The processes involved in neutron activation analysis: (1) irradiation of the nucleus with a low-energy thermal neutron, (2) absorption of the thermal neutron into the target nucleus, (3) decay with the immediate release of a gamma ray to form a radioactive nucleus, and (4) radioactive decay to emit a second gamma ray and a beta particle – an electron – to form a stable nucleus.

Source: Retrieved from Wikimedia Commons; used per Creative Commons Attribution.

requires a source of thermal neutrons, and this usually means access to a nuclear reactor, but this is becoming more readily available.

12.3.10 Uses of Neutron Activation Analysis in Forensic Science

NAA analysis has been used in a variety of forensic cases, primarily when only very small or rare samples are available, to detect extremely low concentrations of trace elements, or when non-destructive analysis is required.

One forensic application of NAA has been in the identification of explosives. By analyzing the trace components of samples taken after an explosion, NAA has been shown to be a valuable tool in tracking the source of the explosive material back to the original manufacturer. It can also be used in tracking explosive materials found prior to their detonation.

NAA has been used to examine the ultra-trace elemental compositions of hair, body tissues, soils, paints, plastics, and glass samples. Recent work has also been done on bone samples of unidentified people with the idea that the trace elemental composition found in the bones themselves may lead to the geographic region where the person lived, since different places on the Earth have different trace element compositions. Food grown and consumed in these areas would be expected to "imprint" their trace elemental composition within the bone, forming a type of geographic "fingerprint" of where the person lived. Measuring this trace elemental composition of the bone sample and comparing it with known geographic trace levels could be used to support the matching of a person with a specific locale where they had lived for a period of time.

BOX 12.6   "MAN WITH THE GOLDEN HELMET": BUT WHO PAINTED IT?

For decades, the painting in a museum in Berlin called the "Man with the Golden Helmet" represented the epitome of Rembrandt and was one of the pillars of the museum. However, within art circles, experts debated whether it was really the work of Rembrandt. There were some unusual features of the work that helped fuel this debate. Recently, the Rembrandt Project in the Netherlands examined the painting using neutron activation analysis. The results have strongly suggested that the work is not by the hand of Rembrandt but rather by an unknown contemporary of his.

FIGURE 12.33 *Man with the Golden Helmet*, attributed to Rembrandt van Rijn (1606–1669).

Source: Retrieved from Wikimedia Commons; used per Creative Commons Attribution.

NAA has an important place in forensic examinations of rare works of art. It provides non-destructive testing for ultra-trace elemental compositions that can be used to support or refute a claim of authenticity of a work of art. How many other great works that we've attributed to the masters are really by other artists? Only time and analytical chemistry may tell.

12.3.11 Auger, ESCA, and Other Related Forms of Atomic Spectroscopy

There are many other forms of atomic spectroscopy that have not yet made a significant impact in forensic science, but their potential remains to provide information as future needs develop. These forms of spectroscopy are typically conceptually similar to the analyses that we've already discussed. The general process for many of these methods involves a particle, such as an electron, colliding with an inner electron of an atom in the sample to knock it away. The higher-level electrons then cascade down to emit characteristic wavelengths of light or an energetic particle that provides an identification of the element present in the sample.

For example, in Auger spectroscopy, a beam of electrons is aimed at a sample. An electron from the beam can collide with an inner electron in a target atom to excite it to a higher energy level but not enough energy to strip it entirely away from the atom. Once in this state, however, the electron can fall back to the ground state and, in the process, provide enough energy to emit another electron from the atom with a characteristic energy. Information, such as elemental composition at different depths from the surface of the sample, can be readily determined, as shown in Figure 12.34.

ESCA spectroscopy – or Electron Spectroscopy for Chemical Analysis – is similar to the Auger process in some ways. In the ESCA technique, high-energy photons (rather than electrons) are aimed at the sample and provide enough energy to knock an inner electron away from the atom. The energy of this ejected electron is then analyzed, as in Auger spectroscopy, and similar chemical information can be gained about the compound.

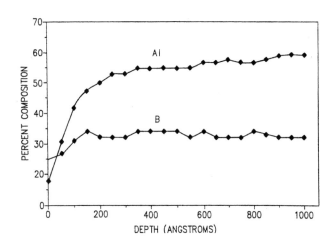

FIGURE 12.34 Auger depth profile of an aluminum boride thin film on glass.

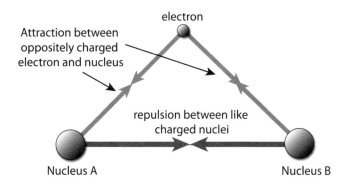

FIGURE 12.35 Electron-nuclear attractions and nuclear-nuclear repulsions in the hydrogen atom.

12.4 MOLECULAR SPECTROSCOPY

12.4.1 Introduction: Basic Quantum Mechanics for Molecules

So far, we have focused on the interactions of individual atoms with electromagnetic radiation. But light is also a very powerful tool for both determining the identity and measuring the properties of larger atomic assemblies: molecules. Molecules, in the simplest sense, are groupings of atoms that are held together in very specific arrangements to form compounds that typically have properties that are quite different from the elements that make them up. The unique properties of molecules derive largely from how the electrons from the individual atoms work together to form a more stable arrangement than that of the free atoms. In other words, there must be an energetic advantage for atoms to group themselves together into these well-defined arrangements rather than existing solely as separate, unconnected atoms.

The energy holding atoms together as molecules can be thought of as a balancing act between the attractive forces of differently charged objects with the repulsive forces of like-charged objects. We know that a positive charge is attracted by a negative charge while two positive charges repel each other. Therefore, when a negatively charged electron is placed between two positively charged nuclei, as shown in Figure 12.35, each nucleus is strongly attracted to the negatively charged electron. The net result of this attraction is that the two nuclei are themselves pulled together by the electron that they share in common. The two nuclei are drawn toward each other until the repulsive force between these like-charged nuclei becomes too great to allow them to approach each other any closer. The result is that the unit of the two nuclei and the electron form a tightly bound trio that is lower in energy than

if they were simply free atoms, thereby providing the driving force for making a stable molecule. In a molecule made up of many atoms, there can be many of these types of interactions holding the entire assembly together in a carefully balanced network.

Knowledge of the behavior of the electrons in molecules, therefore, is the key to understanding molecular properties, including how they interact with light. The electrons, in turn, can be best understood by the same quantum mechanical ideas that we developed in Section 12.2 for individual atoms.

Consider, for a moment, the simplest of all molecules – hydrogen (H_2). From quantum mechanics, we know that the electrons in the two hydrogen atoms can be considered as *waves* – we call these wave descriptions of electrons in atoms *orbitals*. Each possible orbital of an atom is similar to a different standing wave possibility in the jump rope analogy presented previously in Figure 12.14.

Waves can be added together, just as ripples on a pond add when they run into each other. Waves can add by lining up the crest of one wave with the crest of another to reinforce each other and form a larger wave, called in-phase or constructive interference, as illustrated in Figure 12.36. Alternatively, waves can add together by placing the crest of one wave directly on top of the trough, or lowest point, of a second wave. When this happens, the waves destructively interfere with each other and effectively cancel each other out (Figure 12.36).

As with all waves, when two electron waves (orbitals) are brought together, they can overlap to add together as normal waves do: constructively or destructively. If we start with two completely isolated hydrogen atoms that are far apart from each other and then bring them together, the electron waves will begin to overlap, as shown in Figure 12.37. When the waves overlap, they can add constructively or destructively to form a new composite wave. What this means for molecule formation is that, if the waves add constructively, the electron will spend more of its time *between* the two nuclei (the place where the waves reinforce each other), pulling the nuclei toward each other to hold the atoms of the molecule together by a *chemical bond*. If the waves add destructively, the electrons are pushed *away* from the space between the two nuclei and out to the far "edges" of the atoms – exposing the two nuclei to their mutually repulsive like-charges and forcing them apart. This is

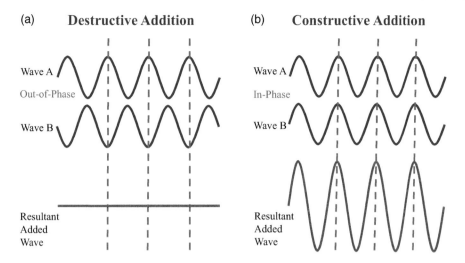

FIGURE 12.36 Addition of Waves: The addition of two waves, *A* and *B*, together can be in-phase, or constructively added, (b) or out-of-phase, destructively added (a).

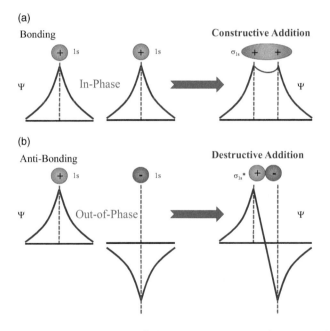

FIGURE 12.37 Addition of electron waves (orbitals): Waves of two individual hydrogen atoms (a) can be added together constructively to reinforce each other (top right) or destructively to cancel each other where they overlap (bottom right) to form the hydrogen molecule, H_2. Electrons placed in the resulting constructively formed molecular wave (orbital) hold the molecule together while electrons in the destructively added wave push the molecule apart. The top shows the bonding orbital where the electron resides more between the two atoms; (b) the anti-bonding arrangement where the electron spends more of its time away from the space between the nuclei, leading to an arrangement where the nuclei repel each other.

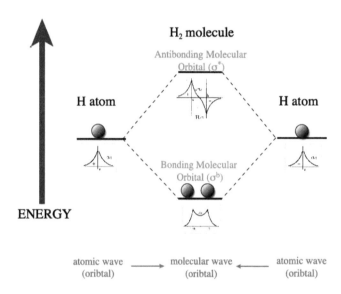

FIGURE 12.38 The electron waves of two hydrogen atoms can come together to form a bonding (lower energy) or an antibonding (higher energy) arrangement.

called an *antibonding* arrangement or orbital (usually denoted with an asterisk "*" next to the name of the new antibonding waves). It is called antibonding since it pushes the atoms away from each other and is the conceptual opposite of the bonding arrangement. These two types of bonding environments are

shown in Figure 12.37. When the two H atomic waves, or orbitals, are added together, the resulting new waves are no longer just atomic orbitals but extend their wave features over more than one atom and are, therefore, called *molecular orbitals*.

Energetically, the two possible arrangements, bonding and antibonding molecular orbitals, play the defining role in determining how molecules behave and even what molecules can form in the first place. The bonding arrangement, where the waves reinforce each other and draw the atoms closer together, is *lower* in energy than when they destructively add, causing the nuclei to repel each other. This is demonstrated in Figure 12.38, where the waves for the hydrogen atom's electrons are shown at each side of the diagram, and the waves (orbitals) for the newly formed H_2 molecule are depicted in the middle of the diagram. Since each hydrogen atom has just one electron, the hydrogen molecule (H_2) contains a total of two electrons. These two electrons completely occupy the lowest bonding molecular orbital in the H_2 molecule; quantum mechanics dictates that each molecular orbital can contain a maximum of only two electrons. Notice that the two electrons in the H_2 molecule, depicted in the center of Figure 12.38, are at a *lower* energy than their starting positions in the two isolated hydrogen atoms (located at the sides of the figure).

As can be imagined, there are many ways and orientations in which atoms can come together to form chemical bonding and antibonding arrangements that produce stable molecules. Quantum mechanics, however, defines the rules as to exactly how this can happen and what types of new molecular orbitals can be formed. In the very simple H_2 molecule, there are only two possibilities – the two molecular orbitals shown in Figures 12.37 and 12.38: bonding (denoted σ^b) and antibonding (denoted σ^*) orbitals. Each of these molecular orbitals has its own unique energy level, quantized exactly as are the energy levels in atoms with only certain allowed, fixed energy levels. As molecules become more complex, the same basic ideas hold true except that there are many more possibilities of how the atomic waves (orbitals) can add together, giving rise to many molecular orbitals, each with its own quantized energy levels. Electrons fill these possible molecular orbitals from the lowest energy to the highest energy, just as a drinking glass fills with water from the bottom to the top. In Figure 12.38, the two electrons in H_2 fill the lowest energy bonding molecular orbital, the H_2 molecule's ground state (labeled σ^b – "b" for bonding). Even going to a slightly more complex molecule, such as carbon monoxide (CO), significantly increases the complexity of the types and number of molecular orbitals that can be formed, as illustrated in Figure 12.39, but the process of forming new molecular orbitals and filling them with electrons is identical

to that used for H_2. In CO, the total number of electrons also fills the molecular bonding orbitals formed from the individual atomic waves (orbitals) from the lowest energy to higher energy.

Just as in atoms, electrons residing in the orbitals of a molecule can absorb a photon of light and become excited to a higher energy level. This idea is the basis of molecular spectroscopy; molecules with electrons in quantized energy levels (molecular orbitals) can absorb or emit light to move between these levels. By measuring the wavelength and intensity of these transitions, we can learn much about the presence and quantity of specific molecules contained within an unknown sample.

12.4.2 Ultraviolet-Visible Spectroscopy (UV-vis)

The part of the electromagnetic spectrum encompassing the ultraviolet and visible regions (between about 150 and 750 nm) contains just the right amount of energy to typically move electrons between energy levels within molecules. For this reason, UV-visible spectrometry is often referred to as electronic spectroscopy. Electrons are excited from a lower level, most often the ground state, to a higher-level energy through the absorption of a photon, as shown in Figure 12.40. Similarly, molecules may emit a photon when they fall down from a higher energy level to a lower one, similar to atomic emission spectroscopy. Usually, in UV-visible spectroscopy, electrons move between only a few orbitals, most often between the highest energy molecular orbitals occupied with electrons (labeled "bonding" in Figure 12.40) and the lowest energy unoccupied (empty) molecular orbitals (labeled as "antibonding").

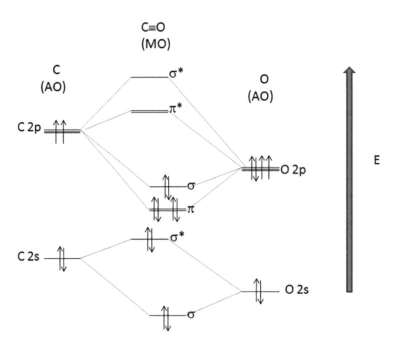

FIGURE 12.39 Molecular orbital diagram for the carbon monoxide molecule (CO).

Source: Used per Creative Commons Share-Alike 3.0 Unported, Author: Jcwf.

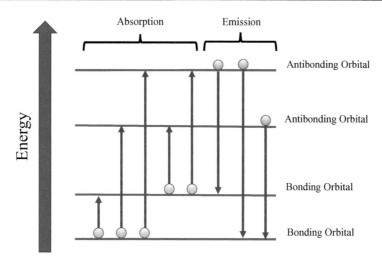

FIGURE 12.40   Molecular orbitals and possible UV-visible transitions for a simple organic molecule.

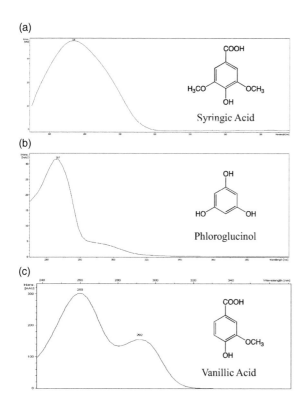

FIGURE 12.41   UV-visible spectra for several organic compounds: syringic acid, phloroglucinol, and vanillic acid.

Source: (a,b) Used per Creative Commons Attribution-Share Alike 3.0 Unported. User: NotWith; (c) Creative Commons Attribution-Share Alike 3.0 Unported, Author: Nono64.

When photons shine on a molecule with energy that exactly matches the difference between two energy levels within the molecule, the photon can be absorbed. A spectrometer measures the wavelength of the light where this absorption occurs along with how much light is absorbed. These measurements provide information for the identification of the molecule. The UV-visible spectra for some common organic molecules are shown in Figure 12.41. The wavelengths and intensities of the peaks in the spectrum help tell what and how much of the chemical is in the sample.

Organic molecules, such as those made by living organisms or the vast majority of the drugs on the market today, are often considered spectroscopically as composed of a collection of special features called *functional groups*. For example, some organic molecules contain an OH group, called an alcohol functional group, attached to the molecular framework, such as CH_3CH_2OH (ethanol). The presence of this OH group imparts certain chemical and physical properties to the molecule. Other organic molecules may contain a bromine atom or a C=O unit as a functional group that provides different chemical features. There are dozens of these special functional groups that are routinely encountered in organic chemistry. When present, these functional groups give their own special "signatures" in spectroscopy and provide "handles" for the identification of an unknown substance. For example, organic bromide compounds absorb light at around 205 nm while a C=O group may absorb at ~290 nm. Identifying the presence of these functional groups in a molecule through spectroscopy helps determine the molecule's identity. Additionally, measuring the amount of light absorbed by these functional groups gives the amount of the substance present, information that is needed in drug assays.

Visible spectroscopy is particularly important in forensic settings for quantifying the color of an object, such as a paint chip, clothing, tinted glass, and many other forms of colored evidence. It is one thing to say that an object appears red, but it may be something more useful forensically to say that the object absorbs light at 510 nm, separating it from another red object that absorbs at 520 nm. Our eyes perceive color as the wavelength of light scattered or reflected from an object *but not absorbed* by the object. When white light shines on an object, molecules within it may absorb some of the wavelengths of the light, effectively removing these wavelengths from the beam. The remainder of the wavelengths pass through the object unchanged and can be reflected into our eyes to be perceived as color. For example, if white light shines on a leaf, pigment

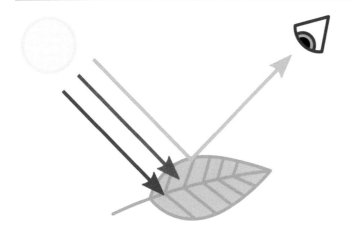

FIGURE 12.42 Absorption of blue and red light from the sun but not green light makes the leaf appear green to our eyes.

Source: Used per Creative Commons Attribution-Share Alike 4.0 International; Author: Nefronus.

molecules in the leaf absorb the red and blue light but *not* the green wavelengths (Figure 12.42). The green light is then reflected off the leaf's surface, and we perceive the color of the leaf as green. The perceived color is the *complementary color* of that which is absorbed. For example, using Figure 12.43, if green light is absorbed by an object, the complementary color of green

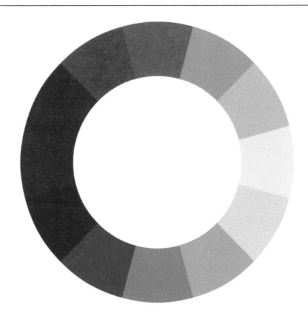

FIGURE 12.43 Complimentary colors: when white light passes through a substance, it can absorb certain characteristic wavelengths of the light – the complimentary colored light not absorbed will pass through to be perceived as color.

Source: Retrieved from Wikimedia Commons; used per Creative Commons Attribution.

BOX 12.7   THE MASTER'S TOUCH … OR SOMEONE ELSE'S?

In the world of fine art, the history of a painting or sculpture is important, referred to as provenance. Spectroscopy can be used not only to distinguish a fake from the real article, but it can also reveal where and how people have "touched up" the work to enhance its value, aesthetic appeal, or repair damage.

For example, the painting shown in Figure 12.44, entitled "The Virgin and Child," was painted by Dirck Bouts (1410/1420–1475). The photograph, shown at left, displays how the painting appears under normal visible light illumination. Using ultraviolet illumination, however, dark spots are easily seen on the woman's face (right). These spots come from places where the painting has been retouched. Knowing this can help restorers return the work to its original state.

FIGURE 12.44 *The Virgin and Child*, painted by Dirck Bouts (1410/1420–1475).

Source: Courtesy of ACE by permission.

is red (opposite green on the color wheel) and red will be the observed color of the object. [Note: this conceptual process is different from mixing paints or inks to make colors, see Chapter 14.] Obviously, this information has important uses in forensic science in the identification/matching of paint samples, clothing, and pigments – anything that appears colored. Pigments, dyes, and other color-absorbing materials will be presented in more detail in Chapter 14, but the color analysis of these important forms of forensic evidence relies on UV-visible spectroscopy.

12.4.3 Infrared Spectroscopy (IR)

Infrared spectroscopy, unlike most of the other forms of spectroscopy that we've discussed, does not deal with the transitions of electrons between large energy levels within atoms or molecules. Infrared radiation, with longer wavelengths than visible light, does not contain enough energy to cause electronic transitions to occur. Instead, infrared radiation only has enough energy to excite specific quantized vibrations within the molecule.

Molecules are held together by bonds between the atoms, as described previously. In a very simple sense, these bonds may be considered as similar to tiny springs attached holding the two bonded atoms together. These atoms can then vibrate through the spring's action. The amount of energy needed to cause these vibrations depends on the strength of the spring, or actually the chemical bond; the stronger the bond, the more energy that is needed to cause the vibration to occur. This is similar to comparing the energy needed to compress a very weak spring from a watch with a spring from a truck's suspension; it's relatively easy to compress the weak spring but very difficult to move the truck spring (Figure 12.45). The strength of a chemical bond depends on several factors, such as the identity of the two atoms involved, the number of electrons they share between them, the types of bonding connections to other atoms, the three-dimensional shape of the molecule, and others. These factors all contribute to making different chemical bonds vibrate with a wide range of allowed energies.

The vibrational energies found within molecules are quantized, just as electronic levels are quantized. Since vibrational energies are small with respect to the electronic energy levels, however, each electronic level contains a number of quantized vibrational energy levels. If a photon of light has exactly the right amount of energy to excite the molecule to a higher-energy vibration, then the photon will be absorbed.

As it turns out, quantum mechanics dictates what types of vibrations are allowed for a molecule and what energy is required to cause a vibration to occur. Besides receiving the right energy, in order for a vibration to be "allowed" (and absorb light energy), there must also be a change in the electronic "center of charge" of the molecule when the vibration occurs, something like a change in the "center of gravity" for an object but with an electronic charge instead. For example, consider the simple molecule carbon dioxide (CO_2). CO_2 is a linear molecule, as shown in Figure 12.46, that has three possible ways in which it can vibrate. The first vibration, called a symmetric stretch (Figure 12.46a), has the two outer oxygen atoms moving in and out at the same time; both move in together and both move out together. When this happens, there

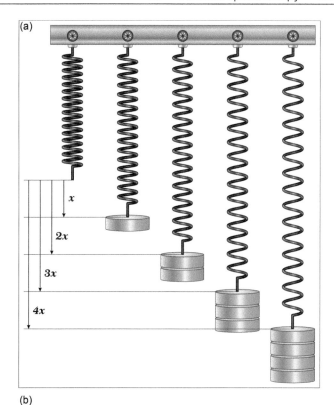

FIGURE 12.45 Different sized springs: (a) It's far easier to compress a smaller spring than a larger spring. (b) Different amounts of energy are needed to cause atoms connected by a chemical bond to vibrate by compression and expansion along the direction of the bond.

Source: Shutterstock and Retrieved from Wikimedia Commons; used per Creative Commons Attribution.

is no change in the electronic center of gravity of the molecule and so it cannot absorb light. The second vibration, shown in Figure 12.46b, is called an asymmetric stretch; one oxygen atom moves in closer to the central carbon atom while at the same instant the other oxygen atom moves farther away. There *is* a change in the electronic center of gravity for this vibration so infrared light is absorbed. The final vibration, depicted in Figure 12.46c, is actually made up of two vibrations that are exactly the same but simply rotated by 90° (only one is shown). This type of vibration, called a bending mode, also can absorb infrared light. Thus, two out of the three different vibrations possible for CO_2 can absorb IR light. As expected, the infrared spectrum for CO_2, shown in Figure 12.47, displays just two absorptions – one for each of the "allowed" vibrations of the molecule.

CO_2 is indeed a very simple molecule but serves to illustrate the way vibrational spectroscopy works at the molecular level. Most molecules of interest are much more complicated, containing dozens or even hundreds of atoms held together in

(a)

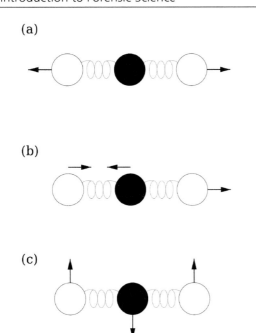

(b)

(c)

FIGURE 12.46 Ways that the CO_2 molecule can vibrate, called vibrational modes.

Source: Retrieved from Wikimedia Commons; used per Creative Commons Attribution.

(a)

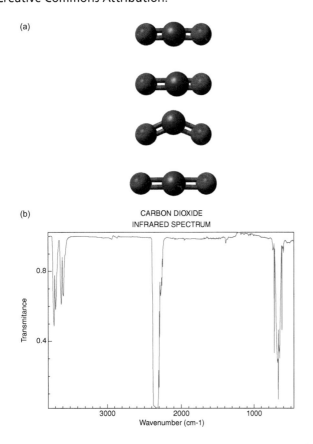

(b) CARBON DIOXIDE
INFRARED SPECTRUM

FIGURE 12.47 (a) Allowed vibrational movements (modes) for CO_2 and (b) the Infrared spectrum for CO_2 shows the two active vibrational modes that are in the IR and can absorb light.

Source: NIST and Retrieved from Wikimedia Commons; used per Creative Commons Attribution.

complex shapes that influence how they can vibrate and absorb infrared light. This can result in very complicated spectra. But it is this very complexity that makes infrared spectroscopy so useful in identifying compounds. Each different compound gives rise to a unique spectrum all its own, such as that shown in Figure 12.48 for *n*-propanol, a simple organic alcohol. This complexity works something like a fingerprint. If a fingerprint contained only one or two lines, it wouldn't be very useful, but since it contains hundreds of lines with many features, it is very useful in identifying a person. Infrared spectroscopy is similar in that its complexity allows us to unambiguously distinguish one compound from another.

BOX 12.8   STRANGE CONVENTIONS?

In infrared spectroscopy, the spectra are not usually shown in graphs of light absorbed or emitted versus the wavelength (λ), as in other forms of spectroscopy. Instead, the wavelength is plotted as $1/\lambda$ as "reciprocal centimeters" (cm^{-1}):

$$cm^{-1} = \frac{1}{\lambda}$$

Also, typical IR spectra do not plot the amount of light absorbed by the sample but rather show the percent of light that passes through the sample, called percent transmittance. (Don't blame me, I didn't make this up!)

Some combinations of atoms are so common in organic chemistry, and give rise to infrared absorptions at specific wavelengths that they are diagnostic of the presence or absence of a particular functional group. For example, finding an IR absorption at 1,700 cm^{-1} is a very strong indicator that a C=O group is present in the molecule, thereby eliminating all possible molecules except those that contain this grouping. Table 12.2 presents just a few infrared absorptions that are diagnostic for specific organic functional groups.

The region of the infrared spectrum, from about 500 to 1,500 cm^{-1}, is usually very complicated and is often referred to

TABLE 12.2 Table correlating selected infrared absorption frequencies with organic functional groups

FREQUENCY (CM⁻¹)	VIBRATIONAL MODE	ORGANIC FUNCTIONAL GROUP
3,300–3,500 cm⁻¹	N–H stretch	Amines
3,200–3,500 cm⁻¹	O–H stretch	Alcohols
3,000–3,100 cm⁻¹	C–H stretch	Alkenes
2,850–3,000 cm⁻¹	C–H stretch	Alkanes
2,260–2,222 cm⁻¹	C≡N stretch	Cyanides, nitriles
2,100–2,200 cm⁻¹	C≡C stretch	Alkynes
2,000–1,650 cm⁻¹	C–H bending	Aromatics
1,665–1,760 cm⁻¹	C=O stretch	Ketones, aldehydes, esters, acids
1,640–1,680 cm⁻¹	C=C stretch	Alkenes
1,550–1,500 cm⁻¹	N–O stretch	Nitro-compounds

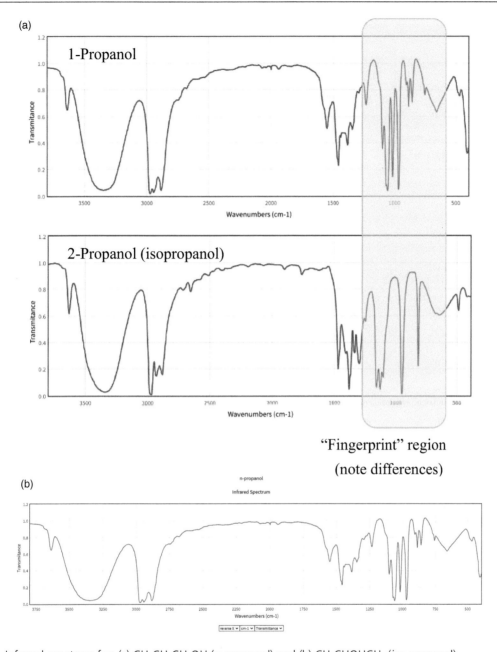

(a)

1-Propanol

2-Propanol (isopropanol)

"Fingerprint" region
(note differences)

(b)

n-propanol

Infrared Spectrum

FIGURE 12.48   Infrared spectrum for: (a) $CH_3CH_2CH_2OH$ (*n*-propanol) and (b) $CH_3CHOHCH_3$ (*iso*-propanol).

Sourced: (a) Use per Creative Commons Attribution 2.0 Generic. User: ChiralJon. (b) US Secretary of Commerce; NIST.

as the "fingerprint" region. This region is especially important since even small modifications in the structure of a compound will result in noticeable changes in the absorptions of this region. For example, shown in Figure 12.48 are the IR spectra for two isomers of C_3H_8O. While parts of the spectra are very similar, the fingerprint region for each isomer is quite different, allowing us to quickly and easily distinguish between the two compounds.

12.4.4 Forensic Applications of Infrared Spectroscopy

Infrared spectroscopy is an important tool for forensic chemical analysis, and a few of these uses include:

- **Alcohol Analysis**: Many current field breath-alcohol analyzers are based on measuring the infrared wavelengths absorbed by ethyl alcohol. The amount of IR light absorption provides a direct measurement of the amount of alcohol in someone's breath, leading to a breath-alcohol concentration (BAC) determination (Chapter 13). One manufacturer of such an analyzer reports that "IR (spectro)photometry represents the most significant advancement in IR breath analysis in 20 years … [the] technology is virtually non-sensitive to any potentially interfering substance in the breath of a subject" (Figure 12.49).

- **Identification and Verification of Unknown Compounds**: IR spectra provide key analytical data for the identification and verification of unknown compounds by comparing the measured spectra of an unknown with databases containing the spectra of tens of thousands of known compounds. This can be accomplished very rapidly through computer-based searching techniques. The method provides rapid identification for drugs, poisons, pollutants, and other types of organic samples.
- **Fiber Analysis**: Today, many fibers are made of polymers of organic compounds. IR spectroscopy provides the best method for identifying the chemical composition of these polymeric materials.
- **Paint and Ink Analysis**: Individual layers of paint can be analyzed by IR spectroscopy to identify the pigments, dyes, and binders in the sample through comparison with known reference samples. Similarly, inks, dyes, and other related materials can be identified using IR.

12.4.5 Microwave, Terahertz, X-Ray, and Related Spectroscopies

Other forms of molecular spectroscopy are gaining application in specialized areas of forensic analysis.

Microwave spectroscopy primarily measures the energy necessary to rotate molecules. These quantized rotational energy levels are present in each vibrational level of a molecule, just as many vibrational levels exist on each electronic level. However, these rotational energy levels are very close together and require even less energy to excite than infrared vibrational activity. Thus far, microwave spectroscopy has not made much of an impact in forensic analysis.

At the longer wavelength end of the spectrum, beyond the infrared but shorter than the microwave region, is terahertz radiation (usually between 0.1 and 10 mm). The main application of terahertz spectroscopy has been in imaging people for the detection of concealed weapons, such as at airports, border crossings and similar security situations, as shown in Figure 12.50. Terahertz radiation can easily pass through clothing, wood, plastic, and ceramics, among others. However, they are blocked by metal, water, and certain chemicals of particular interest, such as explosives. Terahertz radiation has been able to "see" inside sealed envelopes, packages, and through clothing to not only detect but also to help identify the contents. There is still a great deal of work needed to make this technology practical, including addressing public concern about "invasion of privacy" rights.

FIGURE 12.49 An infrared-based alcohol breath analysis instrument for field use.

Source: Used per Creative Commons Attribution-Share Alike 4.0 International; User: Keith Nothacker.

FIGURE 12.50 A terahertz (THz) image of suspect showing the presence of a concealed weapon in the suspect's pocket.

Source: NIST.

Finally, X-rays have also been used to identify materials of interest. However, this technique has already been presented in detail.

12.5 MASS SPECTROMETRY: THE WORKHORSE OF FORENSIC ANALYSIS

12.5.1 Introduction to Mass Spectrometry (MS)

Mass spectrometry has developed into one of the most important tools available to the forensic chemist today for discovering chemical information about a sample. The method is usually very fast, convenient, reliable, unambiguous, and readily available in forensic laboratories, making it the current "gold standard" of forensic molecular identification.

The basic principles of mass spectrometry are different from the types of spectroscopies that have been discussed already. Mass spectrometry (MS) does *not* rely upon measuring the energy changes that occur when an atom or molecule moves between two energy states. Instead, mass spectrometry uniquely identifies molecules both based on their molecular masses, the sum of the atomic weights of the individual atoms making up the molecule, and how molecules uniquely break into fragments.

The underlying concepts of mass spectrometry are rather straightforward. The process begins by putting the molecule of interest into the vapor phase in a very good vacuum system.

A beam of high-energy electrons is then focused directly on the target molecule, stripping off an electron through collisions between electrons in the beam and those in the molecule (called electron impact ionization, EI). When a negatively charged electron is removed from a neutral molecule in this way, the result is the formation of a positively charged molecule, called an ion, that can then be accelerated down an evacuated tube simply by applying an electrical voltage along the length of the tube, as shown in Figure 12.51. As these charged molecular ions are flying down the tube, they pass through a strong magnetic field that serves to deflect their path from a straight line into a curved trajectory. The degree of deflection of the ions depends upon how "heavy" they are. Finally, the deflected molecules collide with a detector placed at the end of the tube at positions dependent on their masses, shown schematically in Figure 12.52.

The amount of deflection from a straight-line trajectory that a charged molecule displays depends on several factors, including the strength of the magnet, the mass and charge of the molecule, and the velocity of the molecule as it flies down the tube. If all these factors are kept constant *except* the mass of the molecule, we can relate the amount of deflection observed for a molecule directly to its mass. A very simple analogy can help to illustrate this concept. Consider, for instance, a bowling ball and a feather that are somehow propelled down a bowling alley at the same speed (Figure 12.53a). Halfway down the alley, a fan is set up blowing across the lane (perpendicular to the direction that the objects are traveling). When the rather massive bowling ball passes by the fan, it is not deflected from its straight-line course very much at all and proceeds to the end of the lane largely along its original trajectory. In contrast, however, when the light feather passes by the fan, its trajectory is changed quite considerably, and it is deflected far from

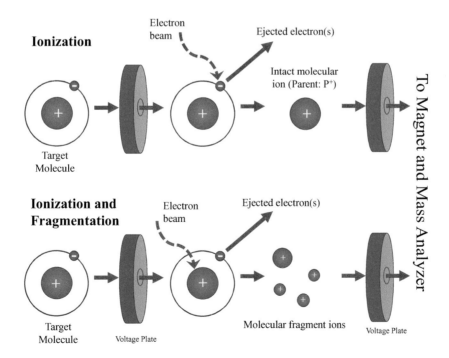

FIGURE 12.51 Ionization and acceleration of molecules and fragments in a mass spectrometer.

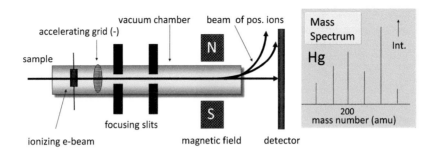

FIGURE 12.52   Simplified arrangement of a magnetic mass spectrometer.

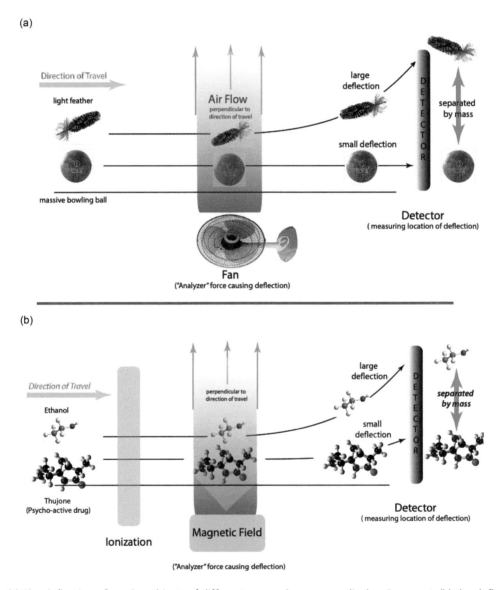

FIGURE 12.53   (a) The deflection of moving objects of different masses by a perpendicular air current; (b) the deflection of moving, charged molecules of different masses by a perpendicular magnetic field.

its original course. In other words, for objects moving down the bowling alley according to this arrangement, the amount of deflection from their original straight-line path depends on how heavy the object is: the more massive an object, the less it is deflected, while the lighter the object, the more deflection will be observed. If we conceptually replace the bowling ball and feather with molecules of different masses Figure 12.53b,

and replace the fan with a strong magnetic field positioned across the direction of the molecule's travel, a very similar effect is observed at the molecular scale. In the figure, the rather light (small) ethanol molecule (C_2H_6O) is deflected a great deal from its straight-line course, while the roughly five times heavier thujone molecule ($C_{10}H_{16}O$, a psychoactive drug) is deflected to a far smaller degree. The net result is that these

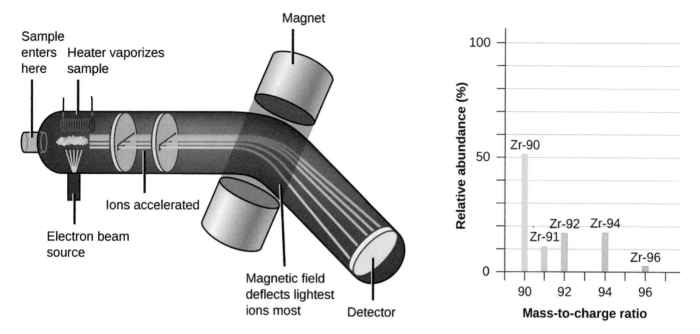

FIGURE 12.54 Schematic diagram of how a magnetic mass spectrometer operates: (1) molecules are placed into an evacuated tube, (2) heated gently to put them into the gas phase, (3) the molecules are ionized – an electron is removed – through collisions with other electrons from a high-energy electron beam and the positively charged molecules are (4) accelerated down the tube by high-voltage plates where the molecules are separated according to their varying masses by a magnetic field before (5) finally striking a detector that records their positions.

molecules are separated by the magnetic field based on their molecular masses.

A mass spectrometer works by providing a way to move charged molecules down the length of a tube and then to deflect them to varying degrees depending on their masses. A typical mass spectrometer is shown schematically in Figure 12.54. The data from the experiment are plotted as the intensity of the detector's signal (number of molecules hitting the detector at a time) versus mass. One refinement of our picture, however, is that we do not actually measure directly the mass of the molecule but rather measure something called the *mass-to-charge ratio* instead (m/e or sometimes called m/z, where m is the mass and e or z is the charge). This is because of the interconnected relationship between mass and charge in bringing about the observed deflection ($m/e = H^2 r^2/2V$, where H is the magnetic field strength, r is the radius of the deflection, and V is the voltage used to accelerate the ions). Usually, however, this is not a problem since the experimental setup is arranged such that only a single electron is typically stripped off the molecule to give a singly charged molecule, making the charge (the "e" of m/e) equal to 1 and the measured m/e ratio actually the same as the mass of the molecule. It is possible, however, for a molecule to be double-ionized, and that would give a measured mass half of its actual mass ($m/2$), although this is not common since it's much more difficult to remove a second electron from a positively charged molecule than to remove the first electron from the neutral molecule.

Today, there are actually many types of mass spectrometers that use the principles just described but employ design variations on the theme. For example, some spectrometers employ a tiny opening in front of a small, fixed detector to

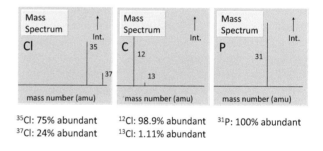

^{35}Cl: 75% abundant ^{12}Cl: 98.9% abundant ^{31}P: 100% abundant
^{37}Cl: 24% abundant ^{13}Cl: 1.11% abundant

FIGURE 12.55 Mass spectra of elemental samples of chlorine (Cl), carbon (C), and phosphorus (P).

measure one mass at a time and simply vary the magnetic field strength to bring into "focus" different masses that sweep across the detector's opening as the field changes. A similar effect can also be employed by keeping the magnetic field strength fixed but varying the accelerating voltage to sweep the mass-separated ions across the detector. Despite the dozens of design variations, they all rely on the same idea of generating ions, separating them by their masses, and detecting the ions based on their masses.

The mass spectrum for an element or molecule consists of a series of lines on a plot of intensity versus mass (amu). For example, the mass spectrum for elemental phosphorus consists of a single line at 31 amu, corresponding to the atomic weight of phosphorus (Figure 12.55). Other elements, such as chlorine and carbon, give rise to multiple lines. These lines correspond to different isotopes of the element (isotopes are atoms with the same number of protons but *different* numbers

Isotopes of Carbon

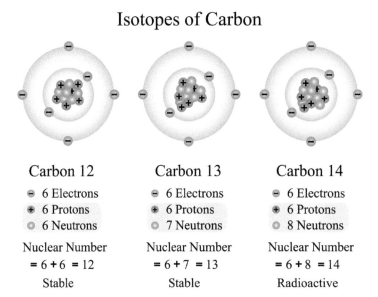

Carbon 12	Carbon 13	Carbon 14
⊖ 6 Electrons	⊖ 6 Electrons	⊖ 6 Electrons
⊕ 6 Protons	⊕ 6 Protons	⊕ 6 Protons
○ 6 Neutrons	○ 7 Neutrons	○ 8 Neutrons
Nuclear Number	Nuclear Number	Nuclear Number
= 6 + 6 = 12	= 6 + 7 = 13	= 6 + 8 = 14
Stable	Stable	Radioactive

FIGURE 12.56   Isotopes of carbon: all have six protons but have differing numbers of neutrons that lead to different masses that are observed separately in the mass spectrum.

Source: Shutterstock.com.

of neutrons), as illustrated in Figure 12.56. The height of each line (signal intensity) gives the relative amount of the various isotopes present.

If this were all the information that was obtainable from a mass spectrum, it would be useful but rather limited in scope. Fortunately, mass spectrometry provides far more information than just the molecular mass. So far, we have considered only what happens when the electron collides with a molecule and simply knocks away an electron, resulting in a charged molecule that's only missing one electron – otherwise, the molecule is completely intact and the mass of the charged molecule and the starting molecule are essentially the same. This charged, but otherwise intact molecule, is called the *molecular or parent ion* (P^+). It turns out, however, that this is far too limiting a picture of what actually happens during the mass spectral experiment.

When the electron beam hits the target molecule, besides causing the molecule to simply lose an electron, it can also fragment the molecule into a variety of smaller charged molecular pieces, called *fragment ions*. This is similar to when a cue ball is used to break the starting triangular setup in a billiards game, as shown in Figure 12.57. A wide variety of patterns of balls on the table can result from the single action of the cue ball on the original arrangement. Molecular ions, created by the energetic electrons, may also fragment into smaller positively charged "fragment" ions. For example, in the molecule methanol (grain alcohol, CH_3OH), several types of fragmentations can happen when it is hit by the electron beam. Examples of these chemical possibilities are shown in the equations below:

$$CH_3OH + e^- \text{------}> CH_3OH^{+\cdot} \text{ (molecular ion)}$$

$$CH_3OH^{+\cdot} \text{------}> CH_2{=}OH^+ + H^\cdot \text{ (fragment ions)}$$

$$CH_3OH^{+\cdot} \text{------}> CH_3^+ + OH^\cdot \text{ (fragment ions)}$$

The mass spectrum for methanol, as depicted in Figure 12.58, displays several lines, each corresponding to a particular fragment with a different mass. For example, the molecular ion, $CH_3OH^{+\cdot}$, with a mass of 32 amu, can fragment to produce several smaller fragments: $CH_2 = OH^+$ (mass of 31), HCO^+ (mass 29), and CH_3^+ (mass 15). Each of these fragments appears in the resulting mass spectrum at m/e positions corresponding to their fragment masses.

Molecules can fragment into a variety of different pieces depending on their molecular structures. As a molecule becomes more complex, so does the number of ways it can fragment. The fragmentation patterns observed in the spectrum – both the mass locations and the relative intensities of the peaks – combine to form a unique mass spectral "signature" of the compound. For example, the commonly encountered drug cocaine ($C_{17}H_{21}NO_4$) can break apart to form a variety of fragment ions (Figure 12.59). The way molecules break apart can yield relatively complex spectral patterns that would be nearly impossible to confuse with another compound, even one that is quite closely related chemically (Figure 12.60).

A typical mass spectrum can often be analyzed to unambiguously identify a particular chemical compound. Typically, several steps are employed, including: (1) identifying the parent ion (the highest mass in the spectrum, corresponding to the molecular weight of the compound), (2) looking for patterns in observed fragment ions and comparing those patterns with the molecule's structural features (e.g., a Parent$^+$ – 15 peak would indicate the loss of a CH_3 group from the molecule, a P^+ – 17 peak might suggest the presence of an OH functional group in the molecule, etc.), and (3) comparing the "fine details" of the spectrum, including the mass location and intensity of the peaks present, with the spectrum of a standard reference compound.

FIGURE 12.57   Cue ball "fragmenting" the opening arrangement of billiard balls.

Source: Shutterstock.com.

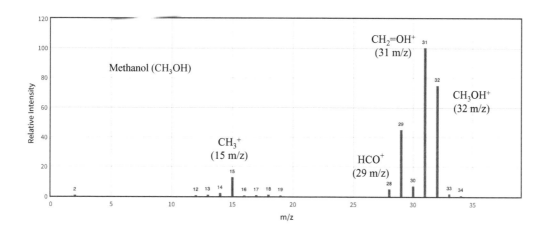

FIGURE 12.58   Fragmentation and mass spectrum of methanol (CH_3OH).

Source: NIST.

Consider, for example, the mass spectrum of *n*-octane (C_8H_{18} or $CH_3CH_2CH_2CH_2CH_2CH_2CH_2CH_3$), shown in Figure 12.60. The molecular weight of the intact molecule is 114 amu, observed as the highest peak at 114 m/e in the spectrum. The next highest peak is at 99 amu, indicating a loss of 15 amu from the P^+ peak. This can be recognized (after some practice) as arising from the loss of a methyl group (CH_3) from the molecule, expected since the structure of octane contains a CH_3 group at the "end" of the molecule. The next five highest mass peaks, at 85, 71, 57, 43, and 29 amu, are all spaced 14 amu apart – exactly the mass of a CH_2 unit. This is consistent with the structure of the octane molecule, where the "inner" CH_2 groups can be removed one-by-one to give the lower mass peaks (P^+ – CH_3CH_2 at mass 85, P^+ – $CH_3CH_2CH_2$ at mass 71, P^+ – $CH_3CH_2CH_2CH_2$ at mass 57, and so on). There are still a number of smaller peaks in the spectrum that serve as a "fingerprint" for the compound, setting it apart from all other molecules and unambiguously identifying the spectrum as belonging to *n*-octane. The details of an MS fragmentation pattern can be used to identify even very closely related compounds. For example, the two very closely related isomers of hexadecane with the same molecular formula ($C_{16}H_{34}$), as shown in Figure 12.61, display very different mass spectra.

BOX 12.9   MASS SPECTROMETRY TERMS

- **Molecular Ion**: The +1 charged ion of the entire, intact molecule, corresponding to the molecular weight of the molecule.
- **Fragment Ion**: Charged ions that are fragments of the parent molecule.
- **Base Peak**: The most intense peak in the mass spectrum.
- **Parent Peak**: The peak corresponding to the complete molecule; same as the molecular ion.
- **Mass-to-charge** (*m/z*): The measured mass as a ratio to its charge.

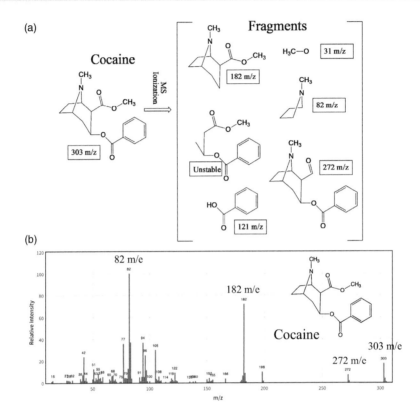

FIGURE 12.59 Several possible fragmentation paths (a) and the complete mass spectrum of cocaine (b), each line corresponding to the mass of a fragment formed.

Source: Spectrum image source: NIST.

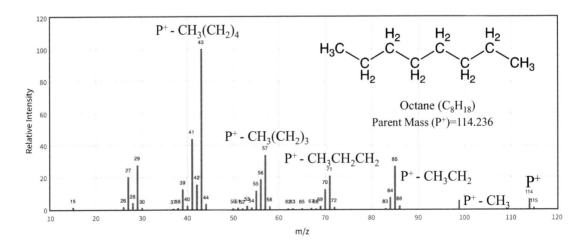

FIGURE 12.60 Mass spectrum of *n*-octane ($CH_3CH_2CH_2CH_2CH_2CH_2CH_2CH_3$).

Source: Spectrum image source: NIST.

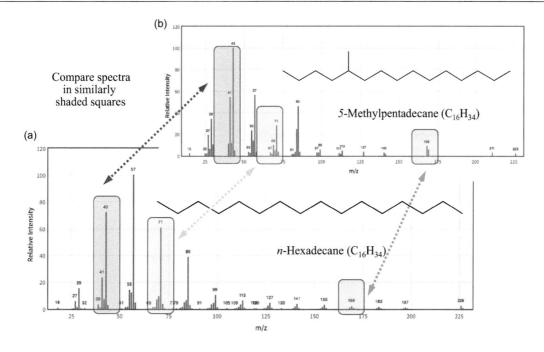

FIGURE 12.61 Mass spectra of isomeric compounds: (b) MS of *n*-hexadecane ($C_{16}H_{34}$) and (a) 5-methylpentadecane ($C_{16}H_{34}$) showing the differences in the spectra of two very closely related compounds with the same molecular formula.

Spectrum image source: NIST.

Occasionally, the parent ion of a molecule is not sufficiently stable to make it all the way to the detector. In these instances, no parent ion is observed in the spectrum, potentially complicating the interpretation of the spectrum. However, there are a variety of techniques that can help identify the total mass of the molecule even when the peak for the parent ion is not present. These include the use of gentler forms of ionization.

Fortunately for forensic work, the mass spectra of several hundred thousand compounds have been measured and entered into computer databases. By comparing the spectrum obtained from an unknown compound with those in the database, it is often possible to unambiguously identify the compound within just a few seconds. For example, Figure 12.62 shows the mass spectrum of an unknown compound and the spectra of four other compounds suspected as possibilities for the unknown. By simply comparing the spectrum of the unknown with the spectra of the four possibilities, the identity of the unknown compound is clear: caffeine.

Mass spectral data can also be used for quantitative analysis by relating the level of signal from the detector for a particular peak to the concentration of the molecule in the unknown sample. This method is commonly used for assaying the amount of drugs, poisons, and alcohol in body tissue and fluid samples.

Spectrometers currently in use are very sensitive instruments. Detecting both negative and positive ions is routinely possible, and instruments employing a variety of ionization techniques have been developed to gain spectra of even very "stubborn" compounds. For example, solids that are difficult to put into the gas phase can be heated, bombarded with fast atoms, laser irradiated, or subjected to a number of other approaches to prod them into the gas phase. In contrast, fragile molecules that would be destroyed in the electron beam can be treated more gently to reduce their complete fragmentation by ionizing other molecules first, which, in turn, gently ionize the fragile molecule (called chemical ionization). Nonetheless, all these spectrometers work on the principles already described and provide a versatile array of techniques to gain unmatched chemical and structural information about an unknown compound.

12.5.2 GC-Mass Spectrometry (GC/MS)

A mass spectrum is readily interpretable only for a single, pure compound, but as we learned in the previous chapter, forensic samples are rarely found as pure compounds. In order to analyze the composition of a mixture, the various components must first be separated from one another and then analyzed individually by the mass spectrometer. Fortunately, there are very convenient ways of accomplishing this multi-step process by linking a chromatographic system directly to a mass spectrometer. While many types of chromatography are used today for separations, the gas chromatograph-mass spectrometer duet is by far the most common, providing detailed information on complex mixtures of compounds rapidly and reliably.

Chromatography, as described in detail in Chapter 11, is used to separate the components of a mixture by taking advantage of the differing strengths of interaction between a solid material (stationary phase) and the various compounds in the

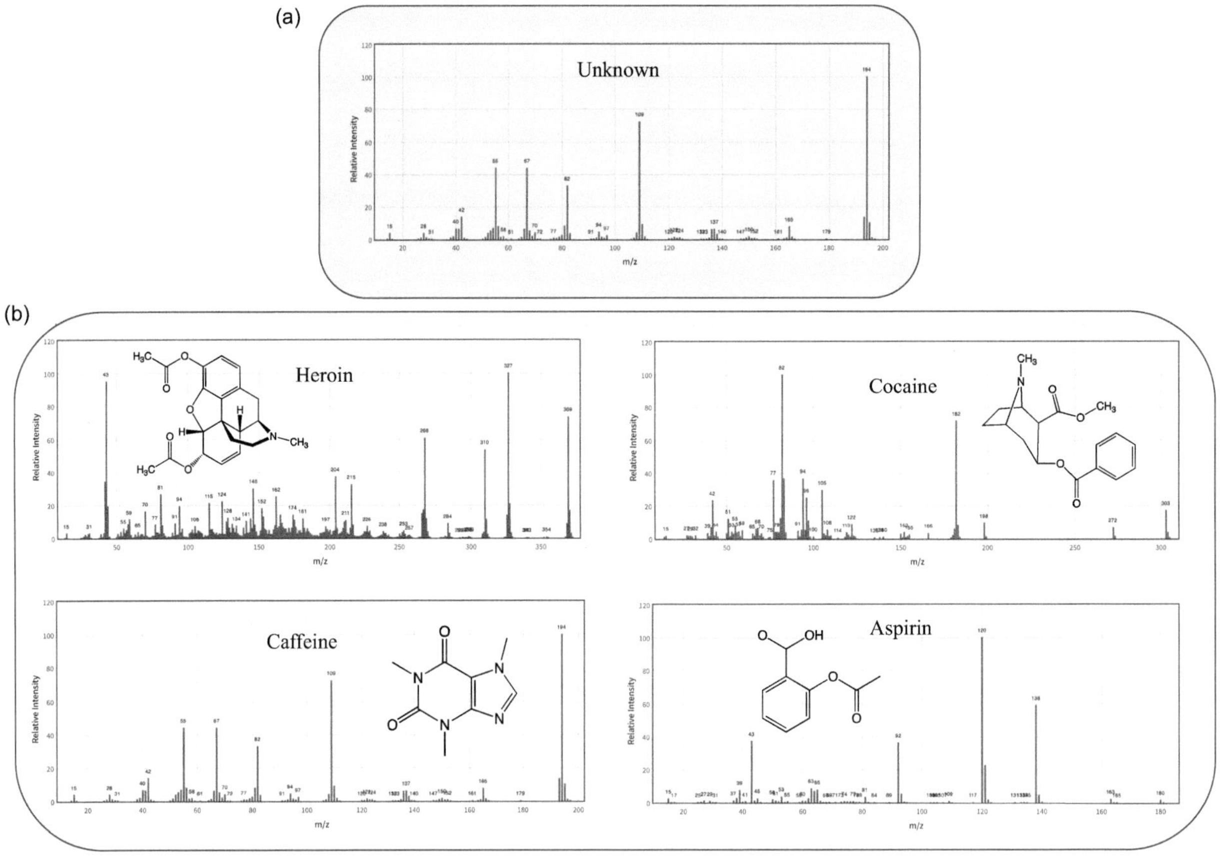

(a)

(b)

FIGURE 12.62   Mass spectrum (a) of an unknown compound and the reference mass spectra of four known substances for comparison (b). What is the identity of the top unknown sample?

Spectrum image source: NIST.

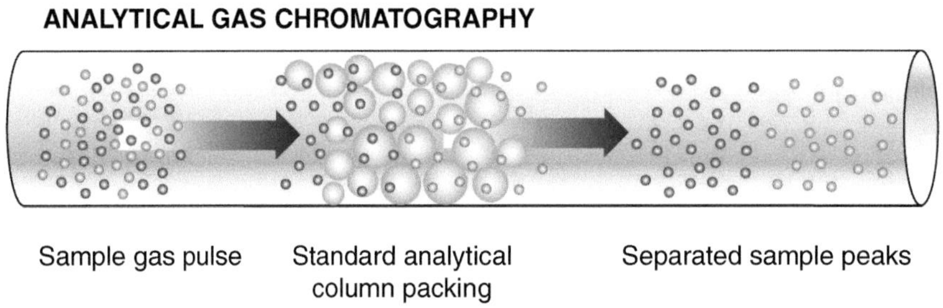

ANALYTICAL GAS CHROMATOGRAPHY

Sample gas pulse   Standard analytical   Separated sample peaks
                        column packing

FIGURE 12.63   Separation of components of a mixture using gas chromatography.

mixture that are swept along past it by a mobile phase. The greater interaction a compound has with the stationary phase, the more slowly it will progress along the tube; remember the analogy of the hornets and the honey bees with the flowerbed (Section 11.3). In gas chromatography, the mobile phase is a gas stream and the stationary phase is usually a long, very thin glass tube that may be coated on its inside with substances to enhance its interactions with certain types of molecules (e.g., coating with wax, amines, etc.). The forensic mixture is injected into the gas stream, which carries it along past the stationary phase, as shown in Figure 12.63. By the time the

components reach the end of the tube, they have been separated from each other and emerge from the end of the tube at different times, called their *retention times*. For example, complex mixtures of compounds can be quickly separated into their individual components, as shown in Figure 12.64, by using GC with each compound displaying its own distinctive retention time.

The real strength of the technique comes, however, when it is teamed directly with a mass spectrometer. In essence, the end of the GC column is hooked directly into the front end of the mass spectrometer (Figure 12.65). As each separated component

(a)

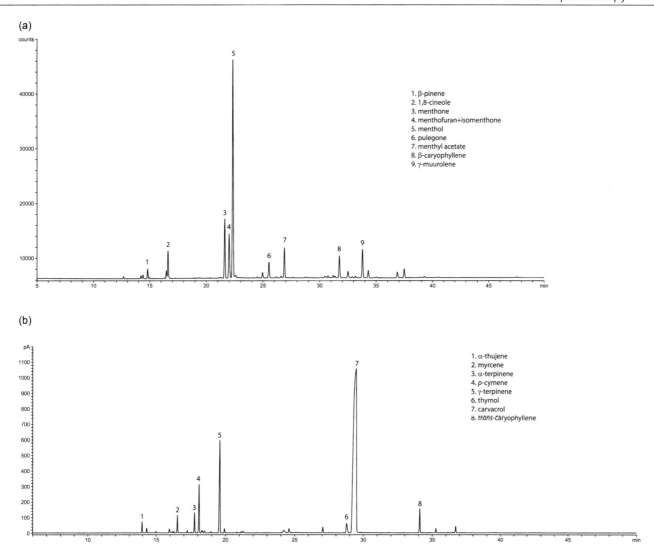

1. β-pinene
2. 1,8-cineole
3. menthone
4. menthofuran+isomenthone
5. menthol
6. pulegone
7. menthyl acetate
8. β-caryophyllene
9. γ-muurolene

(b)

1. α-thujene
2. myrcene
3. α-terpinene
4. p-cymene
5. γ-terpinene
6. thymol
7. carvacrol
8. trans-caryophyllene

FIGURE 12.64 GC plot of a complex mixture showing the separation into individual compounds of extracts of (a) peppermint (*Mentha x piperita*) and (b) oregano (*Origanum heracleoticum*). Each line represents a different chemical in the mixture.

Source: Images courtesy Shutterstock.com.

emerges from the end of the GC tube, it is immediately injected into the ionization chamber of the mass spectrometer to begin the mass analysis process. This gives rise to a separate mass spectrum for *each* pure component separated from the mixture, allowing us to identify each compound. Additionally, measuring the area under the GC peak gives us an accurate determination of how much of each compound is in the sample. This process is illustrated in Figure 12.66. The entire process can be summarized by the steps: (1) components separate by GC, (2) identify each component by MS, and (3) quantify.

The tandem chromatography-mass spectrometer arrangement has been extended to other chromatographic techniques to broaden the range of their uses. For example, some samples are difficult to put in the gas phase, such as larger molecules or biological molecules. For these types of samples, a liquid chromatographic system can be used. For example, the electrospray system, as illustrated in Figure 12.67, can be used for the analysis of very large biomolecules with molecular weights that run into the thousands.

10.5.3 Mass Spectrometry of Forensic Samples

The use of mass spectrometry, especially when coupled to a chromatographic system, is applicable to a wide array of forensic applications and is an excellent confirmatory chemical test. It would be impossible to present all the areas in which MS analysis has had a significant impact in forensic science, but a few key areas will be highlighted in this section.

GC-MS analysis is often the method of choice for the identification and quantification of drugs and various chemicals in samples. This testing may be used for integrity, background, and compliance testing in the workplace or elsewhere. This type of testing serves as a screen for monitoring drug use and usually requires just the identification of any drug or drug metabolites in body fluids or tissues that show the unauthorized use of banned materials (e.g., drugs and steroids in urine, blood, tissues, etc.). If the presence of the drug is detected, that is all the information

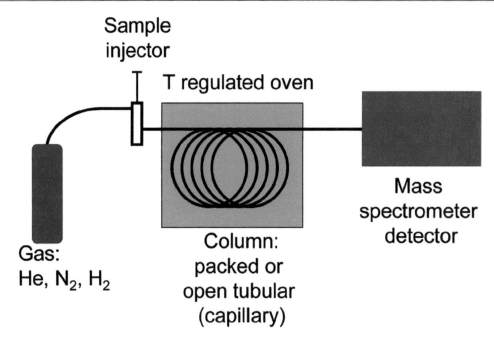

FIGURE 12.65   Arrangement of a GC-mass spectrometer.

Source: Used per Creative Commons Attribution-Share Alike 3.0 Unported. User: K. Murray (Kkmurray).

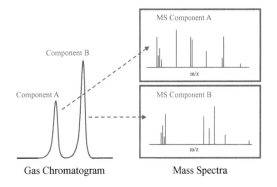

FIGURE 12.66   MS analysis of each peak in the GC as it emerges from the end of the GC column.

that is required to take action. Drug metabolites can be found in many body tissues, including in a person's hair, providing a relatively long timeline of drug use or poison administration.

Mass spectrometry-based testing is often needed to determine both the identity *and* the amount of a particular substance in a person's body. As an indispensable tool for toxicology, it is able to match spectral features among hundreds of thousands of possibilities in just seconds. For example, the GC-MS analysis of blood-alcohol and drug levels can often provide the best data in DUI and performance-modifying drug cases. Samples taken during an autopsy are also analyzed by GC-MS for the presence and levels of poisons, toxins, drugs, and biochemical markers associated with certain diseases and injuries. Clinical medical practitioners need rapid and reliable MS-based methods for determining substances in a person's body when treating a patient – and this

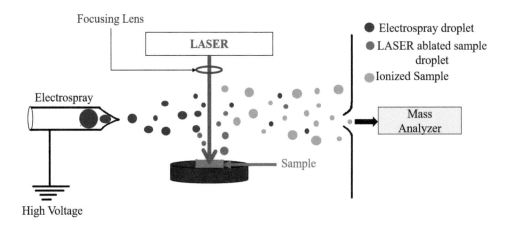

FIGURE 12.67   Electrospray MS setup and spectrum for large biomolecules.

Source: Used per Creative Commons Attribution-Share Alike 4.0 International. User: Anowar Hossain Khan.

may also involve forensic considerations, such as the actions of a chronic abuser of alcohol or drugs. Using chemical ionization, a very gentle way of ionizing a molecule, can help in rapidly screening drug samples since it results in a very prominent $P^+ + 1$ peak (one larger than the molecular ion) without very much fragmentation at all, greatly simplifying the spectrum and giving a quick idea of what drugs might be in the sample.

Mass spectral analysis is often the best analytical method for determining chemical trace levels. Environmental samples can be analyzed for pollutants and contaminants when bringing criminal actions against suspected polluters. Inks and paints, extracted from a document or automobile finish, can be analyzed to determine if the pigments are consistent with the story the suspect tells. The residue left behind at a fire can be analyzed for the presence of accelerants expected from an arson fire.

Finally, stable isotope MS analysis has also recently been gaining prominence in forensic investigations. With this method, it is possible to trace biological, mineral, and nuclear samples back to their place of origin in the world. For example, plant matter can be analyzed to determine if a marijuana sample was originally grown in California or South America. Using this approach, samples can be traced back to their geographic sources, drugs can be mapped to their points of original growth and harvest, and gunpowder residue can be traced to its manufacturer. The technique works by measuring the ratios of certain elemental isotopes in a sample. These isotopic ratios tend to vary from place to place and from manufacturer to manufacturer and can be used for comparative analysis.

An analogy of how one variant of the technique works for drug analysis is presented in Figure 12.68. Consider a jar with many jelly beans of different flavors. We'd like, however, to know how many cherry jelly beans there are in the jar but can't count them directly (this is similar to the problem of determining how much of a substance is in a person's blood or tissues). So, instead, we add ten blueberry jelly beans to the jar and mix everything up (step 1). Then, we extract a one-ounce sample of the jelly beans (step 2). We then sort and count the number of each flavor of jelly beans in the extracted ounce (step 3). In this example, we find that there are three cherry and two blueberry jelly beans in our one-once extractant, or a cherry-to-blueberry ratio of 3/2 (step 4). Then, by simple math,

1. Add a "marked" reference

2. Extract measured sample (e.g., 1 oz.)

3. Count different colors

> 3 cherry (red), 2 blueberry (blue), 2 banana (yellow), 2 watermelon (green), 1 grape (purple)

4. Calculate

> Observe the found cherry to blueberry ratio = 3/2
> Know number of blueberry added to total amount in jar
> Calculate, using 3/2 ratio, the amount of cherry in the jar

FIGURE 12.68 An analogy of how isotope analysis works.

we can estimate the number of red cherry jelly beans in the entire jar without counting its contents directly. This process can be similarly done using labeled chemicals or drugs (the blueberries added to the whole sample).

Stable isotope analysis is conducted using very sensitive mass spectrometers. This type of isotope analysis has been used to determine where a person has lived from their bones, teeth, and hair. One example is to look at the ratio of the ^{18}O isotope to the ^{16}O and ^{17}O isotopes. This ratio varies from place to Since the $^{18}O/^{17}O/^{16}O$ ratio in the water and food consumed by a person is reflected in their bones, teeth, and hair the tap water oxygen isotopic ratio is very similar to the ratio found in people's teeth), it may be possible to determine a person's place of origin or where they have lived for a period of time by measuring the isotopic ratio in unknown remains (see Box 12.10).

While more investigation needs to be done before this technique gains widespread forensic application, it holds the promise of becoming a valuable tool in the forensic arsenal (Table 12.3).

BOX 12.10 PLACE OF ORIGIN: IT'S IN YOUR BONES

The ratio of the stable isotopes of oxygen, ^{16}O, ^{17}O, and ^{18}O, as well as those of hydrogen, ^{1}H and ^{2}H, changes from place to place on the Earth. These ratios are quite sensitive to a number of physical forces and conditions, such as evaporation, condensation, atmospheric temperature, and local geology. For example, water molecules containing the ^{1}H or ^{16}O isotopes are generally found inland and along temperature, altitude, and latitude gradients. Natural variations in these factors lead to the observed variation in the ratios across the planet.

The isotopic ratios of the oxygen and hydrogen isotopes found within a person also vary and are directly related to the isotopic ratio found in the water and food that a person consumes. Since these ratios change from place to place, the ratios of these isotopes found in a person's bones, teeth, and hair can be used as a marker to help predict where the person came from originally and where they have lived for a period of time.

For example, the oxygen isotopic ratio of a hair sample from an unknown murdered woman was used to help identify her remains in 2000 when her body was found near the Great Salt Lake. By examining the oxygen isotopic ratio in her hair, investigators were able to track where the victim had traveled and lived. Scientists from the University of Utah found that the woman had traveled in Idaho, Washington, and Oregon within the previous two years. This information led

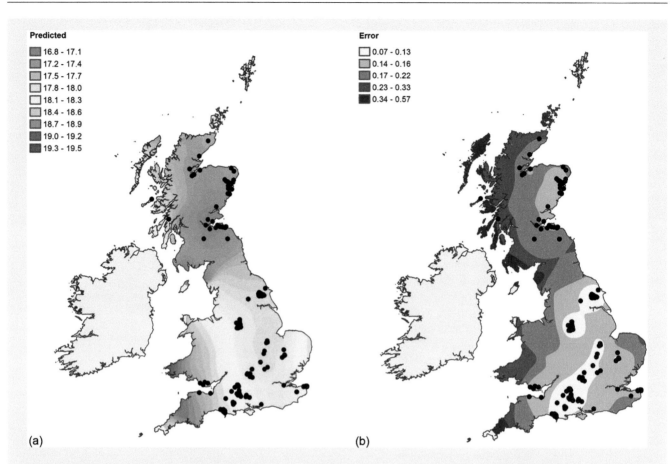

Predicted

- 16.8 - 17.1
- 17.2 - 17.4
- 17.5 - 17.7
- 17.8 - 18.0
- 18.1 - 18.3
- 18.4 - 18.6
- 18.7 - 18.9
- 19.0 - 19.2
- 19.3 - 19.5

Error

- 0.07 - 0.13
- 0.14 - 0.16
- 0.17 - 0.22
- 0.23 - 0.33
- 0.34 - 0.57

(a)

(b)

FIGURE 12.69 Prediction (a) and standard error surface (b) of the spatial variation in δ18Op values in Britian.

Source: Used per Creative Commons Attribution 4.0 International License, Maura Pellegrini, John Pouncett, Mandy Jay, Mike Parker Pearson and Michael P. Richards.

investigators to a missing person, Nikole Bakoles, who also fit many of the attributes found in the remains. Ms. Bakoles had lost touch with her family before 2000, and it wasn't until 2003 that a missing person report was filed. A DNA analysis was then able to confirm the identity of the remains as that of the missing person.

Another example comes from the crash of Flight 1549 in New York City in 2009, which has become known as the "Miracle on the Hudson." This airliner landed in the Hudson River, just off Manhattan, after it struck a flock of geese at 2,900 ft just after takeoff from LaGuardia Airport. The pilot was forced to make an extraordinary and successful emergency landing in the Hudson River. Scientists at the Smithsonian Museum Conservation Institute used stable hydrogen isotopic analysis to examine the feathers from the geese that struck the airplane. The goal was to determine if the geese were permanently resident around the airport or were part of a migratory flock. The researchers found that the isotope values of the geese were most similar to migratory Canada geese from the Labrador region, and were significantly different from those residing year-round near New York City. This knowledge is essential for wildlife professionals to develop policies and techniques that will reduce the risk of future bird-airplane collisions.

TABLE 12.3 Selected features of some common analytical methods

TECHNIQUE	QUALITATIVE OR QUANTITATIVE	SAMPLE SIZE REQUIRED	DETECTION LEVELS	DESTRUCTIVE	INSTRUMENTAL AVAILABILITY
Atomic absorption	Quant.	0.001 g	10^{-4} g/L	Yes	Simple
Atomic emission	Qual.*	0.001 g	10^{-4} g/L	Yes	Moderate
Neutron activation	Qual. and Quant.	0.001 g	1×10^{-9} g	No	Difficult
Ultraviolet-visible	Quant.	0.001 g	10^{-3} g	No	Simile
Infrared	Qual.	0.001 g	10^{-3} g	No	Simple
Mass spectrometry	Qual*	0.1 mL–10^{-8} mL	10^{-9} g	Yes	Simple

Note: *Primarily used qualitatively but can also provide quantitative information if standardized and calibrated.

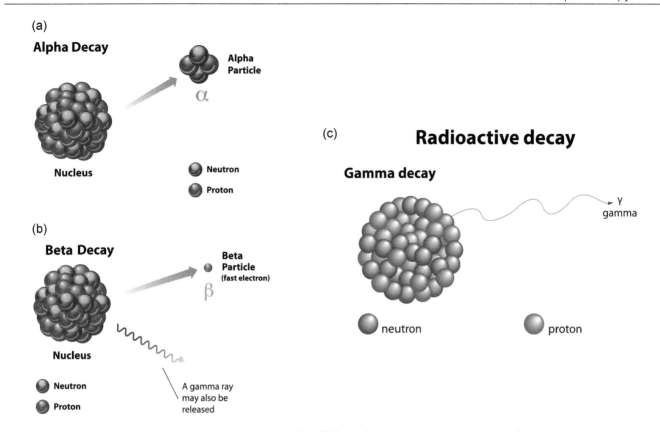

FIGURE 12.70 Types of radioactive decay: (a) alpha emission, (b) beta decay, and (c) gamma emission [red spheres are protons, blue are neutrons and black are electrons].

Source: All images courtesy Shutterstock.com.

12.6 RADIOCHEMICAL ANALYSIS

12.6.1 Introduction

On occasion, it is valuable to know how old a piece of evidence is for the purposes of an investigation, especially biological items such as wood, paper, vellum, human remains, and fibers. This can range from dating a historical document, work of art, or wooden artifact to determining if a set of human remains requires forensic and criminal attention or is simply of historic interest. Questions such as these can often be answered by measuring the amount of naturally occurring radioactive substances in the sample.

12.6.2 Radioactivity

Radioactive materials are everywhere – all around us and within us. But what does radioactivity mean and how can it be used as part of a forensic investigation?

A radioactive substance contains atoms with unstable nuclei that emit particles and/or electromagnetic radiation spontaneously, ultimately forming stable nuclei. This emission process is commonly called *radioactive decay*. There are several ways that an unstable nucleus can transform itself into a stable atom, but among the most common processes are alpha, beta, and gamma emission. These three types of radioactive decay are shown in Figure 12.70.

Alpha emission (α) is the ejection of a helium nucleus, containing two neutrons and two protons, from the radioactive nucleus to form a new atom that is four mass units lighter and shifted by two elements to the *left* in the periodic table due to the loss of the two protons. For example, atoms of ^{241}Am can emit an alpha particle to become a ^{237}Np atom.

A second type of radioactive decay results from the emission of an electron, called *beta (β) emission*, conceptually converting a neutron in the nucleus into a proton by the removal of an electron from the *nucleus*. This transforms the atom into the element one step to the *right* in the periodic table.

The third type of radioactive decay, *gamma (γ) radiation*, results from the emission of a high-energy photon of electromagnetic radiation in the gamma ray region (wavelengths less than 1×10^{-11} m; more than 100,000 times smaller than the wavelength of visible light).

Radioactive decay occurs spontaneously at a rate determined solely by a particular nucleus. This means that the rate at which a substance radioactively decays is not influenced by temperature, sunlight, pressure, or any other factors that we can control – it is a process that occurs at a rate that depends only on the radioactive material. We can describe this rate by defining a very simple but useful term: the *half-life*. The half-life of an isotope is simply the amount of time that it takes for half of a sample to undergo radioactive decay (written as $t_{1/2}$). For example, the half-life of ^{14}C is 5,570 years. This means

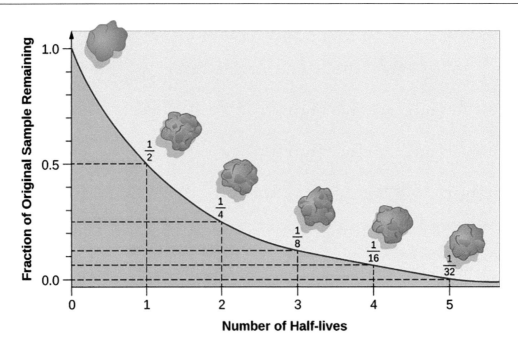

FIGURE 12.71   Decay of a radioactive material (14C) through five half-lives.

Source: Used per Creative Commons Attribution. User: Andrew Fraknoi, David Morrison, and Sidney Wolff. © 1999–2018, Rice University.

that if we started with 10 g of 14C, after 5,570 years only 5 g of 14C would remain. After waiting another half-life period of 5,570 years, or 11,140 years in total after the start, there would be only 2.5 g of 14C remaining, and so on. This is illustrated graphically in Figure 12.71.

BOX 12.11   RADIO-COIN TOSS?

To understand radioactive decay, try this simple experiment. Take a number of coins (maybe 50 or 100 coins) and, after shaking them up, toss them onto the table. Count, record, and remove all the "heads-up" coins and make a stack. This toss represents one half-life. Repeat the process of shaking, tossing, counting, removing all the "heads-up" coins, and stacking in a separate pile – each toss is one additional half-life – until there are no more coins. When you're done, plot the number of tails coins remaining after each toss (vertical axis) versus toss number (half-life, horizontal axis). How does this plot compare to the one shown in Figure 12.71? [you can do the same thing with M&M candies – removing all the ones with the M&M logo facing up just as you did with the "heads" coins].

Since the rate of radioactive decay is not affected by everyday environmental factors, such as temperature and pressure, then if we know (or assume) how much radioactivity was present at the start and we know how much is present now, we can simply figure out how much time has elapsed for this much decay to have occurred. Using the example from above, if we knew that there were 10 g of 14C at the start of the decay process and that now only 1.25 g are left, we know that three half-lives must have elapsed (division in half three times). Three half-lives for 14C would equate to $3 \times 5,570$ years or 16,710 years. Using these ideas, it is possible for us to determine the age of an unknown object as long as there is a radionuclide with the right half-life (not too long nor too short relative to the time frame that we're interested in, but just the right length of time – a Goldilocks situation) and how much of it was present at the start.

12.6.3 Radiocarbon Dating

The most common radionuclide (radioactive isotope of an element) used for dating objects, such as wood, human remains, and inks, is the 14-carbon isotope (a 14C nucleus contains six protons and eight neutrons). This is a particularly convenient nucleus for dating once-living materials since they are composed largely of carbon *and* there is essentially a constant proportion of radioactive carbon in the living biosphere. 14C, the most abundant, radioactive carbon isotope, has a half-life (5,570 years); just the right length.

The process begins high in the upper reaches of the Earth's atmosphere where high-energy cosmic radiation first comes into contact with the molecules in our atmosphere (Figure 12.72). The cosmic radiation creates a high-energy neutron that bombards a non-radioactive nitrogen-14 nucleus

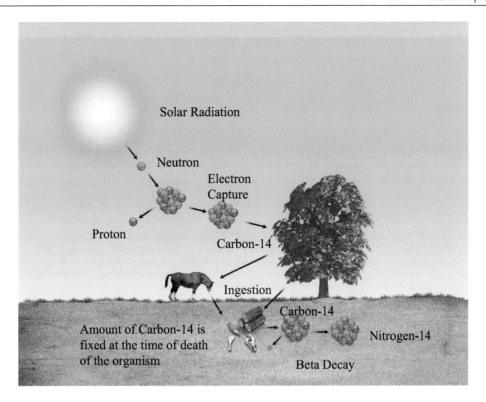

FIGURE 12.72 ^{14}C cycle from solar source through to radioactive decay. Carbon-14 is a radioactive isotope of the carbon, created continuously in the upper atmosphere by the action of cosmic rays on nitrogen-14 (shown at upper left). This radiocarbon-14 is incorporated into living materials through photosynthesis and passed down the food chain. Ultimately, the carbon-14 decays back to nitrogen-14 (shown at lower right). This radioactive decay continues at a steady rate after an organism dies, when it no longer takes up carbon from the environment. This allows the time since death to be calculated from the relative abundance of 14-carbon remaining in the sample.

Image Source: Mikkel Juul Jensen/Science Photo Library. Used with permission

(N_2 molecules make up about 80% of our atmosphere), converting the ^{14}N into a radioactive ^{14}C nucleus with the emission of a proton, basically trading a neutron for a proton while keeping the nuclear mass the same and shifting the atom one element to the left

$$^{14}_{7}N + ^{1}_{0}n \rightarrow ^{14}_{6}C + ^{1}_{1}p$$

This is a continuous and ongoing process, converting ^{14}N into ^{14}C as the sun shines on the Earth. The radioactive ^{14}C that is formed then makes its way into the biosphere, primarily as $^{14}CO_2$ that is absorbed into photosynthesizing plants. This radio-^{14}C is then incorporated into a variety of organic compounds, especially glucose, the building block of cellulose, starch and a variety of cellular proteins. These ^{14}C-enriched compounds ultimately end up in animals, soils, other plants, and the rest of the living world through the food chain, as illustrated in Figure 12.73. The amount of ^{14}C in the world at any one time is balanced, however, by the continual and natural decay of the ^{14}C back into ^{14}N through beta decay:

$$^{14}_{6}C \rightarrow ^{14}_{7}N + ^{0}_{-1}e + \text{Energy}$$

The amount of ^{14}C in the biosphere is, therefore, in a steady state or in equilibrium; the same amount of ^{14}C that is produced daily from ^{14}N solar irradiation decays back into ^{14}N from ^{14}C beta decay, ready to begin the cycle once again. Therefore, the percentage of ^{14}C in relation to all the carbon in the biosphere remains constant over time.

As long as an organism is living, it is exchanging carbon with the world around it. This means that the proportion of radioactive to non-radioactive carbon in all living organisms is also essentially constant; we have the same relative proportion of ^{14}C in our bodies as all other living organisms. When an organism dies, however, it stops consuming carbon sources and, at the time of death, the amount of ^{14}C in the organism is fixed – no more is added. The number of ^{14}C nuclei in the dead organism decays over time. Therefore, it is a straightforward process to determine the age of an organic artifact since we know how much ^{14}C all living organisms have in them and we can measure how much ^{14}C is actually in a particular now dead, but once alive, item. Using the method described above (see Box 12.12), we can calculate how many half-lives have gone by to get the age of the sample. Because of the length of the half-life of ^{14}C, the method is typically good to about ±50 years for dating objects up to about 40,000 years old.

BOX 12.12   HOW TO CALCULATE THE AGE OF AN ARTIFACT

Using the ideas of radioactive decay, we can now calculate how old an object is using the equation:

$$t = \frac{\left[\ln(N_{final}/N_{initial})\right]}{(-0.693)} \times t_{\frac{1}{2}}$$

(where t = is the age of the object in years, N_{final} is the amount of ^{14}C radioactivity at the current time, $N_{initial}$ is the amount of ^{14}C radioactivity at the beginning – moment of death of the organism, and $t_{\frac{1}{2}}$ is the half-life, which for ^{14}C is 5,570 years).

So, if you measured the ^{14}C radioactivity of an artifact as three counts per minute and a living plant measured 15 counts per minute, the equation would look like:

$$t = \frac{\left[\ln(3/15)\right]}{(-0.693)} \, (5{,}570 \text{ years}) = 12{,}900 \text{ years}$$

(Note: "ln" means "natural logarithm" and probably is a button on your calculator.)

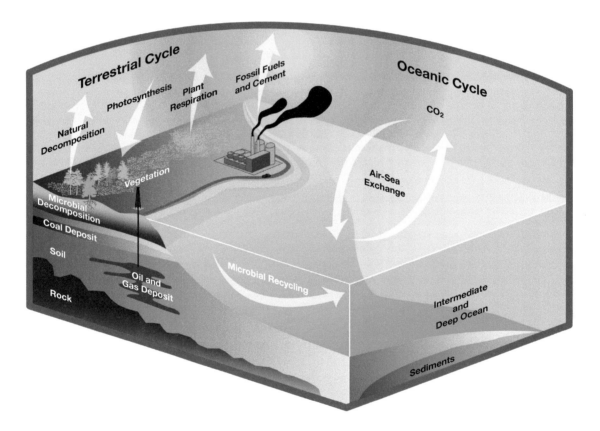

FIGURE 12.73   Carbon cycle showing how $^{14}CO_2$ can be incorporated throughout the living biosphere and used for radiocarbon dating.
Source: US Department of Energy.

Forensic anthropologists and pathologists periodically encounter cases where it is difficult to determine how long a person has been dead due to the poor state of preservation or other complicating factors. Radiocarbon dating may be helpful in classifying remains as recent or historic, with obvious impact on legal investigations. Recently, the lens of the eye, a relatively long-lasting structure, has also been shown to give useful dating for deaths through radio-^{14}C dating.

Radiocarbon dating has been extensively used for determining the age and, therefore, the authenticity of documents, museum artifacts, musical instruments, paintings (mainly from the canvas or wood backing), mummies, and many other once-living objects.

While an increasingly common technique in forensic investigations, radiocarbon dating can provide age information that is unobtainable by any other methods.

BOX 12.13   A CRIME CASE OR A HISTORIC INSIGHT?

In 2003, the extraordinarily well-preserved remains of a murder victim was pulled from a bog in Ireland. He was clearly the victim of deliberate and planned violence; he had a broken nose, cracked skull, lacerations on his abdomen, in addition to the noose around his neck. But who was he and where should the "criminal" investigation begin.

Radiocarbon dating, however, showed that the body belonged to an Iron Age man, nearly 2,300 years old. Archeologists now debate whether the wounds seen were from a ritualistic sacrifice or from the punishment inflicted on an ancient criminal. Nonetheless, despite the amazing preservation, this is more a case for the history books than for a criminal investigation.

FIGURE 12.74   Bog body of the *Clonycavan Man* at National Museum of Ireland, Dublin, from around the 4th or 3rd century BC.

Source: Used per Creative Commons Attribution-Share Alike 2.0 Generic. User: Mark Healey.

QUESTIONS FOR FURTHER PRACTICE AND MASTERY

12.1   What is the wavelength of a photon of light that has a frequency of 3×10^6 Hz?

12.2   What is the relationship between the frequency of light and its energy?

12.3   What must an electron do to move from a lower energy level to a higher energy level?

12.4   What is meant by the terms ground state and excited state for an electron?

12.5   What is an absorption spectrum?

12.6   What is meant by characteristic wavelength?

12.7   What are some of the typical forensic uses for atomic absorption spectroscopy (AAS)?

12.8   What is atomic emission spectroscopy (AES)?

12.9   Which method, AAS or AES, is more sensitive and why?

12.10   What information does the presence of trace elements in glass or metals provide the forensic chemist?

12.11   What are some of the advantages in using neutron activation analysis? What is the major disadvantage of this technique?

12.12   How are atoms held together in molecules?

12.13   Explain the process that gives rise to molecular bonding orbitals and molecular antibonding orbitals.

12.14   What are organic functional groups? How do they play a role in UV-visible spectroscopy?

12.15 How does the use of infrared light in spectroscopy differ from the use of visible or UV light?

12.16 IR spectra are often very complex. How does this complexity work in favor of the forensic chemist?

12.17 Which field analysis method is used in breath-alcohol concentration determination?

12.18 How does a mass spectrometer work?

12.19 What are fragment ions and how do they contribute to the uniqueness of a compound's mass spectrogram?

12.20 What is stable isotope mass spectroscopy? What are some of the uses of this process?

12.21 What are the three principal types of radioactive decay?

12.22 What is the basis for using ^{14}C to date organic compounds?

EXTENSIVE QUESTIONS

12.23 What is the wavelength of light emitted when an electron falls from level 5 ($n = 5$) to level 1 ($n = 1$)?

12.24 A forensic technician collects a sample of an unknown white powder and sends it to the lab for analysis. As the lab technician who will analyze this sample, what analytical procedures might you follow in order to identify the substance or substances in the unknown sample?

12.25 Complete the following reactions:

    a. $^{238}U \rightarrow {}^4He + ?$
    b. $^{210}Bi \rightarrow \beta- + ?$
    c. $^{234}Th \rightarrow {}^{230}Ra + ?$

12.26 A forensic anthropologist is given a piece of cloth taken from a body discovered at a construction site. The anthropologist needs to determine its age in order to determine if it is of historical significance or should be considered for a criminal investigation. The amount of ^{14}C is analyzed and found to be 25.0% of the normal amount found in living organic material. How old is the cloth and should a criminal investigation be started ($t_{1/2}$ of ^{14}C = 5,570 years)?

GLOSSARY OF TERMS

absorption: in spectroscopy, it is the uptake of light by a substance, accompanied by an increase in the energy of the substance's molecules or atoms.

alpha emission: the ejection of a helium nucleus, containing two neutrons and two protons (^4_2He), from a radioactive nucleus to form a new atom that is four mass units lighter and shifted two elements to the *left* in the periodic table.

antibonding: a type of chemical bonding that inhibits attraction between atoms and whose energy increases as atoms are brought closer together, resulting in a net repulsion between the atoms.

asymmetric: without the balance of symmetry.

atomic mass (weight): the mass of an atom that is expressed in the standard unit of atomic mass units (amu): approximately equal to the number of protons and neutrons in the atom.

atomic mass unit (amu): the unit of mass that weighs one-twelfth of the mass of a carbon-12 atom. Used to express atomic and molecular weights.

atomic number: the number of protons in the nucleus of an atom.

Balmer series: a series of bright lines in the emission spectrum of Hydrogen involving electronic transitions from higher energy levels into the lower $n = 2$ level.

base peak: the most intense peak in a mass spectrum.

beta emission: the emission of an electron from a radioactive nucleus, transforming the atom to the element one step to the *right* in the periodic table.

bonding: a type of chemical interaction between atoms where the energy decreases as atoms are brought closer together (until nuclear repulsion becomes important), resulting in a net attractive force between the atoms.

carbon cycle: the process whereby carbon is exchanged between living and non-living components in a cyclic arrangement.

chromatography: the process of separating the components of a mixture that relies on the differential affinities of the various components with some medium, such as a solid, gas or liquid.

color: the way that our eyes and brain *perceive* different wavelengths of light in the visible range.

complimentary color: pairs of colors that, when mixed in the proper proportions, produce a neutral color (e.g., black or white). Sometimes referred to as "opposite" colors.

detector: an instrument, or part of an instrument, designed to sense the presence of something of interest, such as electromagnetic radiation or radioactivity.

duality of nature: a basic principle of quantum mechanics whereby all particles and waves have *both* wave and particulate properties. The property exhibited depends on which property is experimentally measured.

electromagnetic radiation: radiation that is made up of perpendicular electrical and magnetic waves that oscillate as they move through space.

electron impact ionization: the ejection of an electron from an atom or molecule caused by an impact with a high-energy electron.

emission: the discharge of electromagnetic radiation or radioactivity as an atom or molecule goes from a higher to a lower energy state.

excited state: a higher energy level, above the ground state, of an atom or molecule.

fragment ion: a smaller, charged "piece" or fragment of a molecule.

frequency: the number of waves that pass a fixed point per unit of time.

functional group: the part of a molecule that defines its chemical structure and is responsible for a characteristic set of reactions and properties.

gamma emission: the emission of a high-energy photon of electromagnetic radiation in the gamma ray region, usually from a radioactive nucleus.

gas chromatography: a form of chromatography, used for separating mixtures into its individual components, that uses a gas as the mobile phase.

ground state: the lowest energy state of an atom or molecule.

half-life: the amount of time necessary for one-half of the original sample to change, decompose or decay away.

Heisenberg Uncertainty Principle: the principle that states that we can never know simultaneously both the position and the momentum (related to velocity) of an object with complete certainty.

infrared spectroscopy: the measurement of the absorption/emission of light between about 500 and 4,000 cm^{-1} (2,500–20,000 nm) that causes quantized vibrations in molecules.

ionization: the removal of an electron from an atom or molecule.

isomers: chemical compounds with the same molecular formula but with different arrangements of the atoms and displaying different properties.

isotope: two or more atoms with the same number of protons but *different* numbers of neutrons.

mass spectrometry: an instrumental method that separates ionized, gas-phase molecules and molecular fragments by their masses and records the distribution of the observed masses in a mass spectrum.

mass-to-charge ratio (m/e or sometimes m/z): the relationship between mass and charge given by the equation: $m/e = H^2r^2/2V$. Typically, this is the mass measurement shown in a mass spectrum.

mobile phase: in chromatography, the component that moves the solute past a fixed medium.

molecular ion: see "Parent Ion".

molecular formula: the chemical formula that shows the number and kind of each atom in a molecule.

molecular weight: the mass of a molecule that is expressed in the standard unit of atomic mass units (amu) and determined by the sum of the atomic masses of all of the atoms that make up the molecule.

molecular orbital: an orbital that extends across part or an entire molecule.

neutron activation analysis: the analytical method that measures the characteristic energy emitted from atoms after bombardment with thermal neutrons to determine the atomic composition of the sample.

nuclide: a type of atom defined by its number of protons and neutrons along with its quantum state.

orbital: the mathematical representation of the probability of finding an electron in a region of space.

parent ion: the peak in the mass spectrum corresponding to the complete molecule, usually the highest mass peak in the spectrum.

quantization: the act of restricting or limiting the possible values that an item may display to a finite set, usually determined by a set of rules described in quantum mechanics.

quantum mechanics: the field of chemistry and physics that mathematically deals with the motion and properties of subatomic particles, atoms and molecules.

radioactivity: the spontaneous emission of particles and/or electromagnetic radiation in nuclear decay.

radioactive decay: the disintegration of unstable nuclei with the emission of particles and/or electromagnetic radiation.

radiocarbon dating: the analytical method usually used for determining the age of once-living, carbon-containing materials based on the amount of radioactive carbon-14 measured in the sample.

retention factor (Rf): a measure of the degree of interaction of a substance in chromatography with the stationary phase: determined by dividing the distance the substance traveled by the distance the mobile phase traveled during a period of time.

spectroscopy: the study of the interaction of electromagnetic radiation with matter as a function of its wavelength or frequency.

standing wave: a vibration system where certain portions of the waves do not vibrate or move (remain fixed) while other components around them vibrate.

stationary phase: in chromatography, the component that remains fixed (does not move) during a separation.

symmetric: an arrangement where there is correspondence between two or more points on an object or figure (similarity in shape, size, and relative positions between points in a figure or object).

ultraviolet-visible spectroscopy: the measurement of the absorptions of light between about 150 and 750 nm.

voltage: the unit of electrical potential difference.

visible light: electromagnetic radiation that can be detected by the human eye, typically from between 280 nm and 750 nm.

wavelength: the distance measured between like points of successive waves, such as the distance between the crest of one wave to the crest of the following wave.

wavenumber: the measure of energy in reciprocal centimeters (cm^{-1}) as given by cm$^{-1} = 1/\lambda$.

BIBLIOGRAPHY

Robert D. Blackledge (Ed.), *Forensic Analysis on the Cutting Edge: New Methods for Trace Evidence Analysis*, Wiley-Interscience, 2007.

John M. Chalmers, Howell G.M. Edwards, and Michael D. Hargreaves (Eds.), *Infrared and Raman Spectroscopy in Forensic Science*, Wiley, 2012.

Heinrich D. Holland and Karl K. Turekian (Eds.), *Treatise on Geochemistry, Vol. 14. Stable Isotopes in Forensics Applications*, Leslie A. Chesson, Brett J. Tipple, John D. Howa, Gabriel J Bowen, Janet E. Barnette, Thure E. Cerling, J.R. Ehleringer, Elsevier Ltd, 2014.

J. Michael Hollis, *Modern Spectroscopy* (4th Ed.), Wiley, 2004.

Lawrence Kobilinsky (Ed.), *Forensic Chemistry Handbook*, Wiley, 2011.

Wolfram Meier-Augenstein, *Stable Isotope Forensics: Methods and Forensic Applications of Stable Isotope Analysis* (2nd Ed.), Wiley, 2017.

Kenton J. Moody, Ian D. Hutcheon, and Patrick M. Grant, *Nuclear Forensic Analysis*, CRC Press, 2005.

Donald L. Pavi, Gary M. Lampman, George S. Kriz, and James A. Vyvyan, *Introduction to Spectroscopy* (4th Ed.), Brooks Cole, 2008.

Francis Rouessac and Annick Rouessac, *Chemical Analysis: Instrumentation Methods and Techniques*, Wiley, 2007.

Robert M. Silverstein, Francis X. Webster, and David Kiemle, *Spectrometric Identification of Organic Compounds* (7th Ed.), Wiley, 2005.

Douglas A. Skoog, F. James Holler, Stanley R. Crouch, *Principles of Instrumental Analysis* (6th Ed.), Brooks Cole, 2006.

Jehuda Yinon, *Advances in Forensic Applications of Mass Spectrometry*, CRC Press, 2004.

Jehuda Yinon, *Forensic Applications of Mass Spectrometry*, Volume 3, CRC Press, 1995.

Forensic Toxicology

13

13.1 INTRODUCTION TO FORENSIC TOXICOLOGY

What is there that is not a poison? All things are poison and nothing without poison. Solely the dose determines that a thing is not a poison.

Paracelsus (a.k.a. Philippus Theophrastus Aureolus Bombastus von Hohenheim, 1493–1541)

LEARNING GOALS AND OBJECTIVES

Forensic Toxicology deals with how drugs, toxins, and poisons act on our bodies and how our bodies respond and act on the foreign chemical. After completing this chapter, you should be able to:

- Describe pharmacodynamics and understand how a drug or poison works on a body.
- Explain pharmacokinetics and how a drug or poison is worked upon by a body.
- Define what is meant by the terms drugs, medicines, pharmaceuticals, poisons, and toxins.
- Discuss what is meant by toxicity and how it is measured.
- Describe the difference between poison, toxin, and venom.
- Illustrate what is meant by a drug pathway in the body and what is ADME.
- Explain how drugs and poisons are metabolized.
- Illustrate how new drugs are discovered and what is meant by "off-label" uses.
- Show what is meant by a corrosive and a metabolic poison and how they work.
- Describe the scope and nature of the worldwide drug problem.
- List example durgs that are narcotics, hallucinogens, stimulants, depressants, and steroids.
- Explain what is meant by "club drugs" and Drug-Facilitated Sexual Assault (DFSA).
- Describe the *Controlled Substance Act* and how drugs are assigned to the schedules.
- List some of the chemical properties of ethanol (alcohol).
- Discuss how alcoholic beverages are produced, consumed, and abused.
- Relate information about the toxicological properties of alcohol (ethanol).
- Describe what is meant by BAC and how it is measured.
- Illustrate what is meant by presumptive and confirmatory drug testing.
- Explain what is meant by the half-life and clearance time of a drug or poison.
- Describe the role of a forensic toxicologist.

13.1.1 Introduction

Drugs are everywhere around us and in us in today's society (Figure 13.1). They have a more profound effect on our everyday lives than ever before in history. Drugs help to keep us healthy, diagnose and manage diseases, reduce pain, cure infections, stem the spread of infectious illnesses, combat epidemics, and repair body tissues. They also change our moods, help us to sleep better, make it easier to lose weight, and reduce our stress and anxiety levels. We expect and rely on drugs to solve our everyday physical and psychological needs, both large and small. Even the food we eat is treated with drugs and other chemicals to make it more abundant, safe, and inexpensive. Through all this, we require our drugs to be safe, effective, fast-acting, inexpensive, and readily available. Humans today form a worldwide society that has developed and flourished largely because of the amazing advances in pharmaceutical medicines, agricultural chemicals, food additives, and bulk chemicals.

Pharmaceuticals – chemicals developed primarily to fill medical needs – can come from either natural sources, known by local healers for generations, or may derive from man-made processes at the end of a long and expensive discovery, testing, and manufacturing enterprise, monitored by stringent quality control measures. We look to science and technology to find new and better cures and remedies for both long-known and newly emerging needs, and we hold our governments responsible for keeping us safe in the process. Bringing a new drug, herbicide, pesticide, or food additive to market, therefore,

Age 0-4	Age 4-12	Age 12-24	Age 25-64	Age 65 and Over
Amoxicillin	Ibuprofen	Albuterol	Folic Acid	Everything else

FIGURE 13.1 We live in a time dominated by drugs for good and ill. (Left to Right): (Infant) Amoxicillin, (Toddler) Ibuprofen, (Teenager) Albuterol/Fluoxetine, (Adult) Folic Acid, and (Elderly) Everything else.

Source: Shutterstock.com

requires a complex partnership between science, technology, policy, ethics, business, and the law.

Today, the global pharmaceutical industry continues to rapidly grow, with over $1 trillion in sales annually that are expected to continue to grow at between 4% and 7% per year into the foreseeable future. Thousands and thousands of medications are now available for all sorts of preventative, diagnostic, and therapeutic uses. Tens of millions of new compounds are screened every year in the never-ending quest for better and more effective medications to prevent, combat, or treat diseases to help us live healthier, happier, and longer lives (Figure 13.2).

Our lives are also intimately intertwined with a vast array of chemicals designed to make our personal environment safer, kill unwanted pests, treat infestations, and protect our foods. Poisons and toxins fulfill a significant societal and personal need and have helped deal with many problems that have plagued humankind since the beginning of time. But they also, like pharmaceuticals, come with considerable risks and present difficult problems.

Because of the ready availability of drugs and related chemicals, it is not surprising that many of these compounds find their way into "off-label" uses – the use of drugs and poisons designed originally to fill a narrow medical need but later "repurposed" for a totally different and often harmful purpose. Drugs designed for well-focused biomedical healthcare needs are used for recreation, crime, or personal gain.

Chemicals intended to reduce the threat to our crops from pests can be used to intentionally injure someone. Abused compounds range from anxiety-reducing drugs, such as diazepam (Valium) and fluoxetine (Prozac), to psychoactive drugs, such as LSD and marijuana, to date-rape drugs to facilitate personal assault, such as Rohypnol and MDMA (Ecstasy), to the ubiquitous mood-changing abuse of alcohol, with tens of thousands of examples in between (Figure 13.3). Our worldwide legal systems – police, courts, and prisons – are clogged with cases either directly or indirectly involving drugs and chemicals of abuse. One recent estimate suggested that between 80% and 90% of all criminal cases involved some type of drug or alcohol usage that either caused or aggravated the criminal activity.

Because of the pervasive influence of inappropriately used and consumed drugs, poisons, and other chemicals, the field of toxicology plays a central role in every forensic laboratory. Toxicology is the study of the effects of chemicals on living organisms, including both how the chemical affects a person as well as how the body responds and acts upon the chemical. Forensic toxicology specifically deals with the study of substances that are used in a manner in conflict with the law.

In this chapter, we will explore the field of forensic toxicology. We must begin, of course, by looking at how drugs and poisons are developed and how they are intentionally designed to work helpfully in the body. Then, we will examine how

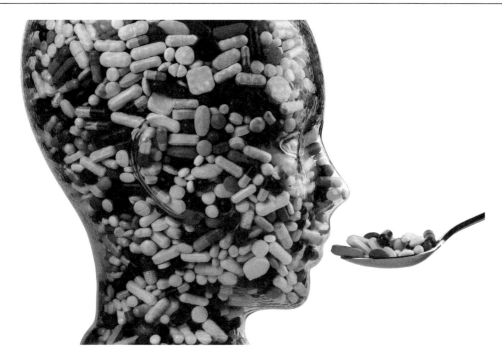

FIGURE 13.2   Prevalence of drug use.

Source: Shutterstock.com

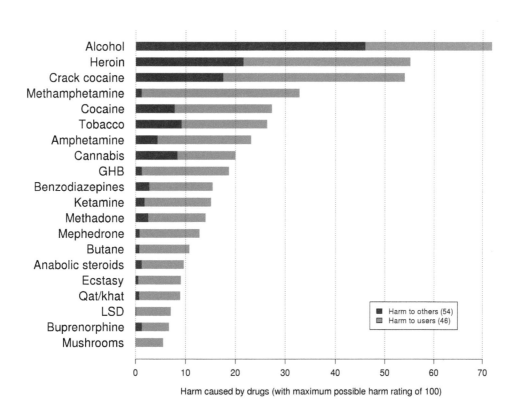

FIGURE 13.3   Illicit drugs and chemicals surround our lives. In this plot, experts were asked to rank both illegal and legal drugs on measures related to the drug's harm to both the user and to society. These measures included damage to health, drug dependency, economic costs, and crime. Note that alcohol is ranked as the most harmful, not only to society but also to the user.

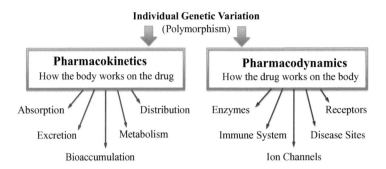

FIGURE 13.4   Relationships between pharmacodynamics, pharmacokinetics, and genetics.

these substances are abused in a criminal fashion for decidedly "off-label" uses. Next, because of its immense consumption, we will examine separately the toxicology of one specific substance: alcohol. Finally, we will explore how forensic toxicology is practiced in real life.

13.2 TOXICOLOGY BASICS AND PHARMACEUTICALS

13.2.1 Introduction

Toxicology involves the study of how people and other living organisms interact with drugs and poisons. These interactions can be divided into two main categories: how a drug works on an organism, called *pharmacodynamics*, and how an organism works on the drug, called *pharmacokinetics*. The relationship between these two areas, and how genetics play an underlying role, is illustrated in Figure 13.4.

13.2.2 Pharmacodynamics

Pharmacodynamics, the study of changes caused by a drug in a person, deals specifically with how a chemical can affect the internal functioning of an organism. There are many modes of action that allow chemicals to work on the body, and each mode specifically determines how a drug or poison can cause an effect. Drugs can bond directly to cells and biomolecules, destroy tissues, replace needed naturally occurring substances, or reduce the production of unwanted chemicals, among others. For example, the drug Orinase can boost the body's production of insulin, while Lipitor reduces its manufacture of cholesterol. The difficult balance in medicine is to select the right drug in the correct amount to cause only the medically desired effect without doing any harm. Anti-cancer drugs are typically aimed at destroying cancerous cells using a cell poison, called a cytotoxin, without killing other surrounding healthy cells. The extent to which a drug causes unwanted side effects may limit its usefulness. Cancer drugs are designed to

kill the most rapidly growing cells, especially cancer cells, but they also effectively kill other fast-growing cells in the body, such as hair follicle and stomach lining cells, leading to hair loss and nausea. Each drug has its own set of side effects that can range from insignificant to severe. It relates to the old axiom to be avoided, that the medicine cured the disease but killed the patient.

BOX 13.1   DRUG NAMES: WHAT DOES IT ALL MEAN?

The array of names used for drugs is absolutely bewildering! There are so many names and endless variations of names for each drug, and even separate names for mixtures of drugs, that it takes an expert to keep track of them. But why are there so many names for the same chemical?

Names for a drug arise from the different audiences and uses for the compound. Dr. George Johnson (txtwriter.com) says it reminds him of T.S. Eliot's poem on *The Naming of Cats* (the basis of the Broadway play *Cats*), where every cat needs three names. One name is a "sensible everyday name," one a "particular name," and one a "private name." When considering drugs, for instance, take the often abused drug Rohypnol. Here's some of its many names and why there are so many:

- A "Sensible Name" – A name that everyone can remember and that the various drug companies can use to market the drug, such as the name *Rohypnol*.
- A "Particular Name" – A name for pharmacists and doctors to use, one that tells something about the family of drugs it belongs to, something like your family name. The "particular name" for Rohypnol is *flunitrazepam*.
- A "Private Name" – just for chemists, who need to be able to put a chemical structure unambiguously to a compound just from the name without ever having seen the compound before. They must be able to figure out the structure from *just*

the name. So Rohypnol is called *6-(2-fluoroph enyl)-2-methyl-9-nitro-2,5-diazabicyclo[5.4.0] undeca-5,8,10,12-tetraen-3-one* [$C_{16}H_{12}FN_3O_3$].

- And one more, a "Nickname" (not from Elliot's characterization, however) – The very familiar or "street names." For Rohypnol, these include *"rowies," "rophy", "ruffles," "roachies," "roofies," "ruffies,"* and dozens of others that seem to change almost daily.

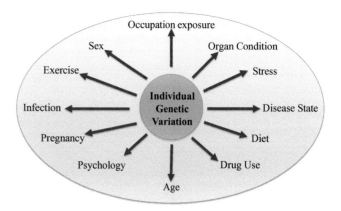

FIGURE 13.5   How a drug may be affected by an individual person's body – pharmacokinetics.

13.2.3 Pharmacokinetics

Pharmacokinetics can be described simply as how a body acts on a chemical, such as a drug or poison, and how the chemical moves through a person's system and is eventually eliminated from the body. Pharmacokinetics must, therefore, consider the key steps in the drug's movement that include absorption, bioavailability, distribution, metabolism, and excretion. For example, pharmacokinetics follows the path of a drug through a person's body from the time it is first administered until it is ultimately excreted, including how it might be metabolized by the body into other molecules, called *metabolites*. These metabolites may each have their own separate effects and actions on the body and are frequently employed as chemical "signatures"; when detected, they are clear evidence of the use of the original drug.

Metabolism refers to the chemical processes in our bodies that convert food into energy and all the other compounds required for life. Drugs, like other chemicals, are metabolized by the body along quite specific pathways. How a body breaks down and processes a drug depends both upon the chemical properties of the drug and on factors specific to a person. For instance, factors including genetics, age, gender, diseases present, body impairment and function, tobacco or drug use, exercise, environmental exposures, and others may change the rate and ultimate outcome of how a drug is metabolized in a person's body. Some of these person-based variables are shown in Figure 13.5. For example, for some people Valium (diazepam) might have the desired effect of anxiety reduction, while in others there may be no effect at all, and still others may experience unacceptable side effects and reactions from life-threatening reactions. Since the Valium taken in each case is chemically identical, any difference in the effect it has from person to person must depend upon the genetic and biochemical makeup of each individual; these are pharmacodynamic effects. The genetic component of these different outcomes for drugs in a person is illustrated in Figure 13.6. Ultimately, however, diazepam is metabolized by specific enzymes found in the liver, and the predictable metabolites are excreted by the kidneys (Figure 13.7), pharmacokinetic effects. For example, over time, the body eliminates diazepam and forms the metabolite desmethyldiazepam, which is then slowly eliminated, as illustrated in Figure 13.8.

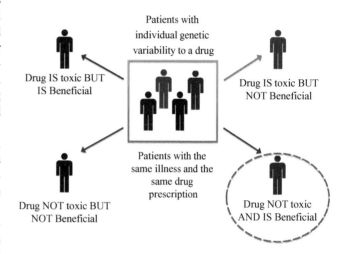

FIGURE 13.6   The role of genetics (pharmacogenetics) in drug pharmacokinetics and pharmacodynamics.

One useful concept related to pharmacokinetics is the half-life of the drug ($t_{1/2}$), meaning the time it takes for the body to eliminate half of the drug present. This time interval can range from hours to days or longer and is affected by the same factors that are shown in Figure 13.5. For forensic casework, the half-life of a drug limits how long we can detect a drug, or its metabolites, in the body after use, a question of obvious legal importance.

The most common place where drugs and poisons are metabolized by the body is in the liver, where highly specific enzymes reside that are charged with the task of recognizing, grabbing, and modifying chemicals that are foreign to our bodies (Figure 13.7). The presence and action of these enzymes are largely controlled by our DNA and there is great variation among people regarding these enzymes. For example, it has been shown that about 50% of people have DNA modifications that influence how liver enzymes metabolize some of the most common drugs. This leads to very different effects from person to person on both the pharmacodynamics and pharmacokinetics of a particular drug (Figure 13.6). The large percentage of drugs that are therapeutically ineffective for

ENZYME FUNCTION
(synthesis)

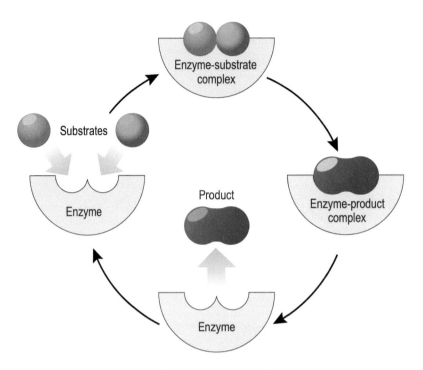

FIGURE 13.7 Enzyme metabolism of a drug or poison (called the substrate) into new products (called metabolites).

Source: Shutterstock.com

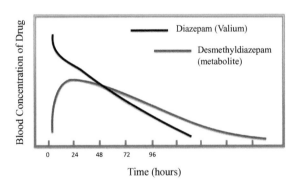

FIGURE 13.8 Metabolism of diazepam (Valium) into desmethyldiazepam, showing how diazepam is removed from the blood *via* metabolism [the black line is the amount of diazepam in the body, and the red line represents desmethyldiazepam].

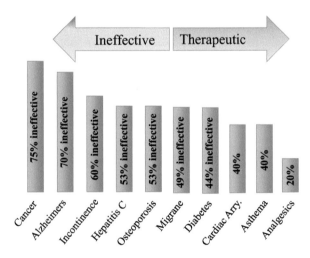

FIGURE 13.9 The relationship between effective (therapeutic) and ineffective outcomes of commonly prescribed medications for various illnesses.

different people is illustrated in Figure 13.9. This effect may lead to not only ineffective treatments but also to potentially life-threatening adverse drug reactions, estimated as the cause of 100,000 deaths and 2.2 million serious drug reactions in the United States annually. The fields of genetic toxicology and precision healthcare (personalized at the level of each person's own DNA composition) explore these individual responses to drugs and have the prospect of someday allowing doctors to

prescribe drugs tailored for specific individuals based upon their unique DNA codes, thereby greatly reducing ineffective and adverse drug reactions and maximizing the beneficial effects of therapy.

Drugs may be natural or synthetic chemical compounds that are used for physiological (body) or psychological (mind) effects. In common *forensic* usage today, unfortunately, there is a distinction made between the terms "drug" and "medicine" by the general public, although in the medical world they are actually very similar, though not identical. Popular use of the term "medicine" refers to those chemicals taken to help deal with a generally accepted medical condition (e.g., therapy, prevention, or diagnosis), while the term "drug" implies chemicals that are taken for originally unintended or uncontrolled uses. In U.S. law, however, a drug, the broader of the two terms, is defined as a "substance intended for use in the diagnosis, cure, mitigation, treatment, or prevention of disease, or a substance intended for use as a component of a medicine," while a medicine is more narrowly defined as a "substance used specifically in treating a disease." Nonetheless, the main issues in forensics usually relate to the abusive use of drugs and other chemicals, as legally defined by society.

Poisons, in contrast, are usually defined as compounds designed with the specific purpose of killing cells or organisms: cytotoxins. They act in a variety of ways, as will be examined in the following sections. However, as you've probably guessed, drugs can behave as poisons and poisons can be used as drugs.

13.2.4 Medicinal Toxicology

To paraphrase the 15th-century physician Paracelsus, *everything* is a poison, it only depends upon the dose. *Dose* refers to the amount of a substance taken into the body over a short period of time. Actually, Paracelsus was quite correct in saying that anything can be considered a poison in the right dosage, even water (too much water dilutes key components of blood, such as potassium and sodium, leading to heart and kidney failure). Often, there can be a fine line between the correct therapeutic dosage to treat a problem and a toxic dosage causing harm. For example, the life-saving, plant-derived heart medicines digitalis (from foxglove) and atropine (from deadly nightshade, Figure 13.10) in the right dosages help compromised hearts function better, while just slightly more than the beneficial dosage is fatal.

Toxicity also depends on how long a person is exposed to the chemical. *Acute toxicity* refers to a single dosage, while *chronic toxicity* refers to effects spread over a longer period of time. Effects of an acute exposure are usually seen within the first several minutes to days after exposure, while chronic effects may take months or even years to become evident. Typically, the doses for acute exposure are higher than those resulting in chronic exposure, and the immediate symptoms are much more noticeable and severe. For example, acute toxicity of aspirin occurs at levels above 150 mg/kg of a person's body weight (the amount found in about 20 of the 500 mg "extra-strength" tablets for a 150 lb person; see LD_{50} below). Chronic toxicity for aspirin, however, is usually below 100 mg/kg taken over many days or weeks. Acute poisoning symptoms frequently include nausea, abdominal pain, organ

FIGURE 13.10   Deadly nightshade (*Atropa belladonna*) provides a life-saving heart medicine, atropine, but a slightly too large or too small a dose can be deadly or ineffective, respectively.

Source: Prof. Dr. Otto Wilhelm, Thomé Flora von Deutschland, Österreich und der Schweiz, Gera, Germany, 1885.

failure, and may be life-threatening, as shown in Figure 13.11, while chronic symptoms may not be immediately apparent but may include lethargy, dizziness, weakness, and later on, liver and kidney damage. Acute symptoms may often be reversible while chronic symptoms typically are not, with much of the damage done before the presence of the toxin is even known.

A measure of the toxicity of a substance is its *lethal dose*, or LD value. Usually, the lethal dose is given as an LD_{50} value, or the amount of a substance necessary to kill 50% *of a population*. It is important to note that the LD_{50} value for a chemical refers to its effect distributed over an *entire* population and does not give the probability of any particular individual dying from a given level of exposure (a person with a sensitivity to a chemical may have a very low tolerance and a very high chance of death from even a small exposure). Other LD values are sometimes used instead of LD_{50}; in each case, the subscript refers to the percentage of the population killed, such as LD_{90} and LD_{95}, referring to the dosages needed to kill 90% and 95% of a population, respectively.

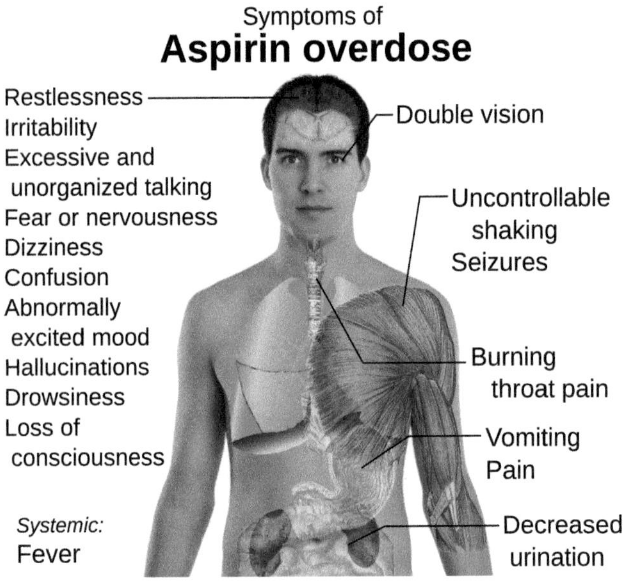

Symptoms of
Aspirin overdose

Restlessness
Irritability
Excessive and
  unorganized talking
Fear or nervousness
Dizziness
Confusion
Abnormally
  excited mood
Hallucinations
Drowsiness
Loss of
  consciousness

Double vision

Uncontrollable
  shaking
Seizures

Burning
  throat pain

Vomiting
Pain

Systemic:
Fever

Decreased
  urination

FIGURE 13.11   Symptoms of acute aspirin toxicity.

Source: Retrieved from Wikimedia Commons; used per Creative Commons Attribution.

TABLE 13.1 LD_{50} values for several common chemical and drugs

SUBSTANCE	LD_{50} (MG/KG)
Water	90,000
Sugar (Sucrose)	29,700
Table Salt (NaCl)	3,000
Aspirin	1,750
Detergent	1,260
Ethanol	1,000
Morphine	500
Caffeine	200
Heroin	150
Lead	20
Cocaine	17.5
Cyanide	10
Nicotine	2
Strychnine	0.8
Batrachotoxin[†]	0.002
Tetanus or Botulinus	0.000001

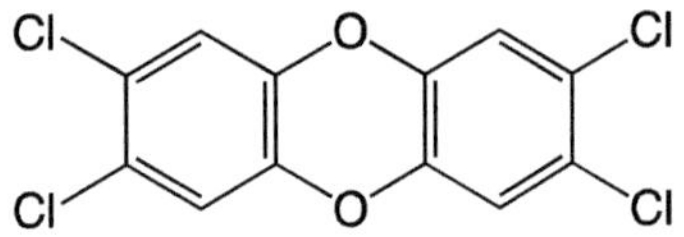

Species	LD_{50} (mg /Kg)
Guinea Pig	0.0006
Monkey	0.07
Rabbit	0.115
Hamster	3.5

FIGURE 13.12 LD_{50} values for dioxin for different species.

It is, of course, never ethical to experiment directly on human subjects to determine LD_{50} values, although occasionally these levels are known for humans from accidental exposures. Typically, however, animals are used to determine the LD_{50} values, and then estimates are made for humans from these data. It is important to note that LD_{50} values for a particular chemical are very species-specific, so the choice of which animal provides the best model for humans is always up for debate, as seen in Figure 13.12 for the LD_{50} values for the

chemical dioxin in different animals. It is very important to note that LD values refer *only* to doses that cause death – many chemicals cause varying degrees of harm at much lower than lethal dose levels, such as temporary or permanent biological and psychological impairment, organ damage, drug dependence, and altered biochemical functioning of the body. For example, the LD_{50} value of methanol (wood alcohol, CH_3OH) is ~810 mg/kg, while the dose necessary to cause blindness is greater than ten times less.

Some LD_{50} values for various commonly encountered drugs and toxins are shown in Table 13.1. Larger LD_{50} values mean that the chemical is less toxic; a larger dose must be given to reach a toxic level. LD_{50} values are reported in terms of milligrams of the chemical per kilogram of body weight and refer to acute exposures, those taken in one dose. These ideas mean that the larger the body, the more of the chemical that must be administered to get the same toxic result (see Box 13.2). For example, it's clear that for beverage alcohol (ethanol, C_2H_5OH), vastly different amounts are needed to reach life-threatening, toxic levels; 110 g (~6 beers taken quickly) for a 240 lb person to just 20 g (~1 beer) for a 44 lb child are required to reach lethal levels.

BOX 13.2   USING LD_{50} VALUES: BODY WEIGHT EFFECTS

LD_{50} values, in mg of chemical per kg of body weight, relate to the size of the person since larger bodies tolerate more of a chemical. It is easy to calculate what the LD_{50} dosage would be for a particular-sized person. Here's an example using ethanol, or "drinking" alcohol (C_2H_5OH):

GENERAL EQUATIONS:

$$LD_{50} = \frac{Y \text{ mg of substance}}{1 \text{ kg body weight}}$$

$$LD_{50}.Z \text{ mg} = (X \text{ kg body weight})(LD_{50}) = (X \text{ kg body weight})\left(\frac{Y \text{ mg of substance}}{1 \text{ kg body weight}}\right)$$

FOR A 150 LB PERSON (68 KG):

$$LD_{50} = (68 \text{ kg body weight})\left(\frac{1,000 \text{ mg EtOH}}{1 \text{ kg body weight}}\right) = 68,000 \text{ mg} = 68 \text{ g EtOH}$$

FOR A 240 LB PERSON (60 KG):

$$LD_{50} = (\sim 110 \text{ kg body weight})\left(\frac{1,000 \text{ mg EtOH}}{1 \text{ kg body weight}}\right) = 110,000 \text{ mg} = 110 \text{ g EtOH}$$

FOR A 44 LB CHILD (20 KG):

$$LD_{50} = (20 \text{ kg body weight})\left(\frac{1,000 \text{ mg EtOH}}{1 \text{ kg body weight}}\right) = 20,000 \text{ mg} = 20 \text{ g EtOH}$$

(Note: ~17 g of alcohol is what is found in one 12 oz beer (6% alcohol) and 1 oz of ethanol weighs about 23.2 g.)

Some surprising results also come out of LD calculations by comparing different compounds for the same size person (see Box 13.3). For example, nicotine, found in cigarettes, is five times more toxic than cyanide. Furthermore, the tetanus toxin is 10 million times more toxic than cyanide, such that a grain of the toxin, barely large enough to see, could be fatal.

BOX 13.3   MORE LD_{50} CALCULATIONS

Cyanide (for 150 lb human - ~ 68 kg):
(68 kg)(10 mg/kg) = 680 mg (0.68 g)
Nicotine (for 150 lb human; e.g., from cigarettes):
(68 kg)(2 mg/kg) = 136 mg (0.14 g)
(note: 1 cigarette delivers ~ 2 mg nicotine)
Strychnine (for 150 lb human - ~ 68 kg):
(68 kg)(0.8 mg/kg) = 54 mg (0.05 g)
Batrachotoxin (for 150 lb human - ~ 68 kg):
(68 kg)(0.002 mg/kg) = 0.136 mg (0.0001 g)
Tetanus Toxin (for 150 lb human - ~ 68 kg):
(68 kg)(0. 000001 mg/kg) = 0.068 mg!

(**Note**: For comparison, there are 500 mg in a typical "extra-strength" Tylenol tablet.)

Previous exposure to a chemical can also have a profound effect upon the response a person has to later exposures. In general, there are three ways that a prior exposure can play a role.

- **Sensitization**: Prior exposure may lead to a heightened response the second time someone is exposed to a compound. This often involves an immune-type response on the second exposure to even very small amounts, well below toxic levels. This can lead to an overly strong response, such as whole-body involvement in anaphylactic shock that can lead to rapid death (Figure 13.13). This type of allergic response can occur with any type of allergen but is often seen in exposures to food, insect stings, snakebites, poisons, and medication (drugs).
- **Tolerance**: The body may adapt to chronic exposure to a compound, leading to an increased acceptance (tolerance) of the chemical by the body, as illustrated in Figure 13.14. When this happens, an

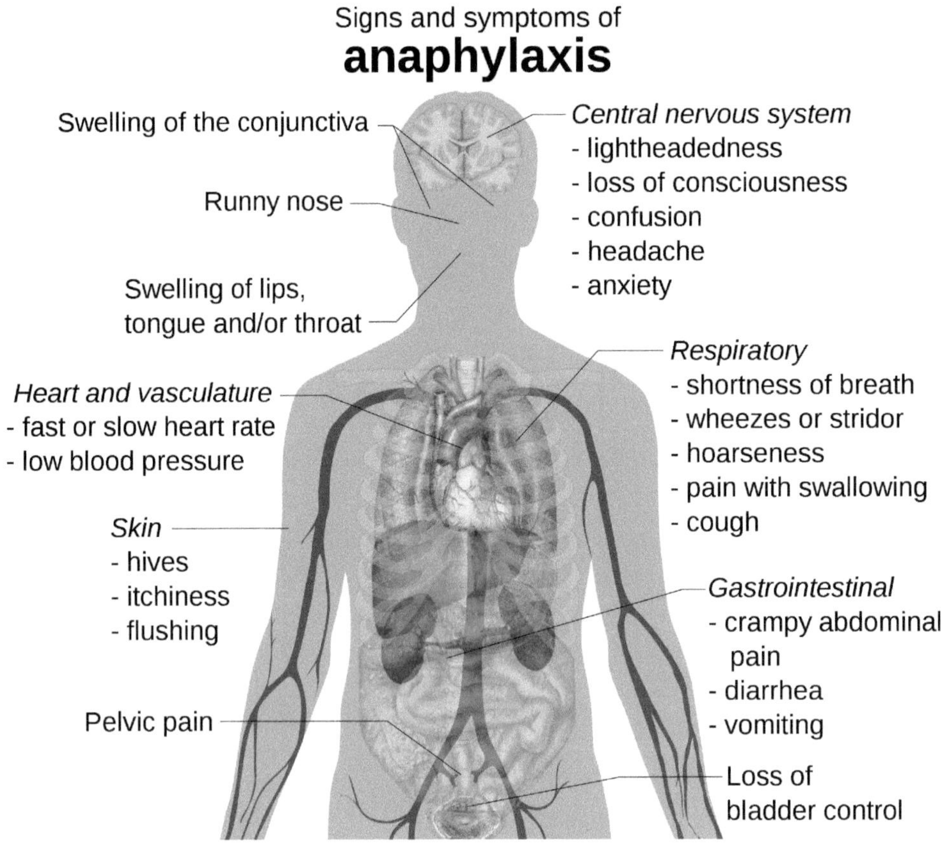

Signs and symptoms of
anaphylaxis
Swelling of the conjunctiva
Runny nose
Swelling of lips,
tongue and/or throat
Heart and vasculature
- fast or slow heart rate
- low blood pressure
Skin
- hives
- itchiness
- flushing
Pelvic pain
Central nervous system
- lightheadedness
- loss of consciousness
- confusion
- headache
- anxiety
Respiratory
- shortness of breath
- wheezes or stridor
- hoarseness
- pain with swallowing
- cough
Gastrointestinal
- crampy abdominal
pain
- diarrhea
- vomiting
Loss of
bladder control

FIGURE 13.13 Symptoms of anaphylactic shock, a response to prior sensitization to a drug or poison.

Source: Retrieved from Wikimedia Commons; used per Creative Commons Attribution.

Progressive Model
Steady-state Model
Dose required for minimum response
Time (weeks)

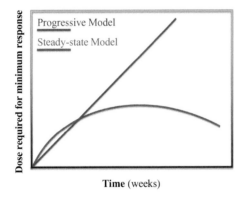

FIGURE 13.14 Amount of drug needed to achieve the same response from a patient; more drug is needed over time just to have the same effect (blue line).

increased dose is needed just to reach the same original effect from the earlier lower dose. Many abused drugs, such as heroin, amphetamines, morphine, barbiturates, and alcohol, follow this pattern of increased tolerance in the user. When coupled with a built-up dependence on the compound, the body's response creates a vicious circle of the abuser requiring the drug in ever-increasing dosages just to have the same effect.

- **Bioaccumulation**: If a compound is not eliminated from the body but instead is stored in tissues, then over time enough of the poison can accumulate to cause significant problems. Heavy metals, especially, interact with living tissues to result in this type of toxicity.

13.2.5 Drugs, Poisons, and the Human Body

Drugs and poisons, like all chemicals, follow specific pathways through the body (pharmacokinetics), sometimes causing dramatic physiological changes in the process (pharmacodynamics). As mentioned before, a drug's pathway can be considered to have four distinct steps: absorption → distribution → metabolism → elimination (called "ADME").

Absorption: In order for a chemical to affect a person, it must first make its way into the bloodstream (Figure 13.15). There are a variety of ways to start this process, including:

- **Ingestion**: Ingestion means that the compound enters the gastrointestinal system through the mouth (orally). This can happen through contaminated food, drink or in medicinal formulations. Compounds taken in by this route must make it through the

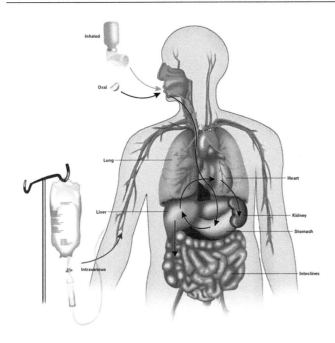

FIGURE 13.15 Methods for drugs to enter the body: ingestion, injection (intravenous), inhalation, and skin contact.

Source: Kim and De Jesus (2024).

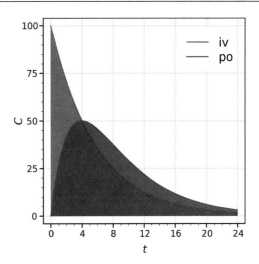

FIGURE 13.16 Differences in bioavailability – the amount of a drug in the bloodstream available to do its job – depend on how it is absorbed, with injection (labeled IV) being very fast and yielding higher concentrations than oral (ingestion) or absorption (labeled po), which results in a slower, more prolonged process with lower drug concentrations. The area under the curve indicates how much of the drug is in the bloodstream.

Source: Retrieved from Wikimedia Commons; used per Creative Commons Attribution.

formidable battery of digestive chemicals, starting in the mouth and continuing into the stomach and intestines. Eventually, if the drug survives this harsh treatment and makes it into the stomach and small intestine, it can be absorbed into the bloodstream, mostly through the small intestines (80%–90%). Because of the number of barriers that a chemical must pass through, the *bioavailability* – the amount of the compound that reaches the bloodstream – is lower and more drawn out over time for oral ingestion than for direct injection (Figure 13.16).

- **Injection**: An injection inserts the compound either directly into the bloodstream or into nearby tissue, bypassing most of the complications arising from digestive and other natural barriers designed to keep unwanted foreign chemicals out of our bloodstream. This method can result in a rapid bioavailability of the full dose of the chemical to the body and usually results in a high concentration of the drug quickly in the blood stream, especially when injected directly into a blood vessel. The injection can be directly into a blood vessel (intravenous), into muscle (intramuscular), into deeper skin layers (subcutaneous), or into the surface skin layers (intradermal), as shown in Figure 13.17. Many drugs of abuse are administered by injection since it delivers the maximum dose in the shortest amount of time.
- **Inhalation**: The lungs are organized to allow for the rapid and easy transport of molecules between the bloodstream and the air; O_2 is transferred into and CO_2 is transferred out of the body *via* the lungs. Breathing a compound into the lungs, either a drug (e.g., asthma medicines) or a poison (e.g., carbon monoxide, hydrogen cyanide, etc.), delivers the compound to lung tissue for rapid absorption. The compound is then absorbed through the thin lining of the lungs to enter the bloodstream rather quickly.
- **Skin or Mucus Membrane Contact**: A compound can be absorbed directly through the skin or mucus linings, such as lining the nose, under the tongue, or in the rectum. Examples of this type of delivery include transdermal patches (e.g., for seasickness and assistance in stopping smoking), suppositories (to deliver antibiotics or analgesics through the rectum), nasal mists (e.g., flu vaccines), and sublingual medications (e.g., under-the-tongue heart drugs).

No matter how a drug or poison is delivered, it must eventually make its way from its point of initial administration into the bloodstream. As mentioned before, the body has a number of protective barriers that limit this from happening. For example, when taken orally, a drug is first transported *via* a special blood vessel ("portal vein") directly from the intestines to the liver, bypassing entirely the body's bloodstream loop (Figure 13.18). There, it must first go through an initial screening pass in the liver – called the "first-pass effect" – before entering the bloodstream. The amount of a compound that actually makes it into the bloodstream, its bioavailability, is thus regulated by the liver. Other delivery methods bypass the liver, although all but direct injection have hurdles to pass before the chemical can make its way into the bloodstream.

INJECTION TECHNIQUES

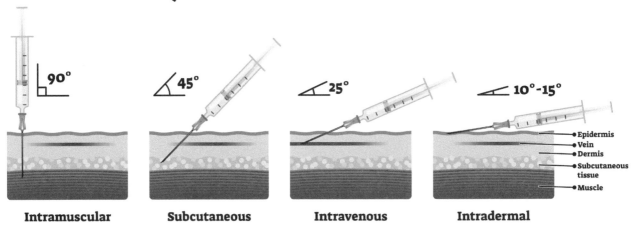

FIGURE 13.17   Methods of administering drugs by injection through the skin: into muscle (intramuscular) into the deeper skin layers (subcutaneous), into a blood vessel (intravenous), or into the surface skin layers (intradermal).

Source: Shutterstock.com.

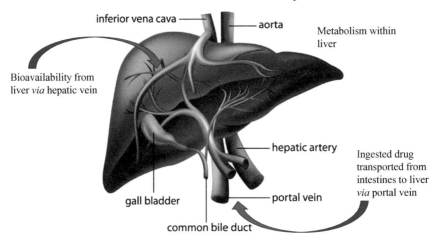

FIGURE 13.18   First pass of ingested drugs from the intestines is transported by the portal vein to the liver for preliminary screening before making its way into the bloodstream.

Source: iStockphoto. Credit: blueringmedia.

Distribution: Once in the bloodstream, absorbed chemicals are rapidly carried throughout the body (Figure 13.19). On average, red blood cells make a complete circuit of the body in about 60 seconds at speeds of up to ~12 ft/s in the larger vessels, carrying drugs, poisons, and everything else associated with a living organism along with it. This distribution can be affected by circulation problems and the presence of other molecules, such as fats and proteins, that grab onto the drug. In order to cause a desired effect, however, a chemical must make it to the specific "target" cells (organ). If the drug is not specific for a particular target organ, however, it can be taken up by other organs, often leading to a variety of unwanted side effects or a decrease in its effectiveness. Some organs have their own "defensive" mechanisms that might slow or prevent a drug or poison from entering. One such formidable obstacle is the *blood-brain barrier*, a very effective roadblock of tightly packed capillaries that prevents most drugs and poisons from entering the highly sensitive brain. This barrier selectively allows only very small molecules to pass in or out, such as oxygen, glucose, and waste products, while stopping larger molecules from entering, including hormones, viruses, bacteria, and drugs. This barrier usually works quite well to keep the brain safe and functioning properly, but it presents a

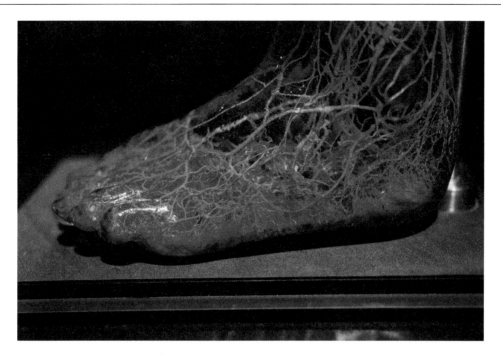

FIGURE 13.19 Photo showing the amazing complexity of the blood vessels that distribute chemicals throughout the body in seconds, including drugs and poisons. Shown is a real foot where all the bone and tissue have been removed, leaving behind only the "plastinated" blood vessels.

Source: Shutterstock.com.

significant challenge when designing drugs that target the tissues of the brain.

In general, compounds entering the body must ultimately make it either into or onto the right cells to cause an effect, often utilizing complex mechanisms that cells have developed.

Metabolism: Once at its destination and finished with its "work" on cells and organs, the drug enters a process where it is transformed into manageable waste products. This operation, called metabolism, forms a variety of products, called *metabolites*, and actually begins the moment the compound enters the bloodstream, as shown in Figure 13.20 for aspirin. While some of this breakdown takes place in the target organ and in the bloodstream, it is the liver where the majority of this decomposition occurs. The liver, the largest organ in the body, continuously screens and removes unwanted chemicals from the body, an enormous but absolutely vital task. This is accomplished by a host of very specialized proteins, called enzymes (Figure 13.7), which break apart, join together, and transform these chemicals into products that can be readily eliminated from the body.

Sometimes, the drug administered is not what causes the medicinal effect. Sometimes, a metabolite of the initial drug is responsible for the primary action. For example, while codeine may be what is administered, it is the metabolite of codeine, called morphine, that causes most of the therapeutic effect.

Elimination (excretion): The metabolites resulting from a chemical's transformation in the liver can take several pathways out of the body. Most water-soluble compounds travel through the kidneys and are eliminated in the urine, although some move from the liver directly into bile that is eliminated in the intestines (Figure 13.21). Fat-soluble substances, must first be turned into water-soluble compounds before they can enter the waste stream and be eliminated. Some compounds may also be eliminated directly either through the skin or into the lungs to be expired while breathing out.

As you can see, a drug or poison has a rather torturous pathway from the outside world, through the body, and then back outside once again, probably transformed into different compounds along the way. Each of these steps, as we shall see later, has very important implications in forensic toxicology.

13.2.6 Medicinal Chemistry

Most abused compounds, with the major exceptions of alcohol and plant-based compounds, are usually drugs designed for other purposes that are instead used for unintended "off-label" applications. For this reason, it is helpful when considering any forensic issues involving drugs to have a basic understanding of how pharmaceuticals are developed for medicinal uses.

The actual production of the medications available to us today is only the last and probably easiest step in a long path of discovery, development, and testing. Drug companies, universities, and foundations expend enormous effort to discover new compounds that are more effective, have fewer side effects, and are easier to make than existing medications.

Aspirin
Salicyclic acid
Gentisic acid
Gentisuric acid

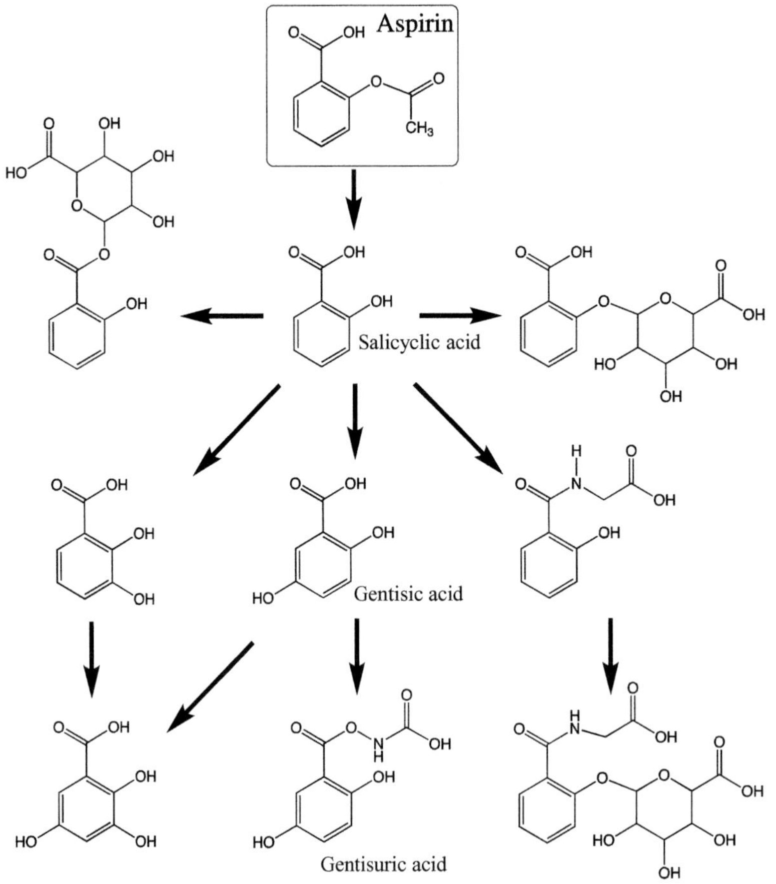

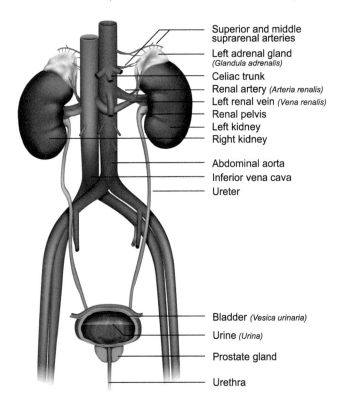

FIGURE 13.20 Aspirin and its metabolites that the body breaks down aspirin into for elimination.

Superior and middle suprarenal arteries
Left adrenal gland (Glandula adrenalis)
Celiac trunk
Renal artery (Arteria renalis)
Left renal vein (Vena renalis)
Renal pelvis
Left kidney
Right kidney
Abdominal aorta
Inferior vena cava
Ureter
Bladder (Vesica urinaria)
Urine (Urina)
Prostate gland
Urethra

FIGURE 13.21 Urinary system, responsible for eliminating water-soluble waste products through the kidneys.

Source: Shutterstock.com.

New drugs typically come from several approaches to drug discovery and design. These include:

- **Ethnopharmacology**: explores traditional folk remedies to identify new drugs (Figure 13.22). These cultural and traditional treatments are researched, collected, and attempts made to isolate the active ingredient(s) in the laboratory. Once isolated, it is necessary to conduct stringent testing to determine if the remedy truly works or if it lacks true medical validity. Important drugs such as aspirin, digitalis, quinine, and morphine were developed using this approach.
- **Fortuitous**: This method could also be called "accidental" since new drugs arising from this approach are discovered either while looking for something else or are the result of unintended circumstances. The key, of course, is that *someone must realize* what they have actually stumbled upon. The classic, world-changing example of this comes from the discovery of penicillin (see Box 13.4).
- **Chemical Modification**: An existing drug can be chemically modified to reduce side effects or to improve its effect by systematically changing parts of the molecule and seeing if the desired properties are improved or reduced.
- **Targeted Drug Discovery**: This approach uses a planned method to find new drugs. For example,

FIGURE 13.22 Wormwood (*Artemisia absinthium*), an ancient traditional medicine, contains effective agents for stimulating digestive processes.

Source: C. A. M. Lindman, Bilder ur Nordens Flora, 1901.

if the underlying biochemistry of a disease is understood, it might be possible to design a drug that interrupts the progression of the disease on a molecular level. Additionally, a drug may need to have only a few correct functional groups at just the right places in the molecule to be effective. Recognizing what are the active portions of a drug molecule can allow chemists to change the molecule in some places while keeping the active portion intact. This can lead to improvements in the action of the drug, as illustrated for morphine in Figure 13.23.

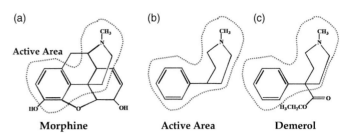

FIGURE 13.23 The active portion of morphine (a, within dotted circular line), the part of the structure of morphine needed to cause its pain-reducing effects, is only part of the molecule. Maintaining this active region (b) and adding other chemical pieces to the active region can result in a new molecule (Demerol, c) that is more easily produced, keeps much of morphine's medical properties, and is less addictive. This is referred to as "conserving" the active region of the molecule.

- **Combinatorial (screening) Methods**: Today, vast libraries containing millions of closely related compounds are prepared and rapidly screened to see if any of these have desired medicinal activity. Once candidates are found that show some activity, new libraries are built upon close relatives of these "first-generation" compounds and similarly screened. This approach allows new generations of drugs to be identified and refined very rapidly. The new and emerging areas of bioinformatics, biotechnology and related approaches are redefining drug discovery, offering opportunities to develop new drugs in ways never before possible.

Once a new candidate drug is discovered through one of the methods above, a long process of refinement, testing, evaluation, and validation begins. It may take ten years and more than a billion dollars to bring a promising new drug from discovery to pharmacy shelves. This process includes the synthesis and purification of the compound, safety and efficacy testing (including toxicity), multi-phased clinical trials, and regulatory evaluations.

BOX 13.4 FLEMING'S VACATION

In 1928, Alexander Fleming, a researcher studying bacteria, was ready for an extended break. In his rush to leave, he didn't quite clean up all of his experiments as well as he might have, certainly an understandable shortcoming when heading for vacation. After his return, just as he was about to dispose of an old petri dish containing some of his bacteria cultures, he grew curious when he observed that a bacterial culture that had accidentally been contaminated with mold grew *no* bacteria. The key, of course, was that he *noticed* this oddity rather than just washing up the dishes. But this chance discovery, one that would change modern life, was only one of a number of chance circumstances that led to the discovery. If any of these events had been missed, Fleming's important contribution – Penicillin, the antibiotic that has saved millions of lives – would never have happened.

Some of these chance events leading to the discovery of the antibiotic properties of Penicillin were:

- Fleming left some petri dishes uncleaned when he left for an extended vacation.
- A researcher on the floor below Fleming was studying a rare strain of mold (*Penicillium notatum*).
- Fleming was working on *Staphylococcus* sp. at the time (a bacterium especially sensitive to Penicillin).

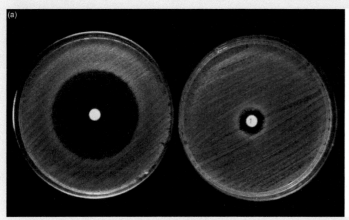 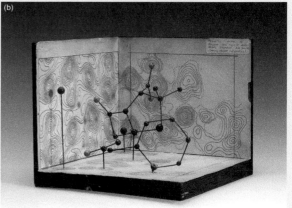

FIGURE 13.24   The structure of penicillin by Dorothy Hodgkin (a). (b) Petri dish cultures of two strains of *Staphylococcus aureus* bacteria. A white pellet of penicillin drug is placed in the center of each dish. At left, one bacterial strain shows sensitivity to the penicillin drug by forming a clear zone of inhibited growth around the pellet. At right, a second strain of bacteria shows resistance to the penicillin, and its growth is not inhibited by the drug pellet.

Source: (a) Used per Creative Commons Attribution-Share Alike 2.0. User: Science Museum London/Science and Society Picture Library. (b) John Durham/ Science Photo Library. Used with permission.

- Mold spores drifted from the floor below, into Fleming's lab, and contaminated some of his unwashed Petri dishes due to inadequate lab ventilation.
- The uncommonly cool weather first slowed the growth of the bacteria but promoted the growth of the mold.
- After a period that was just the right length, the warm weather returned permitting the growth of the bacteria and slowing the mold's growth.
- Fleming returned from vacation and noticed antibacterial action.

It still took over a decade after this discovery, and the work of many others, to make Penicillin a drug that could be mass-produced in a safe and effective form. When Fleming accepted the Nobel Prize for medicine, he truly said, "Nature makes penicillin; I just found it."

13.3 POISONS AND TOXINS

13.3.1 Introduction

POISONS are compounds that primarily function by killing cells. For centuries, poisoning was a feared and especially common method of "doing away" with someone. Medieval royalty had food testers, alchemists worried about finding antidotes for poisons, and professional assassins were well-stocked in methods to poison an unsuspecting victim without a trace. Conspiracy theories about the poisoning of influential people have accompanied unexpected deaths for centuries, although until the development of our modern methods of toxicology, death by poison could rarely be proven.

Poisons remain a visible part of our lives. Our childhood tales are filled with poisoning cases: *Snow White* and her poisoned apple, *Sleeping Beauty's* poisoned spinning wheel, and the Grimm's fairy tale of the *Poisoned Combs*, to name just three. As has been frequently pointed out, our literature, TV, and movies are made far more interesting through the effects of poisons on good and bad characters alike. In literature, poisoning is a common theme with such infamous examples as Shakespeare's *Hamlet*, Arthur Conan Doyle's *The Sign of Four*, Lemony Snicket's *A Series of Unfortunate Events*, Robert Graves' *I, Claudius*, Agatha Christie's *Cards on the Table*, and even *Metamorphoses* by Ovid (written in 8 AD). The comic movie from the 1940s, starring Cary Grant, called *Arsenic and Old Lace* tells the tale of two old spinsters who use arsenic and other poisons to help lonely, elderly gentlemen on their way to a happier life. In the classic movie, *The Court Jester*, Danny Kaye has to contend with the rhyme "The pellet with the poison's in the vessel with the pestle; the chalice from the palace has the brew that is true!" Even comic book superheroes have derived their powers from a toxic poisoning event: Spiderman, the Mutant Ninja Turtles, Daredevil, and many others. We are fascinated by poisons!

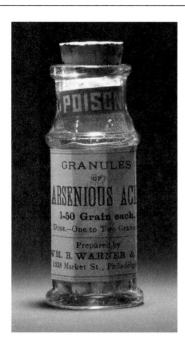

FIGURE 13.25 Arsenic-containing medicine from about 1900.

Source: NIH.

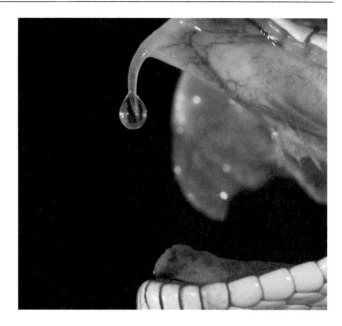

FIGURE 13.26 Rattlesnake showing venom from the fangs.

Source: Shutterstock.com.

Part of the mystique of poisons arises because they often come from very common, easily obtained sources that may mimic the symptoms of natural diseases and leave no traces behind – the magic bullet (Figure 13.25). The very tiny doses of poisons necessary to cause great harm can usually be disguised in the food or drink of unsuspecting victims. Symptoms can develop rapidly or be more insidious and develop slowly over many months, depend upon the way the poison acts. For example, low doses of arsenic, the so-called "inheritance powder," result in weakness, confusion, disorientation, digestive problems, and other low-grade symptoms in chronic doses. Over time, these symptoms, while ultimately leading to death, may simply be attributed to the inevitable decline of a person from natural causes. An entire "cult" grew up in Medieval Europe where would-be assassins were trained in how to use arsenic and other poisons to achieve their political, economic, and personal goals. Wives were schooled on how to poison their husbands, businessmen were taught to use poisons on rivals, and challengers even learned how to carefully poison wet nurses with less than lethal doses in order to murder the young heirs they nursed.

Toxins are distinguished as a special subset of poisons that are produced specifically by living organisms, such as snakes (e.g., cobra, rattlesnake), bacteria (e.g., botulinus, tetanus, *E. coli*), and certain plants (e.g., ricin, atropine, digitoxin, etc.). Sometimes, a further distinction is made by calling a toxin that is injected directly into a victim (as opposed to ingestion) a venom, such as from a snakebite or insect sting (Figure 13.26). A venomous organism, such as a black widow spider or a rattlesnake, is one that uses poison to defend itself while a poisonous organism is one that unintentionally causes harm through ingestion, inhalation, or skin contact. So, a snake may produce venom, while a mushroom may be dangerous due to the toxin that it contains.

Many poisons, however, have both healing and harming properties. Arsenic is still used medicinally to treat a variety of problems, including cancer and sleeping sickness. Digitalis is a strong heart medication, but anything more than the prescribed dose may be fatal.

Today, accidental and intentional poisoning cases are all too common and form an important part of the work of a forensic toxicologist. The pathologist and toxicologist must understand how various poisons are administered and how they affect the body. This knowledge helps them recognize the symptoms and determine if poisoning might have been the cause of death, and if so, whether the poisoning was accidental or intentional.

13.3.2 Method of Action

Poisons act in a variety of ways on the human body, but, in general, their modes of action can be used to classify them into two general categories: corrosive poisons or metabolic poisons.

13.3.3 Corrosive Poisons

Corrosive poisons are substances that act to destroy tissues through a "brute force" approach. These substances physically destroy tissues upon direct contact and usually act quickly. The most common corrosive poisons are strong acids and bases. These chemicals often work to rapidly catalyze destructive reactions in the tissues. Corrosive poisons typically hydrolyze fats, proteins, and other biological chemicals by adding the chemical components of water to sensitive bonds, literally digesting biomolecules by breaking larger molecules into smaller ones. For example, large fat molecules are broken into

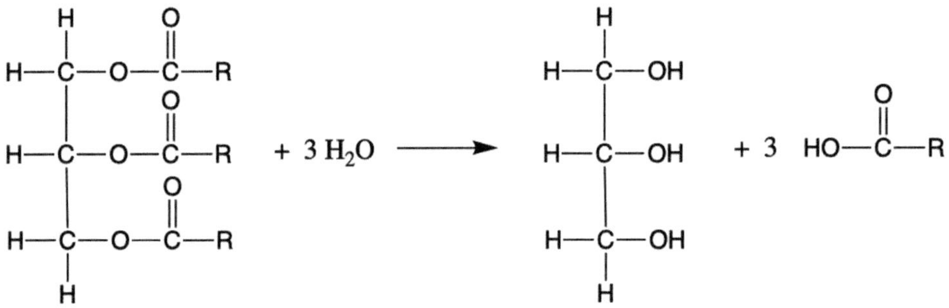

FIGURE 13.27   Hydrolysis reaction of a fat (left molecule) into the much smaller glycerol and three carboxylic acid molecules by the acid-catalyzed reactions of corrosive poisons.

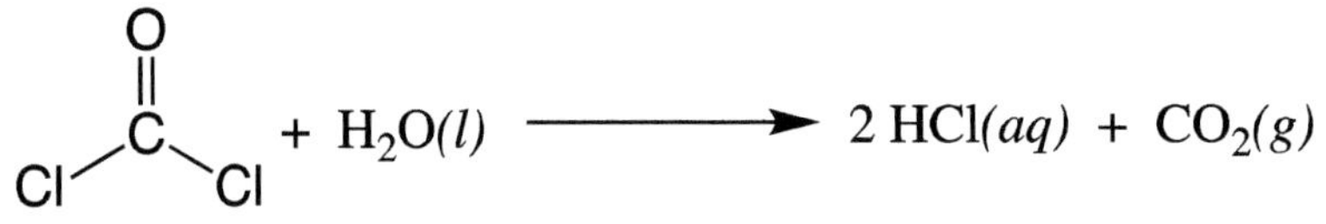

FIGURE 13.28   The reaction of phosgene ($Cl_2C=O$) with water to produce hydrochloric acid.

the much smaller molecules of glycerol and carboxylic acids by acid-catalyzed hydrolysis reactions (Figure 13.27).

In contrast, some strong acids, such as sulfuric acid, rapidly dehydrate or remove water from tissues, generating of a significant amount of heat. Cells die quickly when these dehydrating agents rupture cell membranes, denature DNA, and destroy proteins. If enough acid is present, the heat generated can be quite significant and also cause the thermal destruction of tissues. Some corrosive poisons, such as nitric acid and hydrogen peroxide, act as strong oxidizing agents capable of breaking strong chemical bonds.

Strong acids are common corrosive poisons and include sulfuric acid, hydrochloric acid, and nitric acid. Strong bases, sometimes called caustic poisons, include sodium hydroxide, potassium hydroxide, and lithium hydroxide.

Luckily, most common corrosive poisons provide clear warning signals that alert people when they come into contact with a dangerous compound. For example, just 0.01% of ammonia in the air causes choking and respiratory distress, prompting people to seek fresh air before it becomes fatal. Most acids and bases interact with the nerve endings in the skin, sending strong pain signals that alert the person that immediate action is necessary.

There are some corrosive poisons, however, that don't provide noticeable warning signals until damage has proceeded rather far and, because of this, are particularly dangerous. For example, hydrofluoric acid (HF), widely used in the electronics and glass industries and produced annually in amounts of over 1 million tons, destroys tissues and bone but usually does not send pain signals upon immediate tissue exposure. This is because HF interferes with normal nerve functioning, and it is only when the acid reaches much deeper tissue levels and bone that clear pain signals are first perceived by the body. HF is also absorbed more rapidly into tissues than other mineral acids, making its way to deep tissues and into the bloodstream very quickly. However, most of the toxicity from HF actually occurs from the action of the fluoride ion (F^-) that binds very effectively to calcium in the blood.

Some corrosive poisons are particularly problematic because of the compounds they produce in the body, rather than the direct action of the poison itself. Phosgene (Cl_2CO), a WWI poisonous gas still used in the plastics industry today, is a gas that, when inhaled into the lungs, reacts with the water there to form hydrochloric acid *inside the lungs* (Figure 13.28). The body then attempts to counteract the presence of the acid in the lungs by diluting it – usually a good response to reduce damage from acid exposure. But in this case, the body rapidly moves fluids into the lungs from other tissues, causing pulmonary edema (fluid in the lungs) that essentially drowns the victim in their own water. Unfortunately, phosgene does not produce well-recognized warning signals upon exposure; it smells faintly of new-mown hay and the reaction in the lungs is relatively slow. This means that by the time a victim begins to realize they have been exposed, most of the damage has been done.

Corrosive poisons are often contained in many common household items and are easy to obtain. A few examples are given in Table 13.2. These compounds are produced on the megaton scale annually, and their ready availability results in both accidental and intentional exposures.

13.3.4 Metabolic Poisons

Metabolic poisons are those that act by affecting the biochemical functioning of cells and tissues. Unlike corrosive poisons, metabolic poisons may not leave any visible marks behind on exposed tissues and may be overlooked. These poisons act in

TABLE 13.2 Common corrosive poisons

COMPOUND	COMMON NAMES	HOME USES
Sulfuric acid (H_2SO_4)	Vitriol, sour water	Rain repellent (auto), laundry perfume/dye-free detergent, drain opener, car battery
Hydrochloric acid (HCl)	Muriatic acid, spirit of salt	Toilet cleaner/disinfectant, rust and stain remover, laundry odor eliminator, tile cleaner, yard and garden muriatic acid cleaner, fish pond treatment
Potassium hydroxide (KOH)	Potash, caustic potash, potassium hydrate	Batteries, automotive cleaner, tile sealer, household cleaning solution, oven/BBQ cleaner, drain opener, lawn "food", non-aerosol hairspray, pesticides
Sodium hydroxide (NaOH)	Ascarite, caustic soda, lye, soda lye	Batteries, car wash, pipe cleaner, wood stripper, household cleaner, mildew remover, drain opener, disinfectant

many ways that are ultimately toxic to cells, including blocking vital chemical reactions, promoting damaging reactions, directly decomposing biological molecules, or competing with cells for needed chemicals. The checklist of how these metabolic poisons work is very long, but a few examples will illustrate both the range of ways in which these compounds may have their toxic effects and to illustrate the most common modes of action encountered with these poisons.

Carbon Monoxide (mode of action: competition with O_2, asphyxiation): Carbon monoxide (CO), a colorless, odorless, and tasteless gas, is classified as a metabolic poison. Carbon monoxide is produced by the incomplete combustion of organic materials, such as from an improperly working furnace or an automobile with a malfunctioning catalytic converter. These sources may produce large amounts of carbon monoxide without detection or noticeable warning signals to a victim.

Carbon monoxide works in the human body by binding very tightly to the iron centers of hemoglobin (Hb) molecules in our red blood cells to form carboxyhemoglobin (COHb). Normally functioning hemoglobin binds only rather weakly to oxygen to form oxyhemoglobin (O_2Hb), the molecule that efficiently transports oxygen from the lungs to the cells where the oxygen is released for use in respiration (converting nutrients into energy). This reversible, weak Hb-O_2 bond allows the oxygen to be released just where it's needed – a delicate balance between a bond strong enough to hold onto the oxygen long enough to deliver it from the lungs to the cells without losing it en route but weak enough to give up the O_2 when it reaches its cellular destination (Figure 13.29). The problem in CO poisoning, however, is that the carboxyhemoglobin, formed from the reaction of Hb and CO, is over 140 times *more stable* than the oxyhemoglobin complex. This means that the CO displaces oxygen from the Hb very effectively, bonding more tightly than oxygen, and it is only very slowly released from the Hb. The formation of the very stable COHb, therefore, effectively removes the molecules of hemoglobin from service, greatly diminishing the blood's ability to deliver oxygen and starving the cells of oxygen. This may not seem like a big problem, but because of the tight bond between CO and Hb, breathing in air containing only 0.1% of carbon monoxide for just four hours converts over 60% of the Hb in blood to carboxyhemoglobin,

reducing by 60% the blood's ability to transport oxygen. CO is not, however, a cumulative poison, and if the exposure is caught in time and the victim is given plenty of oxygen, all the CO is eventually released from the Hb, allowing it to once again function normally (although permanent damage and death can result from O_2 starvation before the Hb is restored to function).

CO poisoning is a silent killer; it gives no warning signals and can overtake a person either while sleeping or awake without their notice (Figure 13.30). It is also a common method of suicide – neither painful nor difficult, the victim just feels sleepy and never awakens. Common in CO poisoning is a "cherry pink" complexion of tissues, as shown in Figure 13.31, that arises from the bright red color of the carboxyhemoglobin.

Cyanide (mode of action: interference with metabolic pathways causing asphyxiation): Cyanide, CN^-, is a common chemical used in manufacturing, pest control, electroplating, and plastics production. While commonly thought of as the hydrogen cyanide gas (HCN), cyanide is also found in a variety of plants and seeds, especially cherry syrup, flax, apricot pits, cashews, corn, and chickpeas. Even though it is found in these natural sources, accidental cyanide poisoning from natural sources is very rare since very large quantities of the plant matter are required to reach a dangerous level. Cyanide poisoning can occur, however, from the use of alternative cancer remedies employing amygdalin (sometimes called bitter almond, laetrile, or Vitamin B_{17} in the marketplace), which is found in almonds and apricot pits (note that medical authorities have called this form of cancer treatment one of the worst "cancer quack promotion(s) in history"). Antidotes to cyanide poisoning are available, such as sodium nitrite ($NaNO_2$) followed by sodium thiosulfate ($Na_2S_2O_3$), but it must be administered very quickly after exposure to have any chance of being effective.

Cyanide is a very fast-acting poison when introduced into the body, often having a noticeable effect within seconds. Once in the body, it causes asphyxiation (deprivation of oxygen) but in a manner quite different from that of carbon monoxide poisoning. Cyanide interferes with enzymes in the body, particularly with an enzyme called cytochrome c oxidase, so

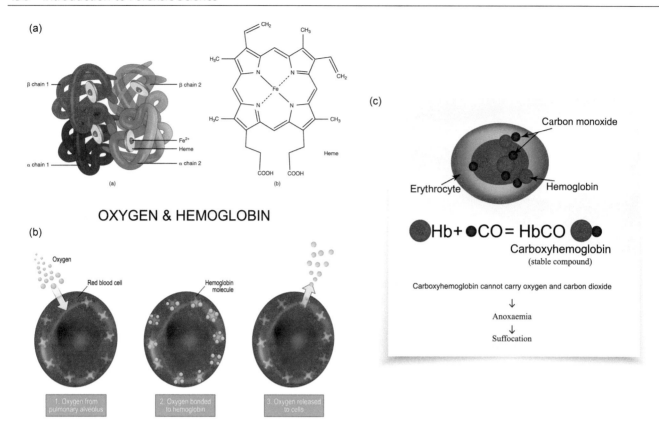

FIGURE 13.29 Carbon monoxide (CO) poisoning action. (a) molecule of hemoglobin (Hb), showing the four iron atoms as red spheres, (b) normal function of Hb in O_2 transport, and (c) CO displaces oxygen from the Hb in the red blood cells, thereby interrupting the blood's ability to carry oxygen from the lungs to the body's cells.

Source: (a) Used with permission Creative Commons Attribution 3.0 Unported; OpenStax College from Anatomy & Physiology, Connexions Web site. http://cnx.org/content/col11496/1.6/, Jun 19, 2013. (b) Credit iStockphoto.com. Credit: ttsz. (c) Shutterstock.com.

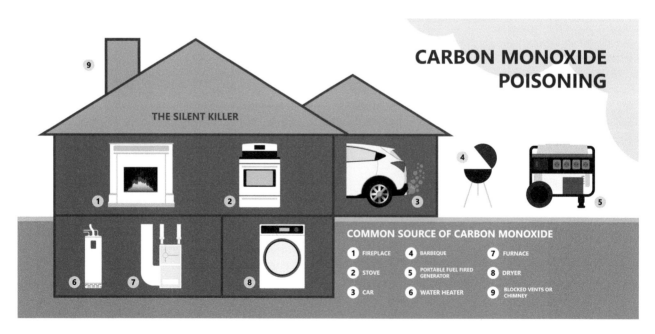

FIGURE 13.30 Common household sources of CO poisoning.

Source: Shutterstock.com.

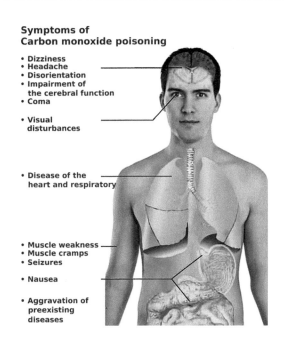

Symptoms of Carbon monoxide poisoning

- Dizziness
- Headache
- Disorientation
- Impairment of the cerebral function
- Coma

- Visual disturbances

- Disease of the heart and respiratory

- Muscle weakness
- Muscle cramps
- Seizures

- Nausea

- Aggravation of preexisting diseases

FIGURE 13.31 Symptoms of carbon monoxide poisoning, including a "cherry red" coloration in a non-fatal poisoning exposure.

Source: Retrieved from Wikimedia Commons; used per Creative Commons Attribution.

that, even while the cells are receiving a sufficient supply of oxygen from the lungs, they cannot use it; the metabolic pathway for respiration in the cell is shut down by cyanide's effect upon the necessary proteins and enzymes. Sufficient dosages of cyanide can cause death in minutes. A pink complexion, similar to that seen in CO poisoning, results from the bright red color of a cyanide-hemoglobin complex. Lower doses of cyanide can lead to confusion, vertigo, weakness, and, through accumulation over time, coma, and death.

Cyanide poisoning rarely occurs accidentally but is commonly used in both suicide and intentional poisoning cases because of its fast action and ready availability in tablet form.

Heavy Metal Poisons (mode of action: inactivation of enzymes and biomolecules): While there is no suitable, single definition of a heavy metal, they are usually defined in toxicology as elements in the periodic table that fall into the classification of a metal or metalloid. These include arsenic, mercury, lead, cadmium, iron, nickel, and others. These elements are all around us: in our food, in the air, and in the products that we use. Arsenic gives the green color to "pressure" treated lumber and stops decay, mercury is found in fluorescent light bulbs and medical vaccines, lead is used in car batteries, bullets, and pewters, and cadmium is found in pigments and alloys. Older

BOX 13.5 PAIN RELIEF MURDERS

Twelve-year-old Mary Kellerman, who lived on the outskirts of Chicago, awoke one morning not feeling very well and took an extra-strength Tylenol (Acetaminophen) capsule to help. Soon afterwards, she died from what was later determined to be cyanide poisoning. Nearby, Adam Janus also died from taking cyanide-laced Tylenol, as did his brother and

FIGURE 13.32 Tylenol murders: Surveillance photo of victim Paula Price purchasing the cyanide-tainted Tylenol.

sister-in-law who had gathered for his funeral when they took Tylenol from the same bottle that Adam had used (unknown as the poison's source at the time). Eventually a total of seven people from the Chicago area died from poisoning by cyanide hidden in Tylenol caplets (Figure 13.32). To this day, the crime remains unsolved but led to the US Congress passing tough anti-tampering laws.

Four years later, in Washington state, a frighteningly similar scenario began to unfold. Bruce Nickell and, Sue Snow both died from cyanide poisoning arising from tampered Excedrin tablets. Attention in the case quickly focused on Stella Nickell, Bruce's wife. She had purchased two bottles of Excedrin from two different stores, and both were found to contain cyanide. Only three other bottles in the entire state were found to contain cyanide, making it improbable that she had randomly purchased two contaminated bottles from different sources. Other pieces of the puzzle soon began to fall into place. Stella herself alerted police to the poisoned tablets after her husband's death even though it was initially attributed to emphysema. Police quickly realized that if Bruce had died of poisoning instead of emphysema, Stella would collect twice the insurance money, so it was in her financial best interest to reveal the cyanide-laced tablets. It turned out that Stella had recently bought a large amount of cyanide-containing fish-tank algae remover; so much, in fact, that the pet store had to make a special order. A book on poisons was also found in the local library with Stella's fingerprints on the pages describing cyanide poisoning, and she had talked for years about killing her husband.

Stella Nickell, convicted by a jury of murdering her husband, still insisted on her innocence while serving time.

Many other high-profile cases of cyanide murder/suicide have been reported, including those of Rosemarie Essa, Jim Jones, and the Jonestown murder/suicide of more than 900 people, Hitler's generals, and Rasputin.

paints containing lead still present a significant problem when eaten by children. Some of these heavy metal poisons, especially arsenic and thallium, are poisons of choice for homicide.

Heavy metals may enter the body through food, from the air, or by direct absorption through the skin. Once in the body, they react with the oxygen or sulfur-containing groups in enzymes to form tightly bound chemical complexes, rendering the enzymes incapable of doing their normal jobs, as illustrated in Figure 13.33. These metals accumulate in tissues and are not readily eliminated, making repeated low-level exposures particularly problematic. Symptoms of chronic exposure vary from mild headache and diarrhea to confusion and impaired motor and language skills. Exposure in young children is especially critical, where even small chronic amounts of heavy metals may significantly impact their mental development. Toxicologists typically measure the amount of heavy metals by either urine or blood analysis.

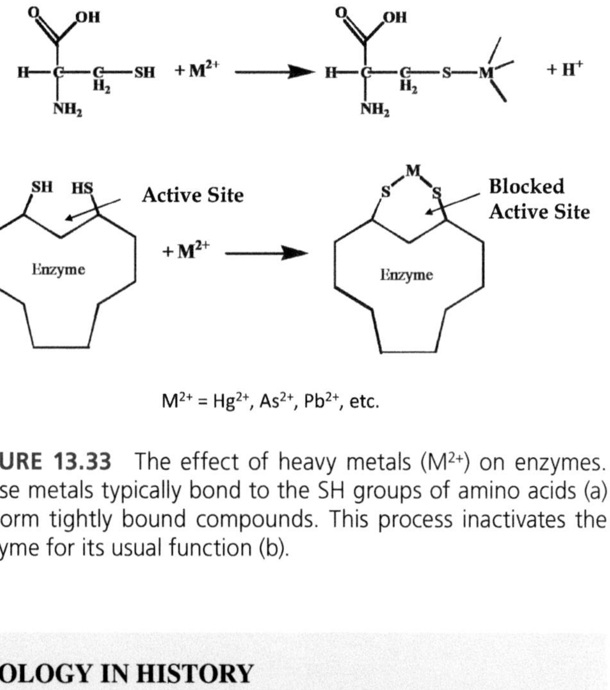

$M^{2+} = Hg^{2+}, As^{2+}, Pb^{2+},$ etc.

FIGURE 13.33 The effect of heavy metals (M^{2+}) on enzymes. These metals typically bond to the SH groups of amino acids (a) to form tightly bound compounds. This process inactivates the enzyme for its usual function (b).

BOX 13.6   MERCURY TOXICOLOGY IN HISTORY

Mercury is the only metal that is a liquid at room temperature, which has long fascinated people. It has also led to some significant problems. Low levels of mercury are stored in our tissues for very long periods and can lead to mental and physical impairment.

In older times, manufacturers of hats used liquid mercury to help mold and stiffen the felt into the right shape. They often suffered from symptoms of mercury poisoning: shakiness, aggressiveness, mood changes, irrationality, and antisocial behavior. The likely origin of the term "mad as a hatter" derives from this obvious connection between hat-making and occupational mercury poisoning. The classic example of a mad hatter is, of course, the character of that name from Lewis Carroll's *Alice in Wonderland* who fits the definition of mad both from the standpoint of irrationality as well as bad temper.

FIGURE 13.34   Lewis Carroll's Mad Hatter from *Alice in Wonderland* (1865) is a classic example of mercury poisoning. Credit: The Mad Hatter, illustration by John Tenniel, 1865.

Strychnine (mode of action: kills nerve cells – a neurotoxin): Strychnine is an example of a large class of chemicals called *neurotoxins* – molecules that interfere with the normal functioning of nerve cells. Normal nerve cells operate by turning on and off very rapidly to send electrical signals throughout the body. Different chemicals in a nerve cell turn the signal "switch" on and other chemicals turn it off very quickly, ready to send the next signal, something like a Morse code for the body. Strychnine and most other neurotoxins work by stopping the nerves from turning off and relaxing after firing, resulting in severe muscle spasms and nerve tiring. Over time, the muscles tire, and neurons (nerve cells) "burn out" from prolonged operation. Initial symptoms include paralysis, severe pain, and intense spasms. The action of strychnine eventually leads to complete exhaustion and failure of the muscles to work, including the muscles needed for pumping the heart and for breathing. Strychnine is readily available and is still used as a pesticide (most commonly as rat poison).

There are many classes and types of neurotoxins, including toxins and venom from thousands of plants (e.g., horse chestnut and Buckeye tree), animals (e.g., bees, scorpions, spiders, snakes, and fish), and bacteria (e.g., botulinum toxin – the

most potent of all known poisons), including the Japanese pufferfish toxin (tetrodotoxin) shown in Figure 13.35. Chemical warfare agents, the so-called "nerve gases" such as *sarin*, are also mostly potent neurotoxins.

Other Poisons (various modes of action): Some poisons, while not neurotoxins, act by emulating important biological molecules but without their beneficial action. For example, dioxins (a class of chlorine-containing organic molecules) mimic hormones in the body and disrupt the myriad chemical reactions controlled by our hormones. These molecules bind to specific sites in cells called *receptors* and "unlock" access to chemical reactions that may be harmful to the cell. The intentional dioxin poisoning of Ukrainian president Viktor Yushchenko illustrates the devastating effects of these types of biomolecule mimics (Figure 13.36).

These are just a few examples of the various modes of operation of common poisons and toxins in the body, illustrating how they can have cytotoxic effects. The forensic toxicologist needs to know how these chemicals work, the range of symptoms they produce, and how to detect and measure their presence in the body. The analytical methods used for determining the presence of drugs and poisons will be presented in more detail later in this chapter.

FIGURE 13.35   Japanese pufferfish, whose meat is considered a delicacy in some places make the potent neurotoxin *tetrodotoxin*, fatal in amounts of only a few milligrams and 1,250 times more toxic than cyanide. A fatal dose could fit on the head of a pin and typically results in around 50 deaths annually in Japan.

Source: Used per Creative Commons Attribution-Share Alike 4.0 International license, User: Totti.

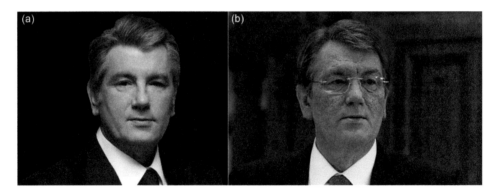

FIGURE 13.36   Viktor Yushchenko, a Ukrainian presidential candidate in 2004, was poisoned with dioxin. The pictures show before (a) and after (b) photos of his poisoning.

Source: (a) Adapted from image of Government of Ukraine. Used per Creative Commons Attribution 4.0 International. b) Used per Creative Commons Attribution-ShareAlike 3.0 Unported. User: Muumi.

BOX 13.7   SERIAL POISONERS

History is full of serial poisoners who ply their trade on unsuspecting victims for personal profit and satisfaction, and the supply doesn't seem to be slowing. A sample of the hundreds of known cases includes:

- *The Council of Ten* in Renaissance Venice poisoned for a fee for private reasons or to protect the "security of the Republic of Venice." They sponsored poison training "schools" and maintained a skilled set of assassins on call.
- *Belle Gunness* (1859–1908) murdered her husband and two children to collect money to buy a farm in Indiana. She may have murdered all her children, boyfriends, and husbands. Later, she lived an early version of the Broadway show *Arsenic and Old Lace* by putting ads in the local newspaper for lonely men, only to dispatch them with poison. After a fire destroyed the farm, the remains of an estimated 49 victims were discovered.
- Poisoner *Donald Harvey* was a nurse in the Cincinnati area who became known as the "Angel of Death" when he pleaded guilty to 37 murders. Official estimates place the total number between 37 and 57 deaths. He claimed that he murdered to "ease the pain" of terminally ill patients.

FIGURE 13.37 Painting entitled *A glass of wine with Caesar Borgia* (1893) by John Collier (1850–1934.) In Renaissance Italy, poisoning was so frequently used to effectively remove rival politicians, religious leaders, and family members that all natural deaths of popes, cardinals, and royalty were considered highly suspect. The most infamous name among poisoners was the Borgia family, who were thought to be involved in using poisons such as arsenic, strychnine and aconite in drinks, gloves, book pages, and other places.

Credit: A Glass of Wine with Caesar Borgia, John Collier, 1893.

- *Genene Jones*, a pediatric nurse in Texas, killed between 11 and 46 children by lethal injection, although she was convicted in 1985 for the killing of just two victims.
- In 2000, *Kristin Rossum* poisoned her husband with fentanyl to indulge in a love affair with her boss at the San Diego Medical Examiner's Office. She staged the death to recreate a scene from her favorite movie, *American Beauty*, with rose petals and their wedding pictures in bed with him.

13.4 DRUGS OF ABUSE

13.4.1 Introduction

While poisons ultimately act by killing cells, drugs typically act either by subtly modifying chemical processes or by supplying missing or removing molecules to our bodies. Drugs are by design intended for therapeutic uses: dealing with medical problems, delivering necessary biomolecules, or reducing problematic symptoms. The level of health and longevity today is largely attributable to the amazing array of drugs available to physicians for dealing with the many diseases and symptoms that we face, with new medications coming to the market at an ever-increasing rate. But today, the term "drug" has come to have vastly different meanings to different people, ranging from their recognition as life-sustaining pharmaceuticals to a view that they are substances taken for recreation and escape.

The same drugs that have been carefully developed to maximize their beneficial therapeutic action may also be taken for uses not originally intended. These compounds, deemed by society as drugs of abuse, are taken in efforts to quickly become stronger, look better, change mood, modify personal outlook, find release and escape from difficult situations, or

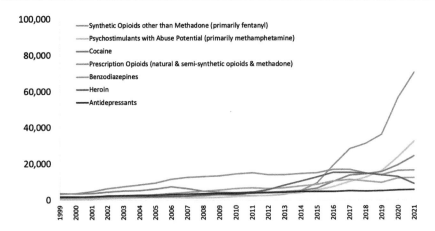

*Includes deaths with underlying causes of unintentional drug poisoning (X40–X44), suicide drug poisoning (X60–X64), homicide drug poisoning (X85), or drug poisoning of undetermined intent (Y10–Y14), as coded in the International Classification of Diseases, 10th Revision. Source: Centers for Disease Control and Prevention, National Center for Health Statistics. Multiple Cause of Death 1999-2021 on CDC WONDER Online Database, released 1/2023.

FIGURE 13.38   National drug-involved overdose deaths by drug-specific category, number among all ages, 1999–2020. The graph illustrates the use of pharmaceuticals for "off-label" abusive uses. Overall, drug overdose deaths rose to 91,799 deaths reported in 2020.

CDC, National Center for Health Statistics.

end lives. Prescription drugs are among the most common of all abused drugs, with hundreds of formulations readily available in-home medicine cabinets, on pharmacy shelves, and for sale illegally on the street. Increasingly, people turn to drugs to find rapid relief from personal problems and for recreational pleasure, often without considering the consequences of their actions, as shown in Figure 13.38.

All commercial drugs, both over the counter and those prescribed by a physician, have been closely scrutinized for their safety and usefulness before they ever reach a consumer. Prescription drugs are manufactured under exceptionally strict quality control standards before they are carefully administered and monitored for a patient, with a well-trained medical professional weighing the dosages needed against any potential side effects. When these drugs are taken for "off-label" uses in an uncontrolled fashion, guided by often dangerously misinformed street lore, the consequences are usually predictably bad, as shown in Figure 13.39. Drugs from street sources may be far from hygienic and commonly contain contaminants, diluents, and poisons, along with the actual identity of the drug itself being suspect. Taking drugs from unknown sources essentially negates the untold efforts and billions of dollars of research expended to ensure a safe and effective product. Under these conditions, people often become addicted to an illicit drug, spiral out of control, and then turn to crime or self-harm to perpetuate their dependence to the exclusion of other aspects of their lives. This is, of course, where forensic science steps in to try to understand which drug(s) contributed to a particular criminal action or observed personal behavior. Drug analysis has, in fact, driven much of the development of forensic laboratories worldwide. All societies are struggling with the effects of illicit drug use and combating the associated personal dereliction, crime, and violence.

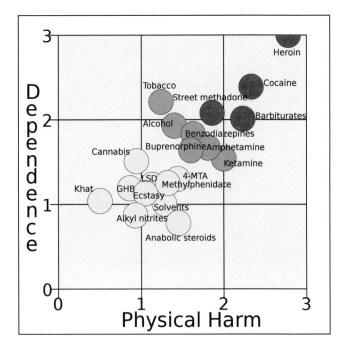

FIGURE 13.39   Relationship of various drugs with dependence and the potential for physical harm.

Source: Used per Creative Commons Attribution 3.0 Unported license; User: Apartmento2 (derivative work translation by: Apartmento2)

The vast majority of crimes today have drug use implications, either necessitated by drug-related demands or committed while under the influence of personality-modifying chemicals. Estimates indicate that greater than 80% of all crimes are somehow drug-related. These are not victim-less crimes but clearly injure the perpetrators themselves, their

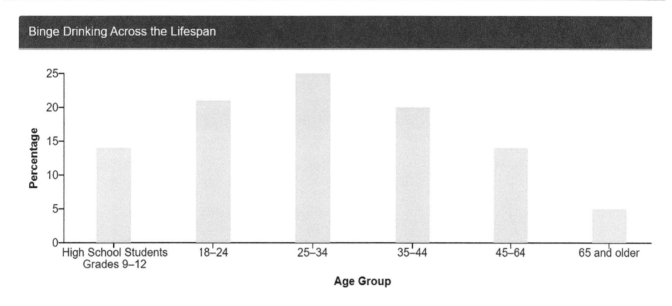

Data Sources: Youth Risk Behavior Surveillance System, 2019 and Behavioral Risk Factor Surveillance System, 2021.

FIGURE 13.40   Alcohol abuse levels (binge drinking) reported by age group (2021).

Source: CDC.

families, friends, co-workers, neighborhoods, and communities. Each year, at least 40 million serious illnesses and injuries result from illicit drug use, including injuries and deaths to innocent bystanders.

Illicit drug use has reached epidemic proportions worldwide. In a recent U.S. government study, over 15 million people aged 12 and over reported using an illicit drug on a regular basis, about 6% of households nationally. One-half of all adults reported use of marijuana at least once in their lifetime, and 41% of high school seniors reported using an illicit drug within the previous year. When those consuming alcohol are added to the list, the number skyrockets to an estimated 100 million Americans, 20 million of whom have a severe alcohol problem (Figure 13.40). While this represents a drop in overall use in the past 30 years, it still touches a very large segment of the population. The United Nations has reported that the annual use of illicit drugs in the 15–64 age group is about 10% of the world's population.

Many people deceive themselves by thinking that drug users come from a different part of society from their own. This is clearly not true. Statistics from the National Criminal Justice Reference Service report that three-quarters of regular drug users have jobs. Drug dependence reaches every social, educational, cultural, age, and income group. As can be seen in Figure 13.41, the levels of drug use cut across all economic backgrounds. It is often true, however, that lower-income abusers may lack sufficient resources to pay for adequate treatment, and communities with a rampant drug trade typically see increases in crime, violence, and failed businesses.

Drug dependence, not just use, also affects all socioeconomic levels. As described in earlier sections, different drugs have varying potential for dependence (Figure 13.39).

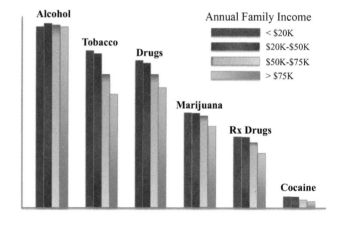

FIGURE 13.41   Percentage of youths aged 12–17 reporting regular substance use by annual family income (U.S. Dept. of Health and Human Services, Substance Abuse and Mental Health Admin.).

The dependence may be physical (physiological), psychological, or both. For example, some drugs such as LSD and marijuana have a relatively lower potential for physical dependence but a relatively high potential for psychological dependence. This means that, while the body may not respond as severely to removing the drug, a person's psychological makeup may drive them very strongly toward continued use. In contrast, the use of some drugs, such as heroin and cocaine, results in a very strong physiological dependence upon the drug, with severe or even life-threatening consequences arising from withdrawal from the drug. As an aside, the risk of overdose death increases dramatically when a person returns to a drug after a period of abstinence and withdrawal. This is because, as mentioned before, with continued use, the body grows accustomed to some drugs and requires continually increasing quantities to achieve the same effect. When someone stops using for a while, their physiological tolerance of the drug "resets" to a lower level. However, if they later return to the drug and administer a dose of the same size as their last dose, their body is now less tolerant of the compound, and an overdose results. Unfortunately, this is a frequent occurrence seen by medical examiner's offices in overdose deaths.

13.4.2 Drug Classifications

Most drugs of abuse fall into just a few general categories, such as: narcotics, hallucinogens, depressants, stimulants, steroids, and club (date-rape) drugs. In the following sections, each of these classes will be explored. However, due to the enormous abuse of alcohol worldwide, alcohol toxicology will be treated separately later in this chapter.

13.4.3 Narcotics

The term narcotic is often misused to indicate all drugs of abuse. However, the correct and proper use of the term deals specifically with a class of drugs that bring relief from pain and cause sleep. Narcotics are specifically analgesic compounds: chemicals that relieve pain by depressing parts of the nervous system. Common members of this group include opium, morphine, heroin, codeine, oxycontin, and methadone, among others. Confusion in the use of the term narcotic, however, still persists in places such as the popular media, law enforcement, and criminal justice, with some state laws still classifying non-narcotic drugs as narcotics, including marijuana (hallucinogen), methamphetamine (stimulant), and cocaine (stimulant).

Most narcotics are derived from naturally harvested opium, the sticky white sap from the opium poppy plant (*Papaver somniferum*, Figure 13.42a) grown all across the world, but especially in Asia. Once the beautiful red flowers drop off, the bulb is intentionally "injured" to allow the opium sap to seep out of the bulb. The opium typically contains about 10-15% morphine, along with some codeine and thebaine, from which a variety of other opiate narcotics can be chemically prepared. Heroin, morphine, codeine, and all opium-derived narcotics are related by their similar chemical structures, as shown in Figure 13.43. Naturally occurring compounds in this chemical family contained in the opium sap are called *opiates* (e.g., morphine, codeine, and thebaine). Those that are made synthetically *from* the naturally occurring opiates are called semi-synthetic opioids (e.g., heroin, hydrocodone, and

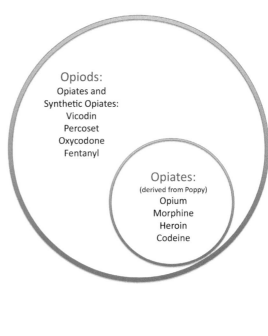

FIGURE 13.42 Opium poppy bulb (a; *Papaver somniferum*) showing opium sap and (b) diagram showing that opiates are a subset of the opiod group.

Source: Retrieved from Wikimedia Commons; used per Creative Commons Attribution.

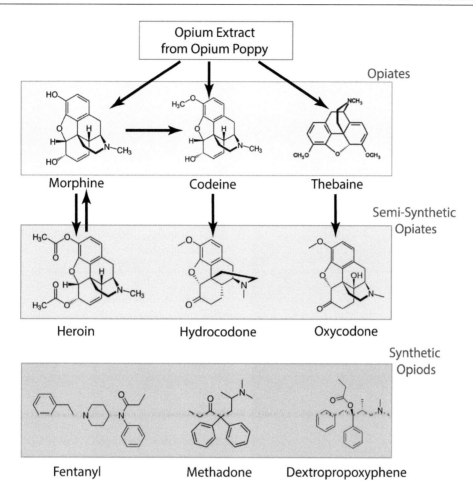

FIGURE 13.43 Opiate narcotics prepared from opium derived from poppy plants (*Papaver somniferum*). About 10–15% of opium is made up of morphine. Naturally occurring opium compounds are opiates, those made synthetically *from* the naturally occurring opiates are semi-synthetic opiates, and those independently prepared are called synthetic opioids.

oxycodone), and those independently prepared in the laboratory are synthetic *opioids* (e.g., fentanyl, methadone, dextropropoxyphene, etc.). The distinction between the opioids and opiates is illustrated in Figure 13.42b. The synthetic opioids usually are not structurally related to the opium-derived compounds and include vicodin, oxycodone, and fentanyl (Figure 13.43, bottom). These opioids have narcotic properties to varying degrees similar to those of the opiates.

Morphine is named, after good reason, for Morpheus, the Greek god of dreams, son of Nyx (goddess of the night), and attendant to Hypnos (god of sleep). It is one of the most powerful analgesics known to medicine and provides relief from deep-seated pain. The chemical structure of morphine allows it to precisely fit into special nerve cell receptors in a "lock-and-key" fashion, effectively blocking pain signals from ever reaching the brain. Morphine is the most commonly prescribed drug for severe pain relief today, but its use is tightly controlled, well beyond the level of most prescription medications. The physician must register with the U.S. Drug Enforcement Administration and report to them how much and to whom it is prescribed – if they prescribe too much, they face legal action. Morphine is also highly addictive and

prolonged use requires ever-increasing dosages to achieve the same effect. A lethal dose of morphine by ingestion is ~120–250 mg for an adult human. When taken orally, about 25% of the morphine makes it into the bloodstream, while nearly 100% is immediately bioavailable when injected intravenously.

Heroin is produced from morphine by chemically replacing morphine's two OH groups with two organic ester groups $(CH_3C(O)O)$ (Figure 13.43). Because of this chemical change, heroin is less water-soluble than morphine and must be injected directly into the bloodstream or made into a salt to increase its water solubility. Once in the bloodstream, however, it is able to pass more quickly across the blood-brain barrier than morphine, causing it to be more potent, faster-acting, but also shorter lived than morphine. When absorbed by tissues, heroin is chemically changed rapidly back into morphine. Long-term use of heroin causes remarkable physical changes, including apathy, loss of appetite, and personal neglect, as illustrated by Figure 13.44. Heroin produces a euphoric effect by suppressing the central nervous system to produce a warm and calming feeling due to blood vessel dilation.

Heroin is administered in a variety of ways, including injection (probably most common), orally, smoking, insufflation

Long-term effects of
Heroin

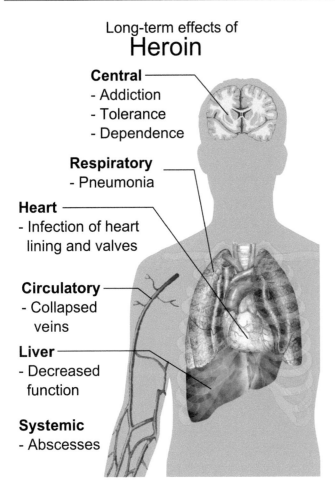

Central
- Addiction
- Tolerance
- Dependence

Respiratory
- Pneumonia

Heart
- Infection of heart lining and valves

Circulatory
- Collapsed veins

Liver
- Decreased function

Systemic
- Abscesses

FIGURE 13.44   Effects on the body of long-term heroin use.

Source: Retrieved from Wikimedia Commons; used per Creative Commons Attribution.

(inhaled), and suppository (anal insertion). Many varieties of heroin are available on the street, differing in purity and the nature of contaminants (Figure 13.45). Street heroin is very commonly diluted by adding a variety of compounds, most commonly caffeine, acetaminophen (e.g., Tylenol), quinine, and lactose (a sugar), with the typical concentration of heroin ranging between only 3% to as much as 50%. Uncertainty in the actual amount of heroin in any given street sample makes it very difficult and dangerous for a user to know how much to inject, with different heroin samples varying more than 1500% in the concentration of its active ingredient. This would be like guessing how much aspirin to take for a headache with a possible range of potency to get the same effect varying between 1 and 20 tablets. Typically, abusers are little concerned with what dosage they are really receiving or the consequences of mixing heroin with the >50 % of unknown material that they inject along with it.

In the body, heroin, like all opiates, is broken down by our metabolism into other compounds that are ultimately excreted from the body. Toxicologists are able to identify these metabolites to verify the use of opiates even after the heroin itself is completely metabolized. This provides a relatively long window of time for demonstrating that opiate use has occurred. As an example, part of the metabolic pathway for heroin and codeine is shown in Figure 13.46.

Codeine, while found in varying degrees in natural opium sap, is also produced directly from morphine by replacing one –OH group with an $-OCH_3$ group (called an *ether*). It is a mild pain reliever but finds most of its prescription use as a cough suppressant (antitussive) by decreasing the activity level in the part of the brain that controls coughing (as do most opiates). Codeine is less addictive than other opiates but it still can cause dependency. In some states and countries (e.g., Canada, Europe),

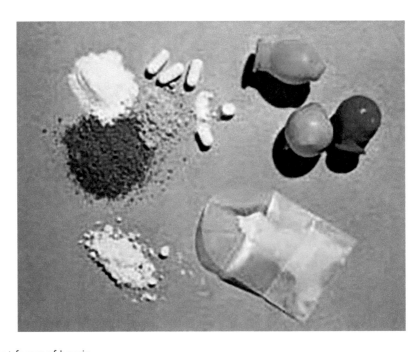

FIGURE 13.45   Different forms of heroin.

Source: Retrieved from Wikimedia Commons; used per Creative Commons Attribution.

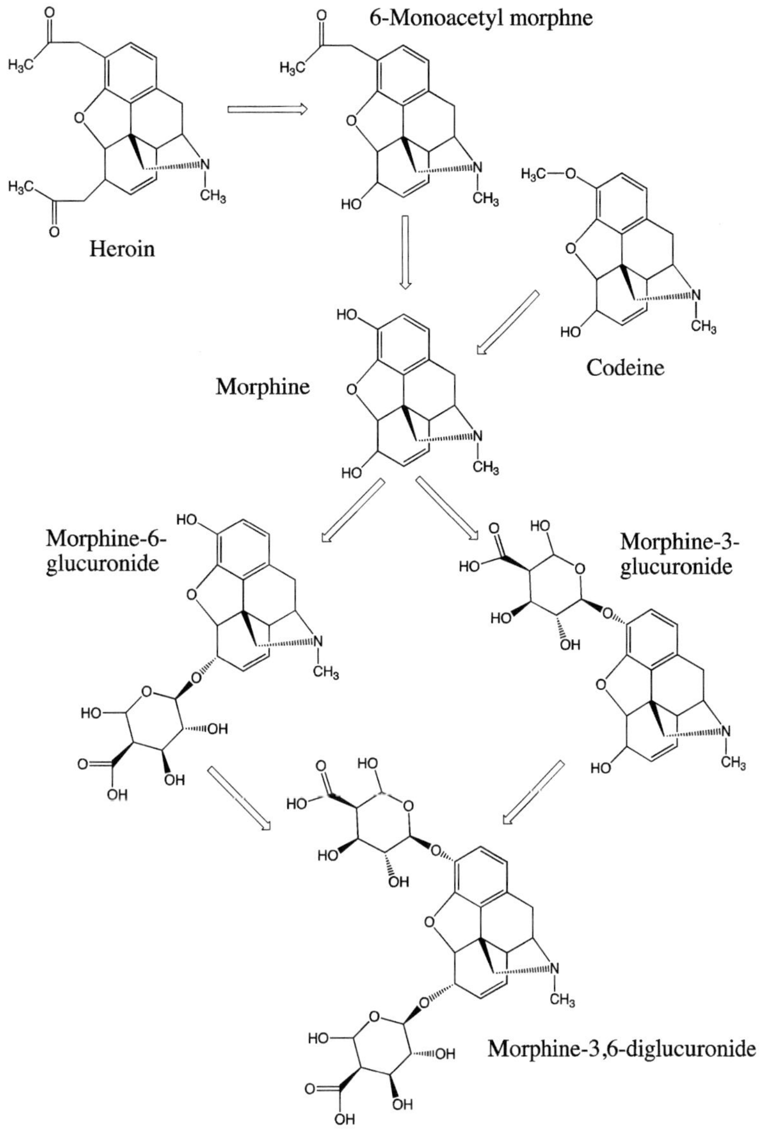

FIGURE 13.46 Compounds produced in the metabolism of heroin and codeine that can be analyzed for to confirm a diagnosis of opiate poisoning.

formulations with low dosages of codeine are available without a prescription, although usually there are restrictions on the total amount that can be purchased. Because of its increasing regulation and lack of potency relative to other opiates, it is typically not a choice of adult abusers but is still of concern for younger abusers since it is found in many household medicine cabinets.

A variety of narcotics are also chemically synthesized in the laboratory. These substances, called opioids, are not derived from opium but are classified *with* opiates because they act in a similar fashion upon the body. Methadone is a completely synthetic opioid that is today used as a substitute drug for opium addicts, although it has pain-reducing properties of its own. Levorphan and dextrorphan are two other synthetic opioids whose action is regulated by a simple modification of their structures (see Box 13.8).

OxyContin (Percocet) and hydrocodone (Vicodin) are medications widely prescribed for mild pain relief. Often,

BOX 13.8   LEFT- AND RIGHT-HANDED MOLECULES?

Sometimes, very subtle modifications in a molecule can dramatically change how it impacts the body. In chemistry, some molecules can have a "twin" that has different properties. For example, levorphanol and dextrorphan, as shown in Figure 13.47, are two molecules with exactly the same chemical components and only differ in that they are simply mirror images of each other. Despite the very similar appearance of their structures, when you try to place one directly on top of the other, they are not the same – just as our right and left hands are mirror images that are not superimposable. When you place one hand on top of the other, the major parts don't line up even though both hands are composed of the exact same parts.

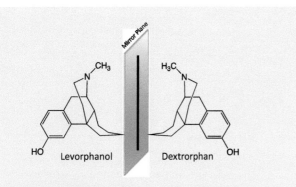

FIGURE 13.47 Handedness in molecules: non-super-imposable mirror images.

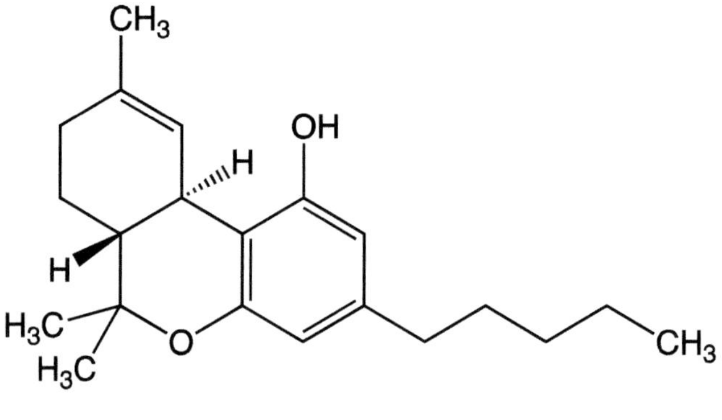

FIGURE 13.48 Structure of THC (Δ⁹-Tetrahydrocannabinol), the primary psychoactive ingredient in marijuana.

So, like our hands, we can say that the two molecules have a "handedness"; the chemical term is *chirality*. Both our hands and levorphanol/dextrophan are chiral. In fact, their names derive from this fact; "levo" comes from the word for left and "dextro" comes from the word for right.

Our bodies have many chiral molecules within them that interact differently with other "handed" molecules; right-handed molecules react differently than left-handed molecules, much like the way our right hand interacts differently with right- and left-handed gloves. For example, levorphanol is a more potent pain killer than morphine and is very addictive while its mirror image, dextrorphan, is completely non-addicting and without any analgesic properties.

these compounds are combined with other drugs, such as acetaminophen (Tylenol), and are available in time-released formulations to provide longer-lasting pain relief. Because of their ready availability, they are also easy targets for abuse. Since OxyContin and hydrocodone are frequently prescribed, abusers have found insidious ways to obtain these drugs, including pharmacy robberies and receiving multiple prescriptions for the same ailment from different, unsuspecting doctors.

13.4.4 Hallucinogens

Hallucinogens are compounds that alter normal thought processes, perceptions of the world, personal awareness, and psychological moods. Commonly encountered examples include marijuana, PCP (phencyclidine), LSD (lysergic acid diethylamide), mescaline, and ecstasy (MDMA or methylenedioxy-methamphetamine). But by far, the most commonly used member of this group is marijuana.

Marijuana (also called cannabis since it derives from the plant *Cannabis sativa*) is the most common of all hallucinogenic drugs used worldwide, according to the UN. Estimates suggest that over half of all adults have tried marijuana at some time in their lives. Controversy remains intense surrounding the legalization of medicinal and recreational marijuana use, with strong advocates on both sides of the debate. A number

FIGURE 13.49 Leaf pattern of *Cannabis sativa* (marijuana).

Credit: Franz Eugen Köhler, Köhler's Medizinal-Pflanzen, 1897.

of states and countries have either reduced or eliminated criminal penalties relating to possession and use of marijuana. Nonetheless, it is still legally classified in many places, including the U.S. federal government, as a substance of abuse with restrictions upon its possession and use, and is therefore one of the most commonly used illicit drug in the United States.

Marijuana contains a psychoactive drug that is quickly metabolized by the body into a number of other chemicals, many of which are psychoactive themselves. Tetrahydrocannabinol (THC) is the primary active ingredient in marijuana (Figure 13.48), although marijuana contains a complex mixture of many compounds, including other cannabinols. Typically, the leaves (Figure 13.49) and dried flowers of the plant are harvested for processing and contain the highest concentrations of THC, ranging in concentration from 5% to 20% THC. Cannabis is used in a variety of forms (Figure 13.50), but most commonly, the dried plant matter is simply smoked, although more recently, other THC-containing products have become popular. The dried female flower parts of *Cannabis* (specifically the trichomes, Figure 13.51) can be processed into a more potent powder form, called kief, that is pressed into cakes or blocks called hashish. The hashish can be further processed through a solvent extraction process to yield a red oil, called hashish oil. The trichomes are often useful in identifying the dried plant material.

Hashish can contain between 15% and 70% THC, while hashish oil can hold up to 90% THC. As with marijuana, these hashish products can be smoked, but many other methods of use are encountered, including vaporization, burning as incense, and cooking into food.

Cannabis is a hearty weed that grows well in many climates. The plants grow to between 5 and 15 ft tall and continue to develop

FIGURE 13.50   Various forms of *Cannabis*-derived products: (a) dried marijuana flowers and leaves, (b) keif, (c) hashish, (d) marijuana cigarettes, (e) marijuana resin, and (f) CBD/Hashish oil.

Source: (c), (d), (e), and (f) Shutterstock.com

FIGURE 13.51   Trichomes of *Cannabis sativa* (marijuana) where THC is concentrated.

Source: Antonio Romero/ Science Photo Library. Used with permission.

as long as they receive more than 12 hours of sunlight daily – less than that, and the plant begins to flower. Since cannabis plants are also used in hemp production (primarily for rope making), varieties of cannabis have been developed that minimize their THC content, allowing them to be used commercially in ropes and not be subject to international drug restrictions. Cannabis has been cultivated specifically for drug use by humans for millennia, with confirmed use dating back to at least 3,000 BCE in regions of Asia and the Middle East. Countries in Europe and the Western Hemisphere began to outlaw the possession and consumption of cannabis, however, only in the early 20th century, with the first laws in the United States probably dating to about 1906.

THC begins to have psychoactive effects on the body at about the 10 mg/kg level. Symptoms of low-level use include lowered blood pressure, increased heart rate, impairment of memory and learning processes, an increase in appetite, and mood shifts (Figures 13.52 and 13.53). THC rapidly crosses the blood-brain barrier and binds to nerve synapses in the brain (synapses are the junctions between nerve cells that complete the electrical connections in the nervous system). This changes the nerve signal pathways in the brain itself, causing euphoric feelings.

THC and its metabolites (especially THC-COOH) can be directly measured by GC/MS in urine, sweat, blood, and other body fluids. The half-life of THC in the body is quite long – about ten days, one of the longest among all illicit drugs. This means that marijuana use can be detected for weeks and even months after use. When used only once, the THC and metabolites generally clear the body to undetectable levels within about a week. Daily use, however, may mean that cannabis use may be detected for as long as three months in urine. THC can be tentatively identified in the field by the Duquenois-Levine and other color tests.

Although less common now than in the past, LSD (Lysergic acid diethylamide) continues to be a widely abused drug (the structure of LSD is in Figure 13.54). LSD was first prepared in the laboratory in 1938 from ergotamine derived from the Ergot fungus and is still usually synthesized from natural sources of lysergic acid. It is a "fragile" molecule that decomposes in light and air but is stable for long periods when kept dry and dark or in solution.

LSD produces altered mental processes, a distorted sense of time and space, hallucinations, and synesthesia (when

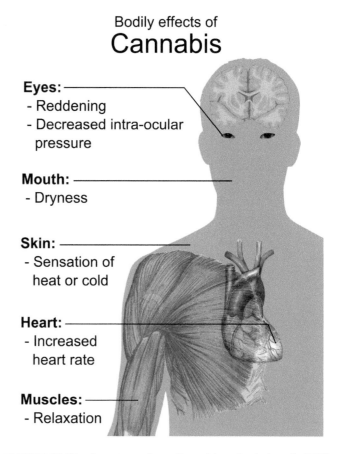

Bodily effects of
Cannabis

Eyes:
- Reddening
- Decreased intra-ocular pressure

Mouth:
- Dryness

Skin:
- Sensation of heat or cold

Heart:
- Increased heart rate

Muscles:
- Relaxation

FIGURE 13.52   Symptoms from *Cannabis sativa* (primarily THC) use.

Source: Retrieved from Wikimedia Commons; used per Creative Commons Attribution.

stimulation of one sensory form leads to stimulation of another sensation, such as when hearing a sound generates a particular visual sensation). LSD is a very potent psychoactive compound, with the typical dose ranging from about 100 to 500 μg and an LD_{50} value of about 0.2 mg/kg. LSD is usually taken orally, with one of the most common forms involving chewing a piece of blotter paper that has been soaked with an LSD-containing

FIGURE 13.53   Effects of drugs on spiders (the drugs were fed to the spiders through doped flies): (from left to right) marijuana, benzedrine, caffeine, and chloral hydrate.

Source: NASA/ Science Photo Library. Used with permission.

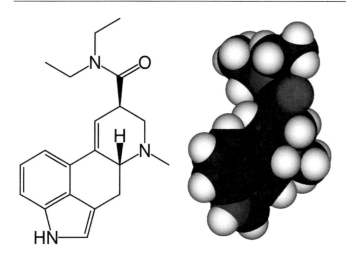

FIGURE 13.54 Structure of LSD; Lysergic acid diethylamide.

Source: Retrieved from Wikimedia Commons; used per Creative Commons Attribution.

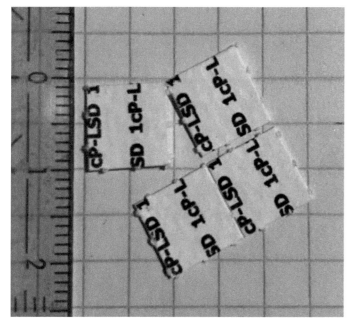

FIGURE 13.55 Sheets of blotter paper soaked with a dilute LSD solution are taken orally to administer the drug.

Source: Retrieved from Wikimedia Commons; used per Creative Commons Attribution.

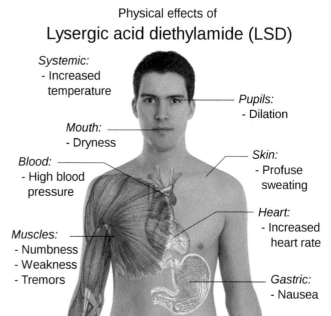

Physical effects of
Lysergic acid diethylamide (LSD)

Systemic:
- Increased temperature

Mouth:
- Dryness

Blood:
- High blood pressure

Muscles:
- Numbness
- Weakness
- Tremors

Pupils:
- Dilation

Skin:
- Profuse sweating

Heart:
- Increased heart rate

Gastric:
- Nausea

FIGURE 13.56 Physiological effects of LSD usage.

Source: Retrieved from Wikimedia Commons; used per Creative Commons Attribution.

with most serotonin receptors. This is believed to excite activity in the cerebral cortex of the brain, the part responsible for memory, consciousness, perception, and thought.

Since the dose of LSD required for an individual is so small (ca. 0.200 mg), LSD is more easily prepared, transported, and sold than most other drugs. LSD and its metabolites are readily detected in blood, urine, and other body fluids, although they are rapidly broken down by light and air. LSD is also fluorescent and glows bluish-white under ultraviolet irradiation.

A variety of other hallucinogens, both synthetic and those derived from natural sources, are commonly available. Phencyclidine (PCP or "angel dust") was initially developed as a synthetic medicinal pharmaceutical but was found to be too dangerous for use as an anesthetic due to a tendency to cause adverse side effects. While not manufactured commercially today, its synthesis is still performed in small illegal laboratories from readily available starting materials. Low doses of the drug produce feelings of euphoria and decreased inhibition. Larger doses can lead to anxiety attacks, violence, auditory hallucinations, and psychosis.

Natural hallucinogens have been used by cultures around the world since before the beginning of recorded history. Mescaline (peyote), isolated from the peyote cactus (Figure 13.57), and psilocybin, found in many species of mushrooms (Figure 13.58), have been used in religious observances worldwide to intensify experiences. These hallucinogens are significantly less potent than LSD and are relatively rarely abused due to their lower potency, increases in body tolerance, and limitations of easily available sources.

MDMA (3,4-Methylenedioxymethamphetamine, also known as "Ecstasy"), a synthetic drug, induces feelings of euphoria and reduced anxiety, similar to many other hallucinogens.

solution (Figure 13.55). The body quickly develops a tolerance for the drug, contributing to its relatively low risk for physiological dependence since it becomes more difficult to achieve the same hallucinogenic effect with continued use. Symptoms of use include pupil dilation, decreased appetite, weakness, nausea, increased heart rate, sweating, and tremors, among others (Figure 13.56). Long-term problems connected with LSD usage include psychosis and continuing hallucinations ("flashbacks"), which can arise years later even from a single dose.

The LSD molecule binds to many types of receptors in the brain, including all dopamine and adrenal receptors, along

MDMA is a very common recreational drug and works by releasing serotonin, dopamine, and other body chemicals to achieve feelings of well-being. The half-life of MDMA in the body is about eight hours, and it is rapidly metabolized and eliminated from the system.

FIGURE 13.57   Peyote cactus (*Lophophora williamsii*) from which mescaline is isolated.

13.4.5 Depressants

These compounds act to depress the functioning of the central nervous system, bringing about calmness and sleep. Many common drugs fall into this category and include tranquilizers, barbiturates, and alcohol. Since alcohol is by far the single most commonly used depressant and abused drug worldwide, it will be treated separately in Section 13.5. These drugs, other than alcohol, are commonly called tranquilizers, sedatives, and "downers." In moderate dosages, these compounds may produce symptoms similar to alcohol intoxication.

Barbiturates are derivatives of barbituric acid and have the potential for both significant physiological and psychological dependence. Still in medical use today, these compounds are prescribed for anesthesia, sedation, and treatment of seizures. Phenobarbital, secobarbital (Seconal), pentobarbital (Nembutal), and amobarbital (Amytal) are probably the most readily available of these drugs but, according to the DEA, are not likely to be heavily abused due to their mode of action and use primarily in hospitals. Some of these barbiturates have been called "truth drugs" since they have been used to reduce inhibitions to such a level that a person provides information they would otherwise not disclose. The most commonly used anesthetic drug today, however, is propofol (Diprivan), which is not a barbiturate.

The use of barbiturates has largely been supplanted by another class of chemicals called benzodiazepines, such as Valium, Halcion, and Xanax (Figure 13.59). These

FIGURE 13.58   The Liberty Cap fungus (*Psilocybe semilanceata*) that produces the psychoactive compound psilocybin.

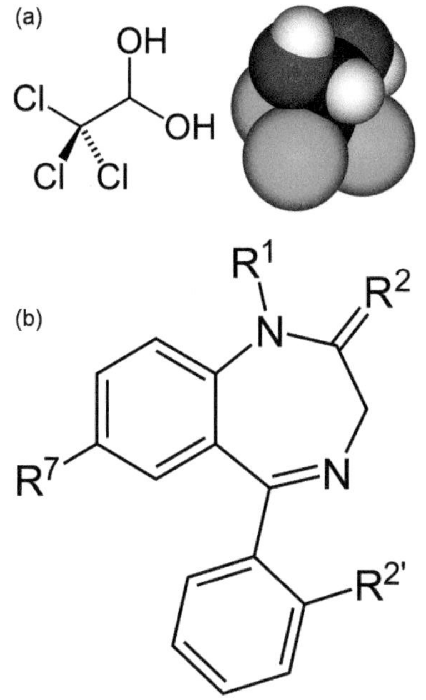

FIGURE 13.59 Chemical structures of the depressants chloral hydrate (a) and benzodiazepine (b).

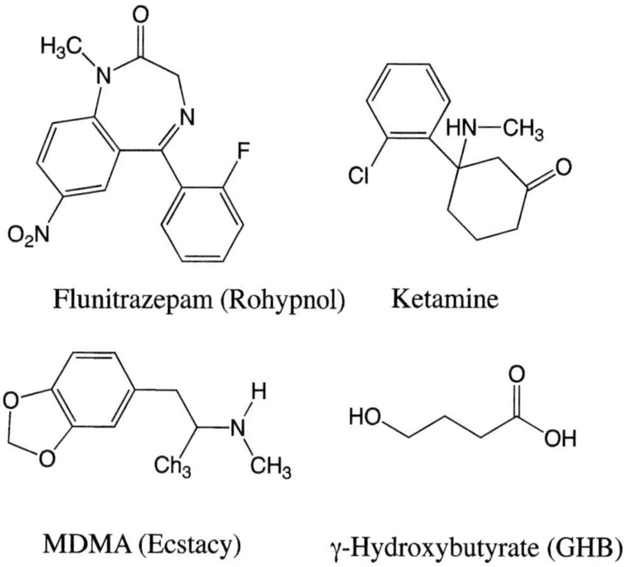

FIGURE 13.60 Common "Club" or "Date-Rape" drugs, including Rohypnol, ketamine, Ecstasy, and GHB.

compounds are among the most commonly prescribed medications currently in the United States, about one out of every five prescriptions written, and are used therapeutically to control seizures, reduce anxiety, and relieve muscle pains and spasms. In high dosages, these compounds act as hypnotic compounds, inducing sleep. These compounds are generally not heavily abused, despite their ready availability, and those who do abuse them often obtain the drug through multiple prescriptions from different doctors. The exceptions to this tend to be adolescents, with access to the drug at home or from street sources, along with heroin and cocaine abusers.

Chloral hydrate, first synthesized in the 1830s, is a strong sedative. In fiction and reality, this compound is the famous "knock-out drops" or "Mickey Finn," since it is very soluble in water and alcohol and is not illegal in all countries. Its medicinal use today is rather limited, largely replaced by other depressants.

A growing health concern, especially among the young, is the use of inhaled volatile gases, such as solvents, propellants, glue, hair sprays, spray paints, cleaning fluids, and similar compounds. While some of these compounds act in other ways, many of them serve as depressants. This includes "glue sniffing" and "huffing" methods of administering chemicals rapidly into the body through the lungs. Solvents are placed into plastic bags or soaked into rags before being inhaled. Unfortunately, these readily available solvents are absorbed very quickly into the blood stream. This activity leads to severe medical problems, such as permanent liver, kidney, heart, and brain damage that can lead to sudden death.

13.4.6 Club or "Date-Rape" Drugs

Several depressants, along with a few drugs from other classes, are specifically being used clandestinely to reduce a person's natural inhibitions and to induce amnesia of what happened while under the influence of the drug. These compounds are often part of drug-facilitated sexual assault cases (DFSA) and include Rohypnol, GHB, ketamine, and MDMA (ecstasy, actually a hallucinogen), as shown in Figure 13.60.

Club drugs are easily obtained, readily concealed, and quickly added to an unsuspecting person's food or drink, as depicted in Figure 13.61. These drugs act by depressing the central nervous system to render the victim incapable of making rational decisions, such as withholding consent for sexual advances. Attackers often rely upon the common amnesia effects of the drug; the victims cannot remember anything that happened while under the drug's influence. Because of this amnesia, victims often only have vague recollections of events and are typically too embarrassed to come forward to report the crime, feeling guilty and somehow responsible for the events.

One of the most common of the club drugs is Rohypnol (flunitrazepam), a member of the benzodiazepine depressant family (Figure 13.62). Rohypnol is ten times more powerful than Valium and acts quickly to impair a victim's judgment, typically within 20–30 minutes of administering the drug, and its effect lasts for hours. It is called by a variety of street names including "forget-me pill," "roofies," "Mind eraser," "Ropies," and dozens of others. Commercial "at-home" kits are now available to help detect the presence of club drugs in a person's drink or food.

Rohypnol is manufactured and prescribed outside the United States as a sleeping aid but it is quite addictive and dangerous when the dosage is not carefully controlled (as it

FIGURE 13.61 Club drugs are easily added to the food and drink of unsuspecting victims to reduce their inhibitions and memory in a drug-facilitated sexual assault (DFSA).

Source: Shutterstock.com.

rarely is in DFSA). When mixed with alcohol, a very common method of delivering the drug, combined effects can rapidly lead to respiratory depression, aspiration, coma, and death.

Another very common club drug is MDMA or "ecstasy," a hallucinogen mentioned earlier. This drug is also highly

addictive and extended use can have severe biological effects including increased blood pressure and heart rate, muscle spasms, kidney failure, and a significantly increased chance of heart attack and stroke. Abuse of this drug is one of the major causes of cardiac arrest in otherwise healthy young people.

13.4.7 Stimulants

Stimulants have essentially the opposite effect of depressants and work, as the name implies, by increasing a person's alertness and activity. Common stimulants include cocaine, nicotine, caffeine, and the large family of amphetamine-related compounds. The use of some of these compounds, such as nicotine and caffeine, to increase alertness is quite common and generally accepted in society, while the use of others, such as cocaine, is illegal in most places in the world. Like some other classes of drugs, stimulants often bring a feeling of well-being, reduced appetite, and increased levels of "energy."

Cocaine (benzoylmethylecgonine) is a very powerful stimulant that acts upon the central nervous system. It is derived from the leaves of the coca plant and was first isolated in 1855. Initially used as an anesthetic, one of the first ever produced (Figure 13.63), it eventually found its way in 1886 into a formulation along with caffeine in wine. Later the wine was dropped, sugar was added as a sweetener, and the drink was named Coca-Cola. The drink was advertised as employing "the valuable tonic and nerve stimulant properties of the coca plant and cola nuts." After 1906, however, the cocaine was removed from the drink to comply with U.S. laws.

Cocaine functions by interfering with the reabsorption of neurotransmitters, such as dopamine and serotonin, by the

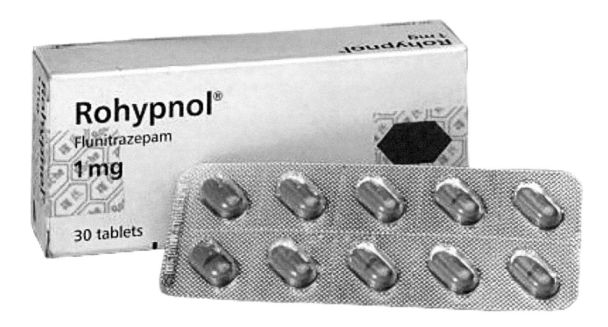

FIGURE 13.62   Rohypnol drug commonly used in drug-facilitated sexual assault.

Source: Used per Creative Commons Attribution-Share Alike 4.0 International license. User: Jermund9.

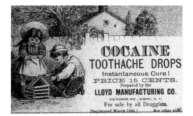

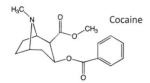

FIGURE 13.63 Cocaine was once readily available before the long-term severe medical issues associated with its use were understood. The structure of cocaine is shown below the advertisement.

Source: Retrieved from Wikimedia Commons; used per Creative Commons Attribution.

FIGURE 13.64 Cocaine powder as the hydrochloride salt.

Source: U.S. DEA.

FIGURE 13.65 Crack cocaine "rocks."

Source: U.S. DEA.

Cocaine is still extracted from coca leaves using organic solvents and is chemically converted into its hydrochloride salt, although it is found in a number of different "forms" on the street. The hydrochloride form is readily water-soluble and can be directly injected or "snorted" (Figure 13.64) to introduce it rapidly into the blood stream. Crack cocaine (Figure 13.65) is the "freebase" form of the drug (not the hydrochloride salt) that can then be heated or smoked; the name "crack" comes from the sound often heard as the solid drug is heated. Cocaine is, however, sensitive to high temperatures, so smoking the drug decreases the amount of active drug delivered. Street samples of cocaine are often diluted with other compounds, most commonly lidocaine, sugar, phenacetin, or caffeine.

Amphetamines, often called "speed" or "uppers," are commonly prescribed for medical problems including appetite suppression and as stimulants. A variety of amphetamines are known, such as those shown in Figure 13.66. These compounds cause the body to release reserves of the neurotransmitters dopamine and noradrenaline that act quickly on the central nervous and sympathetic systems to produce feelings of exhilaration, self-assurance, motivation, and enhanced focus, as depicted in Figure 13.67. Amphetamines tend to cause prolonged "highs" resulting from the blockage of dopamine re-uptake and inhibition of the enzymes that metabolize dopamine; both of these effects work to keep the dopamine around longer and cause a longer effect. After the drug wears off, however, severe depression and deep fatigue usually result, primarily due to depletion of neurotransmitter reserves caused by their rapid release from the drug's action in the first place. It takes time for the body to build the reserves back up, during

body, resulting in a buildup of these compounds and leading to an overstimulation of the neurons. This buildup leads to a longer exposure of the nervous system to these neurotransmitters, especially in the pleasure centers of the brain, resulting in a feeling of euphoria, well-being, and abundant energy. Cocaine is very addictive and can also cause acute cardiovascular (heart) and cerebrovascular (brain) emergencies. Physical effects can include constricted blood vessels, dilated pupils, increased heart rate, and others. Because of this, there is at least a 24-fold increase in the risk of acute myocardial infarction (a form of heart attack) one hour after cocaine use, with the risk independent of the size of the dose taken; any dose increases substantially the risk. Cocaine is also a vasoconstrictor, reducing blood flow through blood vessels, leading to changes in skin and other bodily functions. Cocaine use provides "highs" that are often short-lived, leading the user into more frequent use of the drug to regain the feelings of exhilaration. It is a very addictive drug with tolerance rapidly built up by the body, resulting in more drug required to achieve the same relative effect.

Amphetamine
3,4-Methylenedioxy-amphetamine (MDA)
3,4-Methylenedioxyethyl-amphetamine (MDEA)
Methamphetamine
3,4-Methylenedioxy-methamphetamine (MDMA, Ecstacy)
3,4-Methylenedioxy-phenyl-2-butanamine (MBDB)
Ephedrine
Pseudoephedrine

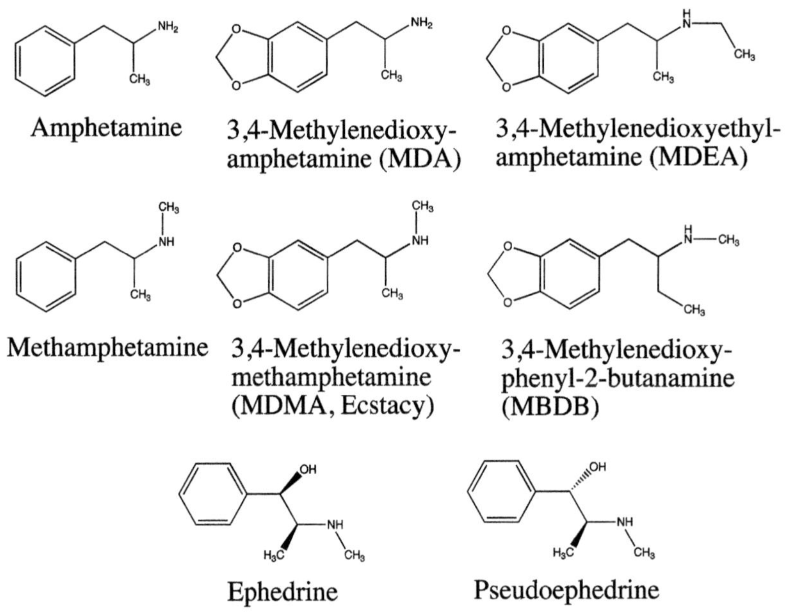

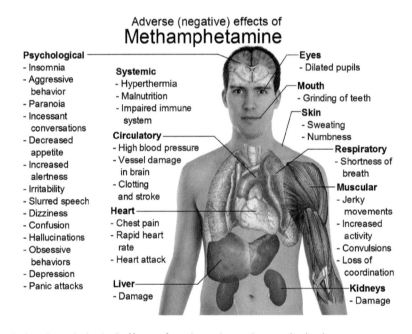

FIGURE 13.66 Chemical structures of some common amphetamines.

Adverse (negative) effects of
Methamphetamine
Psychological
- Insomnia
- Aggressive behavior
- Paranoia
- Incessant conversations
- Decreased appetite
- Increased alertness
- Irritability
- Slurred speech
- Dizziness
- Confusion
- Hallucinations
- Obsessive behaviors
- Depression
- Panic attacks
Systemic
- Hyperthermia
- Malnutrition
- Impaired immune system
Circulatory
- High blood pressure
- Vessel damage in brain
- Clotting and stroke
Heart
- Chest pain
- Rapid heart rate
- Heart attack
Liver
- Damage
Eyes
- Dilated pupils
Mouth
- Grinding of teeth
Skin
- Sweating
- Numbness
Respiratory
- Shortness of breath
Muscular
- Jerky movements
- Increased activity
- Convulsions
- Loss of coordination
Kidneys
- Damage

FIGURE 13.67 Physiological and psychological effects of methamphetamine on the body.

Source: Retrieved from Wikimedia Commons; used per Creative Commons Attribution.

which time the person feels very poorly. This would be akin to spending all one's money on payday at a fancy restaurant, only to starve afterward until the next payday arrives.

Amphetamines are one of the most societally problematic drugs due to the increases in violent and antisocial behavior promoted by the drug's use. The compound is synthesized in dangerous "home" laboratories ("meth labs") by inexperienced, amateur chemists (Figure 13.68). Addiction drives users into depression, weight loss, insomnia, psychosis, and other behavioral problems, accompanied by a greatly increased risk of cardiovascular and cerebrovascular problems. Amphetamine use is also associated with a rapid increase in the body's tolerance to the drug.

13.4.8 Steroids

Steroids are organic ring molecules that naturally promote muscle growth and repair, regulate metabolism and immune function, and control blood properties (e.g., blood volume, electrolyte balance, etc.). Steroids include both naturally occurring compounds in the human body, such as hormones (e.g., androgens, progesterones, testosterones, estrogens, etc.) and cholesterol, as well as chemicals derived from other sources, such as anabolic steroids and corticosteroids. Their structures are all built upon a basic five-ring pattern, as shown in Figure 13.69, differing only by the chemical groups attached to this framework.

FIGURE 13.68 Clandestine methamphetamine laboratory – a dangerous operation! The workers pack bags of newly synthesized "crystal meth" into shipping containers for distribution.

Source: Shutterstock.com.

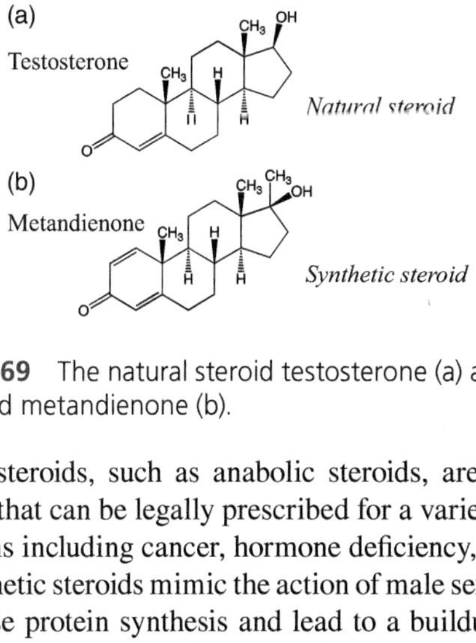

FIGURE 13.69 The natural steroid testosterone (a) and the synthetic steroid metandienone (b).

Some steroids, such as anabolic steroids, are controlled substances that can be legally prescribed for a variety of medical problems including cancer, hormone deficiency, and AIDS. These synthetic steroids mimic the action of male sex hormones that increase protein synthesis and lead to a buildup of tissue mass and muscle. The use of these performance-enhancing steroids, however, has been banned by most athletic organizations, but the problem of their use remains significant. The National Institute on Drug Abuse reported that 3.4% of all high school seniors have used steroids at least once in the preceding year. Professional athletes seem to be especially susceptible to steroid use, with an increasing number of high-profile cases occurring each year. These steroids work by allowing athletes to train harder and longer and to recover from these workouts faster, resulting in a rapid enhancement of their natural abilities.

Steroid use appears to be addictive and can lead to significant health risks (Figure 13.70), including increased risk for cancer, severe mood swings, increases in violent and aggressive behavior, renal failure (kidneys), and severe acne (Figure 13.71). In males, anabolic steroids essentially shut down male hormone production in the body, resulting in sexual dysfunction, testicular atrophy (shrinkage and dysfunction), hair loss, and enlargement of breasts. In females, anabolic steroids promote the development of typically "male" features, including growth of facial hair, increase in pattern baldness, cessation of menstrual cycles, deepening of the voice, and muscle growth. Since the liver is the primary organ for the removal of these compounds, taking large doses of steroids can result in liver inflammation, hepatitis, cirrhosis, tumors, and irreversible liver failure.

BOX 13.9   TYPES OF DRUGS

- **Narcotics**: bring relief from pain and induce sleep. Often incorrectly used in reference to any socially unacceptable drug. Narcotics are analgesic: relieve pain by depressing the nervous system (e.g., opium, morphine, heroin, codeine, opiates – oxycontin, methadone).
- **Hallucinogens**: alter normal thoughts, perceptions, and moods (e.g., PCP, LSD, mescaline, MDMA, ecstasy).
- **Depressants**: depress functions of the central nervous system, reduce anxiety, and aid in bringing about calmness and sleep (e.g., alcohol, barbiturates, tranquilizers).
- **Stimulants**: increase alertness, mental activity, and focus (e.g., cocaine, amphetamines).
- **Club/Date-Rape Drugs:** reduce inhibitions and awareness, may cause amnesia (e.g., Rohypnol, ecstasy (MDMA), GHB, ketamine).
- **Steroids**: promote muscle growth and repair (e.g., androgen, testosterone, anabolic steroids).

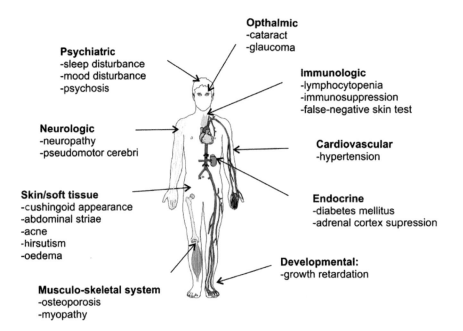

FIGURE 13.70   Potential problems from the use of steroids, such as methylprednisolone.

Source: Used per Creative Commons Attribution-Share Alike 4.0 International license. Timmermans et al. (2019).

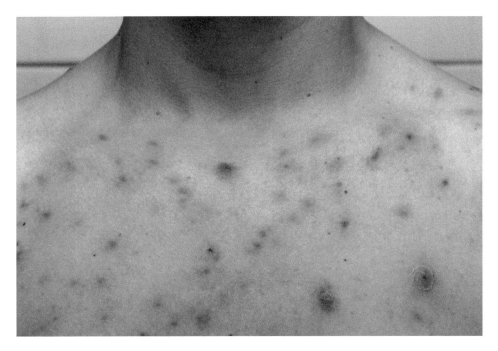

FIGURE 13.71   Steroid-use induced acne.

Source: Gerber et al. (2008). © 2008 Elsevier Ltd. All rights reserved. Used with permission.

13.4.9 Drug Laws

Drug use and trafficking is clearly a global problem, with many different approaches taken to deal with the problem. Most countries have laws governing the manufacture, sale, distribution, and use of certain drugs. These laws vary greatly between nations based upon prevailing social, cultural, and religious norms. Between 1989 and 1999, 66 countries developed comprehensive national drug policies; many more continue to work on legislation. The United Nations Office on

TABLE 13.3 Information about the classification (schedules) of drugs in the United States

	SCHEDULE I	*SCHEDULE II*	*SCHEDULE III*	*SCHEDULE IV*	*SCHEDULE V*
Potential for dependence and abuse	High	High (lower than Schedule I)	Moderate: lower than either Schedule I or II drugs	Low	Very Low
Medical use	No currently accepted medical use for treatment	Current accepted medical use but with severe restrictions on prescribing	Current accepted medical use for treatment	Current accepted medical use in treatment	Current accepted medical use in treatment
Restrictions	Illegal in any quantities	Requires special reporting and administration	Prescription required	Prescription required	Over-the-counter medications; limited restrictions
Examples	Heroin, LSD, marijuana, methaqualone, GHB	Morphine, PCP, cocaine, methadone, OxyContin, fentanyl, Adderall, Ritalin, methamphetamine	Codeine, hydrocodone, some barbiturates, ketamine, anabolic steroids	Librium, Darvon, Xanax, Valium	Cough medicine, Lyrica, Motofen (atropine), NSAIDs
Criminal sentences	Very Severe, especially when accompanied by violence – including life imprisonment	Severe when not used within strict guidelines of medical oversight	Moderate	Moderate	Variable: from low to moderate

Drugs and Crime (UNODC) continues its engagement in defining and controlling the worldwide manufacture, sale, and use of drugs for recognized medical applications, with a focus on criminal law enforcement when these and other drugs are used illicitly. In Europe, drug use is usually considered more of a health issue than a criminal issue, although the trafficking, sale, or use of chemicals that lead to harm and dependency typically carry criminal penalties. While there is a great deal of variation from country to country, the focus in Europe is on: (1) police enforcement limiting the supply of illicit drugs by arresting dealers and stemming importation, (2) educators teaching anti-drug information, and (3) doctors dealing with addiction and chemical dependency problems.

In the United States, the Controlled Substance Act (CSA), Title II of the larger Comprehensive Drug Abuse Prevention and Control Act of 1970, established the legal foundation for the government's goal of fighting the national drug abuse problem: the "War on Drugs." Importantly, it pulled together several existing, and often confusing and conflicting, laws that control the manufacture and distribution of many types of drugs. The CSA provides criminal guidelines for possessing different amounts of chemicals defined as *controlled substances*, with an attempt to distinguish users from those who distribute the drug. In the United States alone, there are an estimated 1.8 million drug arrests each year.

The CSA law classifies all drugs into five groups, called *schedules*, which arrange drugs based primarily on their accepted medical usages and potential for abuse (with some

exceptions for particular substances). A summary of the features of these schedules is given in Table 13.3.

Schedule I drugs are those that are deemed the most dangerous, carry a very high potential for abuse, lack any current accepted medical use, and do not have an accepted safe method for using the drug, even under careful professional medical supervision. No prescriptions can be written for these substances and their manufacture is tightly overseen by the DEA (Drug Enforcement Administration, Figure 13.72). Drugs in this class include heroin, marijuana, LSD, the date-rape drug GHB, and the hallucinogens psilocybin and mescaline (with some exceptions for indigenous community uses).

Schedule II drugs are those that also have a high potential for abuse and dependence but have at least some generally accepted medical applications (generally accepted by the medical community and confirmed by the Department of Justice). These medications, when prescribed by a physician, carry severe restrictions on when and how they might be used. Morphine, a Schedule II drug, is most often prescribed and administered in a hospital setting where strict oversight is possible, and access to the drug by personnel is carefully monitored. Other drugs in this schedule include cocaine, methadone, Oxycontin, a variety of amphetamines, high concentration codeine, phencyclidine, and Ritalin (often prescribed for attention deficit disorder, ADD, in children).

Schedule III drugs have a lower potential for abuse and addiction than compounds in either Schedule I or II and have well-accepted medical uses. These drugs are still highly

FIGURE 13.72 In the United States, the Drug Enforcement Administration (DEA) of the Department of Justice (DoJ) is charged with overseeing the Controlled Substance Act (CSA).

Source: DEA.

regulated but are prescriptible by a physician and available from a pharmacist, although the number of refills of these prescriptions is controlled. Drugs in this group include anabolic steroids, the common date-rape drug ketamine, hydrocodone, codeine compounded with a pain reliever (such as ibuprofen or acetaminophen), and a variety of intermediate-acting barbiturates.

Schedule IV drugs are those that carry a relatively low potential for abuse and have a medically accepted application. These drugs also have a low potential for either psychological or physiological dependence. This category contains many common prescriptions that may be refilled up to five times within a six-month period and includes many long-acting barbiturates, moderate analgesics, stimulants, and antipsychotic drugs, among many others.

Schedule V drugs are those that have a low potential for abuse and dependence and have well established medical uses. These drugs can only be distributed for medical purposes and include a number of over-the-counter medications like cough suppressants and anti-diarrheal medications.

While there have been a number of tests of the constitutionality of the CSA, it has thus far been upheld by the Supreme Court. The classification of drugs into a particular drug schedule is subject to legislation and occasionally changes over time. For example, the placement of the date-rape drug GHB on Schedule I was legislated in 2000 although when used as a medication under the trade name *Xyrem* it remains a Schedule III drug (one of several multiply-listed drugs). The CSA is federal law, but states may have a different set of classifications. For example, while marijuana remains a Schedule I drug in the Federal CSA system, a number of states have either legalized or decriminalized its possession and use.

13.5 ALCOHOL

13.5.1 Introduction

Alcohol has been a part of human society for a very long time. Some historians have attributed the rise of civilization to the development of methods for producing alcohol since it provides a safe storage of a mobile form of calorie-containing nutrition for long periods – freeing mankind from the perpetual preoccupation with searching for the next meal. Current best guesses place the first widespread preparation of alcohol-containing foodstocks between 5,000 and 10,000 years ago. Certainly by 700 BC the Greeks had a thriving wine industry that was later refined by the ancient Romans. Historically, winemaking was focused in the Mediterranean region, while beer production was mostly concentrated in the cooler, northern parts of Europe where it was generally too cold to grow grapes. But human ingenuity has developed alcohol-producing methods using different fermentable materials in virtually every part of the globe.

As much as alcohol has been a stepping-stone in mankind's freedom to explore beyond the next meal, there have also been societal problems arising from the overindulgence of alcohol from the beginning of recorded civilization. Today, alcohol is the number one abused drug worldwide, causing more deaths and injuries than any other compound.

In this section, we begin by briefly exploring the chemistry and production of alcohol, followed by a discussion of its pharmacodynamics, pharmacokinetics, and legal considerations.

13.5.2 Alcohol Properties

Organic alcohols are compounds that contain something called a hydroxyl functional group, or an OH group, drawn in red in Figure 13.73. Three of the most common alcohols shown in the Figure (methanol, ethanol, and isopropanol) have relatively simple chemical structures, consisting of small organic fragments attached to OH units.

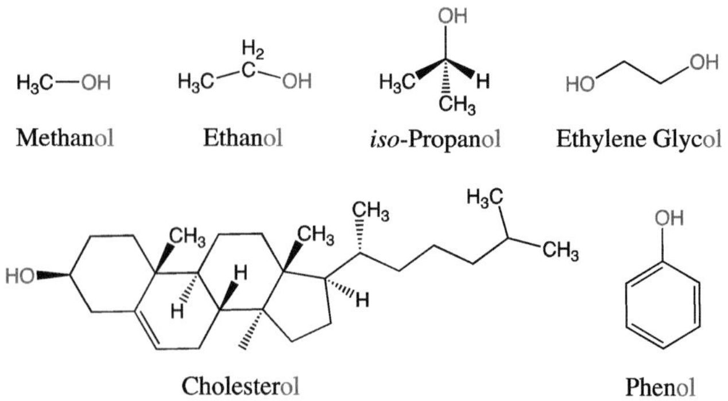

FIGURE 13.73 Chemical structures of several common alcohols (the alcohol functional group is highlighted in red in the structures).

Methanol (CH_3OH), sometimes called wood alcohol or wood spirits, is a colorless, low-boiling liquid (b.p. = 65°C) that is not suitable for human consumption. Its name derives from early production methods that involved burning or distilling wood. Methanol is, however, very toxic with an LD_{50} of only 428 mg/kg. Biological problems result, however, at levels well below the LD values. For example, ingestion of only 10 mL of methanol can cause permanent blindness by destruction of the optic nerve. It is used primarily as a solvent for chemical reactions, in forming plastics, and in cleaning solutions.

Isopropanol (C_3H_7OH), often called rubbing alcohol (although most commercially available "rubbing alcohol" actually contains between 70% and 99% ethanol), is also quite toxic (LD_{50} = ~ 3,500 mg/kg) and, like methanol, is not suitable for human consumption. As little as 100 mg directly applied can cause severe eye problems and poisoning can result from ingestion and inhalation as well as direct absorption through the skin. Isopropanol is used in large-scale commercial processes as either a solvent or as a cleaning compound. In the body, it is broken down into acetone and causes depression of the central nervous system, leading to nausea, anesthesia, dizziness, coma, and death.

Ethanol (C_2H_5OH), the alcohol consumed in all alcoholic beverages, is also a clear, colorless liquid (b.p. 78°C). It is a volatile, flammable, colorless compound that, in pure form, has a slight odor and causes a burning sensation when consumed. Ethanol dissolves in water at all proportions (called "miscible"), and water-ethanol mixtures form something called an *azeotrope*, meaning that, using normal distillation methods, there is always at least 4% water remaining in distilled ethanol. To obtain pure ethanol (called absolute alcohol), another chemical is added that "denatures" the alcohol, allowing it to be distilled as a pure compound. Denatured alcohol, however, is not suitable

for consumption. Ethanol concentrations in beverages are usually referred to as its "proof," which, in the United States, is twice the percent composition of the alcohol. For example, a solution containing 50% ethanol is called 100 proof alcohol. Ethanol is classified as both a poison and a drug (LD_{50} = 7,060 mg/kg), and it acts as a strong central nervous system depressant.

15.5.3 Alcohol Production

In order to understand the forensic and legal aspects of alcohol consumption, an understanding of the sources of the alcohol consumed is first necessary. While ethanol can be made from petrochemicals and cellulose, by far the most common method for its production for human consumption comes from the fermentation of natural sugars. Fermentation uses strains of yeast to metabolize sugars into carbon dioxide and ethanol.

$$C_6H_{12}O_6 ------> 2\ CH_3CH_2OH + 2\ CO_2$$
sugar ethanol carbon dioxide

The fermentation typically occurs under anaerobic conditions, minimizing the presence of oxygen. The conditions for maximizing the yeast's production of ethanol are carefully controlled, although the toxicity of the ethanol itself usually limits the highest concentration of ethanol that can be produced before killing the yeast and stopping the process. Typically, the maximum concentration of ethanol from natural fermentation is about 15% ethanol by volume.

Nationally, U.S. ethanol production surmounted ~18 billion gallons in 2020 – although the vast majority of this production was directed toward fuel uses (Figure 13.74). The U.S.

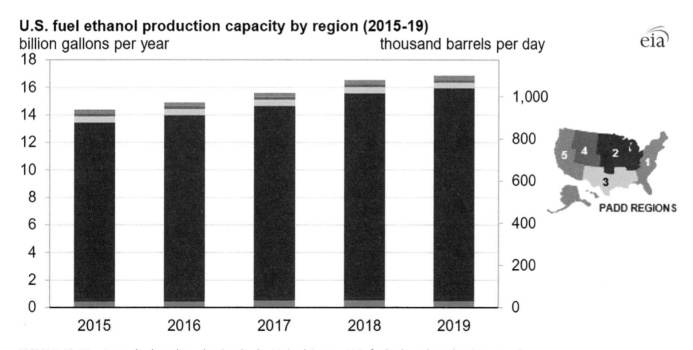

FIGURE 13.74   Annual ethanol production in the United States: U.S. fuel ethanol production capacity.

Source: U.S. Energy Information Administration, U.S. Fuel Ethanol Plant Production Capacity Report.

per capita annual consumption of alcoholic beverages is about 2.5 gallons per person.

Virtually any source of sugar can and has been used to produce ethanol by fermentation, including corn, fruit juices, grains, potatoes, beets, cane sugar, and honey. The source of the sugar dictates what type of alcoholic beverage is produced. The flavor, color, and consistency of an alcoholic beverage come mostly from other chemicals in the mixture, rather than from the alcohol. These other substances, called *congeners*, primarily arise as byproducts of the fermentation process but may also simply be present from the original sugar source.

Beer is probably the oldest alcoholic beverage ever produced (Figure 13.75) and, worldwide, is the third most commonly consumed drink behind water and tea. Beer is usually produced from the fermentation of grains, most commonly barley, which is steeped in water to make it germinate first (called a "malt"). The malt is boiled with hops (flower clusters

(a)

(b)

FIGURE 13.75 Beer production from a hieroglyph and statue from ancient Egypt (~2400 BCE).

Source: (b) Creative Commons Attribution-Share Alike 4.0 International license. User: ArchaiOptix.

FIGURE 13.76 Hop flower cluster (*Humulus lupulus*).

Source: Used per Creative Commons Attribution 4.0 International license, User: Mbrickn.

of the hop plant, Figure 13.76) to form a "wort" to add flavor and aroma. Finally, the wort is fermented by the addition of yeast to produce the beer. Today, beer making is a very complex and carefully controlled multi-step process, as illustrated in Figure 13.77. There are a number of types of beer, depending on how the brewing takes place. Beer with a higher alcoholic content is called ale, while a stout is a beer flavored with roasted grain. Lager is a beer that has been allowed to age for a relatively long time. Most beers have an alcohol content ranging between 1% and 6% ethanol (by volume). Curiously, "lite" beer has a lower caloric content primarily because it simply has a lower alcohol content.

Cider comes from the fermentation of apples, pressed to release the fruit juice. If the fermentation is stopped before all the sugar is consumed, a "sweet cider" results, while "sparkling cider" is produced when the carbon dioxide byproduct of the fermentation is trapped inside the bottle (although today, sparkling cider is often prepared by injecting carbon dioxide into the bottle after fermentation has ended).

Wine is most often prepared from the fermentation of grapes and fruits and is often a very complex and carefully controlled process (summarized in Figure 13.78), one that generations of producers have developed into an art form. In general, red wines are produced by fermenting the grapes with the

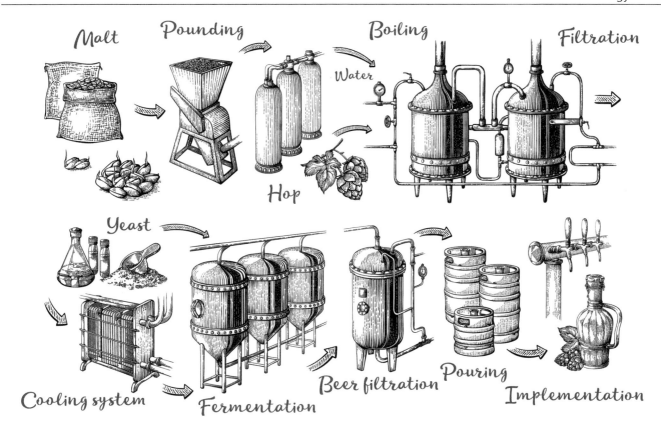

FIGURE 13.77   Steps in the production of beer.

Source: Shutterstock.com.

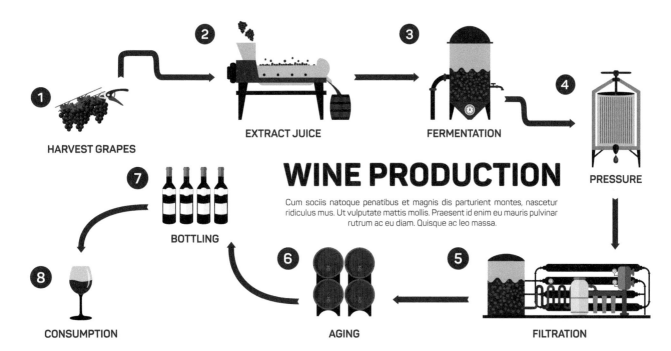

FIGURE 13.78   Simplified steps in winemaking.

Source: Shutterstock.com.

skins left in the fermentation mixture, while white wines come from mixtures in which the skins have been removed prior to fermentation. Wine production typically involves a slower fermentation and aging process, often lasting for months or years. Wines typically have alcohol contents ranging from 9% to 16%.

When alcoholic mixtures are distilled, the alcohol content is increased. Spirits are defined as alcoholic preparations with at least a 20% alcohol content. The distillation process often changes the flavor properties of the beverage by removing or altering some of the congeners found in the liquid.

A variety of other alcoholic beverages are produced and vary by what is used as the sugar source, how it is fermented and processed, how it is aged (or not), and how the final product is bottled and stored. Some common examples are given in Box 13.10. To avoid confusion in nomenclature, the term "alcohol" will be used here as it is commonly employed and refers to ethanol (CH_3CH_2OH).

BOX 13.10   OTHER ALCOHOLIC BEVERAGES

- *Brandy* is grape wine distilled to increase the alcohol content. Brandy is aged for long periods in wooden casks until it is "mature."
- *Gin* is made from malted barley (germinated barley grain) and rye that is flavored with juniper or other plant flavorings. Gin can also be made from corn or molasses.
- *Rum* is distilled from fermented sugar cane or molasses and aged in wooden barrels.
- *Whiskey* is made from fermented grain mash, aged in wooden casks. Fermentation is usually started by adding the residue from previous fermentations.
- *Sherry* is a "fortified" wine in which brandy is added to the wine to increase its alcohol content to between 15% and 18% ethanol. The term "sherry," however, can only be legally used for products originating in the Jerez region in southern Spain; any similar products made elsewhere must simply be called "fortified wine."

Many other types of alcoholic beverages exist, including those from native cultures around the world: mare's milk, honey drinks, plant infusions of all kinds, including those that are produced by chewing and spitting back into the "mother" liquor.

13.5.4 Alcohol Toxicology

Alcohol is primarily consumed orally (by mouth), although it can also pass directly through the skin or be inhaled. Most of the alcohol ingested is absorbed either in the stomach (~20%) or in the small intestines (~80%). Once absorbed, it is very rapidly distributed throughout the body and equilibrated in all body fluids.

The biological effects of alcohol only occur once the alcohol reaches the blood stream and the body's tissues. Several factors influence the rate of alcohol absorption into the blood stream, including:

- **Gastric Emptying**: This term refers to the rate at which the contents of the stomach are moved into the intestinal tract. Alcohol absorption is much faster in the upper portions of the small intestines than in the stomach. Therefore, moving the stomach's alcoholic contents into the intestines speeds up the transfer of alcohol into the bloodstream.
- **Food and Drugs**: Alcohol absorption is much faster when the stomach is empty, as the alcohol more rapidly passes into the small intestines: faster gastric emptying. Estimates indicate that the rate of alcohol absorption is about three times slower after eating, especially fatty foods, than when drinking on an empty stomach. Figure 13.79 shows the effect of an empty and full stomach on the blood alcohol concentration (BAC).
- **Physical Condition/Exercise**: Physical exercise typically slows gastric emptying, mainly by diverting blood supplies to the body's muscles rather than to the gastrointestinal system. Additionally, a greater body weight means more fluid volume in the body to dilute the alcohol, leading to lower alcohol concentrations from consuming the same amount of alcohol. Some drugs, such as nicotine, marijuana, and others, also modify the rate of gastric emptying.
- **Amount of Alcohol Consumed**: At first, the rate of alcohol absorption in the stomach is rapid but then quickly declines, even if the amount of alcohol in the stomach remains high. Conversely, the rate of alcohol absorption in the small intestines remains high over time.

Once in the body, alcohol is rapidly distributed to all the body's fluids and organs. It easily crosses biological barriers, including the blood-brain barrier and the placenta. However, the behavioral and physical changes resulting from alcohol consumption are mainly connected with its effects on brain tissue.

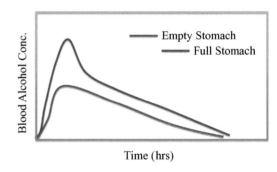

FIGURE 13.79 The effect of food on blood alcohol content (BAC): the red line shows the blood alcohol content (BAC) when alcohol is consumed with an empty stomach and the blue line shows the BAC when the alcohol is consumed after eating a meal.

Brain lobes

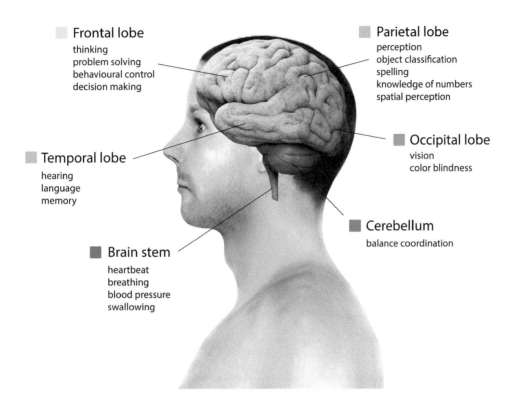

Frontal lobe
thinking
problem solving
behavioural control
decision making

Parietal lobe
perception
object classification
spelling
knowledge of numbers
spatial perception

Occipital lobe
vision
color blindness

Temporal lobe
hearing
language
memory

Cerebellum
balance coordination

Brain stem
heartbeat
breathing
blood pressure
swallowing

FIGURE 13.80 Structures of the brain and the primary responses they control.

Source: Shutterstock.com.

The brain is the terminus of the central nervous system's millions and millions of nerve cells (neurons). Alcohol interacts with the cell membranes of the neurons, altering the electrical transmission of signals in the brain. While alcohol acts like other drugs in stimulating the "reward pathways" of the brain, it also acts quite differently from many other drugs by affecting multiple systems of the brain through a combination of stimulation and inhibition. Alcohol generally acts as a depressant and first affects the front of the brain, the frontal lobe responsible for judgment, concentration, and normal inhibition (Figure 13.80). As the alcohol level increases, the effects move toward the back of the brain, sequentially affecting language control, motor skills, body orientation, and lastly, the visual center of the brain.

Alcohol use, however, does affect all the body's organs, especially when used chronically. A primary target is the liver, the organ responsible for removing most of the alcohol and its metabolism byproducts. Many of the byproducts of the liver's action on alcohol are very toxic to the liver itself. Their presence can lead to alcoholic hepatitis and scarring (cirrhosis) and represents the leading cause of liver-related deaths (see Chapter 8, Figure 8.22). Alcohol also causes damage to other body systems, including the gastrointestinal, cardiovascular, endocrine, immune, and pulmonary systems.

13.5.5 Blood Alcohol Concentration (BAC)

The concentration of alcohol in the body's *tissues* dictates its effect on a person's behavior and physiology. Tissue concentration, in turn, depends directly on the amount of alcohol absorbed into the blood stream. It is rather hard to measure directly the amount of alcohol in a living person's tissues so we rely upon the next best thing: measuring the amount of alcohol in the bloodstream, a measurement called the *blood alcohol content* or concentration (BAC).

The BAC is defined as grams of alcohol in 100 mL of blood (sometimes referred to as milligram percent). For example, a BAC of 0.08% is equal to 0.08 g of alcohol in every 100 mL of blood (100 mL = 1 dL). The effect of a particular BAC level varies from person to person, but some typical BAC levels have been legally associated with certain physiological and behavioral changes, as given in Table 13.4. Different countries have varying BAC thresholds for criminal legal action, especially for driving, ranging from anything greater than 0.00% to 0.15%, although most nations fall in the 0.05%–0.08% range. Some representative values are presented in Table 13.5.

TABLE 13.4 Typical effects of different blood alcohol concentrations (BAC) on the body

BAC (G/DL)	CHANGES IN PERSONALITY	BRAIN REGIONS AFFECTED	IMPAIRED ACTIVITIES
0.01–0.05	Relaxation, reduction of inhibition	Cerebral cortex	Alertness
0.06–0.10	Numbness, nausea, sleeplessness	Cerebral cortex and frontal lobe	Judgment
0.11–0.20	Mood swings, anger, sadness, mania	Cerebral cortex, frontal lobe, and cerebellum	Coordination, motor skills, and visual tracking
0.21–0.30	Aggression, depression, stupor, reduced sensations	Cerebral cortex, frontal lobe, cerebellum, and brain stem	Inappropriate behavior, slurred speech, lack of balance
0.31–0.40	Unconsciousness, coma	Entire brain	Loss of body regulation, difficulty breathing, slowed heart rate
Greater than 0.41	Death		

TABLE 13.5 Selected international legal limits for BAC levels when driving

BAC (G/DL)	COUNTRY
0.00% (0 tolerance)	Russia, Saudi Arabia, Brazil, Canada (new drivers), Hungary
0.02%	China, Poland, Norway, Netherlands, Sweden, Puerto Rico
0.03%	India, Japan, Uruguay
0.04%	Canada (provincial)
0.05%	Austria, Belgium, Denmark, France, Greece, Israel, Italy, Peru, Spain, Thailand, Turkey
0.08%	Canada (criminal), Mexico, New Zealand, Norway, United Kingdom, United States

---

BOX 13.11   THE COST OF ALCOHOL

Alcohol is involved in:

- 68% of manslaughter cases.
- 62% of assault offenders.
- 54% of murders.
- 48% of robberies.
- 44% of burglaries.
- 39% of all fatal crashes.

(National Institute on Drug Abuse and the National Institute on Alcohol Abuse and Alcoholism. 1998. The economic cost of alcohol and drug abuse in the United States 1992. Bethesda, MD: National Institute on Alcohol Abuse and Alcoholism.)

The risks associated with driving after drinking are well documented. Figure 13.81 demonstrates a plot of the relative risk based on the BAC level.

BAC levels represent a balance between the rate at which alcohol is added to the bloodstream through absorption and how much alcohol is metabolized out of the blood by the liver. If the amount added is equal to the amount removed, the BAC will remain relatively constant. If, however, absorption is faster than elimination, the BAC will increase. A variety of factors affect an individual's BAC and include:

- The *amount* of alcohol consumed.
- The *rate* of consumption.
- The individual's body *weight*.
- The person's *gender*: women typically have less water and more fat tissue in their bodies, leading to less alcohol absorption by the fat, less fluid to dilute the alcohol, and higher BACs.
- The type of drink consumed (*alcohol content* of the drink).
- Previous *drinking history* of the individual: chronic alcohol consumption makes the liver more efficient at removing the alcohol until the liver ultimately becomes permanently damaged by the alcohol.
- *Genetic background, age, physical condition, and diseases present*: all can affect how fast the body removes alcohol:an impaired liver is less able to remove alcohol and its function also slows with age.
- Whether the alcohol is taken with or without *food, medications, or other drugs.*

A variety of online, app, and "pocket" calculators for BAC levels are available, allowing an estimation of BAC levels based on known alcohol consumption and a person's body mass. Figure 13.82a illustrates the U.S. standard drink per alcohol type in fluid ounces, and Figure 13.82b depicts the impacts of increased alcohol intake on the body and impairment.

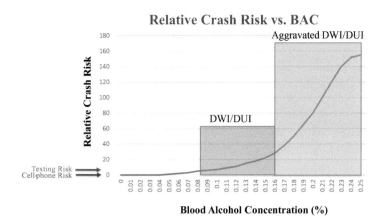

FIGURE 13.81 Relative risk of being involved in an automobile crash plotted against blood alcohol concentration.

Usually, the maximum BAC level is reached between 30 and 90 minutes after consumption, as shown in Figure 13.79. This means, of course, that a person's alcohol level may continue to rise well after they have taken their last drink. This may have dire consequences if a great deal of alcohol is consumed over a short period of time and then the person simply passes out; their BAC level would continue to increase to a dangerous, life-threatening level more than an hour after they passed out and may require emergency medical attention instead of simply "sleeping it off."

13.5.6 Alcohol Elimination

Once the alcohol is in the bloodstream, the liver immediately begins to remove it. The vast majority of alcohol, therefore, leaves the body after it is oxidized by the liver's enzymes (~90%–95%), although some is directly eliminated in sweat, urine, and breath (a central tenet of the "breathalyzer test," Section 13.5.7.).

Once the alcohol enters the liver through the blood, it is converted by an *alcohol dehydrogenase enzyme* into acetaldehyde (CH_3CHO). The acetaldehyde is then converted into acetate ($CH_3CO)_2^-$, a form of acetic acid, by another set of enzymes (acetaldehyde dehydrogenase), as shown in Figure 13.83. Because there are only a fixed number of sites in the liver where this occurs, the rate of alcohol elimination is fixed, typically removing about 0.5 oz (~30 mL) of alcohol per hour (or ~1.5 oz of 80 proof alcohol, 0.015% BAC per hour). In Figure 13.84, the rate of elimination is constant and the amount of time it takes for different amounts of alcohol to be eliminated is shown. The metabolites of alcohol oxidation in the liver are ultimately eliminated in the urine.

Alcohol use has both short and long-term effects on the body's physiology. Besides the immediate impairment and intoxication symptoms, a delayed "hangover" can result. A hangover is a collection of symptoms that includes nausea, headache, increased heart rate, excessive thirst, insomnia, dizziness, diaphoresis (sweating), and unsteadiness. These symptoms arise from the effects of the alcohol, its oxidized metabolites, and the congeners present in the drink. Alcohol consumption upsets the body's water balance, causing thirst. Alcohol metabolites effectively acidify a person's blood, a process called acidosis, which causes the body to experience thirst, nausea, and sweating. It also modifies the body's normal daily rhythms, similar to the effects of "jet lag." Some studies have suggested that a major cause of hangover arises from the congeners in the drink, and the presence of these additional compounds varies greatly from one type of alcohol to another.

13.5.7 Blood Alcohol Content (Concentration) Testing

It is often necessary to determine a person's BAC level and their degree of intoxication for legal considerations. This testing usually occurs in several "stages," beginning with a field sobriety test and concluding with an accurate laboratory BAC measurement.

Field Sobriety: This preliminary form of testing involves a series of behavioral tasks that a person suspected of being intoxicated is requested to perform by a police officer on site. The National Highway Traffic Safety Administration (NHTSA) has developed a battery of three tasks, called the Standardized Field Sobriety Test (SFST), to evaluate impairment as the basis of probable cause for arrest. These tests include (Figure 13.85):

- **Horizontal Gaze Nystagamus (HGN)**: This test examines the involuntary jerking of the eyes as a person looks from side to side. Under normal conditions, this jerking occurs only when someone looks far to the side, but when intoxicated, the jerking movement occurs even when a person looks only slightly to the side (less than 45°). Intoxicated people often have difficulty in "tracking" movements smoothly as they try to follow an object, such as a

(a)

What Is a Standard Drink?

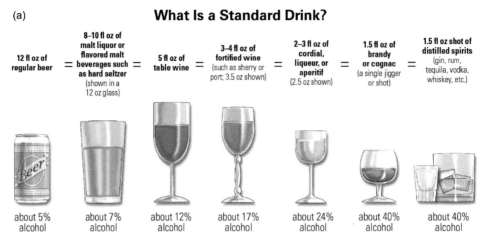

Each drink shown above contains 0.6 fluid ounces of "pure" ethanol and represent one U.S. "standard drink" or "alcoholic drink equivalent."

(b)

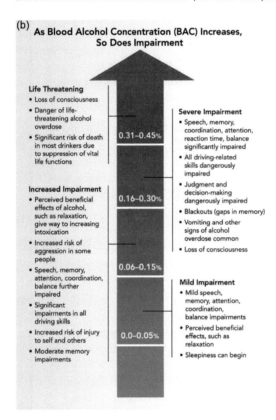

FIGURE 13.82A AND B   (a) What represents one standard U.S. drink and (b) approximate BAC calculation graphic and impairment.

Source: NIH and National Institute on Alcohol Abuse and Alcoholism.

pen or flashlight, with their eyes. The NHTSA study showed that people displaying this response had an 88% chance of being at or above a 0.08% BAC level.

- **Walk and Turn (WAT)**: This test is a "divided attention" test that is usually performed easily by a sober person but is difficult for an impaired person. Typically, the person is instructed to walk in a straight line in a "heel-to-toe" fashion for a specified number of steps, turn, and walk back to where

they started: a series of simultaneous tasks that they must think about (e.g., walking, balance, counting, etc.). An intoxicated person has difficulty doing several actions at once, including listening to multi-step instructions and performing simple tasks.

- **One Leg Stand (OLS)**: In this test, the suspect is asked to balance on one foot while counting until they are told to stop. Signs of impairment include swaying, putting the foot down, and using arms to balance.

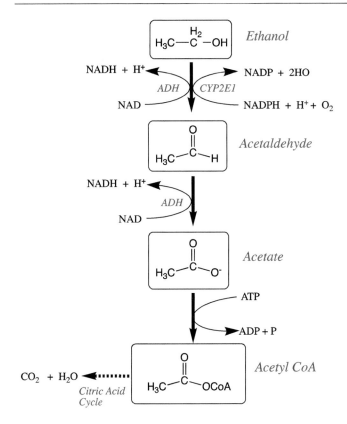

FIGURE 13.83 Metabolic pathways of ethanol (alcohol) metabolism in the liver.

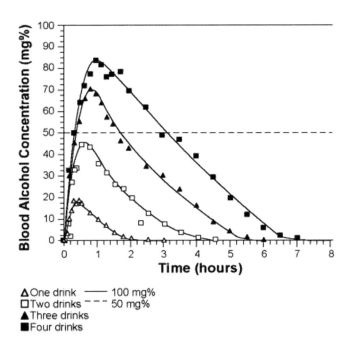

FIGURE 13.84 The rate of alcohol metabolism by the liver.

Source: Images courtesy Shutterstock.com.

△One drink ——— 100 mg%
□Two drinks – – – 50 mg%
▲Three drinks
■Four drinks

Breath Testing: Once a person is suspected of being intoxicated, a breath alcohol test is usually administered by the officer, often called a *breathalyzer* or *intoxilyzer* test, to more accurately measure the BAC level.

FIGURE 13.85 Standardized field sobriety tests (SFST): (a) Horizontal Gaze Nystagmus and (b) a person performing a walk and turn test (WAT).

Source: Shutterstock.com.

Alcohol in the blood circulates rapidly throughout the body, including to the lungs. The lungs contain millions of tiny sacs, called *alveoli*, which provide an efficient way to transfer gases between the air and the circulating blood (Figure 13.86). In the lungs, oxygen from the air becomes dissolved in the blood and carbon dioxide dissolved in the blood escapes into the air. This exchange process is described by something called *Henry's Law*, which states that when a solution containing a dissolved volatile compound, such as O_2, CO_2, or even CH_3CH_2OH (alcohol), is brought into contact with a gas (the air), a fixed equilibrium is established between the amount of the volatile compound in the air and the amount dissolved in the liquid. In other words, while some of the compound (i.e., ethanol) escapes into the air, some of it also redissolves in the liquid (i.e., blood). So, at a fixed temperature and pressure, once equilibrium is reached, there is a set ratio of volatile compound in the air to that in the liquid. In the case of alcohol and blood, this ratio is just about 2,100 to 1. This means that, at the temperature of the breath leaving a person (body temperature), there is always the same amount of alcohol in 1 mL of blood as there is in 2,100 mL of expired air. So, if we can determine the concentration of alcohol in a person's breath, we can work backward to directly relate this to the amount of alcohol in their blood by using the 2,100:1 ratio.

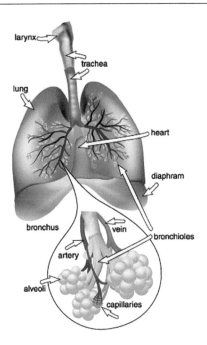

FIGURE 13.86 Structures of the lungs, including the alveoli, responsible for transferring gases between the air and the dissolved compound, such as alcohol in liquid blood.

Source: Shutterstock.com.

There are several methods currently used to determine the amount of alcohol in a person's breath, and therefore how much alcohol is in their blood (BAC). The *breathalyzer* is one method being used, although its use is rapidly being phased out. The breathalyzer works by observing the results of a chemical reaction between the alcohol in a breath sample and a colored compound. Analysis begins when a person blows an air sample into a small chamber. Once in this chamber, the known volume of air in the fixed-sized chamber reacts with a mixture of chemicals, including potassium dichromate and sulfuric acid, with silver nitrate used as a catalyst to speed up the reaction with the alcohol. Here, the alcohol reacts with the red-orange potassium dichromate, turning some of it into the green chromium sulfate compound. The device then electronically compares the color of the solution with a standard; the more green chromium sulfate that is produced, the more alcohol in the breath. A readout then indicates the person's BAC level.

Today, however, this chemical reaction-based system has been replaced by devices that measure the amount of alcohol in the breath directly using infrared spectroscopy (Chapter 12). This superior process does not require chemical reactions and chemical solutions (Figure 13.87). The device, also called either a *Breathalyzer* or an *Intoxilyzer*, measures the infrared light absorbed by the ethanol molecule to determine both the amount of ethanol present and the verification of the identity of the intoxicant from the wavelengths of light absorbed.

Other methods for determining the amount of alcohol in blood are also available and are becoming more common. One such method uses something called a fuel cell. In these devices, the alcohol in a sample of breath passes over a tiny piece of platinum. The alcohol in the sample is oxidized into acetic acid by the action of the platinum electrode, producing a measurable electrical current. The more alcohol that is oxidized, the greater the electrical current generated. By measuring the current, an estimate of the alcohol content of a person's breath can be determined.

FIGURE 13.87 Breathalyzer test for determining the alcohol content of a person's breath being administered.

Source: Shutterstock.com.

FIGURE 13.88   Portable (personal) BAC device.

Source: Retrieved from Wikimedia Commons; used per Creative Commons Attribution.

Today, personal, pocket-sized BAC measuring devices are available at relatively low cost to consumers to help them estimate their own BAC levels, such as the devices shown in Figure 13.88.

There are a number of problems with each of these types of alcohol measuring devices, including false positive readings. For example, the infrared-based devices cannot distinguish between ethanol and acetone (among other compounds). Hypoglycemic diabetic people can generate acetone in their blood as part of their condition, leading to false positive alcohol readings. Accurate tests also require "deep-lung," or alveolar air, where the alcohol in the air and blood are in equilibrium. It is, therefore, important to ensure that "deep-lung" air is sampled. Other problems with breathalyzer devices include difficulties in calibration (standardization of the readings), differences in body temperatures (changing the Henry's Law calculation), diseases present (e.g., acid reflux, diabetes, blood diseases), and certain other chemicals present in a person's breath (e.g., high-alcohol content mouthwashes), among others.

Laboratory (Confirmatory) Testing: The definitive test, however, is usually the analysis of the BAC using gas chromatography-mass spectrometry tandem (GC/MS, Chapter 12). In this method, the amount of alcohol is quantitatively determined by the GC (Figure 13.89), while the unambiguous identification of ethanol in the sample is carried out in the mass spectrometer. There are very few interferences with this method, and it provides the most reliable and accurate BAC level determinations possible. Sometimes, ethyl glucuronide, a metabolite of ethanol breakdown in the body, may also be analyzed in urine samples.

Finally, sometimes a spectrophotometric method may be useful in determining the BAC level, especially as a second

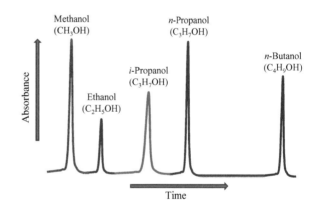

FIGURE 13.89   Gas chromatograph for several common alcohols. The area under the peaks is related to the amount of that compound present in the sample.

Credit: Used with permission and courtesy of Mike Revenson.

confirmatory test. In this method, the ethanol is first enzymatically converted into acetaldehyde, generating a chemical called NAD (nicotinamide adenine dinucleotide; a co-enzyme found in all living cells). The acetaldehyde is trapped as a stable compound using hydrazine (N_2H_4), and the amount of NAD formed is measured in the ultraviolet spectral region. The more NAD present, the higher the alcohol concentration in the sample.

While many products claim to reduce someone's tested BAC levels, these usually don't interfere with GC/MS methods. The only non-medically available "treatment" that is effective in lowering the BAC is simply time; time to allow the liver to process the alcohol out of the bloodstream.

FIGURE 13.90   A far too common occurrence from mixing driving with either alcohol or drug use.

Source: Paul Rapson/Science Photo Library. Used with permission.

13.5.8. Legal Considerations

As described earlier, different countries and states have varying legal thresholds for BAC levels to be considered in civil or criminal violations. These levels often vary depending on the tasks being performed: levels are usually set much lower or even at zero for a bus driver or pilot compared to the higher allowed BAC levels for a private individual to operate a vehicle. Some countries have set the BAC for individual vehicular operation at zero; any detected alcohol in the blood is a criminal violation (Figure 13.90).

The measurement of BAC levels has also been considered by the U.S. Supreme Court. In a landmark 1966 case (*Schmerber v. California*), a patient was being treated in a hospital for injuries from a car accident when medical personnel took blood samples to measure his BAC levels, over the objections of the patient. The defendant (patient) argued that two of his constitutional rights were violated when the samples were taken over his protests: the right against self-incrimination (5th amendment) and the right against unreasonable search and seizure (4th amendment). The Supreme Court ruled against the defendant on both grounds. The Court ruled that the self-incrimination right only pertained to verbal or written testimony and does not carry over to physical evidence. They also ruled that taking the blood sample amounted to a justified emergency situation since the defendant's body was destroying evidence by metabolizing away the alcohol, and there wasn't time for a search warrant to be issued. The decisions noted that the blood samples were taken by medical professionals using safe and accepted procedures. There is also a general recognition that operation of a vehicle on a public road amounts to a person's acceptance of an implied contract between the person and the state, including permission to monitor alcohol levels and other compliance issues.

Finally, sometimes it is necessary to determine the amount of alcohol consumed hours earlier based upon a measured BAC level taken later. When this is required, something called the Widmark equation is used. Simply stated, if you know information such as the person's body weight, the BAC at the later time, the time between the first drink and the measurement, and other information, it is possible to back-calculate the number of drinks consumed at an earlier time. There are, of course, significant limitations in using the Widmark equation, but it has proven useful.

13.6 PRACTICE OF FORENSIC TOXICOLOGY

13.6.1 Introduction

A major part of forensic toxicology deals with determining the presence and amount of certain chemicals found in a sample. These samples can come from a variety of sources, such as from a medical examiner's autopsy, unidentified compounds seized during an arrest, chemicals extracted from pieces of evidence, and many others related to investigations. At times, very little may be known in advance about the sample. But sometimes, particular substances are suspected, based on a person's behavior, which dictates the type of analysis that needs to be performed.

13.6.2 Toxicology and Forensic Medicine

Forensic toxicologists are frequently called upon to answer a number of important questions: what substances are present in a sample, what is the legally defensible identity of a particular chemical substance, how much of each chemical component is present in the sample, when was a drug/poison likely taken, and whether a compound was naturally occurring in the body, accidentally taken, or intentionally put there. Forensic toxicologists employ an impressive arsenal of analytical tools to provide answers to these questions. While these techniques have largely been presented in detail in previous chapters, in summary, they include:

- **Physico-Chemical Methods (Chapter 11):** Measuring the physical properties of a substance (e.g., determination of color, density, refractive index, etc.) and chemical properties (e.g., titration, etc.).
- **Spectroscopic Methods (Chapter 12):** Identifying and quantifying a chemical based on its absorption or emission of certain wavelengths of light.
- **Chromatography/Mass Spectrometry (Chapters 11 and 12):** Separating mixtures into their components using chromatographic techniques followed by the analysis of the components by mass spectrometry.
- **Immunoassay (Chapter 6):** Identifying a compound based on antibody-antigen specific reactions (e.g., ELISA, EMIT, etc.).

Different types of tests are performed depending on the information and level of analysis required. In the field, presumptive tests are often conducted to quickly screen an unknown substance to determine if it contains certain compounds and if it warrants further examination. For example, the Marquis test (Figure 13.91) is a presumptive color-change test. If the color of the solution changes when the Marquis reagent is mixed with a sample, then it is likely to contain alkaloids, compounds such as MDMA, methamphetamine, or LSD. In contrast, confirmatory tests, such as mass spectrometry, immunoassay, or infrared spectrometry, are highly discriminating and can unambiguously identify each substance in the sample with a high degree of certainty.

The work of the toxicologist is complicated by a number of issues that require careful attention. When part of a death investigation, the amount of a drug or poison in the sample might be extremely small and require careful handling and analysis (as little as 1×10^{-9} g might be present). Additionally, the compounds of interest may be part of a very complex mixture that requires painstaking separation into individual components before any analysis can be completed (Figure 13.92).

FIGURE 13.91 Color changes in the presumptive Marquis test for alkaloids. The test contains a mixture of formaldehyde and concentrated sulfuric acid, which is dripped onto the substance being tested. Different compounds produce different colored reactions.

Source: Retrieved from Wikimedia Commons; used per Creative Commons Attribution.

BOX 13.12   USEFUL TERMS

- **Analyte:** The compound that you're analyzing for.
- **Metabolite:** The compound formed from the metabolism or breakdown of a drug.

Information provided by a toxicologist can help the medical examiner answer the question of whether an unexplained or sudden death occurred due to poisoning or drug use and whether it involved an intentional or accidental dose. This determination can, of course, be difficult, but the quantity and type of drug or poison found in the body, along with how it was administered, can provide important information to help the medico-legal investigation team arrive at a defensible determination.

Sierra Vista Hospital
Karl E. Kirschner, P.O. Box 1367, San Luis Obispo, California 93406-1367 | 805 543-6550
David M. Lawrence, M.D., Pathologist
Steven B. Jobst, M.D., Pathologist

TOXICOLOGY REPORT

DRUGS CHECKED QUALITATIVELY

AMI

DRUG SCREEN RESULT: Trace of Hydroxyzine (Vistaril) detected on blood specimen submitted.

CANNABINOID (MARIJUANA) SCREEN: Not done (it requires urine)   NORMAL: Negative

BLOOD ALCOHOL : Negative %   NORMAL: None detected

SPECIMEN IDENTIFICATION: HUBBARD, L. HUBBARD   ROOM:

DATE SPECIMEN RECEIVED: 1/25/86   TYPE OF SPECIMEN: Blood: 2 red vac. 1 gray vac. vitreous fluid

DATE TEST PERFORMED: 1/25 and 1/27/87   DOCTOR:

SPECIMEN SUBMITED BY: Sheriff's Coroner (dr. Kirschner)

TECHNOLOGIST: DA (Silva)   DATE: 1/27/86

An American Medical International, Inc. Health Care Center   Revised: 12/12/84 ERS

FIGURE 13.92 A sample forensic toxicology report form.

Used per Creative Commons Attribution-Share Alike 3.0 Unported license; Credit: Source image by BruceBlaus. Derivative by Mikael Häggström, M.D.

13.6.3 Sample Collection

Biological samples can come from a variety of sources. Samples from a medical examiner's investigation can include body fluids and/or solid organs and tissues. A partial list of these sources is given in Table 13.6.

Blood is a very common fluid used for toxicology testing. However, the location from which the blood is sampled matters. For example, blood taken near the liver or other solid organs may contain much higher concentrations of a drug or poison than blood sampled elsewhere, as the drug may diffuse *post-mortem* out of the organ and into the surrounding blood.

TABLE 13.6 Some common sources of biological toxicology samples

FLUIDS	ORGANS
Blood	Skin
Urine	Lungs
Vitreous Humor	Hair
Oral Fluid	Fingernails
Semen	Liver
Stomach Contents	Kidney
Bile	Bone
Vomit	Other (heart, brain, etc.)
Semen	
Sweat	

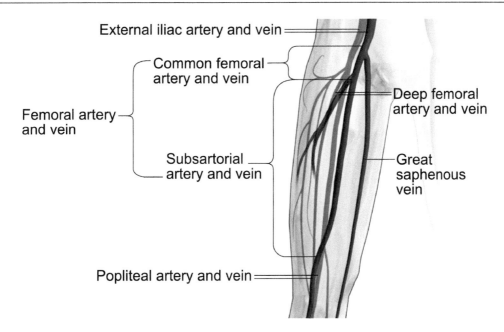

External iliac artery and vein

Common femoral artery and vein

Femoral artery and vein

Deep femoral artery and vein

Subsartorial artery and vein

Great saphenous vein

Popliteal artery and vein

FIGURE 13.93 Femoral artery – usually the preferred place for blood sampling in post-mortem examinations.

Source: Retrieved from Wikimedia Commons; used per Creative Commons Attribution.

Usually, pathologists try to take blood from the femoral artery, located in the leg (Figure 13.93), as it is far from the major organs of the body. Heart, jugular artery, and solid organ samples may also be taken for analysis and comparison.

Urine is good for determining whether a drug was used but it does not usually give a good indication of how much was taken since drug concentration in the urine is greatly affected by many factors, including how long it has been accumulating, how much liquid someone has taken in (hydrated or dehydrated), and how long ago they last voided their bladder. Urine is, however, easily sampled and can be rapidly analyzed for drug presence. This type of analysis is particularly useful and common in workplace, parole, and compliance testing where the amount of a drug is less important than that it is found at all (zero tolerance).

Other body fluids and organs can also be sampled. The vitreous humor (eye fluid) is commonly used since it is easily collected, is quite stable, and correlates very well with blood data.

It is essential that *representative* samples be taken for the analysis. A representative sample is a small amount of material that is taken from the total sample present that possesses the same chemical characteristics of the larger sample. Once the sample is taken, it is important to make sure that the collected samples are appropriately packaged, transported, and stored correctly. Storage of samples must be arranged to avoid sample loss, prevent any chemical reactions or degradation from occurring before the analysis is performed, and eliminate any possible sources of contamination. Reporting statistical information and chain of custody requirements must also adhere to the highest standards to ensure that the toxicological evidence can withstand the scrutiny of the courtroom (Figure 13.92).

Different drugs also reside within the body for varying periods of time. The half-life of a drug or poison is the amount of time it takes for one-half of the chemical to be eliminated, as illustrated for several common drugs in Figure 13.94. Often, however, since we can measure very small amounts of compounds, a drug can be detected for many half-lives in the body's fluids and tissues. Table 13.7 gives typical amounts of time for a given drug to clear the body to undetectable levels (different from the half-lives of the compound).

13.6.4 Toxicology Cases

When working with a medical examiner, a toxicologist may be called upon to provide information concerning a deceased patient (post-mortem toxicology). Typically, these types of investigations include suspected drug-related deaths, road traffic deaths, and homicide cases. Toxicology testing for living suspects may involve drunk/drugged driving, drug-facilitated sexual assault (DFSA), workplace testing, or athletic contesting cases, among others.

Workplace testing usually focuses on determining a person's integrity, their prior drug use, or compliance with job-related regulations. Increasingly, restrictions are being placed on a person's use of drugs outside of their working hours. This trend closely resembles the strict testing and drug compliance rules observed in international athletic events, especially the Olympics (Figure 13.95).

Finally, the practicing forensic toxicologist may be called into court to testify about the various stages of the testing process, from sample collection through analysis and interpretation of the data. A toxicologist may also be called upon to assess the role that a particular drug would have on a person's behavior.

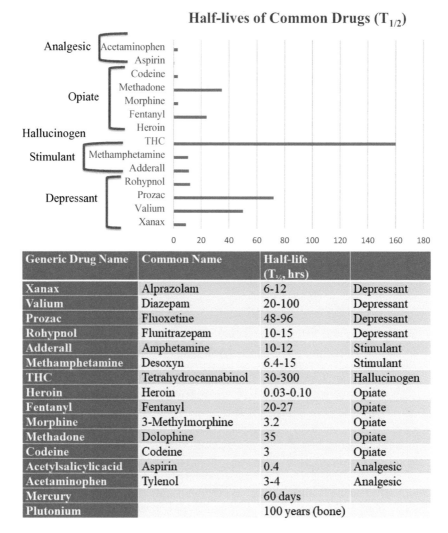

Half-lives of Common Drugs (T₁/₂)

Generic Drug Name	Common Name	Half-life (T₁/₂, hrs)	
Xanax	Alprazolam	6-12	Depressant
Valium	Diazepam	20-100	Depressant
Prozac	Fluoxetine	48-96	Depressant
Rohypnol	Flunitrazepam	10-15	Depressant
Adderall	Amphetamine	10-12	Stimulant
Methamphetamine	Desoxyn	6.4-15	Stimulant
THC	Tetrahydrocannabinol	30-300	Hallucinogen
Heroin	Heroin	0.03-0.10	Opiate
Fentanyl	Fentanyl	20-27	Opiate
Morphine	3-Methylmorphine	3.2	Opiate
Methadone	Dolophine	35	Opiate
Codeine	Codeine	3	Opiate
Acetylsalicylic acid	Aspirin	0.4	Analgesic
Acetaminophen	Tylenol	3-4	Analgesic
Mercury		60 days	
Plutonium		100 years (bone)	

FIGURE 13.94   Half-lives of several common drugs.

TABLE 13.7   Typical times for drugs to clear the body to undetectable levels

DRUG	MINIMUM CLEARANCE TIME	MAXIMUM CLEARANCE TIME
Ethanol (alcohol)	0–4 hours	6–8 hours
Amphetamines	2–7 hours	2–4 days
Anabolic Steroids	4–6 hours	1–3 months
Cannabinoids	6–18 hours	Up to 10 days
Cocaine (metabolite)	1–4 hours	1–4 days
LSD	2 hours	1–4 days
MDMA (ecstasy)	1 hour	2–3 days
Nicotine	4–6 hours	2–3 days
Opiates (Heroin, Morphine, Codeine)	2 hours	2–3 days
Psilocybin	2 hours	1–3 days
Rohypnol	1 hour	8 hours
GHB	1 hour	8 hours

Olympic Drug Testing

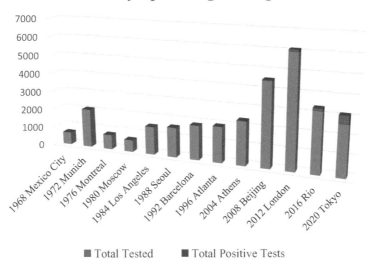

■ Total Tested   ■ Total Positive Tests

FIGURE 13.95   Olympic drug testing since 1968.

QUESTIONS FOR FURTHER PRACTICE AND MASTERY

13.1 What is a narcotic drug?

13.2 Describe how alcohol is eliminated from the body chemically as CH_3CH_2OH.

13.3 Through which organ does most alcohol enter the bloodstream?

13.4 According to the Controlled Substances Act, in which schedules are drugs listed that have the highest potential for abuse and without any accepted current medical use?

13.5 Where is alcohol primarily oxidized by the body?

13.6 Describe the factor(s) that determine the rate at which alcohol is absorbed into the bloodstream.

13.7 What is meant by "off-label" use of drugs and related compounds?

13.8 What is toxicology?

13.9 Define pharmacodynamics and pharmacokinetics.

13.10 What are some of the ways that a drug may act on the body pharmacodynamically?

13.11 What are metabolites?

13.12 What is a drug half-life?

13.13 Why do the same drugs have different effects on different people?

13.14 In the general public's mind, what is the difference between a medicine and a drug?

13.15 What is a poison?

13.16 What is the difference between acute toxicity and chronic toxicity?

13.17 What is meant by an LD value and what does LD_{50} mean?

13.18 What are the three ways prior exposure to a chemical can influence a person's response to a new exposure?

13.19 What does the acronym "ADME" stand for? Describe each step.

13.20 What are the different means of delivering a drug to the body?

13.21 What is bioavailability?

13.22 Which organ "screens" chemicals before they enter the bloodstream?

13.23 What is the blood-brain barrier?

13.24 What are several ways that drugs are discovered or designed?

13.25 Differentiate between a poison, a toxin, and a venom.

13.26 What damage results from corrosive poison?

13.27 What is a metabolic poison?

13.28 What is the biological mechanism of carbon monoxide poisoning? How does the victim appear physically?

13.29 What is the "mode of action" in cyanide poisoning? In heavy metal poisoning?

13.30 What is a neurotoxin?

13.31 What is the" mode of action" for most neurotoxins?

13.32 What are the general designated categories for drug abuse?

13.33 What is a narcotic? What is an opiate?

13.34 What is a hallucinogen? What is the mode of action of a hallucinogen?

13.35 What is a synthetic opiate and an opioid? Give examples.

13.36 For approximately how long after a chronic marijuana smoker stops smoking can the drug be detected in the user's urine?

13.37 LSD, peyote, PCP and psilocybin belong to what classification of drugs?

13.38 What are the effects of depressants on a person physiologically and psychologically?

13.39 What is meant by a "date-rape" drug?

13.40 How does a stimulant, like cocaine, typically produce its "high"?

13.41 How does the biological operation of an amphetamine differ from how cocaine works?

13.42 What are the risks associated with steroid abuse?

13.43 What is the most abused drug worldwide?

13.44 What does "80 proof" mean with respect to an alcohol solution?

13.45 What is a congener?

13.46 What factors affect the rate of absorption of alcohol into the bloodstream?

13.47 What is meant by blood alcohol concentration, BAC? What is the U.S. legal BAC limit?

13.48 What are the three tests used in a field sobriety test?

13.49 How does an IR breathalyzer work?

13.50 How does fuel cell BAC analysis work?

13.51 What are some of the problems with the results of presumptive BAC tests?

13.52 What are some of the methods used as confirmatory tests for BAC?

13.53 What is the only non-medical "treatment" effective at lowering BAC?

13.54 What is the legal importance of the U.S. Supreme Court's decision in *Schmerber v. California* in 1966?

13.55 What is the presumptive Marquis test used to identify?

EXTENSIVE QUESTIONS

13.56 Water has a LD_{50} value of 90,000 mg/kg. How many gallons of water must a 150 lbs person drink to have a 50% chance of dying? (1 lb = 454 g, 1 kg = 2.2 lbs, 1 gallon of water = 8 lbs)

13.57 Explain the five different drug schedules developed by the CSA (Controlled Substance Act). Be sure to include schedule number, potential for abuse and examples of drugs included.

13.58 Describe the effects that increasing levels of absorbed alcohol have on various regions of the brain and the resultant behavioral and motor skill changes in the individual.

13.59 Henry's Law is the basis for many field breathalyzer tests. Explain how Henry's Law is used to determine a presumptive BAC.

13.60 A toxicologist receives several vials of blood collected from a victim of a vehicular accident. The blood samples were collected from the femoral artery, the abdominal cavity near the liver and the carotid artery of the neck. The resultant toxicology showed a very different level of alcohol in the blood from the femoral artery as compared to the blood from the area near the liver, with the alcohol level much lower from the femoral artery. What could account for the higher level in the blood collected near the liver?

13.61 Drugs can be detected in a person's system for varying amounts of time depending upon the drug. What is the maximum detection time for each of the following to show a positive test in a sample? (A) alcohol, (B) marijuana – chronic user, (C) Ecstasy, (D) Rohypnol, (E) opiates, and (F) marijuana – infrequent user.

GLOSSARY OF TERMS

absorption: in spectroscopy, the uptake of light by a substance, accompanied by an increase in the energy of the molecules or atoms of the substance.

acidosis: the acidification of the blood.

acute dose: an amount of a chemical administered over a short period of time.

alcohol: an organic compound with an OH functional group, but the term generally refers to ethanol when referring to consumed alcohol.

alcohol dehydrogenase enzyme: an enzyme in the liver that converts ethanol (CH_3CH_2OH) into acetaldehyde (CH_3CHO).

analgesic: a compound that relieves pain.

analyte: the compound that you are analyzing for.

BAC (Blood Alcohol Content or Concentration): a measure of the amount of alcohol in the bloodstream, usually given in terms of grams of alcohol in 100 mL of blood (g/dl, sometimes referred to as milligram percent).

barbiturates: derivatives of barbituric acid that act as depressants.

bioaccumulation: the accumulation of a substance in the tissues of an organism.

bioavailability: the amount of the compound that reaches the bloodstream.

breathalyzer: a device for measuring the alcohol in a person's expired breath.

breath testing: a method for measuring BAC levels from the alcohol in a person's breath.

chronic exposure: an amount of a chemical administered over a long period of time.

congeners: other substances, besides alcohol, that are found in alcoholic beverages.

Controlled Substance Act (CSA): a law that established the U.S. legal foundation for the criminal guidelines for possessing different amounts of controlled substances.

corrosive poisons: substances that physically destroy tissues upon direct contact and usually act immediately, such as strong acids and bases.

cytotoxin: a substance that is toxic to cells.

depressants: compounds that act to depress the functioning of the central nervous system, bringing about calmness and sleep.

distribution: the spreading of a substance throughout an organism after administration.

dose: the amount of a substance administered at a particular time.

drug: a substance given for medical purposes, such as the prevention, diagnosis or treatment of disease.

elimination: the removal of substances, including metabolic waste products, from the body.

ethanol: the chemical compound CH_3CH_2OH, usually referring to the alcohol used for human consumption or as an additive to fuels.

ethnopharmacology: the exploration of traditional folk remedies for finding new drugs.

fermentation: the use of certain strains of yeast to metabolize sugars into carbon dioxide and ethanol.

field sobriety test: testing that involves a series of behavioral tasks done by a person suspected of being intoxicated.

half-life ($t_{1/2}$): the amount of time necessary for one-half of the original sample to change, be eliminated, decompose or decay away.

hallucinogens: compounds that alter normal thought processes, perceptions, personal awareness, and psychological moods.

Henry's Law: the physical principle that states when a solution containing a dissolved volatile compound is brought into contact with a gas, a fixed equilibrium is set up between the amount of the volatile compound in the gas (air) and the amount dissolved in the liquid.

horizontal gaze nystagamus (HGN): a test that examines the involuntary jerking of the eye as a person looks from side to side, used to gauge levels of alcohol impairment.

ingestion: the oral (mouth) entry of a chemical into the body through the gastrointestinal tract.

injection: the insertion of a compound either directly into the bloodstream or in nearby tissue.

intramuscular: the injection of a substance directly into a muscle.

intravenous: the injection of a substance directly into a blood vessel.

lethal dose (LD_{50}): the amount of a substance administered at one time that is necessary to cause death in a percentage of a population; LD_{50} refers to 50% of a population.

medicine: a drug or chemical used for the prevention, diagnosis, or treatment of disease.

metabolic poisons: compounds that act by affecting the biochemical functioning of cells and tissues.

metabolite: a compound formed from the metabolism/breakdown of a drug.

narcotic: a drug that brings relief from pain and induces sleep.

neuron: nerve cells.

neurotoxins: molecules that interfere with the normal functioning of nerve cells.

opiates: compounds derived from opium sap.

opioids: all drugs, including those made independently in the laboratory, that function similarly to the opiates.

pharmacodynamics: the study of how a drug works on a person's body.

pharmacokinetics: the study of how a person's body processes a drug.

poison: a compound that primarily functions by killing cells.

semi-synthetic opiates: drugs made synthetically from naturally occurring opiates.

side effect: a secondary effect from a medical treatment.

Standardized Field Sobriety Test (SFST): a battery of tasks used to evaluate impairment as the basis of probable cause for arrest.

steroids: compounds that promote muscle growth and repair, regulate metabolism and immune function, and control blood properties.

stimulants: compounds that increase alertness and activity.

subcutaneous: the injection of a substance directly into the skin layers.

synapses: junctions between nerve cells that complete the electrical connections in the nervous system.

synesthesia: an effect that occurs when stimulation of one sensory form leads to stimulation of another sensation.

tolerance: the capacity of an organism to be affected by the administration of a dose of a chemical.

toxicology: the field that deals with the nature and effects of poisons.

toxin: a subset of poisons that are produced specifically by living organisms.

venom: a toxin that is injected directly into a victim.

BIBLIOGRAPHY

Randall C. Baselt, *Disposition of Toxic Drugs and Chemicals in Man* (8th Ed.), Biomedical Publications, 2008.

Peter A. Gerber et al., "The dire consequences of doping", *The Lancet*, 372(6939), 656, 2008.

P.K. Gupta, *Fundamentals of Toxicology, Essential Concepts and Applications*, Academic Press, 2017.

Ernest Hodgson, *A Textbook of Modern Toxicology*, Wiley, 2010.

Christopher P. Holstege, Thomas Neer, Gregory B. Saathoff, and R. Brent Furbee, *Criminal Poisoning: Clinical and Forensic Perspectives*, Jones and Bartlett Publishers, 2010.

Sue Jickells, Adam Negrusz, Anthony C. Moffat, and M. David Osselton, *Clarke's Analytical Forensic Toxicology* (2nd Ed.), Pharmaceutical Press, 2013.

Melanie John Cupp, *Toxicology and Clinical Pharmacology of Herbal Products*, Humana Press, 2010.

J. Kim and O. De Jesus, *Medication Routes of Administration.* StatPearls [Internet] [Updated 2023 August 23]. Treasure Island (FL): StatPearls Publishing, 2024. https://www.ncbi.nlm.nih.gov/books/NBK568677/.

Curtis Klaassen, *Casarett & Doull's Toxicology: The Basic Science of Poisons* (7th Ed.), McGraw-Hill Professional, 2007.

Richard Laing and Jay A. Siegel, *Hallucinogens: A Forensic Drug Handbook*, Academic Press, 2003.

N.T. Lappas and C.M. Lappas, *Forensic Toxicology: Principles and Concepts* (2nd Ed.), Elsevier, 2021.

Barry Levine and Sarah Kerigan, *Principles of Forensic Toxicology* (5th Ed.), American Association for Clinical Chemistry, 2020.

D.K. Molina, *Handbook of Forensic Toxicology for Medical Examiners* (Practical Aspects of Criminal & Forensic Investigations), CRC Press, 2009.

Maryadele O'Neil (Ed.), *The Merck Index: An Encyclopedia of Chemicals, Drugs and Biologicals* (14th Ed.), Merck, 2006.

Kalipatnapu N. Rao, *Forensic Toxicology: Medicolegal Case Studies*, CRC Press, 2012.

Fred Smith and Jay A. Siegel, *Handbook of Forensic Drug Analysis*, Academic Press, 2004.Richard A. Stripp and Lawrence Kobilinsky, *The Forensic Aspects of Poisons* (Inside Forensic Science), Chelsea House Publications, 2007.

S. Timmermans, J. Souffriau, and C. Libert, "A general introduction to glucocorticoid biology". *Frontiers in Immunology*, 10, 1545, 2019. doi: 10.3389/fimmu.2019.01545

John H. Trestrail, *Criminal Poisoning: Investigational Guide for Law Enforcement, Toxicologists, Forensic Scientists, and Attorneys* (Forensic Science and Medicine), Springer, 2007.

A. Wallace Hayes, *Principles and Methods of Toxicology* (5th Ed.), CRC Press, 2007.

Forensic Fire and Explosives

14

14.1 FORENSIC FIRE AND EXPLOSIVES INVESTIGATIONS

The most tangible of all visible mysteries - fire.

Leigh Hunt (1784–1859)

LEARNING GOALS AND OBJECTIVES

Forensic Investigations may deal with the causes of fires and explosions. After completing this chapter, you should be able to:

- Describe what fire is and the roles played by the components in the fire tetrahedron.
- Discuss the different types of information that may be part of a fire investigation.
- Explain what is meant by arson and some of the clues of intentionally set fires.
- Relate what the common explosives used today are and how they are classified.
- Discuss the causes of physical damage from an explosion.
- Describe how the identities of explosives may be determined in the laboratory.

14.1.1 Introduction

Fire has been both a boon and a threat to human civilization throughout history. While providing heat and a means of preparing safe food, it also presented clear threats. Many cities, such as Rome, London, Chicago, and New York, have all experienced devastating fires in their past. In the Middle Ages, William the Conqueror required that all fires be covered and people remain inside after a specified time in the evening, a practice known as "couvre feu" or "cover the fire,"

giving rise to our modern term "curfew." From this need to protect people and property, fire inquiries remain an important aspect of forensic science today. Thus, advances in fire investigation have relied upon the development of increasingly sophisticated and effective tools, processes, and analyses for exploring the crimes and events involving fire and explosions.

Investigations into the cause and nature of fires and explosions require careful observation and reliance upon forensic scientific analysis to unravel the chain of events leading to the event. While fires and explosions release large quantities of energy (Figure 14.1), traces of their origins can remain surprisingly long after they have been extinguished. These investigations explore the physical and chemical components that help explain how these fire and explosions occurred.

14.1.2 Fire Basics

In order to understand how forensic evidence can provide critical insights into the cause and events surrounding a fire or explosion, we first need to understand the basics of fire and combustion.

Fire is defined as the rapid oxidation of substances through combustion reactions, resulting in the release of energy, often in the form of heat and light, and the formation of new chemical products. Specifically, burning is an exothermic chemical reaction – a reaction that gives off energy – that occurs between a fuel and an oxidant. An oxidant (or oxidizing agent) is simply a chemical that can either transfer oxygen atoms to or remove electrons from another chemical compound (Figure 14.2). In combustion reactions, the fuel (the reducing agent) reacts with the oxidant to form new compounds where each element in the fuel is combined with the oxidant. Many chemical oxidants are known, but in most cases, the oxidant in fires is simply atmospheric oxygen (O_2), and the most common fuels are organic compounds, composed primarily of carbon and hydrogen, called *hydrocarbons*. In these reactions, oxygen combines with the carbon and hydrogen of the fuel to produce carbon dioxide (CO_2) and water (H_2O) vapor as products (Figure 14.3), as illustrated by the following equations for representative hydrocarbons:

FIGURE 14.1 Fires combine the necessary ingredients to deliver large amounts of energy very rapidly. This photograph was taken during a major fire involving an abandoned convent in Massueville, Québec, Canada. The fire was so violent that firefighters had to focus their efforts on saving the adjacent church instead of attacking the involved building itself.

Source: Used per Creative Commons Share Alike 3.0, Unported. User: Sylvain Pedneault.

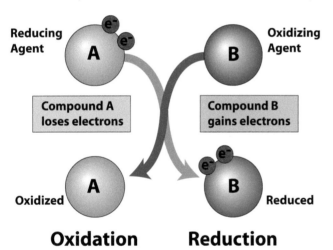

FIGURE 14.2 Oxidation and reduction reactions. A reducing agent is itself oxidized (loses electrons) by reducing something else while an oxidizing agent is reduced (gains electrons) by oxidizing something else (the reducing agent). The process may be thought of as the net transfer of electrons from the reducing agent to the oxidizing agent in the overall reaction.

Source: Shutterstock.com.

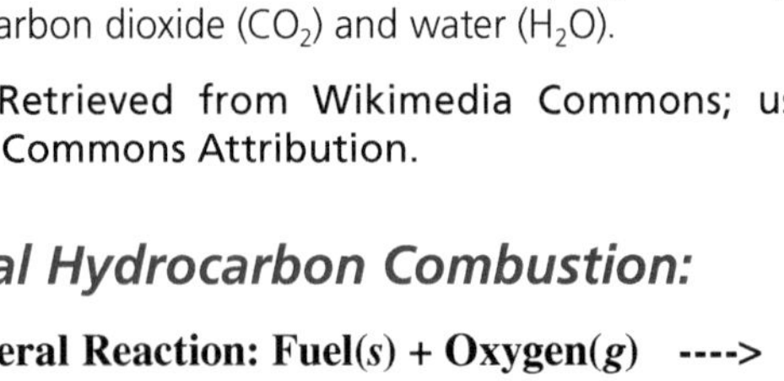

$$CH_4 + 2O_2 \longrightarrow CO_2 + 2H_2O$$

FIGURE 14.3 Combustion of methane (CH_4) with oxygen (O_2) to form carbon dioxide (CO_2) and water (H_2O).

Source: Retrieved from Wikimedia Commons; used per Creative Commons Attribution.

General Hydrocarbon Combustion:

General Reaction: Fuel(s) + Oxygen(g) ----> CO$_2$(g) + H$_2$O(g) + Energy (14.1)

Methane: $CH_4(g) + 2\ O_2(g)$ ----> $CO_2(g) + 2\ H_2O(g) +$ **Energy** $\Delta H°_{comb.} = -54.0$ kJ/g

Gasoline:* $C_8H_{18}(g) + {}^{25}/_2\ O_2(g)$ ----> $8\ CO_2(g) + 9\ H_2O(g) +$ **Energy** $\Delta H°_{comb.} = -47.3$ kJ/g

Wood:* $C_6H_{10}O_5(s) + 6\ O_2(g)$ ----> $6\ CO_2(g) + 5\ H_2O(g) +$ **Energy** $\Delta H°_{comb.} = -15.0$ kJ/g

(*approximate chemical formulas for gasoline and wood (cellulose) are shown here).

BOX 14.1   WHAT IS A FLAME?

When a fire occurs, hot gases are produced from the combustion of the fuel. These hot gases can emit visible light when high-energy electrons from the heated molecules cool to lower energies, emitting a photon of visible light (see Chapter 12).

During burning, some of the potential energy stored in the chemical bonds of the molecules that make up the fuel is released. The energy generated in this process can take the form of heat, light, sound, mechanical, or other forms of energy. In natural organic fuels, for example, energy from the sun is first captured by plants and stored by forming chemical bonds in the molecules that the plants make, such as glucose, cellulose, oils, and many others. Generally, energy is released (exothermic) when chemical bonds form and is required (endothermic) to break bonds. This may seem "backward", but energy is usually released only when new, *stronger* bonds are formed to make products. In photosynthesis, for example, plants break apart the very strong bonds of carbon dioxide and water to make new chemical bonds in the production of glucose and oxygen molecules, as shown in Equation 14.2, an energetically uphill process (Figure 14.4). The energy needed to break the CO_2 and H_2O bonds is supplied to the plants from sunlight. During combustion, the strong bonds of the CO_2 and H_2O products are reformed to release the energy stored in the glucose and oxygen.

$$6H_2O(l) + 6CO_2(g) \text{--->} C_6H_{12}O_6(s) + 6\ O_2(g)\ \Delta H$$
$$= +2803\ kJ/mol \qquad (14.2)$$

This process is similar to storing energy in a book by placing it on a high shelf. Energy is required to lift the book to the shelf and is stored by virtue of the position of the book (potential energy). The energy can be released by pushing the book off the shelf, thereby converting the stored potential energy of position into the kinetic energy of motion. In an analogous fashion, energy is stored in the chemical bonds of the product molecules from photosynthesis. This energy may later be recovered by oxidizing the glucose and oxygen back

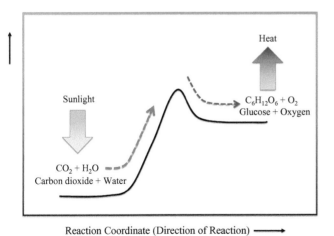

FIGURE 14.4 Energy considerations in the conversion of light energy from the sun into chemical energy stored in the bonds of the products of photosynthesis (reaction moves left to right). The process is reversed (moves right to left) during combustion to liberate the stored energy. Notice that the products of photosynthesis (right) are higher in energy than the starting compounds (left), and likewise, the products of combustion (left) are lower in energy than the starting fuels and oxygen (right).

into CO_2 and H_2O to release energy. Of course, glucose may also be transformed into other molecules by the plant (e.g., linked together to make cellulose), consumed as food by other organisms, or modified through other processes, such as in the geological and chemical processes that lead to the formation of fossil fuels. When these compounds burn as fuels, the long-stored solar energy is finally released in the heat and light that we observe, as illustrated in the cycle shown in Figure 14.5.

Each type of fuel generates a characteristic amount of energy on burning, called the *heat of combustion* for the compound, denoted as $\Delta H^{\circ}_{combustion}$. When given in kJ/g, as shown for the reactions above (1 kJ = 1000 Joules of energy or about the energy in a burning match), the larger the $\Delta H^{\circ}_{comb.}$ value, the more energy that is generated per gram of fuel. From this, we can see that methane can deliver over 3½ times the amount of energy given off by an equal amount of wood. Heats of combustion are also often given in kJ *per mole* of compound burned.

Oxidation reactions are among the most common of all chemical reactions on Earth. Oxygen is one of the few elements known to form compounds with every other element in the periodic table. Everything around us undergoes oxidation reactions to some extent, but why do some chemicals explode, others burn rapidly, some burn slowly, and even others appear to be relatively unreactive? The answer largely has to do with the energy requirements and rates of chemical reactions, which are important considerations to understand for combustion and explosive reactions.

Most chemical reactions require an input of energy to get the process started, even if the products are lower in energy than the reactants, liberating heat when the reaction occurs. In other words, even if the reaction is an energetically downhill process, it requires a "push" to get started. The energy that must be given to get a reaction going is called the *activation energy* of the reaction (E_{Act}, Figure 14.7). This is similar to the energy necessary to start a roller-coaster going or a rock rolling downhill. We must first put in sufficient energy to get the coaster car to the top of the first hill (the activation energy), and once there, the coaster continues its own until the end of the ride. If not enough energy is added to push the car to the top of the hill, it will roll back to where it started and not go on to the end point. It's the same with chemical reactions; enough energy must be added to the reaction to get it over the "hill" of the activation energy so that it can proceed to products; the addition of an insufficient amount of energy will not initiate the reaction and it will just "roll" back to the beginning as unreacted starting materials. Often, this activation energy is used to break chemical bonds in the starting molecules to allow new bonds to form, such as breaking the C–H bonds in the oxidation of methane to form the new C=O bonds in carbon dioxide. The higher the activation energy, the more energy is needed to get a chemical reaction started. For example, in Figure 14.8, the energy profiles for two reactions are shown, one reaction having a much higher activation energy than the other (E_{Act} Reaction 1 > E_{Act} Reaction 2). Reaction 1 would require much more energy to be initially added than reaction 2 for it to reach

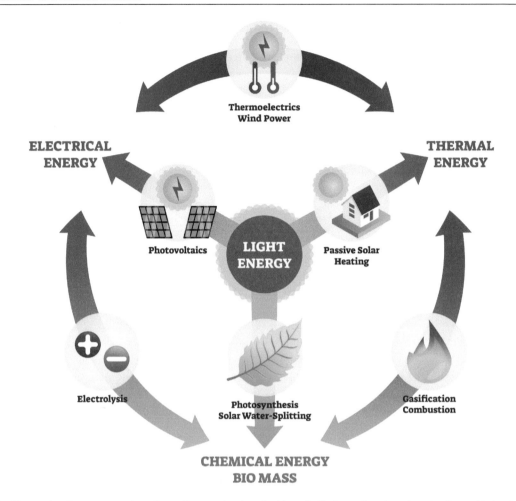

FIGURE 14.5   The cycle of energy capture from the sun in chemical bonds that can be stored and released later to deliver energy through combustion.

Source: Shutterstock.com.

the top of the energy "hill" and have the reaction initiated. Some reactions have sufficiently low activation energies that room temperature is sufficient to provide the needed energy to start the reaction. Other reactions require the input of larger amounts of energy that must be provided by an outside source, such as the energy generated by friction when rubbing a match on sandpaper, directly heating the compound, providing a hot flame or spark, or even from light energy. Finally, some reactions have activation barriers that are so high that very large amounts of energy are required to start the process, such as the oxidation of gold or the ignition of a secondary explosive. Each compound has its own unique activation barrier to oxidation that must be overcome (see Section 14.1.3 on auto-ignition temperature).

BOX 14.2   FIRE FROM THE SKY!

When the German airship Hindenburg burned on May 6, 1937, near Lakehurst, New Jersey, over 7 million cubic feet of hydrogen gas, used to keep the ship afloat, combined rapidly with oxygen:

$$2H_2(g) + O_2(g) ------> 2\,H_2O(g) + Energy\ \Delta H^{\circ}_{comb.} = -484\ kJ/mol$$

This explosion and fire lasted just 34 seconds but liberated over 2.1 billion kJ of energy and produced 160,600 kg (~355,000 lbs) of water as vapor. This is equivalent to 160,600 L of liquid water (~42,500 gal of water) and about the electrical energy needs for 100 average U.S. homes for a year (10^{12} J): all released in seconds. Fire investigators are still trying to piece together what happened to cause the catastrophic results. Theories include both accidental and intentional causes.

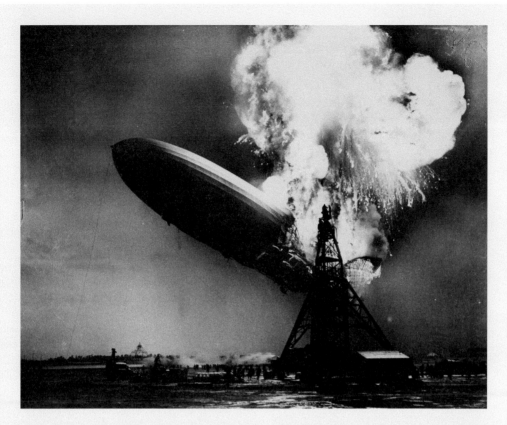

FIGURE 14.6 Explosion and combustion of the Hindenburg on May 6, 1937 near Lakehurst, New Jersey which released about 2.1 billion kJ of energy and produced ~160,600 Kg (~355,000 lbs) of water.

Source: Retrieved from Wikimedia Commons; used per Creative Commons Attribution.

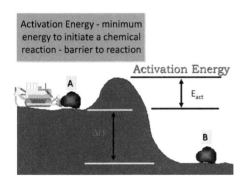

FIGURE 14.7 Activation energy is the amount of energy required to get a reaction started.

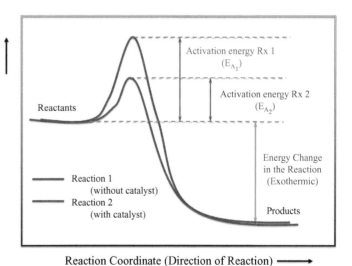

Reaction Coordinate (Direction of Reaction) ⟶

FIGURE 14.8 Activation energies for two different chemical reactions. The activation energy of reaction 1 is much higher than the activation energy required to initiate reaction 2, meaning that less energy is needed to start reaction 2.

Chemical reactions represent a change in matter. Starting materials are converted into products at a specific rate: the amount of change that happens in a given amount of time. The main explanation of why some chemicals explode, while others burn only slowly comes from considering the rates of chemical reactions. Explosive reactions happen at very fast rates while combustion reactions occur much more slowly. A number of important factors contribute to the observed *rate of a chemical reaction* including activation energy, concentration, temperature, molecular orientation (how two molecules

come together), the presence of a catalyst, and the reaction medium. On the molecular level, these factors combine to effectively control how *many* reacting molecules come

(a)   Collision Visualizations

$$Cl + NOCl \longrightarrow Cl_2 + NO$$

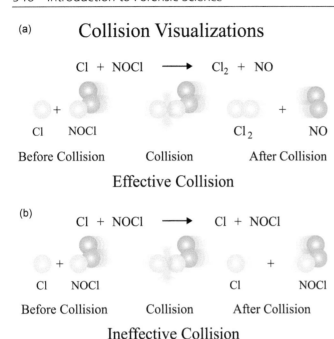

Cl   NOCl Cl_2 NO

Before Collision   Collision   After Collision

Effective Collision

(b)

$$Cl + NOCl \longrightarrow Cl + NOCl$$

Cl   NOCl   Cl   NOCl

Before Collision   Collision   After Collision

Ineffective Collision

FIGURE 14.9 Collision model for chemical reactions. In the reaction (b) the reactants do not have sufficient energy to react while in the reaction (a) they collide with sufficient energy to form new products.

Source: Shutterstock.com.

together during a *time* span with just the right *orientation* and enough *energy* to cause the reaction to occur, a concept called the *collision model* (Figure 14.9). The more collisions of molecules or atoms with the right features in a measure of time, the faster the rate.

Increasing the concentration of the reactants leads to more productive collisions leading to products by crowding the reactants more tightly together and forcing them to collide more frequently. For example, heating steel wool in the air with about 21% oxygen causes it to glow and be slowly oxidized, as shown in Figure 14.10. Taking the steel wool that has been heated to the same temperature and placing it into a pure oxygen atmosphere, however, causes it to burst into flames and react much faster. The observed differences in this example are caused by simply changing the concentration of the oxygen in the two experiments. Similarly, in burning solid objects, such as wood or paper, increasing the surface area of the solid effectively increases the concentration or amount of oxygen that can reach the fuel, thereby increasing the rate. For example, a solid phone book burns rather slowly while a shredded book, where much more oxygen is available to the fuel surface, burns rapidly (Figure 14.11). As the concentration of combustion products increases, however, the oxidation reaction tends to slow down because these products "blanket" the surface, effectively reducing the amount of surface area available for reaction.

Changing the temperature of a reaction also greatly affects its rate. Roughly, the rate of a chemical reaction doubles for every 10°C that the temperature is raised. Increasing the temperature increases the kinetic energy of the molecules – the molecules move faster. This means that more molecular collisions occur per unit of time with enough energy for a productive reaction to occur. This temperature effect is particularly

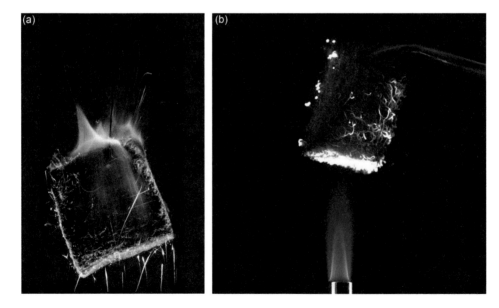

FIGURE 14.10 Steel wool oxidizes slowly in air (a) but much faster when heated in a pure oxygen environment (b). When heated, the small fibers of steel react with air to form iron oxide through an exothermic reaction. When burned in atmospheric air, the steel fibers away from the surface of the wool, where oxygen is used up, melt and are thrown out to ignite when they reach the air – seen as sparks. When heated in a pure oxygen atmosphere, the steel wool oxidizes spectacularly fast due to the much larger supply of oxygen.

Source: (a) Science Photo Library. (b) E.R. Degginger / Science Photo Library. Used with permission.

FIGURE 14.11 Which would burn faster – the intact phone book or the shredded book? The answer has to do with how much oxygen can react with the surfaces of the paper fuel.

Source: Shutterstock.com.

important in considering the spread of fires. As a fire burns, energy is given off to the surroundings mostly as heat. This heat increases the temperature of the fuel and air mixture, in turn speeding up the combustion reaction. This cyclic process continues with the added heat serving to increase the burning rate to give off even more heat that, once again, increases the temperature until the fuel, oxidant or other components are changed or consumed (Figure 14.12). Once the fire starts and the cycle begins, it can very rapidly accelerate from the exothermic combustion process.

Sometimes, a chemical called a catalyst is present that can greatly affect the rate of a reaction. A *catalyst* is a compound that lowers the activation energy of a chemical reaction, thereby increasing its rate, but without being consumed in the reaction. Catalysts function in a variety of ways by helping to bring the reacting molecules together in such a way that leads to productive reactions. Catalysts can weaken bonds in reactants, hold molecules in the right orientations for reactions to occur or alter the path of a chemical reaction. Frequently, burn-rate catalysts (compounds that modify the rate of the combustion reaction) are added to explosives and propellants to increase the combustion rate for a specific purpose.

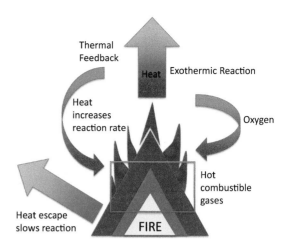

FIGURE 14.12 Feedback process where heat generated from a fire increases the burn rate of the fire in a cyclic loop.

For example, iron oxide (Fe_2O_3) can be added to ammonium perchlorate solid rocket propellants (NH_4ClO_4 – called an AP-type propellant), such as used in the space shuttle's solid rocket booster and in many improvised propelled weapons. These catalysts increase the rate of the combustion reaction and deliver more propulsion per unit of time. Sulfur or other compounds are sometimes added to gunpowder to similarly increase the rate of combustion of the powder. Catalysts may also be added to reduce, control, or suppress combustion, including in certain types of fire-retardant additives found in fabrics, building materials, and fire extinguishers. Detecting the minute presence of these catalysts in explosive residues can provide a great deal of information about their point of manufacture, primary intended use, and how they were employed in the observed blast.

In actuality, combustion reactions are very complex chemical processes that often do not result solely in the reaction products shown by the idealized chemical reactions of Equation 14.1. The incomplete combination of hydrocarbon fuels with oxygen can give carbon monoxide (CO) as the major product instead of carbon dioxide. In fact, the major cause of fire-related deaths comes not from direct burns or heat but from toxic vapors, such as carbon monoxide and smoke (Figure 14.13). Additionally, common impurities in fuels, especially sulfur and nitrogen-containing compounds, can combine to give various oxides, such as SO_3 and NO_3. If temperatures are high enough, even the usually very inert atmospheric nitrogen (N_2) can also combine with oxygen to give a variety of toxic nitrogen oxides (around 1% of products formed in hot fires). As an illustration, some of the additional reactions that are possible when natural gas (mostly methane), with its common impurities, is burned include:

$$CH_4(g) + 2\ O_2(g) \longrightarrow CO_2(g) + 2\ H_2O(g) + \text{Energy}$$
$$\Delta H^\circ_{comb.} = -882\ \text{kJ/mol}$$

$$2\ CH_4(g) + 3\ O_2(g) \longrightarrow 2\ CO(g) + 4\ H_2O(g) + \text{Energy}$$
$$\Delta H^\circ_{comb.} = -1,782\ \text{kJ/mol}$$

$$N_2(g) + O_2(g) \text{---}> 2\,NO(g) + \text{Energy}\ \Delta H^\circ_{comb.} = -90.3\ \text{kJ/mol}$$

$$N_2(g) + 2\,O_2(g) \text{---}> 2\,NO_2(g) + \text{Energy}\ \Delta H^\circ_{comb.} = -33.1\ \text{kJ/mol}$$

$$S(g) + O_2(g) \text{---}> 2\,SO_3(g) + \text{Energy}\ \Delta H^\circ_{comb.} = -296.8\ \text{kJ/mol}$$

…and other reactions are also possible depending on the impurities in the fuel.

When the rate of the reaction is slow, some combustion reactions can still occur through flameless reactions. *Smoldering* (or glowing combustion) is the slow, lower temperature combustion of compounds without a flame, often to give incomplete combustion products (largely carbon monoxide from organic compounds). Wood, cellulose, cotton, tobacco, plastics, dust, and humus are typical substances that can support long-lasting

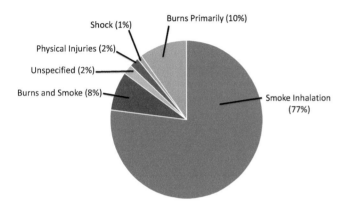

FIGURE 14.13 Causes of fire-related deaths. About 80% of the deaths are from toxic gases and/or smoke (Scotland).

smoldering reactions. Smoldering materials, such as those from tobacco products, can eventually lead to the initiation of fires, especially in furniture, clothing, and bedding. Smoldering also occurs at the end of a fire event after all of the volatile flammable materials have been driven off from solid fuels, such as wood. This is the case often seen in fireplaces when the flames are gone but the coals continue to glow red-hot for a long time (Figure 14.14). Oxidation reactions are still occurring at the surface of the wood, just at a relatively slow rate since the oxygen cannot penetrate beyond the surface into the fuel.

14.1.3 Fire Initiation, Growth, Decay, and Suppression

In order for a fire to begin, grow, and continue, four basic components are required. The close relationship between these four elements is often depicted in the *fire tetrahedron*, as shown in Figure 14.15. These components are heat, oxygen (oxidant), fuel, and a chemical chain reaction.

- **Heat**: For a fire to start and be sustained, a critical temperature (similar to an activation energy) must first be achieved and then maintained. If the temperature drops below this value, the fire will soon go out. The most common firefighting medium, water, acts simply to reduce the temperature of a fire by absorbing large amounts of heat energy in its phase transition from liquid water to gaseous water. Two values are defined to help understand the

FIGURE 14.14 Smoldering, or glowing combustion, occurs with wood fires when all the volatile components of the wood have burned but combustion still occurs at the surface of the fuel.

Source: Shutterstock.com.

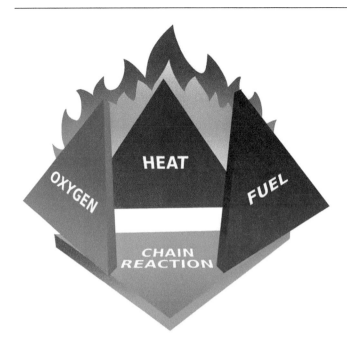

FIGURE 14.15 Fire tetrahedron illustrates the components required for initiating and sustaining a fire.

Source: Retrieved from Wikimedia Commons; used per Creative Commons Attribution.

temperatures needed for the combustion of a specific fuel. The *auto-ignition temperature* (or kindling point) is the minimum temperature at which a substance

will spontaneously ignite *without* an external source of ignition (spark), as shown in Figure 14.16. From a chemical standpoint, once the temperature is high enough to overcome the *activation energy* necessary for the combustion reaction to occur (the auto-ignition temperature), a compound can spontaneously combust. At temperatures below the auto-ignition point, there is not enough energy for the material to oxidize without some external stimulus. Once initiated, heat generated from the oxidation reaction of the fuel then maintains the temperature necessary to support combustion. The *flash point* of a fuel is the lowest temperature at which it will vaporize sufficiently to form an ignitable mixture with air that will combust when an ignition source is supplied (e.g., a spark or flame). If the temperature of a burning fire drops below the flash point of the fuel, the fire will cease burning and extinguish. Each substance has its own characteristic auto-ignition and flash point temperatures, and examples of these values for several common fuels are given in Table 14.1. The flash point for a compound is usually well below the auto-ignition temperature, meaning that the temperature needed to ignite a fire with a spark is much lower than the spontaneous combustion point. It is useful to note, as an example, the very low flashpoint of methane (−221°C) relative to its high auto-ignition temperature (+537°C), a difference of over 750°C! The energy needed to start a combustion reaction can be provided by heat generated by friction (e.g., lighting a match), a spark, electrical discharge, or other means.

FIGURE 14.16 Smoking hay bales that have spontaneously combusted. Hay (mown grass) has an auto-ignition point of 130°F (55°C), but it varies by the moisture content of the hay. This means that it will not burst into flames without an ignition source at temperatures below 55°C.

Source: Shutterstock.com.

TABLE 14.1   Some flash point and auto-ignition temperatures for common fuels

FUEL	FLASH POINT (°C)	AUTO-IGNITION TEMPERATURE (°C)
Gasoline	−43	246
Diesel Fuel	62	210
Vegetable Oil	327	~650
Paper	232	450
Wood	~300	300–450
Methane	−221	537
Ethanol (70%)	16	363

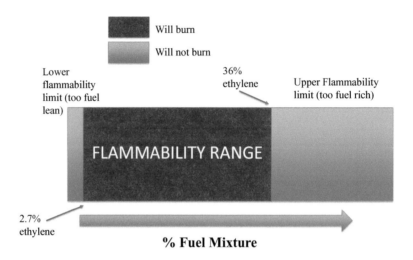

FIGURE 14.17   Ethylene (C_2H_4) has a lower flammability limit of 2.7% ethylene (97.3% air) and an upper flammability limit of 36% ethylene (64% air). As long as the concentration is either below or above these upper and lower limits of air-fuel mixtures, respectively, there is no fire/explosion risk. If, however, the air-fuel mixtures is between these limits, an explosion/fire could occur if a spark is provided.

BOX 14.3   SPONTANEOUS COMBUSTION?

Throughout history, there have been claims that people, animals, and property have spontaneously been consumed by fire that started without any apparent external source of ignition. While human spontaneous combustion has not been verified, there are instances when an object can build up enough heat to reach the auto-ignition point. For example, the microbial decay of hay or similar materials in an enclosed, non-ventilated space can generate enough heat to reach the auto-ignition point of the fuel. Similarly, cloth soaked with certain oils, such as linseed oil, and sealed in a container can generate enough heat from a slow oxidation process to reach the auto-ignition point of the cloth, setting off a spontaneous fire. Spontaneous combustion without an external heat source or spark is exceedingly rare; however, it is not a common source of fires.

- **Oxygen/Oxidizer**: An oxidizer, most often oxygen (O_2) from the air, is needed for a fire to begin and continue. The fuel and the gaseous oxygen must come into contact and mix *in the gas phase* for the combustion reaction to occur. The relative amounts of oxygen and fuel in the gaseous mixture are called the *air-fuel ratio*. There are threshold limits of air-fuel mixtures, referred to as the *flammability limits*, which are required for combustion. Beyond these limits, combustion cannot be sustained, as illustrated in Figure 14.17. This occurs when there is either too much oxygen with too little fuel present in the mixture (lean mixture) or too much fuel and too little oxygen (rich mixture). For example, the lower flammability limit for methane is about 5% methane, the lowest concentration of methane in air that can sustain a flame, and the upper limit of flammability is about 15%. If the concentration of methane is in the range of 5% to 15%, combustion (explosion) can occur. Outside of these limits, the mixture is safe and does not burn even when a flame is available. The air-fuel ratio describes the *gaseous* mixture based on the percentage of the compound mixed with air, and it should be remembered that air is only about 21% oxygen; the rest is composed of inert gases such as nitrogen (~78%) and argon

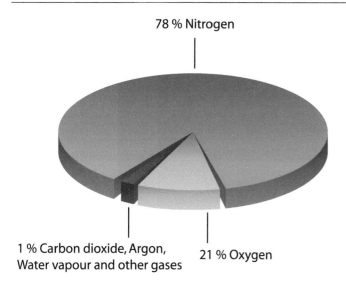

78 % Nitrogen

1 % Carbon dioxide, Argon, Water vapour and other gases

21 % Oxygen

FIGURE 14.18 The average composition of atmospheric air on Earth.

Source: Shutterstock.com.

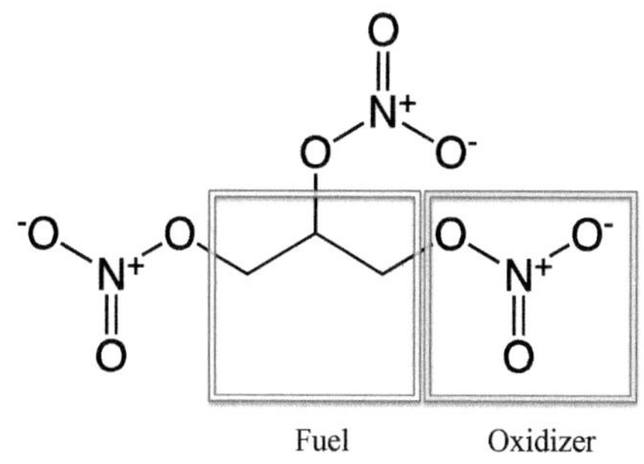

Fuel   Oxidizer

FIGURE 14.19 The structure of nitroglycerine, a major component of dynamite and cordite, contains both fuel components ($C_3H_5O_3$) and oxidizer components (NO_3) within the same molecule, such that no external oxygen source is needed for detonation to occur: $4C_3H_5(ONO_2)_3(l) \longrightarrow 12CO_2(g) + 10H_2O(g) + 6N_2(g) + O_2(g)$.

(~1%) (Figure 14.18). Additionally, none of the solid or liquid components of the fuel are considered in the ratio, only the gaseous portions.

Decreasing the amount of oxygen available to a flame will cause it to burn more slowly while increasing the oxygen content within the flammability limits increases the rate of combustion. Fanning a flame or providing ventilation essentially delivers more oxygen to the flame, causing it to burn faster.

In the case of explosives, the oxidizer often is *not* atmospheric oxygen but rather another compound added as the oxidant. Atmospheric oxygen (~21% of air) just can't supply oxygen fast enough to an explosive compound to generate the extremely fast chemical reactions that characterize explosions. Instead, an oxidizer is added either to the explosive mixture or incorporated into the explosive compound itself so that it has both fuel and oxidizer portions fused into a single molecule. Nitroglycerine, shown in Figure 14.19, is a good example of an explosive that contains both oxidizer and fuel components within the same molecule. Black powder, in contrast, uses a separate compound added to the mixture, such as potassium nitrate (KNO_3, "saltpeter"), that serves as the oxidant.

• **Fuel**: Fuel, as we define it relative to fire and explosives, is any material that stores chemical energy that can be extracted through combustion reactions. Fuels may be in any physical state: solid, liquid, or gas. The burning process with oxygen, however, must occur in the gas phase since O_2 is a gas and, therefore, can only reach the fuel near the interface between the gaseous oxygen and the solid or liquid fuels. For example, a solid or liquid must first be

heated sufficiently for combustible gases to be given off that can be rapidly mixed with and oxidized by the gaseous oxygen in the air. In other words, the fuel must also be a gas in order to react with the gaseous oxidant, oxygen. The flash point of a fuel is simply the temperature at which the solid or liquid fuel generates enough volatile gaseous products to create a concentration of these gases within the flammability limits for combustion for the fuel. Most common fuels come from biological sources: biofuels or fossil fuels. Biofuels are those that come from any carbon source that can be readily replenished and are termed a renewable resource (e.g., plants, microorganisms, animals, wood, ethanol, oils, fats, etc.). Fossil fuels are hydrocarbons (C_xH_y compounds) that are derived from the ancient remains of fossilized plants and animals, such as petroleum, various oils, coal, natural gas, and tars. Fossil fuels are a non-renewable resource since the supply is not replenished; it takes millions of years to convert biological matter into these fossil fuels. Other fuel sources, although not as commonly encountered, can be derived from mineral and other inorganic sources.

BOX 14.4 TYPES OF FIRES

In the United States, fires are classified into groupings depending upon the source of the fuel. The classification of the fire is used to determine the best way to suppress it. The categories of fires are:

• **Class A Fire**: Ordinary combustibles, such as wood, paper, cloth, trash, cardboard, and PVC.
• **Class B Fire**: Flammable liquid or gaseous fuels, such as benzene, gasoline, oil, butane, fuel oil, kerosene, propane, and natural gas.

- **Class C Fire**: Involving live electrical equipment, often caused by short circuits or overheated electrical cables.
- **Class D Fire**: Combustible metals and alloys, such as iron, aluminum, sodium, and magnesium.
- **Class K Fire**: Cooking media that contain vegetable or animal fat and oils.

- **Chemical Chain Reaction**: Combustion reactions occur through a complex chemical process called a *radical chain reaction*. A radical is a molecule or atom that has an unpaired electron in its outermost (valence) layer. Usually, nature tries to pair all electrons in molecules to form stable compounds, and because of this, radicals tend to be very reactive intermediate compounds that try to pair up their electrons by pulling electrons from other molecules. When a radical encounters a non-radical molecule or atom, it reacts by grabbing (abstracting) an electron from that non-radical molecule. The original radical then becomes a more stable non-radical species, while the original non-radical molecule becomes a radical (sounds confusing, but think of it like this: if you had no money and your friend has $1, you could borrow the $1 from them, leaving them now without money (where you started) and you now have $1 (where they started)). This is illustrated schematically in Figure 14.20. The process of a radical pulling an electron from a non-radical to create a new non-radical and a radical can continue in a long series of reactions called a *chain reaction*, similar to that shown in Figure 14.20. These highly reactive radical intermediates can continue to pull

non-radical molecules apart, leading to new products and, in the case of combustion, to the observed oxidized products.

Combustion actually consists of many simultaneous but different radical chain reactions, usually started by oxygen-based radicals. Molecular oxygen (O_2), more correctly called dioxygen, is an unusual molecule in that it's most stable form is a diradical (it has two unpaired electrons in its lowest energy form). The high initiation temperatures required for combustion partly come from the need to convert the stable oxygen diradical into a very reactive electron radical state (spin-paired). This latter, highly reactive form of oxygen then can then abstract a hydrogen atom or other fragments from the fuel molecules to give a variety of new radicals, including the HOO·radical, called the hydroperoxide radical (the dot by the formula indicates an unpaired electron, making it a radical). The radicals formed at the high temperatures of combustion continue the chain reaction until either the fuel is consumed or the temperature drops too low to produce the necessary radicals to continue the chain reaction. Most of these radicals are so short-lived, however, that they cannot be detected but nonetheless lead to the observed combustion products. Anything that can inhibit the formation or remove these radicals from the combustion mixture can effectively shut down the combustion process.

14.1.4 Fire Dynamics

In order for a fire to start and grow, all four components of the fire tetrahedron must be present in the right form. Conversely, to stop a fire, one or more of these basic ingredients must be

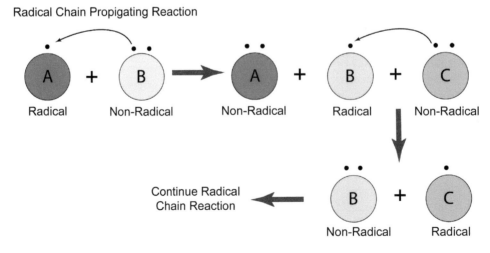

FIGURE 14.20 Radical chain reaction propagating (continuation) steps: the small dots represent valence (outermost) electrons, and the larger spheres (labeled A, B, and C) represent atoms or molecules. Note that species with a pair of electrons are labeled non-radical, while those with unpaired, single electrons are labeled as radicals.

removed. Different firefighting materials and techniques are aimed at reducing or eliminating one of these four components.

- **Heat Suppression**: The most common firefighting agent is water. Water largely acts to cool the fire by absorbing large amounts of energy. Compounds that cool the fire can help to bring it under control by lowering the temperature below the ignition point.
- **Oxidant Suppression**: Carbon dioxide and sodium bicarbonate (solid extinguisher) act to smother the fire by removing oxygen from the equation. This typically requires large amounts of CO_2 to be effective, as much as 75% of the surface of the fuel must be covered with CO_2 to suppress the fire in some instances. CO_2 is denser than air, so it settles to the lowest point to blanket a low-lying fire. Since it does not support combustion and displaces oxygen from the neighborhood of the fuel, it serves as an effective extinguisher. Because of the toxicity of CO_2, however, it is most often employed on smaller fires. In enclosed areas, inert gases such as nitrogen can also be used to remove the oxidant by displacing the oxygen, although this can be very dangerous for any people trapped in the contained space due to the lack of oxygen to breathe.
- **Fuel Suppression**: Typically, the removal of fuel occurs by either physically isolating the fuel source or interrupting the flow of fuel into the fire, such as turning off a gas valve.
- **Chain Reaction Suppression**: A common type of fire extinguisher uses a substance called Halon as the active fire suppressant, one of a family of halomethane compounds such as $CBrF_3$ (Halon 1301) and $CBrClF_2$ (Halon 1211). Halon acts at high temperatures to produce halogen atom radicals (*e.g.*, fluorine, chlorine, bromine, or iodine radicals) that rapidly react with radicals produced in the combustion chemical chain reaction, such as the hydrogen (H·) and hydroperoxide (HOO·) radicals. Removing the chain-continuing radicals interrupts the combustion process, terminating the fire even when sufficient heat, fuel, and oxygen are present.

14.1.5 Fire Stages

Fires often present a predictable pattern of development and damage. Understanding how a "normal" fire behaves gives key insights when investigating fires that may have been set intentionally and deviate from the normal patterns. Fires usually develop through four stages (Figure 14.21):

- **Incipient Stage**: The first stage usually is invisible to a viewer but involves the generation and accumulation of the volatile and combustible gases necessary to support combustion.

- **Smoldering/Growth Stage**: Small amounts of visible smoke may be seen at the beginning of this stage as the heat and mixture of fuel and oxidizer reach a point to support active combustion, initially at a relatively slow rate. As this oxidation reaction continues (smoldering), the temperature rises, increasing the rate of the oxidation reaction. The heat can be transferred by a number of means including radiation, convection, diffusion, and conduction (Figure 14.22). Initially, the fire's growth is controlled by the properties of the fuel but, as the fire grows, it becomes controlled by the amount of oxygen present, often called *ventilation-controlled fire growth*. The reaction rate doubles as the temperature rises about every 10°C, leading to a rapid growth cycle for the fire. To continue to grow, a fire must spread beyond the initial point of ignition to incorporate additional fuel. The "movement" of a fire follows well-understood patterns that can help decipher the initial source and primary cause of a fire.
- **Full Development/Active Fire Stage**: The critical combination of all the necessary elements must be in place to lead to a raging fire. A *flashover* may take place leading into this stage. A flashover is the rapid transition to a fully developed fire by the nearly simultaneous ignition of all the flammable materials within an enclosed space. It occurs when the surfaces in an enclosed space are rapidly heated to the auto-ignition temperature, igniting large amounts of unburned flammable gases that have accumulated from the pyrolysis of the surfaces (Figure 14.23). During the full development stage, firefighters are always conscious of the possibility of an explosive *backdraft* event, especially later in this stage. A backdraft is possible when a fire burns in an enclosed space and uses up much of its oxygen supply, starving the fire of oxygen and causing it to decrease when it still has plenty of gaseous fuel. The backdraft can then occur, often explosively, when oxygen is rapidly reintroduced into the room that has accumulated unburned fuel (from lack of O_2), such as by opening a window or from a roof collapse, leading to a sudden increase of oxygen leading to a flash of combustion.
- **Decay**: This is the final stage of the fire when either the fuel is consumed or, due to firefighting efforts, one or more of the elements of the fire tetrahedron have been removed. After the active flames have been extinguished, the fire may continue to smolder for days.

When dealing with a fire, investigators consider the variables that led to the *rate* at which heat was released during the fire. This important quantity is called the *Heat Release Rate*, or HRR. The variables that affect the HHR include the size of the area burning, the identity of the fuel, the moisture

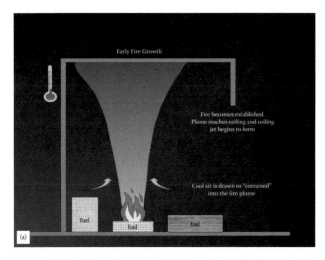

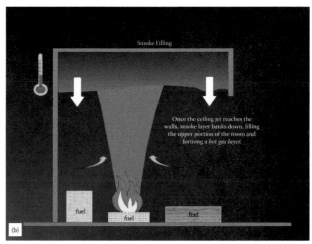

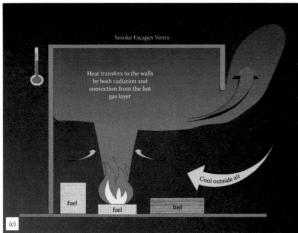

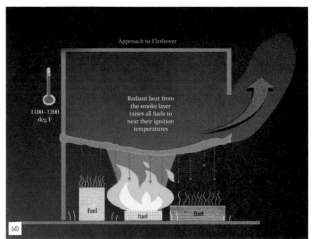

FIGURE 14.21 Developmental stages of a typical fire – the vertical axis is temperature and the horizontal axis is time.

Source: Lentini (2018).

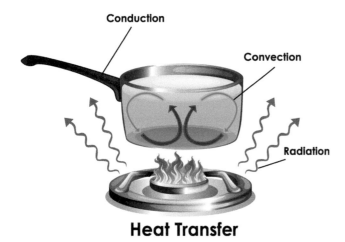

FIGURE 14.22 Methods of transferring heat from a source to its surroundings.

Source: Shutterstock.com.

content of the fuels, the surface area available for combustion (see Figure 14.11), the orientation of the burning materials (e.g., lying on the floor, standing vertically, on the walls, or elevated off of the floor, Figure 14.24), the method for heat transfer (see Figure 14.22), and how efficiently the materials themselves burn. All these factors combine to give an estimate of how much heat *should* be released from a given fire over time. Unusual features, such as a fire hotter in some places than would be expected, can provide fire investigators important information about the source, progression, materials, and nature of the fire.

14.1.6 Fire Investigation

With an understanding of the basics of fire initiation, development and behavior, fire investigators are often asked to piece together evidence to explain the cause and actions of the fire. There are several reasons for this type of investigation. The first is to determine the cause of the fire to help prevent future similar events from happening elsewhere as well as to ensure that the specific fire will not reoccur. The second is to determine if the fire arose from a "natural" or accidental cause or was due to someone's unlawful actions, whether through negligence or intent. Fires arising from either negligence or intent

FIGURE 14.23 A flashover can happen when the surfaces of an enclosed space are heated to the auto-ignition temperature.

Source: iStockPhoto

can lead to criminal prosecution, and the investigator's work forms the foundation of any court case brought forward.

Arson is the criminal act of intentionally setting fire without lawful consent. Arson may be part of other crimes such as covering a homicide, destroying property for insurance fraud, or eliminating questionable records. It may also be determined to be a hate crime, a crime of revenge, or terrorism, among other possibilities. An important part of any investigation is determining if there was a motive for setting the fire. The most common reason for arson is to destroy property to collect insurance money, especially when it would be hard to sell or otherwise collect money for the specific property (see Box 14.5).

Arson investigations usually begin with a direct examination of the fire scene. Investigators must work as quickly as is safely possible after the fire has been extinguished since fire-related evidence can be very transient and short-lived. The combined action of the fire itself and the results of efforts to put out the fire can destroy evidence that might be crucial to the investigation. Working carefully but quickly afterward can help preserve key evidence.

In order to start a fire, an arsonist must somehow arrange the components of the fire tetrahedron to facilitate the rapid initiation and growth of a fire. This might involve gathering ignitable fuel together in one place, providing a heat or ignition source, or adding compounds specifically to facilitate fire initiation (accelerants). An evidence-based demonstration of arson requires investigators to show that somehow one or more of the fire tetrahedron's components have been altered inappropriately or criminally to facilitate a fire. It is important to note that failing to find any natural or accidental cause of a fire is not an acceptable legal argument for determining arson as the cause of the fire. The outcomes of many cases have shown that this line of reasoning does not withstand the rigors of trial.

BOX 14.5 INSURANCE FRAUD THROUGH ARSON

Intentionally setting fire to property for the purpose of collecting insurance money is believed to be the number one reason for arson. Insurance companies must often defend themselves through civil proceedings using the arson defense to avoid paying a settlement. In order to avoid paying, an insurance company must successfully prove arson through "clear, cogent, and convincing evidence" (U.S. Supreme Court, Colorado v. New Mexico, 467 U.S. 310 (1984)). The burden of proof is on the *insurance company* and they must *positively* prove the case against the owner (the presumption is that the owner is innocent of arson until proven guilty). The insurer must prove that the owner committed arson of the property by either direct (physical) or circumstantial evidence. Court precedent requires that the insurer must prove: (1) evidence of arson by someone, (2) motive for the fire by the owner, and (3) evidence specifically implicating the owner (often called "opportunity" evidence).

For example, a claim of arson was upheld in court (*Thomure v. Truck Insurance Exchange*, 8th *Circuit*, *1986*) on the following grounds:

- **Evidence of Arson**: Proof was given that accelerants were poured throughout the house and intentionally lit.
- **Motive**: The insured was in severe financial difficulty and the property had been unsuccessfully up for sale for several years.

- **Opportunity Evidence**: All the inhabitants of the house were unusually away at the time of the fire, the home had been insured for twice its purchase price value, and the owners had claimed very large sums for destroyed personal items. Additionally, the owners had moved household furnishings, firewood, parked cars, and the pet dog well away from the home just before the fire and had stored four gallons of kerosene in a clothes closet.

The court deemed that there was sufficient physical and circumstantial evidence to support the insurance company's claim of arson with the intent to defraud.

Many arson fires involve the use of *accelerants* to set fires. In fire investigations, accelerants are defined as compounds, often hydrocarbons, which facilitate the initiation and growth of a fire, but do not necessarily serve as a main fuel source. This is a somewhat different definition than the usual usage of the chemical term "accelerant," which refers to a catalyst that alters the rate of a chemical reaction without being consumed itself in the reaction (the accelerant is, therefore, technically not a catalyst since it is changed/consumed by the end of the reaction). Nonetheless, common fire-related usage makes little distinction between an accelerant and a fuel and the term is usually meant to describe any added substance that promotes a fire. A list of commonly employed accelerants, along with some of their properties, is given in Box 14.6. The use of accelerants can cause a fire to start faster, burn hotter, and consume the fuel in a different pattern than a typical, naturally occurring fire. Investigators look for traces of these accelerants that remain after the fire as direct physical evidence of arson (see Box 14.6).

Investigators often begin by interviewing the firefighters responding to the blaze, especially asking about any unusual behavior of the fire, even if it is a vague feeling that the fire simply did not behave as they had expected. Clues that might directly suggest arson include multiple points of origin of the fire, the presence of accelerants, unusual burn patterns, quantity and color of the smoke, disabled fire-suppression systems (*e.g.*, sprinklers, hydrants, hoses, etc.), unusual ventilation arrangements, and the condition of the fire scene.

The color of the smoke can help investigators learn what was burning and assess whether the smoke is consistent with fuels normally found in the structure. For example, gasoline tends to produce a yellow flame with thick black smoke, while wood produces a yellow or red flame with gray or light brown smoke (Figure 14.25). If firefighters observe thick black smoke coming from a building when they arrive, this could be an indication that gasoline was involved. If the building would not normally be expected to contain gasoline, such as a residential structure, this would suggest further investigation.

a. 1 second after ignition

b. 10 seconds after ignition

c. 35 seconds after ignition

d. 61 seconds after ignition

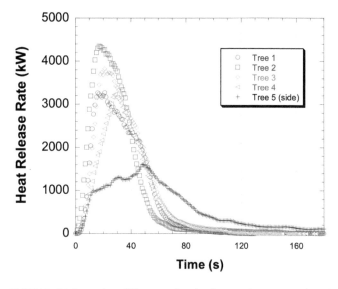

FIGURE 14.24 The difference in the heat release rate (HHR) on the orientation of the fuel. In this study, the HRR of standing and lying down evergreen trees were measured. Trees 1–4 were standing vertically and tree 5 was lying on its side. From the graph of the HRR for Tree 5 (black line), the one lying on its side, it is seen to burn much slower than the rate for the vertically oriented trees.

Source: NIST; Madrzykowski (2008).

Arsonists often know that increasing the supply of oxygen to a fire accelerates its rate of combustion (similar to blowing on glowing kindling in a fireplace or campfire to start the fire).

BOX 14.6   SOME COMMON ARSON ACCELERANTS

Arsonists have been known to use many different accelerants when setting fires. Some of the most commonly employed are (f.p. = flash point and AIT = auto-ignition temperature):

- **Acetone** (C_3H_6O, f.p. –20°C, AIT. 465°C): Acetone is a very volatile liquid with a strong odor that is used as a solvent in varnish, cosmetics, and nail polish remover.
- **Alcohols** (Methyl alcohol [wood alcohol, CH_3OH, f.p. 12°C, AIT 484°C], Ethyl alcohol [grain alcohol, C_2H_5OH, f.p. 13°C, AIT 365°C], and Isopropyl alcohol [rubbing alcohol, C_3H_7OH, f.p. 12°C, AIT 399°C]): These colorless liquids are readily available and find many uses including in beverages (ethanol only), industrial solvents, cleaning materials, fuel additives, and windshield wiper fluids.
- **Carbon Disulfide** (CS_2, f.p. –30°C, AIT 100°C): CS_2 is a colorless liquid with the odor of rotten eggs and is used in the manufacture of rayon and nylon, the vulcanization of rubber and resins, along with uses as a solvent. Because of its low auto-ignition point, it can spontaneously combust when in contact with hot steam pipes.
- **Camping Stove Fuel** (various hydrocarbons, f.p. –33°C, auto-ignition temp. not reported): These light fuels are distilled from petroleum processing and are commonly available as fuel sources for camping stoves and lanterns.
- **Ethyl Ether** ($C_2H_5OC_2H_5$, f.p. –45°C, AIT 180°C): Ether is a very volatile, low-boiling compound (b.p. 34°C) that can form shock-sensitive explosive peroxides upon standing or exposure to light. It is a common organic solvent.
- **Fuel Oils** (*e.g.,* C_9 –C_{23} compounds, such as kerosene, home heating oil, f.p. range from 42°C to 96°C, AIT ranges from 210° to 260°C): Very commonly available materials, but they tend to burn slower due to their lower volatilities.
- **Gasoline** (mixture of hydrocarbons, f.p. –43°C, AIT 280°C): Very flammable and readily available, gasoline is the most common of all accelerants employed by arsonists.
- **Mineral Spirits** (mixed hydrocarbons, f.p. 40°C, AIT 245°C): Commonly employed as paint thinner.
- **Turpentine** ($C_{10}H_{16}$, f.p. 32° to 46°C, AIT 253°C): Commonly used as a paint thinner and in varnishes, soaps, linoleum flooring, and polishes.

FIGURE 14.25   Different colored smoke from a wood fire (a) and a gasoline fire (b).

Source: (a) Used with permission Creative Commons Share Alike 3.0. User, Author: Midol~enwiki. (b) Credit: FEMA.

Finding doors and windows propped open or unusual openings cut into walls or ceiling might suggest the work of an arsonist. Likewise, finding firefighting or fire-suppression equipment disabled, turned off, or missing, which might allow the fire to grow unchecked and slow the firefighting response, provides further evidence.

Investigators especially look at the burn patterns left behind by the fire. Finding multiple places where the fire seems to have simultaneously originated, multiple explosions or flashovers is unusual with a natural fire. Additionally, "natural" fires tend to spread and build in well-recognized patterns. Deviations from these patterns can be evidence for arson. For example, finding a linear burn pattern, such as shown in Figure 14.26, indicates the use of an accelerant that was poured over the floor and then ignited. An "inverted cone" burn pattern (Figure 14.27) is another indication of an unusual burn pattern associated with arson accelerant use. Accelerants poured on floors can leak underneath the floor tiling or through floorboards to show an unusual burn pattern when the tiles or floorboards are removed for inspection, as illustrated in Figure 14.28. Other significant findings can include localized "rusting" (oxidation) on metal items, finding accelerant containers in or near the fire scene, a detectable odor of gasoline, soot plumes in unexpected places, shifted furniture or other flammable items "stacked" together as fuel sources, and other unusual features. Investigators also look to see if specific items had been removed *from* the scene *prior* to the fire, especially sentimental and valuable items. This type of action clearly shows a premeditated plan for setting the fire. Sometimes, evidence of accelerant use can come from the injuries sustained by the arsonist at the fire. Arsonists who use ignitable fluids may be burned on their hands, face, and legs in patterns that could be consistent with. accelerant use (Figure 14.29).

Commercially available handheld hydrocarbon detectors, sometimes called "sniffers," can be useful in screening a fire scene for the possible presence of any accelerants (Figure 14.30). These devices typically function by continuously sampling the air and monitoring the temperature of an internal hot filament for increases in temperature from the presence of oxidizable compounds in the sampled air.

Investigators often use photographers and/or personal observations at the scene to "watch the watchers": to observe any bystanders, voluntary helpers, witnesses, or victims who might be familiar or behave unusually. Some types of arsonists like to watch firefighting operations, even helping firefighters or videotaping the results of their efforts.

Determining the point or points of origin of a fire is very important. Looking for the deepest charring is *not* a good method for determining the origin, contrary to popular notion. Instead, identifying fire plumes, as shown in Figure 14.31, determining the path of the spread of the fire, and witness information can help locate sources.

Arson investigations are very tricky matters to handle correctly. They require very careful observation, reliance upon tested scientific methods and validation, trained experts with experience in understanding fire behavior, and a complete openness to all possibilities. Investigators need to follow the process of the scientific method, be slow and deliberate in coming to a conclusion, and support their conclusion with evidence and logical reasoning. Wrongful convictions and improper findings are damaging to all involved, including those diligent investigators who exercise the proper, competent, and honest methods for investigating fires.

14.1.7 The Fire Scene: Collecting Fire Evidence

A fire scene is most properly considered to be a crime scene until it has been shown to be otherwise. Because of this, all the general care and practices in dealing properly with any potential crime scene must be observed, as outlined in Chapter 2. The most important first consideration must be the safety of the responders, victims, property owners, and the general public. First responders must deal effectively with any potential threats, including rendering assistance to victims, communicating any dangers to the public, establishing a safe perimeter, and other steps to make the scene safe – especially by extinguishing the fire and removing any possibility of re-ignition. Care must be given to the possible presence of any dangerous incendiary devices that might remain after the fire that present a real safety threat.

Once the scene is deemed safe, other standard crime scene processing steps then need to be quickly established. The scene must be carefully documented, especially photographically, noting the position and identification of all items of evidence, burn patterns, and fire damage. Proper search warrants are usually needed for any extensive searches beyond quick searches to establish that the fire scene is no longer dangerous. Proper chain of custody procedures, searching methods, and site control are critical for ensuring that any evidence collected at the site will be admissible in court. Investigators should search carefully for any types of physical evidence that might include incendiary devices (e.g., matches, torches, lighter, firearms, and others, Figure 14.32), impression evidence (e.g., footprints, fingerprints, tool marks, etc.), the location and pattern of debris, the presence of any trace evidence (e.g., hair, fibers, clothing, chemical residues, odors, etc.), and any unusual structural arrangements and burn patterns, as described previously. To the extent possible, potential evidence should be protected and left unmoved until it can be properly documented, cataloged, and collected. It is important, of course, to limit the use of gasoline-powered and similar equipment to avoid contamination of the evidence with gasoline that might be confused with an accelerant associated with arson. If possible, the clothing from a suspect should also be treated as evidence since it may be contaminated with accelerant.

A variety of types of evidence can be collected from a fire scene. Usually, any evidence collected is placed in air tight metal containers to trap volatile gases within the container. The contents of these containers can later be analyzed to see

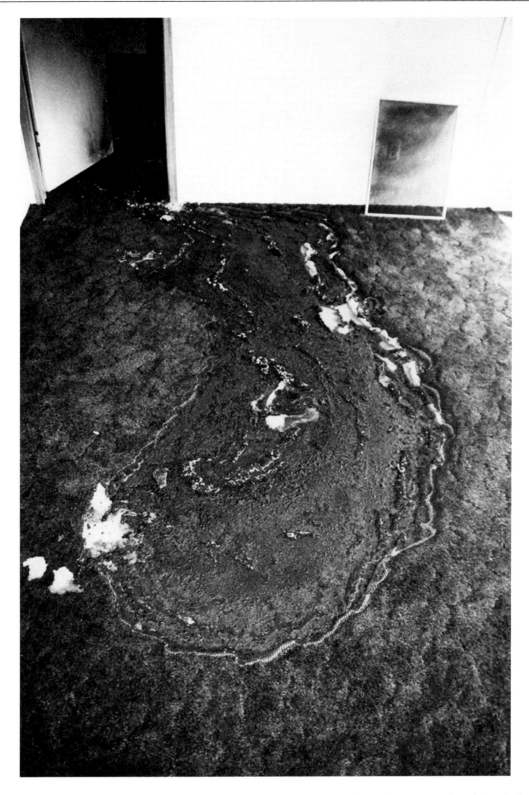

"Obvious pour pattern." The only surface that was burned in this mobile home was the floor. There were no furnish-ings in the house. The carpet was tested and found to be positive for the presence of a medium petroleum distillate such as mineral spirits or charcoal lighter fluid. This is one of the rare cases where visual observation alone can lead to valid conclusions about what caused the pattern.

FIGURE 14.26   The unusual linear burn pattern indicates the use of an accelerant that was spread in the observed burn pattern and ignited intentionally.

Source: Lentini (2018).

FIGURE 14.27 The presence of an inverted cone pattern (center of the right wall) suggests an unusual fire pattern.

Source: Almiral and Furton (2004).

if traces of accelerants or unusual fuels can be found. Typical containers for storing fire evidence are shown in Figure 14.33. Care must be taken to prevent any contamination of the samples and keep them as close to the original condition as possible until they reach the laboratory. Accelerants are most often trapped in porous materials, such as wood, cloth, carpeting, and similar. Collecting these types at samples in suspected points of origin is important since they are often the best places to detect accelerants.

14.1.8 Analyzing Fire Evidence in the Laboratory

One of the most commonly used analyses in the laboratory of fire evidence involves the chemical detection of accelerants collected from the fire scene. This is most often done using GC-Mass Spectrometry (GC/MS). The gas chromatograph separates the many components of the sample, and the mass spectrometer is then used to unambiguously identify each component. This type of analysis is important since most accelerants are quite similar in chemical composition and consist of complex mixtures of many compounds. A GC/MS analysis is required to determine which specific accelerant was employed by identifying the presence and amount of each component in the mixture.

There are several commonly employed methods for obtaining a sample for GC/MS analysis. One method uses a solvent to extract any possible accelerants from the sample. The problem with this method is that it does not concentrate the sample and requires the use of relatively large amounts of solvent (usually CS_2). A second method gently heats the contents of the sealed evidence container to drive any trapped volatile gases in the sample into the gas phase. A syringe is then

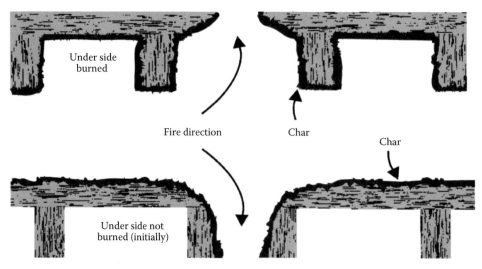

Fire patterns resulting from burning from above and below.

FIGURE 14.28 The unusual burn pattern of heavily burned wood interspersed with unburned wood is evidence that a liquid accelerant was poured on a floor above and leaked down onto the supporting joists. The fire burned where it leaked between the floorboards and, where it did not contact the wood, little burning was observed.

Source: Lentini (2018).

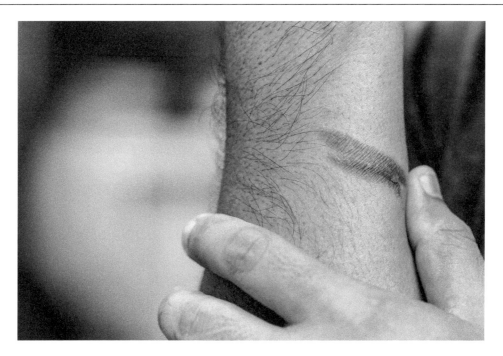

FIGURE 14.29 A pattern of burns on suspects on their hands, legs, or face can be supportive of their involvement in spreading accelerants at the fire scene.

Source: Shutterstock.com.

FIGURE 14.30 Handheld hydrocarbon detector ("sniffer") can be used to help detect the presence of fire accelerants at the fire scene.

Source: Shutterstock.com.

inserted into the top of the can and a volume of the headspace air is removed and injected into the GC/MS for analysis.

Several improved methods have been developed that use an adsorbent, such as activated charcoal, to capture and concentrate any volatile accelerants present. When the contents of the container are heated, the trapped volatile gases are captured by an activated charcoal sample. The charcoal serves to concentrate these gases, which can are then

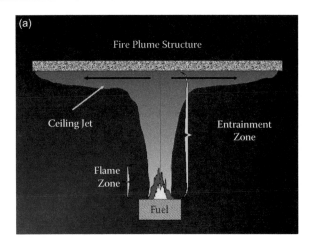
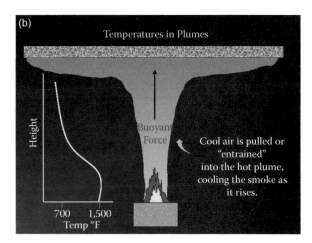

FIGURE 14.31 Identifying the initial location of the fire by observing the ceiling "plume" markings that are usually directly over the initial source (a). The pattern of fire growth from the plume can also help locate the source item (b).

Source: Lentini (2018).

FIGURE 14.32 A "Molotov Cocktail", usually made of a bottle containing kerosene, with a cloth wick, is an incendiary device easily improvised but leaves behind physical evidence that may be traced.

Source: Shutterstock.com.

be recovered by washing it with a solvent (CS_2) and injecting the extract into the GC/MS for analysis. A more recent method called solid-phase microextraction (SPME) utilizes a polymer-coated silica fiber (SiO_2) to concentrate the volatile components. After absorbing the gases, the silica fiber is then placed into the GC instrument directly and heated to release the volatile materials. Typical gas chromatograms for the common accelerants are shown in Figures 14.34 and 14.35, respectively. The "fingerprint" patterns of the GC, coupled with the identification of each component, provide powerful evidence for the presence of accelerants at the fire scene.

BOX 14.7   WRONGFUL CONVICTION? THE WILLINGHAM CASE

In December 1991, a fire ran through the Willingham home in Corsicana, Texas, killing the Willinghams' three daughters. Cameron Todd Willingham, the children's father, escaped with only minor burns. Prosecutors charged Willingham with setting the fatal fire to cover up alleged abuse of the children, despite no positive evidence for the abuse. Cameron Willingham was convicted of arson and homicide based on fire evidence presented, and he was executed on February 17, 2004.

After his execution, there have been major probes into the forensic fire evidence. Experts on both sides of the issue are currently debating the strengths and weaknesses of the evidence presented. An unprecedented commission has been set up by the State of Texas to examine the claims, and the case remains controversial to date. Read the information available about the case and formulate your own conclusions concerning the case.

FIERY LOVE LETTERS

In 2002, Terry Barton was employed by the U.S. Forest Service when she burned a love letter from her estranged husband in the forest, setting off a wildfire outside of Denver. Barton, whose job ironically was to spot illegal fires, called in the blaze to authorities on June 8, 2002. Before it could be extinguished, the fire burned 138,000 acres of forest and destroyed 133 houses and one business. Investigators found the remains of burnt matches and a letter mailed to Barton at the source of the fire. Barton was arrested, convicted, and sentenced to two concurrent six-year terms in prison. The judge, however, refused to require her to pay the government $14.6 million in restitution to cover the costs of the firefighting and restoration in the Pikes Peak National Forest, as the prosecution had requested.

14.2 EXPLOSIVES AND PROPELLANTS

14.2.1 Introduction

Like fire, explosives have been an integral part of human history for both constructive and destructive purposes (Figure 14.36). Explosives today are used to clear the way for new construction, aid in mining for valuable minerals and fuels, and serve as propellants to launch satellites into space.

FIGURE 14.33 Typical containers for storing fire-related evidence.

Source: Lentini (2018).

Unfortunately, explosives have also been used for terrorism, the destruction of property, and a variety of other criminal actions. Explosions can occur accidentally, such as in a natural gas explosion, or intentionally, such as to clear a building site or "blow a safe." Increasingly, worldwide criminal justice systems are also being called upon to investigate the planned or actual use of explosive devices as tools for the political ends of terrorist and militaristic groups. Because of their pervasive use in society for constructive purposes, explosive compounds are often readily available to criminals. Due to their widespread use in criminal actions, investigations involving explosives and propellants form an important part of modern forensic science.

Explosives and propellants are often grouped together under the all-encompassing title of *energetic materials*. Explosives are compounds that react very quickly to produce heat, light, and the rapid outward expansion of gases. Propellants are compounds designed to optimize the production of pressurized gas that can be directed through an opening (*e.g.*, nozzle) to produce thrust. Their main purpose is to drive an object through space, such as a bullet, projectile, or missile. All energetic materials act in the same way by releasing stored potential energy over a very short time, primarily in the form

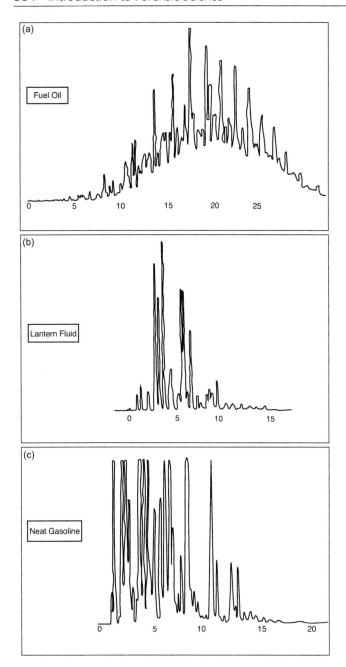

FIGURE 14.34 Gas chromatograms of several common fire accelerants: (a-c) fuel oil, lantern fuel (kerosene), and gasoline.

Source: Redsicker and O'Connor (1996).

of both kinetic and thermal energy. The relative proportion of energy released as thermal, kinetic, or light energy, however, varies greatly among energetic materials. Most often, the reaction driving this highly energetic release is oxidation, the same fundamental reaction-type that occurs in fires and rusting. The main difference between flammable materials, discussed in Section 14.1, and energetic materials is that energetic materials release a great deal of energy over a *very short time* interval from a relatively compact volume of material. In fact, most explosives are designed to result in as near-instantaneous a release of energy as possible upon ignition.

14.2.2 Types of Explosions

Explosions can be classified as either chemical or physical explosions. A physical explosion results in the rapid release of gases from a highly pressurized container or tank. These types of explosions do not necessarily result in the significant production of heat or light, and the released energy is largely kinetic energy, the energy of motion. For example, a damaged residential water heater may detonate when heated if its safety relief valves have been damaged and the tank has no way to release built-up pressure until it suddenly erupts at the weakest structural point. Since liquids are essentially incompressible fluids (meaning that they keep about the same volume even when subjected to very high pressures), the pressure in a sealed tank continues to rise upon heating until it reaches the catastrophic rupture pressure of the container, leading to a pressure-driven explosion. There is usually no chemical reaction associated with physical explosions, although changes in the physical state of the propellant may occur; the water before and after the explosion remains in the same chemical form (H_2O).

A chemical explosive, in contrast, undergoes an extremely rapid chemical reaction that releases both kinetic and thermal energy. Chemical explosives are, by far, the most common type of explosives encountered in forensic investigations.

14.2.3 Chemical Explosives

The basic considerations that have already been discussed for fire generation are also central to an understanding of energetic materials. Chemical explosives must contain a fuel source, an oxidizer, and an initiator that provides the energy necessary to start the reaction (activation energy). One important difference, however, is that explosive reactions are simply far too fast for atmospheric oxygen to deliver the oxidizer quickly enough to sustain the reaction. To solve this problem, explosives usually contain both fuel and oxidizer components either within the same molecule or in two separate chemicals that are mixed together. This was illustrated earlier in the case of nitroglycerin (Figure 14.37).

Chemical explosives vary enormously both in the amount of energy that they release and their mechanism for releasing it. Explosives are usually classified by the rate at which they react. *High explosives* result from very rapid chemical reactions where the explosive charge typically reacts at speeds greater than 1,000 m (1,094 yards) per second. A *detonation* results when high explosives are employed and form supersonic pressure waves (shock waves faster than the speed of sound, 343 m/s). High explosive shock waves from a detonation can move in excess of 8,500 m/sec (19,000 miles per hour). A shock wave rips apart the explosive's molecules, leading to the generation of large amounts of heat and gas (Figure 14.38). High explosives can quickly shatter anything in the path of the resulting powerful shock wave (shattering power is called *brisance*). *Low explosives*, in contrast, involve reactions that occur at rates of less than 1,000 m/s. These

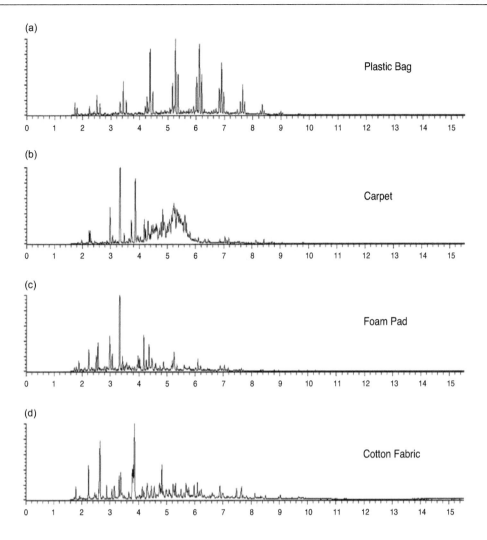

FIGURE 14.35   Gas chromatograms of several common products from the combustion of various household items: (a-d) plastic bag, carpet, foam pad and cotton fabric.

Source: Almiral and Furton (2004).

FIGURE 14.36   Explosion and fire onboard the offshore drilling plat-form (Deepwater Horizon) in the Gulf of Mexico on April 20, 2010.

Source: DHS, U.S. Coast Guard.

FIGURE 14.37   Dynamite, employing nitroglycerin as the explo-sive agent, is a common chemical explosive.

Source: Shutterstock.com.

FIGURE 14.38   In 1965, the U.S. Navy detonated 500 tons of TNT in Operation "Sailor Hat" on the Hawaiian island of Kahoolawe in a weapons test. Note the rapidly expanding shock wave spreading over the water just beyond the ship USS Atlanta and the shock condensation cloud lifting over the explosion.

Source: U.S. DoD, Navy photograph.

FIGURE 14.39   A flame front characterizes the method of propagation for low explosive deflagrations, such as seen at a demonstration at Nellis Air Force Base 2014 airshow.

Source: Shutterstock.com.

explosions are usually referred to as *deflagrations* and are propagated mainly by a flame front rather than a supersonic shock wave (Figure 14.39). These types of explosives produce a much slower, subsonic shock wave (slower than the speed of sound) relative to high explosives. Because of the slower speed of the shock wave, the results of deflagrations tend to be best described as having a "pushing" effect, rather than a shattering effect. However, the results from a low explosive's shock wave and flame front can still be enormously damaging from pressure alone.

TABLE 14.2   Energy and power values for selected high explosives

COMPOUND	ΔHEXPLOSION (KJ/KG)	POWER INDEX (%)[a]	TNT EQUIVALENCE[b]	DETONATION VELOCITY (M/S)
Primary High Explosives				
Lead Azide		12.8	0.16	5,180
Lead Styphnate		20.3	0.19	5,200
Secondary High Explosives				
TNT	3.72	110.3	1.00	6,900
Nitroglycerin		168.0	1.52	7,700
PETN	6.31	165.2	1.50	8,400
RDX	5.62	167.9	1.52	8,750
Picric Acid		100.0	0.91	7,350
HMX	5.60	165.9	1.50	9,100
Tetryl	4.15	129.7	1.18	7,850
ANFO			0.82	5,270

[a] Power Index is the amount of heat (Q) and volume (V) of gas generated by an explosion compared to a standard explosive picric acid). Power Index

$$= \frac{Q \times V}{Q_{(picric\ acid)} \times V_{(picric\ acid)}} 100$$

[b] TNT Equivalence $= \dfrac{Q \times V}{Q_{(TNT)} \times V_{(TNT)}}$.

Note: the standard is gradually changing to RDX instead of TNT.

The relative energy released from an explosive material is often described using several values. For example, the heat of explosion (ΔH explosion or combustion) measures the heat output from an explosion. More commonly, however, the combined heat and volume of gases generated during an explosion are compared with a standard, either picric acid (power index) or trinitrotoluene (TNT equivalence). Selected values of $\Delta H_{explosion}$, power index, TNT equivalence, and detonation velocity of some common high explosives are given in Table 14.2.

14.2.4 Low Explosives

Low explosives usually consist of a flammable fuel with a separate oxidant. Most gun powders, fireworks, and flares contain low explosives, where their main function is as a propellant. Black powder, probably the most common low explosive, uses carbon as the fuel, potassium nitrate as the oxidant, and sulfur as an ignition catalyst to produce carbon dioxide and nitrogen gases from its rapid combustion, according to the simplified reaction.

$$3\ C(s) + S(s) + 2\ KNO_3(s) \longrightarrow 3\ CO_2(g) + N_2(g) + K_2S(s)$$

The actual chemical reaction, however, is much more complicated than the simplified reaction shown above, but the simplified version provides a useful picture of the reaction chemistry. The production of four moles of rapidly expanding, hot CO_2 and N_2 gas is primarily responsible for pushing a projectile

forward, such as when a gun is fired. Several types of gunpowder (e.g., smokeless powders, black powder, flash powder, blasting powder, etc.) have been developed that have different ratios of reactants, along with the inclusion of modifying additives (e.g., nitroglycerine, diphenylamine, etc.) to provide a variety of properties tailored to optimize desired combustion features. For example, smokeless powders are based on nitrocellulose instead of carbon and deliver more power per weight of powder (energy density).

Devices that use low explosives can often be improvised from readily obtainable basic materials or purchased directly from gun stores. In fact, a low explosive can be made from almost any fuel and an oxidizer, such as potassium chlorate or potassium permanganate. These explosives represent a significant threat when used for criminal purposes because of their ready availability and relatively easy preparation.

One of the more common low explosive oxidizers is potassium chlorate ($KClO_3$). This compound is used in several large-scale industrial processes including as a disinfectant, an agricultural fertilizer, and in the production of safety matches and fireworks. Potassium chlorate may be mixed with a great variety of fuels, including sugar, cellulose, starch, Vaseline, and mineral oil, to make an explosive mixture. These readily preparable mixtures can be sealed in an enclosed container, such as a pipe, and ignited by a fuse to create an explosion of great force, such as in a pipe bomb or grenade (Figure 14.40).

Low explosive mixtures also result when natural gas (or another volatile flammable fuel gas) is mixed with oxygen but not ignited. When a source of ignition is finally provided, the entire volume of the mixture ignites almost simultaneously, creating an explosive result. If this process occurs from a gas

FIGURE 14.40   Typical pipe bomb arrangement (improvised explosive device, IED).

Source: U.S. DoD.

leak in an enclosed space, such as in a house or vehicle, the hot, rapidly expanding gases can explosively rip the walls and roof from the structure. Of course, the mixture must have the appropriate air-fuel ratio that lies within the flammability limits required for combustion and, therefore, allows the explosion to occur (see Figure 14.16).

14.2.5 High Explosives

High explosives, typically considered those that detonate at speeds over 1,000 m/s, can be further divided into two groups: primary and secondary explosives (Figure 14.41). *Primary explosives* are those that are sensitive to heat, flame, shock, or friction and typically detonate quickly rather than burn. These compounds are usually employed in relatively small quantities to detonate the otherwise inert secondary explosives. Their use to detonate other larger secondary charges arises from their relative instability to certain stimuli. They are rarely used as a sole explosive due to the difficulty associated with their safe handling and storage. Commonly, they are packaged in small capsules, called *blasting caps* (Figure 14.42), that are inserted into the secondary explosive and detonated by electrical or mechanical means.

Common primary explosives include lead azide ($Pb(N_3)_2$), lead styphnate ($C_6HN_3O_8Pb$), tetrazene ($C_2H_6N_{10} \cdot H_2O$), and diazodinitrophenol (DDNP, $C_6H_2N_4O_5$), as shown in Figure 14.43. Lead azide is the most commonly used primary explosive today. It has a high-ignition temperature, is only

slightly soluble in water, and doesn't react with aluminum, making it especially suitable for use in waterproof detonators made of aluminum capsules. Lead styphnate is generally more stable to shock and friction than lead azide, but it is also quite sensitive to static discharge: it can be discharged even by a static charge from the human body. DDNP is often used in propellants and has the advantage that it does not react with metals. Tetrazene is used as an impact-sensitive primer in self-priming ammunition, replacing the older use of toxic mercury fulminate.

Secondary explosives, in contrast with primary explosives, are those that are relatively stable to heat, shock, electrical discharge, and friction and usually require much more energy to detonate, such as that provided by a primary explosive detonator (blasting cap). Many examples of secondary explosives have been developed for both military and commercial applications. Common examples are TNT (trinitrotoluene, $C_7H_5N_3O_6$), dynamite (nitroglycerin-based explosive), RDX (cyclotrimethylenetrinitramine, $C_3H_6N_6O_6$), PETN (pentaerythritol, $C_5H_8N_4O_{12}$), HMX (octogen or cyclotetramethylenetetranitramine, $C_4H_8N_8O_8$), and ANFO (ammonium nitrate, NH_4NO_3). The structures of these common secondary explosives are illustrated in Figure 14.44.

Dynamite was the first high explosive safely manufactured and commercially available. Its explosive properties were discovered and developed by Alfred Nobel in Sweden in 1867 (see Box 14.8). Commercial dynamite contains an adsorbent, such as diatomaceous earth, sawdust, clay, or wood pulp, that has been soaked in nitroglycerin, often resulting in a content

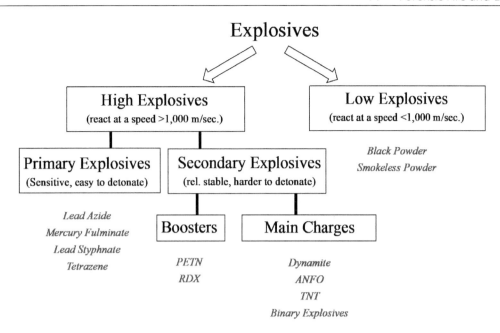

FIGURE 14.41 Classification of high explosives.

FIGURE 14.42 Blasting caps employing a primary high explosive are used to detonate larger secondary explosive charges. These electrical detonators shown vary in their sensitivity and delay time between initiation and detonation.

Source: Used per Creative Commons Attribution-Share Alike 4.0, International. User: DaDoKa.

of about 60% nitroglycerin. It is usually sold in ½ lb sticks of compressed material individually wrapped in waxed paper (Figure 14.37). Typical dynamite is about 60% more powerful than TNT. Today, military dynamite contains no nitroglycerin but contains about 75% RDX and 15% TNT and is generally much safer to store and use. True dynamite is being phased out of use because of the hazard of its manufacture, storage, and handling in favor of newer, less hazardous explosives.

BOX 14.8   A NOBEL IRONY

By 1800, it became clear that black powder was not powerful enough or otherwise suitable for new applications for explosive materials, such as in mining and civil construction. Nitroglycerin was discovered in 1847 but was so shock-sensitive that the inventor, Ascanio Sobrero, abandoned his work. With his father, however, Alfred Nobel launched a family business based on the production of nitroglycerin explosives. After several catastrophic explosions, including one that destroyed the factory and killed his brother Emil in 1864, Alfred set about finding a way to make nitroglycerin safer to manufacture and use. Nobel found that if he mixed nitroglycerin with an inert absorbent, such as *kieselguhr* (diatomaceous earth) or clay, he could produce a far safer and more easily handled material. When he patented his work, he settled upon the name dynamite for his new discovery, based on the Greek word for "power." Further work by Nobel produced variants of dynamite that were more powerful, easier to use, and even safer. Nobel's work with these safer explosives made him very wealthy.

Toward the end of his life, a French newspaper erroneously published Alfred Nobel's obituary in which he was called the "merchant of death." Apparently, Nobel became so concerned with how he would be remembered posthumously that he decided to devote his estate to awarding annual prizes in chemistry, medicine, physics, literature, and peace (fraternity). Today, the Nobel Prize is considered the premier recognition in the sciences.

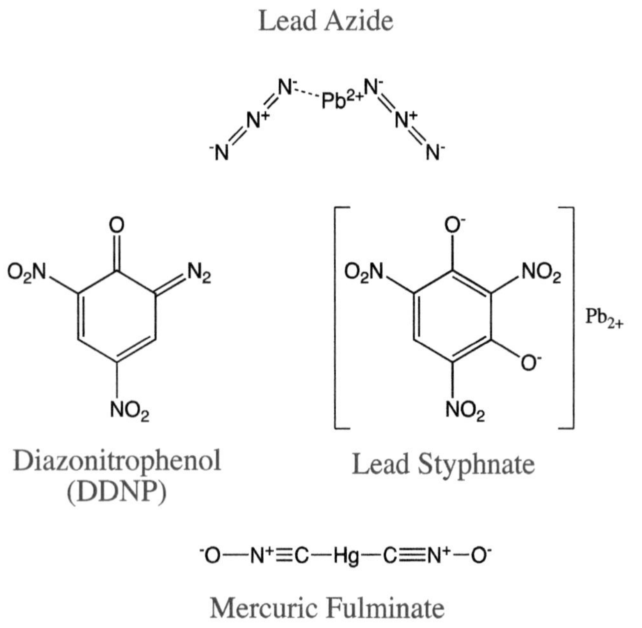

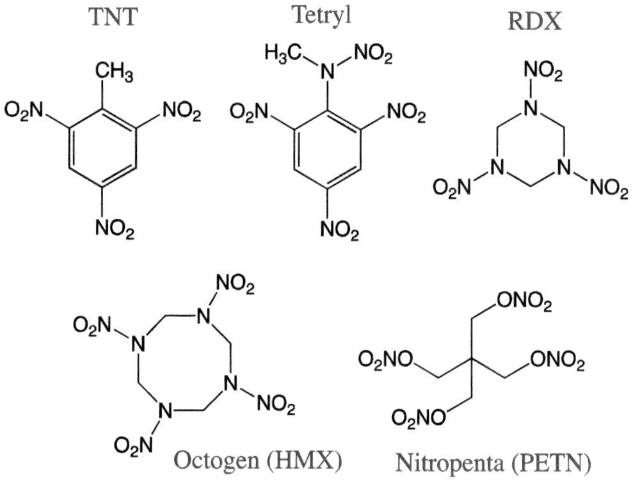

FIGURE 14.44   Examples of high-energy secondary explosives.

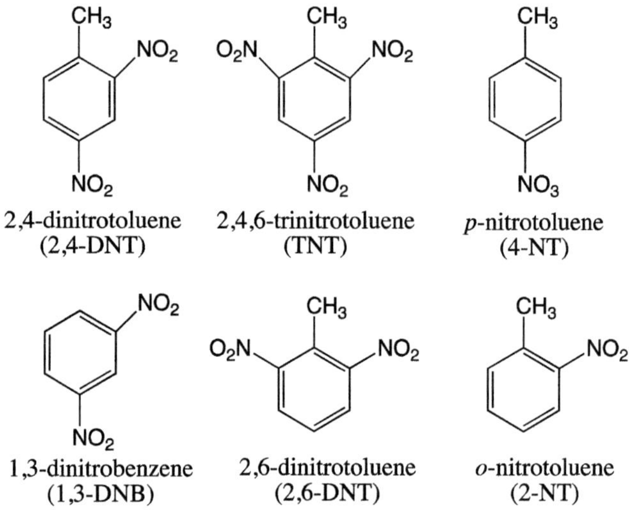

FIGURE 14.45   The structure of TNT and several chemically-related explosive compounds.

One of the most common high explosives is trinitrotoluene (TNT) and its family of structurally related compounds (Figure 14.45). TNT is especially useful because it is very insensitive to shock and friction, greatly decreasing the risk of accidental detonation, and it explodes with a velocity of 6,900 m/s. It is insoluble and insensitive to water, making it useful in wet or moist environments. It is important to note that TNT and dynamite are *not* the same material – dynamite is made from a stabilized mixture of nitroglycerin and an adsorbent, while TNT is an entirely different chemical compound. TNT is commonly employed in both military and commercial uses, although commonly it is mixed with other explosive compounds to tailor its discharge properties for a particular application. The explosive strength of TNT is commonly used as a standard measure of the strength of other high explosives (Table 14.2).

As with low explosives, high explosives can also be improvised from readily obtainable basic materials. For example, ammonium nitrate (NH_4NO_3) is a very common agricultural fertilizer that can also be used as a powerful oxidizer when

FIGURE 14.43   Some common primary explosives.

combined with a fuel, such as heating oil, kerosene, sugar, nitromethane, or diesel fuel (see inset box "Oklahoma City Bombing"). When combined, this mixture forms a strong explosive called ANFO, or ammonium nitrate/fuel oil explosive. Today, ammonium nitrate is one of the most commonly encountered commercial explosive oxidants. The simplicity of manufacture and ready availability of components unfortunately make ANFO a common choice for homemade bombs and for terrorist attacks.

A variety of nitro-based explosives have been developed, largely driven by military requirements. These include PETN, RDX, and HMX. While HMX has been considered the highest-energy secondary explosive available, octanitrocubane ($C_8(NO_3)_8$), a shock-insensitive compound, is thought to be even 20%–25% more powerful. Octanitrocubane is very difficult to synthesize, requiring over 30 synthetic steps in its preparation, making it a very rarely employed explosive. PETN is the most stable of the group and is very powerful with exceptional shattering force (brisance). RDX and HMX, however, are probably the most common shattering shock wave explosives, primarily due to their very high detonation velocities. These explosives

are also commonly mixed with other explosives and modifiers to generate mixtures with tailored explosive properties. For example, C4 is a form of plastic explosive that contains 80% RDX and 20% plasticizer (often polyisobutylene and di(2-ethylhexyl)sebacate). C4 is a putty-like material that can be shaped around an object prior to detonation.

14.2.6 Damage from Explosions

Explosives cause damage through several mechanisms: shock waves, fire (heat), and flying debris. Depending on the specific explosive employed, the relative contribution of these three destructive forces varies significantly. High explosives cause a great deal of damage from shock waves, while low explosives primarily damage using heat and fire.

A shock wave consists of highly compressed gases that travel rapidly outward from the point of detonation. Shock waves may be deflected when they encounter an object, causing localized intensification of the wave many times the original pressure (Figure 14.46). After the passage of the initial

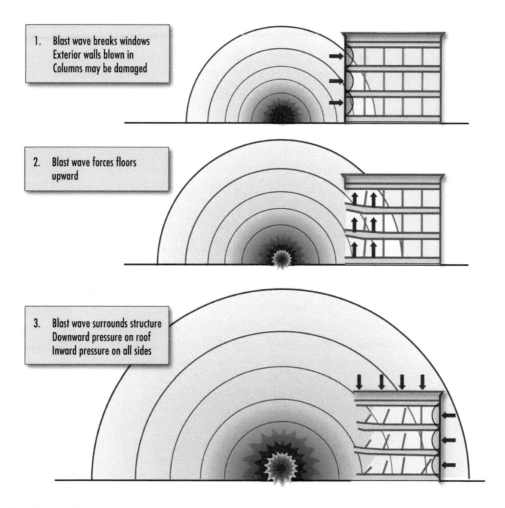

FIGURE 14.46 Shock wave damage to structures.

Source: FEMA, FEMA Risk Management Series No. 428, BIPS-07, January 2012 Edition 2.

TABLE 14.3 Damage from shock waves

DAMAGE	PRESSURE (PSI)
Breakage to window glass	0.1 to 0.22
Minor building damage	0.5–1.1
Sheet metal buckled	1.1–1.8
Concrete wall failure	1.8–2.9
Collapse of wood-frame buildings	>3.0
Damage to reinforced concrete buildings	6–9
Probable destruction of most buildings	10–12

high-pressure front, a negative pressure zone (vacuum) follows. To fill this negative pressure void, a secondary burst of air carrying debris occurs as air rushes back into the negative pressure zone. Shock wave pressures from a high explosive can reach more than 100 lbs per square inch (psi) in the vicinity of the blast. Table 14.3 shows some typical pressures that can cause structural damage. Fatal pressures for humans are about 50 psi. Injuries caused by the pressure front of a shock wave from a high explosive are called primary injuries. Secondary injuries are those that result from flying shrapnel and other objects, while tertiary injuries are those sustained when a person is thrown by the blast wind.

All explosives can cause a significant amount of damage from the heat generated during the blast. The heat from the hot gas can sear objects it encounters as well as ignite fires in its path.

14.2.7 Evidence Collection

Evidence collection is very similar to that described for examining a fire scene with a special emphasis on ensuring that the scene is safe from secondary or unexploded material on the site. Therefore, explosives experts must first clear the site of any potential hazards before the investigation can continue.

As with fire investigation, it is important for investigators to work quickly and efficiently to collect and properly process soils and other materials around the blast site. Any places where explosive residues might collect, especially porous and permeable materials, should be collected for laboratory analysis.

One of the first jobs of an investigator is to determine whether an explosion has occurred and, if so, whether it was accidental or caused by a bomb or similar device. Investigators attempt to piece together the physical evidence with witness accounts to ascertain the consistency with an explosion. Sudden sounds, flashes of light, and flying debris serve as good initial indications that an explosion has occurred. The primary effort will be to determine the cause of the blast and, if it was from a bomb, recovering the explosive device. Fragments of evidence are likely to be widely scattered, possibly even within the bodies of victims and embedded within walls and structures. Suspects'

hands need to be swabbed, and their clothing preserved for evidence of explosive materials and residues. As with fire evidence, there are characteristic damage patterns that experienced investigators will search for. Damage patterns from shock waves and thermal fronts on nearby structures can provide valuable information.

Throughout the process of evidence collection, care must be taken to avoid cross-contamination of the evidence and ensure that proper collection procedures, such as the chain of evidence and photographic records, are followed.

14.2.8 Analysis of Explosive Evidence

Laboratory analysis of explosive materials usually centers on the identification of the explosive or combination of explosives present. Secondly, it might be possible to trace a particular mixture back to an individual manufacturer or local supplier (see below).

One of the most important techniques for identifying explosive materials employs GC/MS analysis. Methods have been developed for separating the various components of an explosive mixture by gas chromatography and then using mass spectrometry to unambiguously identify each component. Each component is separated from the others in the chromatogram and the relative amount of each can be determined by measuring the relative areas under the peaks corresponding to the compound. The mass spectrum for each peak can be measured and compared with that obtained from a database of known spectra for each kind of explosive compound to provide a positive identification of the material, such as the MS of RDX, as shown in Figure 14.47.

A variety of other spectroscopic methods have been used in the identification of explosives. These include Resonance Raman, Infrared (Figure 14.48), and Terahertz spectroscopy. These spectroscopic methods examine characteristic ways that molecules vibrate and measure the energy of these vibrations (Chapter 12). Terahertz techniques specifically focus on vibrations in the wavelength range of 0.1 to 1 mm while both Raman and infrared spectroscopies employ infrared radiation from about 700 to 4,000 nm. Typically, these analyses are conducted by comparing the spectrum of the unknown explosive recovered from the scene with spectra taken from standard reference samples. Terahertz methods are also being used in airports as screening tools to detect explosives hidden in luggage or on a person's body since terahertz radiation does not pose any health risk and can pass through cloth, paper, and similar materials easily, revealing hidden explosives. Ideally, it might be possible to identify the explosive and its location from its terahertz signal from a safe distance.

Electron microscopic analysis of samples may also prove useful in identifying the explosive material. Different explosives leave residues with distinctive structures and shapes. Recently, there has been a push to add taggants to explosive mixtures that would allow the explosive to be identified after

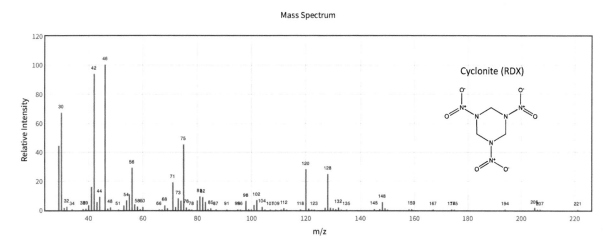

FIGURE 14.47 Tandem MS-MS of Cyclonite (RDX) sample. The peak at 102 m/z is very characteristic of RDX and results from the loss of a CH_2NNO_2 fragment from the parent molecule.

Source: NIST, Mass Spectrometry Data Center.

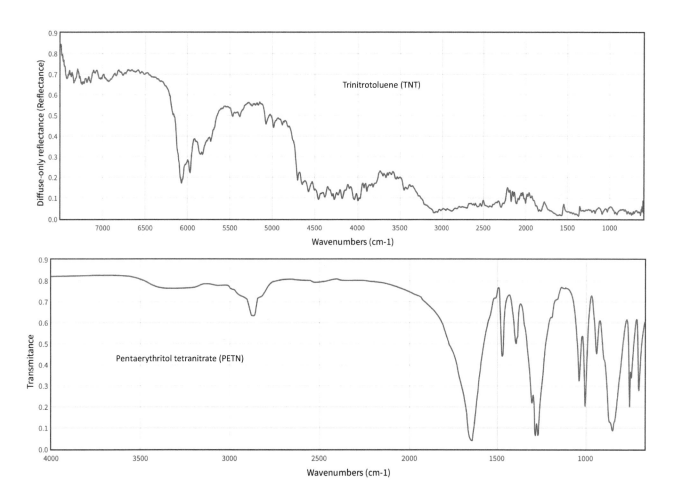

FIGURE 14.48 FT-Infrared spectra for two high explosives: TNT and PETN.

Source: NIST.

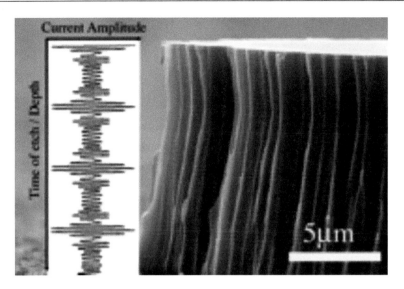

FIGURE 14.49 Exceptionally stable and durable microparticles can be fabricated that serve as "spectral barcodes" that can be encoded with information about the manufacturer and withstand the force of a detonation.

Source: Used with permission and courtesy of Wiley; image by Prof. Michael J. Sailor at UC San Diego.

detonation. A taggant is a microscopic material that is exceptionally durable and can be "imprinted" with permanent information, much like a barcode that identifies its origin and type of explosive present. For example, researchers have developed layered, nanostructured materials that can provide key information through optical methods (Figure 14.49).

Investigations into the causes of explosions require patience, skill, and experience. The work of the field investigator necessitates the support of good laboratory analysis to identify and verify the presence of the compounds involved. By working together, the true nature and cause of an explosion or fire can often be determined with certainty.

BOX 14.9   ACETONE PEROXIDE THREATS

Unfortunately, some explosive materials are a bit too readily obtainable and have been used by terrorists and other criminals. For example, acetone peroxide (TATP) has been used in a number of attacks, including by Richard Reid (dubbed the "shoe bomber") in 2001 on an American Airline flight and by Umar Farouk Abdulmutallab (called the "underwear bomber") on Christmas Day, 2009 on a Northwest Airlines flight. Luckily, neither was able to detonate their TATP-based devices. However, because of the instability and difficulty in detonating this compound, a number of attempts have resulted in severe injuries to the bomb-makers themselves. For example, in 2008, a member of the French anti-speed camera group lost both hands after his TATP bomb exploded prematurely.

OKLAHOMA CITY BOMBING

On April 19, 1995, The Alfred P. Murrah Federal Building in Oklahoma City, Oklahoma, was destroyed by a massive blast. Additionally, the blast damaged or destroyed over 300 nearby buildings and claimed the lives of 168 people, while injuring more than 680 others. Shortly after the blast, Timothy McVeigh was stopped for a traffic violation but was then quickly linked to the OK City blast. Forensic evidence implicated a co-conspirator, Terry Nichols, who was then also quickly arrested. The bomb had been constructed in a rental truck by McVeigh and Nichols and consisted of the contents of 108 bags (23 kg or 50 lbs each) of ammonium nitrate, three 55-gallon drums of liquid nitromethane, several crates of Torvex (a high explosive), 17 bags of ANFO, and various fuses and detonators. McVeigh and Nichols planned the blast to coincide with the end of the siege of a religious cult in Waco, Texas, two years earlier.

The FBI gathered over 3½ tons of evidence and conducted over 28,000 interviews in their investigation of the blast. After a trial, McVeigh was found guilty and executed on June 11, 2001. His co-conspirator, Terry Nichols, was also found guilty and is serving 161 consecutive life terms without the possibility of parole.

FIGURE 14.50 Bombing of the Alfred P. Murrah Federal Building in Oklahoma City on April 19, 1995 using ANFO.
Source: FEMA News Photo.

QUESTIONS FOR FURTHER PRACTICE AND MASTERY

14.1 What are the four basic components required to produce a fire?

14.2 Define endothermic reaction, exothermic reaction, and activation energy.

14.3 What is the role of a catalyst in a chemical reaction?

14.4 What is meant by the auto-ignition temperature?

14.5 What is the fire tetrahedron? What is the function of each part?

14.6 What is meant by the flash point of a substance?

14.7 What is meant by flammability limits?

14.8 How does nitroglycerine differ from black powder with respect to the source of its fuel and oxidant?

14.9 In what state of matter must a fuel be in order for it to air oxidize in combustion?

14.10 What is a radical? How does it figure into the combustion process?

14.11 What is an accelerant? Give examples of some commonly used accelerants.

14.12 Explain how an explosive backdraft occurs?

14.13 What factors determine an HRR, heat release rate?

14.14 What is the legal definition of arson?

14.15 If an arson investigator finds that there are no known natural or accidental causes for a fire, is that enough to prove arson in a court of law? Explain your answer.

14.16 What are some of the things an arson investigator looks for at a fire scene that may indicate arson was involved?

14.17 True or False: The point of origin of a fire is usually found at the spot of the deepest charring.

14.18 What are the duties of a First Responder?

14.19 What types of evidence collection containers are typically used for materials collected at the scene of a fire where arson is suspected?

14.20 Once an evidence sample is in the lab, what analysis technique is usually used to identify the presence of an accelerant?

14.21 What is the distinction when classifying a material as flammable as opposed to energetic?

14.22 What is a physical explosion? Give examples. What is the principal form of energy released in a physical explosion?

14.23 What is the source of energy in a chemical explosion?

14.24 What is brisance?

14.25 What is a deflagration?

14.26 What types of ingredients must be present to make a low explosive?

14.27 Give examples of fuels that are used in low explosives.

14.28 What is a primary high explosive? Why aren't they typically used as the sole explosive?

14.29 What is a secondary high explosive?

14.30 What properties make lead azide suitable as a primary explosive?

14.31 What properties of TNT make it a more suitable explosive than nitroglycerine?

14.32 What is ANFO?

14.33 What is a shock wave? What is a negative pressure zone?

14.34 Distinguish between primary, secondary, and tertiary injuries from a shock wave.

14.35 What properties of terahertz spectroscopy make it ideal for use at airports to check for explosives?

14.36 What is a taggant? What properties must it have?

EXTENSIVE QUESTIONS

14.37 Identify the factors that influence the rate of a chemical reaction and indicate how changing each of these factors impacts the rate of the reaction.

14.38 Explain the process that causes a fire to accelerate as it burns.

14.39 Ray Bradbury's novel, 'Fahrenheit 451', was about a society that burned all books in order to control the thoughts of its people. What is the significance of the title? (Note: °F= 9/5°C + 32)

14.40 Discuss the different firefighting materials and techniques. Indicate why each is effective and when they are used.

14.41 Explain the different classifications of fires.

14.42 Explain the four developmental stages of a fire.

14.43 What are some of the fire anomalies an arson investigator might look for during an investigation?

14.44 A piece of carpeting collected at the scene of a suspected arson fire is sent to the lab in an evidence collection can. What methods can be used to extract any volatile components that may be trapped in the carpet fibers?

14.45 Explain the different properties of a high explosive compared to a low explosive.

GLOSSARY OF TERMS

accelerant: a compound that facilitates the initiation and/or growth of a fire.

activation energy: the energy necessary to overcome the energetic barrier to a chemical reaction.

air-fuel ratio: the relative amounts of air (oxygen) and fuel in a gaseous mixture.

arson: the criminal act of intentionally setting a fire without lawful consent.

auto-ignition temperature (or kindling point): the minimum temperature at which a substance will spontaneously ignite *without* an external source of ignition.

backdraft: when a fire burns in an enclosed space and uses up much of its oxygen supply, starving the fire of oxygen, followed by oxygen rapidly reintroduced to the room with the accumulated unburned fuel, often producing an explosion.

black powder: a mixture of potassium nitrate, carbon, and sulfur (usually in a ~75:15:10 ratio) that burns very rapidly upon ignition.

brisance: the shattering power of a shock wave.

catalyst: a compound that lowers the activation energy of a chemical reaction, thereby increasing its rate, without being consumed in the reaction.

chain reaction: a long series of reactions with initiation, propagation, and termination steps in which the products continue the spread of the reaction.

chemical explosive: a chemical that undergoes an extremely rapid reaction that releases both kinetic and thermal energy.

combustion: the rapid oxidation of a compound, where a fuel reacts with an oxidant to form new compounds with the generation of heat and light.

deflagration: a combustion reaction, often generated by a low explosive, that is propagated mainly by a subsonic flame front (low-intensity pressure wave).

detonation: the very rapid oxidation reaction generated by high explosives that produces highly destructive supersonic pressure waves (shock waves).

dynamite: a mixture of an adsorbent, such as diatomaceous earth, sawdust, clay, or wood pulp, that has been soaked in nitroglycerin.

exothermic reaction: a chemical reaction that liberates heat.

explosive: a compound that reacts very quickly with the production of heat and light that is accompanied by the rapid outward expansion of gases.

fire: the rapid oxidation of substances through combustion reactions with the evolution of energy, often in the form of heat and light, with the formation of new chemical products, usually carbon dioxide and water.

fire tetrahedron: a diagram showing the close relationship between the four elements required for a fire to start and be sustained: fuel, oxygen, heat, and chemical chain reaction.

flammability limits: the upper and lower threshold limits of the air-fuel mixture that are required for combustion to occur.

flash point: the lowest temperature at which a fuel will vaporize sufficiently to form an ignitable mixture with air that will combust when an ignition source is supplied.

flashover: the rapid transition to a fully developed fire by the nearly simultaneous ignition of all the flammable materials in an enclosed space.

fuel: any material that stores chemical energy that can be extracted through combustion reactions with the evolution of energy.

glowing combustion: see "Smoldering."

Halon: an active fire suppressant that is one of a family of halomethane compounds and works by interfering with the chain reaction required for a fire.

Heat of combustion ($\Delta H°combustion$): the characteristic amount of energy released by a compound upon burning, expressed usually in kJ per mole or gram of substance.

heat release rate (HRR): the rate at which heat is released during a fire.

high explosive: a compound that yields very rapid chemical reactions where the charge typically reacts at speeds greater than 1,000 m (1,094 yards) per second.

HMX: a nitro-containing high explosive.

hydrocarbon: a compound composed primarily of carbon and hydrogen.

kinetic energy: the energy of motion.

low explosive: a compound that undergoes reactions that occur at rates less than 1,000 m/sec.

modus operandi: the method a person uses to commit a crime.

oxidant (also known as oxidizing agent or oxidizer): a chemical that can either transfer oxygen atoms to or remove electrons from another chemical compound.

PETN: a nitro-containing high explosive.

photosynthesis: the process where plants break apart the bonds of carbon dioxide and water to make the new bonds in the products of glucose and oxygen.

physical explosion: a process resulting in the rapid release of gases from a highly pressurized container or tank.

primary explosive: a compound that is sensitive to heat, flame, shock, or friction and typically detonates quickly rather than burns.

propellant: a compound that optimizes the production of pressurized gas that can be directed through an opening to produce thrust.

radical: a molecule or atom that has an unpaired electron in its outermost (valence) shell.

rate of a chemical reaction: a measure of how fast a reaction proceeds to products.

RXD: a nitro-containing high explosive.

secondary explosive: an explosive compound that is relatively stable to heat or shock and requires more energy to be detonated, usually provided by a primary explosive.

shock wave: a wave that consists of highly compressed gases that travel rapidly outward from a point of detonation.

smokeless powder: a nitrocellulose-based explosive.

smoldering: the slow, lower temperature combustion of compounds without a flame, often giving incomplete combustion products, such as CO.

Taggant: an exceptionally durable microscopic material that can be "imprinted" with permanent information that identifies the origin and type of explosive present.

TNT: a secondary high explosive made of trinitrotoluene.

BIBLIOGRAPHY

Jai Prakash Agrawal, *High Energy Materials: Propellants, Explosives and Pyrotechnics*, Wiley-VCH, 2010.

Jacqueline Akhavan, *The Chemistry of Explosives*, Royal Society of Chemistry, 2011.

Jose R. Almiral and Kenneth G. Furton, *Analysis and Interpretation of Fire Scene Evidence*, CRC Press, 2004.

Alexander Beveridge (Ed.), *Forensic Investigation of Explosions* (2nd Ed.), CRC Press, 2011.

Chandler, *Fire Investigation*, Delmar Cengage Learning, 2009.

Paul Cooper and Stanley R. Kurowski, *Introduction to the Technology of Explosives*, Wiley-VCH, 1996.

Tenney L. Davis, *The Chemistry of Powder and Explosives*, Angriff Press, 2012. James D. DeHaan and David J. Icove, *Kirk's Fire Investigation* (7th Ed.), Prentice Hall, 2011.

International Association of Arson Investigators, *Fire Investigator: Principles and Practice NFPA 921 and 1033*, Jones and Bartlett Learning, 2010. Thomas M. Klapatke, *Chemistry of High-Energy Materials*, De Gruyter, 2011.

John J. Lentini, *Scientific Protocols for Fire Investigation*, CRC Press, 2006.

John J. Lentini, *Scientific Protocols for Fire Investigation* (3rd Ed.), CRC Press, 2018.

D. Madrzykowski, *Impact of a Residential Sprinkler on the HRR of a Christmas Tree Fire*, NIST, 2008.

National Fire Protection Association, *NFPA 921: Guide for Fire and Explosion Investigations 2011*, Natl Fire Protection Assoc., 2011.

James G. Quintiere, *Principles of Fire Behavior*, Delmar Publishers, 1997.

David R. Redsicker and John J. O'Connor (Eds.), *Practical Fire and Arson Investigation* (2nd Ed.), CRC Press, 1996.

James T. Thurman, *Practical Bomb Scene Investigation* (2nd Ed.), Taylor and Francis, 2011.

PART 4

Physical Properties in Evidence

Physical Properties
Mineralogical, Soil, Glass, and Paint Analysis

15

15.1 PHYSICAL PROPERTIES IN EVIDENCE

LEARNING GOALS AND OBJECTIVES

Physical properties can be used to characterize key features of evidence. After you complete this section of this chapter, you should be able to:

- Describe what is meant by chemical and physical properties and changes.
- Define what is meant by the intrinsic and extrinsic properties of substances.
- Explain what density and viscosity are and how they can be measured.
- Discuss refraction, refractive index, and birefringence, and how they are determined.
- Explain how colors are formed and perceived in additive and subtractive methods.

15.1.1 Introduction

Thus far, we have focused on properties of evidence that relate specifically to their biological and chemical characteristics, especially their unique features and classifications. Characterizing the physical properties of evidence, including glass, soil, and plastic objects, may often be the best way to classify and understand these types of evidence. In this chapter, we will explore some of the physical properties of evidence and examine how these properties provide useful information about the composition, use, and classification of evidence.

15.1.2 Chemical and Physical Properties

In describing matter (something that occupies space and has mass), we define two general types of properties: chemical and physical properties. Each substance has its own unique set of these properties that dictate its behavior and allow us to distinguish it from other substances. *Chemical properties* are those that can be measured only by attempting to change the chemical identity of the material itself through some sort of chemical transformation: a chemical reaction. *Physical properties*, in contrast, are those that can be measured *without* changing a material's chemical identity. Some selected examples of these two types of properties are given in Table 15.1.

Chemical properties are described by changes observed through potential chemical reactions of a substance and are always defined *with respect to* a particular chemical process. For example, the combustion, specific reactivity, or thermal stability properties of a compound are measured by examining their potential reactions with oxygen (combustion) or other specific chemicals (reactivity or stability). In fact, chemical properties are always defined relative to a specific chemical reaction that includes the reactants and reaction conditions. For example, zinc metal is stable to water (no reaction occurs) while unstable toward hydrochloric acid (forming $ZnCl_2$ and H_2

TABLE 15.1 Selected example of chemical and physical properties

CHEMICAL PROPERTY	PHYSICAL PROPERTY
Heat of combustion	Color
Toxicity	Density
Flammability	Melting Point
Corrosion	Boiling Point
Reactivity	Solubility
Stability	State (solid, liquid, gas)
	Hardness
	Temperature

DOI: 10.4324/9781003183709-19

when they come into contact at room temperature). In contrast, lithium metal is unstable toward water, transforming the lithium metal into LiOH with the liberation of H_2. Specifying reaction conditions is necessary for defining chemical properties. A reaction may occur extremely slowly or not at all at 0°C, while it may proceed very quickly at 100°C. Chemical reaction conditions often defined when describing chemical properties may include temperature, concentration, pressure, light irradiation, and the presence or absence of a catalyst.

The measurement of physical properties, in contrast, is not defined relative to any chemical process but is defined as properties related to the state of the matter itself. For example, the measurement of density, melting point, and state (solid,

liquid, or gas) of a substance does not result in changing the material into some other chemical substance. These properties depend on the unique chemical structures and features of the substances themselves, such as how the atoms are arranged in space to form the solid or how much energy is needed to separate the individual molecules or atoms. When a substance undergoes a physical change, it alters its appearance but not its chemical composition. For example, when ice melts – a physical change – it visibly changes from a hard solid to a mobile liquid, but it always remains H_2O. Among the physical properties are density, melting/boiling points, refraction, and color.

BOX 15.1   STATES OF MATTER

Solid: Fixed shape and volume.
Liquid: No fixed shape but fixed volume.
Gas: No fixed volume and no fixed shape.
Plasma: A gas where electrons have moved between atoms to form ionized (charged), gaseous atoms (the most common form of matter in the Universe).

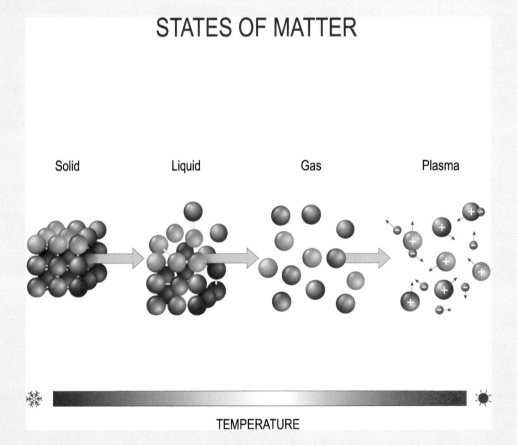

FIGURE 15.1   States of matter: solid, liquid, gas, and plasma.

Source: Shutterstock.com.

15.1.3 Intrinsic and Extrinsic Properties

Some physical properties of a substance depend on how much of the material is present, while others do not (Table 15.2). *Intrinsic properties* are those that remain the same regardless of the quantity of the material present in the sample. These properties are particularly useful in forensic analysis since a small sample can be used to determine the properties of the entire, larger item. Intrinsic properties include melting point, boiling point, density, color, temperature, and luster (shininess); the measured properties are the same regardless of the sample size used. *Extrinsic properties*, however, are those that vary with changes in the amount of material in the sample. Extrinsic properties include mass, volume, and length. Both intrinsic and extrinsic properties are important in forensic analysis; the intrinsic properties of an item can help identify its chemical composition, while the extrinsic measurements can indicate if the item fits a particular scenario. For example, the intrinsic properties of a bullet cartridge can tell what alloy was used in its manufacture, while the extrinsic properties can identify its caliber, type, and manufacturer.

Some physical properties of matter are particularly useful in identifying an unknown material and have found routine uses in forensic settings. These include density, refractive index, birefringence, and color.

15.1.4 Density

Density (ρ, pronounced "row") is very useful in the identification of certain types of materials, especially soil, geological, and glass samples. It is simply defined as the amount of mass of a substance contained in a particular unit of volume, or $d = \rho = m/V$ (d is density, m is mass, and V is volume). Density is most commonly expressed in terms of grams per cubic centimeter, or g/cm^3 (note: $1\ cm^3 = 1\ mL$ or milliliter). The densities of several common substances are given in Table 15.3 and vary greatly. The density of water is $1.00\ g/cm^3$ at $4°C$ since the gram was originally defined as the weight of $1\ cm^3$ of water.

Several ways have been devised to experimentally measure the density of a substance, even for very small samples, such as tiny glass shards and minute soil samples. For liquid samples, the direct determination of density simply requires

TABLE 15.3 Density of selected compounds (g/cm^3)

SUBSTANCE	DENSITY
Air	0.0013
Mica	0.54
Wood	0.85
Ice	0.93
Water	1.00
Flint Glass	1.39*
Window Glass	1.94*
Windshield Glass	2.57*
Quartz	2.64
Aluminum	2.70
Lead	11.3
Gold	19.3

*Values vary considerably by type and composition of the glass.

determining the mass of a known volume of the liquid. For example, the mass of $1\ cm^3$ (mL) of a liquid can be measured directly to give the density. Density measurements for solids are more difficult since determining the volume of a solid accurately can present significant challenges.

For regularly shaped solids, the volume can be measured by determining the dimensions of the object and calculating the volume. In most circumstances, however, this is not possible because of the irregular shapes found for solids, especially for small forensic samples. Three common methods have been employed to determine solid volumes: displacement, flotation, and buoyancy (or up-thrust) measurements:

- **Volume by Displacement**: This method involves the direct measurement of the displacement of a liquid, such as water, by a sample (Archimedes' discovery described in Chapter 4). In this process, the amount of water displaced by a completely submerged solid is measured and is equal to the volume of the unknown solid (Figure 15.2). The major drawbacks of this method are the potential inaccuracies in measuring the volume change upon adding the solid to the water and occasional problems with the solubility of the solid in the liquid. Often, forensic samples are very small, making it exceptionally difficult to determine accurately the very small volume changes when the liquid is displaced. The advantage of this method for larger samples, however, is that it is experimentally very simple.
- **Flotation**: Flotation can be used to approximate the density of a sample. A solid sample will sink through a liquid of lower density than its own, float on top of liquids with higher densities, and be suspended in a liquid that has the same density. In this method, a *gradient column* is employed that contains several different liquids of varying density. The column, as shown in Figure 15.3, is prepared

TABLE 15.2 Intrinsic and extrinsic properties

INTRINSIC PROPERTY	EXTRINSIC PROPERTY
Color	Mass (weight)
Density	Volume
Melting/Boiling Point	Dimensions (length)
Conductivity	Number (quantity)
Temperature	

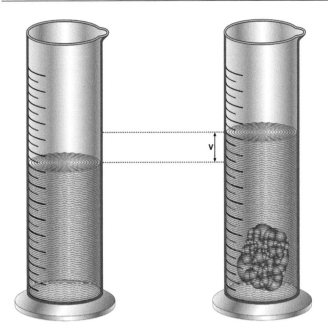

FIGURE 15.2 Determining the volume of an irregularly shaped solid by water displacement.

Source: Shutterstock.com/

by carefully layering the different liquids on top of one another, with the most dense on the bottom to the least dense on the top. The solid to be determined is then dropped onto the top of the column and it will sink until it reaches a liquid layer that has a higher density than its own (Figure 15.4) where it will float on the top of this denser liquid. The density of the solid can then be approximated as less than the density of the liquid it floats upon and greater than the density of the next higher layer that it sank through. For example, if a plastic die is found to float on a maple syrup layer ($d = 1.37$ g/cm^3) and sink in milk ($d = 1.035$ g/cm^3), the relationship of the densities of the three components must then be milk<plastic<maple syrup or the density of the plastic is between 1.03 and 1.37 g/cm^3. The closer together the density of the gradient layers, the more accurately the density of the solid sample can be approximated.

Density gradient techniques are the most common methods employed in forensic determinations. An alternative method is to use a single dense liquid in a column and simply change its density by heating it and noting the temperature where the sample just sinks. Using a known curve that relates the density of the liquid to temperature, the density of the liquid when the sample sank can be determined.

• **Buoyancy**: When a solid object is placed in a liquid, such as water, two opposite forces act on the solid. The first is the gravitational force pulling the sample down through the liquid, as illustrated in Figure 15.5. The second is the density of the liquid

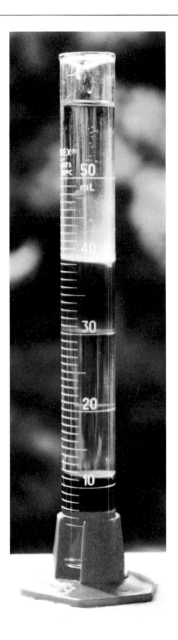

FIGURE 15.3 A liquid density gradient column with (from top to bottom) olive oil, corn oil, wine (dyed red), water (dyed greenish-blue), soap liquid (dyed green), and maple syrup (amber) shown. The liquid with the highest density (maple syrup) is on the bottom and the least dense liquid on top (olive oil).

Source: Used per Creative Commons Attribution 3.0 Unported. User: Kelvinsong.

that acts in the opposite direction to buoy up the sample. Archimedes' principle states that the buoyant force (up-thrust force) experienced by a submerged object is equal to the weight of the liquid displaced by the object. In this method, a solid sample is suspended by a thin wire and submerged in a known weight of water. The weight of the water (and flask) is measured both with and without the submerged solid. Since the weight increase of the water when the object is submerged is equal to the weight of the

FIGURE 15.4 A multi-liquid density column consisting of (from top to bottom): rubbing alcohol (*iso*-propanol, d = 0.785 g/cm³), canola oil (d = 0.914 g/cm³), water (d = 1.00 g/cm³), dish soap (d = 1.02 g/cm³), milk, (d = 1.035 g/cm³), maple syrup (d = 1.37 g/cm³), corn syrup (d = 1.39 g/cm³), and honey (d = 1.42 g/cm³). The floating solids are (top to bottom): balsa wood (d = 0.10 g/cm³), a plastic die (d = 1.37 g/cm³), and a steel nut (d = 7.750 g/cm³).

Source: Giphotostock/Science Photo Library. Used with permission.

water displaced, we can calculate the volume of the water displaced as equal to the volume of the submerged object (remember, we know two of the three variables in the density equation ($d = m/V$): we know the mass of the displaced water and the density of the water, so we can calculate the volume of water displaced). In essence, the water is holding up some of the weight of the object – exactly the weight of the water the object displaces. Therefore, the difference in weight between the two measurements is equal to the volume of the water displaced by the sample, since the density of water is 1.00 g/cm³. For example, if a solid with a 2 mL volume that weighs 5 grams is suspended in the water, the flask and water with the sample will weigh 2 g more than just the flask and water alone (the weight of the water displaced by the 2 mL volume of the sample). Thus, the weight difference is equal to the volume of the sample since the density of water is about 1 g/cm³. Another way to view this is that the 5 g mass of the sample is partially supported and held up by the water (2 grams worth), and the remaining mass (3 g) of the sample is the load on the wire that suspends the solid.

15.1.5 Viscosity

Viscosity, often referred to as the "thickness" of a liquid, is the resistance of a liquid to flow. For example, water is "thin" and flows readily at room temperature, while syrup is "thick" and flows slowly, as illustrated by two fractions of crude oil in Figure 15.6. The less viscous the fluid, the easier it flows. A viscosity measurement can be a useful characterization

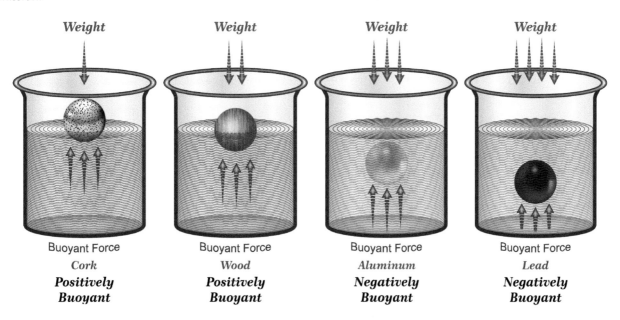

FIGURE 15.5 Determining the density of a solid by buoyancy. The gravitational force pulling the sample downward is noted with the red arrows and the density of the liquid that acts to buoy up the sample, which is dependent upon its density, is shown as blue arrows.

Source: Shutterstock.com.

FIGURE 15.6 The viscosity or "thickness" (resistance to flow) of a liquid can help to determine both its identity and behavior under set conditions: (a) fuel oil, one of the heaviest and most viscous components of crude oil made up of carbon chains 50–70 atoms long, and (b) lubricating oil, a lighter crude oil component, composed of carbon chains only 20–50 atoms long.

Source: (a,b) Paul Rapson/Science Photo Library. Used with permission.

in certain types of forensic evidence, especially in paint, motor oil, lubricants, industrial fluids, and related substances (Figure 15.7).

The viscosity of a liquid sample can be measured in a variety of ways but is usually determined using an instrument called a viscometer. Most viscometers measure the time it takes for a fixed amount of liquid sample to pass either through a hole or a tube. Of course, the viscosity of the liquid sample is greatly affected by its temperature; liquids generally become less viscous when they are heated (compare cold versus hot syrup).

15.1.6 Refractive Index

Light travels at about 3.0×10^8 m/s in a vacuum and slows and bends when it enters a transparent substance. The amount of slowing and, therefore, the observed bending of the light beam depends on the properties of the substance through which the light beam moves. You've seen this effect if you've ever noticed a straight object standing in a glass of water that appears to be bent at the point where it enters the water (Figure 15.8). This effect is caused by the change in the speed of light as it passes from one transparent substance (the air) into another (the water). This effect is referred to as the *refraction* of light by a substance. Every transparent substance, such as glass or plastic, exhibits a characteristic amount of refraction of light called its *refractive index* (RI) that is largely dictated by the substance's density and chemical structure. The refractive index of a substance is defined as the velocity of light in a vacuum divided by the velocity of light in the substance. For example, the refractive index for a diamond is calculated as follows:

$$\text{Refractive Index} = \frac{\text{velocity of light in a vacuum}}{\text{velocity of light in a substance}}$$

$$\text{Refractive Index (diamond)} = \frac{\text{velocity of light in a vacuum}}{\text{velocity of light in a diamond}}$$

$$\text{Refractive Index (diamond)} = \frac{3 \times 10^8 \text{ m/s}}{1.2 \times 10^8 \text{ m/s}}$$

$$\text{Refractive Index (diamond)} = 2.42$$

Every transparent substance has its own characteristic refractive index, and knowing this for a substance can help characterize it. For example, RI can help determine if a small shard of broken glass originated from a window, a headlight or a pair of eyeglasses. The refractive indices and densities for some commonly encountered transparent materials are shown in Table 15.4.

The amount of bending of the light beam that occurs upon entering the substance depends on the refractive index of the two transparent substances the light is moving between (air to water; glass to water) and the angle between the light beam and the line perpendicular to the surface separating the two substances. This is illustrated in Figure 15.9. The refractive index can be easily calculated for a substance by measuring the observed bending angles that occur when the light beam moves from the air into a transparent substance, such as glass (assuming light has about the same speed in a vacuum as in air). The angle between the incoming light beam and a line perpendicular to the surface as it crosses from one medium to another is called the angle of incidence (usually denoted as θ_{air} since the light is measured traveling from air into the transparent material). The angle between the light beam and the perpendicular as it enters a medium is called the angle of refraction ($\theta_{\text{substance}}$).

One method for directly determining the refractive index of a transparent substance involves the physical measurement of the bending of a light beam. A Dutch physicist named Willebrord Snell (1591-1626) long ago derived a relationship between the different angles of light (θ_{air} and $\theta_{\text{substance}}$) as it passes from one transparent medium to

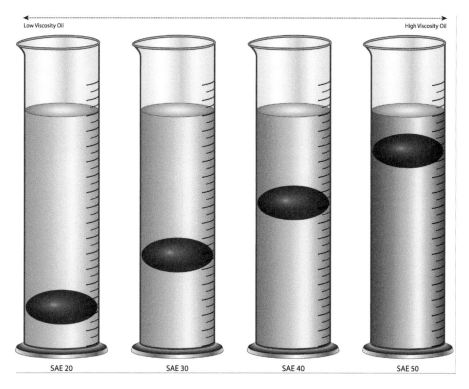

FIGURE 15.7   Viscosities of petroleum oil, as measured by the rate that a small pellet falls in the sample (cm/s).

Source: Shutterstock.com.

FIGURE 15.8   The "illusion" of the bent pencil in a glass of water is used to demonstrate optical refraction due to the difference in the refractive index between water and air.

Source: Ed Degginger/Science Photo Library. Used with permission.

another. This is referred to as Snell's law, which states (see Figure 15.9):

$$\mathrm{RI}_{(material\ leaving)}\ \sin(incident\ angle) = \mathrm{RI}_{(material\ entering)} \\ \times \sin(refractive\ angle)$$

$$\mathrm{RI}_{(air)}\ \sin(\theta_{air}) = \mathrm{RI}_{(substance)}\ \sin(\theta_{substance})$$

By directly measuring the amount of bending that a light beam undergoes upon traveling from the air into a sample, the RI of the sample can be directly determined. That's a lot of math so, since the refractive index of air is approximately 1.00, then Snell's law simplifies to:

$$\mathrm{RI}_{substance} = \frac{\sin\theta_{air}}{\sin\theta_{substance}}$$

Thus, by measuring the values for θ_{air} and $\theta_{substance}$ (Figure 15.9), we can calculate the index of refraction for the sample directly.

A second way to determine the refractive index (RI) of a sample is to place it in various liquids with different refractive indices. When a transparent sample is placed in a liquid with a higher RI, a halo is observed around the edges of the sample, referred to as the *Becke line* (Figure 15.10). As the RI of the liquid is changed, for example by heating the liquid, and its RI approaches the RI of the sample, the Becke line gradually fades until the glass sample can no longer be seen. At this point, the RI of the liquid is the same as the RI of the sample, and the RI of the sample can be determined by knowing the RI of the liquid. If a sample obtained from the crime

TABLE 15.4 Some selected densities and refractive indices (RI) for transparent materials

MATERIAL	DENSITY (G/ML)	REFRACTIVE INDEX
Glasses		
Lead Glass (Soft) [Corning]	3.05	1.560
Borosilicate Pyrex Glass [Corning]	2.23	1.474
Window Glass	2.47–2.56	1.51
Headlight Glass	2.47–2.63	1.47–1.49
Quartz	2.65	1.644
Plastics[1]		
High-Density Polyethylene (HDPE, #2)	0.952–0.965	1.54
Low-Density Polyethylene (LDPE, #4)	0.917–0.940	1.50–1.54
Polypropylene (PP, #5)	0.900–0.910	1.49
Polystyrene (PS, in solid form, #6)	1.04–1.05	1.59–1.60
Minerals		
Diamond (C_n)	3.53	2.42
Zircon ($ZrSiO_4$)	4.65	1.923
Hematite (Fe_2O_3)	7.874	2.940
Quartz (SiO_2)	2.65	1.544
Topaz $Al_2(F,OH)_2SiO_4$	3.55	1.606

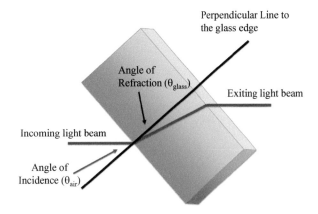

FIGURE 15.9 Angles involved in determining the refractive index (RI) of a solid.

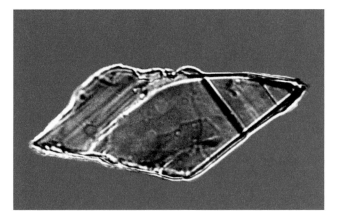

FIGURE 15.10 The RI for a sodium chloride crystal (RI = 1.50) is lower than the RI of the surrounding oil (1.5150) and, therefore, shows a white Becke line around the outside perimeter of the crystal. If the crystal had an RI higher than the oil, the Becke line would look like a black halo.

Source: Dr. Cecil H. Fox/Science Photo Library. Used with permission.

scene and a sample found on the suspect can be placed in the same RI solution, we can quickly see if the two have identical RIs. This type of comparison can most efficiently show that two pieces are dissimilar since the RI of the samples can be quickly compared. A plot of the refractive indices for samples of sheet glass in an FBI study shows the range of RI values (Figure 15.11).

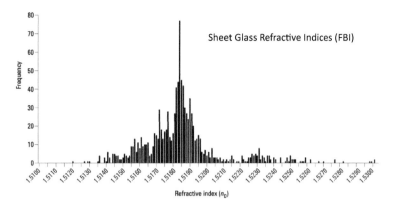

FIGURE 15.11 Distribution of the refractive indices of sheet glass from an FBI database.

Source: Forensic Science Communications, FBI, 2001, 3.

15.1.7 Birefringence

Birefringence is essentially a double refraction phenomenon in certain crystalline materials where the refractive index is different depending on which direction the light goes through the crystal. This phenomenon is common with some types of minerals and plastics. In other words, light travels at different speeds through a birefringent material depending on the actual pathway it takes relative to the orientation of the atoms or molecules in the material. Two examples are shown in Figure 15.12. Birefringence can be used to help identify minerals, fibers, and different types of plastics and polymers, as well as to detect stress in glass and plastics.

15.1.8 Color and Optical Properties

Color is the way our eyes and brain *perceive* different wavelengths of light in the visible range. In our eyes, there are three different types of color receptor cells called cone cells (S, M, and L type cone cells), each responding to its own region of the visible spectrum. Our perception of color results from the differing stimulation of these cone cells. Each color causes a different "mixture" of signals from the three types of cone cells to be sent to the brain. The brain combines the signals to give us our perception of color.

Color can be used to define an object and understand what wavelengths of light the object absorbs, reflects, or transmits. In forensic settings, a color determination can help identify a paint chip, a fiber, a specific ink, or any other colored object. There are, however, several ways that the visible color we perceive for an object can be produced and measured. Two of the most important of these processes are referred to as subtractive and additive color methods.

One very common way that color is produced has to do with something called *subtractive color* mixing. Subtractive mixing

FIGURE 15.12 Examples of birefringent materials (two different refractive indices in the same sample): (a) calcite ($CaCO_3$) and (b) plasticware.

Source: (a) Shutterstock.com; (b) Used per Creative Commons Attribution-Share Alike 4.0 International. User: 3465.

results from mixing pigments together, such as with paints and dyes. In the subtractive process, blending all possible pigments together yields black and the absence of any pigment yields white. The mixing of pigments to produce other colors follows the same basic principles of light reflection and absorption. Each pigment or dye present selectively absorbs some wavelengths of light and transmits others to our eyes. In this system, the three primary colors are usually defined as cyan (blue-green), magenta, and yellow (CMYK system) for the subtractive CMYK color wheel, as shown in Figure 15.13(Right). For example, if we shine white light, as shown in Figure 15.14 (simplified in the drawing as a multicolor beam of light), onto a painted surface that absorbs (subtracts) the blue and green components of the light, then the red wavelengths are not absorbed and are transmitted to our eyes. We then see the surface as colored red. Similarly, if the red and blue wavelengths are absorbed by the pigment molecules and green is transmitted, we perceive the surface as green. Finally, if none of the colors are absorbed, the color of the surface appears white. This situation is probably the most common way that we encounter color from solid objects.

Additive color mixing is essentially the opposite case of subtractive color mixing. White light consists of a mixture of all possible wavelengths, or colors, of light. There are three *primary colors* used to determine the additive nature of light: red, green, and blue (RGB system). In the additive mixing process, if we start with white light containing all three of the primary colors. When we remove one of these primary colors, the remaining two colors add together to give us the perception of a different color. Similarly, adding two beams of differently colored light gives a new additive color. For example, if we filter out the blue light from a white light beam, the colors of red and green remain. Red and green then add together to give yellow light. This relationship is commonly displayed in an additive color wheel, shown in Figure 15.13 (left). Similarly, if we start by adding together a beam of green light and a beam of red light, such as on TV set or in a theater, we perceive yellow light resulting. Adding three beams of red, green, and blue produces white light and filtering all three yields black (no light).

Complementary colors are two colors that, when added together, yield either white light (additive) or a black pigment (subtractive). For example, mixing yellow and blue light gives, white light (additive) while mixing yellow and magenta pigments gives black (subtractive). Complementary colors are displayed on directly opposite sides of the appropriate color wheel (Figure 15.13). Secondary colors are defined as those that arise from mixing together primary colors. In the additive system, the secondary colors are yellow, cyan, and magenta. In the subtractive system the secondary colors are green, orange, and purple.

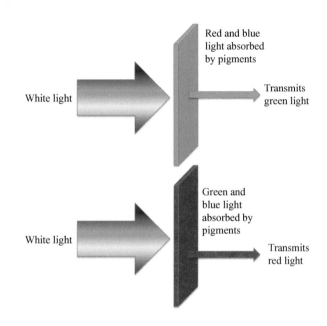

FIGURE 15.14 Subtractive color scheme from shining white light from the left onto different colors of paint. The pigments in each color remove (or subtract) some wavelengths of light from the white light through absorption. The remaining wavelengths of light are then transmitted and detected by our eyes to be interpreted as color.

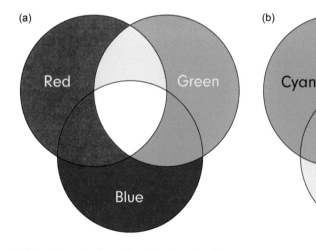

FIGURE 15.13 Additive (a) and subtractive (b) color wheels.

Source: Shutterstock.com.

15.1.9 Electrical Properties and Ductility

Electrical properties can sometimes be helpful in identifying the components of metallic systems, such as telling the difference between aluminum, steel, and zinc or characterizing an alloy (12 K vs 24 K gold). Resistivity can also determine if a circuit or an electrical object is functional. For example, measuring the resistivity of a light bulb filament can easily show if it is intact or damaged from use – providing information about whether the headlight was broken when it was lit, burning out the filament from hot exposure to oxygen, or breaking the bulb when it was turned off, where the filament remains intact. Resistivity is a measure of how strongly a material resists the flow of electric current while conductivity indicates how well a substance conducts an electric current. Ductility refers to the ability of a substance to be stretched into a wire or hammered into thin sheets without shattering. Metals are typically quite ductile, while ceramics shatter when stressed.

15.1.10 Other Measurements

Other physical properties that can be measured and are used in forensic laboratories to help characterize substances include melting point, boiling point, sublimation point, and hardness (Figure 15.15). Most of these properties and their measurement have already been discussed in previous chapters but will be employed in considering glass, mineral, and paint evidence later in this chapter.

15.2 ENVIRONMENTAL FORENSIC EVIDENCE

"It is simplicity itself," he remarked, chuckling at my surprise—"so absurdly simple that an explanation is superfluous; and yet it may serve to define the limits of observation and of deduction. Observation tells me that you have a little reddish mould adhering to your instep. Just opposite the Wigmore Street Office they have taken up the pavement and thrown up some earth, which lies in such a way that it is difficult to avoid treading in it in entering. The earth is of this peculiar reddish tint which is found, as far as I know, nowhere else in the neighbourhood. So much is observation. The rest is deduction."

(Conan Doyle, 1890)

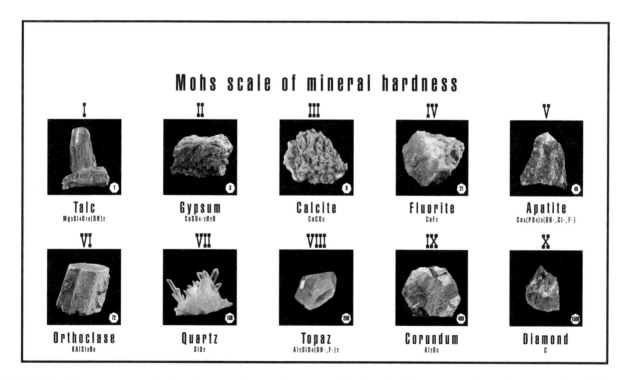

FIGURE 15.15 The measurement of hardness can be used to very quickly identify different minerals, such as those found in forensic soils and geological samples.

Source: Shutterstock.com.

LEARNING GOALS AND OBJECTIVES

Soil, mineral, and other aspects of forensic geology can provide valuable trace forensic evidence. After studying this section, you should be able to

- Explain what is meant by forensic geology and soil analysis.
- Describe how the organic and inorganic components of soils may be analyzed.
- Discuss what types of forensic information may be derived from geological and soil analyses.

15.2.1 Introduction

Environmental evidence can play a key role in criminal investigations by providing connections between a specific place and a suspect or item of evidence from adhered traces. This evidence may take the form of tiny pieces of soil or geological material carried away from a location on a person's clothing, automobile, or directly on their body. Forensic soil and geology, part of the broader field of *environmental forensics*, can also provide unique "fingerprinting" tools useful in tracking the sources of material either around the block or around the world. The primary tools for making the unique link between a specific site and a piece of evidence lie in measuring physical properties to identify these materials.

15.2.2 Forensic Geology

Geology is the detailed study of the Earth and its materials along with the physical processes that act upon them. Geological materials have long been recognized as valuable trace evidence capable of linking a crime scene location with specific pieces of physical evidence. Minute traces of rock, minerals, and soil can provide unique proxy information, useful both in investigations and prosecutions (Figure 15.16). *Proxy indicators*, as discussed in detail in the chapter of forensic ecology (Chapter 10), are small amounts of identifiable material from a specific location that provide, with relatively high accuracy, information about the site from which they originated (see Section 10.2). For example, identifying the mineral composition and particle-size distribution of a sample of sand can tell a great deal about possible locations from which that sand might have originated.

15.2.3 Soil

Soil, commonly called "dirt" when adhered to someone or something, is a mixture of inorganic (mineral) and organic

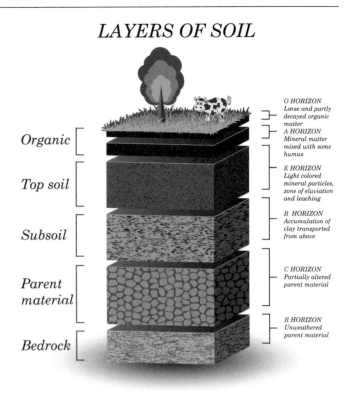

LAYERS OF SOIL

FIGURE 15.16   Typical layers of soils and soil horizons.

Source: Shutterstock.com.

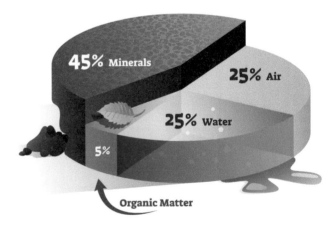

SOIL COMPOSITION

FIGURE 15.17   The typical composition of soils from a woodland environment. These percentages may vary greatly dependinghe environmental source of the soil.

Source: Shutterstock.com.

components that are packed together relatively loosely, containing solid, liquid (usually water), and gaseous (pores containing air) components (Figure 15.17). The inorganic fraction usually consists of very small broken fragments of larger rocks, microcrystallites, minerals, and powdered inorganic compounds. The organic fraction consists of animal, plant, bacteria, and fungi in varying states of decay. Soils can range in makeup from almost entirely organic, such as might be found on a thick forest floor, to a pure inorganic sample, such as the sand found on beaches, mountaintops, and deserts. Soils may also contain material added through the actions of people, both consciously and unwittingly. For example, gardeners often add "exotic" materials (those not found locally), such as peat moss, lime, and organic fertilizers, to make the soil better for growing plants. People, vehicles, and animals can also "track" in minerals and soils from other locations inadvertently, thereby bringing unique non-native "markers" to the locale. All these features can, in theory, combine to make a particular soil profile at a location unique from all others in the world. Occasionally, soil profiles may even differ greatly every few feet at some locations. This extreme soil variation, of course, provides both rich forensic information when characterized, but also presents significant challenges by providing too much variation to be practically workable.

Soils tend to be very heterogeneous and complex mixtures, composed of many different components. Even the same mineral type found in a sample can be present in a wide range of shapes and sizes. Particle sizes in the soil determine many of the physical features of a soil and range from large gravel to very small clay particles. The distribution of the different components and sizes of particles dictates the type of soil present (Figure 15.18).

Soils also contain varying amounts of water and air components. Water can adhere tightly to subsurface components and minerals, including water chemically bound to inorganic compounds that are very difficult to remove, even with extreme heating. The pores in the soil trap different amounts of air, depending on the relative size of the components. The amount of air and water in soil may either aid or slow the decay of the organic components depending on the environmental conditions. Soils are mixed by the action of both living and non-living forces. Animals burrow, plant roots disrupt, and bacteria and fungi "digest" soil components, resulting in a mixing of soils.

Fine soil and mineral samples can be carried for great distances by the wind, water, people, and animals, and can be used for a variety of forensic purposes. These can include identifying the specific components for the purpose of comparing samples, visualizing footprints, and fingerprints, and tracing the path a person took.

Minute mineral and soil traces are often found on pieces of physical evidence but are especially common on clothing, vehicles, shoes, and buried implements, including shovels, weapons, bones, tools, etc., as shown in Figure 15.19. Additionally, some soil components are easily carried for long periods of time directly on people: in their hair, on their skin, under fingernails, in nasal and respiratory passages, and in their intestinal tracts. Samples almost too small to visualize can provide a wealth of information and are readily overlooked by suspects and thus may be preserved unwittingly as incriminating evidence. The mineral components of samples are also difficult to chemically change or destroy. For example, minerals are often not affected by high temperatures or by harsh chemical environments, so they can withstand burning, chemical corrosion, or other severe conditions and remain identifiable as originating from a particular location.

The complexity of soil and geological samples actually aids in connecting a site with a piece of evidence. The more features that can be analyzed and quantified, the greater the certainty in either matching or eliminating a particular location as a possible origin for the sample. The converse is also true; if there is little variation in soil composition for very large areas, such as on a beach, the use of forensic soil analysis can be limited. Geologists with detailed knowledge of local soils and mineral distribution can help track a sample of soil found on a person to a set of possible locations or even to a single location.

There are several key features to consider when using geological and soil samples in forensic investigations, including their physical, chemical, and biological properties. Comparing these properties with those of reference samples taken from known locations can help to link the two samples.

Soil samples are analyzed to determine the identity and amount of each component that makes up the soil. The mineral components are identified by a variety of physical methods. Physical measurements of the shapes and sizes of the particles, along with determinations of density, color (Figure 15.20),

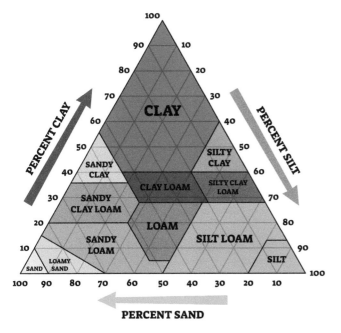

FIGURE 15.18 Components of different types of soils.

Source: Shutterstock.com.

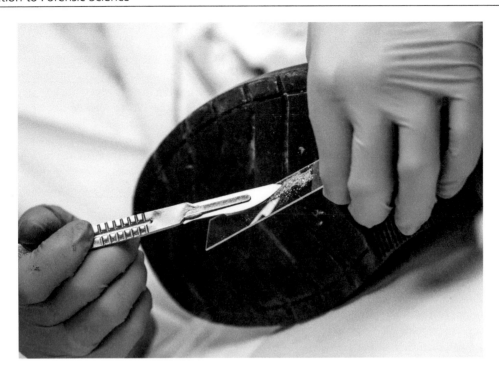

FIGURE 15.19   Soil sample being removed from a shoe as evidence.

Source: Shutterstock.com.

FIGURE 15.20   Using a standard color indexing book (Munsell) to determine the color of a soil or geologic sample.

Source: Used per Creative Commons Attribution 2.0 Generic. © John Kelley, http://SoilScience.info.

refractive index, and birefringence, provide information for distinguishing one sample from another. X-ray diffraction may be used in this characterization. Polarizing light microscopy and particle-size distributions can also be especially effective in identifying and characterizing mineral components in soil (Figure 15.21).

The biological origins of the components in soil are often determined through the use of microscopy. Identification of

FIGURE 15.21   Soil sample being ground up to examine the particles and identify the soil type, as well as other characteristics of that soil. When compared to other soil samples, this evidence could help to place a suspect at a crime scene.

Source: Mauro Fermariello/Science Photo Library. Used with permission.

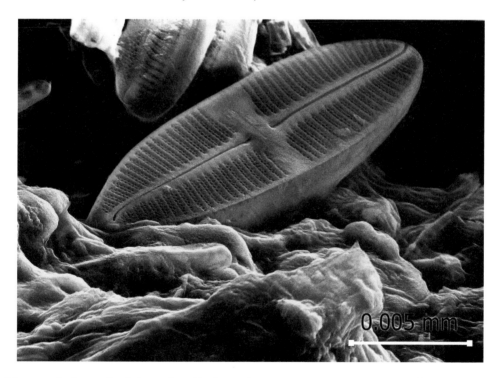

FIGURE 15.22   Microscopic diatom fossils in a mineral/soil sample.

Source: Used per Creative Commons Attribution 4.0 International. User: Gribkov.

ecological markers, such as pollen, leaf fragments, bacteria, fungi, and minute animal remains and fossils (e.g., diatoms), may be used to develop a unique profile of a particular location and used for comparison to an unknown sample (Figure 15.22). The specific organic molecules in the sample are not usually identified, but this has been occasionally reported using HPLC chromatographic and mass spectral measurements for some soil samples.

Minerals and some soils are important in the manufacture of a variety of common items. For example, flowerpots, bricks, insulation for houses and safes, and concrete are just a few

FIGURE 15.23   Undisturbed layering in a soil profile.

Source: Shutterstock.com.

objects made from soils. Soils also make their way into processed foods and consumables. In a recent case, the soil component in an eaten sausage was identified from stomach contents and traced back to a specific packing plant where it was made; this information was then used to determine exactly where that person ate their last meal. It is virtually impossible to eat plant foods without consuming some small fragments of soil.

Examination of soil layers can also be helpful in determining if the soil at a site has been disturbed or altered, such as when digging a grave. In these cases, a "normal" uniform stratigraphic pattern (layering pattern of soil strata, such as shown in Figure 15.23) of a site can be disrupted and indicates where mixing has occurred (Figure 15.24). Identifying disturbed areas is a common technique used by archaeologists and forensic anthropologists to help locate buried remains.

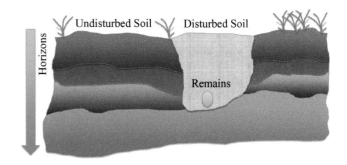

FIGURE 15.24   Disturbed soil layer patterns can provide evidence of a grave site. Regions of disturbed soil and undisturbed soil horizons can be identified, which can lead to buried remains or objects.

BOX 15.2   HIGH FLYING GEOLOGY

Just six months after the United States entered World War II, the United States Geological Survey (USGC) set up a Military Geology Group to help with important Earth Science-related issues, such as gathering information on potential military landing sites, water supplies, and the location of suitable building supplies. In early 1945, this group was asked to help with a rather bizarre question related to actual Japanese attacks on the US West Coast.

Between November 1944 and April 1945, Japan released more than 9,000 incendiary balloons against the West Coast of the United States, with nearly 1,000 reaching the mainland, from Alaska as far south as Mexico and inland as far as Iowa. These paper hydrogen balloons were 32 ft in diameter (9.75 m) and carried two incendiary (fire) bombs and one 15 Kg anti-personnel bomb. While the bombs caused relatively little actual damage, their potential for causing widespread fires and public terror was significant. The U.S. military had no idea where they were being launched from, although they thought it most likely that the balloons came from Japanese ships positioned off the U.S. West Coast. Officials did not believe that these devices could have originated in Japan, nearly 5,500 miles away. Interestingly, the media reported very little about these potentially destructive weapons at the request of the military, a fact that largely contributed to ending the attacks.

These balloon weapons required a substantial amount of ingenious engineering; they needed to stay aloft until dropping their deadly payloads on U.S. targets after launch. The one clue to their production and launch site came from several small bags of sand recovered from the balloons. These sandbags were used as ballast for the balloons, keeping them from going too high by their weight and automatically releasing some sand if the balloon dropped too low. The USGS was given the task of finding the point of origin of the sand in the ballast bags. The sand was carefully analyzed, measured, and "inventoried," especially looking at the diatoms in the sand (skeletons of microscopic algae). Once done, the team then looked to find the possible sources of the sand – but it wasn't quite that easy. The locations near the suspected launch sites on the U.S. coast or on any of the mid-Pacific islands clearly did not have sand anything like that found in the bags. Eventually, they broadened their search and found a surprising but very likely source – the beaches at the northern end of the main island of Japan: Honshu.

Reconnaissance of the Japanese beach site, proposed based on the geological analysis, confirmed it as the production and launch site in Japan. The deployment of these weapons from such a distance was made possible by a discovery by the Japanese that was unknown to the rest of the world at that time: the jet stream. The jet stream is a very high, fast-moving current of air that travels globally from west to east. The Japanese had learned that if they could launch the balloons into the jet stream from Japan, about three days later the balloons would be over the mainland United States. Eventually, the United States destroyed the hydrogen production facility needed for the balloons, and without any evidence of the effectiveness of the incendiary balloons, Japan canceled the operation in mid-1945. An interesting case of geologic detection!

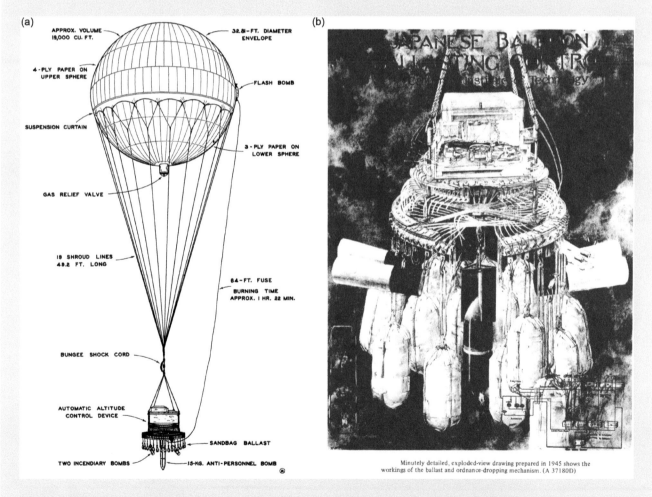

FIGURE 15.25   Schematic drawing (a) and sandbags(b) from the WWII Japanese incendiary bombs.

Source: NIST.

15.3 FORENSIC GLASS AND PLASTIC ANALYSIS

LEARNING GOALS AND OBJECTIVES

Glass and plastics are frequently encountered in forensic science. When you complete this section, you should be able to

- Explain the composition of glass and what types are often encountered.
- Describe how glass is manufactured and how different types may be distinguished.
- Explain what types of forensic glass analyses may be employed.
- Discuss the information that can be gained from the fragmentation patterns of glass.
- Show how glass fragments may be used to determine the direction of the force applied to the glass.
- Define a plastic and explain how plastics can be analyzed for forensic information.

15.3.1 Introduction

Both glass and plastics are so ubiquitous in our society that many crimes involve either their utilization in weapons or as evidence collected from the crime scene. When glass or plastic is broken, such as in an automobile accident or burglary, fragments may be carried away from the scene of the crime on the clothing, shoes, or hair of a suspect. These samples may provide either class information, such as the type of glass or plastic involved, or individual evidence, such as that obtained by uniquely reconstructing a shattered item by fitting the pieces together.

It is often important to determine, if possible, whether a particular sample of glass or plastic found on a suspect or a piece of evidence matches, at least in terms of its chemical and physical properties, a similar piece found at the scene of a crime. While most glasses and plastics may look very similar by visual inspection, they may be quite different in terms of these properties. Glass and plastics can also tell a story of the chain of events that happened during a crime. In this section, we will explore the information that these materials can provide.

15.3.2 Glass

Items made of glass have been valued for millennia, both for their great utility and their aesthetic beauty. Today, glass objects retain this dual role and are pervasive in our lives, with applications from windows and windshields to specialty glasses used in medical practice, fiber optic telecommunications, scientific research, and art.

Glass is primarily composed of silicon dioxide (silica, SiO_2), the same material that makes up sand and is the most common compound found in the Earth's crust. The silica is usually combined with smaller amounts of other compounds to modify the properties of the glass in useful ways. Glass is actually an amorphous solid; a material that is without a regular, repeating crystal structure (Figure 15.26). As an amorphous material, it does move, although exceptionally slowly, so slowly that no appreciable movement can be detected over thousands or even millions of years (see Box 15.3). The properties of glass as a hard and brittle substance come from the inter-connected nature of the SiO_2 network.

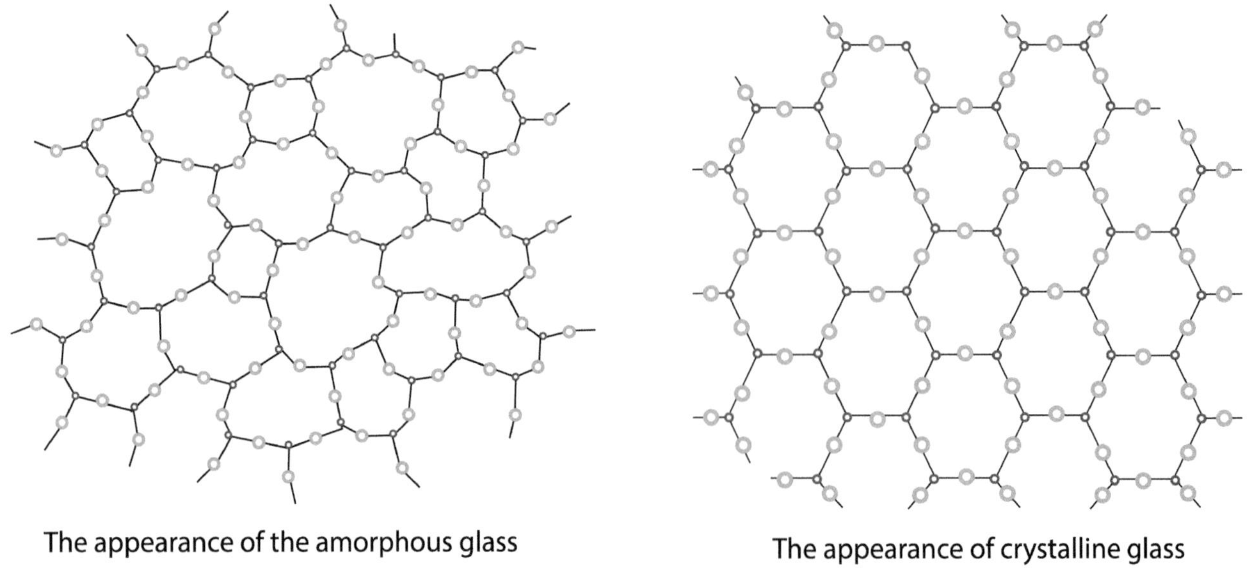

The appearance of the amorphous glass

The appearance of crystalline glass

FIGURE 15.26   Examples of the chemical structures of amorphous and crystalline glass.

Source: Shutterstock.com.

BOX 15.3 DOES GLASS REALLY FLOW?

Glass, as an amorphous solid (by most definitions), actually does flow very, very slowly. Contrary to popular misconception, however, older window glass is not thicker at the bottom due to its flow but rather due to the method that was used to make the window glass. Centuries ago, glass for windows was difficult to make and was prepared by spinning large discs of glass, forcing the glass out from the center toward the edges, making it thinner at the edges than the center. The window panes were then cut from the discs and the thicker portion (closer to the center) was usually installed downward for aesthetic and practical reasons. Glass moves so slowly that it would not be appreciably noticed over many thousands of years in a window frame.

FIGURE 15.27 Blown glass method for producing bottles and other complex shapes using cast iron molds.

Source: Shutterstock.com.

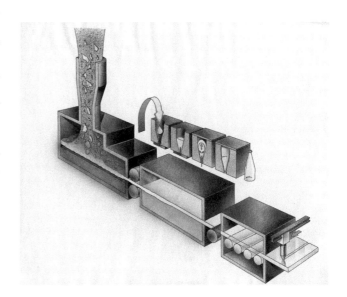

FIGURE 15.28 Float glass method used for producing flat panels of glass, shown along the bottom. The blown method is shown along the top.

Source: DK Images/Science Photo Library. Used with permission.

The properties of glass can be readily modified by adding other chemicals to the molten silica. For example, glass can be colored through the addition of metal salts and related compounds: blue from copper oxide, milky from aluminum oxide, green from cobalt or iron oxide, and red from selenium sulfide, among many others. Glass can also be made more resistant to thermal shock (rapid cooling or heating) by adding boron oxide to the silica to produce *borosilicate* glass. One common trade name for borosilicate glass is the popular *Pyrex* brand, used extensively for cooking where the glass is often heated and cooled very quickly. The most common type of glass, *soda-lime* glass, is used predominantly for window glass, bottles, and jars. It is produced by adding a variety of compounds to the molten silica, including sodium carbonate (Na_2CO_3), lime (CaO), alumina (Al_2O_3), and salts (NaCl or others). Glass destined for windows typically has a higher sodium and/or magnesium content than glass that is made into containers. There is, however, an enormous variation in the amount and identity of these smaller components in glass that may occasionally help to distinguish individual glass samples based on their chemical analysis.

Modern glass is produced in several ways, depending upon the required shape and ultimate purpose of the glass. The oldest technique still employed in large-scale production today is *blown* or spun glass. In this process, a piece of molten glass is blown either into a mold to form shaped materials or formed freehand to generate art-glass pieces, such as goblets, vases, and decorative pieces. The commercial production of bottles and other containers uses an automated molding process in which a small bubble of glass is injected into a mold and blown to take the shape of the mold (Figures 15.27 and 15.28). After cooling, the mold is removed to free the shaped piece. This method is employed to inexpensively produce millions of bottles and complex shapes annually, with all pieces from the same mold having the same exact dimensions.

Flat glass is produced by one of two methods: float glass or rolled glass techniques. In the *float glass* method, a layer of molten glass comes out of a furnace as a continuous sheet that is then floated onto a bed of molten metal, most often tin (Figure 15.28). The glass and the tin do not mix, allowing the glass to form a uniform, perfectly flat, seamless sheet that is cooled sufficiently by the time it reaches the other side of the bed, where it is cut while retaining its flat shape. The cut piece of flat glass then passes through a hot annealing chamber that reduces the stress within the glass piece without allowing it to distort. This method produces glass that is almost completely flat and free of distortions and imperfections.

A second method, called the *rolled glass* technique, uses rollers to press the molten glass into a flat shape. This method often transfers imperfections into the glass from the rollers such that it is not usually used for making clear window glass. Instead, the rollers can be patterned to intentionally give a texture to the final piece of glass, such as for use in shower doors and decorative dividers, as shown in Figure 15.29.

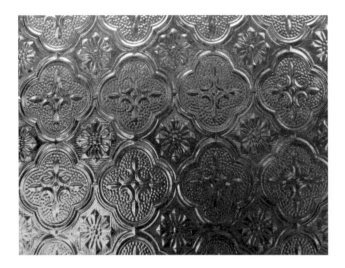

FIGURE 15.29   A sample of rolled glass with an intricate design imprinted into the flat glass.

Source: Used per Creative Commons Attribution-Share Alike 3.0 Unported. User: Menirogar.

The properties of glass can also be modified by treating it after it has been formed. Most glasses become molten between 1200° and 1800°C and soften at about 800°C. However, if glass is held at a somewhat lower temperature, known as the annealing temperature, the stress in the glass is slowly relieved without changing its shape, making it much stronger and resistant to thermal or mechanical shock. The annealing temperature is lower than that necessary to deform the glass but high enough to allow the stresses to relax, usually between 450° and 550°C, depending on the type of glass.

Glass may also be modified in several other ways to make it safer for certain applications; these products are referred to as safety glass. *Tempered glass* is usually heated just to the point where it softens, followed by rapid cooling. Since the outer surface cools much faster than the inside of the glass, the outer surface tension is very high and generates high stress levels throughout the piece, making the glass exceptionally strong. When this type of glass breaks, however, the stresses are relieved rapidly and it fragments into tiny blocks of glass instead of into sharp shards of glass, as shown in Figure 15.30. These smaller block pieces are far less likely to cause injury when broken, making this type of glass usually required for car windows (not windshields) and "public" space glass, such as in buildings and for sports applications. Another type of safety glass is called *laminated glass* where a piece of clear plastic or resin is sandwiched or "laminated" between two pieces of glass (Figure 15.31). When laminated glass breaks, the internal plastic holds the fragments together and greatly reduces the danger of flying glass shards on impact. An example of a broken laminated car windshield is shown in Figure 15.32 where, even though broken, all the pieces remain in place.

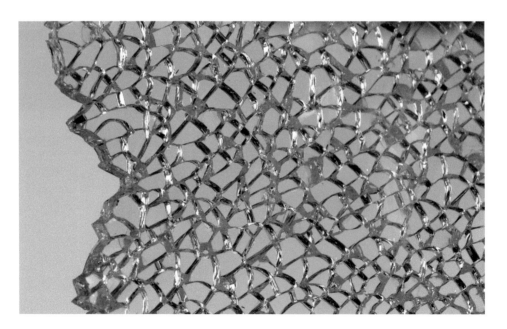

FIGURE 15.30   Broken tempered glass breaks into small pieces of glass rather than into sharp shards, making it safer for use in windows and windshields.

Source: Shutterstock.com.

FIGURE 15.31 Laminated glass showing the plastic sheet sandwiched between two pieces of tempered glass.

Source: Shutterstock.com.

FIGURE 15.32 Broken laminated windshield glass stays together after shattering due to the plastic layer between the two pieces of glass.

Source: Shutterstock.com.

15.3.3 Forensic Characterization of Glass

A primary goal of forensic glass analysis is to fully characterize the features and properties of the sample. The initial characterization usually begins with simple measurements of the dimensions of the piece: thickness, width, and length.

The physical and chemical properties of both glass and plastic then usually include measuring the color, density, and refractive index of the sample. Information about the chemical composition of the glass can be obtained using ultraviolet-visible and infrared spectroscopy, along with inductively coupled plasma-mass spectrometry (ICP-MS). Each of these types of characterizations has already been discussed in previous chapters but generally provides class information that is usually not individualized to the extent that allows two samples to be "matched" uniquely (see Chapter 2).

Sometimes, it is possible to piece a broken glass object back together, similar to putting together a jigsaw puzzle. When a shard found on a suspect or other source can be fitted into a reconstructed, broken glass object, this provides a very strongly individualized connection between the two samples. This method of direct physical matching is tedious but powerful when a fit is found. Depending on the method of production, glass can also have patterns or striations that can be quite individualized. Glass from the side windows of cars can be scratched by dirt deposited on the rubber gasket holding the window in place to form a pattern that can be used to aid matching. Similarly, windshield wiper patterns can be used to help piece a broken windshield together or determine from which side of the car the fragment originated. Matching these patterns provides additional support for connecting the two pieces of evidence together, as shown in Figure 15.33.

When window glass is broken by a small projectile, such as a bullet or stone, it often breaks in a fashion that provides valuable information. Two types of cracks or fractures are usually found around the point where a projectile strikes the piece of flat glass: radial and concentric cracks. *Radial cracks* are those that extend or "radiate" outwards from the central point of impact, producing a star-like pattern (Figure 15.34). *Concentric cracks* are those that form rings that approximately circle the point of impact. These types of fractures are caused by the different stresses put on the glass from the projectile. When a projectile first impacts the glass, initially, the glass flexes a bit until the limit of its flexibility is reached. When this limit is exceeded, the glass first fractures on the side opposite to the force to form a radial crack, as illustrated in

Figure 15.35. As the projectile continues forward and pushes the glass further to cause it to bend even more, the glass then breaks on the same side as the force to relieve the added stress by forming concentric cracks.

It is usually very difficult, if not impossible, to accurately estimate the size and velocity of the actual projectile that caused a particular glass fracture pattern or even what type of projectile caused the impact. Impacts from stones, bullets, or other small projectiles give very similar fracture patterns. Large projectiles may completely fragment the glass. Occasionally, it may be possible to detect traces of gunpowder, soil, or other residue from the projectile to help in its identification – but not often.

It is sometimes important to determine the direction from which the projectile came as it hit the glass, especially when trying to determine the path of deflected bullets and the location of a shooter. When the point of impact remains relatively

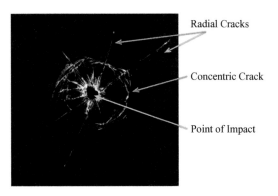

FIGURE 15.34   Radial and concentric cracks on a broken piece of flat glass.

FIGURE 15.33   Two pieces from the end of a broken jar showing matching striations and patterns.

Source: Used with permission and courtesy Scott Rubins.

intact, a crater may be found on the exit side of the glass, as shown in Figure 15.36, forming a much larger exit hole than the entrance hole. When glass breaks, *stress-induced striations*, sometimes called ribs, heckles or conchoidal marks, are usually formed on the edge of the glass, Figure 15.37. These marks form an approximate 90° angle with one surface and very small (acute) angles toward the other surface of the glass. These stress marks can be used to determine from which side the force came and, by a simple relationship, the direction of the projectile. The right angle always faces the surface where the crack originated. In a radial crack, the surface where the crack starts is on the *side opposite* to the force, while in concentric cracks, the fracture starts on the side nearest the force (Figure 15.35). There is a simple rule to help remember this: "The 3Rs: **R**adial fractures form **R**ight angles to **R**everse

(or rear) side to the force." This is illustrated for both radial and concentric fractures in Figure 15.37. This means that, if a radial crack can be identified, the surface next to the right angle is the side *opposite* to the force, and the converse is true for a concentric fracture.

When multiple projectiles, such as bullets, impact glass, it may be valuable to know the order in which the bullets hit the glass. This can be done simply by examining the fracture patterns of the glass and knowing the simple rule that *newer fractures do not cross preexisting fractures*, but rather stop (terminate). It is then a matter of carefully examining the fracture pattern to locate where radial fractures terminate at another, preexisting fracture. In the example shown in Figure 15.38, the crack radiating from bullet impact 2 stops when it encounters the crack radiating from the impact of bullet 1 (Figure 15.38b,

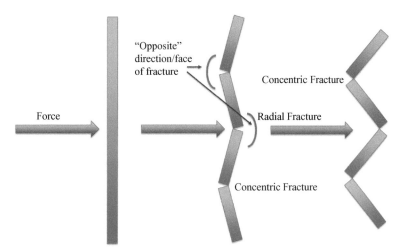

FIGURE 15.35 Glass fractures from projectile stresses that cause the radial and concentric fractures.

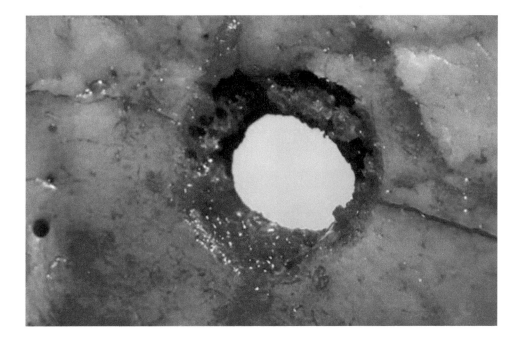

FIGURE 15.36 Crater formation on the exit side of a projectile.

Source: Catanese (2016).

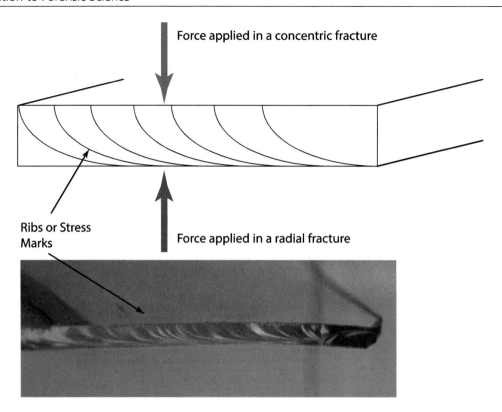

Force applied in a concentric fracture

Ribs or Stress
Marks

Force applied in a radial fracture

FIGURE 15.37   Edge "rib" or stress marks along the edge of broken glass can provide information as to the direction from which the force came.

left of the figure). This means that the crack from bullet 1 was already formed when bullet 2 hit the glass, so the order of impact must be bullet 1 first, then bullet 2. By similar reasoning, impact number 3 must have been first.

Fractures in glass from larger blunt force objects and heat-formed fractures can usually be easily differentiated from those of small projectile impacts by their fracture patterns, since they typically lack the well-defined point of impact.

Sometimes, it is valuable to know whether a bulb or headlight was turned on or off when it was shattered. There are several ways of gaining this information, including looking for small glass particles that melt onto a hot filament or finding oxidation on the filament that occurs when the hot filament is rapidly exposed to air. An example is shown in Figure 15.39.

BOX 15.4   CASE STUDY IN GLASS

In 1988, several jars of Gerber baby food were discovered to contain glass fragments. While it was possible that the contamination arose from a single event, such as a light bulb bursting over the production line, careful analysis showed these glass fragments arose from a number of quite different sources (e.g., headlight, plate glass, light bulb, etc.). The conclusion by the FBI was that several consumers independently placed the fragments into the food jars themselves in the hope of forcing the company to compensate them for the potentially dangerous contamination.

15.3.4 Plastics

Plastics are simply defined as materials that can be molded, but common usage today implies objects made from high molecular weight polymeric compounds. Plastics have an enormous range of physical and chemical properties, from soft, flexible fibers, sheets, and objects (e.g., nylon, Styrofoam, and low-density polyethylene) to extremely dense and strong materials (e.g., PVC, eyeglass plastics, and structural plastics). They have been engineered to replace much of the metal in our vehicles and are used in medicine, telecommunications, and optics along with thousands of other applications. As such, plastics are common forms of forensic evidence. Today, almost all the plastics that we use are made of synthetic polymers.

In previous chapters, we considered the various important aspects of polymer chemistry. In summary, polymers are long chain molecules made up of smaller molecular "building blocks" that are linked together. DNA, cellulose, spider's silk, and the components of most plastics are examples of polymeric materials.

Plastics have many forensic features in common with glass. They can provide class evidence based on their chemical and physical properties or individualized evidence when the characteristics are suitably unique to allow certain identification. Among the key physical properties used to characterize polymers are the determinations of their density and refractive index. Density and RI values for several common plastics are given in Table 15.4.

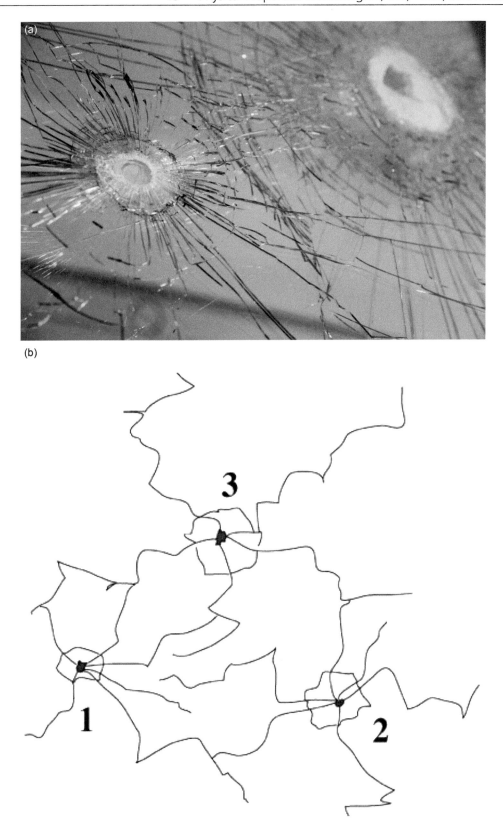

FIGURE 15.38   Bullet-generated fractures in plate glass. (a) The interference of the fragmentation patterns can be used to determine the order of bullet impacts. (b) the order of impact is 3, 1, and finally 2.

Source: (a) Michael Donne/Science Photo Library. Used with permission.

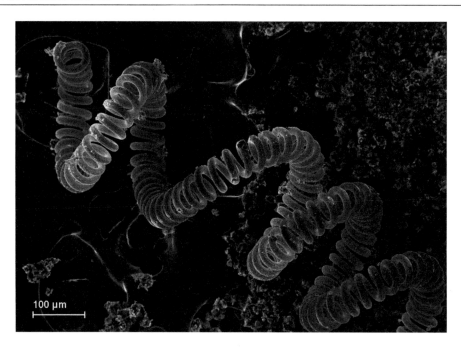

FIGURE 15.39   Small glass particles fused onto a hot headlamp filament that was on when broken.

Source: Used per Creative Commons Attribution-Share Alike 4.0 International. User: Capkuckokos.

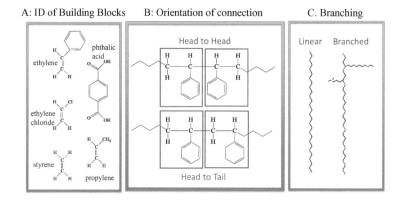

FIGURE 15.40   Several features that control the chemical and physical properties of polymers: (A) the identity of building blocks (ethylene, ethylene chloride, styrene, phthalic acid, and propylene), (B) the mode of connection (the tail-to-tail configuration is not shown), and (C) the branching, if present.

The physical and chemical properties of polymers are controlled by their chemical structures. Changing these chemical features will change the properties of the resulting polymer. While a more complete discussion of the chemistry of polymers is beyond the scope of this book, it is valuable to understand some of the key features that affect the properties of polymers since we can look for these features to help unambiguously identify which polymers are used in a particular piece of plastic. The five chemical features that are most important in controlling the properties of polymers are:

- The chemical structure of the building blocks (monomers) that make up the polymer.
- The mode in which the molecular building blocks are connected together (how the building blocks link: head-to-tail, head-to-head, etc.).
- The length of the polymer chain.
- The type of branching of the chain.

- The three-dimensional arrangement of the chains (e.g., cross-linking, straight, etc.).

Today, most polymers are made up of just five basic chemical building blocks (monomers). These five are illustrated in Figure 13.40(a): ethylene, ethylene chloride, styrene, phthalic acid, and propylene. Most of these are produced synthetically from petroleum feedstocks in enormous quantities. The specific monomer is then put together through a chemical reaction to form the long polymeric chains with the desired properties. Identifying the specific monomers that make up the polymer is a key step in characterizing the polymer.

For monomers that are not symmetric (where the two "ends" of the monomer are chemically different, such as in styrene), it matters exactly how the monomeric units are linked together. Three possibilities exist for these types of monomers: head-to-head, head-to-tail, or tail-to-tail arrangements, as shown in Figure 15.40(b). The polymer can also form straight or branched chains (Figure 15.40(c)), depending on the ability of the chains to connect to other chains. If, for example, a monomer can only connect at two points, only a straight chain can form (such as linking railroad cars together). If, on the other hand, the monomer can connect at three or more points, complex branched chains can result with "tree-like" structures (See Figure 7.65 in Chapter 7 on biopolymers). Branching affects the polymer's properties by changing the ways that the chains can pack together. Consider the analogy of stacking individual pieces of straight lumber versus stacking a collection of cut bushes. The "unbranched" lumber can be packed very tightly and efficiently together, forming a very dense stack. In contrast, the branches of the bushes make it very hard to stack them efficiently; the branches keep the individual bushes from coming close together and leave a great deal of empty space in the resulting stack. Similarly, straight-chain polymers can pack together much more efficiently and closely than branched-chain polymers. For example, ethylene can form either branched or straight-chain polymers. The straight-chain version of polyethylene (PE) allows the chains to pack together efficiently and forms the tough and strong high-density polyethylene (HDPE). In comparison, the branched polyethylene polymeric chains do not pack very well together, forming the soft, pliable low-density polyethylene (LDPE). The differences in the properties in products made from these two forms of polyethylene are illustrated in Figure 15.41.

The lengths of polymer chains can range in size from just a relatively few monomers linked together to many thousands of monomers connected together in a single polymeric molecule. The length of these chains is important to the observed properties of the polymer. For example, as the length of the chain grows, the polymer changes from a liquid to a soft solid to a tough solid.

Finally, the polymeric chains can become twisted and tangled together in a complex three-dimensional arrangement. The degree to which the molecules tangle affects their physical properties, especially how they react to heat. Polymeric molecules can also be chemically linked together through a process called cross-linking. This cross-linking prevents the molecules from moving around or past each other by connecting them together, forming rigid plastics.

The characterization of a polymer requires determining how all these chemical factors come together to form the plastic. It is necessary to know the identity of the building blocks, the degree of branching, and other chemical information to provide an unambiguous forensic identification of the plastic material. While plastics may be colored materials, two colored samples may also be hard to distinguish visually, especially in small fragmentary samples. In this case, ultraviolet and infrared characterization may be particularly important in defining the sample. The harder, more brittle plastics may form impact fractures very similar to those found in glass. Analysis of these patterns can yield information similar to that determined from glass samples. Fortunately, analytical methods, such as those described in Chapter 12, have been developed to answer these important questions.

15.4 PAINTS AND COATINGS

LEARNING GOALS AND OBJECTIVES

Recovered paint samples may be important types of evidence, such as paint chips from automobiles and clothing used during burglaries. When you complete this chapter, you should be able to:

- Describe the general chemical composition of paints and dyes.
- Discuss what types of information paint and coating trace evidence may provide.
- Explain how paints are analyzed in forensic science.

FIGURE 15.41 (a) High-density polyethylene (HDPE) and (b) low-density polyethylene (LDPE).

Source: Shutterstock.com.

15.4.1 Introduction

Painted objects and surfaces are found throughout society today. Cars, homes, furniture, and many other objects are coated with paint to provide both protection and beauty. Small pieces of paint are often unwittingly transferred between objects during vehicular accidents, burglaries, robberies, assaults, homicides, and even through simple contact with freshly painted surfaces during a crime. It should not be surprising, therefore, that paint can form a valuable part of trace forensic analysis.

15.4.2 Paint Composition

Paints are opaque coatings typically composed of three components: pigment, binder (sometimes referred to as medium or vehicle) and diluent (solvent). The *pigment* portion of paint consists of very tiny colored particles of organic and inorganic compounds that give the paint its characteristic hue (Figure 15.42). The medium or *binder* suspends the pigment particles and helps firmly fix them to the surface. Finally, a volatile liquid *solvent*, such as water or an organic liquid, provides a consistency suitable for spreading the paint on the surface. After spreading, the liquid evaporates, leaving behind the pigments and binder to form the residual paint layer.

A *dye* is distinguished from paint in that a dye is usually a soluble compound that binds directly to the material and does not require any medium to bind the coloring to the surface. In contrast, the pigments in paints are usually insoluble materials and have little or no affinity for the surface, so they are suspended in the binder to cause them to adhere to the surface. For example, cloth is dyed, while a metal surface may be painted.

Originally, pigments were prepared from very finely ground, naturally occurring minerals, or inorganic compounds. Modern pigments, with an enormous range of possible colors, continue to be created from both organic and inorganic sources. Historically, dyes came from living sources, such as plant or insect-derived compounds. Today, however, both paints and dyes are created from synthetically prepared organic compounds.

Depending on the end use, a painted surface may require a simple, single coat of paint or a very complex, multilayer process. Automotive finishes are among the most complex, aiming to achieve the desired color depth and sheen. Automobile paint finishes typically start with a primer layer that tightly binds to the metal or plastic unfinished piece of the car (Figure 15.43). The primer serves as a waterproof, stable foundation upon which to build subsequent colored layers and provides additional protection to the surface. Primers are designed to either chemically bind tightly to the surface or have physical properties that promote binding. Next, many coats of different paints of varying thicknesses are independently added on top of the primer. Each coat helps to add the depth and luster required for the finish; some may even have metallic flakes embedded within the layer. Finally, an outer clear coat is applied to the surface to provide protection and add the desired shine to the car's finish. The total process of covering the surface can involve many separate layers, as shown in Figure 15.44.

FIGURE 15.42   Solid pigments used for coloring paints.

Source: Shutterstock.com.

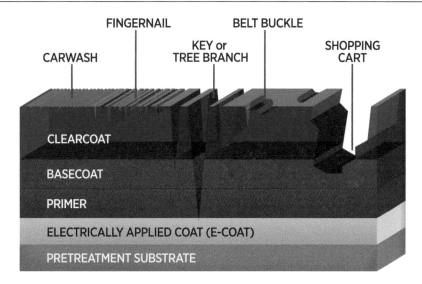

FIGURE 15.43 Typical types of paint coatings used in an automotive finish.

Source: Eastman Chemical Co./K. Irvine, NIST.

FIGURE 15.44 Typical multilayer automotive paint chip showing the complexity of layers built up to form the final product.

Source: Shutterstock.com.

The chemical identity of each of these layers, along with their thicknesses, can provide a very individualized connection between two pieces of paint evidence.

Upon drying, the binder and clear coat often chemically form a cross-linked polymer through air oxidation or ultraviolet light irradiation to form durable, hard surfaces. Two terms are important to distinguish in this process. Drying is simply the evaporation of the solvent from the paint, while curing involves a chemical reaction, such as polymerization, to form the final coating. For example, Lacquers are coatings that use simple evaporation to form the coating,

leaving behind a hard, solid layer. Lacquer coatings will readily dissolve when a solvent is added, however, so they are not usually suitable for coatings that will come in contact with solvents. Enamels, in contrast, form layers of tough, cross-linked polymeric materials when exposed to oxygen. Latex paints are water-based materials with a binder that is composed of very small polymer particles; when the solvent evaporates, the particles fuse together to form the insoluble coating. Variations upon these basic chemistries are possible, yielding an array of different paint products tailored to specific needs and demands.

15.4.3 Forensic Paint Analysis

Paint chip evidence may provide both class and individual characteristics, depending on the circumstances. Information about the chemical composition of a paint layer may come from several sources.

Infrared spectrophotometry is commonly employed to analyze the composition of the layer. In this case, the IR spectrum serves as a spectroscopic "fingerprint" for a paint layer, used in a comparison between two samples. X-ray diffraction has also been used to analyze the paint's components, often allowing analysis of the layer as it is received in the laboratory (*in situ*).

Another key method for the characterization of a paint sample is to analyze its color. As described in Section 15.1, paint pigments absorb part of the visible spectrum of light, allowing only some wavelengths to be reflected (or transmitted) from the surface for us to see. In essence, the pigments act as filters, blocking certain wavelengths of light while the reflected wavelengths are allowed to pass. In this subtractive color scheme, the wavelengths of light that are not absorbed form our perception of the color of the object. For example, if the pigments absorb green and blue light, the color appears red to the observer since the components of red light are reflected. Color or hue is experimentally measured using microspectrophotometers that examine the ultraviolet (190 to 380 nm) and visible (380 to 800 nm) ranges of the spectrum.

Gas pyrolysis mass spectrometry is also used in the analysis of paints. In this process, the paint chip is heated to form volatile gases from the components of the paint. These volatile compounds are measured both by the gas chromatograph (retention time of each fraction) and mass spectrometry (identity of each fraction).

BOX 15.5   HUNTING A "FOX"

In 1985, British serial rapist Malcolm Fairley, known as "the Fox", was caught and convicted largely on the basis of forensic paint analysis. At one particular crime scene in North London, investigators found tiny flakes of a very specific type of yellow paint on a tree about 45 in. (1.14 m) off the ground. The paint was analyzed and determined to be unique to the Austin Allegro car model made between 1973 and 1975 (called "Harvest Yellow"). This color was relatively rare, with only 1500 vehicles of this color ever made in the United Kingdom. Investigators began to visit every registered owner of these cars. When investigators visited Fairley, they found him cleaning a yellow Austin Allegro car that had scratches in the painted surface about 45 in off the ground. Fairley was immediately arrested and reportedly broke down and confessed to police during the trip to the station. Samples taken from the suspect's car were found to match those found at the crime scene. Fairley was convicted and sentenced to six life terms for the attacks, along with an additional 26 years for related offenses. He has, however, already been released under a new identity in the United Kingdom after serving less than 20 years of his 146-year sentence.

FIGURE 15.45   1975 Austin Allegro 2 door.

The physical properties of a paint sample can also be very informative in comparing two samples. The color, order of layers, and thickness of each layer are important factors to consider. Additionally, any impurities, weathering, or defects in the paint help to individualize the sample. Databases are available for automotive paint identification that can enable determination of the make, model, and years of manufacture of the vehicle based on paint evidence.

QUESTIONS FOR FURTHER PRACTICE AND MASTERY

15.1 Explain the difference between chemical and physical properties. Give examples of each.

15.2 What are intrinsic and extrinsic properties?

15.3 What methods are used to determine the volume of an irregularly shaped object?

15.4 Explain the density gradient technique used to determine the density of a substance.

15.5 What is viscosity?

15.6 What is refraction? Why does it happen?

15.7 What is the definition of: (a) angle of incidence, (b) angle of refraction, and (c) refractive index?

15.8 Consider a sample of glass that has an angle of refraction of 24° while the angle of incidence is 18°. What is the refractive index of the glass?

15.9 What is a Becke line? When is it observed?

15.10 What is birefringence?

15.11. What are proxy indicators?

15.12 What are some of the factors that make soil samples unique?

15.13 How does the complexity of a soil sample help a forensic scientist establish or eliminate a connection of the sample to a crime scene?

15.14 What is the difference between float glass and rolled glass? What is tempered glass?

15.15 What is "safety glass"?

15.16 What are radial and concentric cracks in glass?

15.17 True or False: In a stress-induced striation, the 90° angle side always faces the side away from where the crack originated for radial cracks.

15.18 True or False: In a radial crack, the surface where the crack starts is on the opposite side of the applied force.

15.19 True or False: In a concentric fracture, the fracture starts on the side nearest the applied force.

15.20 A car windshield has sustained a series of impacts. What simple rule regarding radial cracks can be used to determine the sequence of the impacts?

15.21 What measurements are usually the first ones made to determine what type of plastic has been sent to the crime lab for analysis?

15.22 What factors go into determining the physical and chemical properties of a polymer?

15.23 What are the typical three components of paint?

15.24 How does a dye differ from a paint?

15.25 What is the difference between drying and curing with respect to paint?

15.26 The use of gas pyrolysis mass spectrometry is used to analyze what components of paints?

15.27 When comparing two paint samples to see if they are similar, what physical properties are compared?

EXTENSIVE QUESTIONS

15.28 In the movie, *Monty Python and the Holy Grail*, a woman is accused of being a witch. To determine if she is indeed a witch, her density is to be determined by comparing her ability to float relative to a duck's ability to float. How does flotation work as a forensic tool to determine the relative density of a sample?

15.29 Explain the difference between additive and subtractive color combinations.

15.30 Light absorption from light sources differs from color perception from pigments. Explain how.

GLOSSARY OF TERMS

additive color mixing: adding together two colors of light to create a different color.

Becke line: the halo observed at the edges of a solid, transparent sample when immersed in a liquid with a higher refractive index (RI) than that of the sample. An optical phenomenon used in measuring the refractive index of an object.

binder: the portion of paint that suspends the pigment particles and helps to firmly fix them to the surface.

birefringence: a double refraction phenomenon in certain crystalline materials where the refractive index is different depending on the direction that the light travels through the material.

blown glass: the product of a process where molten glass is blown either into a mold to form shaped objects or formed freehand to generate art-glass pieces.

borosilicate glass: glass with boron oxide added to the silica to improve its ability to withstand rapid changes in temperature.

buoyancy: a method to determine the volume of an irregularly shaped object by determining the mass of the water (or liquid) displaced by the submerged object.

chemical properties: The properties that can be measured only by attempting to change the chemical identity of the material itself through a chemical transformation.

color: the way that our eyes and brain perceive different wavelengths of light in the visible wavelength range.

complimentary color: pairs of colors that, when mixed in the proper proportions, produce a neutral color (e.g., black or white). Sometimes referred to as "opposite" colors.

concentric cracks: the fractures in glass that form rings that approximately circle the point of impact.

conchoidal marks: see "Stress-induced striations."

density (d or ρ): defined as the amount of mass of a material contained in a given unit of volume, or $d = m/V$ (where d is density, m is mass, and V is volume).

dye: a soluble compound that binds directly to the surface and does not require any medium to bind.

extrinsic properties: the properties that change if the amount of material in the sample changes.

float glass method: the method for producing flat glass where a layer of molten glass comes out of a furnace as a continuous flat sheet that is then floated onto a bed of molten metal, most often tin.

floatation: a method for approximating the density of a sample by determining the density of a liquid upon which the sample will float.

geology: the detailed study of the Earth and its materials along with the physical processes that act upon them.

glass: an amorphous solid material, composed primarily of silicon dioxide (SiO_2).

intrinsic properties: the properties that are the same no matter how much material is present in the sample.

laminated glass: a form of safety glass where a piece of clear plastic or resin is sandwiched or "laminated" between two pieces of glass.

paint: an opaque coating that binds to the surface of an object.

paint solvent: the liquid component of paint that provides a consistency suitable for spreading the paint on the surface.

physical properties: properties that can be measured without changing the chemical identity of a material.

pigment: the portion of paint, consisting of very tiny colored particles of organic and inorganic compounds, that gives the paint its characteristic hue.

plastics: materials that can be molded; today they are often made from high molecular weight polymeric compounds.

proxy indicators: small amounts of identifiable material from a specific location that can indicate with relatively high accuracy information about the location from which they originated.

radial cracks: fractures in glass that extend or "radiate" outwards from the central point of impact, producing a "star-like" pattern.

refractive Index: the ratio of the speed of light between two transparent substances (usually the air and another substance, such as glass or plastic), calculated as the velocity of light in vacuum (or air) divided by the velocity of light in the substance. Used to characterize transparent materials.

rolled glass method: the method for producing flat glass that uses rollers to press the molten glass into a flat shape, often imprinting an indented design into the glass.

soda-lime glass: glass produced by adding various compounds to the molten silica, including sodium carbonate (Na_2CO_3), lime (CaO), alumina (Al_2O_3), or salts (NaCl or others).

soil: a mixture of inorganic (mineral) and organic components that are packed together relatively loosely with solid, liquid, and gaseous fractions.

stress-induced striations: rib marks that appear on the edge of broken glass.

subtractive color mixing: the color that occurs when mixing pigments together and arises from one color being removed from white light through absorption by the pigment.

tempered glass: glass that has been either heated or chemically treated to change the stresses within the glass to make it safer upon breaking.

viscosity: the resistance of a liquid to flow.

volume by displacement: a method to determine the volume of an irregularly shaped object by directly measuring the volume of liquid it displaces when submerged.

BIBLIOGRAPHY

Brian Caddy (Ed.), *Forensic Examination of Glass and Paint: Analysis and Interpretation*, CRC Press, 2001.

Charles Catanese, *Color Atlas of Forensic Medicine and Pathology*, CRC Press, 2016.

James M. Curran, Tacha N. Hicks, and John S. Buckleton, *Forensic Interpretation of Glass Evidence*, CRC Press, 2007.

Arthur Conan Doyle, *The Sign of Four*, 1890.

Forensic Glass Examination Guidelines, Scientific Working Group on Materials Analysis (SWGMAT), 2004, www.swgmat.org/Introduction%20to%20Forensic%20Glass%20Examination.pdf

Forensic Paint Analysis and Comparison Guidelines, Scientific Working Group on Materials Analysis (SWGMAT), 2000, www2.fbi.gov/hq/lab/fsc/backissu/july1999/painta.htm

Raymond C. Murray, *Evidence from the Earth: Forensic Geology and Criminal Investigation*, Mountain Press Publ. 2004.

Raymond C. Murray, *Forensic Geology*, Prentice Hall, 1998.Karl Ritz, Lorna Dawson, and David Miller (Eds.), *Criminal and Environmental Soil Forensics*, Springer, 2008.

Alastair Ruffell and Jennifer McKinley, *Geoforensics*, Wiley, 2008.

Firearms, Ballistics, and Impression Evidence

16

16.1 FORENSIC FIREARMS AND BALLISTICS

LEARNING GOALS AND OBJECTIVES

Firearms are frequently used in the commission of criminal acts. After completing this chapter, you should be able to:

- Explain how firearms developed and their basic principles of operation.
- Describe the main features and differences between handguns, long guns, and shotguns.
- Explain what is meant by ballistics and what factors affect the trajectory of a projectile, especially including terminal ballistics.
- Discuss how firearm weapons and ammunition design affect functional aspects of the weapon.

16.1.1 Introduction

Firearms have played a key role in human history and they clearly remain a ubiquitous part of society worldwide today. Everyone who has ever been to the movies or watched television is well acquainted with our fascination with firearms. "Westerns" have made famous the 19th-century revolver-carrying outlaw confronting the rifle-wielding law officers. War movies and urban crime shows frequently depict handgun and automatic weapon use in all types of settings. We see handguns carried by our law officers, long guns by hunters, and even larger weapons by members of the armed services. The use of firearms in both criminal and mass terrorist acts is increasing, while the regulation of firearm access is hotly debated and contested. There is no denying that firearms are a part of our everyday lives (Figure 16.1).

Today, firearms are by far the most common weapon used for deadly assault and are involved in an overwhelming number of robberies and other types of violent and assault crimes (Figure 16.2). When firearms are used in the commission of a real-life crime, forensic science plays a central role in linking a firearm and a criminal together.

16.1.2 Historical Perspective

In order to understand how modern firearms work, it is necessary to roughly understand how these weapons have evolved over the years and how they continue to rapidly change today. It all began with the invention of gunpowder. This first chemical explosive was discovered by Chinese alchemists sometime around the 9th century CE and was used initially in fireworks to "scare away evil spirits." At least by the early 13th century, however, the Chinese had invented and begun using simple versions of firearms, but it wasn't until the start of the 14th century that these weapons began to be developed into more reliable implements of warfare and personal assault. Early weapons were very crude and were referred to simply as "hand cannons" (Figure 16.3), a device that grew out of the much older 10th-century fire-lances; a hollow tube filled with gunpowder at the end of a spear that functioned similarly to a rough flamethrower when ignited. In a modest

FIGURE 16.1 Firearms identification and analysis are important parts of modern forensic science and criminal justice. Connecting a bullet with a specific firearm is often central to the investigation of a shooting event.

Source: Shutterstock.com.

DOI: 10.4324/9781003183709-20

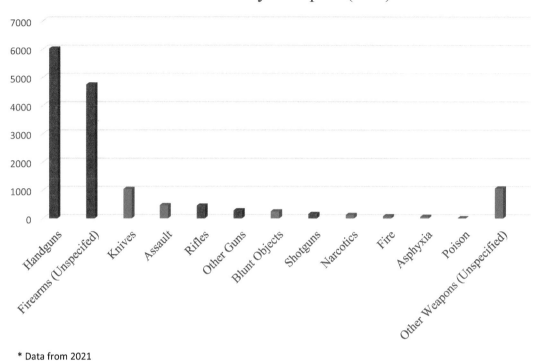

FIGURE 16.2   Relative use of firearm weapons (shown in red) compared to other lethal methods (shown in blue) for homicides in the United States.

FIGURE 16.3 Chinese "hand cannon" from a 15th-century manuscript by Konrad Kyeser von Eichstadt (*Bellifortis,* 1405, also called the *Kyeser Codex*).

Source: Retrieved from Wikimedia Commons; used per Creative Commons Attribution.

advance over the earlier fire-lances, hand cannons worked simply by placing gun powder at the closed end of a tube, tamping projectiles, such as stones or metal shrapnel, into the tube and igniting the gunpowder through a small hole above the powder. Obviously, such weapons were relatively ineffective as firearms because of their extreme inaccuracy, difficulty, and slowness of charging them, and the personal hazards that they presented to the shooter (they tended to explode rather than shoot). They were, however, more effective than bows and arrows and other early weapons in certain situations. For example, hand cannons could be quickly made in relatively large numbers and shot by inexperienced soldiers with only a brief training period, as opposed to arrow-based weapons where it took months to build a good bow or crossbow and sometimes months or even years to master shooting effectively. It didn't take people long to recognize the potential advantages that gunpowder-based weapons provided for assaulting enemies from "safe" distances, beyond the range of retaliatory spears and arrows. The recognition of these battlefield advantages spurred experimentation and new designs in firearm operation. It could well be argued that the history of the world, especially national borders and political regimes, has been shaped by waves of innovation in firearm technology.

Paralleling the early development of better gun mechanics was the necessity to improve the explosive properties of the gunpowder itself. Modifications in the relative amounts of gunpowder's primary components (carbon, sulfur, and potassium nitrate), along with the occasional introduction of small amounts of other chemicals, produced more reliable, faster-burning, and higher-power explosives. These chemical advances required stronger gun chambers made of metal instead of the previously used wooden barrels to withstand the explosive power of the new powder. The use of more regularly shaped projectiles, especially those which prevented the propulsive gas from escaping around the shot without moving it down the barrel, began to be adopted. The combined developments in chemistry and machinery coupled to produce new weapons that could launch their projectiles farther and with much greater accuracy than ever before possible. Once again, each small success drove further experimentation and development toward the realization of the great potential of firearms to alter the balance of power on the field of battle.

Firearms apparently spread either through trade routes or by invasion forces to the Middle East and Europe by the early 1300s. The hand cannons quickly evolved in Europe into much larger bore cannons used to help break sieges and bring down fortifications. Eventually, the rather crude personal hand cannons also gave rise to several new designs, in particular those with greatly improved ignition mechanisms such as the matchlock and wheelock igniters. All these designs, however, were ultimately replaced by the vastly improved flintlock weapons of the early 17th century. These *flintlock* weapons involved a long, hollow metal barrel, higher energy gunpowder, and vastly improved shot and firing mechanisms. The heart of the flintlock firing system made use of a spark created by moving a piece of flint over a steel plate (the "frizzen") to ignite a small primer charge that then set fire to the main explosive charge (Figure 16.4). Flintlock guns, however, suffered from many drawbacks, including poor reliability (e.g., misfires, accidental firing, no firing, barrel fouling, and explosions), the inability to be fired in wet conditions, high maintenance, slow firing, and rather severe safety problems. Despite these difficulties, flintlock muskets fueled the armies of much of the world between the mid-17th and mid-19th centuries, in some places even into the 20th century. In these flintlock guns, most of the familiar

components of modern guns came together for the first time: the long barrel, a highly explosive charge, and an efficient firing mechanism for igniting the charge.

Flintlock muskets and earlier firearms, where the gunpowder, wadding, and bullets all had to be loaded down the barrel of the gun ("*muzzle-loading*"), eventually gave way to *breech-loading* firearms in the mid-19th century. A breech-loading weapon places the ammunition directly into the firing chamber without having to put it down the barrel. The transition point between the older muzzle-loading and the modern breech-loading weapons involved the advent of something called a *percussion cap* (Figure 16.5). These caps were small metal cases that contained a tiny amount of a shock-sensitive explosive, such as mercury fulminate. When the percussion cap was struck with the gun's hammer, the explosive detonated and ignited the main charge of the ammunition. This meant that the shooter did not need to fuss with the complexity of priming the weapon but could simply charge the ammunition, snap on the percussion cap, and shoot. This type of ignition system also led to the development of the first efficient multi-shot revolvers, such as the "Pepper-box" revolver shown in Figure 16.6.

Military uses certainly drove much of the development of firearms, where accuracy, speed of firing, weapon durability, and the need for ever-increasing high-energy projectiles were of paramount importance. It didn't take too long to realize the advantage that could be provided by ammunition that combined a percussion cap igniter directly into a prepackaged unit along with the main explosive charge and bullet. The term ammunition, while originally used to describe anything used as a weapon, has come to most commonly refer collectively

FIGURE 16.4 Mechanism of a flintlock musket showing the flint (held in the upright arm) that strikes the steel plate (just to the right of the flint), forming a shower of sparks that ignites the priming powder when the trigger is pulled.

Source: Shutterstock.com.

to projectiles, explosives (e.g., gunpowder), and fuses taken together. Thus, breech-loading weapons were revolutionized by the advent of *fixed ammunition*: ammunition that combined primer, an accurately measured main charge, and a bullet all enclosed in a single, easily handled, watertight casing or *cartridge* (Figure 16.7). Each intact unit of firearm ammunition is usually referred to as a *round*. A complete fixed cartridge could be loaded directly into the firing chamber exceedingly rapidly as a self-contained, all-in-one unit. Prior to fixed ammunition, the primer, main charge, and bullet all needed to be "loaded" in separate actions, a slow and sometimes unreliable practice under anything but ideal conditions, especially in the heat of battle or adverse weather conditions, especially rain. Advances arising from the industrial revolution, however,

FIGURE 16.5 Percussion caps for breech-loaded weapons that were filled with the shock-sensitive explosive that ignited the main charge when struck by the hammer of the firearm.

Source: Used per Creative Commons Attribution-Share Alike 4.0, International. User: Friedrich Haag.

allowed for the rapid manufacture of millions of "rounds" of standardized fixed ammunition within small dimensional tolerances. This uniform ammunition could be quickly, reliably, and safely placed directly into a firing chamber and did not require operators to load each component individually. The famous Springfield rifles were among the first long guns to take full advantage of this technological breakthrough (Figure 16.8). An important aspect of breech-loading firearms is that the gun's barrel no longer had to be completely smooth; since the bullet and ammunition did not have to pass down the barrel, the barrel could be scored or rifled to vastly improve the accuracy of the weapon (see later sections describing rifling). Muzzle-loading barrels could not be grooved since ammunition would "foul" the grooves as it was loaded, leading to poor weapon functioning.

While fixed ammunition contained all the necessary components for firing, many different designs were explored in actual practice. In the most successful designs, including a large portion of the ammunition still used today, a shock-sensitive compound, such as mercury fulminate, lead styphnate, or a similar compound (see Chapter 14), is placed inside the metallic primer cap (firing cap) which is then snugly fitted into the main charge. Side, pin, rim, and center placements of the firing caps were all tried, although the center cap arrangement predominated both then and now. The net result is the same for all these different designs, however: a hammer strikes the cap, igniting the pressure-sensitive explosive that then ignites the main charge.

Advances in the rapid delivery of fresh ammunition and the extraction of spent cases allowed the development of efficient "repeater," semi-automatic, and fully automatic ("machine gun") weapons, including those that hold many cartridges of ammunition without the need for manual reloading. Today, there is an enormous variation in commercial and military weapons, from small-bore handguns to massive

FIGURE 16.6 Revolvers, such as the 1850s "Pepper-box" revolver with five barrels, became multi-shot, hand-held weapons possible through the use of percussion cap technology.

Source: Shutterstock.com.

FIGURE 16.7 19th-century fixed ammunition with bullet, main charge, and primer all-in-one complete unit.

Source: Retrieved from Wikimedia Commons; used per Creative Commons Attribution.

FIGURE 16.8 The Springfield Trapdoor Rifle from 1873 was one of the first mass-produced breech-loading rifles and was adopted by the U.S. Army.

Source: Used per Creative Commons Attribution-Share Alike 4.0, International. User: Gromitsonabarth.

artillery weaponry. The fastest military automatic machine guns today can shoot up to a staggering 1 million rounds per minute ("Metal Storm" weapon), while high-precision sniper rifles can hit moving targets several miles away with startling accuracy. Guns intended for civilian use are readily available in all shapes and sizes, from tiny derringers to very large hunting rifles, shotguns, and some semi-automatic weapons.

To better understand the weapons encountered in forensic work, Section 16.1.3 describes the major types of modern firearms and their modes of operation.

16.1.3 Firearm Basics

A firearm is usually defined as an assembly consisting of a barrel and a mechanical action that allows a projectile(s) to be propelled forward through the action of an extremely fast combustion reaction. As expected, given such a general definition, there is an enormous range and variety of firearms, spanning from miniature pistols to massive military weapon systems. But all these weapons have several basic features in common: an explosive material is detonated within an enclosed chamber, which provides only one direction for the escape of the

enormous pressure built up from the reaction. The release of this high-pressure gas is channeled to push a projectile down a tube toward a target with great energy. The combustion chamber where the explosion occurs is designed with only one escape route for the pressure; one open side with all the remaining sides sealed, like a box without a top. The projectile tightly fits within the walls of the chamber such that when the explosion occurs, the energy of the escaping gas acts upon the end surface of the projectile to force it down the barrel. All firearm designs must accommodate this basic mode of action in some fashion.

BOX 16.1   REMINDER

A mole is a unit of measure that contains a certain number of things, especially quantities of chemicals. One mole of carbon, sulfur, or CO_2 all contain the same number of items: 6.023×10^{23}. The mole allows us to compare quantities of very small items such as atoms and molecules where the numbers are very large, even in the smallest samples (see Chapter 12 for more on the mole).

(a)

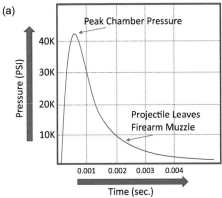

(b)

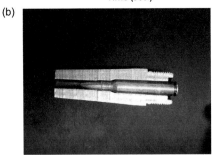

(c)

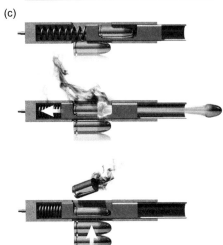

FIGURE 16.9 (a) The pressures generated upon firing a bullet. (b) A cutaway picture of a firearm barrel. (c) A schematic of the design to convert the chemical potential energy of gunpowder into the kinetic energy of the bullet motion, with the ejection of the spent casing.

Source: (b) Courtesy Matt Kurimsky. (c) Claus Lunau/Science Photo image. Used with permission.

The propulsive force given to a projectile most often comes from the rapid combustion of gunpowder. In this reaction, one mole of solid gunpowder may produce up to six moles of hot, expanding gas (depending on the type of powder used). This means that a relatively small volume of solid gunpowder can produce a very large volume of expanding gas. For example, if one gram of carbon were entirely converted to gaseous CO_2 at the combustion temperature of gunpowder (~3300°F), the CO_2 would occupy a volume of about 85 liters (ca. 3 ft³); an increase in volume well over 190,000 times! Since this volume of gas is confined initially to a very small space in the gun chamber, an

enormous pressure develops behind the bullet. For example, the pressure in the chamber of a common 0.223 rifle is on the order of 4,300 atmospheres (that's a pressure 4,300 times the pressure that is found on the surface of the Earth, or about 62,000 pounds per square inch, psi). The typical buildup of high-pressure gas upon firing a firearm is illustrated in Figure 16.9. This huge pressure is quickly relieved as the bullet is forced down the barrel with great energy and velocity.

Over time, gun designers have discovered a variety of innovative ways to modify all the features of firearms in order to maximize particular desired end results, such as accuracy, projectile mass, weapon size, bullet velocity, and terminal ballistics. In forensic science, however, three basic firearm designs are most commonly encountered: the handgun, rifle (long gun), and shotgun.

16.1.4 Handguns

Handguns are smaller firearms designed specifically for operation using one hand and represent a broad class of weapons that includes derringers, pistols, revolvers, and others. Sometimes, the word pistol is used interchangeably with handgun, but technically a pistol is just one specific type of handgun (one with the barrel and chamber in one solid piece). Handguns are the easiest firearms to carry as they are lighter in weight and can be more quickly and easily brought into action. They are, however, far less accurate over longer distances due to their relatively short barrels and, therefore, are most often considered primarily as defensive weapons. In one recent study, it was found that only 11% of handgun shots fired from assailants and 25% of the bullets fired by police hit their intended targets. In a close-in situation, it is far easier to keep a handgun's muzzle pointed at an attacker than a long-barreled rifle during a struggle. The components of typical handguns are shown in Figure 16.10.

Handguns come in a variety of designs that include single-shot and multi-shot variants. Single-shot handguns are usually used for target shooting and hunting. *Revolvers* feed the ammunition to the barrel of the gun by rotating a cylinder that contains several separate firing chambers loaded with filled cartridges. Once fired, the barrel is rotated to align another loaded chamber with the barrel. In this way, it is possible to rapidly fire typically between five and eight shots.

Both semi-automatic and fully automatic handguns have been developed. In a *semi-automatic* weapon, the energy released from one firing is used to mechanically eject the spent case and reload the next fresh round into the firing chamber. One round is fired for each pull of the trigger. In a *fully automatic* weapon, the filled rounds are reloaded as in the semi-automatic weapon, but the weapon continues to fire when the trigger is held down; multiple shots are fired from one trigger pull. Pistols are reloaded through the use of a magazine; a device that is spring-loaded with ammunition that forces a new cartridge into the firing chamber immediately after one round has been fired, as shown in Figures 16.10 and 16.11.

Revolvers tend to be simpler than the automatic weapons, easier to maintain, and are usually capable of firing larger bullets, while automatic weapons typically can shoot more rounds at a time and be reloaded faster.

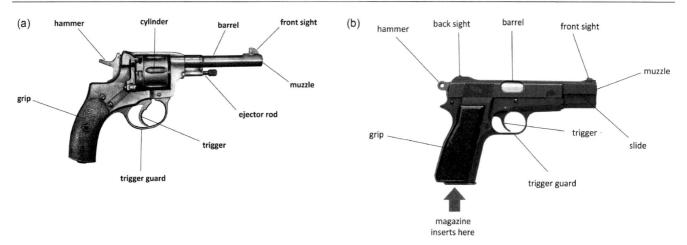

FIGURE 16.10 Parts of a typical revolver (a) and semi-automatic pistol (b) handgun.

Source: Images used with permission from Shutterstock.com.

FIGURE 16.11 Magazine used for reloading a pistol.

Source: Shutterstock.com.

BOX 16.2 "GHOST GUNS"

Today, small firearms are more available than ever. One particular type of weapon, however, is causing great concern with law enforcement and government officials. These are hard-to-trace homemade weapons, often referred to as "ghost guns," made from readily available components, which can be purchased without any background checks or regulations to assemble fully functional weapons. Often, these components are purchased inexpensively from hardware stores or online kits and don't carry serial numbers or other identifiers. Additionally, with advances in the ability to prepare complex items using computer-controlled 3D printing processes (additive manufacturing), functional weapons may be prepared using home-based printing devices. Currently, it is not legally prohibited by federal law to home-make firearms for personal use in the United States, as long as the firearm is not intended to be sold or transferred to someone else, although a recent Supreme Court decision (2023) has upheld federal restrictions on the manufacture of these "ghost" weapons.

16.1.5 Long Guns

Long guns are named for their relatively long barrels and include several types, such as the well-known rifle (Figure 16.12). The longer barrels of these weapons allow them to have far better accuracy over long distances than handguns and fire projectiles faster. Thus, long guns are best known for their accuracy while handguns are best appreciated for their convenience.

One of the major advances in improving the accuracy of firearms came from the discovery that forming spiral groves,

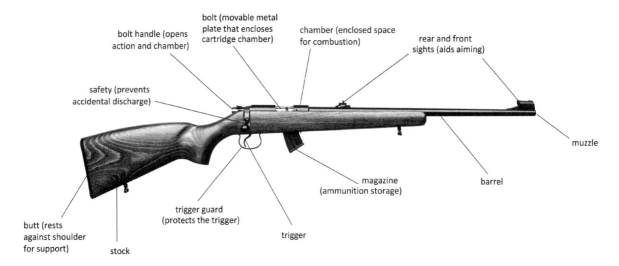

FIGURE 16.12 Parts of a typical rifle (long gun).

Source: Shutterstock.com.

called *rifling*, on the inside of the gun's barrel causes the projectile to spin about its long axis in a motion leading to something called spin or gyroscopic stabilization (Figure 16.13). Spinning an elongated projectile greatly improves its aerodynamic properties, allowing it to go much farther and with much better precision and accuracy. The improved stability and accuracy of a spinning bullet is similar to the stabilizing effect seen in the spinning of a football, "Frisbee" (flying disc) or child's top, as illustrated in Figure 16.14.

The rifling inside a gun's barrel may be described in several ways to provide useful characteristic information about an individual weapon. First, the number of grooves inscribed in the barrel, producing characteristic "lands" and "grooves" (Figure 16.13), may be counted. The *grooves* are the areas where some of the barrel metal has been removed to create a depression, leaving the "higher," untouched *lands* projecting farther into the center of the barrel. For example, the rifled barrel may have six grooves and six lands. Other guns may have between two and eight, or even more, grooves. Second, the handedness of the twist can be either to the right (dextrorotatory) or to the left (levorotatory), causing the bullets to spin in one particular direction. American rifles traditionally spin the bullets to the right while British rifles often are designed to cause left-handed spins. Finally, the length of the barrel necessary for a groove to make one full rotation of the twist (360°), called the twist rate, can be measured. For example, it might take 10 in. of barrel to complete one full rotation (1:10 twist) or 25 in. (1:25 twist), or any of many other possibilities. For example, a Remington .22 rifle has a 1:14 twist rate while a Winchester .243 has a 1:10 twist. The shorter the twist rate distance, the faster the bullet will spin. It is important to note that these rifling features are imprinted in relief on any bullet fired from the gun, greatly aiding in the identification of the gun that fired a particular bullet.

An alternative type of rifling, called polygonal rifling, has recently become common. In this type of weapon, the traditional lands and grooves are replaced by "hills" and "valleys" in a more rounded, polygonal (multi-sided shape),

(a)

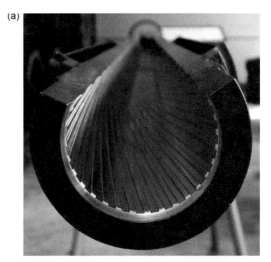

(b)

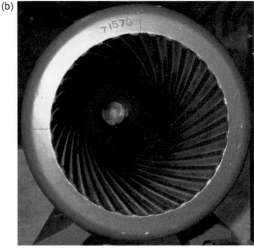

FIGURE 16.13 The inside of a gun barrel showing the grooved rifling that causes the projectile (bullet) to spin when it leaves the barrel.

Credit: **(a) Used per Creative Commons Share Alike 3.0, Unported. User: baku13. (b) Used per Creative Commons Attribution-Share Alike 2.0, Generic. User: David Holt.**

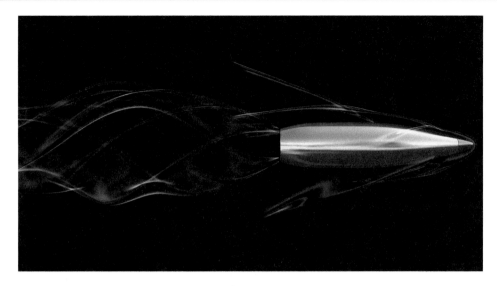

FIGURE 16.14 Spinning a projectile, such as a football, soccer ball, or bullet, greatly improves the aerodynamic performance of the object. The spin on this bullet can be seen from the spiraled trace behind the bullet.

Source: Shutterstock.com.

most often a hexagonal (six-sided) or octagonal (eight-sided) pattern (Figure 16.15). The advantage of polygonal barrels is that they are very fast and inexpensive to manufacture relative to traditionally grooved barrels. The process simply uses a tool (mandrel) with a polygonal shape that is first inserted into the round bore of the barrel. The barrel is then pressed ("cold forged") around the polygonal mandrel to form the shaped bore. These barrels are relatively smooth and have far fewer striations than traditionally grooved barrels since no material is "gouged" out but is instead simply pressed around a mold. Bullets fired from these polygonal barrels do have characteristic striation markings, although they are generally less pronounced than those found for other types of rifling.

Like handguns, long guns come in a variety of shapes and sizes. In many places, there is a minimum legal barrel length, 16" in the United States and Canada, for example. The firing mechanism can also be single-shot, semi-automatic or fully automatic in design.

16.1.6 Shotguns

Shotguns are often considered to be a type of long gun but are distinguished from other long guns by several design features and by the type of projectiles which are fired from them. Shotguns use ammunition that contains either many small pellets, called *shot*, packed into a single cartridge (Figure 16.16), or a single, solid projectile, called a *slug*. Because rifling would prematurely scatter the small pellets, shotgun barrels are smooth and not rifled. The gauge of a shotgun generally refers to the size of the shot used (Figure 16.16). The diameter of the shotgun's barrel is equal to the size of the balls that are needed to weigh one pound. For example, a 12-gauge shotgun's barrel is roughly the same diameter as a single ball weighing 1/12 of a pound, while a 20-gauge shotgun's barrel is the same as that

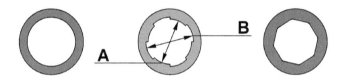

FIGURE 16.15 Cross-sections of polygonal (Right) and traditional (land and grooved) (Middle) land (A) and grooved (B) barrels.

Source: Retrieved from Wikimedia Commons; used per Creative Commons Attribution.

(a)

(b)

FIGURE 16.16 Shotgun cartridge components (a) and cross-section of a typical shotgun cartridge comparison (b).

Source: (b) iStockphoto.com. Credit: Arthit Pornpikanet.

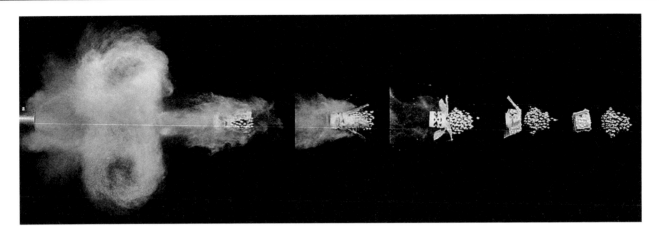

FIGURE 16.17   Sequence of pictures showing shotgun pellets spreading out after leaving the barrel of the gun.

Source: Used per Creative Commons Attribution 3.0 Unported. User: Andrew Davidhazy.

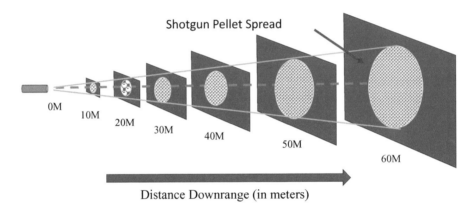

FIGURE 16.18   Scatter of shotgun pellets in relation to the distance from the gun.

of a shot weighing 1/20 of a pound. Once the shot leaves the barrel of the gun, the individual pellets scatter (Figure 16.17). The size of the scatter pattern increases as the distance from the gun increases (Figure 16.18).

Shotguns are particularly useful when precise aim is not important but projectile coverage of an area is desired instead, such as against a rapidly moving or airborne target. Shotguns are also used widely by police and military agencies in urban environments because the potential spread of the projectiles may increase the likelihood of hitting an intermediate range target without accurate aiming.

16.1.7 Air Guns

A commonly encountered family of "firearm-like" weapons that do *not* meet the usual definition for a firearm are air guns. These weapons are probably best considered within this group, however, because of their overall similarity of operation to firearms. Air gun weapons move a projectile solely by the release of stored gas pressure rather than through combustion. This group includes the common BB guns, air rifles, air pistols, and

some types of shotguns that expel projectiles by compressed gas, such as compressed air, CO_2, or nitrogen. These devices date their origin to at least the mid-1500s and have remained popular in certain settings since then.

Air guns have several advantages and drawbacks over conventional firearms. They are typically lightweight, relatively easy to manufacture, and can fire very rapidly and quietly in almost any physical environment, including in very wet conditions. Additionally, they can be readily improvised whenever a pneumatic source can be built (a source of pressurized gas) and don't require the careful storage necessary for powder-based ammunition. Air gun ammunition is most often shaped pellets or round balls that are extremely inexpensive; top-of-the-line "Olympic" air gun ammunition costs about 2¢ each compared with >50¢ each for some of the least expensive firearm ammunition. Compared to firearms, however, they tend to provide far less power and are less accurate over longer distances. Modern air guns are usually intentionally built for lower pressure operation for safety reasons, although air guns are available that can rival certain features of firearms. High-pressure air guns can expel projectiles at velocities over 1,100 ft/s and are popular with both target shooters and small game hunters.

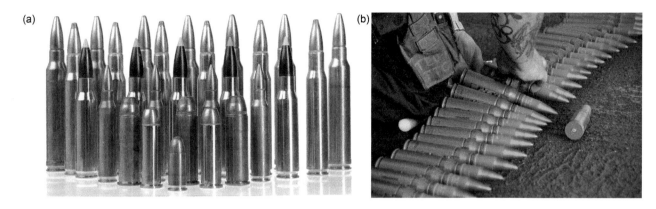

FIGURE 16.19 Some of the many types of ammunition available. These range from small <5 mm ammunition to the blue-tipped ammunition on the right which is nearly 12″ tall (25 mm).

Source: (a) Shutterstock.com; (b) Source: U.S. Navy photo by Mass Communication Specialist 2nd Class Daniel Barker.

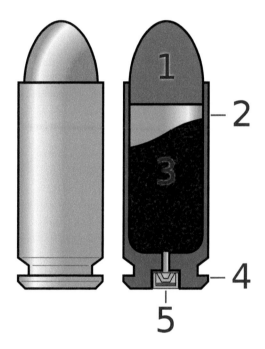

FIGURE 16.20 Typical rifle ammunition components include: (1) bullet, (2) cartridge case, (3) gunpowder, (4) rim holding powder, and (5) primer.

Source: Used per Creative Commons Attribution-Share Alike 3.0, Unported. User: Glrx.

16.1.8 Ammunition

The ammunition for firearms comes in as many variations as the weapons themselves. They vary depending upon which outcome the designers are attempting to optimize: speed, accuracy, distance, or other characteristics (Figure 16.19). Ammunition is most often defined by the size of the gun barrel that it is designed for, usually given as a caliber or mm measurement. *Caliber* is the size of a gun barrel, measured between opposite grooves, and expressed as a fraction of an inch. For example,

a barrel with a diameter of 0.22 in. is referred to as .22 caliber. The diameter can also be expressed in mm (1/1000 of a meter), such as 9 mm. Even though caliber actually refers to the size of the gun's bore, cartridges are referred to by the caliber of the weapon in which they are intended to be used. As described previously, shotguns are usually defined by gauge rather than caliber or mm used for other firearms.

Ammunition is also defined by the amount and type of powder used, the dimensions and shape of the projectile, composition of the bullet (what metals make up the alloy used in the bullet), and other features. An example of typical rifle ammunition is shown in Figure 16.20. Some ammunition is "super-charged," called magnum ammunition, and contains more than the usual complement of explosive propellant.

> **BOX 16.3 SOME HELPFUL FIREARMS DEFINITIONS**
>
> **Action**: Mechanical apparatus of a firearm that loads, fires, and ejects the cartridge.
> **Barrel**: Metal pipe that guides the initial flight of the bullet.
> **Breech:** End of the gun barrel nearest to the action.
> **Breech Block (or Face)**: Back of the firing chamber.
> **Bullet**: Projectile fired from a weapon.
> **Caliber**: Diameter of the gun barrel, expressed in 1/100th of an inch.
> **Cartridge**: Ammunition made up of casing, primer, powder, wadding, and bullet.
> **Chamber**: Enclosure that contains the cartridge when ready to fire.
> **Gauge**: Measure of the diameter of the barrel of a shotgun.
> **Hammer**: The part of the action that drives the firing pin into the primer upon firing.
> **Lands and Grooves**: The spiral grooves and raised positions inside a gun barrel resulting from rifling.

Magazine: Device for holding and delivering cartridges.

Magnum: Type of cartridge containing more than the standard amount of powder, resulting in more power to the bullet.

Muzzle: The end of the gun barrel where the bullet exits the weapon.

Powder: Solid explosive used to propel the bullet.

Primer: Shock-sensitive compound that ignites the main charge of a cartridge upon being struck.

Rifling: The spiral grooves or polygonal interior shape inside a gun barrel that causes the bullet to spin.

Sight: Device on top of a gun that improves aim and accuracy.

Silencer: Device, placed over the muzzle, that reduces the noise emitted when the weapon is discharged.

Stock: Frame holding the barrel and action together which allows aiming and firing.

16.1.9 Ballistics

Ballistics is the study of how projectiles move through space. The field is particularly concerned with how the flight of a projectile can be influenced by features such as projectile shape, the force used to drive the projectile forward, and aerodynamic considerations. Gun and ammunition designers work to understand the factors that affect the flight of projectiles and optimize features that lead to the desired characteristics of the flight. The ballistics of a projectile are usually considered in three "phases": internal (initial), external (intermediate), and terminal ballistics.

Internal Ballistics: Internal, or initial, ballistics deals with the part of a bullet's path that occurs within the gun itself. The explosion of gunpowder in the chamber causes a large force to be applied to the base of the bullet, propelling it forward. Pressure is a measure of the force applied to a given surface area; in this case, the area of the end of the bullet. Rifles usually generate far more pressure than handguns: 70,000 psi for a rifle compared with 40,000 psi for a typical handgun, leading to a much higher force applied to the bullet. Higher pressures require stronger chambers and generate more recoil and combustion byproducts. The force of the expanding gas continues to accelerate the bullet down the entire length of the barrel; the longer the barrel, generally the higher the acceleration and the faster the bullet is traveling when it leaves the firearm.

External Ballistics: External, or intermediate, ballistics focuses on the flight of the bullet from the time it leaves the barrel of the gun until it reaches the target. Several features define the specific flight properties of a bullet, including the energy propelling it forward, the bullet's shape, its mass, and environmental conditions (e.g., wind, rain, etc.).

The ideal situation in gun design would be to convert as much of the energy as possible from the contained explosion into

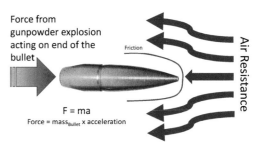

Force from gunpowder explosion acting on end of the bullet

Friction

Air Resistance

F = ma
Force = mass$_{bullet}$ × acceleration

FIGURE 16.21 Effect of air resistance, or drag, in opposing the forward motion of a bullet through the air.

moving the projectile down the barrel. This process represents a conversion of the chemical energy of the gunpowder into the kinetic energy of the projectile. Kinetic energy, the energy of motion, is given by the expression $KE = \frac{1}{2} mv^2$ (where m is the mass and v is the velocity of the projectile) and describes the force moving the projectile in a straight line. The more energy applied to the bullet (the more powder used in the ammunition), the faster a bullet of a given mass will move. Another way to look at this is that as the bullet becomes larger, more explosive force will be needed to move it to a specific velocity.

Opposing the forward motion of a bullet is *drag* or air resistance (Figure 16.21). As a bullet moves through the air, it must displace the air in its path, creating friction that hinders its forward motion. The amount of drag depends largely on the size and shape of the bullet.

Gravity also plays a crucial role in determining a bullet's trajectory. Gravity constantly pulls objects downward with a constant force (Force = mg, where m is mass and g is the gravitational constant). In fact, a bullet simply dropped vertically at the same instant as one fired horizontally from a rifle (at the same height above the ground) will hit the ground at exactly the same moment as the fired bullet (Figure 16.22). A bullet fired at twice the speed of sound will drop about 3 in. in 100 yards and about 30 in. by the time it has traveled 300 yards (Figure 16.23). However, the faster a bullet travels, the less it will drop over a fixed distance because it takes less time to reach the target when moving faster.

Bullets typically do not follow completely straight-line paths to a target but instead "wobble" and rotate, as shown in Figure 16.24. The more wobble and rotation in a bullet generally lead to less accuracy in reaching its target. The design of a bullet has much to do with both how the bullet travels through the air and what happens when it strikes a target (terminal ballistics). For example, a thin, needle-like bullet has reduced air resistance and may travel very rapidly and accurately but imparts very little of its kinetic energy to any object it hits, slicing through the target with less damage. In contrast, a round bullet has far greater air resistance, causing it to travel more slowly and less accurately, but it would deliver most or all its energy into the target, causing far more damage (assuming it actually makes it to the target). Therefore, many bullet designs are available that deal with these conflicting features to optimize a desired outcome.

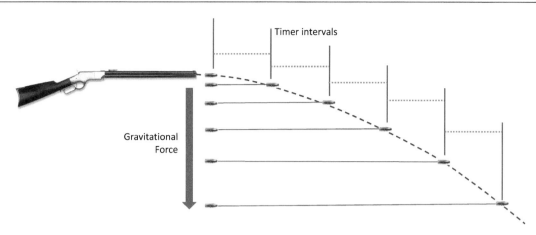

FIGURE 16.22   Two bullets of the same mass, one fired and one dropped vertically at the same moment, will reach the ground at the same instant.

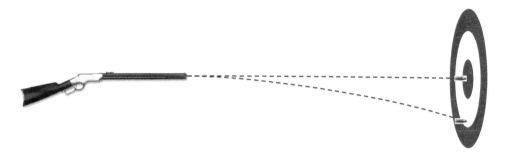

FIGURE 16.23   The downward effect of gravity on the trajectory of a bullet.

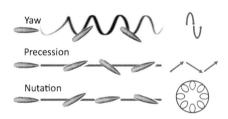

FIGURE 16.24   The "wobble" (yaw) and "rotation" (pitch/roll or precession/nutation) of a typical bullet as it moves along its trajectory.

Terminal Ballistics: Terminal ballistics describes what happens when a bullet hits its target. Biological aspects of a bullet hitting a living object, including tissue damage, have already been presented in detail in Chapter 8. Bullets may tumble, flatten (Figure 16.25), fragment, and melt when they encounter a target (Figure 16.26). The pattern of injury or damage depends upon the shape, speed, and motion of the bullet when it strikes. Significant damage may also result from the impact of shock waves arising from the compression and rarefaction of air along the path of the bullet (Figure 16.27). The more energy that the projectile can impart to its target, the more damage will be done.

FIGURE 16.25   The deformation of a bullet after impact (terminal ballistics).

Source: Courtesy and used with permission of Philip Orlando.

FIGURE 16.26 Slow-motion photograph of a spherical bullet entering and traveling through a water ball.

Source: Shutterstock.com.

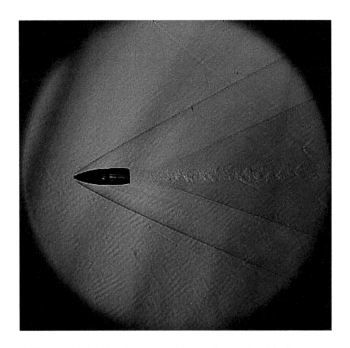

FIGURE 16.27 Shockwave produced from a fired bullet traveling through the air (bullet is at the left of the picture).

Source: Used per Creative Commons Attribution 4.0, International. User: Nathan Boor.

BOX 16.4   RIGHT TO BEAR ARMS

In the United States, the 2nd Amendment to the U.S. Constitution deals with the right of people to own firearms. The Amendment says, "A well regulated militia being necessary to the security of a free State, the right of the People to keep and bear arms shall not be infringed."

A vigorous debate continues today, however, about what the "right to bear arms" phrase in this amendment really means. Some argue that it refers to private individuals, while others contend that it includes only the military use of arms (well-regulated militia). The Supreme Court has historically interpreted this phrase as referring to an *individual's right* to own and carry weapons, within reasonable limits. In both 2008 and 2010, the Supreme Court ruled in two 2nd Amendment cases that the wording protects an individual's right to "possess a firearm, unconnected to service in a militia and to use that firearm for traditionally lawful purposes, such as self-defense within the home." They did, however, also support limitations on what type of weapons fall into this category of "lawful use." However, this intense debate continues today.

16.2 FORENSIC IDENTIFICATION OF FIREARMS

16.2.1 Introduction

Firearm identification may play a valuable role in forensic investigations. Important questions as to how and by whom gun-related crimes were committed may be answered through a detailed examination of the bullets and firearms recovered either from a crime scene or taken from suspects. The Association of Firearm and Toolmark Examiners (AFTE) has defined the field of forensic firearms identification as determining "if a bullet, cartridge case, or other ammunition component was fired by a particular firearm." In this section, we will focus on several of the most important types of firearms investigations that are routinely employed.

16.2.2 Bullet Comparisons

Firearm evidence, especially bullets and ammunition casings, may be recovered from crime scenes. Investigators usually want to know key information such as the type of gun that fired the recovered bullets and the likelihood that they were fired from one specific weapon. If they can link a suspect to a specific weapon that fired the shots, much of an investigation can quickly fall into place. Fortunately, there are several well-established ways that this type of information can be provided.

Bullets recovered from a crime scene can sometimes be measured to provide information about the caliber and the type of ammunition. Additionally, the chemical composition of a bullet, along with the composition of any gunpowder residue and material from the gun barrel, can be analyzed to provide comparative information. This data significantly limits the possible range of weapons that the bullet could have been fired from, along with the possible manufacturers of the ammunition, narrowing the search for the weapon down significantly.

One of the best ways, however, of connecting a bullet with a type of weapon or even with one particular weapon comes from a close examination of the rifling marks that were inscribed upon the bullet as it passed down the gun's barrel. The rifling, the lands and grooves inside the barrel of a gun that cause the bullet to spin upon firing, are made in a variety of ways, all of which are employed today in the manufacture of weapons. Methods may be employed to form the grooves in the metal on the inside of the barrel either all at once or one groove at a time. A broach cutter (Figure 16.28) is used to cut all of the grooves simultaneously by forcing a cutter head down the smooth, drilled-out barrel of the gun while rotating the cutter with a characteristic twist rate. A second method, probably the most commonly employed technique today, employs a hot "button" that is forced down the smooth barrel at very high pressures, *compressing* the metal into the grooved shapes *rather than cutting* the grooves into the metal. Alternatively, a mandrel (a sort of rod-shaped, grooved template) that has raised ribs corresponding to the desired rifling grooves is first inserted into a slightly oversized, smooth barrel, and then the barrel is compressed or hammered into shape around the mandrel, leaving the grooves and lands formed inside the barrel when the mandrel is removed.

When a bullet passes along the barrel of a gun, the softer metal of the bullet is distorted and shaped to match the lands and grooves of the barrel. Examination of the fired bullet can then show imprinted patterns from the firearm that it was fired from, including the number of grooves, the direction of twist (left-handed or right-handed), and the twist rate (Figure 16.29). Investigative agencies, such as the FBI, maintain databases of this type of information for an enormous number of manufactured weapons. This information, coupled with the caliber and overall shape and chemical composition of the bullet, can identify unambiguously the make and model of the weapon that shot the bullet: very useful class characteristics. Similarly, if the number, size, handedness, and twist of a bullet do not *all* match a suspect gun, then that gun can be eliminated as a possible weapon used for firing the bullet. But recovered bullets can also provide individual information as well as class characteristic information about the gun that fired them.

The mechanical process of first drilling out the smooth bore of the gun barrel and then forming the rifling grooves in the barrel leaves tiny random imperfections, called *stria*, in the metal walls of the barrel (Figure 16.30). These imperfections from the manufacturing process are thought to be unique to each individual weapon, a sort of "signature" for the weapon.

FIGURE 16.28 A broach cutter (metal reamer) that forms all of the grooves at once when forced down the barrel of the gun.

Source: Shutterstock.com.

FIGURE 16.29 Marks from a gun barrel's rifling on fired bullets.

Source: Images used courtesy Shutterstock.com.

FIGURE 16.30   Stria, or imperfections, occurring on the barrel of a handgun.

Source: Shutterstock.com.

FIGURE 16.31   Test-firing a suspect gun into a water tank in order to compare the stria on the test-fired bullet with the stria on an unknown bullet.

Source: Used with permission and courtesy of Matt Kurimsky, Onondaga Co. Forensic Laboratory.

Additionally, each time the weapon is fired, the barrel is slightly scratched by the passage of the bullet to form individual characteristics in the pattern of each firearm barrel's imperfections. These tiny imperfections are imprinted in the soft metal of the bullet as it rapidly travels down the barrel when fired. Matching the stria from a fired bullet with the stria inside a particular weapon can provide very convincing evidence that the bullet was actually fired from that particular weapon.

It is, however, exceedingly difficult to directly compare the internal striae on the inside of the barrel directly with those on a fired bullet. Instead, the matching process usually involves test firing a bullet from the suspect gun using ammunition comparable to the crime scene bullet (Figure 16.31). The striae on the test-fired bullet are then compared with those on the unknown bullet using a comparison microscope. Matching these striae can indicate a high probability that the two bullets were fired from the same weapon, as illustrated in Figure 16.32.

It is not uncommon, however, for the stria not to match exactly at every point between the test-fired bullet and the bullet in question. These differences can arise from several causes. Bullets are often distorted or even largely destroyed upon impact, providing only a small amount of surface area suitable for comparison. Also, the striations in a weapon are not permanent features but change slightly with each and every bullet fired. Thus, even two successively fired bullets are expected to have slightly different patterns. Nonetheless, the stria patterns between two bullets fired from the same weapon usually are overwhelmingly the same.

Since shotgun barrels are not rifled and use small shot instead of bullets, striae are not typically useful in shotgun identification. However, if the wad, the paper or plastic piece that pushes the cluster of shot down the barrel upon firing, is recovered, it can often be related back to the gauge of the shotgun and possibly even to the manufacturer of the ammunition.

(a)

(b)

FIGURE 16.32   (a) Comparison of a test-fired and an unknown bullet (note the vertical dividing line between the two bullet images in the center of the picture) and (b) a fragment match to damage on a suspect bullet.

Source: Used with permission and courtesy of Matt Kurimsky, Onondaga Co. Forensic Laboratory.

16.2.3 Other Stria Comparisons

There are a number of other places where the tiny stria imperfections can be imprinted upon various components of fired ammunition and firearms. For example, when a bullet is fired, a firing pin forcefully strikes the detonator in the ammunition

FIGURE 16.33 Matching patterns using a comparison microscope from two cartridge cases, one test fired and the other from an unknown weapon.

Source: Used with permission and courtesy of Matt Kurimsky, Onondaga Co. Forensic Laboratory.

to set off the primer charge. Any pattern on the firing pin can be transferred *via* this impact to the end of the cartridge case. Comparing the firing pin pattern on test-fired and crime scene cartridge casings can link the weapon and the recovered bullet (Figures 16.33 and 16.34).

Relatively recently, some firearm manufacturers have begun to microscopically stamp identification information onto the end of the firing pin. When the cartridge is struck by the pin, the information is transferred from the pin to the casing. This allows for the rapid identification of the make, manufacturer, and sometimes even the manufacturing lot of the weapon that fired the ammunition.

When a bullet is fired, the explosive reaction propels the bullet forward and at the same time it pushes the metal ammunition casing backward with equal force. When this cartridge casing strikes the back of the firing chamber (called the breech block or breech face), any imperfections in the metal surface of the breech are transferred to the end of the casing. Thus, comparing a test-fired and crime scene casing can link a casing with a particular gun (Figure 16.35). In all this work, the comparison microscope provides a convenient method for comparing the test-fired and recovered firearm evidence (Figure 16.36).

In automatic and semi-automatic weapons, a mechanical extractor ejects spent casings after each bullet is fired to allow a new cartridge to be loaded. When this happens, the extractor can scratch the sides of the casing in unique ways that are useful in identifying the type and possibly even the individual weapon, as shown in Figure 16.37.

Of course, fingerprints and other similar markings can also be found on bullet casings and gun handles. It is sometimes quite amazing that criminals may be very careful about fingerprints elsewhere at a crime scene and

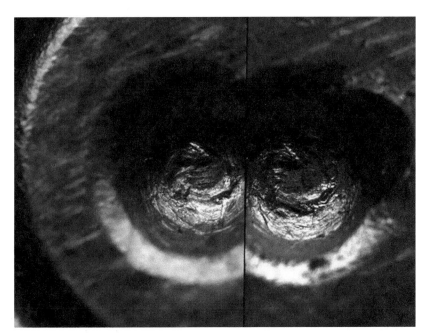

FIGURE 16.34 Microscopic image of a firing pin impression comparison between test-fired and recovered cartridges.

Source: Used with permission and courtesy of Matt Kurimsky, Onondaga Co. Forensic Laboratory.

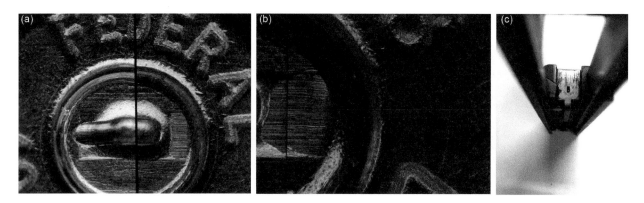

FIGURE 16.35   (a) Breech face marks, (b) firing pin aperture shear marks, and (c) breech block impressions on a Glock handgun.

Source: Used with permission and courtesy of Matt Kurimsky, Onondaga Co. Forensic Laboratory.

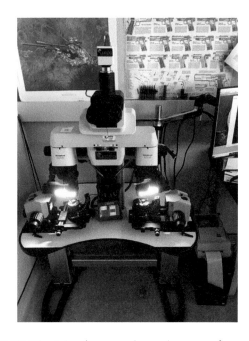

FIGURE 16.36   A Leeds comparison microscope for comparing test-fired and recovered firearm evidence.

Source: Used with permission and courtesy of Matt Kurimsky, Onondaga Co. Forensic Laboratory.

completely forget about transferring their fingerprints to the cartridges when they handle ammunition while loading the gun (Figure 16.38).

16.2.4 Gunshot Residues (GSR)

When a weapon is discharged, not all the powder is dissipated as a gas. Some of the unreacted explosive charge, along with solid combustion byproducts, are discharged from every opening in the gun, especially from the muzzle, into the nearby environment. These telltale residues often coat the hands, clothing, and body of the shooter and victim if they are close enough (Figure 16.39). Swabs taken from potentially contaminated surfaces can be chemically analyzed using a variety of techniques, especially atomic absorption, X-ray diffraction, and scanning electron microscopy, to show that a discharge has taken place nearby (Figures 16.40 and 16.41). Especially useful are analyses for lead, barium, copper, chromium, and antimony (Figure 16.42). Scanning electron microscopy can also be used to compare the shapes of the residue particles and help determine the type of powder used in the ammunition.

When a firearm is discharged, gunshot residue is propelled out of the barrel of the gun. This residue can travel up

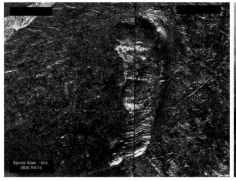

FIGURE 16.37   Marks left by an extractor when a semi-automatic weapon expels a spent ammunition casing.

Source: Used with permission and courtesy of Matt Kurimsky, Onondaga Co. Forensic Laboratory.

FIGURE 16.38 A forensic scientist examining a fired bullet casing using a technique that allows fingerprints to be visualized on metal surfaces. Fingerprints slightly corrode metal surfaces and, when a current is passed through the metal which has been coated in a fine conducting powder, the corroded area attracts the powder.

Source: Brian Bell/Science Photo image. Used with permission.

to about 10 ft and still be detected upon a surface in its path, such as on clothing, a victim's body, or a wall. As the residue moves away from the muzzle (end of the barrel), it tends to spread out. Determining how much spread occurs is usually done by firing a series of test shots at various distances and experimentally measuring the spread and density of the GSR on the surface. Knowing how the residue spreads out, a muzzle-to-target distance can be estimated by measuring the size pattern of any residue present on clothing or any other surface of the target. Often, sufficient information can be gained through simple visual or microscopic inspection of the target material, but chemical analysis is also commonly employed.

GSR can also be chemically identified through the application of a number of different chemical tests. The most common of these are color "spot" tests that detect the nitrates, nitrites, or lead in gunpowder.

Gunshot residue may persist on clothing and hands for a surprisingly long period of time. Many components of GSR are not very water-soluble, and the irregular shapes of particles can firmly lodge themselves within the mesh of clothing and fabrics. Handwashing, however, may be effective in reducing the GSR levels to below detectable quantities. Similarly, vigorous treatment or any inadvertent contact may spread the GSR, causing undesired contamination effects that may reduce the values of the analysis. For this reason, the hands of victims and suspects are often protected at the crime scene by placing bags around them to prevent GSR loss or contamination. This is particularly important in potential suicide cases. Suspects are also tested as soon as possible for GSR contamination, including at different places on their hands and arms that might help to show if and how the weapon was held (Figure 16.40).

FIGURE 16.39 Discharge of unreacted powder and combustion byproducts is released upon firing that can deposit on the shooter.

Source: Used per Creative Commons Share Alike 3.0, Unported. User: Niels Noordhoek.

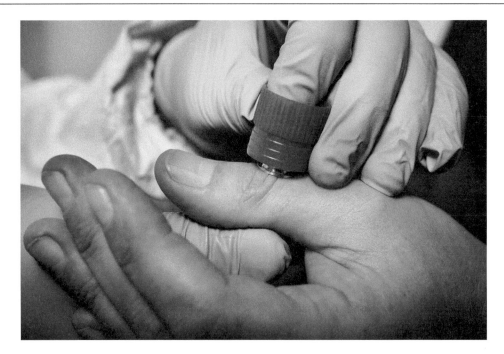

FIGURE 16.40   Swabbing a suspect's fingers for GSR.

Source: Shutterstock.com.

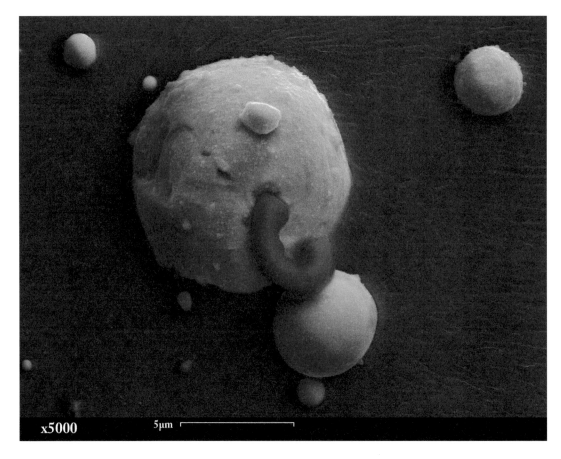

FIGURE 16.41   A scanning electron micrograph of gunshot residue (GSR).

Source: Edward Kinsman/Science Photo image. Used with permission.

16.2.5 Serial Number Restoration

Manufactured firearms are stamped in one or more places with uniquely identifying serial numbers by law. These numbers are registered and may be used to trace the point of manufacture, sale, and ownership of a weapon. They allow police investigators to easily trace weapons back to their owners. Weapons used in criminal activity, however, are often tampered with in attempts to obliterate the identifying serial number by scratching or grinding. It is important to try to restore these illegible numbers to effectively trace a recovered weapon. Fortunately, this is often possible.

When a serial number is stamped into the metal of a firearm, a very hard die containing the serial number is pressed into the metal with a great deal of pressure. When this happens, the crystal structure of the metal underneath the stamped numbers is deeply stressed and distorted by the stamping process. Fortunately, removing the outermost layer of metal through scratching or grinding cannot change the deep modification of the metal's structure that happened during stamping. It is, therefore, possible to restore illegible serial numbers chemically by selectively developing the areas where the metal has been "stressed."

In this process, the "stressed" metal below the die-stamped numbers is more easily etched away chemically than the surrounding block of metal since its structure has been damaged. For example, a water solution containing hydrochloric acid (HCl) and copper (II) chloride etches away the stressed metal faster than the unstressed metal. First, the metal to be restored is cleaned and polished. Then, a hydrochloric acid/$CuCl_2$ solution is applied to the surface. After a period of time, the "stressed" region of the stamped numbers dissolves away to reveal the ID number. An example of the results of this process is shown in Figure 16.43a. An

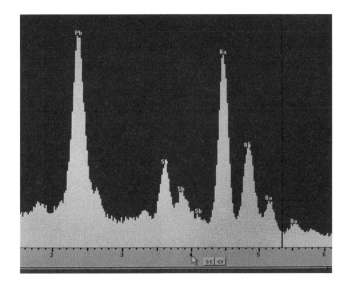

FIGURE 16.42 Elemental analysis of gunshot residue (GSR) by SEM-EDXA. This reveals the elements present, seen as the peaks in the pattern. Peaks are labeled for lead (Pb), antimony (Sb), and barium (Ba). GSR is produced during the firing of a firearm.

Source: Mauro Fermariello/Science Photo image. Used with permission.

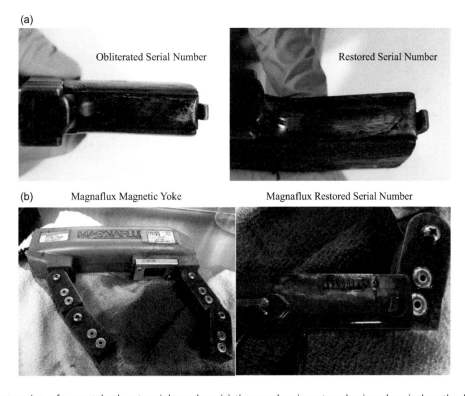

FIGURE 16.43 Restoration of a scratched-out serial number: (a) the number is restored using chemical methods and (b) magnaflux restoration of obliterated serial numbers.

Source: (b) Used with permission and courtesy of Matt Kurimsky, Onondaga Co. Forensic Laboratory.

alternative method uses a magnetic flux to localize magnetic powder in the obliterated serial numbers for visualization (Figure 16.43b).

Unfortunately, the records of serial numbers of older weapons may not be available, or a crime weapon may have been stolen or passed among many people, such that serial numbers, even when present, might not provide much valuable information.

16.2.6 Ballistics

Understanding the trajectory of a bullet can help to reconstruct in detail the events that occurred during a shooting. The paths of the bullets may be determined by carefully measuring and positioning any known endpoints, impact angles, trajectory data in autopsy reports, and other known points (Figure 16.44). This information can then be integrated into a representation of the crime scene; increasingly computer-assisted design (CAD) programs are being used for this purpose, as shown in Figure 16.45. This type of crime scene reconstruction can provide relevant and detailed information about the relative positions of the shooter and victim, the timing of the shots, and the movements of the participants during the incident.

Part of the ballistics testing in the laboratory is also to determine if a particular weapon is both capable of firing

(functionality) and potentially has recently been fired. Obviously, an inoperable weapon could not have been used in a shooting incident.

16.2.7 Integrated Ballistic Identification System (IBIS) and National Integrated Ballistics Information Network (NIBIN)

In 1999, the formerly separate databases maintained by the FBI and ATF were merged to form the National Integrated Ballistics Information Network (NIBIN). In this system, law enforcement partners use the Integrated Ballistic Identification System (IBIS) to input and recover digital images of the markings found on fired bullets and cartridge cases either recovered from crime scenes or from test-fired weapons (Figure 16.46). These digital images are then compared with those previously stored in the NIBIN system. The computer matching system then searches for comparable images that investigators can examine microscopically. Using the NIBIN system, law enforcement investigators are able to "discover links between crimes more quickly, including links that would never have been identified absent the technology." For example, the New York City Police Department has identified thousands of "hits" using the NIBIN system.

FIGURE 16.44   Reconstruction of bullet trajectories at a crime scene.

Source: Phillipe Psaila/Science Photo image. Used with permission.

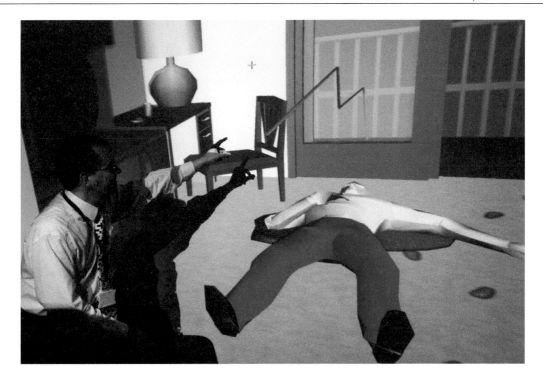

FIGURE 16.45 Ballistics information can provide important information about the location and sequence of events involved in a shooting. This CAD reconstruction shows a dead man lying on a floor with a brown line indicating the trajectory of the bullet that killed the man.

Source: Louise Murray/Science Photo image. Used with permission.

FIGURE 16.46 An image of a recovered cartridge case used for comparison in the NIBIN system.

Source: Used with permission and courtesy of Matt Kurimsky, Onondaga Co. Forensic Laboratory.

BOX 16.5   SACCO AND VANZETTI

On April 15, 1920, an afternoon robbery in Braintree, Massachusetts, left a paymaster and a security guard dead and nearly $16,000 in payroll gone. It was a case that helped change the landscape of criminal justice and immigrant rights in the United States.

Police investigations of the homicides quickly centered on a group of local Italian anarchists and militants. On May 5, 1920, Nicola Sacco and Bartolomeo Vanzetti were arrested when they showed up to claim a car that the police suspected had been used in the assault and robbery: both men were armed, carried anarchist literature, and Vanzetti had unusual ammunition in his pockets, similar to that used during the robbery.

After a highly publicized trial with a near-frenzy of public interest, Sacco and Vanzetti were convicted of the murders. In the following six years, all appeals failed, and the two were executed on August 23, 1927. The public outrage from the proceedings and results of the trial led to some important reforms in the legal process, especially regarding the handling of evidence and what constitutes "expert" testimony.

A major part of the trial centered upon forensic firearm analysis. Many witnesses were presented by both sides, including a large number of "non-experts" that presented pseudo-expert analysis (59 for the prosecution and 99 for the defense in total), some of whom testified regarding the match (or non-match) between a bullet test-fired from Sacco's gun and that found in the body of the victim. Additionally, the prosecution argued that the type of ammunition used in the assault was of an obsolete and rare type, but it matched the unusual collection of ammunition found in Vanzetti's pockets when he was arrested. It has been reported that even some of the defense experts changed their minds on examining the test-firing evidence and agreed that the fatal bullet was fired from Sacco's gun.

Through the years, attention has remained centered upon the central question in the case: *Was the fatal shot fired from Sacco's gun?* In later investigations in 1961 and 1983, using significantly improved ballistic testing methods, the analysis concluded that the fatal shot had indeed been fired from Sacco's gun. Various authors have continued to argue about both guilt and innocence; however, and the debate continues. In 1977, Gov. Michael Dukakis of Massachusetts issued a proclamation that Sacco and Vanzetti had been unfairly tried and convicted. The proclamation did not, however, imply their guilt nor their innocence as a pardon would do. Nonetheless, significant questions remain, and the Sacco and Vanzetti case continues to be actively debated.

FIGURE 16.47   The Saco and Vanzetti Case. (a) Worldwide protests were held to save Sacco and Vanzetti, including in London, England in 1921 and (b) a large mosaic mural from "The Passion of Sacco and Vanzetti" by Ben Shahn (1967) located at Syracuse University.

Source: (b) Used per Creative Commons Share Alike 3.0, Unported. User: DASonnenfeld.

16.3 FORENSIC IMPRESSION EVIDENCE

16.3.1 Introduction

Impression evidence, items that carry lasting and observable marks from contact with another object, comes in many forms. So far, we have discussed how individualistic patterns are transferred from our fingers, hands, feet, and even lips and ears to other objects (Chapter 7), and how analyzing them can aid in identifying one person's actions from among those of all others. Similarly, earlier in this chapter, the analysis of permanent marks on gun barrels, bullets, extractors, and other parts of weapons and ammunition was shown to be a powerful way to establish linkages between a recovered bullet and one particular weapon. But, there are many other types of impression evidence where marks of contact can be effectively used to show that the two particular objects were once in intimate contact. These include footprints, tire tracks, bite marks, and tool marks, among others (Figure 16.48). While these other types of impression evidence could just as suitably be presented elsewhere in this text, they will be covered here due to the similarities that often exist between the techniques used in firearm examinations and those employed in the analysis of impression evidence.

16.3.2 Impression Evidence Basics

Impression evidence arises from imprinting or pressing a patterned or shaped object upon another object to leave behind some sort of image of the original patterned object. Impression evidence provides several key types of forensic information, including:

- Identification of the objects that came into direct contact, both from class characteristics (e.g., make, model, and type) and from individual characteristics (e.g., wear marks, imperfections, unique structural patterns, etc.) that help establish an unambiguous linkage between two items.
- Determination of how many people and objects were involved in an incident.
- Description of the movements of the participants and objects (e.g., weapons, vehicles, furniture, etc.) during the incident.
- Development of a timeline and sequence of actions that occurred during an incident: what happened first, next, and so on.
- Support or lack thereof for eyewitness, suspect, and victim accounts of what occurred.

Impression evidence can take several forms, depending on the types of objects and surfaces involved. Impression information can be either two-dimensional or three-dimensional in nature. Two-dimensional impressions typically result when an object comes into direct contact with a hard surface or material. The hard surface is not indented or molded by contact with the object, but patterns can be transferred to the surface, such as when a fingertip comes into contact with a glass or a vehicle tire rolls over a concrete roadway. The print formed from this type of contact may produce either a positive or negative image (Figure 16.49). A *positive image* is made when the object *leaves something behind* on the surface that can be visualized. This happens when an object is covered with ink, blood, oil, soil, moisture, or another substance that is transferred to the surface, similar to the way printing is done on

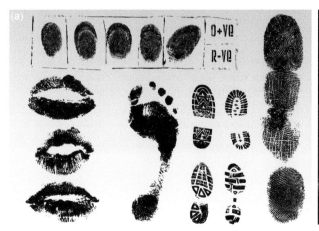

FIGURE 16.48 (a) Types of impression evidence, including fingerprint, footprint, and lip marks can be used to understand a crime scene. (b) Probably the most famous footprint impression evidence in history: the view from the Moon with Earth rising on the horizon showing the footprints of the astronauts who walked there from the Apollo 11 mission.

Source: Images used courtesy Shutterstock.com.

(a)

(b)

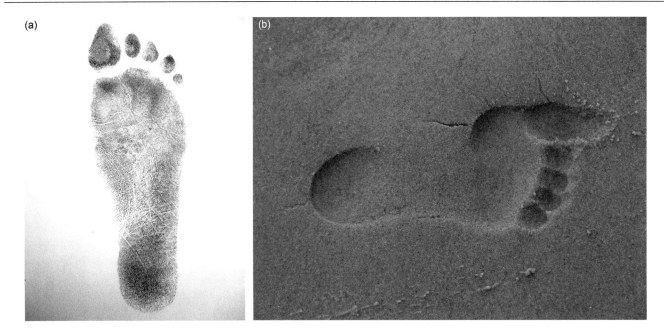

FIGURE 16.49   A positive footprint (a) and negative footprint (b). The positive print occurs from leaving something behind on the surface (such as ink on paper) and the negative print comes from removing materials from the surface, such as removing sand or dust from a surface.

Source: (a) Used per Creative Commons Share Alike 4.0, International. User: Metrónomo.

FIGURE 16.50   Positive image footprint from mud on a floor.

Source: Shutterstock.com.

paper (Figure 16.50). Most fingerprints on an object are positive prints resulting from the transfer of oils and secretions to the surface that remain to be detected later. A *negative image* is formed, in contrast, when some covering *material is removed* from the surface through contact. For example, dust, snow, or blood distributed on the floor in a thin layer can adhere to a tire or shoe and be removed when a vehicle drives over the

area or someone walks across the surface (Figure 16.51). After the contact, the resulting pattern of the tire or shoe remains in areas where the coating has been removed.

Impression evidence can also be three-dimensional in nature. In this case, an object comes into contact with a soft or moldable substance (called a "plastic" material) to leave behind an exact three-dimensional imprint of the original

FIGURE 16.51 Shoe prints form a negative image on a dusty surface by removing (or compacting) some of the dust from the surface.

Source: Shutterstock.com.

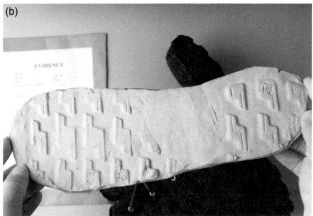

FIGURE 16.52 3-D impression evidence from footwear: (a) a negative imprint in mud can form a positive imprint when cast in a material that hardens after being poured into the negative "mold", and (b) the final casting made from the original impression.

Source: Image courtesy Shutterstock.com.

object. The image formed is actually a negative impression of the original object since "high points" in the original object are recorded as "low points" on the print. Making a casting of the three-dimensional imprint "inverts" the impression to form a positive of the original; high points in the cast correspond to high points in the original, as shown in Figure 16.52.

Impressions can also be divided into three basic types, just as is done with fingerprints: visible, latent, or plastic impressions. *Visible* impressions are those that are readily observable without any visualization aids. Examples include prints from inked fingers, tracks in mud, scratch marks on a door lock, and bite-mark wounds on a victim. *Latent* impressions are those that are not immediately observable but can be "developed" using a variety of techniques to make the image visible. Special light sources, chemical reagents, powders, and spectroscopic techniques have all been used effectively to visualize latent impression patterns. For example, Figure 16.53 shows a latent print from a foot that held minute traces of blood, far below that which can be seen with the unaided eye. The "invisible" minute amounts of blood transferred to the floor from the foot were effectively visualized by chemical treatment and illumination with ultraviolet light. Finally, *plastic* impressions are those that have been formed when an object is imprinted into a soft, moldable material.

The processing of most types of impression evidence usually follows several basic common practices. These steps usually involve localization, photography, documentation, casting (for 3D impressions), and lifting the impression.

Usually, the process begins by sweeping the area to locate and extensively photograph the evidence. Special lighting, fluorescent techniques, and various powders may be used for locating even difficult-to-see impressions. Photographs must have a scale indicator of some sort within the image, and the set of pictures needs to include both wide-field pictures that place the impression within the context of the larger crime scene and close-up detail shots. Pictures are usually taken directly above the impression with the light source moved to different angles relative to the surface. One especially useful technique for finding and photographing impressions uses oblique lighting, where the light comes in at a low (or oblique) angle relative to the surface (Figure 16.54). This technique gives highlights and contrast to the topology of the impression, much as the setting sun causes shadows over hills and valleys to give a clearer three-dimensional picture of a landscape. Forensic photographers also use alternative light sources (ALS) that essentially employ light of different wavelengths (colors) to visualize the components of the impression (Figures 16.55). Since different chemicals, such as drugs, body fluids, dust, minerals,

FIGURE 16.53   Latent footprint visualized by ultraviolet light to make faint traces of blood on the foot visually observable.
Source: Shutterstock.com.

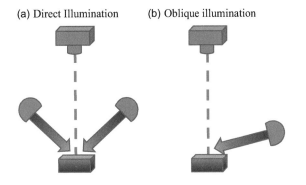

(a) Direct Illumination   (b) Oblique illumination

FIGURE 16.54   Direct (a) and oblique (b) lighting arrangements for photographing impression evidence.

pigments, and others, fluoresce at different wavelengths of light, alternative light sources can be used to selectively visualize and photograph the evidence. Latent impression evidence of many varieties can be visualized using techniques developed for latent fingerprint examination. For example, magnetic powders, visualization reagents (e.g., ninhydrin, crystal violet, and luminol), "super-glue" methods, and others can be effective for footwear, tire tracks, and other forms of latent impressions.

Documentation of the evidence often involves written descriptions and sketches/drawings of the crime scene, relating the positions of the evidence with fixed points of reference. As with other types of documentation for crime scenes, computer-assisted and GPS methods help spatially locate the important aspects of the scene, including footprint and other types of impression evidence.

For three-dimensional impressions, such as footprints, tire tracks, and tool marks, castings are taken whenever possible.

Castings provide actual-sized, permanent reproductions of the original impression, often with great detail, even to the microscopic level depending upon the quality of the original impression. Casts may also preserve detail beyond just the bottom surface of the original object. In deep, three-dimensional impressions, details from the sides of the object that are very difficult to photograph can be well preserved. Casts also provide a permanent record of the short-lived impression and provide tangible support for the photographic records that have been made, allowing later re-visitation to examine the impression further.

Forming castings involves pouring a rather thin liquid material into the impression that slowly sets into a solid material that retains the detailed features of the original pattern. Most often, dental stone or dental silicone are used in preparing these casts, an improvement over the older Plaster of Paris methods. Dental stone, a gypsum-based product, forms a hard, strong solid that doesn't require reinforcement to be very stable – much harder and more durable than Plaster of Paris. Dental silicone forms a rubber-like material that, when set, retains the details of the original impression. Casts can be made from impressions in a variety of conditions and materials. Casts are readily taken from impressions made in sand, mud, soil, cement, and even snow.

Two-dimensional impressions can often be lifted and preserved using techniques developed for fingerprints. Depending on the situation, powders can usually be lifted using clear plastic sheets. Other dry impressions can be lifted using an electrostatic lifting device that allows charged dust and dirt particles to adhere to a charged metal plate, which then accurately transfers the particles to a plastic sheet for preservation and analysis. If the impression is wet, it can either be directly

FIGURE 16.55 An alternative light source (ALS) available for visualizing latent impression evidence.
Source: Shutterstock.com.

lifted using a gel or indirectly lifted first by powdering with fingerprint dusting powder and then lifting the powder as a dry image. In any case, standardized methods have been developed to lift and preserve many types of two-dimensional impression evidence.

16.3.3 Footprints

Footwear impressions, one of the more common types of impression evidence found at crime scenes, can be especially useful in identifying the presence of individual people at a crime scene. Footwear evidence can be found not only on floors, but also on doors, walls and elsewhere when suspects kick these surfaces. Footwear evidence has even been recovered from people's skin in cases of violent assaults. Investigators can also look inside a person's shoes to find skin friction ridge patterns from their footprints, similar to fingerprints but located on the toes and soles of the feet.

Once footwear impressions have been identified, documented, and preserved, forensic analysts then attempt to gain class information by identifying the manufacturer, make, and model of the footwear from the sole pattern (Figure 16.56). This process is greatly aided by databases, such as SICAR and TreadMark, which contain registered patterns and information about thousands of different models of footwear.

Footwear impressions may often be individualized by identifying molding imperfections (Figure 16.57) and wear and damage marks (Figure 16.58) in the sole patterns. These imperfections found on crime scene evidence can then be compared to the shoes of a suspect by looking for similar (or missing) tread pattern damage.

Information based on footwear can also provide a very rough estimate of the approximate height of the wearer since a rough correlation between shoe size and height follows a statistical distribution pattern (and sometimes an approximate stature estimate can be quite useful). Height can also be approximated by measuring the distance between successive footprints and correlating the stride length statistically with limb dimensions: longer strides suggest longer limbs, which suggest a taller stature. The order in which a series of footprints was laid down can also sometimes be determined by looking for overlapping footprints; the most recent footprint impresses its pattern over that of a previously existing print. Finally, whether a person was simply standing or moving and, if moving, the speed at which that person was traveling – whether walking or running – can be estimated by the depth of the toe and heel portions of a print. For example, the footprint impressions of a running person typically have deeper indentations at the toe than at the heel, and overall, the entire impression is deeper when running compared to those made by someone walking.

16.3.4 Tire Tracks

Vehicles of all types have been part of criminal activity. Due to the relatively heavy weight of vehicles and the deeply engraved characteristic patterns found on the tire treads, these impressions are often found marking crime scenes in soil, sand, mud, snow, asphalt, and other surfaces. Tread patterns have also been effectively lifted from victims hit by the vehicle.

In many ways, tire tracks are similar to footwear impressions in that both class and individual characteristics may be

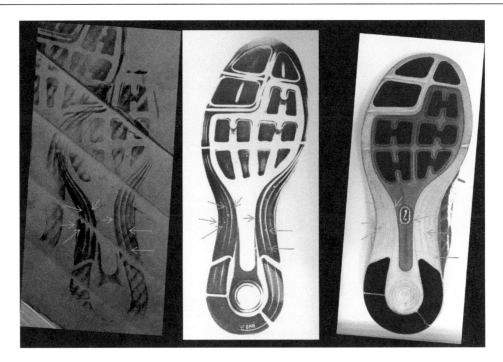

FIGURE 16.56   Visualization of footwear evidence.

Source: Used per Creative Commons Share Alike 4.0, International. User: Zalman992.

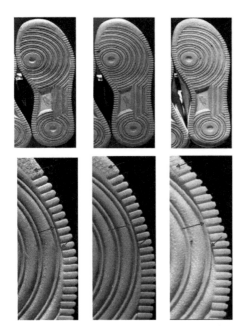

FIGURE 16.57   Differences in new shoes arising from imperfections in the molding process. The arrows depict the mold variations in each of the different shoes along the outside end of the shoe.

Source: FBI, Smith (2009).

identified when comparing recovered tracks with known origin references (Figure 16.59). Because of the variation in the patterns, it is often possible to determine the manufacturer, model, and sometimes even the year of manufacture of a particular tire from its tread design. Three-dimensional imprints

may also show the marks from the sidewalls of the tire, including manufacturer imprints. Measuring the distance along a single track between a repeating identifiable mark, such as a damage mark or worn spot on the tire, can provide the circumference of the tire.

Information that can be used to match a tire track with one specific tire can come from wear and damage patterns. Since tires are made from relatively soft materials and interact at high speeds with hard objects and surfaces, wear is expected for tire treads (Figure 16.60). Damage occurring from irregular road surfaces or from impact with small objects further individualizes a particular tread. Comparing any imperfections found in the tire impression with those on the suspect tire can provide information that may support or refute a connection to the crime scene of that particular tire and, therefore, of one specific vehicle. It is important to note, however, that tires continually wear, and that the patterns may not match exactly if the vehicle has been driven significantly since the time the impression was made.

Tire impressions can also provide information about the vehicle itself. Measuring the distance between two tracks can give information regarding the width (wheelbase) and distance between the axles of the vehicle. Track widths are not always the same between front and rear axles, which can be a further identifying feature when observed. The turning radius of a vehicle may also be estimated in certain cases.

16.3.5 Tool Marks

Tools are commonly employed in criminal acts, from break-ins and vandalism to assaults and robberies. Identifying

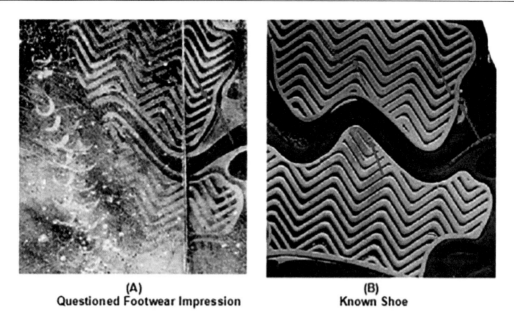

(A)
Questioned Footwear Impression

(B)
Known Shoe

FIGURE 16.58 A comparison identifying characteristics in the impression found at the crime scene (a) with features observed on the sole of the known shoe (b). The arrows indicate the position of unique identifying characteristics from wear and damage to the sole of the shoe.

Source: FBI, Smith (2009).

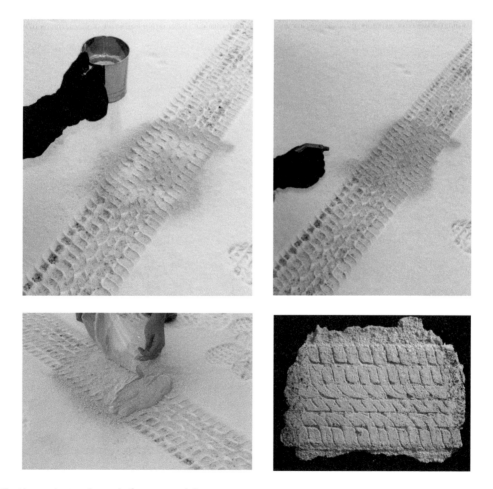

FIGURE 16.59 Casting a tire track made from a track in snow.

Source: Bodziak (2008).

FIGURE 16.60 Typical wear patterns on automobile tires.

Source: Shutterstock.com.

characteristic markings can, as with other types of impression evidence, identify a type or even the specific tool employed in these actions.

Tool mark creation arises in a variety of ways, ranging from screwdrivers and crowbars used to open doors and windows to weapons used in violent crimes (Figure 16.61). Of particular importance is the presence of any striations that might be present in the markings. For example, shown in Figure 16.62 is a microscopic image of the striations on a punch tool. Matching unique imperfections provides strong evidence connecting the two items. Similarly, the details of the cut marks on other soft materials, such as plastics, can also reveal a wealth of data (Figure 16.63).

There are clearly too many other types of impressions to detail here. In essence, any time a harder object comes into contact forcibly with a softer one, the opportunity for transferring an impression is possible. For example, an offender used a fake police badge, placed in a plastic holder of his wallet, to gain access and attack a victim. The criminal discarded the badge but retained the plastic case in his wallet, which later showed the detailed impression of the badge, providing strong evidence of the suspect's connection to the crime.

16.3.6 Bite Marks

In the past, bite marks have been used to help identify attackers in violent crimes, especially sexual assaults. Bite marks have previously been used to identify individual people from the marks left in foodstuffs (e.g., apples, cheese, chocolate),

FIGURE 16.61 Micro-computed tomography image of tool marks on a bone cut in a dismemberment case.

Source: Black et al. (2017).

pencils, leather, chewing gum, and human flesh, among others. Gathering and analyzing bite-mark evidence has involved photographing the gouges or wounds (in the case of human flesh) with appropriate scale markers, as well as taking a cast of a suspect's teeth, usually by a forensic odontologist (dentist). The cast from the suspect's teeth and the bite marks found on a victim or other objects at the crime scene were then compared to establish or refute a connection between the two tooth-mark patterns (Figure 16.64).

Bite marks can also result from non-human attacks. Bite marks from domestic animals are most common with between 1 and 2 million reported annually in the United States, mostly

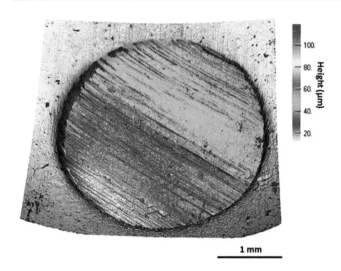

FIGURE 16.62 The 3D topography of a punch toolmark.

Source: NIST.

FIGURE 16.63 Marks made on plastic vacuum tubing with two different types of knives. The striations can be observed on the tubing, showing how it was cut and helping to identify the tool (knife) that created it.

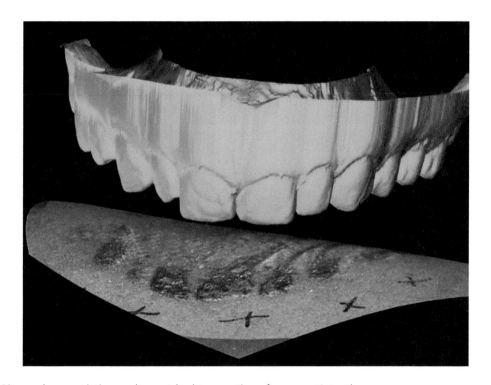

FIGURE 16.64 Bite marks on a victim can be matched to a casting of a suspect's teeth.

Source: NIH.

from dogs. Dogs and other animals have characteristic tooth patterns that can aid in identifying the species, size, and behavior of a particular animal. For example, rodents tend to leave small, parallel marks and typically attack the face, head, fingers, and toes first, while dogs tend to bite around the head and neck and usually attack when defending their territories.

The use of forensic human bite-mark analysis is currently under intense scrutiny, with much work and discussion on the issue. The current practice of individualizing an attacker by this type of analysis does not hold up to scientific scrutiny and provide enough uniqueness to identify a particular assailant. The basic premise is whether there is sufficient variability between the dentition of individual people to make a unique identification possible and whether this information can be extracted from bite-mark wounds on victims so that a meaningful comparison and unambiguous match can be made. At present, bite-mark identification has largely been abandoned from trial practice.

BOX 16.6   THEODORE "TED" BUNDY

Probably the best-known use of bite-mark impression evidence in criminal justice comes from the case of Ted Bundy. Bundy was a serial killer who assaulted and murdered at least 30 young women between 1974 and 1978.

Bundy was arrested in Utah in 1975 on a number of charges not related to the murders before escaping from prison and continuing his spree of assault and murder. Then, in January of 1978, Bundy entered the Chi Omega sorority house at Florida State University and murdered two women and assaulted two others. One of the victims, Lisa Levy, was found with a deep bite-mark wound from the attacker. Bundy was arrested about a month later, after he had committed other assaults and at least one more homicide.

At his trial, Bundy handled much of his own defense (despite having five court-appointed defenders). The crucial evidence that led to his conviction came from an analysis of a bite-mark wound on Levy. Castings of Bundy's teeth were made by odontologists and pictures of his dentition were overlain upon scaled pictures of the victim's bite mark. Odontologists Richard Souviron and Lowell Levine testified that the bite marks on the victim uniquely matched those taken from Bundy's dental castings.

After a brief deliberation, the jury found Bundy guilty of two murders, three counts of attempted first-degree murder, and two counts of burglary. Six months later, Bundy was also tried and convicted of the murder of 12-year-old Kimberly Leach in Orlando, Florida. The judge ordered Bundy executed on the murder convictions.

After exhausting all possible appeals, Bundy finally agreed to talk with investigators where he confessed to (but without ever taking responsibility for) over 30 murders, including some that investigators were not even aware of. Bundy was ultimately executed for his crimes on January 24, 1989. Today, bite mark evidence has largely been excluded from trial practice.

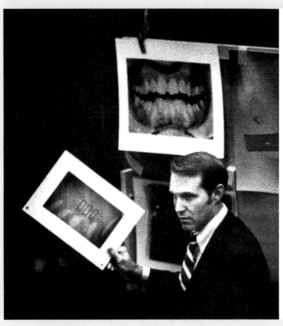

FIGURE 16.65   Ted Bundy's trial evidence and conviction.

Source: Public Domain.

QUESTIONS FOR FURTHER PRACTICE AND MASTERY

16.1   What is meant by the land and groove marks on a bullet?

16.2   What is meant by terminal ballistics?

16.3   Explain the difference between muzzle-loading firearms and breech-loading firearms.

16.4   What is the function of a percussion cap?

16.5   What is fixed ammunition and what are its advantages?

16.6   What is rifling, and what effect does it have on a fired bullet?

16.7   What is the difference between a pistol and a revolver?

16.8   What is the difference between a semi-automatic and a fully automatic weapon?

16.9   What are the lands and grooves in a rifle barrel?

16.10 What is polygonal rifling?

16.11 What is meant by twist rate? What effect does increasing the twist rate have on a fired projectile?

16.12 What are some of the features of a shotgun that distinguish it from a rifle?

16.13 How is the caliber of a gun determined? Why are bullets referred to by caliber?

16.14 What is meant by the term ballistics?

16.15 What are the three "phases" of ballistics for a projectile? Explain each phase.

16.16 What are the typical methods for rifling a gun barrel?

16.17 What information can a forensic scientist determine from examining a fired bullet?

16.18 What are stria and how do they occur?

16.19 What identifying information can be obtained from a bullet casing that may connect it to a particular weapon?

16.20 What is gunshot residue (GSR)?

16.21 A forensic technician studies the GSR pattern at a crime scene. The technician measures the pattern of the GSR on objects leading up to the victim. After conducting a comparison test with the weapon, what conclusions can be drawn about the position of the assailant relative to the victim?

16.22 What two techniques are typically used when trying to restore an illegible gun serial number?

16.23 What is the fundamental principle with regard to metal crystal structure that allows serial number restoration through chemical treatment?

16.24 What is the difference between a positive impression and a negative impression?

16.25 What are the three basic types of impressions? Explain the differences and provide examples.

16.26 What methods are used to process impressions?

16.27 How do alternative light sources aid in photographing impressions?

16.28 What is the preferred medium used for making a forensic casting? What are its advantages over the old Plaster of Paris medium?

16.29 What information about a suspect might be determined from: (a) the size of a shoe print, (b) the distance between shoe prints, and (c) the depth of the heel and toe imprints?

16.30 What identifying markers are looked for when analyzing tire impressions at a crime scene?

16.31 What are tool marks?

16.32 What is the debate in the legal community about bite-mark impressions as admissible evidence?

GLOSSARY OF TERMS

action: the mechanical apparatus of a firearm that loads, fires, and ejects the cartridge.

air gun: weapons that move a projectile solely by the release of stored pressurized gas rather than through combustion.

alternative light sources (ALS): light sources that employ light of different wavelengths to visualize the components of an impression.

ballistics: the study of how projectiles move through space.

barrel: the metal pipe that guides the initial flight of the bullet in a firearm.

breech: the end of the gun barrel nearest to the action.

breech block (or face): the back of the firing chamber.

breech-loading firearm: a weapon in which the ammunition and bullet are placed directly into the firing chamber without it having to put down the barrel.

broach cutter: a tool used to simultaneously cut all the rifling grooves by forcing the cutter head down a smooth, drilled-out gun barrel while rotating the cutter with a characteristic twist rate.

bullet: the projectile fired from a weapon.

button rifling: a process in which a small, shaped form is forced down the smooth gun barrel at very high pressures to form the grooves in a rifled barrel.

caliber: the diameter of the gun barrel in 1/100th of an inch.

cartridge: ammunition made up of casing, primer, powder, wadding, and bullet.

casting: a physical replica of an impression, formed by a moldable material that sets into an actual-sized, permanent reproduction of the original impression.

chamber: the enclosure in a firearm's design that contains the cartridge when ready to fire.

dental stone: a gypsum-based ($CaSO_4 \cdot 2H_2O$) product that, when mixed with water and poured into a mold, sets to form a hard, strong, and stable solid that doesn't require reinforcement.

drag: the force that opposes the forward motion of the bullet created by air resistance.

external (or intermediate) ballistics: the study of the flight of the bullet from the time it leaves the end of the weapon's barrel until it reaches the target.

firearm: an assembly consisting of a barrel and a mechanical action that allows a projectile to be propelled forward through the action of an extremely fast combustion reaction.

firearm identification: the process of determining "if a bullet, cartridge case, or other ammunition component was fired by a particular firearm."

fixed ammunition: ammunition that combines primer, an accurately measured main charge, and the bullet all enclosed in a single, easily handled, watertight casing.

flintlock weapon: firearms that use a spark created by moving a piece of flint over a steel plate ("frizzen") to ignite a small primer charge that then sets fire to the main charge.

fully automatic weapon: a firearm where the filled rounds are reloaded automatically (see semi-automatic weapon), and the weapon continues to fire multiple shots when the trigger is held down.

gauge: a measure of the diameter of the barrel of a shotgun.

gravity: the force that constantly pulls objects downward with a constant force, defined as $F = mg$ (where m is mass and g is the gravitational constant).

grooves: the places where some of a gun's barrel metal has been removed (rifling) or shaped to create a depression.

gunpowder: an explosive chemical mixture of carbon, potassium nitrate and sulfur that undergoes a rapid oxidation reaction and is used to propel projectiles in firearms.

gunshot residue (GSR): deposits of unreacted explosive material and solid combustion byproducts that are discharged from openings in the gun into the nearby environment upon firing.

hammer: the part of the action that drives the firing pin into the primer upon firing.

handgun: a smaller firearm designed for operation using one hand.

impression evidence: items of evidence that carry the lasting and observable marks from contact with another object.

internal (or initial) ballistics: the consideration of the part of a bullet's path that occurs within the firearm itself.

kinetic energy (KE): the energy of motion given by the expression $KE = \frac{1}{2} mv^2$ (where m is the mass and v is the velocity of the moving object).

lands: the portions of the inside surface of a rifled gun barrel that project farthest into the center of the barrel adjacent to grooves.

latent impression: impression evidence that is not immediately observable but which can be made visible using a variety of techniques.

long gun: a category of firearms with relatively long barrels that includes rifles.

magazine: a device for holding and delivering cartridges.

magnum: a cartridge containing more than the standard amount of powder which delivers more power to the bullet.

mandrel: a rod-shaped, grooved template with raised ribs corresponding to the desired rifling grooves; used to compress a gun barrel into shape, leaving the formation of grooves and lands inside the barrel when the mandrel is removed.

muzzle: the very end of the gun barrel where the bullet exits the weapon.

muzzle-loading firearm: a weapon in which the bullets and ammunition are loaded directly down the barrel of the gun.

National Integrated Ballistics Information Network (NIBIN): a database used to compare stored firearm pattern information with unknown (crime scene recovered) patterns.

negative image: an image formed when some material covering a surface is removed by contact.

oblique lighting: light that comes in at a low (or oblique) angle relative to the surface.

percussion cap: a small metal case containing a tiny amount of shock-sensitive explosive, such as mercury fulminate or lead styphnate, that when struck sets off the main charge of the ammunition.

plastic: a moldable material.

plastic impressions: impression evidence that has been formed when an object is imprinted into a soft, moldable material.

polygonal rifling: an alternative to the traditional lands and grooves rifling where "hills" and "valleys" form a more rounded, polygonal pattern.

positive image: an image created when an object leaves something behind on the surface that can be visualized.

powder: the solid explosive used to propel the bullet.

primer: the shock-sensitive compound, today often lead styphnate, that ignites the main charge of a cartridge upon being struck.

revolver: a firearm in which ammunition is moved into place for firing by means of rotating a cylinder that contains a number of separate firing chambers loaded with filled cartridges.

rifling: spiral grooves inside the gun's barrel which cause the projectile to spin about its long axis.

round: an intact and complete unit of ammunition (primer, bullet or "slug" and main charge).

semi-automatic weapon: a firearm in which the energy released from firing mechanically ejects the spent case and reloads the next fresh round into the firing chamber; one round is fired for each pull of the trigger.

serial number restoration: the process of making visible serial numbers stamped into a gun that have been filed or ground away.

shotgun: a type of long gun without rifling that uses ammunition containing either many small pellets (shot) packed into a single cartridge or a single, solid projectile (slug).

shrapnel: fragments of metal from a bomb, shell, or mine.

sight: the device on a gun that improves aim and accuracy.

silencer: a device, placed over the muzzle, that reduces the noise emitted by firing a weapon.

spin (or gyroscopic) stabilization: the rotational movement of an elongated projectile around its long axis which greatly improves its aerodynamic properties, allowing it to go much farther and with increased precision and accuracy.

stock: the frame that holds the barrel and action together to allow aiming and firing.

stria (striations): tiny imperfection marks transferred between two objects that pass with direct contact.

terminal ballistics: the study of what happens when a projectile hits its target.

three-dimensional impression: impressions that occur when an object comes into contact with a soft or moldable substance to leave behind an exact three-dimensional imprint of the original object.

twist rate: the length of a gun barrel in which the rifling makes one full rotation (360°).

two-dimensional impression: impressions that occur when an object comes into direct contact with a hard surface or material that is not indented or molded by contact with the object but onto which patterns can be transferred by the deposition or removal of materials.

visible impressions: impression evidence that is readily observable without any visualization aids.

BIBLIOGRAPHY

Association of Firearm and Tool Mark Examiners, *AFTE Glossary*, 1994.

Sue Black et al., *Criminal Dismemberment: Forensic and Investigative Analysis*, CRC Press, 2017

William J. Bodziak, *Footwear Impression Evidence: Detection, Recovery and Examination* (2nd Ed.), CRC Press, 1999.

William Bodziak, *Tire Tread and Tire Track Evidence: Recovery and Forensic Examination*, CRC Press, 2008.

C. Michael Bowers, *Forensic Dental Evidence* (2nd Ed.), Academic Press, 2010.

Lucien C. Haag, *Shooting Incident Reconstruction*, Academic Press, 2006.

Brian J. Heard, *Handbook of Firearms and Ballistics*, John Wiley and Sons, 1997.

Edward E. Hueske, *Practical Analysis and Reconstruction of Shooting Incidents*, CRC Press, 2005.

Raymond J. Johansen, Raymond Johansen, and C. Michael Bowers, *Digital Analysis of Bite Mark Evidence*, Forensic Imaging Inst., 2000.

David S. Pierce, *Mechanics of Impression Evidence*, Auerbach Publications, 2011.Robert A. Rinker, *Understanding Firearm Ballistics* (6th Ed.), Mulberry House Publ. Com., 2005.

Michael Smith, "The Forensic Analysis of Footwear Impression Evidence", *Forensic Science Communications*, 11(3), July 2009.

Tom Warlow, *Firearms, the Law, and Forensic Ballistics* (2nd Ed.), CRC Press, 2005.

Forensic Document, Photo, Video Analysis, Voice ID and Linguistics

17

17.1 FORENSIC DOCUMENT ANALYSIS

LEARNING GOALS AND OBJECTIVES

Handwritten and printed documents often play important roles in legal applications. After you complete this chapter, you should be able to:

- Discuss questioned document analysis (QD).
- Describe the different types of forensic documents analyzed.
- Expand upon the underlying scientific basis of questioned document analysis.
- Present methods QD analysts employ.
- Describe the types of information gained through a questioned document analysis.
- Explain the limitations of questioned document analysis.

17.1.1 Introduction

Words are important. While many animal and plant species can communicate in some fashion with each other, the ability to use the learned skill of language to reveal to others our thoughts and ideas is at the heart of what makes us uniquely human. We can use words and language to convey both concrete and abstract information that a listener has never heard or even thought about before. But words can also quickly and effectively impart not only factual information and observations to others, but just as easily can convey our personal thinking, emotions, aspirations, discoveries, and ideas. You've probably never heard anyone say "the sleeping yellow kangaroo dreams

of dancing," but yet by reading these words you can quickly understand and imagine what the words mean.

Sometimes, however, the *manner* that we choose to communicate may be almost as important as the thoughts themselves. Over time, humans have developed many creative ways in which to extend and expand our ability to communicate with others far away; a developmental process that continues today.

Verbal language first provided us with the ability to rapidly communicate with those in our immediate neighborhood, a skill with clear survival value: "Look out for the mastodon!" or "this is how to make fire." Later, written language allowed us to communicate with others far distant from us as well as to record information and ideas for later reference. As our needs and desires grew, so did the development of more complex forms of language and communication. However, language has deepened far beyond just a tool of communication; it has become intimately associated with our individual and collective identities, perceptions, and cultures.

The study of language is referred to as *linguistics*, and increasingly forensic linguistics is an important tool for several types of investigations.

Handwriting, and later printing, provided humans with the ability to communicate easily across space and time. Today, we read equally well the words from writers who produced their works last week, last century or even last millennium. But handwriting also holds information quite personal beyond the actual words. Looking at the unconsciously produced subtle features of handwriting can help to identify the author of a particular document. Similarly, we can look at these same handwriting features to determine that a document was not produced by the attributed author but rather by some "hidden" author: a forger (Figure 17.1).

Graphic forms of communication, such as paintings and drawings, were developed long ago and allowed early humans to add individualism to the process of communication while sharing personal information. Beautiful works from many thousands of years ago, such as that shown in Figure 17.2, demonstrate the ability of early humans to tell stories in graphic form. These forms of expression progressed into various forms of artwork, growing out of the simple embellishment of utilitarian objects and experimentation with images into items

DOI: 10.4324/9781003183709-21

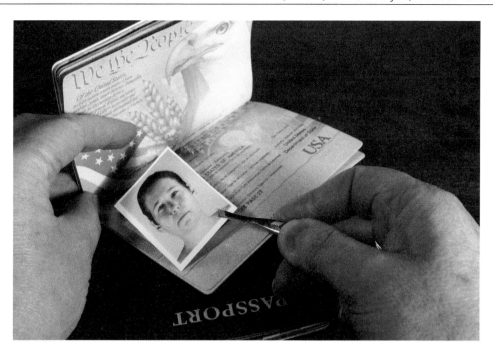

FIGURE 17.1   Determining the origin of a questioned document can be centrally important in a forensic investigation. Uncovering the work of a forger can have long-range legal and criminal implications.

Source: Shutterstock.

FIGURE 17.2   Petroglyphs allowed early man to record events and ideas in personal styles, such as in these cave paintings from at least 10,000 years BCE.

Source: Shutterstock.

FIGURE 17.3   Altered photograph of the Democratic congresswomen of the 113th U.S. Congress where, according to the AP, staff of the office of the Minority Leader of the US House of Representatives digitally added four women who could not arrive at the location in time to join the group portrait in person.

Source: Retrieved from Wikimedia Commons; used per Creative Commons Attribution. 4.0 Author: AndrewBuck.

made solely for their beauty and the feelings that they evoke in others. Today, these graphic forms of communication and expression extend to include both traditional forms of art and imagery as well as photographic, video and digital art. We are often greatly influenced by these images, with almost instant access to visual media produced across the world. Given the availability and ease of use of computer photographic and video altering software, how do we know that what we are looking at is real (Figure 17.3)? Therefore, a key forensic question that is increasingly being asked is whether images are authentic or somehow modified?

Given the central place of various forms of written, oral, and graphic communication in the world today, it is not surprising that these means of expression can play a significant role in forensic investigations. Criminal behavior can sometimes be tracked through a trail of physical and electronic communications, altered visual and graphic items intending to defraud or influence, and voice data that can be used to identify a particular person. The choice of specific language constructions (e.g., grammar, syntax, modulations, etc.) can talk much about the user: are they native speakers, are there hidden meanings in their words, and what was their frame of mind when using the words. Even the mode of communication (e.g., written, oral, photographic, digital, etc.) that someone chooses to use may provide valuable insights nto an investigation.

In this chapter, we will explore the forensic aspects of various forms of human communication through the analysis of questioned documents, altered visual imagery, electronic communication, and forensic linguistics.

17.1.2 Questioned Documents

Documents form the basis of a large part of our communication, providing permanent records of our thoughts, actions, and transactions. They have especially been important for millennia in recording legal, personal, and financial information. Because of the value placed upon the contents and validity of these documents, forgeries that provide false information and give an "unfair" advantage to a forger are also quite common. *Forgery* is defined as the act of preparing or altering a document, signature, financial certificate, work of art, electronic communication, or other valued item with the intention to defraud, damage, or cheat; in other words, to make someone believe that the work was made by a person other than the forger. Clearly, it is of great interest to be able to unambiguously detect and expose these forgeries as frauds to avoid their intended damage and deceit.

In forensic science, the term "questioned document" refers to any document over which there is some legal dispute regarding its origin, authenticity, or authorship. Such documents might include financial checks, currency, wills, anonymous letters, agreements, passports, personal identification records, receipts, messages, and many others. The task of determining whether a physical document is authentic or a forgery usually falls to a questioned document examiner, an expert skilled in the methods of detecting fraudulent written or printed evidence. Electronic communication examination may require the work of a computer or electronic media specialist (discussed separately). The field encompasses many components of document analysis but includes handwriting analysis, signature authenticity, and examination of a variety of printed materials.

17.1.3 Handwriting Analysis

Handwriting is defined as a person's individual style of writing with an implement, such as a pen or pencil. The underlying premise of analyzing a sample of handwriting to determine its authorship is the idea that a *person's handwriting is unique to them*. When we first learn and practice handwriting as children, we are taught to copy forms provided by our teachers as closely as possible to the example. Through repetition

and practice, the act of forming letters and words becomes an unconscious behavior pattern, such as walking or riding a bicycle. As we become more proficient in writing, we develop our own personal writing styles that, while varying somewhat over time and even within a single document, may present distinguishable features that allow for the identification of the author of the document. Under the best conditions, experts believe that the uniqueness provided by handwriting analysis may be as individualistic as our fingerprints.

Teachers of handwriting often use instructional writing models, called copybooks (Figure 17.4). Many copybook styles exist and the choice of which one to use for instruction varies by local preferences and which styles are in "vogue" at the time. Among the most common today are the Palmer, D'Nealian and Zaner-Bloser styles. Because the particular choice of copybook used as the model changes by location and time, a person's handwriting depends upon when and where they *first* learned to write. In other words, the particular writing models that we learn from give rise to the basic *style characteristics* of our writing. Understanding this variation can give insight into when and where the author of a document first learned to write.

The goal of handwriting analysis is usually to either discover information about an unknown author of a handwriting sample (e.g., ransom or threatening letter) or to compare it with a known source to determine if the two documents were written by the same hand (e.g., authentic vs forgery). It is really two separate questions that a document analyst deals with: who wrote a document and/or who didn't write it.

A person's handwriting usually displays several features that collectively help individualize their work: *individual characteristics*. Their handwriting depends on their training, physiology (fine motor skills), and characteristic personal preferences. While it is typical for people to share several individual features in common, it is highly unlikely that they will share in common the dozens of these characteristics found in a typical document.

FIGURE 17.4 The English alphabet written using the D'Nealian cursive script. The gray arrows beside each letter indicate the starting position for drawing each symbol.

BOX 17.1   FORENSIC DOCUMENT ANALYSIS VS GRAPHOLOGY

Forensic document examination deals with identifying individualistic characteristics in a person's handwriting and comparing these features between documents to come to a conclusion about the authorship of a questioned document. Graphology, in contrast, has nothing to do with identification but rather tries to make a connection between the features of a person's handwriting and their personality or character traits. The two fields use very different methods and for quite different purposes. Graphology is today considered to be without scientific support or merit. In a large 1992 study, the meta-analysis of over 200 scientific studies concluded that graphology is unable to predict any kind of personality trait on any known personality test. While graphology has been shown to be without scientific merit, people still rely upon it for important decisions. For example, it has been reported that in France roughly 70% and in the United States between 5% and 10% of companies use graphology for hiring decisions.

Individualizing features are often divided into four main categories: form, arrangement, quality, and content. Some of the key features analyzed for each of these four categories include:

Form:

- **Handwriting Style**: Generally, there are three basic styles of handwriting: block, script, and cursive (Figure 17.5). Block capital writing uses all upper-case (capital) letters that are upright and separated from one another. This is a style often adopted by children just learning to write and is generally the easiest to read and learn. In contrast, script handwriting uses both upper- and lowercase letters that are not joined together and resembles most a printed text (when someone is asked to "print" their name, this is the style most often used). This is often a style that people default to when they are most concerned with legibility. Cursive writing is a style of rapid writing in which most of the letters in a word are joined together, leaving spaces only between words. A number of variants of these basic styles have been developed, although today the script style is becoming more common. An individual may also blend these styles together, resulting in a style that incorporates elements of cursive and script together in their handwriting. A person may also switch between these styles within a document or even within a given sentence.
- **Shape of the Letters**: The formation of individual letters has enormous variation in the roundedness

or sharpness of each character. Some examples are shown in Figure 17.6. A person may also form a letter differently depending on where the letter occurs in a word.

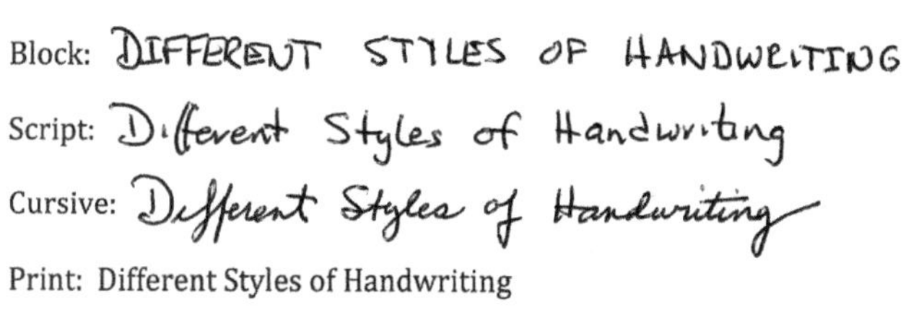

- **Slope and Line Locations of the Writing**: Individual letters may be sloped forward, vertical, or backward relative to the direction of the writing (Figure 17.7). The text may also conform tightly to a straight line (including on a provided line as well as above and below the line), slant upwards, downward, or randomly oriented. The direction of pen movements and strokes can usually be determined from the writing, allowing differentiation between left-handed writing and right-handed writing. For example, counterclockwise circular strokes, such as in the letters "o" and "a", indicate right-handed writing while clockwise indicates a left-handed author.
- **Rhythm of the Writing**: When writing normally, a person may display a certain rhythm or lack of rhythm (arrhythmia) in their style of forming letters and words (Figure 17.8). Rhythm most often refers to a regular repetition or "periodicity" of various writing elements, such as word and letter spacing and the visual "flow" of the words on paper. Features such as the start and end of each letter or word, the pressure on the paper, connectedness of the writing, and the visual flow all contribute to the rhythm of the writing. Handwriting involves the movement of the writer's hand across the page coupled with small motor movements of the hand. The coordination of these movements often follows a pattern that the writer has developed through practice and individualization. Lack of rhythm *may* indicate problems with motor control or result from certain disease states. Many scientists believe that handwriting may be an early indicator of a person's psychological and physiological state. Handwriting in elderly people often degrades due to problems with their fine muscle control and shakiness. Other conditions that are thought to be observable in a person's handwriting include Parkinson's disease, brain damage, alcohol abuse, schizophrenia, Alzheimer's, arthritis, heart disease, and several others. People

Block: DIFFERENT STYLES OF HANDWRITING

Script: Different Styles of Handwriting

Cursive: Different Styles of Handwriting

Print: Different Styles of Handwriting

FIGURE 17.5 Handwriting styles: block, script, and cursive above printed text.

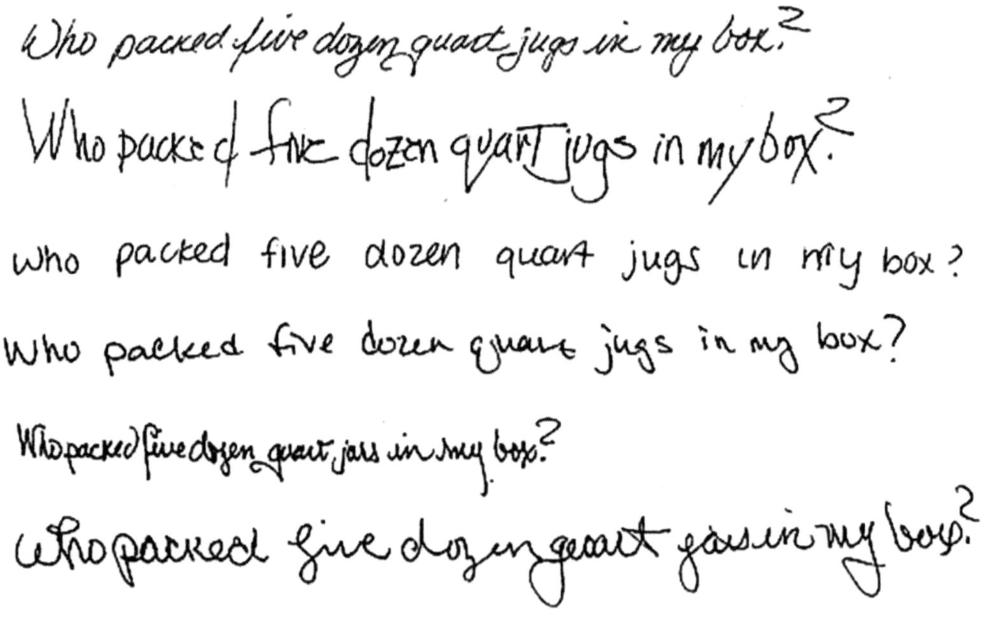

FIGURE 17.6 Handwriting examples showing variations in the shapes of the letters and the slope of the writing.

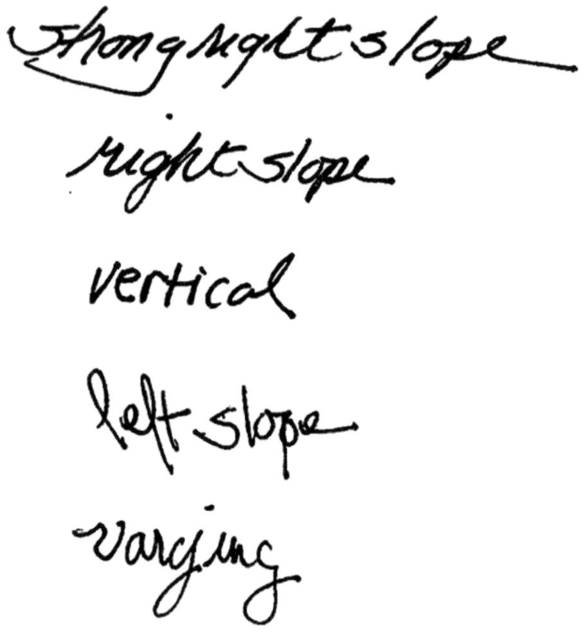

FIGURE 17.7 The slope (slant) of writing is an individual characteristic feature of writing.

FIGURE 17.8 Arrhythmic handwriting: signature of psychopathic mass-murder Charles Manson.

with schizophrenia, for example, show a higher tendency to display writing with strange letter formations, nonsensical words, confusing or illegible text, and rhythmic disorganization of lines and words.

- **Size of the Writing**: The size of the letters, including the relative size of the different letters within a word and the extensions on the letters (the parts of a letter extending below the line or projecting upward, such as found in the letters "g," "t," "h," and "f"), are important individual features. For example, what is the proportion of the "short" letters (e.g., a, c, o, and u) compared with the taller letters (e.g., t, b, d, h, f, and l). Additionally, are the round letters disproportionately wide relative to other letters?

Arrangement:

- **Spacing of the Letters, Words, and Lines**: Both words and letters within words may range from very closely spaced and packed together to more spread out on the page. The closeness of the lines of text and the width of the margin on the page are also important characteristics. When tightly spaced, the writing from one line may overlap with the writing on the following line. It is also usually possible to discern the sequence of the writing, which strokes came first, next, and so on.

Quality:

- **Pressure and Thickness**: The downward pressure and the thickness of the lines, often a function of the pen employed, are characteristics of the writer. Analysts look for the smoothness of the lines and try to gauge the speed of writing from the pressure and thickness of the lines. Slower writing may be a valid indication of forgery, where the writer goes slowly to mentally copy an exemplar of someone's signature. Pauses in writing, sometimes evident from breaks in the writing or places where the pen has been removed from the paper and then restarted can also indicate forgery.

Content:

- **Grammar, Spelling, and Syntax**: The spelling, grammar, capitalization, and punctuation used in a document help reveal the preferences, background, and training of the author. For example, in the famous example of the ransom note in the Lindbergh kidnapping case, the grammar and spelling in the document provided important information about the kidnapper (a German immigrant):

     "Dear Sir! Have 50 000$ redy with 25 000 $ in 20 $ bills 15 000 $ in 10 $ bills and 10 000 $ in 5 $ bills. After 2-4 days we will inform you were to deliver the Mony. We warn you for making anyding public or for notify the Police the child is in gut care."

17.1.4 Handwriting Comparisons

The most commonly encountered questions in handwriting analysis deal with determining the authorship of a document. The key questions generally may be framed in two possible ways: were two documents written by the same hand (identification) or were the two documents written by different people (forgery). Answering these questions requires a comparison of the questioned document with handwriting examples known to have been written by the purported author of the questioned document. The analyst usually places their conclusions into one of nine categories based on how certain they are that the handwriting belonged to the ascribed author:

1. Identification (highest degree of confidence)
2. Highly probable
3. Probable
4. Indications (some evidence for similarities exist but the connection is relatively weak)
5. No conclusion (unable to make a determination)
6. Weak indications (dissimilarities exist, no strong evidence)
7. Probably not (the two documents likely did not come from the same author)
8. Strong probability not (almost certain that the two documents do not match)
9. Elimination (the two documents were definitely written by different authors)

These nine levels help quickly relate the confidence level that the analyst has in their conclusions on the authorship of a questioned document based on the physical evidence available.

BOX 17.2   REQUEST EXEMPLARS AND THE LAW

The U.S. Supreme Court has ruled in several key instances that it is legal to require handwriting exemplars from a suspect, with or without their permission. These decisions have stated that taking these samples, even before a lawyer is appointed for a suspect, does not violate a suspect's 4th or 5th amendment rights (*Gilbert v. California, 1967* and *US v. Mara*, respectively). The Court has ruled that the handwriting of a person is an "identifying physical characteristic outside its [5th amendment] protection." They have also said that requiring an exemplar does not constitute an unreasonable search and seizure, meaning that the person's 4th amendment rights are not violated by requiring a handwriting exemplar.

Handwriting analysis is a slow and time-consuming process built upon the examiner's study and experience of the ways that people form letters and words. When comparing two documents to determine if they were written by the same person or not, individual characteristics are the most important elements to identify, especially dissimilarities. While a single particular handwriting feature may appear in common in the handwriting of many people, it is highly unlikely that two people would share multiple individual features in their handwriting. As more and more characteristic features are identified, the more likely it becomes to uniquely identify or rule out one person as the author of a document. Likewise, as more dissimilarities are noted, the more likely it is that the two documents came from different people.

The process usually begins by locating comparison writing samples of known authorship, referred to as *exemplars*, and carefully sorting through both the exemplars and questioned document to locate and study any individual characteristic features. The collection of as many comparison examples of known authorship as possible leads to greater certainty in the analyst's conclusion. One of the biggest problems frequently encountered comes when dealing with a questioned document that is relatively short or when exemplars are either scarce or without enough variation to allow for a valid comparison. The authors of questioned documents often work diligently to disguise their handwriting by using block letters, unnatural writing styles (sometimes changing hands and slants), carefully copying exemplars, or forcing their writing into unfamiliar sentence structures. Each of these factors can make the analysis of authorship particularly difficult.

Natural variations in a person's handwriting occur all the time, even within the same sentence. Because of these natural differentiations, a significant number of exemplars are needed to more fully understand the *range* of variation. Finding exemplars, however, may be a difficult problem and can require careful investigation.

Exemplars usually fall into two categories: request and non-request samples. *Non-request* samples are those that were written under "natural" conditions, usually before the person's writing was of any legal interest. Examples written close to the time that the questioned document was written are preferred, although usually a person's natural handwriting doesn't change significantly over time. Non-request exemplars are preferred whenever possible. *Request* samples are those provided by a suspect when asked, usually at times when they know that their handwriting is under scrutiny. In these cases, great care must be taken not to influence a writer's handwriting, such as not showing them the questioned document to copy. When taking the exemplars, it is highly desirable to take repeated samples over time, with breaks in between writing sessions. This approach makes it difficult for a person to alter their writing style consciously and consistently. Examiners must be very cautious and aware of the possibility of *simulation* in requested exemplars. *Simulation* refers to an attempt by someone to intentionally disguise their handwriting. Often, however, it is possible to determine if simulation has occurred, either in the exemplar or in the questioned document, especially in longer documents.

Questioned document analysts use a variety of techniques and methods to compare the individual characteristics of documents. One of the most common methods involves the construction of comparison tables. In this process, the examiner begins by taking each and every letter in the document, one at a time, and builds a table showing the natural variations in the letters throughout the document. When they first encounter a letter, they enter the letter's style into the table. The next time they encounter that particular letter, they compare it to the previous entry; if it shows a variation, it is added to the table. For example, every time the letter "a" appears in the document, it is compared to all the variations of "a" found in the comparison table. Each time the same letter is encountered, the examiner must decide if it is the same as a variation already entered on the comparison table or a different variant; different variants are added to the table, while similar ones are not. A sample comparison table for a document is shown in Figure 17.9. This table shows that the examiner found multiple kinds of the letter "b" and four different variants for each of the numerals "5" and "2." There are a number of tables that must be prepared, one for capital letters, one for letters found at the beginning or end of a word, one for letters within a word, one for script letters, and so on, each with its own set of variants. Additionally, tables for numbers and punctuation are also needed. In actual practice, the examiner takes a digital photograph of the document and copies and pastes a digital image of each letter variant into the table, rather than hand drawing it, so as to have an exact replica of the letter in the comparison table.

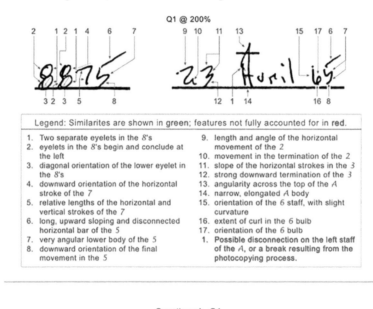

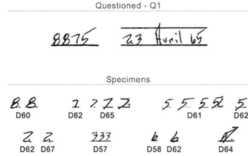

FIGURE 17.9 A letter comparison table showing the range of variation in an exemplar of a person's writing. Toward the bottom of the chart, similar letters and numerals are shown, with differences between the upper and lower portions of the chart indicated.

Source: CRC Bisesi and Kelly, used with permission.

Questioned	Specimen

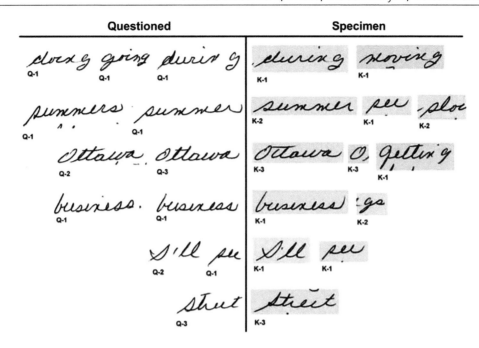

FIGURE 17.10 Letter comparison table for handwriting analysis (the questioned document is on the left, and the exemplar on the right).

Source: CRC Bisesi and Kelly, used with permission.

The process of preparing the comparison tables is completed for all the known exemplars and also separately for the questioned document. At the end of the process, the examiner has a set of tables, one set providing a comprehensive log of photographic images of the known variants of a specific person's handwriting and another set of tables with the variants found solely in the questioned document. The examiner then compares the results in the two sets of tables, looking for similarities and differences. The goal is to achieve a very high probability of either matching the two documents or showing that they were produced by different hands. As a last step, the examiner prepares a final comparison table, such as that shown in Figure 17.10, that combines the results of the individual comparison tables to highlight the differences and similarities found between the exemplars and the questioned document. The example in Figure 17.10 shows that there is a very high probability that the two documents were indeed written by the same person.

Simulation, intentionally disguising one's handwriting such as in creating a forgery or in providing a requested exemplar, may be difficult to discern although there are a number of telltale features that can help detect when it occurs. Ideally, the documents to be compared should be as long as possible to provide a meaningful sample of variants. A lengthier document is also important because, while someone may be able to disguise their handwriting for a short while, over a longer period of writing they eventually get careless, tired, or forgetful and revert back to their native handwriting styles. Finding significant differences, especially stylistic differences, between the beginning and the end of the document can be an important indicator of simulation. Other indicators of simulation include shaky lines, irregular starts and stops in the writing, uneven or heavy pressure on the paper, slow writing, and inconsistent or oddly changing letter characteristics.

BOX 17.3 HITLER DIARIES: A CASE OF QUESTIONED EXEMPLARS

In 1983, the German magazine *Stern* was offered the exclusive rights to publish the previously unknown diaries of Adolph Hitler. These unknown diaries, in 62 volumes supposedly smuggled out of East Germany after their discovery in a wrecked WWII airplane, told a very different story about Hitler's leadership and knowledge of World War II than previously understood. For example, they portrayed Hitler as a more generous and understanding person who had little knowledge of the atrocities carried out by the Third Reich. *Stern* paid 10,000,000 Marks for the journals and announced the discovery and their intent to publish the writings.

Before publication of the diaries, however, *Stern* needed first to verify their authenticity beyond the simple anecdotal information surrounding their discovery. *Stern* submitted samples of the diaries, along with exemplars of Hitler's handwriting from the German Federal Archives, to two of the most respected handwriting experts in the world. Both these experts determined that the exemplars and the diaries positively matched. This news, rather than settling the debate, actually sparked a heated public discussion among historians, publishers and scientists about the diary's origins. To provide more evidence for their claim of authenticity, *Stern* decided to subject the diaries to further testing. Chemical analysis of the diaries, however, showed beyond a doubt that the paper, ink, and glue in their construction were definitely post-WWII materials and that the diaries were forgeries. So, how could the handwriting experts have gotten it so wrong?

As it turns out, the experts got it mostly correct, with one small twist. The forger, Konrad Kujau, had been a prolific forger of Hitler's works for many years, including books, papers, signatures, and paintings. His works were so widespread that when the exemplars were chosen from the National Archives, these too had been forged by Kujau. The experts were actually comparing the diaries against fraudulent exemplars by the same forger. So, the exemplars and the diaries were actually written by the same person – but Kujau and not Hitler. Eventually, scrutiny of the diaries with other Hitler writings, coupled with discrepancies in historical information they contained, further supported the forgery claim. Kujau and his accomplice were ultimately found and convicted of their crimes. It all shows how important good exemplars are!

FIGURE 17.11   Hitler Diaries: (a) Hitler's original signature and (b) Kajau's forged Hitler signature.

Source: Retrieved from Wikimedia Commons; used per Creative Commons Attribution.

17.1.5 Questioned Signatures

Among all forms of handwriting, a person's signature is the most personalized and sometimes the most valuable. We use our signatures to certify our wishes, transfer funds, make agreements, and validate legal documents. Because of the value of signatures as our endorsement of a document, forensic questioned document examiners are often required to determine if a signature is authentic or a forgery.

Generally, analysts look specifically at the accuracy and fluency of a signature in determining its authenticity. The accuracy of a signature relates to how the letters are formed, including any embellishments, and whether it contains individual characteristics that match with the exemplars. Fluency relates to how smoothly and rapidly a signature is made. People often spend years "working" on their signatures to individualize them, and, therefore, can generate intricate and highly personalized signatures quite rapidly. Accuracy and fluency in a forgery actually work against each other; as a forger writes more fluently (rapidly), the accuracy of the signature is usually decreased. In the analysis, it is usually not possible to

determine specifically who the forger was but only whether the signature was, or was not, forged. A famous example, shown in Figure 17.12, illustrates a comparison between an exemplar and two questioned signatures that the FBI determined to be forgeries. The position and ink pooling of a signature relative to the rest of the document can also be important if there is a known tendency for someone to sign in a particular place, as illustrated in Figure 17.13.

There are several common methods that forgers use to produce unauthorized signatures and handwriting. These include:

- **Forged Signature**: In this case, the forger makes no attempt to conceal their own handwriting and simply signs a person's name to a document using the forger's normal handwriting. This is more effective than might be thought since the recipient of the forgery might have no ready frame of reference to even suspect a forgery.
- **Simulated Signature**: These are signatures where a forger first carefully examines an authentic signature and then produces the forgery "freehand,"

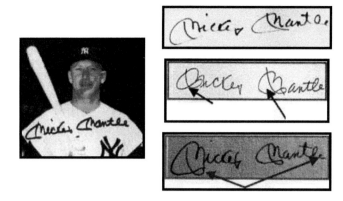

FIGURE 17.12 Questioned signature of famous baseball player Mickey Mantle on a photograph. Mantle's known signature is shown at top, and the lower two were determined by the FBI to be forged versions.

Source: FBI.

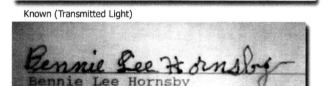

FIGURE 17.13 Examination of a questioned signature showed "pooling" of the ink in the signature. It was later found that the authentic signatures also showed similar "pooling." While this was initially thought to indicate a forgery, it was later shown to be consistent with the writer's normal writing.

Source: CRC Bisesi and Kelly, used with permission.

(a)

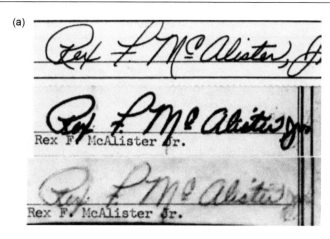

(b) GENUINE

SIMULATIONS

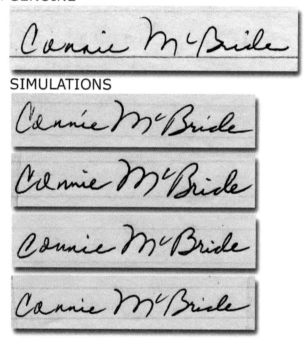

FIGURE 17.14 (a) The authentic Rex McAlister signature is shown at the top and the middle figure is a forgery, with an infrared photograph of the forgery, which showed a faint carbon outline underneath the ink, below. (b) The signatures of Connie McBride show a series of simulations by a skilled forger.

Source: CRC Bisesi and Kelly, used with permission.

without any aid except the forger's skill. The forger may first practice repeatedly to become proficient in producing the signature naturally before making the actual forgery (Fig. 17.14).

- **Traced Forgery**: The forger uses an authentic signature as a template that they carefully follow in making the forgery. There are several ways that this can be done. In one method, the forger places the authentic signature *over the document* that will contain the final forgery. They then trace heavily over the authentic signature, making an indented version of the signature on the underlying forged document. Finally, the forger goes over the indentations on the forged document with a pen to produce the final signature. In another method, the document containing the authentic signature is placed *under the document* that will contain the final forgery. A light is then shone through both documents from below (often using a light-box or window), and the forger follows the authentic signature in pen on the top forged document. In a third method, a pencil version of the authentic signature is first carefully made, either freehand or by using carbon paper. Then, the forger traces directly over the penciled signature in ink. After the ink has dried, the pencil marks can be erased, leaving just the pen signature visible. Each of these methods, however, leaves behind remnants of the tracing method that can be observed through microscopic or spectroscopic study.

- **Intentional Forgery**: In this case, a person intentionally adds forced or unusual features to *their own signature*, intending to disclaim the signature later.
- **Fictitious Signature**: In some instances, both the document and the signer are fictitious, making it challenging to compare the signature with other samples. This might occur when someone uses an alias or attempts to use an official document with an untraceable name for identification or other purposes.
- **Cut-and-paste**: Using computer or photocopying technologies, an authentic signature may be copied from one document and pasted into the forged one. Microscopic examination can often detect this type of forgery as printed rather than handwritten.

BOX 17.4   DETECTING A FORGERY

These some telltale features, which analysts look for in forgeries, include:

- Shaky handwriting
- Unusual pen lifts from the paper
- Slow writing
- Retouching attempts (after the writing has been done to make it look better)
- Resting points (small "dots" where the pen has rested on the paper when interrupted during making a forgery)
- Indentation (evidence of tracing)
- Underlying pencil marks (evidence of tracing)
- Exact match between questioned signature and an exemplar (evidence of tracing since it does not show any natural variation)
- Scaling differences (unusual relative dimensions of the letters and words resulting from a lack of fluency in the writing)

There are a number of challenges, however, in analyzing a signature. Since signatures are relatively short and often embellished, they usually do not display the full range of natural variation in a person's handwriting. Additionally, people never sign their names in exactly the same way twice. For example, if you sign your name multiple times on a single piece of paper, you will find clear differences that distinguish each signature

from all the others. These factors mean that many signature exemplars may be needed to make a valid comparison. Finally, it is important to remember that the legal definition of forgery requires the intent to defraud or mislead; it is not forgery to sign for someone with their full approval and knowledge.

17.1.6   Printed Documents

Today, many people spend far more time typing their communications than handwriting them on paper. In some ways, this makes determining the authenticity of a document's authorship more difficult, but not impossible. It should be noted that determining the authenticity and possibly the source of a typed or printed document is quite different from the field of cybersecurity, verifying computer-based information and communications, as presented in a later chapter.

Typewriter Forensics: Typewriters are rapidly becoming obsolete and today's documents prepared on them are far less commonly encountered in forensic applications. Nonetheless, typewriters are still used in a significant number of homes and offices for producing documents. Additionally, many documents that are legally significant in the present may have been prepared during the "age of typewriters," so the ability to evaluate these documents is still very pertinent today. The forensic identification provided by matching a typed document with a specific typewriter has been well established. Typical questions posed to examiners are what type of typewriter or printer produced a given document (manufacturer, make, and model) and whether a specific machine was used to produce a questioned document.

Typewriters work by manually depressing a key that moves a lever with a raised metal template (a die) of the letter on its end. The typeface die strikes the paper by hitting an inked ribbon that transfers an ink image of the letter to the paper. Typewriters can be either electric or manual, and most commonly use either a separate lever-die combination for each letter (including a printwheel) or a "ball" that contains all the letters (Figure 17.15). Manual typewriters (non-electric) usually have one permanent typeface that cannot be changed readily, while electric units often have interchangeable typeface balls that allow changing fonts. A *font* is a complete set of type in one size and design, as illustrated in Figure 17.16. Today, there are thousands of fonts available for computer-based printing, but both manual and electric typewriters are typically limited to just a few possibilities. The size of a font is usually given in points, a measurement that dates back to the beginning of printing, and today is defined as 72 *points* per inch (or 1 point is equal to $1/72$ in., and 12 points make up the unit called a *pica*), as illustrated in Figure 17.17. To define a particular sample of printing, including typewriting, the class characteristics of font, size, style (e.g., italics, bold, all-capitals, etc.), ribbon-type, and color are all determined.

In the case of a typewriter, the type die gradually becomes worn, dirty, mis-aligned, and even damaged by mis-hits. These imperfections are the source of individual characteristics of one specific typewriter that may connect a sample of typing to that one individual machine. For example, in Figure 17.18, a damaged and worn typeface produces a uniquely modified typed letter. In addition, when the typeface strikes the inked ribbon, transferring the ink to the paper, the ink where the letter strikes is removed from the ribbon. Sometimes, the cloth or paper fibers that make up the ribbon can be seen microscopically in the final

FIGURE 17.15   A typewriter ball transfers images of letters to the paper through an inked ribbon.

Source: Retrieved from Wikimedia Commons; used per Creative Commons 3.0 Unported, Author: Etan J. Tal.

typed letter and matched to the ribbon, as shown in Figures 17.19 and 17.20. Additionally, most typewriters mechanically move the ribbon forward slightly after each letter is struck so that each letter has a fresh ribbon surface to make the print. This means that the ribbon is a type of "ticker-tape" that can be examined to read back the letters and words that were typed on that particular typewriter, as shown in Figure 17.21.

Printer Forensics: Computer-based printing has enormously reduced the use of typewriters in preparing documents. In these systems, the document is first prepared, edited, and stored digitally on the computer, with an enormous range of possible fonts, styles, spacings, sizes, and graphics readily available to the typist. Once prepared, the document may be printed out as many times as desired using one of three main types of computer printers. A *dot-matrix* printer is most similar to a typewriter in that the printer uses an inked ribbon that is struck to produce the images on the paper. Dot-matrix printers, rather than using a single die for each letter, instead use a series of very tiny pins that combine to form the image of a letter on the paper (Figure 17.22). This is the oldest computer printer technology and is largely replaced today by the other printer types. An *inkjet* printer forces ink through a nozzle or many small nozzles (similar to a dot matrix) to form the letters on the page. Finally, in a *laser printer*, a laser beam (an intense beam of light) is used to form a positively charged image of what is to be printed on a rotating metal drum (Figure 17.23). Then, a negatively charged toner powder (the "ink") adheres to the drum only where the positively charged image has been formed. The resulting toner image is then rotated and transferred onto the paper and fused to the surface by the application of heat.

In the examination of printed documents, it is often very difficult to discern information beyond what class or type of printer was used and possibly what software program was employed to create the text (not all fonts are available in specific software packages). It is very difficult to identify an *individual* printer from the documents it prints. In some instances, with laser printers, however, it is possible to identify unique

Script:	*The quick brown fox jumps over the lazy dog.*
Arial Narrow:	The quick brown fox jumps over the lazy dog.
Impact:	**The quick brown fox jumps over the lazy dog.**
Calibri:	The quick brown fox jumps over the lazy dog.
Times New Roman:	The quick brown fox jumps over the lazy dog.
Arial:	The quick brown fox jumps over the lazy dog.
Comic Sans:	The quick brown fox jumps over the lazy dog.
Kristen:	The quick brown fox jumps over the lazy dog.
Arial Black:	**The quick brown fox jumps over the lazy dog.**
COPPERPLATE:	THE QUICK BROWN FOX JUMPS OVER THE LAZY DOG.
Courier:	The quick brown fox jumps over the lazy dog.
Wingdings:	✈︎♒︎❍︎ ◻︎◆︎❒︎⍓︎& &◻︎◻︎◆︎■︎ ✖︎□︎⌧ ☐◆︎◻︎⬧︎ □◆︎❒︎□ ◆︎♒︎❍︎ ●☺︎✲︎⌧ ⬧︎□︎⍓︎⬥︎

FIGURE 17.16   Examples of many different common printing fonts.

Source: Retrieved from Wikimedia Commons; used per GNU General Public License, v3.

2 point	An Introduction to Forensic Science
4 point	An Introduction to Forensic Science
6 point	An Introduction to Forensic Science
8 point	An Introduction to Forensic Science
10 point	An Introduction to Forensic Science
12 point	An Introduction to Forensic Science
14 point	An Introduction to Forensic Science
16 point	An Introduction to Forensic Science
18 point	An Introduction to Forensic Science
20 point	An Introduction to Forensic Science
22 point	An Introduction to Forensic Science
24 point	An Introduction to Forensic Science

FIGURE 17.17 Different sizes of the *Times* font.

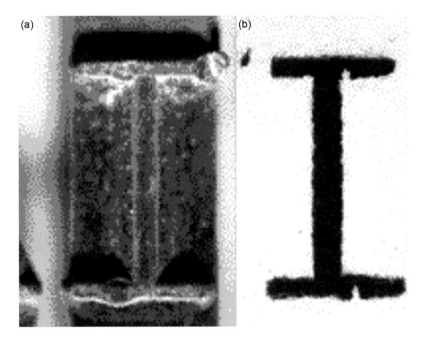

FIGURE 17.18 Damage to the letter "I" typeface (a) and the resulting print (b) shows damage can help to identify letters produced on this typewriter.

Source: FBI.

imperfections located on the image drum that are transferred to the paper. Identifying these imperfections may, in rare instances, provide a method of identifying a single laser printer as the source of a questioned document.

Photocopiers: Photocopiers are very common, readily available to almost everyone, and provide for the rapid duplication of documents, sometimes with extraordinary levels of replication. A typical photocopier operates on essentially the same principles as a laser printer (Figure 17.23) and employs a rotating drum, an intense light source, and toner powder to create an image. Because of wear and microscopic damage to the rotating drum through heavy use, it is sometimes possible to connect a particular photocopied document to one machine by matching these characteristic imperfections on the drum

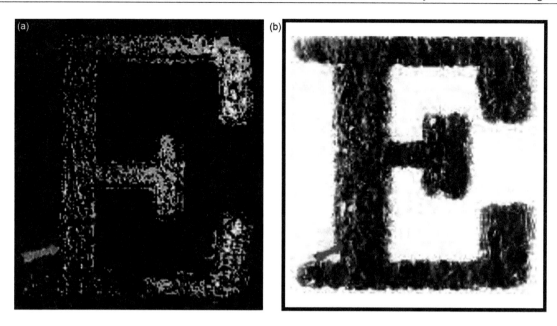

FIGURE 17.19 An example of the transfer of fiber impressions from the inked typewriter ribbon to the paper; (b) Carbon ribbon impression, and (a) the fiber imperfections from the ribbon seen in the typed letter on paper.

Source: FBI.

FIGURE 17.20 Fabric pattern of the typewriter's inked ribbon is seen in the typed letter.

Source: CRC Bisesi and Kelly, used with permission.

FIGURE 17.21 A typewriter ribbon records all the letters typed on that machine. Reading back the ribbon reveals the message typed.

Source: Retrieved from Wikimedia Commons; used per Creative Commons Share-alike 4.0. © Raimond Spekking.

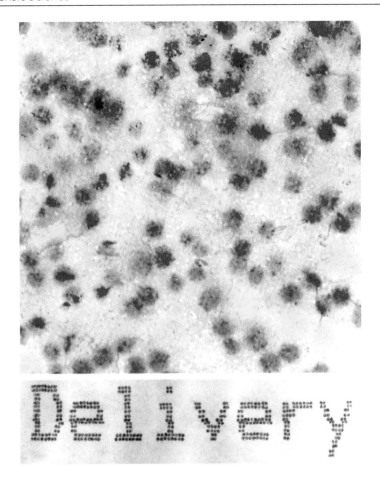

FIGURE 17.22   A dot-matrix printer forms the letter images by using a series of small pins that hit an inked ribbon.

Source: Retrieved from Wikimedia Commons; used per Creative Commons Attribution.

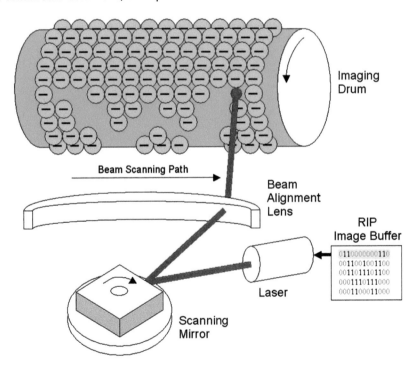

FIGURE 17.23   Steps in laser printing.

Source: Retrieved from Wikimedia Commons; used per GNU Free Documentation License. Author: DMahalko at English Wikipedia.

with the corresponding imperfections in the print. Usually, this requires a microscopic examination of the document and a series of test print exemplars from the photocopier in question for comparison. Additionally, chemical analysis of the toner, the presence of any marks from the paper handling machinery of the copier, and dirt and scratches on the glass of the copier (seen as small specks, called *trash marks*, on the photocopy) help to individualize a particular printer. The trash marks may be particularly useful in quickly linking together a group of documents produced on the same machine.

17.1.7 Other Printed Documents

The detection of forged printed documents, most often counterfeit currencies, bonds and similar valuable items, is an area of enormous concern worldwide. To try to combat counterfeit money and certificate production, governments and corporations continue to develop both traditional and new high-technology safeguards for thwarting the counterfeiter's work (Figure 17.24). Unfortunately, this is a continuing battle as counterfeiters continue to use increasingly sophisticated reproduction methods. Some of the more common anti-counterfeiting measures currently in use include special inks and papers, raised printing, watermarks, micro-printing, embedded identification strips (Figure 17.25), designs that are difficult to reproduce or photocopy, holographic images, color/image shifting printing, and serial numbers, among many others (Figure 17.26). A watermark is a translucent design that is pressed or otherwise ingrained into the fibers of the paper when it is manufactured to leave a faintly visible image when held up to a light source. For example, if most forms of modern currency are held up to the light a faint image will be seen that was invisible before (Figure 17.26). Manufacturers of paper for both commercial and private use also often employ watermarks and frequently change aspects of their own manufacturer's watermark or employ special watermarks designed specifically for one customer that can sometimes be used to establish the date (or range of dates), manufacturer, and purchaser of the original paper. Of course, missing watermarks where they would be expected also can readily expose a counterfeit document. Examiners usually also determine the method used in producing the printed item (e.g., silk-screening, lithography, and others).

A key method for analyzing counterfeit currency involves the use of the comparison microscope. For example, using this technique, an authentic and a questioned bill can be easily compared. A variety of other anti-counterfeit features are also best seen microscopically, as shown in Figure 17.27. Other analytical methods will be discussed in Section 17.1.9.

17.1.8 Obliterated, Altered, Erased, and Indented Writing

Criminals may desire to alter or somehow change existing documents to modify or obliterate their original meanings.

For example, the simple addition or deletion of a single zero at the right of a number changes its value ten-fold. This single action can quickly change a $100 check into a $1,000 check or an IOU from $10,000 to $1,000. Questioned document analysis includes methods that try to restore the original writing their intended meaning and intent.

Obliterated writing occurs when someone tries to conceal original text by adding an opaque substance to block out the ability to visibly read a portion of the document. Techniques have been developed, however, that often allow the original writing to be visualized. These techniques range from simply shining light through the document from behind (Figure 17.28) to the use of high-tech alternative light sources and spectroscopic methods.

Altered writing, including erasures, additions, and deletions, can dramatically change the meaning of a text. If the altered writing has been done by adding writing to the document using a different pen, the chemical differences between the two inks can be spectroscopically differentiated to show what was the original and what was the added text (Figure 17.29). Erasures can also be made visible by using alternative light sources to highlight minute traces of the ink or pencil marks that remain from the original writing.

When writing on a piece of paper that lies on top of other sheets, the pressure of writing can cause indentations on the lower pages, called *indented writing* (or sometimes second-page writing). These faint indentations form an accurate record of what was written on the top document after it is removed (Figure 17.30). Indented writing often happens when writing on pads, diaries, official files (part of a stack of papers), and desk blotters. Matching indented writing on paper in a suspect's possession with that found from a crime provides a valuable link between the suspect and the crime. Similarly, when indented writing does *not* agree with what appears on the written document, then an alteration has most likely been made to the original document.

A number of methods have been developed to visualize indented writing, including oblique lighting (Chapter 16) and using an electrostatic detection apparatus (ESDA). Oblique lighting, which involves light coming in at a low (or oblique) angle relative to the surface of the document, highlights any minute depressions in the paper by causing shadows to form in the indentations. This technique works well for fairly deeply indented paper but may miss more subtle or faint indentations.

Probably the most common method for visualizing indented writing uses an electrostatic detection apparatus (ESDA). In this method, a plastic (Mylar) film is firmly adhered to the surface of the document using a vacuum (Figure 17.31). The paper/Mylar combination is then treated with a high-voltage electrostatic charge. This process yields a charged surface on the plastic with the greatest charge accumulating where the paper has been indented, locating even very faint, microscopic impressions. Toner powder is then spread over the charged plastic surface, and the toner is most strongly attracted to the highest statically charged areas, areas that contain the indentations. After the excess toner has been removed, the visualized indented writing may be either photographed or

$100 Note
Issued 2013 - Present
All U.S. currency remains legal tender, regardless of when it was issued.

Key Security Features

3-D Security Ribbon
Tilt the note back and forth while focusing on the blue ribbon. You will see the bells change to *100s* as they move. When you tilt the note back and forth, the bells and *100s* move side to side. If you tilt it side to side, they move up and down. The ribbon is woven into the paper, not printed on it.

Bell in the Inkwell
Tilt the note to see the color-shifting bell in the copper inkwell change from copper to green, an effect which makes the bell seem to appear and disappear within the inkwell.

Watermark
Hold the note to light and look for a faint image of Benjamin Franklin in the blank space to the right of the portrait. The image is visible from both sides of the note.

Color-Shifting Ink
Tilt the note to see the numeral *100* in the lower right corner of the front of the note shift from copper to green.

Security Thread
Hold the note to light to see an embedded thread running vertically to the left of the portrait. The thread is imprinted with the letters *USA* and the numeral *100* in an alternating pattern and is visible from both sides of the note. The thread glows pink when illuminated by ultraviolet light.

Additional Design and Security Features

 Federal Reserve System Seal
A black seal to the left of the portrait represents the entire Federal Reserve System. A letter and number beneath the left serial number identifies the distributing Federal Reserve Bank.

 Microprinting
Look carefully (magnification may be necessary) to see the small printed text *THE UNITED STATES OF AMERICA* on Benjamin Franklin's jacket collar, *USA 100* around the blank space containing the portrait watermark, *ONE HUNDRED USA* along the golden quill, and small *100s* in the note borders.

 Raised Printing
Move your finger up and down Benjamin Franklin's shoulder on the left side of the note. It should feel rough to the touch, a result of the enhanced intaglio printing process used to create the image. Traditional raised printing can be felt throughout the $100 note, and gives genuine Federal Reserve notes their distinctive texture.

Paper
Federal Reserve note paper is one-fourth linen and three-fourths cotton, and contains red and blue security fibers.

 Portrait and Vignette
The $100 note features a portrait of Benjamin Franklin on the front of the note and a vignette of Independence Hall on the back of the note.

 Symbols of Freedom
Phrases from the Declaration of Independence and the quill the Founding Fathers used to sign the historic document are found to the right of the portrait.

 Gold 100
A large gold numeral *100* on the back of the note helps those with visual impairments distinguish the denomination.

 Treasury Seal
A green seal to the right of the portrait represents the U.S. Department of the Treasury.

 Serial Numbers
A unique combination of eleven numbers and letters appears twice on the front of the note.

 Series Year
The design includes series years 2009 and 2009A.

For more information about U.S. currency visit **www.uscurrency.gov**

FIGURE 17.24 Some of the many constantly changing anti-counterfeit measures used to thwart and detect counterfeit currency, in this case, a $100 U.S. note.

Source: UST.

FIGURE 17.25 An anti-counterfeit strip embedded in the paper of a U.S. $20 bill that fluoresces under UV light.

Source: Retrieved from Wikimedia Commons; used per Creative Commons Attribution.

preserved by placing a second adhesive plastic layer on top of the Mylar, effectively making a "sandwich" containing the toner-highlighted writing. ESDA methods are very sensitive, often revealing writings missed by other methods. Importantly, the unharmed original document may be recovered after the ESDA has been used to visualize the indented writing.

BOX 17.5   ANCIENT WORDS RESTORED

Sometimes, restoring obliterated writing can have non-legal but very important uses. For example, probably the most famous mathematician of all time was Archimedes who lived in ancient Syracuse from about 287 to 212 BCE. One of his greatest achievements and life's work, *the Archimedes Palimpsest*, however, was hidden for safety at a remote Greek monastery following the fall of Constantinople in 1204 AD. After a number of years, its significance was forgotten, and the text was scraped from the parchment pages, turned 90°, folded, and overwritten with the text of a book of prayers. Throughout this time, the manuscript was believed to be lost to history – or so it was thought until 1906. In that year, a Danish scholar recognized the manuscript during his travels and was able to photograph and discern some of the Archimedian text before the volume once again disappeared. Resurfacing in 1998, it was purchased by an unknown buyer, and restoration work began in earnest. Using a variety of light sources, including light from the Stanford Linear Accelerator, the original writings have now been restored. And there was an added bonus. Not only did the Palimpsest contain five complete works of Archimedes, including the only known copies of three of them, but it also contained 4th-century speeches by Hypereides, Aristotle's Categories transcribed by 3rd-century philosopher Alexander of Aphrodisias, and other works.

17.1.9 Analytical Methods

In the analysis of questioned documents, key information can come from the chemical and physical analysis of the paper and inks used in the preparation of the document. From these analyses, the type, age, composition, and even the origin of the ink and paper may sometimes be determined. For example, finding that the ink on a document had a component that was not available when the document was supposedly written rules out the ink or paper as original (see Box 17.3).

Inks are analyzed in a variety of ways, including some methods previously described in this chapter. One of the most common methods involves the chromatographic separation of the different chemical components in the ink (see Section 11.3 for details on chromatography). In summary, chromatography uses the varying interactions of different chemical compounds toward a common material, such as paper or silica gel. For example, compounds that interact only weakly with the paper are pushed along by the movement of a solvent through the paper rather easily. Compounds that interact more strongly with the paper, however, move more slowly. Different inks can be readily separated and analyzed from one another using such chromatographic techniques. Different colored inks are almost always made up of several compounds. For example, blue ink often contains blue, red, purple, magenta, and other colors mixed together in differing proportions to give the characteristic hue of the ink. Separating and analyzing the chemical composition and relative amount of each pigment in the ink can be used to identify the specific ink used in preparing a document (Figure 17.33).

One method becoming increasingly common for examining altered writing is called *hyperspectral imaging*. This type of imaging gathers light from a wide band of the electromagnetic spectrum, typically the visible and near-infrared portion of the spectrum, and breaks it into smaller bands for processing; each band covering a relatively small portion of the spectrum. Each pixel (very tiny part of an image) of the digitized document is analyzed for the amount of light absorbed or reflected at the wavelengths in the band. When the bands for each pixel are analyzed, differences in the chemical compositions in the various locations of the document can be observed, thus locating different types of ink in various places on a questioned document (Figure 17.34). Similarly, hyperspectral imaging can readily detect alterations in a document.

A variety of other spectroscopic methods have been used in analyzing inks and papers. These have primarily included Raman spectroscopy, infrared spectroscopy, and mass spectrometry. Each method provides advantages and disadvantages relative to the information required (see Chapter 12).

The writing on burned and charred documents can sometimes be visualized using spectroscopic methods. The chemical analysis of paper may also provide clues to its components, type, manufacture, and origin. As with other types of physical evidence, pieces of a torn or ripped piece of paper can be fitted back together to show that they were once a single piece (Figure 17.36).

$50 Note
Issued 2004 - Present

All U.S. currency remains legal tender, regardless of when it was issued.

Key Security Features

Security Thread
Hold the note to light to see an embedded thread running vertically to the right of the portrait. The thread is imprinted with the text *USA 50* and a small flag in an alternating pattern and is visible from both sides of the note. The thread glows yellow when illuminated by ultraviolet light.

Watermark
Hold the note to light and look for a faint image of President Grant in the blank space to the right of the portrait. The image is visible from both sides of the note.

Color-Shifting Ink
Tilt the note to see the numeral *50* in the lower right corner on the front of the note shift from copper to green.

Additional Design and Security Features

 Federal Reserve System Seal
A black seal to the left of the portrait represents the entire Federal Reserve System. A letter and number beneath the left serial number identifies the distributing Federal Reserve Bank.

 Microprinting
Look carefully (magnification may be necessary) to see the small printed text *FIFTY, USA,* and *50* inside two of the blue stars to the left of the portrait, *FIFTY* repeated within both side borders of the note, and *THE UNITED STATES OF AMERICA* in President Grant's collar.

 Raised Printing
Move your finger along the note's surface to feel the raised printing, which gives genuine Federal Reserve notes their distinctive texture.

 Paper
Federal Reserve note paper is one-fourth linen and three-fourths cotton, and contains red and blue security fibers.

Color
The note includes subtle background colors of blue and red to both sides of the note.

 Portrait and Vignette
The $50 note features a portrait of President Grant on the front of the note and a vignette of the United States Capitol on the back of the note.

 Symbols of Freedom
Representative of the United States flag, a field of blue stars is located to the left of the portrait, while three red stripes are located to the right of the portrait. A small metallic silver-blue star is located on the lower right side of the portrait.

Green 50
A large green numeral *50* on the back of the note helps those with visual impairments distinguish the denomination.

 Treasury Seal
A green seal to the right of the portrait represents the U.S. Department of the Treasury.

 Serial Numbers
A unique combination of eleven numbers and letters appears twice on the front of the note.

 Series Year
The design includes series years 2004, 2004A, 2006, 2009, and 2013.

For more information about U.S. currency visit **www.uscurrency.gov**

FIGURE 17.26 Many methods are used to help prevent the production of counterfeit bills. For example, micro-printing on a $50 bill shows the words "The United States of America" printed on Pres. Grant's collar. Special paper is used that contains very fine blue and red fibers embedded in the paper (not printed on the surface of the bill). Watermarks, such as the image of Grant when held up to the light, and color-shifting inks are used to stop counterfeiters.

Source: UST.

FIGURE 17.27 Microscopic examinations of a U.S. $100 bill, showing anti-counterfeit features: (a) a Scanning electron microscope (SEM) image of the ink on a new 100 dollar bill, showing the special highly reflective optical ink used on the large 100 patterns and on the liberty bell, (b) SEM image of paper used to print the U.S. $100 dollar bill (notice the fibers in the paper), (c) SEM image of the lenticular array in the U.S.$ 100 dollar bill that shows a different color when the viewing angle of the bill is changed, and (d) security feature using micro-printing that is very difficult to duplicate with a laser or inkjet printer.

Source: All images courtesy and used with permission from Science Photo Library.

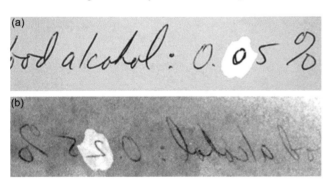

FIGURE 17.28 The obliterated writing on a check by opaque correction fluid (a) can be read (b) by shining infrared or ultraviolet light onto the document or, as in this case, using transmitted light viewed from the reverse side.

Source: CRC Bisesi and Kelly, used with permission.

17.1.10 Legal Challenges to Handwriting Analysis

In recent years, strong challenges have been made in the courts regarding the scientific basis and reliability of forensic questioned document analysis, especially handwriting analysis. While a number of Supreme Court rulings have upheld the place of handwriting analysis in court, controversy still remains around its use in cases, and, at this point, the courts are divided as to its admissibility.

There have been an increasing number of cases where forensic handwriting analysis has been successfully challenged

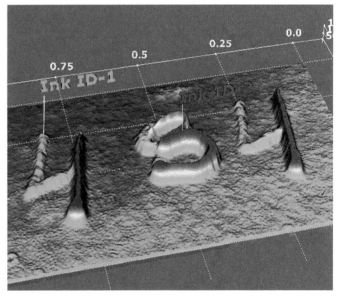

FIGURE 17.29 Hyperspectral imaging can be used to show that two different inks were used in the preparation of a questioned document. The image shows one ink (labeled Ink ID-1) in green while a second, chemically different ink (labeled Ink ID-2) shows up as red. This shows the conversion of the original "131" into "484."

Source: Used with permission courtesy and © ScienceGL, Inc. (www.sciencegl.com).

on the grounds that it does not meet the *Daubert* requirements for good scientific analysis. In an important case (*United States* v. *Saelee*, 2001), a District Court ruled that handwriting analysis was based on a "lack of empirical evidence on

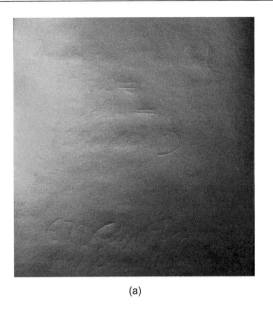

(a)   (b)

FIGURE 17.30   Indented writing.

Source: CRC Kelly and Angel, used with permission.

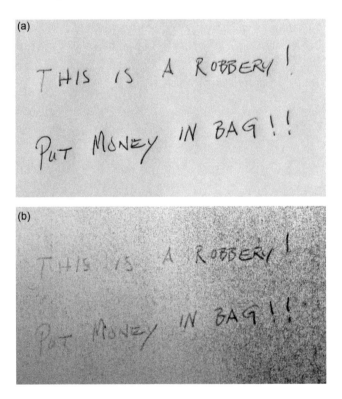

FIGURE 17.31   An electrostatic detection apparatus (ESDA) is being used to visualize indented writing. (a) A handwritten robbery note written on the top-most sheet of a pile of papers. (b) The ESDA image was developed on the sheet of paper positioned beneath the written note at the time of writing.

Source: Retrieved from Wikimedia Commons; used per Creative Common Share-alike 4.0. Author: QDE-can.

the proficiency of document examiners" and "little empirical testing [had been] done on the basic theories upon which the field is based." Additionally, the court found that "not much is known about the error rates of forensic document examiners." Because of this, they ruled that in this case "the handwriting expert's testimony [was] not sufficiently reliable to be admissible." Other court decisions, however, have found handwriting analysis meets acceptable scientific standards and is admissible. In a 2011 study, the handwriting of 1,500 people was analyzed by a computer program and found that the program

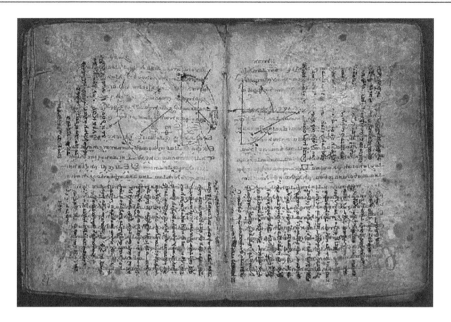

FIGURE 17.32 A page from Archimedes' famous Palimpsest (287–212 BCE). A palimpsest is a manuscript where the original writing has been effaced or obliterated to make room for later writing but of which traces of the original remain. In this case, the book was cut, rotated, and the original writing erased to use as a prayer book. It has now been restored such that the original writings of Archimedes can be read. Archimedes was a Greek mathematician, scientist, engineer, and inventor from the ancient city of Syracuse.

Source: Retrieved from Wikimedia Commons; used per Creative Commons Attribution.

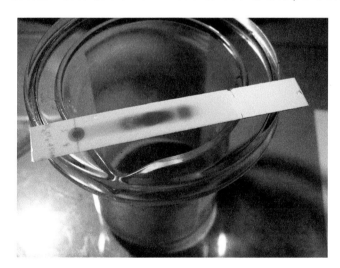

FIGURE 17.33 Thin-layer chromatogram for a sample of black ballpoint pen ink.

Source: Retrieved from Wikimedia Commons; used per Creative Commons Shareli-alike 3.0 Unported. Author: Natrij at English Wikipedia.

was "able to establish with a 98 percent confidence that the writer can be identified." This result, when considering the age, race, sex, and other variables of the writers, was extrapolated to conclude that the estimated confidence of determining the writer of a document for the entire U.S. population was 95%. Handwriting analysis is today employed in many forensic investigations and work is now being done to provide the necessary validation and quantification to allow this form of analysis to stand firmly on a solid scientific foundation.

FIGURE 17.34 Hyperspectral images of Thomas Jefferson's draft of the U.S. Declaration of Independence. The bottom five images show a portion of the writing analyzed at different wavelengths. At some wavelengths (lower two), the word "subject" is seen to underlie Jefferson's overwritten word "citizens," rather significantly changing the tone of the document.

Source: Library of Congress (Fair Use).

BOX 17.6   A MASTER FORGER'S WORK

One of the most famous and gifted American forgers was Joseph Cosey, who did his work during the early part of the 20th century. Cosey specialized in historical documents, from Jefferson to Lincoln. One of the reasons that Cosey's work was so hard to detect was his use of "vintage" materials – paper, pens, and inks that were used at the time that the forged authors lived. Combining these period materials with amazing skill, Cosey was very successful in his trade – but not quite successful enough. He was eventually caught in 1937 and sentenced to three years in prison. It is believed by experts that many of Cosey's forged documents are still in circulation and believed to be authentic.

For example, one of Cosey's most famous forgeries was the signature of President Abraham Lincoln. The top signature is the forgery, and the one below it is the actual signature of Pres. Lincoln. Note that the forgery follows a rather straight line while the original is much more irregular in its baseline. Nonetheless, it is an amazingly good replica.

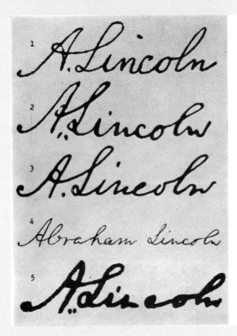

LINCOLN AUTOGRAPHS AND FORGERIES
(Solution to picture queries on page 82)

1. A forgery on a copy of the Wigwam Edition (1860) of Lincoln's life and works. As explained in the text Lincoln was not in the habit of autographing publications of this kind. The regularity of the writing disclosed in the enlargement, makes this the poorest imitation of the lot.

2. A genuine signature affixed to a letter to General H. W. Halleck dated September 19, 1863. Lincoln usually put two dots after "A" but not always.

3. A forgery of Lincoln's name signed to a promissory note dated November 16, 1860. Enlargement discloses this signature to be too nearly perfect. There is something wrong with the "A." Moreover, Lincoln in November, 1860, did not need to borrow $35 on a note.

4. Lincoln seldom signed "Abraham" to a letter but he almost always used his full name on a document. This example is genuine.

5. A forgery by Joseph Cosey. Notice how he used porous paper to blur his lines and thus hide their irregularity.

FIGURE 17.35   President Abraham Lincoln's (1809–1865) signature and forged versions of his signature (*Journal of the Illinois State Historical Society* (1908–1984), 1949 Illinois State Historical Society).

Source: Fair Use.

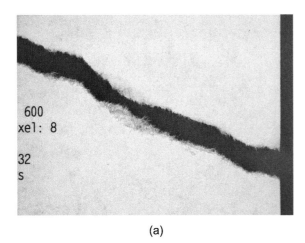
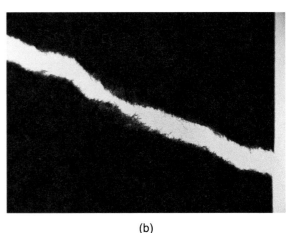

(a)   (b)

FIGURE 17.36   Ripped pieces of paper can be fitted back together to show that the two pieces were once joined together.

Source: CRC Kelly and Angel, used with permission.

BOX 17.7   2001 ANTHRAX ATTACKS

In September 2001, anonymous letters containing deadly anthrax spores were sent to several news agencies and to Congress. Ultimately, five people were killed, and 17 others were infected. The government launched one of the most extensive and far-reaching criminal investigations ever undertaken to find and stop the perpetrator.

One of the key pieces of evidence came from the actual letters containing the spores. All the letters were prepared on a photocopy machine and were different sizes. The letters were carefully analyzed for handwriting, syntax, and hidden meaning to provide important clues in the case. Eventually, the letter evidence and other investigative information, such as analyses of the anthrax origins, led the FBI to conclude in 2008 that a former biodefense worker, Dr. Bruce Ivins, was the sole perpetrator of the crime. Ivins committed suicide on July 27, 2008, and the FBI formally closed the investigation in 2010.

FIGURE 17.37   Envelope from the anthrax letter sent to the office of Sen. Tom Daschle in 2001.

Source: Retrieved from Wikimedia Commons; used per Creative Commons Attribution.

17.2 FORENSIC PHOTOGRAPHIC AND VIDEO ANALYSIS

A picture is worth a thousand words.

(anon.)

LEARNING GOALS AND OBJECTIVES

Photographic images are expected to capture and preserve unbiased information. These images may be useful for the identification of criminals and documentation of the events that occur during the commission of a crime. When you complete this section, you should be able to

- Discuss relevant aspects of video and photographic forensic analysis.
- Describe the uses of photographic images in forensic investigations.
- Expand upon the tools and methods used to analyze photographic evidence.
- Explain some of the limitations and challenges to image analyses.

17.2.1 Introduction

Video and photographic devices seem to be everywhere, from cell phones and personal computers to surveillance cameras in stores, streets, and offices. Whether we are aware of it or not, we are often being watched and recorded by cameras that stand

FIGURE 17.38　Surveillance cameras watch our every move, and such forensic photographic analysis can provide information critical to an investigation. In 2021, it was estimated that there were about 85 million surveillance cameras in the United States and over one billion installed worldwide. It has been estimated that cities in China have about 440 cameras per 1,000 people, while Moscow (Russia) has ~17 cameras per 1,000 and London has about 13 cameras per 1,000 people.

Source: Shutterstock.

constant vigil in recording people and property (Figure 17.38). Cameras watch for shoplifting in stores, traffic violations at road crossings, vandalism outside buildings, robberies in homes, and unauthorized entries to restricted places. Police and others now routinely wear body cameras that record both their actions and those of people they deal with. Because of their prevalence, photographic devices are increasingly capturing important forensic evidence. These images may provide dramatic records of the actions that occurred as part of a crime, leading to the identification of the criminals and tying them to their actions.

Photographic and video records have a powerful impact on people. Because of the power of this influence, images may be altered and modified to improperly manipulate and wrongly change our understandings, beliefs, and feelings about events and people. Modified videos and pictures are quite easily made using readily available computer software and rapidly distributed as authentic renditions of events around the world. These manipulations may range from the subtle enhancement of the appearance of a model to blatant manipulations to add or remove people and objects from a scene.

The role of forensic photographic and video analysis spans a number of areas including image enhancement, authentication, documentation, and analysis. These topics will be briefly presented in this section.

17.2.2 Video Forensic Analysis

Video images captured by surveillance cameras and personal video cameras, especially phone cameras, can play a role in an investigation and later criminal prosecution. Forensic video analysis may come into play in several aspects of inquiry, including:

- Making a record of crime scenes as part of the processing of the scene.
- Recording the events that occurred during the commission of a crime.
- Documenting the authenticity of a video.
- Separating multiplexed video signals from multiple surveillance cameras (images from many cameras recorded on one tape).
- Enhancing and clarifying video images for the identification of people and interpretation of events.
- Enlarging or highlighting specific areas of interest.

In previous chapters, still and video photography have been described as tools for documenting both the overall features of a crime as well as recording the close-up details of the identified evidence. The crime scene photographic record needs to be taken when the scene is as close to pristine condition as possible, before other types of forensic processing have begun. Photographic images also form a permanent record that can later be used to document the steps employed in evidence location and collection.

Video recordings have been shown to be faithful but often incomplete reporters of criminal actions. Surveillance and personal video recordings have been frequently used in court to identify perpetrators and to document beyond question the extent and sequence of their criminal actions. Often, criminals do not consider the presence of hidden cameras or the likelihood that images taken by accomplices of their actions will make it into the hands of the police.

Video images taken by surveillance cameras at crimes are, unfortunately, often of very poor quality and may show only a limited perspective of the scene. This may arise through the use of inexpensive and poorly maintained equipment, overuse of tapes (sometimes recorded over hundreds of times), unsteady camera handling (phone cameras), poor lighting conditions, limited view locations, rapid motion action, and low-resolution images. In these instances, investigators may turn to computer enhancement techniques to make obscured images in the video visible and understandable.

In the video enhancement process, the video is usually first digitized (if it is not already) onto a computer system. This allows specially developed software to adjust, manipulate, and enhance the images in a scientifically acceptable and court-admissible manner. It is especially important during this process that a proper chain of custody be established, beginning with the original recording and including a detailed log of exactly how the images were manipulated. Many software programs automatically maintain this log, along with the original recording, for later verification in court of how the enhancements were performed.

Surveillance systems often use multiple cameras that feed into a single recorder. The recorder "multiplexes" these images onto one video recorder, usually by recording just a few frames from each camera at a time or encoding superimposed images from all the cameras together. The resulting tape is unwatchable in the multiplexed form because of the very fast switching that

FIGURE 17.39 Reconstruction of car number plate LUE 991L: blurred original and maximum entropy reconstruction - a computer enhancement technique.

Source: Science Photo Library.

happens between cameras or because of the confusion of super-imposed images; to be viewed, the forensic software must first de-multiplex the images – putting all the scrambled images from one camera back into one sequence. Complicating this de-multiplexing task is the fact that different security systems have varying ways of performing the multiplexing operation, and each requires a particular software package for the de-multiplexing operation. Once completed, the de-multiplexed images may allow investigators to follow a person from one camera to another camera to establish a record of their movements.

Sometimes, video images are too dark or lack sufficient contrast to be able to pick out useful information. When not enough light is present, the image from a video camera is usually filled with "noise," random "sparkles" (sometimes called "snow") in the picture that result from increased amplification of thermal and electronic background signals in the camera's imaging system. Forensic video software must first be used to brighten up this type of image, but this brightening process also increases the noise levels as well. To combat this, the enhancement software **frame averages** several adjacent images by "adding" together a number of sequential frames of the recording. In the frame averaging process, the random noise that changes locations from frame to frame is canceled out while the faint images from real objects remain unchanged and are increased in signal intensity. For example, in Figure 17.39, the dark car license plate image is difficult to see the details in the original image, but through the computer enhancement, the image appears readable.

BOX 17.8   KEYS TO VIDEO EVIDENCE

Managing video evidence can be challenging. Here are a few practices that should be considered when using videos:

- Search for all video cameras that might have captured the event.
- Work quickly; many surveillance systems have auto-erase functions that clear tapes weekly or monthly.
- Check timing recorded on the cameras since they may be inaccurate.
- Confiscate both the recorder (tape) *and* the camera.
- Maintain a proper chain of custody and a log of all enhancement operations for the recording.
- Utilize a forensic video expert to enhance and clarify video images of interest.

(Adapted from the National Center for Audio and Video Forensics (NCAVF); www. ncavf.com/advice/top-tips-for-security-camera-evidence)

Sometimes, video information is not legible because of blurring caused by either a rapidly moving object or by a camera moving too quickly. This often occurs because the shutter speed of the camera (the speed with which the camera creates each new frame) is slower than the speed needed to resolve the blurred object. To "de-blur" such images, forensic video software determines the speed and direction of the object or camera and corrects to keep a portion of the image

FIGURE 17.40   De-blurred image of a moving vehicle makes the license plate readable.

Source: NASA.

stationary in the picture, thereby allowing frame averaging or similar processes to enhance the image, as shown in Figure 17.40.

The images captured by a stationary camera might only record a small portion of an object of interest at a time, such as a vehicle, boat, or plane moving past the camera. It is often desirable, however, to have a picture of the entire object for identification. This is accomplished by aligning multiple images, each capturing a portion of the entire object, to create a "panorama mosaic" picture. To illustrate the process, Figure 17.41 shows how NASA has taken many separate images of the Martian landscape and overlapped them carefully to give a picture covering km of terrain.

17.2.3 Forensic Photographic Analysis

There are two main roles of still photography in forensic science: site/evidence documentation and photographic analysis and enhancement. In previous chapters, the key role of photography in documenting both crime scenes and individual pieces of evidence has been emphasized (Figure 17.42). These images form a permanent record of the evidence that can be revisited periodically as an investigation progresses as well as used in court to connect the evidence with the scene. The Scientific Working Group on Imaging Technology (SWGIT) provided guidelines and best practice information on photographic techniques for legal applications. As with all types of evidence, proper chain of custody procedures must be followed for *each* picture, including an identification number for the shot. Photographic evidence, however, has the added requirement that it must also provide information about where and when the picture was taken, the relative orientation of the photo within the crime scene, and technical information such as shutter opening, focal length, magnification (e.g., wide-angle

FIGURE 17.41   A panoramic mosaic image of the Martian landscape showing the Jezero Crater, from the Perseverance mission.

Source: NASA.

FIGURE 17.42 Surveillance camera images of the September 11, 2001 airplane attack on the Pentagon (a) at the instance of impact and (b) the response after impact.

Source: Retrieved from Wikimedia Commons; FBI images.

vs telephoto), shutter speed, film characteristics (when film is used), and other relevant photographic information. Each photograph must also include some type of scale marker, such as a ruler or object of known dimensions (e.g., coin or similar standard-sized object), which allows the observer to judge the size of the item in the image. This is clearly a very specialized area of expertise that requires significant experience and training to take usable forensic photographic records.

BOX 17.9 JANUARY 6TH INSURRECTION VIDEOS ANALYSIS

On January 6, 2021, a group of attackers stormed the U.S. Capitol Building in a discredited protest of the outcome of the 2020 presidential election, threatening elected officials gathered to certify the results of the election and causing over $30M in damages, according to the Capitol architect. In addition, five people died either shortly before, during, or following the event with numerous injuries reported, including 138 police officers.

Photographic evidence, from both official Capitol Hill surveillance cameras and videos filmed and later posted by witnesses and the attackers themselves, has formed the basis of the identification, arrest, and trials for many of these assailants. Thus far, over 1,000 people have been identified, arrested, and charged because of their criminal actions on that day, largely found and tried based on the strength of the photographic record.

FIGURE 17.43 January 6, 2020 insurrection video analysis was instrumental in identifying participants in the U.S. Capitol assault in Washington DC.

Source: Shutterstock.

Photography may also be used to capture invisible images by recording infrared, ultraviolet, X-ray, or other wavelengths of light either illuminating an object or emitted by an object. The evidence photographed may range from microscopic-sized objects to crime scenes that may span over miles of terrain. Specialized fields of forensic photography include medicolegal, microscopic, alternative light source, spectroscopic, underwater, impression, and aerial photography. Photographers are also called upon to prepare graphical presentations and present expert testimony for court proceedings.

Increasingly, digital cameras are being used to record crime scenes and evidence photographs. These cameras allow for rapid picture taking, accommodate thousands of images without changing memory chips, and allow for the immediate viewing of the images on-site. Since digital images may also be deleted from the camera's memory easily, once taken, an image should not be deleted, even if it is out of focus or of poor quality. Deleting images opens up the photographer to questions by the opposing counsel about why they were deleted. Was it because they showed exculpatory evidence that would exonerate a defendant?

As with video images, photographic images can be modified and enhanced to reveal otherwise hidden information. Dark pictures may be brightened and enhanced to reveal previously hidden details (e.g., license plates, suspect's faces, weapons, etc.). Photographs may be digitally sharpened to help identify suspects. An entire range of computer-based enhancements is possible using simple software applications.

Photographic images may also be altered with the intent to cheat or deceive. One important role of forensic photography, therefore, is to authenticate images and expose fraudulently made or manipulated pictures. Photographs taken with older film-based cameras and darkroom printing techniques could be altered, but the process was typically rather difficult and relatively easy to detect. The advent of modern digital cameras and image-altering software, however, has made it quite simple to create sophisticated altered images. While these altered images are occasionally found in artwork and commercial advertisements, they most often come under the purview of forensic experts when they are designed specifically to conceal, misdirect, or defraud viewers.

One way to identify altered photographs is to examine the "specular highlights" in various parts of the photograph. Specular highlights are the bright spots on the surface of the subject in the picture that result from strong illumination, such as from the sun or artificial lighting. For example, the shadows and bright spots for different objects in a picture can be analyzed for intensity, color, and, most importantly, the direction of the light source. If the light sources do not match up, the photograph has likely been altered. Additionally, backgrounds can be "cloned": exact copies of small portions of the picture pasted at other locations in the picture. These are identified by finding identical "pieces" in several places in the photograph. A great variety of other photographic alterations are possible, and sophisticated tools have been developed to locate such deceptions (Figure 17.44).

FIGURE 17.44 An altered photograph claimed in 2020 to show former U.S. Secretary of State and 2016 presidential candidate Hillary Clinton shaking hands with al-Qaeda leader Osama bin Laden. The image was shown to be altered to add bin Laden to the scene, who was killed by U.S. forces in 2011, but not before millions had viewed and believed the photograph's veracity worldwide. The original version of the picture showed Clinton with Indian musician Shubhashish Mukherjee at an event in 2004.

Source: AFP.

Age Progression to:
55 years old

Rachel Trlica   **Renee Wilson**   **Julie Ann Moseley**

FIGURE 17.45   Age progression photographs of Rachel Trlica, Renee Wilson and Julie Ann Moseley produced by the National Center for Missing and Exploited Children (NCMEC). The small pictures in the bottom left of each age-progressed picture show the girls at the times of their missing.

Source: Retrieved from Wikimedia Commons; used per Creative Commons Share-Alike 4.0 International. Author: http://www.missingkids.com/home.

One photographic tool that investigators sometimes employ to find missing or abducted children is to create an age progression or regression from a known photograph. For example, if a child has been missing for years, the police take a younger photograph of the child and "age" the image so that people might have an idea of what the child would look like today (Figure 17.45). Similarly, age-progressed photographic renderings of suspects, who have long been sought, might aid in finding them.

Clearly, photography may play a key role in a forensic investigation. With proper use and expertise, it can provide invaluable information to the criminal justice system.

17.3 FORENSIC VOICE RECOGNITION AND LINGUISTICS

LEARNING GOALS AND OBJECTIVES

Language can inform legal decisions through voice recognition and the specific usage of language in written and spoken forms. When you complete this section, you should be able to

- Discuss the basics of voice recognition.
- Show how voice recognition may be experimentally done.

- Demonstrate how forensic linguistics can inform legal considerations.
- Describe some of the limitations of forensic voice recognition and linguistics.

17.3.1 Introduction

The ability to speak provides us with the capacity to communicate rapidly and efficiently with others. The production of speech requires the complex and coordinated movements of rather sophisticated structures in our throats, necks, heads, and mouths. However, there are subtle differences in the shapes and sizes of these many sound-producing structures between people that give rise to the individual sound quality of a particular person's spoken voice. We've all experienced hearing the voice of an unseen person, such as on the telephone, radio, or television, and instantly knowing the identity of that person from their voice alone. This ability forms the basis of the field of forensic voice recognition.

In forensic science, voice recognition and linguistics may help identify a speaker by their voice or speech patterns. For example, voice recognition analysis can aid in identifying a person through a threat left on someone's voicemail or answering machine, the audio from a robbery captured on a surveillance camera, or a kidnapper's call to make ransom arrangements. Linguistics can also provide important insights into the questioned interpretation of the meaning of a recorded confession or the authenticity of verbal legal instructions. In instances such as these, an analysis of an audio record may provide crucial information about the identity and intent of the speaker.

17.3.2   Forensic Voice Recognition

Voice recognition for forensic applications is usually considered to have two main uses: voice identification and voice verification. Voice identification focuses on determining who is the speaker on a recording from among a group of possibilities. The group might consist of just a few suspects or include many possibilities. Voice verification, however, deals with determining if a recorded voice belongs to one particular person and involves a comparison of the questioned voice with a known exemplar for that person. Less frequently, voice recognition deals with intelligibility enhancement, security authentication, and other applications.

The physical process of speech requires the carefully choreographed movements of many organs and tissues in the human body, including the brain, nervous system, lungs, larynx, tongue, jaw, and mouth (Figure 17.46). The human voice physically begins with the production of a positive air pressure in the lungs to generate a steady stream of air outward through the trachea (windpipe). This causes the thin tissues of the vocal cords in the larynx to rapidly vibrate (Figure 17.47), producing alternating slight increases and decreases in air pressure, called sound waves (Figure 17.48). The faster the vibration, the higher the perceived pitch of the sound will be. The rate at which these vibrations occur is called the frequency, which refers to the number of sound waves to passing a fixed point in a given amount of time. The sound created in the larynx is modified as it passes through the remainder of the vocal tract. The jaw, lips, tongue, palate, nasal cavity, and other organs modulate the produced sound waves into the audible patterns that we recognize as speech.

The subtle qualities of a sound, sometimes called timbre, depend largely on the specific size and shape of the throat, mouth, and nasal cavity, which vary significantly from person to person. As the sound passes through these areas, it causes the residual air in the cavities to vibrate more or less based on the complex natural frequencies of the space. When this happens, some frequencies of the original sound are reinforced, making them sound louder, while simultaneously reducing others, leading to a smaller contribution of these frequencies to the overall sound. These differences allow us to distinguish the sound of a trombone from a piano playing the same note. It's also the reason we can differentiate one person's voice from another's. Each sound produced from these instruments or a person consists of a combination of many different sound frequencies; when added together, they produce the unique sound that we hear, called a waveform. For example, shown in Figure 17.49 are the different frequencies (waveform) and their intensities (amplitudes) that add together to produce the sound for the word "baby." Changes to the relative amount

HUMAN DIGESTIVE SYSTEM

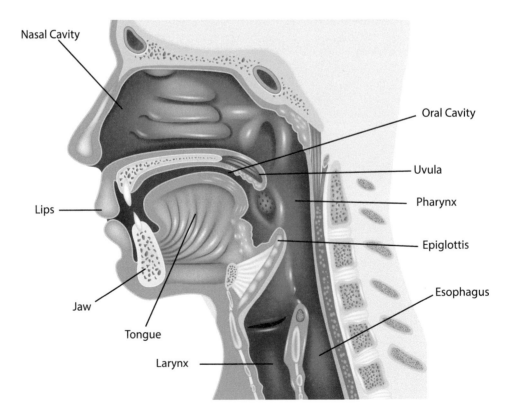

FIGURE 17.46   Some of the organs and tissues involved in voice production.

Source: Shutterstock.

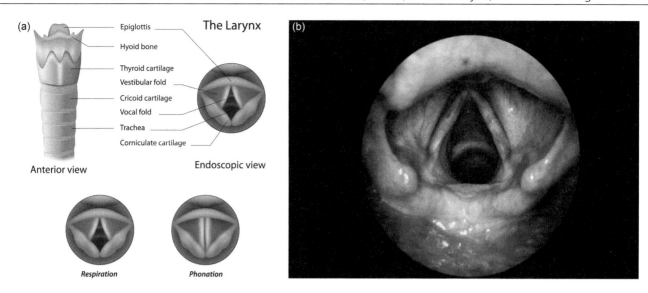

FIGURE 17.47 (a) The Larynx, including the vocal cords and glottis, and (b) an endoscopic image of a resting healthy larynx (voice box) and the resting vocal cords (the inverted v-shaped structure in the center left and right). The vocal cords are responsible for the production of sound by vibrating as air is expelled from the lungs.

Source: (a) Shutterstock, (b) Science Photo Library.

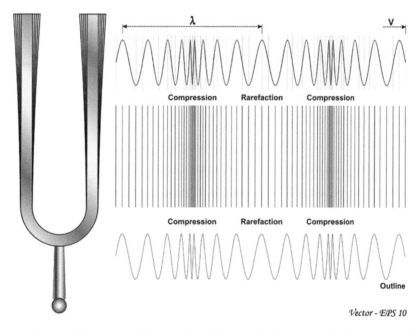

FIGURE 17.48 Formation of increased (compressed) and reduced (rarefied) air pressure by vibration, such as from a tuning fork or the vocal cords, to produce sound.

Source: Shutterstock.

of each individual frequency that contributes to the final mix alter the quality of the sound that we hear.

The differences in the size and shape of a person's vocal cavities, coupled with the characteristic ways they modulate and articulate their words, produce a sound pattern that experts believe is unique to each person. The probability that two people have exactly the same physical makeup in their sound-generating structures and employ the same speech articulations is believed to be extremely small. Scientists have

developed a method to measure and graphically display the different frequencies that exist in the subtleties of our speech, called a *sound spectrograph* or *voiceprint*.

A spectrogram displays three key components of speech in a single plot (Figure 17.50). The vertical axis (middle plot, Figure 17.50) is used to display the different frequencies that make up the sound, while the horizontal axis shows the time elapsed during the measurement. The degree of darkness of the line at a particular point indicates the intensity of that particular frequency at that moment, a darker line indicates a louder frequency, while a lighter line indicates less contribution of that frequency to the overall sound. Putting all of these features together for a given word or sentence produces a voiceprint that captures the individual features of a person's speech, as correlated at the bottom of Figure 17.50.

Voice spectrograms have been used extensively in legal settings, with well over 7,000 reported instances of voice recognition in forensic investigations and court cases. An example of how this is done is illustrated in Figure 17.51. In the top two spectrograms of the figure, the voiceprint of a speaker can be compared with a recorded voiceprint for identification verification, determining whether the two voice patterns were made by the same person.

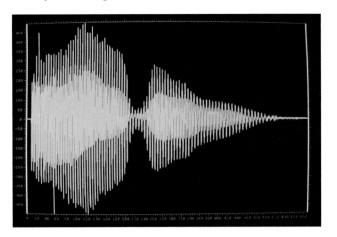

FIGURE 17.49   Sound frequencies that add together to give the characteristic sound of the word "baby," produced on a speech synthesizer.

Source: Science Photo Library.

Research reported by NIST suggests that voice spectrograms might be as individual as a person's fingerprints. However this is still under debate since natural variations are observed in voiceprints of the same person saying the same phrase at different times. Several large-scale studies, including one involving 250 speakers at Michigan State University and one by the FBI using 2,000 test subjects, have reported that high-confidence identifications could be reached in just about 35% of the cases examined and that the error rates in these analyses were near 0.3% for false identifications and 0.5% for false eliminations (FBI study). Because of concerns raised with the methods employed in these studies, however, it has been suggested that these error rates should only be considered as the minimum potential error rates. It has been proposed that at least 20 unique indicators are required to make a valid voice identification, although there is also controversy here. Variations in instrumentation, operator skill, analyst experience, potential analyst bias, disguised voices, and other issues often cast doubt on the validity of voiceprint identifications. Voiceprint identifications are currently being challenged in a number of courts, and some areas have specific restrictions upon their use.

Voice recognition work sometimes includes efforts to improve the intelligibility of speech found on a damaged or noisy recording. Experts have developed a number of computer-based methods to remove some of the noise and artifacts on recordings to enhance the ability to understand the speech on the tape.

17.3.3   Forensic Linguistics

Linguistics, the study of language, is increasingly being used in legal settings for understanding legal texts, informing judicial processes, and interpreting the meaning of specific language

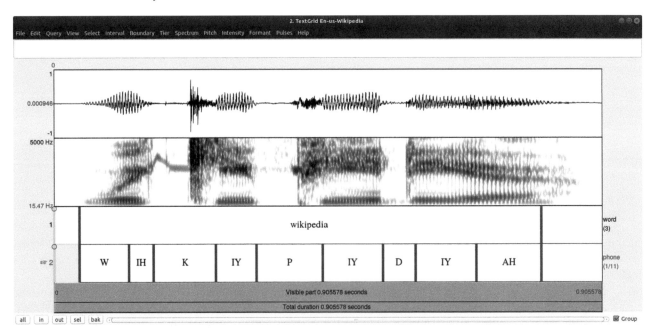

FIGURE 17.50   A voiceprint of a person saying "W-ih-k-iy-p-iy-d-iy-ah" or the word "Wikipedia".

Source: Retrieved from Wikimedia Commons; used per GNU General Licence, v3. Author: Wugapodes.

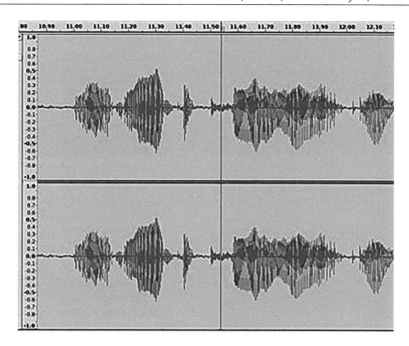

FIGURE 17.51 Voice spectrographs may be able to aid police investigators in identifying a person by matching their voice sample (shown above) to voice data records, in a method similar to matching fingerprints.

Source: NIST.

in criminal cases. Applications may include cases relating to the ability of certain suspects to understand their legal rights, the specific wording of criminal confessions, the meaning of certain statements made by participants during the commission of a crime, and the protection of the commercial rights of corporations for certain words and phrases, to name just a few.

One common application of forensic linguistics involves interpreting the language of the law, including written judgments, statutes, and legal agreements (e.g., contracts, mortgages, wills, etc.). Since linguistics deals with how meaning and intent may be communicated between people, linguists can help to interpret the meaning behind the legal prose in documents that can sometimes be particularly confusing to lay readers. Specific language is also important when communicating with juries regarding their instructions as well as in understanding courtroom testimony. How lawyers phrase questions, and how these questions are understood by those testifying can play a key role in the proceedings.

Language plays an important role in various aspects of the pre-trial criminal justice system, including interrogating witnesses and suspects, collecting statements, and obtaining confessions. This role is especially critical when dealing with bilingual or non-native speakers, as phrasing, tense, and voice (e.g., active or passive) may have subtly different meanings across languages.

Forensic linguists are occasionally asked to clarify the meaning of someone's words or to explain why a particular phrasing was used. For example, in one case (Derek Bentley Case, UK 1952), a police officer asked a cornered criminal to give him their gun. An accomplice allegedly then said to the gunman "Let him have it!" The policeman was then shot and killed. But what did the accomplice actually mean – hand the officer the gun or shoot the officer? The entire prosecution of the accomplice rested upon how that phrase was interpreted. The answer to this question would mean the difference between the accomplice advocating for surrender or promoting homicide (the accomplice was convicted).

BOX 17.10   TRADEMARKS TO GENERIC LANGUAGE

Linguists have been called to testify as to when a trademark becomes so widely used that it loses its legal protection. A number of common terms in our language today have made the transition to generic usage, including:

- **Aspirin**: Acetylsalicylic acid and owned originally by Bayer AG.
- **Band-Aids:** Protective skin covers, owned originally by Johnson and Johnson.
- **Coke**: Cola-containing drink, registered in 2003 by Coca-Cola Corp. but debated.
- **Escalator**: Moving stairs, originally owned by Otis Elevator Co.
- **Google**: To search the internet, owned by Google Inc.
- **Heroin**: An opiate drug, originally a trademark of Bayer AG.
- **Thermos**: An insulating container, originally owned by Thermos GmbH.
- **Yo-Yo**: Originally a trademark of Duncan Co.
- **Zipper**: Interlocking fabric connectors, originally owned by B.F. Goodrich.

Linguists may also become involved in trademark disputes, such as determining how trademarks and legally protected words may be translated into another language. Additionally, when a trademark becomes part of the common generic language, it loses its legal protection and corporate ownership. For example, many people use the word "Xerox" generically to mean making a photocopy, although the term was originally intended solely to relate to the copiers produced by the Xerox Corporation. Similar terms might include "to google" as a generic term (to search for something on the internet), having a "coke" (meaning a generic cola), or aspirin (meaning acetylsalicylic acid, originally a trademark owned by Bayer).

Forensic aspects of language clearly play key roles in many types of legal processes. Given the continued evolution of both language and the means by which we choose to communicate, the field seems destined to continue informing legal proceedings in the future.

BOX 17.11 THE GREAT ESCAPE

In the 1963 movie *The Great Escape* depicting the escape of prisoners from a German POW camp, a tunnel is constructed from a barracks within the camp to an area beyond the containment fence. Two of the prisoners eventually make their way in disguise to a bus leaving the area. They are captured, however, when a suspicious Gestapo agent wishes them "good luck" in English. When one of the prisoners unconsciously responds to the Gestapo agent in English, they are captured. This illustrates an interesting application of forensic linguistics in determining a person's native language.

QUESTIONS FOR FURTHER PRACTICE AND MASTERY

17.1 What is the definition of forgery?

17.2 What gives rise to an individual's basic style characteristics in their handwriting?

17.3 What are the three basic handwriting styles?

17.4 A counterclockwise circular stroke when writing the letter, O, usually indicates the author is using which hand?

17.5 When examining a questioned document, what specific features is the document analyst looking for?

17.6 When comparing a suspect sample of handwriting to a known sample from a given author, the analyst will

assign it one of nine categories of certainty. What do those nine different categories describe?

17.7 What is the significance of the U.S. Supreme Court decision in *Gilbert v. California, 1967* and *United States v. Mara*?

17.8 What are non-request exemplars?

17.9 What are some of the problems analysts face when collecting requested exemplars of a suspect's handwriting? What measures are taken to minimize some of these problems?

17.10 What does the term, simulation, mean with respect to handwriting?

17.11 What are comparison tables and how are they constructed?

17.12 What are some of the signs that indicate an exemplar is a simulation?

17.13 When analyzing a signature for authenticity, what is meant by accuracy and fluency?

17.14 What is the difference between a forged signature, a simulated signature, and a traced signature?

17.15 What is: (a) a font, (b) a pica, and (c) a ribbon with reference to a typewriter?

17.16 What are the differences between dot-matrix, inkjet, and laser jet printers?

17.17 What is a possible way to connect a copied document to a particular copy machine?

17.18 What are "trash marks"?

17.19 What are common anti-counterfeiting measures currently in use with U.S. currency?

17.20 What might chemical and physical analysis of a questioned document determine about the ink and the paper used in that document?

17.21 What methods are used to compare ink samples?

17.22 What is hyperspectral imaging and what is it used for?

17.23 What are some of the common difficulties that forensic scientists face when analyzing surveillance video?

17.24 What is multiplexing?

17.25 What does the acronym SWGIT stand for?

17.26 What information must be included with every photograph that is being used as evidence?

17.27 What are specular highlights? How do they help determine if a photograph has been altered?

17.28 What are the two main uses of voice recognition for forensic applications?

17.29 What parts of the body are involved in producing speech?

17.30 What is timbre? What factors contribute to timbre?

17.31 What is a sound spectrograph?

17.32 What three key components of sound are displayed on a sound spectrograph?

17.33 There are several valid concerns over the reliability of voice prints as evidence. What are some of these concerns and what reliability percentage has the FBI assigned to voice print evidence?

EXTENSIVE QUESTIONS

17.34 Explain the four main categories of individualizing features in handwriting.

17.35 Explain the oblique lighting method of analyzing indented writing as well as the electrostatic detection apparatus method.

17.36 A video of a crime being committed is sent to the lab for analysis. The quality of the video is poor. It is dark with lots of noise, is blurry and has several partial images of the suspect's getaway vehicle. Explain what the lab can do to make the video much more useful to investigators.

GLOSSARY OF TERMS

age regression and progression photography: the process of taking a picture of a person and simulating their appearance at either a younger or older age by software manipulation of the picture.

altered writing: the changes made to a document that include erasures, additions, and deletions.

block capital writing: a method of writing that uses all upper-case (capital) letters which are upright and separated from one another.

chromatography: a method that uses the varying interactions of different chemical compounds toward a common material to separate the components of a mixture.

copybook: an instructional handwriting model.

counterfeit: an imitation made to be mistaken for a genuine article, such as counterfeit money.

cursive writing: a method of rapid writing in which most of the letters in a word are joined together, leaving spaces only between words.

de-multiplexing: the process of separating multiplexed images into separate images, such as those obtained from a single source (camera).

dot-matrix printer: a printer, similar to a typewriter, that uses very tiny pins combined to form the image of a letter onto paper.

electrostatic detection apparatus (ESDA): a device that uses a high-voltage electrostatic charge to visualize indented writing.

exemplar: a writing sample of known authorship.

fictitious signature: an instance where either or both the document and the signer are imaginary, such that there are no exemplars and the signature cannot readily be compared with other samples.

font: a complete set of type in one design:

forgery: the act of preparing or altering a document, signature, financial certificate, work of art, or other item with the intention to defraud, damage, misrepresent, or cheat.

frame averaging: when several adjacent images are added together to reduce random noise and enhance the image on the recording.

frequency: the number of waves that pass a fixed point per unit of time.

graphology: a pseudoscientific field that tries to form a connection between the features of a person's handwriting and their personality or character traits.

handwriting: a person's individual style of writing with an implement.

handwriting style: a basic system or process of handwriting such as block, script, or cursive.

hyperspectral imaging: an imaging system that gathers light from a wide band of the electromagnetic spectrum and breaks it into smaller bands for processing, each band covering a relatively small portion of the spectrum.

indented writing: when writing on a piece of paper that lies on top of another material causes indentations in the underlying material.

inkjet printer: A printer that forces ink through an array of tiny nozzles to form letters and images on the page.

intentional forgery: when a person intentionally adds forced or unusual features into their own signature such that they can later disclaim the signature as their own.

larynx: the muscular and cartilaginous organ at the upper portion of the trachea, containing the vocal cords, often called the voice box.

laser printer: a printer that uses a laser beam to form a positively charged image of what is to be printed on a rotating metal drum. Toner is then adhered to the charged areas of the drum and transferred to paper.

linguistics: the study of language.

multiplexed images: a sequential or superimposed compilation of images from multiple camera feeds combined onto a single record.

non-request exemplar: a handwriting sample of known origin that is written under "natural" conditions, usually before the person's writing was of any legal interest.

obliterated writing: writing where the original text is concealed by adding an opaque substance to block out the ability to visibly read a portion of the document.

panoramic mosaic: a picture that is prepared by aligning multiple images that each capture a portion of the entire object.

photography: the process of capturing and producing images by the action of light on film or a detector.

point: the size of a font defined as 72 points per inch.

questioned document: any document over which there is some legal dispute regarding its origin, authenticity, or authorship.

request exemplar: an authentic writing sample provided when asked.

rhythm: the regular repetition or "periodicity" of various writing elements, such as word and letter spacing and the visual "flow" of the words on paper.

script handwriting: a method of writing that uses both upper and lowercase letters that are not joined together and resembles most a printed text.

signature: a person's individualized writing of their name.

simulation: an attempt by someone to disguise their handwriting.

sound spectrograph: a device that records the intensities of different frequencies of sound as a function of time, usually as someone speaks.

specular highlights: the bright spots that result from strong illumination, such as from the sun or artificial lighting, on the surface of the subject in the picture.

traced forgery: the use of an authentic signature as a template that is carefully followed in making the forgery.

trash marks: dirt and scratches on the window of a photocopier that are seen as small specks on the copy.

typewriter: a mechanical device that produces print by striking an ink image onto the paper.

voice recognition: the analysis of aspects of voice production and speech that can be used for voice identification and voice verification.

voiceprint: see *sound spectrograph*.

writing style characteristics: handwriting based on a particular writing model.

BIBLIOGRAPHY

Malcolm Coluthard and Alison Johnson (Eds.), *The Routledge Handbook of Forensic Linguistics*, Routledge, 2016.

Malcolm Coulthard, Alison Johnson, and David Wright, *An Introduction to Forensic Linguistics* (2nd Ed.), Routledge, 2016.

David Ellen and Stephen Day, *Scientific Examination of Documents: Methods and Techniques* (4th Ed.), CRC Press, 2018.

John Gibbons, *Forensic Linguistics: An Introduction to Language in the Justice System*, Wiley-Blackwell, 2003.

Ordway Hilton, *Scientific Examination of Questioned Documents*, CRC Press, 1992.

Jan S. Kelly and Mirian Angel, *Forensic Document Examination in the 21st Century*, CRC Press, 2021,

Jan S. Kelly and Brian S. Lindblom (Eds.), *Scientific Examination of Questioned Documents* (2nd Ed.), CRC Press, 2006.

Katherine M. Koppenhaver, *Forensic Document Examination, Principles and Practice*, Humana Press, 2010.

Gerald R. McMenamin, *Forensic Linguistics: Advances in Forensic Stylistics*, CRC Press, 2002.

John Olsson, *Forensic Linguistics: An Introduction to Language, Crime and the Law* (2nd Ed.), Continuum, 2008.

John Olsson, *Wordcrime: Solving Crime Through Forensic Linguistics*, Continuum, 2012.

Steven A. Slyter, *Forensic Signature Examination*, Charles C. Thomas Publ. Ltd., 1996.

Michael Wakshull, *Forensic Document Examination for Legal Professionals: A Science-Based Approach*, Q9 Consulting, Inc., 2019.

Forensic Engineering and Computer Science

18

Scientists investigate that which already is; engineers create that which has never been.

Albert Einstein (1879–1955)

LEARNING GOALS AND OBJECTIVES

Forensic engineering deals with the application of the principles of engineering to legal problems. After completing this chapter, you should be able to:

- Describe the role that forensic engineering plays in forensic investigations.
- Discuss how an engineering failure analysis may be performed.
- Explain what is meant by structural load, factor of safety, and margin of safety.
- Illustrate the types of information that can be derived from a reverse engineering process.
- Describe how engineering contributes to crime scene reconstructions.
- Answer what is meant by conservation of energy and conservation of momentum.
- Show how energy and momentum calculations may be used in vehicular accident analysis.
- Explain how measuring skid marks provides information in accident reconstructions.
- Describe the role of computer engineering in forensic science.
- Illustrate how emerging fields, such as artificial intelligence and social-media forensics, are shaping forensic investigations.

18.1.1 Introduction

We are surrounded by an amazing complexity of devices, materials, and structures that have been designed and manufactured through the ingenuity, creativity, and hard work of humans. For most of us, the majority of our lives are spent engaged with the products of various engineering disciplines, from the devices that cook our food, to the homes and offices that we live and work in, to the transportation that moves us rapidly and safely around, to the computers that allow us to work and communicate, and even to our leisure-time activities with a multitude of engineered forms of entertainment (e.g., computer games, smart devices, videos, recreational vehicles, digital arts, and many others). Engineers also oversee the building of roads and bridges, processing and packaging of foods, production of safer vehicles, safely treating waste products, and providing clean water. We take most of these things for granted, often not even noticing their existence until, of course, they malfunction. We are fascinated with devices and machines: fast cars, mobile communication, on-demand entertainment, convenient food preparation, biomedical equipment, and so many others. But because of the many vital roles that these structures and technologies play in our lives, it should not be surprising that various forms of engineering may also be part of forensic investigations, especially in the areas of structural failure analysis and crime scene reconstruction. Increasingly, engineered technologies and structures play a more direct role in the commission of crimes themselves, especially in computer-based crimes.

Engineering is the field that takes fundamental scientific, economic and practical knowledge and applies that understanding to the design and construction of structures, devices, materials, and processes that directly impact human lives. The word "engineering" fittingly dates back to the Latin word *ingenium*, meaning an "innate character, nature or talent" or, in other words, using an understanding of nature for practical purposes. Ancient engineers developed basic tools, such as the pulley, inclined plane, lever, and wheel, to construct useful structures for homes, markets, water delivery systems, roads, and temples. In fact, the rise and fall of human civilizations

DOI: 10.4324/9781003183709-22

FIGURE 18.1 A modern reconstruction of the *Antikythera Mechanism*. Originally built between 150 and 100 BCE to calculate the positions of the sun, moon, and planets for any date, it is an extraordinary example of early engineering.

Source: Retrieved from Wikimedia; photo by Giovanni Dall'Orto.

have often been attributed directly to the development of new engineering concepts and methods. The rise of ancient civilizations such as Egyptian, Roman, Greek, Chinese, and Mayan have all been appropriately attributed to the innovative structures, tools, and weapons that they were able to design and construct. Through their works, these cultures were able to shape and extend their empires, primarily because they effectively used feats of engineering to harness their physical environments (Figure 18.1). This reliance on engineering, of course, continues today, where much of what we rely on in our modern daily lives are the products of advances in engineering.

Today, engineering encompasses a host of different disciplines that include aerospace, biomedical, chemical, civil, computer, electrical, materials, mechanical and nuclear engineering, among other specialties. Each of these disciplines focuses on developing a particular type of material, device, or process for a specific desired outcome. Structural and civil engineers deal with the design and construction of larger-scale works, such as buildings, roads, water and sewage systems, canals and bridges that enhance public health, safety and living conditions. Electrical and computer engineers focus primarily on the design of electricity-based technologies, such as electrical circuitry, computers, power generators, and telecommunications. Mechanical and aerospace engineers design and build mechanical systems that are intended to lead to enhanced manufacturing processes, vehicles, robots, aircraft, and weapon systems. Chemical and biomedical engineers work to develop processes and technologies that convert small-scale laboratory chemical and biological discoveries into either large-scale productions or enhanced medical treatments, therapies, and devices. Through the work of these many disciplines, we have learned to control our personal, local, and global environments with amazing skill and complexity.

The discipline of forensic engineering has developed in parallel with modern engineering itself and cuts across disciplinary boundaries. As engineers have learned to apply new techniques over time, they have also sought to analyze what happened when their structures failed. Often this process was focused on learning from these failures in order to gain an understanding of how to build safer and better structures in the future. These investigations were also used, however, to hold the engineers and building contractors responsible for the safety and function of their works. Among our oldest known laws are those dealing specifically with faulty construction projects (see Box 18.1). In the 19th century, forensic engineering formally began to be increasingly used to inform courts regarding negligent or intentionally fraudulent building and design practices. Today, engineers have several important roles to play in court. While forensic engineering has many different aspects, two of the most important are failure analysis and crime scene analysis and reconstruction. These two areas will be the primary focus of the information presented in this chapter.

BOX 18.1   ANCIENT CODES FOR ENGINEERS

Society has long held designers and builders responsible for the function and safety of their products. The famous *Code of Hammurabi*, containing laws laid down almost 4,000 years ago, describes the severe penalties that an engineer could expect if they cheated or failed in their work:

> If a builder builds a house for someone, and does not properly construct it, and the house that he built falls down and kills the owner, then the builder shall be put to death. If it kills the son of the owner, the son of the builder shall be put to death.
> … Since he did not construct it properly, the builder shall rebuild the house at his own expense.

FIGURE 18.2 Hammurabi's code from a stone stele, one of the oldest known deciphered writings, contains building codes and punishments for violating these codes, among other laws (shown is a modern casting from the original).

Similarly, in the Bible, Deuteronomy 22:8 says:

> When you build a new house, you must build a railing around the edge of its flat roof. That way you will not be considered guilty of murder if someone falls from the roof.

Engineered systems have also found their way into the actual commission of crimes. For example, vehicles may be considered evidence in hit-and-run cases, and weapon systems certainly play a common role in criminal activity.

Increasingly, computers and the internet are being used to launch cyberattacks and assaults on individuals, corporations, and even entire nations. Fraud, identity theft, deception, and harassment are constant challenges based on engineered computer systems. And newly emerging fields, including artificial intelligence (AI), cyber surveillance, espionage, fake news, and hacking/phishing, are rapidly changing the landscape for forensic investigators. In the latter sections of this chapter, we will briefly introduce the growing field of computer and internet forensic engineering.

18.1.2 Forensic Engineering Failure Analysis

Forensic failure analysis deals with trying to determine why certain processes, materials, structures, or components failed in the performance of their intended function. This type of analysis can span the entire discipline of engineering and applied science to include investigations such as examining the reasons for a building collapse; the failure of an individual component within a complex system, such as a power cable, pipe, computer chip, or electrical circuit; looking for the causes of an explosion; and investigating how

a manufacturing process either did not produce the desired product or somehow got out of control. In fact, any type of structure, process, or engineered system may be the subject of a detailed forensic failure analysis.

There are generally two goals in forensic failure analysis that drive an examination of the causes of a failure. First, it might be important to decide who was responsible for the failure in order to bring either criminal charges or levy financial damages against them. In this setting, the engineering analysis may inform the court regarding the underlying causes and sequence of events that led to the observed failure along with a comparison of the normal practices expected in the field compared with the practices used in the failed system. If the failed system is found to be below the normal expectations and standards of performance and safety, civil and criminal liability may be assigned. Second, it might be of particular value to modify specific designs or practices in order to prevent similar failures from happening in the future: we try to learn from these failures to avoid repeating the same mistakes. While the *methods* of investigating failures for these two purposes may be nearly identical, the ultimate *use* of the information discovered might be quite different.

Forensic engineering makes use of many of the investigative tools and techniques described in previous chapters. For example, a spectroscopic or microscopic analysis of a failed component might reveal a flaw in a manufacturing process that could lead to a complete system failure (Figure 18.3). This type of analysis usually seeks to discover the chain of events, sometimes extending over many years and involving the contributions of many people from different companies, that must have occurred in a stepwise fashion to yield the observed failure. For example, the full forensic story behind a sudden bridge collapse might start with the identification of a relatively minor design error that was later compounded by faulty materials, improper construction, substitution of below specification building components (e.g., thinner structural steel, weaker cables, or a lower grade of cement than the engineer specified), or poor maintenance. Each of these items, while not individually sufficient to bring the bridge down by itself, nonetheless contributed in a sequential fashion to arrive at a final catastrophic result. The specific methods, tools, and expertise required for these investigations ultimately depend on the nature of the analysis required. The examination of a damaged pipe in a gas explosion may require a microscopic or X-ray analysis of the pipe, while the investigation of a dam collapse might require examination of engineering schematic diagrams and blueprints, contractor notes, aerial photography, maintenance logs, and computer modeling to reach a reasonable understanding of the events that occurred (see Box 18.2).

BOX 18.2   FAILURE OF THE VAL DI STAVA TAILINGS DAM

In July 1985, the upper bank of an earthen dam in Northern Italy collapsed and cascaded into a lower dam, which then also gave way. In the resulting massive wave of water, mud, and debris that hurtled down the Stava valley, 268 people were killed, and over 62 buildings and 8 bridges were completely destroyed before the outflow finally reached the Avisio River.

The cause of the failure was, of course, carefully investigated and found to arise from a number of cumulative factors. Both dams had several key design flaws that included being built upon relatively marshy soil with an upper bank that prevented proper drainage, compounded by improperly installed drainage pipes. Additionally, the dams were enlarged from a planned 9 to 25 m tall (lower dam); too tall for that type of dam, and the two dams were built too close to one another. After their construction in 1961 and 1969, the dams had minimal inspection and maintenance and, when inspected for safety in 1974, were found to be "at the limits" of safety. Despite this, the mine owners provided a "positive security" report that allowed them to enlarge the upper dam to 34 m.

In the reconstructed sequence of events, investigators found that, due to a malfunctioning drainage pipe, the pressure on the unstable upper dam caused its collapse. The added pressure of the contents from the first dam cascading into the lower dam caused that lower dam to fail also, sending 180,000 cubic meters of material down the Stava Valley at speeds approaching 90 km/h.

A trial was held in 1992 that led to the conviction of ten people on manslaughter charges, including company officials and government overseers. The companies were also found liable for damages from their misdeeds.

FIGURE 18.3   Image of foam insulation (a) and a colored X-ray image of part of the space shuttle Discovery (b) showing cracks on the external fuel tank that led to the explosion of the shuttle.

Source: NASA.

Forensic Structural Failure Analysis: One of the most common forms of forensic failure analysis involves determining the reasons for damage or destruction of a large-scale permanent structure. Here, engineers are faced with determining the cause of a sudden structural failure that may have developed slowly over many decades of wear, use, and hidden damage. Investigations can be slowed since older structures may lack blueprints or may have been built in many phases, with each piecemeal addition added to the existing structure without consideration of the potential problems such additions may cause.

In analyzing the unexpected collapse of a structure, engineers usually consider three types of forces that act upon the structure: static loads, dynamic loads, and cyclic loads. Loads are forces that are represented as *vectors*, meaning that they are quantities that have both a magnitude component (such as the force or pressure acting on a building) and direction (the direction in which the force is applied, such as gravity downward, wind sideways, etc.), as illustrated in Figure 18.4. At the simplest level, the difference between a static and a dynamic load is whether that load changes over time: static loads refer to the forces on a building that vary relatively little over time, while dynamic loads may vary greatly over time. During the design phase, however, both static and dynamic loads are most often treated as static loads when calculating the stresses and forces acting on a building. Cyclic loads are those that change predictably over a period of time, such as those forces that occur because of vibrations or heating/cooling cycles.

Successful constructions must first deal with the effects of gravity; all structures must be able to support the weight of the building itself (e.g., brick walls, concrete floors, roof,

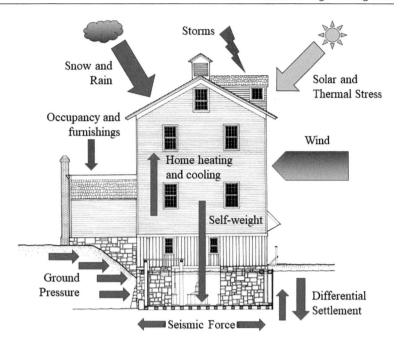

FIGURE 18.4 Building loads usually considered in failure analysis. These include: static loads (e.g., plumbing, self-weight, etc.), dynamic loads (e.g., furniture, wind, rain, snow, ground pressure, etc.), and cyclic loads (e.g., solar, home heating, etc.).

TABLE 18.1 Examples of static and dynamic loads placed upon a structure by various components.

SAMPLE STATIC (DEAD) LOADS		SAMPLE DYNAMIC (LIVE) LOADS		
MATERIAL	LOAD (POUNDS PER SQ FT OF MATERIAL)	CATEGORY	DESCRIPTION	LOAD (POUNDS PER SQ FT OF ITEM/MATERIAL)
Asphalt shingles	2	Hospital	Wards and rooms	40
Brick (4" wall)	40	Libraries	Reading rooms	60
Concrete block	55		Book stacks	125
Earth (moist)	100	Manufacturing	Light	75
Glass (¼" thick)	3.3		Heavy	125
Gypsum wallboard	1.8	Offices		50
Harwood floor	2.5	Schools	Classrooms	40
Plywood	1.4	Stores		100
Steel decking	2.5	Auditoriums	Fixed seating	50
Water	62*		Moveable seating	100
Suspended ceiling	1		Stage areas	125
Plaster (½" thick)	4.5	Garages	Vehicle storage	50

*pounds per cubic foot. Values excerpted from Barry Onouye and Kevin Kane: Statics and Strength of Materials for Architecture and Building Construction, second edition; Prentice-Hall, 2001.

supports, etc.) along with any built-in furnishings, plumbing, electrical components, fire systems and the effects of normal weather conditions. *Static loads* refer to the combined weight, and therefore the downward gravitational force, imposed on a building from these relatively unchanging, or only very slowly changing, features.

Dynamic loads, also called live loads, in contrast, are those that may vary greatly with time and include such things as the weights of movable furniture, occupants (people), snow loads accumulated on the roof, wave and flood action, machinery brought into the structure and any other movable weights

that can be brought into the structure. Dynamic loads may act on any structure, including buildings, bridges, dams, towers, and others. For example, bridges experience dynamic loads that vary depending largely upon how many cars and trucks cross the bridge at any given time. Vertical live loads for structures, those loads acting principally downward, include people, movable building furnishings, vehicles, movable equipment, snow, and rain. Lateral live loads, those that act principally horizontally in a side-ways fashion, may involve forces derived from wind, earthquake, and water and soil forces (particularly for portions of a building located below ground). There are

FIGURE 18.5 Expansion joints on a bridge allow the structure to expand and contract in response to dynamic and cyclic loads placed upon the bridge.

Source: Shutterstock.com.

also forces that may randomly act in any direction that include impacts, movements of the foundation, and the shifting and "settling" of the structure itself. Some examples of both static and dynamic loads are given in Table 18.1.

Cyclic loads, sometimes considered as a specific example of dynamic loads, involve forces that are repeated over and over periodically and can lead to fatigue and damage in building materials. Fatigue is the cumulative and progressive alteration of materials that results in eventual damage from the repetition of certain types of movements or pressures. Fatigue occurs from the cyclic addition and removal of stresses and loads to a structural component. A load is a force placed on a material, while stress is the response of the material to the load (e.g., lots of homework is a load that causes stress in students in response to the load). The maximum amount of stress placed on a material during fatigue is often much less than that needed to simply break the material but high enough to cause compression and relaxation to occur. Generally, the greater the stress applied to a material, the shorter that material's useful lifetime will be. Cyclic loads cause stresses that, if above a certain threshold, will ultimately weaken the material by forming microscopic cracks and fractures. As the cyclic stress-relaxation process continues, the tiny cracks continue to grow until they reach a critical size necessary to cause the entire structure to suddenly fail.

FIGURE 18.6 Fatigue fracture. This photograph of a failed bolt shows a characteristic fatigue fracture where the darker areas arise from the slow formation of tiny micro-cracks resulting from repeated expansion and compression of the bolt. Each cycle causes a tiny displacement or disruption of the crystalline structure of the metal that is cumulative. The lighter areas show where the final sudden fracture occurred.

Source: Retrieved from Wikimedia; used per Creative Commons 4.0 International. User: Want Hui-li, Qin Si-feng.

Structures, such as bridges and buildings, must be designed to accommodate cyclic movements and stresses safely. For example, the Golden Gate Bridge in San Francisco experiences cyclic (daily) thermal stress as the bridge is warmed by the sun each day and cooled each night (Figure 18.5). Because of this thermal cycling, the bridge contracts at night and expands during the day, causing the center of the span to move up and down as much as 16 ft (4.8 m) daily. Vibrations are often considered as cyclic loads that can rapidly weaken a structure to the breaking point through fatigue (Figure 18.6). A classic example is the destruction of the Tacoma Narrows Bridge (see Box 18.3). Cyclic vibrations can occur from earthquakes, road vibrations from traffic, trains, machinery (e.g., jackhammers, compressors, motors, jet engines, etc.), aerodynamic wind effects, and even lines of people marching in step across a bridge.

BOX 18.3   THE LAST RIDE OF "GALLOPING GERTIE"

The first Tacoma Narrows Bridge, constructed over part of the Puget Sound in the State of Washington, opened for business on July 1, 1940. When it opened, it was the third longest suspension bridge in the world. Curiously, during its construction, the bridge was known to move vertically in windy conditions, giving rise to its nickname of "Galloping Gertie" by construction workers.

The morning of November 7, 1940, after little more than four months of operation, the bridge's main span began to vibrate in response to a 40-mile-per-hour wind at a rate of 0.2 Hz (one oscillation every 5 seconds) with an amplitude of 28 ft (the amount that the span moved up and down)! Eventually, the bridge collapsed from this extreme cyclic stress, sending 600 ft of the roadway into the Puget Sound 190 ft below.

FIGURE 18.7   The Tacoma Narrows Bridge, over Puget Sound in Washington, nicknamed "Galloping Gertie," collapsed on the morning of November 7, 1940.

Engineers continue to debate the underlying cause of the bridge's collapse today, but it is safe to say that it was pulled apart by the cyclic vibrational stresses placed upon the bridge's building materials. Many engineers believe that the fundamental reason for the bridge's collapse was due to something called aerodynamic instability, similar to the flutter of an airfoil, power cable, or even a stop sign in heavy wind. It occurs when structural stiffness, aerodynamic properties, and applied forces combine to cause rotations and vibrations that can lead to structural failure.

The total load placed on a structure is ultimately transferred to the earth, but structures are designed to distribute and transfer their loads in a variety of ways. For example, a typical residential home transfers the loads from the roof, floors, and most of its contents first to the outer walls of the structure and then to the ground, as shown in Figure 18.8. Damage to these outer load-bearing walls often leads to the partial or total collapse of the building, as illustrated in Figure 18.9. For example, many buildings constructed in the late 1800s to early 1900s were simple "box" structures, built primarily of locally produced materials such as brick, mortar (the bonding material used to hold bricks together) and wood. The most frequently employed design used outer brick walls, held together with inexpensive lime mortar, to transfer the weight of the structure to the ground, coupled with horizontal wooden beams (joists) that fitted into notches in the brick walls to hold and transfer the weight of the floors and contents to the outer walls. These buildings often had flat, gently sloping roofs constructed of wooden beams and planking covered with felt and tar to aid rainwater runoff. Over long use and poor maintenance, however, rainwater can penetrate at the juncture of the roof's brick walls and the flat wooden decking. The rainwater runs down along the inside wall of the building, often undetected behind the framed interior walls of the building. During this long-term process, the chemical components of the mortar gradually leach away, thereby weakening the outer load-bearing walls. At some point when enough of the strength of the mortar has been removed, the wall suddenly collapses without any visible warning to the occupants of the building since the damage is largely hidden behind the interior walls.

Structures deal with the distribution and transfer of loads in various ways. Some modern skyscrapers, for example, consist of a massive central core that bears most of the weight of the floors, allowing complex outer shapes and unusual architectural designs, while others use a combination of internal and external support structures (Figure 18.10). For example, suspension bridges transfer the weight through the support towers, while rigid bridges use various types of trusses to distribute and transfer the weight. Many different truss support designs have been devised, depending on the structure's load requirements and the available building materials, as shown in Figure 18.11.

BOX 18.4   MILWAUKEE'S MILLER BASEBALL PARK CRANE COLLAPSE

On July 14, 1999, while placing a nearly 1,000,000-pound section for the roof of a new baseball stadium under construction in Milwaukee, Wisconsin, the crane, known as "Big Blue", collapsed, resulting in the deaths of three people and causing millions of dollars in damages. Big Blue was an enormous crane over 500 ft tall carrying 2.4 million pounds of counterweights and run by three operators. The crane was designed to handle this load well – so why did it collapse?

The forensic engineering company ESI was called in to investigate the collapse. The engineers investigated many aspects of the accident including:

- The materials used in the structure of the crane.
- The physical evidence remaining within the wreckage.
- The winds present at the time of the collapse.
- The loads placed on the crane and the roof section.
- The strength and stiffness of the crane.
- The ground supporting the crane.
- The effects of roof load dynamics on the crane.

From their detailed analysis, the forensic engineers determined that the accident resulted from the unfortunate combination of a number of smaller factors that collectively contributed to the collaspe. No single factor was sufficient on its own to cause the collapse, but when all combined, they led to the observed tragedy. These factors included: the wind speed and direction, the strength of the soil underneath the massive crane, the flexibility of the crane, the design of the crane, and the actions of the three operators.

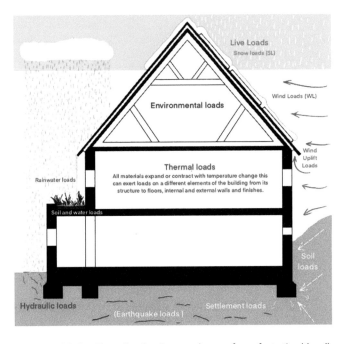

FIGURE 18.8 The distribution and transfer of static (dead), dynamic (live) and cyclic (environmental and thermal) loads to the external walls in a residential building and then to the ground.

Architects and engineers usually design structures with a large capacity to hold both expected and *unplanned* loads. The *factor of safety* (FS) of a structure describes its ability to withstand loads beyond those anticipated from the total of static and dynamic loads. The FS is usually expressed as a ratio of the largest load that a structure can endure to the expected actual load (design load):

$$\text{Factor of Safety} = \frac{\text{Material Strength}}{\text{Design Load}} \quad (18.1)$$

A factor of safety value of 2.0 indicates that the structure should be able to hold about twice the expected load before failure would occur. Engineers usually use a "worst-case" scenario when calculating the factor of safety for a structure. Required factors of safety

values for structural components vary but often range between 3 and 10 or more, meaning that the structure should hold at least three to ten times the expected total load for the structure. For example, if the total load (dynamic plus static) on a structure is calculated to be 100,000 pounds, then a FS value of three means that the structure's design must be specified to handle at least 300,000 pounds of load. Structures in areas of earthquake, hurricane and other potentially high dynamic load environments may require even greater factors of safety. Evaluating the designed FS for structural components along with accurately estimating the expected total loads on a structure are key steps in forensic structural failure analysis. Looking at how a structure failed can point to either design or construction flaws (or both) that somehow compromised the safety requirements of the structure. An engineer may use an FS value of 5.0 for a building component but, during construction, a substitute material might be used that only has an FS value of 3 for the given application. For example, in the catastrophic collapse of the Skywalk in the Hyatt Regency Hotel in Kansas City, Missouri, a modified design was substituted during construction that compromised the FS of the suspension system holding up the skywalk. The result was a collapse that killed 114 people and cost over $120 million in claims and damages.

A second safety value that engineers use when making their designs, called the *Margin of Safety* (MoS), describes the ratio of the actual strength of the structure to the *required* strength of the structure. There are several definitions of MoS that depend on the specific engineering application (e.g., civil, aerospace, mechanical, etc.) but most relate to the ratio of the load that the structure is able to take before it fails to the load that it is required to withstand, usually dictated by law or common practice, and is often given by the equation (Equation 18.2):

$$\text{Margin of Safety (MoS)} = \frac{\text{actual load capacity}}{\text{load capacity required}} - 1 \quad (18.2)$$

For example, a MoS of zero means that the component exactly meets the required load capacity, and a value below zero means that it *did not* meet the requirement. Note that the required load capacity in the MoS calculation may already have a factor of

FIGURE 18.9 Collapse of a building's outer wall that was weakened by damage to the outer load-bearing walls from poor maintenance.

Source: Shutterstock.com.

FIGURE 18.10 Unusual architectural designs are possible through the careful direction of the internal loads within the building to the Earth.

Source: Shutterstock.com.

safety several times larger than the expected actual load for the structure; it is the load *capacity* (how much it can actually hold) and not the total of dynamic and static loads placed on the structure that is used in this calculation. In determining MoS, it is also the *legal* load capacity required that is used in the calculation. This may seem confusing, but the legal capacity is basically a measure of the amount of load that a structure *can* withstand compared to the legal requirements of what it *must* withstand.

Forensic System Failure Analysis: Sometimes, the catastrophic failure of an engineered system is brought about by the failure of just one or several smaller components that make up the entire system. Such failure can result in a significant

Roof Truss Types

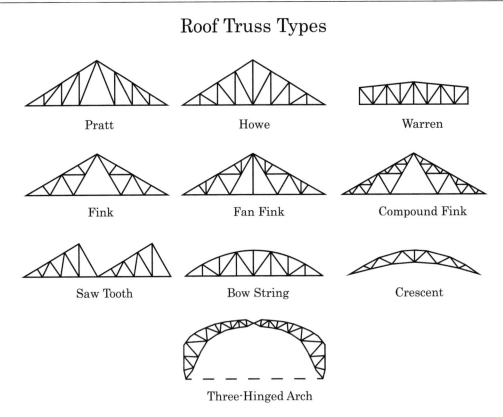

FIGURE 18.11   Examples of building trusses used to carry and distribute loads to end ground supports.

Source: Shutterstock.com.

loss of life, property or revenue and may involve criminal or civil litigation focused upon forensic evidence of improper design, illegal construction, or poor operational practices. Forensic failure analysis investigations may also provide information specifically for insurance claims where the underlying cause of the failure needs to be determined before a proper settlement can be completed. Insurance investigations rarely ever make it into court and are typically settled between the parties but nonetheless may require the same level of forensic investigation as those cases that do find their way into court. System failure analysis investigations may require that forensic engineers explore the causes of failure for vehicles, machinery, or industrial processes (e.g., chemical manufacturing productions). These failures may be due to a wide range of causes that include improperly designed or poorly constructed systems, undetected wear and stress faults, poor maintenance practices, overtaxing a system or component beyond its engineered capabilities (exceeding the designed Margin of Safety), physical damage from impacts, accidents, corrosion, fire, and human error in their operation. This type of analysis requires an intimate understanding and working knowledge of the key features and use practices for the failed system or component. The investigation often employs a combination of digging out background information (e.g., blueprints, maintenance logs, legal requirements, standards, etc.), carrying out detailed site investigations, completing computer modeling simulations, and running multidisciplinary laboratory analyses before a reasonable answer is reached.

Failure analysis is most often focused on determining the root cause, or failure mechanism responsible for the observed problem. Engineers frequently use a technique known as *reverse engineering* to help determine these root causes. Reverse engineering refers to starting with a finished product or end result and then carefully "taking it apart" in a piece-by-piece fashion to determine how it works and how it was constructed: "working backward." For example, an engineer may start with a finished and working clock and take it completely apart to learn the secrets of its operation and design. Engineers and scientists in industry may do this with a competitor's product to see how the competition solved a particular problem or made a better product. Forensic reverse engineering, however, specifically deals with beginning at the point of the failure and then working backward to the root cause of the failure, examining the design, manufacturing process, and functioning of each component individually and collectively. By understanding both the expected operation as well as the role that each component played in the observed failure, it can help work through the sequence of events that led to the problem.

System failure analysis may also play a central role in investigations that involve piecing together intentionally designed criminal devices, such as bombs and weapon systems, that have been used to destroy much larger structures, such as a building, ship, or aircraft. The incredibly detailed, difficult, and time-consuming task of piecing together the remains of an airplane that exploded in mid-air, for example, may be the only way to locate the exact position within the aircraft where the explosion originated. Determining this location may aid in identifying whether the explosion was caused by an intentionally detonated device, a mechanical failure (e.g., material flaw, fatigue, stress failure, etc.), an unexpected impact (including a firearm discharged within the craft followed by explosive decompression), or through human error (e.g., an improperly closed door, misaligned cargo weight, or a wrench inadvertently left in an engine during repairs). If the investigation is able to identify the characteristic features that arise from the detonation of an explosive device onboard, locating the position of the device precisely within the structure may allow it to be traced back to its point of origin and creator. A superb example of this was presented earlier in the case of the "Lockerbie Bombing Crime Scene" in Chapter 2. In this case, investigators were able to pinpoint the exact location of the bomb, hidden within a transistor radio case in a

suitcase in the forward cargo hold of the aircraft. Knowing this, they were able to trace the suitcase and its contents back to the point when it was placed onboard the aircraft. By locating several articles of clothing that were in the suitcase containing the bomb, investigators were able to trace the suitcase and its contents back to the perpetrators responsible for the crime thousands of miles away through an amazing example of investigative determination, diligence, and skill.

A component failure analysis may also provide the only detailed description possible of the sequence of events that led to an observed catastrophic result. Analyses of these types helped investigators piece together how the events unfolded that led to the destruction of the World Trade Center in New York City, the Oklahoma City bombing, and the explosion of the space shuttle *Challenger* (see Box 18.5), among many others.

BOX 18.5   THE LOSS OF THE SPACE SHUTTLE *CHALLENGER*

NASA's flagship program for many years was its space shuttle program, aimed at providing a rapid, inexpensive, and reusable space-delivery system for exploration and economic development. The enormously successful shuttle program ultimately flew 135 missions from 1981 until mid-2011 before being retired to allow for the development of newer space vehicles.

On January 28, 1986, a "routine" launch of the shuttle *Challenger*, however, ended in disaster. Seventy-three seconds into the launch, the spaceship exploded, completely disintegrating over the Atlantic Ocean, and killing all seven crew members onboard. This disaster led NASA to halt all shuttle flights for 32 months until a complete investigation could be completed and design changes implemented to prevent any similar problems with shuttle launches in the future.

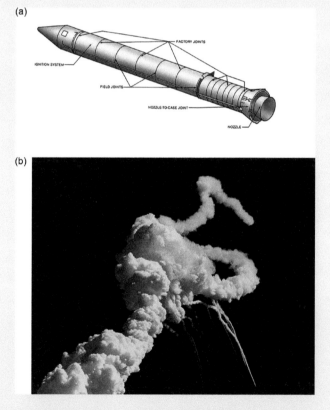

FIGURE 18.12   Space Shuttle *Challenger*: (a) a schematic drawing of the solid rocket booster and (b) the catastrophic destruction of *Challenger* from a faulty seal in the solid rocket booster.

Source: NASA.

The problem, of course, was that the space shuttle was an enormously complicated vehicle with millions of parts. Complicating this was the fact that the shuttle used over 1.3 million pounds of liquid oxygen and 2.2 million pounds of solid rocket fuel. Within all this complexity and explosive chemicals, investigators needed to find the "needle in the haystack."

After an extensive recovery effort and investigative process, the cause of the failure was found to come from a single O-ring in the solid rocket booster engine on the shuttle. The O-ring was designed to provide a necessary flexible joint between sections of the powerful solid rocket boosters and was constructed of materials that could withstand the very high temperatures present during launch. But it was found that the weather on the day of the launch was unusually cold, causing the O-ring to crack. Once in flight, the crack opened to allow hot gases from the booster engine to cut through the rocket, explosively igniting the entire remaining fuel supply. The failure of this one, relatively small component, therefore, was the cause of the loss of the entire shuttle vehicle and crew.

18.1.3 Forensic Engineering and Crime Scene Reconstruction

Each engineering discipline can make important contributions to creating a crime scene reconstruction that sheds light on the sequence of events that occurred during the commission of a criminal act. In Chapter 2, the use of common engineering tools, such as computer-aided design (CAD) programs and total surveying stations (Figures 18.13 and 18.14), was described as modern applications of technology to criminal investigations. These and other engineering techniques have changed the way crime scenes are processed, analyzed, and presented to juries.

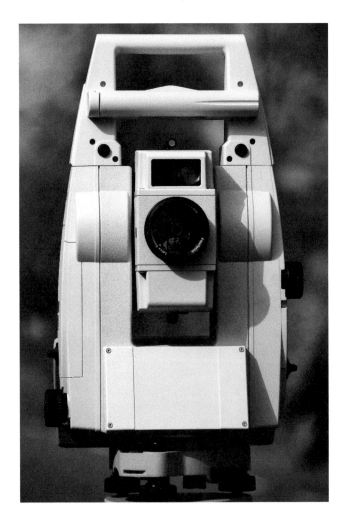

FIGURE 18.13   A Leica Viva TS16 total station that can rapidly take a large number of measurements at a crime scene. These measurements are then used to create a very detailed map of the crime scene on the computer that can be analyzed and observed from many different perspectives.

Source: Retrieved from Wikimedia; used per Creative Commons Share Alike 4.0 International. User: Alex P. Kok.

7.62x39mm and .45Auto fired from a moving vehicle

FIGURE 18.14   The modeled crime scene of an outdoor drive-by shooting using a 3D laser scanner and then back-extrapolating the flight paths of the bullets to find the region of their origin.

Source: Image used with permission and courtesy of Mike Haag of the Albuquerque P.D. Crime.

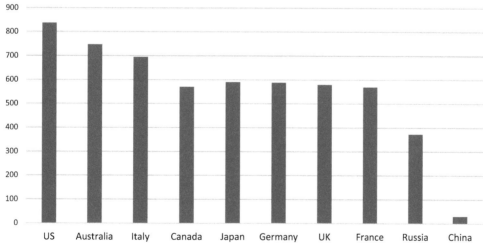

FIGURE 18.15   A plot showing the number of passenger vehicles by country per 1,000 persons of driving age inhabitants (2020).

There is probably no place where the practical use of engineering tools and expertise in crime scene reconstruction is more evident, however, than in vehicular accident investigations.

Forensic Vehicular Accident Reconstruction: The past 100 years have seen an extraordinary explosion in the availability and use of motorized vehicles worldwide. Cars and trucks come in all sizes, shapes, and designs to fit an enormous range of practical and recreational uses. In the United

States alone, there is nearly one vehicle for every person in the country with over 285 million registered passenger vehicles reported in the United States in 2019 (excluding buses, motorcycles, and trains) (Figure 18.15).

During the early 20th century, the number and severity of vehicular accidents rapidly grew as the density of vehicles swelled, higher speeds became possible, and extensive new high-speed roadways were constructed. A 2019 WHO estimate reported that about 1.4 million people were killed

Causes of Vehicular Fatalities

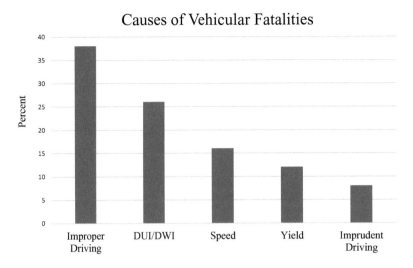

FIGURE 18.16   Typical contributing causes for fatal vehicular accidents (DMV).

worldwide and 50 million injured in vehicular accidents. Traffic fatalities are the leading cause of deaths worldwide among children in the 10- to 19-year-old age group and for the 25- to 35-year-old population in the United States. These accidents arise from a variety of causes that include human, vehicular, environmental, and road design factors, as illustrated in Figure 18.16. Because of this range of contributing causes, there is usually a need to determine the exact circumstances and reasons for a vehicular accident. Fortunately, this type of information may often be best provided through an engineering approach to the reconstruction of the accident.

Many tools and techniques may be employed when investigating a vehicular accident to answer key questions, including:

- the relative positions of the vehicles and surroundings.
- the speed of the vehicle(s) involved.
- the direction and trajectory of the vehicles and passengers both before and after the impact (especially if passengers were thrown from the vehicle).
- the point and angle of impact.
- the items involved in the impact (e.g., vehicles, people, trees, telephone poles, etc.).
- the actions of the drivers (e.g., when and where the brakes were applied).
- the start and end points of the collision.

As it turns out, each of these questions can usually be addressed with a high degree of accuracy using several basic principles of physics and engineering. Most vehicular accident reconstruction usually begin with a consideration of energy and momentum.

Energy and Momentum: Vehicular accidents involve objects in motion that collide, transfer their energies, and eventually come to rest. The movements of all objects, including vehicles, are best described through the application of some simple and basic ideas of physics and engineering. Two terms are of particular importance in these descriptions: energy and momentum.

In previous chapters, concepts about energy, and especially the conversion of energy between its various forms, were presented. Motion (kinetic energy), heat, light, sound, and even mass are all examples of the different forms that energy may take. *Kinetic energy* is the energy associated with the motion of an object and is given by the very simple expression:

$$\text{Kinetic Energy (KE)} = \frac{1}{2} mv^2 \tag{18.3}$$

(where m is the mass, and v is the velocity of the object)

This relationship should make common sense, we understand intuitively that when an object moves faster, it has greater energy. Similarly, as an object increases in mass at a specific speed, the energy associated with its motion likewise increases. From Equation 18.3, however, it can be seen that when the velocity of an object doubles, its energy quadruples, since the energy increases as the square of the velocity. Similarly, from Equation 18.3, we see that doubling the mass of an object doubles its energy. These simple relationships have enormous importance when considering vehicular accident damage. A car traveling at 40 mph has four times the kinetic energy as the same car traveling at 20 mph and will require roughly four times the distance to stop. For example, a car going 20 mph will skid about 19 ft before coming to a complete stop, while the same car going 40 mph (double the speed) will require about 76 ft to stop (Figure 18.17). When you add in a person's average reflex time to react and apply the brakes, the total stopping distance at 40 mph is over 160 ft.

The transfer of energy between its many forms is governed by the physical law called the *Conservation of Energy* that states that, while energy may be converted between its different forms, the total energy of an isolated system *must remain constant*. For example, when an object in motion strikes an immovable object, the kinetic energy of the moving body is changed mostly into heat, light, sound, and work energy, the products that we observe from a collision. This is called an inelastic collision, where some or all the kinetic energy is converted into other forms of energy (see Box 18.6). During an emergency stop or collision, the kinetic energy of a

BOX 18.6   COLLISIONS DEFINITIONS

Elastic Collision: A collision where the amount of kinetic energy is the same before and after the collision.

Inelastic Collision: A collision where some or all the kinetic energy is converted into other forms of energy, such as work, sound, or thermal energy.

Force (F): The impetus given to an object and calculated as mass times acceleration (F = ma).

Work (W): the movement of a mass through a distance and defined as force times distance (W = Fd).

Gravitational Acceleration (g): A constant indicating how fast an object is accelerated by Earth's gravity.

Frictional Coefficient (f): A numeric value that indicates the resistance an object encounters when moving over a surface.

ABBREVIATIONS:

m = mass
v = velocity
d = distance
K = crush coefficient for the car
x = crush depth measured
S = speed at start of skid

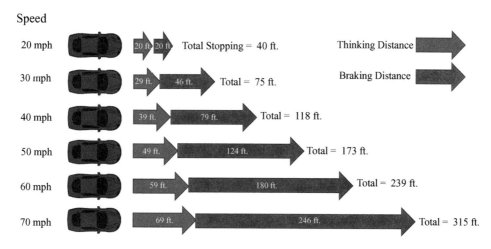

FIGURE 18.17   Approximate distances required to stop for a car at various speeds, including the distances traveled while thinking (responding) and while braking.

vehicle is *irreversibly* converted into work energy in a one-way process - it cannot be converted backward into kinetic energy later. *Work* (W) is defined simply as the product of the force applied to an object times the distance that the object moves by the action of force. *Force* (F), the impetus used to move the object, is given by the product of an object's mass times its acceleration. The two equations that mathematically define work and force are:

$$W = Fd \qquad (18.4)$$

(where F is the force, and d is the distance through which the object is moved)

$$F = ma \qquad (18.5)$$

(where F is the force, m is the mass, and a is the acceleration)

When a car rapidly applies and locks its brakes until it stops, the car's initial kinetic energy is *completely* converted into work, frictional heat, or other forms of energy. When the car stops, it has zero kinetic energy; all of its initial kinetic energy has changed into other forms of energy. This is a statement of the idea of *conservation of energy* where the total energy of the system before the brakes were applied (when the car is moving) must be equal to the total energy after it has completely stopped. This can be stated using several simple equations (18.6–18.8):

$$\text{Energy}_{\text{before}} = \text{Energy}_{\text{afterward}} \qquad (18.6)$$

$$E_{\text{initial}} = E_{\text{final}} \qquad (18.7)$$

$$E_{\text{final}} - E_{\text{initial}} = 0 \qquad (18.8)$$

The three equations above all say exactly the same thing but in slightly different ways – they all say that energy has been conserved. We've neither lost nor gained any energy, just changed it into different forms as the car stops.

BOX 18.7   PHYSICS BRAIN TEASER

Question: If a bulldozer pushes with all its power against a wall that it cannot budge, even a little bit, does the bulldozer do any work?

Answer: No, since the object being pushed did not move through any distance, no work was done. Remember $w = f\,d$ and if d (distance) is zero, then the product is zero; no work is done.

When the brakes of a vehicle are quickly applied, a major way that the kinetic energy of the vehicle can be reduced is through skidding (Figure 18.18). A skid occurs when the tires of a vehicle stop rotating while the car continues to move forward. During this process, some of the rubber from the tires is worn away from the tire's surface, leaving behind a dark streak of rubber on the surface of the road. Eventually, friction (and any collision) brings the car to a stop. The measured length of a vehicle's skid marks can be used to provide an estimate of the vehicle's speed when it began to skid using the physics we've discussed so far.

BOX 18.8   FRICTIONAL FACTORS IN REAL LIFE

The friction coefficients that appear in a number of the equations used in vehicular accident reconstruction are important values to get correct. Tables for friction coefficients have been constructed but to use these in an actual scene often requires too much estimation and uncertainty. To get around this, the friction coefficient is usually measured under the actual conditions of the accident. To do this, a police officer usually drives a patrol car at a fixed speed over the roadway in question and then locks their brakes to cause a skid. Since the velocity of the police car and its skid mark are known in this case, the only missing variable from the equation $(v = (2\,g\,f\,d)^{\frac{1}{2}})$ – the friction coefficient (f) – can be calculated for the actual conditions of the crash.

Let's consider that the energy transferred when a skidding car stops goes entirely into friction. The work done through skidding, like all other forms of work, is then determined simply by the force *times* the distance traveled *times* a frictional coefficient (a value that relates to how well energy can be transferred between the two "rubbed" surfaces, in this case the car's tires and the road surface). The energy (E) done as work in this process is given by:

$$E_{work} = Ffd \tag{18.9}$$

(where F = force, f = frictional coefficient, and d = distance)

Since we know from Equation 18.5 that force also equals mass times acceleration, $F = m\,g$ (in this case, the acceleration must be replaced by the constant of gravitational acceleration, g, because of the action of gravity), we can substitute m times g into Equation 18.9 for force to get:

$E_{work} = F\,f\,d$ then replace F in this equation with (m g) to get:

$$E_{work} = (m\,g)\,fd \tag{18.10}$$

So, finally, we can put it all together. During skidding, a car starts with a certain amount of kinetic energy (Equation 18.3) that is entirely converted into the work energy of the skid that brings the car to a stop (Equation 18.10). Since *all* the initial kinetic energy of the car is transferred to the work energy of the skid (KE at the end of the skid is zero), we can set these two equations for KE (Equation 18.3) and E_{work} (Equation 18.10) equal to each other, or:

Equation 18.3 = Equation 18.10

$$E_{\text{initial kinetic}} = E_{\text{skid work}} \tag{18.11}$$

$$\tfrac{1}{2}mv^2 = m\,g\,f\,d \tag{18.12}$$

If we simplify this with the use a little algebra and solve this equation for the velocity of the car at the start of the skid (v), we come up with:

$$v = (2\,g\,f\,d)^{\frac{1}{2}} \tag{18.13}$$

(Equation for speed at the start of skid without impact.)

The equation above (Equation 18.13) gives us a very easy way to calculate the minimum velocity necessary for a car to skid the measured distance (d) [note: g and f in the above equations are constants: $g = 32.17$ ft/s^2 and f is 0.75 for dry pavement (or the value measured on the scene as described by the police car above); f depends upon the surface being skidded over and, to a small extent, on the characteristics of the tires involved]. Equation 18.13 is sometimes called the "skid formula." An example of how it can be readily used to determine the speed of a vehicle at the beginning or at any point along a skid is given in the inset boxes "Example of Skid Mark Calculations."

It is important to note that this formula works *only* when the vehicle skids to a stop without hitting anything heavy. If a collision with a heavy object occurs, such as another vehicle or roadway object, then a more complicated formula must be used that takes into account the fact that some of the kinetic energy of the skidding car is transferred to the object struck in the collision, energy that is *not* transferred to the work of the skid through friction.

One common method to determine the amount of energy transferred upon collision uses a *crush depth* measurement.

FIGURE 18.18   Skid marks from rapid braking. (a) Photo on the right shows a continuous skid while the photo on the left (b) shows skid marks from the vehicle wheels bouncing on the pavement.

Source: (a) Used with permission and courtesy of Science Photo Library; (b) Shutterstock.com.

**BOX 18.9   EXAMPLE OF SKID MARK CALCULATIONS
(WITHOUT A COLLISION – SIMPLE STOP)**

In an accident where a car struck a pedestrian, the investigators wanted to know how fast the car was going when it hit the person. In the investigation, it was found that the skid mark was 150 ft long and that the pedestrian was struck 75 ft before the car came to a stop (end of the skid mark).

Using Equation 18.13 (the skid formula), we can calculate the car's speed when it hit the pedestrian (v = velocity):

$$v = (2\, g\, f\, d)^{1/2} \tag{18.13}$$

Substitute into the formula using $g = 32.17$ ft/s^2 and f is 0.75 to get,

$$v = [2\,(32.17\text{ ft/s}^2)\,(0.75)\,(75\text{ ft})]^{1/2}$$

$$v = [3{,}619]^{1/2}$$

$$v = 60.2 \text{ ft/s or } 41.0 \text{ mph when it struck the pedestrian.}$$

In order to calculate the speed of the car at the beginning of the skid, the same process is used:

$$v = (2\, g\, f\, d)^{1/2}$$

$$v = [2\,(32.17\text{ ft/s}^2)\,(0.75)\,(150\text{ ft})]^{1/2}$$

$$v = [7.238]^{1/2}$$

$$v = 85.1 \text{ ft/s or } 58.0 \text{ mph the skid started.}$$

For example, based on measurements from test vehicles, a particular type of car might be found to require 4,500 pounds of force to crush in the front of the vehicle by a distance of 1 in. This means that 4,500 pounds of force derived from the car's kinetic energy must be used to cause the 1-in. indentation. By measuring both the length of the skid marks and the amount of crush observed on a vehicle, the speed of the vehicle can be determined at all points along the vehicle's path. In this case, all the kinetic energy of the car is *still* transferred away as it comes to a stop, but the transferred energy is now distributed between the frictional work of the skid and the energy necessary to cause the observed crush (Figure 18.19). The revised equation which is used to calculate the speed of the vehicle at the beginning of the skid when some of the kinetic energy is used to crush in the car is shown in Equation 18.14:

$$\text{Kinetic Energy} = \text{Skid Energy} + \text{Crush Energy} \quad (18.14)$$

$$\tfrac{1}{2}\,mv^2 = m\,g\,f\,d + Kx \quad (18.15)$$

(where K is the measured crush coefficient for the car, x is the crush depth measured from the crashed car, and m is the mass of the car (not the weight) that is calculated by $m = F/g$ where F/g is the force weight of the vehicle).

Crush energy is simply the amount of kinetic energy transferred from the striking car to the impacted structure (e.g., another vehicle, bridge, etc.), which caused the observed indentation in the struck object. Once again, if we use a little algebra and solve Equation 18.15 for v (velocity), we come up with the equation for the speed at the start of a skid with impact and crush factor:

$$v = [2\,g\,d\,f + 2\,(K/m)\,x]^{\frac{1}{2}} \quad (18.16)$$

An example of how Equation 18.16 can be used to determine the speed of a vehicle involved in a collision at the beginning of a skid is given in Box 18.10.

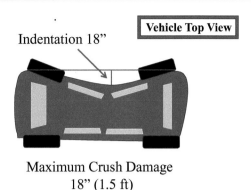

Maximum Crush Damage
18" (1.5 ft)

FIGURE 18.19 Measuring the crush distance from a collision in order to calculate the speed of the striking vehicle prior to the collision.

Using the appropriate formula for a given situation, it is relatively easy to determine if the vehicle was traveling faster than the posted speed limit prior to the accident – information that may carry important legal implications. These equations (Equation 18.13 for skids without a collision and 18.16 for skids with a collision) can be simplified even further by combining all the constants together to give the most common form of the equations employed by police investigators, shown in the box called "Simplified Formulas."

The speeds calculated by conservation of energy methods described above are usually considered to provide the *minimum* speed necessary to cause the observed length of the skid mark. This is because a number of variables can lead to shorter than expected measured skid marks, such as the difficulty in determining the beginning of the skid since the marks may be rather faint (until the tire rubber heats sufficiently to melt). Additionally, these formulas assume that once applied, the brakes remain "locked" on, and the skid is continuous until the vehicle comes to a complete stop.

Examining the skid marks themselves may also provide valuable information. For example, it is usually possible to tell

---

BOX 18.10   EXAMPLE OF SKID MARK CALCULATION (WITH A COLLISION)

In an accident, a 1-ton (2,000 lb force weight) car skidded for 150 ft before striking a concrete bridge abutment. If the car front end was crushed in by 6 in. and had a crush coefficient of 5,000 lb/in., we can use Equation 18.15 to calculate the car's speed when it started the skid:

Kinetic Energy = Skid Energy + Crush Energy

$v = [2\,g\,d\,f + 2\,(K/m)\,x]^{\frac{1}{2}}$

$v = [2\,(32.17\text{ ft/s}^2)(150\text{ ft})(0.75) + 2\,(5.000\text{ lb/in.}/62.1\text{ s}^2\text{lbf/ft})(6\text{ in.})]^{\frac{1}{2}}$ (see note below)

$v = [7.238 + 966]^{\frac{1}{2}}$

$v = 90.5$ ft/s or 61 mph at the start of the skid

[Note that the equation uses the mass calculated by dividing the force (2,000 lbf by g since lb is defined as force $= m\,g$.]

BOX 18.11   SIMPLIFIED FORMULAS

By adding in all the constants together and putting everything in the common distance unit of feet, the two key Equations, 18.13 and 18.15, can be simplified. Equation 18.13 becomes:

Minimum Speed Formula without collision = S_1

$$S_1 = \sqrt{(30)(d_1)(f)}$$

(where S_1 is the initial speed at the start of the skid (in mph), d_1 is the distance of the skid before stopping, and f is the frictional coefficient).

Equation 18.15 (with collision) simplifies to:

Striking vehicle at the start of the skid = S_c

$$S_c = \sqrt{\left[(30)(d_1)(f)\right] + \left[(30)(d_2)(cf)\right]}$$

(where S_c is the initial speed at the start of the skid (in mph), d_1 is the distance of the skid before impact, f is the frictional coefficient, d_2 is the depth of the crush in ft, and cf is the crush factor in lb/ft).

FRONT SKID MARK   **REAR SKID MARK**

FIGURE 18.20   The difference between front and rear tire skid marks.

Source: U.S. Department of Defense.

the difference between the front and rear tires from the pattern they produce (Figure 18.20). Front tire skid marks usually appear darker on the outer edge and lighter in the center, while rear tires show the reverse pattern, darker in the center and lighter on the outside edges of the skid mark. Sometimes, the tire tracks are not continuous. Broken patterns can occur for a variety of reasons including tire skipping due to bouncing, gaps where the brakes are applied and released and reapplied, or through antilock brake use. Examples of the information obtainable from the patterns observed are illustrated in Figure 18.21.

There are times, such as in head-on or glancing collisions, or simply when there are physical problems associated with measuring the skid marks, that these simple formulas do not work. In those cases, conservation of momentum methods are usually employed.

BOX 18.12 FRICTIONAL COEFFICIENT (F)

The frictional coefficient that appears in skid formulas relates to how well energy can be transferred between the two "rubbed" surfaces. Different surfaces have different coefficients and, therefore, affect the stopping distance of the vehicle. The table below gives some examples of how different frictional coefficients affect stopping distance.

SPEED (MPH)	ASPHALT (F = 0.75)	CONCRETE (F = 0.90)	SNOW (F = 0.30)	GRAVEL (F = 0.50)
30	40 ft	33 ft	100 ft	60 ft
40	71 ft	59 ft	178 ft	107 ft
50	111 ft	93 ft	278 ft	167 ft
60	160 ft	133 ft	400 ft	240 ft

Source: Modified from James O. Harris, "Determining Vehicle Speeds From SkidMarks", https://www.scribd.com/document/396158789/Skid-Mark-Evidence-pdf

In the table, the frictional coefficients are approximate. In actual practice, a test skid is used to calculate *f*. In this test, a vehicle of known speed and mass is caused to skid to a stop at the scene. The length of the skid is then measured and the *f* calculated from the known speed.

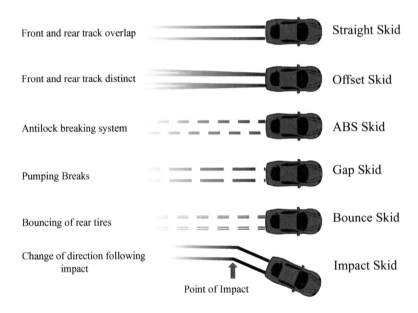

FIGURE 18.21 Different skid mark patterns tell investigators about the sequence of events, trajectory, and speed in a skid.

Conservation of momentum: *Momentum* is defined as the mass times the velocity of an object, or:

$$p = m v \tag{18.17}$$

(where *p* is the momentum, *m* is the mass, and *v* is the velocity of the object).

On closer inspection, it may seem like this momentum equation is very similar to the kinetic energy equation that was defined earlier as ½ the mass of an object times its velocity squared ($KE = \frac{1}{2} mv^2$) – both involve the mass and velocity of an object. What's the difference? The difference is that momentum is a *vector* quantity, while KE is a scalar quantity – meaning that momentum must be defined as a mass moving *in a particular direction* while KE says nothing about direction. As with energy, a conservation law says that momentum, while it can be transferred between objects, is conserved. This means the total momentum before a collision must equal the total momentum after any collision. Therefore, when two vehicles collide, there is no net change in the total momentum of the system, and they have the same total amount of momentum before and after the collision. Additionally, Newton's third law says that when two objects collide, such as vehicles, they exert equal and opposite forces on each other. Examples of this concept are illustrated by practical experiences such as playing billiards (observing the results of the impact of the cue ball with target balls) or in Newton's cradle (Figure 18.22).

FIGURE 18.22 Classic demonstration of the principle of conservation of momentum. Newton's cradle, shown here, has five steel balls that are initially at rest and touching. At the start, one ball is raised and released to strike the other stationary balls. The momentum of the moving ball before the collision is mv and the momentum of the stationary balls is zero. After the collision, the momentum of the moving ball is transferred along to the stationary ball at the far end of the line that then flies away with the momentum of the originally moving ball (mv), leaving four balls once again stationary (*mv* = 0).

Source: Shutterstock.com.

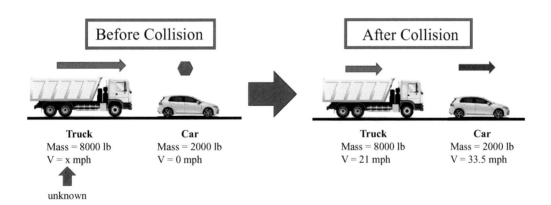

FIGURE 18.23 Momentum transfer and conservation of momentum in a truck–car collision.

As an example of how these ideas of conservation of momentum might be used in vehicular reconstruction, consider the following situation (Figure 18.23). The driver of a truck does not see a stopped car ahead and rear-ends the parked car. The 2,000 lb parked car skids 50 ft after impact, while the 8,000 lb truck, applying the brakes immediately upon impact, skids only 20 ft. Investigators would like to know what the speed of the truck was before the collision.

Using the idea of conservation of momentum, the total momentum of the two impacting vehicles must be the same both before and after the collision. The stopped car has a pre-collision momentum of zero, while the truck has all the momentum (mv). After the collision, the two vehicles both immediately have *some* momentum since they both skid

forward. In order to determine the speed of the truck before the collision, we must first calculate the speed of the two vehicles and their momentum *immediately after* the impact using the skid formula (Equation 18.13) and their total momentum (Equation 18.17). Here's how it works in a stepwise fashion:

Step 1: Calculate the velocity of the car immediately after the impact (assuming an asphalt roadway with $f = 0.75$) [**Note**: since the English system is used primarily in the United States, these units will be used here. The process works, of course, equally well using the metric system]:

$$v = (2\,g\,f\,d)^{\frac{1}{2}}$$

$v = [2\ (32.17\ ft/s^2)\ (0.75)\ (50\ ft)]^{\frac{1}{2}}$

$v = (2,412\ ft/s)^{\frac{1}{2}}$

$v = 49.1\ ft/s\ or\ 33.5\ mph$

Step 2: Calculate the velocity of the truck immediately after the impact:

$v = (2\ g\ f\ d)^{\frac{1}{2}}$

$v = [2\ (32.17\ ft/s^2)\ (0.75)\ (20\ ft)]^{\frac{1}{2}}$

$v = (965\ ft/s)^{\frac{1}{2}}$

$v = 31.0\ ft/s\ or\ 21.1\ mph$

Step 3: Calculate the momentum of the car immediately after the impact:

$p = m\ v$ (note *m* here must be weight/*g*)

$p = (2,000\ lb/32.17\ ft/s^2)(49.1\ ft/s)$

$p = 3,052\ ft\ lbs/s$

Step 4: Calculate the momentum of the truck immediately after the impact:

$p = m\ v$ (note *m* here must be weight/*g*)

$p = (8,000\ lb/32.17\ ft/s^2)(30.0\ ft/s)$

$p = 7,460\ ft\ lbs/s$

We now can figure out the *total* momentum immediately after the collision by simply adding together the momentum of the car and the truck:

$P_{total} = P_{car} + P_{truck}$

$P_{total} = 3,052\ ft\ lbs/s + 7,460\ ft\ lbs/s$

$P_{total} = 10,512\ ft\ lbs/s$

Since the momentum of the car was zero before the impact, all this post-impact momentum (p_{total}) must have come from the truck. This is shown schematically in Figure 18.23. We can now simply use the equation for momentum ($p = m\ v$) to calculate the speed of the truck just before the collision, this time substituting in the total momentum for *p* and the mass of the truck for *m*:

$p = m\ v$

$v = p/m$ (note *m* here must be weight/*g*)

$v = (10,512\ lbf/s)\ /\ (8,000\ lbs/32.17\ ft/s^2)$

$v = 42.3\ ft/s = \sim29\ mph$

The truck was, therefore, moving at least 29 mph just before the impact. While this simple example shows how the process works, more complicated arrangements of impact angles and momentum require a more sophisticated analysis. However, the fundamental ideas and concepts still apply and are the basis of all such determinations.

Using the two ideas of energy and momentum from physics, engineers can learn a great deal about both the positions and speeds of vehicles and other objects both before and after a collision. This information allows them to construct a detailed sequence of events that can help assign the cause, and potentially the blame, for the accident.

Skid marks and the starting and end points of the "participants" of a crash are only part of the evidence that must be collected at the scene of a vehicular accident. Figure 18.24 shows some of the other types of evidence that often play a part in accident scene reconstructions. Investigators must also be well aware of factors that can compromise the evidence such as weather conditions and the disruption of the scene by EMT personnel as they render necessary medical aid. Finally, officers must work quickly to process and release the roadway back to normal vehicular use. Despite these factors, crash site reconstructions can be extremely accurate and provide a detailed picture of the sequence of events that occurred during a crash where no other record is available.

Automated systems carried on an individual vehicle can provide direct data about accidents. When airbags were first installed in automobiles, their deployment was controlled by rather simple computer chips. As the technology matured, not only did the onboard computer reduce the incorrect

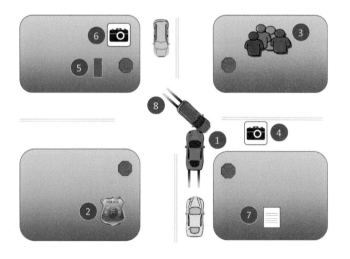

FIGURE 18.24 Data sources for investigating a vehicular accident: (1) crash-site walk-thru, (2) interviews and reports from first responders, (3) eyewitness interviews, (4) initial photographs of the scene, (5) record evidence locations with markers and total station measurements, (6) re-photograph of the scene with evidence markers, (7) official report, and (8) skid mark analysis.

deployment of the airbags, but it also increasingly recorded actual real-world data on the chip that provided engineers with valuable information for designing safer vehicles. Today, most vehicles carry "black-box" recorders that not only control the deployment of complex safety features when a crash occurs but also record a variety of data about the car's operation before a crash, such as vehicle speed, brake pedal deployment, turn-signal use, engine speed, seat-belt use, and accelerator pedal position. These data have been successfully used in courtroom situations as impartial witnesses to the last seconds before an impact. Since 2014 in the United States, all new cars have been required to carry black box recorders to monitor both the actions of the car and driver just before and during a crash. Courts are increasingly making use of these automated and reliable computer "witnesses" to vehicular accidents.

Most vehicles are now produced with other onboard instruments that are finding use in forensic investigations. For example, GPS systems are very commonly found in vehicles, both built-in and added later. These systems can record both the position and speed of a vehicle very accurately, and not just for the seconds directly preceding a crash, but for an entire trip that may last many hours or even days (Figure 18.25). Additionally, many GPS systems have cameras that can photograph events surrounding a crash. Some vehicles also carry onboard communications systems, such as GM's *OnStar*, that can automatically notify a dispatcher when an accident occurs. The dispatch records of these conversations between the vehicle's occupants, dispatchers and first responders may also find valuable application in courtroom proceedings. These records can be used to establish an accurate timeline of events, from the moment of the crash through the early response phase of the accident.

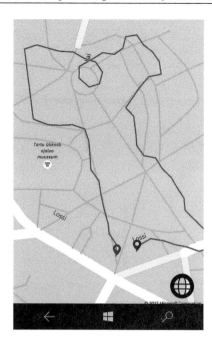

FIGURE 18.25 The log from a car's GPS system shows a person's routes, stops, speeds and other information that can be used as part of a criminal investigation.

Source: Retrieved from Wikimedia. Used per Creative Commons Share Alike 4.0 International. User: TiKaTreib.

These latter examples show some of the potential of automated computer-based recording systems. But, of course, computers can present both opportunities and challenges to forensic investigation, as will be presented in the following section.

BOX 18.13 FAILURE ANALYSIS OF THE WORLD TRADE CENTER

On the fateful morning of September 11, 2001, a disbelieving world watched as two fully fueled Boeing 767 aircraft sequentially smashed into the sides of the north and south towers of the World Trade Center (WTC) in New York City as part of a coordinated attack of four jetliners on buildings in New York City and Washington, DC. The towers withstood the initial assault of the crash and fire before the north and south towers ultimately collapsed after 102 and 56 minutes, respectively. There were 2,606 victims in the towers and there were an additional 246 passengers in the planes and 411 emergency workers on the ground killed. Amazingly, an estimated 14,000 workers in the two towers were able to escape before their collapse. The remaining two jetliners crashed in a field in rural Pennsylvania and the Pentagon in Washington DC, killing an additional 40 in PA and 189 in the Pentagon (both passengers and victims on the ground).

It was important after the disaster to fully understand the reasons for the collapse of the towers through a detailed and complete forensic failure analysis, both to prevent future similar tragedies but also to fully process the WTC crime scene (a process that continues over two decades later), including the identification and return of the remains of the victims to their families. Central to the investigation was an understanding of the contributing causes and the chain of events, from an engineering perspective, that led to the collapse.

In order to understand the destruction of the twin towers, it was necessary to understand first their design and construction. The towers were built in the mid-1960s to early 1970s and were a new departure from older designs for skyscrapers. Rather than using a conventional heavily reinforced outer-frame structure, the towers were designed using a relatively lightweight central core and "perimeter tube" design. The design employed 244 relatively small exterior steel columns and a dense, strong central core structure (27 m × 40 m core) in the middle of the building. The central core, containing elevators, stairs, and service components, held the primary weight of the towers (the towers weighed about 500,000 t; relatively light for a 64-million-square-ft, 411 m-tall building). This design allowed the towers to be relatively open – more than

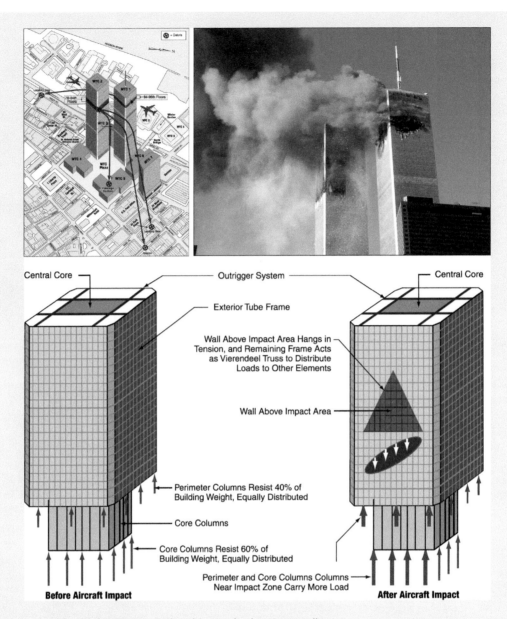

FIGURE 18.26 World Trade Center terrorist bombing and subsequent collapse.

Source: FEMA/DHS.

95% air – with plenty of windows. The beauty of the design was that if some of the outer perimeter columns were lost or weakened, the structure would simply shift some of the weight to the adjacent columns without a problem – it was a very *redundant* and highly *resilient* structure. It was also designed to withstand huge lateral (sideways) loads from wind, even those from a 225 km/h hurricane.

When the aircraft impacted the towers, the buildings well withstood the force of the crash. Each fully fueled aircraft, however, spilled between 40,000 to 90,000 L of jet fuel into the towers that then quickly ignited. Contrary to early speculation, however, the fire was not sufficiently hot to melt the steel beams of the tower, but they were hot enough to cause critical damage. The fire, technically called a diffuse flame, was an air-fed, fuel-rich mixture (evidenced by the black, sooty smoke that came from the fire) that probably reached only a maximum temperature of about 650°C, well below the 1500°C needed to melt steel. However, steel begins to soften at about 425°C and loses about half of its strength by 650°C. Engineers, nevertheless, have determined that, because of the designed margin of safety and load features of the buildings, the towers would still have been able to readily survive even if their steel supports lost over half of their structural strength. It was well within their designed capacity to stand up even to this type of structural compromise. The problem, however, was that other factors combined with the reduced strength of the steel supports to cause the collapse.

When the fire burned in the tower, it primarily heated just one side of the steel beams, especially the floor beams. The sides of the beams *away* from the flames, however, remained significantly cooler. This difference in temperature caused distortions in the long, slender steel beams of the floor supports, causing them to buckle. When the floors buckled, the clips that held the floor supports (joists) to the outer support columns and the building's core were most vulnerable and presumably separated from the supports when the floors and walls bowed. This caused one floor to collapse onto the floor below it. The added load from the floor that came down from above then exceeded the capacity of the lower floor, which also gave way. In this manner, the entire structure collapsed similar to dominoes falling in a row. Because of the enormous inertia and momentum of the mass of the upper floors, the building collapsed essentially straight down without leaning over, reaching a speed of over 200 km/h when it hit the bottom about ten seconds later (free fall would have taken eight seconds). The towers then collapsed primarily from two causes: a weakening of the steel supports by the heat from the fire and the buckling of the floors and supports from uneven heating causing the floors to give way.

The design of the WTC was not flawed but, in fact, provided a structure that held up amazingly well to the enormous and unexpected stresses caused by the impact and subsequent fire. The perimeter tube design protected vital components of the tower, stiffened its structure from lateral stress (wind), and provided a redundant method for shifting load when damage occurred. The towers lasted between one and two hours before their ultimate collapse, allowing thousands of workers to successfully escape. No designer or engineer would ever be expected to anticipate that such a massive amount of jet fuel would be ignited within the building in such a short time.

18.2 COMPUTER AND INTERNET FORENSICS, CYBERSECURITY, AND AI

LEARNING GOALS AND OBJECTIVES

Computer and internet forensics focus on the analysis of electronic digital information associated with criminal behavior. The related area of cybersecurity deals with keeping confidential information safe and secure. When you complete this this section, you should be able to

- Explain what is meant by computer and software engineering.
- Discuss how computers and the internet may be used for criminal behavior.
- Describe methods used to track and analyze computer-based crime.
- Discuss special legal considerations that are involved with computer-based crime.
- Explain what is meant by cybersecurity and informatics and why they are important.

18.2.1 Introduction

Few inventions in human history have changed life so radically as the computer. Many of us are now so wedded to electronic, computer-driven devices, such as laptop computers, smartphones, electronic tablets, PDAs, cameras, televisions, and many other digital devices, that their absence for even a few hours causes significant distress and disruption to the ways in which we normally function. Additionally, the rapid expansion of the internet, the worldwide computer communications network, has provided unimagined connectivity and communication opportunities to people virtually around the world. A person now only needs a relatively inexpensive computer and a simple telecommunications link to instantly broadcast their messages, upload information, communicate with others, retrieve data from anywhere, and commit cybercrime. Pictures and video images from events captured by smartphones and digital video cameras are nearly instantly broadcast globally, whereas before it took hours or even days for such information to be widely disseminated. We now expect to be able to watch events unfold across the city, country, or world on our personal TV, computer, or cellphone screen essentially as it happens.

In most places, the development of computer hardware and software is considered to be a subfield of engineering. Often, the field is divided into *computer engineering*, which deals with the design, development, and fabrication of computer hardware (e.g., circuitry, computer systems, storage media, etc.), and *computer software engineering*, which focuses on the design and development specifically of computer software (e.g., programs, applications, operating systems, communication protocols, etc.).

The advent of the personal computer and high-speed internet, while bringing incredible opportunities and changing the way that we live, has also brought the potential for great abuse and misuse. Because of the rapid ongoing development of new technologies, computer and internet crime bring with them unique challenges not faced by any other field of forensic science. Computer misuse can extend beyond the typical local nature of criminal action to include acts of

FIGURE 18.27 Computer forensics presents many unique features to an investigation. Here, a police expert examines a hard drive in search of criminal evidence.

Source: Shutterstock.com.

terrorism and computer-based international assaults against entire countries and corporations by even a single individual located perhaps across the globe from their intended targets. Fake and manipulated pictures, fraudulent reports, and misleading information can be very damaging and exceptionally dangerous. Unfortunately, unethical, and criminal people have learned how to effectively manipulate others through the use of these fake information streams and worldwide platforms. Nonetheless, investigators and agencies are now developing the tools and expertise to locate, preserve, process, and use computer and media-based forensic information effectively in criminal and civil cases (Figure 18.27).

BOX 18.14   SHARON LOPATKA HOMICIDE

The death of Sharon Lopatka in 1996 presented a number of "firsts" for computer crime investigators. Lopatka had set up an internet business, called "Classified Concepts," that provided a number of computer-based services from ad writing to psychic readings but also ventured from the mainstream to offer strange fetish items for sale on the internet. While living with her husband, Lopatka became involved with a much darker side of the internet and ultimately came up with the idea of using her internet business to find a man who would torture and ultimately kill her in a "consensual" homicide case. After exchanging emails for months with several people, all of whom backed out as soon as they realized that Sharon was serious, she identified and "negotiated" with 45-year-old computer analyst Robert "Bobby" Glass who agreed to perform the homicide. On October 13, 1996, she told her husband that she was going to meet friends in Georgia but instead had arranged to meet Glass in North Carolina. After several days of torture, Glass ultimately strangled Lopatka on October 16, 1996, with a nylon cord.

When her husband found a note soon after she had departed indicating a different and bizarre reason for the trip, he immediately called the police. Investigators seized and searched Lopatka's computer records and emails, which quickly led them to Bobby Glass and North Carolina. After issuing a search warrant, investigators found Lopatka's body 75 ft from Glass's trailer home in a shallow grave.

The case went to trial, Glass pleaded guilty to voluntary manslaughter and was sentenced to 36–53 months for the homicide conviction. Two weeks before his ultimate release in 2002, however, he suffered a fatal heart attack in prison.

This case was one of the first where the internet was used to arrange for a homicide. The intense media coverage of the case led to an active debate about internet censorship and freedoms that continues today.

18.2.2 Computer Crime

Computer forensics deals with the identification, preservation, analysis, and documentation of digital information derived primarily from computers and their storage media devices. There are a great many areas of abuse and types of crimes that may involve computer forensics. These investigations may include:

- Cyber stalking, bullying, and harassment.
- Child and other illegal forms of pornography and sexual solicitation.
- Assault and attack (e.g., denial of service, destruction of data, computer virus release, disruption of function, etc.).
- Employee internet abuse and industrial/international espionage.
- Traditional crime information sources (e.g., drug deal records, money laundering, embezzlement, fraud, deception, etc.).
- Deliberate unauthorized "hacking" into other computer systems and assessment of damage done.
- Illegal and unethical modification of sensitive and securely stored data and transmissions (see Section 18.2.5 on Cybersecurity).
- Defamation and libel attacks.
- Internet of Things (IoT), cloud, and network forensics.

It is important to note at the outset that, because of the rapid advances in computer-based technologies, the case law and legislation dealing with computer forensics are very rapidly changing. New challenges, barely imaginable today, may become central players in the near future. Understandably, this chapter can only deal primarily with the basic principles and fundamental aspects of computer-related forensics.

18.2.3 Computer Investigations

Computer data can be relatively fragile and fleeting. The simple act of just opening a file changes the file by overwriting the time and date that it was last opened. Digital information is often not well protected and usually very easily deleted, modified, and transmitted directly by the action of the computer's user as well as through automated programming that periodically deletes data and cleans storage media. Both deliberate destruction of electronic information and routine alteration can allow criminals to hide their tracks relatively easily. Additionally, the nature of the internet provides anonymity to users that makes it very difficult to track messages and actions back to their electronic sources. Even if the source can be traced to a particular computer, there remains the problem of tying one particular person to the action performed on a specific computer. This personal connection might be straightforward to establish if the computer is a single-user system but becomes far more difficult if the computer is part of an

unsupervised multi-user platform, such as in a public or corporate computer cluster (e.g., computer clusters in a library, company, university, internet café, and others). Additionally, users can frequently change their profiles, computer account information, usernames, passwords, service carriers, and take other measures to stay one step ahead of investigators and remain hidden.

BOX 18.15   SOME USEFUL DEFINITIONS

Internet: A computer communications network that connects computers together worldwide.

Persistent Data: Data stored on a hard drive that remains after a computer is turned off.

Volatile Data: Data stored in memory (often RAM) that is lost when the computer powers off.

Wiretap: Monitoring of communications transmissions.

Byte: A piece of digital information made up of eight bits. Kb is a kilobyte (1,000 bytes) and MB is a megabyte (1,000,000 bytes).

Bit: The smallest piece of digital data, either a "1" or a "0."

CD-ROM: Compact Disk Read-Only Memory.

Cloud Computing: Involving "cloud"-computing: the delivery, storage, and extraction of data using the internet.

IoT: Internet of Things.

Operating System: The software that controls and runs the basic functions of a computer.

RAM: Random Access Memory.

ROM: Read Only Memory, digital memory that cannot be written over but can be read by a computer.

Partition: A subdivision of a hard drive.

Probably the most important aspect of investigating computer-based crime is the availability of an appropriately trained expert analyst. Analysts in this field are required to have both extensive and specialized computer expertise along with detailed training in forensic investigations. Computer forensic investigations require following a protocol that can withstand the rigors of a courtroom environment. Guidelines have been established by a number of groups, but especially by the Scientific Working Group on Digital Evidence (SWGDE, see www.swgde.org for a wealth of linked information), to assist in establishing proper steps and methods for investigating these crimes. Seizing and collecting computer hardware and software may require a specific search warrant, although the tests described in Chapter 2 are usually still applicable. For example, digital evidence that can be defined as in "plain view" may be obtainable without a warrant, but with some significant limitations. For example, if a computer is turned on at a crime scene with incriminating evidence in plain view on the desktop, then it can be recovered without a warrant. Similarly, if a warrant is issued to search a computer for evidence of fraud and an investigator finds a folder entitled "child pornography" on the desktop, this is usually considered in plain view and can be opened. In order to explore the folder beyond a very cursory look, however, the issuance of a specific search warrant would still be required to properly search and seize any criminal evidence. Computer evidence is often also governed by laws not usually found for other types of forensic evidence, such as wiretap, electronic communications, and stored information laws. Unfortunately, because of the relative newness of the field and the continuing rapid development of computer systems and software, the laws relating to computer evidence are still largely in flux and undergoing continual change. Nonetheless, good practices are now generally established for digital evidence investigations.

Computer crime investigations generally follow well-recognized steps that include collection, preservation, analysis, and reporting, with proper and detailed documentation running through all these steps. The first tasks of any computer investigation, therefore, must be to collect and preserve as much of the data as possible. Whenever a crime scene is identified as having the potential to provide digital evidence, investigators must act quickly to prevent the modification and deletion of data, either directly by the user's actions or through the computer's automated "clean-up" processes. If a computer is still active and powered on, simply turning it off may result in the loss of any information stored in the computer's RAM memory. RAM, or random access memory, is a type of short-term memory that is usually erased when the computer is turned off. Sometimes, though, RAM-stored information can still be accessed for a period of time after the computer is turned off since the electric charge in a computer's circuitry is not dissipated immediately but may take hours or even days under certain conditions to discharge, especially in low-temperature conditions or with higher voltage systems. Other evidence that might be seized may include the computer hardware, external storage media, interfaces, and backup data.

The forensic investigator typically first makes a *static image* (or copy) of the computer's hard drive and any external storage media at the very beginning of the preservation phase. This process protects the original data from both accidental and intentional modification during the processing and analysis itself. It also provides legal verification for the analysis by preserving the original data in a pristine form. Investigators then use the copy rather than the original for their analysis, processing, and documentation.

The analysis portion of the investigation can be extremely complicated and technical in nature. One technique commonly employed deals with the recovery of deleted files. When a file is deleted, many computer operating systems simply remove that file's name and computer "address" from its file directory listing, but it might not immediately erase the actual file. This action simply breaks the link between the file and its directory listing without actually removing the data from the disk. It may be possible, then, to search the hard drive to reconstruct the deleted file from different sectors of the computer's memory. Using a technique known as file carving, an entire drive can be searched to locate key identifying information from deleted files, which can then be used to reconstruct the original file. Today, a number of programs are available to investigators that have been specifically designed to recover and analyze computer data. In special circumstances, investigators can even use a scanning electron microscope (SEM) to physically read the individual magnetic domains on a portion of a computer disk to reconstruct a file. Computer users, however, have become more aware of these deleted file recovery techniques and increasingly are using overwriting software (writing random data over the deleted files) and other techniques to prevent file reconstruction, a process known as anti-forensics (see Box 18.17 on "anti-forensics").

Investigations may search for specific file names, content labels on files, keywords, or types of information stored on the system. A computer may have millions of stored files, most of

BOX 18.16   ENRON'S COMPUTERS

In late 2001, Enron – a very large oil company with over $60 billion in assets – financially collapsed and filed for bankruptcy (the largest in U.S. history), leaving employees without jobs and, in many cases, without retirement funds. What inflamed the situation even more was that it seemed that the corporate executives of Enron were not affected personally as other Enron workers had been. Other "flags" quickly emerged that suggested the collapse was far more than the fiscal failure of a corporation. In response, Congress launched a probe into the collapse of Enron.

The congressional inquiry demanded documents from the company including email communications and other computer-based documents. Early in the investigation, however, it was learned that many records associated with Enron's dealings had been destroyed or deleted, both by the company itself and by its auditors (Arthur Andersen and Company). Fortunately, forensic investigators were able to recover some of the key deleted files from Arthur Andersen Co.'s computer backup system. For example, a recovered file showed that Enron had set up an "off-shore" web site to store hidden files associated with Enron's California dealings. Other emails directed employees to delete and destroy emails and files, even after a federal subpoena had been issued for the information. One particular email from JP Morgan Chase described a secret Enron loan called a "prepay." When investigators followed this email chain, they found other messages, such as: "Enron loves these deals as they are able to hide funded debt from their equity analysts because they (at the very least) book it as deferred [revenue] or (better yet) bury it in their trading liabilities" and "Five [billion] in prepays!!!!!!!!!!!!!!!" with the reply being "Shut up and delete this email."

Partially from the computer forensics work, a number of the top executives at Enron stood trial and were ultimately criminally convicted.

BOX 18.17 ANTI-FORENSICS

Cyber criminals have found ways to thwart prosecutions using a number of tools called *antiforensics*. These programs are designed specifically to make it as difficult as possible to retrieve or track information from a computer. These programs may function simply by changing the hidden identifying "header" for a file, interrupting information transfer. Another tool involves splitting up a file into tiny pieces and then attaching those pieces at the ends of other files as hidden data that is retrievable and reassembled only by the antiforensics software. Encryption can also be used to prevent others from reading a particular file. In encryption, a file's contents are converted into a string of seemingly meaningless symbols, letters, and numbers according to a complex set of rules (the key). Without the rules, it is very difficult or impossible to translate the information in the file back into a readable form. Other programs function by overwriting and deleting files if any unauthorized entry into the computer system is detected.

which have little to do with the purpose of the investigation. A key step, therefore, involves filtering out data with evidentiary value from the vast amount of irrelevant information.

One important computer forensic method is to extract the history of internet use from the computer's web browser or from its email (or similar) communications log, even if these histories have been deleted. Sometimes, central computer records kept on a server (not the individual computer) can be compared with information on an individual machine to look for anomalies that might indicate misuse. These central sources may also provide temporary automatic backup for an individual computer that may be searched for files deleted on the local computer. These centrally stored records may be kept for days or weeks (or even longer) after they have been deleted on the individual computer.

The careful documentation of all the steps performed, equivalent to the chain of custody for other forms of evidence, is critical if the computer forensic analysis is to stand up in court. Once the analysis is complete, the investigator must also effectively communicate the results of the analysis, a task that might be complicated by the technical complexity of the computer analysis itself.

18.2.4 Investigative Tools

The law enforcement community must rely upon adequate tools for identifying and analyzing the many aspects of computer crime. A number of ever-updating forensic software packages have been developed that facilitate these investigations. Disk imaging software can be used to record both the structure and the contents of a hard drive without changing the hard drive itself. This allows the investigator to process and search the data stored on the drive by using the imaged

data, preventing any compromise of the original data itself. Some software tools can reconstruct the storage drive bit by bit. "Hashing" tools can be used to compare original hard drives with any copies made, allowing a determination of the copy as an identical match or altered version compared to the original.

File recovery programs have been developed that search for particular files and types of digital data. Once the files or data are found, these programs then work to try to restore data and rebuild the original file. Sometimes, only part of the file can be recovered but this fragment can still play a useful forensic role. Encryption decoding software has also been developed for restoring encrypted or password-protected data.

18.2.5 Cybersecurity and Network Forensics

Every day, hundreds of billions of financial transactions, personal communications, and other types of sensitive data pass through computer-mediated pathways. For example, one banking company alone reportedly processes billions of financial transactions and records daily. Each of these records must be authenticated, logged, and acted upon in some proper and legal fashion. Additionally, trillions of records are stored and routinely accessed that contain an enormous variety of sensitive information; information to which only properly authorized people should have access. The problem, of course, is providing proper and easy access to people authorized to use the stored information while preventing access to those who should not have access. The field of *cybersecurity* deals specifically with providing integrity and trust to both stored data and sensitive information that passes through computer-mediated channels.

The goal of the field is to protect digital data from corruption, theft, modification, or accidental loss. Many of the tools described already play a role in cybersecurity. These protective measures may include both physical barriers (e.g., locked rooms, physical protection of the computer, dongle use, etc.) and software tools (e.g., authentication, verification, and tracing methods). This is a large and rapidly growing field, with new discoveries and methods continually being developed and refined.

The field of cyberforensics also deals with the newly emergent areas of IoT systems and network forensics. IoT refers to the "Internet of Things" and involves the networking of "everyday" devices that contain embedded sensors, software, and internet connectivity. These devices include smart home appliances (e.g., refrigerators, toasters, televisions, home security cameras, etc.), health implants, smart meters, personal assistant devices (e.g., Siri, Alexa, PDAs, etc.), home environmental systems (e.g., heating/cooling), traffic signals, smart cameras, and many others. Devices that exchange data with the internet can serve as entry points to their controlling interconnected computer systems in a variety of cybercrime activities, including spying, identification theft, blackmail, and others. IoT forensics deals with extracting legal evidence from these types of devices.

IoT is related to the field of *cloud forensics* which deals with extracting information from "cloud-based" information storage and retrieval systems. Cloud systems deliver services, such as data storage, database access, networking, software access, and intelligence, purely over the internet ("the cloud"). Companies and individuals may heavily rely on these services for inexpensive and reliable data storage and retrieval, along with easy software maintenance and access. Cloud computing primarily provides three types of computing services: Infrastructure-as-a-Service (IaaS), Platforms-as-a-Service (PaaS), and Software-as-a-Service (SaaS) uses. IaaS applications provide users with access to inexpensive servers and data storage, PaaS systems provide managed application software, and SaaS uses typically deliver services such as software updates, bug fixes, and other general software maintenance (e.g., auto-updates to smart phone and computer operating systems). Cloud forensics deals with discovering and documenting any uses of the "cloud" for criminal activity, including data breaches, identity theft, and illegal surveillance. While investigations involving cloud computing may use similar tools employed in network and digital forensics, the task of obtaining evidence may be significantly more complex due to the distributed nature of the cloud.

18.2.6 Informatics

Increasingly, many areas of forensic science have developed extensive databases of stored information that can be quickly and accurately searched for matching properties to help identify something. *Informatics* is a field with several definitions but basically encompasses the collection, classification, storage, and retrieval of archival knowledge and information. Some of these databases commonly encountered in forensic science include:

- DNA (e.g., the Combined DNA Index System [CODIS, US], National DNA Database [NDNAD, UK]).
- Drugs (e.g., Ident-A-Drug, RxList, PharmInfoNet: includes registry information, tablet labeling information, toxicological information, etc.).
- Fingerprints (e.g., Integrated Automatic Fingerprint Identification System [IAFIS]).
- Fire (e.g., Ignitable Liquids Reference Collection [ILRC, the National Center for Forensic Sciences]).
- Firearm Information (e.g., Integrated Ballistic Identification System [IBIS] and National Integrated Ballistics Information Network [NIBIN]: databases of bullet and cartridge case markings, extractor marking registry, gunpowder ID, etc.).
- Glass (e.g., Glass Evidence Reference Database: information on >700 glass samples provided by manufacturers, distributors, and vehicle junkyards).
- Ink (e.g., International Ink Library [U.S. Secret Service and the Internal Revenue Service]: includes more than 9,500 inks dating from the 1920s).

- Paint (e.g., National Automotive Paint File [FBI] and Paint Data Query [Canadian RCMP]: automotive paint data from domestic and foreign car manufacturers).
- Handwriting (e.g., Forensic Information System for Handwriting [FISH, US Secret Service] and the Forensic Handwritten Document Retrieval System [CEDAR–FOX]).
- Medical and dental records.
- Shoeprints (e.g., TreadMark™, SoleMate, etc.).
- Spectroscopy (e.g., mass spectral libraries, infrared absorption data, UV/Vis absorption data, Chem Finder, etc.).
- Tire tracks (e.g., TreadMate).
- Toolmarks (e.g., NIBIN, Toolmark database [Iowa State University], etc.).

Many other forensic databases are currently in development, and those that exist are continually expanded and refined.

Forensic databases are used for several purposes, as described in Chapter 2. In summary, however, they can provide two key types of information: identification and comparison. An *identification analysis* aims to identify the relevant features of a piece of evidence with as much certainty as possible to achieve an unambiguous identification of the material. In contrast, a *comparison analysis* seeks to associate a standard reference sample of known origin with a sample of unknown origin. Typically, two types of comparison analysis are frequently encountered: *one-to-many matching* (comparing an unknown sample with a very large pool of known possibilities) and *one-to-one matching* (comparing an unknown sample with just one reference sample, usually used for verification or authentication).

Fortunately, computers are very good at all these types of analysis, providing rapid and reliable identification and comparison of unknown samples with information stored in a database.

18.2.7 Artificial Intelligence (AI)

The development of forensic science over the years has been strongly driven by new technological advances and scientific discoveries. The recent advent of sophisticated computer-based methods, such as artificial intelligence (AI) and machine learning (ML), has the potential to revolutionize and transform both our criminal justice system, including forensic science, and society at large.

Artificial intelligence focuses on using computers to perform tasks commonly associated with human thinking, including the ability to reason, discover meaning, learn from past experiences, and adapt to new circumstances. Machine learning is very similar, using computer programs to produce models from large datasets to perform complicated tasks. A subset of ML, referred to as *deep learning*, uses established artificial neural networks structured similarly to those of the human brain to perform complex tasks. All these methods utilize vast data sets and known existing patterns, including the enormous ocean of information available on the internet, to perform their

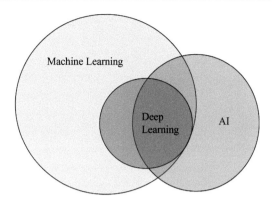

FIGURE 18.28 Relationship between machine learning (ML), artificial intelligence (AI), and deep learning (DL).

work. The close relationship between AI, ML, and deep learning is illustrated in Figure 18.28.

AI approaches are becoming pervasive in society today, with everyday applications including healthcare (e.g., automated diagnoses from vast patient record banks, optimizing medical resources, and reviewing patient treatment plans), business (e.g., developing marketing plans, designing effective supply chains, and verifying credentials in financial transactions), and as personal assistants (e.g., Siri, Alexa, etc.). Given the complexity of criminal investigations, it shouldn't be surprising that AI techniques are finding increasing use in forensic science, with an expectation of explosively rapid growth of the technology in criminal activity. Some of the current uses, and concerns, of AI-based methods in forensics include:

Evidence Processing: Evidence collected and analyzed from a crime scene may include a large quantity of diverse types of information. Deep learning methodologies are helping to find specific objects or patterns that may otherwise go unnoticed by investigators by checking potential relationships between huge numbers of disparate objects and facts. Additionally, document analysis may be expedited through machine learning's natural language processing (NLP) algorithms that analyze huge amounts of text to identify relevant information. This includes the use of AI in analyzing mountains of digital evidence exceptionally rapidly, such as emails, text messages, electronic files, and unusual internet activity patterns. Such methods also form an increasing part of evaluating national security risks and personal threats. AI electronic surveillance algorithms are being used to continuously monitor online social media and other computer platforms in attempts to identify potential threats and criminal activity before they become significant problems.

Policing Methodologies: Machine learning models may be employed to predict criminal behavior patterns, thereby aiding law enforcement agencies in allocating resources more efficiently. By analyzing huge amounts of historical crime data, these models can identify patterns and locations that might not be otherwise obvious.

DNA Analysis: AI is contributing to DNA analysis by automating the process of identifying matches in DNA profiles and processing complex sequencing data. Additionally,

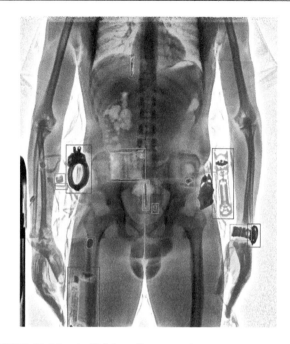

FIGURE 18.29 Artificial Intelligence software was used to rapidly detect the presence and assess the threat of objects in an X-ray image from a body scanner.

Source: Retrieved from Wikimedia. Used per Creative Commons Share Alike 4.0 International. User: Mirddincom.

this approach may be useful in identifying undiscovered connections between otherwise seemingly unrelated cases.

Biometric Information: AI approaches to facial recognition and surveillance, fingerprint matching, and voice analysis, among others, are enhancing investigators' abilities in rapidly identifying suspects and victims (Figure 18.29). Future uses may include AI analysis of both written and spoken language to detect threat sentiment, personal emotion, deception, and other language patterns that may suggest criminal intent or activity (Figure 18.30).

Forensic Medicine: AI methods can assist in evaluating autopsy data and framing expert opinions. This, in the future, may include procedures such as the analysis of toxins, detection of pathological changes in body organs, predictions of weapons used in an assault, and time since death calculations. The primary challenge to using AI approaches in forensic medicine is the development of high-quality datasets for analysis and establishing the validity of AI methods in court. For example, determining the cause of death by drowning may be one of the most challenging tasks from post-mortem images. Recent studies have successfully used deep learning approaches to classify subjects into drowning or non-drowning cases by analyzing post-mortem lung CT images. Similar applications have been reported for age estimation of human remains, gender evaluation, and personal identification, especially in mass disaster situations (Figure 18.31).

It is very important to note that, despite the assistance AI-based methods may bring to an investigation, their use also raises some very significant ethical concerns. AI algorithms may be biased because they build on systemic biases present

FIGURE 18.30   Artificial Intelligence software can be used to rapidly estimate the emotional state of a person.

Source: Shutterstock.com images.

FIGURE 18.31   An apparent image of a young woman, computer-generated using AI techniques. This person does not exist but was generated using an analysis of many portraits.

Source: Retrieved from Wikimedia. User: Owsmcgee. Image generated by StyleGA.

in historical data. This is particularly important in predictive policing methods and the use of AI in pretrial detention and post-conviction sentencing determinations. AI approaches are only as unbiased and accurate as the datasets they employ. Additionally, since the method frequently employs both public and private databases, personal privacy infringement is a real concern. The outcome of AI analyses can also be purposefully manipulated through intentional alterations of input datasets. AI methods are often further limited by a lack of common sense, an inability to extend predictions to unknown experiences, an inability to consider context (e.g., sarcasm, irony, etc.), and a lack of creativity and intuition, which are common to human investigators.

AI is currently most effective when it serves to complement human expertise rather than replace it in decision-making processes. By identifying patterns and trends from huge data sets, AI can aid in investigations by enhancing efficiency and

accuracy as well as providing new leads in otherwise missed directions.

It is not difficult to predict that AI-based methods will become an increasingly prevalent presence in criminal activity and as a tool in the future of forensic science.

18.2.8 Conclusions

Computers represent an enormous tool with incredible opportunities for the future. They can also, however, present a significant opportunity for criminal threats to both individuals and society. As rapidly as computers are developing, new tools are being invented to detect, recover, and analyze digital, AI, and networked forms of evidence. The use of digital evidence in court is currently in flux, but it clearly will increasingly find a central role in forensic investigations.

BOX 18.18 FORENSIC ENGINEERING EQUATIONS

Conservation of Energy: $E_{final} - E_{initial} = 0$

Conservation of Momentum: $p_{final} - p_{initial} = 0$ (where p is momentum).

Factor of Safety (FS): $FS = \dfrac{\text{material strength}}{\text{design load}}$

Force (F): $F = m\,a$ (where F is the force, m is the mass, and a is the acceleration).

Kinetic Energy (KE): $KE = \frac{1}{2}\,mv^2$ (where m is the mass, and v is the velocity of the object).

Margin of Safety (MoS): $MoS = \dfrac{\text{actual load capacity}}{\text{load capacity}} - 1$

Momentum: $p = m\,v$ (where p is the momentum, m is the mass, and v is the velocity of the object).

Skid Equation (without impact): $v = (2\,g\,f\,d)^{\frac{1}{2}}$

Skid Equation (with impact): $v = [2\,g\,d\,f + 2\,(K/m)\,x]^{\frac{1}{2}}$

Simplified Skid Formula (S_1): $S_1 = S_1 = \sqrt{(30)(d_1)(f)}$ (where S_1 is the initial speed at the start of the skid (in mph), d_1 is the distance of the skid before stopping, and f is the frictional coefficient).

Simplified Skid Formula with Crush (S_c): $S_c = S_c = \sqrt{\left[(30)(d_1)(f)\right] + \left[(30)(d_2)(cf)\right]}$ (where S_c is the initial speed at the start of the skid (in mph), d_1 is the distance of the skid before impact, f is the frictional coefficient, d_2 is the depth of the crush in ft, and cf is the crush factor in lb/ft).

Work (W): $W = F\,d$ (where F is the force, and d is the distance through which the object is moved).

Work Energy (E_{work}): $E_{work} = F\,f\,d$ (where F is the force, f is the frictional coefficient, and d is the distance).

QUESTIONS FOR FURTHER PRACTICE AND MASTERY

18.1 In a forensic failure analysis, there are generally two goals. What are those two goals, and why are they important?

18.2 When considering the unexpected collapse of a structure, forensic engineers consider three types of forces that act on the structure. Describe these three forces.

18.3 What is a vector?

18.4 Classify each of the following as either a static or dynamic load: (a) brick façade of a building, (b) roof, (c) traffic on a bridge, (d) snow on a roof, (e) plumbing in a building, (f) people in an arena at a convention, (g) wind, (h) furniture in a building.

18.5 What causes fatigue in a metal?

18.6 What is meant by a compression-relaxation cycle?

18.7 What is meant by the Factor of Safety for a structure? What is the typical FoS range required for a structure?

18.8 What is the Margin of Safety?

18.9 What is reverse engineering?

18.10 How many times more kinetic energy does a 2,000 lb vehicle traveling at 60 mph have than a 1,000 lb vehicle traveling at 30 mph?

18.11 A car struck and seriously injured a pedestrian. The driver applied the brakes and left a skid with an overall length of 120 ft If the pedestrian was struck 80 ft before the end of the skid mark, how fast was the car going when it struck the pedestrian? ($g = 32.7$ ft/s^2 and $f = 0.75$)

18.12 A 2,000 lbs vehicle with a crush coefficient of 4,000 lbs/in. strikes a bridge abutment and the front end is crushed in 4 in. If there is a 200 ft skid mark leading to the bridge abutment, how fast was the vehicle going at the start of the skid? ($g = 32.17$ ft/s^2, $f = 0.75$, $K = 4,000$ lbs/in., $m = 62.1$s^2 lbf/ft)

18.13 What information may be determined from skid mark patterns?

18.14 What is the difference between a vector quantity and a scalar quantity?

18.15 What are the steps that are usually followed in a computer crime investigation?

18.16 What is "file carving" and how is it used in file recovery?

18.17 What is the field of cybersecurity?

18.18 What is meant by the terms: (a) artificial intelligence, (b) machine learning, and (c) deep learning?

18.19 Describe forensic investigations involving IoT and cloud computing.

18.20 What are some of the areas that AI is playing a role in forensic science?

EXTENSIVE QUESTIONS

18.21 Explain what is meant by static loads, dynamic loads, and cyclic loads.

18.22 There are many possible causes of system failures in vehicles, machinery, and industrial processes. List as many of these possible causes of system failures as you can.

18.23 In the forensic reconstruction of a vehicular accident, what are the key questions that must be answered?

18.24 A 2,500 lbs car is parked on the side of the road. A 10,000 lb truck rear ends the car and the car skids forward 80 ft while the truck skids 30 ft after impact. How fast was the truck going when it struck the car? Assume $f = 0.75$ for the asphalt roadway.

18.25 Cyber forensics is a relatively new area of criminal investigations. What difficulties are faced by computer forensic investigators? Include in your discussion issues with warrants, collection of digital data, identifying a particular computer as the source of the data, and tying a single user to a particular computer.

18.26 What are some of the ethical concerns involved with using AI and related methods in forensic science and policing?

GLOSSARY OF TERMS

anti-forensics: approaches designed to make it as difficult to retrieve or track information from a computer.

artificial intelligence (AI): using computers to perform tasks commonly associated with human thinking, including the ability to reason, discover meaning, learn from past experiences and adapt to new circumstances.

bit: the smallest piece of digital data, either a "1" or a "0."

byte: a piece of digital information made up of eight bits: a kilobyte (Kb) is 1,000 Bytes and a megabyte (MB) is 1,000,000 Bytes.

CD-ROM: Compact Disk Read-Only Memory.

cloud forensics: deals with extracting information from "cloud-based" information storage and retrieval systems.

comparison analysis: a method that attempts to associate a standard reference sample of known origin with a sample of unknown origin.

computer engineering: the subfield of engineering that deals with the design, development, and fabrication of computer hardware (e.g., circuitry, computer systems, storage media, etc.).

computer software engineering: the subfield of engineering that focuses on the design and development of computer software (e.g., applications, operating systems, communication protocols, etc.).

conservation of energy: the principle that states that energy may be converted between its different forms, but the total energy of an isolated system must remain constant.

conservation of momentum: the principle that states that the total momentum of an isolated system must remain constant.

crush depth: the distance that a given part of a vehicle is indented from a collision.

crush energy: the amount of energy required to cause an observed indentation in a material, such as a vehicle. Usually given by $E = Kx$ (where K is the measured crush coefficient for the vehicle, x is the crush depth measured from the crashed vehicle).

cybersecurity: the field that deals with providing integrity and trust to both stored data and information passing through computer-mediated channels.

cyclic load: forces on a structure that occur repeatedly and can lead to fatigue and damage to building materials; sometimes considered a specific example of a dynamic load. Cyclic loads may occur from vibrations or heating/cooling cycles, for example.

deep learning: using computers to generate artificial neural networks, structured similarly to those of the human brain, to perform complex tasks.

dead load: see Static load.

design load: the expected actual load planned for a building.

dynamic loads: combined weight imposed upon a structure that may vary greatly over time. Also called live loads.

elastic collision: a collision where the amount of kinetic energy is the same before and after the collision.

engineering: the field that takes fundamental scientific, economic, and practical knowledge and applies it to the design and construction of structures, devices, materials, and processes.

factor of safety (FS): a value that reflects the ability of a structure to hold loads beyond those anticipated from the total of static and dynamic loads.

fatigue: a cumulative and progressive process that results in eventual damage to building materials, often through the repetition of certain types of movements or pressures.

force (F): the impetus given to an object and defined as mass times acceleration.

forensic engineering: the field dealing with the legal investigation of how materials, processes, structures, and objects fail in their intended function. The field also informs legal proceedings regarding accident reconstruction, tracking cyber-crime, and related functions.

forensic failure analysis: investigations that deal with trying to determine why certain processes, materials, structures, or components fail in the performance of their intended function.

frictional coefficient (f): a numeric value that indicates the resistance an object encounters when moving over another surface.

gravitational acceleration (g): a constant on Earth indicating how fast an object is accelerated by gravity.

identification analysis: a method for identifying the relevant features of a piece of evidence with as much certainty as possible, leading to an unambiguous identification of the material.

inelastic collision: a collision where some or all the kinetic energy is converted into other forms of energy, such as work, light, or thermal energy.

internet: a computer communications network that connects computers worldwide.

IoT: Internet of Things.

irreversible process: a process that can only proceed in one direction.

kinetic energy: the energy associated with the motion of an object and determined by the expression: $KE = 1/2 \; mv^2$.

live loads: see Dynamic loads.

machine learning: computer programs that produce models from large data sets to perform complicated tasks.

margin of safety (MoS): the ratio of the actual strength of the structure to the required strength of the structure.

operating system: the software that controls and runs the basic functions of a computer.

partition: a subdivision of a hard drive.

persistent data: data stored on a hard drive that remains after a computer is turned off.

RAM: Random Access Memory.

reverse engineering: a process that starts with a finished product or end result and then takes it "apart" piece-by-piece to determine how it works, was constructed, or failed.

ROM: Read Only Memory, digital memory that cannot be written over but can be read by a computer.

skid: a skid occurs when the tires of a vehicle stop rotating while the vehicle continues to move forward.

static load: refers to the combined weight imposed upon a structure from relatively unchanging, or only very slowly changing, features of a structure. Sometimes called a dead load.

volatile data: data stored in memory (often RAM) that is lost when the computer powers off.

wiretap: monitoring of communications transmissions.

work (W): energy used to move a mass through a distance and defined as force times distance.

BIBLIOGRAPHY

Charles J. Brooks, *Cybersecurity Essentials*, Sybex, 2018.

Kenneth L. Carper, *Forensic Engineering*, (2nd Ed.) CRC Press, 2001.

Jacob Field and Kenneth L. Carper, *Construction Failure*, John Wiley and Sons, 1997.

Colin Gagg, *Forensic Engineering: The Art and Craft of a Failure Detective*, CRC Press, 2020.

Gerard Johnsen, *Digital Forensics and Incident Response: Incident response techniques and procedures to respond to modern cyber threats* (2nd Ed.) Packt Publishing, 2020.

Mattys Levy, Mario Salvadori, and Kevin Woest, *Why Buildings Fall Down: How Structures Fail*, W.W. Norton and Co., 2002.

Gary L. Lewis, *Guidelines for Forensic Engineering Practice*, ASCE Publications, 2003.

Richard A. Marquise, *Scotbom: Evidence and the Lockerbie Investigstion*, Algora Publishing, 2006.

Randall K. Noon, *Introduction to Forensic Engineering*, CRC Press, 1992.

Randall K. Noon, *Forensic Engineering Investigation*, CRC Press, 2001.

Erdal Ozkaya, *Cybersecurity: The Beginner's Guide: A comprehensive guide to getting stared n cybersecurity*, Packt Publishing, 2019.

Stephen E. Petty, *Forensic Engineering: Damage Assessments for Residential and Commercial Structures*, CRC Press, 2013.

Robert T. Ratey, *Forensic Structural Engineering Handbook*, McGraw-Hill Professional Publ., 2000.

PART 5

Behavioral Forensic Evidence

Behavioral Forensic Science 19

19.1 BEHAVIORAL FORENSIC SCIENCES

LEARNING GOALS AND OBJECTIVES

The field of behavioral forensic science primarily focuses on the relationships between the fields of psychology and sociology and the criminal justice system. After completing this chapter, you should be able to:

- Explain what is meant by the terms forensic psychology and forensic sociology.
- Describe how psychology is used before (investigative phase), during (criminal phase) and after (sentencing phase) trials.
- Illustrate how criminal profiling is done and what its strengths and limitations are.
- Discuss what is meant by legal competency and what its implications are.
- Describe the roles that a forensic psychologist might play in the legal system.
- Discuss the tools available to assess mental illness and how they are employed.
- Explain what is meant by a forensic psychological autopsy.

19.1.1 Introduction to Forensic Behavioral Science: Forensic Psychology and Sociology

Most forms of forensic evidence are readily amenable to direct physical measurement and quantitative analysis. In fact, forensic science is historically based on observable evidence that relies upon quantifiable scientific data which does not require significant amounts of subjective interpretation. However, behavioral science often deals with more subjective types of information that probe the underlying reasons for the outwardly observable patterns of a person's individual thoughts, intentions, and behavior. The field also deals with how people function both individually and collectively within larger groups and societies. Nevertheless, the behavioral sciences are now increasingly making use of measurable data to understand and predict personal reasoning and actions, partially in response to the field's growing application in legal practice (Figure 19.1).

What exactly are the behavioral sciences? The behavioral sciences are fields of scientific exploration that examine the underlying reasons behind observed personal and societal human behavior. This broad term encompasses the work of several fields, but especially those of psychology and sociology.

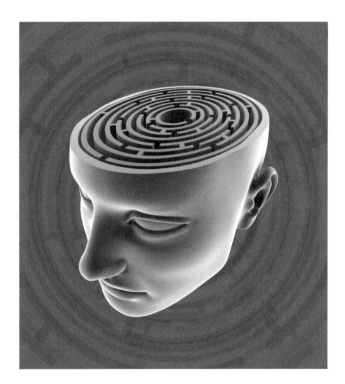

FIGURE 19.1 The forensic behavioral sciences seek to provide insights into a person's thinking and behavior. Forensic psychology deals primarily with how people function individually, while forensic sociology focuses on collective behaviors within larger groups and societies.

Source: Shutterstock.com

Psychology is focused on understanding human behavior through the examination of a person's individual thoughts and mental processes. The field explores mental functioning from many different perspectives and covers a number of sub-disciplines. For example, a neurobiological approach to psychology looks at the molecular and cellular components of the brain and nervous system to discover how memory, emotion, perception, reasoning, and other personal traits are stored and processed at fundamental levels: molecules, cells, and organs. Clinical psychology, in contrast, aims to apply generally accepted concepts of psychology to prevent and treat mental distress and dysfunction, as well as to promote personal mental health and well-being. Cognitive psychology examines how a person's underlying mental activity affects their memory, perception, problem-solving, reasoning, learning, language, and other brain functions. Social psychology focuses on how individual people deal with others in social settings and how groups, in turn, affect the thought processes of an individual. These are just a few of the many branches of modern psychology (Figure 19.2). Other sub-disciplines of psychology include abnormal, comparative, developmental, educational, sport, and school psychology. The growing field of forensic psychology, of course, deals with the application of psychological theories and practices to legal questions.

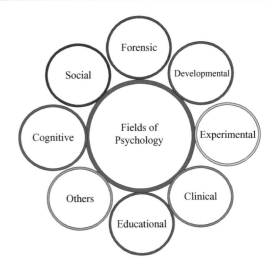

FIGURE 19.2   Psychology covers many related areas of behavioral science, including forensic psychology.

A characteristic trait of humans is that individuals tend to cluster together to form larger units to collectively provide for the basic needs of individuals (e.g., safety, shelter, nutrition, child-raising, etc.) as well as for other purposes, such as companionship, common interests, and pleasure. The field of *Sociology* examines how individuals and groups collectively function and behave within the context of larger societies. It also explores how individuals form social networks that operate together as complex organizations. Sociologists may focus on families, businesses, governments, cultures, political organizations, and social movements, among other types of human groups. While psychology may be thought of as focusing on the individual, sociology tends to focus instead on the functioning of a society. In a forensic setting, sociologists may address issues related to domestic abuse syndrome, family dynamics, group-based thinking, cultural pressures, context, and social group involvements, such as cults, networks, clubs, and "fringe" organizations. Understanding how an individual affects a society and, in turn, how the society affects a particular individual may have very important legal implications.

BOX 19.1   SELECTED JOURNALS IN FORENSIC PSYCHOLOGY

- *American Journal of Forensic Psychiatry*
- *American Journal of Forensic Psychology*
- *Criminal Behavior and Mental Health*
- *Journal of Child Sexual Abuse*
- *Journal of Forensic Neuropsychology*
- *Journal of Forensic Psychology Practice*
- *Journal of Police and Criminal Psychology*
- *Journal of Psychiatry and Law*
- *Law and Psychology Review*
- *Psychiatry, Psychology and Law*
- *Psychology, Crime and Law*
- *Sexual Abuse*
- *Law and Human Behavior*
- *Criminal Justice and Behavior*
- *Behavioral Sciences and the Law*
- *Journal of Interpersonal Violence*
- *Journal of American Academy of Psychiatry and Law*
- *Psychology, Public Policy and Law*
- *Journal of Family Violence*
- *International Journal of Law and Psychiatry*
- *Journal of Forensic Psychiatry*
- *Journal of Threat Assessment*
- *Violence Against Women*
- *Archives of General Psychiatry*
- *American Journal of Psychiatry*
- *Development and Psychopathology*

19.1.2 Background for Behavioral Forensic Sciences

Perhaps nowhere in forensic science is the inherent tension between science and the law more clearly seen than when considering the behavioral sciences. While both science and the law seek accurate information and logical deduction through generally accepted means of analysis, there are still many fundamental differences between the two fields. As described in the very beginning of this book, legal questions usually have a finite time for active consideration before a decision must be rendered. Science, on the other hand, deals with questions in an open-ended fashion; there is not a timeline for coming to a definitive conclusion but rather a process is employed of continual and ongoing experimentation, analysis, and refinement. The clinical behavioral sciences typically also involve an ongoing, open-ended process when working with an individual that is not easily amenable to a strict timetable. The law also seeks "hard" physical data, usually derived through direct measurement of a material, to provide a basis for making supportable decisions. In the behavioral sciences, however, unbiased and definitive tests and data in a forensic setting are often difficult or at times even impossible to obtain and, once obtained, may be difficult to interpret unambiguously. Nonetheless, the behavioral sciences are routinely called upon to provide vital information in conducting investigations and deciding legal questions.

BOX 19.2   SELECTED APPLICATIONS FOR FORENSIC PSYCHOLOGY

CIVIL:

- Child custody
- Civil commitment
- Deprivation of parental rights
- Employment litigation
- Guardianship
- Personal injury
- Threat assessment
- Testamentary capacity (wills, documents, etc.)
- Worker's compensation

CRIMINAL:

- Interrogations
- Criminal (offender) profiling
- Juvenile waiver (from juvenile to adult court)
- Juvenile sentencing
- Competence to stand trial
- Competence to be sentenced
- Competence to waive Miranda rights
- Insanity defense
- Diminished capacity
- Sentencing
- Commitment of sex offenders
- Role of alcohol in the crime
- Others

(Source: Adapted from Packer, 2008)

19.1.3 Forensic Psychology

At the outset, an important distinction must be made between the practice of clinical psychology and forensic psychology. Clinical psychology focuses on the *diagnosis and treatment* of mental and behavioral disorders in people. Diagnoses are often made slowly, evolving, and changing over time as the consultation process between the patient and psychologist continues. Treatments similarly evolve over time as the long-term *cooperative* process between the psychologist and patient develops, most often with the patient's willing participation stemming from their desire to find help for their problems. Clinical psychology is not an exact science and may involve multiple,

successive approaches and "restarts" during the course of treatment in dealing with a person's problems. The treatment approach for an individual person continues to evolve as they change and progress.

Forensic psychology, in sharp contrast to clinical psychology, focuses solely on the *diagnosis* of mental and behavioral problems at a particular time without *any* concern toward the person's treatment and eventual recovery. Additionally, the forensic diagnosis determined for a person is not expected to change or evolve over the course of a trial. Forensic work is not concerned with the person's mental welfare or with their best interests; rather, it seeks to understand their mental and behavioral state when the crime was committed, when they are tried, or when they are sentenced. In fact, any consideration toward providing treatment, therapy, or advice for a patient from a forensic psychologist as part of a trial is considered unethical and is strictly forbidden as a conflict of interest. Forensic psychological investigations are, therefore, not carried out for the subject's benefit but solely to inform the court. In summary, in clinical psychology, there are *patients* working toward their effective treatment, while in forensic psychology, there are *subjects*, often defendants, presented for evaluation.

BOX 19.3   PSYCHIATRIST OR PSYCHOLOGIST?

The two terms, "psychiatrist" and "psychologist", are frequently encountered in forensic work, but what's the difference between them? While there are important similarities, there are also key differences.

Both psychiatrists and psychologists are mental health professionals who may practice diagnostic psychology and psychotherapy in the treatment of mental illnesses and disorders. Both have extensive education and training, must be licensed by states before they can practice, and may be involved professionally with forensic cases. Both can treat a full range of mental diseases and disorders, from very mild to severe illnesses.

Psychiatrists are first trained as medical doctors and then, typically, go on to four or more years of residency training in mental health. As MDs, psychiatrists can prescribe medicines and may focus on the medication management aspects of an illness, although many psychiatrists also do psychotherapy.

Psychologists are often Ph.D. (or Psy.D.) scientists with at least two years of specialized internship in clinical training. They usually focus on psychotherapy and typically cannot prescribe medications (except in a few states). While psychologists usually rely more heavily on testing than psychiatrists, both professions use various forms of psychological testing.

The differences in forensic and clinical psychological approaches are quite evident when considering how the two disciplines are practiced. Most legal systems employ an *adversarial* approach between the opposing sides of an issue as a means of getting at the key information of the case. Clinical behavioral science, however, usually employs a *cooperative* approach, without "opposing sides," in dealing with people. In clinical settings, the patient and the psychologist (or psychiatrist) work together cooperatively to design and implement a patient's treatment plan. There is usually a well-understood recognition by the patient in clinical settings that their cooperation with the psychologist will lead to an end result that they personally desire. In forensic psychology, however, the subject is often very aware that full cooperation with the psychologist might clearly work against them and they, accordingly, often seek to be evasive, misleading, or even hostile in their dealings with the forensic psychologist. Ethically, forensic subjects must be told in advance that their evaluation is solely for legal purposes and not for their treatment. There is usually no advantage, therefore, for the person to cooperate with the forensic psychologist since there is no treatment option in the forensic process and the results may land them in jail or lead to confinement in a mental institution. This, of course, complicates the job of the forensic psychologist or psychiatrist since the subject is often intentionally working against the purposes of the examination.

Despite these issues and problems, the legal system is making increasing use of the behavioral sciences. Psychological professionals are often called upon to aid in interrogating witnesses, empaneling juries, evaluating minors, testifying in court, and assisting with sentencing, among other duties. In the following sections, some select uses of the behavioral sciences in forensic settings will be presented.

19.1.4 Applications of Forensic Psychology

The use of forensic psychology in legal settings encompasses a range of activities, from aiding in the investigative process, through informing courtroom proceedings, to providing post-trial opinions regarding sentencing and the treatment and/or commitment of defendants. Each of these uses may employ different psychological tools and expertise but is expected to rely upon generally established and accepted principles. While it is impossible to be complete, a few of the most common applications of forensic psychology are described in this chapter.

The use of forensic psychology in criminal cases may be divided into three broad areas based on when the information and expertise are required: pretrial, during trial and post-trial phases of the criminal justice process. Pretrial applications include criminal personality profiling, interrogation and interview techniques, threat analyses, crime scene reconstruction, motive discernment, and case linkages. Trial uses include jury selection, competency to stand trial evaluation, evaluation of insanity and diminished capacity defenses, assessment of the defendant's mental state at the time of the crime, the role of drugs or alcohol in the crime, and advice on defense/prosecution case presentations in court. If a defendant is found incompetent to stand trial, the forensic psychologist may also

advise the court about the steps that need to be taken to make the defendant competent to stand trial. Post-trial uses often center upon sentencing options open to the court: should the defendant be committed to a civil or forensic mental institution and/or be required to take medication. Additionally, the forensic psychologist/psychiatrist may be called upon to monitor the treatment and progress of an incompetent defendant and to decide if there is a chance for them to become competent within a reasonable time.

19.1.5 Pretrial Uses of Forensic Psychology

During the investigative phase, psychological techniques can play a role in identifying the likely perpetrator of the crime and in building a sustainable case against them. This process is often referred to as the *criminal investigative analysis* (CIA) method and contributes information in a number of ways.

Crime Scene Analysis: The evaluation of a crime scene from the perspective of a criminal's behavior can provide specific insights into how and why the crime was committed as well as what type of person might commit a particular crime. Crimes require *both* a criminal intent, *mens rea* (Latin term for "guilty mind"), and a criminal act, *actus reus* ("guilty act"), on the part of the offender. Understanding the linkage between these two aspects can inform the investigative process. Moreover, understanding the criminal act can provide valuable insights into the guilty mind that produced the act.

In the behavioral *criminal investigative analysis* (CIA) process, the investigator first assembles all the information obtained from the crime scene, along with any other relevant input, such as witness statements, police reports, medical interventions to aid victims, and any known prior linked activities or similar crimes. The investigator then tries to find the psychological thread tying all these items together. Answers to critical questions may be found through this type of behavior-based analysis, including:

- Why did the event occur?
- Was it planned or spontaneous?
- How was the criminal contact initiated?
- Why did it happen at that particular location and at that time?
- What was exchanged between the offender and the victim?
- How did the participants act during the exchange?
- What was the perpetrator thinking during the crime?
- How did the participants view their roles during the crime?
- What motivated the actions of the perpetrator (and sometimes the victim) after the crime?

This analysis may uncover prior relationships between the victim and the offender, even unconscious ones, and reveal the level of criminal refinement and judgment of which the offender is capable. The analysis may also allow investigators to clear through the forest of irrelevant information to focus on the truly relevant evidence and behaviors. This process can also point to the existence of missing evidence, for which an intentional search can then be made. The CIA method can help investigators assess a suspect's mental and physical ability to commit the crime (means), their motivation for performing the crime, and their specific opportunity to carry out the crime, sometimes summarized popularly as the *means, motive, and opportunity*. Piecing all this information together may provide insights into the criminal's personality, mental state, and character that can be used by investigators to reduce the field of possible suspects and, in the best scenario, lead ultimately to one particular person.

Many aspects of the CIA method, such as profiling and victimology, are often not acceptable in courtroom proceedings as evidence. The intended use of CIA is to provide direction for investigators into productive avenues of inquiry, especially when few other leads may be available, and to help them search for and build a credible case against possible perpetrators for criminal prosecution.

Victimology: The relatively recent use of ideas from the field of victimology, or the study of victims, in criminal cases involves looking for links between the background, life, lifestyle, occupation, education, age, habits, physical and sexual characteristics, and other features of a victim with the criminal action that has been directed against them. It may be thought of as "victim profiling" and is conceptually the reverse of "criminal profiling" that focuses behavioral inquiry on the criminal. Investigators try to learn as much as possible about the victims themselves in the search for hidden relationships between the victims and the offender. For example, understanding a victim's lifestyle, beliefs, and personality can help shed light on questions such as why the attack was initiated on the chosen victim rather than against someone else, and why they were attacked in a particular manner or place.

BOX 19.4 VICTIMOLOGY

Possible ways a person can harm another:

1. **Physical Abuse**: Hitting, punching, pulling hair, slapping, grabbing, biting, kicking, bruising, burning, twisting, throwing, killing.
2. **Sexual Abuse**: Any unwanted sexual contact, sexual intercourse without consent, rape, forced sexual perversion, forced unprotected sex, and forced sex with other people or animals.
3. **Verbal Abuse**: Derogatory comments, insults, humiliations, constant put-downs (usually with the victim told they are physically unattractive, inferior, incompetent, unable to succeed on their own and are not a good role model). The intent is to keep the victim under total control.
4. **Psychological/Emotional Abuse**: Manipulation and/or intimidation over extended periods

that are intended to destroy the other's self-esteem or sense of self, including destroying or depriving someone of self-esteem, property, personal needs, food, sleep, or the comfort of pets.
5. **Spiritual Abuse**: Occurs as a deep sense of betrayal by religious traditions or other moral agents of the community when the victim feels that faith did not protect them or that the moral code of society has failed them.
6. **Economic Abuse**: Insisting victims turn over their money, possessions, or wealth, requiring them to beg for necessities, giving them insufficient allowance for basics, or refusing to let them participate in financial decisions for themselves.
7. **Social Abuse**: Jokes, criticisms, or put-downs, usually about appearance, sexuality, or intelligence; false accusations, suspiciousness, constant monitoring and control of the victim's activities or access to information; isolation.

(Source: Adapted from O'Connor, 2011)

The way in which a victim is chosen may provide critical insights into the criminal's thinking and mental state. One key question to answer is whether the choice of the victim was carefully considered or was purely by chance. The victim may be a complete stranger to the criminal but yet be very carefully chosen, such as is often the case where serial killers prey upon victims that have very specific physical or personal traits. It is important to note that the criminal investigative use of victimology is *entirely different* from assigning "moral guilt" to the victim for the crime directed against them by their actions or some aspect of their traits. For example, a serial killer might target young, blond-haired women as prey, so that a victim cannot be thought at all morally responsible for the crime directed against them due to their physical traits, lifestyle, or personality. This aspect of victimology is an *extremely* controversial area of study as researchers probe the validity and potential destructiveness of the idea of victim "proneness."

Interrogations and Interviews: Interviews of witnesses and interrogations of suspects play a central role in the criminal investigative process. Properly handled, interrogations can provide a wealth of information, even leading to confessions, while their improper or ineffectual use can be disastrous to a case. Most interrogations rely upon an understanding of human personalities and behaviors in an attempt to gain information, detect lying, and obtain confessions from suspects.

The successful interrogation of suspects generally relies upon two types of information: crime scene evidence, especially behavioral evidence, and background information about the suspect. Interviewers must first do their "homework" thoroughly. The crime scene itself, when properly analyzed for behavioral cues, may give insights into the perpetrator's personality, mental state, and motives for the crime. During the interrogation, the suspect's compatibility with the behavioral evidence obtained from the crime scene can lead investigators to either a stronger or weaker belief that the suspect was involved in the crime. For example, if a fairly high level of sophistication was needed to perform the crime, the ability of the suspect to achieve this level of sophistication can be evaluated. If it becomes clear during the interrogation that the crime was well beyond the suspect's mental means to plan and carry out, then it becomes highly unlikely that the suspect was involved. If, in contrast, it is observed that their mental composition lends itself to the particular type and process of the crime, then they become a more likely suspect.

One goal of an interrogation may be to obtain a confession from the suspect. Knowing more about the suspect's thoughts, beliefs, feelings, and mental background can prepare an interviewer to conduct a successful interrogation. Most common types of criminal personalities employ one of three kinds of interrogation defense mechanisms: *rationalization, projection, and minimization* (RPM). When an investigator can recognize that a suspect is employing one or more of these defense tactics, they can use that information to draw the suspect into providing valuable information or a confession.

Rationalization involves the criminal providing themselves with reasonable explanations to justify their actions in ways that favorably reflect on them and allow them to "save face" in their own estimation. Interviewers can build upon this behavior by empathizing and agreeing with the suspect that their actions were quite reasonable, understandable, and even justified by the situation, building a sense of confidence and rapport between the interviewer and the subject. It's important to note that the interrogator provides a comfort level to the suspect on a psychological basis and *not* in any legal sense.

Projection deals with the criminal placing blame for the crime on someone else, *i.e.*, projecting the blame onto others, often the victim. Interviewers can encourage this type of blame projection by suggesting that the crime was reasonable based upon the provocation received through the actions or words of someone else, especially the victim.

Minimization allows criminals to reduce both their involvement in the crime and the actual seriousness of the crime itself, thereby reducing their internal responsibility for the crime, possibly to the point that they believe themselves to be the true victim through shifting the responsibility for the crime to the actual victim. Interviewers can reinforce this mechanism by using words such as "accident," "mistake," "unavoidable," or "minor" and avoid words such as "murder," "assault," and "violent" when talking to the suspect. A murder is still a murder, but the perpetrator can lessen their internal guilt by convincing themselves that it was a mistake or an unintentional accident (see Box 19.5).

BOX 19.5   THE INTERVIEWER'S ART

Investigators often ask, 'Do any magic words exist for obtaining confessions?' The answer is an unequivocal yes. Certain words and phrases, such as '*accidents happen...*,' '*anyone in this situation could have...*,' '*everybody makes mistakes...*,' can give offenders a dignified way to admit their involvement in a crime and provide investigators with a proven approach to obtaining confessions.

In a case presented in this article, a 16-year-old stepdaughter was reportedly missing from her home. The stepfather, "Brad," had been on bad terms with the daughter, "Valerie," and had separated from the girl's mother just days before the missing report was filed. Investigators used the Rationalization-Projection-Minimization (RPM) concepts to obtain a confession from Brad for the daughter's homicide. Here are some of the ways investigators used an understanding of the RPM defense mechanisms to establish a relationship with Brad and obtain the confession:

- **Rationalization**: "Brad, being suddenly placed in the situation of having a wife and teenager in your home must have been stressful. Any man would have seen the need to define the rules for a teenager, like curfews, use of the car, whom she dated. Constant tension existed in the house, ending with your wife's taking her daughter's side and forcing you out of the picture."
- **Projection**: "Brad, if only Valerie's mother had set clear rules when Valerie was growing up, she wouldn't be such a defiant teenager. If her mother had backed your reasonable rules for Valerie, maybe Valerie would have understood. If Valerie hadn't openly ridiculed and taunted you, you would have held your temper as you usually do. It was Valerie who started this."
- **Minimization**: "I have looked at this case very carefully, Brad. This was probably an accident. You didn't intend to do this. You wish you could change it and would change it if possible. It was not a planned, intentional act; it just happened. This is not like you. You normally don't act this way."

Using these approaches, investigators were able to obtain a confession from a difficult suspect.

(Source: Excerpted from Napier and Adams, 1998)

FIGURE 19.3 The interrogation of suspects is usually performed in carefully arranged rooms designed to place the suspect in an appropriate psychological and physical position to maximize the advantage of the interviewer.

Source: Photo image retrieved from Wikimedia. Used per Creative Commons 3.0 Unported. User: nesnad

Many methods of interrogation have been developed that rely upon manipulating the physical environment, psychological mood, and perceptions of the suspect (Figure 19.3). One common approach is the *Reid Technique*, which uses nine steps in carrying out an interrogation. These steps include confrontation, story (theme) development, stopping suspect denials, overcoming suspect objections, holding the suspect's attention, loss of the suspect's resolve, providing alternatives to the suspect, holding a conversation with the suspect, and obtaining the confession. These techniques have been employed extensively by police and law enforcement agencies for successful suspect interviews.

Interrogations are, of course, open to controversy surrounding issues of coercion and deception, especially when a confession is obtained, and the possibility of violating a suspect's civil rights. Significant strides have been made in recent years, however, to protect the personal rights of the suspect while still providing investigative latitude to the police during the interrogation process. Nonetheless, care must be exercised to restrict interrogations to within the bounds of what is deemed locally to be an acceptable, ethical, and admissible process.

Eyewitnesses: Forensic psychologists are sometimes asked to evaluate the reliability of potential eyewitnesses during an investigation. Eyewitness testimony is well known to be among the most unreliable forms of evidence and is increasingly being excluded from trials. Nonetheless, a good eyewitness can help, and a mistaken one can harm an investigation. The brain has an amazing ability to fill in the "blanks" with information that may seem completely factual to a witness when the memory is actually incomplete or faulty. This tendency is compounded by the fact that witnessing a crime is a stressful event. When placed under stress, the brain may "forget" a great deal of information or fail to notice fully-visible but unexpected items (inattentional blindness) and replace them with fabricated memories. Some witnesses

try especially hard to be "helpful" to the police, especially victims and family members, but this added stress can easily lead to either constructed information or altered memories without the witness even knowing it. Such witnesses may easily be inadvertently led to recall events that they believe are true but actually never happened. These problems all contribute to incorrect or misleading witness testimony that psychologists try to identify and place in perspective during an investigation.

False Confessions: Made-up and untrue confessions are relatively common in high-profile cases, and forensic psychology can be used to help discern true from false confessions. These false confessions may arise for many reasons. The confessor may suffer from a mental illness, be under the influence of drugs, desire attention, or simply be confused and tired. Sometimes, a criminal may confess to a crime to protect someone else or provide an "alibi" for themselves from another, more severe crime, such as confessing to a robbery to avoid the accusation that they committed a murder at the same time but in another location. Other false confessors may admit to a crime they didn't do simply to end a difficult or intimidating interrogation. Often, a psychological evaluation can discover underlying reasons that might lead to the false confession or expose inconsistencies between the confession and the physical evidence recovered. In some cases, the police may release only some of the information about a crime to the public to quickly evaluate a false confession.

Profiling: Probably one of the most familiar, and often incorrectly portrayed, psychological tools used in television and movie plots is psychological criminal profiling. Criminal profiling, sometimes called "offender profiling" or "criminal investigative analysis" (FBI term), in its broadest sense, is usually defined as the application of accepted behavioral science concepts to provide information about a criminal's behavioral patterns and personal characteristics from known information about a serial crime. This information, if assembled properly by trained and ethical practitioners, can assist with the reconstruction of the crime scene, aid in identifying the offender, and provide evidence during the trial. The primary goal is usually to provide information about the characteristics of an unknown criminal by the way they plan, execute, and interact with the victims of their crimes. The profile does not typically identify any specific criminal but rather focuses on identifying the kind of person most likely to have committed the crime.

BOX 19.6   EARLY PROFILING EFFORTS

Profiling in one form or another has been around for at least a millennium. The first real psychological profiles based upon empirical behavioral research, however, began in the 1940s.

An interesting early use of scientific psychological profiling occurred during World War II in 1943 when Dr. Walter C. Langer was asked by the U.S. Government to develop a psychological profile of German leader Adolph Hitler in an attempt to predict and understand his next moves in the war. Dr. Langer published the results of his analysis years later in 1972 in his book *The Mind of Adolph Hitler.*

Dr. Langer analyzed anything he could find about Hitler: speeches, writings, accounts, past actions, interviews with acquaintances, and other sources. From these, he determined that Hitler was meticulous, often manic, delusional, and sadistic, suffered from an Oedipus complex, and had urolagnia. He also feared germs, always crossed a room diagonally while whistling, and liked Wagnerian opera and dangerous circus acts.

From these and many other pieces of information, Dr. Langer predicted that Hitler's mental state was badly deteriorating in 1943. He also predicted that if the war went against him, he would not try to escape to another country nor allow himself to be captured but would rather commit suicide or be intentionally killed by an aid. Today it is widely believed that Hitler killed himself in his private bunker in Berlin on the eve of the allied occupation of the city.

The criminal profiling process has undergone enormous revision since its first systematic application in the 1970s, although it had been used sporadically earlier. One of the most famous and earliest examples came from the description of George Metsky as New York City's "Mad Bomber" from the 1940s and 1950s (see Box 19.7). This kind of profiling usually involves a multi-step process, such as the FBI method outlined in Figure 19.4. It is a relatively recent application of behavioral science to the law and continues to undergo development and refinement.

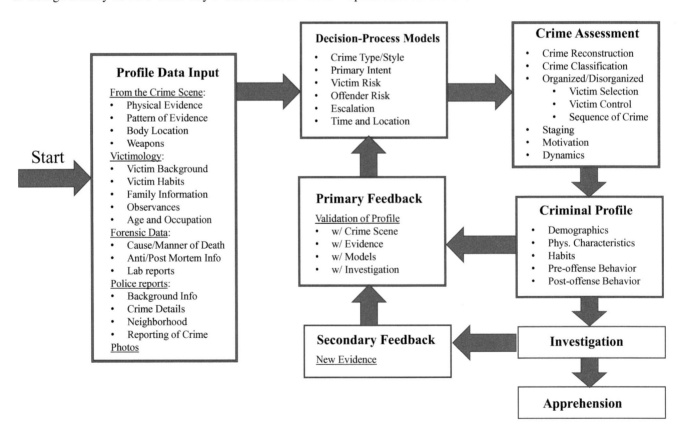

FIGURE 19.4   Method developed by the FBI for formulating a criminal profile from available information and evidence.

Source: Figure redrawn and excerpted from Douglas et al. (1986).

BOX 19.7   NEW YORK'S "MAD BOMBER": THE BEGINNINGS OF PSYCHOLOGICAL PROFILING

One of the first uses and dramatic early successes of criminal psychological profiling occurred in the 1940s and 1950s in New York City. For 16 years, the city was terrorized by a series of 33 pipe bombs placed across the city, of which 22 exploded. The first bomb, placed in 1940, carried the note "Con Edison Crooks – This is for you" (Note: Con Edison is the primary electrical supplier for New York City). After intense investigative efforts, all leads led to a dead end.

Finally, psychologists were called in to try to rekindle the investigation. Psychologists carefully compiled all that was known in the case and, using the best research and concepts of the era, compiled a list of characteristics that the unknown bomber was expected to display, including:

- A male of average build (historically, most bombers were males).
- Forty to fifty years old, since paranoia develops slowly.
- Precise, neat, and careful – determined from his letters.
- A foreign-born, educated person (but not college).
- A loner with few friends, little interest in women, and probably living with his mother in Connecticut (from proximity considerations).
- When caught would probably be wearing a double-breasted suit.

Police published details of the profile, seeking information from the public and asking the bomber to turn himself in. The bomber responded with another letter that gave more information about his grievances against Con Edison. Eventually, through several published letters, the police were able to determine from the bomber that he had been injured on the job and been turned down for compensation, even giving the date of his injury as September 5, 1931. Eventually, they located the files of a former Con Edison employee, George Metesky, the details of which matched remarkably well with the details given by the bomber, including the date of injury. Metesky was arrested and provided the police with an accounting of all the bombs, even a number of bombs that they had never found. George Metesky was found to be "incurably insane" (terminology of the era) and committed to a state mental hospital in 1957. Later, Metesky was released in 1971 and lived to an age of 90 before passing away in 1994. When arrested, he was wearing the predicted double-breasted suit.

FIGURE 19.5   Photo of serial bomber George Metesky, wearing a double-breasted suit, when he was arrested in 1957.

Source: Library of Congress.

Criminal profiling has found uses in providing leads for many types of serial crimes such as in hostage situations, anonymous threatening letters and messages, stalking, serial homicides, sexual attacks, arson, kidnapping, and others. The technique has probably gained its greatest attention in assisting with serial violent attacks. In these situations, the crimes often appear to be "motiveless" and random, striking fear and even panic in the area residents. Because of their seemingly random nature, useful investigative leads may be very limited in serial crimes. This is in contrast with other types of violent crimes where an array of known suspects with understandable, and even clearly apparent, motives for committing the crime are available. Criminal profiling in serial attacks, however, holds that these events are actually not motiveless crimes but rather are crimes where the motive is known only to the criminal, and sometimes not even consciously understood by the criminal themselves. So, while the criminal may not know their victims or have planned the crime ahead of time, the choice of victim and method of attack are not random but fit a set of required features in the criminal's mind. There are underlying patterns of behavior in committing the crime that, as more data is obtained, help to paint a detailed picture of the criminal and the motives behind the particular serial events.

BOX 19.8   SON OF SAM

During the summers of 1976 and 1977, a serial killer, referred to as the "Son of Sam," seemingly at random shot 13 people, killing 6. The victims were usually young women, and they and their companions were attacked in secluded locations. In an attempt to discover suspects or motives for these crimes, police turned to criminal profiling.

Psychologists who analyzed the case profiled the criminal as a paranoid schizophrenic (a person who suffers from symptoms such as delusions, auditory hallucinations, anxiety, emotional emptiness, and anger) who believed that he was the victim of a demonic possession.

From a chance lead of a parking ticket given near a crime scene and information from the profile, police were led to David Berkowitz on August 10, 1977. When confronted by the police, Berkowitz's comment was "You got me. What took you so long?".

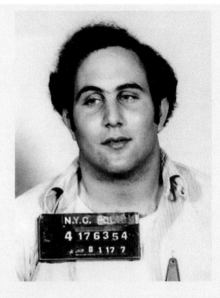

FIGURE 19.6   David Berkowitz, aka "Son of Sam."

Source: Retrieved from Wikimedia Commons; used per Creative Commons Attribution.

Developing a criminal profile usually involves several stages, beginning with the collection of all possible types of information that might be relevant to the case. In the FBI approach, the first stage of the process is referred to as the *profiling data input stage*. This stage relies upon information collected at the crime scene and information about the victim's background, personality, and traits, along with interviews, medical information, and any possible relationships with other similar crimes (see Box 19.9). Subsequent stages in developing the profile usually include the *decision process model stage*, where the collected information is arranged into patterns (e.g., victim and perpetrator's risk assessment, intent of the perpetrator, crime type, etc.), the *crime assessment stage*, where the information is used to reconstruct the events of the crime focusing on how each participant behaved and reacted before and during the crime, the *criminal profile stage*, where the psychologist tries to determine the criminal's behavioral composition and personality and to formulate this analysis into a useful investigative plan, and finally, the *investigative stage*, where the plan based on the profile is used to generate and pursue leads. These stages are focused, of course, on arriving at the end game of apprehending the criminal.

BOX 19.9   LINKAGE ANALYSIS

One type of criminal profiling involves looking for possible links between several crimes. The process involves trying to understand the behavior of the offender to see if similar features can be found in different crimes. The analysis often employs gathering both physical and psychological evidence, including determining the *modus operandi*, victimology, crime scene similarities, and any "signatures" of the criminal.

Psychologists typically break the crime itself down into several phases for detailed analysis. The *Antecedent phase* involves the time up to the commission of the crime. Psychologists try to determine what plan the offender had before the crime occurred and what was the "trigger" that caused them to act when and where they did. The *method and manner phase* evaluates what actually happened during the crime, focusing on how the victim was chosen, and what method and manner was employed during the crime. This phase usually involves trying to determine

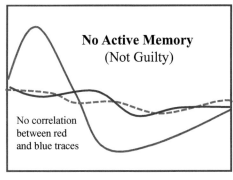

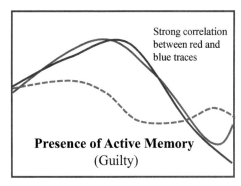

Simulated Brain Fingerprint Patterns

FIGURE 19.7   Brain fingerprinting.

the *modus operandi* of the criminal (MO, translated as "mode of operating"). The MO refers to the method, habits and tendencies of the offender in committing the crime: how it was done. The next phase is the *evidence disposal phase*. In homicides, this usually refers to the disposal of the body but in other types of crimes it deals with how, if at all, the criminal changed or destroyed the evidence of their deeds after the crime. The final phase is the *post-offense behavior phase*, which explores if and how the criminal becomes involved with the investigation itself, such as through letters to the police, interactions with the media, clandestinely observing their crimes (e.g., as a spectator, scrapbooks, etc.) or other ways. For example, arsonists frequently stay close to their criminal works by spectating, video recording, or closely following news reports to "re-experience" their crimes.

The field of criminal or offender profiling is undergoing continuous development to improve its reliability and establish standards for its practice. Current trends are focused on employing solid, generally accepted psychological principles in preparing the profile rather than relying heavily upon the investigative field experience of the profiler. Additionally, statistical methods based on empirical studies of serial crimes are making significant contributions to the field. Care must be taken not to shut down other lines of investigation, however, when a match is found between the profile and a suspect, as "false positive" matches and errors in profiles are still relatively common (see the case of Richard Jewell in the Olympic Park bombing in Atlanta in 1996: Kent Alexander and Kevin Salweh, 2019.).

Other Pretrial Uses: Occasionally, specialized psychological tools are employed in investigations. Some of these are rarely admissible in court but may be useful in helping investigators either focus their efforts or uncover new leads on an otherwise "cold" trail. Two of these techniques have received more attention than the others: hypnosis and brain fingerprinting. Their use, however, remains somewhat controversial and may or may not be admissible in court proceedings.

Hypnosis: Hypnosis, rather than being the sleep state often portrayed in movies, instead involves a state of heightened awareness and concentration, deep relaxation, inner absorption, and enhanced suggestibility. A number of important misconceptions exist about hypnosis. For example, in hypnosis, the truth is that you cannot be compelled to do anything

against your intrinsic nature, be forced into a hypnotic state, or be trapped in a trance state. The technique does, however, allow access to hidden or repressed memories and emotions. The problem, of course, is that it is also very easy for an analyst to inadvertently plant altered or new memories in a person's hypnosis-suggestible mind, often without the analyst even knowing that it was being done.

Forensic hypnosis has been used in a number of high-profile cases, such as the Ted Bundy, Boston Strangler, Hillside Murders, and Sam Sheppard cases. It has been used to relax witnesses to allow them to remember forgotten information and to look for evidence of malingering or deception in suspects, among other uses. Guidelines have been established to help standardize hypnotic forensic investigations.

Brian Fingerprinting: Brain fingerprinting is very different from hypnosis. Brain fingerprinting uses very rapid measurements of the brain's electrical signals ("brain waves") in response to various stimuli, such as words, pictures, or sounds, to determine if a particular memory preexists within a person's mind. Based on the patterns of these signals, a determination can be made as to whether the relevant information is stored in the subject's memory or not (Figure 19.7). Thus far, brain fingerprinting has been deemed admissible in many court proceedings and has also found use during investigations.

19.1.6 Trial Uses of Forensic Psychology

Once a case moves to the judicial system for prosecution, psychology continues to play an important role in the proceedings. The usual role is to inform the court about the mental state and competencies of the defendant. Recent uses, however, have also included assisting legal teams with juror selection and advice about how best to present their cases.

Jury Selection: The fair and proper selection of a jury is central to our constitutional criminal justice system. The process of empaneling a jury, as might be expected, is a key step in the legal process (Figure 19.8). Typically, the two "sides" in a case are allowed to question and, with limitations, indicate whether prospective jurors are acceptable or unacceptable to them. During this process, each side focuses on finding

FIGURE 19.8 Famous scene from the film *12 Angry Men* by Sidney Lumet. This film illustrated the importance of the psychological characteristics of jury members.

Source: Retrieved from Wikimedia Commons; used per Creative Commons Attribution.

jurors that will be most sympathetic to their case without being disqualified by the other side and while staying within legal boundaries (i.e., disqualification cannot usually be made on the basis of race, gender, age, religion, disability, sexual orientation, etc.). Increasingly, forensic psychologists are involved in important cases by advising legal teams about the acceptability or unacceptability of an individual juror and how to determine their acceptability. This process is sometimes referred to as the *scientific jury selection* (SJS) *method*.

In the selection process, each potential juror is usually subjected to the *voir dire* process (from the Old French "to speak the truth"). Usually, each side is allowed to ask potential jurors open-ended questions that allow the juror to freely talk about their experiences, beliefs, background, and feelings. Psychologists then help the legal teams to understand the thinking behind the answers given in court by the potential jurors. They look for predictive characteristics in these answers that can give insight into the potential juror's personal attitudes and openness to their case. For example, consultants try to determine a potential juror's prevailing bias-related attitudes (e.g., age, gender, or racial biases), previous personal histories and attitudes toward the police and crime, and a potential juror's attitudes toward the specific type of crime and defendant in the case.

Forensic psychologists may also look to the community as an indicator of how individual jurors will behave when making their decisions. They may employ demographics, statistics, concepts from group psychology and sociology, area resident attitude surveys, and even perform mock trials conducted in the area to understand better how prospective jurors may be either inclined or disinclined toward their case. More generally, psychologists may prepare a list of personal attributes found in jurors that would view their case most favorably. Through these tools, the psychologist tries to inform the legal team regarding the acceptability of specific jurors and what types of in-court presentations might be most effective in making their case to the jury.

BOX 19.10   REASONS FOR INCOMPETENCE

Common mental disorders that may lead to a determination of incompetence to stand trial include:

- Organic brain syndromes (brain abnormalities such as strokes, tumors, etc.).
- Cognitive or severe memory problems.
- Severe neuroses, such as paranoia or severe anxiety.
- Psychoses or schizophrenia.
- Mental retardation arising from congenital, developmental, trauma, and infective causes.

Competency to Stand Trial (CST): The 5th and 14th Amendments to the U.S. Constitution, as well as the laws of many other nations, require that a defendant "shall not be deprived of life, liberty, or property, without *due process of law*" and equal protection. The courts have ruled repeatedly that this due process clause requires defendants to demonstrate suitable mental capacity to understand the charges brought against them and to reasonably assist in their own defense. Therefore, to stand trial, the U.S. Supreme Court has defined adequate competency only when a defendant has *both* "sufficient present ability to consult with his lawyer with a reasonable degree of rational understanding" and a "rational as well as factual understanding of the proceedings against him." This competency determination specifically evaluates a defendant's competency *at the time of trial* and does not consider the person's mental state at the time the crime was committed. The standards and the interpretation of what it actually means to have "sufficient present ability" and "rational as well as factual understanding", however, are usually left to each state and court to determine. The final decision, however, usually rests with the trial judge and is usually based upon the psychological information provided to the court by the forensic psychologist or psychiatrist. Typically, when found incompetent to stand trial, a person is committed either to a mental institution or to a physician's care until such time as they are determined to be competent. Once deemed competent, they are then usually eligible to stand trial (see Box 19.11).

BOX 19.11   RESTORING COMPETENCE

In 1987, Kenneth L. Curtis first struck his former girlfriend, Donna Kalson, with his truck and then shot and killed her before attempting suicide by shooting himself in the head in a murder-suicide attempt. Despite extensive medical trauma and with the .32-caliber bullet permanently lodged in his brain, Curtis survived the wound but with severe disability and permanent brain damage. Nonetheless, he was charged with Kalson's homicide. Prior to trial, however, he was deemed incompetent to stand trial due to mental defect, and the charges were dismissed. Curtis was ultimately released rather than confined to an institution.

Eleven years later, in 1998, the wheelchair-bound Curtis was discovered enrolled in college as a pre-med student with a 3.3 GPA after completing 48 credits of study; his tuition was partially paid for by the State Department of Social Services.

Curtis was rearrested, found competent to stand trial – largely based on his good grades in college – and pleaded guilty to manslaughter, receiving the maximum allowable sentence of 20 years in prison.

It has been estimated that around 60,000 competency evaluations are performed each year in the United States to aid courts in determining a defendant's ability to stand trial. These evaluations, however, may also have important uses beyond simply determining whether a defendant is fit to be tried in court. For example, in the United States, it has been estimated that around 90% of all criminal cases involve guilty pleas by defendants that never formally come to trial. In these instances, a person must be deemed competent by the court to either plead guilty to a crime or waive their access to a defense attorney. Customarily, it has been up to the defense, however, to seek a competency evaluation in such cases. In the United States, a person must also be determined to be competent before they can be executed, in capital punishment states. If they are deemed incompetent for execution, they must be provided with treatment aimed at restoring their competency before they can be executed, which may include the use of psychoactive medications. Of course, there is a debate as to whether it is completely ethical to medically treat a person simply to restore competency only to allow their execution to proceed, although most medical organizations and professionals believe that it is proper to treat a person regardless of their legal circumstances.

One quite specific application of a competency determination involves the right of a defendant to represent themselves in court, a process legally called *pro se* (from Latin meaning "for themselves"). Before a defendant can be allowed to represent themselves, however, they must first be warned of the dangers and risks of representing themselves without counsel, have knowledge of the charges and punishment they face, understand the rules of evidence and courtroom practice, and be competent to understand what they will face during the trial. Once deemed competent and able to understand the legal issues at stake, a judge cannot deny *pro se*, even if they disagree with how the defendant would present their case.

BOX 19.12   *PRO SE* COMPETENCE?

In legal history, there can be found a number of high-profile cases where the defendant has decided to represent themselves in court (*pro se*), usually with disastrous results. Often, this self-representation, ensured by the Constitution's 6th Amendment, stems from a defendant's paranoia regarding the competency of their appointed legal team, a disagreement as to how to

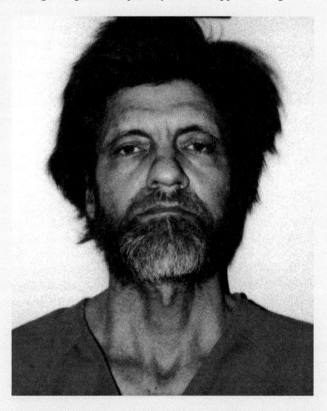

FIGURE 19.9   Convicted "Unabomber" Ted Kaczynski (1942–2023).
Source: FBI.

defend their case, or from delusions regarding their own legal abilities. Classic examples of this come from the cases of Ted Kaczynski (the "Unabomber,"), Joe Hunt, and killers Ted Bundy, Charles Manson, and Colin Ferguson, among others.

In the case of the "Unabomber" Ted Kaczynski, a series of bombs were mailed between 1978 and 1995 which injured 23 people and killed 3. Eventually, a suspect known as "Unabomber" (because frequent targets were universities) was identified and captured through leads gleaned from his published manifesto. At trial, Kaczynski asked to represent himself when his defense team decided upon an insanity defense. Kaczynski was found competent to stand trial by the judge but deemed not competent to represent himself. When forced to accept legal help, rather than agreeing with his defense team's strategy of an insanity defense, he agreed to plead guilty to 13 of the crimes. He died in prison in 2023.

For a different outcome in a case where a defendant was allowed to represent themselves, look up the case of Colin Ferguson.

Defenses based upon Mental Diseases or Defects: A number of legal psychological defenses have been recognized as arising from a defendant's mental diseases or defects. Largely, these psychological determinations deal with the defendant's *mental state at the time of the offense* (MSO), and a psychologist's opinion to the court about the defendant's MSO is often critical evidence. Two of these psychological defenses, among others, however, are particularly important: legal insanity and diminished capacity.

Legal Insanity: One of the most popularly portrayed, but in reality, rarely used psychological defenses, is the insanity defense. It is important to note that legal insanity is *solely* a legal construct and is not a psychological definition. Different jurisdictions and courts define legal insanity somewhat differently but most follow, in some fashion, a definition that dates back to an 1843 English law, called the McNaughten Rule, which says that legal insanity can be used as a defense only if:

> at the time of the committing of the act, the party accused was laboring under such a defect of reason, from a disease of the mind, as not to know the nature and quality of the act he was doing; or, if he did know it, that he did not know he was doing what was wrong.

Simply stated, legal insanity is a viable defense only if the person either did not know what they were doing or couldn't tell right from wrong at the time of the crime. In essence, the person admits that they actually did the crime by taking this defense strategy; that issue is not in dispute in the insanity defense. Instead of arguing in court whether or not they actually committed the crime, however, they must then prove that they were in such a mental state when committing the crime that they were not responsible for their actions. If a defendant is not successful in proving their incapacitated mental state at the time of the crime, they will be found guilty and sentenced accordingly since they have already admitted that they performed the crime.

In actual practice, the insanity defense is both rarely used (employed in less than 1% of all felony cases) and even more rarely successful (less than one-fifth of "insanity" cases result in a not guilty by reason of insanity verdict, or about 0.2% of all cases, about 2 in a 1,000 cases overall). Homicide cases also form less than one-third of insanity defense cases.

Additionally, the insanity defense is usually considered *not* to apply to psychopathic and sociopathic criminals, such as serial offenders. These are generally considered to be antisocial personality disorders and do not meet the requirements of a successful insanity defense.

The basis for an insanity defense is quite different from a determination of incompetence to stand trial. The insanity defense deals with a plea of *not guilty* by reason of insanity based on the offender's *mental state at the time of the crime*, while competence deals with whether a person is competent to stand trial due to their mental state *at the time of the trial*. Someone who is deemed incompetent to stand trial is usually held in a mental institution until such a time as they are determined to be competent to stand trial and participate in their own defense. When someone is determined to be not guilty by reason of insanity, they are usually committed to a mental institution until they are deemed safe to themselves and others and are then released. Statistically, however, a defendant found not guilty by reason of insanity spends twice as long confined to a mental institution when compared to a person simply found guilty of the same crime and sentenced to prison. Essentially, no defendants found not guilty by insanity are directly released right after the trial, even under supervision. There are, however, legal limits to how long and under what conditions a person can be committed after conviction. For example, the defendant must be reviewed periodically to determine if continued treatment and/or confinement is necessary and where they should receive that treatment (e.g., forensic hospital, private mental hospital, clinic, supervised out-patient, etc.).

Following the case of John Hinckley (see Box 19.13), the U.S. Congress revised the laws governing the insanity defense to state that a person can be found not guilty of a crime by reason of insanity when they cannot "appreciate" the criminal nature of their act. This was a big change from previous standards that used the term "knowledge" instead of "appreciate" when applied to their understanding of the wrongful behavior of their actions. The use of the term "appreciate" implies a greater understanding by the criminal of their acts as compared with just simple knowledge. The law also forbids psychologists from testifying specifically on whether a person is insane or not. The psychologist can give their opinion about any mental

BOX 19.13   THE JOHN HINCKLEY CASE

One of the few high-profile cases to successfully use the insanity defense was that of John Hinckley. On March 20, 1981, the 25-year-old John W. Hinckley, Jr. partially broke through a police line and fired six shots at President Ronald Reagan who had just concluded a speech in Washington, DC, badly wounding Reagan and three others.

At the time, Hinckley said that he had performed the attempted assassination in order to impress actress Jodie Foster with "the greatest love offering in the history of the world."

When brought to trial in 1982, Hinckley used the insanity defense for the 13 counts he was charged with. The jury ultimately found Hinckley not guilty by reason of insanity and he was committed to St. Elizabeths Hospital. At the hospital, Hinckley was determined to be "unpredictably dangerous" to himself and others. Later, it was determined that Hinckley no longer presented a threat to himself or others and was granted unconditional release on June 15, 2022.

Because of the verdict in the case, Congress and a number of states reviewed their insanity laws and made important changes afterward.

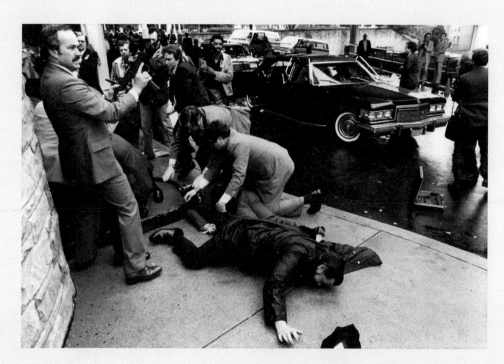

FIGURE 19.10   Chaos outside of the Washington Hilton Hotel after a 1981 assassination attempt on President Reagan by John W. Hinckley, Jr. The President was close to death upon arrival at George Washington University Hospital. Also wounded were White House press secretary James Brady, Secret Service agent Tim McCarthy, and police officer Thomas Delahanty. Brady had permanent brain damage and was disabled until his death in 2014 (33 years later), which was considered a homicide because it was caused by his gunshot injury.

Source: Photo Taken March 30, 1981, Michael Evans – U.S. National Archives and Records Administration.

illness in a suspect and how it might affect their thoughts and actions, but the determination of insanity is reserved solely for the jury, emphasizing the legal and not psychological definition of the term "insanity."

As described before, a crime is considered to have two parts: the guilty act (*actus reus*) and the guilty intent (*mens rea*). Most insanity definitions deal with "cognitive" insanity: the inability to separate right from wrong or a lack of *mens rea*. Some jurisdictions, however, also include a "volitional" definition of insanity. Volitional insanity arises in otherwise mentally healthy people who become so unbalanced at the time of the crime that they are *unable* to stop themselves or comply with the law even though they may know the difference between right and wrong (they are unable to fight an irresistible impulse). Most courts, however, restrict the definition of insanity to cognitive insanity.

Diminished Capacity: A special form of the insanity defense is often referred to as the *diminished capacity defense.* The term, while interpreted differently by various courts and jurisdictions, usually means that the offender had a reduced ability to understand the crimes that they committed; they could not form the needed *mens rea* or did not act knowing the consequences of their actions, but did not fully meet the requirements of legal insanity. As with the insanity defense, the defendant clearly admits to the crime but then seeks some level of protection because their mental state at the time of the crime was altered or impaired. Some states allow this defense only to reduce the degree of the charge on conviction but cannot lead to a not guilty verdict. For example, a first-degree murder charge may be reduced to third-degree murder or manslaughter if the diminished capacity defense is successful. First-degree murder requires premeditation, deliberation, and the intent to kill while lesser charges, such as second-degree murder or manslaughter, reduce these requirements. A diminished capacity defense usually must show that a person lacked one of the three key ingredients (premeditation, deliberation, and intent) required for a first-degree murder conviction based upon their mental state. Similar to the insanity defense, diminished capacity is rarely used and is not even an option in many jurisdictions.

BOX 19.14   DIMINISHED CAPACITY DUE TO "TWINKIES"

In 1978, former San Francisco Supervisor Daniel J. White shot and killed Mayor George Moscone and Supervisor Harvey Milk.

FIGURE 19.11   Former San Francisco Supervisor Daniel J. White shot and killed Mayor George Moscone and Supervisor Harvey Milk in 1979. Shown is the upper portion of the front page of the *San Francisco Chronicle* on November 28, 1978, the morning after the assassination.

Source: Retrieved from Wikimedia Commons; used per Creative Commons Attribution.

When the case came to trial, White's defense team argued that his mental state at the time of the crime was compromised from his problems with depression and used the diminished capacity defense. They argued that, among other things, White's mental state had driven him to a number of unusual behaviors, including changing his diet to a high-sugar "junk" food diet: "Twinkies." The jury, moved by his confession, agreed with the defense and reduced his conviction from murder to voluntary manslaughter.

After serving five years of his seven-year sentence, White was paroled. Within two years of release, however, White committed suicide by carbon monoxide (CO) poisoning.

Other Uses: Forensic psychology may serve many other functions in the courtroom. As mentioned earlier, psychologists may be asked to present their opinions about the credibility of witnesses and the possible lying by witnesses and the defendant. Malingering (the faking or exaggeration of symptoms), deceit, exaggeration, and other types of fraud and misrepresentation are very important challenges in courtroom deliberations as conflicting "stories" are evaluated by the jury to determine who is actually telling the truth. The testimony of a psychologist can help uncover these attempts to present untruths as reality.

19.1.7 Post-trial Uses of Forensic Psychology

Forensic psychologists may be called upon to assist the court in their work after the criminal phase of the trial has concluded. For example, a psychologist may be asked for their opinion when the court determines the appropriate sentence to levy on the convicted criminal. The ability of a defendant to be rehabilitated and their understanding of and remorse for their crimes may be taken into account during sentencing. In this type of determination, the psychologist may interview the defendant, their family members, and friends, review the defendant's past medical records, and evaluate potential triggers for their abnormal behaviors. The psychologist may be asked to identify any special needs of a convicted person so that the court can determine which institution is best for treatment or which medications to require.

Psychologists may be asked to provide an opinion as to the defendant's dangerousness to themselves or others and what is the probability of their re-committing criminal acts. These considerations are particularly important when considering parole appeals, probation requirements, and responding to violations. In death sentence convictions, a psychologist is called upon to testify as to whether the defendant is competent to understand the death sentence and if not, what could be done to make them competent to be executed.

When a defendant is found incompetent to stand trial, forensic psychologists are involved in determining what steps are necessary to bring them back to competency and to monitor or even oversee the person's clinical treatments.

19.1.8 Forensic Psychological Testing

Over the years, psychologists have developed a number of analytical tools to assist in assessing a person's individual psychological makeup. These tests try to measure more quantitatively various aspects of a person's personality, psychopathology (mental illness, distress, or abnormal behavior), and mental function. One of the goals of these tests is to place any psychological diagnosis of a person on a less subjective and a more objective basis. Psychological tests, however, form just one part of the process of a person's clinical evaluation and are usually balanced with other information such as a subject's medical history, conversations held with the subject, information from their friends and family members, concurrent physical testing (e.g., MRI, CT, and blood testing), prior legal involvements, and other methods.

The forensic assessment of a person's behavior usually makes significant use of objective tests based on standard and normative assessments (using comparisons with a large body of test data from healthy populations). While there is some debate about the validity of using these standard psychological tools in legal settings, most forensic psychologists and courts find these tests useful in making fair determinations in psychological assessments.

BOX 19.15   SELECTED PSYCHOLOGICAL TESTS EMPLOYED IN FORENSIC PSYCHOLOGY

Projective Tests:
- Rorschach test
- Thematic apperception test (TAT)
- Arrangement tests
- Picture drawing tests
- Bender-Gestalt test.

Personality Inventories:
- California Psychological Inventory (CPI)
- Millon Clinical Multiaxial Inventory (MCMI)
- Minnesota Multiphasic Personality Inventory (MMPI)
- Quality of Life Inventory (QLI).

Intelligence and Cognitive Tests:
- Wechsler General Intelligence Scale Revised
- Wechsler Memory Scale Revised.

Brain Function Impairment:
- Halstead-Reitan Neuropsychological Battery
- Luria-Nebraska Neuropsychological Battery.

Specific Disorders Tests:
- Beck Depression Inventory
- Psychopathy Checklist Revised
- Structured Interview of Reported Symptoms.

The psychological tests that are most commonly used in legal applications fall into two categories: general psychological tests and specialized forensic tests. General psychological tests measure aspects of a person's personality, intellectual functioning, memory abilities, brain function, the type and level of any impairment present, and the presence of specific disorders (e.g., tests for depression, substance dependence, schizophrenia, etc.). Most specialized forensic tests, in contrast, focus only on determining a person's ability to function in certain situations, such as their competency to stand trial, understand their legal rights and the charges brought against them, aid in their defense, serve as parents or guardians, or make proper medical decisions.

General Psychological Tests: Many tests have been established and broadly accepted within the psychological community as being valid and useful in assessing various components of a person's personality, mental health, and behavior. These general tests include: (1) projective tests, (2) personality inventories, (3) intelligence and cognitive tests, (4) brain function and impairment tests, and (5) tests for specific disorders.

- *Projective Tests*: These tests aim to evaluate a subject's personality and thought processes by exploring how the test subject thinks about themselves and their world. Projective tests attempt to get the subject to "project" themselves into a new situation, an ambiguous image, or a new set of circumstances. The responses of the subject are then compared with a "normal" set of test responses to look for patterns or deviations from the typical response. Projective tests also aim to uncover any abnormal fantasies and obsessions that may influence the person's thoughts and actions. Several specific tests have been developed to provide this information:

- **Rorschach Test**: Probably the best-known projective test is the Rorschach, or "ink blot," test that typically shows the subject a series of ten ambiguous, symmetrical ink blots printed on cards, such as that shown in Figure 19.12, and then asks them what they see in the patterns. The main idea of this test is that the subject's inner feelings, thoughts, and perceptions will be projected onto the vague shapes to reveal their inner hidden thinking. The analysis comes by comparing the subject's answers to "normal" answers previously collected when the cards were shown to many test subjects, including people with known mental disorders. The analyst carefully records not only the actual response of the test subject to each card but also notes the amount of time that they took in considering the shape, what aspect of the shape they focused on, and the relationships between answers for different cards. For example, if the subject saw threatening or authoritative figures in all or most of the cards, that would suggest a paranoid response.

- **Thematic Apperception Test (TAT)**: In this test, subjects are shown images of people in various relatively random settings and asked to describe what they see and believe is going on or led up to the scenes shown in the pictures. The analysis of the subject's responses can indicate how they "project" themselves into the story of the scene; do they see conflict, threat, malice, happiness, or other attributes in the pictures. A typical TAT picture is shown in Figure 19.13, for which a subject might be asked to describe what has happened, what is happening now, how the people in the drawing are feeling, and what will happen next. Answers to a series of these pictures can provide insight into the subject's thought processes, moods, fantasies, and perceptions. For example, consistently seeing violent themes in the drawings can suggest a leaning toward violent emotions and actions, while sexual descriptions can suggest abnormal sexual obsessions or problems.

- **Arrangement Tests**: A number of tests have been developed that require a subject to put pictures or shapes into some order that tells a story. For example, they might be presented with three facial expressions of the same person, asked to arrange these in any order that they choose, and then tell a brief story based on this arrangement. For example, a subject may be given a set of images of the same person, as shown in Figure 19.14 and asked to arrange them to tell a

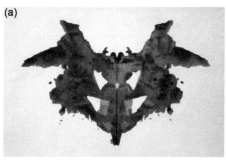
(a)

(b)

FIGURE 19.12 Two of the ten Rorschach cards often used in a projective test: shown are the 1st (a) and 4th (b) Rorschach cards. The 1st card in the series is commonly perceived as a bat (53%) or a butterfly (29%). The 4th image is commonly seen as an animal skin or a large threatening figure from a perspective that looks upwards. People with depression may especially dwell on the perceived dark and threatening attributes of this 4th card.

Source: Retrieved from Wikimedia Commons; used per Creative Commons Attribution.

FIGURE 19.13 A typical Thematic Apperception Test (TAT) drawing.

Source: Science Photo Library.

story. The ordering and nature of the story can provide the analyst with information about the person's perceptions and inner feelings.

- **Picture Drawing Tests**: In this projective test, a subject is asked to draw freehand a representation of themselves, others, objects, or scenes.

Depending on how they draw attention to or away from certain features or even the nature of what they choose to include in the drawing, information can be gained about their inner thinking processes. This is a particularly common test for younger subjects, as shown in Figure 19.15.

FIGURE 19.14   Multiple images of the same person showing different emotions that can be arranged by a subject in any order to tell a story in an arrangement projective psychological test.

Source: Shutterstock.com.

FIGURE 19.15   Self-drawing by a 10-year-old. The subject's inclusion, attention to, or away from certain features can be used to help understand their inner thinking processes.

Source: Shutterstock.com.

- *Personality Inventories*: These types of tests use standardized methods to determine a subject's personality type and provide an overall personality profile of the subject. The tests typically aim to assess a subject's attitudes, emotions, beliefs, social skills, and thought processes, making up their outward personality and dictating their actions. The tests are usually compared with extensive pools of test results from many subjects. Inventories may be used to look for specific disorders or to objectively corroborate diagnoses made using projective tests. For example, specialized inventories may be used to provide evidence that a subject is malingering (exaggerating symptoms) or psychopathic (displayings little regard for the rights of others including antisocial, amoral, or egocentric behavior).

One commonly used approach evaluates five broad factors describing personality traits that can be measured through psychological testing, often referred to as the five-factor model, NEO, or OCEAN test: **O**penness to new experience, **C**onscientiousness, **E**xtraversion, **A**greeableness, and **N**euroticism (see Box 19.16). *Openness* to new experience, sometimes called intellect and imagination, looks at the breadth and scope of a person's interests and their ability to be imaginative. *Conscientiousness* evaluates the level of organization and ability of a person to plan effectively and be thorough. *Extraversion* focuses on the traits of talkativeness, energy, confidence, and assertiveness. *Agreeableness* traits include sympathy, affection, kindness, and helpfulness. Finally, *neuroticism*, or emotional stability, looks at a person's levels of anxiety, moodiness, nervousness, and anger.

BOX 19.16   FEATURES OF THE NEO PERSONALITY INVENTORY

Neuroticism identifies individuals who are prone to psychological distress.
- **Anxiety, anger, hostility, depression, self-consciousness, impulsiveness, vulnerability.**

Extraversion (or extroversion): Quantity and intensity of energy directed outwards into the social world:
- **Warmth, gregariousness, assertiveness, activity, excitement seeking, and positive emotion.**

Openness to Experience: The active seeking and appreciation of experiences for their own sake:
- **Fantasy, aesthetics, feelings, actions, ideas, and values.**

Agreeableness: The kinds of interactions an individual prefers from compassion to tough mindedness:
- **Trust, straightforwardness, altruism, compliance, modesty, and tender mindedness.**

Conscientiousness: Degree of organization, persistence, control and motivation in goal-directed behavior:
- **Competence, order, dutifulness, achievement, striving, self-discipline, and deliberation.**

(Source: Excerpted and adapted from Costa and McCrae, 1992)

Other theories and methods, such as the *International Personality Item Pool* (IPIP) and the *Ten-Item Personality inventory*, are also commonly used in evaluating personality traits.

A number of tests have been developed to help quantitatively build personality inventories. These include:

- **NEO PI-R Test**: This inventory test evaluates 240 items that relate to the five-factor model. Each of the five major categories is broken down into six smaller categories for evaluation. For example, a person's agreeableness is broken down into six sub-categories: trust, straightforwardness, altruism, compliance, modesty, and tender mindedness.
- **Minnesota Multiphasic Personality Inventory** (MMPI): This test provides an assessment of an adult's psychopathology and mental disorders. The test is made up of over 500 statements covering a wide range of topics, such as attitudes on religion, political ideas, education, and others, that the subject is required to respond to with true, false, or "cannot say" responses. The test is designed to identify traits that are known to be associated with specific groups of mental patients.

- **Intelligence and Cognitive Function Tests**: These tests explore a person's intellectual and cognitive (thinking) capacity. The tests may be of forensic use since a person's intelligence may bear centrally upon the legal issue of a criminal's responsibility for a crime and their competency to stand trial. Many forms of intelligence testing have been used over the years, and these tests are continually being revised and reconsidered. Several of the most important include:
    - **Wechsler Intelligence Test**: This highly standardized test, used for subjects 16 years or older, includes both verbal and nonverbal sections.

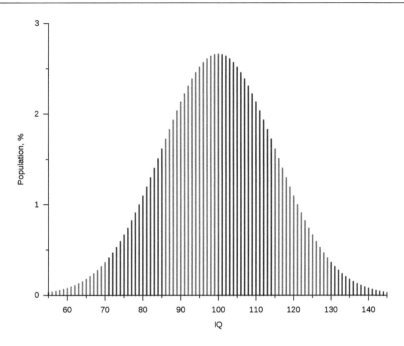

FIGURE 19.16 Distribution of Weschler IQ scores. The test standardizes scores such that the mean score is 100 with each standard deviation from the mean as 15 IQ points. Different colors are used in the plot for each standard deviation above or below the mean.

Source: Retrieved from Wikipedia; used per Creative Commons 2.5 Share-Alike. User: Alessio Damato, Mikhail Ryazanov.

The test is scored so that the mean is established at 100 with a standard deviation of 15 (meaning 68% of the test takers score between 85 and 115, as shown in Figure 19.16). The test also breaks down intelligence into a number of subtests, such as verbal (comprehension, vocabulary, word reasoning), perceptual reasoning (picture concepts, matrix reasoning), working memory (letter-number sequencing), and processing speed (arithmetic, coding).

- **Folstein Test** (Mini Mental State Exam, MMSE): This relatively rapid exam (11 questions) is designed to rapidly screen subjects for cognitive problems and dementia.
- **Brain Function and Impairment Tests**: Tests have been developed to determine the type and extent of brain injury and impairment that may be present in a subject, especially when brain injuries are known to have happened. Two of the most common tests are the Halstead-Reitan Neuropsychological Battery (HRNB) and the Luria-Nebraska Neuropsychological Battery (LNNB). These tests try to determine a person's "biological intelligence" by examining their attention, memory, language, logical-analytic skills and others abilities. These tests, like intelligence testing, may be important in

determining a defendant's responsibility for a crime and their competency to stand trial.
- **Specific Disorder Tests**: As the name implies, a number of very specific tests have been developed to evaluate a patient for certain mental disorders. For example, specific tests have been established for testing for the presence of bipolar disorder, schizophrenia, and personality disorders.

Specialized Forensic Tests: The second broad type of psychological testing, besides general psychological tests, is the specific forensic tests. A number of psychological tests are used that are entirely focused on providing psychological information relative only to a specific legal question. For example, tests have been developed to evaluate a person's ability to understand and rationally waive their *Miranda* rights (warning of potential consequences of making statements to the police). The important distinction between general psychological tests and specific forensic tests is that the specific tests probe questions that are only of legal importance and usually do not relate to clinical diagnoses of the test subject. These assessment tools are limited in scope and may not address all the important features of an evaluation, so most practitioners do not use these tools alone but couple them with other forms of general standardized psychological testing.

19.1.9 Psychological Autopsy

Sometimes, it is quite difficult for a medical examiner to determine confidently the manner of death when considering a possible suicide among other classifications of deaths (e.g., homicide, accidental, natural, and undetermined) in an "equivocal" case. *Equivocal deaths* are those where the reasons and intentions of the victim and/or the circumstances surrounding the death are not clear. For example, distinguishing between an *accidental* drug overdose death and a suicide by *intentional* overdose may require psychological information about the person's intentions that is not readily available to the medical examiner. To aid in manner of death determinations in these types of equivocal cases, psychologists have developed a method for the retrospective analysis of a person's psychological makeup that focuses especially on the identification of suicide risk factors in the person, called a *psychological autopsy* (PA). A working definition of a psychological autopsy (PA) is

a post-mortem investigative procedure requiring the identification and assessment of suicide risk factors present at the time of death, with the goal of enabling a determination of the manner of death to as high a degree of certainty as possible.

(Knoll, 2008)

The use of a psychological autopsy in a forensic setting has usually been found to be admissible by courts due to the wide acceptance of the practice by clinical psychologists. Because of its long-standing use and general acceptance, the psychological autopsy generally is held to meet the Frye standard

for admissibility, although it is most commonly encountered in civil cases. Over the years, various organizations have worked to establish and refine standard protocols for performing a psychological autopsy, although no single standardized protocol exists today.

Psychological autopsies may be employed in a variety of forensic and research investigations, including those listed in Table 19.1. In cases of equivocal death, the results of the PA often greatly influence a medical examiner's ultimate determination of the manner of death. Examples of equivocal deaths where PA analyses are commonly used are given in Table 19.2. The reliance on the findings of the PA is rooted in a large body of supportive clinical data. For example, studies have shown that more than 90% of people who committed suicide suffered from identifiable mental disorders, especially mood and substance dependence disorders. Current theory holds that the risk for suicide arises from the interplay of psychiatric illness with social and situational stresses and circumstances.

The psychological autopsy can be used to aid in the formulation of a criminal profile through victimology. In this application, the technique examines the victim's history to assess whether the victim lived in a situation that would make them particularly vulnerable as a target for a killer.

Criminal cases using PA methods usually deal with determining between a possible suicide and a homicide or a suicide influenced by the abusive behavior of another person. Civil cases often focus on whether the deceased's beneficiaries should receive death benefit payments. For example, many insurance policies prohibit payment of benefits in instances of suicide, although some policies make a distinction between an "insane and a sane" suicide, paying benefits for the former but not for the latter. An *insane suicide* is a

TABLE 19.1   Uses of the psychological autopsy include

- Assist medical examiners with "equivocal" deaths
- Conduct research on suicide
- Handle insurance claims
- Deal with Criminal cases
- Address estate issues and contested wills
- Manage malpractice claims
- Handle Worker's Compensation cases
- Address product liability cases
- Implement organizational suicide prevention efforts
- Promote understanding and grieving among surviving family.

Source: Knoll (2008).

TABLE 19.2   Examples of equivocal deaths where a psychological autopsy might be employed

- Drug related deaths
- Autoerotic asphyxia
- Self-induced asphyxia (e.g., the "choking game")
- Drownings
- Vehicular deaths
- "Russian Roulette" deaths
- "Suicide by Cop" deaths
- Staged death scenes.

Source: Knoll (2008).

strictly legal term, defined by the U.S. Supreme Court, to apply to a decedent when their

> reasoning faculties are so far impaired that he is not able to understand the moral character, the general nature, consequences, and effect of the act he is about to commit, or when he is impelled thereto by an insane impulse, which he has not the power to resist.

In contrast, the Court has defined a *sane suicide* as meaning that the person "in the possession of his ordinary reasoning faculties, from anger, pride, jealousy, or a desire to escape from the ills of life, intentionally takes his own life." The main difference is whether the person fully comprehends that their acts will lead to their death. Other civil uses of PA methods include worker's compensation cases to determine the liability of an employer for the suicide of an employee and in medical malpractice and related cases where the suicide of the person might be deemed to be the result of the patient's treatment or medications.

Psychological autopsies require the analysis of as much relevant information about the deceased person as possible. Key sources of this information often include medical records, including any psychological assessments and treatments, police records, interviews with family members and friends, employment history, written records by the person (e.g., diaries, suicide notes, emails, correspondence, internet use, etc.), family history of psychological problems, autopsy results and police reports. The biological profile of the person (e.g., age, sex, illness, etc.) can also be helpful in evaluating risk factors for suicide by evaluating known risk factors for different populations. Investigators may need to visit the death scene to understand any special relationships between the death setting with potential risk factors or suicidal behaviors. Interviews with family members, friends, co-workers, and acquaintances are usually required for any complete PA evaluation. These interviews are often quite structured, and protocols such as the Structured Clinical Interview for DSM-IV Disorders (SCID) have been developed to assist in the completion of these interviews. The environment and timing of these interviews may be quite important, and usually, a two to six-month interval between the death and the interview is suggested.

The goal of the PA is to provide a detailed picture of the deceased person's personality, behavior, risk factors, and possible motivations for suicide. Table 19.3 presents some of the

TABLE 19.3 Goals of a psychological autopsy when determining whether the decedent was a probable candidate for suicide

- Identify behavior patterns: reactions to stress, adaptability, changes in habits or routine.
- Establish the presence or absence of mental illness.
- Identify possible precipitants.
- Determine the presence or absence of motives.
- Determine the presence or absence of suicidal intent.
- Identify suicide risk factors, both mitigating and aggravating.
- Perform a post-mortem suicide risk assessment.
- Establish whether or not the deceased was a likely candidate for suicide.

Source: Knoll (2008).

goals of the psychological autopsy process. It is important to note that usually no single factor provides a comprehensive evaluation of suicidal risk. Risk-increasing and risk-reducing factors must both be weighed and evaluated within the context of the complex mosaic of the person's psychological composition and the circumstances surrounding their death. The PA is focused to allow the expert to render an opinion, supported by as much quantitative and qualitative evidence as possible, as to "whether or not the decedent was a likely candidate to commit suicide at the time in question," rather than whether the deceased did or did not commit suicide.

19.1.10 Conclusions

The behavioral sciences have a vital role to play in providing forensic evidence in the criminal and civil justice systems, from the initial phases of an investigation through to post-sentencing evaluations that may continue for decades beyond the actual courtroom proceedings. As the behavioral sciences continue to develop assessment tools and tests, they will be increasingly relied upon in criminal and legal settings. It is, however, as important to recognize the limitations of these tools as it is to understand their strengths in evaluating criminal behavior. Nonetheless, forensic behavioral science now represents a vital part of forensic science.

QUESTIONS FOR FURTHER PRACTICE AND MASTERY

19.1 Provide a brief explanation for each of the following terms: (a) behavioral sciences, (b) psychology, and (c) sociology.

19.2 What are some of the sub-disciplines of psychology and briefly describe the focus areas of study for each of these sub-disciplines?

19.3 Describe briefly the difference between clinical psychology and forensic psychology.

19.4 What are some applications of forensic psychology to civil and criminal cases?

19.5 The adversarial system is the method for handling a case in court, while the cooperative approach is the basis of clinical psychology. Describe what each of these two approaches is and how they differ in practice.

19.6 Describe what is meant by the term victimology. List some ways that a person can harm another. What do you think the possible psychological effects of these harmful actions can be on the victim? Should all of these be considered criminal acts and under what circumstances?

19.7 Crimes are thought to have two parts: *mens rea* and *actus reus*. What is meant by these terms, and how do they relate to the common ideas of motive, means and opportunity when considering a criminal act?

19.8   The RPM method involves identifying three kinds of behavior that criminals often employ as a defensive psychological strategy when being interviewed. Describe what the RPM terms of rationalization, projection, and minimization mean and give examples of how people might use these strategies in criminal and non-criminal settings.

19.9   Describe some of the problems in relying upon eyewitness testimony in investigations and in court. Should this type of testimony be allowed into court? If so, do you believe that there should there be restrictions or instructions to the jury on when and how it can be used and why?

19.10   Criminal profiling can provide investigators with new leads in difficult, seemingly random or cold cases. Describe how the process works, including the types of data needed for the analysis and the types of information that it can provide to investigators. What are the limitations of a criminal profile? Should the results of a criminal profile be admissible in court, why or why not?

19.11   How can hypnosis and brain profiling be used in criminal cases? Should these methods be admissible in court, and if so, under what circumstances?

19.12   What is meant by the *voir dire* process of jury selection and how can forensic psychology play a role in these proceedings. Does this seem like a fair and just use of psychological expertise?

19.13   The term "competency to stand trial" is important to courtroom proceedings. What does it mean and how is someone determined to be incompetent to stand trial? Do you believe every defendant should be evaluated for their competency? Support your answer from both practical and philosophic positions.

19.14   What are the requirements to show that someone is legally insane? Why is it so seldom actually used? When used, what time frame does the insanity defense deal with – the time of trial, the time of the crime, or another time? What happens to a person if they use the insanity defense and are unsuccessful in proving their case? What if they are successful? What is the difference between cognitive insanity and volitional insanity?

19.15   When should the diminished capacity defense be considered? What are the requirements to be successful in a diminished capacity defense? What legal restrictions are usually placed on this defense?

19.16   What is meant by malingering, when might it be used in criminal proceedings, and how might it be detected?

19.17   What is a projective psychological test? Give examples and describe their basic features and the types of information that can be derived from these tests. Try the Rorschach test yourself and the picture drawing test of a group of friends and compare your responses from each test to see what patterns you might observe.

19.18   In a personality inventory, what does the acronym OCEAN stand for? What types of information can be gained from a personality inventory, and how might this information be used to inform the court?

19.19   Describe the basic ideas behind intelligence testing and when it might be used in a forensic setting. What are the limitations and strengths of this type of test?

19.20   What is meant by "biological intelligence," and how can brain function tests assess this? What features are analyzed to provide information about the level of brain impairment in brain-damaged people?

19.21   Describe some specific disorder tests and what mental diseases or disorders they assess.

19.22   What are some typical specialized psychological forensic tests and when might they be employed? What are some of the strengths and limitations of these tests?

19.23   What is meant by an "equivocal" death? How can a psychological autopsy be used to determine if an "equivocal" death is a suicide, a homicide, or an accident? How is the psychological autopsy carried out, and what types of information does it typically employ?

19.24   What is meant by the legal terms insane suicide and sane suicide?

GLOSSARY OF TERMS

---

actus reus: Latin term for "guilty act," used to describe the specific act of a criminal event.

adversarial approach to law: when opposing sides of a legal issue present contrasting views, supported by logical arguments, as a means of presenting the key information of a case.

brain fingerprinting: a technique that uses multiple measurements of the brain's electrical signals ("brain waves") in response to various stimuli, such as words, pictures, or sounds, to determine if a particular memory exists within a person's mind.

brain function and impairment test: a psychological test that tries to determine the type and extent of brain function injury and impairment that may be present in a subject.

clinical psychology: a subdiscipline of psychology that focuses on the diagnosis and treatment of mental and behavioral disorders in people.

competence to stand trial: in order to stand trial, a defendant must have both "sufficient present ability to consult with his lawyer with a reasonable degree of rational understanding" and a "rational as well as factual understanding of the proceedings against him."

criminal investigative analysis: see criminal profiling.

criminal profiling: a largely investigative tool where accepted concepts from behavioral science are used to provide information about the criminal's behavioral patterns and personal characteristics based on known information about a serial crime.

diminished capacity: a legal defense where the offender had a reduced ability to understand the crimes that they committed; they could not form the needed *mens rea* or did not act knowing the consequences of their actions, but did not fully meet the requirements of legal insanity.

equivocal deaths: deaths where the reasons and intentions of the victim and/or the circumstances surrounding the death are not clear.

forensic psychology: a subdiscipline of psychology that deals with the application of psychological theories and practices to inform legal questions.

hypnosis: a psychological state characterized by heightened awareness and concentration, deep relaxation, inner absorption, and enhanced suggestibility.

insane suicide: a strictly legal term, defined by the U.S. Supreme Court, to apply to a decedent when their "reasoning faculties are so far impaired that he is not able to understand the moral character, the general nature, consequences, and effect of the act he is about to commit, or when he is impelled thereto by an insane impulse, which he has not the power to resist."

intelligence and cognitive function test: a psychological test that measures a person's intellectual and thought capacity in a variety of sub-areas, such as verbal, perceptual reasoning, working memory, and processing speed.

legal competence: possessing the necessary abilities or legal qualifications required to participate in a legal process.

legal insanity: an entirely legal construct that is usually a viable defense only if the person either did not know what they were doing or couldn't tell right from wrong at the time of the crime.

linkage analysis: the process of trying to understand the behavior of an offender by seeing if similar features can be found in different crimes in an attempt to link these crimes together.

malingering: the faking or exaggeration of symptoms.

mens rea: Latin term for "guilty mind" used to describe the criminal intent of an event.

minimization: a mental escape that allows criminals to reduce both their involvement in and the actual seriousness of the crime, thereby reducing their internal responsibility for the crime.

modus operandi (MO): referring to the method, habits, and tendencies of the offender in committing the crime: how the crime was committed.

neurobiological psychology: a subdiscipline of psychology that examines the molecular and cellular components of the brain and nervous system to discover how memory, emotion, perception, reasoning and other traits are stored and processed at the microscopic level.

personality inventory: a standardized psychological test that is used to determine a subject's personality type and provide an overall personality profile of the person.

projection: a means whereby the criminal places blame for the crime on someone else, projecting the blame, often onto the victim.

projective test: psychological tests that try to evaluate a subject's personality and thought processes by exploring how the test subject thinks about themselves and their world and performed by evaluating that subject's responses to ambiguous images or new situations.

psychological autopsy: a post-mortem investigative procedure requiring the assessment of suicide risk factors at the time of death.

psychology: the field that focuses on understanding human behavior by examining a person's individual thought and mental processes.

rationalization: a mental process in which the criminal justifies their actions by providing explanations that they feel are reasonable and reflect favorably upon themselves.

sociology: the field that examines how individuals and groups function and behave within the context of larger societies and how individuals form social networks that collectively operate together as complex organizations.

specific disorder test: a psychological test developed to evaluate a subject for specific mental disorders.

victimology: the study of the victims in criminal cases that looks for links between the background, life, lifestyle, occupation, education, age, habits, physical characteristics, and other features of a victim with the criminal action directed against them.

BIBLIOGRAPHY

M.J. Ackerman, *Essentials of Forensic Psychological Assessment* (2nd Ed.), John Wiley, 2010.

C.R. Bartol and A.M. Bartol, *Current Perspectives in Forensic Psychology and Criminal Behavior* (3rd Ed.), Sage, 2011.

C.R. Bartol and A.M. Bartol, *Introduction to Forensic Psychology* (3rd Ed.), Sage, 2011.

P.T. (Jr.) Costa and R.R. McCrae, *The Test People*, Hogrefe Ltd., Oxford, 1992.

J.E. Douglas, R.K. Ressler, A.W. Burgess, and C.R. Hartman, "Criminal profiling from crime scene analysis", *Behavioral Sciences & the Law*, 4(4), 401–421, 1986.

S.M. Fulero, *Forensic Psychology* (3rd Ed.), Wadsworth, 2008.

A.M. Goldstein and I.B. Weiner, *Handbook of Psychology, Forensic Psychology* (Vol. 11), John Wiley, 2003.

T. Grisso, *Evaluating Competencies: Forensic Assessments and Instruments*, Springer, 2002.

Jack Kitaeff, *Forensic Psychology*, Pearson, 2010.

J.L. Knoll IV, "The psychological autopsy, part I: applications and methods", *Journal of Psychiatric Practice*, 14, 393, 2008.

G.B. Melton et al., *Psychological Evaluations for the Court*, Guilford Press, 1997.

G.B. Melton, J. Petrila, N.G. Poythress, and C. Slobogin, *Psychological Evaluations for the Courts* (4th Ed.), Guilford Press, 2017.

R.G. Meyer and C.M. Weaver, *Law and Mental Health*, Guilford Press, 2005.

Michael R. Napier and Susan H. Adams, "Magic words to obtain confessions". In *FBI Law Enforcement Bulletin*, Oct. 1998.

T. O'Connor, "Advanced applied victimology". In *MegaLinks in Criminal Justice*, Tom O'Connor (ed.), North Carolina Wesleyan College (Publ.), 2011.

Shairlaine Ortiz, *Forensic Psychology 101: A Quick Guide That Teaches You the Top Key Lesson, About Forensic Psychology from A to Z*, CreateSpace Independent Publishing Platform, 2018.

I.K. Packer, *Evaluation of Criminal Responsibility* (Best Practices in Forensic Mental Health Assessment), Oxford Univ. Press, 2009.

Ira K. Packer, "Specialized practice in forensic psychology: Opportunities and obstacles", *Professional Psychology: Research and Practice*, 39(2), 245–249, 2008.

I.B. Weiner and A.K. Hess, *Handbook of Forensic Psychology* (4th Ed.), John Wiley and Sons, 2013.

P. Zapf and R. Roesch, *Evaluation of Competence to Stand Trial* (Best Practices in Forensic Mental Health Assessment), Oxford Univ. Press, 2008.

Kent Alexander and Kevin Salweh, *The Suspect: An Olympic Bombing, the FBI, the Media, and Richard Jewell, the Man Caught in the Middle*, Harry N. Abrams, Publ., 2019 [ISBN-13: 978-1419734625].

Index

Note: **Bold** page numbers refer to tables and *italic* page numbers refer to figures.

abdomen 261
abrasion 260
absorbance 98
abuse
    economic 729
    physical 729
    psychological/emotional 729
    sexual 729
    social 729
    spiritual 729
    verbal 729
accelerants 556, 557
accidental death 250
accumulated degree-days (ADD/°D) 353–354,
        354, 355
    degree hours (ADH) 353–354, *354, 355*
accuracy, concept of *83,* 83–85, *84*
acetone 557
acetone peroxide (TATP) 574
action 623
activation energy 543, *545,* 549
active bloodstains 177–179, *177–179*
actus reus 728, 739
addition reactions (polymers) 228
additive color mixing 590
administrative searches 39
admissibility of evidence 23, 25, 26, 28
Adventure of the Blanched Soldier, The (Doyle)
        18
Adventure of the Cardboard Box, The (Doyle) 15
adversarial approach to law 727–728
Age of Enlightenment 10
age regression and progression photography 679,
        679
agglutination 170–171
air-fuel ratio 550
air guns 622–623
airport 39
air resistance 624
albumin 162
*The Alchymist, in Search of the Philospher's
        Stone Discovers Phosphorus*
        (painting) *389,* **390**
alcohol 557
    absolute 521
    blood alcohol concentration *see* blood alcohol
        concentration (BAC)
    brandy 524
    ethanol 521, 539
    horizontal gaze nystagamus 527, *529*
    malt 522
    methanol 521
    miscible 521
    production of *521–523,* 521–524
    Schmerber v. California 533
    sherry 524
    toxicology 524–525
Alfred P. Murrah Federal Building 574, *575*
algor mortis 255

allele *vs.* gene *126*
altered writing 665
alternative light source (ALS) *641*
Altmann, Richard 116
Alzheimer's disease 258, 268
amelogenin gene 144
American Academy of Forensic Science (AAFS)
        7, 72, 73
American Board of Criminalistics (ABC) 73
American Chemical Society (ACS) 386
American Society of Crime Lab Directors
        (ASCLD) 7, 73
ammonium nitrate (NH_4NO_3) 570, 571
ammonium nitrate/fuel oil explosive (ANFO) 571
ammunition 615–617, 623
    with bullet 616, *617*
    components *623*
    fixed 616
    types of *623*
amorphous glass, chemical structures of *598*
amplitude 95
amylase 182
anagen phase 214
analytical problem-solving skills 54
ancestry informative markers (AIMs) 139
ANFO 571
angle of impact 177–178
angstrom (Å) 108
annealing 132, 133, 134, 152
anode 282
anthropology
    allometric relationships 309, 332
    American Association of Biological
        Anthropologists 316
    anterior (ventral/front) 301, *306,* 332
    background 300
    biological profile 306–307, 318, 332, 747
    bones *see* bone
    circumstantial identification 307
    collagen *see* collagen
    co-mingled remains 326, *326,* 332
    cribra orbitalia 318
    crime scene processing 41, *41,* 325, 558
    deep 301, 332
    distal 301, *323,* 332
    facial reconstruction *see* facial reconstruction
    Homo sapiens 316
    human skeletal anatomy *see* human skeletal
        anatomy
    inferior 301, 332
    King Richard III 324–325, *325*
    lateral 301, 332
    longitudinal 301, 332
    medial 301, 332
    minimum number of individuals *see*
        minimum number of individuals
        (MNI)
    most likely number of individuals *see* most
        likely number of individuals (MLNI)

ossification 312–313, 332
osteometry 309–310, 332
positive identification 307
posterior (dorsal) 301, 332
post-mortem interval *see* post-mortem
        interval (PMI)
proximal 301, 332
pubic symphysis 311, 314, *315*
sagittal 301, 332
sexual dimorphism 310, 333
superficial 301, 332
superior 301, 332
taphonomy 245, 298, 327–329, 333
antemortem 255
anthrax attacks (2001) 673
anthropometry 10, *10*
antibody 165
anti-forensics 715
antigen 165
Antikythera Mechanism *688*
Antoinette, Marie 151
apocrine gland 193
Applied Biosystems™ 3500 Series Genetic
        Analyzer *138*
Applied Biosystems™ AmpFLSTR™ *138*
AP-type propellant 547
Archimedes 8, *387,* 387–388
    eureka 387
    palimpsest *671*
    principle 584
arch pattern 195
Argentina's children case 151
arrangement tests 742–743, *743*
arrhythmic handwriting *654*
arson 555–556
    insurance fraud 555–556
artery 262
arthropods 342, 344
    adventive species (incidental parasites) 345,
        380
    entomology 337, 342–358, 380
    faunal succession 345, 349, 351, 380
    necrophagous species 344–345, 380
    omnivorous species 345, 380
    parasites 345, 380
    PMI *see* post-mortem interval (PMI)
    predators 345, 348
artificial intelligence (AI) 149, 716–719, *717, 718*
    biometric information 717
    DNA analysis 717
    evidence processing 717
    forensic medicine 717
    policing methodologies 717
Ashworth, Dawn 114
asphyxia 272–273, *272*
Association of Firearm and Toolmark Examiners
        (AFTE) 626
astrological zodiac *64*
astrology 63

atmospheric air *551*
atmospheric oxygen 551
atomic absorption spectroscopy (AAS) *439*, 439–441
atomic emission spectroscopy (AES) *439*, 441–444, *442*
atomic fluorescence spectroscopy (AFS) 444, *444*
attribution 148
authentication 31, 188
auto-ignition temperature 549, **550**, 553
automated biometric identification system (IDENT) 240
automated fingerprint identification system (AFIS) 192, *193*
autopsy
    access and control of remains 260–261
    closure 262
    evaluation and analysis of samples 262
    external examination 261
    information from *259*, 259–260
    removing organs 261–262
    requirement of 257–258, **258**, *258*
    thoracoabdominal and brain cavities, opening of 261, *261*
average/arithmetic mean 66, *66*
Avogadro's Number 81
azimuthal locating 44

backdraft 553
ballistic(s) 624–626
    evidence 104
    external (intermediate) 624, *624*, *625*
    forensic identification of 634, *634*
    internal (initial) 624
    terminal *625*, 625–626, *626*
barrel 623
base pairing 133, 152
Bayesian model 71
Beamish, Douglas 150
Becke line 587
behavioral forensic science *725*, 725–747
    background 726–727
Bell, Joseph 17
bell-shaped distribution *see* normal distribution
Bendectin 25
Bentley, E.C. 19
Bertillon, Alphonse 10
Bertillon measurements *11*
bias 57
bias in forensic science 72–73, 73–74
    cognitive bias 73–74
    confirmation bias 74
    expectation bias 74
    motivational bias 73
    selection bias 74
bifurcation 197
bile 184
Bill of Rights (1791) 36
binder (paint) 608
binding precedent 22, 26
biochemical analysis, of forensic samples *30*
biochemical senses 85
biochemical signals 85
biofuels 551
biological evidence 79–109
    estimating reliability of measurements 83–85
    observation, measurement, and forensic science 79–83, *80*
    tools for *see* biological tools for biological evidence
biological sensors 86

biological tools for biological evidence 85–102, 104–108
    bright field optical microscopy 92, *92*
    comparison microscopy 99–100, *101*, *102*
    comparison of features 102, **103**
    dark field optical microscopy 92–93, *93*
    electron microscopy *see* electron microscopy
    fluorescence microscopy 96–98, *97*
    infrared microscopy 98, *98*, *99*
    microscopy basics 86–87
    optical microscopy 89, *91*, 91–92
    phase contrast microscopy 95–96, *96*
    polarized light microscopy 93–95, *95*
    staining techniques in microscopy 101–102, **102**, *102*
    stereomicroscopy 98–99, *99*, *100*
    working of magnifying lens 87, *89*
    working of microscope 88–91
biomedical imaging 278–280, *278–281*
biometric(s)
    automated biometric identification system (IDENT) 240
    basics of 236
    eye biometrics 238, *238*
    face image data 239, *240*
    hand and finger geometry 237
    history of *235*, 235–236
    methods of 236–237
    new methods and technologies 239–240
    security scan 32
    traits, types of 237–240
    vein geometry analysis 237, *237*–238
    voice analysis 239, *239*
    writing and typing analysis 237
biometric traits
    automated biometric identification system (IDENT) 240
    eye biometrics 238, *238*
    face image data 239, *240*
    hand and finger geometry 237
    new methods and technologies 239–240
    vein geometry analysis *237*, 237–238
    voice analysis 239, *239*
    writing and typing analysis 237
biopolymers 116
birefringence 589, *589*
bit 713
bite marks 644–645, *645*
black powder 567, 569
bladder 263
blasting caps 568, *569*
block capital writing 653
blood
    albumin 162
    analysis in crime detection 156–158, *157*
    blood-based diseases 162–163, *163*
    cellular components of 159–162, *160–162*
    chemistry 158
    components of *154*
    definitions of 158
    liquid components of 158–159, *159*
    red blood cells *155*
blood alcohol
    evidence 39
    test 38
blood alcohol concentration (BAC) 525–532
    breathalyzer 529, *530*, *531*
    breath testing 529, *530*, *531*
    field sobriety 527–531
    horizontal gaze nystagamus 527, *529*
    laboratory (confirmatory) testing 531

    National Highway Traffic Safety Administration 527
    one leg stand 528, *529*
    standardized field sobriety test 527, *529*
    walk and turn 528, *529*
blood pattern analysis 175
    active bloodstains 177–179, *177–179*
    bloodstain patterns analysis *175*, 176
    collecting and preserving blood evidence 181
    passive bloodstains *176*, 176–177
    transfer bloodstains *180*, 180–181
blood testing
    biological sample, individualizing 169–173, *171–172*
    enzyme linked immunosorbent assay 168–169, *169*
    enzyme multiplied immunoassay technique 167–168, *168*
    human blood, determining 165–167, *166–167*
    monoclonal antibodies 169, *170*
    suspicious stain, determining 163–165, *164–166*
blood typing 33, **171**, 173, **173**
bloody handprint 8
blown glass method 599, *599*
blunt force trauma (BFT) 253, 261, 273, 296, 323, 332
    ball-peen hammer *324*
    examples of *273*
    types of 268
body fluid analysis 150
Bogen, Mark 146–147
Bond v. United States, 529 US 334 (2000) 36
bone
    baby's "soft spots"/fontanelles 313
    beveling of 270, 272, *271*, 323, 332
    compact *see* compact bone
    crest 302, 332
    dating of 313
    deciduous teeth *see* deciduous teeth
    deep 301, 332
    diaphysis 302, 312, 332
    endoskeleton 301, 332
    epiphysis 302, 332
    facial reconstruction *see* facial reconstruction
    flat 302
    foramen 302, 332
    fracture, types of 328
    hematoma 321, *322*, 327, 332
    hyoid 265, 302, 324, *324*, 332
    inferior (caudal/lower) 302, 332
    irregular 302
    long 302
    permanent teeth *see* permanent teeth
    post-mortem interval *see* post-mortem interval (PMI)
    remodeling 321, *322*, 333
    scanning electron micrograph 301
    sesamoid 302
    short 302
    sutures 313
    types of 302, *302*, *305*
bone marrow 160–162
border 39, *39*
borosilicate glass 599
botany
    database 360
    DNA analysis 360
    plant drugs 363, **364**, 365
    and plant toxins 364–365
    PMI *see* post-mortem interval (PMI)

tetrahydrocannabinol *see* tetrahydrocannabinol (THC)
boundary 41–43, *43*
boundary conditions 60
brain 266–268, *268–269*
    fingerprinting 735, *735*
    function and impairment tests 745
breech 623
breech block (face) 623
breech-loading firearms 615
Brian fingerprinting 735
bright field optical microscopy 92, *92*, 108
brisance 564
broach cutter 627, *627*
Brown, Robert 23
Buckland, Richard 114
bullet 623
    comparisons 626–628
    firing *618*
Bundy, T. T. 646
buoyancy 584–585, *585*
burning 541, 543
    process 551
button rifling 627
byte 713

caliber 623
California v. Ciraolo (1986) 39
camping stove fuel 557
capillary electrophoresis *135*, 135–136
carbon disulfide 557
carbon monoxide (CO) 547
Carpenter v. United States 40
cartilage *284*, 302–304, *304*, 311, 332
    attachment *324*
    callus 321
    degradation 316, *316*
    in fetus 312
    fibrocartilage 321
    ossification 312, 332
    osteoarthritis *see* osteoarthritis
    rheumatoid arthritis *see* rheumatoid arthritis
cartridge 616, 623
    shotguns 621, *621*
castings 640
catagen phase 215
catalysts 164, 228, 547
cathode 282
C. Auguste Dupin (fictional character) 14, 17
cause of death 253–257, *253–257*
"Cave of Hands," Santa Cruz Province in Argentina *8*
CD-ROM 713
cellulose 225, *225*
certainty 5
chain of custody (CoC) 41, 46–47, *49*, 50
chain reaction 552
chain reaction suppression 553
Challenger space shuttle, loss of 697–698
cheiloscopy 192
chemical, biological, radiological, nuclear, and explosive materials (CBRNE) 13
chemical analysis, of forensic samples *30, 32*
Chemical-Biological Sciences Unit, FBI 13
chemical chain reaction 552
chemical composition 30–31
chemical detectors 86, *87*
chemical properties **581**, 581–582
chemical reactions 543, 545, 546, 547
chemiluminescence 165
chemistry
    acid-base indicator in **418**
    and analytics 385, 386–419
    antibody-antigen interactions in 418
    atomic structure in 394
    Avogadro's number 398
    boiling point in 406
    chemical (classical) method, application of **393**, 413–414, 420
    and chromatography 406–411, *408*, **409**, *409, 410*, 420
    combustion analysis in **393**, 415, 420
    and concentration 393, 421
    and confirmatory test 393, 421
    and conservation of mass 397, 421
    dilution *390*
    distillation 407
    elements 395
    extraction *390, 412*
    extrinsic (extensive) properties 404, 421
    filtration *390*
    heterogeneous mixture 405, **405**, *407*, 421
    homogeneous mixture 405, **405**, *407*, 421
    hornet-honey bee analogy *408*
    immunoassay in 418, 421
    intrinsic (intensive) properties 403, 421
    isotopes 395, *396*, 421
    John Dalton 396
    Marquis test 392
    mobile phase 408–409, *409*, 421
    molar mass 399
    mole 398–400, *399*, 421
    molecular formula 400, 421
    molecular weight 400, 421
    periodic table of elements 395, *395*, 421
    physical (instrumental) method, application of **393**
    physical properties 396, 403, 405, 421
    presumptive test 392, 413, 414, 421
    products of 398, 400, 421
    quantitative analysis of 389–390, 421
    reactants 397–398, 400
    retention factor (*Rf*) 409, 422
    robotic workstation used in *390*
    state of matter 403, *404*
    stationary phase in 408–409, **409**, *409*, 422
    stoichiometry of 398, 422
    Tylenol tablet 390
    use of titration in 415–419, *416*
    volumetric (titrametric) analysis 415–418
chemtrails 62
Chesterton, G.K. 19
chimerism 126–127
Chinese "hand cannon" 613, *614*
Christie, Agatha 19
chromatography 667
chromosomes 119, 121, 122, *122*
circulatory system 262
class evidence characteristics *33*, 33–34
clinical psychology 726, 727
cloud computing 713
cloud forensics *716*
coatings 607–611
code of conduct *72*
Code of Hammurabi 688, *689*
coding regions 121, 122
cognitive bias 73–74
cognitive psychology 726
Cohanim 144
collagen **102**, 193, 242, 301, *301*, 303, 332
collision
    elastic 701
    inelastic 701
    model 546, *546*
color indexing book (Munsell) *594*
color properties 589–590, *590*
Combined DNA Index System (CODIS) 138, 144–146, *145*
combustion reactions 547, 552
communication 650–652
    graphic forms of 650–651
compact bone
    bone remodeling 321
    cortical bone 302
    flat 302
    lamellae *301*
    long 302
    sesamoid 302
    short 302
comparison analysis 31–34, 716
comparison microscopy 99–100, *101, 102*
    of ballistic evidence 104
compartment syndrome 268
competence
    legal 737
    pro se 737, 737–738
    restoring 736–737
competency to stand trial (CST) 736–737
complementary DNA 133
complementary pairs 119
complementary sequence 119
complex DNA mixtures 150
complimentary color 612
compound microscope *90*
computer
    based techniques 49
    crime 713
    engineering 711
    forensics 711–719
    investigations 713–715
computer-aided design (CAD) software 44, *46*, 634, *635*, 698
computerized axial tomography (CAT) 285
computerized skeletal reconstruction *7*
computerized tomography (CT)
    of head wound *7*
    imaging 285–287, *286–288*
computer search strategies 31
computer software engineering 711
concave surface 88, *90*
concentric cracks 602, *602*
conchoidal marks *see* stress-induced striations
condensation reactions 228
cone cells 86, 589
confirmation bias 74
confirmatory evidence 57–59
confirmatory test 164
consent 38, 39
conservation of energy 700, 701, 719
conservation of momentum 706–709, *707, 708*, 719
contact wound 271
contamination prevention *49*
contextual bias 73
contractor trace DNA *see* touch DNA
contradictory evidence 63
contrast 91
contributing cause of death 253
Controlled Substance Act (CSA) 519, *520*
    Schedule I drugs 519, **519**
    Schedule II drugs 519, **519**
    Schedule III drugs 519, **519**
    Schedule IV drugs 519, **519**

Schedule V drugs 519, **519**
contusion 260
convex surface 87, 88, *90*
conveyance scenes 50
coordinate mapping 44
copybooks 652
core 195
coronary arteries 262
coroner 246
cortex 211
Cosey, J. 672
Council of Advisors on Science and Technology 74
counterfeit 665, *666*, *668*
creatine phosphokinase (CPK) 385
Crick, Francis 116
crime detection in literature 13–19
crime labs 12–13
crime scene *50*
    diagram of bird's-eye view and floor plan *45*
    three-dimensional map of *46*
    total station device in mapping *45*
    types 50 *see also* conveyance scenes; indoor scenes; outdoor scenes
crime scene evidence 29–34
    comparison analysis 31–34
    identification analysis 30–31
    types 30
crime scene processing *41*, 41–47
    azimuthal locating 44
    coordinate mapping 44
    electronic methods 44
    evidence collection and preservation 45–47
    recording 43
    search for evidence 44–45
    securing and isolating 42
    triangulation 44, *44*
criminal evidence 35, 37, 38
Criminal Investigation (Gross) 10
criminal investigative analysis (CIA) *see* criminal profiling
criminalistics 10, 59
    definition 8
criminal justice 3, 19, 32, 53
criminal profiling 14, 728–729, 734, 734–735
critical thinking 54
Crofts, Freeman Wills 19
crush depth 702, 704, *704*
crush energy 704
crystalline glass, chemical structures of *598*
CSI Effect 7, 19
cursive writing 653
cut-and-paste signature 660
cuticle 210
cyberforensics 715
cybersecurity 715–716
cyclic loads 690, 692, *692*, *694*
cytosine 119
Czar Nicholas II 145, *146*

Daphnia pulex 93
dark field optical microscopy 92–93, *93*
Daubert Standard 6, 26
Daubert v. Merrell Dow Pharmaceuticals 25, 53, 55
dead loads *see* static loads
DeAngelo, Joseph James 140
death
    cause of 253–257, *253–257*
    manner of *250–252*, 250–253, **252**
decay, studies on

ADD *see* accumulated degree-days (ADD/°D)
algor mortis 255, 257, *257*, 259, 296, 346, 351, 380
apoptosis 346
bloated stage 346, *346*, 347, *347*, **349**, *349*
blowfly 344, 349, *349*, *350*, 351, *352*, *353*, *356*, 357–358, 380
blowfly strike 357
bluebottle fly *(Calliphora vomitoria)* 347, 353–354
controlled rearing 355
decay stage 346, *346*, *347*, 348–349, **349**, *349*, *350*, 355
development of fly stages 354
dry stage 346, *346*, *347*, 348, **349**, *349*
fresh stage 346, *346*, 347, *347*, **349**, *349*
green bottle fly *(Lucilia sericata)* 354, 355, 358, *358*
insect types 348, *350*
isomegalen diagram 355–356, *356*, 380
larval biotherapy 357, *357*
maximum temperature (T_{max}) 355
minimum temperature (T_{min}) 355
myiasis 357, 380
PMI *see* post-mortem interval (PMI)
post-decay stage 346, *346*, *347*, **349**, *349*
rigor mortis 250, 255, 258, 298, 346, 351, 381
scanning electron micrograph 353
scavengers 349, *350*
seasonal differences 347
spiracles 351, 353, 381
decay of fire 553
decedent 260
deciduous teeth 313, 332
    "baby"/temporary teeth 313, *314*, *315*
deep learning 716, *717*
deflagrations 566, *566*
DeForrest, Henry 10
delta 195
de-multiplexing 675
denaturation 132–134, 152
density **583**, 583–585
dental stone 640
deoxyribose sugar 117, *117*, *118*
Department of Justice (DoJ) 7
depth of focus (depth of field) 91
dermis 193
The Detection Club 18, 19
detonation 564, 574
diazodinitrophenol (DDNP) 568
digital evidence 713
digital fingerprint scanner *200*
dihydrogen monoxide (DHMO) *63*
dimethyltryptamine (DMT) 365
diminished capacity 740, *740*
dioxygen 552
direct lighting *640*
Disaster Mortuary Operational Response Team (DMORT) 276, 276–277
dissecting microscope *see* stereomicroscopy
disulfide bonds (biopolymers) 217
Dixon's *Q*-test *see Q*-test
DNA *114*, *120*, 121, 141–142
    analysis *13*, 19
    applications *see* forensic applications of DNA
    background 116
    body fluid analysis 150
    cases for study 150–151
    Combined DNA Index System 144–146
    complex DNA mixtures 150

    evidence 6, 7, 113, 114
    functioning as coding for life 122–124
    as genetic record 113–114
    genome and DNA tandem repeats 124–126
    Innocence Project 146
    methylation 149, *150*
    microbial forensics 147–149
    mitochondrial 141–143, *141–144*
    pattern 33
    persistence 149–150
    phenotyping 140, *141*
    plant and animal DNA typing 143
    polymer 117, *118*, 119, 121, 124
    polymerase 133
    RNA analysis 150
    structure 116–119, 121–122
    technology 13
    tracking and surveillance 150
    transfer 149–150
    X chromosome analysis 150
    Y-chromosome typing 142–143
D'Nealian cursive script *652*
documentation 640
    analytical methods 667
    forensic 650–684
    handwriting analysis 652–655
    obliterated writing 665, *669*
    origin of, determining *651*
    printed 660–665, *661–664*
    questioned 652
documents
    printed 660–665, *661–664*
dot-matrix printer 661, *664*
Doyle, Arthur C. 13, 15, 17, 64
    Adventure of the Blanched Soldier, The 18
    Adventure of the Cardboard Box, The 15
    Study in Scarlet, A 13
drag 624
driving under the influence (DUI) action 38
driving while impaired (DWI) action 38
drowning 272–273, *272*
duality of nature 105
ductility 591
Duguay, Shirley 150
dye 608
dynamic loads **691**, 691–692, *692*, *694*
dynamite *565*, 568–569

eccrine glands 193
ecology
    biomes 336, *336*, 380
    and botany 337, 358–365, 380
    classification of life 340–342, *341*
    ecosystem 334, *335*, 336, 337, *338*, 340, 380
    entomology 337, 342–358, 380
    exoskeleton 342, 380
    five kingdoms 341, *341*
    and geology 337
    investigations in 336, 337–340
    and mycology 337, 369–374, 380
    and palynology 337, 365–369
    PMI *see* post-mortem interval (PMI)
    proxy indicators 337, *338*, 367, 381
    and sedimentology 337
    systematics (taxonomy) 340, 358
    and taxonomy 340, 342, 358, 381
    and zoology 337, 373–375
economic abuse 729
ectoderm 190
edema 260
Einstein, Albert 60

elastic collision 701
elastomers 226–227
electrical properties 591
electric current 81
electromagnetic (EM) radiation *86*, 93, *94*, 281
electromagnetic (EM) spectrum 85, *86*
electronic methods 44
electron microscopy 104–106, *105*, *106*, 108–109
    basics 104–106
        scanning electron microscopes 106, *106–109*
        transmission electron microscopy *106*, 108, *109*
electrostatic detection apparatus (ESDA) 665, 667, *670*
embolism 260
emergency circumstances 38
emergency medical treatment (EMT) 42, *42*
Encyclopedia of DNA Elements (ENCODE) Project 121
energetic materials 563
energy capture cycle *544*
energy dispersive X-ray analysis (EDXA) 106, *108*, 109
engineering 698
English Law 36
English system (measurement) 82, 111
Enron Computers 714
entomology 9
    ADD *see* accumulated degree-days (ADD/°D)
    arthropods *see* arthropods
    beetle 342–357, **349**, *349*, *350*, 353, 380
    chitin 342, 380
    decay, studies on *see* decay, studies on
    maggot mass 348, *348*, 355, 356, 380
    and medicolegal 347–358, 380
    oviposition 347, 351, 380
    puparium *345*, 351, 381
entrance/exit wound 270–272
environmental forensic evidence 591–597
    forensic geology 592
    soil 592–596
enzyme 115, 116, 124, 128, 134, 153, 164
enzyme linked immunosorbent assay (ELISA) 168–169, *169*
enzyme multiplied immunoassay technique (EMIT) 167–168, *168*
epidermis 193
epigenetics 148, 149, *150*
equivocal deaths 746, **746**
error bars 68, *69*
erythrocytes *see* red blood cells (RBC)
ethics in forensic science 72–73
ethyl ether 557
eumelanin 209
event 70
evidence
    characteristics 33
    definition 29
evidence collection 41–50
    crime scene processing 41–47
    crime scene types 50
    and evidence team 48–50
    and law 34–39
    and packaging 46, 47, *47*, **48**
    precedent cases for 40–41
    and preservation 45–47
evidence teams 48–50
    photographer 48–49
    recovery and recorder personnel 49–50
    sketch/map preparer 49

specialists 50
team leader 48
exclusionary rule 37
exemplars 31, 33, 41, 655
exothermic combustion process 547
expectation bias 74
experimentation 72
expert testimony 23, *23*, 25–27
explosions 551
    damage from 571–572
    physical 563
    types of 564
explosive(s)
    analysis of evidence 572, 574
    chemical 564, 566–567
    definition 563
    electron microscopic analysis of 572–573
    evidence collection 572
    high **567**, 568–571
    low 567–568
    reactions 545
    spectroscopic methods for 572
extension 133
external (intermediate) ballistics 624, *624*, *625*
extrinsic properties 583, **583**
eyewitness testimony 10

facial reconstruction 211, 332
    biological profile 318
    computer-based digital 320
    DNA phenotyping 140, *141*
    hand-drawn *319*
    John Emil List Case 330
    magnetic resonance imaging 288, 291–292
    overlay process, using 318–319, *319*, 327, 343
    problems with 319
    3D 318, 319, *319*, 324
    tissue depth markers, using 318–320, *320*
    2D 318, *319*
factor of safety (FS) 694, 719
facts 85
Fairchild, Lydia 126, 127
Fairley, M. 610
false science 53
falsifiability 72
familial DNA 140, **140**
fatal pressures 572
fatigue fracture 692, *692*
Faulds, Henry 10
Federal Bureau of Investigation (FBI) 12, 37, 145
Federal Circuit Court of Appeals 23
Federal Rules of Evidence (1975) 25, 74
feedback process *547*
Feynman, Richard 54
fiber analysis 224
    classification of *232*
    collections of fibers in larger pieces 232–233, *233–235*
    definition of 224, *224*
    forensic analysis 231–232
    natural fibers 224–225, *225*
    polymer fibers, forming 230, 231
    polymers 227–230, *227–231*
    regenerated fibers 226, *226*
    synthetic fibers 226, 226–227
fictitious signature 660
field of view 91
Fierstein, Stuart 5
fine motor skills 652
fingermark *see* fingerprint
fingernails

forensic nails use 223, *224*
    growth of *222*, 222–223
fingerprint(s) 8, 10, *637*, 189–190
    Automated Fingerprint Identification System 192, *193*
    background *191*, 191–192
    comparison of 197–199, *198*
    development and structures of *194*, 194–195, *195*
    digital fingerprint scanner *200*
    ear and lip pattern evidence 208, *208*, *209*
    impression (plastic) prints 205, *205*
    Integrated Automated Fingerprint Identification System 199
    latent prints 200–204, *203–204*
    legal challenges to evidence 205–207
    lifting 205, *205*
    Next Generation Identification System 199, *200*
    observing patterns 200–205
    palm- and footprint evidence 207, *207*
    patterns 32, 33, 195–197, *196–197*
    for personal identification 10, *190*
    recognition *32*
    skin 193–194, *194*
    3D scanned digital fingerprint *201*
    uses of 199–200, *201*
    visible prints 200, *202–203*
    visualized, preserving 205, *205–206*
fire *542*
    analyzing evidence in laboratory 560–562
    components 548, *549*, 552
    definition 541
    dynamics 552–553
    initiation, growth, decay, and suppression 548–552
    investigation 554–558
    related deaths 547, 548
    related injuries 273–274, *274*
    scene 558, 560
    stages 553–554
    tetrahedron 548, *549*, 552, 553, 555
    types 551–552
firearm(s) 613–646
    air guns 622–623
    ballistics 624–626, *624–626*, 634, *634*
    basics 617–618
    buller comparisons 626–628, *627*, *628*
    definition 617
    forensic identification of 613, 626–636
    forensic impression evidence 637–646
    ghost guns 619
    gunshot residues 630–632, *631–633*
    handguns 618–619, *619*
    historical perspective 613–617, *614–617*
    injuries 268–272, *269–272*
    Integrated Ballistic Identification System 634
    long guns 619–621, *620*, *621*
    National Integrated Ballistics Information Network 634, *635*
    serial number restoration *633*, 633–634
    shotguns 621–622, *622*
    stria comparisons 629–630, *629–631*
    weapons, relative use of *614*
first responders 41, 42, *42*
fixed ammunition 616
flame, definition 542
flammability limits 550, 551, 568, 576
flashover 553, *555*
flash point 549, **550**, 551
flintlock weapons 615, *615*

float glass method *599*, 599–600
flotation 583–584, *584*, *585*
fluid dynamics 158
fluorescein 165
fluorescence 96, 165
fluorescence microscopy 96–98, *97*
fluorescent dyes 97
fluorochrome acridine orange *102*
Folstein test 745
font 660
    printing *661*
    size *662*
footprints *637*, *638*, 641, *642*, *643*
force 701, *701*, 719
forensic applications of DNA **116**, 127–140
    DNA phenotyping 140, *141*
    familial DNA 140, **140**
    mini-STR 138–139
    polymerase chain reaction (PCR)-based STR
        methods 132–134
    restriction fragment length polymorphism
        128–131
    short tandem repeats typing 135–138
    single nucleotide polymorphisms 138–139,
        139
forensic ballistics testing *31*
forensic engineering and crime scene
        reconstruction 698–710, *699–701*,
        703–709
    forensic vehicular accident reconstruction
        699, 699–700, *700*
forensic engineering failure analysis 689–698
    structural failure analysis 690–695, **691**, *691*
    system failure analysis 695–697
forensic evidence 6, 7, 19, 26, 30, 40, 79
forensic failure analysis 690–695, **691**, *691*
forensic science
    definition 8
    early development 9
    history 8–13
forensic sociology 725–726
forensic spectroscopy
    antibonding 449, *449*, 450, *451*, 474
    atomic absorption spectroscopy and *see*
        atomic absorption spectroscopy
        (AAS)
    atomic emission spectroscopy *see* atomic
        emission spectroscopy (AES)
    atomic fluorescence spectroscopy *see* atomic
        fluorescence spectroscopy (AFS)
    Balmer series 436, *437*, 474
    Bohr, Niels 433–434, 435
    characteristic wavelengths 440
    electromagnetic radiation in *428*, 428–430,
        474
    electromagnetic waves in *429*
    electron-nuclear attractions *448*
    ESCA spectroscopy 447
    excited state 436, 439, 474
    fragmentation 429, *457*, *461*, *462*
    frequency 429, 475
    gas discharge tube in, use of *427*
    ground state 436, *437*, 438, 475
    Heisenberg uncertainty principle 432, 475
    Herschel, William 424
    infrared spectroscopy application in 453–455,
        475
    and instrumental analysis 423
    Kirchhoff, Gustav 427
    "life-sized" analogies 430
    Lyman series 436, *437*

non-quantized **431**
nuclear-nuclear repulsions *448*
orbitals 448, *449*, 475
Paschen series 436, *437*
photon and 428
quantized 430, *431*, *435*
quantum mechanics in 426, 428, 430–431,
    475
radiocarbon dating 470–473, *472*, 475
radiochemical analysis 469–473
retention times 464
Rydberg constant 436
spectrum 424, *437*
standing waves 434, *434*, *435*
ultraviolet-visible spectroscopy *see*
    ultraviolet-visible spectroscopy
    (UV-vis)
use of neutron activation analysis in *see*
    neutron activation analysis (NAA)
use of paradox in 426
wavelength 428, *428*, 475
forensic testimony *7*
forged signature 658, *659*
forgery 652
    detecting 660
    intentional 660
    traced 659–660
fossil fuels 551
Fourth Amendment to the U.S. Constitution
    36–41
    new technology and 37
frame averaging 675
France, Louis-Charles de 151
Franklin, Rosalind 116
French Secret Service 11
frequency 680
frictional factors, in real life 702
friction coefficient 702, 706
friction ridges 194
fruit of the poisonous tree doctrine 37
Frye, James 23
Frye case 6, 23–25, 53
Frye Standard 25, 26
fuel 551
fuel oils 557
fuel suppression 553
full development/active fire stage of fire 553
fully automatic weapon 618
fuming fingerprint visualization (cyanoacrylate)
    204
furrows 195

gall bladder 263, *264*
Galton, Francis 10
gas chromatograms *565*
gas chromatograph-mass spectrometry (GC/MS)
    560–562, 572
gasoline 557
gauge 623
Gaussian distribution *see* normal distribution
gel electrophorsis 129, *129*, 130, *130*, *131*, 135
gene 119, 121, *123*, 124
General Electric Co. v. Joiner (1995) 26
general hydrocarbon combustion 542
genome 119, 121, 124–126
geology 592
    forensic 592
    high flying 596–597
ghost guns 619
glass 598–601
    amorphous *598*

blown 599, *599*
borosilicate 599
bullet-generated fractures in *605*
case study 604
crater formation in *603*
crystalline *598*
float *599*, 599–600
flow 599
forensic characterization of 601–604,
    602–604
fractures *603*
laminated 600, *601*
particles, in headlamp filament *606*
rolled 600, *600*
soda-lime 599
tempered 600, *600*
glowing combustion *see* smoldering
glycoprotein 170
Goddard, Henry 10
Golden Gate Bridge, San Francisco
    failure of 692
Golden State Killer 140
good science 53, 54
GPS system 709, *709*
GPS tracking device 37
gradient column 583, *584*
graphology *vs.* forensic document analysis 653
gravitational acceleration 624, *625*
Great Escape, The (1963) 684
Green River Killer 151
grooves 620, 623
Gross, Hans 10
    Criminal Investigation 10
Grubbs test *see* G-test
G-test 69
guanine 119
gun mechanics 614–615
gunpowder 613–616, 614, 618, *618*, *623*, 626, 631
gunshot 270–271
gunshot residues (GSR) *107*, 630–632, *631–633*

hair analysis 208
    comparison and identification 221–222
    composition 209
    diseases involving 218, *219*
    and fur 208–222
    growth *214–215*, 214–216
    sex and ancestry differences in hair structure
        216, *216*
    structure 209–214, *209–214*
    toxicology 218–220
    treatment 217–218, *217–219*
Halon 553
Halstead-Reitan Neuropsychological Battery
    (HRNB) 745
hammer 623
handguns 618–619
    fully automatic 618
    magazine *619*
    semi-automatic 618, *619*
    typical *619*
handheld hydrocarbon detector *561*
handwriting 650
    analysis 652–655
    arrangement 654
    arrhythmic *654*
    comparisons 655–657
    content 655
    definition 652
    grammer 655
    legal challenges 669–673

letter comparison table **656**, **657**
line locations of 653
pressure and thickness of lines 654–655
quality 654–655
questioned signatures 658–660
rhythm of 653–654
size of 654
slope of 653, *654*
spacing of letters, words, and lines 654
spelling 655
style 653, *653*
syntax 655
hardness *591*
hashing 715
heart 262, *262*
heat 548
heat of combustion 543
heat release rate (HRR) 553, *556*
heat suppression 553
heat transfer *554*
Heisenberg's Uncertainty Principle 5, 83
hematoma 260
hemoglobin 159
Henry, Edward 10
Henry system 195
Herschel, William 10
heterozygous 126
high degree of certainty 33, 34
high-density polyethylene (HDPE) 607, *607*
high flying geology 596–597
high-velocity impact spatter (HVIS) 177
Hinckley, J. 738, 739
Hindenburg German airship 544, *545*
Hitler diaries 657–658
HMX (octogen/
     cyclotetramethylene-tetranitramine)
     568, 571
homicide 250
homozygous 126
Hsi Duan Yu ("Washing Away of
     Wrongs"/"Injustices Rectified," Sung
     T'ze) 9, 343
human digestive system *680*
Human Genome Project (HGP) 124, 125
human skeletal anatomy 301–303, *302*, *303*
     allometric relationships 309
     anterior (ventral/front) 301, *306*, 332
     appendicular 302, *306*, 310, 332
     axial 302, 306, 310, 332
     cartilage *see* cartilage
     collagen *see* collagen
     compact bone 301–303, *301–303*, 308, *308*,
          321, 332
     cribra orbitalia 318
     endoskeleton 301, 332
     facial reconstruction *see* facial reconstruction
     hydroxyapatite *see* hydroxyapatite
          [$Ca_{10}(PO_4)_6(OH)_2$]
     ligaments 303, *311*, 332
     ossification 312, 332
     post-mortem interval *see* post-mortem
          interval (PMI)
     pubic symphysis 311
     sexual dimorphism 310, 333
     spongy bone *302*, 302–304, *303*, 333
     tendons *see* tendons
     types of bones *305*
hybridization 131, 134
hydrocarbons 541, 556
hydrogen bonding 119, *119*
hydroperoxide radical 552

hydroxyapatite [$Ca_{10}(PO_4)_6(OH)_2$] 301, 332
hyperspectral imaging 667, *669*, *671*
hypervariable regions *see* non-coding regions
hypnosis 735
hypodermis *see* subcutaneous layer

identification analysis 30–31, 716
identification *vs.* authentication 199–200
Identifiler™ *138*
illegally-seized evidence 37
illegal search 37
illicit drug use 13
immunoassay 167
immunology 158
impression evidence
     basics 637–641
     bite marks 644–645, *645*
     castings 640
     documentation 640
     footprints *637*, *638*, 641, *642*, *643*
     forensic 637–646
     latent 639, *640*
     lifting 640–641
     negative image 638, *639*
     photography 639–640, *640*
     plastic 639
     positive image 637, *638*
     three-dimensional impression 638–639, *639*
     tool marks 642–644, *643–645*
     types of 637
     visible 639
impression (plastic) fingerprints 205, *205*
incipient stage of fire 553
incision 260
indented writing 665, *670*
individual evidence characteristics 33, 34, *34*, *35*
indoor scenes 50
inductively coupled plasma-mass spectrometry
     (ICP-MS) 601
inelastic collision 701
informatics 716
infrared (IR) light 98
infrared (IR) microscopy 98, *98*, *99*
infrared radiation (IR) 98
infrared spectroscopy 572, 667
Infrastructure-as-a-Service (IaaS) 716
inkjet printer 661
insane suicide 746–747
Integrated Automated Fingerprint Identification
     System (IAFIS) 199
Integrated Ballistic Identification System (IBIS)
     634
integumentary system 193
intellectual and cognitive function tests 744
intentional forgery 660
internal (initial) ballistics 624
International Personality Item Pool (IPIP) 744
internet 713
Internet of Things (IoT) 713
intrinsic properties 583, **583**
inventory searches 39
inverted cone burn pattern 558, *560*
iodine 204
IPIP *see* International Personality Item Pool
irreversible process 700–701
ischemia 159

January 6, 2020 insurrection video analysis 677
Jeffreys, Alec 6, 114, *115*
Johnson, Denise 146–147
Jones, Antoine 37

Journal of Forensic Science 109
Julius Caesar
     homicide investigation of 8
jury selection 735–736
justice, definition 5

Kastle-Meyer test 164, *164*
Kenniwick man case 151
keratin 209
Khumo Tire case 26
Khumo Tire Company 26
kidney 263, *266*
kieselguhr (diatomaceous earth) 570
kinetic energy (KE) 270, 546, 624, 700–702, 704,
     706, 719
Kossel, Albrecht 116

Lacassagne, Alexandre 10
laceration 260
Lacquer coatings 609
*La Faune des cadavres: Application de
     l'entomologie à la médicine légale*
     ("The Fauna of corpses: Application
     of entomology to forensic medicine",
     Megnin, J. P.) 343
laminated glass 600, *601*
lands 620, 623
Langer, W. C. 732
large intestines 263
larynx *681*
laser printer 661
laser printing *664*
latent fingerprints 200–204, *203–204*
latent impressions 639, *640*
law *vs.* science 5
lead azide 568
lead styphnate 568
Leeuwenhoek, Anton van 87
legal competence 737
legal evidence 34–41
     evidence collection and law 34–39
     precedent cases for evidence collection 40–41
legal insanity 738
legal precedents *22*, 22–23, 26
legal system 5, 7
legitimate expectation of privacy 36, 37
legitimate vehicular violation 37
Leica Viva TS16 total station *698*
length 80
letters
     comparison table **656**, **657**
     shape of 653, *654*
leucocytes *see* white blood cells (WBC)
levels of certainty and proof **64**
lie detector test 6, 23, *24*
lifting 640–641
ligature 260
light intensity 81
light microscope components 88–89, *90*
     arm and base 88
     condenser 88
     focus adjustment 88
     illumination system 88
     objective lens 88
     ocular (eyepiece) lens 88
     sample stage 88
     tube/body 88
light to chemical energy conversion 543, *543*
likelihood ratio (LR) 70–72, **71**
linear burn pattern 558, *559*
linguistics 650

forensic 682–684
linkage analysis 734
lip marks *637*
live loads *see* dynamic loads
liver 263, *264*
lividity 255
livor mortis 255
load capacity 695
Locard, Edmund 10–12, *11*, 18, 56
    Treatise on Criminalistics 11
Locard's Exchange Principle 11–12, 20–21, 29
Lockerbie bombing crime scene 43
locus 121, 136, 137, 139, 144, 145
logical analysis 9, 54, 55
long guns 619–621, *620*, *621*
loop pattern 195
Lopatka, S.
    homicide 712
Lord Kelvin 56, 79, 80
Los Angeles Police Department 12
Louis XVI (king) 151
low-density polyethylene (LDPE) 607, *607*
low-velocity impact spatter (LVIS) 177
luminol 164–165
lungs 262–263, *263*
Luria-Nebraska Neuropsychological Battery
        (LNNB) 745
Lyon Police Department 10

machine learning (ML) 716, *717*
magazine *619*, 624
magic 3D glasses 94
magnetic resonance imaging (MRI) 287–293,
        289–293
magnification power 90
magnum 624
malingering 740
Malvo, Lee Boyd 104
Mann, Lynda 114
manner of death 250–252, 250–253, **252**
Margin of Safety (MoS) 694–695, 719
Marsh, James 10
Marston, William 23, *24*
mass disasters 276
mass spectrometry 667
matrilineal inheritance 141, *142*
McNaughten Rule 738
McVeigh, Timothy 574
median 66–67, *67*
medical death investigation
    autopsy 260–262
    brain 266–268, *268–269*
    cause of death 253–257, *253–257*
    heart 262, *262*
    information from autopsy *259*, 259–260
    kidneys, bladder, and urinary system 263, *266*
    liver and gall bladder 263, *264*
    lungs 262–263, *263*
    major organ systems examining 262–268
    manner of death 250–252, 250–253, **252**
    neck 265, *268*
    pancreas 265, *267*
    requirement of autopsy 257–258, **258**, *258*
    sex organs 265–266
    spleen and lymph system 264, *267*
    stomach and intestines 263, *265*
medical examiner 249
medicolegal death investigations 245–247,
        246–248
medicolegal practice 247–249, *248*
medium velocity impact spatter (MVIS) 177

medulla 212
medullary canal *see* medulla
medullary index (MI) 212
Megnin, J. P.
    *La Faune des cadavres: Application de
        l'entomologie à la médicine légale*
        ("The Fauna of corpses: Application
        of entomology to forensic medicine")
        343
al-Megrahi, Abdul 43
melanin 209
Melendez-Dias case 26–27, *27*
mens rea 728, 739, 740
mental state at the time of the offense (MSO) 738
Merrell Dow Pharmaceutical Company 25
"Metal Storm" weapon 617
Metesky, G. 732, 733
Michigan v. Tyler 40, *40*
microbial forensics 147–149
    in warfare 148
Miescher, Johann 116
Miller Baseball Park, MIlwaukee
    crane collapse 693–694
Mincy v. Arizona 40
mineral spirits 557
minimization 730
minimum number of individuals (MNI) 326
minimum speed formula 705
mini-STR 138–139
Minnesota Multiphasic Personality Inventory
        (MMPI) 744
minutiae 197
mitochondrial DNA (mtDNA) 139, 141–142,
        141–144
mode 67, *67*
modus operandi (MO) 735
mole **617**
Molotov Cocktail *562*
momentum 719
    conservation of 706–709, *707*, *708*
    definition 706
monoclonal antibody(ies) 169, *170*
monomers 227
Morrison, Arthur 19
most likely number of individuals (MLNI) 326
motivational biases 73
Muhammad, John Allen 104
multilayer automotive paint chip *609*
multiplexed images 675
multiplexing 137
Murders in the Rue Morgue, The (Poe) 14
mutations 125
muzzle 624
muzzle-loading firearms 615, 616
mycology
    "corpse-finder" mushroom *(Hebeloma
        radicosum)* 371, *371*
    The Crucible 371
    "death cap" *(Amanita phalloides)* 369, *370*,
        371
    ergotamine *372*, 373
    "European destroying angel" *(Amanita
        virosa)* 369, *370*
    fungi 369–373
    Italian white alba truffle *(Tuber magnatum)*
        369, *370*
    Miller, Arthur 371
    Monerans 342, 380
    PMI *see* post-mortem interval (PMI)
    "shaggy ink cap" *(Coprinus comatus)* 371,
        371

T2 toxin 371
Mystery of Marie Roget, The (Poe) 14

National Association of Medical Examiners
        (NAME) 73
National Code of Ethics and Professional
        Responsibility for the Forensic
        Sciences 73
National Commission on Forensic Science, of
        U.S. Department of Justice (DoJ) 73
National Integrated Ballistics Information
        Network (NIBIN) 634, *635*
National Library of Medicine, at National
        Institutes of Health *14*
National Research Council (NRC), of National
        Academies of Science 74
National Science Foundation (NSF) 60
national security 39
natural death 250
natural fibers 224–225, *225*
natural fires 558
natural language processing (NLP) 717
negative image 638, *639*
NEO PI-R test 744
network forensics 715–716
Neufeld, Peter 146
neurobiological psychology 726
neutron activation analysis (NAA) 445–446,
        446, 475
Newton's cradle 706, *707*
Newton's third law 706
Next Generation Identification System (NGI)
        199, *200*
next generation sequencing (NGS) 149
Nichols, Terry 574
ninhydrin 203–204
NIST 682
nitroglycerin *565*, 569, 570
nitroglycerine 551
Nobel, Alfred 568, 570
Nobel, Emil 570
non-coding regions 121, 122, 124–126
non-overlapping 137
non-radical molecule 552
non-request exemplar 656
non-routine search 39
normal distribution 67
nucleic acids 116
nuclein 116
nucleotides 116, *117*, 119, 135
numerical aperture (NA) 91

oblique lighting *640*
obliterated writing 665, *669*
occult blood 156
OCEAN test 744
Oklahoma City bombing 574
one-to-many matching strategy 31, *31*, 32, *32*, 716
operating system 713
Operation "Sailor Hat" *566*
optical microscopy 89, *91*, 91–92
optical properties 589–590, *590*
Orczy, Baroness Emma 19
Orfila, Mathieu 10
orientation *546*
osteoarthritis 316, 332
    degenerative disease *284*
    in hip joint 316
    knee *284*
    by mechanical wear and tear 316
outcomes 70

outdoor scenes 50
out of phase waves 95, *96*
oxidant (oxidizing agent) 541
oxidant suppression 553
oxidation *542*, 543, 545, *546*, 548
oxidizer 550, 551
oxygen 543, 550

paints 607–611
    coatings, types of *609*
    composition *608*, 608–609, *609*
    forensic analysis 610–611
    solvent 608
palimpsest *671*
palmprint 207
Palo Verde tree case 146–147
palynology
    anemophilous plants 367
    anther 366, 368, 380
    autogamous plants 368
    Locard's principle in 366
    palynomorphs 365–367, 369, 380
    pollen fingerprint use in 367
    pollen structure 366, *367*
    SEM photomicrograph *366*
    sporopollen in 365
    and zoogamous plants 368
Pan Am Flight 103 43, *43*
pancreas 265
panoramic mosaic *676*
partition 713
passive bloodstains *176*, 176–177
pat down search 39
pathology 248
pencil
    refractive index of *587*
pentaerythritol (PETN) 571, *573*
People v. Rosario 41
"Pepper-box" revolver 615, *616*
percussion cap 615, *616*
perimortem 255
permanent cavity damage (tissue crush) 269
permanent teeth 314, *314*, *315*
peroxidase 164
persistent data 713
personal biases 73
personal identification authentication *32*
personality inventories 744, *744*
personal safety *49*
petroglyphs *651*
petroleum oil, viscosities of *587*
Phadebas reagent 182
phase contrast microscopy 95–96, *96*
pheomelanin 209
phosphatidylcholine liposomes *102*
photocopiers 662, 665, *666–669*
photography 44, *46*, 639–640, *640*
    forensic analysis 676–679, *677–679*
photons 93
photosynthesis 543, *543*
phrenology *54*
physical abuse 729
physical detectors 86
physical evidence 3, 5, 9, 30
physical properties
    in evidence **581**, 581–591
pica 660
picture drawing tests 743, *743*
pigment 608, *608*
Pikes Peak National Forest 563
pinnascopy 208

Pitchfork, Colin 114
Pitt, William 35
plain view doctrine 37, 39
plane polarized light 93, 94, *94*
plant and animal DNA typing 143
plasma (blood) 159
plastic impressions 639
plastics 604–607
platelets 162
Platforms-as-a-Service (PaaS) 716
Plus PCR Amplification Kit *138*
Poe, Edgar Allan 14
    Murders in the Rue Morgue, The 14
    Mystery of Marie Roget, The 14
    Purloined Letter, The 14, *15*
polarized light applications 94–95, *95*
polarized light microscopy 93–95, *95*
polarizing lens 94, 98
Poll, Harris 63
polygonal rifling 620–621, *621*
polymer 116
polymerase chain reaction (PCR)-based STR
            methods 127, 128, 132–134, 136
polymer(s) 227–230, *227–231*
    chemical and physical properties of *606*,
            606–607
    fibers 230, *231*
polymorphisms 126
population frequency 136
positive image 637, *638*
positron emission tomography (PET) 280
post-mortem 255
post-mortem interval (PMI) 150, 255, 384
    in bloodstain pattern analysis 176
    degradation of different types of RNA, role
            in 150, 176
    examination of RNA in gene expression, role
            in 150
    in forensic anthropology 321
    in forensic botany 360–361, 364
    in forensic ecology 334–336, *355*, 380
    in forensic entomology 351–357, *355*, *356*
    in forensic medicine 254–257, *255*, 298
    in forensic mycology 369–370
    in forensic serology 155
    in forensic taphonomy 327–329
    in forensic zoology 378
    in RNA analysis 150
    time of death, in analysis of 254–255, *255*,
            298, 321, 351, 360
potassium chlorate (KClO$_3$) 567
potential energy 543
powder 624
precedent cases 22, 23
    for evidence collection 40–41
precision, concept of 83, *83*, 84
prejudicial *vs.* probative evidence 30
presumptive test 163–164
primary explosives 568, *570*
primary injuries 572
primer 624
principle of analysis 21
principle of comparison 21
Principle of Individuality (principle of
            uniqueness) 20, 21
principle of persistency 192
principle of progressive change 21
printed documents 660–665, *661–664*
printer forensics 661–662, *664*
printing 650
privacy intrusions 36

private security officer 36
probability in forensic analysis 64, *65*, 70–72, *71*
    definition 70
    event 70
    likelihood ratio 70–72, **71**
    outcomes 70
    theoretical probabilities 70
probable cause, definition 37
probative *vs.* prejudicial evidence 30
Project Innocence 146
projection 730
projective tests 741–743
propellants 563
pro se competence *737*, 737–738
proximal cause of death *see* contributing cause
            of death
proxy indicators 592
pseudoscience 5, 6, 55, *62*
    based on hearsay 60–61
    definition 59–60
    exaggerated/untestable claims 60
    examples 60
    filling voids of scientific understanding 62
    ideas 63
    not lead to new discoveries/knowledge 62–63
    random disregard of facts/data 61
    reliance on confirmatory experiments 61
    reluctance toward experimentation and
            reproducibility 61
    rely on false authority 62
    vs. science 53, **58**, *61*
    use of terminology 62
psychiatrists 727
psychological autopsy 14
psychological autopsy (PA) **746**, 746–747
    definition 746
    equivocal deaths 746, **746**
    goals of **747**
    uses of **746**
psychological/emotional abuse 729
psychologists 727
psychology *725*, 725–726, *726*, *732*
    applications of 727, 728
    Brian fingerprinting 735
    civil applications of 727
    clinical 726, 727
    cognitive 726
    crime scene analysis 728–729
    criminal applications of 727
    eyewitnesses 731
    false concessions 731
    forensic 725–747
    hypnostic 735
    interrogations 729–731, *731*
    interviews 729–731
    journals 726
    neurobiological 726
    post-trial uses of 741
    pretrial uses of 728–735
    profiling 731–735, *732*, 733
    psychological autopsy **746**, 746–747
    testing 741, 741–745
    trial uses of 735–741
    victimology 729
puncture wound 260
Purloined Letter, The (Poe) 14, *15*
Pyrex brand 599

Q-test 69–70
quack testimony 5, 6
quantity 81

quantum mechanics 105
questioned documents 652
questioned signatures 658–660
Quintillian 8

radial cracks 602, *602*, 603
radical chain reaction 552, *552*
radiograph 283
radioimmunoassay (RIA) 168
radiology *277*, 277–278
    biomedical imaging, history of 278–280, *278–281*
    CT imaging 285–287, *286–288*
    forensic uses of medical X-rays 283–285, *284–286*
    in investigations 281
    magnetic resonance imaging 287–293, *289–293*
    X-ray imaging methods 281–283, *282–283*
Raman spectroscopy 667
Ramsey, JonBenét 139
random error 83, *83*, 84
randon access memory (RAM) 713, *714*
range 68
rate of chemical reaction 546, 556
rationalization 730, *730*
RDX (cyclotrimethylenetrinitramine) 568, 569, 571
read only memory (ROM) 713
real *vs.* virtual image 88, *90*
red blood cells (RBC) *155*, 159–161
reduction *542*
reference sample *see* exemplar
refraction 87, 586
refractive index (RI) 586–589, *587–589*
    of transparent materials **588**
regenerated fibers 226, *226*
Reid, Richard 574
reid technique 731
relevant evidence 29, 30, 44
renewable resource 551
reproductive system 265–266
request examplar 656
resolving power 89–90
Resonance Raman spectroscopy 572
restriction enzymes 128–131, *129*
restriction fragment length polymorphism (RFLP) 125, 127, 128, 128–131
    vs. STR DNA typing methods **138**
retina structure 86, *87*, *88*
reverse engineering 696
revolvers 618, *619*
rheumatoid arthritis 316, *316*
rhythm 653–654
ribonucleic acid (RNA) 116, 119, 150
ribose sugar *118*
ribosome 119
ridge 195
ridge count 195
ridge ending point 197
Ridgway, Gary 151
rifling 619–620, 624
    polygonal 620–621, *621*
right to bear arms 626
rigor mortis 255
ring precipitin test 167
ripped pieces of paper *672*
rod cells 86
rolled glass 600, *600*
roof truss

types of *696*
Roosevelt, Theodore 12
root canal procedure 109
Rorschach test 742, *742*
round 616
Royal Society of Chemistry, United Kingdom 18
Russian Czars 145

Saco, N. 636
saliva 182, *183*
sample *vs.* population 65
SARS-CoV-2 pandemic 148
satellite spatter 176
Sayers, Dorothy L. 19
scanning electron microscope (SEM) 106, *106–109*, 714
Scheck, Barry 146
science
    in criminal investigations 10, 11
    definition 54–55
    vs. law 5, *5*
    vs. pseudoscience 53, **58**, *61*
    tools 54
scientific concepts 54
scientific evidence 3, 5, 7, 18, 23–25, *25*, 53
scientific inquiry 12, 53, 56, 74
scientific jury selection (SJS) 736
scientific knowledge 25
scientific methods 5, 10, 14, 25, 54–59, *59*, 72
    analysis and refinement/hypothesis abandonment 56, 58–59
    definition 55
    experimentation 56–58
    and forensic science 59
    hypothesis 56
    observation 56
    prediction 56
scientific system 5
scientific testimony 23, 25
scientific theory/law 59
scientific validity 23, 60, 63, 208
Scientific Working Group on Digital Evidence (SWGDE) 713
Scientific Working Group on Imaging Technology (SWGIT) 676
script handwriting *652*
search and seizure 36, *36*, 38
searches during legal arrests 38
search patterns 44, *47*
search warrant 36, 36–40, *38*
sea searches 39
sebaceous glands 210
secondary explosives 568
secondary injuries 572
secretor 182
selection bias 74
semen 182–183
semi-automatic weapon 618, *619*
seminal acid phosphatase 183
serial number restoration *633*, 633–634
serology 155
serum (blood) 159
sexual abuse 729
sharp force trauma (SFT) 260, 268, 273, 298, 323–324, *324*, 333
    in bloodstain analysis 177
sheet glass
    refractive index of 588, *589*
Sherlock Holmes (fictional character) 13, 14, *16*, 17–18, *20*

The Sherlock Holmes Museum, Baker Street *15*
shock waves 564, *571*, 571–572, **572**
short tandem repeats (STR) 70, *125*, 126, *126*, 132–134, *136*, *137*, 142
    vs. RFLP **138**
shot 621
shotguns 621–622, *622*
shrapnel 614
SICAR 641
Sickle cell anemia 163
sight 624
signature
    cut-and-paste 660
    fictitious 660
    forged 658, *659*
    questioned 658–660
    simulated 658–659
    traced forgery 659–660
significant figures 83–85, *84*
silencer 624
simulated signature 658–659
simulation 656, *657*
single nucleotide polymorphisms (SNPs) 138–139, *139*
skid 702
    equation 719
    marks 703, *703*, *704–706*
    simplied formula 719
    simplied formula with crush 719
slug 621
small intestines 263
smoke 556, *557*
smokeless powders 567
smoldering 548, *548*, 553
snake oil 60, *61*
Snell, W. 586
Snell's law 586–587
sniffers 558
Snowball the cat case 150–151
Sobrero, Ascanio 570
social abuse 729
Society of Forensic Toxicologists (SOFT) 73
sociology 725–726
soda-lime glass 599
sodium chloride crystal
    refractive index of *588*
Software-as-a-Service (SaaS) 716
soil 592–596
    components *593*
    composition *592*
    disturbed layering *596*
    examination *595*
    horizons *592*
    layers *592*
    sample collection *594*
    undistributed layering *596*
solid, refractive index of *588*
solid-phase microextraction (SPME) 562
"Son of Sam" 734
sound spectrograph 681–682
specialized forensic tests 745, *746*
specialized sample preparation techniques 105
specific disorder tests 745
spectrometers 86, *87*
specular highlights 678
spin (gyroscopic) stabilization 620, *621*
spiritual abuse 729
spleen 264
spongy bone
    irregular 302

long 302
    osteoblasts 302
    osteoclasts 302
    osteocyte 302
    trabecular/cancellous bone 302
spontaneous combustion 550
Springfield rifles 616, *617*
stab wound *see* puncture wound
staining techniques in microscopy 101–102, **102**, *102*
standard deviation (SD) 67–68, *68*
    calculating 68
    equation for 68
Standard Operating Procedures (SOPs) 58
stare decisis (system of justice) 22, 26
Stas, Jean Servais 10
states of matter 582
static image 714
static loads 691, **691**, *694*
statistics in forensic science 64–70, *65*
    average/arithmetic mean 66, *66*
    distribution 67
    error bars 68, *69*
    frequency 68
    median 66–67, *67*
    mode 67, *67*
    Q-test 69–70
    range 68
    standard deviation 67–68, *68*
stereomicroscopy 98–99, *99*, *100*
stock 624
stomach 263
stop and frisk 39
Strand Magazine, The 17
stratum basale 195
stratum corneum 194
"Strengthening Forensic Science in the United
    States: A Path Forward" 74
stress-induced striations 602, *603*
stria (striations) 627, *628*
    comparisons 629–630, *629–631*
striation marks 100, *100*
Structured Clinical Interview for DSM-IV
    Disorders (SCID) 747
Study in Scarlet, A (Doyle) 13
subcutaneous layer 189
substrate 168
subtractive color mixing 589–590, *590*
sudden and unexplained deaths (SUD) 274–275
suicide 250
Sung T'ze
    Hsi Duan Yu ("Washing Away of
        Wrongs"/"Injustices Rectified") 9, 343
super glue fuming *see* fuming fingerprint
    visualization (cyanoacrylate)
surface tension 175
surveillance cameras 673–674, *674*, *677*
sweat 184
synthetic fibers *226*, 226–227
Syracuse University 43
systematic error 83, *83*, 84
Système International d'Unités (SI) System
    80–84, *81*, **82**, *82*

Tacoma Narrows Bridge, failure of 692, *692–693*
taggant 574
tandem repeats 119, 124–126
telogen phase 215–216
temperature 80–81
tempered glass 600, *600*

temporary cavitation damage 269
tendons 333
    connecting muscles to bone 303
    sesamoid bone, embedded within 302
Ten-Item Personality inventory 744
Terahertz spectroscopy 572
terminal ballistics *625*, 625–626, *626*
Terrorist Explosive Device Analytical Center,
    FBI 13
test-fired bullet 32, *33*
testimony 3
tetrahydrocannabinol (THC) 363, 397, 508, *508*
tetrazene 568
thematic apperception test (TAT) 742, *742*
theoretical probabilities 70
therapeutic complication 252–253
thermoplastic 227
Thomure v. Truck Insurance Exchange 555–556
thoracoabdominal cavity 261
thorax 261
three-dimensional impression 638–639, *639*
3D scanned digital fingerprint *201*
thrombocytes *see* platelets
time 81
tool marks 642–644, *643–645*
Torres, Roxanne 40, 41
Torres v. Madrid 40–41
toxicology 10
    acid-catalyzed hydrolysis reactions 494
    and alcohol *see* alcohol
    anaphylaxis 485, *486*
    aspirin toxicity/overdose *484*, 490, *536*
    bioavailability 487, *487*
    blood-brain barrier 488
    "brute force" approach 493
    cannabis 363, 508–512
    chronic toxicity 483
    club/date-rape drugs *513*, 513–514, *514*
    Comprehensive Drug Abuse Prevention and
        Control Act of 1970 519
    Controlled Substance Act *see* Controlled
        Substance Act (CSA)
    CO poisoning 495, *496*
    depressants 512–514, *513*, *514*
    diazepam (Valium) use in 478, 481, *482*
    drug abuse 517–518
    drug dependence 484, 503
    drug-facilitated sexual assault 513, *513*
    enzyme metabolism *482*
    ethnopharmacology 490, 539
    fluoxetine (Prozac) use in 478, *478*
    hallucinogens 508–512, *509*
    inheritance powder 399, 493
    injection techniques used in 487, *487*, *488*,
        539
    liberty cap fungus (*Psilocybe semilanceata*)
        512
    lysergic acid diethylamide 508–512, *511*
    and medicine 533
    methamphetamine 511–512, *516*
    oxycontin (Percocet) 507–508, 519, **519**
    and pharmacodynamics *480*, 480–481, *481*
    and pharmacogenetics 480, 480–483, *481*
    and pharmacokinetics 480, *480*, *481*, 481–483
    phosgene (Cl$_2$CO) 494, *494*
    portal vein 487, *488*
    steroids 516–517, *517*, *518*
    stimulants 514–516
    strychnine *484*, 485, 499
    targeted drug discovery 490–491

THC *see* tetrahydrocannabinol (THC)
United Nations Office on Drugs and Crime
    518–519
water-soluble compounds 489
touch DNA 139
touchstones (streak plates) 386, *386*
traced forgery 659–660
trace evidence 190
tracking and surveillance 150
trademarks to generic language 683
transcription 122, *123*, 124
transfer bloodstains *180*, 180–181
transfusion, blood 157
translation 122, 124, *124*
transmission electron microscopy (TEM) *106*,
    108, *109*
transmitted light microscopy 98
transparent materials
    refractive index of **588**
trash marks 665
trauma
    antemortem 321, 332
    blunt force 273, *273 see also* blunt force
        trauma (BFT)
    DMORT *see* Disaster Mortuary Operational
        Response Team (DMORT)
    perimortem 321, 332
    post-mortem 321, 332
    sharp force 273 *see* sharp force trauma (SFT)
    types of 268–275, *268–277*
    vehicular 273
TreadMark 641
Treatise on Criminalistics (Locard) 11
triangulation 44, *44*
trinitrotoluene (TNT) 569, 570, *570*, *573*
truth, definition 5
turpentine 557
12 Angry Men (1957) *736*
twist rate 620, 627
two-dimensional impression 637
two-photon fluorescence microscopy 98
typewriter forensics 660–661, *661–663*

ultrasound imaging 280
ultraviolet radiation 97
ultraviolet-visible spectroscopy (UV-vis) *451*,
    451–453, 475
unbiased methods 55
uncertainty, concept of 83
United Nations (UN) 7
United States Geological Survey (USGC) 596,
    597
University of Edinburgh Medical School 17
urinary system 263
urine 184, *184*
USA Patriot Act 39
U.S. Constitution
    5th Amendment to 736
    14th Amendment to 736
    right to bear arms, 2nd Amendment to 626
U.S. Forest Service 563
U.S. National Institute of Justice 8
U.S. Supreme Court 22, 25, 26, 36–41, *37*, 39, 55

Val de Stava Tailings Dam, failure of 690
Vanzetti, B. 636
variable number tandem repeats (VNTR) 125, 135
vectors 690
vehicular trauma 273
vellus hair 212

ventilation-controlled fire growth 553
verbal abuse 729
verbal language 650
verification 31
victimology 729, 729
video forensic analysis 674–676, 675, 675, 676
virtopsy *see* virtual autopsy
virtual autopsy 293–294, 295
virtual image 87, 88, 90
viscosity 175, 585–586, 586, 587
visible fingerprints 200, 202–203
visible impressions 639
visible light 85, 91, 93, 96, 97, 104, 105
visible portion 85
visual detectors 85, 86
vitreous humor 184
Vitruvian Man 308
voiceprint 681, 682
voice recognition 680–682, 680–682
voice spectrograms 682, 683
voir dire process 27, 736
volatile data 713

volume by displacement 583, 584
Vucetich, Juan 10

Wagner, E.J. 12
warrantless search 36, 37, 38, 38, 39, 40, 40
Watson, James 116
wavelength of particles 104–105
Wechsler Intelligence Test 744–745, 745
white blood cells (WBC) 161–162
whorl pattern 195
wildlife forensics 143
Wilkins, Maurice 116
William of Ockham 60
Willingham, Cameron Todd 563
Willingham case 563
wiretap 713
work 701, 701, 719
  energy 719
World Trade Center (WTC)
  failure analysis of 709–711
World War I 11
writing style characteristics 653–655

X chromosome analysis 150
Xerox Corporation 684
X-ray microanalysis *see* energy dispersive X-ray
  analysis (EDXA)
X-ray(s) 106
  forensic uses of 283–285, 284–286
  imaging methods 281–283, 282–283

Y-chromosome typing 142–143
Yfiler Plus kit *138*
Y-incision 261
Y-SNPs 139

zoology
  animal cruelty investigations
    374, 374
  demodectic mange 376
  and poaching *375*
  taphonomy 373
  U.S. Fish and Wildlife Services 375
  veterinary medicine 374
  wildlife investigations 374–375